Mitchell International

ACKNOWLEDGMENT

Mitchell International thanks the domestic and import automobile and light truck manufacturers, distributors, and dealers for their generous cooperation and assistance which make this manual possible.

MARKETING

Director
Robert Gradijan

Brand Managers
Catherine Smith
Daniel D. Fleming

EDITORIAL

Manager, Annual Data Editorial
Thomas L. Landis

Manager, Special Product Editorial
Ronald E. Garrett

Senior Editors
Chuck Vedra
Ramiro Gutierrez
John M. Fisher
Tom L. Hall
James A. Hawes
Serge G. Pirino

Technical Editors
Scott A. Olsen
Bob Reel
David W. Himes
Alex A. Solis
Donald T. Pellettera
Michael C. May
Scott A. Tiner
James R. Warren
James D. Boxberger
Bobby R. Gifford
Linda M. Murphy
Tim P. Lockwood
Dave L. Skora
Donald Lawler
Wayne D. Charbonneau
Sal Caloca
Charles "Bud" Gardner
Dan Hankins
Robert L. Eller
Nick DiVerde
Trang Nguyen
Julia A. Kinneer

WIRING DIAGRAMS

Manager
Matthew M. Krimple

TECHNICAL LIBRARIAN

Charlotte Norris

PRODUCT SUPPORT

Manager
Eddie Santangelo

Senior Product Specialist
Robert L. Rothgery

Product Specialists
James A. Wafford

Diagnostic Support Specialist
Jeffrey H. Lenzkes

GRAPHICS

Manager
Judie LaPierre

Supervisor
Ann Klimetz

Published By

MITCHELL INTERNATIONAL
9889 Willow Creek Road
P.O. Box 26260
San Diego, CA 92196-0260

ISBN 0-8470-1103-8

© 1994 Mitchell International
All Rights Reserved

Printed in U.S.A.

Customer Service Numbers:
Subscription/Billing Information:
1-800-648-8010 or 619-578-6550
Technical Information:
1-800-854-7030 or 619-578-6550
Or Write: P.O. Box 26260, San Diego, CA 92196-0260

3 1300 00190 1989

D1405646

GENERAL INFORMATION

How to Use the Engine Performance Section
Engine Performance Safety Precautions
Diagnostic Routine Outline
1980-93 Maintenance Reminder Lights
Using Mitchell's Wiring Diagrams
Trouble Shooting
Engine Overhaul Procedures

General Cooling System Servicing
Gear Tooth Contact Patterns
Drive Axle Noise Diagnosis
Anti-Lock Brake Safety Precauti
Wheel Alignment Theory & Ope
Commonly Used Abbreviations
English-Metric Conversion Chart

ACURA

CHRYSLER/MITSUBISHI

FORD MOTOR CO.

GENERAL MOTORS

GEO

HONDA

HYUNDAI

LATEST CHANGES & CORRECTIONS

NOTE: For Eagle Summit information, see Chrysler/Mitsubishi Contents page.

ACURA Through HYUNDAI

ASIAN VOL.1

1993 MITCHELL® IMPORTED CARS, LIGHT TRUCKS & VANS SERVICE & REPAIR

Mitchell®

The Leader in Professional Estimating and Repair Information

1993 GENERAL INFORMATION
Contents

1993 GENERAL INFORMATION
How To Use The Engine Performance Section

We have designed Mitchell® manuals to make them easy to use by organizing service and repair information by manufacturer. Below is a brief description of how to use ENGINE PERFORMANCE section.

INTRODUCTION

Here you will find out how to identify an engine by its Vehicle Identification Number (VIN). The manufacturer's MODEL COVERAGE chart lists each model and its engine option, fuel system, ignition system and engine code. Engine serial number locations are also shown here.

SERVICE & ADJUSTMENT SPECIFICATIONS

Here you will find easy-to-use tables covering *important* specifications. You can find valuable information like spark plug wire resistance, valve clearance, firing orders, etc.

EMISSION APPLICATIONS

Here you will find a chart listing emission control devices used on each model. These are helpful when performing government-required emissions inspections.

ON-VEHICLE ADJUSTMENTS

Here you will find adjustment procedures for checking/adjusting valves, base ignition timing and idle speed. Use this section when performing routine maintenance.

THEORY & OPERATION

Here you will find information on how various engine system and components work. Before diagnosing a vehicle or system with which you are not completely familiar, read this section.

BASIC DIAGNOSTIC PROCEDURES

This is the *first step* in diagnosing any driveability problem. These procedures can help you avoid skipping a simple step early, like checking base timing, which could be costly in both time and money later. Once all systems are "GO" here, proceed to SELF-DIAGNOSTICS or TROUBLE SHOOTING – NO CODES.

SELF-DIAGNOSTICS

Use this information to retrieve and interpret trouble codes accessed from the vehicle's self-diagnostic system. Once information is retrieved, diagnostic procedures are given to help pinpoint and repair computer system/component faults. Also included are steps for clearing trouble codes, once these faults are repaired. If there is a problem not indicated by trouble codes, proceed to TROUBLE SHOOTING – NO CODES.

TROUBLE SHOOTING – NO CODES

This is where to go when you have a problem that does not have a trouble code or when working on a non-computer controlled vehicle. It can help with symptoms and intermittent testing procedures. Procedures in this information should lead you to a specific component or system test.

SYSTEM & COMPONENT TESTING

Here you will find various tests for engine performance systems and their components, such as air induction (turbochargers and superchargers), fuel control, ignition control and emission systems.

PIN VOLTAGE CHARTS

These are supplied (when available) to quicken the diagnostic process. By checking pin voltages at the electronic control unit, you can determine if the control unit is receiving and/or transmitting proper voltage signals.

SENSOR OPERATING RANGE CHARTS

These are supplied (when available) to determine if a sensor is out of calibration. An out-of-calibration sensor may not set a trouble code, but it will cause driveability problems.

WIRING DIAGRAMS

Here you can identify and trace component circuits or locate shorts and opens in circuits. They can also help you understand how individual circuits function within a system.

VACUUM DIAGRAMS

Here we give you underhood views of vacuum-hose routing which can help you find incorrectly routed hoses. Remember, a vacuum leak on computer-controlled vehicle can cause many driveability problems.

REMOVAL, OVERHAUL & INSTALLATION

After you've diagnosed the problem, this is where to go for the nuts-and-bolts of the job. Here you'll find procedures and specifications for removing, overhauling (if available) and installing components.

- Always refer to Engine Tune-Up Decal in engine compartment before performing tune-up. If manual and decal differ, always use decal specifications.

- Do not allow or create a condition of misfire in more than one cylinder for an extended period of time. Damage to converter may occur due to loading converter with unburned air/fuel mixture.

- Always turn ignition off and disconnect negative battery cable BEFORE disconnecting or connecting computer or other electrical components.

- DO NOT drop or shock electrical components such as computer, airflow meter, etc.

- DO NOT use fuel system cleaning compounds that are not recommended by the manufacturer. Damage to gaskets, diaphragm materials and catalytic converter may result.

- Before performing a compression test or cranking engine using a remote starter switch, disconnect coil wire from distributor and secure it to a good engine ground, or disable ignition.

- Before disconnecting any fuel system component, ensure fuel system pressure is released.

- Use a shop towel to absorb any spilled fuel to prevent fire.

- DO NOT create sparks or have an open flame near battery.

- If any EFI components such as hoses or clamps are replaced, ensure they are replaced with components designed for EFI use.

- Always reassemble throttle body components with new gaskets, "O" rings and seals.

- If equipped with an inertia switch, DO NOT reset switch until fuel system has been inspected for leaks.

- Wear safety goggles when drilling or grinding.

- Wear proper clothing which protects against chemicals and other hazards.

1993 GENERAL INFORMATION
Engine Performance Diagnostic Routine Outline

WHERE TO BEGIN DIAGNOSING A DRIVEABILITY PROBLEM

STEP 1 - PERFORM BASIC INSPECTION

a) Verify Customer Complaint
b) Perform Visual Inspection
   (See *BASIC DIAGNOSTIC PROCEDURES*)
c) Test Engine Sub-Systems
   (See *BASIC DIAGNOSTIC PROCEDURES*)
   - Mechanical Condition (Compression)
   - Ignition Output
   - Fuel Delivery
d) Check Air Induction System For Leaks
e) Check & Adjust Basic Engine Settings
   (See *ON-VEHICLE ADJUSTMENTS*)
   - Ignition Timing
   - Idle Speed

STEP 2 - CHECK FOR TROUBLE CODES

a) If equipped with self-diagnostics, check for trouble codes. (See *SELF-DIAGNOSTICS*)
b) Repair cause of trouble codes.
c) Clear control unit memory.

STEP 3 - DIAGNOSE SYMPTOM

a) If self-diagnostics and trouble codes are not available, identify complaint by symptom.
b) See trouble shooting procedure to identify problem.
   (See *TROUBLE SHOOTING - NO CODES*)

STEP 4 - TEST & REPAIR SYSTEM

a) Perform required tests.
   (See *SYSTEM & COMPONENT TESTING*)
b) Verify complaint is repaired.

NOTE: *Some vehicles are equipped with a computer malfunction indicator light. If light comes on and remains on while driving, the vehicle requires service. After repairing fault(s) and clearing fault code(s), the malfunction indicator light should go out. Some models may use a dual-function indicator light, which is also used to indicate emission component service is due. After performing required service, reset indicator light.*

ACURA

MAINTENANCE REQUIRED LIGHT

Legend & Vigor – **1)** At each 7500 mile service interval, the MAINTENANCE REQUIRED light will change from Green to Yellow. If service is not performed (and light is not reset), the MAINTENANCE REQUIRED light will change from Yellow to Red.

2) When service has been completed, reset MAINTENANCE REQUIRED reminder light. To reset reminder light, turn ignition off. Insert ignition key in slot provided below tachometer. *See Fig. 1.*

90E16612   Courtesy of American Honda Motor Co., Inc.

Fig. 1: Resetting Maintenance Required Light (Accord, Legend & Vigor)

CHRYSLER MOTORS & MITSUBISHI

EGR/MAINTENANCE REQUIRED WARNING LIGHT

1) On some models, an EGR or MAINTENANCE REQUIRED warning light in dash will come on as a reminder to have EGR system serviced (each 50,000 miles), oxygen sensor replaced (each 80,000 miles), or evaporative carbon canister replaced (100,000 miles).

2) After servicing or replacing components, reset mileage counter. On all models except Pickup and Ram-50, reset switch is located on back of instrument cluster. *See Figs. 2 and 4.*

3) On Pickup and Ram-50, reset switch is on lower right corner of instrument cluster, behind instrument cluster face trim. *See Fig. 3.* Slide switch to opposite side to reset indicator light.

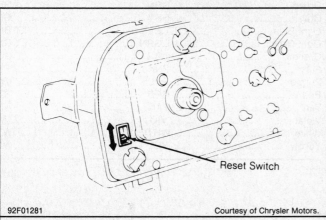

92F01281   Courtesy of Chrysler Motors.

Fig. 2: Locating Warning Light Reset Switch (Colt Vista; Expo & Summit Wagon Are Similar)

4) Remove warning light bulb after 150,000 mile service on Colt Vista. Remove light bulb after 100,000 mile service on Montero. Remove light bulb after 120,000 mile service on Pickup and Ram-50.

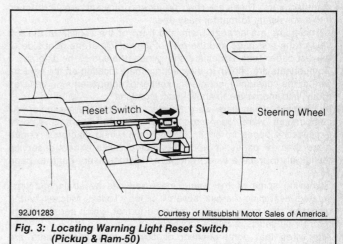

92J01283   Courtesy of Mitsubishi Motor Sales of America.

Fig. 3: Locating Warning Light Reset Switch (Pickup & Ram-50)

93I01433   Courtesy of Mitsubishi Motor Sales of America.

Fig. 4: Locating Warning Light Reset Switch (Montero)

HONDA

MAINTENANCE REQUIRED REMINDER LIGHT

Accord – **1)** At each 7500 mile service interval, the MAINTENANCE REQUIRED light will change from Green to Yellow. If service is not performed (and light is not reset), the MAINTENANCE REQUIRED light will change from Yellow to Red.

2) When service has been completed, reset MAINTENANCE REQUIRED reminder light. To reset reminder light, turn ignition off. Insert ignition key in slot provided to the left of tachometer. *See Fig. 1.*

1993 GENERAL INFORMATION
Using Mitchell's Wiring Diagrams

INTRODUCTION

Mitchell obtains wiring diagrams and technical service bulletins, containing wiring diagram changes, from the domestic and import manufacturers. These are checked for accuracy and are all redrawn into a consistent format for easy use.

All diagrams are arranged with the front of the vehicle at the left side of the first page and the rear of the vehicle at the right side of the last page. Accessories are shown near the end of the diagram. Components are shown in their approximate location on the vehicle. Due to the constantly increasing number of components on vehicles today, it is impossible to show exact locations.

In the past, when cars were simpler, diagrams were simpler. All components were connected by wires, and diagrams seldom exceeded 4 pages in length. Today some wiring diagrams require more than 16 pages. It would be impractical to expect a service technician to trace a wire from page 1 across every page to page 16.

Removing some of the wiring maze reduces eyestrain and time wasted searching across several pages. Today, Mitchell wiring diagrams now follow a much improved format, which permits space for internal details of relays and switches.

Any wires that don't connect directly to their components are identified on the diagram to indicate where they go. There is a legend on the first page of each diagram, detailing component location. It refers you to sub-systems, using grid NUMBERS at the top and bottom of the page and grid LETTERS on each side. This grid system works in a manner similar to that of a road map.

HOW TO USE MITCHELL'S WIRING DIAGRAMS

1) On the first page of the diagram, you will find a listing of major electrical components or systems. Locate the specific component or system you wish to trace. A grid number and letter will follow the component's name.

2) Use the grid NUMBERS (arranged horizontally across the top and bottom of each page) to find the page of the wiring diagram that contains the component you're seeking. When you reach this page, use the grid LETTER/NUMBER combination to find the component's location.

3) Locate the circuit you need to service. The internals are shown for switches and relays to assist you in understanding how the circuit operates.

4) If the wires are not drawn all the way to another component (across several pages), a reference will tell you their final destination.

5) Again, use the legend on the first page of the wiring diagram to determine the grid number and letter of the referenced component. You can then turn directly to it without tracing wires across several pages.

6) The symbols shown in *Fig. 1* are called tie-offs. The first tie-off shown indicates that the circuit goes to the temperature sensor, and is also a ground circuit. The second symbol indicates that the circuit goes to the battery positive terminal. The third symbol leads to a particular component and the location is also given.

7) The lines shown in *Fig. 2* are called options. Which path or option to take depends on what engine or systems the vehicle has.

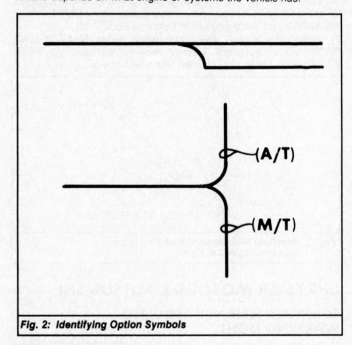

Fig. 2: Identifying Option Symbols

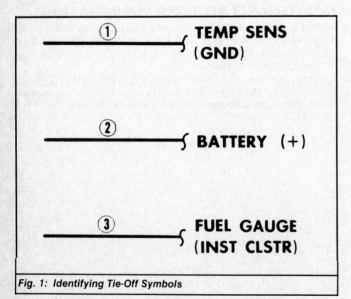

Fig. 1: Identifying Tie-Off Symbols

COLOR ABBREVIATIONS

Color	Normal	Optional
Black	BLK	BK
Blue	BLU	BU
Brown	BRN	BN
Clear	CLR	CR
Dark Blue	DK BLU	DK BU
Dark Green	DK GRN	DK GN
Green	GRN	GN
Gray	GRY	GY
Light Blue	LT BLU	LT BU
Light Green	LT GRN	LT GN
Orange	ORG	OG
Pink	PNK	PK
Purple	PPL	PL
Red	RED	RD
Tan	TAN	TN
Violet	VIO	VI
White	WHT	WT
Yellow	YEL	YL

IDENTIFYING WIRING DIAGRAM SYMBOLS

NOTE: Standard wiring symbols are used on Mitchell diagrams. The list below will help clarify any symbols that are not easily understood at a glance. Most components are labeled "Motor", "Switch" or "Relay" in addition to being drawn with the standard symbol.

 CIRCUIT BREAKER

 COIL (Internal)

 CONNECTOR

 DIODE (In-Line)

 DIODE (Internal)

 DIODE (Light Emitting)

 DEFOGGER GRID

 FUSE

 FUSIBLE LINK

 GROUND

 GLOW PLUG, RESISTOR (In-line), MIRROR HEATER

 INJECTOR, PHOTOCELL

 INTERNAL FUSE, THERMAL LIMITER

 LAMP (Dual Element)

 LAMP (Single Element)

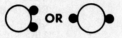 OR MOTOR

 RESISTOR (Internal)

 SENSOR, THERMISTOR

 SOLENOID

 SOLID STATE DEVICE, TRANSISTOR

 SWITCH (Internal)

 TWO PIN SWITCH

 VARIABLE RESISTOR OR POTENTIOMETER

IDENTIFYING WIRING DIAGRAM ABBREVIATIONS

NOTE: Abbreviations in Mitchell Wiring Diagrams are normally self-explanatory. To assist you, we have included a 2-page abbreviation list in this section.

1993 GENERAL INFORMATION
Commonly Used Abbreviations

"A"

A – Amperes
AAP – Auxiliary Accelerator Pump
AB – Air Bleed
ABDC – After Bottom Dead Center
ABS – Anti-Lock Brakes
Abs. – Absolute
AC – Alternating Current
A/C – Air Conditioning
ACCS – A/C Cycling Switch
ACCUM – Accumulator
ACCY – Accessory
A/C – Air Conditioning
ACT – Air Charge Temperature
    Sensor
ADJ – Adjust or Adjustable
ADV – Advance
AFS – Airflow Sensor
AI – Air Injection
AIR or A.I.R. – Air Injection
    Reactor
AIS – Air Injection System
ALCL – Assembly Line
    Communications Link
ALDL – Assembly Line
    Diagnostic Link
Alt. – Alternator or Altitude
Amp. – Ampere
ASCS – Air Suction Control Solenoid
Assy. – Assembly
ASV – Air Suction Valve
A/T – Automatic Transmission/
    Transaxle
ATC – Automatic Temperature
    Control
ATDC – After Top Dead Center
ATF – Automatic Transmission Fluid
ATS – Air Temperature Sensor
Aux. – Auxiliary
Avg. – Average
AXOD – Automatic Transaxle
    Overdrive

"B"

BAC – By-Pass Air Control
BAP – Barometric Absolute
    Pressure Sensor
BARO – Barometric
Batt. – Battery
BBDC – Before Bottom Dead Center
Bbl. – Barrel (Example: 4-Bbl.)
BCM – Body Control Module
BDC – Bottom Dead Center
BHP – Brake Horsepower
Blst. – Ballast
BMAP – Barometric and Manifold
    Absolute Pressure Sensor
BOO – Brake On-Off Switch
B/P – Backpressure
BPS – Barometric Pressure Sensor
BPT – Backpressure Transducer
BTDC – Before Top Dead Center
BTU – British Thermal Unit
BVSV – Bimetallic Vacuum
    Switching Valve

"C"

°C – Celsius
Calif. – California
CANP – Canister Purge
CARB – California Air
    Resources Board
CAT – Catalytic Converter
CB – Circuit Breaker
CBD – Closed Bowl Distributor
CBVV – Carburetor Bowl Vent Valve
cc – cubic centimeter
CCC – Computer Command Control
CCD – Computer Controlled Dwell
CCOT – Cycling Clutch Orifice Tube
CCW – Counterclockwise
CDI – Capacitor Discharge Ignition
CEC – Computerized Engine Control
CID – Cubic Inch Displacement
CIS – Continuous Injection
    System
CIS-E – Continuous Injection
    System-Electronic
cm – Centimeter
CO – Carbon Monoxide
CO_2 – Carbon Dioxide
Cont. – Continued
CONV – Convertible
CP – Canister Purge
CPS – Crank Position Sensor
CTS – Coolant Temperature Sensor
Cu. In. – Cubic Inch
CVC – Constant Vacuum Control
CV – Check Valve or
    Constant Velocity
CW – Clockwise
CYL or Cyl. – Cylinder
C³ I – Computer Controlled
    Coil Ignition
C⁴ – Computer Controlled
    Catalytic Converter

"D"

"D" – Drive
DBC – Dual Bed Catalyst
DC – Direct Current Or Discharge
DDD – Dual Diaphragm Distributor
Def. – Defrost
Defog. – Defogger
DFI – Digital Fuel Injection
Diag. – Diagnostic
DIC – Driver Information Center
DIS – Distributorless Ignition System
DIST – Distribution
DISTR – Distributor
DME – Digital Motor Electronics
    (Motronic System)
DOHC – Double Overhead Cam
DOT – Department of
    Transportation
DP – Dashpot
DRB-II – Diagnostic Readout Box
DVOM – Digital Volt-Ohmmeter

"E"

EAC – Electric Assist Choke
EACV – Electric Air Control Valve
ECA – Electronic Control Assembly
ECM – Electronic Control Module
ECT – Engine Coolant
    Temperature Sensor
ECU – Electronic Control Unit
EDIS – Electronic Distributorless
    Ignition System
EEC – Electronic Engine Control
EECS – Evaporative Emission
    Control System
EFE – Early Fuel Evaporation
EGO – Exhaust Gas Oxygen Sensor
EGR – Exhaust Gas Recirculation
ESA – Electronic Spark Advance
ESC – Electronic Spark Control
EST – Electronic Spark Timing
EVAP – Fuel Evaporative System
EVIC – Electronic Vehicle
    Information Center
EVP – EGR Valve Position Sensor
Exc. – Except

"F"

°F – Fahrenheit (Degrees)
F/B – Fuse Block
FBC – Feedback Carburetor
Fed. – Federal
FI – Fuel Injection
FICD – Fast Idle Control Device
FIPL – Fuel Injector Pump Lever
FPR-VSV – Fuel Pressure Regulator
    Vacuum Switching Valve
Ft. Lbs. – Foot Pounds
FWD – Front Wheel Drive

"G"

g – grams
Gals. – gallons
GND or GRND – Ground
Gov. – Governor

"H"

HAC – High Altitude Compensation
HC – Hydrocarbons
H/D – Heavy Duty
HEGO – Heated Exhaust Gas
    Oxygen Sensor
HEI – High Energy Ignition
Hg – Mercury
Hgt. – Height
HLDT – Headlight
HO – High Output
HP – High Performance
HSC – High Swirl Combustion
HSO – High Specific Output
HTR – Heater
Hz – Hertz (Cycles Per Second)

"I"

IAC – Idle Air Control
IACV – Idle Air Control Valve
IC – Integrated Circuit
ID – Identification
I.D. – Inside Diameter
Ign. – Ignition
In. – Inches
INCH Lbs. – Inch Pounds
in. Hg – Inches of Mercury
Inj. – Injector
IP – Instrument Panel
IPC – Instrument Panel Cluster
ISC – Idle Speed Control
IVSV – Idle Vacuum Switching Valve

"J"

J/B – Junction Block

"K"

KAPWR – Keep Alive Power
k/ohms – kilo-ohms
(1000 ohms)
kg – Kilograms (weight)
kg/cm² – Kilograms Per
Square Centimeter
KM/H – Kilometers Per Hour
KOEO – Key On, Engine Off
KOER – Key On, Engine Running
KS – Knock Sensor
kW – Kilowatt
kV – Kilovolt

"L"

L – Liter
Lbs. – Pounds
LCD – Liquid Crystal Display
L/D – Light Duty
LED – Light Emitting Diode
LH – Left Hand

"M"

mA – Milliamps
MA or MAF – Mass Airflow
MAFS – Mass Airflow Sensor
MAP – Manifold Absolute Pressure
MAT – Manifold Air Temperature
MCU – Microprocessor Control Unit
MCV – Mixture Control Valve
Mem. – Memory
MEM-CAL – Memory Calibration
Chip
mfd. – Microfarads
MFI – Multiport Fuel Injection
MIL – Malfunction Indicator Light
MPI – Multi-Point (Fuel) Injection
mm – Millimeters
MPH – Miles Per Hour
mV – Millivolts

"N"

NA – Not Available
N.m – Newton Meter
No. – Number
Nos. – Numbers
NOx – Oxides of Nitrogen

"O"

O – Oxygen
OC – Oxidation Catalyst
OD – Overdrive
O.D. – Outside Diameter
ODO – Odometer
OHC – Overhead Camshaft
O/S – Oversize
oz. – Ounce
ozs. – Ounces
O_2 – Oxygen

"P"

"P" – Park
PAV – Pulse Air Valve
P/C – Printed Circuit
PCM – Power Train Control Module
PCS – Purge Control Solenoid
PC-SOL – Purge Control Solenoid
PCV – Positive Crankcase
Ventilation
PFI – Port Fuel Injection
PGM-CARB – Programmed
Carburetor
PGM-FI – Programmed
Fuel Injection
PIP – Profile Ignition Pick-up
P/N – Park/Neutral
PRNDL – Park Reverse Neutral
Drive Low
PROM – Programmable
Read-Only Memory
psi – Pounds Per Square Inch
P/S – Power Steering
PSPS – Power Steering
Pressure Switch
PTC – Positive Temperature
Coefficient
PTO – Power Take-Off
Pts. – Pints
Pwr. – Power

"Q"

Qts. – Quarts

"R"

RABS – Rear Anti-Lock Brake
System
RECIRC – Recirculation
RH – Right Hand
RPM – Revolutions Per Minute
RWAL – Rear Wheel
Anti-Lock Brakes
RWD – Rear Wheel Drive

"S"

SBC – Single Bed Converter
SBEC – Single Board
Engine Controller
SEN – Sensor
SES – Service Engine Soon
SFI – Sequential (Port) Fuel Injection
SIL – Shift Indicator Light
SIR – Supplemental Inflatable Restraint
SOHC – Single Overhead Cam
SOL or Sol. – Solenoid
SPFI – Sequential Port
Fuel Injection
SPK – Spark Control
SPOUT – Spark Output
SRS – Supplemental
Restraint System (Air Bag)
SSI – Solid State Ignition
STAR – Self-Test Automatic
Readout
STO – Self-Test Output
SUB-O_2 – Sub Oxygen Sensor
Sw. – Switch
Sys. – System

"T"

TAB – Thermactor Air By-Pass
TAC – Thermostatic Air Cleaner
TAD – Thermactor Air Diverter
TBI – Throttle Body Injection
TCC – Torque Converter Clutch
TCCS – Toyota Computer
Control System
TDC – Top Dead Center
Temp. – Temperature
TFI – Thick Film Ignition
THERMAC – Thermostatic Air
Cleaner
TPS – Throttle Position
Sensor/Switch
TS – Temperature Sensor
TV – Thermovalve
T.V. – Throttle Valve
TWC – Three-Way Catalyst

"V"

V – Valve
Vac. – Vacuum
VAF – Vane Airflow
VAPS – Variable Assist
Power Steering
VCC – Viscous Converter Clutch
VIN – Vehicle Identification Number
VM – Vacuum Modulator
Volt. – Voltage
VOM – Volt-Ohmmeter (Analog)
VRV – Vacuum Regulator Valve
VSS – Vehicle Speed Sensor
VSV – Vacuum Switching Valve

"W"

W/ – With
W/O – Without
WAC – Wide Open Throttle
A/C Switch
WOT – Wide Open Throttle

1993 GENERAL INFORMATION
Trouble Shooting

CHARGING SYSTEM

CHARGING SYSTEM TROUBLE SHOOTING

PROBLEM
Possible Cause   **Action**

NO START CONDITION
Dead Battery .... Check/Replace Battery
Bad Cable Connections .... Clean/Replace Cables
Ignition Switch/Circuit Fault .... Check Switch/Circuit

CHARGING SYSTEM WARNING LIGHT STAYS ON
Loose/Worn Alternator Belt .... Tighten/Replace Belt
Loose Alternator Connections ...... Check/Repair Connections
Warning Light Wiring .... Check/Repair Wiring
Faulty Stator/Diodes .... Test/Repair Alternator
Faulty Voltage Regulator .... Test/Repair Regulator

WARNING LIGHT OFF WITH IGNITION SWITCH ON
Blown Fuse .... Check/Replace Fuse
Faulty Alternator .... Test Alternator
Bad Warning Light Bulb .... Test/Replace Bulb

WARNING LIGHT ON WITH IGNITION SWITCH OFF
Alternator Wiring Short .... Check/Repair Wiring
Faulty Rectifier Bridge .... Test/Repair Alternator

AMMETER INDICATES DISCHARGE
Loose/Worn Alternator Belt .... Tighten/Replace Belt
Loose Alternator Connections ...... Check/Repair Connections
Faulty Ammeter .... Test/Replace Ammeter

NOISY ALTERNATOR
Loose Drive Pulley .... Check/Tighten Pulley Nut
Loose Mounting Bolts .... Tighten Mounting Bolts
Worn/Dirty Alternator
  Bearings .... Clean/Replace Alternator Bearings
Faulty Diodes/Stator .... Replace Diodes/Stator

BATTERY WON'T STAY CHARGED
Defective Battery .... Test/Replace Battery
Accessories Left ON .... Ensure Accessories OFF
Loose/Worn Alternator Belt .... Tighten/Replace Belt
Loose Alternator Connections ...... Check/Repair Connections
Defective Alternator .... Test/Repair Alternator
Short in System .... Check/Repair Short

BATTERY OVERCHARGED
Defective Battery .... Replace Battery
Defective Alternator .... Test/Repair Alternator
Defective Regulator .... Test/Repair Regulator

STARTING SYSTEM

STARTING SYSTEM TROUBLE SHOOTING

PROBLEM
Possible Cause   **Action**

STARTER FAILS TO OPERATE
Dead Battery .... Check/Replace Battery
Bad Connections/Wiring .... Repair Connections/Wiring
Faulty Ignition Switch .... Check Switch Circuit
Faulty Solenoid/Relay .... Replace Solenoid/Relay
Faulty Ground .... Check/Repair Ground

STARTER FAILS TO OPERATE – LIGHTS DIM
Faulty Battery .... Replace Battery
Bad Cable Connections .... Check/Repair Connections
Grounded Starter Windings .... Test/Repair Starter
Faulty Bearing/Bushing .... Replace Bearing/Bushing
Faulty Ground .... Check/Repair Ground
Corroded Terminals .... Clean Terminals

STARTER TURNS – ENGINE DOES NOT
Faulty Starter Drive .... Replace Starter Drive
Broken Drive Housing .... Replace Drive Housing
Faulty Pinion Shaft .... Clean/Repair Shaft
Faulty Flywheel .... Check Flywheel/Starter

STARTING SYSTEM (Cont.)

STARTING SYSTEM TROUBLE SHOOTING (Cont.)

PROBLEM
Possible Cause   **Action**

STARTER DOES NOT CRANK ENGINE
Faulty Starter Drive .... Replace Starter Drive
Broken Drive Housing .... Replace Drive Housing
Missing Flywheel Teeth .... Replace Flywheel
Faulty Ground .... Check/Repair Ground
Frozen Engine .... Check Engine
Liquid-Locked Engine .... Test Cooling System

STARTER ROTATES ENGINE SLOWLY
Faulty Battery .... Replace Battery
Bad Connections/Wiring .... Repair Connections/Wiring
Grounded Starter Windings .... Test/Repair Starter
Faulty Starter Bearings .... Replace Bearings
Faulty Ground .... Check/Repair Ground
Engine Overheated .... Check Cooling System
Timing Too Far Advanced .... Reset Timing
Burned Solenoid Contacts .... Replace Solenoid
High Current Draw .... Test Starter Draw

STARTER ENGAGES ENGINE MOMENTARILY
Timing Too Far Retarded .... Reset Timing
Missing Flywheel Teeth .... Replace Flywheel
Faulty Starter Drive .... Replace Starter Drive
Broken Drive Housing .... Replace Drive Housing
Weak Starter Solenoid .... Replace Starter Solenoid

STARTER DRIVE DOES NOT ENGAGE
Bad Solenoid Contacts .... Replace Solenoid
Bad Solenoid Ground .... Test Solenoid Ground

SOLENOID/RELAY DOES NOT CLOSE
Faulty Battery .... Replace Battery
Bad Connections/Wiring .... Repair Connections/Wiring
Faulty Safety Switch .... Replace Safety Switch
Faulty Solenoid/Relay .... Replace Solenoid/Relay

STARTER DRIVE WILL NOT DISENGAGE
Loose Starter Bolts .... Tighten Starter Bolts
Worn Drive End
  Bushing .... Replace Drive End Bushing
Missing Flywheel Teeth .... Check Flywheel/Drive
Faulty Ignition Switch .... Replace Ignition Switch

SOLENOID CLICKS
Weak Battery .... Charge/Replace Battery
Bad Solenoid Contacts .... Replace Solenoid
Bad Connections/Wiring .... Repair Connections/Wiring
Faulty Solenoid .... Replace Solenoid

HIGH CURRENT DRAW
Dragging Armature .... Replace Starter Bushings
Shorted Armature Windings .... Repair Starter

LOW CURRENT DRAW
Worn Starter Brushes .... Replace Brushes
Weak Brush Springs .... Replace Brush Springs
Faulty Engine Ground .... Check Ground Cable
High Resistance In Positive
  Battery Cable .... Replace Cable

STARTER WHINES DURING CRANKING
Starter Alignment .... Check Starter Alignment
Too Much Distance Between
  Starter Drive & Flywheel .... Ensure Flywheel is Okay
                       Ensure Starter is Correct

STARTER WHINES AFTER STARTING
Starter Alignment .... Check Starter Alignment
Too Little Distance Between
  Starter Drive & Flywheel .... Ensure Flywheel is Okay
                       Ensure Starter is Correct

TUNE-UP

TUNE-UP TROUBLE SHOOTING

PROBLEM
Possible Cause   **Action**

CARBON FOULED PLUGS
Rich Air/Fuel Mixture .... Adjust Air/Fuel Mixture
Faulty Choke .... Replace Choke Assembly
Clogged Air Filter .... Replace Air Filter
Incorrect Idle Speed .... Reset Idle Speed
Faulty Ignition Wiring .... Replace Ignition Wiring
Sticky Valves/Worn Valve Seal .... Check Valve Train
Fuel Injection Operation .... Check Fuel Injection

WET/OIL FOULED PLUGS
Worn Rings/Pistons .... Check Block Condition
Excessive Cylinder Wear .... Rebore/Replace Block

PLUG GAP BRIDGED
Combustion Chamber
Carbon Deposits .... Clean Combustion Chamber

BLISTERED ELECTRODE
Engine Overheating .... Check Cooling System
Loose Spark Plugs .... Clean/Torque Plugs
Over-Advanced Timing .... Reset Timing
Wrong Plug Heat Range .... Install Correct Plug

MELTED ELECTRODES
Incorrect Timing .... Reset Timing
Burned Valves .... Replace Valves
Engine Overheating .... Check Cooling System
Wrong Plug Heat Range .... Install Correct Plug

ENGINE WON'T START
Loose Connections .... Check Connections
No Power .... Check Fuses/Battery

ENGINE RUNS ROUGH
Leaky/Clogged Fuel Lines .... Repair Fuel Lines
Incorrect Timing .... Reset Timing/Check Advance
Faulty Plugs/Wires .... Replace Plugs/Wires

COMPONENT FAILURE
Spark Arcing .... Replace Faulty Part
Defective Pick-Up Coil .... Replace Pick-Up Coil
Defective Ignition Coil .... Replace Ignition Coil
Defective Control Unit .... Replace Control Unit

IGNITION DIAGNOSIS BY SCOPE PATTERN

ALL FIRING LINES ABNORMALLY HIGH
Retarded Ignition Timing .... Reset Ignition Timing
Lean Air/Fuel Mixture .... Adjust Fuel Mixture
High Secondary Resistance .... Repair Secondary Ignition

ALL FIRING LINES ABNORMALLY LOW
Rich Air/Fuel Mixture .... Adjust Air/Fuel Mixture
Arcing Coil Wire .... Replace Coil Wire
Cracked Coil Arcing .... Replace Coil
Low Coil Output .... Replace Coil
Low Compression .... Check/Repair Engine

SEVERAL HIGH FIRING LINES
Fuel Mixture Unbalanced .... Adjust Fuel Mixture
EGR Valve Stuck Open .... Clean/Replace EGR Valve
High Plug Wire Resistance .... Replace Plug Wire
Cracked/Broken Plugs .... Replace Plugs
Intake Vacuum Leak .... Repair Leak

SEVERAL LOW FIRING LINES
Fuel Mixture Unbalanced .... Adjust Fuel Mixture
Plug Wires Arcing .... Replace Plug Wires
Cracked Coil Arcing .... Replace Coil
Low Compression .... Check/Repair Engine
Faulty Spark Plugs .... Replace Plugs

TUNE-UP (Cont.)

TUNE-UP TROUBLE SHOOTING (Cont.)

PROBLEM
Possible Cause   **Action**

CYLINDERS NOT FIRING
Cracked Distributor Cap .... Replace Cap
Shorted Plug Wires .... Replace Plug Wires
Mechanical Engine Fault .... Check/Repair Engine
Spark Plugs Fouled .... Replace Plugs
Carbon Track in Distributor Cap .... Replace Cap

HARD STARTING
Defective Ignition Coil(s) .... Replace Coil(s)
Fouled Spark Plugs .... Replace Plugs
Incorrect Timing .... Reset Ignition Timing

CARBURETOR

CARBURETOR TROUBLE SHOOTING

PROBLEM
Possible Cause   **Action**

ENGINE WON'T START
Choke Not Closing .... Check Choke/Linkage
Choke Linkage Bent .... Check Linkage
Float Dry .... Check/Reset Float Setting

ENGINE STARTS, THEN DIES
Choke Breaker Setting Too Wide .... Check Setting/Adjust
Fast Idle RPM Too Low .... Reset Fast Idle
Fast Idle Cam Index Incorrect .... Reset Fast Idle Cam Index
Vacuum Leak .... Check For Vacuum Leaks
Low Fuel Pump Output .... Repair/Replace Fuel Pump
Low Float Level .... Check/Reset Float Setting

ENGINE QUITS UNDER LOAD
Choke Breaker Setting Incorrect .... Reset Choke Breaker
Fast Idle Cam Index Incorrect .... Reset Fast Idle Cam Index
Hot Fast Idle Speed RPM Incorrect .... Reset Fast Idle RPM

ENGINE IDLES SLOWLY WITH BLACK SMOKE
Choke Breaker Setting Incorrect .... Reset Choke Breaker
Fast Idle Cam Index Incorrect .... Reset Fast Idle Cam Index
Hot Fast Idle RPM Too Low .... Reset Fast Idle RPM

COLD ENGINE STALLS IN GEAR
Choke Breaker Setting Incorrect .... Reset Choke Breaker
Fast Idle RPM Incorrect .... Reset Fast Idle RPM
Fast Idle Cam Index Incorrect .... Reset Fast Idle Cam Index

ACCELERATION SAG OR STALL
Defective Choke Heater .... Replace Choke Heater
Choke Breaker Setting .... Reset Choke Breaker
Float Level Too Low .... Adjust Float Level
Accelerator Pump Defective .... Repair Accelerator Pump

SAG OR STALL AFTER WARM-UP
Defective Choke Heater .... Replace Choke Heater
Faulty Accelerator Pump .... Replace Accelerator Pump
Float Level Too Low .... Adjust Float Level

WARM-UP BACKFIRING/BLACK SMOKE
Choke Stuck Shut .... Check/Replace Choke

TIP-IN HESITATION
Vacuum Leak .... Inspect Vacuum Lines
Accelerator Pump Weak .... Replace Accelerator Pump
Float Level Setting Too Low .... Reset Float Level
Metering Rods Sticking/Binding .... Inspect/Replace Rods
Idle Passages Plugged .... Clean/Rebuild Carburetor

WOT HESITATION
Faulty Accelerator Pump .... Replace Accelerator Pump
Large Vacuum Leak .... Check For Vacuum Leaks
Float Level Too Low .... Reset Float Level
Fuel Delivery Problem .... Inspect Pump, Lines, Filter

FUEL INJECTION

FUEL INJECTION TROUBLE SHOOTING

PROBLEM
Possible Cause   **Action**

ENGINE WON'T START
Cold Start Valve Inoperative .... Test Cold Start Valve
Poor Vacuum/Electrical Connection .... Repair Connections
Contaminated Fuel .... Test Fuel for Water/Alcohol
Bad Fuel Pump Relay/Circuit .... Test Relay/Wiring
Battery Voltage Low .... Charge/Test Battery
Low Fuel Pressure .... Test Press. Regulator/Pump
No Distributor Reference Pulse .... Repair Ignition System
Coolant Temp. Sensor Defective .... Test Temp. Sensor/Circuit
Shorted WOT Switch .... Check/Replace WOT Switch
Defective ECM .... Replace ECM

HARD STARTING
Defective Idle Air Control (IAC) .... Test IAC and Circuit
EGR Valve Open .... Test EGR Valve/Control Circuit
Stalls With A/C On .... Check A/C "On" Signal to ECM
Restricted Fuel Lines .... Inspect/Replace Fuel Lines
Poor MAP Sensor Signal .... Test MAP Sensor/Circuit
Engine Stalls During
  Parking Maneuver .... Check Power Steering Pressure
No Power To Injectors .... Check Injector Fuse/Relay

ROUGH IDLE
Poor MAP Sensor Signal .... Test MAP Sensor/Circuit
Intermittent Fuel Injector
  Operation .... Check Harness Connectors
Erratic Vehicle Speed Sensor
  Inputs .... Harness Too Close to Plug Wires
Poor Temperature Sensor Signal .... Test EGR Valve/Circuit
Poor O$_2$ Sensor Signal .... Test O$_2$ Sensor/Circuit
Faulty PCV System .... Check PCV Valve and Hoses

POOR HIGH SPEED OPERATION
Low Fuel Pump Volume .... Faulty Fuel Pump/Filter
Poor MAP Sensor Signal .... Test Speed Sensor/Circuit

ACCELERATION PING/KNOCK
Poor Knock Sensor Signal .... Test Knock Sensor/Circuit
Poor Baro Sensor Signal .... Test Baro Sensor/Circuit
Improper Ignition Timing .... Adjust Timing
Engine Overheating .... Check Cooling System

TURBOCHARGER

TURBOCHARGER TROUBLE SHOOTING

PROBLEM
Possible Cause   **Action**

Faulty Spark Advance System .... Check Distributor/Ignition
Defective EGR Operation .... Check EGR System
Air Inlet Restriction .... Clear Restriction
Excessive Boost .... Check/Adjust Boost Pressure
Fuel System Fault .... Check Fuel System
Internal Turbo Defect .... Repair/Replace Turbo

LOW ENGINE POWER
Faulty Spark Advance System .... Check Distributor/Ignition
Defective EGR Operation .... Check EGR System
Loose Turbo Bolts .... Check/Tighten Bolts

BLUE EXHAUST SMOKE
Oil Inlet Leak .... Check/Repair Fittings
Oil Drain Leak/Plugged .... Check/Repair Fittings
Turbo Seal Leak .... Check/Replace Seal

GAS ENGINE

GAS ENGINE TROUBLE SHOOTING

PROBLEM
Possible Cause   **Action**

ENGINE LOPES AT IDLE
Leaky Intake Gasket .... Replace Intake Gasket
Blown Head Gasket .... Replace Head Gasket
                                                                Test Cooling System
Worn Timing Chain/Gears .... Replace Timing Chain/Gears
Worn Timing Belt .... Inspect/Replace Belt
Worn Cam .... Inspect Valve Train
Overheated Engine .... Check Cooling System
Clogged PCV System .... Check/Clear PCV System
Leaking EGR Valve .... Check/Replace EGR Valve
Faulty Fuel Pump .... Replace Fuel Pump

ENGINE LACKS POWER
Low Fuel Pressure .... Replace Fuel Pump
Leaky Fuel Pump .... Replace Fuel Pump
Sticky Valves .... Inspect Valve Train
Worn Timing Chain/Gears .... Replace Timing Chain/Gears
Worn Piston Rings .... Check Compression
Weak Valve Springs .... Inspect Valve Train
Worn Cam .... Inspect Cam (Lifters)
Blown Head Gasket .... Replace Head Gasket
                                                                Check Cooling System
Clutch Slipping .... Adjust/Replace Clutch
Overheated Engine .... Check Cooling System
A/T Slipping .... Inspect/Repair A/T
Vacuum Leaks .... Repair Vacuum Leaks
Restricted Exhaust .... Clear Restriction

FAULTY HIGH SPEED OPERATION
Low Fuel Pressure .... Replace Fuel Pump
Leaky Fuel Pump .... Replace Fuel Pump
Sticky Valves .... Inspect Valve Train
Incorrect Valve Timing .... Inspect Valve Train
Intake Manifold Restricted .... Clear Restriction
Worn Distributor Shaft .... Replace Distributor

POOR ACCELERATION
Incorrect Ignition Timing .... Reset Timing
Leaky Valves .... Check Compression
Weak Fuel Pump .... Test/Replace Fuel Pump
Clogged Injectors .... Clean/Replace Injectors
Excessive Intake Valve Deposits .... Clean Valve Deposits

BACKFIRE IN INTAKE MANIFOLD
Improper Ignition Timing .... Adjust Timing
Improper Valve Timing .... Inspect Valve Train
Carbon Tracking/Crossfire .... Inspect Cap/Rotor/Plug Wires
Faulty Plug Wires .... Replace Plug Wires
Defective EGR Valve .... Replace EGR Valve
Lean Fuel Mixture .... Check/Adjust Mixture
Gas in Engine Oil .... Check Fuel System
Sticky Intake Valve .... Check Valve Train
Vacuum Leaks .... Check for Vacuum Leaks

BACKFIRE IN EXHAUST
Vacuum Leak .... Repair Vacuum Leak
Faulty Diverter Valve .... Replace Diverter Valve
Faulty Choke Operation .... Adjust Choke
Exhaust System Leak .... Repair Exhaust Leak
Carbon Tracking/Crossfire .... Inspect Cap/Rotor/Plug Wires

ENGINE DETONATION/PRE-IGNITION
Too Much Timing Advance .... Reset Timing
Faulty Ignition System .... Check Ignition System
Faulty Spark Plugs .... Replace Spark Plugs
Lean Fuel Mixture .... Check Fuel System
Carbon Deposit Build-Up .... Remove Carbon
Low Octane Fuel .... Try Different Fuel
Compression Too High .... Check Compression

GAS ENGINE (Cont.)

GAS ENGINE TROUBLE SHOOTING (Cont.)

PROBLEM
Possible Cause   **Action**

EXCESSIVE OIL CONSUMPTION

Worn Valve Guides/Stems	Inspect Valve Train
Worn Piston Rings	Inspect Engine Block
Worn Cylinder Walls	Inspect Engine Block
Intake Manifold Leak	Replace Gasket
Excessive Bearing Clearance	Inspect Bearings/Crankshaft

NO OIL PRESSURE

Low Oil Level	Add Oil/Check for Leaks
Faulty Oil Pump	Replace Oil Pump
Oil Pick-Up Screen Blocked	Clear Blockage
Loose Oil Pick-Up Tube	Check "O" Ring
Blocked Oil Passages	Inspect Engine Block
Faulty Pressure Relief Valve	Replace Relief Valve
Faulty Oil Light/Gauge	Check Light/Gauge
Worn Engine Bearings	Check/Replace Bearings
Faulty Cooling System	Check Cooling System
Excessive Backpressure	Check Exhaust System

LOW OIL PRESSURE

Low Oil Level	Fill to Proper Level
Faulty Oil Pump	Replace Oil Pump
Oil Pick-Up Screen Blocked	Clear Blockage
Loose Oil Pick-Up Tube	Check "O" Ring
Blocked Oil Passages	Inspect Engine Block
Faulty Pressure Relief Valve	Replace Relief Valve
Faulty Oil Light/Gauge	Check Light/Gauge
Worn Engine Bearings	Check/Replace Bearings

HIGH OIL PRESSURE

Faulty Pressure Relief Valve	Replace Relief Valve
Improper Grade of Oil	Change Oil/Grade
Faulty Oil Light/Gauge	Check Light/Gauge

NOISY MAIN BEARINGS

Low Oil Level	Check Oil Level
Low Oil Pressure	Check Oil Pressure
Worn Main Bearings	Inspect Engine Block
Excessive Crankshaft End Play	Check Main Bearings Check Thrust Washer
Loose Flywheel/Torque Converter	Check Flywheel/Converter
Worn Vibration Damper	Replace Vibration Damper
Worn Crankshaft	Replace Crankshaft/Bearings
Excessive Belt Tension	Check/Loosen Belts

NOISY CONNECTING RODS

Low Oil Level	Check/Fill Oil Level
Low Oil Pressure	Check Oil Pressure
Worn Rod Bearings	Inspect/Replace Bearings
Worn Crankshaft	Check/Replace Crankshaft/Bearings
Misaligned Rod/Cap	Check Rod/Cap
Excessive Belt Tension	Check/Loosen Belts

NOISY VALVE TRAIN

Low Oil Pressure	Check Oil Level/Pressure
Improper Valve Lash	Check Valve Lash
Loose/Worn Timing Belt/Chain/Gears	Check Belt/Chain/Gears
Worn/Bent Push Rods	Check/Replace Push Rods
Worn Rocker Arms	Check/Replace Rocker Arms
Bent Valve	Check Valve Train/Head
Worn Camshaft	Check Camshaft/Bearings
Broken Valve Spring	Replace Valve Spring
Faulty Valve Lifters	Check Lifters/Camshaft
Worn Valve Guides	Check Valve Train
Missing Valve Keeper	Replace Valve Keeper
Loose Rocker Arm Studs	Replace Studs

DIESEL ENGINE

DIESEL ENGINE TROUBLE SHOOTING

PROBLEM
Possible Cause   **Action**

ENGINE WON'T CRANK

Bad Batteries	Test/Replace Batteries
Bad Cable Connections	Clean/Replace Cables
Bad Starter	Test/Repair/Replace Starter
Bad Neutral Safety Switch	Replace Neutral Safety Switch

ENGINE CRANKS SLOWLY

Bad Batteries	Test/Replace Batteries
Bad Cable Connections	Clean/Replace Cables
Bad Starter	Test/Repair/Replace Starter

ENGINE CRANKS NORMALLY, WON'T START

Faulty Glow Plugs	Test/Replace Glow Plugs
Faulty Glow Plug Controller	Test/Replace Controller
No Fuel To Cylinders	Test/Replace Injectors
No Fuel To Injector Pump	Check Fuel Delivery System
Plugged Air Filter	Replace Air Filter
Plugged Fuel Filter	Replace Fuel Filter
Plugged Fuel Tank Filter	Replace Tank Filter
Faulty Fuel Pump	Test/Replace Fuel Pump
Fuel Return System Blocked	Clear Restriction
No Voltage To Fuel Solenoid	Check Fuel Solenoid Wiring
Manual Shut-Off Lever Engaged	Disengage Shut-Off Lever
Incorrect/Contaminated Fuel	Flush/Refill Tank
Incorrect Inj. Pump Timing	Reset Inj. Pump Timing
Low Compression	Check Engine Condition
Faulty Injection Pump	Test/Replace Injection Pump
Fuel Solenoid Closed In RUN Position	Test/Replace Fuel Solenoid

ENGINE STARTS, WON'T IDLE

Incorrect Slow Idle Setting	Adjust Slow Idle Setting
Plugged Air Filter	Replace Air Filter
Faulty Fast Idle Solenoid	Test/Replace Fast Idle Solenoid
Air In Fuel System	Bleed Air From System
Fuel Return System Blocked	Clear Restriction
Glow Plugs Off Too Soon	Test Glow Plugs
Incorrect Inj. Pump Timing	Reset Inj. Pump Timing
No Fuel To Injector Pump	Check Fuel Delivery System
Incorrect/Contaminated Fuel	Flush/Refill Tank
Low Compression	Check Engine Condition
Faulty Injection Pump	Test/Replace Injection Pump

ENGINE STARTS, IDLES ROUGH

Incorrect Slow Idle Setting	Adjust Slow Idle Setting
Plugged Air Filter	Replace Air Filter
Fuel Leak at Injection Line	Repair Fuel Leak
Fuel Return System Blocked	Clear Restriction
Air In Fuel System	Bleed Air From System
Incorrect/Contaminated Fuel	Flush/Refill Tank
Faulty Injector Nozzle	Test/Replace Injector Nozzle
Low Compression	Check Engine Condition

ENGINE SMOKES, CLEARS AFTER WARM-UP

Incorrect Inj. Pump Timing	Reset Inj. Pump Timing
Low Compression	Check Engine Condition
Faulty Injector Nozzle	Test/Replace Injector Nozzle
Air In Fuel System	Bleed Air From System

ENGINE MISFIRES ABOVE IDLE

Plugged Fuel Filter	Replace Fuel Filter
Incorrect Inj. Pump Timing	Reset Inj. Pump Timing
Incorrect/Contaminated Fuel	Flush/Refill Tank

ENGINE WON'T RETURN TO IDLE

Incorrect Fast Idle Setting	Adjust Fast Idle Setting
Faulty Injection Pump	Test/Replace Injection Pump
External Linkage Binding	Check/Repair Linkage
Air In Fuel System	Repair/Bleed Air From System

1993 GENERAL INFORMATION
Trouble Shooting (Cont.)

DIESEL ENGINE (Cont.)

DIESEL ENGINE TROUBLE SHOOTING (Cont.)

PROBLEM
Possible Cause   **Action**

ENGINE LACKS POWER

Restricted Air Intake	Clear Restriction
Faulty EGR Valve	Replace EGR Valve
Restricted Exhaust System	Repair Exhaust System
Blocked Fuel Cap Vent	Replace Fuel Cap
Restricted Fuel Supply From Tank to Injection Pump	Clear Restriction
Incorrect/Contaminated Fuel	Flush/Refill Tank
Faulty Injector Nozzle	Test/Replace Injector Nozzle
Low Compression	Check Engine Condition
Improper Throttle Linkage Adjustment	Adjust Throttle Linkage

CYLINDER KNOCKING NOISE

Injector Nozzles Stuck Open	Test/Replace Injectors
Low Injector Nozzle Pressure	Test/Replace Injectors
Loose Wrist Pin	Disassemble Engine
Piston Slap	Disassemble Engine

ENGINE OVERHEATING

Cooling System Leaks	Repair Cooling System
Loose/Damaged Belt	Tighten/Replace Belt
Plugged Radiator	Rod/Replace Radiator
Defective Fan	Replace Fan
Restricted Airflow Across Radiator	Clear Restriction
Thermostat Stuck Closed	Replace Thermostat
Leaking Head Gasket	Replace Head Gasket Test/Repair Cooling System

ENGINE WON'T SHUT OFF

Injector Pump Fuel Solenoid Does Not Shut Off Fuel Valve	Test/Repair Fuel Solenoid

VACUUM PUMP TROUBLE SHOOTING

PROBLEM
Possible Cause   **Action**

EXCESSIVE NOISE

Loose Pump Mounting	Tighten Pump Mounting
Loose Pump Tube	Tighten Pump Tube
Faulty Pump Valves	Replace Pump Valves

OIL LEAKAGE

Loose End Plug	Tighten End Plug
Bad Seal Crimp	Remove/Recrimp Seal

COOLING SYSTEM

COOLING SYSTEM TROUBLE SHOOTING

PROBLEM
Possible Cause   **Action**

OVERHEATING

Insufficient Coolant	Fill/Pressure Test System
Coolant Leak	Fill/Pressure Test System
Radiator Fins Clogged	Remove/Clean Radiator
Cooling Fan Malfunction	Test Cooling Fan/Circuit
Thermostat Stuck Closed	Replace Thermostat
Clogged Cooling System Passages	Clean/Flush Cooling System
Water Pump Malfunction	Replace Water Pump
Fan Clutch Malfunction	Replace Fan Clutch
Cooling Fan Motor Malfunction	Test Fan Motor
Cooling Fan Relay Malfunction	Test Fan Relay
Faulty Ignition Advance	Check/Replace Advance
Faulty Radiator Cap	Replace Radiator Cap
Broken/Slipping Fan Belt	Replace Fan Belt
Restricted Exhaust	Repair Exhaust System

CORROSION

Impurities in Coolant	Clean/Flush System

COOLING SYSTEM (Cont.)

COOLING SYSTEM TROUBLE SHOOTING (Cont.)

PROBLEM
Possible Cause   **Action**

COOLANT LEAKAGE

Damaged Hose	Replace Hose
Leaky Water Pump Seal	Replace Water Pump
Damaged Radiator Seam	Replace/Repair Radiator
Leaky Thermostat Cover	Replace Thermostat Cover
Cylinder Head Problem	Check Head/Head Gasket
Cylinder Block Problem	Check Cylinder Block
Air in Cooling System	Bleed Cooling System
Leaky Freeze Plugs	Replace Freeze Plugs

RECOVERY SYSTEM INOPERATIVE

Loose/Defective Radiator Cap	Replace Radiator Cap
Overflow Tube Clogged/Leaking	Repair Tube
Recovery Bottle Vent Restricted	Clean Vent

NO HEATER CORE FLOW

Collapsed Heater Hose	Replace Heater Hose
Plugged Heater Core	Clean/Replace Heater Core
Faulty Heater Valve	Replace Heater Valve

CLUTCH

CLUTCH TROUBLE SHOOTING

PROBLEM
Possible Cause   **Action**

CLUTCH CHATTERS/GRABS

Incorrect Pedal Adjustment	Adjust Free Play
Worn Input Shaft Spline	Replace Input Shaft
Binding Pressure Plate	Replace Pressure Plate
Binding Throw-Out Lever	Check Throw-Out Lever Check Throw-Out Bearing Check Bearing Retainer
Uneven Pressure Plate Contact With Flywheel	Align/Replace Worn Parts
Transmission Misaligned	Align Transmission
Worn Pressure Plate	Replace Clutch Assembly
Oil-Saturated Disc	Replace Clutch Assembly Repair Oil Leak
Loose Engine Mounts	Replace Engine Mounts

CLUTCH PEDAL STICKS DOWN

Clutch Cable Binding	Replace Clutch Cable
Weak Pressure Plate Springs	Replace Clutch Assembly
Binding Clutch Linkage	Lubricate Linkage
Broken Clutch Pedal Return Spring	Replace Return Spring

CLUTCH WILL NOT RELEASE

Oil-Saturated Disc	Replace Clutch Assembly Repair Oil Leak
Defective Disc Face	Replace Clutch Assembly
Disc Sticking on Input Shaft Splines	Replace Disc/Input Shaft
Binding Pilot Bearing	Replace Pilot Bearing
Faulty Clutch Master Cylinder	Replace Master Cylinder
Faulty Clutch Slave Cylinder	Replace Slave Cylinder
Blown Clutch Flex Hose	Replace Flexhose
Sticky Throw-Out Bearing Sleeve	Clean/Lube Sleeve
Clutch Cable Binding	Replace Clutch Cable
Broken/Loose Bellhousing	Check Bellhousing

RATTLING/SQUEAKING

Broken Throw-Out Lever Return Spring	Replace Return Spring
Faulty Throw-Out Bearing	Replace Throw-Out Bearing
Faulty Clutch Disc	Replace Clutch Disc
Faulty Pilot Bearing	Replace Pilot Bearing
Worn Throw-Out Bearing	Replace Throw-Out Bearing
Dry Bearing Retainer Slide For Throw-Out Bearing Sleeve	Lubricate Slide

CLUTCH (Cont.)

CLUTCH TROUBLE SHOOTING (Cont.)

PROBLEM
Possible Cause   **Action**

SLIPPING

Faulty Pressure Plate	Replace Clutch Assembly
Worn Clutch Disc	Replace Clutch Assembly
Incorrect Alignment	Realign Clutch Assembly
Faulty Clutch Slave Cylinder	Replace Slave Cylinder

NO PEDAL PRESSURE

Leaky Hydraulic System	Check Clutch Master Cylinder
	Check Clutch Slave Cylinder
	Check Clutch Flexhose
Broken Clutch Cable	Replace Clutch Cable
Faulty Throw-Out Lever	Replace Throw-Out Lever
Broken Clutch Linkage	Repair Clutch Linkage

NOISY CLUTCH PEDAL

Faulty Safety Switch	Check/Replace Switch
Noisy Self-Adj. Ratchet	Replace Ratchet
Dry Throw-Out Bearing	Replace Throw-Out Bearing
Dry Pilot Bearing	Replace Pilot Bearing
Worn Input Shaft	Replace Input Shaft

DRIVE AXLE (RWD)

DRIVE AXLE (RWD) TROUBLE SHOOTING

PROBLEM
Possible Cause   **Action**

KNOCKING OR CLUNKING

Differential Side Gear Clearance	Check Clearance
Worn Pinion Shaft	Replace Pinion Shaft
Axle Shaft End Play	Check End Play
Missing Gear Teeth	Check Diff./Replace Gear
Wrong Axle Backlash	Check Backlash
Misaligned Driveline	Realign Driveline

CLUNKING DURING ENGAGEMENT

Side Gear Clearance	Check Side Gear Clearance
Ring and Pinion Backlash	Check Backlash
Worn/Loose Pinion Shaft	Replace Shaft/Bearing
Bad "U" Joint	Replace "U" Joint
Sticking Slip Yoke	Lube Slip Yoke
Broken Rear Axle Mount	Replace Mount
Loose Drive Shaft Flange	Check Flange

CLICK/CHATTER ON TURNS

Differential Side Gear Clearance	Check Clearance
Worn Clutch Plates [1]	Replace Clutch Plates
Wrong Diff. Lubricant [1]	Change Lubricant

RHYTHMIC KNOCK OR CLICK

Flat Spot on Rear Wheel Bearing	Replace Wheel Bearing

HUM/LOW VIBRATION AT ALL SPEEDS

Faulty Wheel Bearings	Replace Bearings
Faulty "U" Joint	Replace "U" Joint
Faulty Drive Shaft	Balance Drive Shaft
Faulty Companion Flange	Replace Flange
Faulty Slip Yoke Flange	Replace Flange

[1] – Limited slip differential only.

DRIVE AXLE (FWD)

DRIVE AXLE (FWD) TROUBLE SHOOTING

PROBLEM
Possible Cause   **Action**

GREASE LEAKING

Ripped CV Boot	Replace Boot

CLICKING NOISE WHILE CORNERING

Dry/Worn CV Joints	Replace Outer CV Joints

CLUNK ON ACCELERATION

Dry/Worn CV Joints	Replace Inner CV Joints
Worn Trans. Gears/Bearings	Inspect Trans.

VIBRATION/SHUDDER ON ACCELERATION

Dry/Worn CV Joints	Replace CV Joints
Alignment Out	Check Alignment
Incorrect Spring Height	Check Spring Height

SQUEALING OR HUMMING

Dry/Worn CV Joints	Lube/Replace CV Joints
Faulty Wheel Bearing	Replace Wheel Bearing

BRAKE

BRAKE TROUBLE SHOOTING

PROBLEM
Possible Cause   **Action**

CAR PULLS WHILE BRAKING

Faulty Caliper	Rebuild/Replace Caliper
Restricted Brake Hose	Replace Hose
Faulty Rear Brakes	Inspect Rear Brakes
Worn Front Suspension	Check Suspension
Alignment Out	Check Alignment
Incorrect Tire Pressure	Check Pressure
Mismatched Tires	New Tires

HIGH-PITCHED SQUEAL (BRAKES OFF)

Wear Indicators Rubbing	Replace Disc Pads
Faulty Wheel Bearing	Replace Bearing

HIGH-PITCHED SQUEAL (BRAKES ON)

Worn Brake Pads	Replace Disc Pads
Glazed Rotors	Replace Pads/Resurface Rotor

CHATTERING/PULSATING

Faulty Rotors/Drums	Check Runout/Parallelism
Loose Wheel Bearings	Check Bearings
Poorly Installed Pads	Correct Installation

EXCESSIVE PEDAL EFFORT

Faulty Master Cylinder	Rebuild/Replace Cylinder
Faulty Power Booster	Repair/Replace Booster
Worn or Glazed Pads/Shoes	Replace Pads/Shoes
Frozen Caliper Piston	Replace Caliper
Poor Brake Adjustment	Adjust Brakes
Low Fluid Level	Fill Fluid/Inspect System
Air in Lines	Inspect/Bleed System
Heat Boiling Brake Fluid	Re-Route Brake Lines

1993 GENERAL INFORMATION
Trouble Shooting (Cont.)

BRAKE (Cont.)

BRAKE TROUBLE SHOOTING (Cont.)

PROBLEM
Possible Cause   Action

EXCESSIVE PEDAL TRAVEL

Possible Cause	Action
Brake Adjustment	Adjust Brakes
Low Fluid Level	Fill Fluid/Inspect System
Air in Lines	Inspect/Bleed System
Faulty Master Cylinder	Rebuild/Replace Cylinder
Faulty Brake Booster	Repair/Replace Booster
Worn or Glazed Pads/Shoes	Replace Pads/Shoes
Frozen Caliper Piston	Replace Caliper
Booster Actuator Rod Adjustment	Adjust Rod Clearance
Contaminated Fluid	Flush/Bleed System

BRAKES DRAG

Possible Cause	Action
Faulty Master Cylinder	Rebuild/Replace Cylinder
Restricted Brake Lines	Clear Restrictions
Frozen Parking Brake Cables	Replace Cables
Gear Oil-Soaked Pads/Shoes	Repair Oil Leak Replace Pads/Shoes
Brake Fluid-Soaked Pads/Shoes	Repair Fluid Leak Replace Pads/Shoes
Oil Accidentally Mixed With Brake Fluid	Check/Replace All Cylinders/Calipers/Hoses Flush/Bleed System

BRAKES GRAB/UNEVEN ACTION

Possible Cause	Action
Faulty Combination Valve	Replace Combination Valve
Faulty Power Booster	Repair/Replace Booster
Binding Brake Pedal	Check Pedal

WHEEL ALIGNMENT

WHEEL ALIGNMENT TROUBLE SHOOTING

PROBLEM
Possible Cause   Action

PREMATURE TIRE WEAR

Possible Cause	Action
Incorrect Tire Pressure	Check Pressure
Alignment Out	Check Alignment
Worn Front Suspension	Check Suspension
Tires Out of Balance	Balance Tires
Worn Steering Linkage	Check/Replace Linkage
Improper Riding Height	Check/Adjust Riding Height
Uneven/Worn Springs	Replace Springs
Loose/Worn Wheel Bearings	Replace Bearings
Bent Wheel/Rim	Replace Wheel/Rim
Worn/Defective Shocks	Replace Shocks

PULLS TO ONE SIDE

Possible Cause	Action
Incorrect Tire Pressure	Check Pressure
Brake Drag	Inspect Brakes
Mismatched Tires	New Tires
Radial Belt Separation	Replace Tires
Alignment Out	Check Alignment
Frame Bent	Check Frame Damage
Worn Front Suspension	Check Suspension
Worn Steering Linkage	Check/Replace Linkage
Uneven/Worn Springs	Replace Springs
Loose/Worn Wheel Bearings	Replace Bearings

STEERING TOO HARD

Possible Cause	Action
Tight Idler Arm Bushing	Retorque Idler Arm
Tight Ball Joint	Replace Ball Joint
Alignment Out	Check Alignment
Power Steering Fluid Low	Fill/Check Leaks
Power Steering Belt Loose	Tighten Belt
Power Steering Pump Faulty	Repair/Replace Pump
Faulty Steering Gear	Repair/Replace Gear
Faulty Steering Knuckle	Replace Steering Knuckle
Worn Front Suspension	Check Suspension
Incorrect Tire Pressure	Check Pressure

WHEEL ALIGNMENT (Cont.)

WHEEL ALIGNMENT TROUBLE SHOOTING (Cont.)

PROBLEM
Possible Cause   Action

VEHICLE WANDERS

Possible Cause	Action
Incorrect Tire Pressure	Check Pressure
Loose/Worn Wheel Bearings	Replace Bearings
Alignment Out	Check Alignment
Loose Strut Rod (Bushings)	Repair Strut Rod
Faulty Stabilizer Bar	Repair Stabilizer Bar
Worn Spring/Shock	Replace Spring/Shock
Worn Front Suspension	Check Suspension

FRONT END SHIMMY

Possible Cause	Action
Tires Out of Balance	Balance Tires
Radial Belt Separation	Replace Tires
Excessive Wheel Runout	Repair/Replace Wheel
Alignment Out	Check Alignment
Worn Rack Bushings	Replace Bushings
Worn Front Suspension	Check Suspension
Loose/Worn Wheel Bearings	Replace Bearings
Dry/Worn CV Joints	Lube/Replace CV Joints

SUSPENSION

SUSPENSION TROUBLE SHOOTING

PROBLEM
Possible Cause   Action

FRONT END NOISE

Possible Cause	Action
Loose/Worn Wheel Bearings	Replace Bearings
Worn Shocks/Struts	Replace Shocks/Struts
Worn Strut Mountings	Replace Mountings
Loose Steering Gear-to-Frame Mounting Bolts	Check Mounting
Worn Control Arm Bushings	Replace Bushings
Dry Ball Joints	Lubricate Ball Joints

FRONT END SHIMMY

Possible Cause	Action
Tires Out of Balance	Balance Tires
Excessive Wheel Runout	Repair/Replace Wheel
Alignment Out	Check Alignment
Worn Rack Bushings	Replace Bushings
Worn Front Suspension	Check Suspension
Loose/Worn Wheel Bearings	Replace Bearings
Dry/Worn CV Joints	Lube/Replace CV Joints

PULLS TO ONE SIDE

Possible Cause	Action
Incorrect Tire Pressure	Check Pressure
Brake Drag	Inspect Brakes
Mismatched Tires	New Tires
Alignment Out	Check Alignment
Frame Bent	Check Frame Damage
Worn Front Suspension	Check Suspension
Worn Steering Linkage	Check/Replace Linkage
Uneven/Worn Springs	Replace Springs
Loose/Worn Wheel Bearings	Replace Bearings
Power Steering Unbalance	Check Power Steering

SPRING NOISES

Possible Cause	Action
Loose "U" Bolts	Check "U" Bolts
Loose/Worn Bushings	Replace Bushings
Worn/Missing Leaf Spacers	Replace Spacers

CAR LEANS/SWAYS ON CORNERS

Possible Cause	Action
Loose Stabilizer Bar	Replace Bushings
Worn Shocks/Struts	Replace Shocks/Struts
Worn Spring/Shock	Replace Spring/Shock

STEERING COLUMN

STEERING COLUMN TROUBLE SHOOTING

PROBLEM
Possible Cause — **Action**

NOISE IN COLUMN

Possible Cause	Action
Coupling Pulled Apart	Check Coupling
Column Incorrectly Aligned	Align Column
Broken Lower Joint	Replace Joint
Dry Horn Contact Ring	Lube Contact Ring
Dry Column Bearings	Lube/Replace Bearings
Shaft Snap Ring Loose	Seat Snap Ring
Shroud Hits Wheel	Realign Shroud
Lock Plate Ring Loose	Seat Ring
Tight "U" Joint	Replace "U" Joint

STEERING SHAFT BINDS

Possible Cause	Action
Column Misaligned	Align Column
Shroud Misaligned	Align Shroud
Faulty Column Bearings	Replace Bearings
Tight "U" Joint	Replace "U" Joint

SHIFT LEVER BINDS

Possible Cause	Action
Column Misaligned	Align Column
Shroud Misaligned	Align Shroud
Faulty Column Bearings	Replace Bearings
Misadjusted Shifter	Adjust Shifter
Damaged Shift Tube	Replace Tube

EXCESS PLAY IN COLUMN

Possible Cause	Action
Mounting Bracket Loose	Check Bolts
Broken Weld on Jacket	Repair/Replace Column

IGNITION SWITCH STICKS

Possible Cause	Action
Poorly Installed Switch	Check Switch Installation
Worn Key Switch	Replace Key Switch

TILT STEERING COLUMN

TILT STEERING COLUMN TROUBLE SHOOTING

PROBLEM
Possible Cause — **Action**

STEERING WHEEL LOOSE

Possible Cause	Action
Housing/Pivot Pin Loose	Check Clearance
Faulty Anti-Lash Springs	Replace Springs
Upper Bearing Loose	Seat Upper Bearing
Misadjusted Tilt Lock	Adjust Tilt Lock
Loose Support Screws	Tighten Screws
Missing/Broken Bearing Preload Spring	Replace Spring
Housing Jacket Loose	Tighten Screws

PLAY IN COLUMN MOUNT

Possible Cause	Action
Loose Support Screws	Tighten Screws/Bracket
Loose Housing Shoes	Check Housing Shoes
Loose Tilt Pivot Pins	Check Pivot Pins
Loose Shoe Lock Pin	Check Shoe Lock

HOUSING SCRAPES ON BOWL

Possible Cause	Action
Damaged Bowl	Replace Bowl

WHEEL DOES NOT LOCK

Possible Cause	Action
Shoe Seized on Pivot Pin	Check Shoe
Dirty/Damaged Shoe	Clean/Replace Shoe
Faulty Shoe Lock Spring	Replace Spring

WHEEL DOES NOT RETURN

Possible Cause	Action
Bound Pivot Pins	Clean/Replace Pins
Damaged Tilt Spring	Replace Tilt Spring
Turn Signal Switch Wires Too Tight	Reset Wires

NOISE WHEN TILTING

Possible Cause	Action
Worn Upper Tilt Bumpers	Replace Bumpers
Tilt Spring Rubs Housing	Adjust Springs

MANUAL STEERING GEAR

MANUAL STEERING GEAR TROUBLE SHOOTING

PROBLEM
Possible Cause — **Action**

EXCESSIVE STEERING PLAY

Possible Cause	Action
Wheel Bearing Misadjusted	Check Wheel Bearing
Worn/Loose Linkage	Check Linkage
Worn/Loose Ball Joints	Check Ball Joints
Loose Pitman Arm	Check Arm/Gear Splines
Loose Pitman Shaft	Check Gear
Loose Gear Mount	Check Gear Mount
Loose Rack Mount	Check Rack Mount

WHEEL CENTERS POORLY

Possible Cause	Action
Steering Gear Adjusted Too Tightly	Check Gear Free Play
Dry Steering Linkage	Lubricate/Replace Linkage
Dry Ball Joints Bind	Lubricate/Replace Joints
Binding Rack Slide	Inspect Rack
Shaft Contacts Seals	Check Shaft/Replace Seal

POWER STEERING

POWER STEERING TROUBLE SHOOTING

PROBLEM
Possible Cause — **Action**

POWER STEERING PUMP GROWLS/GROANS

Possible Cause	Action
Air In System	Bleed/Check System
Low Fluid Level	Check Fluid/Leaks
High Pressure in Hoses	Clear Restriction
Scored Pump Plates	Check Pump Plates
Worn Cam Ring	Replace Cam Ring

POWER STEERING PUMP RATTLES

Possible Cause	Action
Rotor Slot Vanes Sticking	Clean/Replace Vanes

POWER STEERING PUMP SWISHES

Possible Cause	Action
Faulty Flow Control Valve	Replace Valve

POWER STEERING PUMP SQUAWKS DURING TURN

Possible Cause	Action
Spool Valve "O" Ring Cut	Replace "O" Ring

POWER STEERING PUMP MOANS/WHINES

Possible Cause	Action
Pump Shaft Bearing Scored	Inspect Bearing
Air In Fluid	Fill/Bleed System
Low Fluid Level	Fill/Bleed System
Poor Bracket Alignment	Correct Alignment

POWER STEERING PUMP HISSES DURING TURN

Possible Cause	Action
Internal Leakage in Steering Gear	Check Steering Gear

POWER STEERING PUMP CHIRPS

Possible Cause	Action
Loose Power Steering Belt	Tighten/Replace Belt

POWER STEERING PUMP BUZZES

Possible Cause	Action
Bearing Loose on Shaft	Replace Bearing

POWER STEERING PUMP CLICKS

Possible Cause	Action
Broken Vane Springs	Replace Springs
Worn/Nicked Rotors	Replace Rotors

FLUID FOAMY/MILKY

Possible Cause	Action
Internal Pump Leakage	Reseal Pump
Power Steering Belt Slipping	Tighten/Replace Belt
Pump Output Low	Check Pressure
Faulty Steering Gear	Check Gear

WHEEL SURGES/JERKS

Possible Cause	Action
Low Fluid Level	Check/Fill Fluid
Power Steering Belt Slipping	Tighten/Replace Belt
Pump Output Low	Check Pressure

1993 GENERAL INFORMATION
Engine Overhaul Procedures

DESCRIPTION

Examples used in this article are general in nature and do not necessarily relate to a specific engine or system. Illustrations and procedures have been chosen to guide mechanic through engine overhaul process. Descriptions of cleaning, inspection, and assembly processes are included.

ENGINE IDENTIFICATION

Engine may be identified from Vehicle Identification Number (VIN) stamped on a metal tab. Metal tab may be located in different locations depending on manufacturer. Engine identification number or serial number is located on cylinder block. Location varies with each manufacturer.

INSPECTION PROCEDURES

Engine components must be inspected to meet manufacturer's specifications and tolerances during overhaul. Proper dimensions and tolerances must be met to obtain proper performance and maximum engine life.

Micrometers, depth gauges and dial indicator are used for checking tolerances during engine overhaul. Magnaflux, Magnaglo, dye-check, ultrasonic and x-ray inspection procedures are used for parts inspection.

MAGNETIC PARTICLE INSPECTION

Magnaflux & Magnaglo – Magnaflux is an inspection technique used to locate material flaws and stress cracks. Component is subjected to a strong magnetic field. Entire component or a localized area can be magnetized. Component is coated with either a wet or dry material that contains fine magnetic particles.

Cracks which are outlined by the particles cause an interruption of magnetic field. Dry powder method of Magnaflux can be used in normal lighting and crack appears as a bright line.

Fluorescent liquid is used along with a Black light in the Magnaglo Magnaflux system. Darkened room is required for this procedure. The crack will appear as a glowing line. Complete demagnetizing of component upon completion is required on both procedures. Magnetic particle inspection applies to ferrous materials only.

PENETRANT INSPECTION

Zyglo – The Zyglo process coats material with a fluorescent dye penetrant. Component is often warmed to expand cracks that will be penetrated by the dye. Using darkened room and Black light, component is inspected for cracks. Crack will glow brightly.

Developing solution is often used to enhance results. Parts made of any material, such as aluminum cylinder heads or plastics, may be tested using this process.

Dye Check – Penetrating dye is sprayed on the previously cleaned component. Dye is left on component for 5-45 minutes, depending upon material density. Component is then wiped clean and sprayed with a developing solution. Surface cracks will show up as a bright line.

ULTRASONIC INSPECTION

If an expensive part is suspected of internal cracking, ultrasonic testing is used. Sound waves are used for component inspection.

X-RAY INSPECTION

This form of inspection is used on highly stressed components. X-ray inspection may be used to detect internal and external flaws in any material.

PRESSURE TESTING

Cylinder heads can be tested for cracks using a pressure tester. Pressure testing is performed by plugging all but one of the holes of cylinder head and injecting air or water into the open passage.

Leaks are indicated by the appearance of wet or damp areas when using water. When air is used, it is necessary to spray the head surface with a soap solution. Bubbles will indicate a leak. Cylinder head may also be submerged in water heated to specified temperature to check for cracks created during heat expansion.

CLEANING PROCEDURES

All components of an engine do not have the same cleaning requirements. Physical methods include bead blasting and manual removal. Chemical methods include solvent blast, solvent tank, hot tank, cold tank and steam cleaning of components.

BEAD BLASTING

Manual removal of deposits may be required prior to bead blasting, followed by some other cleaning method. Carbon, paint and rust may be removed using bead blasting method. Components must be free of oil and grease prior to bead blasting. Beads will stick to grease or oil soaked areas causing area not to be cleaned.

Use air pressure to remove all trapped residual beads from component after cleaning. After cleaning internal engine parts made of aluminum, wash thoroughly with hot soapy water. Component must be thoroughly cleaned as glass beads will enter engine oil resulting in bearing damage.

CHEMICAL CLEANING

Solvent tank is used for cleaning oily residue from components. Solvent blasting sprays solvent through a siphon gun using compressed air.

The hot tank, using heated caustic solvents, is used for cleaning ferrous materials only. DO NOT clean aluminum parts such as cylinder heads, bearings or other soft metals using the hot tank. After cleaning, flush parts with hot water.

A non-ferrous part will be ruined and caustic solution will be diluted if placed in the hot tank. Always use eye protection and gloves when using the hot tank.

Use of a cold tank is for cleaning aluminum cylinder heads, carburetors and other soft metals. A less caustic and unheated solution is used. Parts may be left in the tank for several hours without damage. After cleaning, flush parts with hot water.

Steam cleaning, with boiling hot water sprayed at high pressure, is recommended as the final cleaning process when using either hot or cold tank cleaning.

COMPONENT CLEANING

SHEET METAL PARTS

Examples of sheet metal parts are rocker covers, front and side covers, oil pan and bellhousing dust cover. Glass bead blasting or hot tank may be used for cleaning.

Ensure all mating surfaces are flat. Deformed surfaces should be straightened. Check all sheet metal parts for cracks and dents.

INTAKE & EXHAUST MANIFOLDS

Using solvent cleaning or bead blasting, clean manifolds for inspection. If intake manifold has an exhaust crossover, all carbon deposits must be removed. Inspect manifolds for cracks, burned or eroded areas, corrosion and damage to fasteners.

Exhaust heat and products of combustion cause threads of fasteners to corrode. Replace studs and bolts as necessary. On "V" type intake manifolds, sheet metal oil shield must be removed for proper cleaning and inspection. Ensure all manifold parting surfaces are flat and free of burrs.

CYLINDER HEAD REPLACEMENT

REMOVAL

Remove intake and exhaust manifolds and valve cover. Cylinder head and camshaft carrier bolts (if equipped) should be removed only when engine is cold. On many aluminum cylinder heads, removal while hot will cause cylinder head warpage. Mark rocker arm or overhead cam components for location.

Remove rocker arm components or overhead cam components. Components must be installed in original location. Individual design rocker arms may utilize shafts, ball-type pedestal mounts or no rocker arms. For all design types, wire components together and identify according to corresponding valve. Remove cylinder head bolts. Note length and location. Some applications require cylinder head bolts be removed in proper sequence to prevent cylinder head damage. See Fig. 1. Remove cylinder head.

INSTALLATION

Ensure all surfaces and head bolts are clean. Check that head bolt holes of cylinder block are clean and dry to prevent block damage when bolts are tightened. Clean threads with tap to ensure accurate bolt torque.

Install head gasket on cylinder block. Some manufacturers may recommend sealant be applied to head gasket prior to installation. Note that all holes are aligned. Some gasket applications may be marked so that certain area faces upward. Install cylinder head using care not to damage head gasket. Ensure cylinder head is fully seated on cylinder block.

Some applications require head bolts be coated with sealant prior to installation. This is done if head bolts are exposed to coolant passages. Some applications require head bolts be coated with light coat of engine oil.

Install head bolts. Head bolts should be tightened in proper steps and sequence to specification. See Fig. 1. Install remaining components. Tighten all bolts to specification. Adjust valves if required. See VALVE ADJUSTMENT in this article.

NOTE: *Some manufacturers require that head bolts be retightened after specified amount of operation. This must be done to prevent head gasket failure.*

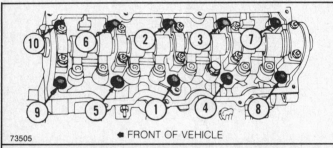

73505   ◆ FRONT OF VEHICLE

Fig. 1: Typical Cylinder Head Tightening or Loosening Sequence

VALVE ADJUSTMENT

Engine specifications will indicate valve train clearance and temperature at which adjustment is to be made on most models. In most cases, adjustment will be made with a cold engine. In some cases, both a cold and a hot clearance will be given for maintenance convenience.

On some models, adjustment is not required. Rocker arms are tightened to specification and valve lash is automatically set. On some models with push rod actuated valve train, adjustment is made at push rod end of rocker arm while other models do not require adjustment.

Clearance will be checked between tip of rocker arm and tip of valve stem in proper sequence using a feeler gauge. Adjustment is made by rotating adjusting screw until proper clearance is obtained. Lock nut is then tightened. Engine will be rotated to obtain all valve adjustments to manufacturer's specifications.

Some models require hydraulic lifter to be bled down and clearance measured. Push rods of different length can be used to obtain proper clearance. Clearance will be checked between tip of rocker arm and tip of valve stem in proper sequence using a feeler gauge.

Overhead cam engines designed without rocker arms actuate valves directly on a cam follower. A hardened, removable disc is installed between the cam lobe and lifter. Clearance will be checked between cam heel and adjusting disc in proper sequence using a feeler gauge. Engine will be rotated to obtain all valve adjustments.

On overhead cam engines designed with rocker arms, adjustment is made at valve end of rocker arm. Ensure valve to be adjusted is riding on heel of cam on all engines. Clearance will be checked between tip of rocker arm and tip of valve stem in proper sequence using a feeler gauge. Adjustment is made by rotating adjusting screw until proper clearance is obtained. Lock nut is then tightened. Engine will be rotated to obtain all valve adjustments to manufacturer's specifications.

CYLINDER HEAD OVERHAUL

CYLINDER HEAD DISASSEMBLY

Mark valves for location. Using valve spring compressor, compress valve springs. Remove valve locks. Carefully release spring compressor. Remove retainer or rotator, valve spring, spring seat and valve. See Fig. 2.

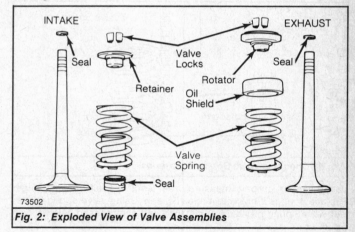

73502

Fig. 2: Exploded View of Valve Assemblies

CYLINDER HEAD CLEANING & INSPECTION

Clean cylinder head and valve components using approved cleaning methods. Inspect cylinder head for cracks, damage or warped gasket surface. Place straightedge across gasket surface. Determine clearance at center of straightedge. Measure across both diagonals, longitudinal center line and across cylinder head at several points. See Fig. 3.

On cast iron cylinder heads, if warpage exceeds .003" (.08 mm) in a 6" span, or .006" (.15 mm) over total length, cylinder head must be resurfaced. On most aluminum cylinder heads, if warpage exceeds .002" (.05 mm) in any area, cylinder head must be resurfaced. Warpage specification may vary by manufacturer. If warpage exceeds specification on some cylinder heads, cylinder head must be replaced.

Cylinder head thickness should be measured to determine amount of material which can be removed before replacement is required. Cylinder head thickness must not be less than the manufacturer's specification.

If cylinder head required resurfacing, it may not align properly with intake manifold. On "V" type engines, misalignment is corrected by machining intake manifold surface that contacts cylinder head. Cylinder head may be machined on surface that contacts intake manifold. Using oil stone, remove burrs or scratches from all sealing surfaces.

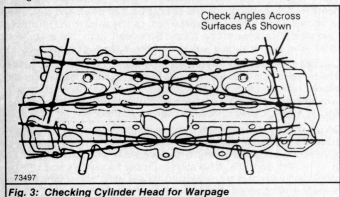

73497

Fig. 3: Checking Cylinder Head for Warpage

VALVE SPRINGS

Inspect valve springs for corroded or pitted valve spring surfaces which may lead to breakage. Polished spring ends caused by a rotating spring indicate that spring surge has occurred. Replace springs showing evidence of these conditions.

Inspect valve springs for squareness using a 90 degree straightedge. See Fig. 4. Replace valve spring if out-of-square exceeds manufacturer's specification.

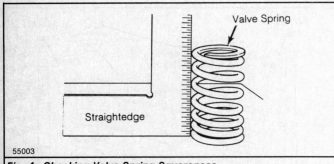

55003

Fig. 4: Checking Valve Spring Squareness

Using vernier caliper, measure free length of all valve springs. Replace springs if not within specification. Using valve spring tester, test valve spring pressure at installed and compressed heights. See Fig. 5.

Usually compressed height is installed height minus valve lift. Replace valve spring if not within specification. It is recommended to replace all valve springs when overhauling cylinder head. Valve springs may need to be installed with color coded end or small coils at specified area according to manufacturer.

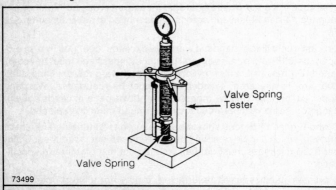

73499

Fig. 5: Checking Valve Spring Pressure

VALVE GUIDE

Measuring Valve Guide Clearance – Check valve stem-to-guide clearance. Ensure valve stem diameter is within specification. Install valve in valve guide. Install dial indicator assembly on cylinder head with tip resting against valve stem just above valve guide. See Fig. 6.

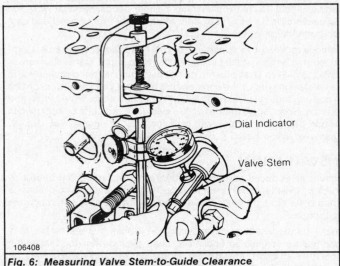

106408

Fig. 6: Measuring Valve Stem-to-Guide Clearance

Lower valve approximately 1/16" below valve seat. Push valve stem against valve guide as far as possible. Adjust dial indicator to zero. Push valve stem in opposite direction and note reading. Clearance must be within specification.

If valve guide clearance exceeds specification, valves with oversize stems may be used and valve guides are reamed to larger size or valve guide must be replaced. On some applications, a false guide is installed, then reamed to proper specification. Valve guide reamer set is used to ream valve guide to obtain proper clearance for new valve.

Reaming Valve Guide – Select proper reamer for size of valve stem. Reamer must be of proper length to provide clean cut through entire length of valve guide. Install reamer in valve guide and rotate to cut valve guide. See Fig. 7.

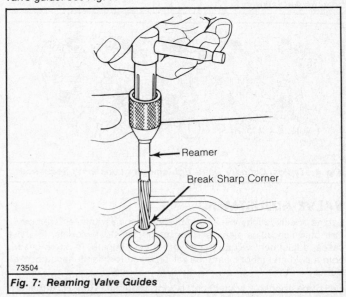

73504

Fig. 7: Reaming Valve Guides

Replacing Valve Guide – Replace valve guide if clearance exceeds specification. Valve guides are either pressed, hammered or shrunk in place, depending upon cylinder head design and type of metal used.

Remove valve guide from cylinder head by pressing or tapping on a stepped drift. See Fig. 8. Once valve guide is installed, distance from cylinder head to top of valve guide must be checked. This distance must be within specification.

Aluminum heads are often heated before installing valve guide. Valve guide is sometimes cooled in dry ice prior to installation. Combination of a heated cylinder head and cooled valve guide ensures a tight guide fit upon assembly. The new guide must be reamed to specification.

Specified Diameter
For Valve Guide

Valve Guide Installer

55007

Fig. 8: Typical Valve Guide Remover & Installer

VALVES & VALVE SEATS

Valve Grinding – Valve stem O.D. should be measured in several areas to indicate amount of wear. Replace valve if not within specification. Valve margin area should be measured to ensure that valve can be ground. See Fig. 9.

If valve margin is less than specification, the valves will be burned. Valve must be replaced. Due to minimum margin dimensions during manufacture, some new type valves cannot be reground. Some manufacturers use stellite coated valves that must NOT be machined. Valves can only be lapped into valve seat.

CAUTION: Some valves are sodium filled. Extreme care must be used when disposing of damaged or worn sodium-filled valves.

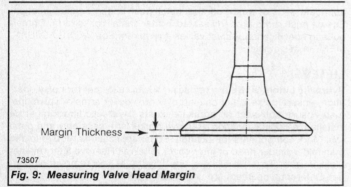

Margin Thickness →

73507

Fig. 9: Measuring Valve Head Margin

Resurface valve to proper angle specification using valve grinding machine. Follow manufacturer's instructions for valve grinding machine. Specifications may indicate a different valve face angle than seat angle.

Measure valve margin after grinding. Replace valve if not within specification. Valve stem tip can be refinished using valve grinding machine.

Valve Lapping – During valve lapping of recently designed valves, be sure to follow manufacturer's recommendations. Surface hardening and materials used with some valves do not permit lapping. Lapping process will remove excessive amounts of the hardened surface.

Valve lapping is done to ensure adequate sealing between valve face and seat. Use either a hand drill or lapping stick with suction cup attached.

Moisten and attach suction cup to valve. Lubricate valve stem and guide. Apply a thin coat of fine valve grinding compound between valve and seat. Rotate lapping tool between the palms or with hand drill.

Lift valve upward off the seat and change position often. This is done to prevent grooving of valve seat. Lap valve until a smooth polished seat is obtained. Thoroughly clean grinding compound from components. Valve-to-valve seat concentricity should be checked. See VALVE SEAT CONCENTRICITY.

CAUTION: Valve guides must be in good condition and free of carbon deposits prior to valve seat grinding. Some engines contain an induction hardened valve seat. Excessive material removal will damage valve seats.

Valve Seat Grinding – Select coarse stone of correct size and angle for seat to be ground. Ensure stone is true and has a smooth surface. Select correct size pilot for valve guide dimension. Install pilot in valve guide. Lightly lubricate pilot shaft. Install stone on pilot. Move stone off and on the seat approximately 2 times per second during grinding operation.

Select a fine stone to finish grinding operation. Various angle grinding stones are used to center and narrow the valve seat as required. See Fig. 10.

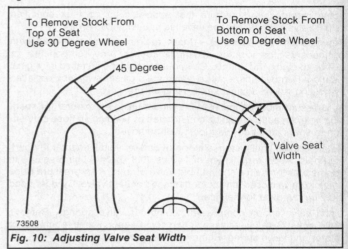

To Remove Stock From
Top of Seat
Use 30 Degree Wheel

To Remove Stock From
Bottom of Seat
Use 60 Degree Wheel

45 Degree

Valve Seat
Width

73508

Fig. 10: Adjusting Valve Seat Width

Valve Seat Replacement – Replacement of valve seat inserts is done by cutting out the old insert and machining an oversize insert bore. Replacement oversize insert is usually cooled and the cylinder head is sometimes warmed. Valve seat is pressed into the head. This operation requires specialized machine shop equipment.

Valve Seat Concentricity – Using dial gauge, install gauge pilot in valve guide. Position gauge arm on the valve seat. Adjust dial indicator to zero. Rotate arm 360 degrees and note reading. Runout should not exceed specification.

To check valve-to-valve seat concentricity, coat valve face lightly with Prussian Blue dye. Install valve and rotate it on valve seat. If pattern is even and entire seat is coated at valve contact point, valve is concentric with the valve seat.

CYLINDER HEAD REASSEMBLY

Valve Stem Installed Height – Valve stem installed height must be checked when new valves are installed or when valves or valve seats have been ground. Install valve in valve guide. Measure distance from tip of valve stem to spring seat. See Fig. 11. Distance must be within specification to allow sufficient clearance for valve operation.

Remove valve and grind valve stem tip if height exceeds specification. Valve tips are surface hardened. DO NOT remove more than .010" (.25 mm) from tip. Chamfer sharp edge of reground valve tip. Recheck valve stem installed height.

VALVE STEM OIL SEALS

Valve stem oil seals must be installed on valve stem. See Fig. 2. Seals are needed due to pressure differential at the ends of valve guides. Atmospheric pressure above intake guide, combined with manifold vacuum below guide, causes oil to be drawn into the cylinder.

Exhaust guides also have pressure differential created by exhaust gas flowing past the guide, creating a low pressure area. This low pressure area draws oil into the exhaust system.

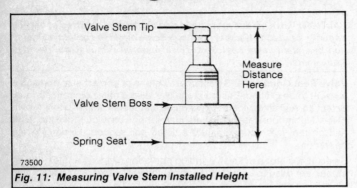

Fig. 11: Measuring Valve Stem Installed Height

Some manufacturers require that special color code or specified height valve stem oil seal be installed in designated area.

Replacement (On-Vehicle) – Mark rocker arm or overhead cam components for location. Remove rocker arm components or overhead cam components. Components must be installed in original location. Remove spark plugs. Valve stem oil seals may be replaced by holding valves against seats using air pressure.

Air pressure must be installed in cylinder using an adapter for spark plug hole. An adapter can be constructed by welding air hose connection to spark plug body with porcelain removed.

Rotate engine until piston is at top of stroke. Install adapter in spark plug hole. Apply a minimum of 140 psi (9.8 kg/cm²) line pressure to adapter. Air pressure should hold valve closed. If air pressure does not hold valve closed, check for damaged or bent valve. Cylinder head must be removed for service.

Using valve spring compressor, compress valve springs. Remove valve locks. Carefully release spring compressor. Remove retainer or rotator and valve spring. Remove valve stem oil seal.

If oversize valves have been installed, oversize oil seals must be used. Coat valve stem with engine oil. Install protective sleeve over end of valve stem. Install new oil seal over valve stem and seat on valve guide. Remove protective sleeve. Install spring seat, valve spring and retainer or rotator. Compress spring and install valve locks. Remove spring compressor. Ensure valve locks are fully seated.

Install rocker arms or overhead cam components. Tighten all bolts to specification. Adjust valves if required. Remove adapter. Install spark plugs, valve cover and gasket.

VALVE SPRING INSTALLED HEIGHT

Valve spring installed height should be checked during reassembly. Measure height from lower edge of valve spring to the upper edge. DO NOT include valve spring seat or retainer. Distance must be within specification. If valves and/or seats have been ground, a valve spring shim may be required to correct spring height. See Fig. 12.

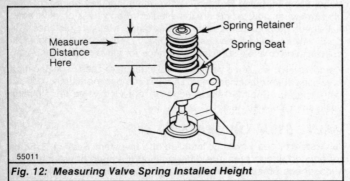

Fig. 12: Measuring Valve Spring Installed Height

ROCKER ARMS & ASSEMBLIES

Rocker Studs – Rocker studs are either threaded or pressed in place. Threaded studs are removed by locking 2 nuts on the stud.

Unscrew the stud by turning the jam nut. Coat new stud threads with Loctite and install. Tighten to specification.

Pressed-in stud can be removed using a stud puller. Ream stud bore to proper specification and press in a new oversize stud. Pressed-in studs are often replaced by cutting threads in the stud bore to accept a threaded stud.

Rocker Arms & Shafts – Mark rocker arms for location. Remove rocker arm retaining bolts. Remove rocker arms. Inspect rocker arms, shafts, bushings and pivot balls (if equipped) for excessive wear. Inspect rocker arms for wear in valve stem contact area. Measure rocker arm bushing I.D. Replace bushings if excessively worn.

The rocker arm valve stem contact point may be reground, using special fixture for valve grinding machine. Remove minimum amount of material as possible. Ensure all oil passages are clear. Install rocker arm components in original location. Ensure rocker arm is properly seated in push rod. Tighten bolts to specification. Adjust valves if required. See VALVE ADJUSTMENT in this article.

PUSH RODS

Remove rocker arms. Mark push rods for location. Remove push rods. Push rods can be steel or aluminum, solid or hollow. Hollow push rods must be internally cleaned to ensure oil passage to rocker arms is cleaned. Check push rods for damage, such as loose ends on steel tipped aluminum types.

Check push rod for straightness. Roll push rod on a flat surface. Using feeler gauge, check clearance at center. Replace push rod if bent. The push rod can also be supported at each end and rotated. A dial indicator is used to detect a bent area in the push rod.

Lubricate ends of push rod and install push rod in original location. Ensure push rod is properly seated in lifter. Install rocker arm. Tighten bolts to specification. Adjust valves if required. See VALVE ADJUSTMENT in this article.

LIFTERS

Hydraulic Lifters – Before replacing a hydraulic lifter for noisy operation, ensure noise is not caused by worn rocker arms or valve tips. Also ensure sufficient oil pressure exists. Hydraulic lifters must be installed in original location. Remove rocker arm assembly and push rod. Mark components for location. Some applications require intake manifold, cylinder head or lifter cover removal. Remove lifter retainer plate (if used). To remove lifters, use a hydraulic lifter remover or magnet. Different type lifters are used. See Fig. 13.

On sticking lifters, disassemble and clean lifter. DO NOT mix lifter components or positions. Parts are select-fitted and are not interchangeable. Inspect all components for wear. Note amount of wear in lifter body-to-camshaft contact area. Surface must have smooth and convex contact face. If wear is apparent, carefully inspect cam lobe.

Inspect push rod contact area and lifter body for scoring or signs of wear. If body is scored, inspect lifter bore for damage and lack of lubrication. On roller type lifters, inspect roller for flaking, pitting, loss of needle bearings and roughness during rotation.

Measure lifter body O.D. in several areas. Measure lifter bore I.D. Ensure components or oil clearance is within specification. Some models offer oversize lifters. Replace lifter if damaged.

If lifter check valve is not operating, obstructions may be preventing it from closing or valve spring may be broken. Clean or replace components as necessary.

Check plunger operation. Plunger should drop to bottom of the body by its own weight when assembled dry. If plunger is not free, soak lifter in solvent to dissolve deposits.

Lifter leak-down test can be performed on lifter. Lifter must be filled with special test oil. New lifters contain special test oil. Using lifter leak-down tester, perform leak-down test following manufacturer's instructions. If leak-down time is not within specifications, replace lifter assembly.

Lifters should be soaked in clean engine oil several hours prior to installation. Coat lifter base, roller (if equipped) and lifter body with ample amount of Molykote or camshaft lubricant. *See Fig. 13.* Install lifter in original location. Install remaining components. Valve lash adjustment is not required on most hydraulic lifters. Preload of hydraulic lifter is automatic. Some models may require adjustment.

NOTE: Some manufacturers require that a crankcase conditioner be added to engine oil and engine operated for specified amount of time to aid in lifter break-in procedure if new lifters or camshaft are installed.

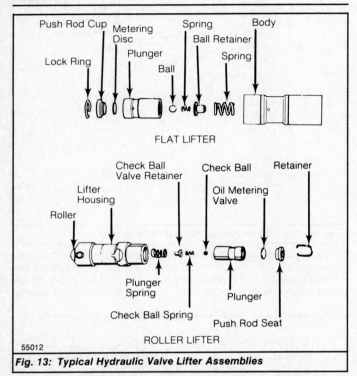

Fig. 13: Typical Hydraulic Valve Lifter Assemblies

Mechanical Lifters – Lifter assemblies must be installed in original locations. Remove rocker arm assembly and push rod. Mark components for location. Some applications require intake manifold or lifter cover removal. Remove lifter retainer plate (if used). To remove lifters, use lifter remover or magnet.

Inspect push rod contact area and lifter body for scoring or signs of wear. If body is scored, inspect lifter bore for damage and lack of lubrication. Note amount of wear in lifter body-to-camshaft contact area. Surface must have smooth and convex contact face. If wear is apparent, carefully inspect cam lobe.

Coat lifter base, roller (if equipped) and lifter body with ample amount of Molykote or camshaft lubricant. Install lifter in original location. Install remaining components. Tighten bolts to specification. Adjust valves. See VALVE ADJUSTMENT in this article.

PISTONS, CONNECTING RODS & BEARINGS

RIDGE REMOVAL

Ridge in cylinder wall must be removed prior to piston removal. Failure to remove ridge prior to removing pistons will cause piston damage in piston ring lands or grooves.

With piston at bottom dead center, place rag in bore to trap metal chips. Install ridge reamer in cylinder bore. Adjust ridge reamer using manufacturer's instructions. Remove ridge using ridge reamer. DO NOT remove an excessive amount of material. Ensure ridge is completely removed.

PISTON & CONNECTING ROD REMOVAL

Note top of piston. Some pistons may contain a notch, arrow or be marked FRONT. Piston must be installed in proper direction to prevent damage with valve operation.

Check that connecting rod and cap are numbered for cylinder location and which side of cylinder block the number faces. Proper cap and connecting rod must be installed together. Connecting rod cap must be installed on connecting rod in proper direction to ensure bearing lock procedure. Mark connecting rod and cap if necessary. Pistons must be installed in original location.

Remove cap retaining nuts or bolts. Remove bearing cap. Install tubing protectors on connecting rod bolts. This protects cylinder walls from scoring during removal. Ensure proper removal of ridge. Push piston and connecting rod from cylinder. Connecting rod boss can be tapped with a wooden dowel or hammer handle to aid in removal.

PISTON & CONNECTING ROD

Disassembly – Using ring expander, remove piston rings. Remove piston pin retaining rings (if equipped). Note direction of piston installation on connecting rod. On pressed type piston pins, special fixtures and procedures according to manufacturer must be used to remove piston pins. Follow manufacturer's recommendations to avoid piston distortion or breakage.

Cleaning – Remove all carbon and varnish from piston. Pistons and connecting rods may be cleaned in cold type chemical tank. Using ring groove cleaner, clean all deposits from ring grooves. Ensure all deposits are cleaned from ring grooves to prevent ring breakage or sticking. DO NOT attempt to clean pistons with wire brush.

Inspection – Inspect pistons for nicks, scoring, cracks or damage in ring areas. Connecting rod should be checked for cracks using Magnaflux procedure. Piston diameter must be measured in manufacturer's specified area.

Using telescopic gauge and micrometer, measure piston pin bore of piston in 2 areas, 90 degrees apart. This is done to check diameter and out-of-round.

Install proper bearing cap on connecting rod. Ensure bearing cap is installed in proper location. Tighten bolts or nuts to specification. Using inside micrometer, measure inside diameter in 2 areas, 90 degrees apart.

Connecting rod I.D. and out-of-round must be within specification. Measure piston pin bore I.D. and piston pin O.D. All components must be within specification. Subtract piston pin diameter from piston pin bore in piston and connecting rod to determine proper fit.

Connecting rod length must be measured from center of crankshaft journal inside diameter to center of piston pin bushing using proper caliper. Connecting rods must be the same length. Connecting rods should be checked on an alignment fixture for bent or twisted condition. Replace all components which are damaged or not within specification.

PISTON & CYLINDER BORE FIT

Ensure cylinder is checked for taper, out-of-round and properly honed prior to checking piston and cylinder bore fit. See CYLINDER BLOCK in this article. Using dial bore gauge, measure cylinder bore.

Measure piston skirt diameter at 90 degree angle to piston pin at specified area by manufacturer. Subtract piston diameter from cylinder bore diameter to determine piston-to-cylinder clearance. Clearance must be within specification. Mark piston for proper cylinder location.

ASSEMBLING PISTON & CONNECTING ROD

Install piston on connecting rod for corresponding cylinder. Ensure reference marking on top of piston corresponds with connecting rod and cap number. *See Fig. 14.*

Lubricate piston pin and install in connecting rod. Ensure piston pin retainers are fully seated (if equipped). On pressed type piston pins, follow manufacturer's recommended procedure to avoid distortion or breakage.

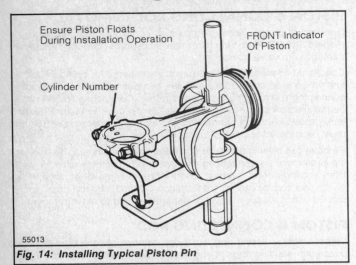

Fig. 14: **Installing Typical Piston Pin**

CHECKING PISTON RING CLEARANCES

Piston rings must be checked for side clearance and end gap. To check end gap, install piston ring in cylinder in which it is to be installed. Using an inverted piston, push ring to bottom of cylinder in smallest cylinder diameter.

Using feeler gauge, check ring end gap. See Fig. 15. Piston ring end gap must be within specification. Ring breakage will occur if insufficient ring end gap exists.

Some manufacturers permit correcting insufficient ring end gap by using a fine file while other manufacturers recommend using another ring set. Mark rings for proper cylinder installation after checking end gap.

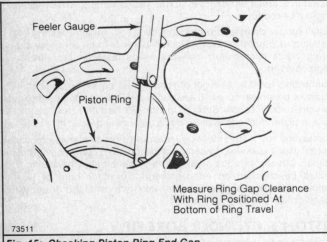

Fig. 15: **Checking Piston Ring End Gap**

For checking side clearance, install rings on piston. Using feeler gauge, measure clearance between piston ring and piston ring land. Check side clearance in several areas around piston. Side clearance must be within specification.

If side clearance is excessive, piston ring grooves can be machined to accept oversize piston rings (if available). Normal practice is to replace piston.

PISTON & CONNECTING ROD INSTALLATION

Cylinders must be honed prior to piston installation. See CYLINDER HONING under CYLINDER BLOCK in this article.

Install upper connecting rod bearings. Lubricate upper bearings with engine oil. Install lower bearings in rod caps. Ensure bearing tabs are

properly seated. Position piston ring gaps according to manufacturer's recommendations. See Fig. 16. Lubricate pistons, rings and cylinder walls.

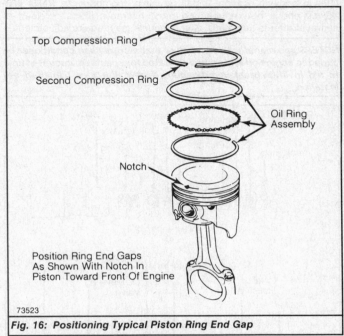

Fig. 16: **Positioning Typical Piston Ring End Gap**

Install ring compressor. Use care not to rotate piston rings. Compress rings with ring compressor. Install plastic tubing protectors over connecting rod bolts. Install piston and connecting rod assembly. Ensure piston notch, arrow or FRONT mark is toward front of engine. See Fig. 17.

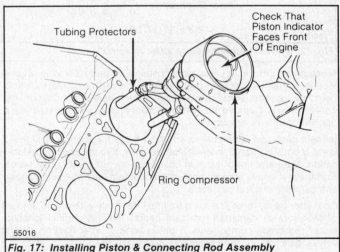

Fig. 17: **Installing Piston & Connecting Rod Assembly**

Carefully tap piston into cylinder until rod bearing is seated on crankshaft journal. Remove protectors. Install rod cap and bearing. Lightly tighten connecting rod bolts. Repeat procedure for remaining cylinders. Check bearing clearance. See MAIN & CONNECTING ROD BEARING CLEARANCE in this article.

Once clearance is checked, lubricate journals and bearings. Install bearing caps. Ensure marks are aligned on connecting rod and cap. Tighten rod nuts or bolts to specification. Ensure rod moves freely on crankshaft. Check connecting rod side clearance. See CONNECTING ROD SIDE CLEARANCE in this article.

CONNECTING ROD SIDE CLEARANCE

Position connecting rod toward one side of crankshaft as far as possible. Using feeler gauge, measure clearance between side of connecting rod and crankshaft. *See Fig. 18.* Clearance must be within specification.

Check for improper bearing installation, wrong bearing cap or insufficient bearing clearance if side clearance is insufficient. Connecting rod may require machining to obtain proper clearance. Excessive clearance usually indicates excessive wear at crankshaft. Crankshaft must be repaired or replaced.

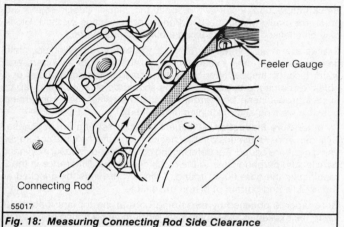

Feeler Gauge

Connecting Rod

55017

Fig. 18: Measuring Connecting Rod Side Clearance

MAIN & CONNECTING ROD BEARING CLEARANCE

Plastigage Method – Plastigage method may be used to determine bearing clearance. Plastigage can be used with an engine in service or during reassembly. Plastigage material is oil soluble.

Ensure journals and bearings are free of oil or solvent. Oil or solvent will dissolve material and false reading will be obtained. Install small piece of Plastigage along full length of bearing journal. Install bearing cap in original location. Tighten bolts to specification.

CAUTION: DO NOT rotate crankshaft while Plastigage is installed. Bearing clearance will not be obtained if crankshaft is rotated.

Remove bearing cap. Compare Plastigage width with scale on Plastigage container to determine bearing clearance. *See Fig. 19.* Rotate crankshaft 90 degrees. Repeat procedure. This is done to check journal eccentricity. This procedure can be used to check oil clearance on both connecting rod and main bearings.

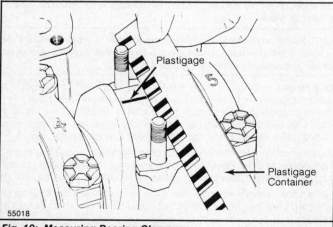

Plastigage

Plastigage Container

55018

Fig. 19: Measuring Bearing Clearance

Micrometer & Telescopic Gauge Method – A micrometer is used to determine journal diameter, taper and out-of-round dimensions of the crankshaft. See CLEANING & INSPECTION under CRANKSHAFT & MAIN BEARINGS in this article.

With crankshaft removed, install bearings and caps in original location on cylinder block. Tighten bolts to specification. On connecting rods, install bearings and caps on connecting rods. Install proper connecting rod cap on corresponding rod. Ensure bearing cap is installed in original location. Tighten bolts to specification.

Using a telescopic gauge and micrometer or inside micrometer, measure inside diameter of connecting rod and main bearings bores. Subtract each crankshaft journal diameter from the corresponding inside bearing bore diameter. This is the bearing clearance.

CRANKSHAFT & MAIN BEARINGS

REMOVAL

Ensure all main bearing caps are marked for location on cylinder block. Some main bearing caps have an arrow stamped on them. The arrow must face timing belt or timing chain end of engine. Remove main bearing cap bolts. Remove main bearing caps. Carefully remove crankshaft. Use care not to bind crankshaft in cylinder block during removal.

CLEANING & INSPECTION

Thoroughly clean crankshaft using solvent. Dry with compressed air. Ensure all oil passages are clear and free of sludge, rust, dirt, and metal chips.

Inspect crankshaft for scoring and nicks. Inspect crankshaft for cracks using Magnaflux procedure. Inspect rear seal area for grooving or damage. Inspect bolt hole threads for damage. If pilot bearing or bushing is used, check pilot bearing or bushing fit in crankshaft. Inspect crankshaft gear for damaged or cracked teeth. Replace gear if damaged. Check that oil passage plugs are tight (if equipped).

Using micrometer, measure all journals in 4 areas to determine journal taper, out-of-round and undersize. *See Fig. 20.* Some crankshafts can be reground to the next largest undersize, depending on the amount of wear or damage. Crankshafts with rolled fillet cannot be reground and must be replaced.

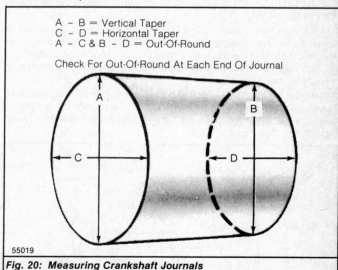

A – B = Vertical Taper
C – D = Horizontal Taper
A – C & B – D = Out-Of-Round

Check For Out-Of-Round At Each End Of Journal

A

B

C

D

55019

Fig. 20: Measuring Crankshaft Journals

Crankshaft journal runout should be checked. Install crankshaft in "V" blocks or bench center. Position dial indicator with tip resting on the main bearing journal area. *See Fig. 21.* Rotate crankshaft and note reading. Journal runout must not exceed specification. Repeat procedure on all main bearing journals. Crankshaft must be replaced if runout exceeds specification.

1993 GENERAL INFORMATION
Engine Overhaul Procedures (Cont.)

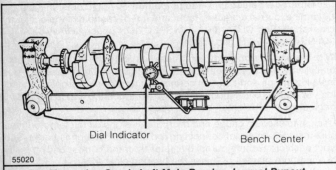

Dial Indicator

Bench Center

55020

Fig. 21: Measuring Crankshaft Main Bearing Journal Runout

INSTALLATION

Install upper main bearing in cylinder block. Ensure lock tab is properly located in cylinder block. Install bearings in main bearing caps. Ensure all oil passages are aligned. Install rear seal (if removed).

Ensure crankshaft journals are clean. Lubricate upper main bearings with clean engine oil. Carefully install crankshaft. Check each main bearing clearance using Plastigage method. See MAIN & CONNECTING ROD BEARING CLEARANCE in this article.

Once clearance is checked, lubricate lower main bearing and journals. Install main bearing caps in original location. Install rear seal in rear main bearing cap (if removed). Some rear main bearing caps require sealant to be applied in corners to prevent oil leakage.

Install and tighten all bolts except thrust bearing cap to specification. Tighten thrust bearing cap bolts finger tight only. Some models require that thrust bearing must be aligned. On most applications, crankshaft must be moved rearward then forward. Procedure may vary with manufacturer. Thrust bearing cap is then tightened to specification. Ensure crankshaft rotates freely. Crankshaft end play should be checked. See CRANKSHAFT END PLAY in this article.

CRANKSHAFT END PLAY

Dial Indicator Method – Crankshaft end play can be checked using dial indicator. Mount dial indicator on rear of cylinder block. Position dial indicator tip against rear of crankshaft. Ensure tip is resting against flat surface.

Pry crankshaft rearward. Adjust dial indicator to zero. Pry crankshaft forward and note reading. Crankshaft end play must be within specification. If end play is not within specification, check for faulty thrust bearing installation or worn crankshaft. Some applications offer oversize thrust bearings.

Feeler Gauge Method – Crankshaft end play can be checked using feeler gauge. Pry crankshaft rearward. Pry crankshaft forward. Using feeler gauge, measure clearance between crankshaft and thrust bearing surface. See Fig. 22.

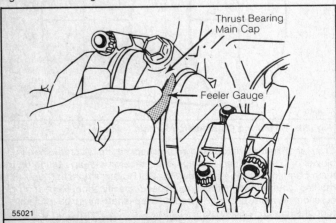

Thrust Bearing Main Cap

Feeler Gauge

55021

Fig. 22: Checking Crankshaft End Play

Crankshaft end play must be within specification. If end play is not within specification, check for faulty thrust bearing installation or worn crankshaft. Some applications offer oversize thrust bearings.

CYLINDER BLOCK

Block Cleaning – Only cast cylinder blocks should be hot tank cleaned. Aluminum cylinder blocks should be cleaned using cold tank method. Cylinder block is cleaned in order to remove carbon deposits, gasket residue and water jacket scale. Remove oil gallery plugs, freeze plugs and cam bearings prior to block cleaning.

Block Inspection – Visually inspect the block. Check suspected areas for cracks using the Dye Penetrant inspection method. Block may be checked for cracks using the Magnaflux method.

Cracks are most commonly found at the bottom of cylinders, main bearing saddles, near expansion plugs and between cylinders and water jackets. Inspect lifter bores for damage. Inspect all head bolt holes for damaged threads. Threads should be cleaned using tap to ensure proper head bolt torque. Consult machine shop concerning possible welding and machining (if required).

Cylinder Bore Inspection – Inspect bore for scoring or roughness. Cylinder bore is dimensionally checked for out-of-round and taper using dial bore gauge. For determining out-of-round, measure cylinder parallel and perpendicular to the block center line. Difference in the 2 readings is the bore out-of-round. Cylinder bore must be checked at top, middle and bottom of piston travel area.

Bore taper is obtained by measuring bore at the top and bottom. If wear has exceeded allowable limits, block must be honed or bored to next available oversize piston dimension.

Cylinder Honing – Cylinder must be properly honed to allow new piston rings to properly seat. Cross-hatching at correct angle and depth is critical to lubrication of cylinder walls and pistons.

A flexible drive hone and power drill are commonly used. Drive hone must be lubricated during operation. Mix equal parts of kerosene and SAE 20W engine oil for lubrication.

Apply lubrication to cylinder wall. Operate cylinder hone from top to bottom of cylinder using even strokes to produce 45 degree cross-hatch pattern on the cylinder wall. DO NOT allow cylinder hone to extend below cylinder during operation.

Recheck bore dimension after final honing. Wash cylinder wall with hot soapy water to remove abrasive particles. Blow dry with compressed air. Coat cleaned cylinder walls with lubricating oil.

Deck Warpage – Check deck for damage or warped gasket surface. Place a straightedge across gasket surface of the deck. Using feeler gauge, measure clearance at center of straightedge. Measure across width and length of cylinder block at several points.

If warpage exceeds specifications, deck must be resurfaced. If warpage exceeds manufacturer's maximum tolerance for material removal, replace block.

NOTE: Some manufacturers recommend that a total amount of material (cylinder head and cylinder block) can only be removed before components must be replaced.

Deck Height – Distance from crankshaft center line to block deck is called the deck height. Measure and record front and rear main journals of crankshaft. To compute this distance, install crankshaft and retain with center main bearing and cap only. Measure distance from crankshaft journal to block deck, parallel to cylinder center line.

Add one half of main bearing journal diameter to distance from crankshaft journal to block deck. This dimension should be checked at front and rear of cylinder block. Both readings should be the same.

If difference exceeds specification, cylinder block must be repaired or replaced. Deck height and warpage should be corrected at the same time.

Main Bearing Bore & Alignment – For checking main bearing bore, remove all bearings from cylinder block and main bearing caps. Install main bearing caps in original location. Tighten bolts to specification.

Using inside micrometer, measure main bearing bore in 2 areas 90 degrees apart. Determine bore size and out-of-round. If diameter is not within specification, block must be align-bored.

For checking alignment, place a straightedge along center line of main bearing saddles. Check for clearance between straightedge and main bearing saddles. Block must be align-bored if clearance exists.

Expansion Plug Removal – Drill hole in center of expansion plug. Remove with screwdriver or punch. Use care not to damage sealing surface.

Expansion Plug Installation – Ensure sealing surface is free of burrs. Coat expansion plug with sealer. Using wooden dowel or pipe of slightly smaller diameter, install expansion plug. Ensure expansion plug is evenly located.

Oil Gallery Plug Removal – Remove threaded oil gallery plugs using appropriate wrench. Soft press-in plugs are removed by drilling into plug and installing a sheet metal screw. Remove plug with slide hammer or pliers.

Oil Gallery Plug Installation – Ensure threads or sealing surface is clean. Coat threaded oil gallery plugs with sealer and install. Replacement soft press-in plugs are installed with a hammer and drift.

CAMSHAFT

CLEANING & INSPECTION

Clean camshaft with solvent. Ensure all oil passages are clear. Inspect cam lobes and bearing journals for pitting, flaking or scoring. Using micrometer, measure bearing journal O.D.

Support camshaft at each end with "V" blocks. Position dial indicator with tip resting on center bearing journal. Rotate camshaft and note camshaft runout reading. If reading exceeds specification, replace camshaft.

Check cam lobe lift by measuring base circle of camshaft using micrometer. Measure again at 90 degree angle to tip of cam lobe. Cam lift can be determined by subtracting base circle diameter from tip of cam lobe measurement.

Different lift dimensions are given for intake and exhaust cam lobes. Reading must be within specification. Replace camshaft if cam lobes or bearing journals are not within specification.

Inspect camshaft gear for chipped, eroded or damaged teeth. Replace gear if damaged. On camshafts using thrust plate, measure distance between thrust plate and camshaft shoulder. Replace thrust plate if not within specification.

CAMSHAFT BEARINGS

Removal & Installation – Remove camshaft rear plug. Camshaft bearing remover is assembled with shoulder resting against bearing to be removed according to manufacturer's instructions. Tighten puller nut until bearing is removed. Remove remaining bearings, leaving front and rear bearings until last. These bearings act as a guide for camshaft bearing remover.

To install new bearings, puller is rearranged to pull bearings toward the center of block. Ensure all lubrication passages of bearing are aligned with cylinder block. Coat new camshaft rear plug with sealant. Install camshaft rear plug. Ensure plug is even in cylinder block.

CAMSHAFT INSTALLATION

Lubricate bearing surfaces and cam lobes with ample amount of Moly-kote or camshaft lubricant. Carefully install camshaft. Use care not to damage bearing journals during installation. Install thrust plate retaining bolts (if equipped). Tighten bolts to specification. On overhead camshafts, install bearing caps in original location. Tighten bolts to specification. On all applications, check camshaft end play.

CAMSHAFT END PLAY

Using dial indicator, check camshaft end play. Position dial indicator on front of engine block or cylinder head. Position indicator tip against

camshaft. Push camshaft toward rear of cylinder head or engine and adjust indicator to zero.

Move camshaft forward and note reading. Camshaft end play must be within specification. End play may be adjusted by relocating gear, shimming thrust plate or replacing thrust plate depending on each manufacturer.

TIMING CHAINS & BELTS

TIMING CHAINS

Timing chains will stretch during operation. Limits are placed upon amount of stretch before replacement is required. Timing chain stretch will alter ignition timing and valve timing.

To check timing chain stretch, rotate crankshaft to eliminate slack from one side of timing chain. Mark reference point on cylinder block. Rotate crankshaft in opposite direction to eliminate slack from remaining side of timing chain. Force other side of chain outward and measure distance between reference point and timing chain. *See Fig. 23.* Replace timing chain and gears if not within specification.

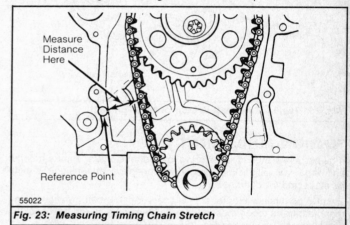

Fig. 23: Measuring Timing Chain Stretch

Timing chains must be installed so timing marks on camshaft gear and crankshaft gear are aligned according to manufacturer. *See Fig. 24.*

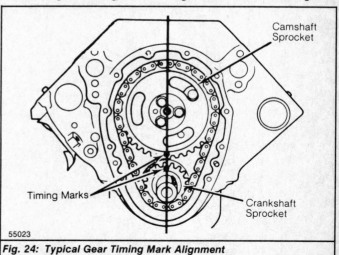

Fig. 24: Typical Gear Timing Mark Alignment

TIMING BELTS

Cogged tooth belts are commonly used on overhead cam engines. Inspect belt teeth for rounded corners or cracking. Replace belt if it is cracked, damaged, missing teeth, or oil soaked.

Used timing belt must be installed in original direction of rotation. Inspect all sprocket teeth for wear. Replace all worn sprockets.

1993 GENERAL INFORMATION
Engine Overhaul Procedures (Cont.)

Sprockets are marked for timing purposes. Engine is positioned so that crankshaft sprocket mark will be upward. Camshaft sprocket is aligned with reference mark on cylinder head or timing belt cover and then timing belt can be installed. *See Fig. 25.*

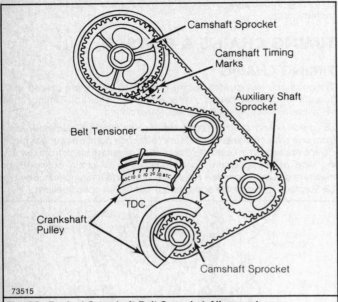

Fig. 25: **Typical Camshaft Belt Sprocket Alignment**

TENSION ADJUSTMENT

If guide rails are used with spring loaded tensioners, ensure at least half of original rail thickness remains. Spring loaded tensioner should be inspected for damage.

Ensure all timing marks are aligned. Adjust belt tension using manufacturer's recommendations. Belt tension may require checking using tension gauge. *See Fig. 26.*

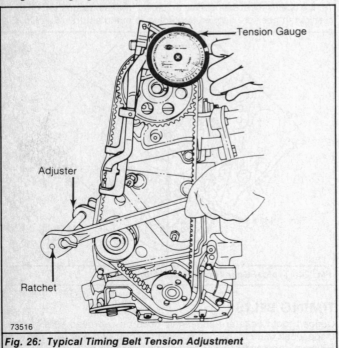

Fig. 26: **Typical Timing Belt Tension Adjustment**

TIMING GEARS

TIMING GEAR BACKLASH & RUNOUT

On engines where camshaft gear operates directly on crankshaft gear, gear backlash and runout must be checked. To check backlash, install dial indicator with tip resting on tooth of camshaft gear. Rotate camshaft gear as far as possible. Adjust indicator to zero. Rotate camshaft gear in opposite direction as far as possible and note reading.

To determine timing gear runout, mount dial indicator with tip resting on face edge of camshaft gear. Adjust indicator to zero. Rotate camshaft gear 360 degrees and note reading. If backlash or runout exceeds specification, replace camshaft and/or crankshaft gear.

REAR MAIN OIL SEAL INSTALLATION

One-Piece Type Seal – For one-piece type oil seal installation, coat block contact surface of seal with sealer if seal is not factory coated. Ensure seal surface is free of burrs. Lubricate seal lip with engine oil and press seal into place using proper oil seal installer. *See Fig. 27.*

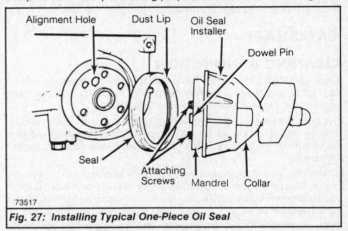

Fig. 27: **Installing Typical One-Piece Oil Seal**

Rope Type Seal – For rope type rear main oil seal installation, press seal lightly into seat area. Using seal installer, fully seat seal in bearing cap or cylinder block.

Trim seal ends even with cylinder block parting surface. Some applications require sealer to be applied on main bearing cap prior to installation. *See Fig. 28.*

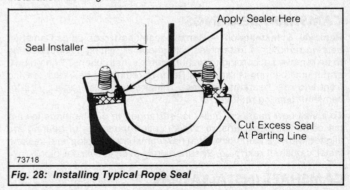

Fig. 28: **Installing Typical Rope Seal**

Split-Rubber Type Seal – Follow manufacturer's procedures when installing split-rubber type rear main oil seals. Installation procedures vary with manufacturer and engine type. *See Fig. 29.*

OIL PUMP

ROTOR TYPE

Mark oil pump rotor locations prior to removal. *See Fig. 30.* Remove outer rotor and measure thickness and diameter. Measure inner rotor

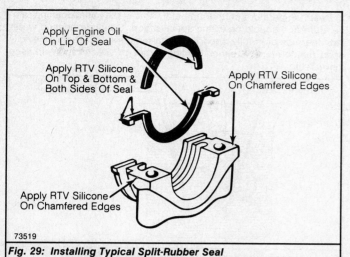

Fig. 29: Installing Typical Split-Rubber Seal

thickness. Inspect shaft for scoring or wear. Inspect rotors for pitting or damage. Inspect cover for grooving or wear. Replace worn or damaged components.

Measure outer rotor-to-body clearance. Replace pump assembly if clearance exceeds specification. Measure clearance between rotors. *See Fig. 31.* Replace shaft and both rotors if clearance exceeds specification.

Install rotors in pump body. Position straightedge across pump body. Using feeler gauge, measure clearance between rotors and straightedge. Pump cover wear is measured using a straightedge and feeler gauge. Replace pump if clearance exceeds specification.

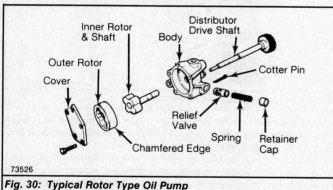

Fig. 30: Typical Rotor Type Oil Pump

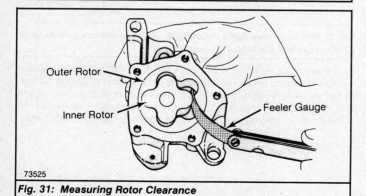

Fig. 31: Measuring Rotor Clearance

GEAR TYPE

Mark oil pump gear location prior to removal. *See Fig. 32.* Remove gears from pump body. Inspect gears for pitting or damage. Inspect cover for grooving or wear. Measure gear diameter and length. Measure gear housing cavity depth and diameter. *See Fig. 33.* Replace worn or damaged components.

Measure pump cover wear using a straightedge and feeler gauge. Replace pump or components if warpage/wear exceeds specification. Check pump mating surface for scratches or grooves.

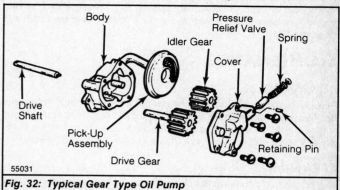

Fig. 32: Typical Gear Type Oil Pump

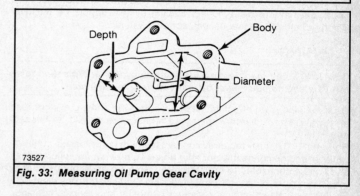

Fig. 33: Measuring Oil Pump Gear Cavity

BREAK-IN PROCEDURE

ENGINE PRE-OILING

Pre-oil engine prior to operation to prevent engine damage. A lightly oiled oil pump will cavitate unless oil pump cavities are filled with engine oil or petroleum jelly.

Engine pre-oiling can be done using pressure oiler (if available). Connect pressure oiler to oil pressure sending unit hole. Operate pressure oiler until oil fills crankcase. Check oil level while pre-oiling.

If pressure oiler is not available, disconnect ignition system. Remove oil pressure sending unit and install oil pressure test gauge. Using starter motor, rotate engine starter until gauge shows normal oil pressure for several seconds. DO NOT crank engine for more than 30 seconds to avoid starter motor damage. Ensure oil pressure has reached the furthest point from oil pump.

NOTE: If installing new lifters and camshaft, some manufacturers recommend adding a "crankcase conditioner" to engine oil.

INITIAL START-UP

Start engine and run at low RPM. Check for coolant, fuel and oil leaks. Stop engine. Recheck coolant and oil level. Fill if necessary.

CAMSHAFT

Break-in procedure is required when new or reground camshaft has been installed. Operate and maintain engine speed between 1500-2500 RPM for approximately 30 minutes.

PISTON RINGS

Piston rings require a break-in procedure to ensure seating of rings to cylinder walls. Follow piston ring manufacturer's recommended break-in procedure.

1993 GENERAL INFORMATION
General Cooling System Servicing

DESCRIPTION

The basic liquid cooling system consists of a radiator, water pump, thermostat, electric or belt-driven cooling fan, pressure cap, heater, and various connecting hoses and cooling passages in the block and cylinder head.

MAINTENANCE

DRAINING

Remove radiator cap and open heater control valve to maximum heat position. Open drain cocks or remove plugs in bottom of radiator and engine block. In-line engines usually have one plug or drain cock, while "V" type engines will have 2, one in each bank of cylinders.

CLEANING

A good cleaning compound can remove most rust and scale. Follow manufacturer's instructions in the use of cleaner. If considerable rust and scale have to be removed, cooling system should be flushed. Clean radiator air passages with compressed air.

FLUSHING

CAUTION: Some manufacturers use an aluminum and plastic radiator. Flushing solution must be compatible with aluminum.

Back flushing is an effective means of removing cooling system rust and scale. The radiator, engine and heater core should be flushed separately.
Radiator – To flush radiator, connect flushing gun to water outlet of radiator and disconnect water inlet hose. To prevent flooding engine, use a hose connected to radiator inlet. Use air in short bursts to prevent damage to radiator. Continue flushing until water runs clear.
Engine – To flush engine, remove thermostat and replace housing. Connect flushing gun to water outlet of engine. Flush using short air bursts until water runs clean.
Heater Core – Flush heater core as described for radiator. Ensure heater control valve is set to maximum heat position before flushing heater.

REFILLING

To prevent air from being trapped in engine block, engine should be running when refilling cooling system. After system is full, continue running engine until thermostat is open, then recheck fill level. Do not overfill system.

TESTING

THERMOSTAT

1) Remove and visually inspect thermostat for corrosion and proper sealing of valve and seat. If okay, suspend thermostat and thermometer in a 50/50 mixture of coolant and water. *See Fig. 1.* DO NOT allow thermostat or thermometer to touch bottom of container. Heat water until thermostat begins to open.

2) Read temperature on thermometer. This is the initial opening temperature and should be within specification. Continue heating water until thermostat is fully open and note temperature. This is the fully open temperature. If either reading is not to specification, replace thermostat.

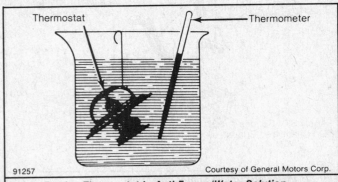

Fig. 1: *Testing Thermostat in Anti-Freeze/Water Solution*

PRESSURE TESTING

A pressure tester is used to check both radiator cap and complete cooling system. Follow pressure tester manufacturer's instructions and test components as follows:
Radiator Cap – Visually inspect radiator cap, then dip cap into water and connect to tester. Pump tester to bring pressure to upper limit of cap specification. *See Fig. 2.* If cap fails to hold pressure or releases at higher pressure than specification, replace cap.

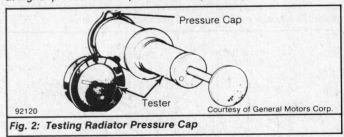

Fig. 2: *Testing Radiator Pressure Cap*

Cooling System – **1)** With engine off, clean radiator filler neck seat. Fill radiator to correct level. Attach tester to radiator and pump until pressure is at upper level of radiator rating.
2) If pressure drops, inspect for external leaks. If no leaks are apparent, detach tester and run engine until normal operating temperature is reached. Reattach tester and observe. If pressure builds up immediately, a possible leak exists from a faulty head gasket or crack in head or block.

NOTE: Pressure may build up quickly. Release excess pressure or cooling system damage may result.

3) If there is no immediate pressure build up, pump tester to within system pressure range (on radiator cap). Vibration of gauge pointer indicates compression or combustion leak into cooling system. Isolate leak by shorting each spark plug wire to cylinder block. Gauge pointer should stop or decrease vibration when leaking cylinder is shorted.

INSPECTION

Clean lubricant from internal parts, then rotate gears and inspect for wear or damage. Mount a dial indicator to housing and check backlash at several points around ring gear. Backlash must be within specifications at all points. If no defects are found, check gear tooth contact pattern.

GEAR TOOTH CONTACT PATTERN

NOTE: Drive pattern should be well centered on ring gear teeth. Coast pattern should be centered but may be slightly toward toe of ring gear teeth.

1) Paint ring gear teeth with a marking compound. Apply some form of load to differential case to resist rotation. Rotate pinion gear until ring gear has made one full revolution

2) Rotate pinion gear in opposite direction to complete one full revolution of ring gear. Examine ring gear teeth for contact pattern. Correct as necessary by moving appropriate shims. Backlash between drive gear and pinion must be maintained within specified limits until correct tooth pattern is obtained.

ADJUSTMENTS

GEAR BACKLASH & PINION SHIM CHANGES

NOTE: Change in tooth pattern is directly related to change in shim and/or backlash adjustment.

1) With no change in backlash, moving pinion further from ring gear moves drive pattern toward heel and top of tooth, and moves coast pattern toward toe and top of tooth.

2) With no change in backlash, moving pinion closer to ring gear moves drive pattern toward toe and bottom of tooth, and moves coast pattern toward heel and bottom of tooth.

3) With no change in pinion shim thickness, an increase in backlash moves ring gear further from pinion. Drive pattern moves toward heel and top of tooth, and coast pattern moves toward heel and top of tooth.

4) With no change in pinion shim thickness, a decrease in backlash moves ring gear closer to pinion gear. Drive pattern moves toward toe and bottom of tooth, and coast pattern moves toward toe and bottom of tooth.

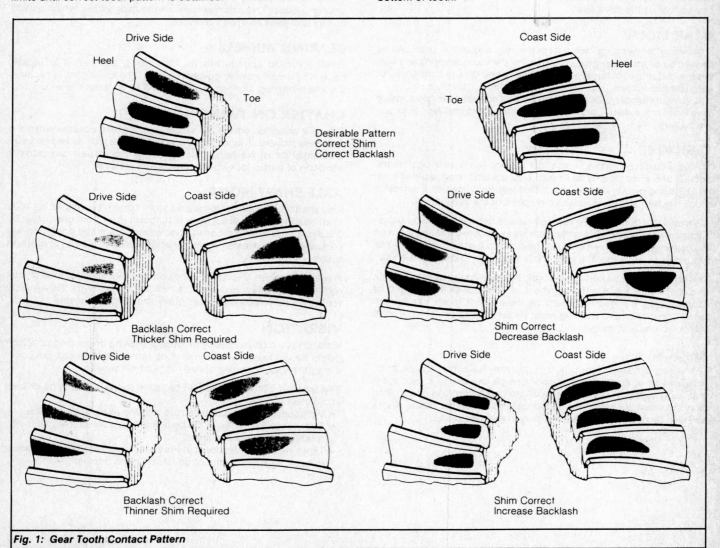

Fig. 1: Gear Tooth Contact Pattern

1993 GENERAL INFORMATION
Drive Axle Noise Diagnosis

UNRELATED NOISES

Some driveline trouble symptoms are also common to the engine, transmission, wheel bearings, tires, and other parts of the vehicle. Make sure that cause of trouble actually is in the drive axle before adjusting, repairing, or replacing any of its parts.

NON-DRIVE AXLE NOISES

A few conditions can sound just like drive axle noise and have to be considered in pre-diagnosis. The 4 most common noises are exhaust, tires, CV/universal joints and trim moldings.

In certain conditions, the pitch of the exhaust gases may sound like gear whine. At other times, it may be mistaken for a wheel bearing rumble.
Tires, especially radial and snow tires, can have a high-pitched tread whine or roar, similar to gear noise. Also, some non-standard tires with an unusual tread construction may emit a roar or whine.

Defective CV/universal joints may cause clicking noises or excessive driveline play that can be improperly diagnosed as drive axle problems.

Trim and moldings also can cause a whistling or whining noise. Ensure that none of these components are causing the noise before disassembling the drive axle.

GEAR NOISE

A "howling" or "whining" noise from the ring and pinion gear can be caused by an improper gear pattern, gear damage, or improper bearing preload. It can occur at various speeds and driving conditions, or it can be continuous.
Before disassembling axle to diagnose and correct gear noise, make sure that tires, exhaust, and vehicle trim have been checked as possible causes.

CHUCKLE

This is a particular rattling noise that sounds like a stick against the spokes of a spinning bicycle wheel. It occurs while decelerating from 40 MPH and usually can be heard until vehicle comes to a complete stop. The frequency varies with the speed of the vehicle.

A chuckle that occurs on the driving phase is usually caused by excessive clearance due to differential gear wear, or by a damaged tooth on the coast side of the pinion or ring gear. Even a very small tooth nick or a ridge on the edge of a gear tooth is enough to cause the noise.

This condition can be corrected simply by cleaning the gear tooth nick or ridge with a small grinding wheel. If either gear is damaged or scored badly, the gear set must be replaced. If metal has broken loose, the carrier and housing must be cleaned to remove particles that could cause damage.

KNOCK

This is very similar to a chuckle, though it may be louder, and occur on acceleration or deceleration. Knock can be caused by a gear tooth that is damaged on the drive side of the ring and pinion gears. Ring gear bolts that are hitting the carrier casting can cause knock. Knock can also be due to excessive end play in the axle shafts.

CLUNK

Clunk is a metallic noise heard when an automatic transmission is engaged in Reverse or Drive, or when throttle is applied or released. It is caused by backlash somewhere in the driveline, but not necessarily in the axle. To determine whether driveline clunk is caused by the axle, check the total axle backlash as follows:
1) Raise vehicle on a frame or twinpost hoist so that drive wheels are free. Clamp a bar between axle companion flange and a part of the frame or body so that flange cannot move.
2) On conventional drive axles, lock the left wheel to keep it from turning. On all models, turn the right wheel slowly until it is felt to be in drive condition. Hold a chalk marker on side of tire about 12" from center of wheel. Turn wheel in the opposite direction until it is again felt to be in drive condition.
3) Measure the length of the chalk mark, which is the total axle backlash. If backlash is one inch or less, clunk will not be eliminated by overhauling drive axle.

BEARING WHINE

Bearing whine is a high-pitched sound similar to a whistle. It is usually caused by malfunctioning pinion bearings. Pinion bearings operate at driveshaft speed. Roller wheel bearings may whine in a similar manner if they run completely dry of lubricant. Bearing noise will occur at all driving speeds. This distinguishes it from gear whine, which usually comes and goes as speed changes.

BEARING RUMBLE

Bearing rumble sounds like marbles being tumbled. It is usually caused by a malfunctioning wheel bearing. The lower pitch is because the wheel bearing turns at only about 1/3 of driveshaft speed.

CHATTER ON TURNS

This is a condition where the whole front or rear vibrates when the vehicle is moving. The vibration is plainly felt as well as heard. Extra differential thrust washers installed during axle repair can cause a condition of partial lock-up that creates this chatter.

AXLE SHAFT NOISE

Axle shaft noise is similar to gear noise and pinion bearing whine. Axle shaft bearing noise will normally distinguish itself from gear noise by occurring in all driving modes (drive, cruise, coast and float), and will persist with transmission in neutral while vehicle is moving at problem speed.

If vehicle displays this noise condition, remove suspect axle shafts, replace wheel seals and install a new set of bearings. Re-evaluate vehicle for noise before removing any internal components.

VIBRATION

Vibration is a high-frequency trembling, shaking or grinding condition (felt or heard) that may be constant or variable in level and can occur during the total operating speed range of the vehicle.

The types of vibrations that can be felt in the vehicle can be divided into 3 main groups:
• Vibrations of various unbalanced rotating parts of the vehicle.
• Resonance vibrations of the body and frame structures caused by rotating of unbalanced parts.
• Tip-in moans of resonance vibrations from stressed engine or exhaust system mounts or driveline flexing modes.

NOTE: Refer to appropriate Anti-Lock Brake System (ABS) article for description, operation, depressurizing, testing, system bleeding, trouble shooting and servicing of specific system. Failure to depressurize ABS could lead to physical injury.

- NEVER open a bleeder valve or loosen a hydraulic line while ABS is pressurized.

- NEVER disconnect or reconnect any electrical connectors while ignition is on. Damage to ABS control unit may result.

- DO NOT attempt to bleed hydraulic system without first referring to the appropriate article in your Mitchell service and repair manual.

- ONLY use specially designed brake hoses/lines on ABS equipped vehicles.

- DO NOT tap on speed sensor components (sensor, sensor rings). Speed rings must be pressed into hubs, NOT hammered into hubs. Striking these components can cause demagnetization or a loss of polarization, affecting the accuracy of the speed signal returning to the ABS control unit.

- DO NOT mix tire sizes. Increasing the width, as long as tires remain close to the original diameter, is acceptable. Rolling diameter must be identical for all 4 tires. Some manufacturers recommend tires of the same brand, style and type. Failure to follow this precaution may cause inaccurate wheel speed readings.

- DO NOT contaminate speed sensor components with grease. Only use recommended coating, when system calls for an anti-corrosion coating.

- When speed sensor components have been removed, ALWAYS check sensor-to-ring air gaps when applicable. These specifications can be found in each appropriate article.

- ONLY use recommended brake fluids. DO NOT use silicone brake fluids in an ABS equipped vehicle.

- When installing transmitting devices (CB's, telephones, etc.) on ABS equipped vehicles, DO NOT locate the antenna near the ABS control unit (or any control unit).

- Disconnect all on-board computers, when using electric welding equipment.

- DO NOT expose the ABS control unit to prolonged periods of high heat (185°F/85°C for 2 hours is generally considered a maximum limit).

1993 GENERAL INFORMATION
Wheel Alignment Theory & Operation

PRE-ALIGNMENT INSTRUCTIONS

Before adjusting wheel alignment, check the following:

- Ensure each axle uses tires of same construction and tread style, equal in tread wear and overall diameter. Using a dial indicator, verify that radial and axial runout of tires is not excessive. Inflation should be at manufacturer's specifications. *See Fig. 1.*
- Ensure steering linkage and suspension does not have excessive play. Check for wear in tie rod ends and ball joints. Springs must not be sagging. Check that control arm and strut rod bushings do not have excessive play.
- Vehicle must be on level floor with full fuel tank, no passenger load, spare tire in place and no load in trunk. Bounce front and rear end of vehicle several times. Confirm vehicle is at normal riding height.
- Ensure steering wheel is centered with wheels in straight ahead position. If required, shorten one tie rod adjusting sleeve and lengthen opposite sleeve (equal amount of turns). *See Fig. 2.*
- Ensure that wheel bearings have correct preload and that lug nuts are tightened to manufacturer's specifications. Adjust camber, caster and toe-in using this sequence. Follow instructions of the alignment equipment manufacturer.

CAUTION: DO NOT attempt to correct alignment by straightening parts. Damaged parts must be replaced.

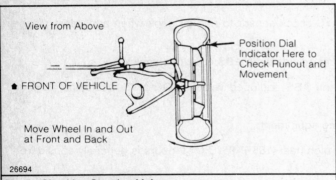

Fig. 1: Checking Steering Linkage

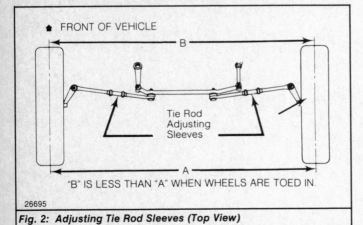

Fig. 2: Adjusting Tie Rod Sleeves (Top View)

CAMBER

1) Camber is the tilting of the wheel, outward at either top or bottom, as viewed from front of vehicle. *See Fig. 3.*

2) When wheels tilt outward at the top (from centerline of vehicle), camber is positive. When wheels tilt inward at top, camber is negative. Amount of tilt is measured in degrees from vertical.

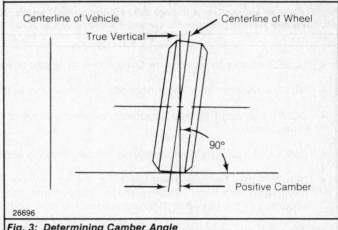

Fig. 3: Determining Camber Angle

CASTER

1) Caster is tilting of front steering axis either forward or backward from vertical, as viewed from side of vehicle. *See Fig. 4.*

2) When axis is tilted backward from vertical, caster is positive. This creates a trailing action on front wheels. When axis is tilted forward, caster is negative, causing a leading action on front wheels.

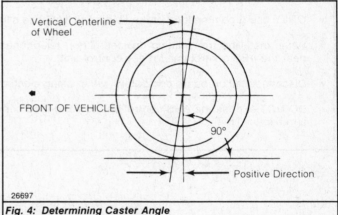

Fig. 4: Determining Caster Angle

TOE-IN ADJUSTMENT

Toe-in is the width measured at the rear of the tires subtracted by the width measured at the front of the tires at about spindle height. *See Fig. 5.* Toe-in specification is Dimension A less Dimension B. A positive figure would indicate toe-in and a negative figure would indicate toe-out. If the distance between the front and rear of the tires is the same, toe measurement would be zero. Use the following procedures to adjust toe-in:

1) Measure toe-in with front wheels in straight ahead position and steering wheel centered. To adjust toe-in, loosen clamps and turn adjusting sleeve or adjustable end on right and left tie rods. *See Figs. 2 and 5.*

2) Turn equally and in opposite directions to maintain steering wheel in centered position. Face of tie rod end must be parallel with machined surface of steering rod end to prevent binding.

3) When tightening clamps, make certain that clamp bolts are positioned so there will be no interference with other parts throughout the entire travel of the steering linkage.

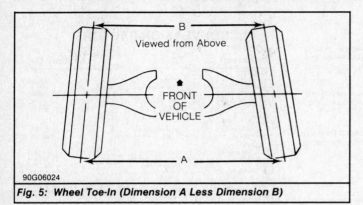

Fig. 5: Wheel Toe-In (Dimension A Less Dimension B)

TOE-OUT ON TURNS

1) Toe-out on turns (turning radius) is a check for bent or damaged parts, and not a service adjustment. With caster, camber, and toe-in properly adjusted, check toe-out with weight of vehicle on wheels.

2) Use a full floating turntable under each wheel, repeating test with each wheel positioned for right and left turns. Incorrect toe-out generally indicates a bent steering arm. Replace steering arm, if necessary, and recheck wheel alignment.

STEERING AXIS INCLINATION

1) Steering axis inclination is a check for bent or damaged parts, and not a service adjustment. Vehicle must be level and camber should be properly adjusted. *See Fig. 6.*

2) If camber cannot be brought within limits and steering axis inclination is correct, steering knuckle is bent. If camber and steering axis inclination are both incorrect by approximately the same amount, the upper and lower control arms are bent.

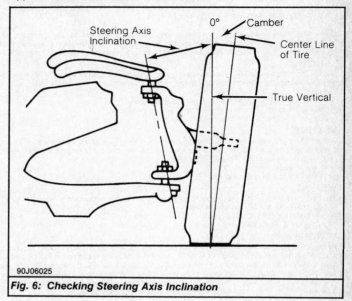

Fig. 6: Checking Steering Axis Inclination

1993 GENERAL INFORMATION
English-Metric Conversion Chart

METRIC CONVERSIONS

Metric conversions are making life more difficult for the mechanic. In addition to doubling the number of tools required, metric-dimensioned nuts and bolts are used alongside English components in many new vehicles. The mechanic has to decide which tool to use, slowing down the job. The tool problem can be solved by trial and error, but some metric conversions aren't so simple.

Converting temperature, lengths or volumes requires a calculator and conversion charts, or else a very nimble mind. Conversion charts are only part of the answer though, because they don't help you "think" metric, or "visualize" what you are converting. The following examples are intended to help you "see" metric sizes:

LENGTH

Meters are the standard unit of length in the metric system. The smaller units are 10ths (decimeter), 100ths (centimeter), and 1000ths (millimeter) of a meter. These common examples might help you to visualize the metric units:

- A meter is slightly longer than a yard (about 40 inches).
- An aspirin tablet is about one centimeter across (.4 inches).
- A millimeter is about the thickness of a dime.

VOLUME

Cubic meters and centimeters are used to measure volume, just as we normally think of cubic feet and inches. Liquid volume measurements include the liter and milliliter, like the English quarts or ounces.

- One teaspoon is about 4 cubic centimeters.
- A liter is about one quart.
- A liter is about 61 cubic inches.

WEIGHT

The metric weight system is based on the gram, with the most common unit being the kilogram (1000 grams). Our comparable units are ounces and pounds:

- A kilogram is about 2.2 pounds.
- An ounce is about 28 grams.

TORQUE

Torque is somewhat complicated. The term describes the amount of effort exerted to turn something. A chosen unit of weight or force is applied to a lever of standard length. The resulting leverage is called torque. In our standard system, we use the weight of one pound applied to a lever a foot long, resulting in the unit called a foot-pound. A smaller unit is the inch-pound (the lever is one inch long). Metric units include the meter kilogram (lever one meter long with a kilogram of weight applied) and the Newton-meter (lever one meter long with force of one Newton applied). Some conversions are:

- A meter kilogram is about 7.2 foot pounds.
- A foot pound is about 1.4 Newton-meters.
- A centimeter kilogram (cmkg) is equal to .9 inch pounds.

PRESSURE

Pressure is another complicated measurement. Pressure is described as a force or weight applied to a given area. Our common unit is pounds per square inch. Metric units can be expressed in several ways. One is the kilogram per square centimeter (kg/cm²). Another unit of pressure is the Pascal (force of one Newton on an area of one square meter), which equals about 4 ounces on a square yard. Since this is a very small amount of pressure, we usually see the kiloPascal, or kPa (1000 Pascals). Another common automotive term for pressure is the bar (used by German manufacturers), which equals 10 Pascals. Thoroughly confused? Try the examples below:

- Atmospheric pressure at sea level is about 14.7 psi.
- Atmospheric pressure at sea level is about 1 bar.
- Atmospheric pressure at sea level is about 1 kg/cm².
- One pound per square inch is about 7 kPa.

WE ENCOURAGE PROFESSIONALISM

THROUGH TECHNICIAN CERTIFICATION

CONVERSION FACTORS

To Convert	To	Multiply By
LENGTH		
Millimeters (mm)	Inches	.03937
Inches	Millimeters	25.4
Meters (M)	Feet	3.28084
Feet	Meters	.3048
Kilometers (Km)	Miles	.62137
AREA		
Square Centimeters (cm²)	Square Inches	.155
Square Inches	Square Centimeters	6.45159
VOLUME		
Cubic Centimeters	Cubic Inches	.06103
Cubic Inches	Cubic Centimeters	16.38703
Liters	Cubic Inches	61.025
Cubic Inches	Liters	.01639
Liters	Quarts	1.05672
Quarts	Liters	.94633
Liters	Pints	2.11344
Pints	Liters	.47317
Liters	Ounces	33.81497
Ounces	Liters	.02957
WEIGHT		
Grams	Ounces	.03527
Ounces	Grams	28.34953
Kilograms	Pounds	2.20462
Pounds	Kilograms	.45359
WORK		
Centimeter Kilograms	Inch Pounds	.8676
Pounds/Sq. Inch	Kilograms/Sq. Centimeter	.07031
Bar	Pounds/Sq. Inch	14.504
Pounds/Sq. Inch	Bar	.06895
Atmosphere	Pounds/Sq. Inch	14.696
Pounds/Sq. Inch	Atmosphere	.06805
TEMPERATURE		
Centigrade Degrees	Fahrenheit Degrees	$(C° \times \frac{9}{5}) + 32$
Fahrenheit Degrees	Centigrade Degrees	$(F° - 32) \times \frac{5}{9}$

Inches	Decimals	mm
1/64	.016	.397
1/32	.031	.794
3/64	.047	1.191
1/16	.063	1.588
5/64	.078	1.984
3/32	.094	2.381
7/64	.109	2.778
1/8	.125	3.175
9/64	.141	3.572
5/32	.156	3.969
11/64	.172	4.366
3/16	.188	4.763
13/64	.203	5.159
7/32	.219	5.556
15/64	.234	5.953
1/4	.250	6.350
17/64	.266	6.747
9/32	.281	7.144
19/64	.297	7.541
5/16	.313	7.938
21/64	.328	8.334
11/32	.344	8.731
23/64	.359	9.128
3/8	.375	9.525
25/64	.391	9.992
13/32	.406	10.319
27/64	.422	10.716
7/16	.438	11.113
29/64	.453	11.509
15/32	.469	11.906
31/64	.484	12.303
1/2	.500	12.700
33/64	.516	13.097
17/32	.531	13.494
35/64	.547	13.891
9/16	.563	14.288
37/64	.578	14.684
19/32	.594	15.081
39/64	.609	15.478
5/8	.625	15.875
41/64	.641	16.272
21/32	.656	16.669
43/64	.672	17.066
11/16	.687	17.463
45/64	.703	17.859
23/32	.719	18.256
47/64	.734	18.653
3/4	.750	19.050
49/64	.766	19.447
25/32	.781	19.844
51/64	.797	20.241
13/16	.813	20.638
53/64	.828	21.034
27/32	.844	21.431
55/64	.859	21.828
7/8	.875	22.225
57/64	.891	22.622
29/32	.906	23.019
59/64	.922	23.416
15/16	.938	23.813
61/64	.953	24.209
31/32	.969	24.606
63/64	.984	25.003
1	1.000	25.400

MITCHELL INTERNATIONAL
9889 Willow Creek Road
P.O. Box 26260
San Diego, CA 92196-0260

Contents

1993 ACURA CONTENTS

1993 MODEL COVERAGE

MODEL	BODY CODE	ENGINE	ENGINE ID	FUEL SYSTEM	IGNITION SYSTEM [1]
Integra	DB2	1.7L (B17A1)	[2]	PGM-FI	Magnetic
	[3]	1.8L (B18A1)	[2]	PGM-FI	Magnetic
Legend	[4]	3.2L (C32A1)	[2]	PGM-FI	DIS
Vigor	CC2	2.5L (G25A1)	[2]	PGM-FI	Magnetic

[1] – Timing is computer controlled.
[2] – Engine and body code are identified by the fourth, fifth and sixth characters of the VIN.
[3] – DA9-Hatchback; DB1-Sedan.
[4] – KA8-Coupe; KA7-Sedan.

VIN DEFINITION

JH4KA554XPC000001

① ② ③ ④ ⑤ ⑥ ⑦ ⑧ ⑨ ⑩ ⑪ ⑫ ⑬ ⑭ ⑮ ⑯ ⑰

① Indicates Nation of Origin.
② Indicates Manufacturer.
③ Indicates Model.
④ ⑤ ⑥ **Indicates Engine/Body Code.**
⑦ Indicates Body & Transmission Type.
⑧ Indicates Model Series.
⑨ Indicates Check Digit.
⑩ **Indicates Model Year.**
⑪ Indicates Assembly Plant.
⑫ ⑬ ⑭ ⑮ ⑯ ⑰ Indicates Production Sequence.

MODEL YEAR VIN CODE APPLICATION

VIN Code	Model Year
M	1991
N	1992
P	1993

ENGINE CODE LOCATION

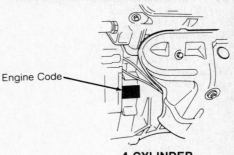

4-CYLINDER

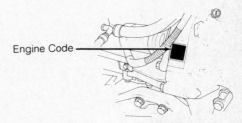

5-CYLINDER

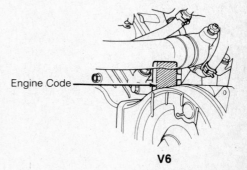

V6

92J26186

Courtesy of American Honda Motor Co., Inc.

1993 ENGINE PERFORMANCE
Emission Applications

1993 ACURA

Model, Engine & Fuel System	Emission Control Systems & Devices
Integra	
1.7L 4-Cyl. SFI	**PCV, EVAP, TWC, FR, SPK,**[1] **O**$_2$**, CEC, MIL,** EVAP-PCSV
1.8L 4-Cyl. SFI	**PCV, EVAP, TWC, FR,**[2] **EGR, SPK,**[1] **O**$_2$**, CEC, MIL,** [2] EGR-SOL, [2] EGR-PS, EVAP-PCSV
Legend	
3.2L V6 SFI	**PCV, EVAP, TWC, FR, EGR, SPK, PAIR,**[1] **O**$_2$**, CEC, MIL,** PAIR-ASVL, PAIR-ASCS, EGR-CVCV, EGR-SOL, EGR-PS, EVAP-PCSV
Vigor	
2.5L 5-Cyl. SFI	**PCV, EVAP, TWC, FR, EGR, SPK,**[1] **O**$_2$**, CEC, MIL,** EGR-CVCV, EGR-SOL, EGR-PS, EVAP-PCSV

[1] – Heated oxygen sensor.
[2] – Auto. trans. only.

NOTE: For quick reference, major emission control systems and devices are listed in bold type; components and other related devices are listed in light type.

CEC – Computerized Engine Controls
EGR – Exhaust Gas Recirculation
EGR-CVCV – EGR Constant Vacuum Control Valve
EGR-PS – EGR Position Sensor
EGR-SOL – EGR Solenoid
EVAP – Fuel Evaporative System
EVAP-PCSV – EVAP Purge Cut-Off Solenoid Valve
FR – Fill Pipe Restrictor
O$_2$ – Oxygen Sensor

MIL – Malfunction Indicator Light
PAIR – Pulsed Secondary Air Injection
PAIR-ASCS – Air Suction Control Solenoid
PAIR-ASVL – Air Suction Valve
PCV – Positive Crankcase Ventilation
SFI – Sequential Fuel Injection
SPK – Spark Controls
TWC – Three-Way Catalyst

Integra, Legend, Vigor

INTRODUCTION

Use this article to quickly find specifications related to servicing and on-vehicle adjustments. This is a quick-reference article to use when you are familiar with an adjustment procedure and only need a specification.

CAPACITIES

BATTERY SPECIFICATIONS

Application	Amp Hr. Rating
Integra	70
Legend	70 Or 80
Vigor	55, 70 Or 80

FLUID CAPACITIES

Application	Quantity
Auto. Transaxle (Dexron-II)	
Integra	
Fluid Change	3.2 Qts. (3.0L)
Overhaul	6.7 Qts. (6.3L)
Legend	
Fluid Change	3.5 Qts. (3.3L)
Overhaul	9.2 Qts. (8.7L)
Vigor	
Fluid Change	2.6 Qts. (2.5L)
Overhaul	7.6 Qts. (7.2L)
Cooling System (Includes Heater)	
Integra	5.3 Qts. (5.0L)
Legend	8.0 Qts. (7.5L)
Vigor	6.3 Qts. (6.0L)
Crankcase (Includes Filter)	
Integra	
1.7L	4.2 Qts. (4.0L)
1.8L	4.0 Qts. (3.8L)
Legend	5.0 Qts. (4.7L)
Vigor	4.5 Qts. (4.3L)
Differential (SAE 90 GL4 or 5)	[1] 1.1 Qts. (1.0L)
Man. Transaxle (SAE 10W-40 API SE or SF)	
Integra	2.3 Qts. (2.2L)
Legend	2.4 Qts. (2.3L)
Vigor	1.9 Qts. (1.8L)

[1] – Except Integra, which has an integral transaxle/differential.

QUICK-SERVICE

SERVICE INTERVALS & SPECIFICATIONS

REPLACEMENT INTERVALS

Component	Miles
Air Filter	30,000
Anti-Lock Brake System High Pressure Hose	60,000
Automatic Transmission Fluid	30,000
Brake Fluid	30,000
Cam Timing Belt	90,000
Coolant	45,000
Differential	30,000
Engine Oil & Filter	7500
Fuel Filter	60,000
Manual Transmission Oil	30,000
Spark Plugs	
Integra (Except GSR) & Vigor	30,000
Integra GSR & Legend	60,000

BELT ADJUSTMENT

Application	[1] Deflection – In. (mm)
A/C Compressor	
Integra	9/32-11/32 (7-9)
Legend	5/16-13/32 (8-10.5)
Vigor	1/4-11/32 (6-9)
Alternator	
Integra	9/32-13/32 (7-10.5)
Legend	3/8-29/64 (9.5-11.5)
Vigor	19/64-3/8 (7.5-9.5)
Power Steering	
Integra	3/8-29/64 (9.5-11.5)
Legend	29/64-17/32 (11.5-13.5)
Vigor	1/4-11/32 (6.5-9)

[1] – Deflection is with 22 lbs. (10 kg) pressure applied midway on longest belt run.

MECHANICAL CHECKS

ENGINE COMPRESSION

ENGINE COMPRESSION [1]

Application	Specification
Integra	
Compression Ratio	
GSR	9.7:1
Except GSR	9.2:1
Compression Pressure at 250 RPM	
Standard	185 psi (13.0 kg/cm²)
Minimum	135 psi (9.5 kg/cm²)
Legend	
Compression Ratio	9.6:1
Compression Pressure at 200 RPM	
Standard	192 psi (13.5 kg/cm²)
Minimum	142 psi (10.0 kg/cm²)
Vigor	
Compression Ratio	9.0:1
Compression Pressure at 250 RPM	
Standard	206 psi (14.5 kg/cm²)
Minimum	135 psi (9.5 kg/cm²)

[1] – Maximum variation between cylinders is 28 psi (2 kg/cm²).

VALVE CLEARANCE

NOTE: Legend models are equipped with hydraulic lifters. No adjustments are required.

VALVE CLEARANCE ADJUSTMENT [1]

Application	In. (mm)
Integra	
1.7L	
Intake	.006-.007 (.15-.18)
Exhaust	.007-.008 (.18-.20)
1.8L	
Intake	.003-.005 (.08-.13)
Exhaust	.006-.008 (.15-.20)
Vigor	
Intake	.009-.011 (.24-.28)
Exhaust	.011-.013 (.28-.32)

[1] – Adjust valves when engine is cold.

IGNITION SYSTEM

IGNITION COIL

IGNITION COIL RESISTANCE – Ohms @ 77°F (25°C)

Application	Primary	Secondary
Integra	.6-.8	12,800-19,200
Legend	.9-1.1	[1]
Vigor	.03-.05	10,800-16,200

[1] – Information is not available from manufacturer.

1993 ENGINE PERFORMANCE
Service & Adjustment Specifications (Cont.)

DISTRIBUTOR SENSORS
DISTRIBUTOR SENSOR RESISTANCE

Application	Ohms
Integra	
CRANK Sensor	350-700
CYL Sensor	350-700
TDC Sensor	350-700
Legend	
CRANK Sensor	650-900
CYL Sensor	650-900
Vigor	
CRANK Sensor	650-850
CYL Sensor	650-850
TDC Sensor	650-850

HIGH TENSION WIRE RESISTANCE
HIGH TENSION WIRE RESISTANCE

Application	Ohms
All Models	25,000 Maximum

SPARK PLUGS
SPARK PLUG TYPE

Application	NGK	Nippondenso
Integra		
Normal Driving	ZFR5F-11	KJ16CR-L11
Hot Climates [1]	ZRF6F-11	KJ20CR-L11
Legend		
Normal Driving	PFR6G-11	PK20PR-L11
Hot Climates [1]	PFR7G-11	PK22PR-L11
Cold Climates	PFR5G-11	PK16PR-L11
Vigor		
Normal Driving	BKR5E-N11	K16PR-L11
Hot Climates [1]	BKR6E-N11	K20PR-L11

[1] – Also for continuous high-speed driving.

SPARK PLUG SPECIFICATIONS

Application	Gap In. (mm)	Torque Ft. Lbs. (N.m)
All Models	.043 (1.1)	13 (18)

FIRING ORDER & TIMING MARKS

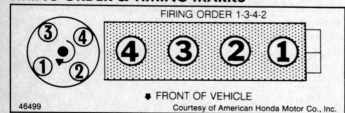

FIRING ORDER 1-3-4-2

▲ FRONT OF VEHICLE

46499   Courtesy of American Honda Motor Co., Inc.

Fig. 1: Firing Order & Distributor Rotation (Integra)

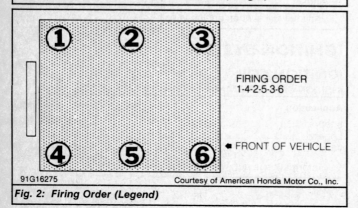

FIRING ORDER 1-4-2-5-3-6

◄ FRONT OF VEHICLE

91G16275   Courtesy of American Honda Motor Co., Inc.

Fig. 2: Firing Order (Legend)

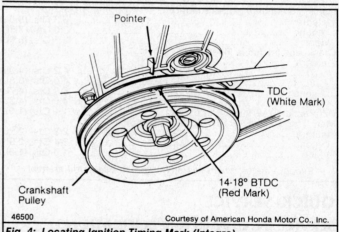

◄ FRONT OF ENGINE

FIRING ORDER 1-2-4-5-3   WIRE-TO-CAP ORDER 1-2-3-C-5-4

92G26183   Courtesy of American Honda Motor Co., Inc.

Fig. 3: Firing Order & Distributor Rotation (Vigor)

IGNITION TIMING
IGNITION TIMING (Degrees BTDC @ RPM)

Application	[1] Man. Trans.	[2] Auto. Trans.
Integra		
1.7L	14-18 @ 750-850	14-18 @ 750-850
1.8L	14-18 @ 700-800	14-18 @ 700-800
Legend		
Coupe	13-17 @ 630-730	13-17 @ 580-680
Sedan	13-17 @ 600-700	13-17 @ 550-650
Vigor	13-17 @ 650-750	13-17 @ 650-750

[1] – Manual transmission in Neutral.

[2] – Automatic transmission in Neutral or Park.

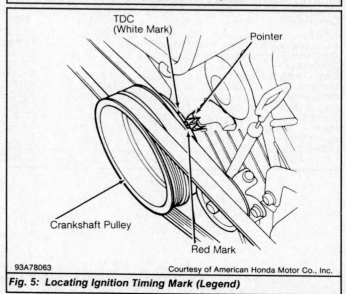

Pointer

TDC (White Mark)

14-18° BTDC (Red Mark)

Crankshaft Pulley

46500   Courtesy of American Honda Motor Co., Inc.

Fig. 4: Locating Ignition Timing Mark (Integra)

TDC (White Mark)

Pointer

Crankshaft Pulley

Red Mark

93A78063   Courtesy of American Honda Motor Co., Inc.

Fig. 5: Locating Ignition Timing Mark (Legend)

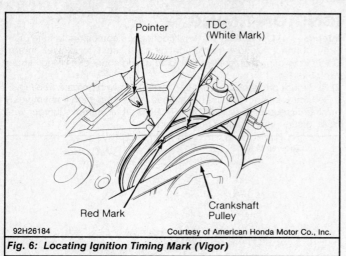

Pointer   TDC (White Mark)

Red Mark   Crankshaft Pulley

92H26184   Courtesy of American Honda Motor Co., Inc.

Fig. 6: Locating Ignition Timing Mark (Vigor)

FUEL SYSTEM

FUEL PUMP

NOTE: *Fuel pump performance is a measurement of fuel pressure and volume availability, not regulated fuel pressure.*

FUEL PUMP PERFORMANCE

Application	Pressure psi (kg/cm²)	Min. Vol. In 10 Sec. Pts. (L)
Integra		
1.7L	[1] 40 (2.8)	.44 (.21)
1.8L	[1] 35 (2.5)	.48 (.23)
Legend		
Coupe	[1] 40 (2.8)	.63 (.30)
Sedan	[1] 33 (2.3)	.48 (.23)
Vigor	[1] 35 (2.5)	.48 (.23)

[1] – Approximate. See REGULATED FUEL PRESSURE table.

REGULATED FUEL PRESSURE

Application	At Idle W/O Vacuum psi (kg/cm²)	At Idle W/ Vacuum psi (kg/cm²)
Integra		
1.7L	48-56 (3.4-3.9)	39-46 (2.8-3.3)
1.8L	41-48 (2.9-3.4)	33-39 (2.3-2.8)
Legend		
Coupe	44-51 (3.1-3.6)	36-43 (2.5-3.0)
Sedan	35-41 (2.5-2.9)	29-35 (2.1-2.4)
Vigor	43-50 (3.0-3.5)	33-41 (2.3-2.9)

INJECTOR RESISTANCE

INJECTOR RESISTANCE SPECIFICATIONS

Application	Ohms
Integra	10-13
Legend & Vigor	1.5-2.5

IDLE SPEED & MIXTURE

IDLE SPEED SPECIFICATIONS

Application	RPM
Integra	
1.7L	[1] 750-850
1.8L	[1] 700-800
Legend	
Coupe	
Automatic Trans.	[1] 580-680
Manual Trans.	630-730
Sedan	
Automatic Trans.	[1] 550-650
Manual Trans.	600-700
Vigor	[1] 650-750

[1] – Automatic transmission in Neutral or Park.

IDLE CO LEVEL

Application	CO Level
All Models	0.1%

FAST IDLE SPEED

FAST IDLE SPEED SPECIFICATIONS

Application	RPM
Integra	1000-2000
Legend	1300-1700
Vigor	1400

THROTTLE ANGLE SENSOR

NOTE: **Throttle angle sensor is not adjustable. For testing procedures, refer to SELF-DIAGNOSTICS or SYSTEM & COMPONENT TESTING article.**

1993 ENGINE PERFORMANCE
On-Vehicle Adjustments

Integra, Legend, Vigor
ENGINE MECHANICAL

Before performing any on-vehicle adjustments to fuel or ignition system, ensure engine mechanical condition is okay.

VALVE CLEARANCE

NOTE: Legend is equipped with hydraulic lifters. Adjustments are not required.

Integra – 1) Cylinder head temperature must be less than 100°F (38°C). Remove valve cover, timing belt covers and distributor cap.
2) Align pointer on timing belt lower cover with TDC (White mark). UP marks on both camshaft sprockets should be at top of cam gears. Distributor rotor should point to No. 1 spark plug wire on cap. Adjust valves on cylinder No. 1.
3) Rotate crankshaft counterclockwise 180 degrees to bring No. 3 piston to TDC on compression stroke. Adjust valves on cylinder No. 3.
4) Rotate crankshaft counterclockwise 180 degrees to bring No. 4 piston to TDC on compression stroke. Adjust valves on cylinder No. 4.
5) Rotate crankshaft counterclockwise 180 degrees to bring No. 2 piston to TDC on compression stroke. Adjust valves on cylinder No. 2.

VALVE CLEARANCE ADJUSTMENT (INTEGRA)

Application [1]	In. (mm)
1.7L	
Intake	.0059-.0075 (.150-.190)
Exhaust	.0067-.0083 (.170-.210)
1.8L	
Intake	.0031-.0047 (.080-.120)
Exhaust	.0063-.0079 (.160-.200)

[1] – Adjust valves when engine is cold.

Vigor – 1) Engine temperature must be less than 100°F (38°C). Remove cylinder head cover. Align No. 1 mark on camshaft sprocket with mark on cam holder. See Fig. 1.
2) Loosen adjustment screw lock nut. Adjust valves on cylinder No. 1. Tighten lock nut. Recheck clearance. Repeat procedure if clearance changes.
3) Rotate crankshaft 144 degrees. Align No. 2 mark on camshaft sprocket with mark on cam holder. Repeat adjustment procedure on cylinder No. 2. Tighten lock nut. Recheck clearance. Repeat procedure on cylinders No. 4, 5 and 3 in this order.

VALVE CLEARANCE ADJUSTMENT (VIGOR)

Application [1]	In. (mm)
Intake	.009-.011 (.24-.28)
Exhaust	.011-.013 (.28-.32)

[1] – Adjust valves when engine is cold.

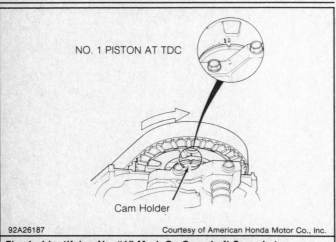
NO. 1 PISTON AT TDC

Cam Holder

92A26187   Courtesy of American Honda Motor Co., Inc.

Fig. 1: Identifying No. "1" Mark On Camshaft Sprocket (Vigor – No. "2" Through "5" Marks Are Similar)

IGNITION TIMING

Integra – 1) Operate engine until cooling fan comes on. Locate Light Gray connector under right side of dash, next to blower motor. Connect terminals of ignition timing adjusting connector using jumper wire. See Fig. 2.
2) Red mark on crankshaft pulley should align with pointer. See Fig. 3. If Red mark and pointer are not aligned, adjust base ignition timing by turning distributor. See IGNITION TIMING table. Remove jumper wire from ignition timing adjusting connector.

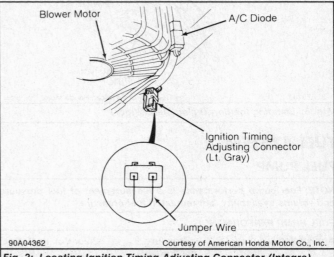
Blower Motor

A/C Diode

Ignition Timing
Adjusting Connector
(Lt. Gray)

Jumper Wire

90A04362   Courtesy of American Honda Motor Co., Inc.

Fig. 2: Locating Ignition Timing Adjusting Connector (Integra)

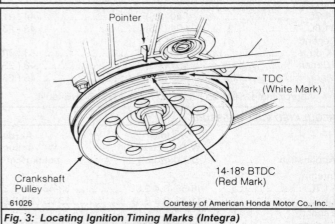
Pointer

TDC
(White Mark)

14-18° BTDC
(Red Mark)

Crankshaft
Pulley

61026   Courtesy of American Honda Motor Co., Inc.

Fig. 3: Locating Ignition Timing Marks (Integra)

IGNITION TIMING (Degrees BTDC @ RPM)

Application	[1] M/T	[2] A/T
Integra		
1.7L	14-18 @ 750-850	14-18 @ 750-850
1.8L	14-18 @ 700-800	14-18 @ 700-800
Legend		
Coupe	13-17 @ 630-730	13-17 @ 580-680
Sedan	13-17 @ 600-700	13-17 @ 550-650
Vigor	13-17 @ 650-750	13-17 @ 650-750

[1] – Manual transmission in Neutral.
[2] – Automatic transmission in Neutral or Park.

Legend & Vigor – 1) Operate engine until cooling fan comes on. Locate ignition timing adjusting connector under right side of dash. Connect terminals of connector using a jumper wire. See Fig. 4.
2) Connect timing light. With engine at idle, Red mark on crankshaft pulley should align with pointer. See Fig. 5. If Red mark and pointer are not aligned, adjust timing. See IGNITION TIMING table.

3) Adjust ignition timing by turning adjusting screw on ignition timing adjuster. *See Fig. 6*. Remove control box cover. Using a 3/16" drill bit, drill out 2 rivets from adjuster. Remove cover.

4) Turn adjusting screw counterclockwise to retard timing or clockwise to advance timing. After adjustment, install cover to ignition timing adjuster using new rivets. Remove jumper wire from ignition timing adjusting connector.

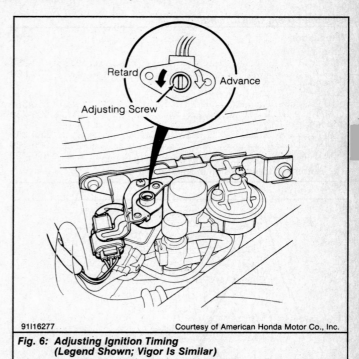

Fig. 6: Adjusting Ignition Timing
(Legend Shown; Vigor Is Similar)

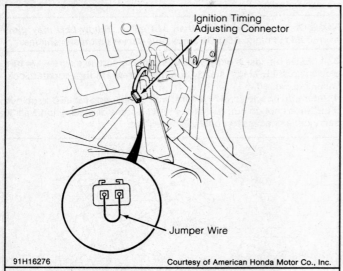

Fig. 4: Locating Ignition Timing Adjusting Connector
(Legend Shown; Vigor Is Similar)

hood fuse box for 10 seconds to reset ECU. Start engine and allow to idle for one minute. Check idle speed. Idle speed should be as specified. See IDLE SPEED SPECIFICATIONS table.

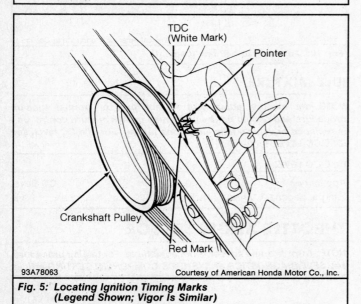

Fig. 5: Locating Ignition Timing Marks
(Legend Shown; Vigor Is Similar)

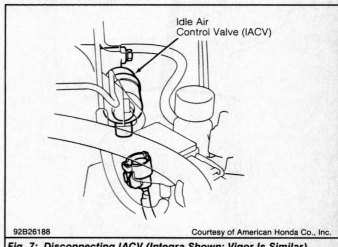

Fig. 7: Disconnecting IACV (Integra Shown; Vigor Is Similar)

IDLE SPEED & MIXTURE

IDLE SPEED

Integra & Vigor – 1) Operate engine until cooling fan comes on. Turn engine off. Connect tachometer. Disconnect 2-wire connector from Idle Air Control Valve (IACV). *See Fig. 7*.

2) Restart engine and hold at 1000 RPM momentarily. Let engine return to idle. Check base idle speed with M/T in Neutral (A/T in "N" or "P") and all accessories, including cooling fan, off. Base idle speed should be 550-650 RPM for Integra and 500-600 RPM for Vigor. If necessary, turn screw to adjust base idle speed. *See Fig. 8*.

3) Turn ignition off. Reconnect 2-wire IACV connector. Remove BACK-UP fuse (7.5-amp on Integra; 10-amp on Vigor) in main under-

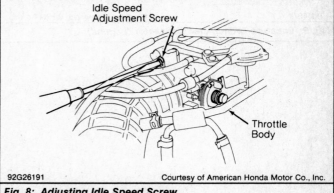

Fig. 8: Adjusting Idle Speed Screw
(Integra Shown; Vigor Is Similar)

IDLE SPEED SPECIFICATIONS

Application	RPM
Integra	
1.7L	[1] 750-850
1.8L	[1] 700-800
Legend	
Coupe	
A/T	[1] 580-680
M/T	630-730
Sedan	
A/T	[1] 550-650
M/T	600-700
Vigor	[1] 650-750

[1] – Automatic transmission in Neutral or Park.

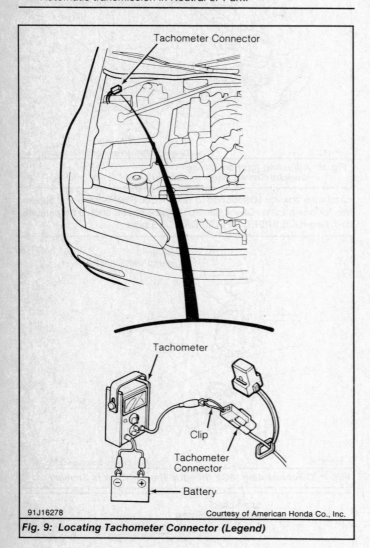

Fig. 9: Locating Tachometer Connector (Legend)

91J16278   Courtesy of American Honda Co., Inc.

Legend – 1) Operate engine until cooling fan comes on. Connect tachometer. *See Fig. 9.* Check base idle speed with M/T in Neutral (A/T in "N" or "P") and all accessories, including cooling fan, off. Base idle speed should be as specified. See IDLE SPEED SPECIFICATIONS table.

2) Connect jumper wire at ignition timing adjusting connector. *See Fig. 4.* Check Yellow LED on ECM (M/T) or PCM (A/T), located under passenger seat.

NOTE: On engines with less than 310 miles, Yellow LED may glow even if idle is okay. DO NOT adjust idle screw on these vehicles.

3) If LED is off, idle is okay. If LED is blinking, turn idle screw 1/4 turn clockwise. If LED is on steady, turn idle screw 1/4 turn counterclockwise. *See Fig. 10.*

4) After turning idle screw 1/4 turn, wait 30 seconds for LED to go out. If LED does not go out, repeat 1/4 turn (in same direction) and wait 30 seconds, as necessary, until LED goes out.

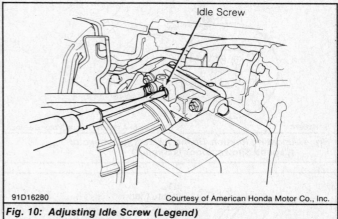

91D16280   Courtesy of American Honda Motor Co., Inc.

Fig. 10: Adjusting Idle Screw (Legend)

IDLE MIXTURE

NOTE: Idle mixture adjustment is not part of normal tune-up procedure and should not be performed unless mixture control unit is replaced or vehicle fails emissions testing. For idle CO level, see IDLE CO LEVEL table.

IDLE CO LEVEL

Application	CO Level
Integra, Legend & Vigor	0.1%

THROTTLE ANGLE SENSOR

NOTE: Throttle angle sensor is not adjustable. For testing procedure, see SELF-DIAGNOSTICS or SYSTEM & COMPONENT TESTING article.

Integra, Legend, Vigor
INTRODUCTION

This article covers basic description and operation of engine performance-related systems and components. Read this article before diagnosing vehicles or systems with which you are not completely familiar.

AIR INDUCTION SYSTEM

BY-PASS CONTROL SYSTEM (LEGEND)

Intake manifold has 3 air intake paths: short, medium and long. Increased engine torque over a broad range is achieved by switching paths. High torque at less than 3300 RPM is achieved by using a single long intake path. High torque at higher RPM is achieved by using both medium and long intake paths. Maximum horsepower is achieved by using all 3 intake paths.

By-Pass Low & High Control Solenoid Valves – When engine RPM is less than 3300 RPM, signal from PCM activates by-pass low and high control solenoid valves to prevent opening of additional intake paths. Intake air goes through the single long intake path. When engine speed is 3300-4000 RPM, by-pass low solenoid valve is shut off, allowing intake air to go through both long and medium intake paths. At engine speeds greater than 4000 RPM, PCM switches off both solenoid valves and intake air goes through all intake paths.

BY-PASS CONTROL SYSTEM (VIGOR)

Intake manifold has 2 air intake paths: long and short. Increased engine torque over a broad range is achieved by switching paths. High torque at low RPM is achieved by using the long intake path only. High torque at higher RPM is achieved by using both intake paths.

By-Pass Control Solenoid Valve – When engine RPM is less than 4900 RPM, signal from PCM activates by-pass control solenoid valve and intake air goes through long intake path. When engine speed is more than 4900 RPM, by-pass solenoid valve is shut off and intake air goes through both intake paths.

VARIABLE VALVE TIMING

VARIABLE VALVE TIMING & LIFT ELECTRONIC CONTROL SYSTEM (VTEC)

Integra 1.7L – VTEC uses 3 different intake cam lobes and rocker arms, synchronizer pistons, and a spool valve. See Fig. 1. Low lift cam lobes operate primary and secondary (outer) rocker arms. High lift cam lobe operates connecting (middle) rocker arm. PCM controls spool valve and synchronizer pistons.

At low speed, primary and secondary rocker arms control intake valve timing, lift and duration. Connecting rocker arm remains disengaged and has no effect on engine operation. At high RPM with heavy engine load, PCM activates spool valve and oil pressure is applied to synchronizer pistons located in primary and secondary rocker arms. This locks primary, connecting and secondary rocker arms together so they are driven as a single unit by high lift cam lobe.

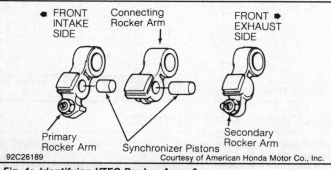

FRONT INTAKE SIDE   Connecting Rocker Arm   FRONT EXHAUST SIDE

Primary Rocker Arm   Synchronizer Pistons   Secondary Rocker Arm

92C26189   Courtesy of American Honda Motor Co., Inc.

Fig. 1: Identifying VTEC Rocker Arms & Synchronizer Piston Assembly (Integra 1.7L)

COMPUTERIZED ENGINE CONTROLS

POWERTRAIN CONTROL MODULE (PCM)

PCM contains memories for fuel injection timing and duration, idle speed control, ignition timing control, PCM back-up functions, and other control functions. The PCM is located under the carpet, in passenger-side footwell.

NOTE: Components are grouped into 2 categories. The first category is INPUT DEVICES, which are components that control or produce voltage signals monitored by the PCM. The second category is OUTPUT SIGNALS, which are components controlled by the PCM.

INPUT DEVICES

Vehicles are equipped with different combinations of input devices. Not all devices are used on all models. To determine the input device usage on a specific model, see WIRING DIAGRAMS article. The available input signals are:

A/C Switch Signal – Signals PCM when A/C is turned on. PCM uses this input to change engine RPM to compensate for extra engine load.

A/T Shift Position Signal – Informs PCM when automatic transmission is in Neutral or Park.

Alternator FR Signal – Sends signals to inform PCM that alternator is charging.

Barometric Pressure Sensor – Converts atmospheric pressure into electrical signals. Barometric pressure sensor is inside PCM.

Battery Voltage (IGN 1) – When ignition switch is ON position, a battery voltage signal (ignition circuit) is sent to PCM.

Brake Switch Signal – Signals PCM that brake pedal has been depressed. PCM uses this input signal to control idle speed.

Coolant Temperature Sensor – Coolant temperature sensor is a thermistor. The resistance of thermistor decreases as coolant temperature increases. PCM uses input to determine air/fuel mixture, timing and idle speed.

Clutch Switch – Signals PCM that clutch is engaged.

Crank Sensor – See IGNITION TIMING CONTROL under IGNITION SYSTEM.

Cylinder (CYL) Sensor – See IGNITION TIMING CONTROL under IGNITION SYSTEM.

EGR Position Sensor – See EGR POSITION SENSOR under EMISSION SYSTEMS.

Heated Oxygen Sensor (HO2S) – Detects oxygen content in exhaust gas and sends this information to PCM. PCM uses input from sensor to vary duration of fuel injection. Legend has 2 HO2S sensors. See OXYGEN SENSOR HEATER under EMISSION SYSTEMS.

Intake Air Temperature (TA) Sensor – TA sensor is a thermistor. Resistance of thermistor decreases as intake air temperature increases. PCM uses input from sensor to determine air/fuel mixture.

Ignition Output – Detects ignition signal. PCM will set a trouble code if PCM does not receive an ignition signal.

Knock Sensor(s) – If knock sensor detects detonation, ignition timing is retarded.

MAP Sensor – Converts manifold absolute pressure into electrical signals and sends this information to PCM. PCM uses input to determine air/fuel mixture.

Power Steering Pressure Signal – Signals PCM of high power steering load. PCM increases idle speed through Idle Air Control Valve (IACV).

Starter Signal – Signals PCM of engine start-up (cranking). PCM uses this to control IACV to promote easy starting.

TDC Sensor – See IGNITION TIMING CONTROL under IGNITION SYSTEM.

Throttle Position Sensor – Throttle position sensor is a potentiometer connected to throttle valve shaft. As throttle opening changes, sensor varies voltage signal to PCM. PCM uses signal to determine fuel injection duration.

Vehicle Speed Sensor (VSS) – Sensor monitors vehicle speed and generates signal to PCM. Signal produces 4 pulses (switch closures to ground) per revolution of speedometer cable. PCM uses input from sensor to determine timing and fuel injection.

Variable Valve Timing & Lift Electronic Control System (VTEC) Pressure Switch Signal – Signals PCM to indicate oil pressure in VTEC. PCM uses information to determine activation of VTEC synchronizer pistons through solenoid. If failure occurs, PCM will set a trouble code.

OUTPUT SIGNALS

Vehicles are equipped with different combinations of computer-controlled components. Not all components listed below are used on every vehicle. For theory and operation of each output component, refer to indicated system.

A/C Compressor Clutch Relay Signal – See IDLE SPEED under FUEL SYSTEM.

By-Pass Control Solenoid Valve(s) – See appropriate BY-PASS CONTROL SYSTEM under AIR INDUCTION SYSTEM.

Malfunction Indicator Light (MIL) – See SELF-DIAGNOSTIC SYSTEM.

EGR Control Solenoid – See EMISSION SYSTEMS.

EVAP Purge Cut-Off Solenoid Valve – See EMISSION SYSTEMS.

Fuel Injectors – See FUEL CONTROL under FUEL SYSTEM.

Fuel Pressure Regulator Cut-Off Solenoid Valve – See FUEL DELIVERY under FUEL SYSTEM.

Fuel Pump Main Relay – See FUEL DELIVERY under FUEL SYSTEM.

Idle Air Control Valve – See IDLE SPEED under FUEL SYSTEM.

Ignitor Unit – See IGNITION SYSTEM.

Oxygen Sensor Heater – See EMISSION SYSTEMS.

PAIR Air Suction Control Solenoid Valve – See EMISSION SYSTEMS.

FUEL SYSTEM

FUEL DELIVERY

Fuel Pump – Fuel pump is located inside fuel tank. When engine is started, main relay operates fuel pump. The pump has a relief valve to prevent excess pressure build-up. If discharge side is blocked, relief valve opens to by-pass fuel from discharge side to inlet side. When engine is turned off, the pump stops. A check valve in the fuel pump maintains fuel pressure in fuel line.

Fuel Pump Main Relay – Main relay is located on left side of firewall. Main relay contains 2 individual relays. First relay operates with ignition on and supplies battery voltage to PCM, injectors and second relay (fuel pump power). PCM controls second relay for 2 seconds after ignition is turned on and whenever engine is running.

Fuel Pressure Regulator – Fuel pressure regulator maintains constant fuel pressure to injectors. When the difference between fuel pressure and manifold pressure exceeds 36-50 psi (2.6-3.5 kg/cm²), the diaphragm is pushed upward and excess fuel is fed back into fuel tank. A vacuum-operated diaphragm inside regulator maintains fuel pressure at a specific range, allowing for changes in engine load.

At idle, intake manifold vacuum is high, causing diaphragm to be pulled up, thus reducing fuel pressure. When throttle is depressed, intake manifold vacuum decreases and regulator spring overcomes manifold vacuum. This causes fuel pressure to increase.

Fuel Pressure Regulator Cut-Off Solenoid Valve – When coolant temperature exceeds 221°F (105°C) or intake air temperature exceeds 176°F (80°C), pressure regulator cut-off solenoid valve cuts vacuum to pressure regulator. This ensures high fuel pressure to injectors and prevents vapor lock.

Injector Resistor – Resistor reduces current supplied to injectors to prevent damage to injector coils.

FUEL CONTROL

Fuel Injectors – When current is applied to solenoid coil, valve lifts up and pressurized fuel is injected close to intake valve. PCM controls injector timing and length of time injector is opened. Injector is sealed by an "O" ring and a seal ring at each injector end (top and bottom).

Fuel Cut-Off – During deceleration, with the throttle valve closed and engine speed more than 1000 RPM, current to the fuel injectors is stopped. Current is also stopped when engine speed exceeds 8100 RPM on 1.7L, 7000 RPM on 1.8L, 7100 RPM on 2.5L and 6500 RPM on 3.2L.

Throttle Body – The throttle body is a single-barrel side-draft type. The lower portion of the throttle valve is heated by engine coolant. The idle adjusting screw (preset at factory) increases or decreases by-pass air. Canister/purge port is located on top of throttle body.

IDLE SPEED

NOTE: *For other input components in idle speed circuit, see INPUT DEVICES under COMPUTERIZED ENGINE CONTROLS.*

Idle speed is controlled by Idle Air Control Valve (IACV) and fast idle control valve. IACV varies amount of air by-passing into intake manifold according to input signals received from PCM. When IACV is activated, valve operates to maintain proper idle speed. On Integra, a dashpot slows the closing of throttle valve during gear shifting (M/T) and deceleration.

A/C Compressor Clutch Relay – Relay signals PCM when A/C circuit is operating. PCM then sends signal to IACV to maintain proper idle speed.

Air Boost Valve (Integra 1.8L A/T & Legend) – Additional air enters intake manifold during engine cranking, helping engine start easier.

Electronic Idle Air Control Valve (IACV) – To maintain proper idle speed, IACV varies amount of air by-passing throttle body according to signals received from PCM.

Fast Idle Control Valve – Thermowax plunger controls valve. When engine is cold, thermowax contracts plunger, allowing additional air to be by-passed into intake manifold and increase engine speed. Valve closes when engine reaches operating temperature.

Power Steering Pressure Switch – Switch signals PCM to increase engine idle speed when power steering load is high.

IGNITION SYSTEM

IGNITOR UNIT

Battery voltage is supplied through ignition switch to ignition coil(s) and ignitor unit. The PGM-FI control unit uses input signals from TDC/crank (or crank/CYL) sensor, throttle position sensor, coolant sensor and MAP sensor to directly activate the ignitor. When activated, ignitor triggers ignition coil(s). On Integra and Vigor, induced voltage from ignition coil is then distributed to each spark plug by the distributor.

DIRECT IGNITION SYSTEM (DIS)

Battery voltage is supplied through ignition switch to PCM (ECU), ignitor unit, ignition coils and spark plugs. *See Fig. 2.* PCM triggers ignitor unit based upon signals from CRANK/CYL and other sensors. Each spark plug is fired directly by one of 6 coils. Ignitor controls each coil.

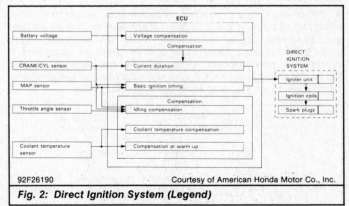

92F26190   Courtesy of American Honda Motor Co., Inc.

Fig. 2: Direct Ignition System (Legend)

IGNITION TIMING CONTROL

NOTE: *For other inputs, see INPUT DEVICES under COMPUTERIZED ENGINE CONTROLS.*

A microcomputer in the PCM controls the ignition timing according to engine speed and vacuum pressure in the intake manifold. Engine speed and vacuum pressure are transmitted to PCM by signals from crank sensor, cylinder (CYL) sensor, TDC sensor (Integra and Vigor), throttle position sensor, coolant temperature sensor, knock sensor(s), and MAP sensor.

The PCM contains memory for ignition timing at various engine speeds, manifold pressure and coolant temperature. When these conditions have been processed, PCM sends signals to ignitor unit to control ignition timing.

Crank Sensor – Determines timing for fuel injection and ignition of each cylinder. It also detects engine RPM.

Cylinder (CYL) Sensor – Detects position of No. 1 cylinder for sequential fuel injection to each cylinder.

Knock Sensor(s) – Detects detonation. When detonation is detected, ignition timing is retarded.

TDC Sensor (Integra & Vigor) – Determines ignition timing at start-up (cranking) and when crank position signal is abnormal.

EMISSION SYSTEMS

EGR System – The EGR system reduces oxides of nitrogen (NOx) emissions by recirculating exhaust manifold gas to intake manifold and into the combustion chambers. System is composed of EGR valve, Constant Vacuum Control Valve (CVCV), EGR position sensor and EGR control solenoid valve.

EGR Position Sensor – PCM contains data for ideal EGR valve lifts for varying operating conditions. The EGR position sensor detects amount of EGR valve lift and sends the information to PCM. PCM compares this information (actual EGR valve lift) with ideal EGR valve lift. If the 2 signals differ, PCM closes EGR control solenoid valve to reduce vacuum applied to EGR valve.

EVAP – This system prevents fuel tank vapors from escaping into the atmosphere.

EVAP Purge Cut-Off Solenoid Valve – When coolant temperature is less than 140-158°F (60-70°C), PCM supplies voltage to the purge cut-off solenoid valve to cut vacuum to purge control valve.

Oxygen Sensor Heater – Oxygen sensor heater stabilizes sensor operation, allowing more accurate determination of exhaust oxygen content. PCM uses this information to determine injector pulse duration.

Positive Crankcase Ventilation (PCV) – PCV system prevents crankcase blow-by gas from escaping into the atmosphere. The plunger in the PCV valve is lifted in proportion to the intake manifold vacuum, drawing the blow-by gases into the intake manifold.

Pulse Secondary Air (PAIR) Injection System (Legend) – System uses an vacuum operated air suction valve. When the air suction valve is activated, manifold vacuum lifts the diaphragm off the air valve. Exhaust gas pulsations draw fresh air from air cleaner into exhaust manifold through the air suction valve.

PAIR Air Suction Control Solenoid Valve (Legend) – The PAIR Air Suction Control Solenoid Valve (PAIR-ASCSV) supplies vacuum to the suction valve when engine speed is greater than 1500 RPM and vehicle speed is greater than 9 MPH. PCM delays activation of PAIR-ASCSV until engine is warm.

SELF-DIAGNOSTIC SYSTEM

MALFUNCTION INDICATOR LIGHT & LED INDICATOR

PCM supplies ground for the Malfunction Indicator Light (MIL) for about 2 seconds when ignition is turned on. When a defect is detected in signal from a sensor, PCM activates the MIL and stores fault code in memory. On Legend, LED indicator light is on PCM and is used in idle adjustment procedure.

MISCELLANEOUS CONTROLS

NOTE: Although not true engine performance-related systems, some controlled devices may affect driveability if they malfunction.

TRANSMISSION CONTROL

NOTE: For other input components, see INPUT DEVICES under COMPUTERIZED ENGINE CONTROLS.

A/T Control Solenoid Valves – On Legend, various engine sensor inputs to the PCM are used to control the A/T shift control and torque converter lock-up control solenoid valves. This provides precise timing for the gear shifts and torque converter lock-up system. On Integra and Vigor , Transmission Control Module (TCM) controls shift solenoids and torque converter lock-up solenoids.

Integra, Legend, Vigor

INTRODUCTION

The following diagnostic steps will help prevent overlooking a simple problem. This is also where to begin diagnosis for a no-start condition.

The first step in diagnosing any driveability problem is verifying the customer's complaint with a test drive under the conditions the problem reportedly occurred.

Before entering self-diagnostics, perform a careful and complete visual inspection. Most engine control problems result from mechanical breakdowns, poor electrical connections or damaged/misrouted vacuum hoses. Before condemning the computerized system, perform each test listed in this article.

NOTE: Perform all voltage tests with a Digital Volt-Ohmmeter (DVOM) with a minimum 10-megohm input impedance, unless stated otherwise in test procedure.

PRELIMINARY INSPECTION & ADJUSTMENTS

VISUAL INSPECTION

Visually inspect all electrical wiring, looking for chafed, stretched, cut or pinched wiring. Ensure electrical connectors fit tightly and are not corroded. Ensure vacuum hoses are properly routed and are not pinched or cut. See VACUUM DIAGRAMS article to verify routing and connections (if necessary). Inspect air induction system for possible vacuum leaks.

MECHANICAL INSPECTION

Compression – Check engine mechanical condition with a compression gauge, vacuum gauge, or an engine analyzer. See engine analyzer manual for specific instructions.

WARNING: DO NOT use ignition switch during compression tests on fuel injected vehicles. Use a remote starter to crank engine. Fuel injectors on many models are triggered by ignition switch during cranking mode, which can create a fire hazard or contaminate the engine's oiling system.

ENGINE COMPRESSION [1]

Application	Specification
Integra	
Compression Ratio	
GSR	9.7:1
Except GSR	9.2:1
Compression Pressure At 250 RPM	
Standard	185 psi (13.0 kg/cm²)
Minimum	135 psi (9.5 kg/cm²)
Legend	
Compression Ratio	9.6:1
Compression Pressure At 200 RPM	
Standard	192 psi (13.5 kg/cm²)
Minimum	142 psi (10.0 kg/cm²)
Vigor	
Compression Ratio	9.0:1
Compression Pressure At 250 RPM	
Standard	206 psi (14.5 kg/cm²)
Minimum	135 psi (9.5 kg/cm²)

[1] – Maximum variation between cylinders is 28 psi (2 kg/cm²).

Exhaust System Backpressure – The exhaust system can be checked with a vacuum or pressure gauge. If using a pressure gauge, remove HO2S sensor or air injection check valve (if equipped). Connect a 0-5 psi pressure gauge and run engine at 2500 RPM. If exhaust system backpressure is greater than 1 3/4 - 2 psi, exhaust system or catalytic converter is plugged.

If using a vacuum gauge, connect vacuum gauge hose to intake manifold vacuum port and start engine. Observe vacuum gauge. Open throttle part way and hold steady. If vacuum gauge reading slowly drops after stabilizing, check exhaust system for restriction.

FUEL SYSTEM

WARNING: ALWAYS relieve fuel pressure before disconnecting any fuel injection-related component. DO NOT allow fuel to contact engine or electrical components.

FUEL PRESSURE

Basic diagnosis of fuel system should begin with determining fuel system pressure.

NOTE: Before disconnecting battery, obtain activation code to reset anti-theft stereo (if equipped).

Relieving Fuel Pressure – Remove negative battery cable. Loosen fuel tank filler cap. Place clean shop rag around fuel filter. Slowly loosen 6-mm service bolt on top of fuel filter one complete turn to relieve system pressure. Always replace washer under 6-mm bolt after loosening.

Pressure Testing – **1)** After relieving fuel pressure, connect Fuel Pressure Gauge (07406-0040001) at 6-mm service bolt location. Reconnect negative battery cable. Start engine and note fuel pressure on gauge. See REGULATED FUEL PRESSURE table. If vehicle will not start, but has spark and no fuel pressure, inspect fuel pump relay. See appropriate FUEL PUMP RELAY procedure.

2) Disconnect vacuum hose from pressure regulator (fuel pressure gauge should rise), and check for manifold vacuum. If vacuum is not present, check for restriction in vacuum port or hose. Plug vacuum hose, and note fuel pressure on gauge. See REGULATED FUEL PRESSURE table.

3) If pressure is higher than specified, check for pinched or clogged fuel return line between fuel rail and fuel tank. If no problem is found in fuel line, replace pressure regulator.

4) If pressure is lower than specified, check for plugged fuel filter. If filter is not plugged, lightly pinch off fuel return line. If fuel pressure does not rise, replace fuel pump. If fuel pressure rises, replace pressure regulator.

REGULATED FUEL PRESSURE

Application	At Idle W/O Vacuum psi (kg/cm²)	At Idle W/ Vacuum psi (kg/cm²)
Integra		
1.7L	48-56 (3.4-3.9)	39-46 (2.8-3.3)
1.8L	41-48 (2.9-3.4)	33-39 (2.3-2.8)
Legend		
Coupe	44-51 (3.1-3.6)	36-43 (2.5-3.0)
Sedan	35-41 (2.5-2.9)	29-35 (2.1-2.4)
Vigor	43-50 (3.0-3.5)	33-41 (2.3-2.9)

Fuel Pump Relay (Integra) – **1)** Remove fuel pump relay, located under left side of dash. Connect battery voltage to terminal No. 4, and ground terminal No. 8 of relay. *See Fig. 1.*

2) Check continuity between relay terminals No. 5 and 7. If continuity exists, go to next step. If continuity does not exist, replace relay.

3) Connect battery positive to relay terminal No. 5, and ground terminal No. 2. Check continuity between relay terminals No. 1 and 3. If continuity exists, go to next step. If continuity does not exist, replace relay.

4) Connect battery positive to relay terminal No. 3, and ground terminal No. 8. Check continuity between relay terminals No. 5 and 7. If continuity exists, relay is okay. If continuity is not present, replace relay.

Fuel Pump Relay (Legend) – **1)** Remove fuel pump main relay located under left side of dash. Connect battery voltage to terminal No. 4, and ground terminal No. 8 of relay. *See Fig. 2.*

2) Check continuity between relay terminals No. 5 and 7. If continuity exists, go to next step. If continuity does not exist, replace relay.

3) Connect battery positive to relay terminal No. 6, and ground terminal No. 2. Check continuity between relay terminals No. 1 and 3. If continuity exists, go to next step. If continuity does not exist, replace relay.

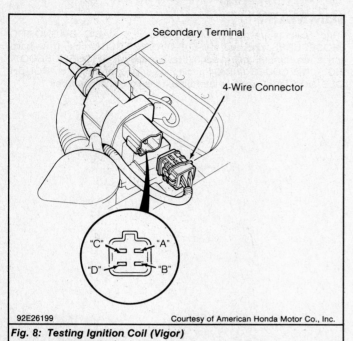

92E26199   Courtesy of American Honda Motor Co., Inc.

Fig. 8: Testing Ignition Coil (Vigor)

PCM Input Signals – **1)** Timing control and triggering of fuel injectors are based on input signals from TDC/CRANK/CYL sensors. These sensors are Permanent Magnet (PM) generator pick-up coils.

2) Using a DVOM (preferably with bar-graph function) on low-volt scale, check each sensor for pulse voltage signal at indicated PCM harness terminals with engine cranking. See PCM INPUT SIGNAL & RESISTANCE TEST TERMINALS table. If pulse signal is present, sensor is okay. If pulse signal is not present, go to step **3)**.

3) Turn ignition off. Disconnect PCM connector. Check wiring harness and connectors. Check resistance of each sensor at indicated PCM harness terminals. See PCM INPUT SIGNAL & RESISTANCE TEST TERMINALS table. If resistance is within specification, go to step **4)**. If resistance is not within specification, go to step **5)**.

PCM INPUT SIGNAL & RESISTANCE TEST TERMINALS

Application	PCM Terminals [1]	Ohms
Integra		
CRANK	B15 & B16	350-700 Ohms
CYL	B11 & B12	350-700 Ohms
TDC	B13 & B14	350-700 Ohms
Legend		
CRANK No. 1	B15 & B16	650-900 Ohms
CRANK No. 2	B14 & B13	650-900 Ohms
CYL No. 1	B12 & B11	650-900 Ohms
CYL No. 2	B9 & B10	650-900 Ohms
Vigor		
CRANK	B15 & B16	650-850 Ohms
CYL	B11 & B12	650-850 Ohms
TDC	B13 & B14	650-850 Ohms

[1] – *See Fig. 9.*

B1   C1   D1
A1   A25   B15   C11   D21
A2   A26   B16   C12   D22
B2   C2   D2

NOTE: TERMINALS C1-C12 NOT USED ON INTEGRA

92B26196   Courtesy of American Honda Motor Co., Inc.

Fig. 9: Identifying PCM Connector Terminals

4) Check continuity to ground on each terminal. If continuity exists, disconnect sensor connector, and recheck appropriate PCM terminal for continuity to ground. If continuity still exists, repair short to ground in harness. If continuity does not exist, replace sensor assembly.

5) Disconnect sensor connector. Check resistance of sensor. *See Fig. 10, 11 or 12.* If resistance is within specification, repair open, short or corrosion in sensor harness between PCM and sensor. See PCM INPUT SIGNAL & RESISTANCE TEST TERMINALS table. If sensor resistance is not within specification, replace sensor assembly.

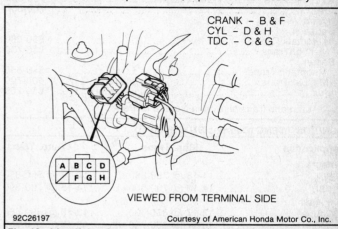

CRANK – B & F
CYL – D & H
TDC – C & G

A B C D
F G H

VIEWED FROM TERMINAL SIDE

92C26197   Courtesy of American Honda Motor Co., Inc.

Fig. 10: Identifying Sensor Connector Terminals (Integra)

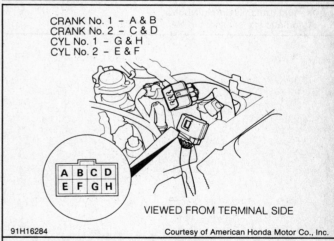

CRANK No. 1 – A & B
CRANK No. 2 – C & D
CYL No. 1 – G & H
CYL No. 2 – E & F

A B C D
E F G H

VIEWED FROM TERMINAL SIDE

91H16284   Courtesy of American Honda Motor Co., Inc.

Fig. 11: Identifying Sensor Connector Terminals (Legend)

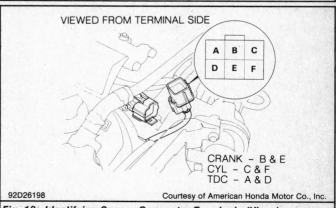

VIEWED FROM TERMINAL SIDE

A B C
D E F

CRANK – B & E
CYL – C & F
TDC – A & D

92D26198   Courtesy of American Honda Motor Co., Inc.

Fig. 12: Identifying Sensor Connector Terminals (Vigor)

1993 ENGINE PERFORMANCE
Basic Diagnostic Procedures (Cont.)

IDLE SPEED & IGNITION TIMING

Ensure idle speed and ignition timing are set to specification. See IDLE SPEED SPECIFICATIONS and IGNITION TIMING tables. For adjustment procedures, see ON-VEHICLE ADJUSTMENTS article.

IDLE SPEED SPECIFICATIONS

Application	RPM
Integra	
1.7L	[1] 750-850
1.8L	[1] 700-800
Legend	
Coupe	
Automatic Trans.	[1] 580-680
Manual Trans.	630-730
Sedan	
Automatic Trans.	[1] 550-650
Manual Trans.	600-700
Vigor	[1] 650-750

[1] – Automatic transmission in Neutral or Park.

IGNITION TIMING (Degrees BTDC @ RPM)

Application	[1] Man. Trans.	[2] Auto. Trans.
Integra		
1.7L	14-18 @ 750-850	14-18 @ 750-850
1.8L	14-18 @ 700-800	14-18 @ 700-800
Legend		
Coupe	13-17 @ 630-730	13-17 @ 580-680
Sedan	13-17 @ 600-700	13-17 @ 550-650
Vigor	13-17 @ 650-750	13-17 @ 650-750

[1] – Manual transmission in Neutral.
[2] – Automatic transmission in Neutral or Park.

SUMMARY

If no faults were found while performing BASIC DIAGNOSTIC PROCEDURES, proceed to SELF-DIAGNOSTICS article. If no hard codes are found in self-diagnostics, proceed to TROUBLE SHOOTING – NO CODES article for diagnosis by symptom (i.e., ROUGH IDLE, NO START, etc.) or intermittent diagnostic procedures.

Integra, Legend, Vigor

INTRODUCTION

If no faults were found while performing BASIC DIAGNOSTIC PROCEDURES, proceed with self-diagnostics. If no fault codes or only pass codes are present after entering self-diagnostics, proceed to TROUBLE SHOOTING – NO CODES article for diagnosis by symptom (i.e., ROUGH IDLE, NO START, etc.).

SELF-DIAGNOSTIC SYSTEM

MALFUNCTION INDICATOR LIGHT (MIL)

All models have a Malfunction Indicator Light (MIL). As a bulb check, light will glow when ignition is on and engine is not running. MIL will also glow when a system failure is detected; a corresponding trouble code will set in Engine Control Module (ECM) memory.

Hard Failures – Hard failures cause malfunction indicator light to glow and remain on until problem is repaired. If light comes on and remains on (light may flash) during vehicle operation, determine cause of malfunction using appropriate TROUBLE CODES procedures. If a sensor fails, ECM will use a substitute value in its calculations to continue engine operation. In this condition, known as limp-in mode, vehicle runs but driveability will not be optimum.

Intermittent Failures – Intermittent failures may cause MIL to flicker or glow and go out after intermittent fault goes away. However, corresponding trouble code will be retained in ECM memory. If related fault does not reoccur within a certain time frame, related trouble code will be erased from ECM memory. Intermittent failures may be caused by sensor, connector or wiring related problems. See INTERMITTENTS in TROUBLE SHOOTING – NO CODES article.

RETRIEVING CODES

NOTE: Before starting tests, ensure engine is in good mechanical condition and adjusted to specifications.

NOTE: For wiring diagrams, see WIRING DIAGRAMS article. For vacuum diagrams, see VACUUM DIAGRAMS article.

MIL may come on indicating a hard or intermittent failure. Locate 2-pin self-diagnostic connector behind glove box. *See Fig. 1 or 2.* Connect diagnostic connector terminals using jumper wire. Turn ignition on. Observe MIL. Light indicates a system trouble code by number of blinks.

Single-digit trouble codes (1-9) are indicated by individual short blinks. Double-digit trouble codes (10-59) are indicated by a series of long and short blinks: number of long blinks equal first digit; number of short blinks equal second digit. See TROUBLE CODE IDENTIFICATION. If codes other than those listed are indicated, substitute a known good ECM and recheck.

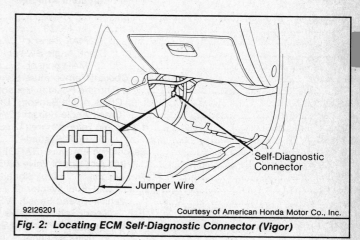

92I26201   Courtesy of American Honda Motor Co., Inc.

Fig. 2: Locating ECM Self-Diagnostic Connector (Vigor)

CLEARING CODES

NOTE: On Vigor, note programmable radio station setting before removing BACK-UP fuse.

Ensure ignition is off. To reset ECM on Integra and Vigor, remove BACK-UP fuse (7.5-amp on Integra; 10-amp on Vigor) from underhood fuse/relay box for 10 seconds. On Legend, remove ACG fuse (No. 15, 7.5-amp) from left underdash fuse box for 10 seconds.

ECM LOCATION

ECM is located on right side of vehicle, in footwell, under carpet.

SUMMARY

If no hard fault codes (or only pass codes) are present, driveability symptoms exist, or intermittent codes exist, proceed to TROUBLE SHOOTING – NO CODES article for diagnosis by symptom (i.e., ROUGH IDLE, NO START, etc.) or intermittent diagnostic procedures.

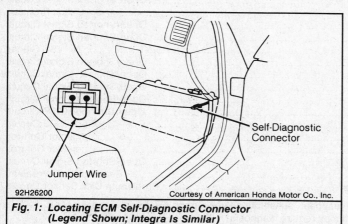

92H26200   Courtesy of American Honda Motor Co., Inc.

Fig. 1: Locating ECM Self-Diagnostic Connector (Legend Shown; Integra Is Similar)

1993 ENGINE PERFORMANCE
Self-Diagnostics (Cont.)

TROUBLE CODE IDENTIFICATION

NOTE: To identify trouble codes, see appropriate TROUBLE CODE
IDENTIFICATION table.

TROUBLE CODE IDENTIFICATION (INTEGRA)

Code [1]	System Affected	Probable Cause
0	ECM	No Signal To ECM
1	HO2S	HO2S Circuit Problem
3	MAP Sensor	MAP Sensor Problem
4	Crank Angle Sensor	Open/Shorted Signal Circuit
5	MAP Sensor	Open/Shorted Signal Circuit
6	Coolant Temperature Sensor	Open/Shorted Signal Circuit
7	Throttle Position Sensor	Open/Shorted Signal Circuit
8	Crank Angle Sensor (TDC)	Open/Shorted Signal Circuit
9	Crank Angle Sensor (CYL)	Open/Shorted Signal Circuit
10	Intake Air Temperature (TA) Sensor	Problem With Sensor
12 (1.8L A/T)	EGR System	Faulty EGR Valve
13	Barometric Pressure (BARO) Sensor	BARO Circuit Problem
14	Idle Air Control Valve (IACV)	Open/Shorted Signal Circuit
15	Ignition Output Signal	Open/Shorted Signal Circuit
16	Fuel Injector	Open/Shorted Signal Circuit
17	Vehicle Speed Sensor (VSS)	Open/Shorted Signal Circuit
21 (1.7L)	Spool Solenoid Valve	Open/Shorted Signal Circuit
22 (1.7L)	Valve Timing Oil Pressure Switch	Open/Shorted Signal Circuit
23 (1.7L)	Knock Sensor	Open/Shorted Signal Circuit
41	HO2S Heater	Open/Shorted Signal Circuit
43	Fuel Supply System	Open/Shorted HO2S Circuit

[1] – If codes other than these are indicated, repeat self-diagnosis. If codes reappear, substitute a known good ECM and recheck codes.

TROUBLE CODE IDENTIFICATION (LEGEND)

Code [1]	System Affected	Probable Cause
0	ECM	No Signal To ECM
1	Left HO2S Sensor	Open/Shorted Signal Circuit
2	Right HO2S Sensor	Open/Shorted Signal Circuit
3	MAP Sensor	MAP Sensor Electrical Problem
4	Crank Angle Sensor No. 1	Sensor Circuit Problem
5	MAP Sensor	MAP Sensor Mechanical Problem
6	Coolant Temperature Sensor	Open/Shorted Signal Circuit
7 [2]	Throttle Position Sensor	Open/Shorted Signal Circuit
9	Cylinder Position Sensor No. 1	Problem In CYL Sensor Circuit
10	Intake Air Temperature (TA) Sensor	Open/Shorted Signal Circuit
12	EGR System	No EGR Action
13	Barometric Pressure (BARO) Sensor	Open/Shorted Signal Circuit
14	Idle Air Control Valve (IACV)	IACV Circuit Problem
15	Ignition Output Signal	Open/Shorted Signal Circuit
16	Fuel Injector	Open/Shorted Signal Circuit
17 [2]	Vehicle Speed Sensor (VSS)	No VSS Signal
18	Ignition Timing Adjuster	Open/Shorted Signal Circuit
23	Left Knock Sensor	Open/Shorted Signal Circuit
41	Left HO2S Heater	Open/Shorted Signal Circuit
42	Right HO2S Heater	Open/Shorted Signal Circuit
43	Left Fuel Supply System	Open/Shorted HO2S Circuit
44	Right Fuel Supply System	Open/Shorted HO2S Circuit
45	Left Fuel Metering	Injector Control
46	Right Fuel Metering	Injector Control
53	Right Knock Sensor	Open/Shorted Signal Circuit
54	Crank Angle Sensor No. 2	Sensor Circuit Problem
59	Cylinder Position No. 2 Sensor	Problem In CYL Sensor Circuit

[1] – If codes other than these are indicated, repeat self-diagnosis. If codes reappear, substitute a known good ECM and recheck codes.

[2] – If S4 on automatic transaxle indicator panel also blinks, A/T control unit may require diagnosis.

TROUBLE CODE IDENTIFICATION (VIGOR)

Code [1]	System Affected	Probable Cause
0	ECM	No Signal To ECM
1	HO2S	HO2S Circuit Problem
3	MAP Sensor	MAP Sensor Problem
4	Crank Angle	Open/Shorted Signal Circuit
5	MAP Sensor	Open/Shorted Signal Circuit
6 [2]	Coolant Temperature Sensor	Open/Shorted Signal Circuit
7 [2]	Throttle Position Sensor	Open/Shorted Signal Circuit
8	Crank Angle Sensor (TDC)	Open/Shorted Signal Circuit
9	Crank Angle Sensor (CYL)	Open/Shorted Signal Circuit
10	Intake Air Temperature (TA) Sensor	Sensor Problem
12	EGR System	Faulty EGR Valve (A/T)
13	Barometric Pressure (BARO) Sensor	BARO Circuit Problem
14	Idle Air Control Valve (IACV)	Open/Shorted Signal Circuit
15	Ignition Output Signal	Open/Shorted Signal Circuit
16	Fuel Injector	Open/Shorted Signal Circuit
17 [2]	Vehicle Speed Sensor (VSS)	Open/Shorted Signal Circuit
18	Ignition Timing Adjuster	Open/Shorted Signal Circuit
20 [3]	Electrical Load Detector (ELD)	Open/Shorted Signal Circuit
23	Knock Sensor No. 1	Open/Shorted Signal Circuit
30 Or 31 [3]	A/T FI Signal	Open/Shorted Signal Circuit
41	HO2S Heater	Open/Shorted Signal Circuit
43	Fuel Supply System	Open/Shorted HO2S Circuit
45	Fuel Metering	Incorrect Fuel Metering
53	Knock Sensor No. 2	Open/Shorted Signal Circuit

[1] – If codes other than these are indicated, repeat self-diagnosis. If codes reappear, substitute a known good ECM and recheck codes.

[2] – If S$_4$ on automatic transaxle indicator panel also blinks, A/T control unit may require diagnosis.

[3] – MIL will not come on if malfunction is in A/T FI or Electrical Load Detector circuit. Fault code will, however, be stored in ECM memory.

TROUBLE CODES (INTEGRA)

CODE 0 OR NO CODES

No MIL – 1) Turn ignition on. If oil pressure light is on, go to next step. If light is off, inspect fuse No. 23. If fuse No. 23 is okay, repair open circuit in Yellow wire between fuse and instrument cluster.

2) If oil pressure light is on, turn ignition off. Connect ECM test harness connector between ECM and ECM connectors. Jumper ECM terminal A13 to body ground. *See Fig. 3.* Turn ignition on. If MIL is now on, go to next step. If light is off, replace MIL bulb or repair open in Green/Orange wire between ECM terminal A13 and instrument cluster.

3) Measure voltage individually between ground and ECM terminals A23 and A24. If more than one volt is present on either terminal, repair open in that wire between ECM and ground terminal G101, located at thermostat housing. *See Fig. 4.* If less than one volt is present on each terminal, replace ECM and retest.

MIL Stays On – 1) Check ECM for fault codes. See RETRIEVING CODES under SELF-DIAGNOSTIC SYSTEMS. Service codes as necessary. If no codes are present, remove jumper from service connector and start engine. If engine starts, go to step **2)**. If engine does not start, inspect ECM fuse in underhood fuse/relay box. If fuse is okay, go to step **4)**.

2) Turn ignition off. Connect ECM Test Harness (07LAJ-PT3010A) between ECM and ECM connectors. *See Fig. 3.* Turn ignition on. Measure voltage between terminals D4 (+) and D22 (–). If voltage is not 5 volts, repair short to body ground between ECM terminal D4 and self-diagnostic connector. If 5 volts are present, connect jumper wire between self-diagnostic connector terminals. Measure voltage between terminals D4 and D22. If 5 volts are present, repair open circuit D4 (Brown wire) or D22 (Green/White wire) between ECM and self-diagnostic connector. If voltage is not 5 volts, go to step **3)**.

3) Ensure jumper wire is removed from self-diagnostic connector. Turn ignition off. Disconnect connector "A" from ECM. Turn ignition on. If MIL goes out, repair short circuit in Green/Orange wire between ECM terminal A13 and MIL. If MIL remains on, replace ECM and retest.

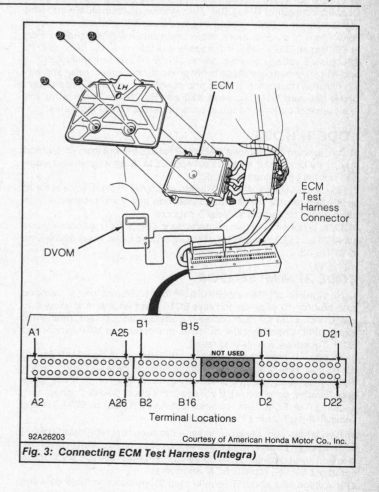

92A26203   Courtesy of American Honda Motor Co., Inc.

Fig. 3: Connecting ECM Test Harness (Integra)

Fig. 4: Identifying Ground Terminal G101 (Integra)

92J26202   Courtesy of American Honda Motor Co., Inc.

4) Ensure jumper wire is removed from self-diagnostic connector. Inspect fuse No. 24 in underdash fuse/relay box. Replace fuse if necessary. If fuse is okay, turn ignition on. Disconnect 3-pin connectors from MAP sensor, throttle position sensor and EGR valve lift sensor (1.8L). If MIL goes out, replace sensor that caused light to go out. If MIL stays on, go to step **5)**.

5) Turn ignition off. Connect ECM Test Harness (07LAJ-PT3010A) between ECM and ECM connectors. See Fig. 3. Leave connector "D" disconnected from ECM. Using an ohmmeter, check for continuity between terminals D19 and D20. If continuity is not present, go to next step. If continuity is present, check for short to body ground in following circuits:

- D19 (Yellow/Red wire) between ECM and MAP sensor.
- D20 (Yellow/White wire) between ECM and throttle position sensor.
- D20 (Yellow/White wire) between ECM and EGR valve lift sensor (1.8L A/T).

6) Ensure all wiring harness connectors are connected to sensors. Connect connector "D" to ECM. Turn ignition on. Individually measure voltage between body ground and terminals A26 and B2. See Fig. 3. If voltage is one volt or more, repair open circuit A26 (Black/Red wire) or B2 (Brown/Black wire). If voltage is less than one volt, go to step **7)**.

7) Measure voltage between terminal A26 (−) and terminals A25 (+) and B1 (+). If battery voltage is not present, check main relay and wiring harness connector. If relay and connector are okay, repair open circuit between ECM terminals A25 and B1 (Yellow/Black wire) and main relay. If battery voltage is present, replace ECM and retest.

CODE 1: HO2S

1) Turn ignition off. Remove BACK-UP fuse (7.5-amp) from underhood fuse/relay box for 10 seconds to reset ECM. Start engine, and warm it to normal operating temperature.

2) Road test vehicle. With M/T in 4th gear (A/T in 2nd), accelerate at wide open throttle for at least 5 seconds and then decelerate, with throttle fully closed, for at least 5 seconds.

3) If MIL is not on, problem is intermittent. Check for poor connections at HO2S and ECM connector. If MIL is on and Code 1 is indicated, go to CODE 43.

CODE 3: MAP SENSOR

1) Turn ignition off. Remove BACK-UP fuse (7.5-amp) from underhood fuse box for 10 seconds to reset ECM. Start engine, and allow it to idle. Check ECM for fault codes. If Code 3 is not present, problem is intermittent. Check for poor or loose connections at MAP sensor and ECM. Test drive vehicle and retest.

2) If Code 3 is present, turn ignition off. Disconnect 3-pin MAP sensor connector. Turn ignition on. Measure voltage between MAP sensor Yellow/Red wire (positive) and body ground. See Fig. 5. If voltage is about 5 volts, go to step **4)**. If voltage is not about 5 volts, connect connector "D" of ECM Test Harness (07LAJ-PT3010A) to ECM, leaving vehicle wiring harness disconnected.

3) Turn ignition on. Measure voltage between test terminals D19 (+) and D21 (−). If about 5 volts are present, repair open circuit in D19 (Yellow/Red wire) between ECM connector and MAP sensor. If voltage is not about 5 volts, replace ECM and retest.

4) If voltage was about 5 volts in step **2)**, measure voltage between Yellow/Red (+) and Green/White (−) wires at MAP sensor. If voltage

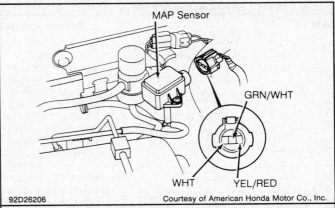

Fig. 5: Locating MAP Sensor & Identifying Connector Terminals (Integra)

92D26206   Courtesy of American Honda Motor Co., Inc.

is not about 5 volts, repair open in Green/White wire between ECM terminal D21 and MAP sensor. If voltage is about 5 volts, measure voltage between White (+) and Green/White (−) wire terminals at MAP sensor.

5) If voltage is about 5 volts, go to step **6)**. If voltage is not about 5 volts, measure voltage between test harness terminals D17 and D21. See Fig. 3. If about 5 volts are present, repair open or short in circuit D17 (White wire) between ECM connector and MAP sensor. If voltage is not about 5 volts, substitute a known good ECM and recheck. If voltage is about 5 volts, replace original ECM and retest. If voltage is not about 5 volts, replace MAP sensor.

6) Turn ignition off. Reconnect 3-pin MAP sensor connector. Connect ECM Test Harness (07LAJ-PT3010A) between ECM and ECM connectors. See Fig. 3. Turn ignition on. Measure voltage between test terminals D17 and D21. If voltage is not about 3 volts, replace MAP sensor. If about 3 volts are present, replace ECM and retest.

CODE 4, 8 OR 9: TDC/CRANK/CYL SENSOR

1) Turn ignition off. Remove BACK-UP (7.5-amp) fuse from underhood fuse/relay box for 10 seconds to reset ECM. Check ECM for fault codes. If Code 4, 8 or 9 is not present, problem is intermittent. Check for poor connections at ECM and distributor. Test drive vehicle and retest.

2) If MIL is on and indicates Code 4, 8 or 9, turn ignition off. Disconnect 8-pin connector from TDC/CRANK/CYL sensor connector at distributor. Check resistance between terminals of each sensor. See Fig. 6. See INPUT SIGNAL & RESISTANCE TEST TERMINALS table. If resistance is not 350-700 ohms, replace distributor sub-assembly. If resistance is 350-700 ohms, go to step **3)**.

INPUT SIGNAL & RESISTANCE TEST TERMINALS

Sensor	Code	ECM Terminal	Sensor Terminal
CRANK	4	B15	B
CRANK	4	B16	F
CYL	9	B11	D
CYL	9	B12	H
TDC	8	B13	C
TDC	8	B14	G

3) Check continuity to body ground on each terminal. If continuity exists, replace distributor sub-assembly. If continuity does not exist, reconnect 8-pin connector. Leaving ECM disconnected, connect ECM Test Harness (07LAJ-PT3010A) to ECM harness connectors. Check resistance between ECM test harness terminals. See INPUT SIGNAL & RESISTANCE TEST TERMINALS table.

4) If resistance is not 350-700 ohms, repair open in faulty circuit. If resistance is 350-700 ohms, check for continuity to body ground on test terminals B11, B13 and B15. If continuity exists on any terminal, repair short circuit. If continuity does not exist, replace ECM and retest.

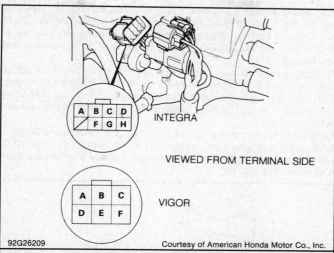

VIEWED FROM TERMINAL SIDE

92G26209   Courtesy of American Honda Motor Co., Inc.

Fig. 6: Identifying TDC/CRANK/CYL Sensor Connector Terminals (Integra & Vigor)

CODE 5: MAP SENSOR

1) Turn ignition off. Remove BACK-UP fuse (7.5-amp) from underhood fuse/relay box for 10 seconds to reset ECM. Start engine and observe MIL. If light is off, problem is intermittent. Check all electrical connections and vacuum hoses. Test drive vehicle and retest.

2) If MIL is on and indicates Code 5, turn ignition off. Connect hand-held vacuum pump to MAP hose at throttle body. See Fig. 7. Apply vacuum. If vacuum holds, go to next step. If vacuum does not hold, attach vacuum pump to MAP sensor. Apply vacuum. If vacuum does not hold, replace MAP sensor. If vacuum holds, check MAP hose for cracks, splits and looseness. Repair as necessary.

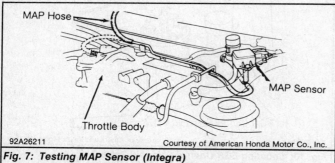

92A26211   Courtesy of American Honda Motor Co., Inc.

Fig. 7: Testing MAP Sensor (Integra)

3) Connect "T" fitting in vacuum hose between MAP sensor and throttle body. Start engine. If vacuum is not present, remove restriction from throttle body. If vacuum is present, turn ignition off. Connect ECM Test Harness (07LAJ-PT3010A) between ECM and ECM connectors. See Fig. 3. Turn ignition on. Measure voltage between test terminals D17 (+) and D21 (-).

4) If voltage is not about 3 volts, replace MAP sensor. If voltage is about 3 volts, start engine and allow it to idle. Recheck voltage between terminals D17 and D21. If voltage is not about one volt at idle, replace MAP sensor. If voltage is about one volt, replace ECM and retest.

CODE 6: COOLANT SENSOR

1) Turn ignition off. Remove BACK-UP (7.5-amp) fuse from underhood fuse/relay box for 10 seconds to reset ECM. Start engine and observe MIL. If light is off, problem is intermittent. Check for poor and loose connections at coolant sensor, shock tower connectors (1.8L), ECM and Transmission Control Module (TCM), if equipped. Test drive vehicle and retest.

2) If MIL is on and indicates Code 6, operate engine until cooling fan comes on. Turn engine off. Disconnect connector from coolant sensor. Measure resistance between sensor terminals. If resistance is not 200-400 ohms, replace coolant sensor.

3) If resistance is 200-400 ohms, turn ignition on. Measure voltage between Red/White wire terminal (+) and body ground. If about 5 volts are present, go to step **6)**. If voltage is not about 5 volts, go to step **4)**.

4) On A/T models, disconnect 18-pin connector from TCM. Turn ignition on. Recheck voltage at Red/White wire terminal. If voltage is about 5 volts, replace TCM. If voltage is not about 5 volts, turn ignition off and reconnect TCM. On all models, connect connector "D" of ECM Test Harness (07LAJ-PT3010A) to ECM, leaving vehicle wiring harness disconnected. Turn ignition on. Measure voltage between test terminals D13 (+) and D22 (-).

5) If voltage is about 5 volts, repair open or short in Red/White wire between ECM terminal D13 and coolant sensor. If voltage is not about 5 volts, replace ECM and retest.

6) If voltage was about 5 volts in step **3)**, measure voltage between Red/White (+) and Green/White (-) wire terminals. If voltage is not about 5 volts, repair open in Green/White wire between ECM connector terminal D22 and coolant sensor. If about 5 volts are present, replace ECM and retest.

CODE 7: THROTTLE POSITION SENSOR

1) Turn ignition off. Remove BACK-UP fuse (7.5-amp) from underhood fuse/relay box for 10 seconds to reset ECM. Check ECM for fault codes. If Code 7 is not present, problem is intermittent. Check for poor or loose connections at throttle position sensor, TCM (if equipped), left and right shock towers (1.8L), and ECM connectors. Test drive vehicle and retest.

2) If MIL is on and indicates Code 7, turn ignition off. Disconnect 3-pin connector from throttle position sensor. Turn ignition on. Measure voltage between Yellow/White (+) and Green/White (-) wire terminals. If voltage is not about 5 volts, go to step **6)**. If about 5 volts are present, turn ignition off. Reconnect sensor connector. Connect ECM Test Harness (07LAJ-PT3010A) between ECM and ECM connectors. See Fig. 3.

3) Turn ignition on. Measure voltage between test terminals D11 (+) and D22 (-). Voltage should be about 0.5 volt at closed throttle and about 4.5 volts at wide open throttle. Transition from 0.5 to 4.5 volts (as throttle is opened) should be smooth. If voltage and operation is correct, replace ECM and retest.

4) If sensor voltages are not correct on M/T models, go to next step. If sensor voltages are not correct on A/T models, disconnect 18-pin connector from Transmission Control Module (TCM). Recheck voltages. If voltages and operation are correct, replace TCM. If voltages and operation are not correct, go to next step.

5) On all models, replace throttle position sensor or repair open or short in Red/Blue wire between ECM terminal D11, TCM (if equipped) and throttle position sensor.

6) If voltage between Yellow/White (+) and Green/White (-) wire terminals in step **2)** was not about 5 volts, measure voltage between Yellow/White wire terminal (+) and body ground. If about 5 volts are present, repair open in Green/White wire between ECM terminal D22 and throttle position sensor.

7) If voltage is not about 5 volts, turn ignition off. Connect ECM Test Harness (07LAJ-PT3010A) between ECM and ECM connectors. See Fig. 3. Turn ignition on. Measure voltage between test terminals D20 (+) and D22 (-). If about 5 volts are present, repair open in Yellow/White wire terminal between ECM connector terminal D20 and throttle position sensor. If voltage is not about 5 volts, replace ECM and retest.

CODE 10: AIR TEMPERATURE (TA) SENSOR

1) Turn ignition off. Remove BACK-UP fuse (7.5-amp) from underhood fuse/relay box for 10 seconds to reset ECM. Check ECM for fault codes. If Code 10 is not present, problem is intermittent. Check for poor connections at ECM, air temperature sensor and wiring harness connectors.

2) Test drive vehicle and retest. If Code 10 is present, turn ignition off. Disconnect 2-pin connector from sensor connector. Using ohmmeter, measure resistance at sensor terminals. If resistance is not 400-4000 ohms, replace air temperature sensor. If resistance is 400-4000 ohms, turn ignition on. Measure voltage between Red/Yellow wire terminal and body ground.

3) If voltage is not about 5 volts, go to step **4)**. If about 5 volts are present, measure voltage between Red/Yellow (+) and Green/White (–) wire terminals at sensor. If voltage is not about 5 volts, repair open in Green/White wire between ECM terminal D22 and air temperature sensor. If about 5 volts are present, replace ECM and retest.

4) Turn ignition off. Connect ECM Test Harness (07LAJ-PT3010A) connector "D" to ECM, leaving wiring harness disconnected. See Fig. 3. Turn ignition on. Measure voltage between test terminals D15 (+) and D22 (–). If about 5 volts are present, repair open or short in Red/Yellow wire between ECM connector terminal D15 and air temperature sensor. If voltage is not about 5 volts, replace ECM and retest.

CODE 12: EGR SYSTEM (1.8L A/T)

1) Turn ignition off. Remove BACK-UP fuse (7.5-amp) from underhood fuse/relay box for 10 seconds to reset ECM. Warm engine until cooling fan comes on. Road test vehicle about 10 minutes, keeping engine speed about 1700-2500 RPM. Check for fault codes. If Code 12 is not present, problem is intermittent. Check ECM, EGR valve and shock tower wiring harness connectors for poor connections.

2) Test drive vehicle and retest. If Code 12 is present, start engine. Disconnect No. 16 hose from EGR valve. See Fig. 8. Connect vacuum gauge to hose. If no vacuum is present, go to step **4)**. If vacuum is present, disconnect 4-pin connector from control box, located on right side of firewall. Check vacuum again on No. 16 hose. If vacuum is present, check vacuum hose routing.

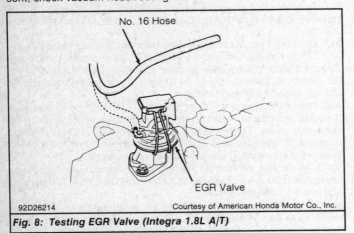

92D26214   Courtesy of American Honda Motor Co., Inc.
Fig. 8: Testing EGR Valve (Integra 1.8L A/T)

3) If routing is okay, replace EGR control solenoid valve. If vacuum is not present, turn ignition off. Remove connector "A" from ECM. Using an ohmmeter, check for continuity between Red wire terminal of 4-pin connector and ground. If continuity is present, repair short in Red wire between EGR control solenoid valve and ECM connector terminal A11. If continuity is not present, replace ECM and retest.

4) If vacuum was not present during first vacuum test in step **2)**, install vacuum pump on EGR valve. With engine idling, apply 8 in. Hg to EGR valve. If engine does not stall/run rough or EGR valve does not hold vacuum, replace EGR valve.

5) If engine stalls/runs rough and EGR valve holds vacuum, disconnect 4-pin connector from control box. Measure voltage between Black/Yellow wire terminal and body ground. If battery voltage is not present, repair open in Black/Yellow wire between solenoid valve and fuse No. 24 (15-amp) in underdash fuse/relay box.

6) If battery voltage is present, install "T" fitting into No. 16 hose. See Fig. 8. Attach vacuum gauge to "T" fitting. Start engine, and allow it to idle. Connect battery voltage to terminal "B" at control box. See Fig. 9. While observing vacuum gauge, connect terminal "D" to negative battery terminal.

7) If gauge reads 8 in. Hg within one second, go to step **9)**. If gauge does not read 8 in. Hg within one second, turn ignition off. Inspect EGR vacuum hoses for leaks, restrictions and misrouting. Repair as necessary. If hoses are okay, disconnect lower hose on EGR control solenoid valve.

8) Connect vacuum gauge to hose. Start engine, and allow it to idle. If 6-10 in. Hg is not present, replace Constant Vacuum Control (CVC) valve. See Fig. 10. If 6-10 in. Hg is present, replace EGR control solenoid valve. See Fig. 10.

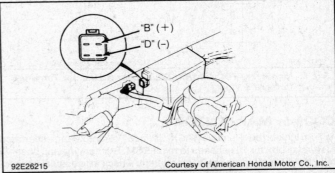

92E26215   Courtesy of American Honda Motor Co., Inc.
Fig. 9: Identifying Control Box Connector Terminals (Integra 1.8L A/T)

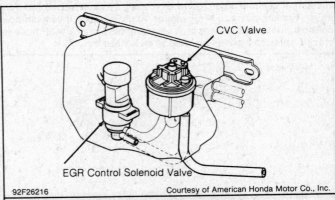

92F26216   Courtesy of American Honda Motor Co., Inc.
Fig. 10: Locating EGR Control Solenoid Valve & Constant Vacuum Control Valve (Integra 1.8L A/T)

9) If gauge read 8 in. Hg in step **7)**, turn ignition off. Ensure EGR control solenoid valve 2-pin connector is attached. Disconnect 3-pin connector from EGR valve lift sensor. Turn ignition on. Measure voltage between Yellow/White (+) and Green/White (–) wire terminals. If voltage is not about 5 volts, go to step **12)**. If voltage is about 5 volts, go to step **10)**.

10) Turn ignition off. Connect 3-pin connector to EGR valve lift sensor. Connect ECM Test Harness (07LAJ-PT3010A) between ECM and ECM connectors. See Fig. 3. Measure voltage between test terminals D12 (+) and D22 (–). If 1.2 volts are present, observe voltmeter and apply 8 in. Hg to EGR valve. Voltage should increase to about 4.3 volts. If voltage is correct, go to step **11)**. If voltage is not correct, repair open or short in Yellow wire between EGR valve and ECM connector terminal D12.

11) If voltage does not consistently increase and decrease as vacuum increases and decreases, replace EGR valve. If voltage consistently increases and decreases with vacuum, reconnect No. 16 hose to EGR valve. Start engine, and allow it to idle. Connect a jumper wire between test terminals A11 and A26. See Fig. 3. If engine does not stall or run rough, repair open in Red wire between ECM connector terminal A11 and EGR control solenoid valve. If engine stalls or runs rough, replace ECM and retest.

12) With 3-pin connector removed from EGR valve, measure voltage between Yellow/White wire terminal and body ground. If about 5 volts are present, repair open in Green/White wire between EGR valve and ECM connector terminal No. D22. If voltage is not 5 volts, connect connector "D" of ECM Test Harness (07LAJ-PT3010A) to ECM, leaving vehicle wiring harness disconnected.

13) Turn ignition on. Measure voltage between test terminals D20 (+) and D22 (–). If about 5 volts are present, repair open in Yellow/White wire between EGR valve and ECM connector terminal No. D20. If voltage is not about 5 volts, replace ECM and retest.

CODE 13: BAROMETRIC (BARO) SENSOR

NOTE: Barometric sensor is built into ECM. Circuit testing is not required.

1) Turn ignition off. Remove BACK-UP fuse (7.5-amp) from underhood fuse/relay box for 10 seconds to reset ECM. Check ECM for fault codes. If Code 13 is not present, problem is intermittent. Check for poor connections at ECM connector and Transmission Control Module (TCM) connector (if equipped). Test drive vehicle and check again.

2) If Code 13 is present on M/T models, go to step **4)**. If Code 13 is present on A/T models, turn ignition off. Connect ECM Test Harness (07LAJ-PT3010A) to ECM, leaving ECM wiring harness disconnected. *See Fig. 3.* Disconnect 18-pin connector from TCM. Check for continuity between test terminal D8 and body ground.

3) If continuity is present, repair short in Red/White wire between ECM connector terminal D8 and TCM. If continuity is not present, substitute a known good TCM. If MIL goes off and Code 13 is not present, replace original TCM. If MIL stays on and/or Code 13 is still present, go to next step.

4) Replace ECM and retest.

CODE 14: IDLE AIR CONTROL VALVE (IACV)

1) Turn ignition off. Remove BACK-UP fuse (7.5-amp) from underhood fuse/relay box for 10 seconds to reset ECM. Check ECM for fault codes. If Code 14 is not present, start engine and allow it to idle. Disconnect 2-pin connector from IACV. If engine speed is not reduced, replace IACV. If engine speed is reduced, problem is intermittent. Check for poor connections at ECM, IACV and wiring harness. Test drive vehicle and retest.

2) If Code 14 is present, disconnect 2-pin connector from IACV. Turn ignition on. Measure voltage between Yellow/Black wire and body ground. If battery voltage is not present, repair open in Yellow/Black wire between IACV and main relay. If battery voltage is present, turn ignition off. Reconnect 2-pin connector.

3) Attach connector "A" of ECM Test Harness (07LAJ-PT3010A) to ECM wiring harness, leaving ECM disconnected. *See Fig. 3.* Turn ignition on. Using a jumper wire, touch test terminal A9 to test terminal A23 several times. If IACV does not click, repair open or short circuit in Blue/Yellow wire between IACV and terminal A9 of ECM connector. If IACV clicks, replace ECM and retest.

CODE 15: IGNITION OUTPUT SIGNAL

1) Turn ignition off. Remove BACK-UP fuse (7.5-amp) from underhood fuse/relay box for 10 seconds to reset ECM. Check ECM for fault codes. If Code 15 is not present, problem is intermittent. Check for poor connections at ECM, ignitor unit and wiring harness connections. Test drive vehicle and retest.

2) If Code 15 is present, turn ignition off. Disconnect 2-pin connector from distributor. Turn ignition on. Measure voltage between Black/Yellow wire and body ground. If battery voltage is not present, repair open in Black/Yellow wire between ignition switch and distributor 2-pin connector. If battery voltage is present, go to step **3)**.

3) Turn ignition off. Reconnect 2-pin connector to distributor. Connect ECM Test Harness (07LAJ-PT3010A) between ECM and ECM connectors. *See Fig. 3.* Turn ignition on. Measure voltage between test terminal A26 (–) and test terminals A21 (+) and A22 (+).

NOTE: A short in Yellow/Green wire between ignitor unit and ECM may damage ignitor unit. Recheck ignitor unit.

4) If voltage is not about 10 volts, check for open or short in Yellow/Green wire between ignitor unit and ECM terminal A21 or A22. If wire is okay, replace ignitor. If about 10 volts are present, replace ECM and retest.

CODE 16: FUEL INJECTOR CIRCUIT

NOTE: If engine will not start, crank engine for 10 seconds or more, if necessary, to set code.

1) Turn ignition off. Remove BACK-UP fuse (7.5-amp) from underhood fuse/relay box for 10 seconds to reset ECM. Check ECM for fault codes. If Code 16 is not present, problem is intermittent. Check for poor connections at ECM, fuel injector and wiring harness connectors. Test drive vehicle and retest.

2) If Code 16 is present, start engine. Using a stethoscope, check for clicking sound at each injector. If injector does not click, turn ignition off. Disconnect 2-pin injector connector from affected injector. Measure resistance between injector terminals. Resistance should be 10-13 ohms. If resistance is not 10-13 ohms, replace injector. If resistance is okay, go to step **3)**.

3) Turn ignition on. Measure voltage between fuel injector harness Yellow/Black wire and body ground. If battery voltage is not present, repair open in Yellow/Black wire between fuel injector and main relay. If battery voltage is present, turn ignition off. Reconnect fuel injector connector.

4) Connect ECM Test Harness (07LAJ-PT3010A) between ECM and ECM harness connectors. *See Fig. 3.* Turn ignition on. Check voltage between A23 (–) and following test terminals.

- Injector No. 1: A1 (+)
- Injector No. 2: A3 (+)
- Injector No. 3: A5 (+)
- Injector No. 4: A2 (+)

If battery voltage is not present, repair open in wire between injector and affected ECM connector terminal (A1, A2, A3 or A5). If battery voltage is present, replace ECM and retest.

CODE 17: VEHICLE SPEED SENSOR (VSS)

1) Turn ignition off. Remove BACK-UP fuse (7.5-amp) from underhood fuse/relay box for 10 seconds to reset ECM. Road test vehicle. While in 2nd gear, accelerate until engine speed reaches 4000 RPM and then, with throttle fully closed, decelerate to 1500 RPM.

2) Check ECM for fault codes. If Code 17 is not present, problem is intermittent. Check for poor connections at ECM, underdash fuse box and underdash wiring harness connectors. Test drive vehicle and retest.

3) If Code 17 is present, raise and support vehicle. Connect ECM Test Harness (07LAJ-PT3010A) between ECM and ECM wiring harness connectors. *See Fig. 3.* Place transaxle in Neutral. Turn ignition on. Slowly rotate left front wheel and measure voltage between test terminals A26 (–) and B10 (+). If voltage pulses 0-12 volts, replace ECM and retest.

4) If voltage did not pulse 0-12 volts in step **3)**, turn ignition off. Disconnect connector "B" from ECM. Turn ignition on. Block right front wheel and rotate left front wheel while measuring voltage between test terminals A26 and B10. *See Fig. 3.*

5) If voltage does not pulse 0-12 volts, repair short or open in Yellow/Red wire between ECM terminal B10 (+) and VSS or cruise control unit. If wire is okay, replace VSS. If voltage pulses 0-12 volts, replace ECM and retest.

CODE 21: SPOOL SOLENOID VALVE (1.7L)

1) Turn ignition off. Remove BACK-UP fuse (7.5-amp) from underhood fuse/relay box for 10 seconds to reset ECM. Warm engine until cooling fan comes on. Road test vehicle. While in 1st gear, accelerate until engine speed reaches 6000 RPM and hold for at least 2 seconds.

Repeat procedure 3 times. Check ECM for fault codes. If Code 21 is not present, problem is intermittent. Check for poor connections at spool valve and ECM connector.

2) If Code 21 is present, turn ignition off. Disconnect spool valve 1-pin connector. Check resistance between connector terminal and body ground. If resistance is not 14-30 ohms, replace spool valve. If 14-30 ohms are present, connect ECM Test Harness (07LAJ-PT3010A) between ECM and ECM connectors. See Fig. 3.

3) Check for continuity between spool valve connector and test terminal A4. If continuity is not present, repair open in wire between spool valve and ECM connector. If continuity is present, check for continuity between spool valve connector terminal and body ground.

4) If continuity is present, repair short in wire between spool valve and ECM connector. If continuity is not present, replace ECM and retest.

CODE 22:
VALVE TIMING OIL PRESSURE SWITCH (1.7L)

1) Turn ignition off. Remove BACK-UP fuse (7.5-amp) from underhood fuse/relay box for 10 seconds to reset ECM. Warm engine until cooling fan comes on. Road test vehicle. While in 1st gear, accelerate until engine speed reaches 6000 RPM and hold for at least 2 seconds. Repeat procedure 3 times. Check ECM for fault codes. If Code 22 is not present, problem is intermittent. Check for poor connections at valve timing oil pressure switch and ECM connector.

2) If Code 21 is present, turn ignition off. Disconnect switch 2-pin connector. Check for continuity between Black wire terminal and body ground. If continuity is not present, repair open in Black wire between switch connector and body ground. If continuity is present, connect ECM Test Harness (07LAJ-PT3010A) between ECM and ECM connectors. See Fig. 3.

3) Check for continuity between test terminal D6 and Blue/Black wire terminal. If continuity is not present, repair open in Blue/Black wire between switch connector and ECM. If continuity is present, check for continuity between test terminal D6 and body ground. If continuity is present, repair short in Blue/Black wire between switch connector and ECM. See Fig. 3. If continuity is not present, go to step 4).

4) Remove 10-mm plug and attach oil pressure gauge. With engine at normal operating temperature, check oil pressure at 1000, 3000 and 5000 RPM. If pressure is below 7 psi (0.5 kg/cm²), replace spool valve. If pressure is 7 psi (0.5 kg/cm²) or more, check for continuity between switch terminals.

5) If continuity is not present, replace valve timing oil pressure switch. If continuity is present, remove spool valve connector. Connect battery voltage to spool valve connector terminal. Start engine. Check oil pressure at 5000 RPM.

6) If oil pressure is less than 57 psi (4 kg/cm²), replace spool valve. If oil pressure is 57 psi (4 kg/cm²) or more, check continuity between switch terminals at 5000 RPM. If continuity is present, replace oil pressure switch. If continuity is not present, replace ECM and retest.

CODE 23: KNOCK SENSOR (1.7L)

NOTE: Repair any engine knocking sounds before performing test.

1) Turn ignition off. Remove BACK-UP fuse (7.5-amp) from underhood fuse/relay box for 10 seconds to reset ECM. Warm engine until cooling fan comes on. Set engine speed at 3000-4000 RPM for 10 seconds. Check ECM for fault codes. If Code 23 is not present, problem is intermittent. Check for poor connections at ECM, knock sensor and wiring harness connectors.

2) Test drive vehicle and retest. If Code 23 is present, turn ignition off. Connect ECM Test Harness (07LAJ-PT3010A) to ECM connectors, leaving ECM disconnected. See Fig. 3. Disconnect knock sensor connector. Check for continuity between test terminal D3 and body ground. If continuity is present, repair short in Red/Blue wire between ECM terminal D3 and knock sensor.

3) If continuity is not present, check for continuity between test terminal D3 and knock sensor connector Red/Blue wire terminal. If continuity is not present, repair open in Red/Blue wire between ECM connector terminal D3 and knock sensor.

4) If continuity is present, reconnect knock sensor. Replace ECM with a known good unit. Warm engine to normal operating temperature. Set engine speed at 3000-4000 RPM for 10 seconds. Check ECM for fault codes. If Code 23 is not present, replace original ECM. If Code 23 is present, replace knock sensor.

CODE 41: HO2S HEATER

1) Turn ignition off. Remove BACK-UP fuse (7.5-amp) from underhood fuse/relay box for 10 seconds to reset ECM. Check ECM for fault codes. If Code 41 is not present, problem is intermittent. Check for poor connections at ECM, HO2S and wiring harness connectors.

2) Test drive vehicle and retest. If Code 41 is present, turn ignition off. Disconnect 4-pin HO2S connector. Measure resistance between HO2S terminals "C" and "D". See Fig. 11. If resistance is not 10-40 ohms, replace sensor. If resistance is 10-40 ohms, go to step 3).

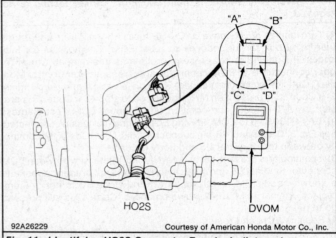

92A26229   Courtesy of American Honda Motor Co., Inc.

Fig. 11: Identifying HO2S Connector Terminals (Integra)

3) Check for continuity between body ground and HO2S terminals "C" and "D". If continuity is present, replace sensor. If continuity is not present, check for continuity between terminal "D" and terminals "A" and "B". If continuity is present, replace sensor.

4) If continuity is not present, turn ignition on. Measure voltage between Yellow/Black (+) and Orange/Black (−) wire terminals at HO2S wiring harness connector. See Fig. 11. If battery voltage is not present, go to step 7). If battery voltage is present, disconnect connector "A" from ECM. Measure voltage between Yellow/Black (+) and Orange/Black (−) wires at HO2S wiring harness connector.

5) If battery voltage is present, repair short circuit in Orange/Black wire between ECM connector terminal A6 and HO2S. If battery voltage is not present, reconnect HO2S. Connect connector "A" of ECM Test Harness (07LAJ-PT3010A) to vehicle wiring harness, leaving ECM disconnected.

6) Connect ammeter between test terminals A6 (+) and A23 (−). Monitor ammeter for 5 minutes. If current is less than 0.1 amp, replace HO2S. If current is not less than 0.1 amp, replace ECM and retest.

7) If battery voltage did not exist in step 4), measure voltage between Yellow/Black wire terminal (+) at HO2S wiring harness connector and body ground. If battery voltage does not exist, repair open in Yellow/Black wire between HO2S and main relay. If battery voltage exists, turn ignition off. Reconnect HO2S wiring harness connector.

8) Connect connector "A" of ECM Test Harness (07LAJ-PT3010A) to ECM wiring harness, leaving ECM disconnected. Turn ignition on. Measure voltage between test terminals A6 (+) and A23 (−). If battery voltage does not exist, repair open in Orange/Black wire between ECM connector terminal A6 and HO2S. If battery voltage exists, replace ECM and retest.

CODE 43: FUEL SUPPLY SYSTEM

1) If referred here from CODE 1, go to step 2). If Code 43 exists, turn ignition off. Remove BACK-UP fuse (7.5-amp) from underhood fuse/

relay box for 10 seconds to reset ECM. Warm engine until cooling fan comes on. With transmission in Neutral, raise engine speed to 3000 RPM and hold for 2 minutes. Check ECM for fault codes. If Code 43 does not exist, problem is intermittent. Check for poor connections at ECM, HO2S and wiring harness connectors.

2) If Code 43 is present, turn ignition off. Connect ECM Test Harness (07LAJ-PT3010A) between ECM and ECM connectors. *See Fig. 3.* Wait 2 minutes. Install jumper wire between test terminals A6 and A26. Turn ignition on while measuring voltage between terminals D14 (+) and A26 (−).

3) If 0.1 volt or less is present as ignition is turned on, go to step **5)**. If more than 0.1 volt is present as ignition is turned on, disconnect HO2S connector. Measure voltage between HO2S wiring harness connector Green/White and White wire terminals.

4) If more than 0.1 volt is present, replace HO2S. If 0.1 volt or less is present, repair open circuit in Green/White or White wire between HO2S and ECM connector.

5) If 0.1 volt or less was present as ignition was turned on in step **3)**, disconnect HO2S connector. Measure voltage between test terminals D14 (+) and A26 (−). If more than 0.1 volt is present, replace HO2S. If 0.1 volt or less is present, disconnect connector "D" from wiring harness. Measure voltage between test terminals D14 (+) and A26 (−). If more than 0.1 volt is present, repair short in White wire between ECM connector and HO2S. If 0.1 volt or less is present, replace ECM and retest.

TROUBLE CODES (LEGEND)

CODE 0 OR NO CODES

No MIL – **1)** Turn ignition on. If oil pressure light is on, go to next step. If light is off, inspect fuse No. 13. Replace fuse and repair short as necessary. If fuse No. 13 is okay, repair open circuit in Yellow wire between fuse and instrument cluster.

2) Turn ignition off. Connect ECM Test Harness (07LAJ-PT3010A) between ECM and ECM connectors. *See Fig. 12.* Connect test terminal A13 to ground. Turn ignition on. If MIL is now on, go to next step. If light is off, replace light bulb or repair open in Blue wire between ECM terminal A13 and instrument cluster.

3) Individually measure voltage between ground and test terminals A23 and A24. If more than one volt is present on any terminal, check open in wire between ECM and ground terminal G101 (at intake manifold). *See Fig. 13.* If less than one volt is present on each terminal, replace ECM and retest.

MIL Stays On – **1)** Check ECM for fault codes. See RETRIEVING CODES under SELF-DIAGNOSTIC SYSTEM. Service codes. If no codes are present, remove jumper wire from self-diagnostic connector. Start engine. If engine does not start, go to step **6)**. If engine starts, turn ignition off. Connect ECM Test Harness (07LAJ-PT3010A) between ECM and ECM connectors. *See Fig. 12.*

2) Turn ignition on. Measure voltage between terminals C9 (+) and A26 (−) of ECM connectors. If voltage is about 5 volts, go to next step. If voltage is not about 5 volts, repair short to body ground in White wire between ECM terminal C9 and self-diagnostic connector.

3) Connect jumper wire to self-diagnostic connector. If about 5 volts are now present, check for open in White wire between self-diagnostic connector and ECM. Check for open in Black wire between self-diagnostic connector and ground.

4) If about 5 volts are not present, remove jumper wire from self-diagnostic connector. Turn ignition off. Disconnect connector "A" of ECM. Turn ignition on. If MIL is on, repair short to ground in Blue wire between terminal A13 and instrument cluster. *See Fig. 12.*

5) If MIL is not on, replace ECM and retest.

6) If engine did not start, check fuses No. 5 (20-amp) and IG COIL (30-amp) in underdash fuse box. Replace bad fuses. Turn ignition on. Install jumper wire between self-diagnostic connector terminals. Individually disconnect 3-pin connectors on MAP and EGR valve lift sensors.

7) If MIL goes out, replace sensor causing MIL to go out. If MIL is on, connect jumper wire to self-diagnostic connector. Disconnect throttle position or ignition timing adjuster connector. Check to see if

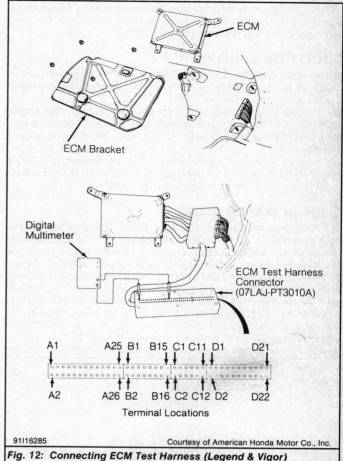

91I16285   Courtesy of American Honda Motor Co., Inc.

Fig. 12: Connecting ECM Test Harness (Legend & Vigor)

92B26204   Courtesy of American Honda Motor Co., Inc.

Fig. 13: Identifying Ground Terminal G101 (Legend)

ECM flashes Code 7 or 18. If Code 7 is indicated, replace throttle position sensor. If Code 18 is indicated, replace ignition timing adjuster.

8) If Code 7 or 18 is not indicated, turn ignition off. Remove jumper wire. Connect ECM Test Harness (07LAJ-PT3010A) between ECM and ECM connectors. *See Fig. 12.* Disconnect connector "D" from ECM side only. Individually check for continuity between body ground and terminals D19 and D20.

9) If continuity exists, repair short to ground in Yellow/White wire between ECM terminal D19 or D20 and MAP sensor, ignition timing adjuster, throttle position sensor or EGR valve lift sensor.

10) If continuity does not exist, reconnect connector "D". Reconnect all sensor connectors. Turn ignition on. Individually measure voltage between ECM body ground and terminals A26 and B2. *See Fig. 12.* If voltage is more than one volt, repair open in Brown/Black wire (A26) or Brown/Black wire (B2) between affected terminal and ground G101 at intake manifold. *See Fig. 13.*

11) If voltage was less than one volt, individually measure voltage between ECM terminal A26 (−) and terminals C1 (+) and A25 (+). *See Fig. 13.* If battery voltage is present, turn ignition off, replace ECM and retest. If battery voltage is not present, repair open in Yellow/Black wire circuit between main relay and ECM terminals A25 and C1. If circuit is okay, check main relay and connector.

CODE 1 OR 2: HO2S

1) Turn ignition off. Remove ACG fuse (No. 15, 7.5-amp) from underdash fuse box for 10 seconds to reset ECM. Start engine, and warm it until cooling fan comes on.

2) Road test vehicle. Place M/T in 4th gear (A/T in 2nd). With engine speed at 1200 RPM, accelerate at wide open throttle for at least 5 seconds and then decelerate with throttle fully closed for at least 5 seconds.

3) Check ECM for fault codes. If no codes are present, problem is intermittent. Check for poor connections at HO2S and ECM connector. If Code 1 or 2 is present, go to CODE 43 OR 44.

CODE 3: MAP SENSOR

1) Turn ignition off. Remove ACG fuse (No. 15, 7.5-amp) from underdash fuse box for 10 seconds to reset ECM. Start engine. Connect jumper wire to self-diagnostic connector. Observe MIL. If Code 3 is not present, problem is intermittent. Check for poor or loose connection at MAP sensor and ECM connector. Test drive vehicle and retest.

2) If Code 3 is present, turn ignition off. Disconnect 3-pin connector at MAP sensor. Turn ignition on. Measure voltage between Yellow/White wire terminal (+) and body ground. See Fig. 14. If about 5 volts is present, go to step **4)**. If voltage is not about 5 volts, turn ignition off. Connect connector "D" of ECM Test Harness (07LAJ-PT3010A) to ECM, leaving vehicle wiring harness disconnected.

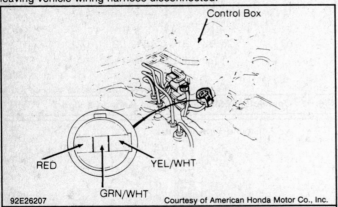

Fig. 14: Identifying MAP Sensor Connector Terminals (Legend)

3) Turn ignition on. If voltage is about 5 volts, repair open in Yellow/White wire between ECM terminal D19 and MAP sensor. If voltage is not about 5 volts, turn ignition off, replace ECM and retest.

4) If voltage was about 5 volts in step **2)**, measure voltage between Yellow/White and Green/White wires at MAP sensor. See Fig. 14. If voltage is not about 5 volts, repair open in Green/White wire between ECM connector terminal D21 and MAP sensor. If voltage is about 5 volts, measure voltage between Red (+) and Green/White (–) wire terminals at MAP sensor.

5) If voltage is not about 5 volts, go to step **7)**. If about 5 volts are present, turn ignition off. Reconnect MAP sensor. Install ECM Test Harness (07LAJ-PT3010A) to ECM and vehicle wiring harness. See Fig. 12. Turn ignition on.

6) Measure voltage between test terminals D17 (+) and D21 (–). If voltage is not about 3 volts, replace MAP sensor. If about 3 volts are present, replace ECM and retest.

7) If voltage was not about 5 volts in step **5)**, turn ignition off. Connect connector "D" of ECM Test Harness (07LAJ-PT3010A) to ECM, leaving vehicle wiring harness disconnected.

8) Turn ignition on. Measure voltage between test terminals D17 (+) and D21 (–). If voltage is about 5 volts, repair open or short in circuit D17 (Red wire) between ECM connector and MAP sensor. If voltage is not about 5 volts, replace ECM and retest.

CODE 4, 9, 54 OR 59: CRANK/CYL SENSOR

1) Turn ignition off. Remove ACG fuse (No. 15, 7.5-amp) in underdash fuse box for 10 seconds to reset ECM. Start engine. Connect jumper wire to self-diagnostic connector. Observe MIL. If Code 4, 9, 54 or 59 is not present, problem is intermittent. Check for poor and loose connections at CRANK/CYL sensor assembly connector and ECM connector. Test drive vehicle and retest.

2) If Code 4, 9, 54 or 59 is present, turn ignition off. Disconnect 8-pin connector from CRANK/CYL sensor. Check wiring harness and terminals. Check resistance of each sensor at indicated terminals. See INPUT SIGNAL & RESISTANCE TEST TERMINALS table. See Fig. 15. If resistance is not 650-900 ohms, replace CRANK/CYL sensor assembly. If resistance is 650-900 ohms, go to step **3)**.

INPUT SIGNAL & RESISTANCE TEST TERMINALS

Sensor	Code	ECM Terminal	Sensor Terminal
CRANK 1	4	B15	A
		B16	B
CRANK 2	54	B14	C
		B13	D
CYL 1	9	B12	G
		B11	H
CYL 2	59	B9	E
		B10	F

3) Check continuity to body ground on each terminal. If continuity exists, replace CRANK/CYL sensor assembly. If continuity does not exist, reconnect 8-pin connector. Connect ECM Test Harness (07LAJ-PT3010A) to ECM harness connectors, leaving ECM disconnected. Check resistance between ECM test harness terminals. See INPUT SIGNAL & RESISTANCE TEST TERMINALS table.

4) If resistance is not 650-900 ohms, repair open in faulty circuit. If resistance is 650-900 ohms, check for continuity to body ground on terminals B9, B11, B13 and B15. If continuity exists on any terminal, repair short circuit. If continuity does not exist, replace ECM and retest.

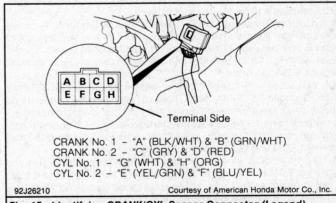

CRANK No. 1 – "A" (BLK/WHT) & "B" (GRN/WHT)
CRANK No. 2 – "C" (GRY) & "D" (RED)
CYL No. 1 – "G" (WHT) & "H" (ORG)
CYL No. 2 – "E" (YEL/GRN) & "F" (BLU/YEL)

Fig. 15: Identifying CRANK/CYL Sensor Connector (Legend)

CODE 5: MAP SENSOR

1) Turn ignition off. Remove ACG (No. 15, 7.5-amp) from underdash fuse box for 10 seconds to reset ECM. Start engine. Connect jumper wire to self-diagnostic connector. Observe MIL. If light is off, problem is intermittent. Check all electrical connections and vacuum hoses. Test drive vehicle and retest.

2) If MIL is on and indicates Code 5, turn ignition off. Remove MAP hose at throttle body base. Connect a hand-held vacuum pump to MAP sensor, and apply vacuum. If vacuum does not hold, replace MAP sensor. If vacuum holds, connect vacuum hose and go to step **3)**.

3) Connect "T" fitting in vacuum hose between MAP sensor and throttle body base. See Fig. 16. Start engine. If vacuum is not present, remove restriction from throttle body. If vacuum is present, turn ignition off. Connect ECM Test Harness (07LAJ-PT3010A) between ECM and ECM connectors. See Fig. 12. Turn ignition on. Measure voltage between test terminals D17 (+) and D21 (–).

4) If voltage is not about 3 volts, replace MAP sensor. If voltage is about 3 volts, start engine and allow it to idle. Recheck voltage between terminals D17 and D21. If voltage is not about one volt at idle, replace MAP sensor. If voltage is about one volt, replace ECM and retest.

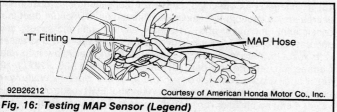

"T" Fitting — MAP Hose

92B26212   Courtesy of American Honda Motor Co., Inc.

Fig. 16: Testing MAP Sensor (Legend)

CODE 6: COOLANT SENSOR

1) Turn ignition off. Remove ACG fuse (No. 15, 7.5-amp) from under-dash fuse box for 10 seconds to reset ECM. If light is off, problem is intermittent. Check for poor and loose connections at coolant sensor, ECM and right shock tower. Test drive vehicle and retest.
2) If MIL is on and indicates Code 6, operate engine until cooling fan comes on. Turn engine off. Disconnect connector from coolant sensor. Measure resistance between sensor terminals. If resistance is not 200-400 ohms, replace coolant sensor.
3) If resistance is 200-400 ohms, turn ignition on. Measure voltage between Red/White wire terminal (+) and body ground. If voltage is about 5 volts, go to step **5)**. If voltage is not about 5 volts, connect connector "D" of ECM Test Harness (07LAJ-PT3010A) to ECM, leaving vehicle wiring harness disconnected. Turn ignition on. Measure voltage between test terminals D13 (+) and D22 (-). *See Fig. 12.*
4) If voltage is about 5 volts, repair open or short in Red/White wire between ECM terminal D13 and coolant sensor. If voltage is not about 5 volts, replace ECM and retest.
5) If voltage was about 5 volts in step **3)**, measure voltage between Red/White (+) and Green/White (-) wire terminals. If voltage is not about 5 volts, repair open in Green/White wire between ECM connector terminal D22 and coolant sensor. If voltage is about 5 volts, replace ECM and retest.

CODE 7: THROTTLE POSITION SENSOR

1) Turn ignition off. Remove ACG fuse (No. 15, 7.5-amp) from under-dash fuse box for 10 seconds to reset ECM. Check ECM for fault codes. If Code 7 is not present, problem is intermittent. Check for poor and loose connections at throttle position sensor, right shock tower harness connector and ECM connectors. Test drive vehicle and retest.
2) If Code 7 is present, turn ignition off. Disconnect 3-pin connector from throttle position sensor. Turn ignition on. Measure voltage between Yellow/White (+) and Green/White (-) wire terminals. If voltage is not about 5 volts, go to step **5)**. If about 5 volts are present, turn ignition off. Reconnect sensor connector. Connect ECM Test Harness (07LAJ-PT3010A) between ECM and ECM connectors. *See Fig. 12.*
3) Turn ignition on. Measure voltage between test terminals D11 (+) and D22 (-). Voltage should be about 0.5 volt at closed throttle and about 4.5 volts at wide open throttle. Transition from 0.5 to 4.5 volts (as throttle is opened) should be smooth.
4) If voltage is correct, replace ECM and retest. If voltages are not correct, replace throttle position sensor or repair open or short in Red/Blue wire between ECM terminal D11 and throttle position sensor.
5) If voltage between Yellow/White (+) and Green/White (-) wire terminals in step **2)** was not about 5 volts, measure voltage between Yellow/White (+) wire terminal and body ground. If voltage is about 5 volts, repair open in Green/White wire between ECM terminal D22 and throttle position sensor. If voltage is not about 5 volts, turn ignition off.
6) Connect ECM Test Harness (07LAJ-PT3010A) between ECM and ECM connectors. *See Fig. 12.* Turn ignition on. Measure voltage between test terminals D20 (+) and D22 (-). If voltage is about 5 volts, repair open in Yellow/White wire terminal between ECM connector terminal D20 and throttle position sensor. If voltage is not about 5 volts, replace ECM and retest.

CODE 10, AIR TEMPERATURE (TA) SENSOR

1) Turn ignition off. Remove ACG fuse (No. 15, 7.5-amp) from under-dash fuse box for 10 seconds to reset ECM. Check ECM for fault codes. If Code 10 is not present, problem is intermittent. Check for poor and loose connections at air temperature sensor, wiring harness and ECM connectors. Test drive vehicle and retest.
2) If Code 10 is present, turn ignition off. Disconnect 2-pin connector from sensor connector. Using an ohmmeter, measure resistance at sensor terminals. If resistance is not 400-4000 ohms, replace air temperature sensor. If resistance is 400-4000 ohms, turn ignition on. Measure voltage between Red/Yellow wire terminal and body ground.
3) If voltage is not about 5 volts, go to step **4)**. If about 5 volts are present, measure voltage between Red/Yellow (+) and Green/White (-) wire terminals at sensor. If voltage is not about 5 volts, repair open in Green/White wire between ECM terminal D22 and air temperature sensor. If about 5 volts are present, replace ECM and retest.
4) Turn ignition off. Connect ECM Test Harness (07LAJ-PT3010A) connector "D" to ECM, leaving wiring harness disconnected. *See Fig. 12.* Turn ignition on. Measure voltage between terminals D15 (+) and D22 (-). If voltage is about 5 volts, repair open or short in Red/Yellow wire between ECM connector terminal D15 and air temperature sensor. If voltage is not about 5 volts, replace ECM and retest.

CODE 12: EGR SYSTEM

1) Turn ignition off. Remove ACG (No. 15, 7.5-amp) from fuse in under-dash fuse box for 10 seconds to reset ECM. Warm engine until cooling fan comes on. Road test vehicle about 10 minutes, keeping engine speed about 1700-2500 RPM. Check for fault codes. If Code 12 is not present, problem is intermittent. Check for poor connections at ECM, EGR valve, control box and shock tower wiring harness connectors.
2) Test drive vehicle and retest. If Code 12 exists, start engine. Disconnect No. 11 hose from EGR valve. *See Fig. 17.* Start engine. Connect vacuum gauge to hose. If vacuum is not present, go to step **4)**. If vacuum is present, disconnect 4-pin connector from control box, located on right side of firewall. Check vacuum again on No. 11 hose. If vacuum is present, check vacuum hose routing. If routing is okay, replace EGR control solenoid valve.

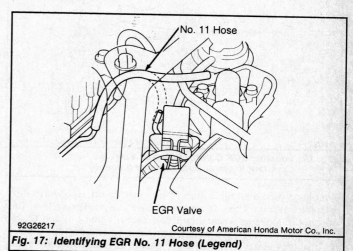

No. 11 Hose

EGR Valve

92G26217   Courtesy of American Honda Motor Co., Inc.

Fig. 17: Identifying EGR No. 11 Hose (Legend)

3) If vacuum is not present, turn ignition off. Remove connector "A" from ECM. Using an ohmmeter, check for continuity between White wire terminal of 4-pin connector and ground. If continuity is present, repair short in White wire between EGR control solenoid valve and ECM connector terminal A11. If continuity is not present, replace ECM and retest.
4) If vacuum was not present during first vacuum test in step **2)**, install vacuum pump on EGR valve. With engine idling, apply 8 in. Hg to EGR valve. If engine does not stall or run rough or EGR valve does not hold vacuum, replace EGR valve.
5) If engine stalls or runs rough and EGR valve holds vacuum, disconnect 4-pin connector from control box. Measure voltage between

Black/Yellow wire terminal and body ground. If battery voltage is not present, repair open in Black/Yellow wire between solenoid valve and FUEL PUMP fuse (No. 22, 20-amp) in underdash fuse box.

6) If battery voltage is present, install "T" fitting into No. 11 hose. Attach vacuum gauge to "T" fitting. Start engine, and allow it to idle. Connect battery voltage to terminal "A" of control box connector. *See Fig. 18.* While observing vacuum gauge, connect terminal "B" to negative battery terminal.

7) If gauge reads 6 in. Hg within one second, go to step **9)**. If gauge does not read 6 in. Hg within one second, turn ignition off. Inspect hoses for leaks, restrictions and misrouting. Repair as necessary. If hoses are okay, disconnect lower hose on EGR control solenoid valve.

8) Connect vacuum gauge to hose. *See Fig. 21.* Start engine, and allow it to idle. If 4.8-6.8 in. Hg is not present, replace Constant Vacuum Control (CVC) valve. *See Fig. 19.* If 4.8-6.8 in. Hg is present, replace EGR control solenoid valve. *See Fig. 19.*

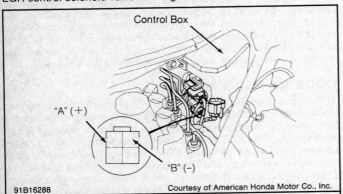

91B126288   Courtesy of American Honda Motor Co., Inc.
Fig. 18: Identifying Control Box Connector Terminals (Legend)

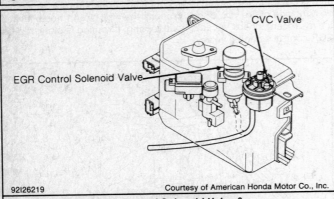

92I26219   Courtesy of American Honda Motor Co., Inc.
Fig. 19: Locating EGR Control Solenoid Valve & Constant Vacuum Control Valve (Legend)

9) If gauge read 6 in. Hg in step **7)**, turn ignition off. Reconnect 4-pin connector at control box. Disconnect EGR valve position sensor. Turn ignition on. Measure voltage between Yellow/White (+) and Green/White (−) wires. If about 5 volts are present, go to step **12)**.

10) If voltage is not about 5 volts, measure voltage between Yellow/White wire (+) and body ground. If about 5 volts are present, repair open in Green/White wire between EGR valve lift sensor and ECM connector D22. If voltage is not about 5 volts, turn ignition off.

11) Connect ECM Test Harness (07LAJ-PT3010A) connector "D" to ECM, leaving vehicle wiring harness disconnected. Turn ignition on. Measure voltage between test terminals D20 (+) and D22 (−). *See Fig. 12.* If voltage is about 5 volts, repair open in Yellow/White wire between ECM connector terminal D20 and EGR valve lift sensor. If voltage is not about 5 volts, replace ECM.

12) If voltage was about 5 volts in step **9)**, turn ignition off. Reconnect 3-pin connector at EGR valve lift sensor. Connect ECM Test Harness (07LAJ-PT3010A) between ECM and ECM connectors. *See Fig. 12.*

Turn ignition on. Measure voltage between test terminals D12 (+) and D22 (−). Voltage should be 1.2 volts with no vacuum and 4.3 volts with 6 in. Hg vacuum applied to EGR valve. If voltage is not as specified, repair open or short in Black/White wire between EGR valve lift sensor and ECM connector terminal D12.

13) If voltage is as specified, check if it consistently increases and decreases as vacuum increases and decreases. If vacuum does not consistently increase and decrease as vacuum increases and decreases, replace EGR valve. If voltage increases and decreases with vacuum, reconnect No. 11 hose. Start engine. Allow it to idle. Connect jumper wire between test terminals A11 and A26. *See Fig. 12.*

14) If engine does not stall or run rough, repair open in White wire between ECM connector terminal A11 and EGR control solenoid valve. If engine stalls or runs rough, replace ECM and retest.

CODE 13: BAROMETRIC (BARO) SENSOR

NOTE: Barometric sensor is built into ECM. Circuit testing is not required.

Turn ignition off. Remove ACG fuse (No. 15, 7.5-amp) from underdash fuse box for 10 seconds to reset ECM. Check ECM for fault codes. If Code 13 is not present, problem is intermittent. Check for poor connections at ECM connector. Test drive vehicle and check again. If Code 13 is present, replace ECM and retest.

CODE 14: IDLE AIR CONTROL VALVE (IACV)

1) Turn ignition off. Remove ACG fuse (No. 15, 7.5-amp) from underdash fuse box for 10 seconds to reset ECM. Check ECM for fault codes. If Code 14 is not present, start engine and allow to idle. Disconnect 2-pin connector from IACV. If engine speed is not reduced, replace IACV. If engine speed is reduced, problem is intermittent. Check for poor connections at ECM, IACV and wire harness connectors. Test drive vehicle and retest.

2) If Code 14 is present, turn ignition off. Disconnect 2-pin connector from IACV. Turn ignition on. Measure voltage between Yellow/Black wire and body ground. If battery voltage is not present, repair open in Yellow/Black wire between IACV and main relay. If battery voltage is present, turn ignition off. Reconnect 2-pin connector.

3) Attach connector "A" of ECM Test Harness (07LAJ-PT3010A) to ECM wiring harness, leaving ECM disconnected. *See Fig. 12.* Turn ignition on. Using a jumper wire, touch test terminal A9 to test terminal A23 several times. If IACV does not click, repair open or short circuit in Blue/Red wire between IACV and ECM connectors. If wire is okay, replace IACV. If IACV clicks, replace ECM and retest.

CODE 15: IGNITION OUTPUT SIGNAL

1) Turn ignition off. Remove ACG fuse (No. 15, 7.5-amp) from underdash fuse box for 10 seconds to reset ECM. Check ECM for fault codes. If Code 15 is not present, problem is intermittent. Check for poor connections at ECM, ignitor unit, wiring harness connectors and G102 ground terminal (located at valve cover). Test drive vehicle and retest.

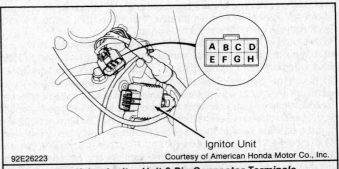

92E26223   Courtesy of American Honda Motor Co., Inc.
Fig. 20: Identifying Ignitor Unit 8-Pin Connector Terminals (Legend)

2) If Code 15 is present, turn ignition off. Disconnect 8-pin connector from ignitor unit. Using ohmmeter, check for continuity between terminals "C" and "F". *See Fig. 20.* If continuity is not present, repair open in Black wire between ground terminal G102 and 8-pin connector.

3) If continuity is present, disconnect 6-pin connector from ignitor unit. *See Fig. 21.* Connect ECM Test Harness (07LAJ-PT3010A) to ECM wiring harness connectors, leaving ECM disconnected. *See Fig. 12.* Check for continuity between body ground and test terminals A21, A22, B3, B4, B6 and B8. If continuity is present at any terminal, repair short circuit.

4) If continuity is not present, check for continuity between ignitor unit 6-pin connector terminal and corresponding terminal at ECM connectors. See ECM/IGNITOR UNIT CONNECTOR TERMINAL IDENTIFICATION table. If continuity is not present, repair open circuit. If continuity is present, substitute a known good ignitor. If symptom/condition goes away, replace original ignitor. If symptom/condition does not go away, replace ECM and retest.

ECM/IGNITOR UNIT CONNECTOR TERMINAL IDENTIFICATION

Ignitor Unit Connector Terminals	ECM Connector Terminals	Wire Color
A	B8	Blue
B	A22	Brown
C	A21	Pink
D	B3	Red
E	B4	Gray
F	B6	Green

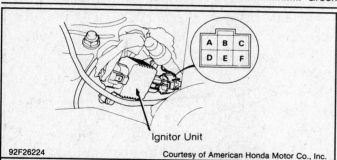

```
A B C
D E F
```

Ignitor Unit

92F26224   Courtesy of American Honda Motor Co., Inc.

Fig. 21: Identifying Ignitor Unit 6-Pin Connector Terminals (Legend)

CODE 16: FUEL INJECTOR CIRCUIT

1) Turn ignition off. Remove ACG fuse (No. 15, 7.5-amp) fuse from underdash fuse box for 10 seconds to reset ECM. Check ECM for fault codes. If Code 16 is not present, problem is intermittent. Check for poor connections at ECM, fuel injectors, fuel injector resistor and wiring harness connectors. Test drive vehicle and retest.

2) If Code 16 is present, start engine. Using a stethoscope, check for clicking sound at each injector. If injector does not click, turn ignition off. Disconnect 2-pin injector connector from affected injector. Measure resistance between injector terminals. If resistance is not 1.5-2.5 ohms, replace injector. If resistance is 1.5-2.5 ohms, go to next step.

3) Turn ignition on. Measure voltage between fuel injector wiring harness connector Red/Black wire and body ground. If battery voltage is present, go to step **6)**. If battery voltage is not present, turn ignition off.

4) Disconnect 8-pin connector at injector resistor. Turn ignition on. Measure voltage between Yellow/Black wire terminal (+) and body ground. If battery voltage is not present, repair open in Yellow/Black wire between injector resistor and main relay. If battery voltage is present, disconnect injector resistor connector.

5) Measure resistance between terminal "E" and all other terminals. *See Fig. 22.* If resistance is not 5-7 ohms, replace injector resistor. If resistance is 5-7 ohms, repair open in Red/Black wire between 2-pin connector and injector resistor.

6) If battery voltage was present in step **3)**, turn ignition off. Reconnect fuel injector connector. Connect ECM Test Harness (07LAJ-PT3010A)

between ECM and ECM connectors. *See Fig. 12.* Turn ignition on. Check voltage between A23 (–) and following test terminals.

- Injector No. 1: A1 (+)
- Injector No. 2: A3 (+)
- Injector No. 3: A5 (+)
- Injector No. 4: A2 (+)
- Injector No. 5: A4 (+)
- Injector No. 6: A6 (+)

If battery voltage is not present, repair open in wire between injector and ECM connector terminal A1, A2, A3, A4, A5 or A6. If battery voltage is present, replace ECM and retest.

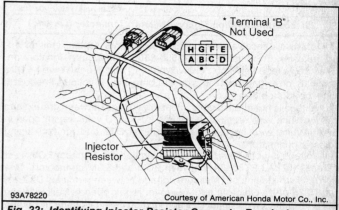

* Terminal "B" Not Used

```
H G F E
A B C D
```

Injector Resistor

93A78220   Courtesy of American Honda Motor Co., Inc.

Fig. 22: Identifying Injector Resistor Connector Terminals (Legend)

CODE 17: VEHICLE SPEED SENSOR (VSS)

1) Turn ignition off. Remove ACG fuse (No. 15, 7.5-amp) from underdash fuse box for 10 seconds to reset ECM. Road test vehicle. While in 2nd gear, accelerate until engine speed reaches 4000 RPM and then, with throttle fully closed, decelerate to 1500 RPM.

2) Check ECM for fault codes. If Code 17 is not present, problem is intermittent. Check for poor connections at ECM, VSS and wiring harness connectors. Test drive vehicle and retest.

3) If Code 17 is present, raise and support vehicle. Connect ECM Test Harness (07LAJ-PT3010A) between ECM and ECM wiring harness connectors. *See Fig. 12.* Place transaxle in Neutral. Turn ignition on. Block right front wheel and slowly rotate left front wheel. Measure voltage between test terminals A26 (–) and C2 (+). If voltage pulses 0-12 volts, replace ECM and retest.

4) If voltage does not pulse 0-12 volts, turn ignition off and disconnect connector "C" from ECM. Turn ignition on. Rotate left front wheel. If voltage does not pulse 0-12 volts, repair short or open in Yellow/Red wire between ECM terminal C2 (+) and VSS. If wire is okay, replace VSS. If voltage pulses 0-12 volts, replace ECM and retest.

CODE 18: IGNITION TIMING ADJUSTER

1) Turn ignition off. Remove ACG fuse (No. 15, 7.5-amp) from underdash fuse box for 10 seconds to reset ECM. Check ECM for fault codes. If Code 18 is not present, problem is intermittent. Check for poor connections at ECM connector and ignition timing adjuster connector. Test drive vehicle and retest.

2) If Code 18 is present, turn ignition off. Disconnect ignition timing adjuster 3-pin connector from control box. *See Fig. 23.* Measure resistance between terminals "A" and "C" of ignition timing adjuster.

3) Resistance should be 3500-6500 ohms. If resistance is as specified, go to step **4)**. If resistance is not 3500-6500 ohms, replace ignition timing adjuster.

4) Measure and record resistance between terminals "A" and "B" on timing adjuster side of harness connector. Measure and record resistance between terminals "B" and "C" on same side of connector. Add both resistance values together.

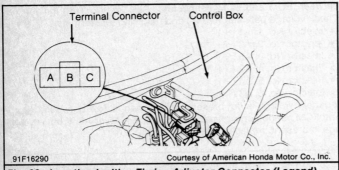

Fig. 23: *Locating Ignition Timing Adjuster Connector (Legend)*

5) If total resistance value is not 3500-6500 ohms, replace ignition timing adjuster. If resistance is 3500-6500 ohms, turn ignition on. Measure voltage between Yellow/White (+) and Green/White (–) wire terminals on wiring harness side of connector. If voltage is about 5 volts, go to step **8).**

6) If voltage is not about 5 volts, measure voltage between ground and Yellow/White wire terminal. If voltage is about 5 volts, repair open in Green/White wire between ECM terminal D22 and ignition timing adjuster connector.

7) If voltage is not about 5 volts, turn ignition off. Connect ECM Test Harness (07LAJ-PT3010A) between ECM and ECM connectors. *See Fig. 12.* Turn ignition on. Measure voltage between terminals D20 (+) and D22 (–). If voltage is about 5 volts, repair open in Yellow/White wire between ECM terminal D20 and ignition timing adjuster. If voltage is not about 5 volts, replace ECM and retest.

8) If voltage between Yellow/White and Green/White wire terminals in step **5)** was about 5 volts, turn ignition off. Reconnect ignition timing adjuster connector. Connect ECM Test Harness (07LAJ-PT3010A) between ECM and ECM connectors. *See Fig. 12.*

9) Turn ignition on. Measure voltage between ECM terminals D8 (+) and D22 (–). If voltage is not 0.5-4.5 volts, repair open or short in Blue/Yellow wire between ECM connector terminal D8 and ignition timing adjuster. If voltage is 0.5-4.5 volts, replace ECM and retest.

CODE 23 OR 53: KNOCK SENSOR

NOTE: Repair any engine knocking sounds before performing test.

1) Turn ignition off. Remove ACG fuse (No. 15, 7.5-amp) from under-dash fuse box for 10 seconds to reset ECM. Warm engine until cooling fan comes on. With transmission in Neutral, hold engine speed at 3000-4000 RPM for 10 seconds. Check for fault codes. If Code 23 or 53 is not present, problem is intermittent. Check for poor connections at ECM, knock sensor and wiring harness connectors. Test drive vehicle and retest.

2) If Code 23 or 53 is present, turn ignition off. Connect ECM Test Harness (07LAJ-PT3010A) to ECM harness connectors, leaving ECM disconnected. *See Fig. 12.*

3) Disconnect knock sensor connector. Check for continuity between test terminal D3 (right sensor) or D4 (left sensor) and body ground. If continuity is not present, go to step **4).** If continuity is present, repair short in Red/Blue wire between ECM connector terminal D4 and left knock sensor or short in White wire between ECM connector D3 and right knock sensor. *See Fig. 24.*

4) Check continuity between test terminal D4 and Red/Blue wire terminal at left knock sensor connector or between test terminal D3 and White wire terminal at right knock sensor connector. If continuity is not present, repair open in wire between ECM terminal D3 or D4 and knock sensor.

5) If continuity is present, reconnect knock sensors. Replace ECM with a known good unit. Warm engine until cooling fan comes on. With transmission in Neutral, hold engine speed at 3000-4000 RPM for 10 seconds. Check ECM for fault codes. If Code 23 or 53 is present, replace knock sensor. If Code 23 or 53 is not present, replace ECM.

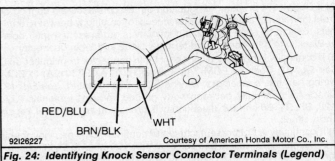

Fig. 24: *Identifying Knock Sensor Connector Terminals (Legend)*

CODE 41 OR 42: HO2S HEATER

1) Turn ignition off. Remove ACG fuse (No. 15, 7.5-amp) from under-dash fuse box for 10 seconds to reset ECM. Check ECM for fault codes. If Code 41 or 42 is not present, problem is intermittent. Check connections at ECM, HO2S and wiring harness connectors. Test drive vehicle and retest.

2) If Code 41 or 42 is present, turn ignition off. Disconnect 4-pin HO2S connector. Measure resistance between HO2S terminals "C" and "D". *See Fig. 25.* If resistance is not 10-40 ohms, replace sensor. If resistance is 10-40 ohms, go to next step.

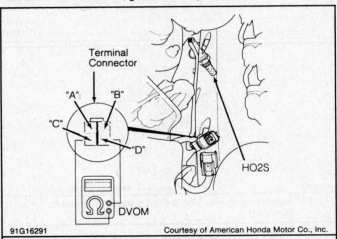

Fig. 25: *Identifying HO2S Connector Terminals (Legend Shown; Vigor Is Similar)*

3) Check continuity between body ground and all HO2S terminals. If continuity is present between any sensor terminal and ground, replace HO2S. If continuity is not present between sensor terminals and ground, check for continuity between terminal "A" and terminals "C" and "D". *See Fig. 25.* If continuity is present, replace HO2S.

4) If continuity is not present, turn ignition on. Measure voltage between HO2S wiring harness connector Black/Yellow wire and Green/Blue wire (left sensor) or Green/Red wire (right sensor). If battery voltage is present, go to step **5).** If battery voltage is not present, measure voltage between Black/Yellow terminal and body ground. If battery voltage is present, go to step **5).** If battery voltage is not present, check FUEL PUMP fuse (No. 22, 20-amp). If fuse is okay, repair open in Black/Yellow wire between HO2S and FUEL PUMP fuse.

5) Turn ignition off. Connect HO2S connector. Connect connector "A" of ECM Test Harness (07LAJ-PT3010A) to vehicle wiring harness, leaving ECM disconnected. Turn ignition on. Measure voltage between test terminal A23 (–) and test terminal A10 (+) for left HO2S or test terminal A12 (+) for right HO2S. *See Fig. 12.*

6) If battery voltage exists, replace ECM and retest. If battery voltage is not present, repair open in Green/Blue wire (left sensor) or Green/Red wire (right sensor) between ECM connector and HO2S.

7) If battery voltage was present in step **4)**, turn ignition off. Disconnect connector "A" from ECM. Turn ignition on. Measure voltage between HO2S wiring harness connector Black/Yellow wire and Green/Blue wire (left sensor) or Green/Red wire (right sensor). If battery voltage is present, repair short in Green/Blue or Green/Red wire between ECM connector and HO2S. If battery voltage exists, replace ECM and retest.

CODE 43 OR 44: FUEL SUPPLY SYSTEM

1) If referred here from CODE 1, go to step **2)**. Turn ignition off. Remove ACG fuse (No. 15, 7.5-amp) from underdash fuse box for 10 seconds to reset ECM. Warm engine until cooling fan comes on. With transmission in Neutral, hold engine speed at 3000 RPM for 2 minutes. Check ECM for fault codes. If Code 43 or 44 is present, go to next step. If Code 43 or 44 is not present, problem is intermittent. Check for poor connections at ECM, HO2S and wiring harness connectors. Test drive vehicle and retest.

> NOTE: If driveability problems are present, test fuel-related components. See SYSTEM & COMPONENT TESTING article.

2) Turn ignition off for at least 2 minutes. Connect ECM Test Harness (07LAJ-PT3010A) between ECM and ECM harness connectors. See Fig. 12.
3) If Code 43 is present, install a jumper wire between test terminals A10 and A26. Attach a digital voltmeter to test terminals A26 (–) and D14 (+). If Code 44 is present, install a jumper wire between test terminals A12 and A26. Attach a digital voltmeter to test terminals A26 (–) and D16 (+). Turn ignition on.
4) Voltage should be .6-.8 volt when ignition is turned on, then drop to less than 0.1 volt within 2 minutes. If voltage is correct, go to step **6)**. If voltage is not correct, disconnect HO2S connector. Measure voltage between HO2S wiring harness connector terminals "A" (+) and "B" (–). See Fig. 25.
5) If more than 0.1 volt is present, reconnect HO2S electrical connector. Warm engine until cooling fan comes on. With transmission in Neutral, raise engine speed to 3000 RPM and hold for 2 minutes. Measure voltage between test harness terminals D14 (+) or D16 (+) and A26 (–). Voltage should be more than 0.5 volt at wide open throttle and less than 0.5 volt when throttle is quickly released. If voltage is as specified, test fuel-related components. See SYSTEM & COMPONENT TESTING article. If voltage is not as specified, replace HO2S.
6) If voltage was correct in step **4)**, disconnect HO2S connector. Measure voltage between test terminal D14 (left sensor) or D16 (right sensor) and A26. If more than 0.1 volt is present, replace HO2S. If voltage is 0.1 volt or less, disconnect connector "D" from vehicle wiring harness.
7) Measure voltage between test terminals D14 (+) or D16 (+) and A26 (–). If more than one volt is present, repair short in Red/Blue wire (right sensor) or White wire (left sensor) between HO2S and ECM connector. If voltage is one volt or less, replace ECM and retest.

CODE 45 OR 46: FUEL METERING SYSTEM

1) Turn ignition off. Remove ACG fuse (No. 15, 7.5-amp) from underdash fuse box for 10 seconds to reset ECM. Start engine, and allow cooling fan to come on. Road test using following procedure:
- With transaxle in D_3 (A/T) or 3rd gear (M/T), cruise at exactly 35 MPH for 10 seconds.
- Release throttle. Allow vehicle to decelerate to less than 30 MPH.
- Accelerate to exactly 35 MPH and cruise for 10 seconds.
- Repeat procedure 10 times.
- Stop vehicle. Turn ignition off.
- Start vehicle. Repeat acceleration/deceleration procedure 5 times.

2) Check ECM for fault codes. If Code 45 or 46 is not present, problem is intermittent and cannot be duplicated at this time.
3) If Code 45 or 46 is present, turn ignition off. Check fuel pressure. See BASIC DIAGNOSTIC PROCEDURES article. Repair if necessary. If fuel pressure is okay, install a known good MAP sensor. Repeat step **1)** and check ECM for fault codes. If Code 45 or 46 is not present, replace original MAP sensor. If Code 45 or Code 46 is present, go to step **4)**.
4) If Code 45 is present, install known good injectors on left side of engine. If Code 46 is present, install known good injectors on right side of engine. If Code 45 and 46 are present, install known good injectors on both sides of engine.
5) Repeat step **1)** and check ECM for fault codes. If codes are not present, replace original fuel injectors. If code is present, inspect fuel line between fuel injectors and fuel filter. If restriction is found, replace or repair as necessary. If restriction is not found, replace ECM and retest.

TROUBLE CODES (VIGOR)

CODE 0 OR NO CODES

No MIL – 1) Turn ignition on. If oil pressure light is on, go to next step. If light is off, inspect BACK-UP fuse (10-amp) located in underdash fuse box. Replace fuse and repair short as necessary. If BACK-UP fuse is okay, repair open circuit in Yellow wire between fuse and instrument cluster.
2) Turn ignition off. Connect ECM Test Harness (07LAJ-PT3010A) between ECM and ECM connectors. See Fig. 12. Connect test terminal A13 to ground. Turn ignition on. If MIL is now on, go to next step. If light is off, replace light bulb or repair open in Green/Red wire between ECM terminal A13 and instrument cluster. See Fig. 12.
3) Individually measure voltage between body ground and test terminals A23 and A24. If more than one volt is present on either terminal, repair open in wire between ECM and ground terminal G101 (located on left side of engine). See Fig. 26. If less than one volt is present on each terminal, replace ECM and retest.

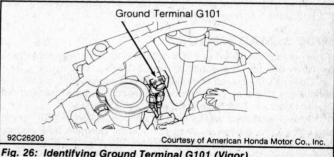

Ground Terminal G101

92C26205
Courtesy of American Honda Motor Co., Inc.
Fig. 26: Identifying Ground Terminal G101 (Vigor)

MIL Stays On – 1) Check ECM for fault codes. See RETRIEVING CODES under SELF-DIAGNOSTIC SYSTEM. Service codes. If codes are not present, remove jumper wire from self-diagnostic connector. Start engine. If engine does not start, go to step **6)**. If engine starts, turn ignition off. Connect ECM Test Harness (07LAJ-PT3010A) between ECM and ECM connectors. See Fig. 12.
2) Turn ignition on. Measure voltage between test terminals D4 (+) and D22 (–). If about 5 volts (M/T models) or 11 volts (A/T models) are present, go to step **3)**. If voltage is not about 5 volts (11 volts on A/T models), repair short to body ground in Brown wire between ECM connector terminal D4, Transmission Control Module (TCM), ABS control unit and self-diagnostic connector. See Fig. 12.
3) Connect jumper wire to self-diagnostic connector. Measure voltage between test terminals D4 and D22. If about 5 volts (11 volts on A/T models) are present, check for open in Brown or Green/White wire between self-diagnostic connector and ECM.
4) If voltage is not about 5 volts (11 volts on A/T models), remove jumper wire from self-diagnostic connector. Turn ignition off. Disconnect connector "A" of ECM. Turn ignition on.
5) If MIL is on, repair short to ground in Green/Red wire between terminal A13 and MIL. If MIL is not on, replace ECM and retest.
6) If engine did not start in step **1)**, check ECM fuse (10-amp) in underhood fuse/relay box and ECM fuse (15-amp) in underdash fuse box.

Replace fuses if necessary. Turn ignition on. Individually disconnect 3-pin connectors on EGR valve lift sensor, MAP sensor and throttle position sensor.

7) If MIL goes out, replace sensor causing MIL to go out. If MIL is on, connect jumper wire between self-diagnostic connector terminals. Disconnect ignition timing adjuster connector. Check if ECM flashes Code 18. If Code 18 is indicated, replace ignition timing adjuster.

8) If Code 18 is not indicated, turn ignition off. Remove jumper wire. Connect ECM Test Harness (07LAJ-PT3010A) between ECM and ECM connectors. *See Fig. 12.* Disconnect connector "D" from ECM side only. Individually check for continuity between body ground and terminals D19 and D20.

9) If continuity exists, repair short to body ground in Yellow/White wire between ECM terminal D19 or D20 and MAP sensor, ignition timing adjuster, throttle position sensor or EGR position sensor. If continuity does not exist, reconnect connector "D" and all sensor connectors.

10) Turn ignition on. Individually measure voltage between ECM terminal A26 (–) and terminals B1 (+) and A25 (+). If battery voltage is not present, repair open in Yellow/Black wire circuit between main relay and ECM terminals A25 and B1. If circuit is okay, check main relay and connector. If battery voltage is present, turn ignition off, replace ECM and retest.

CODE 1: HO2S

1) Turn ignition off. Remove BACK-UP fuse (10-amp) from underhood fuse/relay box for 10 seconds to reset ECM. Start engine, and warm it to normal operating temperature.

2) Road test vehicle. With transmission in 4th gear (A/T in 2nd), accelerate at wide open throttle for at least 5 seconds and then decelerate, with throttle fully closed, for at least 5 seconds.

3) Check ECM for fault codes. If Code 1 is not present, problem is intermittent. Check for poor connections at ECM connector and HO2S. If Code 1 is present, go to CODE 43.

CODE 3: MAP SENSOR

1) Turn ignition off. Remove BACK-UP fuse (10-amp) from underhood fuse/relay box for 10 seconds to reset ECM. Start engine, and let it idle. Check ECM for fault codes. If Code 3 is not present, problem is intermittent. Check for poor or loose connections at MAP sensor and ECM connectors. Test drive vehicle and retest.

2) If Code 3 is present, turn ignition off. Disconnect 3-pin MAP sensor connector. Turn ignition on. Measure voltage between MAP sensor Yellow/White wire (+) and body ground. *See Fig. 27.* If voltage is about 5 volts, go to step **4)**. If voltage is not about 5 volts, connect connector "D" of ECM Test Harness (07LAJ-PT3010A) to ECM, leaving vehicle wiring harness disconnected.

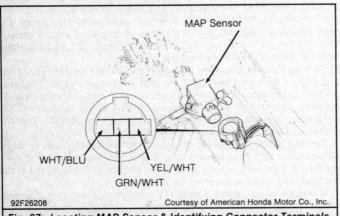

MAP Sensor

WHT/BLU

YEL/WHT

GRN/WHT

92F26208   Courtesy of American Honda Motor Co., Inc.

Fig. 27: Locating MAP Sensor & Identifying Connector Terminals (Vigor)

3) Turn ignition on. Measure voltage between test terminals D19 (+) and D21 (–). If about 5 volts are present, repair open circuit in D19 (Yellow/White wire) between ECM connector and MAP sensor. If voltage is not about 5 volts, replace ECM and retest.

4) If voltage is about 5 volts in step **2)**, measure voltage between Yellow/White (+) and Green/White (–) wires at MAP sensor. If voltage is not about 5 volts, repair open in Green/White wire between ECM terminal D21 and MAP sensor. If voltage is about 5 volts, measure voltage between White/Blue (+) and Green/White (–) wire terminals at MAP sensor.

5) If voltage is about 5 volts, go to step **7)**. If voltage is not about 5 volts, turn ignition off. On A/T models, disconnect Transmission Control Module (TCM) 22-pin connector. Turn ignition on. If about 5 volts are now present, replace TCM. If about 5 volts are still not present, turn ignition off. Go to next step.

6) On all models, connect ECM Test Harness (07LAJ-PT3010A) connector "D" only to ECM, leaving vehicle wiring harness disconnected. Measure voltage between test harness terminals D17 and D21. If about 5 volts are present, repair open or short in circuit D17 (White/Blue wire) between TCM (A/T), ECM and MAP sensor. If voltage is not about 5 volts, replace ECM and retest.

7) Turn ignition off. Reconnect 3-pin MAP sensor connector. Connect ECM Test Harness (07LAJ-PT3010A) between ECM and ECM connectors. *See Fig. 12.* Turn ignition on. Measure voltage between test terminals D17 and D21. If voltage is not about 3 volts, replace MAP sensor. If about 3 volts are present, replace ECM and retest.

CODE 4, 8, OR 9: TDC/CRANK/CYL SENSOR

1) Turn ignition off. Remove BACK-UP fuse (10-amp) from underhood fuse/relay box for 10 seconds to reset ECM. Check ECM for fault codes. If Code 4, 8 or 9 is not present, problem is intermittent. Check for poor connections at ECM, distributor and connector C308 at left shock tower. Test drive vehicle and retest.

2) If MIL is on and indicates Code 4, 8 or 9, turn ignition off. Disconnect 6-pin connector from TDC/CRANK/CYL sensor connector at cylinder head. Check resistance between terminals of each sensor. *See Fig. 6.* See INPUT SIGNAL & RESISTANCE TEST TERMINALS table. If resistance is not 650-850 ohms, replace sensor assembly. See REMOVAL, OVERHAUL & INSTALLATION article. If resistance is 650-850 ohms, go to step **3)**.

INPUT SIGNAL & RESISTANCE TEST TERMINALS

Sensor	Code	ECM Terminal	Sensor Terminal
CRANK	4	B15	E
CRANK	4	B16	B
CYL	9	B11	F
CYL	9	B12	C
TDC	8	B13	D
TDC	8	B14	A

3) Check continuity to body ground on each terminal. If continuity exists, replace sensor assembly. See REMOVAL, OVERHAUL & INSTALLATION article. If continuity does not exist, reconnect 6-pin connector. Connect ECM Test Harness (07LAJ-PT3010A) to ECM harness connectors, leaving ECM disconnected. Check resistance between terminals of each sensor at ECM test harness. See INPUT SIGNAL & RESISTANCE TEST TERMINALS table.

4) If resistance is not 650-850 ohms, repair open in faulty circuit. If resistance is 650-850 ohms, check for continuity to body ground on test terminals B11 and B13. If continuity exists on any terminal, repair short circuit. If continuity does not exist, replace ECM and retest.

CODE 5: MAP SENSOR

1) Turn ignition off. Remove BACK-UP fuse (10-amp) from underhood fuse/relay box for 10 seconds to reset ECM. Check ECM for fault codes. If Code 5 is not present, problem is intermittent. Check all vacuum hoses and connections. Test drive vehicle and retest.

2) If Code 5 is present, turn ignition off. Connect hand-held vacuum pump to MAP hose at throttle body. *See Fig. 28.* Apply vacuum. If vacuum holds, go to step **3)**. If vacuum does not hold, attach vacuum pump to MAP sensor. Apply vacuum. If vacuum does not hold, replace MAP sensor. If vacuum holds, check MAP hose for cracks, splits and looseness. Repair as necessary.

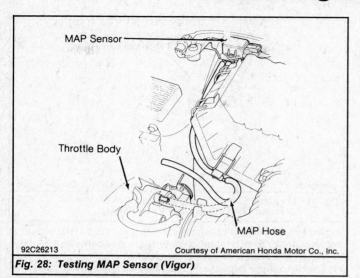

MAP Sensor

Throttle Body

MAP Hose

92C26213   Courtesy of American Honda Motor Co., Inc.

Fig. 28: Testing MAP Sensor (Vigor)

3) Connect "T" fitting in vacuum hose between MAP sensor and throttle body. Start engine. If vacuum is not present, remove restriction from throttle body. If vacuum is present, turn ignition off. Connect ECM Test Harness (07LAJ-PT3010A) between ECM and ECM connectors. See Fig. 12. Turn ignition on. Measure voltage between test terminals D17 (+) and D21 (–).

4) If voltage is not about 3 volts, replace MAP sensor. If voltage is about 3 volts, start engine and allow it to idle. Recheck voltage between test terminals D17 and D21. If voltage is not about one volt at idle, replace MAP sensor. If voltage is about one volt, replace ECM and retest.

CODE 6: COOLANT SENSOR

1) Turn ignition off. Remove BACK-UP (10-amp) fuse from underhood fuse/relay box for 10 seconds to reset ECM. Check ECM for fault codes. If Code 6 is not present, problem is intermittent. Check for poor and loose connections at coolant sensor, ECM and wiring harness. Test drive vehicle and retest.

2) If Code 6 is present, operate engine until cooling fan comes on. Turn engine off. Disconnect connector from coolant sensor. Measure resistance between sensor terminals. If resistance is not 200-400 ohms, replace coolant sensor.

3) If resistance is 200-400 ohms, turn ignition on. Measure voltage between sensor Yellow/Green wire terminal (+) and body ground. If about 5 volts are present, go to step **6)**. If voltage is not about 5 volts, go to step **4)**.

4) On A/T models, disconnect 22-pin connector from Transmission Control Module (TCM). Turn ignition on. Recheck voltage at Yellow/Green wire terminal. If voltage is about 5 volts, replace TCM. If voltage is not about 5 volts, turn ignition off and reconnect TCM. On all models, connect connector "D" of ECM Test Harness (07LAJ-PT3010A) to ECM, leaving vehicle wiring harness disconnected. Turn ignition on. Measure voltage between terminals D13 (+) and D22 (–). See Fig. 12.

5) If about 5 volts are present, repair open or short in Yellow/Green wire between ECM terminal D13, TCM (if equipped) and coolant sensor. If voltage is not about 5 volts, replace ECM and retest.

6) If voltage was about 5 volts in step **3)**, measure voltage between sensor Yellow/Green and Green/White wires. If voltage is not about 5 volts, repair open in Green/White wire between ECM connector terminal D22 and coolant sensor. If about 5 volts are present, replace ECM and retest.

CODE 7: THROTTLE POSITION SENSOR

1) Turn ignition off. Remove BACK-UP fuse (10-amp) from underhood fuse/relay box for 10 seconds to reset ECM. Check ECM for fault codes. If Code 7 is not present, problem is intermittent. Check for poor and loose connections at throttle position sensor, wiring harness connectors and ECM connector. Test drive vehicle and check again.

2) If Code 7 is present, turn ignition off. Disconnect 3-pin connector from throttle position sensor. Turn ignition on. Measure voltage between Yellow/White (+) and Green/White (–) wire terminals. If voltage is not about 5 volts, go to step **6)**. If about 5 volts are present, turn ignition off. Reconnect sensor connector. Connect ECM Test Harness (07LAJ-PT3010A) between ECM and ECM connectors. See Fig. 12.

3) Turn ignition on. Measure voltage between test terminals D11 (+) and D22 (–). Voltage should be about 0.5 volt at closed throttle and about 4.5 volts at wide open throttle. Transition from 0.5 to 4.5 volts (as throttle is opened) should be smooth. If sensor voltages are not correct, go to next step. If voltage is correct, replace ECM and retest.

4) On A/T models, disconnect 22-pin connector from Transmission Control Module (TCM). Recheck voltages. If voltages are correct, replace TCM. If sensor voltages are not correct, go to next step.

5) On all models, replace throttle position sensor or repair open or short in Red/Yellow wire between ECM terminal D11, TCM (if equipped) and throttle position sensor.

6) If voltage between Yellow/White (+) and Green/White (–) wire terminals in step **2)** was not about 5 volts, measure voltage between Yellow/White wire terminal (+) and body ground. If voltage is about 5 volts, repair open in Green/White wire between ECM terminal D22 and throttle position sensor. If voltage is not about 5 volts, turn ignition off.

7) Connect ECM Test Harness (07LAJ-PT3010A) between ECM and ECM connectors. See Fig. 12. Turn ignition on. Measure voltage between test terminals D20 (+) and D22 (–). If voltage is about 5 volts, repair open in Yellow/White wire terminal between ECM connector terminal D20 and throttle position sensor. If voltage is not about 5 volts, replace ECM and retest.

CODE 10: AIR TEMPERATURE (TA) SENSOR

1) Turn ignition off. Remove BACK-UP fuse (10-amp) from underhood fuse/relay box for 10 seconds to reset ECM. Check ECM for fault codes. If Code 10 is not present, problem is intermittent. Check for poor connections at ECM connector, air temperature sensor and wiring harness. Test drive vehicle and retest.

2) If Code 10 is present, turn ignition off. Disconnect 2-pin connector from sensor connector. Using an ohmmeter, measure resistance at sensor terminals. If resistance is not 400-4000 ohms, replace air temperature sensor. If resistance is 400-4000 ohms, turn ignition on. Measure voltage between White/Yellow wire terminal and body ground.

3) If voltage is not about 5 volts, go to step **4)**. If voltage is about 5 volts, measure voltage between White/Yellow (+) and Green/White (–) wire terminals at sensor. If voltage is not about 5 volts, repair open in Green/White wire between ECM connector terminal D22 and air temperature sensor. If voltage is about 5 volts, replace ECM and retest.

4) Turn ignition off. Connect ECM Test Harness (07LAJ-PT3010A) connector "D" to ECM, leaving wiring harness disconnected. See Fig. 12. Turn ignition on. Measure voltage between terminals D15 (+) and D22 (–). If voltage is about 5 volts, repair open or short in White/Yellow wire between ECM connector terminal D15 and air temperature sensor. If voltage is not about 5 volts, replace ECM and retest.

CODE 12: EGR SYSTEM

1) Turn ignition off. Remove BACK-UP fuse (10-amp) from underhood fuse/relay box for 10 seconds to reset ECM. Warm engine until cooling fan comes on. Road test vehicle for about 10 minutes, keeping engine speed about 1700-2500 RPM. Check ECM for fault codes. If Code 12 is not present, problem is intermittent. Check for poor connections at ECM, control box, EGR valve position sensor and wire harness connectors. Test drive vehicle and retest.

2) If Code 12 is present, start engine. Disconnect No. 1 hose from EGR valve. See Fig. 29. Connect vacuum gauge to hose. If no vacuum is present, go to step **4)**. If vacuum is present, disconnect 4-pin connector from control box. Check vacuum again on No. 1 hose. If vacuum is present, check vacuum hose routing. If routing is okay, replace EGR control solenoid valve.

3) If vacuum is not present, turn ignition off. Remove connector "A" from ECM. Using an ohmmeter, check for continuity between Red wire terminal of control box connector and ground. If continuity is present,

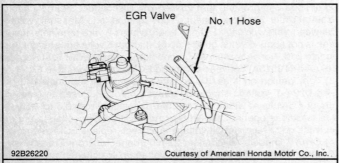

Fig. 29: Identifying EGR No. 1 Hose (Vigor)

repair short in Red wire between EGR control solenoid valve and ECM connector terminal A11. If continuity is not present, replace ECM and retest.

4) If vacuum was not present during first vacuum test in step **2)**, install vacuum pump on EGR valve vacuum port. With engine idling, apply 6 in. Hg to EGR valve. If engine does not stall or run rough or EGR valve does not hold vacuum, replace EGR valve.

5) If engine stalls or runs rough and EGR valve holds vacuum, turn ignition off and disconnect 4-pin connector from control box, located on firewall, behind intake manifold. Turn ignition on. Measure voltage between Black/Yellow wire terminal and body ground. If battery voltage is not present, repair open in Black/Yellow wire between solenoid valve and ECM fuse (No. 2, 15-amp) located in underdash fuse box. If battery voltage is present, install "T" fitting into No. 1 hose.

6) Attach vacuum gauge to "T" fitting. Start engine, and allow it to idle. Connect battery voltage to terminal "B" of 4-pin connector. See Fig. 30. While observing vacuum gauge, connect terminal "D" to negative battery terminal.

7) If gauge reads 6 in. Hg within one second, go to step **9)**. If gauge does not read 6 in. Hg within one second, turn ignition off. Inspect EGR hoses for leaks, restrictions and misrouting. Repair as necessary. If hoses are okay, disconnect lower hose on EGR control solenoid valve.

8) Connect vacuum gauge to disconnected hose. Start engine, and allow it to idle. If about 6 in. Hg is not present, replace Constant Vacuum Control (CVC) valve. See Fig. 31. If about 6 in. Hg is present, replace EGR control solenoid valve. See Fig. 31.

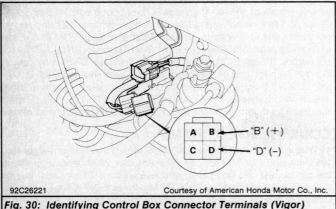

Fig. 30: Identifying Control Box Connector Terminals (Vigor)

9) If gauge read 6 in. Hg in step **7)**, turn ignition off. Reconnect 4-pin connector to control box. Disconnect 3-pin connector to EGR valve lift sensor. Turn ignition on. Measure voltage between Yellow/White (+) and Green/White (–) wire terminals. If voltage is not about 5 volts, go to step **12)**. If voltage is about 5 volts, go to step **10)**.

10) Turn ignition off. Connect 3-pin connector to EGR valve lift sensor. Connect ECM Test Harness (07LAJ-PT3010A) between ECM and ECM connectors. See Fig. 12. Turn ignition on. Measure voltage between test terminals D12 (+) and D22 (–). Voltage should be about 1.2 volts with no vacuum and about 4.3 volts with 6 in. Hg vacuum

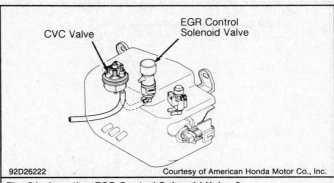

Fig. 31: Locating EGR Control Solenoid Valve & Constant Vacuum Control Valve (Vigor)

applied to EGR valve. If voltage is correct, go to step **11)**. If voltage is incorrect, repair open or short in White/Black wire between EGR valve lift sensor and ECM connector terminal D12.

11) Check if voltage consistently increases and decreases as vacuum increases and decreases. If voltage does not consistently increase and decrease with vacuum, replace EGR valve. If voltage increases and decreases with vacuum, reconnect No. 1 hose to EGR valve. Start engine, and allow it to idle. Connect a jumper wire between test terminals A11 and A26. See Fig. 12. If engine does not stall or run rough, repair open in Red wire between ECM connector terminal A11 and EGR control solenoid valve. If engine stalls or runs rough, replace ECM and retest.

12) If about 5 volts were not present in step **9)**, measure voltage between Yellow/White wire terminal of EGR valve position sensor 3-pin connector and body ground. If about 5 volts are present, repair open in Green/White wire between EGR valve lift sensor and ECM connector terminal D22. If voltage is not about 5 volts, connect connector "D" of ECM Test Harness (07LAJ-PT3010A) to ECM, leaving vehicle wiring harness disconnected.

13) Turn ignition on. Measure voltage between test terminals D20 (+) and D22 (–). If about 5 volts are present, repair open in Yellow/White wire between EGR valve and ECM connector terminal No. D20. If voltage is not about 5 volts, replace ECM and retest.

CODE 13: BAROMETRIC (BARO) SENSOR

NOTE: Barometric sensor is built into ECM. Circuit testing is not required.

Turn ignition off. Remove BACK-UP fuse (10-amp) from underhood fuse/relay box for 10 seconds to reset ECM. Check ECM for fault codes. If Code 13 is not present, problem is intermittent. Check for poor connections at ECM connector. Test drive vehicle and check again. If Code 13 is present, replace ECM and retest.

CODE 14: IDLE AIR CONTROL VALVE (IACV)

1) Turn ignition off. Remove BACK-UP fuse (10-amp) from underhood fuse/relay box for 10 seconds to reset ECM. Check ECM for fault codes. If Code 14 is not present, start engine and allow it to idle. Disconnect 2-pin connector from IACV. If engine speed is not reduced, replace IACV. If engine speed is reduced, problem is intermittent. Check for poor connections at ECM, IACV and wiring harness connectors. Test drive vehicle and retest.

2) If Code 14 is present, turn ignition off. Disconnect 2-pin connector from IACV. Turn ignition on. Measure voltage between Yellow/Black wire and body ground. If battery voltage is not present, repair open in Yellow/Black wire between IACV and main relay. If battery voltage is present, turn ignition off. Reconnect 2-pin connector.

3) Attach connector "A" of ECM Test Harness (07LAJ-PT3010A) to ECM wiring harness, leaving ECM disconnected. See Fig. 12. Turn ignition on. Using a jumper wire, touch test terminal A9 to test terminal A23 several times. If IACV does not click, repair open or short circuit in Black/Blue wire between IACV and ECM connector. If wire is okay, replace IACV. If IACV clicks, replace ECM and retest.

CODE 15: IGNITION OUTPUT SIGNAL

NOTE: If engine does not start, crank engine for at least 20 seconds to allow code to set in ECM memory.

1) Turn ignition off. Remove BACK-UP fuse (10-amp) from underhood fuse/relay box for 10 seconds to reset ECM. Check ECM for fault codes. If Code 15 is not present, problem is intermittent. Check for poor connections at ECM and ignitor unit. Test drive vehicle and check again.

2) If Code 15 is present, turn ignition off. Disconnect 4-pin connector from ignitor unit, located next to ignition coil. Turn ignition on. Measure voltage between Black/Yellow wire and body ground. If battery voltage is not present, repair open in Black/Yellow wire between ignition coil and ignition switch. If battery voltage is present, measure voltage between Black/Yellow wire and Black wire terminal at ignitor unit connector.

3) If battery voltage does not exist, repair open in Black wire between ignitor unit and ground terminal G101, located on left side of engine. *See Fig. 26.* If battery voltage exists, turn ignition off. Reconnect 4-pin connector to ignitor. Connect ECM Test Harness (07LAJ-PT3010A) between ECM and ECM wiring harness connectors.

4) Turn ignition on. Measure voltage between test terminal A26 (–) and test terminals A21 (+) and A22 (+). If voltage is not about 10 volts, check for open or short in Yellow/Green wire between ignitor unit and ECM terminals A21 or A22. If wire is shorted, ignitor may also be damaged. If wire is okay, replace ignitor. If about 10 volts are present, replace ECM and retest.

CODE 16: FUEL INJECTOR CIRCUIT

NOTE: If engine does not start, crank engine for at least 10 seconds to allow code to set in ECM memory.

1) Turn ignition off. Remove BACK-UP fuse (10-amp) from underhood fuse/relay box for 10 seconds to reset ECM. Check ECM for fault codes. If Code 16 is not present, problem is intermittent. Check for poor connections at ECM, fuel injectors, fuel injector resistor and wiring harness connectors. Test drive vehicle and retest.

2) If Code 16 is present, start engine. Using a stethoscope, check for clicking sound at each injector. If injector does not click, turn ignition off. Disconnect 2-pin injector connector from affected injector. Measure resistance between injector terminals. If resistance is not 1.5-2.5 ohms, replace injector. If resistance is 1.5-2.5 ohms, go to next step.

3) Turn ignition on. Measure voltage between fuel injector wiring harness connector Red/Black wire and body ground. If battery voltage is present, go to step **6)**. If battery voltage is not present, turn ignition off. Disconnect 8-pin connector at injector resistor.

4) Turn ignition on. Measure voltage between Yellow/Black wire terminal (+) and body ground. If battery voltage is not present, repair open in Yellow/Black wire between injector resistor and main relay. If battery voltage is present, disconnect injector resistor connector.

5) Measure resistance between terminal "A" and all other terminals. *See Fig. 32.* If resistance is not 5-7 ohms, replace injector resistor. If resistance is 5-7 ohms, repair open in Red/Black wire between 2-pin connector and injector resistor.

6) If battery voltage was present in step **3)**, turn ignition off. Reconnect fuel injector connector. Connect ECM Test Harness (07LAJ-PT3010A) between ECM and ECM wiring harness connectors. *See Fig. 12.* Turn ignition on. Check voltage between A23 (–) and following test terminals.

- Injector No. 1: A1 (+)
- Injector No. 2: A3 (+)
- Injector No. 3: A5 (+)
- Injector No. 4: A2 (+)
- Injector No. 5: A4 (+)

If battery voltage is not present, repair open in wire between injector and ECM connector terminal A1, A2, A3, A4 or A5 . If battery voltage is present, replace ECM and retest.

Injector Resistor

92H26226

Courtesy of American Honda Motor Co., Inc.

Fig. 32: Identifying Injector Resistor Connector Terminals (Vigor)

CODE 17: VEHICLE SPEED SENSOR (VSS)

1) Turn ignition off. Remove BACK-UP fuse (10-amp) from underhood fuse/relay box for 10 seconds to reset ECM. Road test vehicle. While in 2nd gear, accelerate until engine speed reaches 4000 RPM and then, with throttle fully closed, decelerate to 1500 RPM.

2) Check ECM for fault codes. If Code 17 is not present, problem is intermittent. Check for poor connections at ECM, VSS and wiring harness connectors. Test drive vehicle and retest.

3) If Code 17 is present, raise and support vehicle. Connect ECM Test Harness (07LAJ-PT3010A) between ECM and ECM connectors. *See Fig. 12.* Turn ignition on. Block right front wheel. Slowly rotate left front wheel. Measure voltage between test terminals A26 (–) and B10 (+). If voltage pulses between 0-12 volts, replace ECM and retest.

4) If voltage does not pulse 0-12 volts, turn ignition off. Disconnect test harness "B" connector from ECM, leaving wiring harness connected. Turn ignition on. Slowly rotate left front wheel while measuring voltage between test terminals A26 and B10.

5) If voltage does not pulse 0-12 volts, repair open or short in Orange wire between ECM connector terminal B10 (+) and VSS or cruise control unit. If wire is okay, replace VSS. If voltage pulses 0-12 volts, replace ECM and retest.

CODE 18: IGNITION TIMING ADJUSTER

1) Turn ignition off. Remove BACK-UP fuse (10-amp) from underhood fuse/relay box for 10 seconds to reset ECM. Check ECM for fault codes. If Code 18 is not present, problem is intermittent. Check for poor connections at ECM connector and ignition timing adjuster connector. Test drive vehicle and retest.

2) If Code 18 is present, turn ignition off. Disconnect ignition timing adjuster 3-pin connector from control box. *See Fig. 33.* Measure resistance between terminals "A" and "C" of ignition timing adjuster.

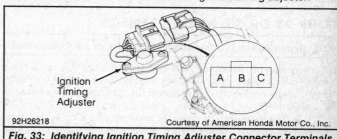

Ignition Timing Adjuster

92H26218

Courtesy of American Honda Motor Co., Inc.

Fig. 33: Identifying Ignition Timing Adjuster Connector Terminals (Vigor)

3) If resistance is 3500-6500 ohms, go to step **4)**. If resistance is not 3500-6500 ohms, replace ignition timing adjuster.

4) Measure and record resistance between terminals "A" and "B" on timing adjuster side of harness connector. Measure and record resistance between terminals "B" and "C" on same side of connector. Add both resistance values together. If total resistance is not 3500-6500 ohms, replace ignition timing adjuster.

5) If resistance is 3500-6500 ohms, turn ignition on. Measure voltage between Yellow/White (+) and Green/White (–) wire terminals on harness side of connector. If voltage is not about 5 volts, go to step **8)**.

6) If voltage is about 5 volts, measure voltage between body ground and Yellow/White wire terminal. If voltage is about 5 volts, repair open in Green/White wire between ECM terminal D22 and ignition timing adjuster connector.

7) If voltage is not 5 volts, turn ignition off. Connect ECM Test Harness (07LAJ-PT3010A) between ECM and ECM connectors. See Fig. 12. Turn ignition on. Measure voltage between ECM terminals D20 (+) and D22 (–). If voltage is about 5 volts, repair open in Yellow/White wire between ECM connector terminal D20 and ignition timing adjuster. If voltage is not about 5 volts, replace ECM and retest.

8) If voltage in step **5)** was not about 5 volts, turn ignition off. Reconnect ignition timing adjuster 3-pin connector. Connect ECM Test Harness (07LAJ-PT3010A) between ECM and ECM connectors. See Fig. 12.

9) Turn ignition on. Measure voltage between ECM terminals D8 (+) and D22 (–). If voltage is not 0.5-4.5 volts, repair open or short in Brown wire between ECM connector terminal D8 and ignition timing adjuster. If voltage is 0.5-4.5 volts, replace ECM and retest.

CODE 20: ELECTRIC LOAD DETECTOR (ELD)

1) Turn ignition off. Remove BACK-UP fuse (10-amp) from underhood fuse/relay box for 10 seconds to reset ECM. Start engine, and allow it to idle. Turn headlights on. Check ECM for fault codes. If Code 20 is not present, problem is intermittent. Check for poor connections at ECM connector and ELD connector. Test drive vehicle and retest.

2) If Code 20 is present, turn ignition off. Disconnect ELD 3-pin connector, located in underhood fuse/relay box. Turn ignition on. Measure voltage between connector Black/Yellow and Black wire terminals. If battery voltage is present, go to step **4)**. If battery voltage is not present, go to step **3)**.

3) Measure voltage between Black/Yellow wire terminal and body ground. If battery voltage is present, repair open in Black wire between 3-pin connector and ground. If battery voltage is not present, repair open in Black/Yellow wire between 3-pin connector and ECM fuse (No. 2, 15-amp).

4) If battery voltage was present in step **2)**, measure voltage between ELD connector Green/Red wire terminal and body ground. If voltage is not 4.5-5.0 volts, repair open or short in Green/Red wire between ECM terminal D10 and ELD. If 4.5-5.0 volts are present, turn ignition off. Reconnect 3-pin connector to ELD. Connect ECM Test Harness (07LAJ-PT3010A) between ECM and ECM connectors. See Fig. 12. Turn ignition on.

5) Measure voltage between test terminals A26 and D10 as follows:
- With headlight switch in first position, 1.8-2.8 volts should exist.
- With headlight switch in second position, 0.8-1.8 volts should exist.
If voltage is not as specified, replace ELD. If voltage is as specified, replace ECM and retest.

CODE 23 OR 53: KNOCK SENSOR

NOTE: Repair any engine knocking sounds before performing test.

1) Turn ignition off. Remove BACK-UP fuse (10-amp) from underhood fuse/relay box for 10 seconds to reset ECM. Warm engine until cooling fan comes on. With transmission in Neutral, hold engine speed at 3000-4000 RPM for 10 seconds. Check for fault codes. If Code 23 or 53 is not present, problem is intermittent. Check for poor connections at ECM, knock sensor and wiring harness connectors. Test drive vehicle and retest.

2) If Code 23 (knock sensor No. 1) or Code 53 (knock sensor No. 2) exists, turn ignition off. Connect ECM Test Harness (07LAJ-PT3010A) to ECM wiring harness connectors, leaving ECM disconnected. See Fig. 12. Disconnect knock sensor connector No. 308, located on left shock tower.

3) Check for continuity between test terminal C1 (sensor No. 2) or C3 (sensor No. 1) and body ground. If continuity is not present, go to next step. If continuity is present, repair short in Red/Blue wire (knock sensor No. 1) or Orange/White wire (knock sensor No. 2) between ECM connector and knock sensor. See Fig. 34.

4) Disconnect knock sensor connector No. 308. See Fig. 34. Check continuity between test terminal C3 and Red/Blue wire terminal at knock sensor connector No. 308 (knock sensor No. 1) or between test

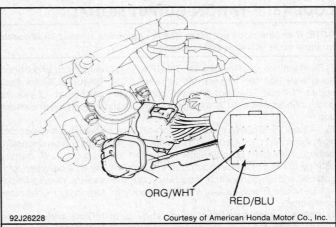

terminal C1 and Orange/White wire terminal at knock sensor connector No. 308. If continuity is not present, repair open in wire between ECM connector and knock sensor.

5) If continuity is present, replace ECM with a known good unit. Warm engine until cooling fan comes on. With transmission in Neutral, hold engine speed at 3000-4000 RPM for 10 seconds. Check ECM for fault codes. If Code 23 or 53 is present, replace appropriate knock sensor. If Code 23 or 53 is not present, replace original ECM.

CODE 30 OR 31: A/T FI SIGNAL

1) Turn ignition off. Remove BACK-UP fuse (10-amp) from underhood fuse/relay box for 10 seconds to reset ECM. Test drive vehicle for at least 5 miles, allowing transaxle to upshift and downshift. Check ECM for fault codes. If Code 30 or 31 is not present, problem is intermittent. Check for poor connections at Transmission Control Module (TCM) or ECM connectors. Test drive vehicle and retest.

2) If Code 30 or 31 is present, turn ignition off. Connect ECM Test Harness (07LAJ-PT3010A) to ECM wiring harness connectors, leaving ECM disconnected. See Fig. 6. Disconnect 22-pin connector from TCM. Using an ohmmeter, check for continuity between body ground and test terminal B3 (Code 30) or B4 (Code 31).

3) If continuity is present, repair short in White/Green (Code 30) or White/Red (Code 31) wire between ECM connector and TCM. If continuity is not present, check White/Green wire or White/Red wire continuity between ECM and TCM wiring harness connectors. Repair wire if continuity is not present. If continuity is present, replace ECM and retest.

CODE 41: HO2S HEATER

1) Turn ignition off. Remove BACK-UP fuse (10-amp) from underhood fuse/relay box for 10 seconds to reset ECM. Check ECM for fault codes. If Code 41 is not present, problem is intermittent. Check for poor connections at ECM connector and HO2S. Test drive vehicle and retest.

2) If Code 41 is present, turn ignition off. Remove HO2S covers. Disconnect 4-pin HO2S connector. Measure resistance between HO2S terminals "C" and "D". See Fig. 25. If resistance is not 10-40 ohms, replace sensor. If resistance is 10-40 ohms, go to step **3)**.

3) Check continuity between body ground and HO2S terminals "C" and "D". If continuity is present, replace sensor. If continuity is not present, check for continuity between terminal "D" and terminals "A" and "B". See Fig. 34. If continuity is present, replace sensor. If continuity is not present, go to step **4)**.

4) Turn ignition on. Measure voltage between Yellow/Black (+) and Pink/White (–) wire terminals at HO2S wiring harness connector. If battery voltage is not present, go to step **7)**. If battery voltage is present, disconnect connector "A" from ECM. Measure voltage between Yellow/Black and Pink/White wire terminals at HO2S wiring harness connector.

Fig. 34: Identifying Knock Sensor Connector No. 308 Terminals (Vigor)

ORG/WHT   RED/BLU

92J26228   Courtesy of American Honda Motor Co., Inc.

5) If battery voltage is present, repair short circuit in Pink/White wire between ECM connector terminal A6 and HO2S. If battery voltage is not present, turn ignition off. Reconnect HO2S. Connect connector "A" of ECM Test Harness (07LAJ-PT3010A) to vehicle wiring harness, leaving ECM disconnected.

6) Connect ammeter between test terminals A6 (+) and A23 (–). Turn ignition on. Monitor ammeter for 5 minutes. If current is less than 0.1 amp, replace HO2S. If current is not less than 0.1 amp, replace ECM and retest.

7) If battery voltage was not present in step **4)**, measure voltage between Yellow/Black wire terminal at HO2S wiring harness connector and body ground. If battery voltage is not present, repair open in Yellow/Black wire between HO2S and main relay. If battery voltage is present, turn ignition off. Reconnect HO2S wiring harness connector.

8) Connect connector "A" of ECM Test Harness (07LAJ-PT3010A) to ECM wiring harness, leaving ECM disconnected. Turn ignition on. Measure voltage between test terminals A6 (+) and A23 (–). If battery voltage is not present, repair open in Pink/White wire between ECM connector terminal A6 and HO2S. If battery voltage is present, replace ECM and retest.

CODE 43: FUEL SUPPLY SYSTEM

NOTE: If driveability problems are present, test fuel-related components. See SYSTEM & COMPONENT TESTING article.

1) If referred here from CODE 1, go to next step. Turn ignition off. Remove BACK-UP fuse (10-amp) from underhood fuse/relay box for 10 seconds to reset ECM. Warm engine until cooling fan comes on. With transmission in Neutral, raise engine speed to 3000 RPM and hold for 2 minutes. Check ECM for fault codes. If Code 43 is present, go to next step. If Code 43 is not present, problem is intermittent. Check for poor connections at ECM and HO2S connectors. Test drive vehicle and retest.

2) Turn ignition off. Connect ECM Test Harness (07LAJ-PT3010A) between ECM and ECM harness connectors. *See Fig. 12.* Wait 2 minutes. Install jumper wire between test terminals A6 and A26. Turn ignition on while measuring voltage between test terminals D14 (+) and A26 (–).

3) If 0.1 volt or less is present as ignition is turned on, go to step **5)**. If more than 0.1 volt is present as ignition is turned on, remove HO2S cover. Disconnect HO2S connector. Measure voltage between HO2S wiring harness connector terminals "A" and "B". *See Fig. 25.*

4) If 0.1 volt or less is present, repair open circuit in White wire between HO2S and ECM connector. If more than 0.1 volt is present, reconnect HO2S electrical connector. Warm engine until cooling fan comes on. With transmission in Neutral, raise engine speed to 3000

RPM and hold for 2 minutes. Measure voltage between test harness terminals D14(+) and A26(–). Voltage should be more than 0.5 volt at wide open throttle and less than 0.5 volt when throttle is quickly released. If voltage is as specified, test fuel-related components. See SYSTEM & COMPONENT TESTING article. If voltage is not as specified, replace HO2S.

5) If 0.1 volt or less was present as ignition was turned on in step **3)**, remove HO2S cover. Disconnect HO2S connector. Measure voltage between test terminals D14 (+) and A26 (–). If more than 0.1 volt is present, replace HO2S. If 0.1 volt or less is present, disconnect ECM connector "D" from wiring harness.

6) Measure voltage between test terminals D14 (+) and A26 (–). If more than 0.1 volt is present, repair short in White wire between ECM connector and HO2S. If 0.1 volt or less is present, replace ECM and retest.

CODE 45: FUEL METERING SYSTEM

1) Turn ignition off. Remove BACK-UP fuse (10-amp) from underhood fuse/relay box for 10 seconds to reset ECM. Start engine, and allow cooling fan to come on. Road test using following procedure:

- With transaxle in D_3 (A/T) or 3rd gear (M/T), cruise at exactly 35 MPH for 10 seconds.
- Release throttle, Allow vehicle to decelerate to less than 30 MPH.
- Accelerate to exactly 35 MPH and cruise for 10 seconds.
- Repeat procedure 10 times.
- Stop vehicle. Turn ignition off.
- Start vehicle. Repeat acceleration/deceleration procedure 5 times.

2) Check ECM for fault codes. If Code 45 is not present, problem is intermittent and cannot be duplicated at this time.

3) If Code 45 is present, turn ignition off. Check fuel pressure. See BASIC DIAGNOSTIC PROCEDURES article. Repair if necessary. If fuel pressure is okay, install known good MAP sensor. Repeat step **1)**. Check ECM for fault codes. If Code 45 is not present, replace original MAP sensor. If Code 45 is present, go to step **4)**.

4) Install known good fuel injectors. Repeat steps **1)** and **2)**. If Code 45 is not present, replace original fuel injectors. If Code 45 is still present, inspect fuel line between fuel injectors and fuel filter. If restriction is found, replace or repair as necessary. If no restriction is found, replace ECM and retest.

1993 ENGINE PERFORMANCE
Trouble Shooting – No Codes

Integra, Legend, Vigor

INTRODUCTION

Before diagnosing symptoms or intermittent faults, perform steps in BASIC DIAGNOSTIC PROCEDURES and SELF-DIAGNOSTICS articles. Use this article to diagnose driveability problems existing when a hard fault code is not present.

NOTE: *Some driveability problems may have been corrected by manufacturer with a revised computer calibration chip or computer control unit. Check with manufacturer for latest chip or computer application.*

Symptom checks can direct technician to malfunctioning component(s) for further diagnosis. A symptom should lead to a specific component, system test or adjustment.

Use intermittent test procedures to locate driveability problems that do not occur when vehicle is being tested. These test procedures should also be used if a soft (intermittent) trouble code was present but no problem was found during self-diagnostic testing.

NOTE: *For specific testing procedures, see SYSTEM & COMPONENT TESTING article. For specifications, see ON-VEHICLE ADJUSTMENTS or SERVICE & ADJUSTMENT SPECIFICATIONS article.*

SYMPTOMS

SYMPTOM DIAGNOSIS

Symptom checks cannot be used properly unless problem occurs while vehicle is being tested. To reduce diagnostic time, ensure steps in BASIC DIAGNOSTIC PROCEDURES and SELF-DIAGNOSTICS articles were performed before diagnosing a symptom. Symptoms available for diagnosis include following.

- Engine Will Not Start
- Difficult Cold Start
- Fast Idle Out Of Specification
- Rough Idle When Warm
- Idle RPM High When Warm
- Idle RPM Low When Warm
- Stalling During Warm-Up
- Stalling After Warm-Up
- Misfire Or Rough Operation
- Emission Test Failure
- Lack Of Power

Recommended system and component checks may not apply to all vehicles.

ENGINE WILL NOT START

Ensure steps for spark and fuel testing in BASIC DIAGNOSTIC PROCEDURES article have been performed. Test ECU power and ground circuits. On Legend, also check coolant temperature sensor.

DIFFICULT COLD START

Check coolant temperature, MAP and CRANK/CYL (Legend) or TDC/CRANK/CYL (Integra and Vigor) sensors. Check ECU, injectors and idle control system components.

FAST IDLE OUT OF SPECIFICATION

Check idle control system components and fuel supply system. Check coolant temperature and throttle angle sensors.

ROUGH IDLE WHEN WARM

Check EACV operation, injectors, EGR system and other emission components. Check MAP, O_2, CRANK/CYL (Legend) or TDC/CRANK/CYL (Integra and Vigor), throttle angle and intake air temperature sensors.

IDLE RPM HIGH WHEN WARM

Check EACV and idle control system components. Check MAP sensor, air intake system and emission systems.

IDLE RPM LOW WHEN WARM

Check EACV, air intake system, MAP sensor, injectors, EGR system and idle control system components.

STALLING DURING WARM-UP

Check EACV, air intake system, idle control system components, fuel supply system and EGR system. Check MAP, CRANK/CYL (Legend) or TDC/CRANK/CYL (Integra and Vigor), coolant temperature and throttle angle sensors.

STALLING AFTER WARM-UP

Check EGR system, EACV, air intake system and fuel supply system. Check MAP, throttle angle, CRANK/CYL (Legend) or TDC/CRANK/CYL (Integra and Vigor), and vehicle speed sensors.

MISFIRE OR ROUGH OPERATION

Check each injector at idle. Check fuel supply, EACV, ignition output signal and EGR system. Check MAP, O_2, CRANK/CYL (Legend) or TDC/CRANK/CYL (Integra and Vigor), and throttle angle sensors.

EMISSION TEST FAILURE

Check injectors and all emission control components. Check MAP, O_2, CRANK/CYL (Legend) or TDC/CRANK/CYL (Integra and Vigor), and coolant temperature sensors.

LACK OF POWER

Check for binding brakes or plugged exhaust. Check fuel supply system, emission control components, injectors, air intake system and EGR system. Check MAP, throttle angle, coolant temperature and vehicle speed sensors. On Integra 1.7L, check spool timing valve and valve timing oil pressure switch.

INTERMITTENTS

INTERMITTENT PROBLEM DIAGNOSIS

Intermittent fault testing requires duplicating circuit or component failure to identify problem. These procedures may lead to computer setting a fault code (on some systems) which may help in diagnosis.

If problem vehicle does not produce fault codes, use DVOM to pinpoint faults. Monitor voltage or resistance values while attempting to reproduce conditions causing intermittent fault. A status change on DVOM indicates area of fault.

When monitoring voltage, ensure ignition switch is in ON position or engine is running. Ensure ignition switch is in OFF position or negative battery cable is disconnected when monitoring circuit resistance.

TEST PROCEDURES

Intermittent Simulation – To reproduce conditions creating intermittent fault, use following methods:
- Lightly vibrate component.
- Heat component.
- Wiggle or bend wiring harness.
- Spray component with water mist.
- Remove/apply vacuum source.

Monitor circuit/component voltage or resistance while simulating intermittent. If engine is running, monitor for self-diagnostic codes. Use test results to identify a faulty component or circuit.

Integra, Legend, Vigor

INTRODUCTION

Before testing separate components or systems, perform procedures in BASIC DIAGNOSTIC PROCEDURES article. Since many computer-controlled and monitored components set a trouble code if they malfunction, also perform procedures in SELF-DIAGNOSTICS article.

NOTE: Testing individual components does not isolate shorts or opens. Perform all voltage tests with a Digital Volt-Ohmmeter (DVOM) with a minimum 10-megohm input impedance, unless stated otherwise in test procedure. Use ohmmeter to isolate wiring harness shorts or opens.

AIR INDUCTION SYSTEMS

AIR INTAKE SYSTEM

NOTE: Many tests can be performed only with Engine Control Module (ECM) Test Harness (O7LAJ-PT3010A). Terminals on ECM test harness connectors match terminals on ECM and wire harness connectors. This allows the technician to test continuity and resistance of vehicle wire harness and devices. Sensor input values can also be monitored while engine is in operation. To identify ECM terminals, see Fig. 1. Integra does not use terminals C1-C12.

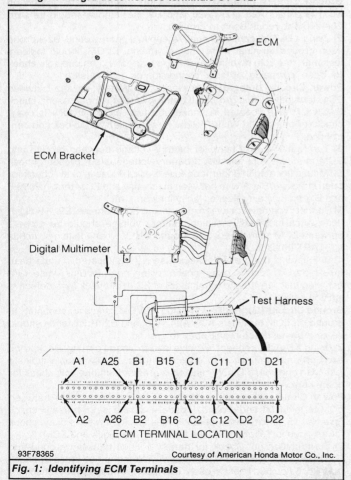

93F78365   Courtesy of American Honda Motor Co., Inc.

Fig. 1: Identifying ECM Terminals

Intake Air By-Pass (IAB) Control Solenoid Valves (Legend) – 1) IAB control solenoid valves are located at right front of engine compartment. Check IAB valve shaft for binding, sticking, and smooth movement. If necessary, clean linkage and shafts with carburetor cleaner.

2) Start engine and let idle. Remove vacuum hose No. 2 from IAB low control diaphragm. *See Fig. 2.* Connect vacuum gauge to hose. If vacuum is not present, go to step **6)**. If vacuum is present, go to step **3)**.

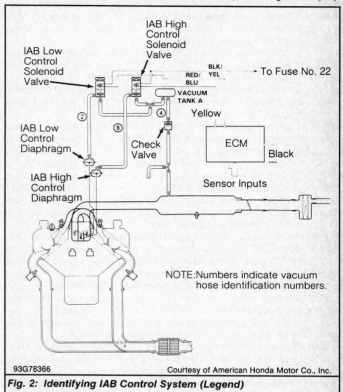

93G78366   Courtesy of American Honda Motor Co., Inc.

Fig. 2: Identifying IAB Control System (Legend)

3) Disconnect vacuum hose No. 8 from IAB high control diaphragm. Connect vacuum gauge to hose. If vacuum is present, go to next step. If vacuum is not present, go to step **11**.
4) Increase engine speed to 3300 RPM. Check for vacuum at hose No. 2. If vacuum is not present, go to next step. If vacuum is present, go to step **16)**.
5) Increase engine speed to 4000 RPM. Check for vacuum at hose No. 8. If vacuum is not present, system is okay. If vacuum is present, go to step **18)**.
6) Remove vacuum hose No. 4 at IAB low control solenoid. Connect vacuum gauge to hose. If vacuum is present, go to next step. If vacuum is not present, check vacuum lines between solenoid, vacuum tank and intake manifold. *See Fig. 2.* Repair as necessary and recheck.
7) Turn ignition off. Unplug 6-wire connector from IAB low control solenoid. Turn ignition on. Measure voltage between Black/Yellow (positive) and Red/Blue (negative) wire terminals. If battery voltage is present, replace by-pass low control solenoid valve. If voltage is not present, go to next step.
8) Measure voltage between Black/Yellow wire terminal and body ground. If battery voltage is not present, repair open in Black/Yellow wire between solenoid 6-wire connector and fuse No. 22. If battery voltage is present, go to next step.
9) Turn ignition off. Install ECM test harness connector between ECM and ECM harness connector. Check Red/Blue wire for continuity between ECM terminal A14 and solenoid connector.
10) If continuity does not exist, repair open in Red/Blue wire. If continuity exists, substitute a known-good ECM and retest. If symptom goes away, replace ECM.
11) Remove vacuum hose No. 4 at IAB high control solenoid. Connect vacuum gauge to hose. If vacuum is present, go to next step. If vacuum is not present, check vacuum line between solenoid and intake manifold. Repair as necessary and recheck.
12) Turn ignition off. Unplug 6-wire connector from IAB high control solenoid. Turn ignition on. Measure voltage between Black/Yel

(positive) and Red/Blue (negative) wire terminals. If battery voltage is present, replace IAB high control solenoid valve. If voltage is not present, go to next step.

13) Measure voltage between Black/Yellow wire terminal and body ground. If battery voltage is not present, repair open in Black/Yellow wire between solenoid 6-wire connector and fuse No. 22. If battery voltage is present, go to next step.

14) Turn ignition off. Install ECM test harness connector between ECM and ECM harness connector. Check Yellow wire for continuity between ECM terminal A18 and solenoid connector.

15) If continuity does not exist, repair open in Yellow wire. If continuity exists, substitute a known-good ECM and retest. If symptom goes away, replace ECM.

16) Turn ignition off. Unplug 6-pin connector from IAB low control solenoid. If vacuum is present, replace IAB low control solenoid valve. If vacuum is not present, go to next step.

17) Unplug connector "A" from ECM. Check Red/Blue wire for short to ground. Repair as necessary. If Red/Blue wire is okay, substitute a known-good ECM and retest. If symptom goes away, replace ECM.

18) Unplug 6-pin connector from by-pass high control solenoid valve. If vacuum is present, replace by-pass high control solenoid valve. If vacuum is not present, go to next step.

19) Unplug connector "A" from ECM. Check Yellow wire between connector and ECM terminal A18 for short to ground. Repair as necessary. If Yellow wire is okay, substitute a known-good ECM and retest. If symptom goes away, replace ECM.

Intake Air By-Pass (IAB) Control Solenoid Valve (Vigor) – 1) IAB control solenoid valve is located on top of intake manifold. Start and idle engine. Disconnect vacuum hose No. 13 from by-pass control diaphragm. *See Fig. 3.* Connect vacuum gauge to hose. If vacuum exists, go to step **6)**. If vacuum does not exist, go to next step.

2) Unplug 2-pin connector from by-pass control solenoid valve. Measure voltage between Black/Yellow and Blue/Red wire terminals of harness connector. If battery voltage exists, repair vacuum leak or blockage between intake manifold and diaphragm. If vacuum is okay, replace by-pass control solenoid valve. If battery voltage does not exist, go to next step.

3) Measure voltage between harness connector Black/Yellow wire terminal and body ground. If battery voltage does not exist, repair open in Black/Yellow wire between connector and fuse No. 2. If battery voltage exists, go to next step.

4) Turn ignition off. Reconnect wiring to by-pass control solenoid valve. Connect test harness to main wire harness only. DO NOT connect it to ECM.

5) Turn ignition on. Connect jumper wire between ECM terminals A17 and A26. If solenoid clicks when jumper wire is connected, substitute a known-good ECM and recheck operation. If solenoid valve does not

click, repair open circuit between harness connector Blue/Red wire and ECM terminal A17.

6) Increase engine speed to 4900 RPM. Check for vacuum at hose No. 13. If there is no vacuum, system is okay. If vacuum exists, unplug 2-pin connector from by-pass control solenoid valve. If vacuum now exists, replace by-pass control solenoid valve. If vacuum does not exist, go to next step.

7) Turn ignition off. Unplug connector "A" from ECM. Check Blue/Red wire for short to ground between ECM terminal A17 and by-pass control solenoid valve connector. Repair as necessary. If Blue/Red wire is okay, substitute a known-good ECM and recheck operation. If symptom goes away, replace ECM.

COMPUTERIZED ENGINE CONTROLS
ENGINE CONTROL UNIT (ECM)

NOTE: Integra M/T uses Engine Control Module (ECM); Integra A/T uses Powertrain Control Module (PCM), which also controls transmission functions. When working on A/T models, all references to ECM also applies to PCM.

NOTE: On all models, ECM is located under a cover panel, in front passenger footwell.

Ground Circuits (Integra) – 1) Measure resistance to ground on ECM terminals A23, A24, A26, and B2. Resistance should be zero ohms. If not, repair open to ground.

2) Using a DVOM, connect negative lead to a good ground. Backprobe each ground terminal. With engine running, DVOM should indicate less than one volt. If voltmeter reading is greater than one volt, check for open, corrosion, or loose connection on ground lead.

Power Circuits (Integra) – 1) Check for battery voltage between ECM terminal D1 and ground. If battery voltage is not present, check BACK UP fuse (located in underhood fuse block). If fuse is okay, check for an open in White/Yellow wire between fuse block and control unit.

2) Turn ignition on. Check for battery voltage between ground and ECM terminals A25 and B1. If battery voltage is not present, check ECM fuse (located in underhood fuse block). If fuse is okay, check for open in Yellow/Black wire between main relay and ECM terminals A25 and B1, faulty main relay, or faulty ignition switch.

3) Connect voltmeter between ground and ECM terminal B9. Hold ignition switch in START position. Battery voltage should be present between ECM terminal B9 and ground ONLY when ignition switch is in START position.

4) If voltage is not present, check fuse No. 18 (located in underdash fuse block). If fuse is okay, check for an open in Blue/White wire between fuse No. 18 and terminal B9 of ECM, or check for a defective ignition switch.

Ground Circuits (Legend) – 1) Using a DVOM, check for continuity to ground on ECM terminals A23, A24, A26, and B2. Resistance should be zero ohms. If not, repair open to ground.

2) Using a DVOM, connect negative lead to a good ground. Backprobe each ground terminal. With engine running, DVOM should indicate less than one volt. If DVOM reading is greater than one volt, check for open, corrosion, or loose connection on ground lead.

Power Circuits (Legend) – 1) Check for battery voltage between ECM terminal D1 and ground. If battery voltage is not present, check fuse No. 15 (located in underdash fuse block). If fuse is okay, check for an open in Yellow/Blue wire between fuse block and ECM.

2) Turn ignition on. Check for battery voltage between ground and ECM terminals A25 and C1. If battery voltage is not present, check fuse No. 5 (located in underdash fuse block). If fuse is okay, check for an open in Yellow/Black wire between main relay and ECM terminals A25 and B1, defective main relay, or defective ignition switch.

3) Connect DVOM between ECM terminal C11 and ground. Hold ignition switch in START position. Battery voltage should be present between ECM terminal C11 and ground ONLY when ignition switch is in the START position.

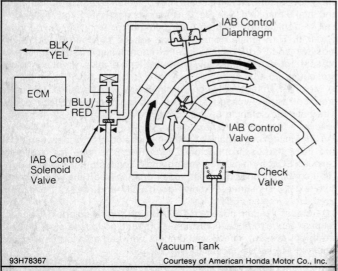

BLK/YEL

ECM

BLU/RED

IAB Control Diaphragm

IAB Control Valve

Check Valve

IAB Control Solenoid Valve

Vacuum Tank

93H78367   Courtesy of American Honda Motor Co., Inc.

Fig. 3: *Identifying By-Pass Control Components (Vigor)*

4) If battery voltage is not present, check fuse No. 14 (located in under-dash fuse block). If fuse is okay, check for an open in Blue/White wire between fuse No. 18 and terminal C11 of ECM, or check for a defective ignition switch.

Ground Circuits (Vigor) – 1) Measure resistance to ground on ECM terminals A23, A24, A26, and B2. Resistance should be zero ohms. If resistance is not zero ohms, repair open to ground.

2) Using a DVOM, connect negative lead to a good ground. Backprobe each ground terminal. With engine running, DVOM should indicate less than one volt. If DVOM reading is greater than one volt, check for open, corrosion, or loose connection on ground lead.

Power Circuits (Vigor) – 1) Check for battery voltage between ECM terminal D1 and ground. If battery voltage is not present, check BACK UP fuse (located in underhood fuse block). If fuse is okay, check for an open in White/Green wire between fuse block and control unit.

2) Turn ignition on. Check for battery voltage between ground and ECM terminals A25 and B1. If battery voltage is not present, check ECM fuse (located in underhood fuse block). If fuse is okay, check for open in Yellow/Black wire between main relay and ECM terminals A25 and B1, defective main relay, or defective ignition switch.

3) Connect voltmeter between ground and ECM terminal B9. Hold ignition switch in START position. Battery voltage should be present between ECM terminal B9 and ground ONLY when ignition switch is in START position.

4) If battery voltage is not present, check fuse No. 18 (located in under-dash fuse block). If fuse is okay, check for an open in Blue/Red wire between fuse No. 9 and terminal B9 of control unit, or check for a defective ignition switch.

ENGINE SENSORS & SWITCHES

ATMOSPHERIC PRESSURE (PA) SENSOR

Sensor is located inside ECM. Check for diagnostic trouble code stored in ECM memory. See SELF-DIAGNOSTICS article.

CLUTCH SWITCH

Legend – Turn ignition off. Unplug 2-wire connector (Pink and Black wires) from clutch switch, located on clutch pedal. With clutch pedal depressed, check continuity of switch. If no continuity exists, replace clutch switch.

COOLANT TEMPERATURE (TW) SENSOR

TW sensor is threaded into upper front side of engine on Integra, and upper right of engine on Legend and Vigor. Unplug 2-wire connector (Red/White and Green/White wires) from sensor. Resistance should be as specified in COOLANT TEMPERATURE (TW) SENSOR RESISTANCE table.

COOLANT TEMPERATURE (TW) SENSOR RESISTANCE [1]

Temperature – °F (°C)	Ohms
-4 (-20)	15,000-18,000
68 (20)	2000-4000
176 (80)	
Integra & Vigor	200-400
Legend	300-400

[1] – Measure resistance across sensor terminals.

CRANK/CYL/TDC SENSORS

1) On Integra, CRANK/CYL/TDC sensors are located within distributor. On Legend, sensors are located under upper left timing belt cover. On Vigor, sensors are under upper timing cover. To test sensor and wiring connections, turn ignition off. Probe appropriate ECM harness terminals to check for resistance of each sensor. See CRANK/CYL/TDC SENSOR RESISTANCE table. If resistance is not as specified, go to step 3).

2) If resistance is as specified, check for continuity to ground at each terminal. If continuity exists, unplug sensor connector and recheck appropriate ECM terminal for continuity to ground. If continuity still exists, repair short to ground in harness. If continuity does not exist, replace sensor assembly.

3) Unplug harness connector at sensor. *See Fig. 4, 5 or 6.* Measure sensor resistance at connector. See CRANK/CYL/TDC SENSOR RESISTANCE table. If sensor resistance is as specified, repair open, short, or corrosion in sensor harness between ECM and sensor. If sensor resistance is not as specified, replace sensor assembly.

CRANK/CYL/TDC SENSOR RESISTANCE

Application	ECM Terminals	Ohms
Integra & Vigor		
CRANK	B15 & B16	350-700
CYL	B11 & B12	350-700
TDC	B13 & B14	350-700
Legend		
CRANK No. 1	B15 & B16	600-950
CRANK No. 2	B14 & B13	600-950
CYL No. 1	B12 & B11	600-950
CYL No. 2	B9 & B10	600-950

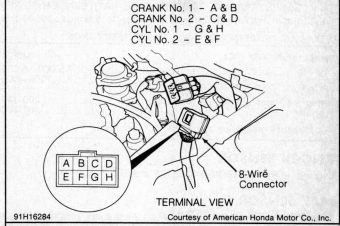

CRANK – B & F
TDC – C & G
CYL – D & H

VIEW FROM TERMINAL SIDE

92G25243

Courtesy of American Honda Motor Co., Inc.

Fig. 4: Identifying TDC/CRANK/CYL Sensor Connector (Integra)

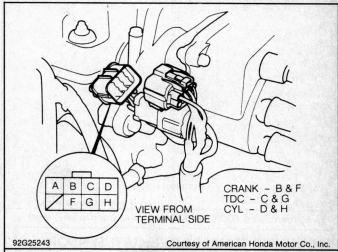

CRANK No. 1 – A & B
CRANK No. 2 – C & D
CYL No. 1 – G & H
CYL No. 2 – E & F

8-Wire Connector

TERMINAL VIEW

91H16284

Courtesy of American Honda Motor Co., Inc.

Fig. 5: Identifying CRANK/CYL Sensor Connector (Legend)

EGR VALVE LIFT SENSOR

Integra A/T – 1) EGR lift sensor is part of EGR valve, located on top of engine. Turn ignition on. Measure voltage between terminals Yellow/White wire (positive) and Green/White wire (negative) by backprobing EGR valve lift sensor connector. If voltage is not about 5 volts, repair open in Yellow/White or Green/White wire between ECM and EGR valve.

2) Measure voltage between Yellow wire (positive) and Green/White wire (negative) by backprobing EGR valve lift sensor 4-wire connector. If voltage is about 1.2 volts, slowly apply 8 in. Hg vacuum to EGR valve. Completely release and reapply vacuum several times. Voltmeter should indicate about 4 volts with vacuum applied. If voltage is not as specified, replace EGR valve.

Legend – 1) EGR lift sensor is part of EGR valve, located on top of engine. Connect test harness between EGR valve lift sensor and engine wire harness. Turn ignition on. Measure voltage between Red and Green wire terminals. If voltmeter does not indicate approximately 5 volts, repair Yellow/White or Green/White wire between ECM and EGR lift sensor.

2) Measure voltage between terminals of White wire (positive) and Green wire (negative). If voltage is about 1.2 volts, slowly apply 8 in. Hg vacuum to EGR valve. Completely release and reapply vacuum several times. Voltmeter should indicate about 4 volts with vacuum applied. If voltage is not as specified, replace EGR valve.

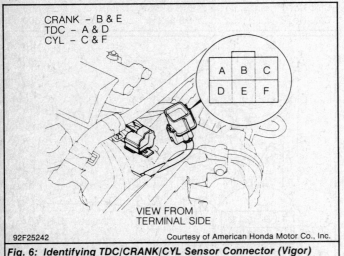

```
CRANK – B & E
TDC   – A & D
CYL   – C & F

        A  B  C
        D  E  F

VIEW FROM
TERMINAL SIDE
```

92F25242   Courtesy of American Honda Motor Co., Inc.

Fig. 6: Identifying TDC/CRANK/CYL Sensor Connector (Vigor)

INTAKE AIR TEMPERATURE (IAT) SENSOR

Unplug IAT sensor 2-wire connector, located on throttle body. Measure resistance between sensor terminals at specified temperatures. See INTAKE AIR TEMPERATURE (IAT) SENSOR RESISTANCE table. Replace IAT sensor if resistance is not as specified.

INTAKE AIR TEMPERATURE (TA) SENSOR RESISTANCE [1]

Temperature – °F (°C)	Ohms
–4 (–20)	15,000-18,000
68 (20)	2000-4000
176 (80)	
Integra & Vigor	200-400
Legend	300-400

[1] – Measure resistance across sensor terminals.

KNOCK SENSOR

Legend – See SELF-DIAGNOSTICS article.

MAP SENSOR

1) MAP sensor is located on firewall on Integra, inside control box on firewall (Legend) or left side of engine compartment (Vigor). Unplug connector from MAP sensor. Turn ignition on. Measure voltage between Yellow/Red and Green/White wires on Integra, or between Yellow/White and Green/White wires on Legend and Vigor. If voltmeter does not indicate about 5 volts, repair wiring between MAP sensor and ECM. If wiring is okay, replace ECM. If voltmeter indicates about 5 volts, go to next step.

2) Turn ignition off. Connect test harness between ECM and vehicle wire harness. Turn ignition on. Measure voltage between terminals 7 and 21. If voltage is not as specified in MAP SENSOR VOLTAGE

table, check sensor output wire between MAP sensor and ECM. Wire is White on Integra, Yellow/White on Legend and White/Blue on Vigor. If wire is okay, replace MAP sensor.

MAP SENSOR VOLTAGE

In. Hg Vacuum Applied	Volts
0	2.8-3.0
5	2.3-2.5
10	1.8-2.0
15	1.3-1.5
20	.8-1.0
25	.3-.5

OXYGEN SENSOR

Oxygen sensor(s) is threaded into exhaust manifold(s). Turn ignition off. Connect test harness between ECM and vehicle wire harness. Connect voltmeter between terminals specified in OXYGEN SENSOR TEST TERMINALS table. Turn ignition on. If voltmeter does not indicate .4 - .5 volt when ignition is first turned on, and less than .1 volt in less than 2 minutes, check wiring between ECM and oxygen sensor. If wiring is okay, replace oxygen sensor.

OXYGEN SENSOR TEST TERMINALS

Model	Terminals
Integra & Vigor	A26 & D14
Legend	
Left Oxygen Sensor	A26 & D14
Right Oxygen Sensor	A26 & D16

POWER STEERING PRESSURE (PSP) SWITCH

1) Unplug PSP switch connector, located near front of engine. Check continuity through PSP switch. With front wheels stationary, switch should be closed. Turn steering wheel left and right, and ensure switch is open. If continuity is not as specified, replace PSP switch.

2) To check wiring harness, unplug PSP switch 2-wire connector. Turn ignition on. Check for battery voltage between PSP switch terminals. If no voltage is present, repair open in wire(s). If wires are okay, substitute a known-good ECM. If problem goes away, replace ECM.

THROTTLE POSITION (TP) SENSOR

1) Unplug connector from TP sensor, located on throttle body. Turn ignition on. Measure voltage between Yellow/White (positive) and Green/White (negative) wire terminals. If voltage is not about 5 volts, check wiring between TP sensor and ECM. If wiring is okay, replace ECM.

2) If voltage is about 5 volts, turn ignition off. Reconnect wire harness to throttle angle sensor. Connect test harness between ECM and vehicle wire harness. Turn ignition on. Measure voltage between test harness terminals D11 and D22. Voltage should be about .5 volt with throttle valve at full-closed position, and about 4.5 volts with throttle valve at full-open position. As throttle opens, voltage should increase smoothly from .5 volt to 4.5 volts.

3) If voltage is not as specified, check for short or open in Red/Blue wire (Integra and Legend) or Red/Yellow wire (Vigor) between ECM and TP sensor. Repair as necessary. If wire is okay, replace TP sensor.

VEHICLE SPEED SENSOR (VSS)

1) VSS is located at left front wheel. Connect test harness between ECM and VSS harness connectors. Block rear wheels. Set parking brake. Raise and support front of vehicle. Connect voltmeter between test harness terminals A26 and B10 (Integra and Vigor) or between terminals A26 and C2 (Legend).

2) Turn ignition on. Slowly rotate left front wheel. Voltage should pulsate between zero and 5 volts. If voltage pulsates as specified, go to step 3). If voltage does not pulsate as specified, check for open or short in Yellow/Red wire between ECM terminal B16 and speed sensor. If wire is okay, replace faulty VSS or ECM.

3) Substitute a known-good ECM, and retest. If problem goes away, replace ECM.

RELAYS & SOLENOIDS

RELAYS

NOTE: *The fuel pump relay is an integral component of the main relay.*

Fuel Pump Relay (Integra) – **1)** Remove main relay, located near underdash fuse block. Check for continuity between relay terminals No. 5 and 7. *See Fig. 7.* If continuity exists, replace relay. If continuity does not exist, go to step **2)**.

2) Check for continuity between relay terminals No. 1 and 3. If continuity exists, replace relay. If continuity does not exist, go to step **3)**.

3) Using a fused jumper wire, connect positive battery terminal to relay terminal No. 4. Connect relay terminal No. 8 to ground. Check for continuity between relay terminals No. 5 and 7. If continuity exists, go to step **4)**. If continuity does not exist, replace relay.

4) Connect positive battery terminal to relay terminal No. 5. Ground terminal No. 2. Check for continuity between relay terminals No. 1 and 3. If continuity exists, go to step **5)**. If continuity does not exist, replace relay.

5) Connect battery positive terminal to relay terminal No. 3. Connect battery negative terminal to relay terminal No. 8. Check for continuity between relay terminals No. 5 and 7. If continuity exists, relay is okay. If continuity does not exist, replace relay.

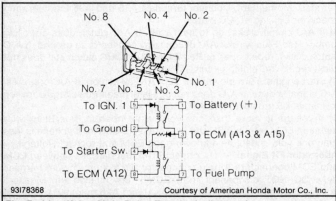

Fig. 7: Identifying Main Relay Terminals (Integra)

Fuel Pump Relay (Legend & Vigor) – **1)** Remove main relay, located at left side of cowl. Check for continuity between relay terminals No. 1 and 3. *See Fig. 8.* If continuity exists, replace relay. If continuity does not exist, go to step **2)**.

2) Check for continuity between relay terminals No. 5 and 7. If continuity exists, replace relay. If continuity does not exist, go to step **3)**.

3) Using a fused jumper wire, connect positive battery terminal to relay terminal No. 4. Connect relay terminal No. 8 to ground. Check for continuity between relay terminals No. 5 and 7. If continuity exists, go to step **4)**. If continuity does not exist, replace relay.

4) Connect positive battery terminal to relay terminal No. 6. Connect negative battery terminal to relay terminal No. 2. Check for continuity between relay terminals No. 1 and 3. If continuity exists, go to step **5)**. If continuity does not exist, replace relay.

5) Connect positive battery terminal to relay terminal No. 3. Connect negative battery terminal to relay terminal No. 8. Check for continuity between relay terminals No. 5 and 7. If continuity exists, relay is okay. If continuity does not exist, replace relay.

SOLENOIDS

Air Suction Control Solenoid Valve (Legend) – See AIR INJECTION under EMISSION SYSTEMS & SUB-SYSTEMS.

By-Pass Control Solenoid Valves (Legend) – See AIR INTAKE SYSTEM under AIR INDUCTION SYSTEMS.

EGR Control Solenoid Valve – See EXHAUST GAS RECIRCULATION (EGR) under EMISSION SYSTEMS & SUB-SYSTEMS.

Fuel Pressure Regulator Cut-Off Solenoid Valve – See FUEL DELIVERY under FUEL SYSTEM.

Idle-Up Solenoid (Integra A/T) – See IDLE CONTROL SYSTEM.

Purge Cut-Off Solenoid Valve – See FUEL EVAPORATION under EMISSION SYSTEMS & SUB-SYSTEMS.

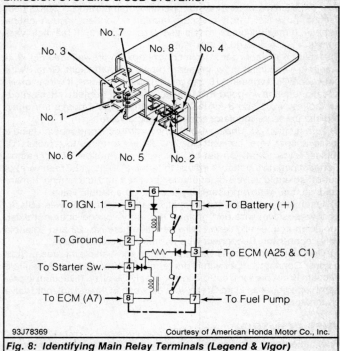

Fig. 8: Identifying Main Relay Terminals (Legend & Vigor)

FUEL SYSTEM

FUEL DELIVERY

NOTE: *For fuel system pressure testing, see BASIC DIAGNOSTIC PROCEDURES article.*

Fuel Pressure Regulator Cut-Off Solenoid Valve (Integra With 1.8L Engine) – **1)** Fuel pressure regulator cut-off solenoid valve is located near top center of firewall. Start and warm engine to normal operating temperature. Disconnect vacuum hose No. 1 from cut-off solenoid valve. Connect a vacuum gauge to hose. If manifold vacuum is present, go to step **4)**.

2) If manifold vacuum is not present, unplug connector from cut-off solenoid valve. If manifold vacuum is now present, go to next step. If manifold vacuum is still not present, check vacuum hoses No. 1 and 20 for leaks or obstruction. If hoses are okay, replace cut-off solenoid valve.

3) Check for short to ground in Green/Yellow wire between ECM terminal A10 and cut-off solenoid valve connector. If wire is okay, substitute a known-good ECM and retest. If problem disappears, replace original ECM.

4) Unplug connector from cut-off solenoid valve. Using a fused jumper wire, connect positive battery terminal to terminal "C" (Black/Yellow wire) of cut-off solenoid valve side of connector. Connect negative battery terminal to terminal "D" (Green/Yellow wire) of cut-off solenoid valve side of connector. Start and idle engine. If manifold vacuum is present, replace cut-off solenoid valve.

5) If manifold vacuum is not present, measure voltage between Black/Yellow (positive) wire and ground. If battery voltage is not present, repair open in Black/Yellow wire between fuse No. 24 and cut-off solenoid valve connector. Reconnect wire harness to cut-off solenoid valve.

6) Connect test harness between ECM and vehicle harness. Start engine. Connect jumper wire from terminal A10 to ground. If manifold vacuum is not present, cut-off solenoid valve is okay. If vacuum is present, repair open in Green/Yellow wire between ECM and cut-off solenoid valve connector.

Pressure Regulator Control Solenoid Valve (Legend) – **1)** Pressure regulator control solenoid valve is located in control box on firewall. *See Fig. 9.* Warm engine to operating temperature. Disconnect vacuum hose No. 1 from pressure regulator. Connect vacuum gauge to hose. If manifold vacuum is present, go to step **3)**. If manifold vacuum is not present, go to next step.

2) Unplug 4-pin connector from control box on firewall. *See Fig. 9.* If manifold vacuum is now present, repair shorted Light Green wire between ECM terminal A19 and control box connector. If wire is okay, substitute a known-good ECM. If vacuum is not present, check vacuum hoses No. 1 and 3 for leaks or obstructions. If hoses are okay, replace pressure regulator control solenoid valve.

3) Turn ignition off. Unplug 4-pin connector from control box. Using a fused jumper wire, connect positive battery terminal to terminal "C" (Black/Yellow wire) of cut-off solenoid valve side of connector. Connect negative battery terminal to terminal "D" (Light Green wire) of cut-off solenoid valve side of connector. Start and idle engine. If manifold vacuum is now present, replace cut-off solenoid valve.

4) If manifold vacuum is not present, measure voltage between Black/Yellow (positive) wire and ground. If battery voltage does not exist, repair open in Black/Yellow wire between fuse No. 22 and solenoid valve connector. Reconnect wire harness to solenoid valve.

5) Connect test harness between ECM and vehicle harness. Start engine. Connect jumper wire from terminal A19 to ground. If manifold vacuum is not present, cut-off solenoid valve is okay. If vacuum is present, repair open in Light Green wire between ECM and solenoid valve connector.

FUEL CONTROL

Fuel Injector – Unplug electrical connector from fuel injector. Measure resistance between fuel injector terminals. Resistance should be 10-13 ohms on Integra, or 1.5-2.5 ohms on Legend and Vigor.

Fuel Pressure Regulator – See FUEL SYSTEM in BASIC DIAGNOSTIC PROCEDURES article.

Fuel Pump – See FUEL SYSTEM in BASIC DIAGNOSTIC PROCEDURES article.

Fuel Pump Relay – See RELAYS under RELAYS & SOLENOIDS.

Injector Resistor (Legend & Vigor) – Injector resistor assembly is located on left side of engine compartment. Unplug injector resistor connector. Measure resistance between each injector resistor terminal and Yellow/Black power wire terminal. If resistance is not 5-7 ohms, replace injector resistor.

IDLE CONTROL SYSTEM

Air Conditioning Signal (Integra) – **1)** Connect ECM test harness between ECM and ECM connectors. Unplug connector "B" from main harness only. DO NOT disconnect from ECM. Turn ignition on.

2) Measure voltage between ECM terminals B5 (positive) and A26 (negative). *See Fig. 1.* If voltage is not about 5 volts, substitute a known-good ECM and recheck.

3) If voltage is about 5 volts, reconnect connector "B" to main wiring harness. Momentarily connect terminals A15 and A26 together and check for clicking of A/C clutch.

4) If A/C clutch clicks, go to next step. If A/C clutch does not click, jumper Yellow wire of A/C clutch relay connector to ground. If A/C clutch clicks, repair open in Yellow wire. If A/C clutch still does not click, repair A/C clutch circuit.

5) Start engine. Turn blower on. Turn A/C switch on. If A/C operates, A/C signal is okay. If A/C does not operate, measure voltage between terminals B5 (positive) and A26 (negative).

6) If voltage is more than one volt, repair open in Blue/Red wire between ECM terminal B5 and A/C pressure switch. If voltage is less than one volt, substitute a known-good ECM, and recheck voltage.

Air Conditioning Signal (Legend) – **1)** Connect ECM test harness

between ECM and ECM connectors. Unplug connector "C" from main harness only. DO NOT disconnect from ECM. Turn ignition on.

2) Measure voltage between ECM terminals C3 (positive) and A26 (negative). *See Fig. 1.* If voltage is not about 10 volts, substitute a known-good ECM, and recheck voltage.

3) If voltage is about 10 volts, reconnect connector "C" to main wiring harness. Momentarily connect terminals A15 and A26 together, and check for clicking of A/C clutch.

4) If A/C clutch clicks, go to next step. If A/C clutch does not click, jumper Red/Blue wire of A/C clutch relay connector to ground. If A/C clutch clicks, repair open in Red/Blue wire. If A/C clutch still does not click, repair A/C clutch circuit.

5) Start engine, and turn blower on. Turn A/C switch on. If A/C operates, A/C signal is okay. If A/C does not operate, measure voltage between terminals C3 (positive) and A26 (negative).

6) If voltage is more than one volt, repair open in Blue/Black wire between terminal C3 and cooling fan control unit. If voltage is less than one volt, substitute a known-good ECM, and recheck voltage.

Air Conditioning Signal (Vigor) – **1)** Connect ECM test harness between ECM and ECM connectors. Unplug connector "B" from main harness only. DO NOT disconnect from ECM. Turn ignition on.

2) Measure voltage between ECM terminals B5 (positive) and A26 (negative). *See Fig. 1.* If voltage is not about 10 volts, substitute a known-good ECM, and recheck voltage.

3) If voltage is about 10 volts, reconnect connector "B" to main wiring harness. Momentarily connect terminals A15 and A26 together, and check for clicking of A/C clutch.

4) If A/C clutch clicks, go to next step. If A/C clutch does not click, jumper Red/Blue wire of A/C clutch relay connector to ground. If A/C clutch clicks, repair open in Red/Blue wire. If A/C clutch still does not click, repair A/C clutch circuit.

5) Start engine. Turn blower on. Turn A/C switch on. If A/C operates, A/C signal is okay. If A/C does not operate, measure voltage between terminals B5 (positive) and A26 (negative).

6) If voltage is more than one volt, repair open in Blue/Black wire between ECM terminal B5 and A/C pressure switch. If voltage is less than one volt, substitute a known-good ECM and recheck voltage.

Alternator FR Signal – **1)** Connect ECM test harness between ECM and ECM connectors. Unplug connector "D" from main wire harness only. DO NOT disconnect from ECM. Turn ignition on. Measure voltage between terminals D9 (positive) and A26 (negative). *See Fig. 1.* If voltage is not about 5 volts, substitute a known-known ECM and recheck.

2) If voltage is about 5 volts, turn ignition off. Reconnect connector "D" to main harness. Start and warm engine to operating temperature. Measure voltage between ECM terminals D94 (positive) and A26.

3) Turn headlights and rear defogger on. If voltage does not decrease, go to next step. If voltage decreases, alternator FR signal is okay. Remove alternator sensor fuse for 10 seconds to reset ECM.

4) Turn ignition off. Unplug connector "D" from ECM only. Disconnect negative battery cable. Check for continuity between ECM test harness terminal D9 and ground. If no continuity exists, go to step **6)**. If continuity exists, unplug Green connector from alternator.

5) Check again for continuity between ECM test harness terminal D9 and ground. If continuity does not exist, check alternator for possible failure. If continuity is present, repair Blue wire (Integra) or White/Red wire (Legend and Vigor) between alternator and ECM terminal D9.

6) Connect Blue wire (Integra) or White/Red wire (Legend and Vigor) to body ground. Check for continuity between ECM terminal D9 and ground. If continuity exist, service alternator. If continuity does not exist, repair Blue wire (Integra) or White/Red wire (Legend and Vigor) between alternator and ECM terminal D9.

Automatic Transmission Shift Position Signal – **1)** While watching shift indicator, shift transmission gear lever to each position. If shift indicator lights up correctly for all positions, turn ignition off.

2) Connect ECM test harness between ECM and ECM connectors. Unplug connector "B" from main harness only. DO NOT disconnect from ECM. Turn ignition on. Measure voltage between ECM terminals B7 (positive) and A26. *See Fig. 1.*

3) If voltage is about 5 volts (Integra and Vigor) or 10 volts (Legend), reconnect connector "B" to main wiring harness. Go to next step. If voltage is not as specified, substitute a known-good ECM and retest.

4) Turn ignition off. Reconnect wire harness to ECM. Place transmission in Neutral. Start engine. Measure voltage between terminals B7 (positive) and A26 (negative) with transmission selector in Park and Neutral positions. If voltage is more than one volt, repair open in Green wire (Integra), Light Green wire (Legend) or Yellow/Green wire (Vigor) between ECM terminal B7 and gauge assembly. If voltage is less than one volt, go to next step.

5) Set transmission selector to Drive position. Measure voltage between terminals B7 (positive) and A26 (negative). If voltage is not about 5 volts (Integra) or 10 volts (Legend and Vigor), repair short circuit in Light Green wire between ECM terminal B7 and combination meter.

6) If voltage is about 5 volts (Integra) or 10 volts (Legend and Vigor), repair short circuit in Green wire (Integra), Light Green wire (Legend) or Yellow/Green wire (Vigor) between ECM terminal B7 and gauge assembly. If voltage is as specified, shift position signal is okay.

Brake Switch Signal – 1) Ensure stoplights operate properly. Connect ECM Test Harness (07LAJ-PT3010A) to ECM main harness. DO NOT connect test harness to ECM. Measure voltage between test harness terminals D2 (positive) and A26 (negative). *See Fig. 1.*

2) Depress brake pedal. If battery voltage is present, switch is okay. If battery voltage is not present, repair open in Green/White wire and ECM terminal D2.

Clutch Signal Switch (Legend) – 1) Unplug connector at clutch switch, located on clutch pedal. Check continuity between clutch switch terminals. If continuity is not present, replace clutch switch. If continuity is present, turn ignition on and measure voltage between Pink (positive) wire terminal and ground.

2) If battery voltage is present, repair open in Black wire between clutch switch and ground connector. If battery voltage is not present, repair open in Pink wire between ECM and switch.

NOTE: Fast idle thermovalve is factory adjusted and should not be disassembled.

Fast Idle Thermovalve – 1) Fast idle thermovalve opens an air passage, which by-passes throttle plate. This allows more air for a fast idle speed. Coolant warms thermovalve and closes air passage. Ensure fast idle thermovalve is closed when engine is at operating temperature.

2) To check fast idle thermovalve, remove air hose from pipe to thermovalve. Start engine. With coolant temperature less than 86°F (30°C) and engine at idle, vacuum should be present at pipe to thermovalve. If vacuum is not present, replace fast idle thermovalve and retest.

3) Warm engine until cooling fan comes on. Check if thermovalve is completely closed. Vacuum should not be present at pipe to thermovalve. If vacuum is present, check coolant level and for air in coolant system. If coolant system is okay, replace fast idle thermovalve and retest.

Intake Air Control Valve (IACV) – 1) Turn ignition off. Unplug 2-wire connector on IACV. Turn ignition on. Measure voltage between Yellow/Black wire terminal of IACV connector and ground. If battery voltage is not present, repair open in Black/Yellow wire between IACV connector and main relay. If battery voltage is present, go to step 2).

2) Connect ECM test harness connector "A" to main wire harness only. DO NOT connect to ECM. Turn ignition on. Momentarily connect and disconnect jumper wire between terminals A9 and A23 on Integra, or between terminals A9 and A26 on Legend and Vigor. *See Fig. 1.* If IACV clicks, substitute a known-good IACV and recheck symptom. If IACV does not click, check Yellow/Blue wire (Integra), Blue/Red wire (Legend) or Black/Blue wire (Vigor) between IACV and ECM terminal A9. If wire is okay, replace IACV.

Manual Transmission Neutral Switch – 1) Connect ECM test harness between ECM and ECM connectors. Turn ignition on. Place transmission in Neutral, and measure voltage between ECM terminals B7 (positive) and A26 (negative). *See Fig. 1.* If voltage is about 10 volts, go to step 4). If voltage is not about 10 volts, go to next step.

2) Disconnect ECM connector "B" from ECM test harness only. DO NOT disconnect from ECM. If voltage is now approximately 10 volts, go to next step. If voltage is not approximately 10 volts, substitute a known-good ECM and recheck. If voltage is now approximately 10 volts, replace original ECM.

3) Reconnect ECM connector "B". Unplug neutral switch 2-wire connector, located on side of transmission. If voltage is now approximately 10 volts, replace neutral switch. If voltage is not approximately 10 volts, repair open in White wire between ECM terminal B7 and neutral switch, or Black wire between neutral switch and ground.

4) Place transmission into gear. If voltage is not about 10 volts, manual transmission neutral switch is okay. If voltage is about 10 volts, disconnect neutral switch 2-wire connector.

5) Connect jumper wire between White wire terminal and Black wire terminal of neutral switch. If voltage is not about 10 volts, replace neutral switch. If voltage is about 10 volts, repair open in White wire between ECM and manual transmission neutral switch or Black wire between neutral switch and ground (located at intake manifold).

Power Steering Pressure (PSP) Switch Signal (Integra & Vigor) – 1) Connect ECM test harness between ECM and vehicle harness connector. Turn ignition on. Measure voltage between ECM terminals B8 (positive) and A26 (negative). *See Fig. 1.* If voltage is less than one volt, go to step 3).

2) If voltage is greater than one volt, unplug 2-wire connector on PSP switch located on power steering pump. Connect jumper between Red and Black wire terminals. If less than one volt is present, replace PSP switch. If voltage is greater than one volt, repair open in Red wire (between ECM terminal B8 and PSP switch) or Black wire and ground connection.

3) Start engine. Turn steering wheel slowly. Measure voltage between ECM terminals B8 (positive) and A26 (negative) while wheel is being turned. If battery voltage exists, PSP signal is okay. If battery voltage is not present, go to next step.

4) Turn ignition off. Unplug PSP switch connector. If voltage is present, replace PSP switch. If voltage is not present, repair short in Red wire between ECM terminal B8 and PSP switch.

Power Steering Pressure (PSP) Switch Signal (Legend) – 1) Connect ECM test harness between ECM and ECM connectors. Measure voltage between terminals B5 (positive) and D22 (negative). If voltage is less than one volt, go to step 3). If battery voltage exists, disconnect 2-wire connector on PSP switch located on power steering pump. Connect jumper between Green and Green/White wire terminals.

2) If battery voltage is present, replace PSP switch. If less than one volt is present, repair open in Green wire (between ECM terminal B5 and PSP switch) or Green/White wire leading to ECM terminal D22.

3) Start engine. Turn steering wheel slowly. Measure voltage between ECM test harness terminals B5 (positive) and D22 (negative) while wheel is being turned. If battery voltage exists, PSP signal is okay.

4) If battery voltage is not present, disconnect ECM test harness connector "B" to main wire harness only. DO NOT disconnect from ECM. Turn ignition on. If 12 volts is not present, try a known-good ECM. If problem goes away, replace ECM.

5) If battery voltage exists, reconnect connector "B" to main harness. Unplug connector from PSP switch. Check Green wire for battery voltage. If battery voltage is present, replace P/S oil pressure switch. If battery voltage is not present, repair short in Green wire between ECM terminal B5 and PSP switch.

Starter Signal (Integra & Vigor) – Connect ECM test harness between ECM and harness connector. Measure voltage on ECM test harness terminals B9 (positive) and A26 (negative) with ignition switch in START position. *See Fig. 1.* If battery voltage is present, starter signal is okay. If voltage is not present, inspect fuse No. 18. If fuse is okay, repair open in Blue/White wire between ECM and fuse No. 18.

Starter Signal (Legend) – Connect ECM test harness between ECM and ECM connectors. Check voltage on ECM test harness terminals C11 (positive) and A26 (negative) with ignition switch in ON position. *See Fig. 1.* If battery voltage is present, starter signal is okay. If voltage is not present, inspect fuse No. 14. If fuse is okay, repair open in Black/White wire between ECM and fuse No. 14.

1993 ENGINE PERFORMANCE
System & Component Testing (Cont.)

Air Boost Valve (Integra 1.8L With A/T) – **1)** Air boost valve is located next to throttle body. Turn ignition off. Disconnect vacuum hose from intake manifold. Connect vacuum pump to hose. Apply vacuum to air boost valve. Replace valve if it holds vacuum.

2) Remove vacuum pump. Reconnect hose to intake manifold. Start and idle engine. Reconnect vacuum pump/gauge to hose. If vacuum exists, replace air boost valve. If there is no vacuum, air boost valve is okay.

IGNITION SYSTEM

NOTE: For basic ignition checks, see BASIC DIAGNOSTIC PROCEDURES article.

TIMING CONTROL SYSTEM

Ignition Timing Adjuster (Legend & Vigor) – **1)** Unplug ignition timing adjuster 3-pin connector. On Legend, ignition timing adjuster is located next to control box on firewall. *See Fig. 9*. On Vigor, ignition timing adjuster is located on left side of engine compartment, outboard of fuel injector resistor. *See Fig. 9*. Measure resistance between "A" and "C" terminals of ignition timing adjuster.

2) Resistance should be 3500-6500 ohms. If resistance is as specified, go to step **3)**. If resistance is not as specified, replace ignition timing adjuster.

3) Measure and record resistance between "A" and "B" terminals on timing adjuster side of harness. Measure and record resistance between "B" and "C" terminals on same side of connector. Add resistance values together. If total of resistance values is not 3500-6500 ohms, replace ignition timing adjuster.

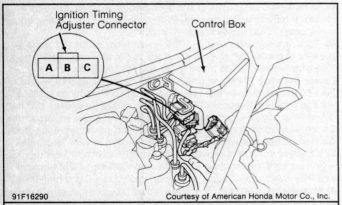

91F16290   Courtesy of American Honda Motor Co., Inc.

Fig. 9: Identifying Ignition Timing Adjuster Connector (Legend Shown; Vigor Similar)

EMISSION SYSTEMS & SUB-SYSTEMS

AIR INJECTION

Pulsed Secondary Air Injection (PAIR) System (Legend) – **1)** PAIR valve is located at top rear of engine. Check all vacuum hose routing. Start and warm engine until cooling fan comes on. Disconnect vacuum hose No. 7 from PAIR valve. *See Fig. 10*. Connect vacuum gauge to hose.

2) If no vacuum is present, go to step **3)**. If vacuum is present, disconnect 6-wire connector at PAIR control solenoid, located at right front of engine compartment. *See Fig. 11*. If vacuum is still present, replace PAIR control solenoid. If vacuum goes away, check for short in Gray wire between 6-pin connector and ECM terminal A17. If wire is okay, substitute a known-good ECM and retest. If problem goes away, replace ECM.

3) Block rear wheels. Raise and support front of vehicle. Start engine. Place transmission in 2nd gear (M/T) or in "2" (A/T). Check for vacuum during deceleration from greater than 9 MPH and 1500 RPM. If vacuum is present, go to step **6)**.

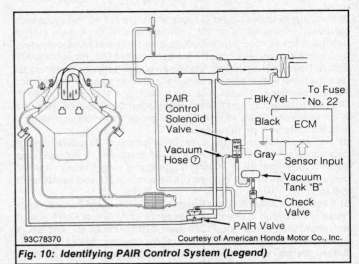

93C78370   Courtesy of American Honda Motor Co., Inc.

Fig. 10: Identifying PAIR Control System (Legend)

93D78371   Courtesy of American Honda Motor Co., Inc.

Fig. 11: Identifying PAIR Control Solenoid Valve (Legend)

4) If no vacuum is present, turn ignition off. Unplug 6-wire connector at PAIR control solenoid. Start engine. Connect voltmeter to Black/Yellow (positive) and Gray (negative) wire terminals of PAIR control solenoid valve. Observe voltmeter reading during deceleration from greater than 9 MPH and 1500 RPM. If voltage is present, replace PAIR control solenoid valve. If voltage is not present, go to next step.

5) Check Black/Yellow wire (between connector and fuse No. 22) and Gray wire (between connector and ECM terminal A17) for opens or shorts. If no problems are found, substitute a known-good ECM and retest. If problem goes away, replace ECM.

6) Connect vacuum hose No. 7. Check for suction noise from PAIR valve during operation at speeds greater than 9 MPH and 1500 RPM. If suction noise is not present, replace PAIR valve. If suction noise is present, system is okay.

FUEL EVAPORATION

Charcoal Canister – Connect vacuum gauge to canister purge air hose located at bottom of canister. Start engine, and increase engine speed to 3500 RPM. Vacuum gauge should indicate 0-4 in. Hg within one minute. If reading is not as specified, replace charcoal canister.

Purge Control Solenoid Valve (Integra) – **1)** Purge control solenoid valve is located on left side of firewall. Ensure coolant temperature is less than 165°F (74°C). Remove vacuum hose No. 7 from purge control diaphragm valve, located on top of canister. Attach vacuum gauge to hose. Start and idle engine. If vacuum is not present, go to step **3)**. If vacuum is present, go to next step.

2) Unplug connector from purge control solenoid valve. Measure voltage between harness terminals of Black/Yellow wire (positive) and Green wire (negative). If battery voltage is present, check vacuum hose for leaks or obstruction. If hose is okay, replace purge control solenoid valve. If battery voltage is not present, check Black/Yellow wire between connector and fuse No. 24, and Green wire between ECM terminal A20 and connector. If wires are okay, substitute a known-good ECM and retest.

3) Warm engine until cooling fan comes on. Check for vacuum. If vacuum is present, go to step **5)**. If vacuum is not present, unplug connector from purge control solenoid valve. If vacuum is now present, go to next step. If vacuum is not present, check vacuum hose. If hose is okay, replace purge control solenoid valve.

4) Check Black/Yellow wire between connector and fuse No. 24, and Green wire between ECM terminal A20 and connector. If wires are okay, substitute a known-good ECM and retest.

5) Reconnect hose. Remove fuel filler cap. Connect vacuum gauge to canister purge line. Start and operate engine at 3000 RPM. If vacuum does not appear within one minute, replace canister. If vacuum appears within one minute, purge control solenoid valve is okay. Go to 2-WAY VALVE procedure.

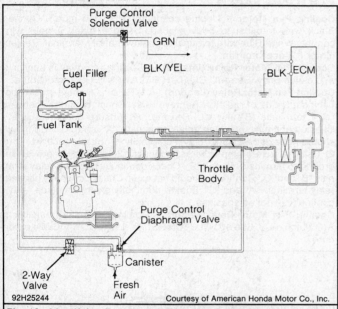

Fig. 12: Identifying Evaporative Emission Control System (Integra)

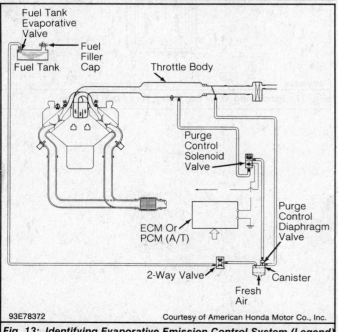

Fig. 13: Identifying Evaporative Emission Control System (Legend)

2-Way Valve – 1) Remove fuel filler cap. *See Fig. 12, 13 or 14.* Remove vapor hose from fuel tank side of 2-way valve, and install "T" fitting. Connect vacuum gauge to "T" fitting and vacuum pump to hose end.

2) Slowly apply vacuum while observing vacuum gauge. Vacuum should stabilize momentarily between .2 and .6 in. Hg. If vacuum does not stabilize (valve opens) in specified range, replace 2-way valve and retest.

3) Move vacuum hose from vacuum to pressure fitting side of vacuum pump. Slowly pressurize vapor line while observing gauge. If pressure stabilizes between .4 and 1.4 in. Hg, valve is okay. If pressure does not stabilize in specified range, replace 2-way valve, and retest.

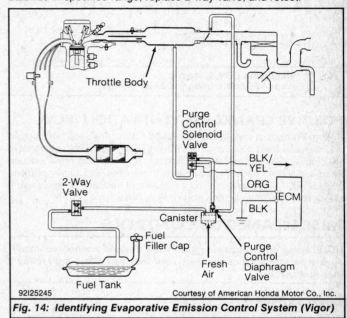

Fig. 14: Identifying Evaporative Emission Control System (Vigor)

EXHAUST GAS RECIRCULATION (EGR)

Constant Vacuum Control (CVC) – Start engine. Verify manifold vacuum is present at CVC valve, located inside control box on firewall. Disconnect CVC vacuum hose at EGR cut-off solenoid. Connect vacuum gauge. If vacuum is not about 8 in. Hg, replace CVC valve.

EGR Control Solenoid Valve – 1) Disconnect vacuum hose at EGR valve. *See Fig. 15.* Connect vacuum gauge to hose. Warm engine until cooling fan comes on. Increase engine speed to about 3000 RPM. Observe vacuum gauge. If vacuum is present, solenoid is okay. If vacuum is not present, go to step **2)**.

2) Disconnect connector from EGR control solenoid valve. Turn ignition on. Connect voltmeter negative lead to ground. Backprobe Black/Yellow wire terminal at connector. If voltage is not present, check for blown fuse or open or short in EGR control solenoid Black/Yellow power supply wire.

3) If voltage is present, increase engine speed to about 3000 RPM. Check for voltage across solenoid terminals. If voltage exists but vacuum is not present, check for restricted hose. If hose is okay, replace defective solenoid.

4) If voltage is not present, check for open in ground wire to solenoid. See WIRING DIAGRAMS article. If ground wire is okay, substitute a known-good ECM and retest. If problem goes away, replace original ECM.

EGR Valve – 1) Warm engine to normal operating temperature. Disconnect vacuum hose from EGR valve. *See Fig. 15.* Connect vacuum pump to EGR valve. With engine at idle, apply vacuum to EGR valve. EGR valve should hold vacuum, and engine should die.

2) If engine does not die and/or vacuum does not hold, replace EGR valve. If engine does not die but vacuum holds, remove EGR valve and check for plugged valve or passages. Clean or replace EGR valve as necessary.

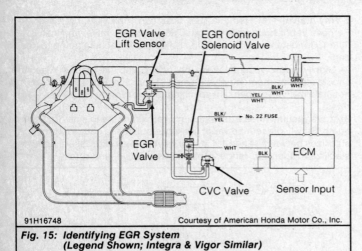

Fig. 15: Identifying EGR System
(Legend Shown; Integra & Vigor Similar)

POSITIVE CRANKCASE VENTILATION (PCV)

Ensure crankcase ventilation hoses and connections are not clogged and no leaks exist. Start engine. With engine at idle, pinch and release PCV hose. Clicking noise should occur. If no clicking noise occurs, ensure manifold vacuum is present. If manifold vacuum is present, replace PCV valve and recheck. If manifold vacuum is not present, check for restricted vacuum port or PCV hose.

MISCELLANEOUS CONTROLS

NOTE: Some of the following controlled devices are not technically engine performance components, but they can affect driveability if they malfunction.

A/C CLUTCH

A/C Clutch Relay (Integra) – Relay is located above compressor. Remove relay. Check continuity between terminals No. 1 and 3. *See Fig. 16.* If continuity exists, replace relay. Using jumper wires, connect 12-volt battery power and ground to terminals No. 2 and 4. Continuity should exist between terminals No. 1 and 3. If continuity is not present, replace relay.

A/C Clutch Relay (Legend & Vigor) – Relay is located in relay block, at right rear of engine compartment. Remove relay. Check continuity between terminals "A" and "B". *See Fig. 16.* If continuity exists, replace relay. Using fused jumper wires, connect 12-volt battery power and ground to terminals "C" and "D". Continuity should exist between terminals "A" and "B". If continuity is not present, replace relay.

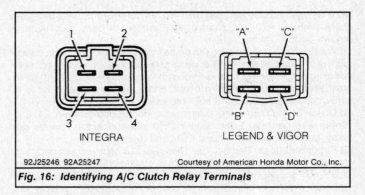

Fig. 16: Identifying A/C Clutch Relay Terminals

COOLING FAN

Cooling Fan Motor – Unplug connector from fan motor. Connect Black wire terminal to body ground. Using a fused jumper wire, connect White/Blue wire terminal to positive battery terminal. Replace motor if it does not run.

Cooling Fan Motor Relay (Integra) – Cooling fan relay is similar to A/C clutch relay. See A/C CLUTCH RELAY (INTEGRA) procedure.

Cooling Fan Motor Relay (Legend) – **1)** Relay is located in relay box behind left side of radiator. Remove relay. Check continuity between relay terminals "B" and "C". *See Fig. 17.* Ensure continuity exists. Check continuity between relay terminals "A" and "C". Continuity should not exist. Replace relay if continuity is not as specified.

2) Using a fused jumper wires, connect 12-volt battery power and ground to terminals "D" and "E". Check continuity between relay terminals "B" and "C." Continuity should not exist. Check continuity between relay terminals "A" and "C". Ensure continuity exists. Replace relay if continuity is not as specified.

Cooling Fan Motor Relay (Vigor) – Cooling fan relay is similar to A/C clutch relay. See A/C CLUTCH RELAY (LEGEND & VIGOR) procedure.

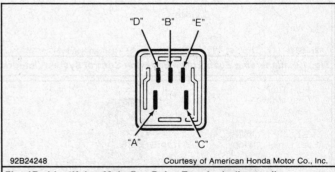

Fig. 17: Identifying Main Fan Relay Terminals (Legend)

1993 ENGINE PERFORMANCE
Pin Voltage Charts

Integra, Legend, Vigor

INTRODUCTION

NOTE: Unless stated otherwise in testing procedures, perform all voltage tests using a Digital Volt-Ohmmeter (DVOM) with a minimum 10-megohm input impedance. Voltage readings may vary slightly due to battery condition or charging rate.

Pin voltage charts are supplied to reduce diagnostic time. Checking pin voltages at the Programmed Fuel Injection Engine Control Module (PGM-FI ECM) determines whether it is receiving and transmitting proper voltage signals. Diagnostic charts may also help determine if ECM harness is shorted or open. *See Figs. 1-14.*

Terminal ID.	Function/Description	Voltage Value (DC Volts Unless Otherwise Specified)
A1	Injector No. 1	Battery Voltage With KOEO [1]
A2	Injector No. 4	Battery Voltage With KOEO [1]
A3	Injector No. 2	Battery Voltage With KOEO [1]
A4	VTEC Solenoid	N/A
A5	Injector No. 3	Battery Voltage With KOEO [1]
A6	Oxygen Sensor Heater	N/A
A7	Fuel Pump Relay	Battery Voltage For 2 Sec. After KOEO [1]
A8	Fuel Pump Relay	Battery Voltage For 2 Sec. After KOEO [1]
A9	Idle Air Control Valve (IACV)	N/A
A10	BLANK	N/A
A11	BLANK	N/A
A12	BLANK	N/A
A13	MIL (CHECK ENGINE) Light	Battery Voltage With KOEO [1]
A14	BLANK	N/A
A15	A/C Clutch Relay	Battery Voltage With KOEO [1]
A16	BLANK	N/A
A17	BLANK	N/A
A18	BLANK	N/A
A19	BLANK	N/A
A20	Purge Control Solenoid Valve	Battery Voltage With KOEO [1]
A21	Ignitor	N/A
A22	Ignitor	N/A
A23	Power Ground	Less Than One Volt With KOEO [1]
A24	Power Ground	Less Than One Volt With KOEO [1]
A25	Fuel Pump Relay	Battery Voltage With KOEO [1]
A26	Shield Ground	N/A

Wire colors (left margin, top to bottom):
Brown, Yellow, Red, Green/Yellow, Light Blue, Orange/Black, Green/Black, Green/Black, Blue/Yellow, Green/Orange, Yellow, Green, Yellow/Green, Yellow/Green, Black, Black, Yellow/Black, Black/Red

[1] – KOEO – Key On, Engine Off.

25	23	21	19	17	15	13	11	9	7	5	3	1
26	24	22	20	18	16	14	12	10	8	6	4	2

CONNECTOR "A"
VIEWED FROM HARNESS SIDE

93C78347

Courtesy of American Honda Motor Co., Inc.

Fig. 1: Identifying Connector "A" Terminals & Pin Voltage Chart (Integra 1.7L)

1993 ENGINE PERFORMANCE
Pin Voltage Charts (Cont.)

Terminal ID.	Function/Description	Voltage Value (DC Volts Unless Otherwise Specified)
B1	Fuel Pump Relay	Battery Voltage With KOEO [1]
B2	Ground	Less Than One Volt [1]
B3	BLANK	N/A
B4	BLANK	N/A
B5	A/C Switch	N/A
B6	BLANK	N/A
B7	Gear Position Indicator (A/T)	N/A
B8	Oil Pressure Switch	N/A
B9	Fuel Pump Relay	Battery Voltage With KOEO [1]
B10	Vehicle Speed Sensor	Zero And 5 Volts As Left Front Wheel Rotates
B11	CYL Sensor "P"	N/A
B12	CYL Sensor "M"	N/A
B13	TDC Sensor "P"	N/A
B14	TDC Sensor "M"	N/A
B15	CRANK Sensor "P"	N/A
B16	CRANK Sensor "M"	N/A

Yellow/Black
Brown/Black
Blue/Red
Green
Red
Blue/White
Yellow/Red
Orange
White
Orange/Blue
White/Blue
Blue/Green
Blue/Yellow

[1] – KOEO – Key On, Engine Off.

| 15 | 13 | 11 | 9 | 7 | 5 | 3 | 1 |
| 16 | 14 | 12 | 10 | 8 | 6 | 4 | 2 |

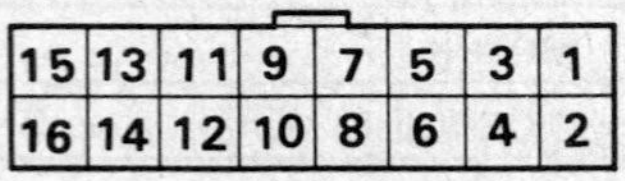

CONNECTOR "B"
VIEWED FROM HARNESS SIDE

93D78348

Courtesy of American Honda Motor Co., Inc.

Fig. 2: Identifying Connector "B" Terminals & Pin Voltage Chart (Integra 1.7L)

	Terminal ID.	Function/Description	Voltage Value (DC Volts Unless Otherwise Specified)
White/Yellow	D1	Vehicle Power	Battery Voltage At All Times
Green/White	D2	Brake Signal	Battery Voltage With Brake Applied
Red/Blue	D3	Knock Sensor	N/A
Brown	D4	Service Check Connector	N/A
	D5	BLANK	N/A
Blue/Black	D6	VTEC Pressure Switch	N/A
Light Blue	D7	Data Link Connector	N/A
Red/White	D8	TCM (A/T)	N/A
Blue	D9	Alternator	N/A
	D10	BLANK	N/A
Red/Blue	D11	Throttle Position Sensor	.5 Volt Closed; 4.5 Volts Open
	D12	BLANK	N/A
Red/White	D13	Engine Coolant Temperature Sensor	N/A
White	D14	Oxygen Sensor	.4-.5 Volt When Ignition Is First Turned On, Decreasing To Less Than .1 Volt In Less Than 2 Minutes
Red/Yellow	D15	Intake Air Temperature (TA) Sensor	N/A
Blue/White	D16	TCM (A/T)	N/A
White	D17	MAP Sensor	3-5 Volts Depending On Atmospheric Pressure
	D18	BLANK	N/A
Yellow/Red	D19	MAP Sensor Reference	Approximately 5 Volts
Yellow/White	D20	Throttle Position Sensor Reference	5 Volts
Green/White	D21	MAP Sensor Signal Ground	Approximately Zero
Green/White	D22	Signal Ground	Approximately Zero

| 21 | 19 | 17 | 15 | 13 | 11 | 9 | 7 | 5 | 3 | 1 |
| 22 | 20 | 18 | 16 | 14 | 12 | 10 | 8 | 6 | 4 | 2 |

CONNECTOR "D"
VIEWED FROM HARNESS SIDE

93E78349

Courtesy of American Honda Motor Co., Inc.

Fig. 3: Identifying Connector "D" Terminals & Pin Voltage Chart (Integra 1.7L)

	Terminal ID.	Function/Description	Voltage Value (DC Volts Unless Otherwise Specified)
Brown →	A1	Injector No. 1	Battery Voltage With KOEO [1]
Yellow →	A2	Injector No. 4	Battery Voltage With KOEO [1]
Red →	A3	Injector No. 2	Battery Voltage With KOEO [1]
	A4	BLANK	N/A
Light Blue →	A5	Injector No. 3	Battery Voltage With KOEO [1]
Orange/Black →	A6	Oxygen Sensor Heater	N/A
Green/Black →	A7	Fuel Pump Relay	12 Volts For 2 Seconds After KOEO [1]
Green/Black →	A8	Fuel Pump Relay	12 Volts For 2 Seconds After KOEO [1]
Blue/Yellow →	A9	Idle Air Control Valve (IACV)	N/A
Green/Yellow →	A10	Pressure Regulator Control Solenoid	Battery Voltage With KOEO [1]
Red →	A11	EGR Solenoid Control Valve	Battery Voltage With KOEO [1]
	A12	BLANK	N/A
Green/Orange →	A13	MIL (CHECK ENGINE) Light	Battery Voltage With KOEO [1]
	A14	BLANK	N/A
Yellow →	A15	A/C Clutch Relay	Battery Voltage With KOEO [1]
	A16	BLANK	N/A
	A17	BLANK	N/A
	A18	BLANK	N/A
	A19	BLANK	N/A
Green →	A20	Purge Control Solenoid Valve	Battery Voltage With KOEO [1]
Yellow/Green →	A21	Ignitor	N/A
Yellow/Green →	A22	Ignitor	N/A
Black →	A23	Power Ground	Less Than One Volt With KOEO [1]
Black →	A24	Power Ground	Less Than One Volt With KOEO [1]
Yellow/Black →	A25	Fuel Pump Relay	Battery Voltage With KOEO [1]
Black/Red →	A26	Shield Ground	N/A

[1] – KOEO – Key On, Engine Off.

25	23	21	19	17	15	13	11	9	7	5	3	1
26	24	22	20	18	16	14	12	10	8	6	4	2

CONNECTOR "A"
VIEWED FROM HARNESS SIDE

93I78350

Courtesy of American Honda Motor Co., Inc.

Fig. 4 Identifying Connector "A" Terminals & Pin Voltage Chart (Integra 1.8L)

	Terminal ID.	Function/Description	Voltage Value (DC Volts Unless Otherwise Specified)
Yellow/Black	B1	Fuel Pump Relay	Battery Voltage With KOEO [1]
Brown/Black	B2	Ground	Less Than One Volt [1]
	B3	BLANK	N/A
	B4	BLANK	N/A
Blue/Red	B5	A/C Switch	N/A
	B6	BLANK	N/A
Green	B7	Park/Neutral Signal (A/T)	N/A
Red	B8	Oil Pressure Switch	N/A
Blue/White	B9	Fuel Pump Relay	12 Volts With Switch In START Position
Yellow/Red	B10	Vehicle Speed Sensor	Zero And 5 Volts As Left Front Wheel Rotates
Orange	B11	CYL Sensor "P"	N/A
White	B12	CYL Sensor "M"	N/A
Orange/Blue	B13	TDC Sensor "P"	N/A
White/Blue	B14	TDC Sensor "M"	N/A
Blue/Green	B15	CRANK Sensor "P"	N/A
Blue/Yellow	B16	CRANK Sensor "M"	N/A

[1] – KOEO – Key On, Engine Off.

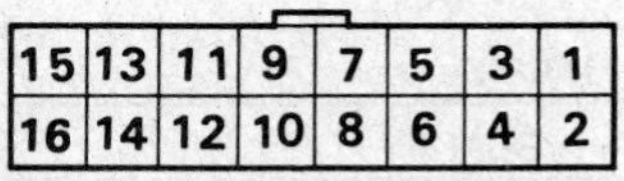

15	13	11	9	7	5	3	1
16	14	12	10	8	6	4	2

CONNECTOR "B"
VIEWED FROM HARNESS SIDE

93J78351

Courtesy of American Honda Motor Co., Inc.

Fig. 5: Identifying Connector "B" Terminals & Pin Voltage Chart (Integra 1.8L)

	Terminal ID.	Function/Description	Voltage Value (DC Volts Unless Otherwise Specified)
White/Yellow →	D1	Battery Power	Battery Voltage At All Times
Green/White →	D2	Brake Signal	Battery Voltage With Brake Applied
	D3	BLANK	N/A
Brown →	D4	Service Check Connector	N/A
	D5	BLANK	N/A
	D6	BLANK	N/A
Light Blue →	D7	Data Link Connector	N/A
Red/White →	D8	TCM (A/T)	N/A
Blue →	D9	Alternator	N/A
	D10	BLANK	N/A
Red/Blue →	D11	Throttle Position Sensor	.5 Volt Closed; 4.5 Volts Open
Yellow →	D12	EGR Valve Lift Sensor	One Volt Closed; 4.5 Volts Open
Red/White →	D13	Engine Coolant Temperature Sensor	N/A
White →	D14	Oxygen Sensor	.4-.5 Volt When Ignition Is First Turned On, Decreasing To Less Than .1 Volt In Less Than 2 Minutes
Red/Yellow →	D15	Intake Air Temperature (TA) Sensor	N/A
Blue/White →	D16	TCM (A/T)	N/A
White →	D17	MAP Sensor	3-5 Volts Depending On Atmospheric Pressure
	D18	BLANK	N/A
Yellow/Red →	D19	MAP Sensor Reference	Approximately 5 Volts
Yellow/White →	D20	Throttle Position Sensor Reference	5 Volts
Green/White →	D21	MAP Sensor Signal Ground	Approximately Zero
Green/White →	D22	Signal Ground	Approximately Zero

21	19	17	15	13	11	9	7	5	3	1
22	20	18	16	14	12	10	8	6	4	2

CONNECTOR "D"
VIEWED FROM HARNESS SIDE

93A78352

Fig. 6: Identifying Connector "D" Terminals & Pin Voltage Chart (Integra 1.8L)

	Terminal ID.	Function/Description	Voltage Value (DC Volts Unless Otherwise Specified)
Brown	A1	Injector No. 1	Battery Voltage With KOEO [1]
White/Blue	A2	Injector No. 4	Battery Voltage With KOEO [1]
Red	A3	Injector No. 2	Battery Voltage With KOEO [1]
Black/Red	A4	Injector No. 5	Battery Voltage With KOEO [1]
Orange	A5	Injector No. 3	Battery Voltage With KOEO [1]
Yellow	A6	Injector No. 6	Battery Voltage With KOEO [1]
Green/Black	A7	Fuel Pump Relay	N/A
	A8	BLANK	N/A
Blue/Red	A9	Electronic Air Control Valve	Battery Voltage With KOEO [1]
Green/Blue	A10	Left Oxygen Sensor Heater Circuit	N/A
White	A11	EGR Control Solenoid Valve	N/A
Green/Red	A12	Right Oxygen Sensor Heater Circuit	N/A
Blue	A13	MIL (CHECK ENGINE) Light Circuit	N/A
Red/Blue	A14	By-Pass Low Control Solenoid Valve	Battery Voltage At Idle With KOER [2]
Red/Blue	A15	A/C Clutch Relay	N/A
	A16	BLANK	N/A
Gray	A17	Air Suction Control Solenoid Valve	N/A
Yellow	A18	By-Pass High Control Solenoid Valve	Battery Voltage At Idle With KOER [2]
Light Green	A19	Pressure Regulator Control Solenoid Valve	N/A
Light Green	A20	Purge Cut-Off Solenoid Valve	N/A
Pink	A21	Ignition Control Module (ICM)	N/A
Brown	A22	Ignition Control Module (ICM)	N/A
Black	A23	Ground	Less Than One Volt
Black	A24	Ground	Less Than One Volt
Yellow/Black	A25	Idle Air Control Valve (IACV)	N/A
Brown/Black	A26	Knock Sensor Circuit	N/A

[1] – KOEO – Key On, Engine Off.
[2] – KOER – Key On, Engine Running.

25	23	21	19	17	15	13	11	9	7	5	3	1
26	24	22	20	18	/	14	12	10	8	6	4	2

CONNECTOR "A"
VIEWED FROM HARNESS SIDE

93B78353

Courtesy of American Honda Motor Co., Inc.

Fig. 7: Identifying Connector "A" Terminals & Pin Voltage Chart (Legend)

	Terminal ID.	Function/Description	Voltage Value (DC Volts Unless Otherwise Specified)
	B1	BLANK	N/A
Brown/Black →	B2	Ground	Less Than One Volt
Red →	B3	Ignition Control Module (ICM)	N/A
Gray →	B4	Ignition Control Module (ICM)	N/A
Green →	B5	Power Steering Pressure Switch Signal	Less Than Battery Voltage With Front Wheels Straight Ahead; Battery Voltage While Slowly Turning Steering Wheel With KOER [1]
Green →	B6	Ignition Control Module (ICM)	N/A
Light Green [2] →	B7	Park/Neutral Switch	N/A
Blue →	B8	Ignition Control Module (ICM)	N/A
Blue/Green →	B9	CYL Sensor No. 2 Circuit	N/A
Blue/Yellow →	B10	CYL Sensor No. 2 Circuit	N/A
Orange/Blue →	B11	CYL Sensor No. 1 Circuit	N/A
White/Blue →	B12	CYL Sensor No. 1 Circuit	N/A
Orange →	B13	CRANK Sensor No. 2 Circuit	N/A
White →	B14	CRANK Sensor No. 2 Circuit	N/A
Orange/Blue →	B15	CRANK Sensor No. 1 Circuit	N/A
White/Blue →	B16	CRANK Sensor No. 1 Circuit	N/A

[1] – KOER – Key On, Engine Running.
[2] – White wire on M/T models.

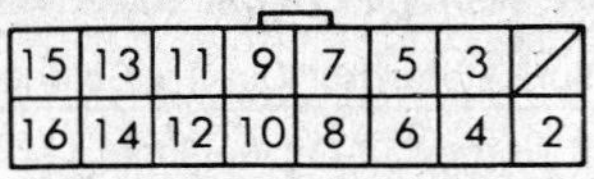

```
15 13 11  9  7  5  3  /
16 14 12 10  8  6  4  2
```

CONNECTOR "B"
VIEWED FROM HARNESS SIDE

93C78354

Courtesy of American Honda Motor Co., Inc.

Fig. 8: Identifying Connector "B" Terminals & Pin Voltage Chart (Legend)

	Terminal ID.	Function/Description	Voltage Value (DC Volts Unless Otherwise Specified)
Yellow/Black →	C1	Ignition Power From Main Relay	Battery Voltage With KOEO [1]
Yellow/Red →	C2	Vehicle Speed Sensor	Zero And 5 Volts As Left Front Wheel Rotates
Blue/Black →	C3	Cooling Fan Control Unit	N/A
Blue →	C4	Tachometer Signal	N/A
Red/Blue →	C5	Cooling Fan Switch Circuit	N/A
	C6	BLANK	N/A
Pink →	C7	M/T Clutch Switch	N/A
	C8	BLANK	N/A
White →	C9	Service Check Connector	N/A
	C10	BLANK	N/A
Black/White →	C11	Start Signal	Battery Voltage In START Position
	C12	BLANK	N/A

[1] – KOEO – Key On, Engine Off.

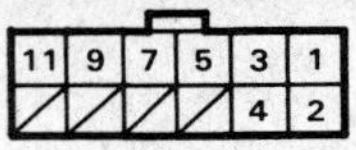

```
11  9  7  5  3  1
        4  2
```

CONNECTOR "C"
VIEWED FROM HARNESS SIDE

93D78355

Courtesy of American Honda Motor Co., Inc.

Fig. 9: Identifying Connector "C" Terminals & Pin Voltage Chart (Legend)

1993 ENGINE PERFORMANCE
Pin Voltage Charts (Cont.)

Wire Color	Terminal ID.	Function/Description	Voltage Value (DC Volts Unless Otherwise Specified)
Yellow/Blue	D1	Vehicle Power From Fuse No. 15	Battery Voltage At All Times
Green/White	D2	Brake Switch Signal Input	Battery Voltage With Brake Applied KOEO [1]
White	D3	Right Knock Sensor Circuit	N/A
Red/Blue	D4	Left Knock Sensor Circuit	N/A
	D5	BLANK	N/A
	D6	BLANK	N/A
	D7	BLANK	N/A
Blue/Yellow	D8	Ignition Timing Adjuster Connector	N/A
White/Red	D9	Alternator Charging Signal	N/A
	D10	BLANK	N/A
Red/Blue	D11	Throttle Position Sensor Signal	About .3 Volt With KOEO [1] At Closed Throttle; About 4.5 Volts At WOT
Black/White	D12	EGR Valve Lift Sensor Signal	About 1.2 Volts At Warm Idle
Red/White	D13	Coolant Temperature Sensor Signal	0.5-4.5 Volts (Varies With Temperature)
White	D14	Left Oxygen Sensor Signal	.4-.5 Volt When Ignition Is First Turned On, Decreasing To Less Than .1 Volt In Less Than 2 Minutes
Red/Yellow	D15	Intake Air Temperature Sensor Signal	0.5-4.5 Volts (Varies With Temperature)
Red/Blue	D16	Right Oxygen Sensor Signal	.4-.5 Volt When Ignition Is First Turned On, Decreasing To Less Than .1 Volt In Less Than 2 Minutes
Red	D17	MAP Sensor Signal	3.0-4.5 Volts (Varies With Manifold Pressure)
	D18	BLANK	N/A
Yellow/White	D19	MAP Sensor Power	About 5 Volts With KOEO [1]
Yellow/White	D20	Sensor Power (Except MAP Sensor)	About 5 Volts With KOEO [1]
Green/White	D21	MAP Sensor Ground	Approximately Zero
Green/White	D22	Sensor Ground (Except MAP Sensor)	Approximately Zero

[1] – KOEO – Key On, Engine Off.

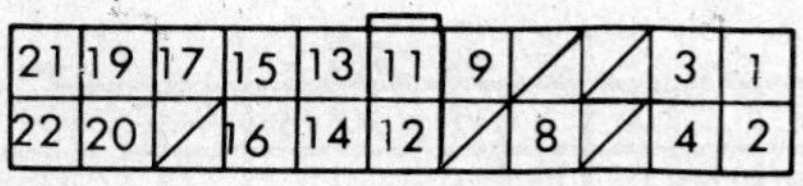

CONNECTOR "D"
VIEWED FROM HARNESS SIDE

93E78356

Courtesy of American Honda Motor Co., Inc.

Fig. 10: Identifying Connector "D" Terminals & Pin Voltage Chart (Legend)

	Terminal ID.	Function/Description	Voltage Value (DC Volts Unless Otherwise Specified)
Brown →	A1	Injector No. 1	Battery Voltage With KOEO [1]
Yellow →	A2	Injector No. 4	Battery Voltage With KOEO [1]
Red →	A3	Injector No. 2	Battery Voltage With KOEO [1]
Green →	A4	Injector No. 5	Battery Voltage With KOEO [1]
Blue →	A5	Injector No. 3	Battery Voltage With KOEO [1]
Pink/White →	A6	Oxygen Sensor Heater	N/A
Green/Black →	A7	Fuel Pump Relay	12 Volts For 2 Seconds After KOEO [1]
Green/Black →	A8	Fuel Pump Relay	12 Volts For 2 Seconds After KOEO [1]
Black/Blue →	A9	Idle Air Control Valve (IACV)	N/A
Orange →	A10	Purge Control Solenoid Valve	Battery Voltage With KOEO [1]
Red →	A11	EGR Solenoid Control Valve	Battery Voltage With KOEO [1]
Lt. Green/Yellow →	A12	Cooling Fan Control Unit	N/A
Green/Red →	A13	MIL (CHECK ENGINE) Light	Battery Voltage With KOEO [1]
	A14	BLANK	N/A
Red/Blue →	A15	A/C Clutch Relay	Battery Voltage With KOEO [1]
White/Green →	A16	Alternator	N/A
Blue/Red →	A17	Intake Air By-Pass Control Solenoid	N/A
Pink →	A18	TCM (A/T)	N/A
	A19	BLANK	N/A
Yellow/Green →	A20	BLANK	N/A
Yellow/Green →	A21	Ignition Control Module (ICM)	N/A
Black →	A22	Ignition Control Module (ICM)	N/A
Black →	A23	Power Ground	Less Than One Volt With KOEO [1]
Yellow/Black →	A24	Power Ground	Less Than One Volt With KOEO [1]
Black/Red →	A25	Fuel Pump Relay	Battery Voltage With KOEO [1]
	A26	Shield Ground	Approximately Zero

[1] – KOEO – Key On, Engine Off.

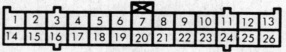

CONNECTOR "A"
VIEWED FROM HARNESS SIDE

93F78357

Fig. 11: Identifying Connector "A" Terminals & Pin Voltage Chart (Vigor)

	Terminal ID.	Function/Description	Voltage Value (DC Volts Unless Otherwise Specified)
Yellow/Black →	B1	Fuel Pump Relay	Battery Voltage With KOEO [1]
Brown/Black →	B2	Ground	Less Than One Volt [1]
White/Green →	B3	A/T Control Unit	N/A
White/Red →	B4	A/T Control Unit	N/A
Blue/Black →	B5	A/C Pressure Switch	N/A
	B6	BLANK	N/A
Yellow/Green →	B7	Park/Neutral Switch	N/A
Red →	B8	Power Steering Pressure Switch	N/A
Blue/Red →	B9	Start Signal	12 Volts With Switch In START Position
Orange →	B10	Vehicle Speed Sensor	Zero And 5 Volts As Left Front Wheel Rotates
Orange →	B11	CYL Sensor "P"	N/A
White →	B12	CYL Sensor "M"	N/A
Orange/Blue →	B13	TDC Sensor "P"	N/A
White/Blue →	B14	TDC Sensor "M"	N/A
Blue/Green →	B15	CRANK Sensor "P"	N/A
Blue/Yellow →	B16	CRANK Sensor "M"	N/A

[1] – KOEO – Key On, Engine Off.

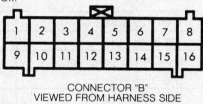

CONNECTOR "B"
VIEWED FROM HARNESS SIDE

93G78358

Courtesy of American Honda Motor Co., Inc.

Fig. 12: Identifying Connector "B" Terminals & Pin Voltage Chart (Vigor)

	Terminal ID.	Function/Description	Voltage Value (DC Volts Unless Otherwise Specified)
Orange/White →	C1	Knock Sensor (Rear)	N/A
	C2	BLANK	N/A
Red/Blue →	C3	Knock Sensor (Front)	N/A
	C4-C12	BLANK	N/A

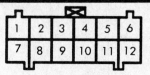

CONNECTOR "C"
VIEWED FROM HARNESS SIDE

93H78359

Courtesy of American Honda Motor Co., Inc.

Fig. 13: Identifying Connector "C" Terminals & Pin Voltage Chart (Vigor)

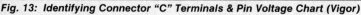

	Terminal ID.	Function/Description	Voltage Value (DC Volts Unless Otherwise Specified)
White/Green →	D1	Battery Power	Battery Voltage At All Times
Green/White →	D2	Brake Signal	Battery Voltage With Brake Applied
Brown →	D3	BLANK	N/A
	D4	Service Check Connector	N/A
	D5	BLANK	N/A
	D6	BLANK	N/A
Brown →	D7	BLANK	N/A
White/Red →	D8	Ignition Timing Adjuster	N/A
Green/Red →	D9	Alternator	N/A
Red/Yellow →	D10	Electronic Load Detector	N/A
White/Black →	D11	Throttle Position Sensor	.5 Volt Closed; 4.5 Volts Open
Yellow/Green →	D12	EGR Valve Lift Sensor	1.0 Volt Closed; 4.5 Volts Open
White →	D13	Engine Coolant Temperature Sensor	N/A
	D14	Oxygen Sensor	.4-.5 Volt When Ignition Is First Turned On, Decreasing To Less Than .1 Volt In Less Than 2 Minutes
White/Yellow →	D15	Intake Air Temperature Sensor	N/A
White/Blue →	D16	BLANK	N/A
Blue/White →	D17	MAP Sensor	3-5 Volts Depending On Atmospheric Pressure
Yellow/White →	D18	A/T Control Unit	N/A
Yellow/White →	D19	MAP Sensor Reference Voltage	5 Volts
Green/White →	D20	Throttle Position Sensor	Approximately Zero
Green/White →	D21	MAP Sensor	Approximately Zero
	D22	Oxygen Sensor Heater	N/A

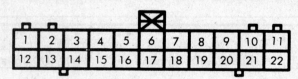

CONNECTOR "D"
VIEWED FROM HARNESS SIDE

93A78360

Fig. 14: Identifying Connector "D" Terminals & Pin Voltage Chart (Vigor)

Integra, Legend, Vigor

INTRODUCTION

Sensor operating range information can help determine if a sensor is out of calibration. An out-of-calibration sensor may not set a trouble code, but it may cause driveability problems.

NOTE: Unless stated otherwise in test procedure, perform all voltage tests using a Digital Volt-Ohmmeter (DVOM) with a minimum 10-megohm input impedance.

COOLANT TEMPERATURE (TW) SENSOR RESISTANCE [1]

Temperature – °F (°C)	Ohms
–4 (–20)	15,000-18,000
68 (20)	2000-4000
176 (80)	
Integra & Vigor	200-400
Legend	300-400

[1] – Measure resistance across sensor terminals.

DISTRIBUTOR SENSOR RESISTANCE [1]

Application	Ohms
Integra	
CRANK Sensor	350-700
CYL Sensor	350-700
TDC Sensor	350-700
Legend	
CRANK Sensor	600-950
CYL Sensor	600-950
Vigor	
CRANK Sensor	650-850
CYL Sensor	650-850
TDC Sensor	650-850

[1] – See SYSTEM & COMPONENT TESTING article to identify sensor terminals.

EGR POSITION SENSOR VOLTAGE [1]

Position	Approximate Volts
Fully Closed	1.0
Fully Open	4.5

[1] – On Integra, measure voltage between terminals C8 (positive) and C12 (negative). On Legend and Vigor, measure voltage between terminals D12 (positive) and D22 (negative). Voltage should increase smoothly as vacuum is applied.

INTAKE AIR TEMPERATURE (TA) SENSOR RESISTANCE [1]

Temperature – °F (°C)	Ohms
–4 (–20)	15,000-18,000
68 (20)	2000-4000
176 (80)	
Integra & Vigor	200-400
Legend	300-400

[1] – Measure resistance across sensor terminals.

MAP SENSOR VOLTAGE [1]

Vacuum Applied (In. Hg)	Volts
0	2.8-3.0
5	2.3-2.5
10	1.8-2.0
15	1.3-1.5
20	.8-1.0
25	.3-.5

[1] – On Integra, measure voltage between ECU terminals C11 (positive) and C12 (negative). On Legend and Vigor, measure voltage between ECU terminals D17 (positive) and D21 (negative).

OXYGEN SENSOR VOLTAGE [1]

Condition	Volts
Lean	.1
Rich	.9

[1] – Measure voltage between ground and O_2 sensor terminal using a high-impedance DVOM.

THROTTLE POSITION SENSOR VOLTAGE [1]

Position	Approximate Volts
Fully Closed	0.1-0.5
Fully Open	4.5-4.8

[1] – On Integra, measure resistance between terminals C7 (positive) and C12 (negative). On Legend, measure resistance between terminals D11 (positive) and D22 (negative). Voltage should increase smoothly as throttle is opened.

VEHICLE SPEED SENSOR VOLTAGE [1]

Model	Approximate Volts
Integra, Legend & Vigor	[2]

[1] – On Integra and Vigor, measure voltage between terminals B10 (positive) and A26 (negative). On Legend, measure voltage between terminals C2 (positive) and A26 (negative).

[2] – Rotate left front wheel slowly. Voltage should pulse between zero and 5 volts.

1993 ENGINE PERFORMANCE
Vacuum Diagrams

Integra, Legend, Vigor

INTRODUCTION

This article contains underhood views or schematics of vacuum hose routing. Use these vacuum diagrams during the visual inspection in BASIC DIAGNOSTIC PROCEDURES article. This will assist in identifying improperly routed vacuum hoses, which cause driveability and/or computer-indicated malfunctions.

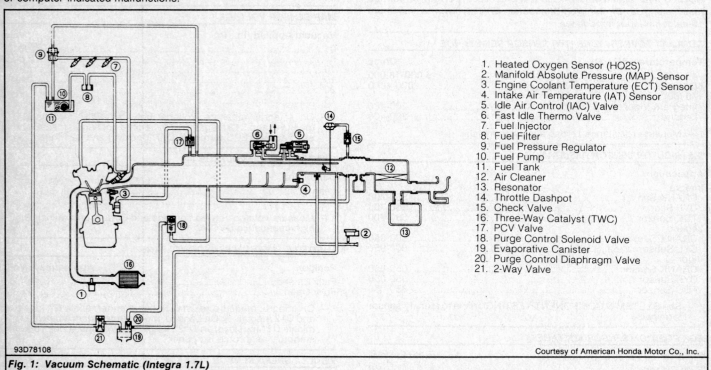

1. Heated Oxygen Sensor (HO2S)
2. Manifold Absolute Pressure (MAP) Sensor
3. Engine Coolant Temperature (ECT) Sensor
4. Intake Air Temperature (IAT) Sensor
5. Idle Air Control (IAC) Valve
6. Fast Idle Thermo Valve
7. Fuel Injector
8. Fuel Filter
9. Fuel Pressure Regulator
10. Fuel Pump
11. Fuel Tank
12. Air Cleaner
13. Resonator
14. Throttle Dashpot
15. Check Valve
16. Three-Way Catalyst (TWC)
17. PCV Valve
18. Purge Control Solenoid Valve
19. Evaporative Canister
20. Purge Control Diaphragm Valve
21. 2-Way Valve

93D78108

Courtesy of American Honda Motor Co., Inc.

Fig. 1: Vacuum Schematic (Integra 1.7L)

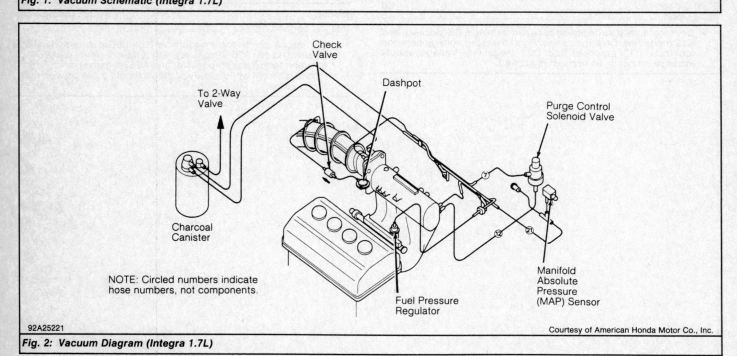

NOTE: Circled numbers indicate hose numbers, not components.

92A25221

Courtesy of American Honda Motor Co., Inc.

Fig. 2: Vacuum Diagram (Integra 1.7L)

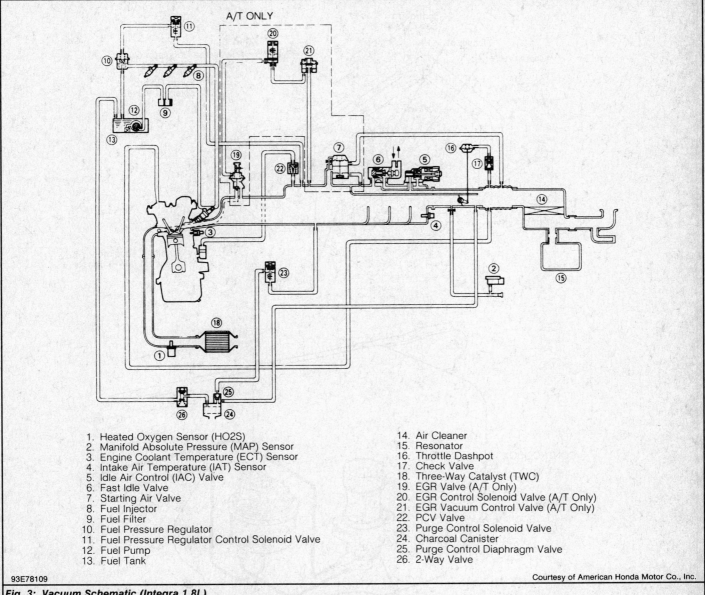

A/T ONLY

1. Heated Oxygen Sensor (HO2S)	14. Air Cleaner
2. Manifold Absolute Pressure (MAP) Sensor	15. Resonator
3. Engine Coolant Temperature (ECT) Sensor	16. Throttle Dashpot
4. Intake Air Temperature (IAT) Sensor	17. Check Valve
5. Idle Air Control (IAC) Valve	18. Three-Way Catalyst (TWC)
6. Fast Idle Valve	19. EGR Valve (A/T Only)
7. Starting Air Valve	20. EGR Control Solenoid Valve (A/T Only)
8. Fuel Injector	21. EGR Vacuum Control Valve (A/T Only)
9. Fuel Filter	22. PCV Valve
10. Fuel Pressure Regulator	23. Purge Control Solenoid Valve
11. Fuel Pressure Regulator Control Solenoid Valve	24. Charcoal Canister
12. Fuel Pump	25. Purge Control Diaphragm Valve
13. Fuel Tank	26. 2-Way Valve

93E78109

Courtesy of American Honda Motor Co., Inc.

Fig. 3: Vacuum Schematic (Integra 1.8L)

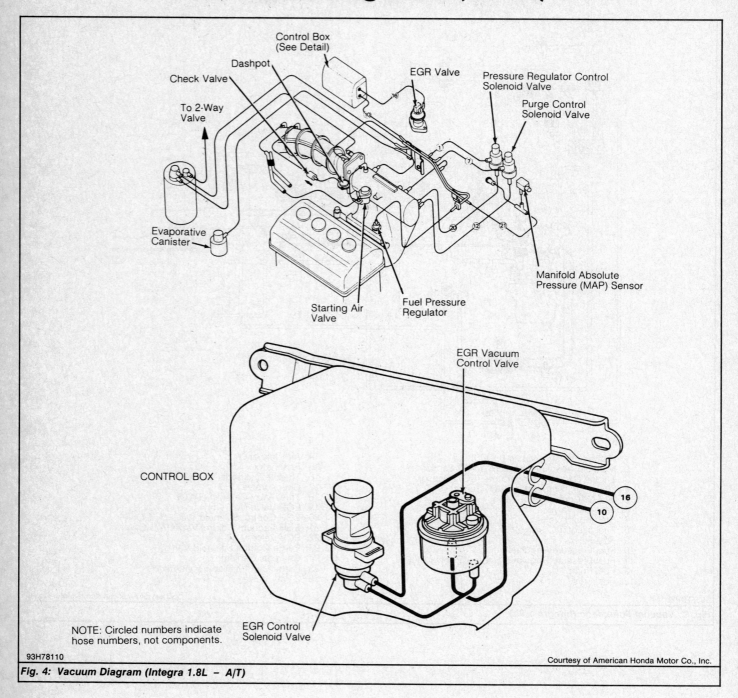

Fig. 4: Vacuum Diagram (Integra 1.8L — A/T)

NOTE: Circled numbers indicate hose numbers, not components.

93H78110

Courtesy of American Honda Motor Co., Inc.

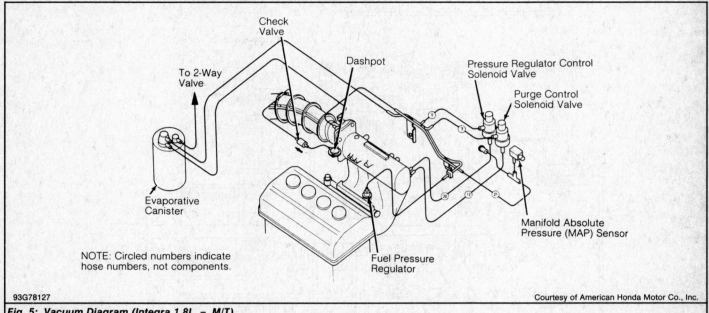

NOTE: Circled numbers indicate hose numbers, not components.

93G78127

Courtesy of American Honda Motor Co., Inc.

Fig. 5: Vacuum Diagram (Integra 1.8L – M/T)

1993 ENGINE PERFORMANCE
Vacuum Diagrams (Cont.)

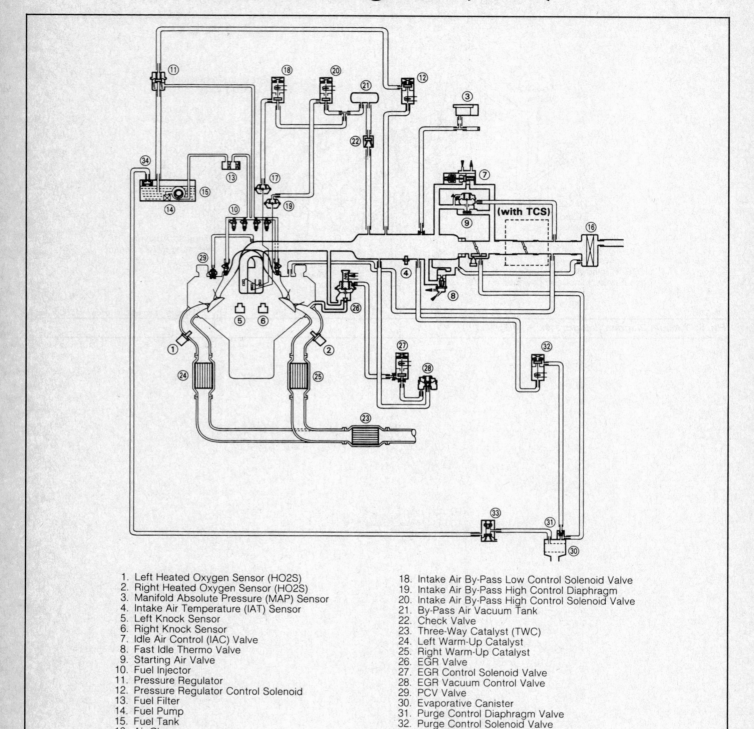

1. Left Heated Oxygen Sensor (HO2S)
2. Right Heated Oxygen Sensor (HO2S)
3. Manifold Absolute Pressure (MAP) Sensor
4. Intake Air Temperature (IAT) Sensor
5. Left Knock Sensor
6. Right Knock Sensor
7. Idle Air Control (IAC) Valve
8. Fast Idle Thermo Valve
9. Starting Air Valve
10. Fuel Injector
11. Pressure Regulator
12. Pressure Regulator Control Solenoid
13. Fuel Filter
14. Fuel Pump
15. Fuel Tank
16. Air Cleaner
17. Intake Air By-Pass Low Control Diaphragm

18. Intake Air By-Pass Low Control Solenoid Valve
19. Intake Air By-Pass High Control Diaphragm
20. Intake Air By-Pass High Control Solenoid Valve
21. By-Pass Air Vacuum Tank
22. Check Valve
23. Three-Way Catalyst (TWC)
24. Left Warm-Up Catalyst
25. Right Warm-Up Catalyst
26. EGR Valve
27. EGR Control Solenoid Valve
28. EGR Vacuum Control Valve
29. PCV Valve
30. Evaporative Canister
31. Purge Control Diaphragm Valve
32. Purge Control Solenoid Valve
33. 2-Way Valve
34. Fuel Tank Evaporative Valve

93J78111

Courtesy of American Honda Motor Co., Inc.

Fig. 6: Vacuum Schematic (Legend Coupe)

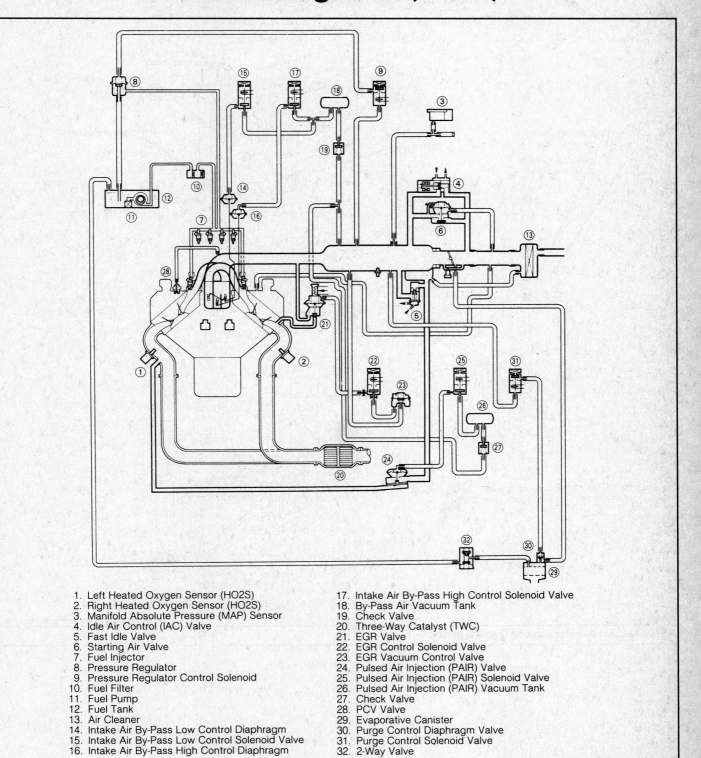

1. Left Heated Oxygen Sensor (HO2S)	17. Intake Air By-Pass High Control Solenoid Valve
2. Right Heated Oxygen Sensor (HO2S)	18. By-Pass Air Vacuum Tank
3. Manifold Absolute Pressure (MAP) Sensor	19. Check Valve
4. Idle Air Control (IAC) Valve	20. Three-Way Catalyst (TWC)
5. Fast Idle Valve	21. EGR Valve
6. Starting Air Valve	22. EGR Control Solenoid Valve
7. Fuel Injector	23. EGR Vacuum Control Valve
8. Pressure Regulator	24. Pulsed Air Injection (PAIR) Valve
9. Pressure Regulator Control Solenoid	25. Pulsed Air Injection (PAIR) Solenoid Valve
10. Fuel Filter	26. Pulsed Air Injection (PAIR) Vacuum Tank
11. Fuel Pump	27. Check Valve
12. Fuel Tank	28. PCV Valve
13. Air Cleaner	29. Evaporative Canister
14. Intake Air By-Pass Low Control Diaphragm	30. Purge Control Diaphragm Valve
15. Intake Air By-Pass Low Control Solenoid Valve	31. Purge Control Solenoid Valve
16. Intake Air By-Pass High Control Diaphragm	32. 2-Way Valve

93I78112

Fig. 7: Vacuum Schematic (Legend Sedan)

1993 ENGINE PERFORMANCE
Vacuum Diagrams (Cont.)

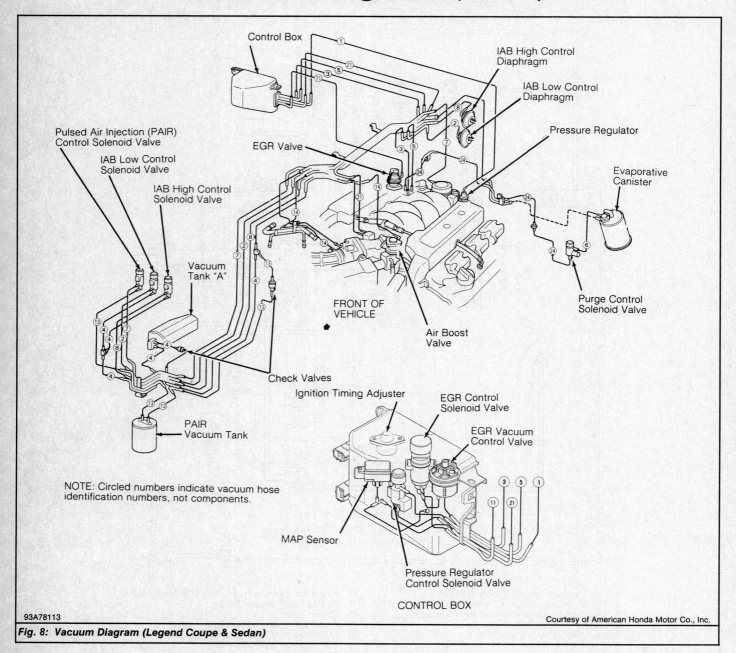

Control Box

IAB High Control
Diaphragm

IAB Low Control
Diaphragm

Pressure Regulator

Pulsed Air Injection (PAIR)
Control Solenoid Valve

IAB Low Control
Solenoid Valve

IAB High Control
Solenoid Valve

EGR Valve

Evaporative
Canister

Vacuum Tank "A"

FRONT OF
VEHICLE

Air Boost
Valve

Purge Control
Solenoid Valve

Check Valves

Ignition Timing Adjuster

EGR Control
Solenoid Valve

EGR Vacuum
Control Valve

PAIR
Vacuum Tank

NOTE: Circled numbers indicate vacuum hose
identification numbers, not components.

MAP Sensor

Pressure Regulator
Control Solenoid Valve

CONTROL BOX

93A78113

Courtesy of American Honda Motor Co., Inc.

Fig. 8: Vacuum Diagram (Legend Coupe & Sedan)

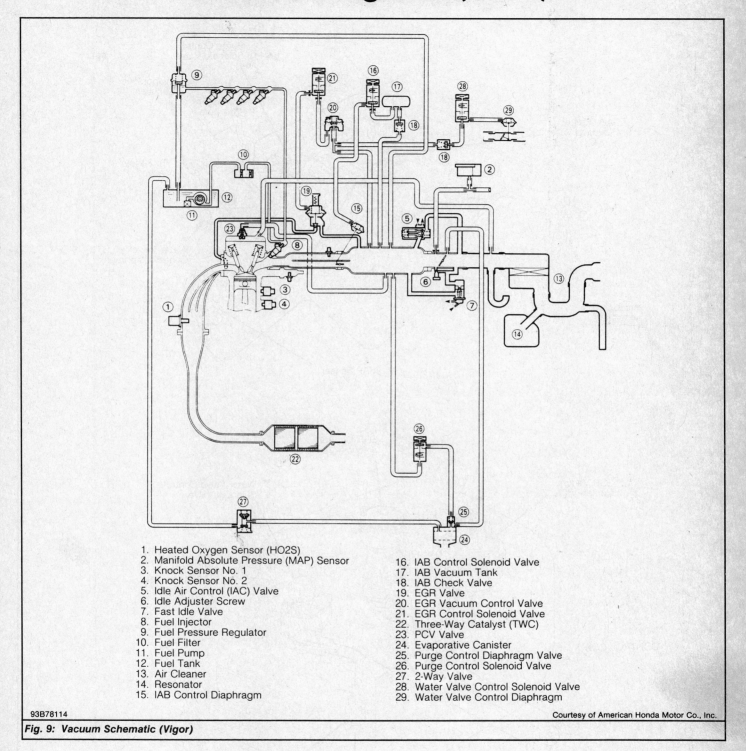

1. Heated Oxygen Sensor (HO2S)
2. Manifold Absolute Pressure (MAP) Sensor
3. Knock Sensor No. 1
4. Knock Sensor No. 2
5. Idle Air Control (IAC) Valve
6. Idle Adjuster Screw
7. Fast Idle Valve
8. Fuel Injector
9. Fuel Pressure Regulator
10. Fuel Filter
11. Fuel Pump
12. Fuel Tank
13. Air Cleaner
14. Resonator
15. IAB Control Diaphragm

16. IAB Control Solenoid Valve
17. IAB Vacuum Tank
18. IAB Check Valve
19. EGR Valve
20. EGR Vacuum Control Valve
21. EGR Control Solenoid Valve
22. Three-Way Catalyst (TWC)
23. PCV Valve
24. Evaporative Canister
25. Purge Control Diaphragm Valve
26. Purge Control Solenoid Valve
27. 2-Way Valve
28. Water Valve Control Solenoid Valve
29. Water Valve Control Diaphragm

93B78114

Fig. 9: Vacuum Schematic (Vigor)

1993 ENGINE PERFORMANCE
Vacuum Diagrams (Cont.)

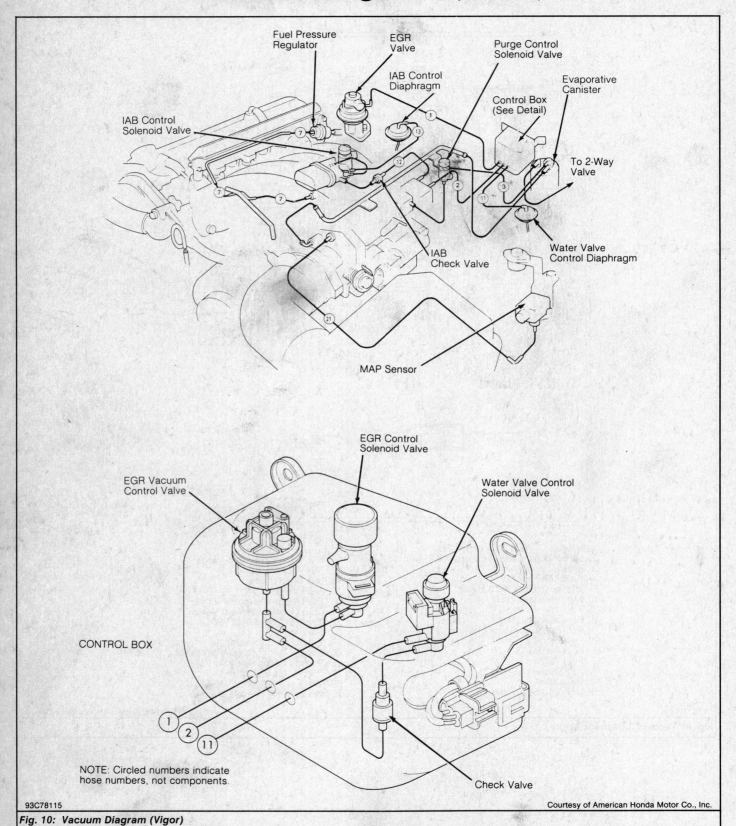

93C78115

Courtesy of American Honda Motor Co., Inc.

Fig. 10: Vacuum Diagram (Vigor)

Integra, Legend, Vigor

INTRODUCTION

Removal, overhaul and installation procedures are covered in this article. If component removal and installation is primarily an unbolt and bolt-on procedure, only a torque specification may be furnished.

IGNITION SYSTEM

DISTRIBUTOR

Removal & Installation (Integra) – **1)** Mark spark plug wires, distributor housing and cylinder head for installation reference. Unplug electrical connectors. Remove hold-down bolts and distributor.
2) Lubricate and install new "O" ring. *See Fig. 1.* Install distributor, aligning reference marks. Align distributor coupling with slot in camshaft. Connect wiring. Adjust ignition timing.

Removal & Installation (Vigor) – Note location of each spark plug wire. Disconnect wires from distributor cap. Remove hold-down bolts, distributor and seal. *See Fig. 2.* Coat new seal with engine oil. Align lugs on distributor drive with grooves in camshaft. Install hold-down bolts loosely. Connect wires. Adjust ignition timing. Tighten hold-down bolts.

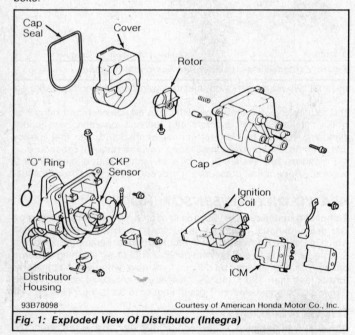

Fig. 1: Exploded View Of Distributor (Integra)

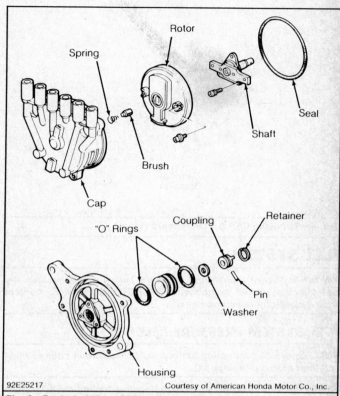

Fig. 2: Exploded View Of Distributor (Vigor)

CRANKSHAFT POSITION (CKP) SENSOR

Removal & Installation (Integra) – CKP sensor is an integral component of distributor. See DISTRIBUTOR.
Removal & Installation (Legend) – Rotate engine clockwise until No. 1 piston is at top dead center. Remove upper timing belt covers. *See Fig. 3.* Remove timing belt from camshaft pulleys. Remove left camshaft pulley. Remove left backing plate. Remove CKP sensor. To install, reverse removal procedure. Check camshaft timing and ignition timing.

CRANKSHAFT POSITION (CKP) & CYLINDER POSITION (CYP) SENSORS (VIGOR)

Removal & Installation – Rotate engine pulley counterclockwise until No. 1 cylinder is at top dead center. Remove upper timing belt cover. Remove timing belt from camshaft pulley. Remove CYP sensor. *See Fig. 4.* Remove camshaft pulley. Remove back cover. Remove CKP sensor. To install, reverse removal procedure. Recheck camshaft timing and ignition timing.

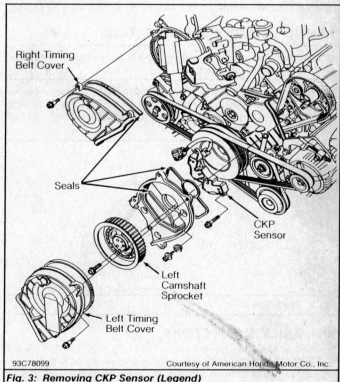

Fig. 3: Removing CKP Sensor (Legend)

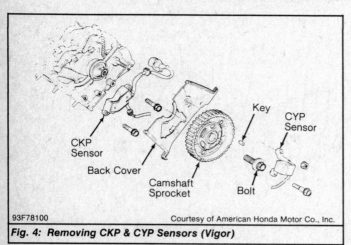

93F78100   Courtesy of American Honda Motor Co., Inc.

Fig. 4: Removing CKP & CYP Sensors (Vigor)

FUEL SYSTEM

WARNING: Always relieve fuel pressure before disconnecting any fuel injection-related component. DO NOT allow fuel to contact engine or electrical components.

FUEL SYSTEM PRESSURE RELEASE

NOTE: Before disconnecting battery, obtain activation code to reset anti-theft stereo (if equipped).

Relieving Fuel Pressure – Remove negative battery cable. Loosen fuel tank filler cap. Place clean shop rag around fuel filter. Slowly loosen 6-mm service bolt on top of fuel filter one complete turn to relieve system pressure. Always replace washer under bolt after loosening.

ENGINE CONTROL MODULE (ECM)

NOTE: Before disconnecting battery, obtain activation code to reset anti-theft stereo (if equipped).

Removal & Installation – Remove negative battery cable. Remove carpet from right footwell. Remove ECM cover. *See Fig. 5.* Unplug electrical connectors. Remove ECM. To install, reverse removal procedure.

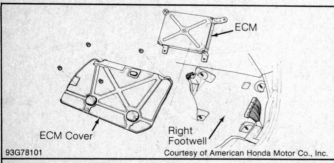

93G78101   Courtesy of American Honda Motor Co., Inc.

Fig. 5: Removing ECM

FUEL RAILS & INJECTORS

Removal – **1)** Relieve fuel pressure. See FUEL SYSTEM PRESSURE RELEASE. On Legend and Vigor, remove engine harness cover(s). On Legend refer to illustration. *see Fig. 6.* On all models, unplug injector electrical connectors. Place a rag over pressure regulator fuel return hose.

2) Disconnect vacuum hose and fuel return hose from pressure regulator. Disconnect fuel line from fuel rail. Remove fuel rail retaining nuts and fuel rail. Remove injectors from intake manifold.

Installation – **1)** Slide new cushion rings onto injectors. Install new "O" rings coated with clean engine oil onto injectors. Insert injectors

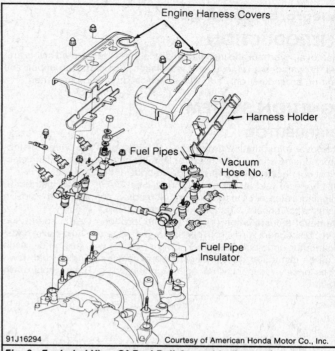

91J16294   Courtesy of American Honda Motor Co., Inc.

Fig. 6: Exploded View Of Fuel Rail Assembly (Legend)

into fuel rail. Align marks on injectors with corresponding marks on fuel rail.

2) Coat new injector seal rings with clean engine oil. Insert rings into intake manifold. Install injectors and fuel rail assembly onto intake manifold. Replace fuel line-to-fuel rail washers. Tighten fuel line-to-fuel rail nuts. To complete installation, reverse removal procedure.

3) Pressurize fuel system by turning on ignition with engine off for 2 seconds. Repeat fuel pressurizing procedure 3 times. Check for fuel leaks.

HEATED OXYGEN SENSOR (HO2S)

Removal & Installation – Oxygen sensor is mounted in exhaust pipe just below exhaust header. It is equipped with a permanent pigtail which must be protected from damage when sensor is removed. Ensure sensor is free of contaminants. Avoid using cleaning solvents of any type. Sensor may be difficult to remove when engine temperature is less than 120°F (48°C). Always use anti-seize compound on threads before installation. Tighten sensor to 33 ft. lbs. (45 N.m).

THROTTLE BODY

Removal & Installation – Disconnect throttle cable at throttle body. Label and disconnect hoses and wiring from throttle body. Drain coolant. Remove retaining nuts or bolts and throttle body. To install, reverse removal procedure.

THROTTLE POSITION SENSOR

Removal & Installation – Throttle angle sensor is located on throttle body. Unplug electrical connector. Remove throttle angle sensor. To install, reverse removal procedure.

TORQUE SPECIFICATIONS
TORQUE SPECIFICATIONS

Application	Ft. Lbs. (N.m)
Distributor Hold-Down Bolts	16 (22)
Fuel Filter Service Bolt	11 (15)
Fuel Line-To-Fuel Rail Nuts	16 (22)
Oxygen Sensor	33 (45)
Throttle Body Bolts & Nuts	16 (22)
	INCH Lbs. (N.m)
CKP Sensor (Legend & Vigor)	108 (12)
CYP Sensor (Vigor)	108 (12)

1993 ENGINE PERFORMANCE
Wiring Diagrams

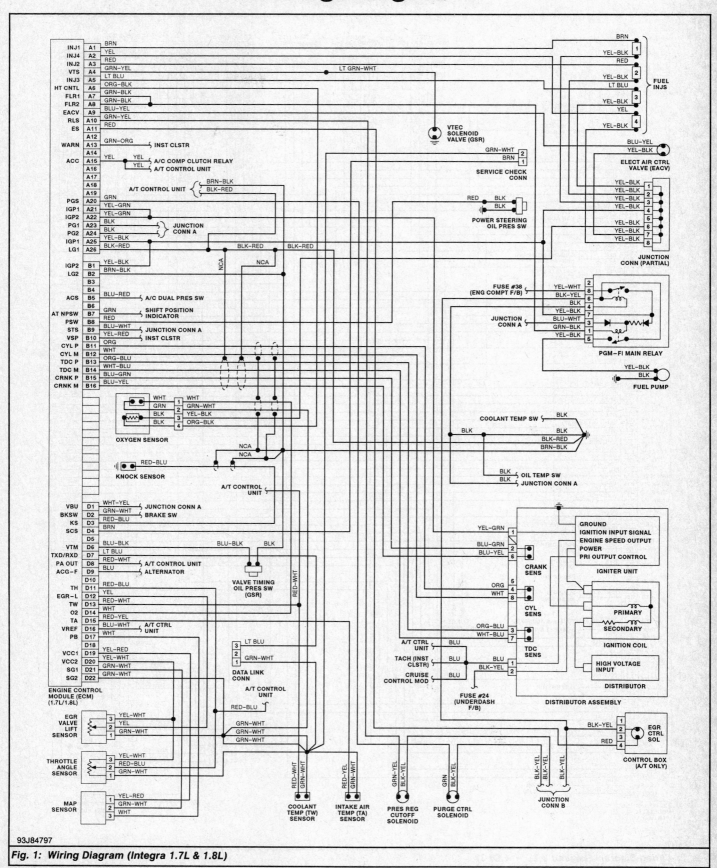

Fig. 1: Wiring Diagram (Integra 1.7L & 1.8L)

93J84797

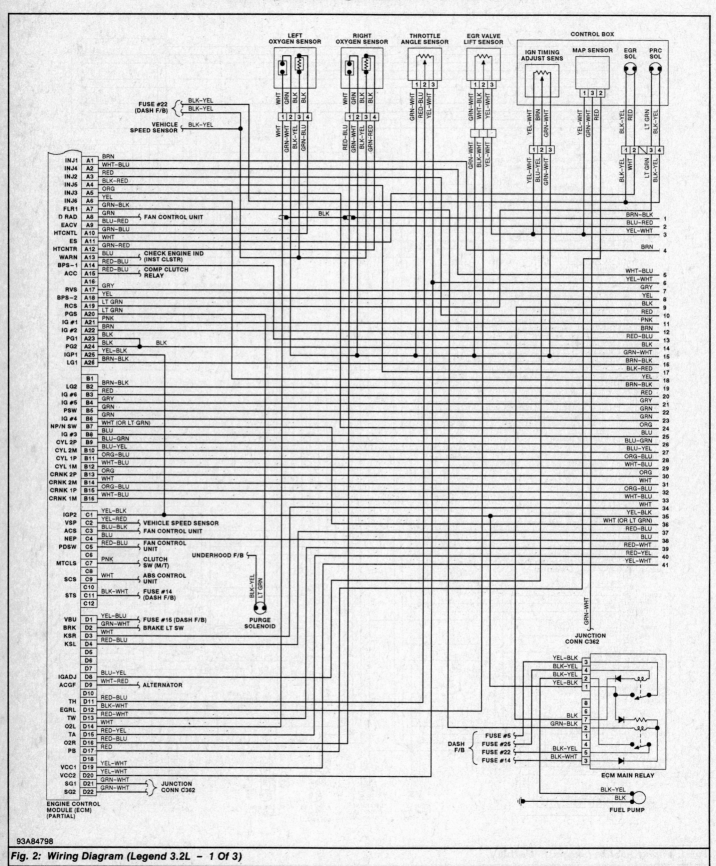

Fig. 2: Wiring Diagram (Legend 3.2L – 1 Of 3)

93A84798

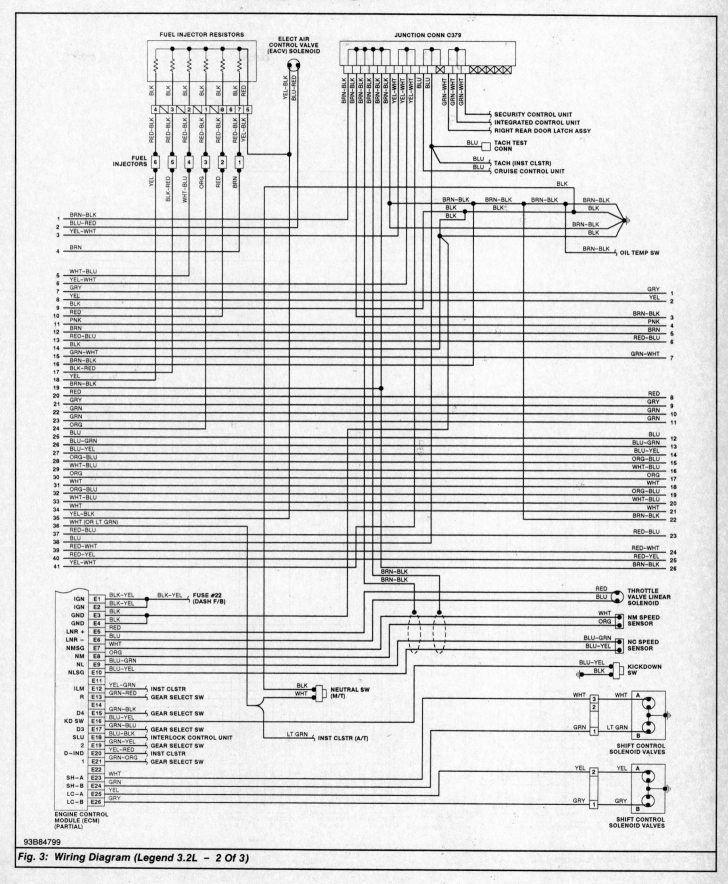

Fig. 3: *Wiring Diagram (Legend 3.2L – 2 Of 3)*

93B84799

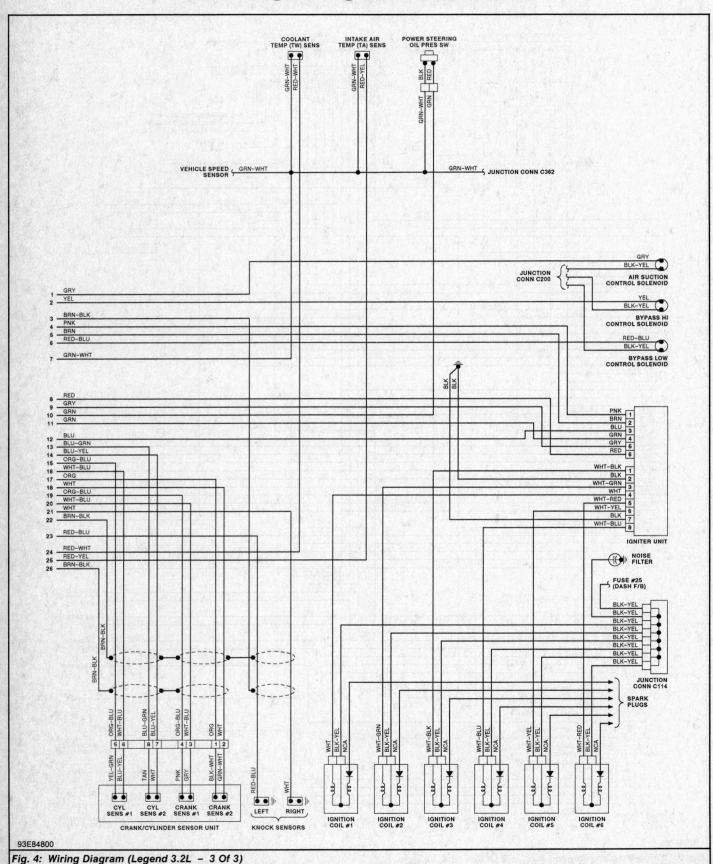

Fig. 4: Wiring Diagram (Legend 3.2L – 3 Of 3)

93E84800

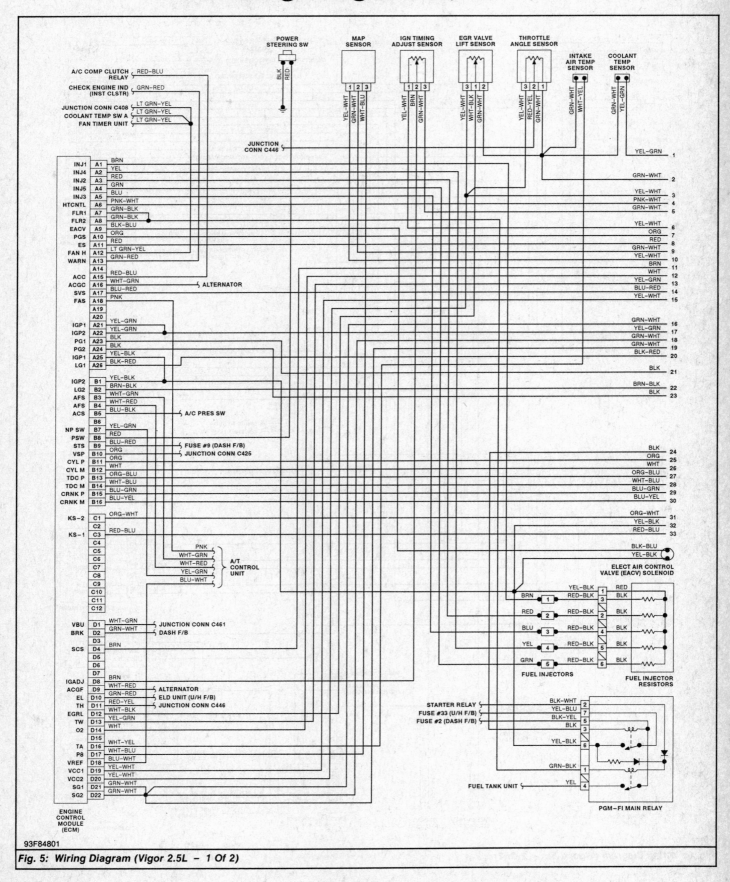

Fig. 5: Wiring Diagram (Vigor 2.5L - 1 Of 2)

93F84801

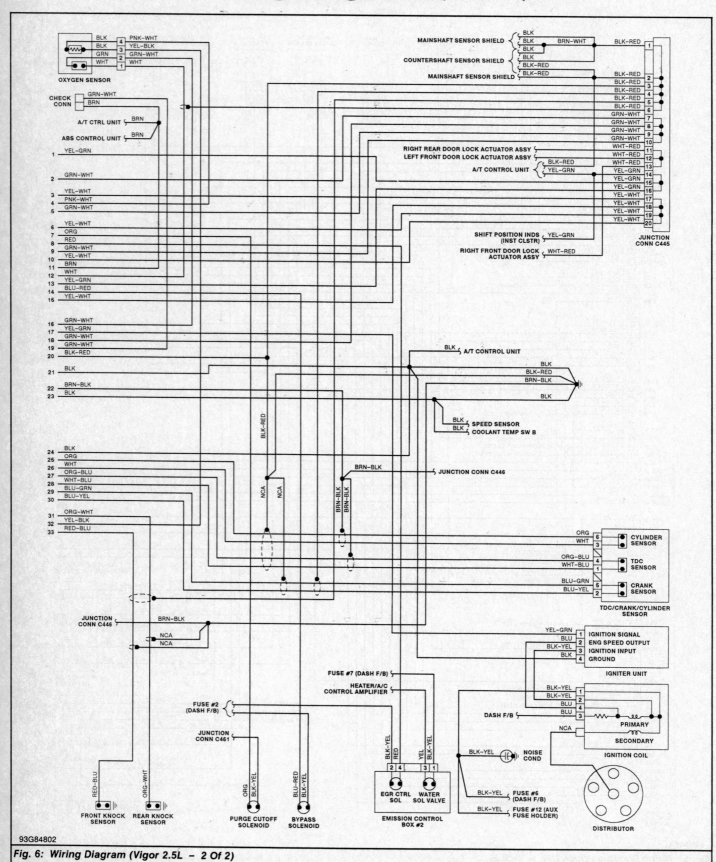

Fig. 6: Wiring Diagram (Vigor 2.5L – 2 Of 2)

93G84802

Integra, Legend, Vigor

DESCRIPTION

Nippondenso 3-phase alternators use 4 positive and 4 negative diodes to rectify current. An internal Integrated Circuit (IC) voltage regulator controls charging system voltage. *See Figs. 1-3.*

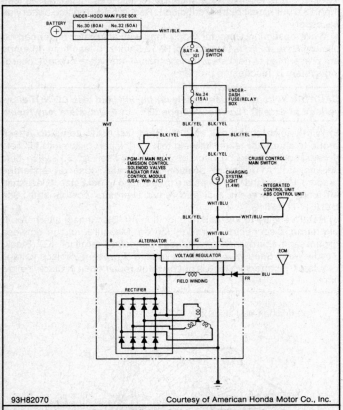

93H82070   Courtesy of American Honda Motor Co., Inc.

Fig. 1: Charging System Wiring Schematic (Integra)

ADJUSTMENTS

BELT ADJUSTMENT

Application	Deflection[1] In. (mm)
A/C Compressor	
Integra	0.28-0.35 (7.0-9.0)
Legend	0.32-0.40 (8.0-10.0)
Vigor	0.24-0.35 (6.0-9.0)
Alternator	
Integra	0.35-0.41 (9.0-10.5)
Legend	0.37-.55 (9.5-11.5)
Vigor	0.30-0.37 (7.5-9.5)
Power Steering	
Integra	0.37-0.47 (9.5-12.0)
Legend	0.45-0.53 (11.5-13.5)
Vigor	0.26-0.35 (6.0-9.0)

[1] – Deflection is with 22 lbs. (10 kg) pressure applied midway on longest belt run.

TROUBLE SHOOTING

NOTE: See TROUBLE SHOOTING article in GENERAL INFORMATION.

ON-VEHICLE TESTING

PRELIMINARY INSPECTION

Check alternator wiring harness connections and drive belt tension. Ensure battery is fully charged. On Integra, ensure fuse No. 24 (15-amp) in dash fuse box is good. *See Fig. 1.* On Legend, ensure fuses

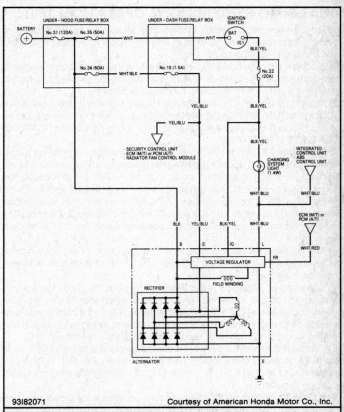

93I82071   Courtesy of American Honda Motor Co., Inc.

Fig. 2: Charging System Wiring Schematic (Legend)

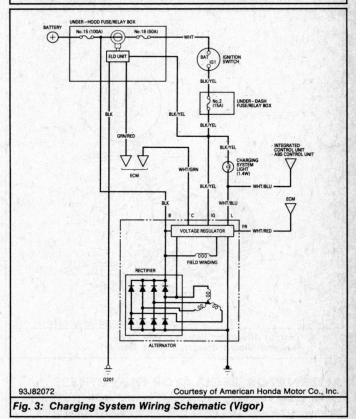

93J82072   Courtesy of American Honda Motor Co., Inc.

Fig. 3: Charging System Wiring Schematic (Vigor)

No. 15 (7.5-amp) and No. 22 (20-amp) in underdash fuse box are good. *See Fig.* 2. On Vigor, ensure fuse No. 2 (15-amp) in underdash fuse box is good. *See Fig.* 3.

CHARGING SYSTEM LIGHT OPERATION TEST

1) Turn ignition on. Charging system light should come on. If charging system light comes on, go to next step. If charging system light does not come on, go to step **6**).

2) Start engine. Charging system light should turn off. If charging system light stays on, go to next step. If charging system light turns off, charging system light circuit is functioning properly.

3) Turn ignition off. Disconnect alternator 4-pin harness connector. Turn ignition on. If charging system light is on, turn ignition off and go to next step. If charging system light is off, go to ALTERNATOR/REGULATOR OUTPUT TEST.

4) Disconnect ABS control module 18-pin connector. On Integra, disconnect integrated control module from under-dash fuse box. On Legend, disconnect integrated control module 22-pin connector. On Vigor, disconnect integrated control module 16-pin connector.

5) On all models, turn ignition on. If charging system light is on, repair short to ground in White/Blue wire. See Figs. 1, 2 and 3. After making repairs, reconnect control module connectors and reset ECM to clear and codes.

6) Turn ignition off. Check fuse No. 24 (Integra), fuse No. 22 (Legend) or fuse No. 2 (Vigor). If fuse is good, go to next step. If fuse is blown, replace fuse.

7) Disconnect alternator 4-pin harness connector. Turn ignition on. Measure voltage between ground and alternator 4-pin harness connector terminal "IG" (Black/Yellow wire). See Fig. 4. Battery voltage should be present. If battery voltage is present, go to next step. If battery voltage is not present, repair open in Black/Yellow wire.

8) Connect a fused jumper wire between ground and alternator 4-pin harness connector terminal "L" (White/Blue wire). See Fig. 4. Charging system light should turn on. If charging system light turns on, replace voltage regulator.

9) If charging system light does not turn on, check for blown charging system light bulb and replace as necessary. If bulb is good, repair open in White/Blue wire.

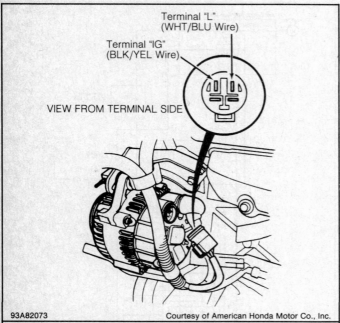

Fig. 4: Testing Alternator Ignition Feed Circuit
(Legend Shown; Integra & Vigor Similar)

ALTERNATOR/REGULATOR OUTPUT TEST

1) Test system using an alternator tester with integral carbon pile (to apply electrical load to system). Hook up tester according to manufacturers instructions. Turn tester selector to STARTING position. Start engine and bring to operating temperature. Raise engine speed to 2000 RPM and hold. Observe voltmeter. If voltage is greater than 15.2 volts, replace voltage regulator.

2) If voltage is less than 15.1 volts, return engine to idle. Ensure all accessories are off. Turn tester selector to CHARGING position. Remove inductive pick-up and zero ammeter. Connect inductive pick-up over alternator battery terminal (ensure arrow points away from alternator). See Fig. 5.

3) Raise engine speed to 2000 RPM and hold. Observe voltmeter. If voltage is greater than 13.9 volts, go to next step. If voltage is less than 13.9 volts, test battery condition. Recharge or replace battery as necessary.

4) While observing ammeter, apply load with alternator tester carbon pile until battery voltage drops to 12-13.5 volts. If less than 40 amps are present, go to next step. If more than 40 amps are present, charging system is functioning properly.

CAUTION: Voltage will rise rapidly during full field test. DO NOT allow voltage to exceed 18 volts. Damage to electrical system may result.

5) With engine speed still at 2000 RPM, full field alternator. Attach probe to alternator tester full field test lead. Insert probe into full field access hole located on back of alternator. See Fig. 5. Switch field selector to "A" (ground) position briefly and observe amperage reading. If more than 40 amps are present, go to next step. If less than 40 amps are present, test and repair alternator components. See BENCH TESTING.

6) Return engine to idle and turn ignition off. Disconnect alternator 4-pin harness connector. Turn ignition on. Measure voltage between ground and alternator 4-pin harness connector terminal "IG" (Black/Yellow wire). See Fig. 4. If battery voltage is present, replace voltage regulator. If battery voltage is not present, repair open in Black/Yellow wire.

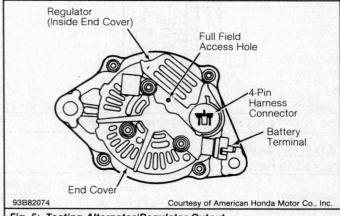

Fig. 5: Testing Alternator/Regulator Output
(Integra Shown; Legend & Vigor Similar)

BENCH TESTING

ROTOR

Ensure bearing rotates smoothly. Connect ohmmeter between slip rings and rotor and rotor shaft. See Fig. 6. Continuity should not exist. Connect ohmmeter between slip rings. Continuity should be present. If continuity is not as specified, replace rotor.

STATOR

Using ohmmeter, check continuity between stator leads. See Fig. 7. Continuity should be present between all stator leads. Check continuity between stator leads and coil core. Continuity should not be present between stator leads and coil core. If continuity is not as specified, replace stator.

RECTIFIER DIODES

NOTE: Use an ohmmeter capable of checking diodes.

1) Check for continuity between terminal "B" and terminals P1-P5 and between terminal "E" and terminals P1-P5. See Fig. 7. Note ohmmeter reading.

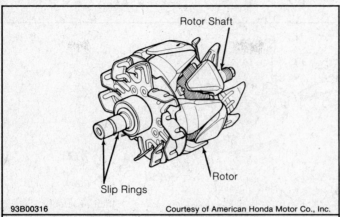

Fig. 6: Identifying Typical Rotor Components

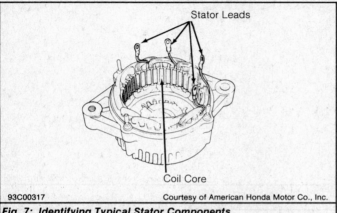

Fig. 7: Identifying Typical Stator Components

2) Reverse leads, and repeat test. Continuity should be present in one direction and not in other. If continuity is not as specified, replace rectifier assembly.

COMPONENT REPLACEMENT

Brushes – Brush holder is accessed by removing end cover and removing 2 retaining screws. Ensure brushes slide smoothly in holder assembly. Check brush holder and brushes for cracks or other

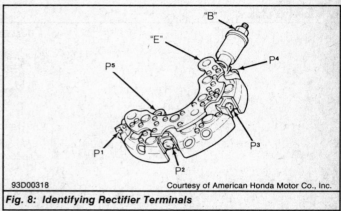

Fig. 8: Identifying Rectifier Terminals

damage. Minimum brush length should be .22" (5.5 mm) on Integra or .06" (1.5 mm) on Legend and Vigor. If brushes are damaged or worn, replace brush holder assembly.

REMOVAL & INSTALLATION

CAUTION: Before disconnecting battery, obtain activation code to reset anti-theft stereo (if equipped).

ALTERNATOR

Removal & Installation (Integra) – **1)** Disconnect negative battery cable. Raise and support vehicle. Remove front wheels. Remove left front axle shaft. See FWD AXLE SHAFTS article in DRIVE AXLES. Disconnect wiring harness connector and White wire from alternator.
2) Remove alternator belt. Remove lower mounting bolt, and swing alternator upward. Remove alternator mounting bracket. Remove alternator adjusting nut and upper through bolt. Remove alternator. To install, reverse removal procedure.
Removal & Installation (Legend) – Disconnect battery cables. Remove battery and battery tray. Remove lower alternator mounting bolt and adjusting rod assembly. Remove alternator from mounting bracket to access wiring on back of alternator. Disconnect wiring harness connector and Black wire from alternator. Remove alternator. To install, reverse removal procedure.
Removal & Installation (Vigor) – Disconnect battery cables. Disconnect wiring harness connector and Black wire from alternator. Remove upper and lower alternator mounting bolts. Remove alternator. To install, reverse removal procedure.

OVERHAUL

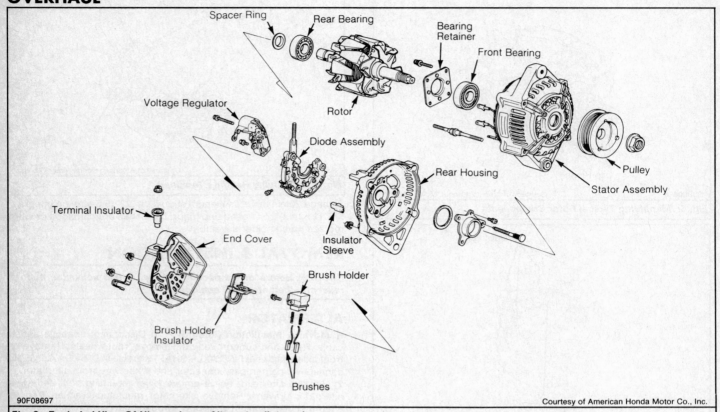

Fig. 9: Exploded View Of Nippondenso Alternator (Integra)

Courtesy of American Honda Motor Co., Inc.

90F08697

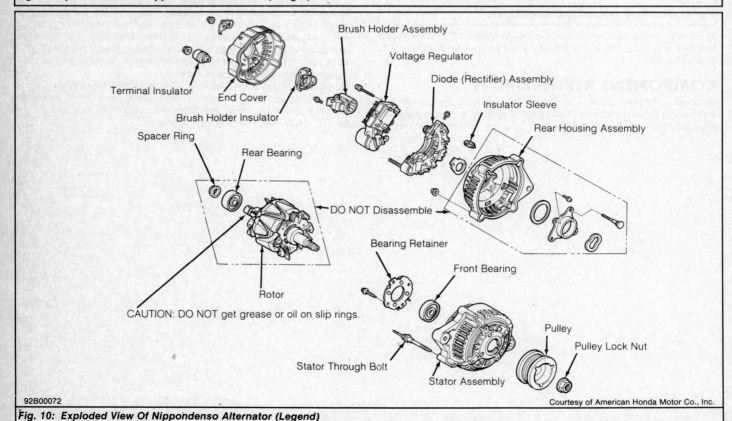

Fig. 10: Exploded View Of Nippondenso Alternator (Legend)

Courtesy of American Honda Motor Co., Inc.

92B00072

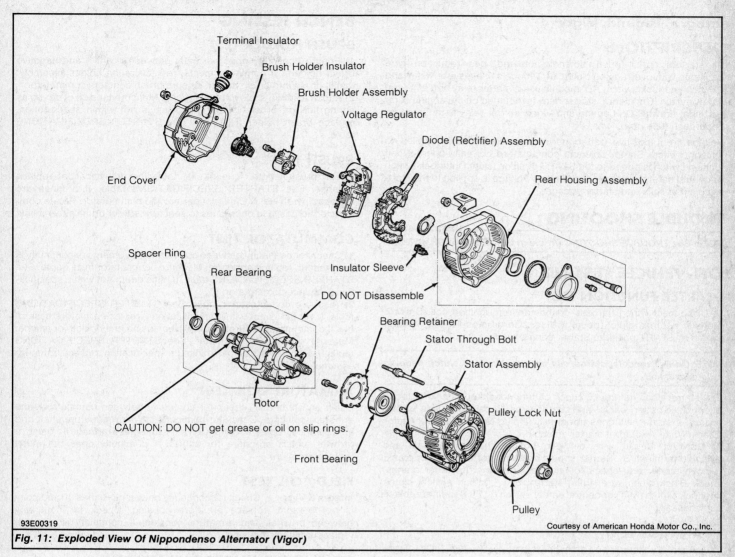

Terminal Insulator
Brush Holder Insulator
Brush Holder Assembly
Voltage Regulator
Diode (Rectifier) Assembly
Rear Housing Assembly
End Cover
Insulator Sleeve
Spacer Ring
Rear Bearing
DO NOT Disassemble
Bearing Retainer
Stator Through Bolt
Stator Assembly
Rotor
Pulley Lock Nut
CAUTION: DO NOT get grease or oil on slip rings.
Front Bearing
Pulley

93E00319

Courtesy of American Honda Motor Co., Inc.

Fig. 11: Exploded View Of Nippondenso Alternator (Vigor)

Integra, Legend, Vigor

DESCRIPTION

All starters are 4-brush, solenoid-actuated, gear-reduction type equipped with overrunning clutch. M/T models use a starter relay and a clutch interlock switch. A/T models use a starter relay and a neutral safety switch. On Integra, starter relay is mounted on the engine compartment firewall. On Legend and Vigor, starter relay is mounted on underdash fuse box.

Voltage from positive battery terminal is continuously applied to ignition switch. Starter solenoid contacts are normally open. When ignition switch is turned to the START position (clutch interlock switch or neutral safety switch closed), battery voltage is applied to the starter solenoid coils and starter engages.

TROUBLE SHOOTING

NOTE: See TROUBLE SHOOTING article in GENERAL INFORMATION.

ON-VEHICLE TESTING

STARTER FUNCTION TEST

1) Disconnect wiring harness connector from ignition coil. On M/T models, depress clutch pedal to floor. On all models, turn ignition switch to START position. Starter should crank.

NOTE: On M/T models, starter will not crank unless clutch pedal is fully depressed.

2) If starter does not crank, check battery condition. Check for loose or corroded battery cables and starter wires. Repair or replace as necessary. If starter still does not crank, unplug terminal "S" connector (Black/White wire) from starter solenoid.
3) Connect jumper wire between positive battery terminal and solenoid terminal "S". Starter should crank. If starter does not crank, remove starter and check for internal problems. If starter cranks, check Black/White wire, fuse, starter relay, ignition switch, clutch interlock switch (M/T) or neutral safety switch (A/T). Repair or replace as necessary.

CRANKING TEST

1) Connect a voltmeter and ammeter to battery. See Fig. 1. On Integra and Vigor, disconnect connector from distributor. On Legend, disconnect 8-pin and 6-pin connectors from ignition control module. Ignition control module is located on right side of engine compartment.
2) On all models, use remote starter switch to crank engine. Check cranking voltage and current draw. Ensure voltage is at least 8 volts. Current draw should be less than 350 amps. Cranking speed should be above 100 RPM.

BENCH TESTING

BRUSH HOLDER TEST

1) Ensure continuity does not exist between positive and negative brush holders. If continuity exists, replace brush holder assembly. Install brush into brush holder. Ensure brush contacts commutator.
2) Attach a spring scale to brush spring. Measure tension of spring as spring lifts off brush. If spring tension is not within specification, replace brush holder assembly. See STARTER SPECIFICATIONS table.

BRUSH TEST

Check brush length. If length is not within specification, replace brushes. See STARTER SPECIFICATIONS table. If brushes are replaced, wrap No. 600 sandpaper around commutator. Rotate commutator across face of brushes to seat new starter brush assemblies.

COMMUTATOR TEST

1) Check for continuity between commutator segments. If continuity is not present, replace armature. Measure commutator mica depth. See STARTER SPECIFICATIONS table. If mica depth not within specifications, replace commutator.
2) Measure commutator runout. See STARTER SPECIFICATIONS table. If runout is not within specifications, replace armature assembly. If commutator is burnt or dirty, clean using emery cloth or a lathe. Measure commutator diameter. See STARTER SPECIFICATIONS table. If diameter is less than minimum specification, replace armature assembly.

ARMATURE COIL TEST

Using an ohmmeter, check for continuity between commutator and armature coil core. Check for continuity between armature shaft and armature coil core. If continuity exists, replace armature. Using a growler, check armature for shorts. If continuity does not exist, replace armature.

FIELD COIL TEST

Integra & Vigor – Check for continuity between brushes. If continuity is not present, replace armature housing. Check for continuity between brushes and armature housing. If continuity is present, replace armature housing.

SOLENOID PLUNGER INSPECTION

Integra – Check contact points and face of starter solenoid plunger for burning and pitting. If surfaces are rough, recondition using a strip of No. 600 sandpaper.

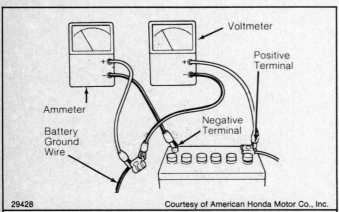

29428   Courtesy of American Honda Motor Co., Inc.

Fig. 1: Connecting Voltmeter & Ammeter For Cranking Test

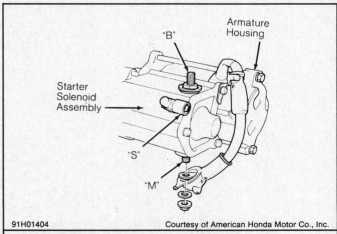

91H01404   Courtesy of American Honda Motor Co., Inc.

Fig. 2: Identifying Solenoid Terminals (Integra)

STARTER SOLENOID TEST

Integra – Check starter solenoid for continuity between terminal "S" and armature housing (ground). *See Fig. 2.* Check continuity between terminals "S" and "M". Continuity should be present. If continuity is not present, replace solenoid.

Legend & Vigor – Remove starter solenoid from starter. With starter solenoid plunger in released position, continuity should exist between terminals "M" and "S" and solenoid housing (ground). *See Fig. 3.* With starter solenoid plunger pushed in, continuity should exist between terminals "B", "M" and "S" and solenoid housing. If continuity is not present, replace solenoid.

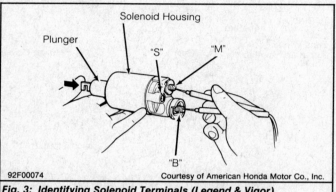

92F00074   Courtesy of American Honda Motor Co., Inc.

Fig. 3: Identifying Solenoid Terminals (Legend & Vigor)

OVERHAUL

NOTE: See exploded views of starters. See Figs. 4-8.

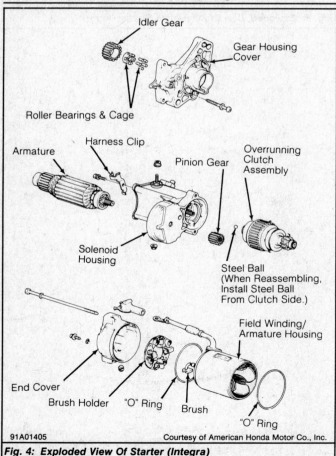

91A01405   Courtesy of American Honda Motor Co., Inc.

Fig. 4: Exploded View Of Starter (Integra)

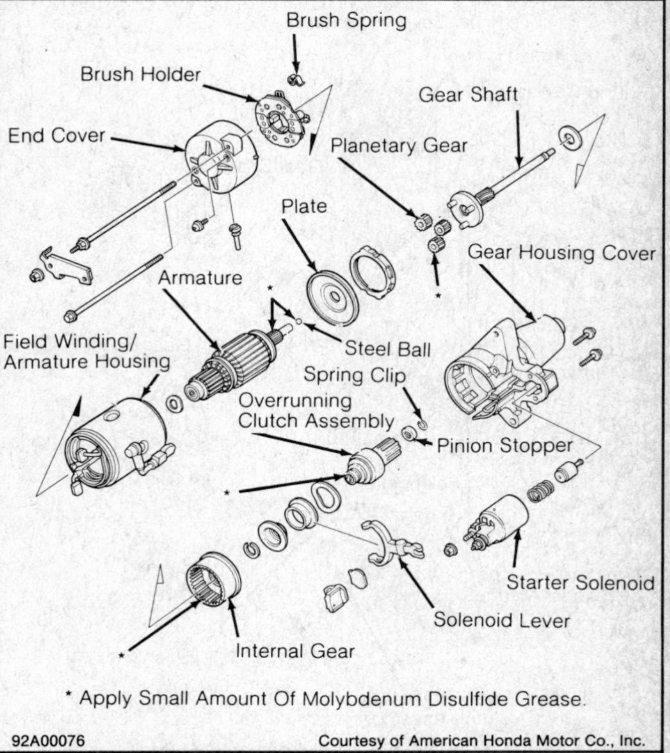

* Apply Small Amount Of Molybdenum Disulfide Grease.

92A00076   Courtesy of American Honda Motor Co., Inc.

Fig. 5: Exploded View Of Starter (Legend)

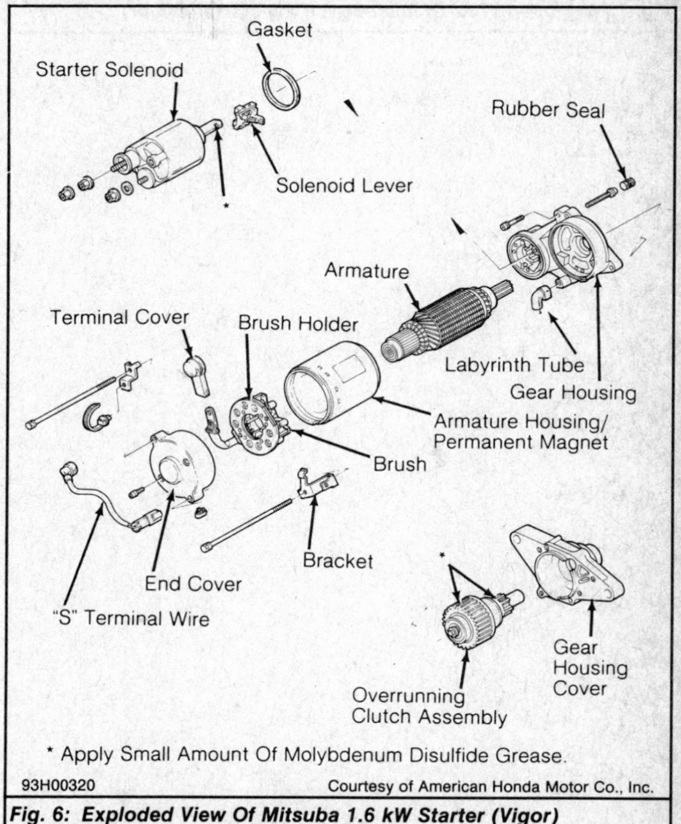

* Apply Small Amount Of Molybdenum Disulfide Grease.

93H00320   Courtesy of American Honda Motor Co., Inc.

Fig. 6: Exploded View Of Mitsuba 1.6 kW Starter (Vigor)

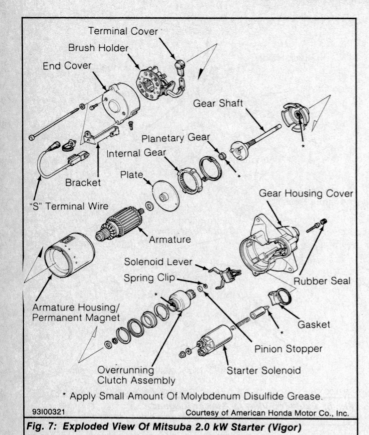

Fig. 7: Exploded View Of Mitsuba 2.0 kW Starter (Vigor)

* Apply Small Amount Of Molybdenum Disulfide Grease.

93I00321   Courtesy of American Honda Motor Co., Inc.

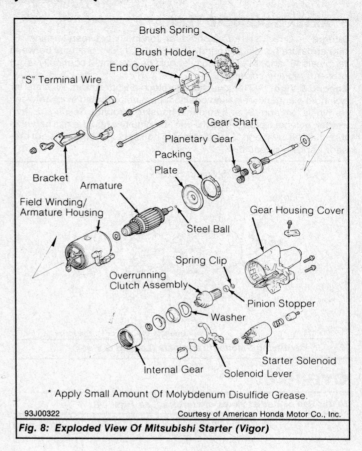

Fig. 8: Exploded View Of Mitsubishi Starter (Vigor)

* Apply Small Amount Of Molybdenum Disulfide Grease.

93J00322   Courtesy of American Honda Motor Co., Inc.

STARTER SPECIFICATIONS

STARTER SPECIFICATIONS

Application	Specification
Carbon Brush	
Length (Standard)	
Integra	0.59-0.61" (15.0-15.5 mm)
Legend	0.71" (18.0 mm)
Vigor	
Mitsuba 1.6 KW	0.62-0.64" (15.8-16.2 mm)
Mitsuba 2.0 KW	0.66-0.68" (16.8-17.2 mm)
Mitsubishi 2.0 KW	0.71" (18.0 mm)
Length (Minimum)	
Integra	0.39" (10.0 mm)
Legend	0.43" (11.0 mm)
Vigor	
Mitsuba 1.6 KW	0.43" (11.0 mm)
Mitsuba 2.0 KW	0.43" (11.0 mm)
Mitsubishi 2.0 KW	0.43" (11.0 mm)
Spring Tension	
Integra	3.8-5.3 Lbs. (1.7-2.4 Kg)
Legend	6.55-8.00 Lbs. (2.97-3.63 Kg)
Vigor	
Mitsuba 1.6 KW	3.57-3.97 Lbs. (1.60-1.80 Kg)
Mitsuba 2.0 KW	3.75-4.19 Lbs. (1.70-1.90 Kg)
Mitsubishi 2.0 KW	6.55-8.00 Lbs. (2.97-3.63 Kg)
Commutator	
Diameter (Standard)	
Integra	1.177-1.181" (29.9-30.0 mm)
Legend	1.256-1.263" (31.9-32.1 mm)
Vigor	
Mitsuba 1.6 KW	1.102-1.106" (28.0-28.1 mm)
Mitsuba 2.0 KW	1.259-1.263" (32.0-32.1 mm)
Mitsubishi 2.0 KW	1.256-1.263" (31.9-32.1 mm)
Diameter (Minimum)	
Integra	1.14" (29.0 mm)
Legend	1.24" (31.5 mm)
Vigor	
Mitsuba 1.6 KW	1.083" (27.7 mm)
Mitsuba 2.0 KW	1.24" (31.5 mm)
Mitsubishi 2.0 KW	1.24" (31.5 mm)
Runout (Standard)	
Integra	0.001" (0.02 mm)
Legend	0.002" (0.05 mm)
Vigor	
Mitsuba 1.6 KW	0.0008" (0.02 mm)
Mitsuba 2.0 KW	0.0008" (0.02 mm)
Mitsubishi 2.0 KW	0.002" (0.05 mm)
Runout (Maximum)	
Integra	0.002" (0.05 mm)
Legend	0.004" (0.10 mm)
Vigor	
Mitsuba 1.6 KW	0.002" (0.05 mm)
Mitsuba 2.0 KW	0.002" (0.05 mm)
Mitsubishi 2.0 KW	0.004" (0.10 mm)
Mica Depth (Standard)	
Integra	0.019-0.031" (0.5-0.8 mm)
Legend	0.019-0.031" (0.5-0.8 mm)
Vigor	
Mitsuba 1.6 KW	0.016-0.020" (0.40-0.50 mm)
Mitsuba 2.0 KW	0.016-0.020" (0.40-0.50 mm)
Mitsubishi 2.0 KW	0.02-0.03" (0.5-0.8 mm)

STARTER SPECIFICATIONS (Cont.)

Application	Specification
Mica Depth (Minumum)	
Integra	0.008" (0.2 mm)
Legend	0.008" (0.2 mm)
Vigor	
Mitsuba 1.6 KW	0.006" (0.15 mm)
Mitsuba 2.0 KW	0.006" (0.15 mm)
Mitsubishi 2.0 KW	0.008" (0.02 mm)
Pinion Gap	
Integra	[1]
Legend & Vigor	0.02-0.08" (0.5-2.0 mm)
No Load At 11 Volts	
Maximum Amps	
Integra	90
Legend	140
Vigor	
Mitsuba 1.6 KW	80
Mitsuba 2.0 KW	90
Mitsubishi 2.0 KW	140
Minimum RPM	
Integra	3000
Legend	3800
Vigor	
Mitsuba 1.6 KW	2600
Mitsuba 2.0 KW	2200
Mitsubishi 2.0 KW	3800

[1] - Specification is not provided by manufacturer.

STARTER SPECIFICATIONS (Cont.)

Application	Specification

TORQUE SPECIFICATIONS

Torque Specifications

Application	Ft. Lbs. (N.m)
Starter Mounting Bolts	
Integra	33 (45)
Legend	55 (75)
Vigor	
Lower	55 (75)
Upper	33 (45)

	INCH Lbs. (N.m)
Battery Terminal Nut	
All Models	89 (10)

WIRING DIAGRAMS

NOTE: For wiring diagrams, see WIRING DIAGRAMS article.

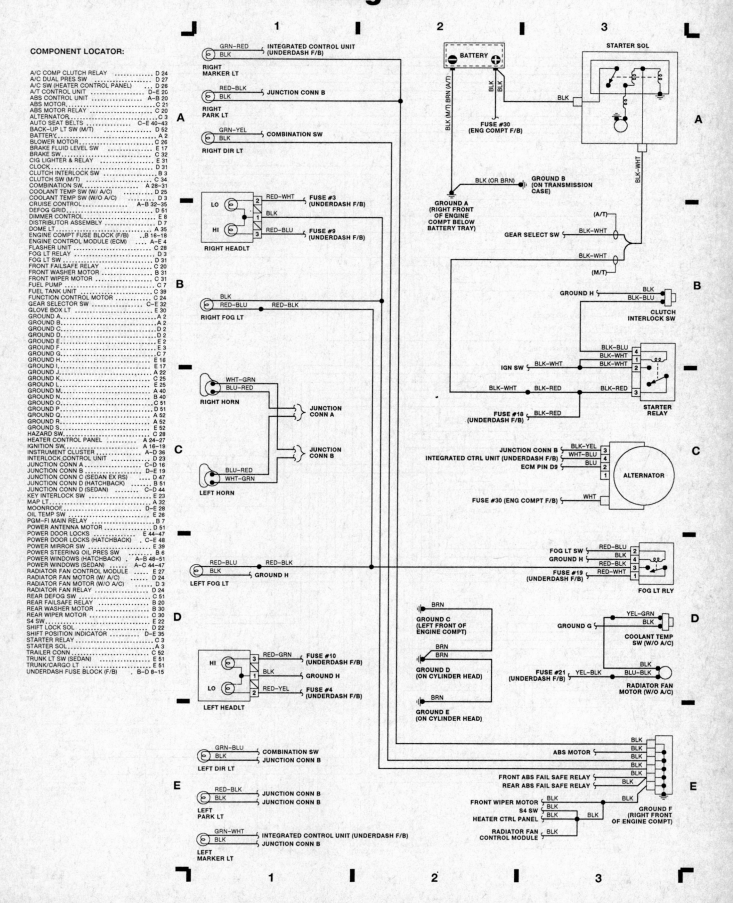

1993 WIRING DIAGRAMS
Integra (Cont.)

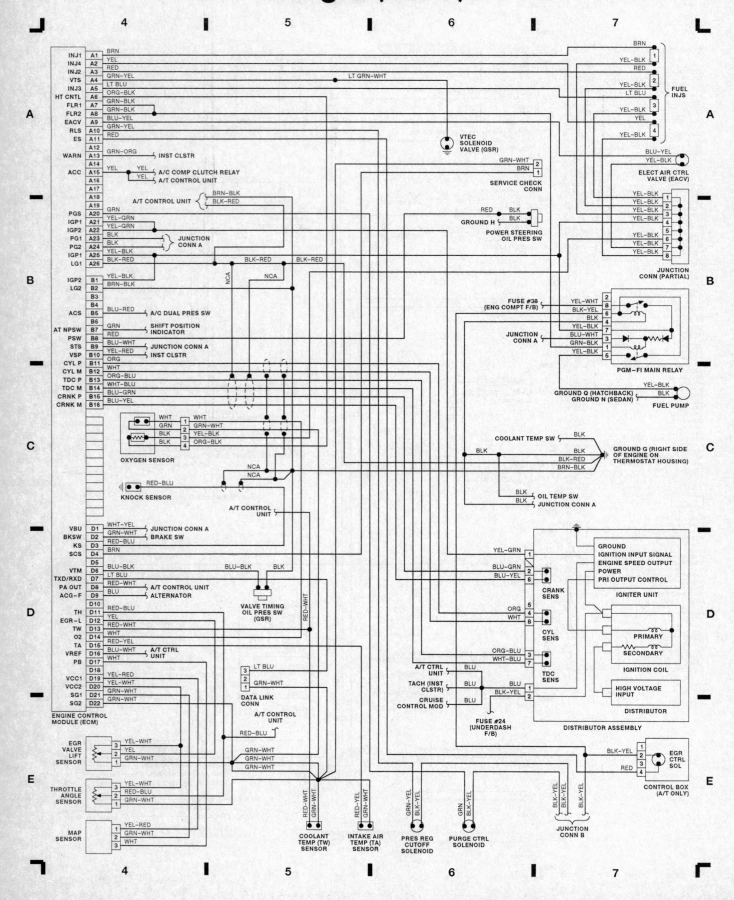

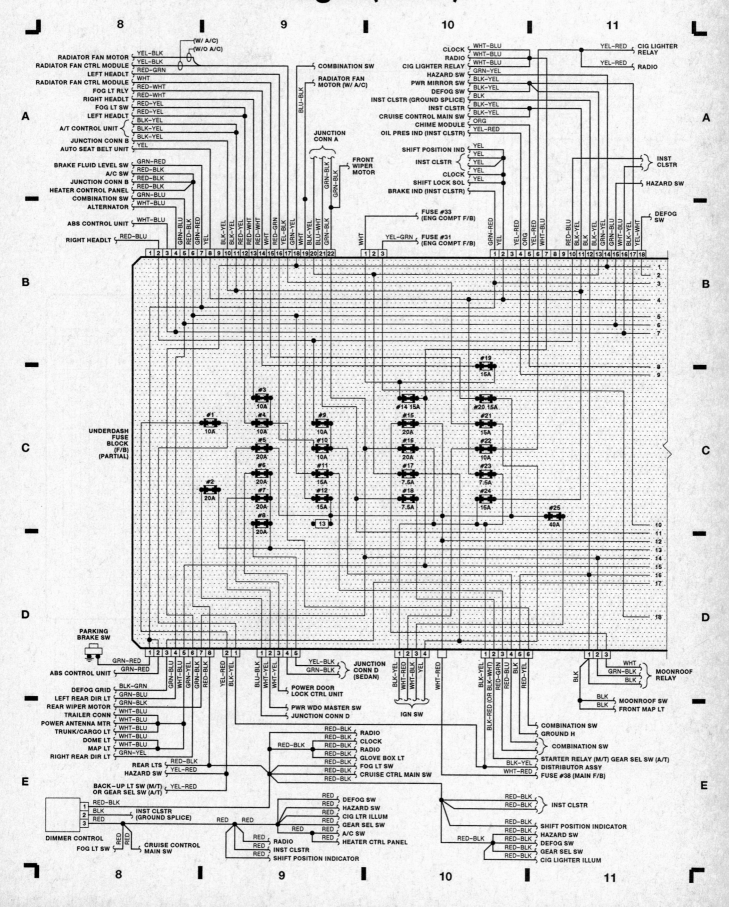

1993 WIRING DIAGRAMS
Integra (Cont.)

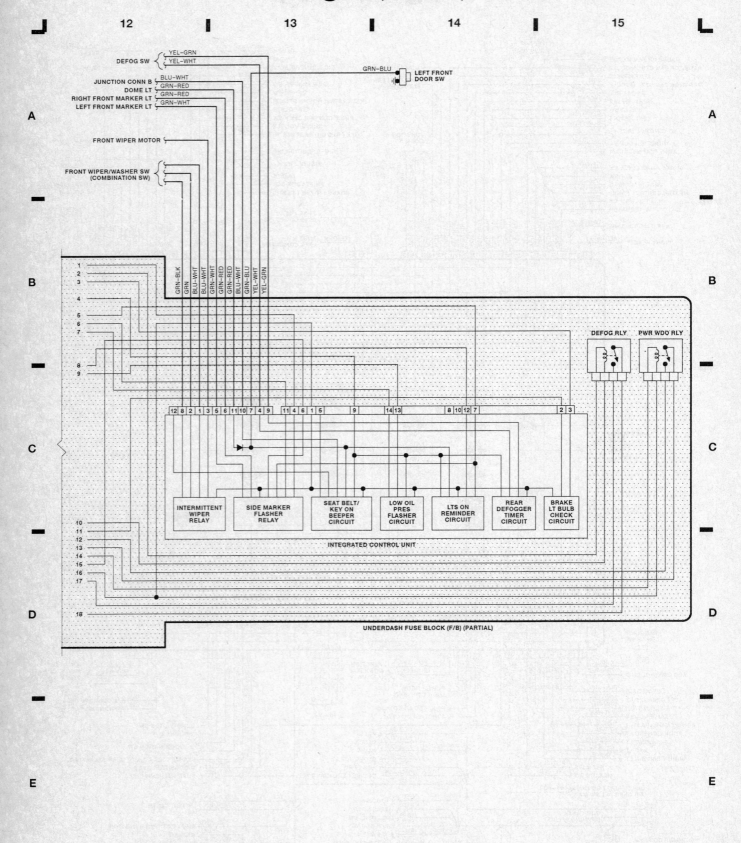

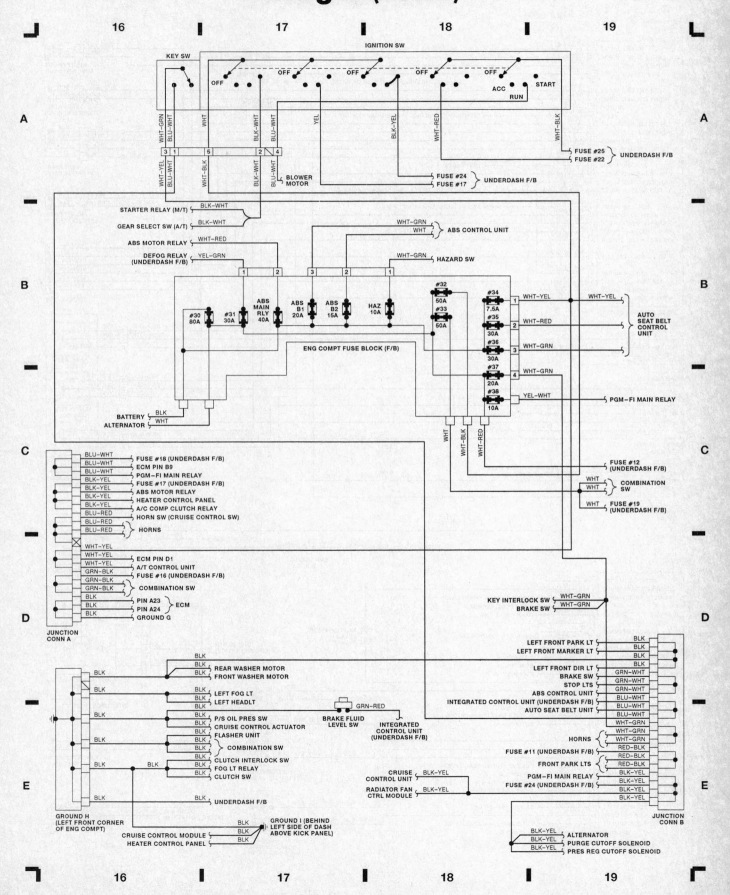

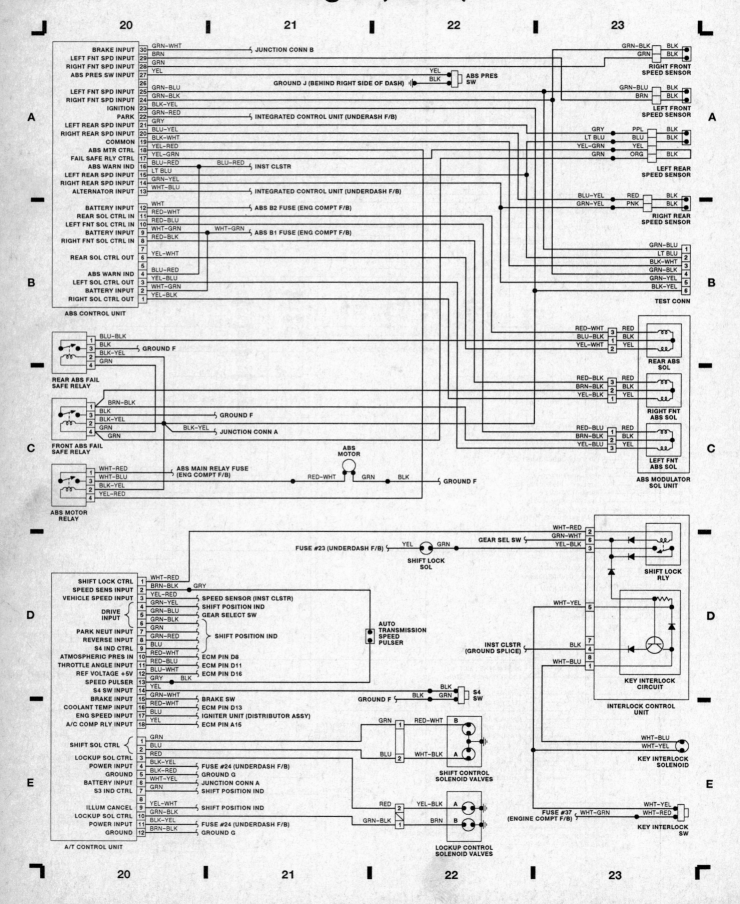

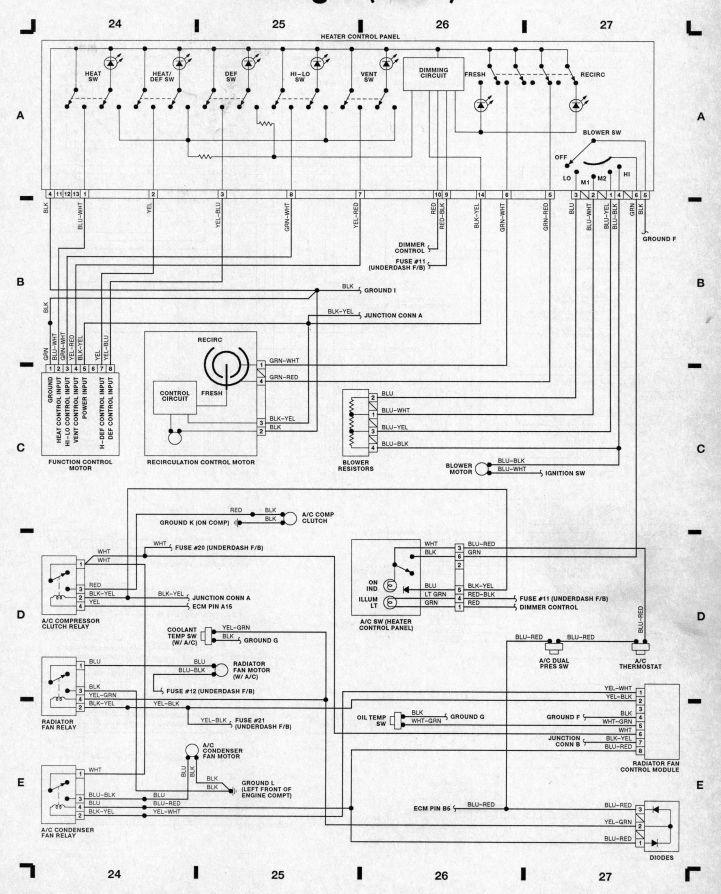

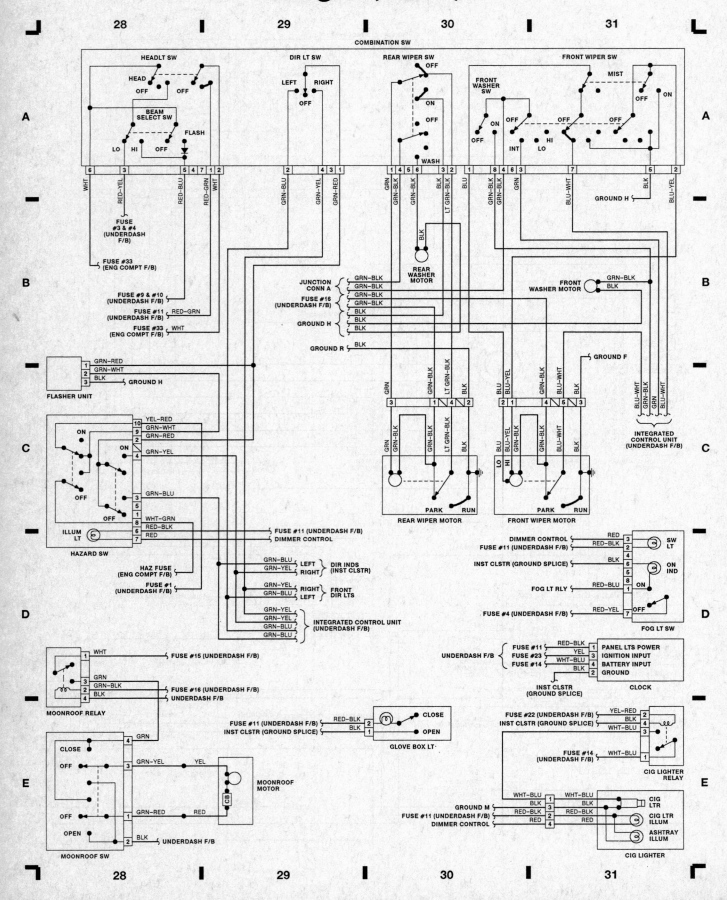

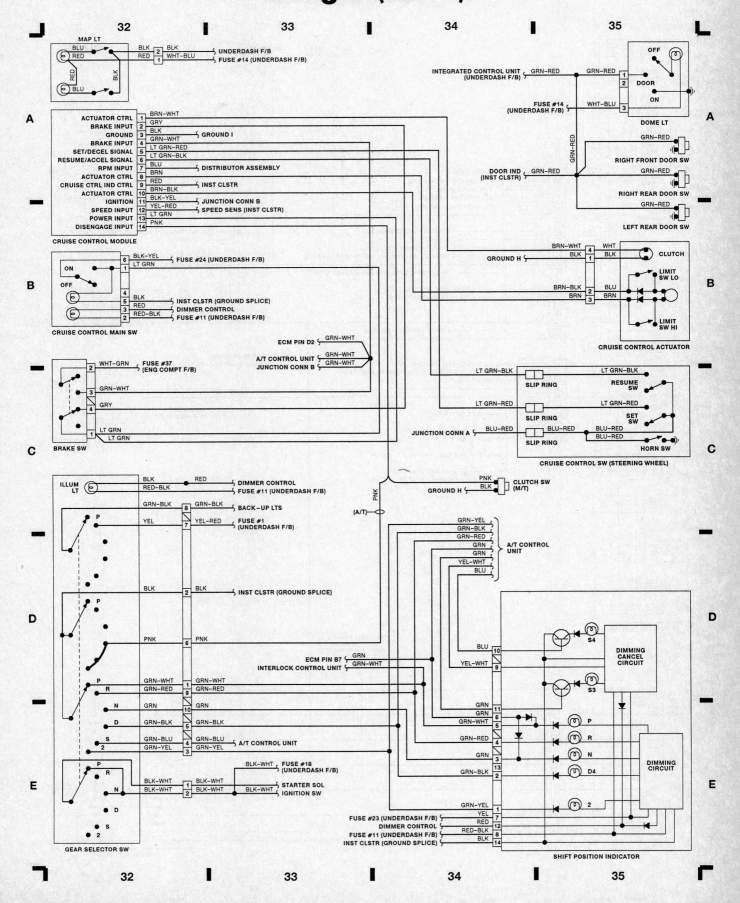

1993 WIRING DIAGRAMS
Integra (Cont.)

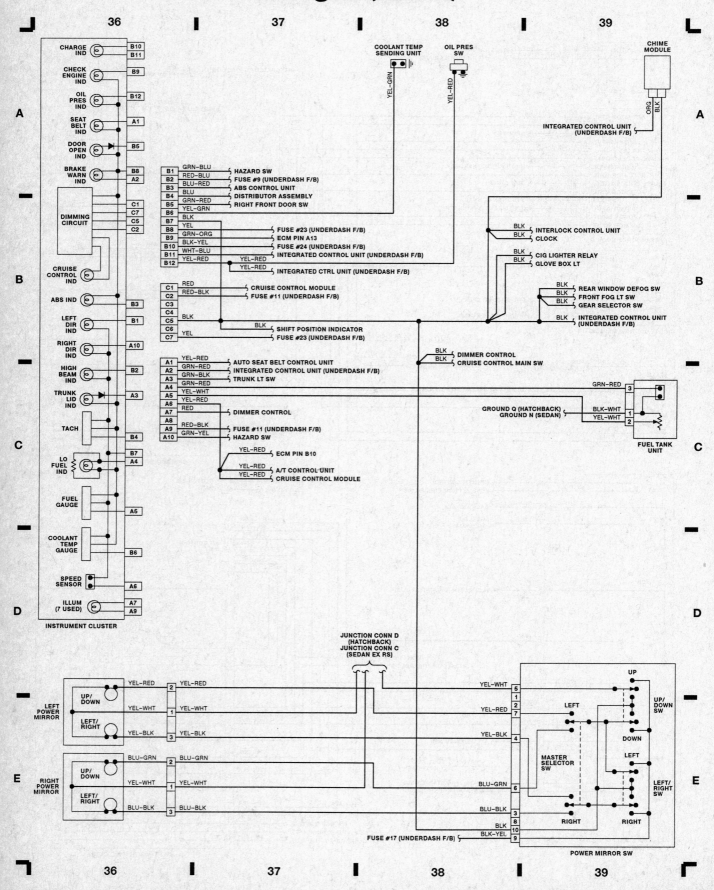

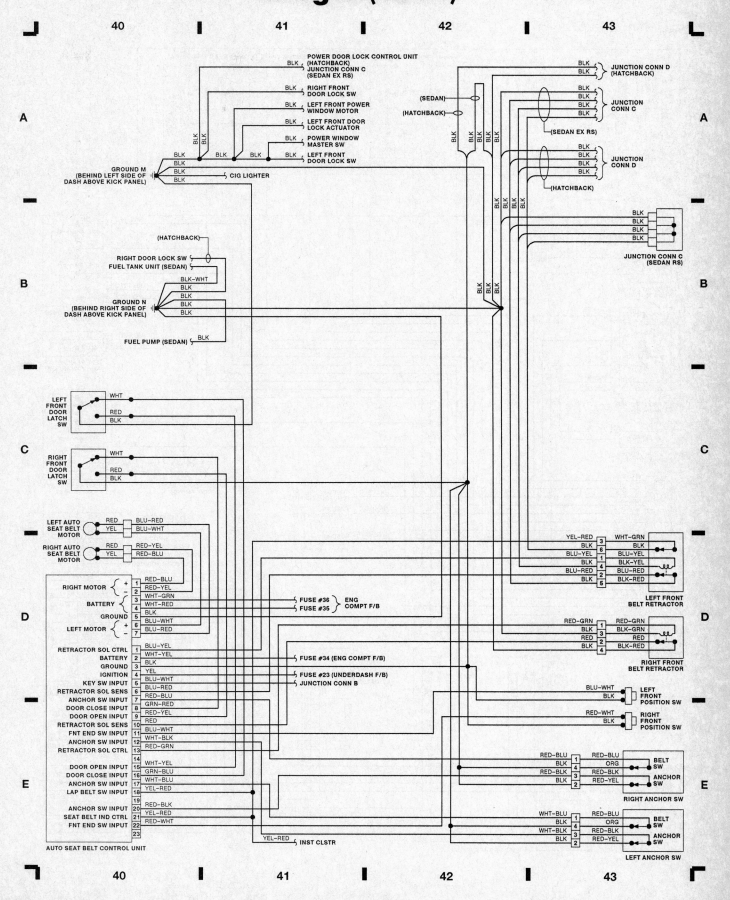

1993 WIRING DIAGRAMS
Integra (Cont.)

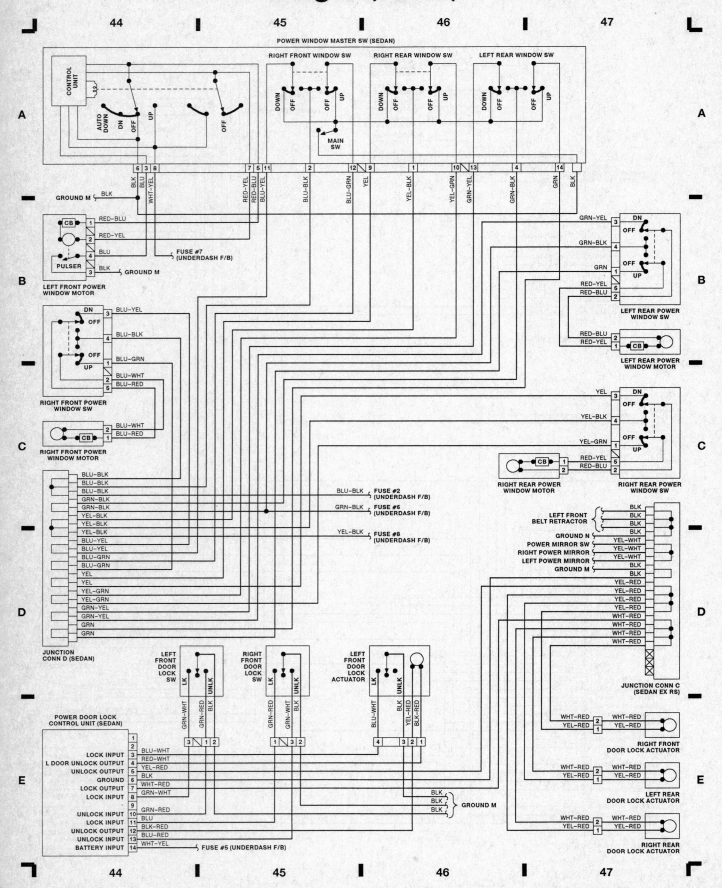

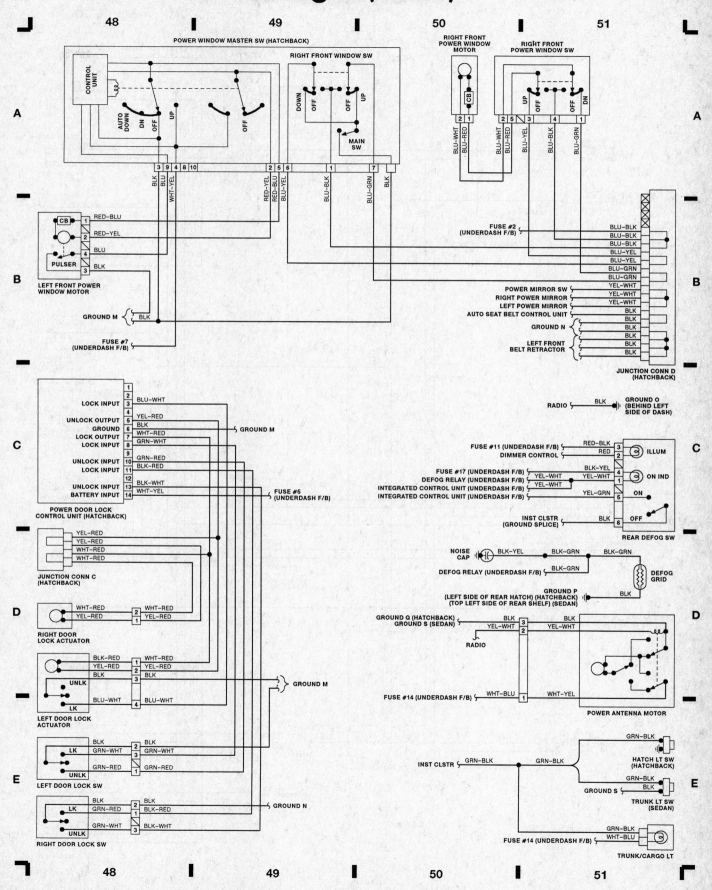

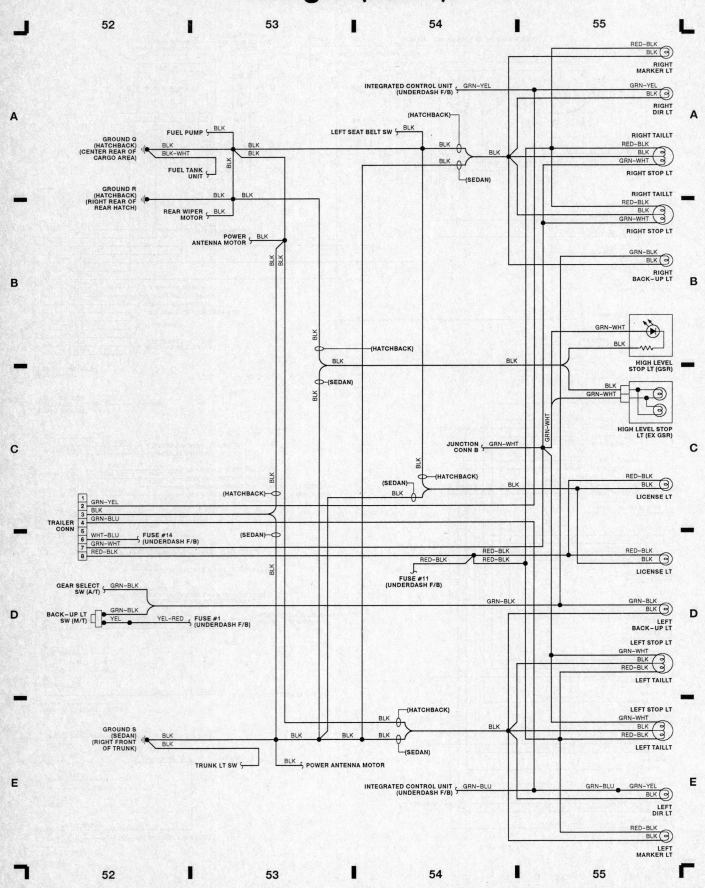

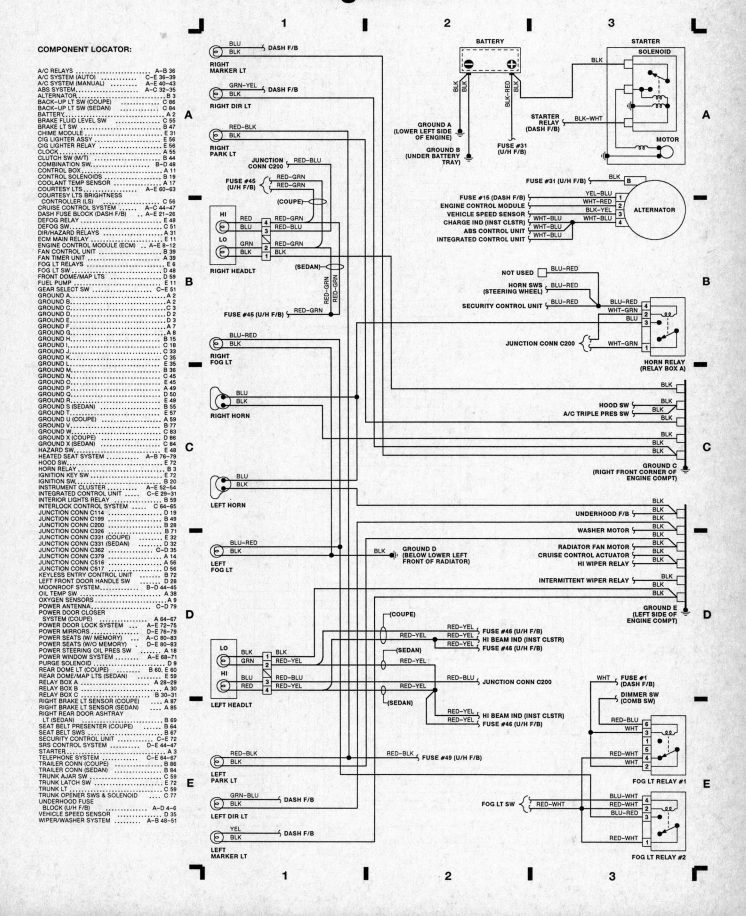

COMPONENT LOCATOR:

A/C RELAYS .... A–B 36
A/C SYSTEM (AUTO) .... C–E 36–39
A/C SYSTEM (MANUAL) .... A–E 40–43
ABS SYSTEM .... A–C 32–35
ALTERNATOR .... B 3
BACK-UP LT SW (COUPE) ..... C 86
BACK-UP LT SW (SEDAN) ..... C 84
BATTERY .... A 2
BRAKE FLUID LEVEL SW ...... C 55
BRAKE LT SW .... B 47
CHIME MODULE .... E 31
CIG LIGHTER ASSY .... E 56
CIG LIGHTER RELAY .... E 56
CLOCK .... A 55
CLUTCH SW (M/T) .... B 44
COMBINATION SW .... B–D 48
CONTROL BOX .... A 11
CONTROL SOLENOIDS .... B 19
COOLANT TEMP SENSOR ...... A 17
COURTESY LTS .... A–E 60–63
COURTESY LTS BRIGHTNESS
  CONTROLLER (LS) .... C 56
CRUISE CONTROL SYSTEM .... A–C 44–47
DASH FUSE BLOCK (DASH F/B) . A–E 21–26
DEFOG RELAY .... E 48
DEFOG SW .... C 51
DIR/HAZARD RELAYS .... A 31
ECM MAIN RELAY .... E 11
ENGINE CONTROL MODULE (ECM) .. A–E 8–12
FAN CONTROL UNIT .... B 39
FAN TIMER UNIT .... A 39
FOG LT RELAYS .... E 6
FOG LT SW .... D 48
FRONT DOME/MAP LTS .... D 59
FUEL PUMP .... E 111
GEAR SELECT SW .... C–E 51
GROUND A .... A 2
GROUND B .... A 2
GROUND C .... C 3
GROUND D .... D 2
GROUND E .... D 3
GROUND F .... A 7
GROUND G .... A 8
GROUND H .... B 15
GROUND I .... C 18
GROUND J .... C 33
GROUND K .... C 35
GROUND L .... E 35
GROUND M .... B 36
GROUND N .... C 45
GROUND O .... E 45
GROUND P .... A 49
GROUND Q .... D 50
GROUND R .... E 49
GROUND S (SEDAN) .... B 55
GROUND T .... E 57
GROUND U (COUPE) .... A 59
GROUND V .... B 77
GROUND W .... C 83
GROUND X (COUPE) .... D 86
GROUND X (SEDAN) .... E 84
HAZARD SW. .... E 48
HEATED SEAT SYSTEM .... A–B 76–79
HOOD SW. .... E 72
HORN RELAY .... B 3
IGNITION KEY SW .... E 72
IGNITION SW. .... B 20
INSTRUMENT CLUSTER .... A–E 52–54
INTEGRATED CONTROL UNIT .. C–E 29–31
INTERIOR LIGHTS RELAY ..... B 59
INTERLOCK CONTROL SYSTEM . C 64–65
JUNCTION CONN C114 .... D 19
JUNCTION CONN C199 .... B 49
JUNCTION CONN C200 .... B 28
JUNCTION CONN C326 .... B 71
JUNCTION CONN C331 (COUPE) . E 32
JUNCTION CONN C331 (SEDAN) . D 32
JUNCTION CONN C362 .... C–D 35
JUNCTION CONN C379 .... A 14
JUNCTION CONN C516 .... A 56
JUNCTION CONN C517 .... D 56
KEYLESS ENTRY CONTROL UNIT . B 72
LEFT FRONT DOOR HANDLE SW . D 28
MOONROOF SYSTEM .... B–D 44–45
OIL TEMP SW .... A 38
OXYGEN SENSORS .... A 9
POWER ANTENNA .... C–D 79
POWER DOOR CLOSER
  SYSTEM (COUPE) .... A 64–67
POWER DOOR LOCK SYSTEM .. A–E 72–75
POWER MIRRORS .... D–E 76–79
POWER SEATS (W/ MEMORY) .. A–C 80–83
POWER SEATS (W/O MEMORY) . D–E 80–83
POWER STEERING OIL PRES SW . A 18
POWER WINDOW SYSTEM ..... A–E 68–71
PURGE SOLENOID .... D 9
REAR DOME LT (COUPE) ...... B 60, E 60
REAR DOME/MAP LTS (SEDAN) . E 59
RELAY BOX A .... A 28–29
RELAY BOX B .... A 30
RELAY BOX C .... B 30–31
RIGHT BRAKE LT SENSOR (COUPE) . A 87
RIGHT BRAKE LT SENSOR (SEDAN) . A 85
RIGHT REAR DOOR ASHTRAY
  LT (SEDAN) .... B 69
SEAT BELT PRESENTER (COUPE) . B 64
SEAT BELT SWS .... B 67
SECURITY CONTROL UNIT .... C–E 72
SRS CONTROL SYSTEM .... D–E 44–47
STARTER .... A 3
TELEPHONE SYSTEM .... C–E 64–67
TRAILER CONN (COUPE) ...... B 86
TRAILER CONN (SEDAN) ...... B 84
TRUNK AJAR SW .... C 59
TRUNK LATCH SW .... E 72
TRUNK LT .... C 59
TRUNK OPENER SWS & SOLENOID . C 57
UNDERHOOD FUSE
  BLOCK (U/H F/B) .... A–D 4–6
VEHICLE SPEED SENSOR (ECM) . D 35
WIPER/WASHER SYSTEM ...... A–B 48–51

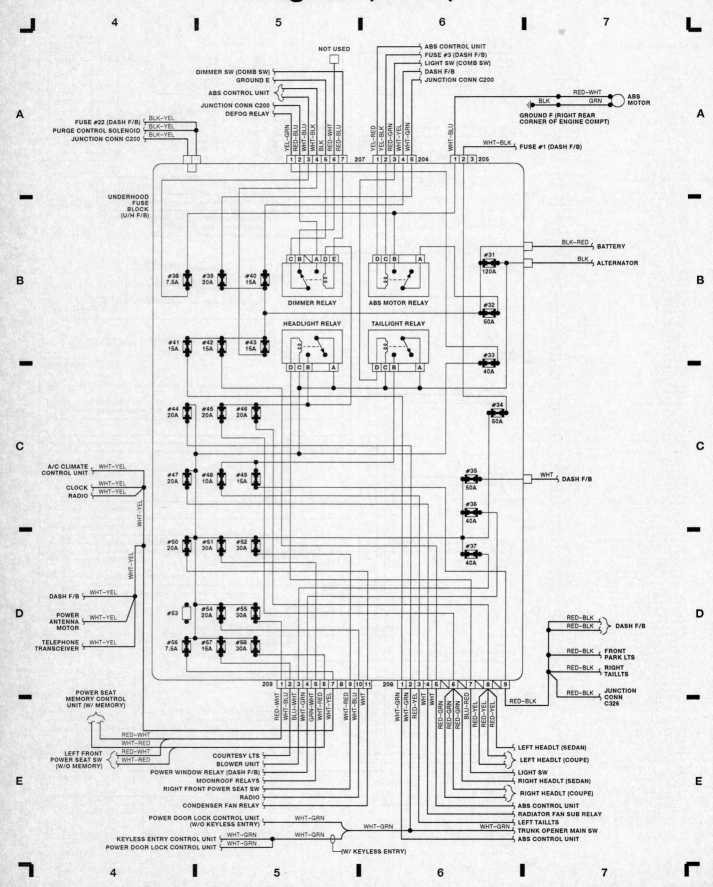

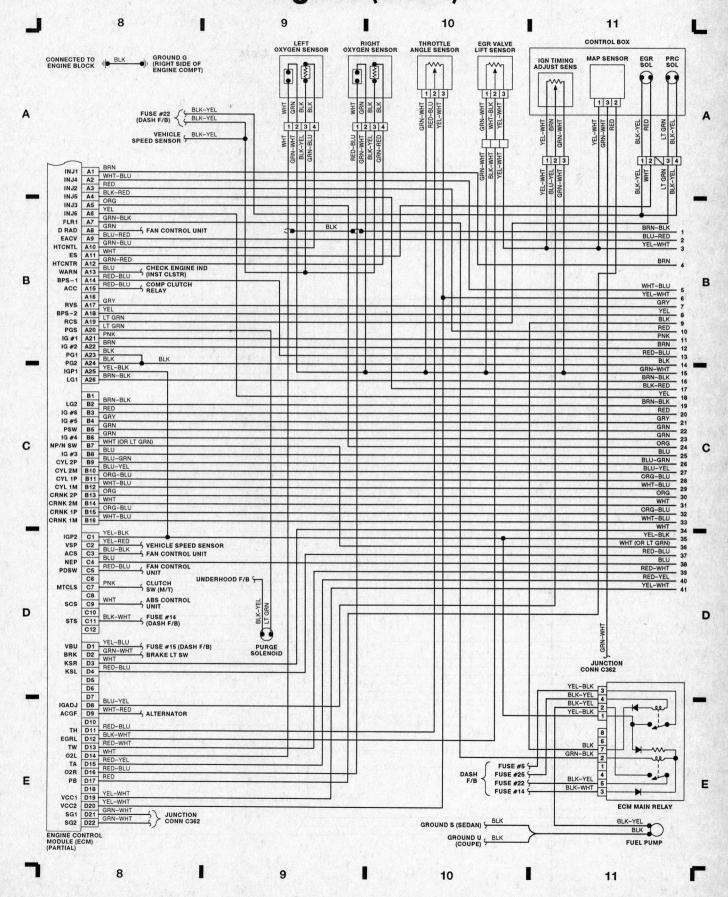

1993 WIRING DIAGRAMS
Legend (Cont.)

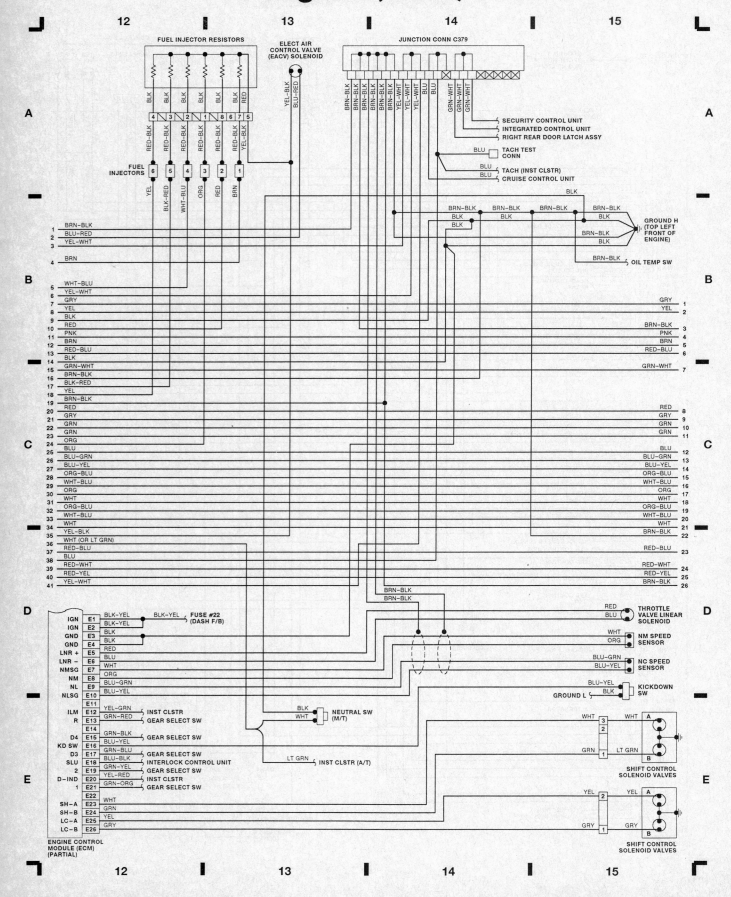

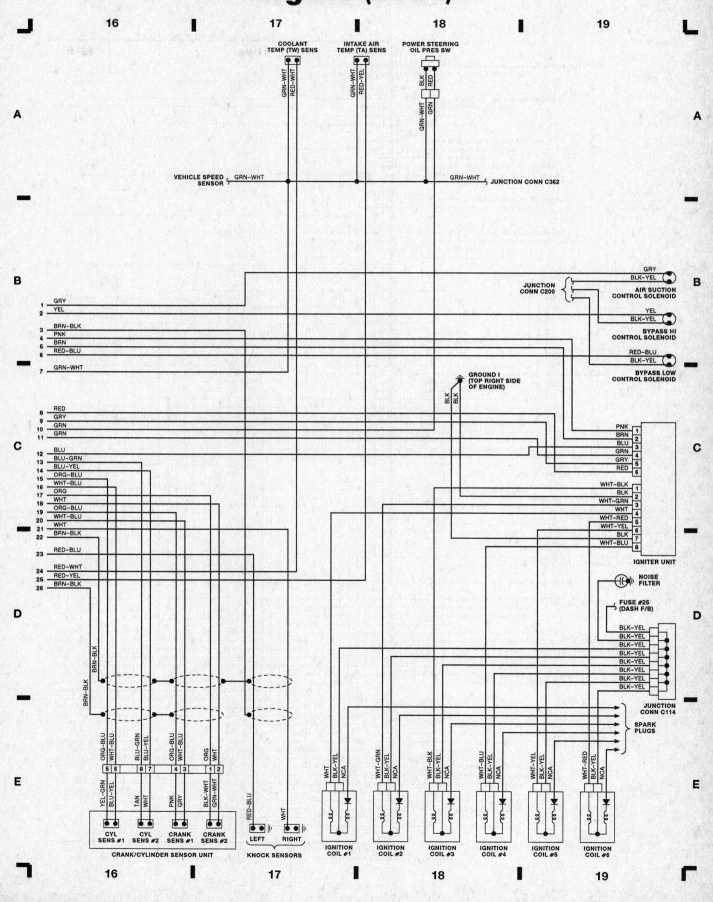

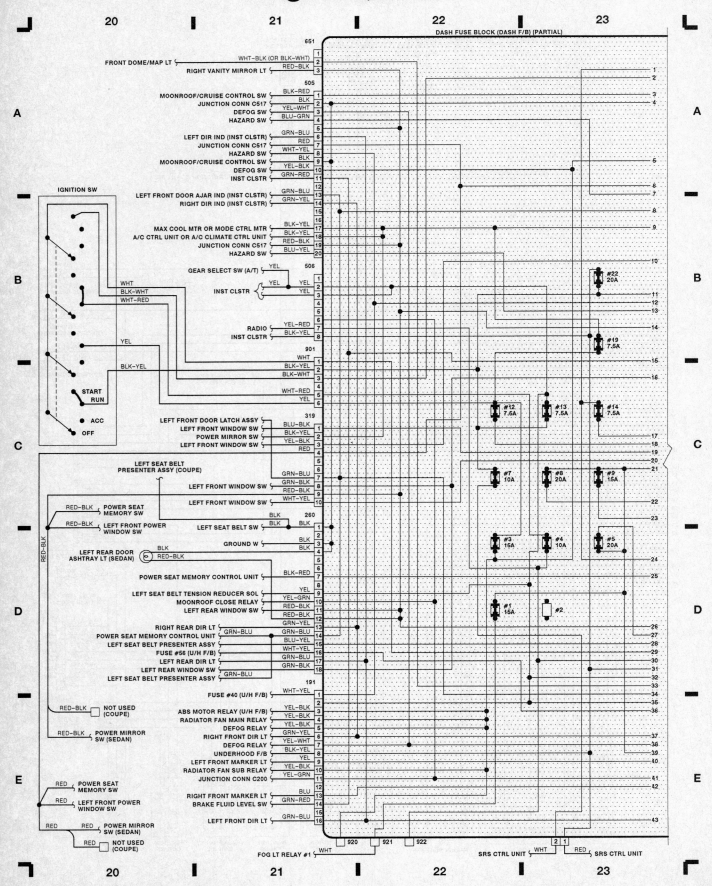

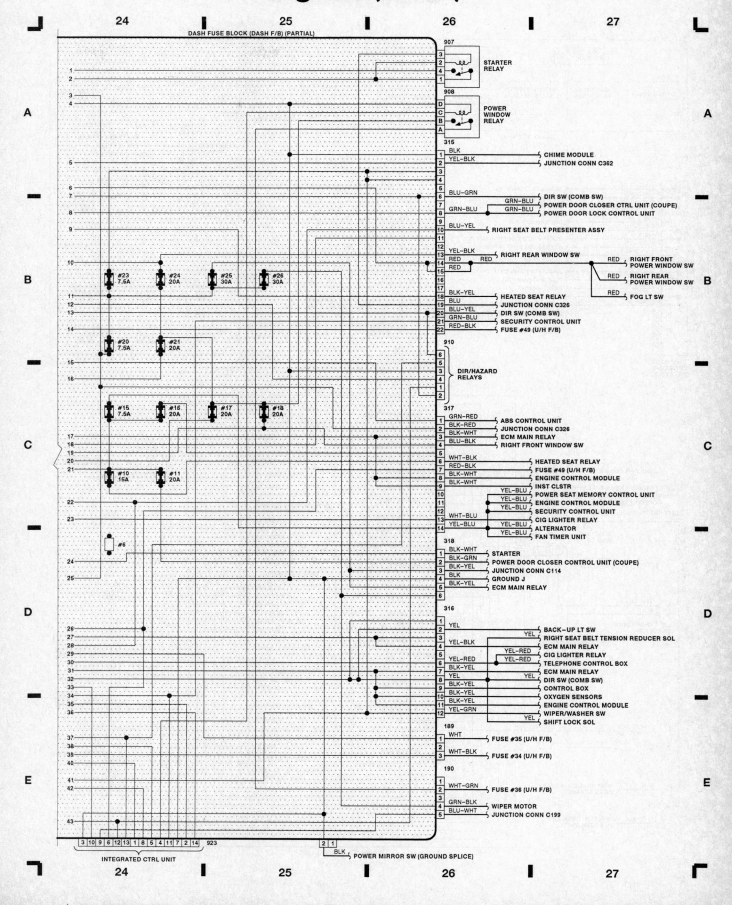

DASH FUSE BLOCK (DASH F/B) (PARTIAL)

907 STARTER RELAY

908 POWER WINDOW RELAY

315
1 BLK — CHIME MODULE
2 YEL-BLK — JUNCTION CONN C362
6 BLU-GRN — DIR SW (COMB SW)
7 GRN-BLU — POWER DOOR CLOSER CTRL UNIT (COUPE)
8 GRN-BLU — POWER DOOR LOCK CONTROL UNIT
10 BLU-YEL — RIGHT SEAT BELT PRESENTER ASSY
13 YEL-BLK — RIGHT REAR WINDOW SW
14 RED — RED — RIGHT FRONT POWER WINDOW SW
15 RED — RIGHT REAR POWER WINDOW SW
RED — FOG LT SW
18 BLK-YEL — HEATED SEAT RELAY
19 BLU — JUNCTION CONN C326
20 BLU-YEL — DIR SW (COMB SW)
21 GRN-BLU — SECURITY CONTROL UNIT
22 RED-BLK — FUSE #49 (U/H F/B)

910 DIR/HAZARD RELAYS

317
1 GRN-RED — ABS CONTROL UNIT
2 BLK-RED — JUNCTION CONN C326
3 BLK-WHT — ECM MAIN RELAY
4 BLU-BLK — RIGHT FRONT WINDOW SW
6 WHT-BLK — HEATED SEAT RELAY
7 RED-BLK — FUSE #49 (U/H F/B)
8 BLK-WHT — ENGINE CONTROL MODULE
BLK-WHT — INST CLSTR
10 YEL-BLU — POWER SEAT MEMORY CONTROL UNIT
11 YEL-BLU — ENGINE CONTROL MODULE
12 YEL-BLU — SECURITY CONTROL UNIT
13 WHT-BLU — CIG LIGHTER RELAY
14 YEL-BLU — ALTERNATOR
YEL-BLU — FAN TIMER UNIT

318
1 BLK-WHT — STARTER
2 BLK-GRN — POWER DOOR CLOSER CONTROL UNIT (COUPE)
3 BLK-YEL — JUNCTION CONN C114
4 BLK — GROUND J
5 BLK-YEL — ECM MAIN RELAY

316
1 YEL — BACK-UP LT SW
3 YEL — RIGHT SEAT BELT TENSION REDUCER SOL
4 YEL-BLK — ECM MAIN RELAY
5 YEL-RED — CIG LIGHTER RELAY
6 YEL-RED — TELEPHONE CONTROL BOX
7 BLK-YEL — ECM MAIN RELAY
8 YEL — DIR SW (COMB SW)
9 BLK-YEL — CONTROL BOX
10 BLK-YEL — OXYGEN SENSORS
11 BLK-YEL — ENGINE CONTROL MODULE
12 YEL-GRN — WIPER/WASHER SW
YEL — SHIFT LOCK SOL

189
1 WHT — FUSE #35 (U/H F/B)
2 WHT-BLK — FUSE #34 (U/H F/B)

190
1 WHT-GRN — FUSE #36 (U/H F/B)
4 GRN-BLK — WIPER MOTOR
5 BLU-WHT — JUNCTION CONN C199

Fuses:
#23 7.5A #24 20A #25 30A #26 30A
#20 7.5A #21 20A
#15 7.5A #16 20A #17 20A #18 20A
#10 15A #11 20A
#6

923
3 10 9 6 12 13 1 8 5 4 11 7 2 14
INTEGRATED CTRL UNIT

2 1 BLK
POWER MIRROR SW (GROUND SPLICE)

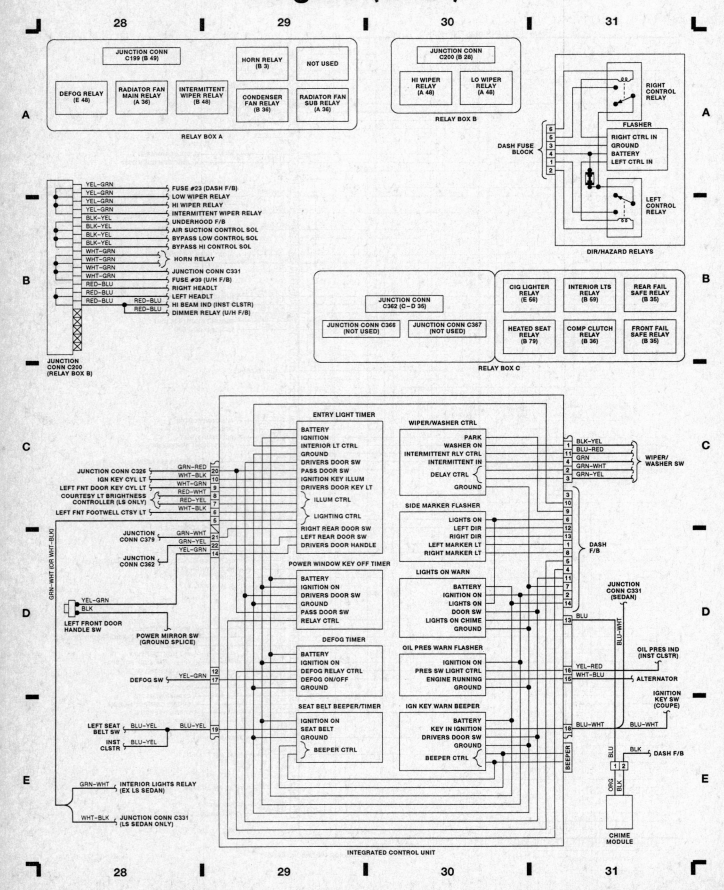

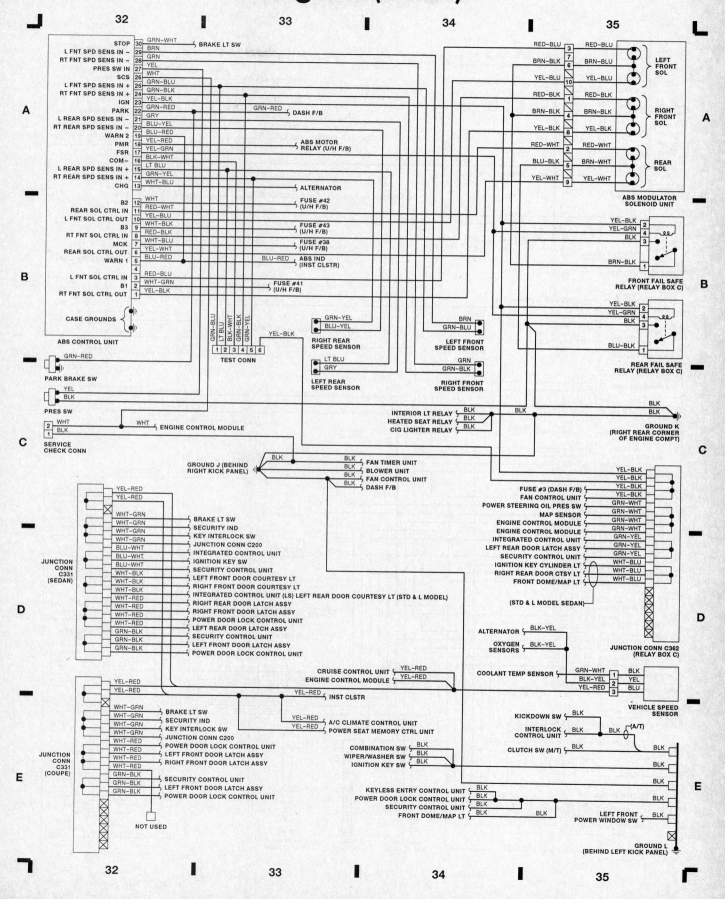

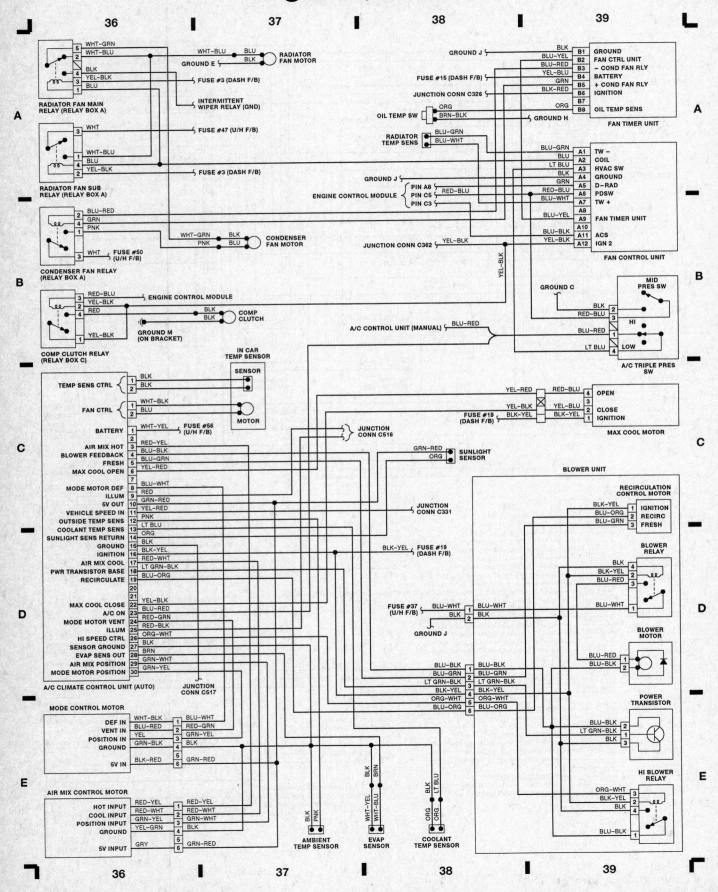

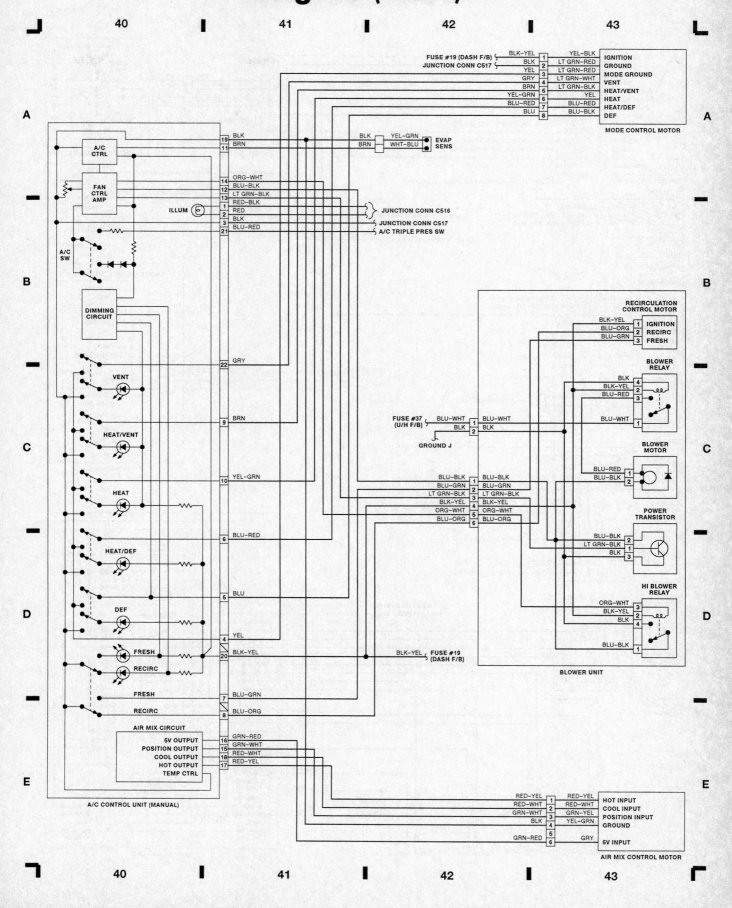

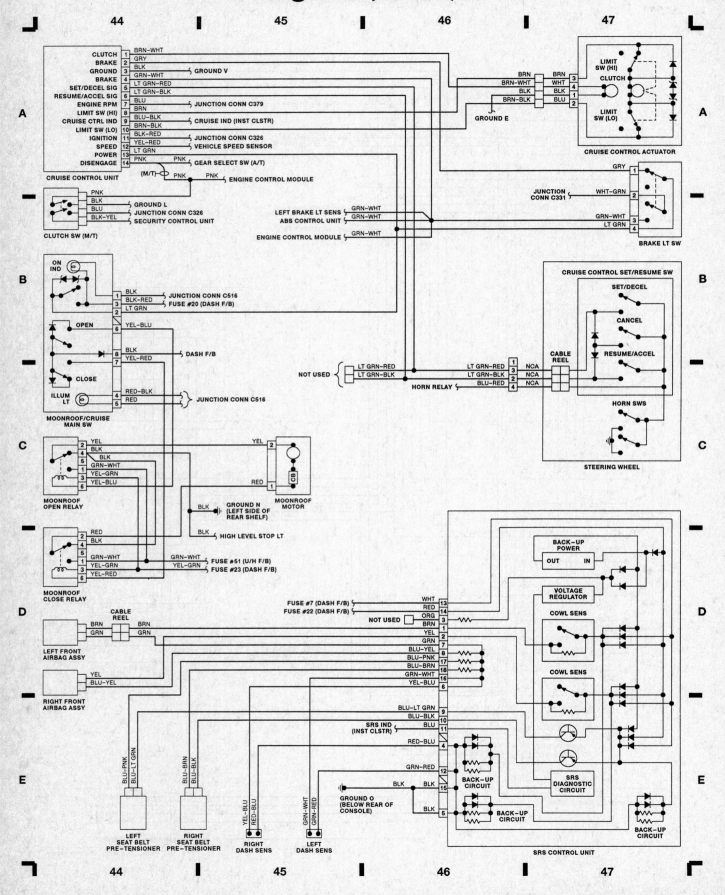

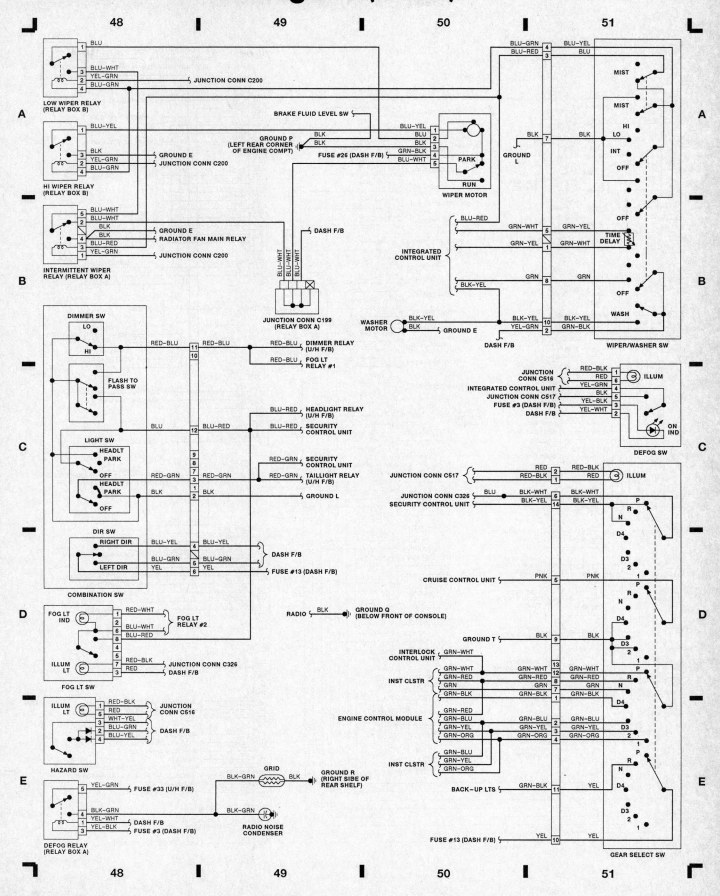

1993 WIRING DIAGRAMS
Legend (Cont.)

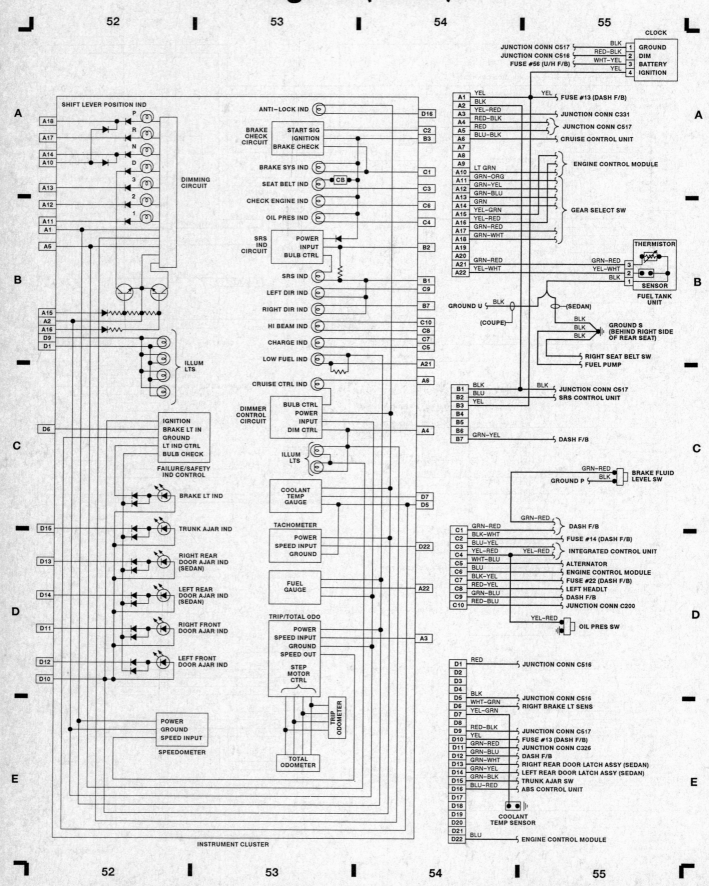

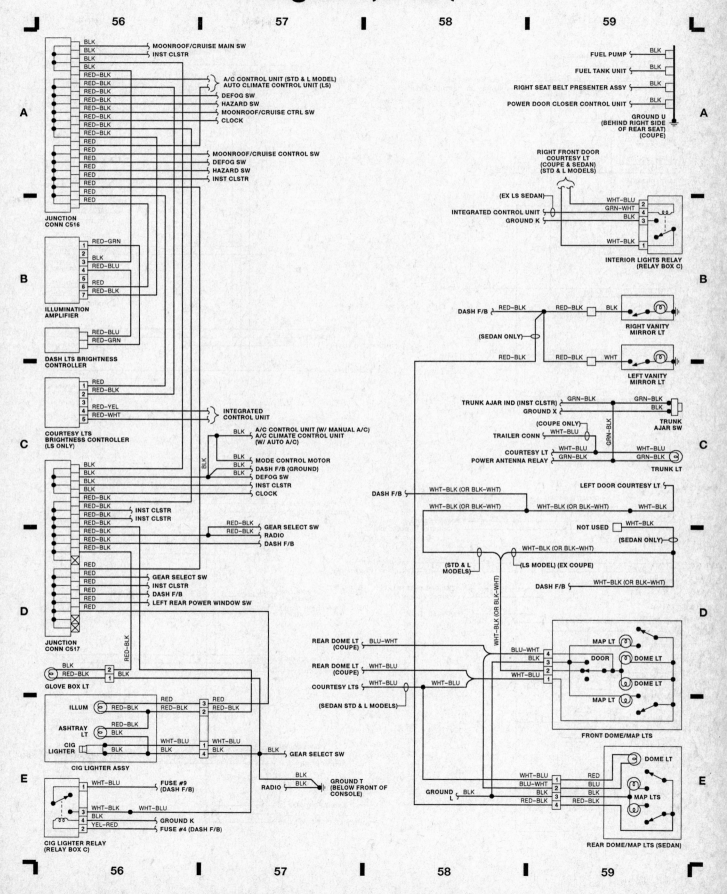

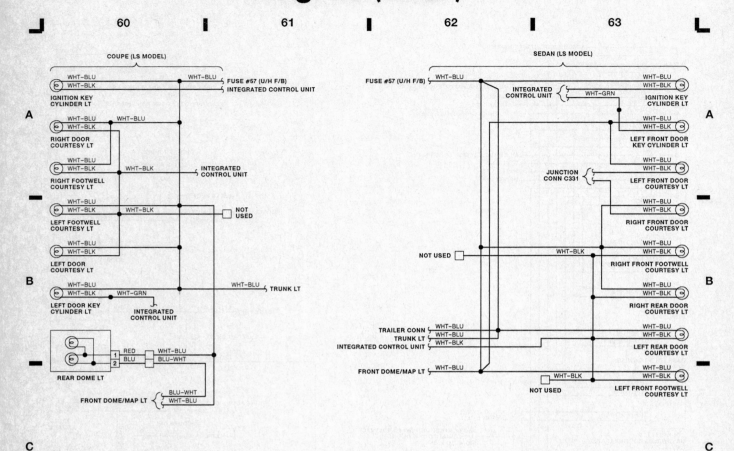

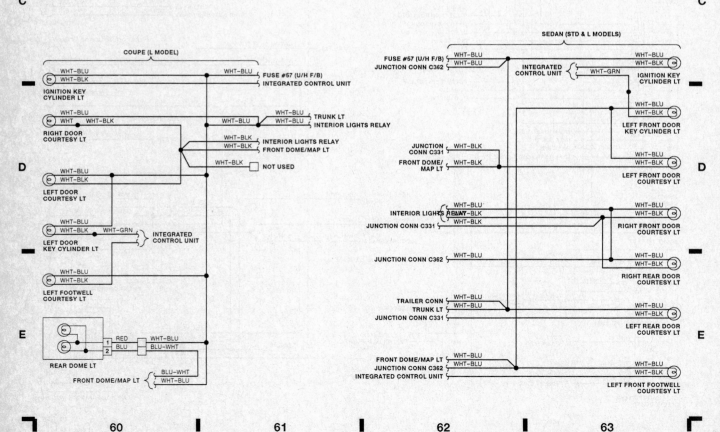

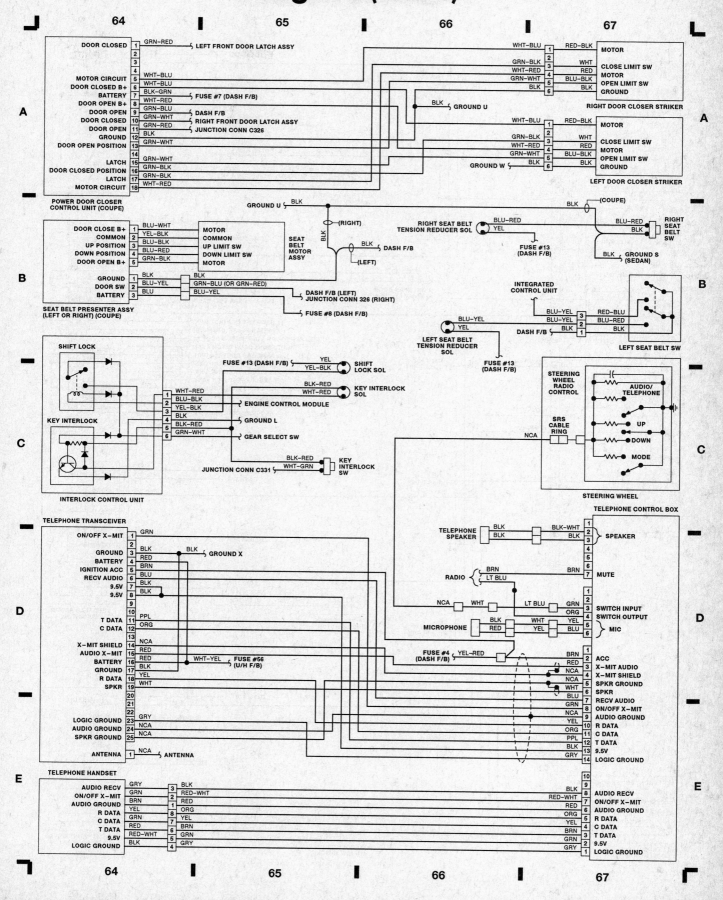

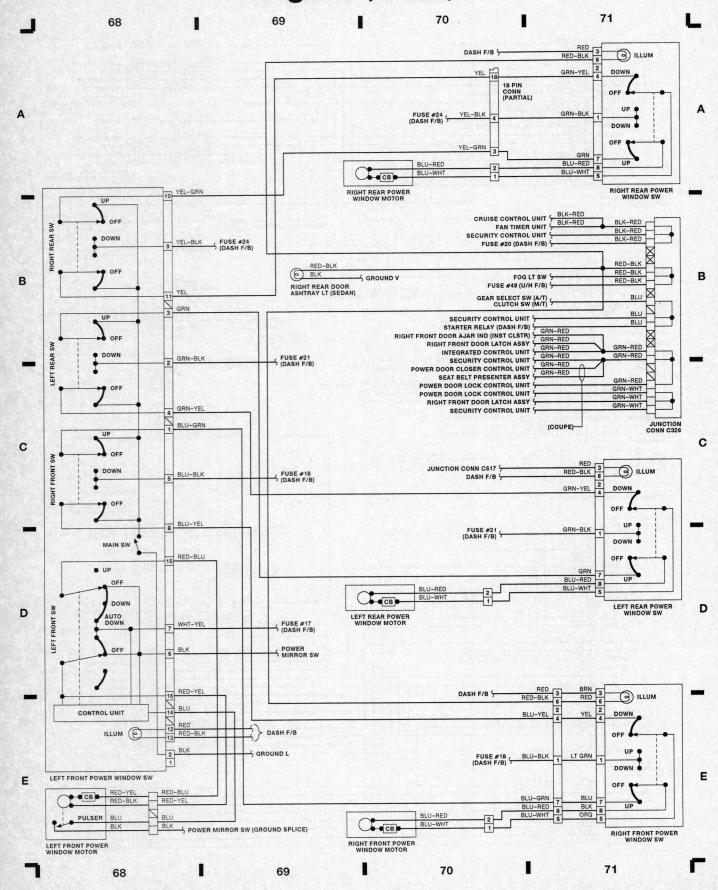

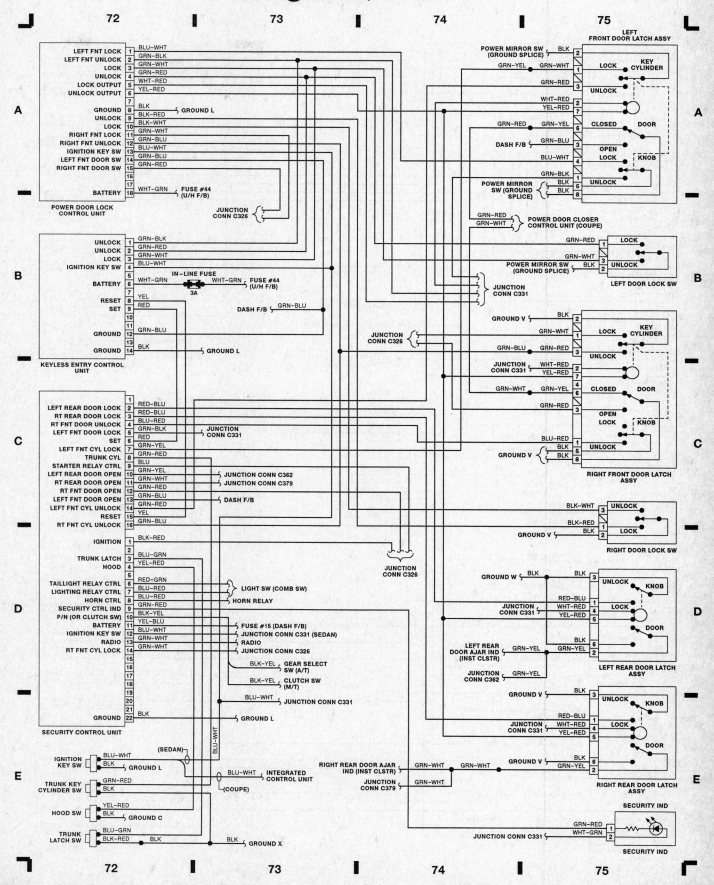

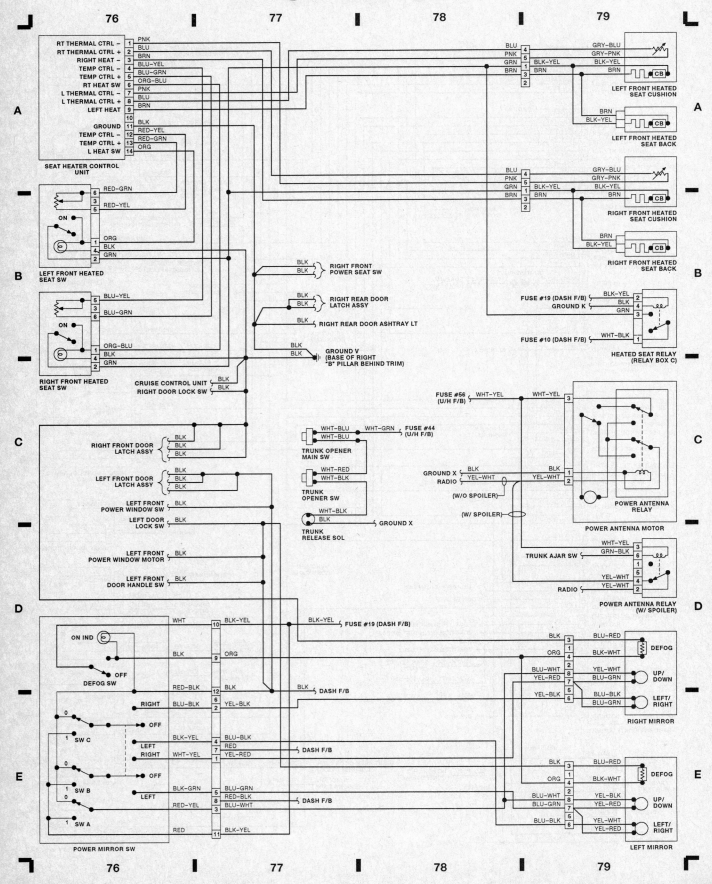

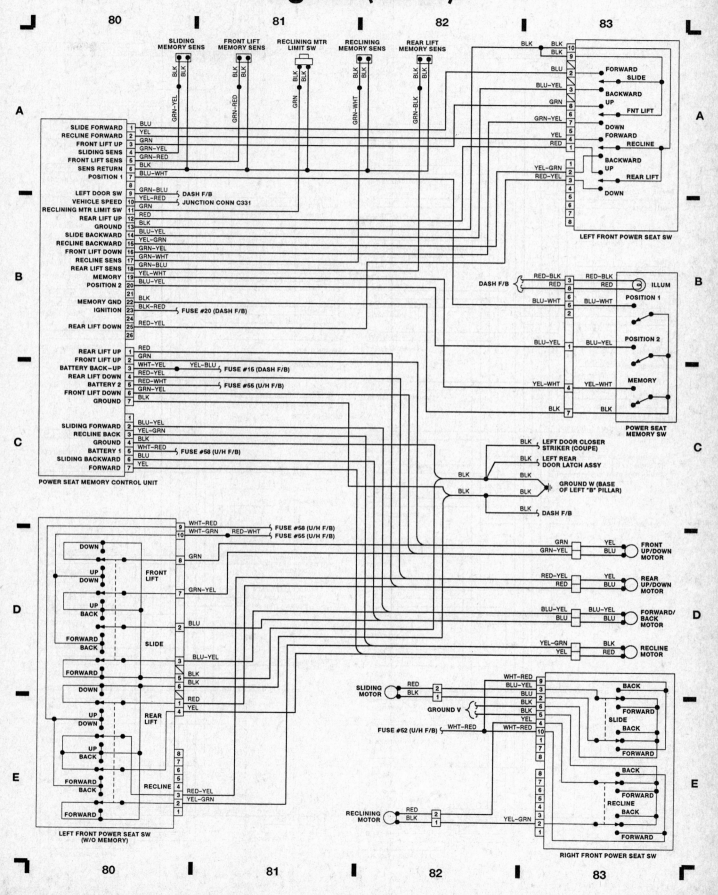

POWER SEAT MEMORY CONTROL UNIT

LEFT FRONT POWER SEAT SW

POWER SEAT MEMORY SW

LEFT FRONT POWER SEAT SW (W/O MEMORY)

RIGHT FRONT POWER SEAT SW

1993 WIRING DIAGRAMS
Legend (Cont.)

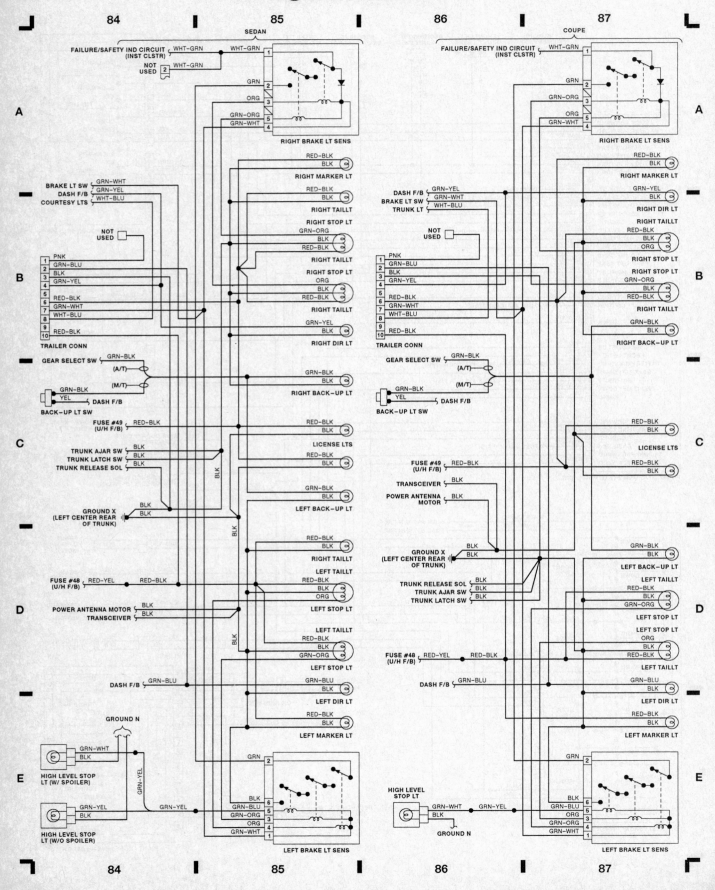

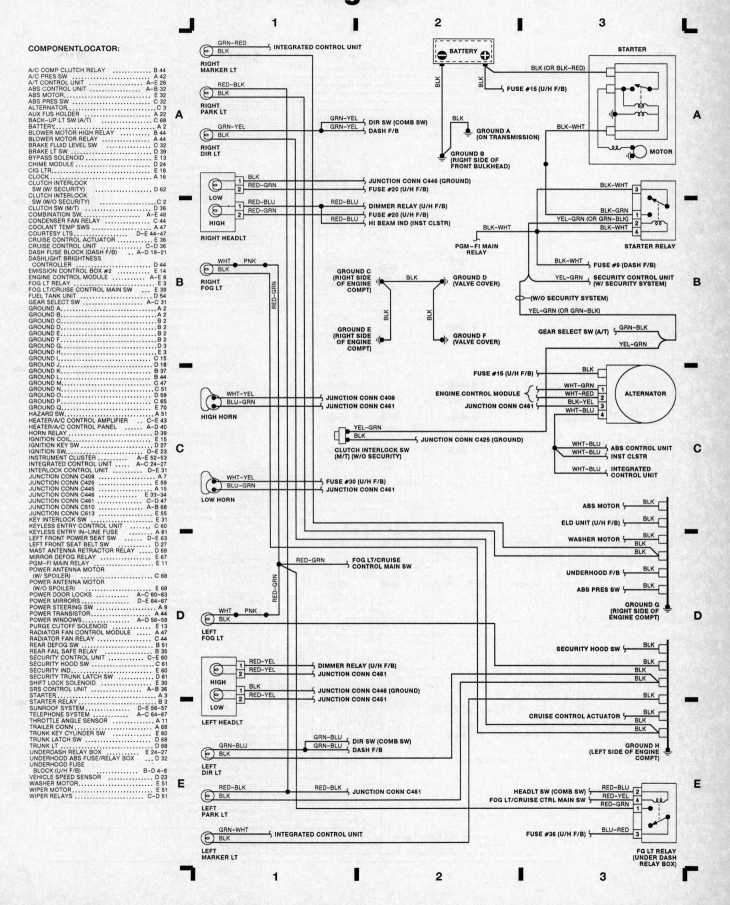

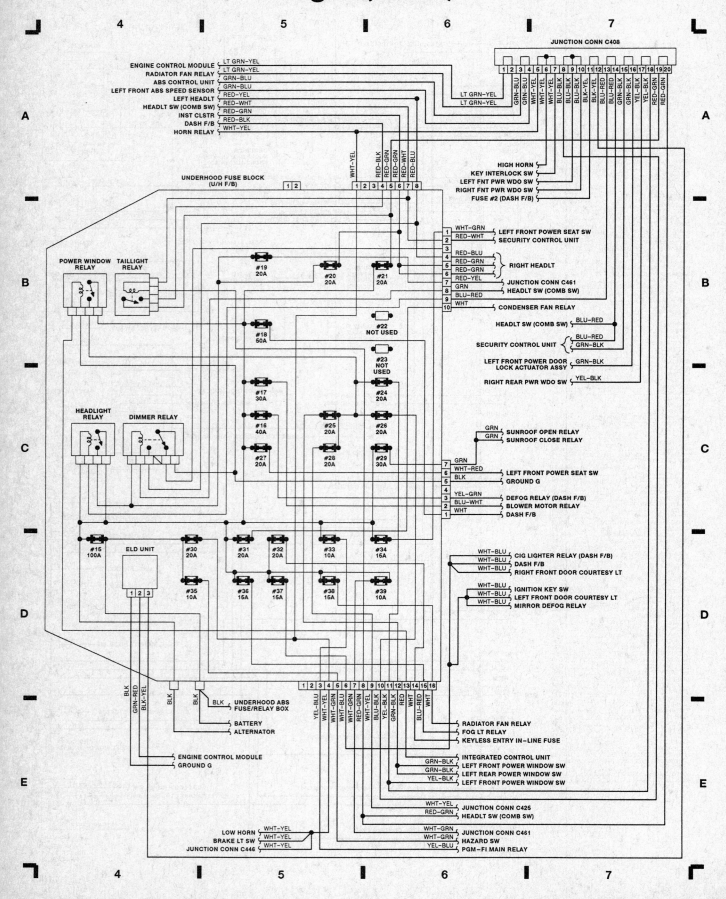

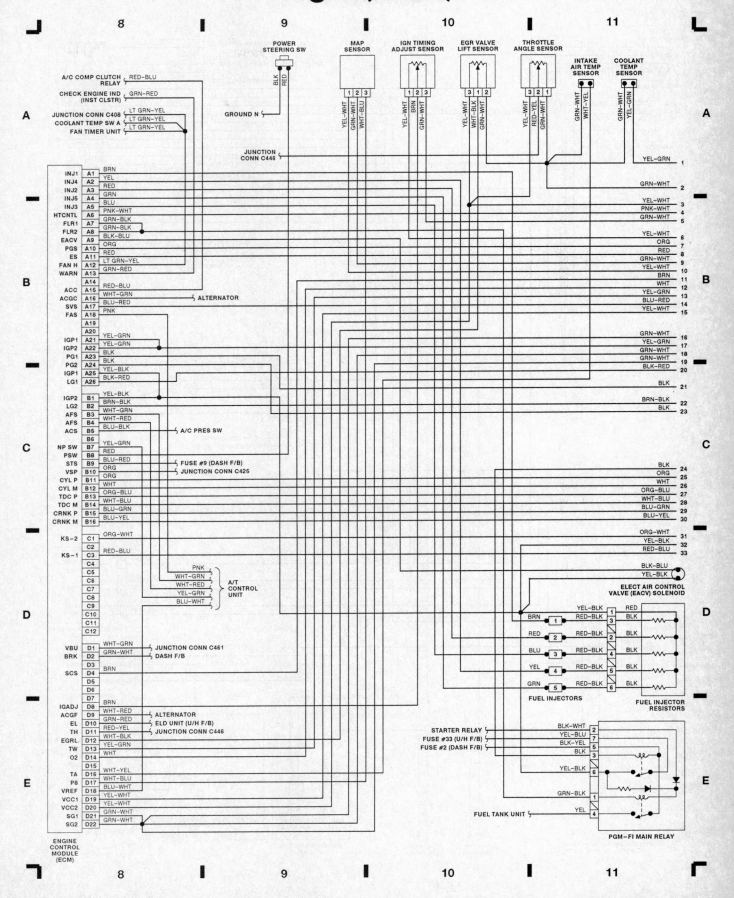

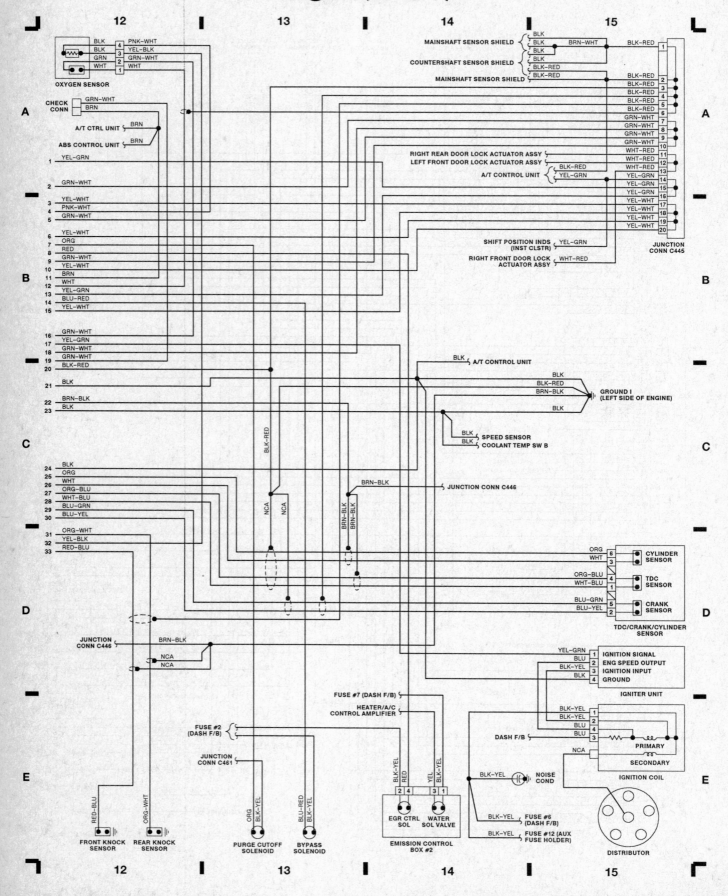

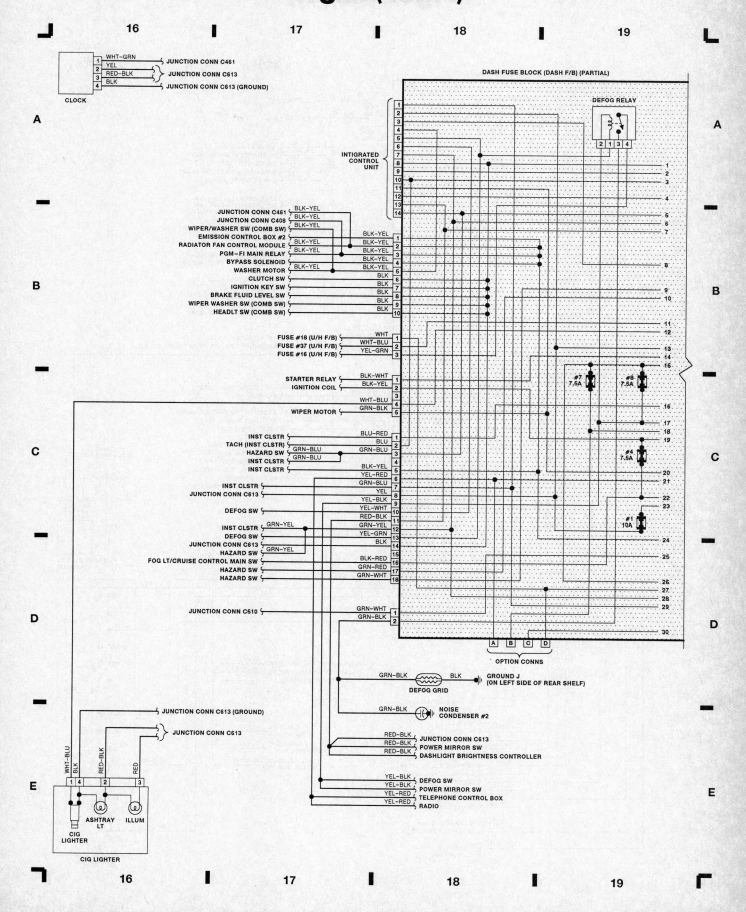

20 21 22 23

DASH FUSE BLOCK (DASH F/B) (PARTIAL)

CIG LIGHTER RELAY

DIR/HAZ RELAY

FLASHER UNIT

#12 7.5A

AUX FUSE HOLDER

BLK-YEL — IGNITION COIL
BLK-YEL — HAZARD SW

YEL-RED — WIPER LOW RELAY
YEL-RED — INTERMITTENT WIPER RELAY
YEL-RED — WIPER HIGH RELAY
YEL-RED — WIPER/WASHER SW (COMB SW)
YEL-RED — SHIFT LOCK SOLENOID

RED-BLK — TAILLIGHT RELAY (U/H F/B) (W/ SECURITY) HEADLT SW (COMB SW) (W/O SECURITY)

1	RED-BLK	RED-BLK	JUNCTION CONN C461
2	RED-BLK		GEAR SELECT SW
3	GRN-YEL		INTERMITTENT WIPER RELAY
4	GRN		WIPER/WASHER SW (COMB SW)
5	BLK		GROUND O
6	BLU	BLU	JUNCTION CONN C425
7	BLU		A/T CONTROL UNIT
8	BLU		CRUISE CONTROL UNIT
9	BLU		IGNITION COIL
10	BLU	BLU	INTERMITTENT WIPER RELAY
11			
12	YEL-RED		
13	GRN-RED		DIR SW (COMB SW)
14	YEL		BACK-UP LT SW (M/T) GEAR SELECT SW (A/T)
15	YEL		
16			

#9 7.5A #10 7.5A #11 10A

#5 10A #6 30A

#2 15A #3 10A

1	GRN-WHT	YEL-BLK	A/C COMP CLUTCH RELAY
2			BRAKE LT SW
3	YEL-BLK	YEL-BLK	RADIATOR FAN CONTROL MODULE
4	YEL-BLK	YEL-BLK	A/C COMP CLUTCH RELAY
5	GRN-YEL		RIGHT FRONT DIR LT
6			
7	BLK-RED		JUNCTION CONN C461
8	GRN-WHT	GRN-WHT	A/T CONTROL UNIT
9	GRN-WHT		CRUISE CONTROL UNIT
10	GRN-WHT	GRN-WHT	ENGINE CONTROL MODULE
11		GRN-WHT	ABS CONTROL UNIT
12	BLU-RED		ENGINE CONTROL MODULE
13			
14	WHT-BLU		FUSE #37 (U/H F/B)
15			
16	GRN-BLU		LEFT FRONT DIR LT
17	BLK-YEL		
18			

JUNCTION CONN C425
GROUND I

BLK YEL ORG
1 2 3

VEHICLE SPEED SENSOR

1	YEL	
2	WHT	WHT
3	WHT-BLK	
4		
5	BLK-YEL	
6	BLK-WHT	YEL
7		

1 2 3 4 5 6 7 8 9 10 11 12

GRN-BLU
GRN-YEL
GRN-BLU
YEL-RED
RED-BLK
WHT-BLU

1 2
GRY
GRY

SRS CONTROL UNIT

HEATER/A/C CONTROL AMPLIFIER — BLK-YEL
BLOWER MOTOR HIGH RELAY — BLK-YEL
BLOWER MOTOR RELAY — BLK-YEL

JUNCTION CONN C446 — BLK-YEL
HEATER/A/C CONTROL PANEL — BLK-YEL
EMISSION CONTROL BOX #2 — BLK-YEL

OFF
ACC
RUN
START
OFF

BLK-WHT

OFF

BLK-YEL

OFF

WHT-BLK

IGNITION SW

WHT-BLU — DOME LT
WHT-BLU — TRUNK LT
WHT-BLU — TRANSCEIVER
WHT-BLU — POWER ANTENNA MOTOR
RED-BLK — JUNCTION CONN C510
YEL-RED — SUNROOF CLOSE RELAY
YEL-RED — SUNROOF OPEN RELAY
GRN-BLU — LEFT REAR DIR LT
GRN-BLU — TRAILER CONN
GRN-YEL — RIGHT REAR DIR LT
GRN-YEL — TRAILER CONN

GRN-BLU — LEFT FRONT DOOR COURTESY LT
GRN-BLU — SECURITY CONTROL UNIT

GRN-BLU — LEFT FRONT DOOR SW

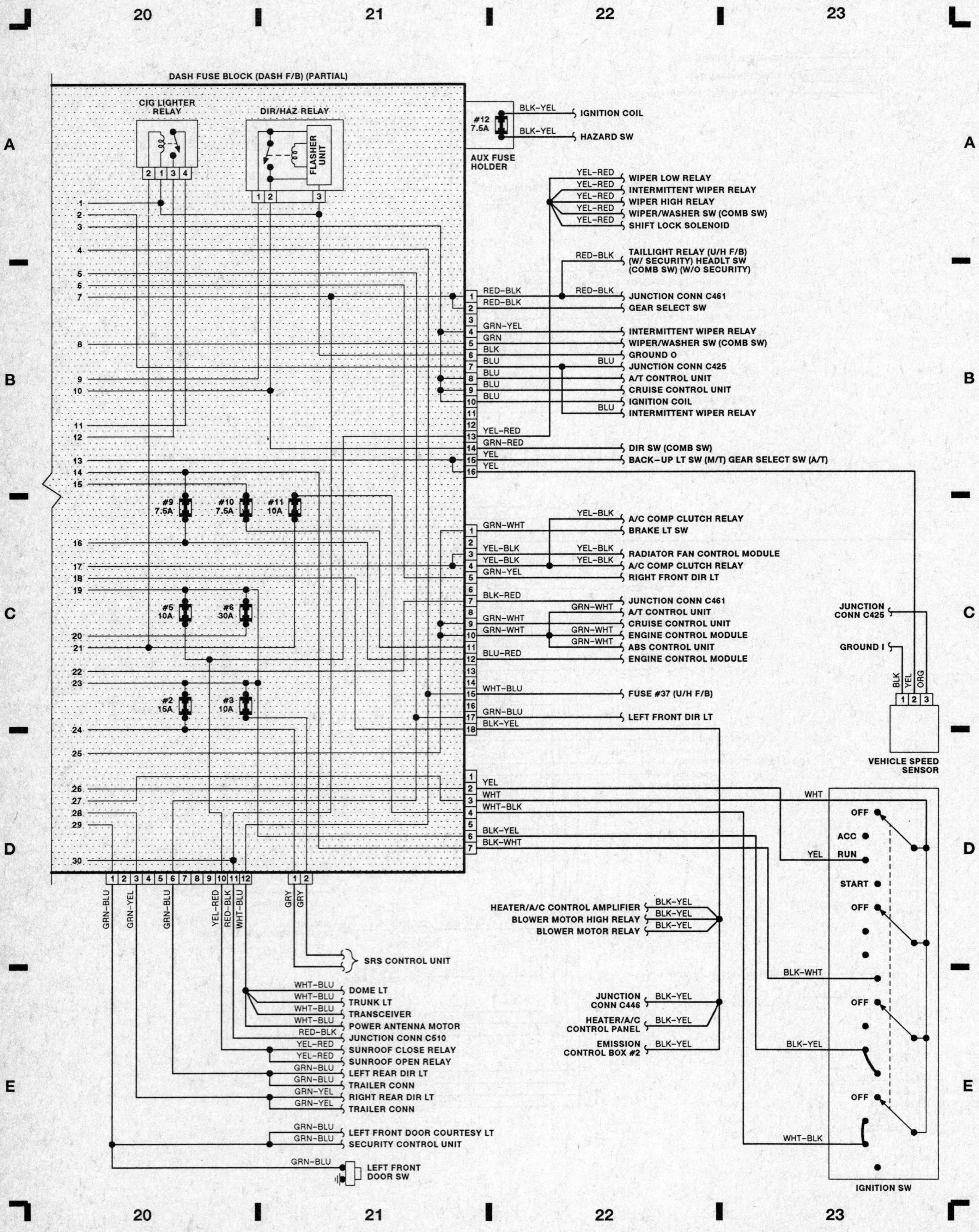

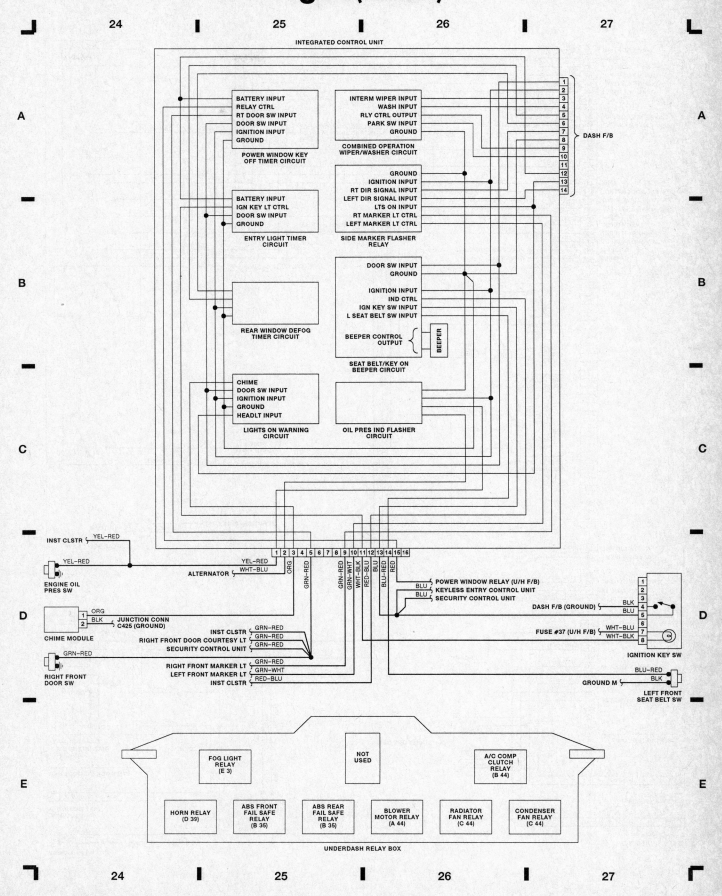

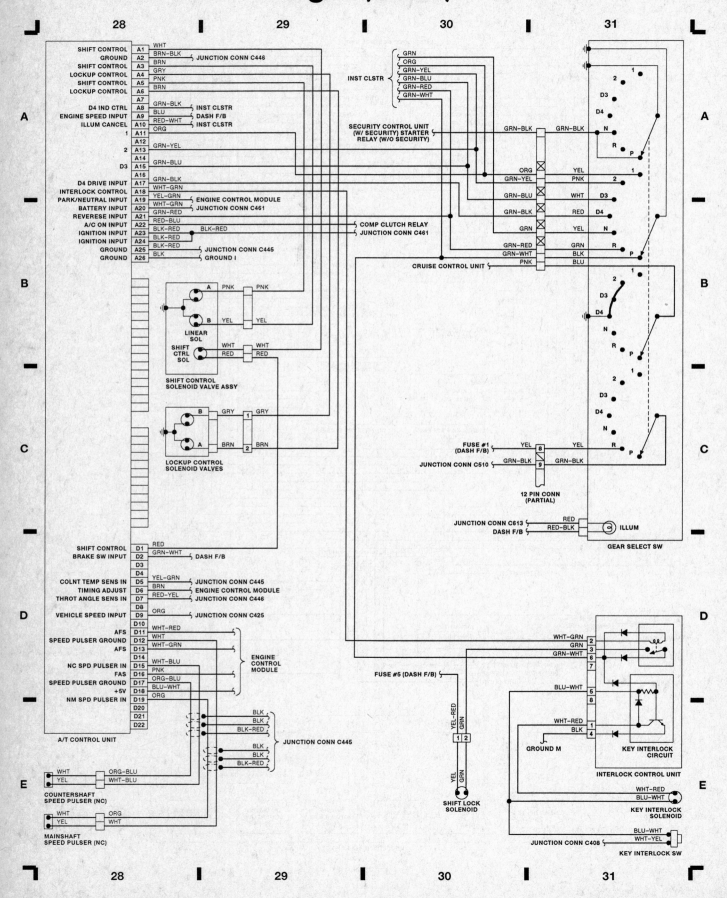

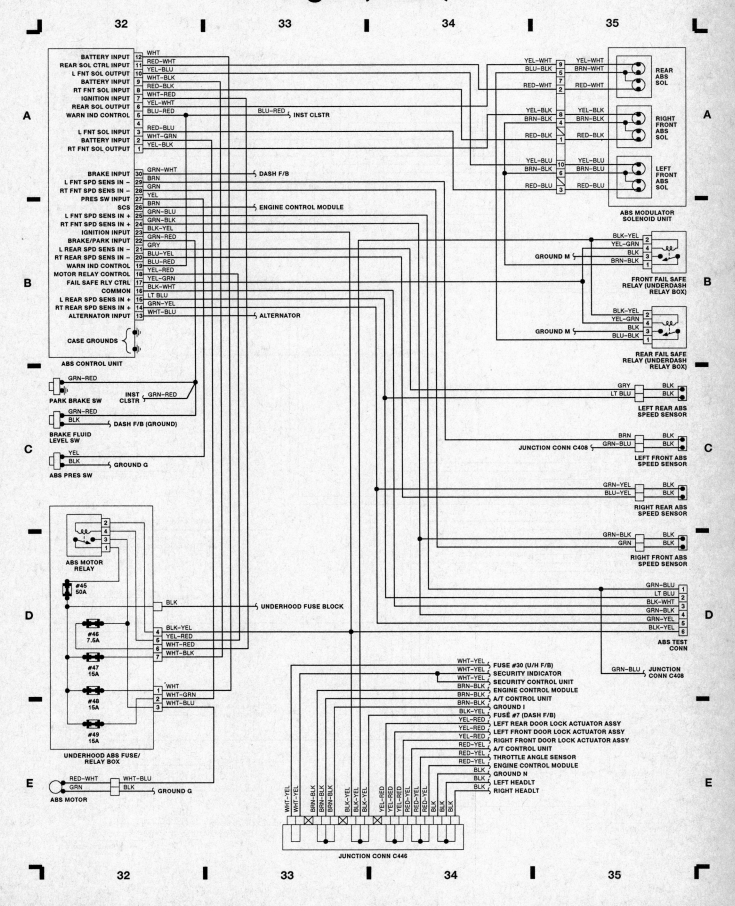

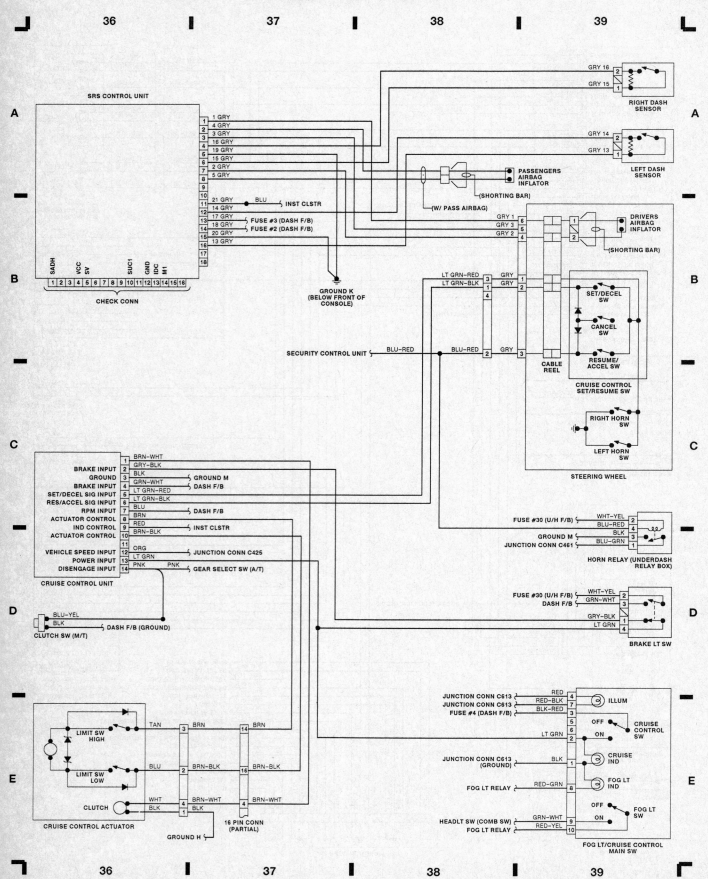

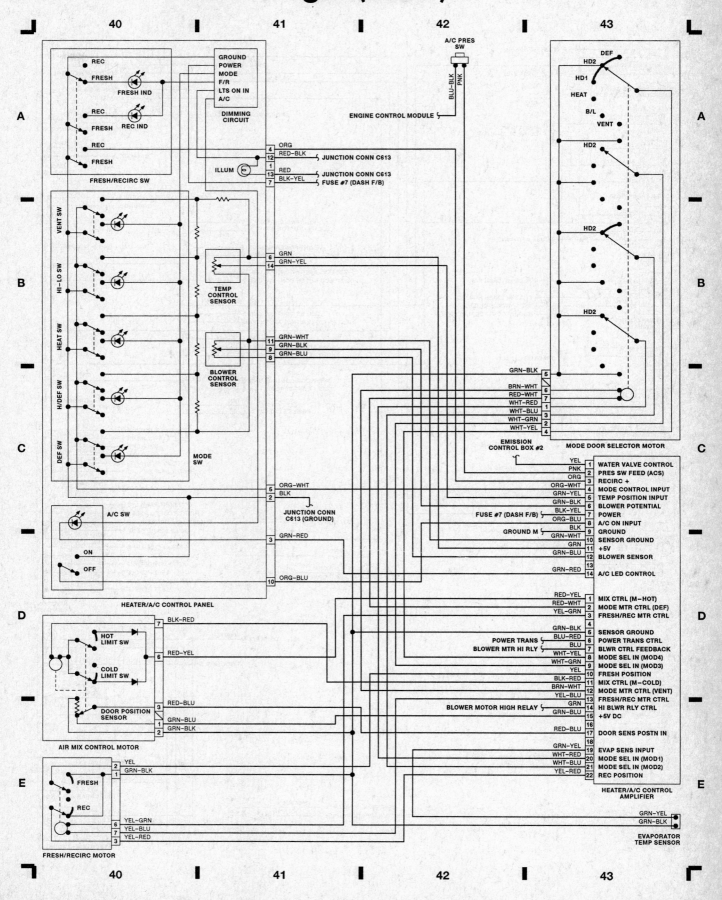

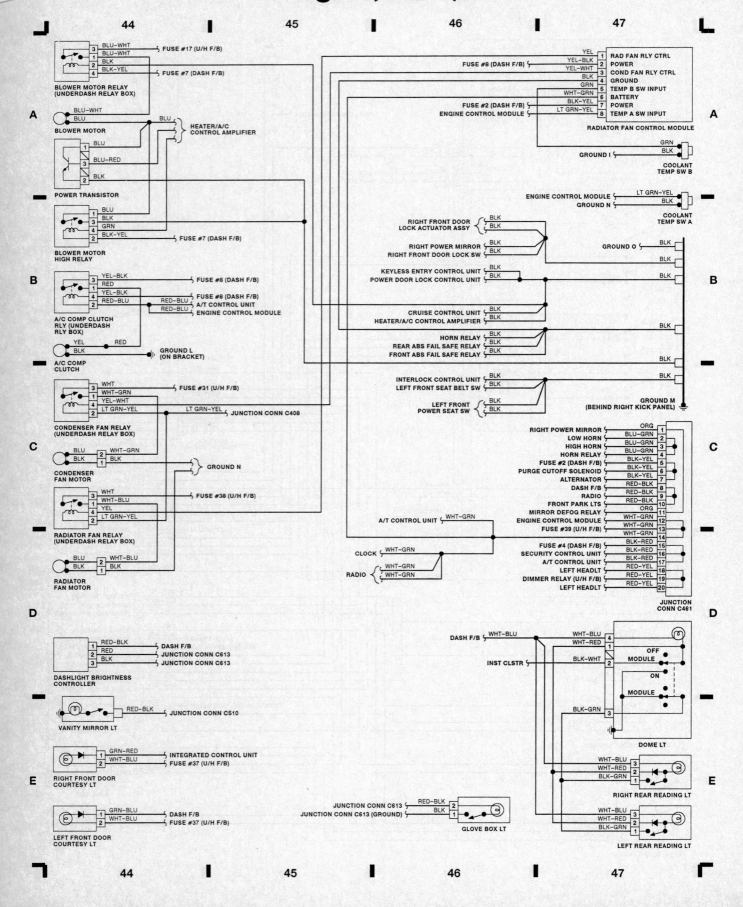

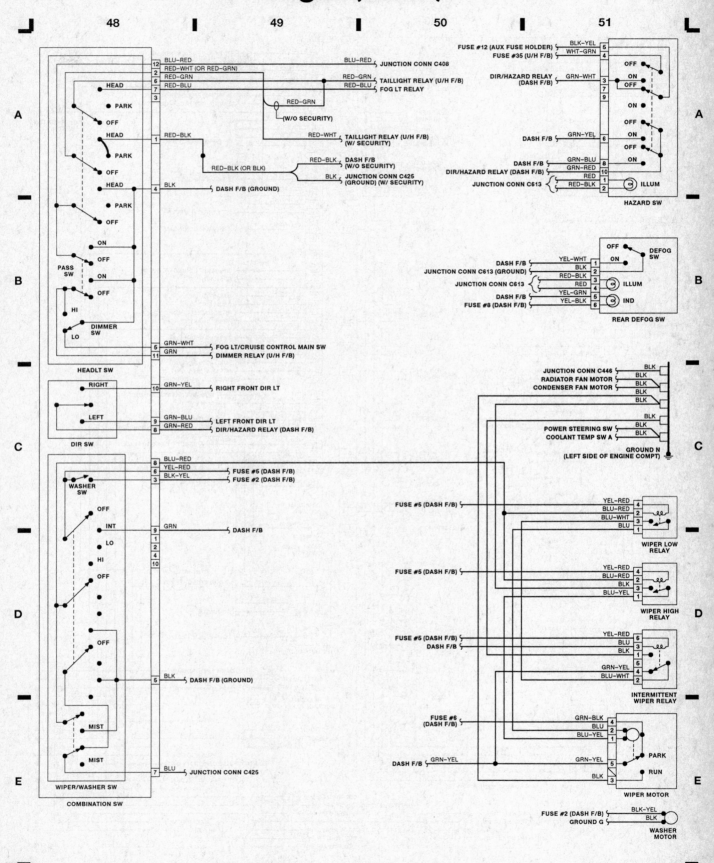

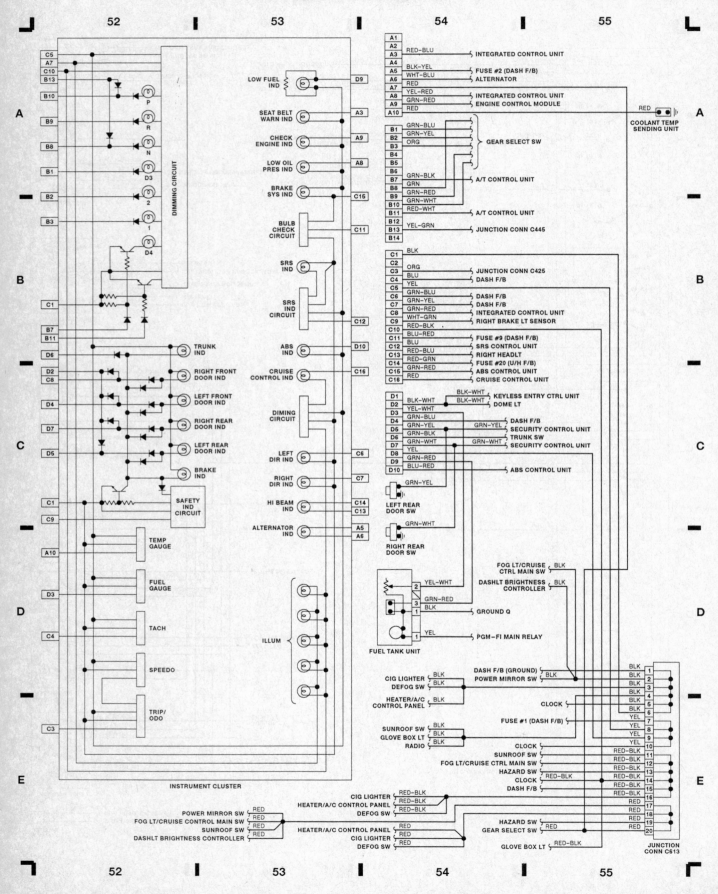

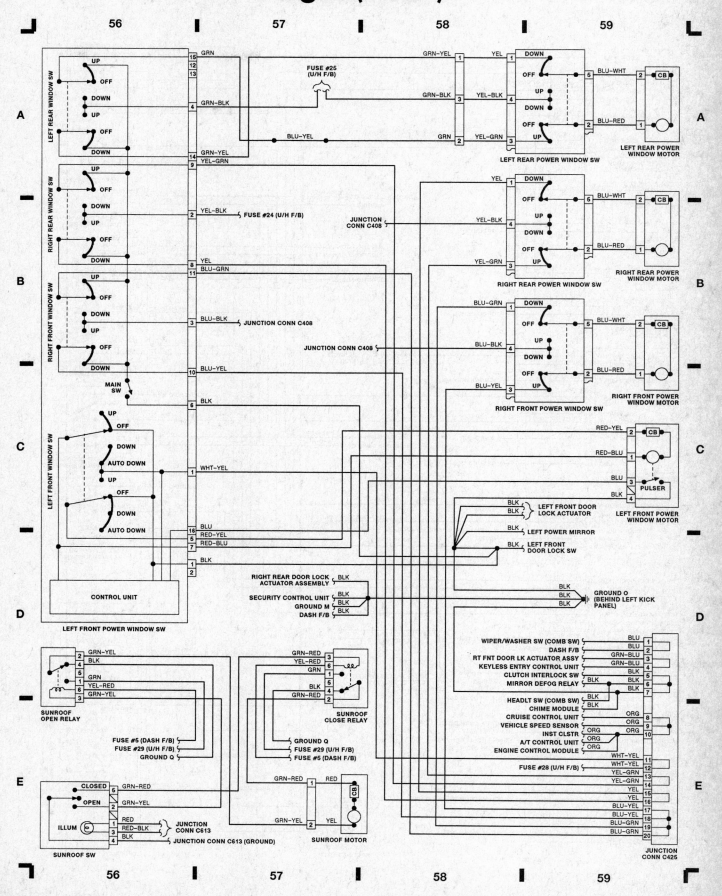

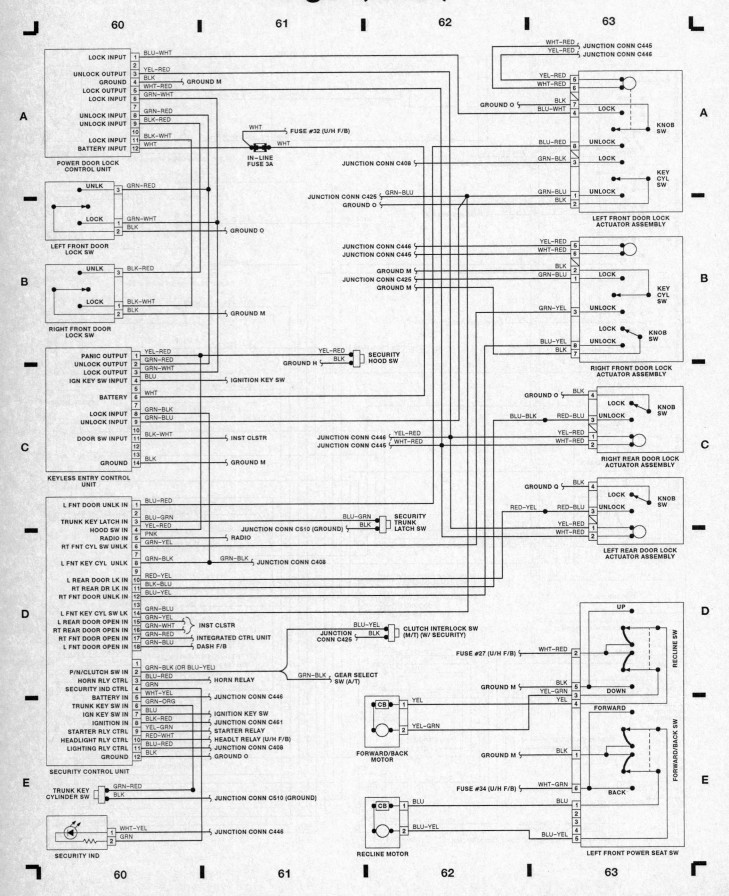

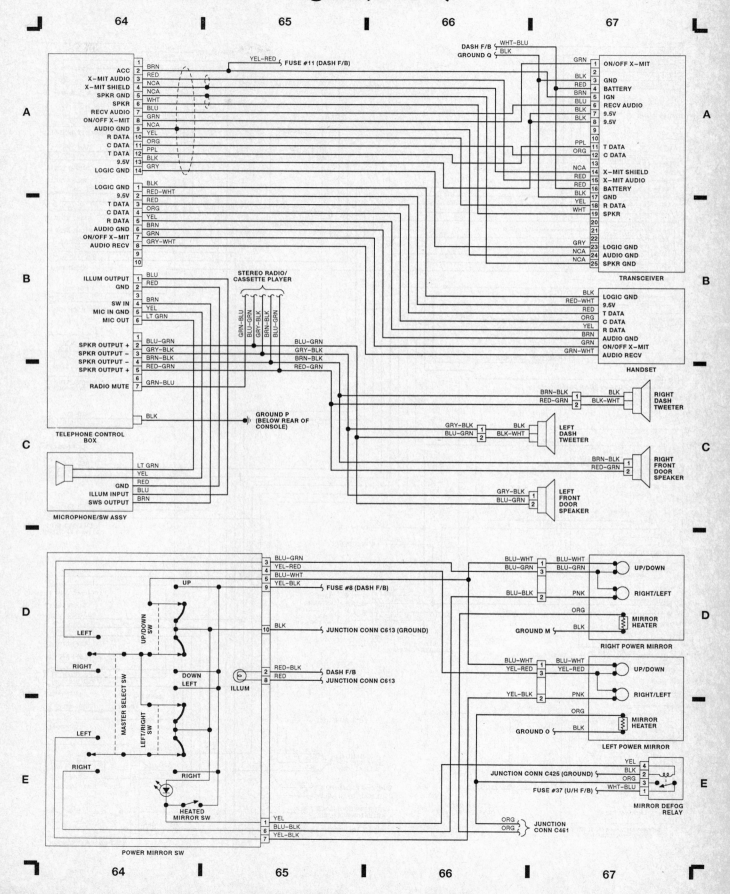

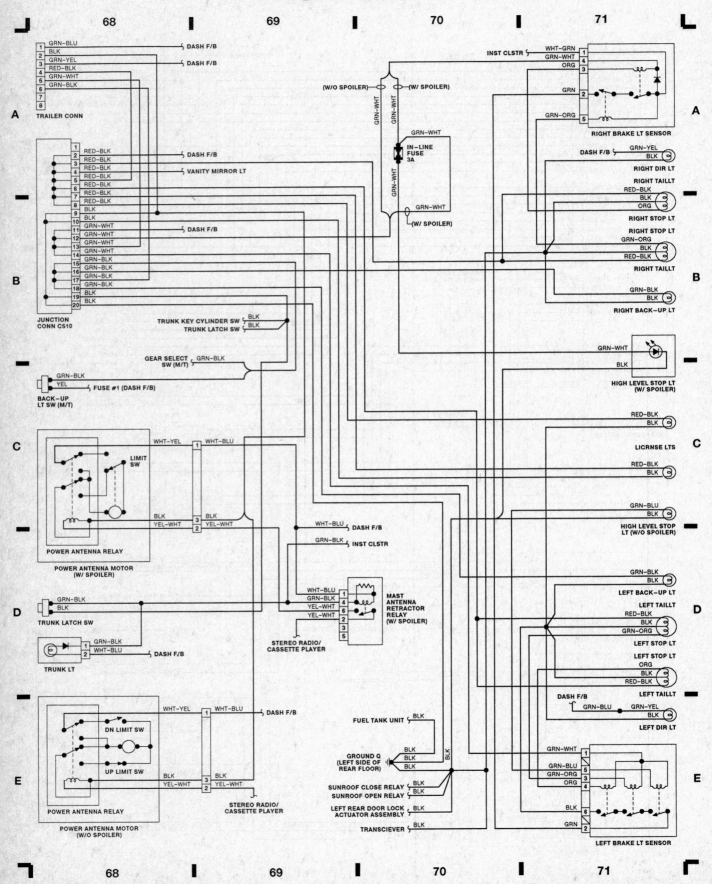

Legend, Vigor

NOTE: On Legend and Vigor, radio/cassette or radio/CD player contains an anti-theft protection circuit. Whenever battery is disconnected, radio will go into anti-theft mode. When battery is reconnected, radio will display CODE and will be inoperative until proper code number is entered by vehicle owner.

WARNING: To avoid injury from accidental air bag deployment, read and carefully follow all WARNINGS and SERVICE PRECAUTIONS.

NOTE: For information on air bag DIAGNOSIS & TESTING or DISPOSAL PROCEDURES, see MITCHELL® AIR BAG SERVICE & REPAIR MANUAL, DOMESTIC & IMPORTED MODELS.

DESCRIPTION & OPERATION

The Supplemental Restraint System (SRS) will activate to protect the driver and passenger when the car receives a sufficient front end impact. System includes left and right impact sensors, SRS unit with cowl sensor and driver-side and passenger-side air bags. *See Fig. 1, 2 or 3.* Legend is equipped with seat belt pretensioners, which are electrically linked with the SRS air bag. In a front-end collision, pretensioner instantly retracts belt to firmly restrain occupant.

SYSTEM OPERATION CHECK

When ignition is turned on, SRS indicator light should come on and then go off after about 6 seconds. If indicator light does not come on, comes on while vehicle is driven or does not go out after about 6 seconds, inspect system as soon as possible.

SERVICE PRECAUTIONS

Observe these precautions when working with air bag systems:
- Disable SRS before servicing any SRS or steering column component. Failure to do so could result in accidental air bag deployment and possible personal injury. See DISABLING & ACTIVATING AIR BAG SYSTEM.
- Wait at least 3 minutes after deactivating air bag system. System maintains air bag system voltage for about 3 minutes after battery is disconnected. Servicing air bag system before 3 minutes may cause accidental air bag deployment and possible personal injury.
- After an accident, inspect all SRS components, including harness and brackets. Replace any damaged or bent components even if

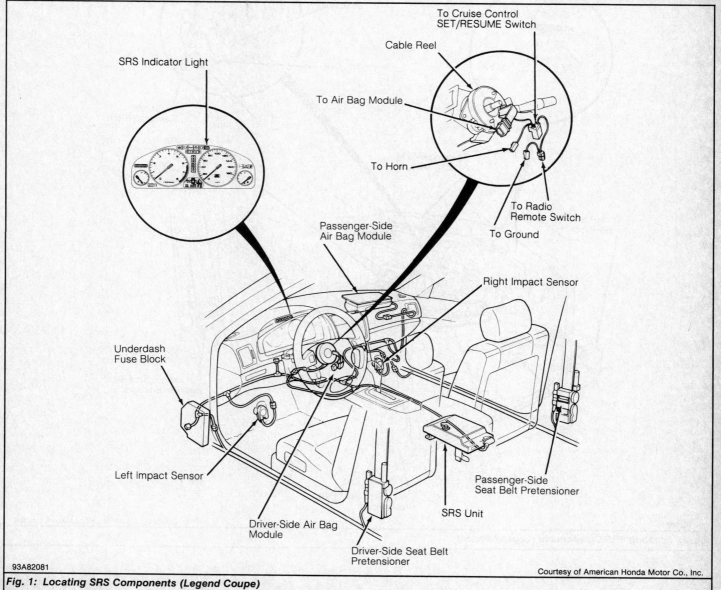

93A82081

Fig. 1: Locating SRS Components (Legend Coupe)

1993 ACCESSORIES & EQUIPMENT
Air Bag Restraint System (Cont.)

a deployment did not occur. Check steering column, knee bolster, instrument panel steering column reinforcement plate and lower brace for damage. DO NOT service any component or wiring. Replace any damaged or defective components or wiring.

- After repairs, turn ignition on from passenger side of vehicle (on single air bag models). Verify SRS indicator light works properly and no system faults are indicated. See SYSTEM OPERATION CHECK.
- Always wear safety glasses when servicing or handling an air bag.
- Air bag module must be stored in its original special container until ready for service. Store air bag module and container in a clean, dry place, away from extreme heat, sparks and sources of high electrical energy.
- When placing a live air bag module on a bench or other surface, always face air bag and trim cover up, away from surface. This will reduce motion of module if it is accidentally deployed.

- NEVER allow any electrical source near inflator on back of air bag module.
- When carrying a live air bag module, point trim cover away from your body to minimize injury in case of accidental air bag deployment.
- DO NOT probe a wire through insulator; this will damage wire and eventually cause failure due to corrosion.
- When performing electrical tests, always use test harnesses recommended by manufacturer. DO NOT use test probes directly on component connector pins or wires.
- DO NOT use electrical equipment not specified by manufacturer.
- If SRS is not fully functional for any reason, DO NOT operate vehicle until system is repaired. DO NOT remove any component or in any way disable system from operating normally. If SRS is not functional, park vehicle until repairs can be made.

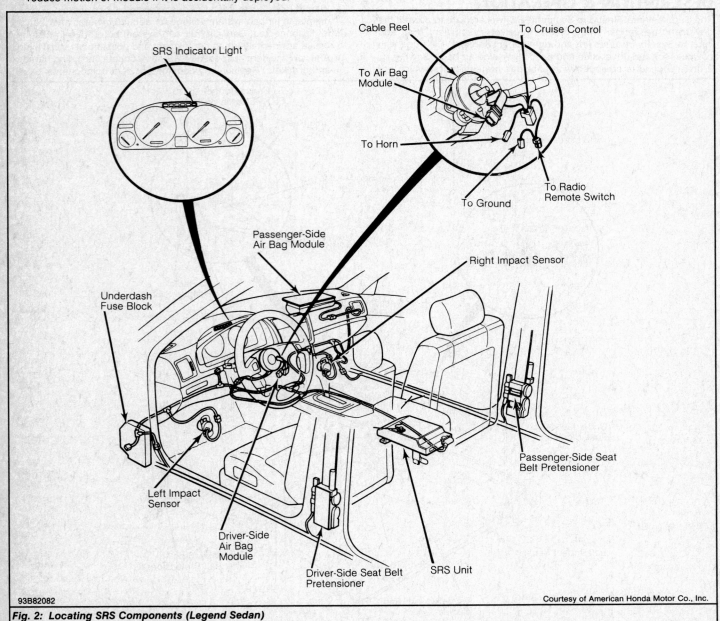

93B82082

Courtesy of American Honda Motor Co., Inc.

Fig. 2: Locating SRS Components (Legend Sedan)

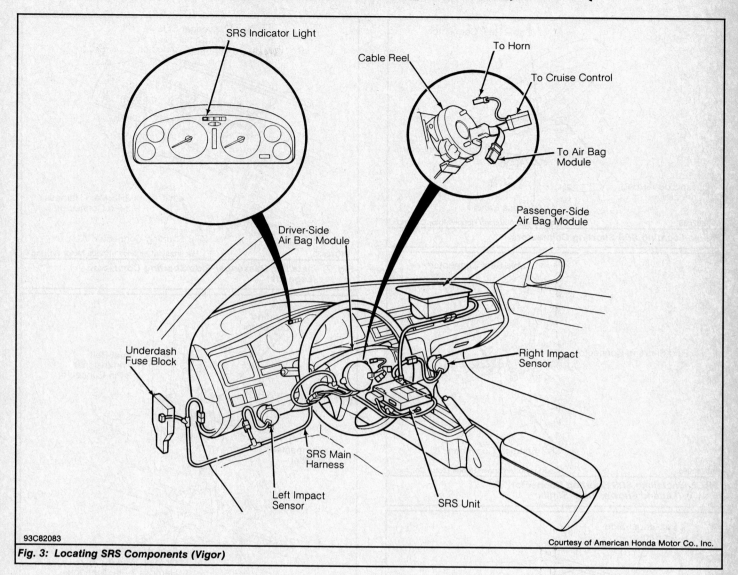

Fig. 3: Locating SRS Components (Vigor)

93C82083

Courtesy of American Honda Motor Co., Inc.

DISABLING & ACTIVATING AIR BAG SYSTEM

WARNING: *Wait at least 3 minutes after deactivating air bag system. System maintains voltage for about 3 minutes after battery is disconnected. Servicing air bag system before 3 minutes may cause accidental air bag deployment and possible personal injury.*

DISABLING SYSTEM

Legend – 1) Turn ignition off. Wait at least 3 minutes to allow capacitor in back-up circuit to discharge. This will prevent a malfunction of seat belt pretensioner. Disconnect battery cables. Remove access panel from under driver-side air bag. *See Fig. 4.* Remove Red shorting connector.

2) Unplug 3-pin connector between air bag and cable reel. Connect Red shorting connector to air bag side of connector. Connect SRS Shorting Connector "A" (07MAZ-SP00200) to cable reel side of connector. *See Fig. 5.*

3) For passenger-side air bag, remove glove box. Unplug connector between passenger-side air bag and SRS main harness. Connect Red shorting connector to air bag side of passenger-side air bag connector. *See Fig. 6.*

4) Connect SRS Shorting Connector "A" to SRS main harness half of 3-pin connector. *See Fig. 7.*

5) Remove quarter trim panel. Remove Red shorting connector from connector holder. Unplug seat belt pretensioner connector. Connect Red shorting connector to seat belt pretensioner half of connector. *See Fig. 8.*

Vigor – 1) Turn ignition off. Wait at least 3 minutes to allow capacitor in back-up circuit to discharge. Disconnect battery cables. Remove access panel from under air bag. *See Fig. 4.* Remove Red shorting connector. Unplug connector between air bag and cable reel. Connect Red shorting connector to air bag side of connector.

2) For passenger-side air bag, remove glove box. Remove Red shorting connector from holder. Unplug connector between passenger-side air bag and SRS main harness. Connect Red shorting connector to air bag side of passenger-side air bag connector. *See Fig. 9.*

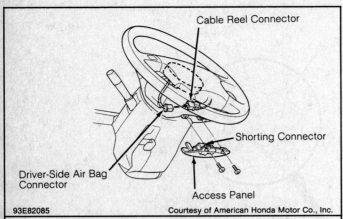

Cable Reel Connector

Shorting Connector

Driver-Side Air Bag Connector

Access Panel

93E82085   Courtesy of American Honda Motor Co., Inc.

Fig. 4: Locating SRS Shorting Connectors

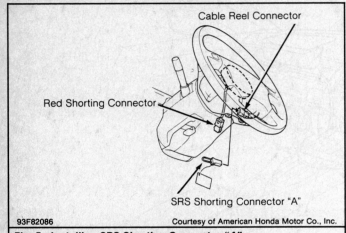

Cable Reel Connector

Red Shorting Connector

SRS Shorting Connector "A"

93F82086   Courtesy of American Honda Motor Co., Inc.

Fig. 5: Installing SRS Shorting Connector "A"
(Legend Shown; Vigor Similar)

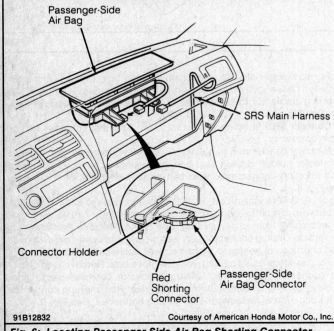

Passenger-Side Air Bag

SRS Main Harness

Connector Holder

Red Shorting Connector

Passenger-Side Air Bag Connector

91B12832   Courtesy of American Honda Motor Co., Inc.

Fig. 6: Locating Passenger-Side Air Bag Shorting Connector
(Legend)

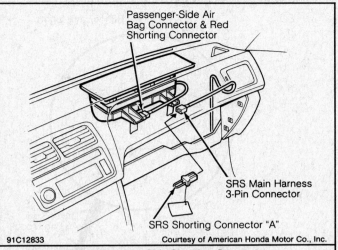

Passenger-Side Air Bag Connector & Red Shorting Connector

SRS Main Harness 3-Pin Connector

SRS Shorting Connector "A"

91C12833   Courtesy of American Honda Motor Co., Inc.

Fig. 7: Installing Passenger-Side Shorting Connector
(Legend)

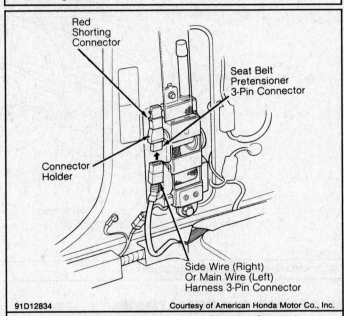

Red Shorting Connector

Seat Belt Pretensioner 3-Pin Connector

Connector Holder

Side Wire (Right) Or Main Wire (Left) Harness 3-Pin Connector

91D12834   Courtesy of American Honda Motor Co., Inc.

Fig. 8: Locating Seat Belt Pretensioner Shorting Connector
(Legend)

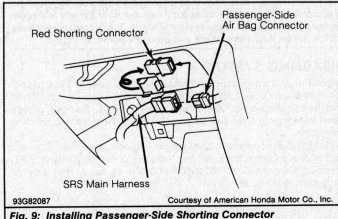

Red Shorting Connector

Passenger-Side Air Bag Connector

SRS Main Harness

93G82087   Courtesy of American Honda Motor Co., Inc.

Fig. 9: Installing Passenger-Side Shorting Connector
(Vigor)

ACTIVATING SYSTEM

Legend – 1) Remove shorting connectors from passenger-side air bag connector (if equipped) and SRS main harness connector. Reconnect passenger-side air bag connector (if equipped) to SRS main harness connector. Reinstall glove box.

2) Remove shorting connectors from driver-side air bag connector and from cable reel connector. Reconnect driver-side air bag connector to cable reel connector. Attach shorting connector to access panel. Reinstall access panel.

3) Remove shorting connectors from seat belt pretensioners. Attach shorting connectors to their holders. Reconnect side harness connector to right pretensioner.

4) Reconnect main wire harness to left pretensioner. Reinstall quarter trim panel. Reconnect battery. Check SRS indicator light to verify system functions properly. See SYSTEM OPERATION CHECK.

Vigor – 1) Remove shorting connector from passenger-side air bag connector. Attach shorting connector to holder. Reconnect passenger-side air bag connector to SRS main harness connector. Reinstall glove box.

2) Remove shorting connector from cable reel connector. Reconnect air bag and cable reel connectors. Attach shorting connector to access panel. Reinstall access panel. Reconnect battery. Check SRS indicator light to verify system functions properly. See SYSTEM OPERATION CHECK.

REMOVAL & INSTALLATION

WARNING: Failure to follow air bag service precautions may result in accidental deployment and personal injury. See SERVICE PRECAUTIONS. After component replacement, perform a system operation check to verify proper system operation. See SYSTEM OPERATION CHECK.

IMPACT SENSORS

Removal – 1) Before proceeding, follow air bag service precautions. See SERVICE PRECAUTIONS. Disable SRS. See DISABLING & ACTIVATING AIR BAG SYSTEM.

2) Impact sensors are located in left and right footwell areas. To remove left impact sensor, remove left footrest and left door sill molding. Pull carpet back. Remove sensor cover and sensor. *See Fig. 10.*

3) To remove right impact sensor, remove right door sill molding and pull back carpet. Remove Electronic Control Unit (ECU). *See Fig. 11.* Remove 2 mounting bolts and impact sensor.

CAUTION: Install sensor wires so they are not pinched and do not interfere with other vehicle parts during sensor installation. Replace a sensor if it is dented, cracked or deformed. For system to operate correctly, right and left impact sensors must be installed on correct sides.

Installation – Install sensor and sensor cover. On left side, install carpet, molding and footrest. On right side, install ECU, carpet and molding. On both sides, tighten sensor mounting bolts to specifica-

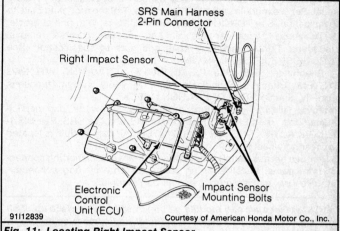

Fig. 11: *Locating Right Impact Sensor*

tion. See TORQUE SPECIFICATIONS table at end of article. To complete installation, reverse removal procedure. Reactivate air bag system. Check SRS indicator light to verify system is functioning properly. See SYSTEM OPERATION CHECK.

AIR BAG MODULE

Removal (Legend) – 1) Before proceeding, follow air bag service precautions. See SERVICE PRECAUTIONS. Disable SRS. See DISABLING & ACTIVATING AIR BAG SYSTEM. Driver-side air bag module is located on steering wheel hub. Passenger-side air bag module (if equipped) is located in right side of instrument panel.

2) To remove driver-side air bag, remove Torx bolts from under steering wheel, radio remote switch cover and cruise control SET/RESUME switch cover. Remove driver-side air bag.

CAUTION: Place air bag module on bench with pad surface up. If air bag is stored with pad down, accidental deployment could propel unit with enough force to cause serious injury.

3) To remove passenger-side air bag (if equipped), remove 4 mounting nuts and 2 mounting bolts. *See Fig. 12.* Remove bracket. Remove 4 mounting screws from passenger-side air bag module. Carefully lift air bag assembly from dashboard.

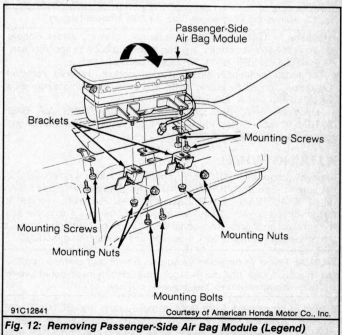

Fig. 12: *Removing Passenger-Side Air Bag Module (Legend)*

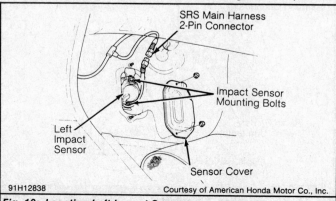

Fig. 10: *Locating Left Impact Sensor*

Installation – 1) Place driver-side air bag assembly onto steering wheel. Secure module with NEW Torx bolts. Tighten mounting bolts to specification. See TORQUE SPECIFICATIONS table at end of article.

2) To install passenger-side air bag module, reverse removal procedure. Tighten mounting bolts and nuts to specification. See TORQUE SPECIFICATIONS table.

3) Reactivate SRS. See DISABLING & ACTIVATING AIR BAG SYSTEM. Check SRS indicator light to verify system functions properly. See SYSTEM OPERATION CHECK.

Removal (Vigor) – 1) Before proceeding, follow air bag service precautions. See SERVICE PRECAUTIONS. Disable SRS. See DISABLING & ACTIVATING AIR BAG SYSTEM. Air bag module is located on steering wheel hub.

2) Remove access panel below air bag. Remove Red shorting connector from panel. Install shorting connector onto air bag connector. Remove Torx mounting bolts and air bag module.

CAUTION: Place air bag module on bench with pad surface up. If air bag is stored with pad down, accidental deployment could propel unit with enough force to cause serious injury.

---

3) To remove passenger-side air bag, remove glove box. Remove 4 mounting nuts from bracket. *See Fig. 13.* Remove bracket and one mounting nut from passenger-side air bag module. Carefully lift air bag assembly from dashboard.

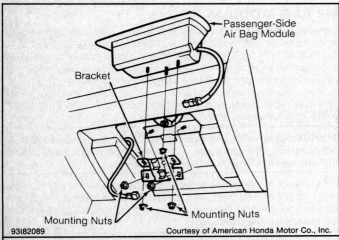

93182089   Courtesy of American Honda Motor Co., Inc.

Fig. 13: Removing Passenger-Side Air Bag Module (Vigor)

Installation – 1) Place air bag module onto steering wheel. Secure module with NEW Torx bolts. Tighten mounting bolts to specification. See TORQUE SPECIFICATIONS table at end of article.

2) To install passenger-side air bag module, reverse removal procedure. Tighten mounting bolts and nuts to specification. See TORQUE SPECIFICATIONS table.

3) Reactivate SRS. See DISABLING & ACTIVATING AIR BAG SYSTEM. Check SRS indicator light to verify system functions properly. See SYSTEM OPERATION CHECK.

STEERING WHEEL

Removal (Legend) – 1) Before proceeding, follow air bag service precautions. See SERVICE PRECAUTIONS. Disable SRS. See DISABLING & ACTIVATING AIR BAG SYSTEM. Put front wheels in straight-ahead position. Remove access panel below air bag. Remove Red shorting connector from panel. Install shorting connector onto air bag connector. Remove Torx mounting bolts and air bag module.

CAUTION: Place air bag module on bench with pad surface up. If air bag is stored with pad down, accidental deployment could propel unit with enough force to cause serious injury.

---

2) Unplug connectors from horn, remote audio and SET/RESUME switches. Remove steering wheel retaining nut. Remove steering wheel by pulling steadily upward while rocking steering wheel from side to side.

Installation – 1) Ensure front wheels are in straight-ahead position. Center cable reel. See CABLE REEL CENTERING under ADJUSTMENTS. Install steering wheel. Install NEW steering wheel retaining nut. Ensure steering wheel shaft engages cable reel. Install NEW Torx bolts.

2) To complete installation, reverse removal procedure. Reactivate SRS. See DISABLING & ACTIVATING AIR BAG SYSTEM. Check SRS indicator light to verify system functions properly. See SYSTEM OPERATION CHECK. Enter anti-theft code into radio.

Removal (Vigor) – 1) Ensure front wheels are in straight-ahead position. Before proceeding, follow air bag service precautions. See SERVICE PRECAUTIONS. Disable SRS. See DISABLING & ACTIVATING AIR BAG SYSTEM. Remove air bag retaining bolt cover. Remove SET/RESUME switch cover. Remove Torx bolts and air bag module.

CAUTION: Place air bag module on bench with pad surface up. If air bag is stored with pad down, accidental deployment could propel unit with enough force to cause serious injury.

---

2) Unplug connectors from horn and SET/RESUME switches. Remove steering wheel retaining nut. Pull steadily upward while rocking steering wheel from side to side.

Installation – 1) Ensure front wheels are in straight-ahead position. Center cable reel. See CABLE REEL CENTERING under ADJUSTMENTS. Install steering wheel. Install NEW steering wheel retaining nut. Ensure steering wheel shaft engages cable reel. Install NEW Torx bolts.

2) To complete installation, reverse removal procedure. Reactivate SRS. See DISABLING & ACTIVATING AIR BAG SYSTEM. Check SRS indicator light to verify system functions properly. See SYSTEM OPERATION CHECK.

CABLE REEL

Removal – 1) Before proceeding, follow air bag service precautions. See SERVICE PRECAUTIONS. Disable SRS. See DISABLING & ACTIVATING AIR BAG SYSTEM. Ensure front wheels face straight ahead.

2) Cable reel is located under steering wheel, in upper steering column. *See Fig. 1, 2 or 3.* Remove upper and lower steering column covers. Unplug connector between cable reel and SRS main harness. Remove air bag assembly from steering wheel. See AIR BAG MODULE under REMOVAL & INSTALLATION. Remove steering wheel nut.

3) Unplug connectors from horn, radio remote switch, ground and cruise control switches. Remove cable reel 3-pin connector from its clips. *See Fig. 14.* Remove steering wheel from column. Remove 4 bolts and cover under steering column. Remove cable reel and cancel sleeve. *See Fig. 15.*

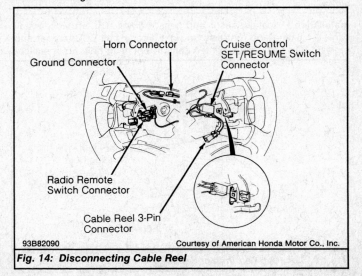

93B82090   Courtesy of American Honda Motor Co., Inc.

Fig. 14: Disconnecting Cable Reel

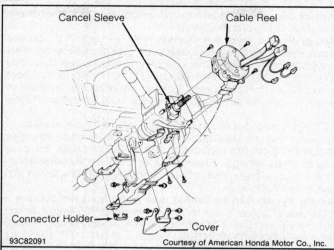

Fig. 15: Removing Cable Reel & Cancel Sleeve

Installation – **1)** Align cancel sleeve grooves with projections on cable reel. *See Fig. 16.* Carefully install cable reel and cancel sleeve onto steering column shaft. Reinstall cover. Install steering column upper and lower covers. Center cable reel. See CABLE REEL CENTERING under ADJUSTMENTS.

2) After cable reel is centered, install steering wheel. Reattach cruise control and cable reel connectors to their clips. Connect horn connector, radio remote switch connector and ground connector.

3) Install steering wheel nut and driver-side air bag module. Tighten steering wheel nut and air bag mounting bolts to specification. See TORQUE SPECIFICATIONS table. Connect cable reel harness to SRS main harness. Attach connector holder to steering column.

4) To complete installation, reverse removal procedure. Reactivate SRS. See DISABLING & ACTIVATING AIR BAG SYSTEM. Check SRS indicator light to verify system is functioning properly. See SYSTEM OPERATION CHECK.

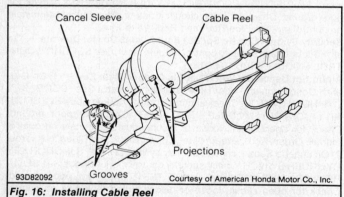

Fig. 16: Installing Cable Reel

SRS UNIT

Removal (Legend) – Before proceeding, follow air bag service precautions. See SERVICE PRECAUTIONS. Disable SRS. See DISABLING & ACTIVATING AIR BAG SYSTEM. SRS unit is located under armrest of center console. *See Fig. 17.* Remove center console. Unplug SRS unit 18-pin connector. Remove 4 SRS unit mounting bolts. Remove SRS unit.

Installation – To install, reverse removal procedure. Tighten SRS unit bolts to specification. See TORQUE SPECIFICATIONS table at end of article. Reactivate SRS. See DISABLING & ACTIVATING AIR BAG SYSTEM. Check SRS indicator light to verify system is functioning properly. See SYSTEM OPERATION CHECK.

Removal (Vigor) – **1)** Before proceeding, follow air bag service precautions. See SERVICE PRECAUTIONS. Disable SRS. See DISABLING & ACTIVATING AIR BAG SYSTEM.

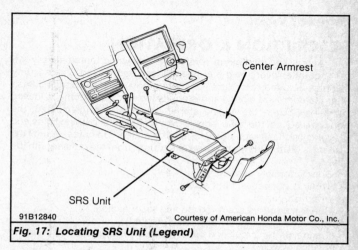

Fig. 17: Locating SRS Unit (Legend)

2) SRS unit is located behind heater control panel. Remove center console. Remove heater control panel. Remove radio panel. Unplug main harness connector from SRS unit. Remove retaining bolts and SRS unit.

Installation – To install, reverse removal procedure. Tighten SRS unit bolts to specification. See TORQUE SPECIFICATIONS table at end of article. Reactivate SRS. See DISABLING & ACTIVATING AIR BAG SYSTEM. Check SRS indicator light to verify system functions properly. See SYSTEM OPERATION CHECK.

ADJUSTMENTS

CABLE REEL CENTERING

After installing cable reel onto steering column shaft, rotate cable reel clockwise until it stops. Rotate cable reel counterclockwise about 2 turns until Yellow gear tooth lines up with mark on cover and arrow on cable reel label points straight up. *See Fig. 18.* Install steering wheel. Attach cruise control and cable reel connectors to their clips.

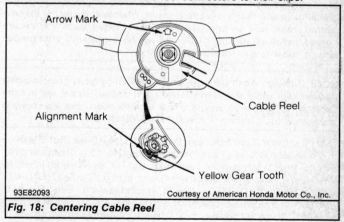

Fig. 18: Centering Cable Reel

TORQUE SPECIFICATIONS

TORQUE SPECIFICATIONS

Application	Ft. Lbs. (N.m)
Impact Sensor Mounting Bolt	16 (22)
Pretensioner Lower Mounting Bolt	24 (33)
Shoulder Harness Anchor Bolt	24 (33)
Steering Wheel Nut	36 (50)
	INCH Lbs. (N.m)
Air Bag Mounting Bolt/Nut	84 (10)
Pretensioner Upper Mounting Bolt	84 (10)
SRS Unit	84 (10)

Legend, Vigor

DESCRIPTION & OPERATION

The Acura security alarm system is activated automatically 15 seconds after everything has been closed and locked. The security alarm system indicator light, located on driver's side door, will flash after the doors are closed and properly locked. If any of the following conditions occur, the engine starter circuit will be interrupted, the horns will sound, the headlights, side marker lights, parking lights and tail lights will flash repeatedly for approximately 2 minutes, or until the system is disarmed by unlocking either door from the outside with the key.

- Door is forcibly opened.
- Trunk is opened without a key.
- Hood is opened.
- Battery terminals are removed and reconnected.
- Hood/trunk opener in vehicle is operated.
- Engine starter circuit and battery circuit are bypassed by breaking ignition switch.

TROUBLE SHOOTING

CAUTION: Legend and Vigor are equipped with Supplemental Restraint System (SRS). SRS wiring harness is routed close to instrument cluster, steering wheel and related components. All SRS wiring harnesses are covered by Yellow outer insulation. DO NOT use electrical test equipment on these circuits. Before working on anti-theft components, disable air bag system. See AIR BAG RESTRAINT SYSTEM article in ACCESSORIES & EQUIPMENT.

WARNING: Wait about 3 minutes after disabling air bag system. Back-up power circuit, capacitor internal to SRS module, maintains system voltage for about 3 minutes after battery is disconnected. Servicing air bag system before 3 minutes may cause accidental air bag deployment and possible personal injury.

NOTE: On Legend and Vigor, radio/cassette or radio/CD player contains an anti-theft protection circuit. Whenever battery is disconnected, radio will go into anti-theft mode. When battery is reconnected, radio will display CODE and will be inoperative until proper code number is entered by vehicle owner.

NOTE: Different wires with the same color have been given a suffix number. For example, Yellow/Green[1] and Yellow/Green[2] are not the same wires. For wire and terminal identification, see appropriate chassis wiring diagram in WIRING DIAGRAMS.

Security Alarm Can't Be Set (Indicator Light Does Not Flash) –
1) On Legend Coupe, check for blown fuses No. 15 (7.5-amp) and No. 20 (7.5-amp) in under-hood fuse block and No. 39 (20-amp) in under-dash fuse block. Check security indicator light (LED). See SECURITY INDICATOR LIGHT (LED). Check ignition switch. See IGNITION SWITCH in STEERING COLUMN SWITCHES article. Check for poor grounds. Check for open circuit, loose or disconnected terminals on control module Yellow/Blue, Black/Red, White/Green, Red/Green[3] and Blue/White wires.
2) On Legend Sedan, check for blown fuses No. 15 (7.5-amp) and No. 20 (7.5-amp) in under-hood fuse block and No. 39 (20-amp) in under-dash fuse block. Check security indicator light (LED). See SECURITY INDICATOR LIGHT (LED). Check ignition switch. See IGNITION SWITCH in STEERING COLUMN SWITCHES article. Check for poor grounds. Check for open circuit, loose or disconnected terminals on control module Yellow/Blue, Black/Red, White/Green, Red/Green and Blue/White wires.
3) On Vigor, check for blown fuses No. 4 (7.5-amp) in under-dash fuse block and No. 30 (20-amp) in under-hood fuse block. Check security indicator light (LED). See SECURITY INDICATOR LIGHT (LED). Check ignition switch. See IGNITION SWITCH in STEERING COLUMN SWITCHES article. Check for poor ground. Check for open circuit, loose or disconnected terminals on control module White/Yellow, Black/Red, Green and Blue wires.

Security System Does Not Operate – 1) On Legend Coupe and Sedan, check Starting system. Check A/T gear position switch or M/T clutch interlock switch. Check security control module input. See SECURITY CONTROL MODULE INPUT TEST. Check for poor ground. Check for open circuit, loose or disconnected terminals on control module Black/White (A/T) or Blue (A/T), and Black/Yellow wires.
2) On Vigor, check Starting system. Check A/T gear position switch or M/T clutch interlock switch. Check security control module input. See SECURITY CONTROL MODULE INPUT TEST. Check for poor ground. Check for open circuit, loose or disconnected terminals on control module Black/White, Green/Black (A/T), Yellow/Green and Blue/Yellow (M/T) wires.

Security System Can Be Set But Horn Alarm Does Not Operate –
1) On Legend Coupe, check for blown fuse No. 39 (20-amp) in under-dash fuse block. Check horn circuit. Check security control module input. See SECURITY CONTROL MODULE INPUT TEST. Check for poor ground. Check for open circuit, loose or disconnected terminals on control module White/Green, Blue and Blue/Red[1] wires.
2) On Legend Sedan, check for blown fuse No. 39 (20-amp) in under-dash fuse block. Check horn circuit. Check security control module input. See SECURITY CONTROL MODULE INPUT TEST. Check for poor ground. Check for open circuit, loose or disconnected terminals on control module White/Green, Blue and Blue/Red wires.
3) On Vigor, check for blown fuse No. 30 (20-amp) in under-hood fuse block. Check horn circuit. Check security control module input. See SECURITY CONTROL MODULE INPUT TEST. Check for poor ground. Check for open circuit, loose or disconnected terminals on control module White/Yellow, Blue/Green[3] and Blue/Green wires.

Security System Can Be Set But Headlight Alarm Does Not Operate – 1) On Legend Coupe and Sedan, check lighting system. Check security control module input. See SECURITY CONTROL MODULE INPUT TEST. Check for open circuit, loose or disconnected terminals on control module Blue/Red[2] and Red/Green wires.
2) On Vigor, check lighting system. Check security control module input. See SECURITY CONTROL MODULE INPUT TEST. Check for poor ground. Check for open circuit, loose or disconnected terminals on control module Blue/Red[1] and Red/White wires.

Security System Can Be Set But Both Alarms Do Not Operate – On all models, check security control module input. See SECURITY CONTROL MODULE INPUT TEST.

Alarm Not Cancelled When Door Is Opened With Key – 1) On Legend Coupe, check door key cylinder switch. See DOOR KEY CYLINDER SWITCH. Check security control module input. See SECURITY CONTROL MODULE INPUT TEST. Check for poor ground. Check for open circuit, loose or disconnected terminals on control module Green/Red[2], Green/Blue[2], Green/Black and Blue/Red[3] wires.
2) On Legend Sedan, check door key cylinder switch. See DOOR KEY CYLINDER SWITCH. Check security control module input. See SECURITY CONTROL MODULE INPUT TEST. Check for poor ground. Check for open circuit, loose or disconnected terminals on control module Green/Red[2], Green/Blue[1], Green/Black and Blue/Red[3] wires.
3) On Vigor, check for blown fuse No. 4 (7.5-amp) in under-dash fuse block. Check security control module input. See SECURITY CONTROL MODULE INPUT TEST. Check for poor ground. Check for open circuit, loose or disconnected terminals on control module Blue/Red[1], Green/Yellow[2], Green/Black[2] and Blue/Red wires.

Alarm Not Cancelled When Key Is Inserted In Ignition Switch – 1) On Legend Coupe and Sedan, check for blown fuse No. 20 (7.5-amp) in under-hood fuse block. Check ignition switch. See IGNITION SWITCH in STEERING COLUMN SWITCHES article. Check security control module input. See SECURITY CONTROL MODULE INPUT TEST. Check for open circuit, loose or disconnected terminals on control module Black/Red and Blue/White wires.
2) On Vigor, check for blown fuse No. 4 (7.5-amp) in under-dash fuse block. Check ignition switch. See IGNITION SWITCH in STEERING COLUMN SWITCHES article. Check security control module input. See SECURITY CONTROL MODULE INPUT TEST. Check for open circuit, loose or disconnected terminals on control module Blue/Red and Blue wires.

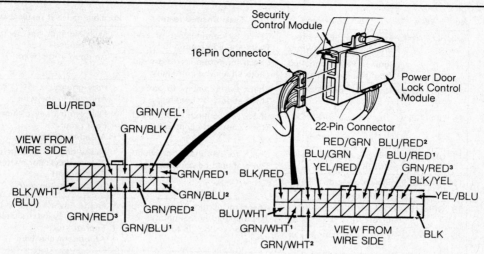

No.	Wire	Test condition	Test: Desired result	Possible cause if result is not obtained
1	BLK	Under all conditions	Check for continuity to ground: There should be continuity.	• Poor ground • An open in the wire
2	YEL/BLU	Under all conditions	Check for voltage to ground: There should be battery voltage.	• Blown No. 15 (7.5 A) fuse • An open in the wire
3	GRN/RED³	Under all conditions	Connect to ground: Security indicator should come on.	• Blown No. 39 (20 A) fuse • Faulty security indicator • An open in the wire
4	BLK/RED	Ignition switch to ON (II)	Check for voltage to ground: There should be battery voltage.	• Blown No. 20 (7.5 A) fuse • An open in the wire
5	BLK/WHT (BLU)	Ignition switch to START (III)	Check for voltage to ground: There should be battery voltage.	• Faulty starter cut relay • An open in the wire
6	BLK/YEL	Ignition switch to START (II) and: Clutch pedal pushed (M/T) Shift lever in P (A/T)	Attach to ground: Starter should crank the engine.	• Blown No. 35 (50 A) fuse • Faulty starting system • Faulty starter cut relay • Faulty clutch interlock switch (M/T) • Faulty A/T gear position switch (A/T) • An open in the wire
7	BLU/RED¹	Under all conditions	Attach to ground: All horns should sound.	• Blown No. 39 (20 A) fuse • Faulty horn relay • Either horn faulty • Poor ground • An open in the wire
8	BLU/RED²	Under all conditions	Attach to ground: Headlights should come on.	• Faulty headlight relay • Faulty lighting system • An open in the wire
9	RED/GRN	Under all conditions	Connect to ground: Taillights should come on.	• Faulty taillight relay • Faulty taillight system • An open in the wire
10	YEL/RED	Hood open	Check for continuity to ground: There should be continuity.	• Faulty hood switch. Misadjusted hood switch • Poor ground • An open in the wire
		Hood closed	Check for continuity to ground: There should be no continuity.	
11	BLU/GRN	Trunk lid open	Check for continuity to ground: There should be continuity.	• Faulty security trunk latch switch • Poor ground • An open in the wire
		Trunk lid closed	Check for continuity to ground: There should be no continuity.	
12	GRN/BLU¹	Driver's door open	Check for continuity to ground: When the door is open, there should be continuity, and when the door is closed, there should be no continuity.	• Faulty driver's door or passenger's door switch • An open in the wire
		Driver's door closed		
13	GRN/RED³	Passenger's door open		
		Passenger's door closed		

(BLU): M/T

93I82121

Courtesy of American Honda Motor Co., Inc.

Fig. 1: *Security Control Module Input Test (Legend Coupe – 1 Of 2)*

No.	Wire	Test condition	Test: Desired result	Possible cause if result is not obtained
14	BLU/WHT	Ignition key is inserted into the ignition switch	Check for continuity to ground: There should be continuity.	• Faulty ignition key switch • Poor ground • An open in the wire
		Ignition key is removed from the ignition switch	Check for continuity to ground: There should be continuity.	
15	GRN/WHT	Under all conditions	Check for continuity to ground: There should be continuity.	• Poor ground • An open in the wire
16	GRN/RED[1]	Trunk key in UNLOCK	Check for continuity to ground: There should be continuity.	• Faulty trunk key cylinder switch • Poor ground • An open in the wire
17	GRN/RED[2]	Driver's door key in UNLOCK	Check for continuity to ground: There should be continuity.	• Faulty driver's door or passenger's door key cylinder switch • Poor ground • An open in the wire
18	GRN/BLU[2]	Passenger's door key in UNLOCK		
19	GRN/YEL[1]	Driver's door key in LOCK	Check for continuity to ground: There should be continuity, as the door keylock is turned in LOCK.	• Faulty driver's door or passenger's door key cylinder switch • Poor ground • An open in the wire
20	GRN/WHT[2]	Right front door key in LOCK		
21	GRN/BLK	Driver's door lock knob in UNLOCK	Check for continuity to ground: There should be continuity.	• Faulty driver's door lock knob switch (Built into the actuator) • Poor ground • An open in the wire
22	BLU/RED[1]	Passenger's door lock knob in UNLOCK	Check for continuity to ground: There should be continuity.	• Faulty passenger's door lock knob switch (Built in the actuator) • Poor ground • An open in the wire

93J82122   Courtesy of American Honda Motor Co., Inc.

Fig. 2: Security Control Module Input Test (Legend Coupe – 2 Of 2)

Alarm Not Cancelled When Trunk Is Opened With Key – 1) On Legend Coupe and Sedan, check trunk key cylinder switch. See TRUNK KEY CYLINDER SWITCH. Check trunk latch switch. See TRUNK LATCH SWITCH. Check security control module input. See SECURITY CONTROL MODULE INPUT TEST. Check for poor ground. Check for open circuit, loose or disconnected terminals on control module Green/Red[1] and Blue/Green wires.
2) On Vigor, check trunk key cylinder switch. See TRUNK KEY CYLINDER SWITCH. Check trunk latch switch. See TRUNK LATCH SWITCH. Check security control module input. See SECURITY CONTROL MODULE INPUT TEST. Check for poor ground. Check for open circuit, loose or disconnected terminals on control module Green/Orange and Blue/Green wires.

Alarm Does Not Operate When Hood Is Opened – On all models, check hood switch. See HOOD SWITCH. Check security control module input. See SECURITY CONTROL MODULE INPUT TEST. Check for poor ground. Check for open circuit, loose or disconnected terminals on control module Yellow/Red wire.

Alarm Does Not Operate When Door Is Opened – 1) On Legend Coupe, check door switch. See DOOR KEY SWITCH, FRONT PASSENGERS DOOR LOCK KNOB SWITCH and REAR DOOR LOCK KNOB LOCK SWITCH. Check security control module input. See SECURITY CONTROL MODULE INPUT TEST. Check for poor ground. Check for open circuit, loose or disconnected terminals on control module Green/Blue[1] and Green/Red[3] wires.
2) On Legend Sedan, check door switch. See DOOR KEY SWITCH, FRONT PASSENGERS DOOR LOCK KNOB SWITCH and REAR DOOR LOCK KNOB LOCK SWITCH. Check security control module input. See SECURITY CONTROL MODULE INPUT TEST. Check for poor ground. Check for open circuit, loose or disconnected terminals on control module Green/Blue, Green/Red[3], Green/Yellow and Green/White[1] wires.
3) On Vigor, check door switch. See DOOR KEY SWITCH, FRONT PASSENGERS DOOR LOCK KNOB SWITCH and REAR DOOR LOCK KNOB LOCK SWITCH. Check security control module input. See SECURITY CONTROL MODULE INPUT TEST. Check for poor ground. Check for open circuit, loose or disconnected terminals on control module Green/Yellow[1], Green/White, Green/Blue[2] and Green/Red wires.

TESTING
SECURITY CONTROL MODULE INPUT TEST

NOTE: Different wires with the same color have been a suffix number. For example, Yellow/Green[1] and Yellow/Green[2] are not the same wires.

Legend – Remove driver's side instrument panel lower cover. Disconnect security system control module 16-pin and 22-pin connectors. Inspect connectors to ensure terminals are making good contact. If terminals are bent, loose or corroded, repair as necessary and recheck system. If terminals are okay, use a Digital Volt/Ohmmeter to perform SECURITY CONTROL MODULE INPUT TEST. *See Figs. 1, 2, 3, and 4.* If input test is okay, replace control module.

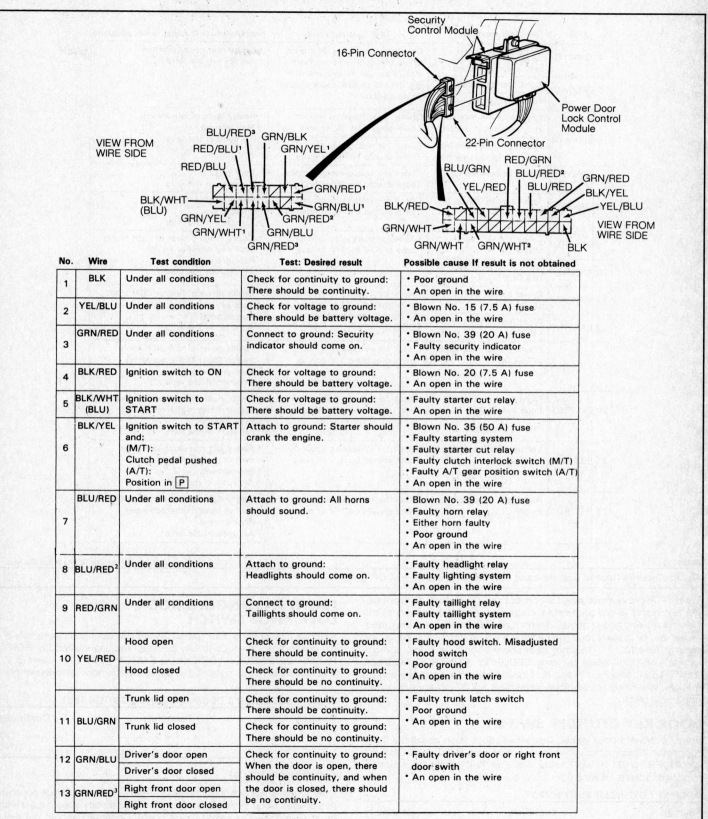

No.	Wire	Test condition	Test: Desired result	Possible cause If result is not obtained
1	BLK	Under all conditions	Check for continuity to ground: There should be continuity.	• Poor ground • An open in the wire
2	YEL/BLU	Under all conditions	Check for voltage to ground: There should be battery voltage.	• Blown No. 15 (7.5 A) fuse • An open in the wire
3	GRN/RED	Under all conditions	Connect to ground: Security indicator should come on.	• Blown No. 39 (20 A) fuse • Faulty security indicator • An open in the wire
4	BLK/RED	Ignition switch to ON	Check for voltage to ground: There should be battery voltage.	• Blown No. 20 (7.5 A) fuse • An open in the wire
5	BLK/WHT (BLU)	Ignition switch to START	Check for voltage to ground: There should be battery voltage.	• Faulty starter cut relay • An open in the wire
6	BLK/YEL	Ignition switch to START and; (M/T): Clutch pedal pushed (A/T): Position in P	Attach to ground: Starter should crank the engine.	• Blown No. 35 (50 A) fuse • Faulty starting system • Faulty starter cut relay • Faulty clutch interlock switch (M/T) • Faulty A/T gear position switch (A/T) • An open in the wire
7	BLU/RED	Under all conditions	Attach to ground: All horns should sound.	• Blown No. 39 (20 A) fuse • Faulty horn relay • Either horn faulty • Poor ground • An open in the wire
8	BLU/RED[2]	Under all conditions	Attach to ground: Headlights should come on.	• Faulty headlight relay • Faulty lighting system • An open in the wire
9	RED/GRN	Under all conditions	Connect to ground: Taillights should come on.	• Faulty taillight relay • Faulty taillight system • An open in the wire
10	YEL/RED	Hood open	Check for continuity to ground: There should be continuity.	• Faulty hood switch. Misadjusted hood switch • Poor ground • An open in the wire
10	YEL/RED	Hood closed	Check for continuity to ground: There should be no continuity.	
11	BLU/GRN	Trunk lid open	Check for continuity to ground: There should be continuity.	• Faulty trunk latch switch • Poor ground • An open in the wire
11	BLU/GRN	Trunk lid closed	Check for continuity to ground: There should be no continuity.	
12	GRN/BLU	Driver's door open	Check for continuity to ground: When the door is open, there should be continuity, and when the door is closed, there should be no continuity.	• Faulty driver's door or right front door swith • An open in the wire
12	GRN/BLU	Driver's door closed		
13	GRN/RED[3]	Right front door open		
13	GRN/RED[3]	Right front door closed		

(BLU): M/T

93A82123

Courtesy of American Honda Motor Co., Inc.

Fig. 3: Security Control Module Input Test (Legend Sedan – 1 Of 2)

No.	Wire	Test condition	Test: Desired result	Possible cause If result is not obtained
14	GRN/YEL	Left rear door open	Check for continuity to ground: When the door is open, there should be continuity, and when the door is closed, there should be no continuity.	• Faulty rear door switches • An open in the wire
		Left rear door closed		
15	GRN/WHT[1]	Right rear door open		
		Right rear door closed		
16	BLU/WHT	Ignition key is inserted into the ignition switch	Check for voltage to ground: There should be 1V or less.	• Faulty ignition key switch • Poor ground • An open in the wire
		Ignition key is removed from the igniton switch	Check for voltage to ground: There should be 1V or more.	
17	GRN/WHT or LT GRN	Under all conditions	Check for voltage to ground: There should be 1V or less.	• Poor ground • An open in the wire
18	GRN/RED[1]	Trunk key in UNLOCK	Check for voltage to ground: There should be 1V or less.	• Faulty trunk key • Poor ground • An open in the wire
19	GRN/RED[2]	Driver's door key in UNLOCK	Check for voltage to ground: There should be 1 V or less.	• Faulty driver's door or right front door key cylinder switch • Poor ground • An open in the wire
20	GRN/BLU[1]	Right front door key in UNLOCK		
21	GRN/YEL[1]	Driver's door key in LOCK	Check for voltage to ground: There should be 1 V or less, as the door keylock is turned in LOCK.	• Faulty driver's door or right front door key cylinder switch • Poor ground • An open in the wire
22	GRN/WHT[2]	Right front door key in LOCK		
23	GRN/BLK	Driver's door lock knob in UNLOCK	Check for voltage to ground: There should be 1 V or less.	• Faulty driver's door lock knob switch (built in the actuator) • Poor ground • An open in the wire
24	BLU/RED[3]	Right front door lock knob in UNLOCK	Check for voltage to ground: There should be 1 V or less.	• Faulty right front door lock knob switch (built in the actuator) • Poor ground • An open in the wire
25	RED/BLU	Left rear door lock knob in UNLOCK	Check for voltage to ground: There should be 1 V or less.	• Faulty left rear door lock knob switch (built in the actuator) • Poor ground • An open in the wire
26	RED/BLU[1]	Right rear door lock knob in UNLOCK	Check for voltage to ground: There should be 1 V or less.	• Faulty right rear door lock knob switch (built in the actuator) • Poor ground • An open in the wire

93B82124   Courtesy of American Honda Motor Co., Inc.

Fig. 4: Security Control Module Input Test (Legend Sedan – 2 Of 2)

Vigor – Remove glove box. Disconnect security system control module 12-pin and 18-pin connectors. Inspect connectors to ensure terminals are making good contact. If terminals are bent, loose or corroded, repair as necessary and recheck system. If terminals are okay, remove fuse No. 37 (15-amp) from under-hood fuse block. Using a Digital Volt/Ohmmeter, perform SECURITY CONTROL MODULE INPUT TEST. See Figs. 5 and 6. If input test is okay, replace control module. When test is complete, install fuse No. 37 (15-amp) in under-hood fuse block.

DOOR KEY CYLINDER SWITCH

Remove driver's door panel. Disconnect door latch assembly 8-pin connector. Check continuity between terminals listed in DOOR KEY CYLINDER SWITCH TEST table. See Fig. 7. If continuity is not as specified in table, replace door latch assembly.

DOOR KEY CYLINDER SWITCH TEST

Position	Terminals	Continuity
Lock	2 & 3	Yes
Unlock	1 & 2	Yes

FRONT PASSENGER'S DOOR LOCK KNOB SWITCH

Remove passenger's door panel. Disconnect door latch assembly 8-pin connector. Check continuity between terminals listed in FRONT PASSENGER'S DOOR LOCK KNOB SWITCH TEST table. See Fig. 7. If continuity is not as specified in table, replace door latch assembly.

FRONT PASSENGER'S DOOR LOCK KNOB SWITCH TEST

Position	Terminals	Continuity
Lock	4 & 5	Yes
Unlock	4 & 5	No

HOOD SWITCH

Open hood. Disconnect hood switch 2-pin connector. Check continuity between hood switch 2-pin connector. Continuity should exist with hood switch lever released (hood open). Continuity should not exist with hood switch lever pushed down (hood closed). If continuity is not as specified, replace hood switch assembly.

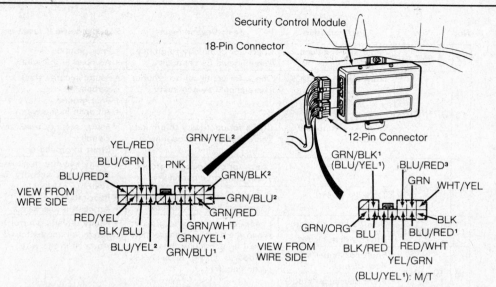

No.	Wire	Test condition	Test: Desired result	Possible cause if result is not obtained
1	BLK	Under all conditions.	Check for continuity to ground: There should have continuity.	• Poor ground • An open in the wire.
2	WHT/YEL	Under all conditions.	Check for voltage to ground: There should be battery voltage.	• Blown No. 30 (20 A) fuse (in the under-hood fuse/relay box). • An open in the wire.
3	GRN	Ignition switch ON.	Connect to ground: Security indicator should come on.	• Blown No. 30 (20 A) fuse (in the under-hood fuse/relay box). • Faulty security indicator. • An open in the wire.
4	BLK/RED	Ignition switch ON.	Check for voltage to ground: There should be battery voltage.	• Blown No.4 (7.5 A) fuse (in the under-dash fuse/relay box). • An open in the wire.
5	YEL/GRN	Ignition switch at START.	Check for voltage to ground: There should be battery voltage.	• Fualty starter cut relay. • An open in the wire.
6	BLU/RED³	Under all conditions.	Connect to ground: All horns should sond.	• Blown No. 30 (20 A) fuse (in the under-hood fuse/relay box). • Faulty horn relay. • Either horn faulty. • Poor ground • An open in the wire.
7	BLU/RED¹	Under all conditions.	Connect to ground: Headlights should come on.	• Faulty headlight relay. • Faulty headlight system. • An open in the wire.
8	RED/WHT	Under all conditions.	Connect to ground: taillights shoud come on.	• Faulty taillight relay. • Faulty taillight system. • An open in the wire.
9	GRN/BLK (BLU/YEL²)	Ignition switch On and; (M/T): clutch pedal pushed (A/T): A/T gear position P .	Check for continuity to ground: There should be continuity.	• Faulty clutch interlock switch (M/T) • Faulty A/T gear position switch (A/T). • An open in the wire.
10	YEL/RED	Hood open.	Check for continuity to ground: There should be continuity.	• Faulty hood switch (Misadjusted hood switch). • Poor ground • An open in the wire.
		Hood closed.	Check for continuity to ground: There should be no continuity.	
11	BLU	Ignition key is inserted into the ignition switch.	Check for continuity to ground: There should be continutiy.	• Faulty ignition key switch. • Poor ground • An open in the wire.
		Ignition key is removed from the ignition switch.	Check for continuity to ground: There should be no continuity.	

93E82119

Courtesy of American Honda Motor Co., Inc.

Fig. 5: Security Control Module Input Test (Vigor – 1 Of 2)

1993 ACCESSORIES & EQUIPMENT
Anti-Theft System (Cont.)

No.	Wire	Test condition	Test: Desired result	Possible cause if result is not obtained
12	PNK	Under all conditions.	Check for continuity to ground: There should be continuity.	• Poor ground • An open in the wire.
13	GRN/ORG	Trunk key in UNLOCK.	Check for continuity to ground: There should be continuity.	• Faulty security trunk key cylinder swtich. • Poor ground • An open in the wire.
		Trunk key in neutral position.	Check for continuity to ground: There should be no continuity.	• Faulty security trunk key cylinder switch. • Short to ground.
14	BLU/GRN	Trunk lid open.	Check for continuity to ground: There should be continuity.	• Faulty security trunk latch switch. (Misadjusted security trunk latch switch). • Poor ground • An open in the wire.
		Trunk lid closed.	Check for continuity to ground: There should be no continuity.	
15	GRN/BLU[2]	Driver's door opened.	Check for continuity to ground: When the door is opened, there should be continuity, and when the door is closed, there should be no continuity.	• Faulty driver's door or front passenger's door switches. • An open in the wire.
		Driver's door closed.		
16	GRN/RED	Front passenger's front door opened.		
		Front passenger's door closed.		
17	GRN/YEL[1]	Left rear door opened.	Check for continuity to ground: When the door is opened, there should be continuity, and when the door is closed, there should be no continuity.	• Faulty left rear door or right rear door switches. • An open in the wire.
		Left rear door closed.		
18	GRN/WHT	Right rear door opened.		
		Right rear door closed.		
19	GRN/BLK[2]	Driver's door key in UNLOCK.	Check for continuity to ground: There should be continuity.	• Faulty driver's door or front passenger's door key switches. • Poor ground • An open in the wire.
20	GRN/TEL[2]	Front passenger's front door key in UNLOCK.		
21	GRN/BLU[1]	Driver's door key in LOCK.	Check for continuity to ground: There should be continuity, as the door keylock is turned in LOCK.	• Faulty driver's door or front passenge's door key switches. • Poor ground • An open in the wire.
		Front passenger's front door key in LOCK.		
22	BLU/RED[2]	Driver's door lock knob in UNLOCK.	Check for continuity to ground: There should be continuity.	• Faulty driver's door lock knob switch (Built in the actuator). • Poor ground • An open in the wire.
23	BLU/YEL[2]	Front passenger's front door lock knob in UNLOCK.	Check for continuity to ground: There should be continuity.	• Faulty front passenger's door lock knob switch (Built in the actuator). • Poor ground • An open in the wire.
24	RED/YEL	Left rear door lock knob in UNLOCK.	Check for continuity to ground: There should be continuity.	• Faulty left rear door lock knob switch (Built in the actuator). • Poor ground • An open in the wire.
25	BLK/BLU	Right rear door lock knob in UNLOCK.	Check for continuity to ground: There should be continuity.	• Faulty right rear door lock knob switch (Built in the actuator). • Poor ground • An open in the wire.

(BLU/YEL[1]): M/T

93H82120

Courtesy of American Honda Motor Co., Inc.

Fig. 6: Security Control Module Input Test (Vigor – 2 Of 2)

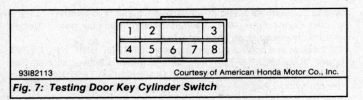

93I82113   Courtesy of American Honda Motor Co., Inc.

Fig. 7: Testing Door Key Cylinder Switch

REAR DOOR LOCK KNOB SWITCH

Remove rear door panel. Disconnect door latch assembly 4-pin connector. Check continuity between terminals listed in REAR DOOR LOCK KNOB SWITCH TEST table. *See Fig. 8.* If continuity is not as specified in table, replace door latch assembly.

REAR DOOR LOCK KNOB SWITCH TEST

Position	Terminals	Continuity
Lock	4 & 5	No
Unlock	4 & 5	Yes

93A82115   Courtesy of American Honda Motor Co., Inc.

Fig. 8: Testing Rear Door Lock Knob Switch

SECURITY INDICATOR LIGHT (LED)

Remove door panel. Remove screw from security indicator light. Apply battery positive to security indicator light 2-pin connector terminal "A" and battery negative to security indicator light 2-pin connector terminal "B". *See Fig. 9.* Indicator light should turn on. If indicator light does not turn on, replace security light assembly.

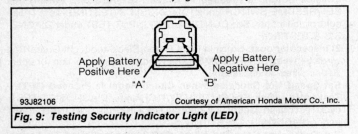

Apply Battery Positive Here "A"   Apply Battery Negative Here "B"

93J82106   Courtesy of American Honda Motor Co., Inc.

Fig. 9: Testing Security Indicator Light (LED)

TRUNK KEY CYLINDER SWITCH

Open trunk and remove trunk rear trim panel. Disconnect trunk key cylinder switch 2-pin connector. Check continuity between trunk key cylinder switch 2-pin connector terminals "A" and "B". *See Fig. 10.* Continuity should exist with trunk key lock is turned to UNLOCK position. Continuity should not exist when key lock is released. If switch does not operate as specified, replace trunk key cylinder switch assembly.

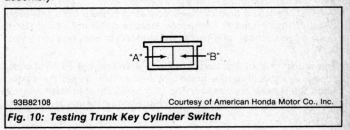

"A"   "B"

93B82108   Courtesy of American Honda Motor Co., Inc.

Fig. 10: Testing Trunk Key Cylinder Switch

TRUNK LATCH SWITCH

Open trunk and remove trunk rear trim panel. Disconnect trunk latch switch 6-pin connector. Check continuity between trunk latch switch 6-pin connector terminals "A" and "B". *See Fig. 11.* Continuity should exist with trunk lid open. Continuity should not exist with trunk latch in closed position (trunk lid closed). If switch does not operate as specified, replace trunk latch switch assembly.

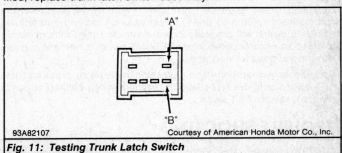

"A"

"B"

93A82107   Courtesy of American Honda Motor Co., Inc.

Fig. 11: Testing Trunk Latch Switch

Open trunk and remove trunk rear trim panel. Disconnect trunk latch switch 2-pin connector. Check continuity between trunk latch switch 2-pin connector terminals. Continuity should exist with trunk lid open. Continuity should not exist with trunk latch in closed position (trunk lid closed). If switch does not operate as specified, replace trunk latch switch assembly.

WIRING DIAGRAMS

See appropriate chassis wiring diagram in WIRING DIAGRAMS.

1993 ACCESSORIES & EQUIPMENT
Cruise Control Systems

Integra, Legend, Vigor

DESCRIPTION

The cruise control unit receives command signals from cruise control main switch and cruise control SET/RESUME or SET/RESUME/CANCEL switch. It also receives operating signals from brakelight switch, Programmed Fuel Injection Electronic Control Unit (PGM-FI ECU), speed sensor, and clutch switch (M/T) or shift position switch (A/T).

The cruise control unit compares actual vehicle speed to selected speed. A signal from the brakelight switch disengages the system when the brakes are applied. The clutch switch, shift lever position switch, and cancel switch also send disengage signals to the cruise control unit.

OPERATION

The cruise control system maintains any speed greater than 30 MPH. To set, press SET switch at desired speed. Pressing main switch to off will cancel cruise control system operation and erase vehicle speed from memory.

If system is disengaged temporarily by brakelight switch, clutch switch, or shift lever position switch, press RESUME switch. With RESUME switch pressed and speed memory retained, vehicle automatically returns to previous set speed. Pressing and holding RESUME switch will gradually increase vehicle speed without having to press accelerator pedal. When RESUME switch is released, system is reprogrammed for new speed.

For gradual deceleration without pressing brake pedal, press and hold SET switch until desired speed is reached. When desired speed is reached, release SET switch.

TROUBLE SHOOTING

CAUTION: Legend and Vigor are equipped with Supplemental Restraint System (SRS). SRS wiring harness is routed close to instrument cluster, steering wheel, and related components. All SRS wiring harnesses are covered by Yellow outer insulation. DO NOT use electrical test equipment on these circuits. Before working on steering column components, disable air bag system. See AIR BAG RESTRAINT SYSTEM article in ACCESSORIES & EQUIPMENT.

INTEGRA

Preliminary Checks – Before trouble shooting by symptom, ensure fuses No. 23 and No. 24 located in underdash fuse box are okay. Also check fuses No. 30, No. 32, and No. 37, located in underhood main fuse box. Replace fuses as necessary. Ensure horn and tachometer operate properly.

NOTE: When diagnosing vehicle by symptom, check possible failures in the order given.

Cruise Control Cannot Be Set – **1)** Check ground connection G301, located in left side of engine compartment next to windshield washer fluid reservoir. Check ground connection G401, located behind left kick panel. Check cruise control unit inputs. See CONTROL UNIT INPUT TEST under DIAGNOSIS & TESTING. Test main switch. See MAIN SWITCH under DIAGNOSIS & TESTING.
2) Test SET/RESUME switch. See SET/RESUME SWITCH under DIAGNOSIS & TESTING. Test brakelight switch. See BRAKELIGHT SWITCH under DIAGNOSIS & TESTING. Test clutch switch on M/T vehicles. See CLUTCH SWITCH under DIAGNOSIS & TESTING. Test shift lever position switch on A/T vehicles. See SHIFT LEVER POSITION SWITCH under DIAGNOSIS & TESTING.
3) Inspect the Black/Yellow wire between underdash fuse No. 24 and cruise control unit, and Light Green wire between main switch, cruise control unit, and brakelight switch. Repair wires as necessary.
Cruise Control Can Be Set, But Indicator Light Does Not Come On – **1)** Check for defective cruise control indicator bulb. Replace as necessary. Check ground connection G301, located at left side of

engine compartment next to windshield washer fluid reservoir. Check ground connection G401, located behind left kick panel. Repair ground connections as necessary.
2) Check cruise control unit inputs. See CONTROL UNIT INPUT TEST under DIAGNOSIS & TESTING. Check gauge dimming circuit. See DIMMER CONTROL CIRCUIT under DIAGNOSIS & TESTING. Inspect the following wires for open circuit: Yellow wire between underdash fuse No. 23 and gauge dimming circuit, and Red wire between gauge dimming circuit and cruise control unit. Repair as necessary.
Cruise Speed Noticeably Higher Or Lower Than Setting – **1)** Check vehicle speed sensor and speedometer cable. See VEHICLE SPEED SENSOR (VSS) in INSTRUMENT PANELS article. Ensure speedometer cable does not bind when rotated.
2) Test actuator assembly and cable free play. See ACTUATOR ASSEMBLY under DIAGNOSIS & TESTING and ACTUATOR CABLE under ADJUSTMENTS. Test cruise control unit inputs. See CONTROL UNIT INPUT TEST under DIAGNOSIS & TESTING.
Excessive Hunting When Trying To Achieve Set Speed – **1)** Test actuator assembly. See ACTUATOR ASSEMBLY under DIAGNOSIS & TESTING. Test vehicle speed sensor and speedometer cable. See VEHICLE SPEED SENSOR (VSS) in INSTRUMENT PANELS article.
2) Ensure speedometer cable does not bind when rotated. Test cruise control unit inputs. See CONTROL UNIT INPUT TEST under DIAGNOSIS & TESTING.
Steady Speed Not Held, Even On Flat Road – **1)** Test vehicle speed sensor and speedometer cable. See VEHICLE SPEED SENSOR (VSS) in INSTRUMENT PANELS article. Ensure speedometer cable does not bind when rotated.
2) Test actuator assembly. See ACTUATOR ASSEMBLY under DIAGNOSIS & TESTING. Test cruise control unit inputs. See CONTROL UNIT INPUT TEST under DIAGNOSIS & TESTING.
Car Does Not Decelerate Or Accelerate Accordingly When Set Or Resume Button Is Pressed – **1)** Test SET/RESUME switch. See SET/RESUME SWITCH under DIAGNOSIS & TESTING. Test cruise control unit inputs. See CONTROL UNIT INPUT TEST under DIAGNOSIS & TESTING.
2) Inspect for open cirucit in Light Green/Black and Light Green/Red wires between SET/RESUME switch and cruise control unit for open. Repair wires as necessary.
Set Speed Not Canceled When Clutch Pedal Is Pressed (M/T) – Test clutch switch. See CLUTCH SWITCH under DIAGNOSIS & TESTING. Test cruise control unit inputs. See CONTROL UNIT INPUT TEST under DIAGNOSIS & TESTING.
Set Speed Not Canceled When Shift Lever Is Moved To Neutral (A/T) – Test shift lever position switch. See SHIFT LEVER POSITION SWITCH under DIAGNOSIS & TESTING. Test cruise control unit inputs. See CONTROL UNIT INPUT TEST under DIAGNOSIS & TESTING.
Set Speed Not Canceled When Brake Pedal Is Pressed – Test brakelight switch. See BRAKELIGHT SWITCH under DIAGNOSIS & TESTING. Test cruise control unit inputs. See CONTROL UNIT INPUT TEST under DIAGNOSIS & TESTING.
Set Speed Not Canceled When Main Switch Is Turned Off – Test main switch. See MAIN SWITCH under DIAGNOSIS & TESTING. Test cruise control unit inputs. See CONTROL UNIT INPUT TEST under DIAGNOSIS & TESTING.
Set Speed Not Resumed When Resume Button Is Pressed With Main Switch On, But Set Speed Temporarily Canceled – **1)** Test SET/RESUME switch. See SET/RESUME SWITCH under DIAGNOSIS & TESTING. Test cruise control unit inputs. See CONTROL UNIT INPUT TEST under DIAGNOSIS & TESTING.
2) Inspect for open circuit in Light Green/Black and Light Green/Red wires between SET/RESUME switch and cruise control unit. Repair wires as necessary.

LEGEND

Preliminary Tests – Before trouble shooting by symptom, ensure fuses No. 13 and No. 20, located in underdash fuse box are okay. Also check fuses No. 35 and No. 39, located in underhood main fuse box. Replace fuses as necessary. Ensure horn and tachometer operate properly.

Cruise Control Cannot Be Set – 1) Check ground connection G152, located at left front corner of engine compartment. Check ground connection G251, located at base of left "B" pillar. Check ground connection G301, located behind left kick panel. Check ground connection G304, located at base of right "B" pillar. Repair ground connections as necessary. Check cruise control unit inputs. See CONTROL UNIT INPUT TEST under DIAGNOSIS & TESTING. Test main switch. See MAIN SWITCH under DIAGNOSIS & TESTING.

2) Test SET/RESUME/CANCEL switch. See SET/RESUME/CANCEL SWITCH under DIAGNOSIS & TESTING. Test brakelight switch. See BRAKELIGHT SWITCH under DIAGNOSIS & TESTING. Test clutch switch on M/T vehicles. See CLUTCH SWITCH under DIAGNOSIS & TESTING. Test shift lever position switch on A/T vehicles. See SHIFT LEVER POSITION SWITCH under DIAGNOSIS & TESTING.

3) Inspect the following wires for open circuit. Repair wires as necessary.
- Blue/Red wire between horns and SET/RESUME/CANCEL switch.
- Light Green/Red wire between SET/RESUME/CANCEL switch and cruise control unit.
- Blue wire between ignition system and cruise control unit.
- Yellow wire between underdash fuse No. 13 and dimming circuit for gauges.
- Black/Red wire between underdash fuse No. 20 and main switch (1991 only).
- Black/Red wire between underdash fuse No. 20, main switch, and cruise control unit connector.
- Light Green wire between main switch, brakelight switch, and cruise control unit.
- Gray wire between brakelight switch and cruise control unit.
- Brown wire between actuator assembly and cruise control unit.
- Brown/Black wire between actuator assembly and cruise control unit.
- Brown/White wire between actuator assembly and cruise control unit.
- Pink wire between clutch switch (M/T) or shift lever position switch (A/T) and cruise control unit.
- Yellow/Red wire between speed sensor and cruise control unit.

Cruise Control Can Be Set, But Indicator Light Does Not Come On – 1) Check for defective cruise control indicator bulb. Replace as necessary. Check ground connection G251, located at base of left "B" pillar. Check ground connection G301, located behind left kick panel. Repair ground connections as necessary.

2) Check cruise control unit inputs. See CONTROL UNIT INPUT TEST under DIAGNOSIS & TESTING. Check dimming circuit for gauges. See DIMMER CONTROL CIRCUIT under DIAGNOSIS & TESTING. Inspect the following wires for open circuit: Yellow wire between underdash fuse No. 13 and dimming circuit for gauges, and Blue/Black wire between dimming circuit for gauges and cruise control unit connector. Repair wires as necessary.

Cruise Speed Noticeably Higher Or Lower Than Setting – 1) Check for tachometer signal on cruise control unit connector (Blue wire). If tachometer signal exists, go to next step. If tachometer signal does not exist, check Blue wire for an open or short. Repair as necessary. If Blue wire is not open or shorted, check for tachometer signal. Repair as necessary.

2) Test actuator assembly. See ACTUATOR ASSEMBLY under DIAGNOSIS & TESTING. Check cruise control unit inputs. See CONTROL UNIT INPUT TEST under DIAGNOSIS & TESTING.

Excessive Hunting When Trying To Achieve Set Speed – 1) Test actuator assembly. See ACTUATOR ASSEMBLY under DIAGNOSIS & TESTING. Check for tachometer signal on cruise control unit connector (Blue wire). If tachometer signal exists, test cruise control unit inputs. See CONTROL UNIT INPUT TEST under DIAGNOSIS & TESTING.

2) If tachometer signal does not exist, check Blue wire for an open or short. Repair as necessary. If Blue wire is not open or shorted, check for ignition system failure (no tachometer signal). Repair as necessary.

Steady Speed Not Held, Even On Flat Road – 1) Check for tachometer signal on cruise control unit connector (Blue wire). If tachometer

signal exists, go to next step. If tachometer signal does not exist, check Blue wire for an open or short. Repair as necessary. If Blue wire is not open or shorted, check for ignition system failure (no tachometer signal). Repair as necessary.

2) Test actuator assembly. See ACTUATOR ASSEMBLY under DIAGNOSIS & TESTING. Test cruise control unit inputs. See CONTROL UNIT INPUT TEST under DIAGNOSIS & TESTING.

Car Does Not Decelerate Or Accelerate Accordingly When Set Or Resume Button Is Pressed – 1) Test SET/RESUME/CANCEL switch. See SET/RESUME/CANCEL SWITCH under DIAGNOSIS & TESTING. Test cruise control unit inputs. See CONTROL UNIT INPUT TEST under DIAGNOSIS & TESTING.

2) Inspect the following wires for open circuit: Light Green/Black wire between SET/RESUME/CANCEL switch and cruise control unit, and Light Green/Red wire between SET/RESUME/CANCEL switch and cruise control unit. Repair wires as necessary.

Set Speed Not Canceled When Clutch Pedal Is Pressed (M/T) – Test clutch switch. See CLUTCH SWITCH under DIAGNOSIS & TESTING. Test cruise control unit inputs. See CONTROL UNIT INPUT TEST under DIAGNOSIS & TESTING.

Set Speed Not Canceled When Shift Lever Is Set To Neutral (A/T) – Test shift lever position switch. See SHIFT LEVER POSITION SWITCH under DIAGNOSIS & TESTING. Test cruise control unit inputs. See CONTROL UNIT INPUT TEST under DIAGNOSIS & TESTING.

Set Speed Not Canceled When Brake Pedal Is Pressed – Test brakelight switch. See BRAKELIGHT SWITCH under DIAGNOSIS & TESTING. Test cruise control unit inputs. See CONTROL UNIT INPUT TEST under DIAGNOSIS & TESTING.

Set Speed Not Canceled When Main Switch Is Turned Off – Test main switch. See MAIN SWITCH under DIAGNOSIS & TESTING. Test cruise control unit inputs. See CONTROL UNIT INPUT TEST under DIAGNOSIS & TESTING.

Set Speed Not Resumed When Resume Button Is Pressed, But Set Speed Temporarily Canceled – Test SET/RESUME/CANCEL switch. See SET/RESUME/CANCEL SWITCH under DIAGNOSIS & TESTING. Test cruise control unit inputs. See CONTROL UNIT INPUT TEST under DIAGNOSIS & TESTING.

VIGOR

Preliminary Tests – Before trouble shooting by symptom, ensure fuses No. 1 and No. 4, located in underdash fuse box are okay. Also check fuses No. 15, No. 18, and No. 30, located in underhood main fuse box. Replace fuses as necessary. Ensure horn and tachometer operate properly.

Cruise Control Cannot Be Set – 1) Check ground connection G401, located behind left kick panel. Check ground connection G251, located at base of left "B" pillar. Check ground connection G402, located behind right kick panel. Repair ground connections as necessary. Check cruise control unit inputs. See CONTROL UNIT INPUT TEST under DIAGNOSIS & TESTING. Test main switch. See MAIN SWITCH under DIAGNOSIS & TESTING.

2) Test SET/RESUME/CANCEL switch. See SET/RESUME/CANCEL SWITCH under DIAGNOSIS & TESTING. Test brakelight switch. See BRAKELIGHT SWITCH under DIAGNOSIS & TESTING. Test clutch switch on M/T vehicles. See CLUTCH SWITCH under DIAGNOSIS & TESTING. Test shift lever position switch on A/T vehicles. See SHIFT LEVER POSITION SWITCH under DIAGNOSIS & TESTING.

3) Inspect the following wires for open circuit. Repair wires as necessary.
- Blue/Red wire between horns and SET/RESUME/CANCEL switch.
- Light Green/Red wire between SET/RESUME/CANCEL switch and cruise control unit.
- Blue wire between ignition system and cruise control unit.
- Black/Red wire between underdash fuse No. 4 and main switch.
- Light Green wire between main switch, brakelight switch, and cruise control unit.
- Gray wire between brakelight switch and cruise control unit.
- Orange wire between vehicle speed sensor and cruise control unit.

- Brown wire between actuator assembly and cruise control unit.
- Black wire between actuator assembly and ground.
- Brown/Black wire between actuator assembly and cruise control unit.
- Brown/White wire between actuator assembly and cruise control unit.
- Pink wire between clutch switch (M/T) or shift lever position switch (A/T) and cruise control unit.

Cruise Control Can Be Set, But Indicator Light Does Not Come On –
1) Check for defective cruise control indicator bulb. Replace as necessary. Check ground connection G401, located behind left kick panel. Check ground connection G402, located behind right kick panel. Repair ground connections as necessary.
2) Check cruise control unit inputs. See CONTROL UNIT INPUT TEST under DIAGNOSIS & TESTING. Check gauge dimming circuit. See DIMMER CONTROL CIRCUIT under DIAGNOSIS & TESTING. Inspect the following wires for open circuit: Yellow wire between underdash fuse No. 1 and gauge dimming circuit, and Redwire between gauge dimming circuit for gauges and cruise control unit. Repair wires as necessary.

Cruise Speed Noticeably Higher Or Lower Than Setting – **1)** Check for signal on Orange wire from vehicle speed sensor. If signal exists, go to next step. If signal does not exist, check Orange wire for an open or short. Repair as necessary. If Orange wire is not open or shorted, check vehicle speed sensor. Repair as necessary.
2) Test actuator assembly. See ACTUATOR ASSEMBLY under DIAGNOSIS & TESTING. Check cruise control unit inputs. See CONTROL UNIT INPUT TEST under DIAGNOSIS & TESTING.

Excessive Hunting When Trying To Achieve Set Speed – **1)** Test actuator assembly. See ACTUATOR ASSEMBLY under DIAGNOSIS & TESTING. Check for signal from vehicle speed sensor (VSS) at cruise control unit connector (Orange wire). If signal exists, test cruise control unit inputs. See CONTROL UNIT INPUT TEST under DIAGNOSIS & TESTING.
2) If VSS signal does not exist, check Orange wire for an open or short. Repair as necessary. If Orange wire is not open or shorted, check VSS. See VEHICLE SPEED SENSOR (VSS) in INSTRUMENT PANELS article. Repair as necessary.

Steady Speed Not Held, Even On Flat Road – **1)** Check for signal from vehicle speed sensor (VSS) at cruise control unit (Orange wire). If signal exists, go to next step. If signal does not exist, check Orange wire for an open or short. Repair as necessary. If Orange wire is not open or shorted, check for VSS system failure. See VEHICLE SPEED SENSOR (VSS) in INSTRUMENT PANELS article. Repair as necessary.
2) Test actuator assembly. See ACTUATOR ASSEMBLY under DIAGNOSIS & TESTING. Test cruise control unit inputs. See CONTROL UNIT INPUT TEST under DIAGNOSIS & TESTING.

Car Does Not Decelerate Or Accelerate Accordingly When Set Or Resume Button Is Pressed – **1)** Test SET/RESUME/CANCEL switch. See SET/RESUME/CANCEL SWITCH under DIAGNOSIS & TESTING. Test cruise control unit inputs. See CONTROL UNIT INPUT TEST under DIAGNOSIS & TESTING.
2) Inspect the following wires for open circuit: Light Green/Black wire between SET/RESUME/CANCEL switch and cruise control unit, and Light Green/Red wire between SET/RESUME/CANCEL switch and cruise control unit.

Set Speed Not Canceled When Clutch Pedal Is Pressed (M/T) – Test clutch switch. See CLUTCH SWITCH under DIAGNOSIS & TESTING. Test cruise control unit inputs. See CONTROL UNIT INPUT TEST under DIAGNOSIS & TESTING.

Set Speed Not Canceled When Shift Lever Is Set To Neutral (A/T) – Test shift lever position switch. See SHIFT LEVER POSITION SWITCH under DIAGNOSIS & TESTING. Test cruise control unit inputs. See CONTROL UNIT INPUT TEST under DIAGNOSIS & TESTING.

Set Speed Not Canceled When Brake Pedal Is Pressed – Test brakelight switch. See BRAKELIGHT SWITCH under DIAGNOSIS & TESTING. Test cruise control unit inputs. See CONTROL UNIT INPUT TEST under DIAGNOSIS & TESTING.

Set Speed Not Canceled When Main Switch Is Turned Off – Test main switch. See MAIN SWITCH under DIAGNOSIS & TESTING. Test cruise control unit inputs. See CONTROL UNIT INPUT TEST under DIAGNOSIS & TESTING.

Set Speed Not Resumed When Resume Button Is Pressed, But Set Speed Temporarily Canceled – Test SET/RESUME/CANCEL switch. See SET/RESUME/CANCEL SWITCH under DIAGNOSIS & TESTING. Test cruise control unit inputs. See CONTROL UNIT INPUT TEST under DIAGNOSIS & TESTING.

ADJUSTMENTS

ACTUATOR CABLE

1) Ensure actuator cable operates smoothly without binding or sticking. Start and warm engine to normal operating temperature. Measure actuator rod movement before cable pulls on accelerator lever (engine speed starts to increase). This is amount of cable free play. *See Fig. 1.* See ACTUATOR CABLE FREE PLAY SPECIFICATIONS table.

ACTUATOR CABLE FREE PLAY SPECIFICATIONS

Application	In. (mm)
Integra & Vigor	0.37-0.49 (9.5-12.5)
Legend	0.14-0.26 (3.5-6.5)

2) If free play is not as specified, loosen lock nut and turn adjusting nut as necessary. Tighten lock nut and recheck free play. Test drive vehicle and verify actual speed is within 2 MPH of set speed. If necessary, check throttle cable free play.

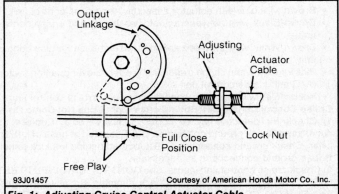

93J01457   Courtesy of American Honda Motor Co., Inc.

Fig. 1: **Adjusting Cruise Control Actuator Cable**

BRAKE PEDAL HEIGHT

1) Loosen brakelight switch lock nut. Back off switch until it no longer touches brake pedal. Loosen brake pedal push rod lock nut. Screw push rod in or out until pedal height from floor is to specification. See BRAKE PEDAL HEIGHT SPECIFICATIONS table. Tighten lock nut.
2) Screw in brakelight switch until plunger is fully pressed (threaded end touching pad on pedal arm). Back off switch 1/2 turn and tighten lock nut firmly. Ensure brakelights work when brake pedal is pressed.

BRAKE PEDAL HEIGHT SPECIFICATIONS

Application	In. (mm)
Integra	
A/T	6.3 (160)
M/T	6.1 (155)
Legend	8.4 (213)
Vigor	
A/T	7.6 (194)
M/T	7.8 (199)

CABLE REEL CENTERING

Legend & Vigor – After installing clockspring onto steering column shaft, rotate clockspring clockwise until it stops. Rotate clockspring counterclockwise about 2 turns until Yellow gear tooth aligns with mark on cover and arrow on clockspring label points straight up. *See Fig. 2.* Install steering wheel. Attach cruise control and cable reel connectors to their clips.

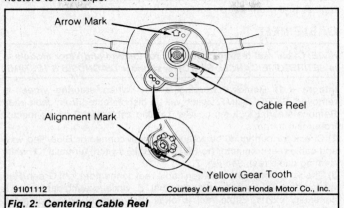

91I01112   Courtesy of American Honda Motor Co., Inc.

Fig. 2: Centering Cable Reel

CLUTCH PEDAL HEIGHT

Integra – 1) Measure clutch pedal disengagement height and pedal free play. Adjust clutch free play by turning nut on clutch cable near transmission. Ensure there is 0.16-0.20" (4-5 mm) free play at tip of release arm near transmission.

2) Turn clutch pedal switch in or out to bring clutch pedal stroke to 5.6-5.8" (142-147 mm). Tighten lock nut. Pedal height should be 7" (177 mm) from floor. Pedal height is measured from middle of pedal face (with clutch released) to floor behind clutch pedal.

Legend – 1) Loosen clutch pedal switch lock nut. Back off switch until it no longer touches clutch pedal. Loosen clutch master cylinder push rod lock nut. Rotate push rod to obtain a pedal height from floor of 7.8" (199.5 mm) and a stroke of 5.6-5.8" (142-148 mm). Pedal height is measured from middle of pedal face (with clutch released) to floor behind clutch pedal. Tighten clutch master cylinder lock nut.

2) Screw in clutch pedal switch until it contacts pedal. Rotate clutch pedal switch in an additional 1/4 - 1/2 turn. Tighten clutch pedal switch lock nut. Loosen clutch interlock switch lock nut (located behind clutch master cylinder inside vehicle). With clutch pedal fully pressed, measure clearance between clutch pedal and floor. Measure from middle of pedal face to floor behind clutch pedal. Clearance should be a minimum of 3.54" (90 mm).

3) Release clutch pedal 0.6-0.8" (15-20 mm) from fully pressed position and hold pedal at this height. Adjust position of clutch interlock switch so engine will start with clutch pedal at this position. Screw switch inward an additional 1/4 to 1/2 turn. Tighten lock nut.

Vigor – 1) Loosen clutch pedal switch (lower switch) lock nut. Back off switch until it no longer touches clutch pedal. Loosen clutch master cylinder push rod lock nut and turn push rod to obtain a pedal height from floor of 8.2" (208 mm) and a stroke of 5.5-5.9" (140-150 mm). Pedal height is measured from middle of pedal face to floor below clutch pedal. Tighten lock nut.

2) Screw in clutch pedal switch until it contacts pedal, then an additional 1/4 to 1/2 turn. Tighten lock nut. Loosen clutch interlock switch (upper switch) lock nut. With clutch pedal fully pressed, measure clearance between middle of pedal face to floor. Clearance should be a minimum of 4.6" (116 mm).

3) Release clutch pedal 0.6-0.8" (15-20 mm) from fully pressed position and hold pedal at this height. Adjust position of clutch interlock switch so engine will start with clutch pedal at this position. Screw switch in an additional 1/4 to 1/2 turn. Tighten lock nut.

SHIFT LEVER POSITION SWITCH

Integra – 1) Turn ignition off. Shift lever position switch is located on right side of shift lever mechanism. Remove front console. Unplug shift switch 10-pin connector. Ensure shift lever is in "P" position.

2) Loosen shift lever position switch mounting bolts. Slowly slide switch while checking for continuity between switch connector terminals No. 6 and 7. *See Fig. 3.*

3) If continuity does not exist, go to next step. If continuity exists, switch is adjusted properly. Tighten switch mounting bolts. Verify vehicle starts with shift lever in "P" position.

4) If continuity does not exist, inspect shift lever detent and bracket for damage. If no damage exists, replace faulty shift lever position switch.

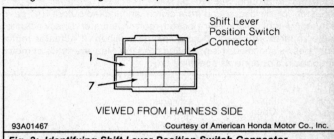

93A01467   Courtesy of American Honda Motor Co., Inc.

Fig. 3: Identifying Shift Lever Position Switch Connector Terminals (Integra)

Legend – 1) Remove front console. Shift lever position switch is located on left side of shift lever mechanism. Unplug shift lever position switch 14-pin connector.

2) Loosen 2 shift lever position switch mounting bolts. Slowly slide switch toward rear of vehicle while checking for continuity between shift lever position switch 14-pin connector terminals No. 9 and 12 *See Fig. 4.*

3) If continuity does not exist, go to next step. If continuity exists, shift lever position switch is okay. Tighten switch mounting bolts. Verify vehicle starts with shift lever in "P" position.

4) If continuity does not exist, check shift lever detent and bracket for damage. If no damage exists, replace shift lever position switch.

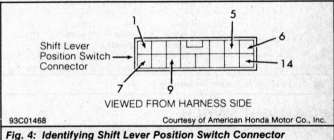

93C01468   Courtesy of American Honda Motor Co., Inc.

Fig. 4: Identifying Shift Lever Position Switch Connector Terminals (Legend)

Vigor – See SHIFT LEVER POSITION SWITCH under DIAGNOSIS AND TESTING.

DIAGNOSIS & TESTING

CAUTION: Legend and Vigor are equipped with Supplemental Restraint System (SRS). SRS wiring harness is routed close to instrument cluster, steering wheel, and related components. All SRS wiring harnesses are covered by Yellow outer insulation. DO NOT use electrical test equipment on these circuits. Before working on steering column components, disable air bag system. See AIR BAG RESTRAINT SYSTEM article in ACCESSORIES & EQUIPMENT.

WARNING: Wait about 3 minutes after disabling air bag system. Back-up power circuit maintains system voltage for about 3 minutes after battery is disconnected. Servicing air bag system before 3 minutes have elapsed may cause accidental air bag deployment and possible personal injury.

NOTE: Radio/cassette or radio/CD player contain an anti-theft protection circuit. Whenever battery is disconnected, radio goes into anti-theft mode. When battery is reconnected, radio displays CODE and is inoperative until proper code number is entered by vehicle owner.

1993 ACCESSORIES & EQUIPMENT
Cruise Control Systems (Cont.)

ACTUATOR ASSEMBLY

1) Unplug 4-pin connector at actuator. Actuator is located on left side of engine compartment. Using jumper wires, connect to terminal "D" of actuator connector to battery voltage, and terminal "A" of actuator connector to ground. *See Fig. 5.*

2) Listen for clicking sound from clutch, and locked output linkage. If actuator output linkage is not locked, replace actuator. Check actuator motor operation in each output linkage position. If actuator motor operates as specified, it is operating properly. Replace actuator motor if it does not operate as specified.

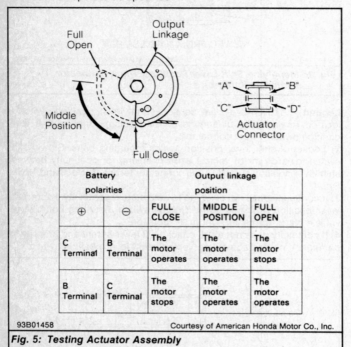

Battery polarities		Output linkage position		
$\oplus$	$\ominus$	FULL CLOSE	MIDDLE POSITION	FULL OPEN
C Terminal	B Terminal	The motor operates	The motor operates	The motor stops
B Terminal	C Terminal	The motor stops	The motor operates	The motor operates

93B01458   Courtesy of American Honda Motor Co., Inc.

Fig. 5: Testing Actuator Assembly

BRAKELIGHT SWITCH

Integra – 1) Unplug connector from brakelight switch. Check for continuity between brakelight switch terminals "A" and "B". *See Fig. 6.* Continuity should exist. Check for continuity between brakelight switch terminals "C" and "D". Continuity should not exist.

2) Press and hold brake pedal. Check for continuity between switch terminals "C" and "D". Continuity should exist. Check for continuity between switch terminals "A" and "B". Continuity should not exist. If switch continuity is not as specified, check brake pedal height. See BRAKE PEDAL HEIGHT under ADJUSTMENTS. If brake pedal height is okay, replace brakelight switch.

Legend & Vigor – 1) Unplug connector from brakelight switch. Check for continuity between switch terminals "A" and "D". *See Fig. 6.* Continuity should exist. Check for continuity between switch terminals "B" and "C". Continuity should not exist.

2) Press and hold brake pedal. Check for continuity between switch terminals "A" and "D". Continuity should not exist. Check for continuity

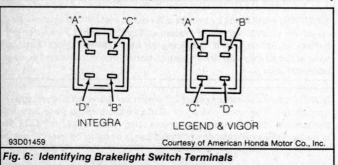

93D01459   Courtesy of American Honda Motor Co., Inc.

Fig. 6: Identifying Brakelight Switch Terminals

between switch terminals "B" and "C". Continuity should exist. If switch continuity is not as specified, check brake pedal height. See BRAKE PEDAL HEIGHT under ADJUSTMENTS. If brake pedal height is okay, replace brakelight switch.

CABLE REEL

NOTE: *Cable reel testing procedure for Legend and Vigor models is in SET/RESUME/CANCEL SWITCH test under DIAGNOSIS & TESTING.*

Integra – 1) Remove steering wheel. When steering wheel is removed, SET/RESUME switch will be disconnected from cable reel. Remove steering column covers. Unplug cable reel 3-pin connector from main harness.

2) Check for continuity between cable reel connector Blue/Red wire and cable reel connector (to SET/RESUME switch) terminal "D" while rotating cable reel. *See Fig. 7.*

3) Check for continuity between cable reel connector Light Green/Red wire and cable reel connector terminal "E" while rotating cable reel. If continuity exists, cable reel is okay. If continuity does not exist, replace cable reel.

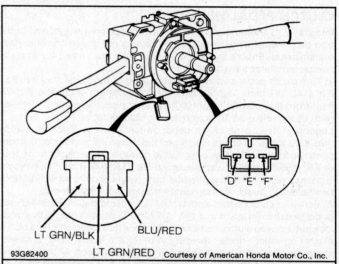

93G82400   Courtesy of American Honda Motor Co., Inc.

Fig. 7: Identifying Cable Reel Connectors & Terminals (Integra)

CLUTCH SWITCH

Unplug connector from clutch switch. Check for continuity between clutch switch terminals. Continuity should exist. Press and hold clutch pedal. Check for continuity between clutch switch terminals. Continuity should not exist. If switch continuity is not as specified, check clutch pedal height. See CLUTCH PEDAL HEIGHT under ADJUSTMENTS. If clutch pedal height is okay, replace clutch pedal switch.

DIMMER CONTROL CIRCUIT

Integra – 1) Turn ignition off. Remove lower dashboard cover. From behind dashboard, push out dimmer switch from dashboard. Unplug dimmer switch connector.

2) Check for continuity between dimmer switch connector Black wire and ground. Continuity should exist. If continuity exists, go to next step. If continuity does not exist, repair open in Black wire or poor ground connection G301, located at left side of engine compartment next to windshield washer fluid reservoir, or ground connection G401, located behind left kick panel.

3) With headlight switch on, check for battery voltage between dimmer switch connector Red/Black wire and ground. If battery voltage exists, go to next step. If battery voltage does not exist, replace blown fuse No. 11, replace headlight switch, or repair open circuit in Red/Black wire.

4) With headlight switch on, use a jumper wire to ground dimmer switch connector Red wire. If instrument lights come on, dimmer switch circuits are okay. Replace dimmer switch. If instrument lights do not come on, repair open circuit in Red/Black wire or Red wire from dimmer switch connector.

Legend – 1) Turn ignition off. Remove 2 screws from instrument cluster bezel. Pull out instrument cluster bezel far enough to unplug electrical connectors (one on left side and 2 on right side). Remove instrument cluster bezel.

2) Measure resistance between dimmer switch terminals "A" and "B" while rotating dimmer dial. *See Fig. 8.* Resistance should vary between zero and 24,000 ohms. If resistance is within specification, go to next step. If resistance is not within specification, replace dimmer switch.

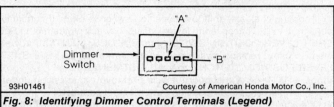

93H01461　　　　　Courtesy of American Honda Motor Co., Inc.

Fig. 8: Identifying Dimmer Control Terminals (Legend)

3) Unplug dashlight brightness control unit 7-pin connector, located behind left side of radio. *See Fig. 9.* Check for continuity between connector Black wire and ground. If continuity exists, go to next step. If continuity does not exist, repair open in Black wire or poor ground connection G251, located at base of left "B" pillar.

4) With headlight switch on, check for battery voltage between 7-pin connector Red/Black wire and ground. If battery voltage exists, go to next step. If battery voltage does not exist, replace blown fuse No. 49, faulty taillight relay, faulty headlight switch, or open circuit in Red/Black wire.

5) With headlight switch on, use a jumper wire to ground 7-pin connector Red wire. If instrument lights come on, go to next step. If instrument lights do not come on, repair open circuit in Red/Black wire or Red wire from 7-pin connector.

6) Measure resistance between 7-pin connector Red/Green wire and Red/Blue wire. Resistance should vary between zero and 24,000 ohms when dimmer control dial is rotated. If resistance is within specification, go to next step. If resistance is not within specification, repair open circuit in Red/Green or Red/Blue wire or replace faulty dashlight brightness control unit.

7) Inspect connection between 7-pin connector and dashlight brightness control unit. If connection is okay, temporarily substitute known good brightness control unit. Check operation of cruise control indicator light.

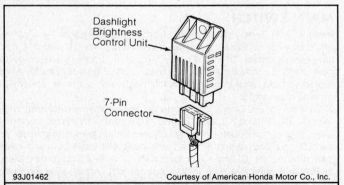

93J01462　　　　　Courtesy of American Honda Motor Co., Inc.

Fig. 9: Dashlight Dimmer Control (Legend)

SET/RESUME SWITCH

Integra – 1) Remove steering wheel. Unplug SET/RESUME switch connector from cable reel. Check for continuity between SET/RESUME switch connector terminals "A" and "C" with SET pressed. *See Fig. 10.* If continuity exists, go to next step. If continuity does not exist, replace SET/RESUME switch. See SET/RESUME SWITCH under REMOVAL & INSTALLATION.

2) Check for continuity between SET/RESUME switch connector terminals "B" and "C" with RESUME pressed. If continuity exists, SET/

RESUME switch is okay. If continuity does not exist, replace SET/RESUME switch. See SET/RESUME SWITCH under REMOVAL & INSTALLATION.

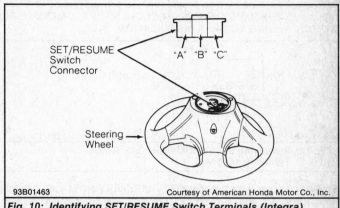

93B01463　　　　　Courtesy of American Honda Motor Co., Inc.

Fig. 10: Identifying SET/RESUME Switch Terminals (Integra)

SET/RESUME/CANCEL SWITCH

NOTE: This test procedure also tests cable reel in steering column.

Legend & Vigor – 1) Disable air bag system. See AIR BAG RESTRAINT SYSTEM article in ACCESSORIES & EQUIPMENT. Connect SRS Test Harness "C" (07MAZ-SP00600) to cable reel 7-pin connector. Check for continuity between SRS Test Harness "C" connector terminal No. 2 (Light Green/Red wire on cable reel harness) and terminal No. 3 (Blue/Red wire on cable reel harness) with SET pressed. *See Fig. 11.* If continuity exists, go to next step. If continuity does not exist, go to step **4)**.

2) Check for continuity between SRS Test Harness "C" connector terminal No. 1 (Light Green/Black wire on cable reel harness) and terminal No. 3 (Blue/Red wire on cable reel harness) with RESUME pressed. If continuity exists, go to next step. If continuity does not exist, go to step **4)**.

3) Check for continuity between SRS Test Harness "C" connector terminal No. 1 (Light Green/Black wire on cable reel harness) and terminal No. 3 (Blue/Red wire on cable reel harness) with CANCEL pressed. Check for continuity between SRS Test Harness "C" connector terminal No. 2 (Light Green/Red wire on cable reel harness) and terminal No. 3 (Blue/Red wire on cable reel harness) with CANCEL pressed. If continuity exists at both sets of terminals, SET/RESUME/CANCEL switch and cable reel are functioning properly. If continuity does not exist, go to next step.

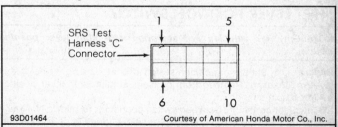

93D01464　　　　　Courtesy of American Honda Motor Co., Inc.

Fig. 11: Identifying SRS Test Harness "C" Terminals (Legend & Vigor)

4) Remove SET/RESUME/CANCEL switch from steering wheel. See SET/RESUME/CANCEL SWITCH under REMOVAL & INSTALLATION. If testing Legend, go to next step. If testing Vigor, go to step **8)**.

5) Check for continuity between SET/RESUME/CANCEL switch terminals "B" and "C" with SET pressed. *See Fig. 12.* If continuity exists, go to next step. If continuity does not exist, replace SET/RESUME/CANCEL switch.

6) Check for continuity between SET/RESUME/CANCEL switch terminals "A" and "C" with RESUME pressed. If continuity exists, go to next step. If continuity does not exist, replace SET/RESUME/CANCEL switch.

7) Check for continuity between SET/RESUME/CANCEL switch terminals "A" and "C" with CANCEL pressed. Check for continuity between SET/RESUME/CANCEL switch terminals "B" and "C" with CANCEL pressed. Go to step **11)** if continuity exists. If continuity does not exist, replace SET/RESUME/CANCEL switch. See SET/RESUME/CANCEL SWITCH under REMOVAL & INSTALLATION.

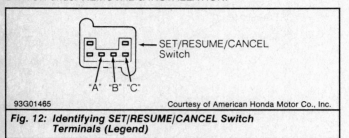

93G01465   Courtesy of American Honda Motor Co., Inc.

Fig. 12: Identifying SET/RESUME/CANCEL Switch Terminals (Legend)

8) Check for continuity between SET/RESUME/CANCEL switch terminals "A" or "A' " and "C" with SET pressed. *See Fig. 13.* If continuity exists, go to next step. If continuity does not exist, replace SET/RESUME/CANCEL switch.

9) Check for continuity between SET/RESUME/CANCEL switch terminals "A" or "A' " and "B" with RESUME pressed. If continuity exists, go to next step. If continuity does not exist, replace SET/RESUME/CANCEL switch.

10) Check for continuity between SET/RESUME/CANCEL switch terminals "A" or "A' " and "B" with CANCEL pressed. Check for continuity between SET/RESUME/CANCEL switch terminals "A" or "A' " and "C" with CANCEL pressed. If continuity exists at both sets of terminals, go to next step. If continuity does not exist, replace SET/RESUME/CANCEL switch. See SET/RESUME/CANCEL SWITCH under REMOVAL & INSTALLATION.

11) Replace cable reel. See CABLE REEL under REMOVAL & INSTALLATION.

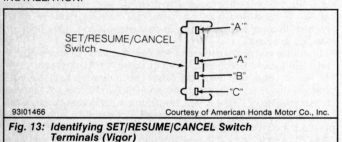

93I01466   Courtesy of American Honda Motor Co., Inc.

Fig. 13: Identifying SET/RESUME/CANCEL Switch Terminals (Vigor)

SHIFT LEVER POSITION SWITCH

NOTE: Only A/T vehicles are equipped with shift lever position switch.

Integra – 1) Shift lever position switch is located on right side of shift lever mechanism. Remove front console. Unplug shift lever position switch 10-pin connector.

2) Check for continuity between switch connector terminals No. 1 and 7 with shift lever in "2", "S", and "D" positions. *See Fig. 3.* If continuity exists in each position, shift lever position switch is okay. If continuity does not exist, go to next step.

3) With DVOM connected to switch connector terminals No. 1 and 7, move shift lever back and forth slightly without pressing shift lever button while in "2", "S", and "D" positions. Continuity should exist in each position.

4) If continuity exists, shift lever position switch is okay. If continuity does not exist, check shift lever position switch adjustment. See SHIFT LEVER POSITION SWITCH under ADJUSTMENTS. If shift lever position switch adjustment is okay, replace shift lever position switch. See SHIFT LEVER POSITION SWITCH under ADJUSTMENTS.

Legend – 1) Shift lever position switch is located on left side of shift lever mechanism. Remove front console. Unplug shift lever position switch 14-pin connector.

2) Check for continuity between switch connector terminals No. 5 and 9 with shift lever in "2", "D_3", and "D_4" positions. *See Fig. 4.* If continuity exists in each position, switch is okay. If continuity does not exist, go to next step.

3) With DVOM connected to switch connector terminals No. 5 and 9, move shift lever back and forth slightly without presssing shift lever button while in "2", "D_3", and "D_4" positions. Continuity should exist in each position.

4) If continuity exists, shift lever position switch is okay. If continuity does not exist, check shift lever position switch adjustment. See SHIFT LEVER POSITION SWITCH under ADJUSTMENTS. If adjustment is okay, replace switch and adjust as necessary. See SHIFT LEVER POSITION SWITCH under ADJUSTMENTS.

Vigor – 1) Raise and support vehicle. Remove transmission undercover. Unplug shift lever position switch 14-pin connector.

2) Check for continuity between switch connector terminal No. 11 and ground with shift lever in "2", "D_3", and "D_4" positions. *See Fig. 14.* If continuity exists in each position, switch is okay. If continuity does not exist, go to next step.

3) With DVOM connected to switch connector terminal No. 11 and ground, move shift lever back and forth slightly without pressing shift lever button while in "2", "D_3", and "D_4" positions.

4) If continuity exists in each position, switch is okay. If continuity does not exist, go to next step.

5) Loosen shift lever position switch bolts. Move switch back and forth while trying to achieve continuity readings specified in steps **2)** and **3)**. If continuity can be achieved, tighten switch bolts. If continuity cannot be achieved as specified in steps **2)** and **3)**, replace faulty shift lever position switch.

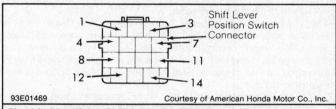

93E01469   Courtesy of American Honda Motor Co., Inc.

Fig. 14: Identifying Shift Lever Position Switch Connector Terminals (Vigor)

MAIN SWITCH

Integra – 1) Remove main switch from instrument panel. With switch off, check for continuity between switch terminals "B" and "C", and between terminals "D" and "E". *See Fig. 15.* If continuity exists, go to next step. If continuity does not exist, replace defective bulb. After replacing bulb, repeat test. If switch continuity is not as specified, replace main switch.

2) Turn switch on. Check for continuity between main switch terminals "A" and "B", "B" and "C", and "D" and "E". If continuity exists, switch is okay. If continuity does not exist, between main switch terminals "A" and "B", replace switch. If continuity does not exist between main switch terminals "B" and "C" or terminals "D" and "E", go to next step.

3) Replace defective bulb inside main switch. After replacing bulb, repeat step **2)**. If continuity is not as specified, replace main switch.

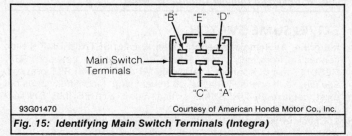

93G01470   Courtesy of American Honda Motor Co., Inc.

Fig. 15: Identifying Main Switch Terminals (Integra)

Legend – 1) Turn ignition off. Remove 2 screws from instrument cluster bezel. Pull out bezel far enough to unplug connectors (one on left side and 2 on right side). Remove bezel.

2) Turn main switch off. Check for continuity between switch terminals "A" and "B", and between "D" and "E". *See Fig. 16*. If continuity exists, go to next step. If continuity does not exist, replace main switch.

3) Turn main switch on. Check for continuity between switch terminals "A" and "B", terminals "B" and "C", and terminals "D" and "E". If continuity exists, main switch is okay. If continuity does not exist, replace switch.

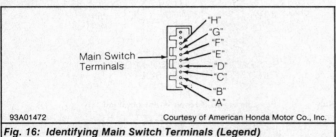

93A01472   Courtesy of American Honda Motor Co., Inc.

Fig. 16: Identifying Main Switch Terminals (Legend)

Vigor – 1) Turn ignition off. Carefully pry main switch from instrument panel. Unplug main switch connector.

2) Turn main switch off. Check for continuity between main switch terminals "A" and "B", and terminals "D" and "E". *See Fig. 17*. If continuity exists, go to next step. If continuity does not exist, replace malfunctioning main switch.

3) Turn main switch on. Check for continuity between main switch terminals "A" and "B", "B" and "C", and "D" and "E". If continuity exists for each terminal pair, switch is okay. If continuity does not exist, replace malfunctioning main switch.

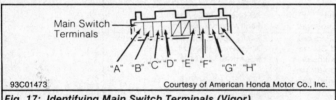

93C01473   Courtesy of American Honda Motor Co., Inc.

Fig. 17: Identifying Main Switch Terminals (Vigor)

CONTROL UNIT INPUT TEST

Integra – 1) Turn ignition off. Remove dashboard lower left cover. Remove left knee bolster. Cruise control unit is located near left kick panel. Unplug cruise control unit 14-pin connector.

2) Using a DVOM, perform cruise control unit input tests in *Fig. 18*. If all input test results are okay, inspect cruise control unit connector for damage and proper fit. If connector is okay and cruise control still malfunctions, replace cruise control unit.

Legend – 1) Cruise control unit is located near right kick panel. Turn ignition off. Remove glove box. Unplug cruise control unit 14-pin connector.

2) Using a DVOM, perform cruise control unit input tests in *Fig. 19*. If all input test results are okay, inspect cruise control unit connector for damage and proper fit. If connector is okay but cruise control still malfunctions, replace cruise control unit.

Vigor – 1) Turn ignition off. Cruise control unit is located under instrument panel above brake pedal bracket. Unplug cruise control unit 13-pin connector.

2) Using a DVOM, perform cruise control unit input tests in *Fig. 20*. If all input test results are okay, inspect cruise control unit connector for damage and proper fit. If connector is okay but cruise control still malfunctions, replace cruise control unit.

REMOVAL & INSTALLATION

CAUTION: Legend and Vigor are equipped with Supplemental Restraint System (SRS). SRS wiring harness is routed close to instrument cluster, steering wheel, and related components. All SRS wiring harnesses are covered by Yellow outer insulation. DO NOT use electrical test equipment on these circuits. Before working on steering column components, disable air bag system. See AIR BAG RESTRAINT SYSTEM article in ACCESSORIES & EQUIPMENT.

WARNING: Wait about 3 minutes after disabling air bag system. Back-up power circuit maintains system voltage for about 3 minutes after battery is disconnected. Servicing air bag system before 3 minutes have elapsed may cause accidental air bag deployment and possible personal injury.

NOTE: Radio/cassette or radio/CD player contain an anti-theft protection circuit. Whenever battery is disconnected, radio goes into anti-theft mode. When battery is reconnected, radio displays CODE and is inoperative until proper code number is entered by vehicle owner.

CABLE REEL

Removal & Installation (Integra) – Remove steering wheel. Remove steering column covers. Unplug cable reel 3-pin connector from vehicle harness. Remove 3 screws from cable reel. Remove cable reel. To install, reverse removal procedure. Discard old steering wheel self-locking nut. Tighten NEW steering wheel self-locking nut to specification. See TORQUE SPECIFICATIONS.

Removal (Legend & Vigor) – 1) Disable air bag system. See DISABLING & ACTIVATING AIR BAG SYSTEM in AIR BAG RESTRAINT SYSTEM article. Ensure front wheels are facing straight-ahead.

2) Cable reel is located under steering wheel, on upper steering column. *See Fig. 21*. Remove lower instrument panel cover below steering column. Remove upper and lower steering column covers. Unplug SRS main harness connector from cable reel connector. Remove connector holder. Remove air bag module. See AIR BAG MODULE in AIR BAG RESTRAINT SYSTEM article.

3) Remove and discard steering wheel nut. Unplug horn connector, radio remote switch connector, cruise control switch connector, and ground connector in center of steering wheel. Release cable reel harness and connectors from retaining clips. *See Figs. 21 and 22*. Pull steering wheel from shaft while guiding cable reel harness and connectors through hole in steering wheel.

4) Remove bolts retaining harness cover under steering column. Remove harness cover. Remove cable reel harness retaining screws under steering column. Remove cable reel retaining screws. Pull cable reel from steering shaft. Remove cancel sleeve.

Installation (Legend & Vigor) – 1) Align cancel sleeve grooves with cable reel projections. *See Fig. 23*. Carefully install cancel sleeve and cable reel onto steering shaft. Install cable reel harness retaining screws. Install harness cover. Install steering column upper and lower covers. Center cable reel. See CABLE REEL CENTERING under ADJUSTMENTS.

2) Route cable reel harness and connectors through steering wheel hole. Install steering wheel. Secure each connector to respective retaining clips and connections in steering wheel.

3) Install NEW steering wheel nut, and tighten to specification. Install air bag module, and tighten mounting screws to specification. See TORQUE SPECIFICATIONS. Connect cable reel to SRS main harness under steering column. Install cable reel connector holder. Install lower instrument panel cover.

4) Activate air bag system. Check SRS indicator light to verify system is okay. See SYSTEM OPERATION CHECK in AIR BAG RESTRAINT SYSTEM article.

1993 ACCESSORIES & EQUIPMENT
Cruise Control Systems (Cont.)

- Numbers 1 through 14 refer to test numbers, not terminal numbers.
- Number 14 (Black/Yellow wire) is used only on 1992 models.
- Ground G301 is located in left side of engine compartment next to windshield washer fluid reservoir.
- Ground G401 is located behind left kickpanel.

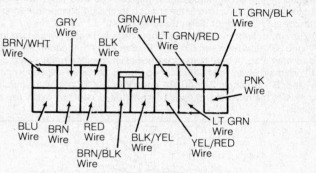

CRUISE CONTROL UNIT CONNECTOR
VIEWED FROM HARNESS SIDE

No.	Terminal	Test condition	Test: Desired result	Possible cause if result is not obtained
1	BLK	Under all conditions.	Check for continuity to ground: There should be continuity.	• Poor ground (G301, G401). • An open in the wire.
2	LT GRN	Ignition switch ON and main switch ON.	Check for voltage to ground: There should be battery voltage.	• An open in the wire. • Faulty main switch. • Blown No.24 (15A) fuse.
3	LT GRN /BLK	Resume switch pushed.	Ground each terminal: Horns should sound as the switch is pushed.	• An open in the wire. • Faulty SET/RESUME switch • Faulty slip ring. • Faulty horn. • Blown No.37 (20A) fuse
4	LT GRN /RED	Set switch pushed.		
5	PNK	M/T: Clutch pedal not pushed. A/T: Shift lever in 2,S or D.	Check for continuity to ground: There should be continuity.	• Poor ground (G301, G401). • An open in the wire. • Faulty or misadjusted clutch switch (M/T). • Faulty shift lever position switch (A/T).
6	BLU	Start the engine.	Check for voltage to ground: There should be battery voltage.	• An open in the wire. • Faulty ignition system.
7	YEL/RED	Raise the front of the car and rotate one wheel or remove the speedometer cable from the transmission and turn slowly by hand.	Check resistance in both directions between the YEL/RED and BLK terminals. There should be continuity in only one direction four times per cable revolution or 23 times per 10 wheel revolutions.	• Faulty speed pulser in speedometer. • An open in the wire. • Poor ground (G301, G401).
8	GRY	Ignition switch ON, main switch ON, and brake pedal pushed, then released.	Check for voltage to ground: There should be O V with the pedal pushed and battery voltage with the pedal released.	• An open in the GRY wire circuit. • Faulty brake light switch.
9	GRN/WHT	Brake pedal pushed, then released.	Check for voltage to ground: There should be battery voltage with the pedal pushed, and O V with the pedal released.	• An open in the GRN/WHT wire circuit. • Blown No.37 (20A) fuse. • Faulty brake light switch.
10	RED	Ignition switch ON.	Attach RED terminals to ground: Indicator light in dash should come on.	• Blown bulb. • An open in the RED wire circuit. • Faulty dimming circuit in gauges. • Blown No.23 (7.5A) fuse.
11	BRN	Connect battery power to the BRN terminal and ground to the BRN/BLK terminal.	Check the operation of the actuator motor: You should be able to hear the motor.	• Faulty actuator. • An open in the wire.
12	BRN/BLK			
13	BRN/WHT	Connect battery power to the BRN/ WHT terminal and ground to body earth.	Check the operation of the magnetic clutch: The clutch should click and the output link should be locked.	• Faulty actuator. • An open in the wire. • Poor ground (G301, G401).
14	BLK/YEL	Ignition switch ON.	Check for voltage to ground: There should be battery voltage.	• An open in the wire. • Blown No.24 (15A) fuse.

93E01474

Courtesy of American Honda Motor Co., Inc.

Fig. 18: Cruise Control Unit Input Test (Integra)

- Numbers 1 through 14 refer to test numbers, not terminal numbers.
- Ground G152 is located at left front corner of engine compartment.
- Ground G251 is located at base of left "B" pillar.
- Ground G301 is located behind left kick panel.
- Ground G501 is located on center floor where center console meets floor inside vehicle.

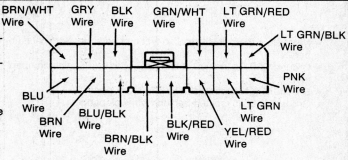

CRUISE CONTROL UNIT CONNECTOR
VIEWED FROM HARNESS SIDE

No.	Wire	Test condition	Test: Desired result	Possible cause if result is not obtained
1	BLK	Under all conditions	Check for continuity to ground: There should be continuity.	• Poor ground (G301) • An open in the wire
2	BLK/RED	Ignition switch to ON	Check for voltage to ground: There should be battery voltage.	• Blown No. 20 (7.5 A) fuse • An open in the wire
3	LT GRN	Ignition switch to ON and main switch to ON	Check for voltage to ground: There should be battery voltage.	• Blown No. 20 (7.5 A) fuse • Faulty main switch • An open in the LT GRN wire
4	LT GRN/ BLK	RESUME button pushed	Ground each terminal: Horns should sound as the switch is pushed.	• Blown No. 39 (20 A) fuse • Faulty SET/RESUME/CANCEL switch • Faulty cable reel • An open in the WHT/GRN, BLU/RED, LT GRN/BLK or GRN/RED wire
5	LT GRN/ RED	SET button pushed		
6	PNK	M/T: Clutch pedal pushed A/T: Shift lever in 2, D_3 or D_4	Check for continuity to ground: There should be continuity. NOTE: There should be no continuity when the clutch pedal is released or when the shift lever is in other positions.	• Faulty or misadjusted clutch switch (M/T) • Faulty A/T gear position switch • Poor ground (G301 or G501) • An open in the wire
7	BLU	Start the engine.	Check for voltage to ground: There should be battery voltage.	• Faulty ignition system or ECM (M/T) or PCM (A/T). • An open in the wire.
8	YEL/RED	Ignition switch to ON and main switch to ON Raise the front of the car and rotate one wheel slowly with the other wheel blocked.	Check for voltage between the YEL/RED ⊕ and BLK ⊖ terminals: There should be 0 – 12 – 0 – 12 V or more repeatedly.	• Faulty vehicle speed sensor (VSS) • An open in the wire • Short to ground
9	GRY	Ignition switch to ON, main switch to ON and brake pedal pushed, then released	Check for voltage to ground: There should be 0 V with the pedal pushed and battery voltage with the pedal released.	• Faulty brake switch • An open in the wire
10	GRN/WHT	Brake pedal pushed, then released	Check for voltage to ground: There should be battery voltage with the pedal pushed, and 0 V with the pedal released.	• Blown No. 39 (20 A) fuse • Faulty brake switch • An open in the wire
11	BLU/BLK	Ignition switch to ON	Attach to ground: Indicator light in the gauge assembly comes on.	• Blown bulb • Blown No. 20 (7.5 A) fuse • Faulty dimming circuit in the gauge assembly • An open in the wire
12	BRN	Connect battery power to the BRN terminal and ground to the BRN/BLK terminal.	Check the operation of the actuator motor: You should be able to hear the motor.	• Faulty actuator • An open in the wire
13	BRN/BLK			
14	BRN/WHT	Connect battery power to the BRN/WHT terminal.	Check the operation of the magnetic clutch: Clutch should click and output link should be locked.	• Faulty actuator • An open in the wire • Poor ground (G152)

Fig. 19: Cruise Control Unit Input Test (Legend)

- Numbers 1 through 14 refer to test numbers, not terminal numbers.
- Ground G301 is located in left front corner of engine compartment.
- Ground G401 is located behind left kick panel.
- Ground G402 is located behind right kick panel.

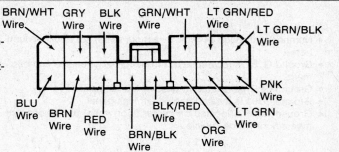

CRUISE CONTROL UNIT CONNECTOR
VIEWED FROM HARNESS SIDE

No.	Wire	Test condition	Test: Desired result	Possible cause if result is not obtained
1	BLK	Under all conditions.	Check for continuity to gound: There should be continuity.	• Poor Ground (G401, G402) • An open in the wire.
2	LT GRN	Ignition switch ON and main switch ON.	Check for voltage to ground: There should be battery voltage.	• Blown No. 4 (7.5 A) fuse (in the under-dash fuse/relay box). • Faulty main switch • An open in the wire.
3	LT GRN/BLK	RESUME button pushed.	Check for voltage to ground: There should be battery voltage.	• Blown No. 30 (20 A) fuse (in the under-hood fuse/relay box). • Faulty SET/RESUME/CANCEL switch. • Faulty horn relay. • Faulty cable reel. • An open in the wire.
4	LT GRN/RED	SET button pushed.		
5	PNK	M/T: Clutch pedal released A/T: Shift lever in 2, D3, or D4.	Check for continuity to ground: There should be continuity. NOTE: There should be no continuity when the clutch pedal is released or when the A/T shift lever is in other positions.	• Faulty or misadjusted clutch switch (M/T). • Faulty A/T gear position switch. • Poor ground (G401, G402). • An open in the wire.
6	BLU	Start the engine.	Check for voltage to ground: There should be battery voltage.	• Faulty ignition system or ECM. • An open in the wire.
7	ORN	Ignition switch ON and main switch ON. Raise the front of the car, rotate one wheel slowly.	Check for voltage between the ORN ⊕ and BLK ⊖ terminals: should be 0—5—0—5 V repeatedly.	• Faulty vehicle speed sensor (VSS) • An open in the wire. • Poor ground (G101).
8	GRY	Ignition switch ON, main switch ON and brake pedal pushed, then released.	Check for voltage to ground: There should 0 V with the pedal pushed and battery voltage with the pedal released.	• Faulty brake switch. • An open in the wire.
9	GRN/WHT	Brake pedal pushed, then released.	Check for voltage to ground: There should be battery voltage with the pedal pushed, and 0 V with the pedal released.	• Faulty brake switch. • An open in the wire.
10	RED	Ignition switch ON.	Connect to ground: Cruise indicator in the gauge assembly comes on.	• Blown bulb. • Blown No. 1 (10 A) fuse (in the under-dash fuse/relay box). • Faulty dimming circuit in the gauge assembly. • An open in the wire.
11	BRN	Connect the battery power to the BRN/WHT terminal and ground to the BRN/BLK terminal.	Check the operation of the actuator motor: You should be able to hear the motor.	• Faulty actuator. • An open in the wire.
12	BRN/BLK			
13	BRN/WHT	Connect the battery power to the BRN terminal.	Check the operation of the magnetic clutch: Clutch should click and output link should be locked.	• Faulty actuator. • Poor ground (G301). • An open in the wire.
14	BLK/RED	Ignition switch ON.	Check for voltage to ground: There should be battery voltage.	• Blown No. 4 (7.5 A) fuse (in the under-dash fuse/relay box). • An open in the wire.

93A82412

Fig. 20: *Cruise Control Unit Input Test (Vigor)*

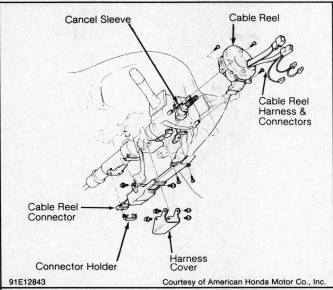

Cancel Sleeve

Cable Reel

Cable Reel Harness & Connectors

Cable Reel Connector

Connector Holder

Harness Cover

91E12843 — Courtesy of American Honda Motor Co., Inc.

Fig. 21: Removing Cable Reel & Cancel Sleeve (Legend & Vigor)

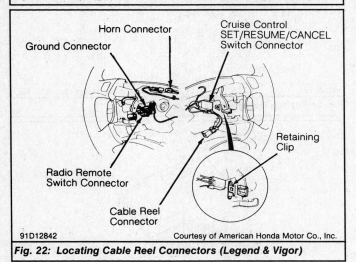

Horn Connector

Ground Connector

Cruise Control SET/RESUME/CANCEL Switch Connector

Retaining Clip

Radio Remote Switch Connector

Cable Reel Connector

91D12842 — Courtesy of American Honda Motor Co., Inc.

Fig. 22: Locating Cable Reel Connectors (Legend & Vigor)

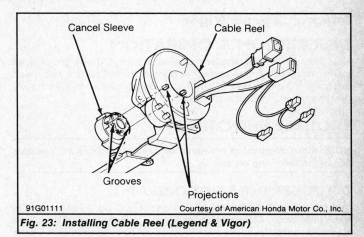

Cancel Sleeve

Cable Reel

Grooves

Projections

91G01111 — Courtesy of American Honda Motor Co., Inc.

Fig. 23: Installing Cable Reel (Legend & Vigor)

SET/RESUME SWITCH

Removal & Installation (Integra) – 1) Remove steering wheel. Discard old steering wheel nut. Unplug SET/RESUME switch connector. Remove retaining screws from back of steering wheel and steering wheel upper cover.

2) Remove retaining screws from front of steering wheel and steering wheel lower cover. Remove retaining screws attaching and SET/RESUME switch. To install, reverse removal procedure. Tighten NEW steering wheel nut to specification. See TORQUE SPECIFICATIONS.

SET/RESUME/CANCEL SWITCH

Removal & Installation (Legend & Vigor) – Carefully pry cover from side of SET/RESUME/CANCEL switch. Remove retaining screws and SET/RESUME/CANCEL switch. To install, reverse removal procedure.

TORQUE SPECIFICATIONS
TORQUE SPECIFICATIONS

Application	Ft. Lbs (N.m)
Steering Wheel Nut [1]	37 (50)
	INCH Lbs. (N.m)
Air Bag Module Torx Screws	88 (10)

[1] – Discard old steering wheel self-locking nut. Use a NEW steering wheel self-locking nut.

WIRING DIAGRAMS

See appropriate wiring diagram in WIRING DIAGRAMS.

Integra, Legend, Vigor

DESCRIPTION & OPERATION

Rear window defogger system consists of a heating wire grid bonded to the inside of window, a dash-mounted control switch, relay, and Integrated Control Unit (ICU). ICU supplies power to grid for 25 minutes or until ignition is turned off.

TROUBLE SHOOTING

NOTE: When diagnosing problems by symptom, check for possible failures in following order.

DEFOGGER DOES NOT OPERATE

Integra – Check fuses No. 17 (7.5 amps) and No. 23 (10 amps) in dash fuse block. Check defogger timer circuit input (in ICU). ICU is located at underdash fuse panel. Check for poor connections. Check for short or open in Yellow or Yellow/White wires.

Legend – Check fuses No. 3 (15 amps) and No. 13 (7.5 amps) in underdash fuse block. Check defogger timer circuit input (in ICU). ICU is located at underdash fuse panel. Check for poor connections. Check for short or open in Yellow, Yellow/White, or Yellow/Black wires.

Vigor – Check fuses No. 1 (10 amps) and No. 8 (7.5 amps) in underdash fuse block. Check defogger timer circuit input (in ICU). ICU is located at underdash fuse panel. Check for poor connections. Check for short or open in Yellow, Yellow/White, or Yellow/Black wires.

INDICATOR LIGHT DOES NOT WORK

Check for burned-out bulb. On Integra, check for poor connections and open in Black/Yellow or Yellow/White wires. On Legend, check for poor connections and open in Yellow/Black or Yellow/White wires. On Vigor, check for poor connections in Yellow, Yellow/White, or Yellow/Black wires.

OPERATION TIME TOO LONG OR TOO SHORT

Check defogger timer circuit input (in ICU). Check for short or open in Yellow/Green and Black wires.

TESTING

DEFOGGER SWITCH TEST

Remove switch from instrument panel. Check for continuity with switch in each position. *See Fig. 1, 2, or 3.* If switch does not function as indicated, replace switch.

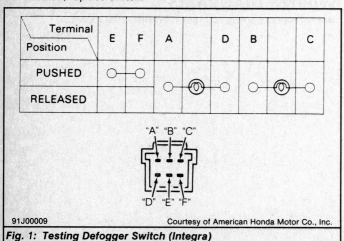

Terminal Position	E	F	A	D	B	C
PUSHED	o—o		o—Ⓤ—o		o—Ⓤ—o	
RELEASED						

91J00009   Courtesy of American Honda Motor Co., Inc.

Fig. 1: Testing Defogger Switch (Integra)

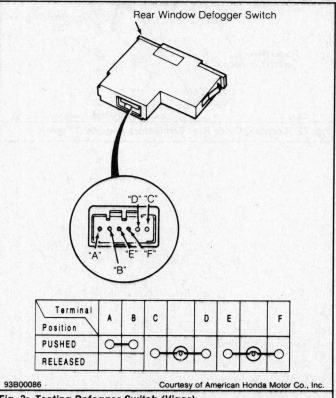

Terminal Position	D	E	C	B	A	F
PUSHED	o—o					
RELEASED			o—Ⓤ—o		o—Ⓤ—o	

92A00380   Courtesy of American Honda Motor Co., Inc.

Fig. 2: Testing Defogger Switch (Legend)

Terminal Position	A	B	C	D	E	F
PUSHED	o—o					
RELEASED			o—Ⓤ—o		o—Ⓤ—o	

93B00086   Courtesy of American Honda Motor Co., Inc.

Fig. 3: Testing Defogger Switch (Vigor)

DEFOGGER RELAY TEST

Unplug defogger relay from dash fuse block. Continuity should not exist between terminals "A" and "B". *See Fig. 4.* Apply battery voltage to terminal "C". Connect terminal "D" to ground. Continuity should exist between terminals "A" and "B".

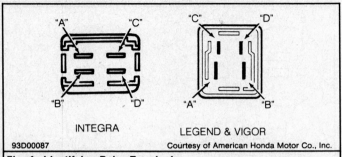

93D00087   Courtesy of American Honda Motor Co., Inc.

Fig. 4: Identifying Relay Terminals

GRID FILAMENT TEST

1) With ignition on, turn on rear window defogger. To locate breaks in grid wire filaments, connect positive lead of voltmeter to middle portion of each filament. Connect negative voltmeter lead to ground.
2) If a grid wire is broken, voltmeter will indicate either zero or battery voltage, depending on location of break. If grid wire is not broken, meter will indicate about 6 volts. To locate break, move probe along grid wire until meter needle moves abruptly.

ON-VEHICLE SERVICE

GRID FILAMENT REPAIR

NOTE: For repair to be effective, broken section must not be longer than one inch (25 mm).

1) Rub area around break with fine steel wool, and then clean with alcohol. Carefully mask area above and below broken portion with masking tape. *See Fig. 5.*

2) Mix repair compound thoroughly. Using small brush, apply heavy coat of repair compound extending 1/8 inch (3 mm) on both sides of break. Allow 30 minutes to dry.
3) Check for proper operation. See GRID FILAMENT TEST under TESTING. Apply second coat of repair compound. Allow 3 hours to dry. Remove tape.

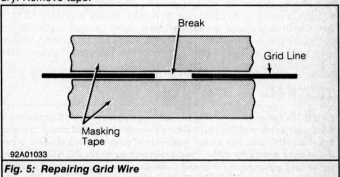

92A01033

Fig. 5: Repairing Grid Wire

REMOVAL & INSTALLATION

DEFOGGER SWITCH

Removal & Installation (Integra) – Remove retaining screws and instrument cluster trim panel. Unplug connector from defogger switch. To install, reverse removal procedure.

Removal & Installation (Legend) – Remove lower instrument panel cover. Remove 2 retaining screws and instrument trim panel. Unplug all connectors from instrument panel. Remove retaining screws and defogger switch. To install, reverse removal procedure.

Removal & Installation (Vigor) – Carefully pry defogger switch from instrument panel. Unplug electrical connector. To install, reverse removal procedure.

DEFOGGER RELAY

Removal & Installation – Defogger relay is on underdash fuse block. Unplug relay to remove. To install, reverse removal procedure.

WIRING DIAGRAMS

See appropriate wiring diagram in WIRING DIAGRAMS.

Integra, Legend, Vigor

DESCRIPTION & OPERATION

All models use conventional analog gauges. Instrument cluster includes speedometer, tachometer, fuel gauge, and temperature gauge. Instrument cluster is equipped with warning lights for charging system, low oil pressure, and Anti-Lock Brake System (ABS). A CHECK ENGINE light, located on instrument cluster, comes on if a computerized engine control fault occurs with engine running. Legend and Vigor are equipped with Supplemental Restraint System (SRS) warning lights.

TESTING

CAUTION: *Legend and Vigor are equipped with Supplemental Restraint System (SRS). SRS wiring harness is routed close to instrument cluster, steering wheel, and related components. All SRS wiring harnesses are covered by Yellow outer insulation. DO NOT use electrical test equipment on these circuits. Before working on steering column components, disable air bag system. See AIR BAG RESTRAINT SYSTEM article in ACCESSORIES & EQUIPMENT.*

FUEL GAUGE

Integra – 1) Turn ignition off. Remove rear seat. Remove fuel pump access cover. Unplug 3-pin connector from fuel gauge sending unit. Connect voltmeter positive lead to terminal "A" (Yellow/White wire). Connect negative voltmeter lead to terminal "B" (Black wire).

2) Turn ignition on. If voltmeter indicates 5-8 volts, go to step **3)**. If voltmeter indicates no voltage, check for blown fuse No. 23 in dash fuse block. Check for open in Yellow, Yellow/White, or Black/White wires. Check for poor ground.

3) Turn ignition off. Connect jumper wire between terminal "A" (Yellow/White wire) and terminal "B" (Black/White wire). Turn ignition on. Gauge needle should start moving toward "F" mark. Turn ignition off within 5 seconds or before gauge needle reaches "F" mark on gauge. Failure to turn ignition off before needle reaches "F" mark may damage fuel gauge.

4) If wiring is okay but fuel gauge needle does not move, replace fuel gauge. If fuel gauge is okay, test fuel gauge sending unit.

Legend & Vigor – 1) Check for blown fuse No. 13 (Legend) or fuse No. 1 (Vigor) at underdash fuse block. Remove access cover in luggage compartment area. Turn ignition off. Unplug 3-pin connector from sending unit.

2) Connect positive voltmeter lead to Yellow/White wire terminal. Connect negative lead to Black wire terminal. Turn ignition on. Voltage should be 5-8 volts. If voltage is as specified, go to step **3)**. If voltage is not as specified, check for poor ground or open in Yellow, Yellow/White, or Black wire.

3) Turn ignition off. Connect jumper wire between Yellow/White and Black wire terminals. Turn ignition on. Fuel gauge needle should move toward "F" mark on gauge. Turn ignition off within 5 seconds or before gauge needle reaches "F" mark. Failure to turn ignition off before needle reaches "F" mark may result in damage to fuel gauge.

4) If wiring is okay but fuel gauge needle does not move, replace fuel gauge. If gauge is okay, test fuel gauge sending unit.

FUEL GAUGE SENDING UNIT

Integra – Remove rear seat. Remove fuel pump access cover. Turn ignition off. Unplug 3-pin connector from fuel gauge sending unit. Using Fuel Sender Wrench (07920-SB20000), remove sending unit. Measure resistance between sending unit terminals "A" and "B" while moving float. *See Fig. 1.* Resistance must be as specified in FUEL GAUGE SENDING UNIT RESISTANCE table.

Legend & Vigor – Remove access cover in luggage compartment area. Turn ignition off. Unplug connector at sending unit. Remove retaining nuts and sending unit. Measure resistance between sending unit terminals "A" and "B". *See Fig. 2 or 3.* Resistance must be as specified in FUEL GAUGE SENDING UNIT RESISTANCE table.

FUEL GAUGE SENDING UNIT RESISTANCE

Float Position	Ohms
Full	2-5
1/2	25-39
Empty	105-110

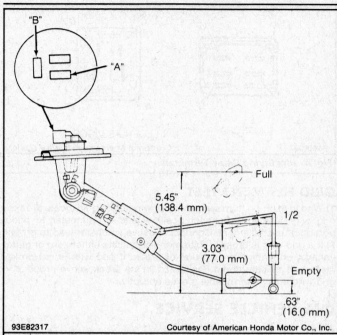

93E82317   Courtesy of American Honda Motor Co., Inc.

Fig. 1: Testing Fuel Gauge Sending Unit (Integra)

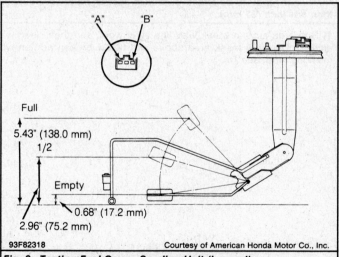

93F82318   Courtesy of American Honda Motor Co., Inc.

Fig. 2: Testing Fuel Gauge Sending Unit (Legend)

TEMPERATURE GAUGE

1) Check for blown fuse No. 23 (Integra) or No. 13 (Legend) in dash fuse block. Turn ignition off. Disconnect Yellow/Green wire from sending unit. Sending unit is threaded into cylinder head. Using a jumper wire, ground sending unit wire.

2) Turn ignition on. Gauge needle should start moving toward "H" mark on gauge. Turn ignition off within 2 seconds or before gauge needle reaches "H" mark. Failure to turn ignition off before needle reaches "H" mark may result in damage to temperature gauge.

3) If temperature gauge needle does not move, check for open circuit in Yellow or Yellow/Green wires. Replace temperature gauge if fuse and wiring are okay. If gauge is okay, check temperature sending unit.

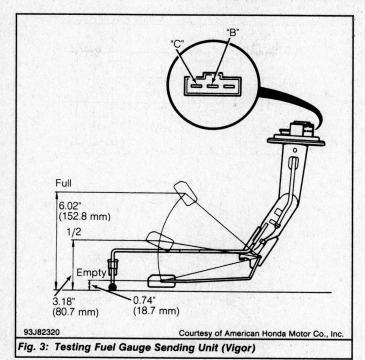

Full

6.02"
(152.8 mm)

1/2

Empty

3.18"
(80.7 mm)

0.74"
(18.7 mm)

"C"   "B"

93J82320   Courtesy of American Honda Motor Co., Inc.

Fig. 3: Testing Fuel Gauge Sending Unit (Vigor)

TEMPERATURE SENDING UNIT

Disconnect Yellow/Green wire from coolant temperature sending unit. Sending unit is threaded into cylinder head. With engine cold, measure resistance between sending unit terminal and ground. With engine warm, repeat resistance measurement. Resistance must be as specified in COOLANT TEMPERATURE SENDING UNIT RESISTANCE table.

COOLANT TEMPERATURE SENDING UNIT RESISTANCE

Temperature °F (°C)	Ohms
133 (56)	142
185-212 (85-100)	32-49

OIL PRESSURE SWITCH

Legend & Vigor – Disconnect Yellow/Red wire from oil pressure switch. Switch is located at front of engine on Legend, and at base of oil filter on Vigor. With engine off, continuity should exist between oil pressure switch terminal and ground. Continuity should not exist with engine running. If switch does not function as specified but oil level and oil pressure are okay, replace oil pressure switch.

VEHICLE SPEED SENSOR (VSS)

Integra – Remove instrument cluster. Connect ohmmeter between terminals "A" and "B" of VSS. *See Fig. 4.* Insert pencil into speedometer cable socket, and rotate it. Replace VSS if continuity does not exist 4 times per revolution.

Legend – 1) Verify fuse No. 22 in underdash fuse block is okay. Speed sensor is located next to oil filter. Unplug 3-pin connector from speed sensor.

2) Check for continuity between Green/White wire and ground. *See Fig. 5.* If continuity exists, go to next step. If continuity does not exist, repair open between speed sensor and Electronic Control Module (ECM) ground. ECU ground is located next to throttle body.

3) With ignition on, check for battery voltage between Black/Yellow wire and ground. If battery voltage exists, go to next step. If battery voltage does not exist, repair open in Black/Yellow wire between speed sensor and underdash fuse box.

4) Measure voltage between Yellow/Red wire and ground. If voltage is about 5 volts, go to next step. If voltage is not about 5 volts, repair short to ground in Yellow/Red wire.

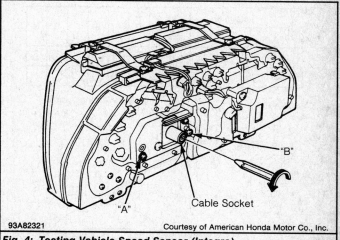

"B"

Cable Socket

"A"

93A82321   Courtesy of American Honda Motor Co., Inc.

Fig. 4: Testing Vehicle Speed Sensor (Integra)

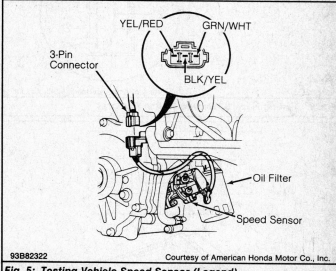

YEL/RED   GRN/WHT

3-Pin Connector

BLK/YEL

Oil Filter

Speed Sensor

93B82322   Courtesy of American Honda Motor Co., Inc.

Fig. 5: Testing Vehicle Speed Sensor (Legend)

5) Reconnect wiring to speed sensor. Raise and support vehicle. Connect voltmeter between sensor connector Yellow/Red wire and ground. With ignition on and transaxle in Neutral, block one front wheel and slowly rotate other front wheel. If voltage does not pulse between zero and 5 volts, replace speed sensor.

Vigor – 1) Verify fuse No. 1 in underdash fuse block is okay. Speed sensor is located next to oil filter. Unplug 3-pin connector from speed sensor.

2) Check for continuity between Black wire and ground. If continuity exists, go to next step. If continuity does not exist, repair open between speed sensor and body ground.

3) With ignition on, measure voltage between Yellow wire and ground. If battery voltage exists, go to next step. If battery voltage does not exist, repair open in Yellow wire between speed sensor and underdash fuse block.

4) Measure voltage between Yellow/Red wire and ground. If voltage is about 5 volts, go to next step. If voltage is not about 5 volts, repair short to ground in Yellow/Red wire.

5) Reconnect wiring to speed sensor. Raise and support vehicle. Connect voltmeter between Orange wire of sensor connector and ground. With ignition on and transaxle in Neutral, block one front wheel and slowly rotate other front wheel. If voltage does not pulse between zero and 5 volts, replace speed sensor.

HAZARD WARNING SWITCH

Check for continuity between specified switch terminals with switch in ON and OFF positions. *See Fig. 6, 7, or 8.*

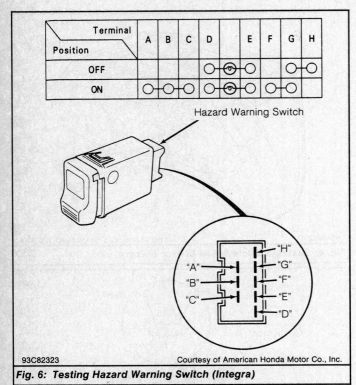

Terminal Position	A	B	C	D	E	F	G	H
OFF				⊙—⊙		⊙—⊙		
ON	⊙—⊙—⊙			⊙—⊙		⊙—⊙—⊙		

Hazard Warning Switch

"A" "B" "C" "D" "E" "F" "G" "H"

93C82323   Courtesy of American Honda Motor Co., Inc.

Fig. 6: Testing Hazard Warning Switch (Integra)

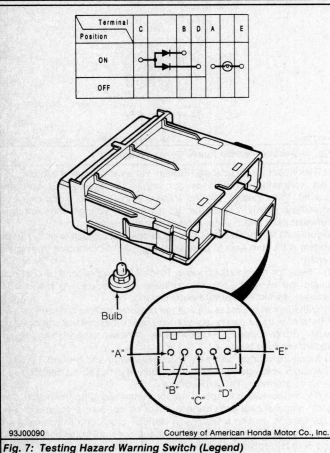

Terminal Position	C		B	D	A		E
ON	⊙		⊙	⊙	⊙		⊙—⊙
OFF							

Bulb

"A" "B" "C" "D" "E"

93J00090   Courtesy of American Honda Motor Co., Inc.

Fig. 7: Testing Hazard Warning Switch (Legend)

Terminal Position	A		B	C	D	E	F	G	H	I
OFF	⊙—⊙—⊙			⊙—⊙						
ON	⊙—⊙—⊙			⊙—⊙				⊙—⊙—⊙		

Bulb

"A" "B" "C" "D" "E" "F" "G" "H" "I"

93B00091   Courtesy of American Honda Motor Co., Inc.

Fig. 8: Testing Hazard Warning Switch (Vigor)

REMOVAL & INSTALLATION
INSTRUMENT CLUSTER

Removal & Installation (Integra) – Disconnect negative battery cable. Remove screws, instrument panel, and trim covers. Unplug switch connectors. Remove instrument cluster retaining screws. Pull instrument cluster to rear. Disconnect speedometer cable. Unplug instrument cluster connectors. Remove instrument cluster. To install, reverse removal procedure.

CAUTION: Legend and Vigor are equipped with Supplemental Restraint System (SRS). Disconnect negative and positive battery cables before removing instrument cluster. All SRS wiring has a Yellow cover. DO NOT use electrical test equipment on SRS circuits.

Removal & Installation (Legend & Vigor) – Disconnect battery cables. Remove lower cover. Remove upper and lower steering column covers. Remove 2 retaining screws and instrument panel trim cover. Unplug switch connectors. Place protective cloth over combination switch. Remove 4 instrument cluster retaining screws. Pull cluster toward rear. Unplug connectors. Remove instrument cluster. To install, reverse removal procedure.

WIRING DIAGRAMS
See appropriate wiring diagram in WIRING DIAGRAMS.

Integra, Legend, Vigor

DESCRIPTION & OPERATION

Power door locks are controlled by driver or front passenger switches which send signals to a control unit. The control unit sends appropriate signals to individual door lock actuators.

On Legend, a switch in the driver's door activates a solenoid which releases the trunk lid.

TROUBLE SHOOTING

CAUTION: Legend and Vigor are equipped with Supplemental Restraint System (SRS). SRS wiring harness is routed close to instrument cluster, steering wheel, and related components. All SRS wiring harnesses are covered by Yellow outer insulation. DO NOT use electrical test equipment on these circuits. Before working on steering column components, disable air bag system. See AIR BAG RESTRAINT SYSTEM article in ACCESSORIES & EQUIPMENT.

INTEGRA

System Does Not Work At All – Check fuse No. 5 in underdash fuse panel. Test control unit inputs. See CONTROL UNIT INPUTS under TESTING. Check for poor ground connections. Check White/Red and White/Yellow wires between fuse panels and control unit.

No Passenger Door Locks With Driver's Switch – Check fuse No. 5 in underdash fuse panel. Test driver's door lock switch. See DOOR LOCK SWITCHES under TESTING. Test control unit inputs. See CONTROL UNIT INPUTS under TESTING. Check for poor ground connections. Check White/Red and Yellow/Red wires between actuators and control unit. Check Blue/White wire between driver's door actuator and control unit.

One Or More Doors Does Not Lock With Driver's Switch –Test appropriate actuator. See ACTUATOR TEST under TESTING. Test driver's switch. Check White/Red and Yellow/Red wires between actuators and control unit.

No Door Locks Or Unlocks With Driver's Switch – Check fuse No. 5 in underdash fuse panel. Test control unit inputs. See CONTROL UNIT INPUTS under TESTING. Check for poor ground connections. Check Green/Red and Green/White wires between driver's switch and control unit. Check White/Red and Yellow/Red wires between actuators and control unit. Check Black/Red and Red/White wires between driver's door actuator and control unit.

One Or More Doors Do Not Lock Or Unlock With Driver's Switch – Test appropriate actuator. See ACTUATOR TEST under TESTING. Check actuator linkage.

No Door Locks Or Unlocks With Passenger's Switch – Check fuse No. 5 in underdash fuse panel. Test passenger's door switch. See DOOR LOCK SWITCHES under TESTING. Test control unit inputs. See CONTROL UNIT INPUTS under TESTING. Check for poor ground connections. Check Blue and Blue/Red wires between passenger's door switch and control unit. On Hatchback, check Black/Red and Black/White wires between passenger's switch and control unit. Check White/Red and Yellow/Red wires between actuators and control unit. Check Black/Red and Red/White wires between driver's door actuator and control unit. Check actuator linkage.

One or More Doors Does Not Lock Or Unlock With Passenger's Switch – Test appropriate actuator. See ACTUATOR TEST under TESTING. Check White/Red and Yellow/Red wires between actuators and control unit. Check Black/Red and Red/White wires between driver's door actuator and control unit.

LEGEND

System Does Not Work At All – Check fuse No. 44 in underhood fuse panel. Test control unit inputs. See CONTROL UNIT INPUTS under TESTING. Check for poor ground connections. Check White/Green wire between fuse panel and control unit.

No Door Locks Or Unlocks With Driver's Switch – Test driver's door lock switch. See DOOR LOCK SWITCHES under TESTING. Test con-

trol unit inputs. See CONTROL UNIT INPUTS under TESTING. Check for poor ground connections. Check Green/White and Green/Red wires between driver's door switch and control unit.

One Or More Doors Does Not Lock Or Unlock With Driver's Switch – Check appropriate actuator and linkage.

No Door Locks Or Unlocks With Passenger's Switch – Test passenger's door switch. See DOOR LOCK SWITCHES under TESTING. Test control unit inputs. See CONTROL UNIT INPUTS under TESTING. Check for poor ground connections. Check Black/Red and Black/White wires between passenger's door switch and control unit.

One or More Doors Does Not Lock Or Unlock With Passenger's Switch – Check appropriate actuator. Check White/Red and Yellow/Red wires between actuators and control unit. Test control unit inputs. See CONTROL UNIT INPUTS under TESTING.

No Door Locks Or Unlocks With Driver's Lock Knob – Test driver's door switch. See DOOR LOCK SWITCHES under TESTING. Test control unit inputs. See CONTROL UNIT INPUTS under TESTING. Check for poor ground connections. Check Green/Black and Blue/White wires between driver's door actuator and control unit.

One Or More Doors Do Not Lock Or Unlock With Driver's Lock Knob – Test appropriate actuator. See ACTUATOR TEST under TESTING. Check actuator linkage. Test control unit inputs. See CONTROL UNIT INPUTS under TESTING.

No Door Locks Or Unlocks With Passenger's Door Key – Test passenger's door key switch. See DOOR KEY SWITCH under TESTING. Test control unit inputs. See CONTROL UNIT INPUTS under TESTING. Check for poor ground connections. Check Green/Blue and Green/White wires between passenger's door key switch and control unit.

One Or More Doors Do Not Lock Or Unlock With Passenger's Door Key – Test appropriate actuator. See ACTUATOR TEST under TESTING. Check actuator linkage. Test control unit inputs. See CONTROL UNIT INPUTS under TESTING.

Driver's Door Doesn't Unlock With Driver's Door Key – Check actuator linkage.

No Doors Unlock With Driver's Door Key – Test driver's door key switch. See DOOR KEY SWITCH under TESTING. Test driver's door lock switch. See DOOR LOCK SWITCHES under TESTING. Check for poor ground connections. Check Green/Red wire between driver's door key switch and control unit. Check Green/Black wire between driver's door actuator and control unit.

Door Locks With Key Inserted And A Front Door Is Open – Check ignition switch. See appropriate STEERING COLUMN SWITCHES article. Test driver's and passenger's door switches. See DOOR LOCK SWITCHES under TESTING. Test control unit inputs. See CONTROL UNIT INPUTS under TESTING. Check for poor ground connections. Check Blue/White wire between ignition switch and control unit. Check Green/Blue wire between passenger's door key switch and control unit.

VIGOR

System Does Not Work At All – Check fuse No. 32 in underhood fuse panel. Test control unit inputs. See CONTROL UNIT INPUTS under TESTING. Check for poor ground connections. Check White wire between fuse panel and control unit.

No Doors Lock With Driver's Lock Knob – Check driver's door actuator linkage.

Passenger Doors Do Not Lock With Driver's Lock Knob – Check fuse No. 32 in underhood fuse panel. Test door lock switch in driver's door actuator. See ACTUATOR TEST under TESTING. Test control unit inputs. See CONTROL UNIT INPUTS under TESTING. Check for poor ground connections. Check Blue/White wire between driver's door actuator and control unit. Check Yellow/Red and White/Red wires between actuators and control unit.

One Or More Doors Do Not Lock With Driver's Lock Knob – Test passenger's door actuator. See ACTUATOR TEST under TESTING. Check Yellow/Red and White/Red wires between actuators and control unit.

No Doors Lock Or Unlock With Driver's Door Switch – Check fuse No. 32 in underhood fuse panel. Test driver's door lock switch. See

DOOR LOCK SWITCHES under TESTING. Test control unit inputs. See CONTROL UNIT INPUTS under TESTING. Check for poor ground connections. Check Green/Red and Green/White wires between driver's door switch and control unit.

One Or More Doors Do Not Lock Or Unlock With Driver's Door Switch – Test passenger's door actuator. See ACTUATOR TEST under TESTING. Check Yellow/Red and White/Red wires between actuators and control unit.

No Doors Lock Or Unlock With Passenger's Door Switch – Check fuse No. 32 in underhood fuse panel. Test passenger's door lock switch. See DOOR LOCK SWITCHES under TESTING. Test control unit inputs. See CONTROL UNIT INPUTS under TESTING. Check for poor ground connections. Check actuator linkage. Check Green/Red and Green/White wires between driver's door switch and control unit. Check Yellow/Red and White/Red wires between actuators and control unit.

One Or More Doors Do Not Lock Or Unlock With Passenger's Door Switch – Test passenger's door actuator. See ACTUATOR TEST under TESTING. Check Yellow/Red and White/Red wires between actuators and control unit.

TESTING

CAUTION: Legend and Vigor are equipped with Supplemental Restraint System (SRS). SRS wiring harness is routed close to instrument cluster, steering wheel, and related components. All SRS wiring harnesses are covered by Yellow outer insulation. DO NOT use electrical test equipment on these circuits. Before working on steering column components, disable air bag system. See AIR BAG RESTRAINT SYSTEM article in ACCESSORIES & EQUIPMENT.

ACTUATOR TEST

CAUTION: To prevent damage to the actuator motor, apply power and ground only momentarily.

Integra (Driver's Door) – **1)** Remove door panel. Unplug connector. Using fused jumper wire, connect battery voltage to actuator connector terminal No. 2. Momentarily connect terminal No. 1 to ground. Actuator should move to lock position. *See Fig. 1.* Check for continuity between connector terminals No. 3 and No. 4. Continuity should exist. **2)** Connect battery voltage to actuator connector terminal No. 1. Momentarily connect terminal No. 2 to ground. Actuator should move to unlock position. Check for continuity between connector terminals No. 3 and No. 4. Continuity should not exist. Replace actuator if operation or continuity is not as specified.

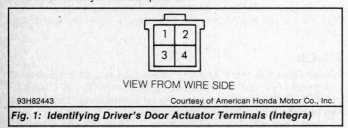
93H82443   Courtesy of American Honda Motor Co., Inc.
Fig. 1: Identifying Driver's Door Actuator Terminals (Integra)

Integra (Passenger's Door) – **1)** Remove door panel. Unplug connector. Using fused jumper wire, connect battery voltage to actuator connector terminal No. 1. Momentarily connect terminal No. 2 to ground. Actuator should move to lock position. *See Fig. 2.*

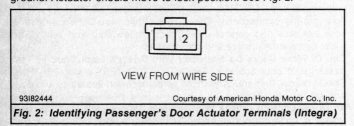
93I82444   Courtesy of American Honda Motor Co., Inc.
Fig. 2: Identifying Passenger's Door Actuator Terminals (Integra)

2) Connect battery voltage to actuator connector terminal No. 2. Momentarily connect terminal No. 1 to ground. Actuator should move to unlock position. Replace actuator if operation is not as specified.

Legend (Driver's Door) – **1)** Remove door panel. Unplug connector. Using fused jumper wire, connect battery voltage to actuator connector terminal No. 2. Momentarily connect terminal No. 5 to ground. Actuator should move to lock position. *See Fig. 3.* Check for continuity between connector terminals No. 6 and No. 7. Continuity should exist. Check for continuity between connector terminals No. 3 and No. 6. Continuity should not exist.

2) Connect battery voltage to actuator connector terminal No. 5. Momentarily connect terminal No. 2 to ground. Actuator should move to unlock position. Check for continuity between connector terminals No. 6 and No. 7. Continuity should not exist. Check for continuity between connector terminals No. 3 and No. 6. Continuity should exist. Replace actuator if operation or continuity is not as specified.

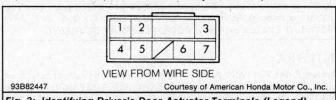
93B82447   Courtesy of American Honda Motor Co., Inc.
Fig. 3: Identifying Driver's Door Actuator Terminals (Legend)

Legend (Front Passenger's Door) – **1)** Remove door panel. Unplug connector. Using fused jumper wire, connect battery voltage to actuator connector terminal No. 2. Momentarily connect terminal No. 5 to ground. Actuator should move to lock position. *See Fig. 4.* Check for continuity between connector terminals No. 3 and No. 6. Continuity should not exist.

2) Connect battery voltage to actuator connector terminal No. 5. Momentarily connect terminal No. 2 to ground. Actuator should move to unlock position. Check for continuity between connector terminals No. 3 and No. 6. Continuity should not exist. Replace actuator if operation or continuity is not as specified.

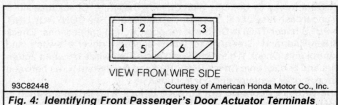
93C82448   Courtesy of American Honda Motor Co., Inc.
Fig. 4: Identifying Front Passenger's Door Actuator Terminals (Legend)

Legend (Rear Door) – **1)** Remove door panel. Unplug connector. Using fused jumper wire, connect battery voltage to actuator connector terminal No. 5. Momentarily connect terminal No. 4 to ground. Actuator should move to lock position. *See Fig. 5.* Check for continuity between connector terminals No. 2 and No. 6. Continuity should not exist.

2) Connect battery voltage to actuator connector terminal No. 4. Momentarily connect terminal No. 5 to ground. Actuator should move to unlock position. Check for continuity between connector terminals No. 2 and No. 6. Continuity should exist. Replace actuator if operation or continuity is not as specified.

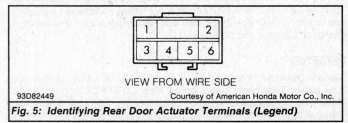
93D82449   Courtesy of American Honda Motor Co., Inc.
Fig. 5: Identifying Rear Door Actuator Terminals (Legend)

Vigor (Driver's Door, With Security System) – **1)** Remove door panel. Unplug connector. Using fused jumper wire, connect battery voltage to actuator connector terminal No. 6. Momentarily connect terminal No. 7 to ground. Actuator should move to lock position. *See Fig. 6.* Check for continuity between connector terminals No. 5 and No. 8. Continuity should exist. Check for continuity between connector terminals No. 4 and No. 5. Continuity should not exist.

2) Connect battery voltage to actuator connector terminal No. 7. Momentarily connect terminal No. 6 to ground. Actuator should move to unlock position. Check for continuity between connector terminals No. 5 and No. 8. Continuity should not exist. Check for continuity between connector terminals No. 4 and No. 5. Continuity should exist. Replace actuator if operation or continuity is not as specified.

93H82450   Courtesy of American Honda Motor Co., Inc.

Fig. 6: Identifying Driver's Door Actuator Terminals (Vigor With Security System)

Vigor (Driver's Door, Without Security System) – 1) Remove door panel. Unplug connector. Using fused jumper wire, connect battery voltage to actuator connector terminal No. 2. Momentarily connect terminal No. 3 to ground. Actuator should move to lock position. *See Fig. 7.* Check for continuity between connector terminals No. 1 and No. 4. Continuity should exist.

2) Connect battery voltage to actuator connector terminal No. 3. Momentarily connect terminal No. 2 to ground. Actuator should move to unlock position. Check for continuity between connector terminals No. 1 and No. 4. Continuity should not exist. Replace actuator if operation or continuity is not as specified.

93I82451   Courtesy of American Honda Motor Co., Inc.

Fig. 7: Identifying Driver's Door Actuator Terminals (Vigor Without Security System)

Vigor (Front Passenger's Door, With Security System) – 1) Remove door panel. Unplug connector. Using fused jumper wire, connect battery voltage to actuator connector terminal No. 6. Momentarily connect terminal No. 7 to ground. Actuator should move to lock position. *See Fig. 8.*

2) Connect battery voltage to actuator connector terminal No. 7. Momentarily connect terminal No. 6 to ground. Actuator should move to unlock position. Replace actuator if operation is not as specified.

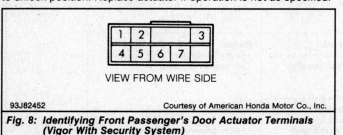

93J82452   Courtesy of American Honda Motor Co., Inc.

Fig. 8: Identifying Front Passenger's Door Actuator Terminals (Vigor With Security System)

Vigor (Front Passenger's Door, Without Security System) – 1) Remove door panel. Unplug connector. Using fused jumper wire, connect battery voltage to actuator connector terminal No. 1. Momentarily

connect terminal No. 2 to ground. Actuator should move to lock position. *See Fig. 9.*

2) Connect battery voltage to actuator connector terminal No. 2. Momentarily connect terminal No. 1 to ground. Actuator should move to unlock position. Replace actuator if operation is not as specified.

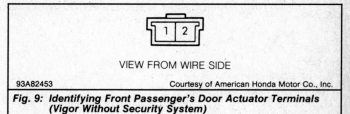

93A82453   Courtesy of American Honda Motor Co., Inc.

Fig. 9: Identifying Front Passenger's Door Actuator Terminals (Vigor Without Security System)

Vigor (Rear Door) – 1) Remove door panel. Unplug connector. Using fused jumper wire, connect battery voltage to actuator connector terminal No. 3. Momentarily connect terminal No. 4 to ground. Actuator should move to lock position. *See Fig. 10.*

2) Connect battery voltage to actuator connector terminal No. 4. Momentarily connect terminal No. 3 to ground. Actuator should move to unlock position.

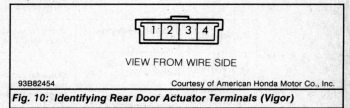

93B82454   Courtesy of American Honda Motor Co., Inc.

Fig. 10: Identifying Rear Door Actuator Terminals (Vigor)

CONTROL UNIT INPUTS

Integra – 1) Turn ignition off. Remove dashboard lower left cover. Remove left knee bolster. Power door lock control unit is located near left kick panel. Unplug power door lock unit 14-pin connector.

2) Using a DVOM, perform power door lock unit input tests in *Fig. 11.* If all input test results are okay, inspect connector and terminals for damage and proper fit. If connector is okay and power door lock still malfunctions, replace power door lock control unit.

Legend – 1) Power door lock control unit is located under instrument panel, to right of steering column. Turn ignition off. Remove instrument panel lower cover. Unplug control unit 18-pin connector.

2) Using a DVOM, perform power door lock control unit input tests in *Fig. 12.* If all input test results are okay, inspect connector and terminals for damage and proper fit. If connector is okay but power door lock still malfunctions, replace power door lock control unit.

Vigor – 1) Turn ignition off. Cruise control unit is located under instrument panel above glove box. Remove glove box. Unplug power door lock control unit 12-pin connector.

2) Using a DVOM, perform power door lock unit input tests in *Fig. 13.* If all input test results are okay, connector and terminals for damage and proper fit. If connector is okay but power door lock still malfunctions, replace power door lock control unit.

DOOR KEY SWITCH

Legend – 1) Remove door panel. Unplug 3-pin connector from actuator. Set switch to lock position. Check for continuity between terminals No. 1 and No. 2. Continuity should not exist. Check for continuity between terminals No. 2 and No. 3. Continuity should exist. *See Fig. 14.*

2) Set switch to unlock position. Check for continuity between terminals No. 1 and No. 2. Continuity should exist. Check for continuity between terminals No. 2 and No. 3. Continuity should not exist.

• Numbers 1 through 9 refer to test numbers, not terminal numbers.

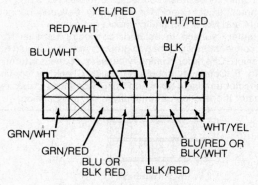

VIEW FROM WIRE SIDE

No.	Terminal	Test condition	Test: Desired result	Possible cause if result is not obtained
1	BLK	Under all conditions.	Check for continuity to ground: There should be continuity.	• Poor ground • An open in the wire.
2	WHT/YEL	Under all conditions.	Check for voltage to ground: There should be battery voltage.	• Blown No.5 (20A) fuse. • An open in the wire.
3	GRN/WHT	Driver's door lock switch in LOCK.	Check for continuity to ground: It should go from battery voltage to 1V or less as the switch is turned.	• Faulty driver's door lock switch. • Poor ground • An open in the wire.
4	GRN/RED	Driver's door lock switch in UNLOCK.		
5	BLU/RED ‹BLK/WHT›	Front passenger's door lock switch in LOCK.	Check for continuity to ground: It should go from battery voltage to 1V or less as the switch is turned.	• Faulty front passenger's door lock switch. • Poor ground • An open in the wire.
6	BLU ‹BLK/RED›	Front passenger's door lock switch in UNLOCK.		
7	BLU/WHT	Driver's door lock knob in LOCK.	Check for continuity to ground: It should go from battery voltage to 1V or less.	• Faulty driver's door actuator. • Poor ground • An open in the wire.
8	RED/WHT and BLK/RED	Connect the WHT/YEL terminal to the RED/WHT terminal, and the BLK/RED terminal to the BLK terminal momentarily.	Check door lock operation: Driver's door should lock as the wires are connected momentarily.	• Faulty driver's door actuator. • An open in the wire.
		Connect the WHT/YEL terminal to the BLK/RED terminal, and the RED/WHT terminal to the BLK terminal momentarily.	Check door lock operation: Driver's door should unlock as the wires are connected momentarily.	
9	WHT/RED and YEL/RED	Connect the WHT/YEL terminal to the WHT/RED[2] terminal, and the YEL/RED terminal to the BLK terminal momentarily.	Check door lock operation: Passenger doors should lock as the wires are connected momentarily.	‹Sedan› • Faulty passenger's door actuator. • An open in the wire.
		Connect the WHT/YEL terminal to the YEL/RED terminal, and the WHT/RED[2] terminal to the BLK terminal momentarily.	Check door lock operation: Passenger doors should unlock as the wires are connected momentarily.	‹Hachback› • Faulty driver's door actuator. • Faulty passenger's door actuator. • An open in the wire.

Fig. 11: Power Door Locks Control Unit Input Test (Integra)

- Numbers 1 through 10 refer to test numbers, not terminal numbers.

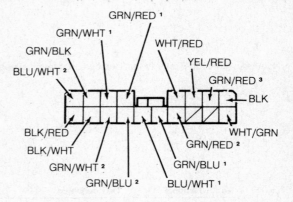

VIEW FROM WIRE SIDE

No.	Wire	Test condition	Test: Desired result	Possible cause if result is not obtained
1	BLK	Under all conditions	Check for continuity to ground: There should be continuity.	• Poor ground • An open in the wire
2	WHT/GRN	Under all conditions	Check for voltage to ground: There should be battery voltage.	• Blown No. 44 (20 A) fuse (in the under-hood fuse/relay box) • An open in the wire
3	GRN/WHT[1]	Driver's door lock switch in LOCK	Check for voltage to ground: It should go from battery voltage to 1 V or less.	• Faulty driver's door lock switch • Poor ground • An open in the wire • Short to ground
	GRN/RED[1]	Driver's door lock switch in UNLOCK		
4	BLK/WHT	Right front door lock switch in LOCK	Check for voltage to ground: It should go from battery voltage to 1 V or less.	• Faulty right front door lock switch • Poor ground • An open in the wire • Short to ground
	BLK/RED	Right front door lock switch in UNLOCK		
5	BLU/WHT[2]	Driver's door lock knob in LOCK	Check for voltage to ground: It should go from battery voltage to 1 V or less.	• Faulty driver's door lock actuator • Poor ground • An open in the wire • Short to ground
	GRN/BLK	Driver's door lock knob in UNLOCK		
6	GRN/BLU[1]	Driver's door open	Check for voltage to ground: It should go from battery voltage to 1 V or less.	• Faulty door switch • Poor ground • An open in the wire
	GRN/RED[2]	Right front door open		
7	BLU/WHT	Ignition key inserted into the ignition switch	Check for voltage to ground: It should go from battery voltage to 1 V or less.	• Faulty ignition key switch • Poor ground • An open in the wire
8	GRN/RED[3]	Driver' door key cylinder in UNLOCK	Check for voltage to ground: It should go from battery voltage to 1 V or less.	• Faulty driver's door key cylinder • Poor ground • An open in the wire
9	GRN/WHT[2]	Right front door key cylinder in LOCK	Check for voltage to ground: It should go from battery voltage to 1 V or less.	• Faulty right fron door key cylinder • Poor ground • An open in the wire
	GRN/BLU[2]	Right front door key cylinder in UNLOCK		
10	WHT/RED and YEL/RED	Connect the YEL/RED terminal to the WHT/GRN terminal, and the WHT/RED terminal to the BLK terminal momentarily.	Check door lock operation: All doors should unlock as the battery is connected momentarily.	• Faulty actuator • An open in the wire
		Connect the WHT/RED terminal to the WHT/GRN terminal, and the YEL/RED terminal to the BLK terminal momentarily.	Check door lock operation: All doors should lock as the battery is connected momentarily.	

93E82457

Courtesy of American Honda Motor Co., Inc.

Fig. 12: Power Door Locks Control Unit Input Test (Legend)

• Numbers 1 through 8 refer to test numbers, not terminal numbers.

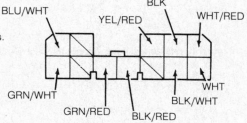

VIEW FROM WIRE SIDE

No.	Terminal	Test condition	Test: Desired result	Possible cause if result is not obtained
1	BLK	Under all conditions.	Check for continuity to gound: There should be continuity.	• Poor ground • An open in the wire.
2	WHT	Under all conditions.	Check for voltage to ground: There should be continuity.	• Blown No. 32 (20 A) fuse (in the under-hood fuse/relay box). • An open in the wire.
3	GRN/WHT	Move the driver's power door lock switch from the neutral position to LOCK.	Check for voltage to ground: There should be less than 1V.	• Faulty driver's power door lock switch. • Poor ground • An open in the wire. • Short to ground. • Faulty control unit.
4	GRN/RED	Move the driver's power door lock switch from the neutral position to UNLOCK.		
5	BLK/RED	Move the front passenger's power door lock switch from the neutral position to LOCK.	Check for voltage to ground: There should be less than 1V.	• Faulty front passenger's power door lock switch. • Poor ground • An open in the wire. • Short to ground. • Faulty control unit.
6	BLK/RED	Move the front passenger's power door lock switch from the neutral position to UNLOCK.		
7	BLU/WHT	Driver's door lock knob in LOCK.	Check for voltage to ground: There should be less than 1V.	• Faulty driver's door actuator. • Poor ground • An open in the wire.
		Driver's door lock knob in UNLOCK.	Check for voltage to ground: There should be battery voltage.	• Faulty driver's door actuator. • Short to ground. • Faulty control unit.
8	WHT/RED or YEL/RED	Connect the WHT terminal to the WHT/RED terminal, and the YEL/RED terminal to the BLK terminal momentarily.	Check door lock operation: All doors should lock as the battery is connected momentarily.	• Faulty passenger's door actuator. • Faulty driver's door actuator. • An open in the wire.
		Connect the WHT terminal to the YEL/RED terminal, and the WHT/RED terminal to the BLK terminal momentarily.	Check door unclok operation: All doors should unlock as the battery is connected mementarily.	

93F82458

Fig. 13: Power Door Locks Control Unit Input Test (Vigor)

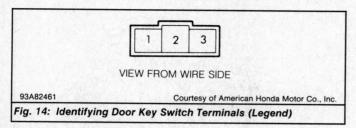

93A82461   Courtesy of American Honda Motor Co., Inc.

Fig. 14: Identifying Door Key Switch Terminals (Legend)

DOOR LOCK SWITCHES

Integra – 1) Remove trim plate. Unplug connector. Set switch to unlock position. Check for continuity between terminals No. 1 and 2. Continuity should not exist. Check for continuity between terminals No. 2 and No. 3. Continuity should exist. *See Fig. 15*

2) Set switch to off position. Check for continuity between terminals No. 1 and 2. Continuity should not exist. Check for continuity between terminals No. 2 and No. 3. Continuity should not exist.

3) Set switch to lock position. Check for continuity between terminals No. 1 and 2. Continuity should exist. Check for continuity between terminals No. 2 and No. 3. Continuity should not exist. Replace switch if continuity is not as specified.

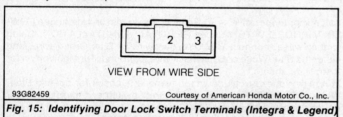

93G82459   Courtesy of American Honda Motor Co., Inc.

Fig. 15: Identifying Door Lock Switch Terminals (Integra & Legend)

Legend – 1) Remove trim plate. Unplug connector. Set switch to unlock position. Check for continuity between terminals No. 1 and 2. Continuity should exist. Check for continuity between terminals No. 2 and No. 3. Continuity should not exist. *See Fig. 54*

2) Set switch to off position. Check for continuity between terminals No. 1 and 2. Continuity should not exist. Check for continuity between terminals No. 2 and No. 3. Continuity should not exist.

3) Set switch to lock position. Check for continuity between terminals No. 1 and 2. Continuity should not exist. Check for continuity between terminals No. 2 and No. 3. Continuity should exist. Replace switch if continuity is not as specified.

Vigor – 1) Remove trim plate. Unplug connector. Set switch to unlock position. Check for continuity between terminals No. 1 and 2. Continuity should exist. Check for continuity between terminals No. 2 and No. 3. Continuity should not exist. *See Fig. 16.*

2) Set switch to off position. Check for continuity between terminals No. 1 and 2. Continuity should not exist. Check for continuity between terminals No. 2 and No. 3. Continuity should not exist.

3) Set switch to lock position. Check for continuity between terminals No. 1 and 2. Continuity should not exist. Check for continuity between terminals No. 2 and No. 3. Continuity should exist. Replace switch if continuity is not as specified.

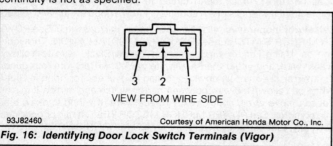

93J82460   Courtesy of American Honda Motor Co., Inc.

Fig. 16: Identifying Door Lock Switch Terminals (Vigor)

TRUNK RELEASE SOLENOID TEST

Legend – Remove trunk inner trim panel. Unplug solenoid connector. Using fused jumper wire, connect battery voltage to solenoid connector terminal "C". *See Fig. 17.* Connect terminal "D" to ground. Replace solenoid if it doesn't operate.

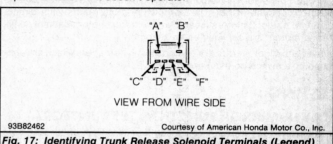

93B82462   Courtesy of American Honda Motor Co., Inc.

Fig. 17: Identifying Trunk Release Solenoid Terminals (Legend)

REMOVAL & INSTALLATION

CAUTION: When battery is disconnected, vehicle computer and memory systems may lose memory data. Driveability problems may exist until computer systems have completed a relearn cycle.

ACTUATORS

Removal & Installation – Remove inner panel. Remove plastic cover. Remove rear channel if necessary. Disconnect linkage. Unplug connector. Remove mounting screws and actuator. To install, reverse removal procedure.

CONTROL UNIT

Removal & Installation (Integra) – Power door lock control unit is located near left kick panel. Turn ignition off. Remove dashboard lower left cover. Remove left knee bolster. Unplug connector. Remove mounting screws and control unit. To install, reverse removal procedure.

Removal & Installation (Legend) – Power door lock unit is located under instrument panel, to right of steering column. Turn ignition off. Remove instrument panel lower cover. Unplug connector. Remove mounting screws and control unit. To install, reverse removal procedure.

Removal & Installation (Vigor) – Cruise control unit is located under instrument panel above glove box. Turn ignition off. Remove glove box. Unplug connector. Remove mounting screws and control unit. To install, reverse removal procedure.

DOOR LOCK SWITCHES

Removal & Installation – Remove trim plate. Unplug connector. Remove switch from trim plate. To install, reverse removal procedure.

WIRING DIAGRAMS

See appropriate chassis wiring diagram in WIRING DIAGRAMS.

Integra, Legend, Vigor

DESCRIPTION & OPERATION

Power mirrors are controlled by a dual control switch located on driver's door panel or instrument panel. The left/right switch directs current to desired mirror. The up/down and left/right switch directs current to one of 2 motors located in the mirror/motor assembly. Mirror and motors are serviced as an assembly.

Legend and Vigor mirrors are equipped with defoggers which are controlled by a switch on the mirror control panel.

TESTING

POWER MIRROR FUNCTION TEST (INTEGRA)

Both Mirrors Inoperative – **1)** Check fuse No. 17 in underdash fuse panel. Replace as necessary. Remove power mirror switch. See POWER MIRROR SWITCH under REMOVAL & INSTALLATION.
2) Turn ignition on. Check for voltage between Black/Yellow wire and ground. See Fig. 1. If battery voltage exists, go to next step. If battery voltage does not exist, repair open Black/Yellow wire between mirror switch and fuse box.
3) Check for continuity between Black wire and ground. If continuity does not exist, repair open circuit in Black wire or poor ground connection. If wiring is okay, substitute known good switch and retest.

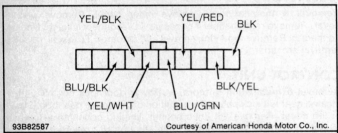

Fig. 1: Identifying Switch Connector Terminals (Integra)

Left Mirror Inoperative – **1)** Remove power mirror switch. See POWER MIRROR SWITCH under REMOVAL & INSTALLATION. Turn ignition on. Using jumper wires, connect Black/Yellow wire to Yellow/Red wire, and either the Yellow/White or Yellow/Black wire to ground.
2) If mirror does not tilt down (or swing left), check for open in Yellow/White or Yellow/Black wire between mirror switch and mirror. If mirror doesn't move at all, check Yellow/Red wire. If wiring is okay, test mirror motor. See POWER MIRROR MOTOR TEST. If mirror operates correctly, test mirror switch. See POWER MIRROR SWITCH TEST.
Right Mirror Inoperative – **1)** Remove power mirror switch. See POWER MIRROR SWITCH under REMOVAL & INSTALLATION. Turn ignition on. Using jumper wires, connect Black/Yellow wire to Blue/Green wire, and either the Yellow/White or Blue/Black wire to ground.
2) If mirror does not tilt down (or swing left), check for open in Yellow/White or Blue/Black wire between mirror switch and mirror. If mirror doesn't move at all, check Blue/Green wire. If wiring is okay, test mirror motor. See POWER MIRROR MOTOR TEST. If mirror operates correctly, test mirror switch. See POWER MIRROR SWITCH TEST.

POWER MIRROR FUNCTION TEST (LEGEND)

Both Mirrors Inoperative – **1)** Check fuse No. 19 in underdash fuse panel. Replace as necessary. Remove power mirror switch. See POWER MIRROR SWITCH under REMOVAL & INSTALLATION.
2) Turn ignition on. Check for voltage between Black/Yellow² wire and ground. See Fig. 2. If battery voltage exists, go to next step. If battery voltage does not exist, repair open Black/Yellow² wire between mirror switch and fuse box.
3) Check for continuity between Black wire and ground. If continuity does not exist, repair open circuit in Black wire or poor ground connection. If wiring is okay, substitute known good switch and retest.

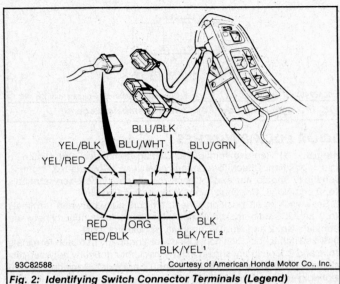

Fig. 2: Identifying Switch Connector Terminals (Legend)

Left Mirror Inoperative – **1)** Remove power mirror switch. See POWER MIRROR SWITCH under REMOVAL & INSTALLATION. Using jumper wires, connect Black/Yellow² wire to Blue/Green wire, and either the Blue/White or Blue/Black wire to ground. Turn ignition on for 2 seconds, then off.
2) If mirror does not tilt down (or swing left), check for open in Blue/White or Blue/Black wire between mirror switch and mirror. If mirror doesn't move at all, check Blue/Green wire. If wiring is okay, test mirror motor. See POWER MIRROR MOTOR TEST. If mirror operates correctly, test switch. See POWER MIRROR SWITCH TEST.
Right Mirror Inoperative – **1)** Remove power mirror switch. See POWER MIRROR SWITCH under REMOVAL & INSTALLATION. Using jumper wires, connect Black/Yellow² wire to Yellow/Red, and either the Blue/White or Yellow/Black wire to ground. Turn ignition on for 2 seconds, then off.
2) If mirror does not tilt down (or swing left), check for open in Blue/White or Blue/Black wire between mirror switch and mirror. If mirror doesn't move at all, check Yellow/Red wire. If wiring is okay, test mirror motor. See POWER MIRROR MOTOR TEST. If mirror operates correctly, test switch. See POWER MIRROR SWITCH TEST.

POWER MIRROR FUNCTION TEST (VIGOR)

Both Mirrors Inoperative – **1)** Check fuse No. 8 in underdash fuse panel. Replace as necessary. Remove power mirror switch. See POWER MIRROR SWITCH under REMOVAL & INSTALLATION.
2) Turn ignition on. Check for voltage between Black/Yellow wire and ground. See Fig. 3. If battery voltage exists, go to next step. If battery voltage does not exist, repair open Black/Yellow wire between mirror switch and fuse box.
3) Check for continuity between Black wire and ground. If continuity does not exist, repair open circuit in Black wire or poor ground connection. If wiring is okay, substitute known good switch and retest.

Left Mirror Inoperative – **1)** Remove power mirror switch. See POWER MIRROR SWITCH under REMOVAL & INSTALLATION. Turn ignition on. Using jumper wires, connect Yellow/Black¹ wire to Yellow/Black² wire, and either the Blue/White or Yellow/Red wire to ground.
2) If mirror does not tilt down (or swing left), check for open in Blue/White or Yellow/Red wire between mirror switch and mirror. If mirror doesn't move at all, check Yellow/Black² wire. If wiring is okay, test mirror motor. See POWER MIRROR MOTOR TEST. If mirror operates correctly, test mirror switch. See POWER MIRROR SWITCH TEST.

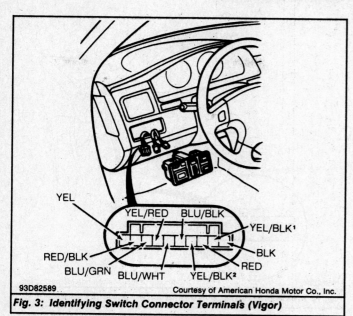

Fig. 3: Identifying Switch Connector Terminals (Vigor)

Right Mirror Inoperative – 1) Remove power mirror switch. See POWER MIRROR SWITCH under REMOVAL & INSTALLATION. Turn ignition on. Using jumper wires, connect Yellow/Black[1] wire to Blue/Black wire, and either the Blue/White or Blue/Green wire to ground.
2) If mirror does not tilt down (or swing left), check for open in Blue/White or Blue/Green wire between mirror switch and mirror. If mirror doesn't move at all, check Blue/Black wire. If wiring is okay, test mirror motor. See POWER MIRROR MOTOR TEST. If mirror operates correctly, test mirror switch. See POWER MIRROR SWITCH TEST.

POWER MIRROR SWITCH TEST

Remove power mirror switch. See POWER MIRROR SWITCH under REMOVAL & INSTALLATION. Check for continuity between specified switch terminals with switch in each position. If continuity is not as specified, replace switch. *See Fig. 4, 5, or 6.* See appropriate POWER MIRROR SWITCH CONTINUITY TEST table.

POWER MIRROR SWITCH CONTINUITY TEST (INTEGRA)

Application	Terminal Numbers
Right Mirror	
Off	3-5-6-10
Up	5-9
Down	3-9
Left	6-9
Right	3-9
Left Mirror	
Off	4-5-7-10
Up	5-9
Down	4-9; 7-9
Left	5-9; 7-9
Right	4-9

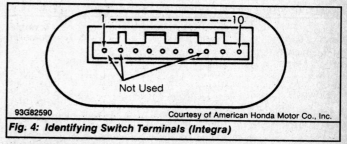

Fig. 4: Identifying Switch Terminals (Integra)

POWER MIRROR SWITCH CONTINUITY TEST (LEGEND)

Application	Terminal Number
Motor Switch	
Right Mirror	
Off	3-4-5-6
Up	3-7
Down	4-7
Left	3-7; 5-7
Right	4-7
Left Mirror	
Off	1-2-3-6
Up	3-7
Down	1-7; 2-7
Left	1-7; 3-7
Right	2-7
Defogger Switch	
On	[1] 6-8-9
Off	No Continuity

[1] – If continuity does not exist between terminals No. 6 and No. 8, replace bulb before condemning switch as defective.

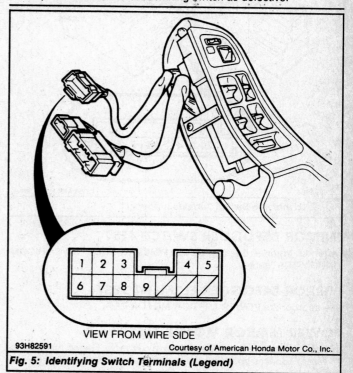

VIEW FROM WIRE SIDE

Fig. 5: Identifying Switch Terminals (Legend)

POWER MIRROR SWITCH CONTINUITY TEST (VIGOR)

Application	Terminal Numbers
Motor Switch	
Right Mirror	
Off	3-5-6-10
Up	3-6-10; 5-9
Down	3-6-9; 5-10
Left	5-6-9; 3-10
Right	3-9
Left Mirror	
Off	4-5-7-10
Up	5-9; 4-7-10
Down	4-7-9; 5-10
Left	5-7-9
Right	4-9; 5-7-10
Defogger Switch	
On	[1] 1-9-10
Off	[1] 9-10

[1] – If continuity does not exist between terminals No. 9 and No. 10, replace bulb before condemning switch as defective.

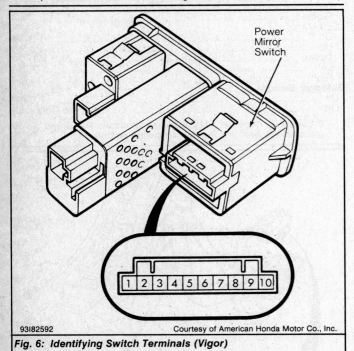

93182592   Courtesy of American Honda Motor Co., Inc.

Fig. 6: Identifying Switch Terminals (Vigor)

MIRROR DEFOGGER SWITCH TEST

Legend & Vigor – See appropriate POWER MIRROR SWITCH CONTINUITY TEST table.

MIRROR DEFOGGER ELEMENT TEST

See appropriate POWER MIRROR MOTOR TEST.

POWER MIRROR MOTOR TEST

Integra – Remove door panel. Unplug connector. Using fused jumper wires, connect specified motor terminals to battery voltage and ground. *See Fig. 7* Replace motor assembly if operation is not as specified. See POWER MIRROR MOTOR TEST (INTEGRA) table.

POWER MIRROR MOTOR TEST (INTEGRA)

Apply 12 Volts To Pin	Ground Pin	Mirror Operation
1	2	Up
2	1	Down
2	3	Left
3	2	Right

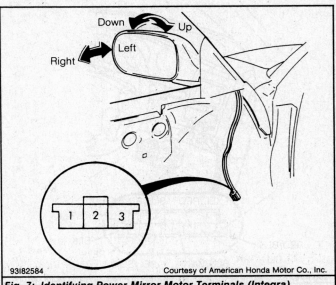

93182584   Courtesy of American Honda Motor Co., Inc.

Fig. 7: Identifying Power Mirror Motor Terminals (Integra)

Legend – Remove cover panel. Unplug connector. Using fused jumper wires, connect specified terminals to battery voltage and ground. *See Fig. 8* Replace motor assembly if operation is not as specified. See POWER MIRROR MOTOR TEST (LEGEND) table.

POWER MIRROR MOTOR TEST (LEGEND)

Apply 12 Volts To Pin	Ground Pin	Mirror Operation
8	7	Up
7	8	Down
7	6	Left
6	7	Right
3	4	Defogger On

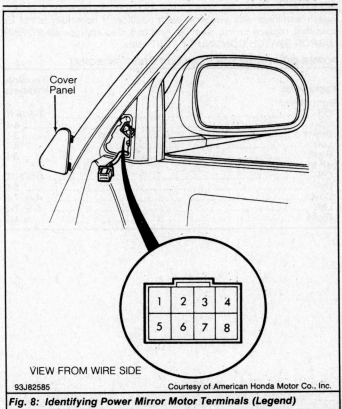

VIEW FROM WIRE SIDE

93J82585   Courtesy of American Honda Motor Co., Inc.

Fig. 8: Identifying Power Mirror Motor Terminals (Legend)

Vigor – Remove cover panel. Unplug connectors. Using fused jumper wires, connect specified terminals to battery voltage and ground. *See Fig. 9.* Replace motor assembly if operation is not as specified. See POWER MIRROR MOTOR TEST (VIGOR) table.

POWER MIRROR MOTOR TEST (VIGOR)

Apply 12 Volts To Pin	Ground Pin	Mirror Operation
1	2	Up
2	1	Down
2	3	Left
3	2	Right
3	4	Defogger On

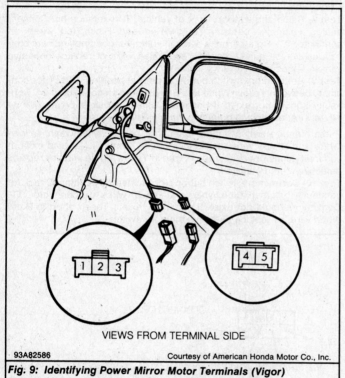

VIEWS FROM TERMINAL SIDE

93A82586 Courtesy of American Honda Motor Co., Inc.

Fig. 9: Identifying Power Mirror Motor Terminals (Vigor)

MIRROR DEFOGGER ELEMENT TEST

See appropriate POWER MIRROR MOTOR TEST table.

REMOVAL & INSTALLATION
POWER MIRROR SWITCH

Integra – Remove instrument panel lower cover. From behind, push switch out from panel. Unplug connector. To install, reverse removal procedure.
Legend – Remove driver's door panel. Unplug connector. Remove switch. To install, reverse removal procedure.
Vigor – From behind, push switch out from panel. Unplug connector. To install, reverse removal procedure.

POWER MIRROR ASSEMBLY

Remove door panel. Carefully pry out cover panel. Hold mirror assembly with one hand while removing mounting screws. Remove mirror assembly. To install, reverse removal procedure. To install, reverse removal procedure.

WIRING DIAGRAMS

See appropriate chassis wiring diagram in WIRING DIAGRAMS.

Legend, Vigor

DESCRIPTION & OPERATION

On Legend, 4 motors provide for front up/down, rear up/down, forward/back, and recline adjustment. A memory feature adjusts the seat to either of 2 preset positions. On Vigor, 2 motors provide front/rear and tilt adjustment.

TROUBLE SHOOTING

See TESTING and WIRING DIAGRAMS

TESTING

NOTE: Different wires with the same color have been given a suffix number. For example, Yellow/Green[1] and Yellow/Green[2] are not the same wires.

CONTROL UNIT INPUT TESTS

Legend – Control unit is located under front center of driver's seat. Unplug connectors. Check all connections and repair as necessary. Different wires of the same color have been assigned a superscript number to distinguish them. For example, the Green/Blue[1] wire is not the same as the Green/Blue[2] wire. *See Fig. 1.*

Test 1) Check for continuity between Black wire on connector "A" and ground. If continuity does not exist, repair Black wire.

Test 2) Check for continuity between Black wire on connector "B" and ground. If continuity does not exist, repair Black wire.

Test 3) Check for battery voltage between White/Red wire on connector "B" and ground. If battery voltage does not exist, replace blown fuse No. 58 in underhood fuse box, or repair open White/Red wire.

Test 4) Check for battery voltage between Red/White wire on connector "A" and ground. If battery voltage does not exist, replace blown fuse No. 55 in underhood fuse box, or repair open Red/White.

Test 5) Check for battery voltage between White/Yellow wire on connector "A" and ground. If battery voltage does not exist, replace blown fuse No. 34 in underhood fuse box, fuse No. 15 in underdash fuse box, or repair open White/Yellow.

Test 6) Check for battery voltage between Black/Red wire on connector "C" and ground. If battery voltage does not exist, replace blown fuse No. 20 in underdash fuse box, or repair open Black/Red.

Test 7) Open driver's door. Check for continuity between Green/Blue[1] wire on connector "C" and ground. If continuity does not exist, replace door switch or repair open in Green/Blue[1] wire. Close driver's door. Check for continuity between Green/Blue[1] on connector "C" and ground. If continuity exists, replace door switch or repair shorted Green/Blue[1] wire.

Test 8) Raise and support front of vehicle. Turn ignition on. Connect analog voltmeter between Yellow/Red and Black/Red wires on connector "C". Rotate front wheels. If voltmeter does not indicate continuous 12-volt pulses, repair Yellow/Red wire, or replace defective vehicle speed sensor.

Test 9) Set memory switch button to neutral position. Check for continuity between Yellow/White and Black[3] wires on connector "C". Continuity should not exist. If continuity exists, repair short in Yellow/White wire, or replace defective memory switch.

Press memory switch button. Check for continuity between Yellow/White and Black[3] wires on connector "C". Continuity should exist. If continuity does not exist, repair open in Yellow/White wire, or replace defective memory switch.

Test 10) Set memory switch button No. 1 to neutral position. Check for continuity between Blue/White and Black[3] wires on connector "C". Continuity should not exist. If continuity exists, repair short in Blue/White wire, or replace defective memory switch.

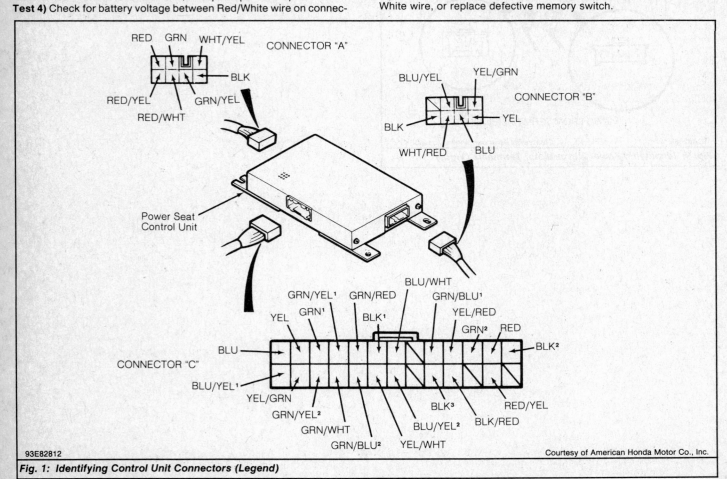

Fig. 1: Identifying Control Unit Connectors (Legend)

93E82812

Courtesy of American Honda Motor Co., Inc.

Press memory switch button No. 1. Check for continuity between Blue/White and Black[3] wires on connector "C". Continuity should exist. If continuity does not exist, repair open in Blue/White wire, or replace defective memory switch.

Test 11) Set memory switch button No. 2 to neutral position. Check for continuity between Blue/Yellow[2] and Black[3] wires on connector "C". Continuity should not exist. If continuity exists, repair short in Blue/Yellow[2] wire, or replace defective memory switch.

Press memory switch button No. 2. Check for continuity between Blue/Yellow[2] and Black[3] wires on connector "C". Continuity should exist. If continuity does not exist, repair open in Blue/Yellow[2] wire, or replace defective memory switch.

Test 12) Set front up/down switch to neutral position. Check for continuity between Green[1] and Black[2] wires on connector "C". Continuity should not exist. If continuity exists, repair short in Green[1] wire, or replace defective memory switch.

Set front up/down switch to up position. Check for continuity between Green[1] and Black[2] wires on connector "C". Continuity should not exist. If continuity exists, repair open in Green[1] wire, or replace defective memory switch.

Test 13) Set front up/down switch to neutral position. Check for continuity between Green/Yellow[2] and Black[2] wires on connector "C". Continuity should not exist. If continuity exists, repair short in Green/Yellow[2] wire, or replace defective memory switch.

Set front up/down switch to down position. Check for continuity between Green/Yellow[2] and Black[2] wires on connector "C". Continuity should not exist. If continuity exists, repair open in Green/Yellow[2] wire, or replace defective memory switch.

Test 14) Set rear up/down switch to neutral position. Check for continuity between Red and Black[2] wires on connector "C". Continuity should not exist. If continuity exists, repair short in Red wire, or replace defective memory switch.

Set rear up/down switch to up position. Check for continuity between Red and Black[2] wires on connector "C". Continuity should exist. If continuity does not exist, repair open in Red wire, or replace defective memory switch.

Test 15) Set rear up/down switch to neutral position. Check for continuity between Red/Yellow and Black[2] wires on connector "C". Continuity should not exist. If continuity exists, repair short in Red/Yellow wire, or replace defective memory switch.

Set rear up/down switch to up position. Check for continuity between Red/Yellow and Black[2] wires on connector "C". Continuity should exist. If continuity does not exist, repair open in Red/Yellow wire, or replace defective memory switch.

Test 16) Set forward/back switch to neutral position. Check for continuity between Blue and Black[2] wires on connector "C". Continuity should not exist. If continuity exists, repair short in Blue wire, or replace defective memory switch.

Set forward/back switch to forward position. Check for continuity between Blue and Black[2] wires on connector "C". Continuity should exist. If continuity does not exist, repair open in Blue wire, or replace defective memory switch.

Test 17) Set forward/back switch to neutral position. Check for continuity between Blue/Yellow and Black[2] wires on connector "C". Continuity should not exist. If continuity exists, repair short in Blue/Yellow wire, or replace defective memory switch.

Set forward/back switch to rear position. Check for continuity between Blue/Yellow and Black[2] wires on connector "C". Continuity should exist. If continuity does not exist, repair open in Blue/Yellow wire, or replace defective memory switch.

Test 18) Set recline switch to neutral position. Check for continuity between Yellow and Black[2] wires on connector "C". Continuity should not exist. If continuity exists, repair short in Yellow wire, or replace defective memory switch.

Set recline switch to forward position. Check for continuity between Yellow and Black[2] wires on connector "C". Continuity should exist. If continuity does not exist, repair open in Yellow wire, or replace defective memory switch.

Test 19) Set recline switch to neutral position. Check for continuity between Yellow/Green and Black[2] wires on connector "C". Continuity should not exist. If continuity exists, repair short in Yellow/Green wire, or replace defective memory switch.

Set recline switch to rear position. Check for continuity between Yellow/Green and Black[2] wires on connector "C". Continuity should exist. If continuity does not exist, repair open in Yellow/Green wire, or replace defective memory switch.

Test 20) Position seat back forward. Check for continuity between Green[2] and Black[1] wires at connector "C". Continuity should exist. If continuity does not exist, repair open in Green[2] or Black[1] wire, or replace defective recline limit switch.

Position Set seat back to rear. Check for continuity between Green[2] and Black[1] wires at connector "C". Continuity should not exist. If continuity exists, repair short in Green[2] or Black[1] wire, or replace defective recline limit switch.

Test 21) Reconnect all wiring. With an analog voltmeter, backprobe 2-pin connector at front up/down motor. With motor running, voltmeter should indicate continuous 5-volt pulses. If voltmeter does not indicate continuous 5-volt pulses, repair Green/Red wire or Black wire, or replace defective memory sensor.

Test 22) With an analog voltmeter, backprobe 2-pin connector at rear up/down motor. With motor running, voltmeter should indicate continuous 5-volt pulses. If voltmeter does not indicate continuous 5-volt pulses, repair Green/Blue[2] wire or Black wire, or replace defective memory sensor.

Test 23). With an analog voltmeter, backprobe 2-pin connector at forward/rear motor. With motor running, voltmeter should indicate continuous 5-volt pulses. If voltmeter does not indicate continuous 5-volt pulses, repair Green/Yellow[1] wire or Black wire, or replace defective memory sensor.

Test 24) With an analog voltmeter, backprobe 2-pin connector recline motor. With motor running, voltmeter should indicate continuous 5-volt pulses. If voltmeter does not indicate continuous 5-volt pulses, repair Green/White wire or Black wire, or replace defective memory sensor.

Test 25 Unplug connector "A". Using jumper wires, connect Green wire to Red/White wire, and Green/Yellow wire to Black wire. Front up/down motor should run. Transpose jumper wires. Motor should run in opposite direction. If motor operation is not as specified, repair appropriate wire or replace defective motor.

Test 26 At connector "A", connect Red wire to Red/White wire, and Red/Yellow wire to Black wire. Rear up/down motor should run. Transpose jumper wires. Motor should run in opposite direction. If motor operation is not as specified, repair appropriate wire or replace defective motor.

Test 27 Unplug connector "B". Using jumper wires, connect Blue wire to White/Red wire, and Blue/Yellow wire to Black wire. Forward/back motor should run. Transpose jumper wires. Motor should run in opposite direction. If motor operation is not as specified, repair appropriate wire or replace defective motor.

Test 28 At connector "B", connect Yellow wire to White/Red wire, and Yellow/Green wire to Black wire. Recline motor should run. Transpose jumper wires. Motor should run in opposite direction. If motor operation is not as specified, repair appropriate wire or replace defective motor.

MOTOR TEST

CAUTION: Disconnect power from motor immediately when motor stops.

Remove seat. Unplug connector from motor. Using jumper wires, connect motor terminals to battery voltage and ground. See WIRING DIAGRAMS for appropriate wire colors. Motor should run smoothly. Transpose jumper wires. Motor should run smoothly in opposite direction. Replace motor if operation is not as specified.

SWITCH TEST

Seat Switch (Legend) – Remove seat. Remove switch. Check for continuity between specified terminals with switch held in each position. Replace switch if continuity is not as specified. See appropriate SEAT SWITCH TEST (LEGEND) table. *See Fig. 2 or 3.*

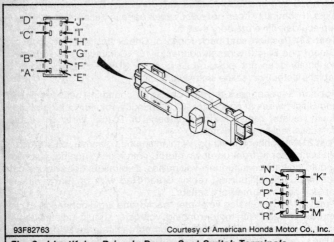

93F82763   Courtesy of American Honda Motor Co., Inc.

Fig. 2: Identifying Driver's Power Seat Switch Terminals (Legend)

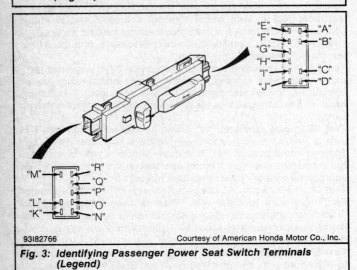

93I82766   Courtesy of American Honda Motor Co., Inc.

Fig. 3: Identifying Passenger Power Seat Switch Terminals (Legend)

DRIVER'S SEAT SWITCH TEST (LEGEND WITH MEMORY)

Switch Position	Terminals
Forward/Back	
Forward	B-I
Neutral	B-C-G-H
Back	C-I
Front Up/Down	
Up	F-G; H-I
Neutral	B-C-G-H
Down	G-I
Rear Up/Down	
Up	A-J
Neutral	A-D-L-M
Down	J-M
Recline	
Forward	D-J
Neutral	A-D-L-M
Back	J-L

DRIVER'S SEAT SWITCH TEST (LEGEND WITHOUT MEMORY)

Switch Position	Terminals
Forward/Back	
Forward	B-I; C-F
Neutral	B-C-F-G-H
Back	C-I; B-F
Front Up/Down	
Up	F-G; H-I
Neutral	B-C-F-G-H
Down	G-I; F-H
Rear Up/Down	
Up	A-J; E-M
Neutral	A-D-E-L-M
Down	A-E; J-M
Recline	
Forward	D-J; E-L
Neutral	A-D-E-L-M
Back	D-E; J-L

PASSENGER'S SEAT SWITCH TEST (LEGEND)

Switch Position	Terminals
Forward/Back	
Forward	B-I; C-F
Neutral	B-C-F
Back	C-I; B-F
Recline	
Forward	D-J; E-L
Neutral	D-E-L
Back	D-E; J-L

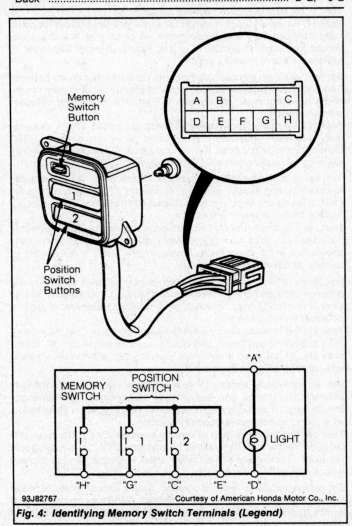

93J82767   Courtesy of American Honda Motor Co., Inc.

Fig. 4: Identifying Memory Switch Terminals (Legend)

Memory Switch (Legend) – Remove driver's door panel. Unplug connector. Remove switch. Check for continuity between specified terminals with switch held in each position. Replace switch if continuity is not as specified. See MEMORY SWITCH TEST (LEGEND) table. *See Fig. 4.*

MEMORY SWITCH TEST (LEGEND)

Switch Position	Terminals
Memory Switch	
On	E-H
Off	No Continuity
Position Switch 1	
On	E-G
Off	No Continuity
Position Switch 2	
On	C-E
Off	No Continuity
Illumination	A-D

Seat Switch (Vigor) – Remove retaining screws and switch. Unplug connectors. Check for continuity between specified terminals with switch in each position. Replace switch if continuity is not as specified. See POWER SEAT SWITCH TEST (VIGOR) table. *See Fig. 5.*

POWER SEAT SWITCH TEST (VIGOR)

Switch Position	Terminals
Forward/Back	
Forward	1-8
Neutral	2-7-8
Back	1-7
Recline	
Forward	4-5
Neutral	3-4-6
Back	3-5

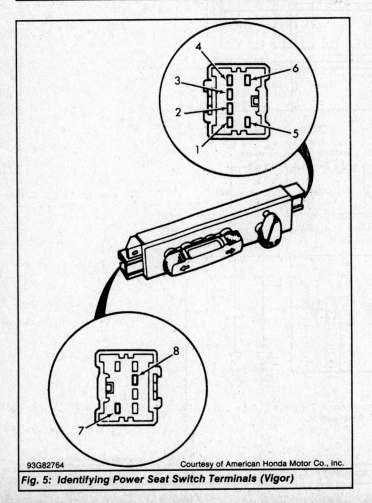

93G82764   Courtesy of American Honda Motor Co., Inc.

Fig. 5: Identifying Power Seat Switch Terminals (Vigor)

REMOVAL & INSTALLATION

CAUTION: When battery is disconnected, vehicle computer and memory systems may lose memory data. Driveability problems may exist until computer systems have completed a relearn cycle.

SEAT ASSEMBLY

Removal & Installation – Position seat fully rearward. Remove front seat track covers and front retaining bolts. Position seat fully forward. Remove rear seat track covers and retaining bolts. Unplug electrical connectors. Remove seat from vehicle.

MOTOR (LEGEND)

CAUTION: Wear protective gloves when removing and installing seat motors.

Removal & Installation (Forward/Back Motor) – Remove seat. Remove seat cushion. Remove slide joint cable. Remove retaining nuts and bolts. Remove motor and gearbox. To install, reverse removal procedure.

Removal & Installation (Recline Motor) – Remove seat. Remove seat cushion. Remove switch plate if necessary. Remove retaining nuts. Remove motor and gearbox. To install, reverse removal procedure. Apply molybdenum grease to gears. Apply thread lock cement to retaining nuts.

Removal & Installation (Up/Down Motor) – Raise rear of seat. Remove seat. Remove seat cushion. Remove harness protector from forward/rear adjuster. Remove springs. Remove plate from forward/rear and up/down adjuster. Unplug connectors. Remove retaining nuts and bolts. Slide pipe brackets inward. Remove motor. To install, reverse removal procedure. Apply molybdenum grease to lead screws. Replace bushings. Apply thread lock cement to retaining bolts.

SEAT ADJUSTER (LEGEND)

CAUTION: Wear protective gloves when removing and installing seat adjuster.

Removal & Installation – Raise front and rear of seat. Remove seat. Remove seat cushion and seat back. Remove switch. Separate recline adjuster from forward/back and up/down adjuster. Remove forward/back joint cable. Remove memory control unit. Remove harness protector. Unplug connectors. Remove lower seat rail caps. Remove any remaining clips and retaining bolts. Remove adjusters. To install, reverse removal procedure. Install new bushings.

MOTOR & SEAT ADJUSTER (VIGOR)

Removal & Installation – Use illustration as a guide. *See Fig. 6.*

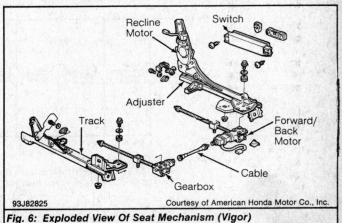

93J82825   Courtesy of American Honda Motor Co., Inc.

Fig. 6: Exploded View Of Seat Mechanism (Vigor)

1993 ACCESSORIES & EQUIPMENT
Power Seats (Cont.)

WIRING DIAGRAMS

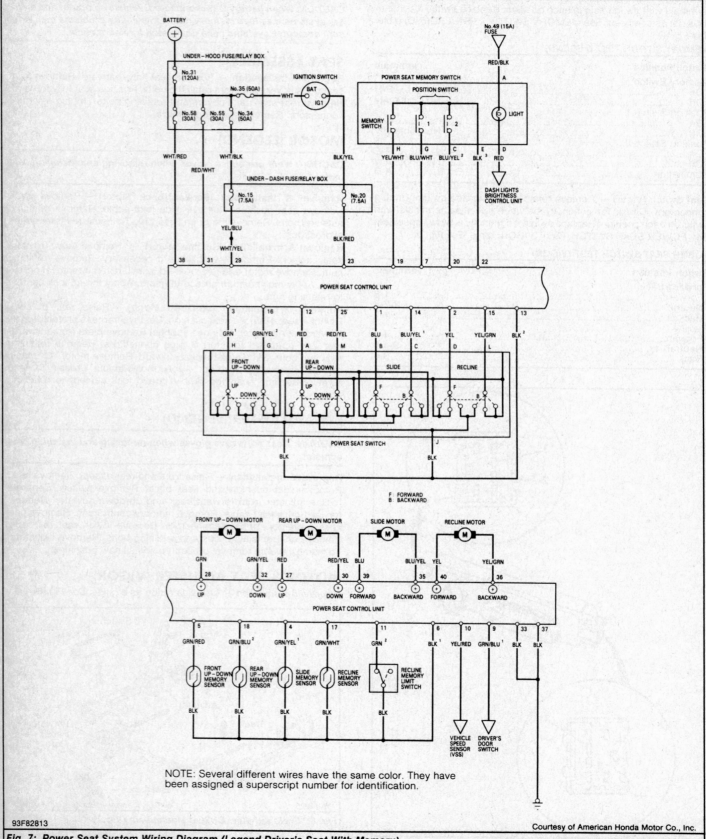

NOTE: Several different wires have the same color. They have been assigned a superscript number for identification.

93F82813

Courtesy of American Honda Motor Co., Inc.

Fig. 7: Power Seat System Wiring Diagram (Legend Driver's Seat With Memory)

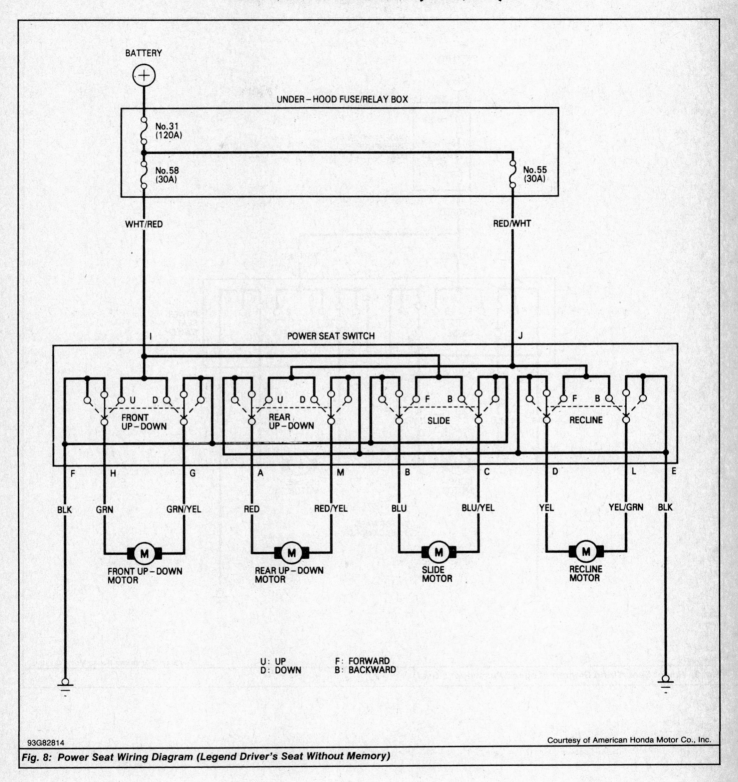

93G82814

Courtesy of American Honda Motor Co., Inc.

Fig. 8: Power Seat Wiring Diagram (Legend Driver's Seat Without Memory)

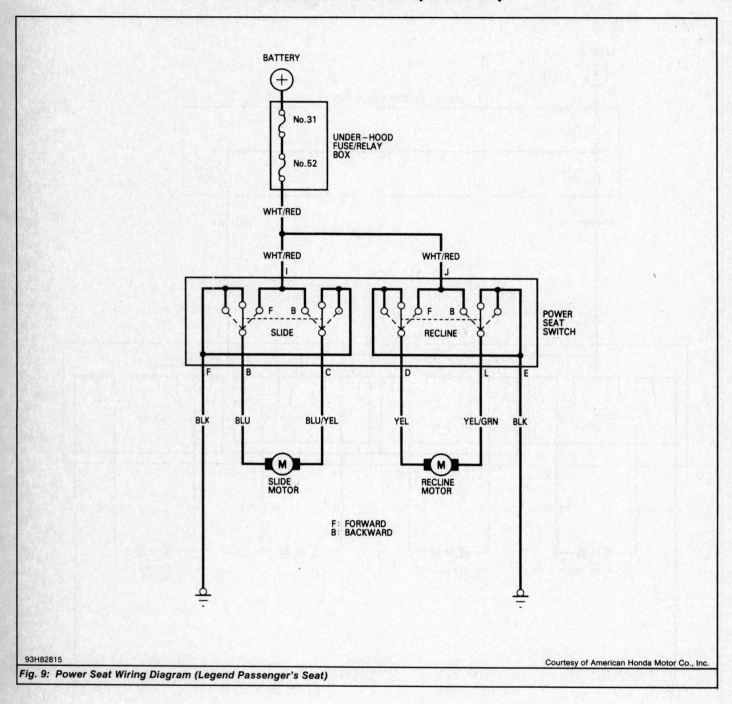

Courtesy of American Honda Motor Co., Inc.

Fig. 9: Power Seat Wiring Diagram (Legend Passenger's Seat)

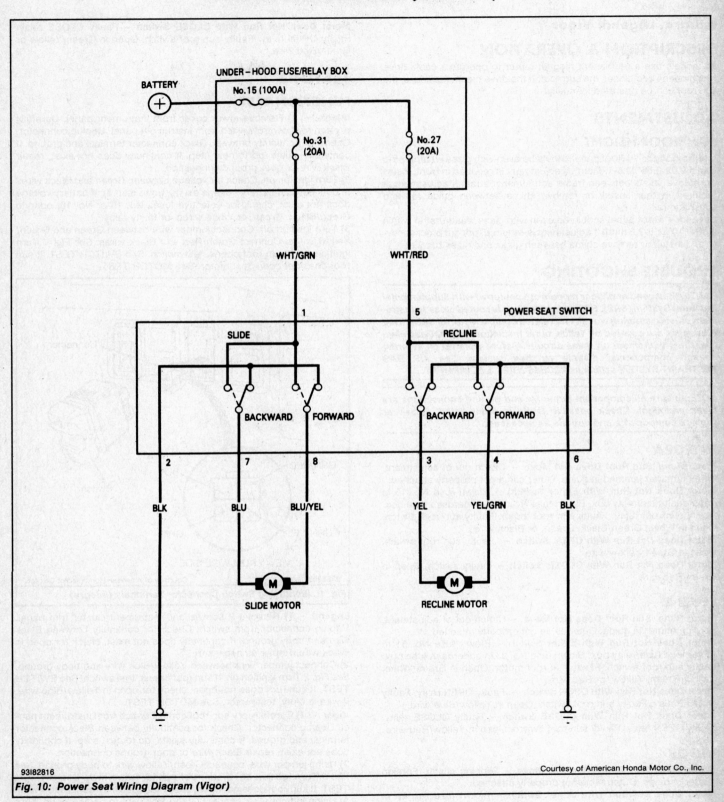

93I82816

Fig. 10: Power Seat Wiring Diagram (Vigor)

Integra, Legend, Vigor

DESCRIPTION & OPERATION

All models use a permanent magnet motor to operate a cable drive which opens and closes the sun roof. If the drive mechanism fails, the sun roof can be operated manually.

ADJUSTMENTS

SUN ROOF HEIGHT

Integra & Vigor – Roof panel should be even with glass weatherstrip within 0.02-0.06" (0.5-1.5 mm). If adjustment is required in front, install or remove shims between frame and sunshade rail. If adjustment is required in rear, install or remove shims between guide rail and sunshade rail.

Legend – Roof panel should be even with glass weatherstrip within 0.06-0.10" (1.5-2.5 mm). If adjustment is required, pry out bracket cover and install or remove shims between glass and glass bracket.

TROUBLE SHOOTING

CAUTION: Legend and Vigor models are equipped with Supplemental Restraint System (SRS). SRS wiring harness is routed close to instrument cluster, steering wheel, and related components. All SRS wiring harnesses are covered by Yellow outer insulation. DO NOT use electrical test equipment on these circuits. Before working on steering column components, disable air bag system. See AIR BAG RESTRAINT SYSTEM article in ACCESSORIES & EQUIPMENT.

NOTE: Ensure all component terminals and ground connections are clean and tight. Check possible faults in order listed. Repair or replace components and circuits as necessary.

INTEGRA

Motor Runs, Sun Roof Does Not Move – Clutch out of adjustment. Foreign matter jammed in guide. Outer cable not properly attached.
Motor Does Not Run With Either Switch) – Blown fuse No. 15 in underdash fuse/relay box. Blown fuse No. 16 in underdash fuse box. Faulty sun roof relay. Faulty sun roof motor. Faulty sun roof switch. Open in White, Green/Black, Green, or Black wire.
Motor Does Not Run With OPEN Switch – Faulty sun roof switch. Open in Green/Yellow wire.
Motor Does Not Run With CLOSE Switch – Faulty switch. Open in Green/Red wire.

LEGEND

Motor Runs, Sun Roof Does Not Move – Clutch out of adjustment. Foreign matter in guide. Outer cable not properly attached.
Motor Does Not Run With Either Switch – Blown fuse No. 51 in underhood fuse/relay box. Blown fuse No. 23 in underdash fuse box. Faulty sun roof switch. Faulty sun roof motor. Open in Green/White, Yellow/Green, Yellow, or Red wire.
Motor Does Not Run With OPEN Switch – Faulty OPEN relay. Faulty CLOSE relay. Faulty sun roof switch. Open in Yellow/Blue wire.
Motor Does Not Run With CLOSE Switch – Faulty CLOSE relay. Faulty OPEN relay. Faulty sun roof switch. Open in Yellow/Red wire.

VIGOR

Motor Runs, Sun Roof Does Not Move – Slipping clutch. Foreign matter in guide. Outer cable not properly attached.
Motor Does Not Run With Either Switch – Blown fuse No. 29 in underhood fuse/relay box. Blown fuse No. 5 in underdash fuse box. Faulty sun roof switch. Faulty sun roof motor. Open in Green, Yellow/Red, Green/Yellow, or Green/Red wire.
Motor Does Not Run With OPEN Switch – Faulty OPEN relay. Faulty CLOSE relay. Faulty sun roof switch. Open in Green/Yellow or Green/Red wire.

Motor Does Not Run With CLOSE Switch – Faulty CLOSE relay. Faulty OPEN relay. Faulty sun roof switch. Open in Green/Yellow or Green/Red wire.

TESTING

FUNCTION TEST

Integra – **1)** Remove lower cover from instrument panel. Carefully pry sun roof control switch from instrument panel. Unplug connector. Check for continuity between Black connector terminal and ground. If continuity exists, go to next step. If continuity does not exist, repair Black wire or poor ground connection.
2) Turn ignition on. Check for voltage between Green and Black wires at connector. If battery voltage exists, go to step 3). If battery voltage does not exist, check for defective fuses No. 15 or No. 16, open in Green/Black, Green, or White wires, or faulty relay.
3) Turn ignition off. Connect jumper wire between Green and Green/Yellow wires. Connect Green/Red and Black wires. *See Fig. 1* Turn ignition on. If sun roof opens, test switch. See SWITCH TEST. If sun roof does not open, test motor. See MOTOR TEST.

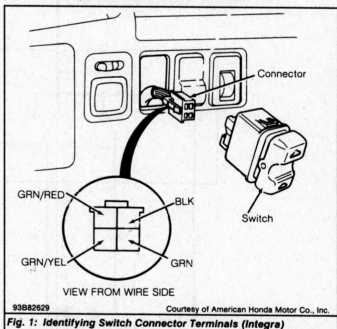

GRN/RED — BLK

GRN/YEL — GRN

VIEW FROM WIRE SIDE

Connector

Switch

93B82629   Courtesy of American Honda Motor Co., Inc.

Fig. 1: Identifying Switch Connector Terminals (Integra)

Legend – **1)** Remove 2 screws and instrument cluster trim panel. Unplug connector from switch. Check for continuity between Black wire and body ground. If continuity does not exist, check for open in Black wire. Repair as necessary.
2) Connect jumper wire between Yellow/Blue wire and body ground. *See Fig. 2* Turn ignition on. If sun roof opens, test switch. See SWITCH TEST. If sun roof does not open, check for open in Yellow/Blue wire. If wire is okay, test motor. See MOTOR TEST.
Vigor – **1)** Carefully pry sun roof control switch from instrument panel. Unplug connector. Check for continuity between Black connector terminal and ground. If continuity exists, go to next step. If continuity does not exist, repair Black wire or poor ground connection.
2) Using jumper wire, connect Green/Yellow wire to body ground. *See Fig. 3* Turn ignition on. If sun roof opens, test switch. See SWITCH TEST. If sun roof does not open, check for open in Green/Yellow wire.
3) Using jumper wire, connect Green/Red wire to body ground. Turn ignition on. If sun roof closes, test switch. See SWITCH TEST. If sun roof does not close, check for open in Green/Red wire. If wiring is okay, test relays and motor. See RELAY TEST and MOTOR TEST.

RELAY TEST

Integra – Remove power window relay from underdash fuse/relay box. Check for continuity between terminals "A" and "B". Continuity should not exist. Using jumper wires, connect terminals "C" and "D" to battery voltage and ground. *See Fig. 4.* Check for continuity between terminals "A" and "B". Continuity should exist. Replace relay if continuity is not as specified.

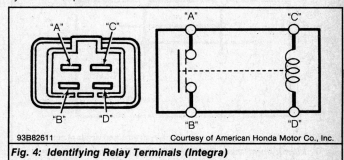

93B82611   Courtesy of American Honda Motor Co., Inc.

Fig. 4: Identifying Relay Terminals (Integra)

Legend & Vigor – **1)** Remove relay from socket. On Legend, relays are located near sun roof motor. On Vigor, relays are located in trunk, on right side. Check for continuity between terminals "A" and "C". Continuity should not exist. Check for continuity between terminals "B" and "C". *See Fig. 5.* Continuity should exist.
2) Using jumper wires, connect terminals "D" and "E" to battery voltage and ground. Check for continuity between terminals "A" and "C". Continuity should exist. Check for continuity between terminals "B" and "C". Continuity should not exist. Replace relay if operation is not as specified.

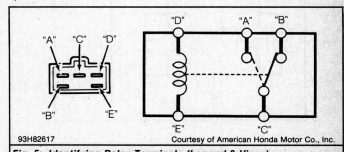

93H82617   Courtesy of American Honda Motor Co., Inc.

Fig. 5: Identifying Relay Terminals (Legend & Vigor)

SWITCH TEST

Remove sun roof switch from instrument panel. See SWITCH under REMOVAL & INSTALLATION. Check for continuity between specified switch terminals with switch in each position. See appropriate POWER SUN ROOF SWITCH CONTINUITY TEST table. If continuity is not as specified, replace switch. *See Fig. 6, 7, or 8.*

POWER SUN ROOF SWITCH CONTINUITY TEST (INTEGRA)

Position	Terminals
Off	"A"-"B"-"C"
Open	"B"-"D"
Close	"C"-"D"

NOTE: *On Legend, the switch contains an internal diode which will cause erroneous no-continuity indications unless the negative terminal of the continuity tester is connected to terminal "H" for "Open" and "Close" checks.*

POWER SUN ROOF SWITCH CONTINUITY TEST (LEGEND)

Position	Terminals
Off	No Continuity
Open	"F"-"H"
Close	"G"-"H"

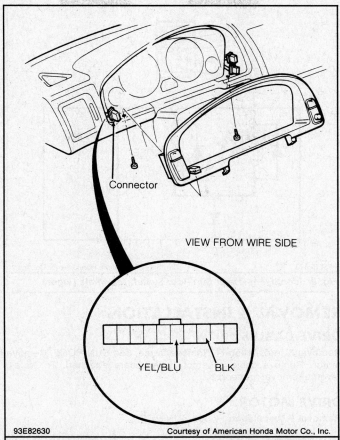

Connector

VIEW FROM WIRE SIDE

YEL/BLU   BLK

93E82630   Courtesy of American Honda Motor Co., Inc.

Fig. 2: Identifying Switch Connector Terminals (Legend)

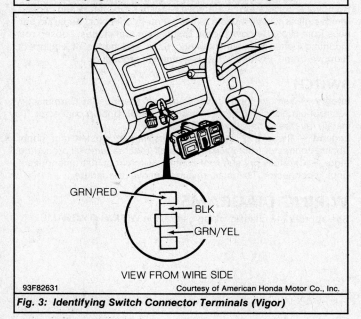

GRN/RED

BLK

GRN/YEL

VIEW FROM WIRE SIDE

93F82631   Courtesy of American Honda Motor Co., Inc.

Fig. 3: Identifying Switch Connector Terminals (Vigor)

MOTOR TEST

Remove headliner. Unplug connector from motor. Using jumper wires, connect battery voltage and ground to motor connector terminals. Check for motor operation. Transpose jumper wires and retest. Replace motor if it does not operate smoothly in both directions.

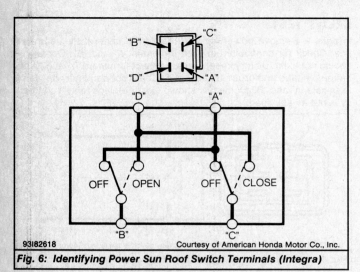

Fig. 6: Identifying Power Sun Roof Switch Terminals (Integra)

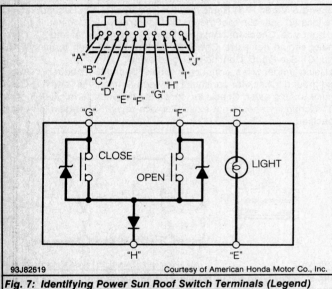

Fig. 7: Identifying Power Sun Roof Switch Terminals (Legend)

NOTE: On Vigor, the switch contains an internal diode which will cause erroneous no-continuity indications unless the negative terminal of the continuity tester is connected to terminal "D" for "Open" and "Close" checks.

POWER SUN ROOF SWITCH CONTINUITY TEST (VIGOR)

Position	Terminals
Off	No Continuity
Open	"B"-"D"
Close	"E"-"D"

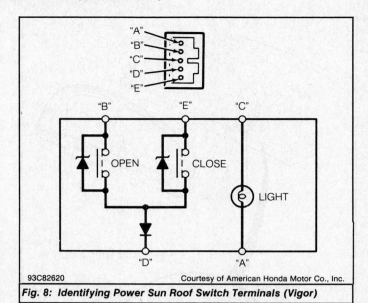

Fig. 8: Identifying Power Sun Roof Switch Terminals (Vigor)

REMOVAL & INSTALLATION

DRIVE CABLES

Removal & Installation – Remove frame. See SUN ROOF. Remove motor. Remove cable assembly with sliders attached. To install, reverse removal procedure.

DRIVE MOTOR

Removal & Installation – See SUN ROOF.

SUN ROOF

Removal & Installation – Remove headliner. On Integra and Legend, remove glass. On all models, unplug motor connector. Separate harness from clips. Remove motor. Disconnect drain tubes. Loosen rear mounting bolts. Remove mounting bolts and hooks (if equipped). Remove frame. To install, reverse removal procedure

SWITCH

Integra – Remove lower cover from instrument panel. Carefully pry sun roof control switch from instrument panel. Unplug connector. To install, reverse removal procedure.
Legend – Remove 2 screws and instrument cluster trim panel. Unplug connector from switch. To install, reverse removal procedure.
Vigor – Carefully pry sun roof control switch from instrument panel. Unplug connector. To install, reverse removal procedure.

WIRING DIAGRAMS

See appropriate chassis wiring diagram in WIRING DIAGRAMS.

Integra, Legend, Vigor

DESCRIPTION & OPERATION

A permanent magnet motor operates each power window. The driver's master switch controls all windows. Passenger switches control only the associated window. If the main switch is in OFF position, only the driver's window operates.

Legend and Vigor power windows may be operated until about 10 minutes after ignition switch is set from the "II" position to the "I" or "0" positions. Time delay function operates as long as neither front door has been opened.

AUTO mode permits driver's window to be fully lowered or raised without holding switch. Pressing switch past its first detent position will engage AUTO mode, fully lowering or raising window. AUTO function is controlled by an integral pulser within the driver's window motor assembly. The pulser cannot be serviced separately.

TROUBLE SHOOTING

CAUTION: *Legend and Vigor are equipped with Supplemental Restraint System (SRS). SRS wiring harness is routed close to instrument cluster, steering wheel, and related components. All SRS wiring harnesses are covered by Yellow outer insulation. DO NOT use electrical test equipment on these circuits. Before working on steering column components, disable air bag system. See AIR BAG RESTRAINT SYSTEM article in ACCESSORIES & EQUIPMENT.*

NOTE: *Ensure all component terminals and ground connections are clean and tight. Check possible faults in order listed. Repair or replace components and circuits as necessary. Some wires have been assigned a superscript to distinguish them from other wires of the same color. For example, the Yellow/Green[1] wire is not the same as the Yellow/Green[2] wire.*

INTEGRA

All Windows Inoperative – Blown fuse No. 16 in underdash fuse box. Faulty power window relay. Open in White/Red or Yellow/Green[1] wire.

Driver's Window Inoperative – Blown fuse No. 7 in underdash fuse box. Faulty driver's window motor. Faulty window regulator. Driver's switch input. Open in White/Yellow wire.

Driver's Window Inoperative In AUTO – Driver's switch faulty. Faulty pulser (in driver's motor). Driver's switch input. Open in Blue wire.

Passenger's Window Inoperative – Blown fuses No. 2 (right front), No. 8. (right rear) and/or No. 6 (left rear) in underdash fuse box. Faulty driver's switch. Faulty passenger's switch. Faulty passenger's window motor. Faulty window regulator. Open in Blue/Black wire (right front), Green/Black[2] wire (left rear), and/or Yellow/Black (right rear) wire.

LEGEND

All Windows Inoperative – Blown fuse No. 36 in underhood fuse box. Blown fuse No. 13 in underdash fuse box. Power window relay. Key-off timer circuit. Open in White/Yellow or White/Green wires.

Driver's Window inoperative – Blown fuse No. 17 in underdash fuse box. Faulty driver's window motor. Faulty window regulator. Faulty master switch. Faulty master switch input. Open in White/Yellow wire.

Driver's Window Inoperative In AUTO – Faulty master switch. Master switch input. Open in Blue wire.

Passenger's Window Inoperative – Blown fuses No. 18 (right front), No. 24 (right rear), and/or No. 21 (left rear) in underdash fuse box. Faulty power window master switch. Faulty passenger's switch. Faulty passenger's window motor. Faulty window regulator. Open in Yellow/Black wire.

VIGOR

All Windows Inoperative – Blown fuse No. 15 in underhood fuse box. Blown fuse No. 37 in underhood relay box. Power window relay. Key-off timer circuit in integrated control unit. Open in Red wire.

Driver's Window Inoperative – Blown fuse No. 28 in underhood fuse box. Faulty driver's window motor. Faulty window regulator. Master switch input. Open in White/Yellow wire.

Driver's Window Inoperative In AUTO – Faulty master switch. Faulty pulser (in driver's motor). Master switch input. Open in Blue wire.

Passenger's Window Inoperative – Blown fuses No. 26 (right front), No. 24. (right rear), or No. 25 (left rear) in underhood fuse box. Faulty power window master switch. Faulty passenger's switch. Faulty passenger's window motor. Faulty window regulator. Open in Yellow/Black wire.

All Windows Inoperative Within 10 Minutes Of Ignition Switch Turned Off – Blown fuse No. 37 in underhood fuse box. Faulty door switches. Faulty key-off timer circuit in integrated control unit.

TESTING

MOTOR TEST

CAUTION: *Disconnect one test immediately when motor stops running.*

Driver's Window Motor Test (Integra) – Remove door panel. Unplug connector from motor. Using fused jumper wire, connect battery voltage to terminal No. 1. Connect terminal No. 2 to ground. See Fig. 1. Motor should run in "up" direction. Transpose jumper wires. Motor should run in "down" direction. Replace motor if it does not run smoothly in both directions.

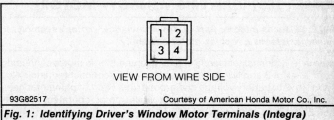

VIEW FROM WIRE SIDE

93G82517   Courtesy of American Honda Motor Co., Inc.

Fig. 1: *Identifying Driver's Window Motor Terminals (Integra)*

Driver's Window Motor Test (Legend & Vigor) – Remove door panel. Unplug connector from motor. Using fused jumper wire, connect terminal No. 1 to battery voltage. Connect terminal No. 2 to ground. See Fig. 2. Motor should run in "up" direction. Transpose jumper wires. Motor should run in "down" direction. Replace motor if it does not run smoothly in both directions.

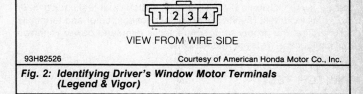

VIEW FROM WIRE SIDE

93H82526   Courtesy of American Honda Motor Co., Inc.

Fig. 2: *Identifying Driver's Window Motor Terminals (Legend & Vigor)*

Passenger Window Motor Test – Remove door panel. Unplug connector from motor. Using fused jumper wire, connect terminal No. 2 to battery voltage. Connect terminal No. 1 to ground. See Fig. 3. Motor should run in "up" direction. Transpose jumper wires. Motor should run in "down" direction. retest. Replace motor if it does not operate in both directions.

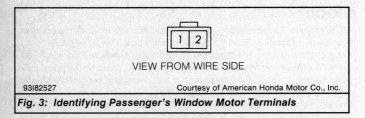

VIEW FROM WIRE SIDE

93I82527   Courtesy of American Honda Motor Co., Inc.

Fig. 3: Identifying Passenger's Window Motor Terminals

POWER WINDOW RELAY TEST

Remove power window relay from underhood fuse/relay box. Check for continuity between terminals "A" and "B". Continuity should not exist. Using jumper wires, connect terminals "C" and "D" to battery voltage and ground. *See Fig. 4.* If continuity does not exist between terminals "A" and "B", replace relay.

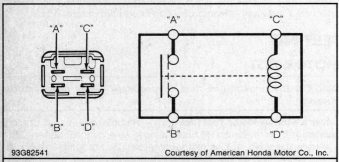

93G82541   Courtesy of American Honda Motor Co., Inc.

Fig. 4: Identifying Power Window Relay Terminals

PULSER TEST (DRIVER'S WINDOW MOTOR)

NOTE: Pulser is integral part of driver's window motor assembly. If pulser is defective, replace motor assembly.

Integra – Connect test leads of analog ohmmeter to motor connector terminals No. 3 and No. 4. Using jumper wires, connect terminals No. 1 and No. 2 to battery voltage and ground. *See Fig. 1.* If ohmmeter needle does not swing back and forth while motor operates, replace motor.

Legend & Vigor – Connect test leads of analog ohmmeter to motor connector terminals No. 1 and No. 2. Using jumper wires, connect terminals No. 3 and No. 4 to battery voltage and ground. *See Fig. 2.* If ohmmeter needle does not swing back and forth while motor operates, replace motor.

SWITCH INPUTS TEST

Turn ignition off. Remove driver's door panel. Unplug connectors from master switch. Using a DVOM, perform switch input tests in *Fig. 5, 6, or 7.* If all input test results are okay, inspect connector and terminals for damage and proper fit. If connector is okay and power windows still malfunction, replace master switch.

SWITCH TEST

Master Switch – Remove power window master switch. See WINDOW SWITCH under REMOVAL & INSTALLATION. Check for continuity between specified switch terminals with switch in each position. If continuity is not as specified, replace switch. *See Fig. 8, 9, or 10.* See appropriate POWER WINDOW MASTER SWITCH TEST table.

NOTE: On Legend, the driver's switch cannot be isolated for testing. Perform SWITCH INPUTS TEST. See Fig. 6. If inputs are normal, but driver's switch does not operate properly, replace master switch assembly.

POWER WINDOW MASTER SWITCH TEST (INTEGRA)

Position	Main Switch	Pin Continuity
Driver's Switch		
Off	[1]	"K"-"L"-"M"
Up	[1]	"K"-"N"
Down	[1]	"M"-"N"
Down (AUTO)	[1]	"M"-"N"
Right Front Switch		
Off	On	"C"-"D"-"O"
	Off	"C"-"H"
Up	On	"C"-"H"
	Off	"C"-"H"
Down	On	"D"-"H"
	Off	"D"-"H"
Left Rear Switch		
Off	On	"A"-"B"-"O"
	Off	"A"-"B"
Up	On	"A"-"G"
	Off	"A"-"G"
Down	On	"B"-"G"
	Off	"B"-"H"
Right Rear Switch		
Off	On	"E"-"F"-"O"
	Off	"E"-"F"
Up	On	"E"-"J"
	Off	"E"-"J"
Down	On	"F"-"J"
	Off	"F"-"J"

[1] – Main switch position does not affect driver's switch operation.

POWER WINDOW MASTER SWITCH TEST (LEGEND)

Position	Main Switch	Pin Continuity
Right Front Switch		
Off	On	"G"-"P"-"Q"
	Off	"G"-"P"
Up	On	"C"-"P"
	Off	"G"-"Q"
Down	On	"C"-"G"; "P"-"Q"
	Off	"C"-"G"
Right Rear Switch		
Off	On	"M"-"N"-"Q"
	Off	"M"-"N"
Up	On	"O"-"M"; "N"-"Q"
	Off	"M"-"O"
Down	On	"N"-"O"; "M"-"Q"
	Off	"N"-"O"
Left Rear Switch		
Off	On	"D"-"E"-"Q"
	Off	"D"-"E"
Up	On	"D"-"F"
	Off	"E"-"Q"
Down	On	"E"-"F"; "D"-"Q"
	Off	"E"-"F"

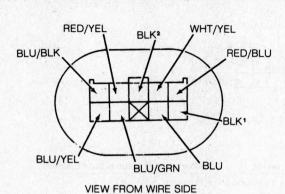

VIEW FROM WIRE SIDE

HATCHBACK

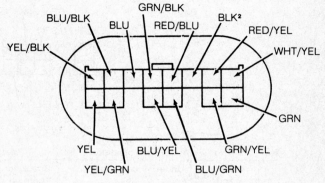

VIEW FROM WIRE SIDE

SEDAN

No.	Terminal	Test condition	Test: Desired result	Possible cause if result is not obtained
1	BLK[1]	Under all conditions.	Check for continuity to ground: There should be continuity.	• Poor ground • An open in the wire.
2	WHT/YEL BLU/BLK YEL/BLK GRN/BLK	Ignition switch is ON.	Check for voltage to ground: There should be battery voltage.	• Blown No.2, 6, 7 or 8 (20A) fuse. • Faulty power window relay. • An open in the wire.
3	RED/BLU and RED/YEL	Connect the WHT/YEL terminal to the RED/BLU terminal, and the RED/YEL to the BLK terminal, then turn the ignition switch ON.	Check the driver's motor operation: It should run.	• Faulty driver's motor. • An open in the wire.
4	BLU/YEL and BLU/GRN	Connect the BLU/BLK terminal to the BLU/YEL terminal, and the BLU/GRN terminal to the BLK terminal, then turn the ignition switch ON.	Check the right front motor operation: It should run.	• Faulty right front motor. • Faulty right front switch. • An open in the wire.
5	YEL and YEL/GRN	Connect the YEL/BLK terminal to the YEL terminal, and the YEL/GRN terminal to the BLK terminal, then turn the ignition switch ON.	Check the right rear motor operation: It should run.	• Faulty right rear motor. • Faulty right rear switch. • An open in the wire.
6	GRN/YEL and GRN	Connect the GRN/BLK terminal to the GRN/YEL terminal, and the GRN terminal to the BLK terminal, then turn the ignition switch ON.	Check the left rear motor operation: It should run.	• Faulty left rear motor. • Faulty left rear switch. • An open in the wire.
7	BLU and BLK[2]	Connect the WHT/YEL terminal to the RED/YEL terminal, and the BLK terminal to the RED/BLU terminal, then turn the ignition switch ON.	Check for resistance between the BLU and BLK terminals: Between 20—50 ohms should be indicated as the driver's motor runs.	• Faulty pulser. • Faulty driver's motor. • An open in the wire

93E82549

Courtesy of American Honda Motor Co., Inc.

Fig. 5: Switch Inputs Test (Integra)

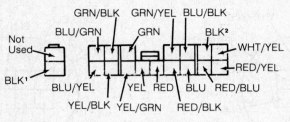

VIEW FROM WIRE SIDE

No.	Wire	Test condition	Test: Desired result	Possible cause if result is not obtained
1	BLK¹ and BLK²	Under all conditions	Check for continuity to gound: There should be continuity.	• Poor ground • An open in the wire
2	WHT/YEL BLU/BLK YEL/BLK GRN/BLK	Ignition switch ON	Check for voltage to ground: There should be battery voltage.	• Blown No. 17 (20 A), 18 (20 A), 21 (20 A), 24 (20 A) fuse • Faulty power window relay • Faulty key-off timer system • An open in the wire
3	RED/BLU and RED/YEL	Connect the WHT/YEL terminal to the RED/BLU terminal, and the RED/YEL terminal to the BLK² terminal, then turn the ignition switch ON.	Check the driver's motor operation: It should run.	• Faulty driver's window motor
4	BLU/YEL and BLU/GRN	Connect the BLU/BLK terminal to the BLU/YEL terminal, and the BLU/GRN terminal to the BLK² terminal, then turn the ignition switch ON.	Check the right front motor operation: It should run.	• Faulty right rear window motor • Faulty right rear switch • An open in the wire
5	YEL and YEL/GRN	Connect the YEL/BLK terminal to the YEL terminal, and the YEL/GRN terminal to the BLK² terminal, then turn the ignition switch ON.	Check the right rear motor operation: It should run.	• Faulty right rear window motor • Faulty right rear switch • An open in the wire
6	GRN/YEL and GRN	Connect the GRN/BLK terminal to the GRN/YEL terminal, and the GRN terminal to the BLK² terminal, then turn the ignition switch ON.	Check the left rear motor operation: It should run.	• Faulty left rear window motor • Faulty left rear switch • An open in the wire
7	BLU and BLK²	Connect the WHT/YEL terminal to the RED/YEL terminal, and the BLK² terminal to the RED/BLU terminal, then turn the ignition switch ON.	Check for voltage between the BLU (+) and BLK² (−) terminals with an analog voltmeter: It should indicate between 3—8 volts as the motor runs.	• Faulty pulser • Faulty driver's window motor • An open in the wire
8	RED/BLK and RED	Combination light switch ON and dash lights brightness controller dial rotated, dash lights should come on full bright.	Check for voltage between the RED/BLK (+) and RED (−) terminals: There should be battery voltage.	• Faulty dash lights brightness control system • An open in the wire

Fig. 6: Switch Inputs Test (Legend)

BLK

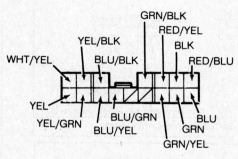

VIEW FROM WIRE SIDE

No.	Terminal	Test condition	Test: Desired result	Possible cause if result is not obtained
1	BLK[2]	Under all conditions.	Check for continuity to gound: There should be continuity.	• Poor ground • An open in the wire.
2	WHT/YEL BLU/BLK YEL/BLK GRN/BLK	Ignition switch ON.	Check for voltage to ground: There should be battery voltage.	• Blown No. 24, 25, 26 or 28 (20 A) fuse (in the under-hood fuse/relay box). • Faulty power window relay. • An open in the wire.
3	RED/BLU and RED/YEL	Connect the WHT/YEL terminal to the RED/BLU terminal, and the RED/YEL terminal to the BLK[2] terminal, then turn the ignition switch ON.	Check the driver's motor operation: It should run.	• Faulty driver's motor. • An open in the wire.
4	BLU/YEL and BLU/GRN	Connect the BLU/BLK terminal to the BLU/YEL terminal, and the BLU/GRN terminal to the BLK[2] terminal, then turn the ignition switch ON.	Check the front passenger's motor operation: It should run.	• Faulty front passenger's motor. • Faulty front passenger's switch. • An open in the wire.
5	YEL and YEL/GRN	Connect the YEL/BLK terminal to the YEL/GRN terminal, and the YEL terminal to the BLK[2] terminal, then turn the ignition switch ON.	Check the right rear motor operation: It should run (the window moves down).	• Faulty right rear motor. • Faulty right switch. • An open in the wire.
6	GRN/YEL and GRN	Connect the GRN/BLK terminal to the GRN terminal, and the GRN/YEL terminal to the BLK[2] terminal, then turn the ignition switch ON.	Check the left rear motor operation: It should run (the window moves down).	• Faulty left rear motor. • Faulty left rear switch. • An open in the wire.
7	BLU and BLK[2]	Connect the WHT/YEL terminal to the RED/YEL terminal, and the BLK[2] terminal to the RED/BLU terminal, then turn the ignition switch ON.	Check for resistance between the BLU and BLK[2] terminals: Between 20-50 ohms should be indicated as the driver's motor runs.	• Faulty pulser. • Faulty driver's motor. • An open in the wire.

Fig. 7: Switch Inputs Test (Vigor)

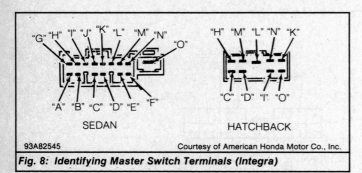

Fig. 8: Identifying Master Switch Terminals (Integra)

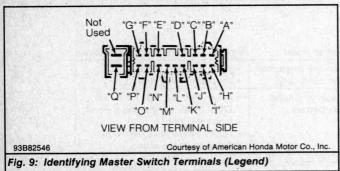

Fig. 9: Identifying Master Switch Terminals (Legend)

POWER WINDOW MASTER SWITCH TEST (VIGOR)

Position	Main Switch	Pin Continuity
Driver's Switch		
Off	1	"H"-"I"-"J"
Up	1	"H"-"N"
Down	1	"J"-"N"
Down (AUTO)	1	"J"-"N"
Right Front Switch		
Off	On	"D"-"E"-"O"
	Off	"D"-"E"
Up	On	"E"-"L"
	Off	"E"-"L"
Down	On	"D"-"L"
	Off	"D"-"L"
Left Rear Switch		
Off	On	"B"-"C"-"O"
	Off	"B"-"C"
Up	On	"C"-"K"
	Off	"A"-"G"
Down	On	"C"-"K"
	Off	"B"-"H"
Right Rear Switch		
Off	On	"F"-"G"-"O"
	Off	"F"-"G"
Up	On	"E"-"J"
	Off	"G"-"M"
Down	On	"F"-"M"
	Off	"F"-"M"

1 – Main switch position does not affect driver's switch operation.

PASSENGER WINDOW SWITCH TEST

Passenger Window Switch Test – Unplug connector from switch. See WINDOW SWITCH under REMOVAL & INSTALLATION. Check for continuity between specified switch terminals with switch in each position. If continuity is not as specified, replace switch. *See Fig. 11.* See PASSENGER POWER WINDOW SWITCH TEST table.

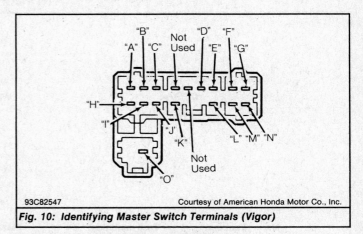

Fig. 10: Identifying Master Switch Terminals (Vigor)

PASSENGER POWER WINDOW SWITCH TEST

Switch Position	Continuity
Integra	
Off	"A"-"B"; "C"-"E"
Up	"A"-"B"; "C"-"E"
Down	"B"-"D"; "C"-"E"
Legend	
Off	"A"-"G"; "D"-"E"; "A"-"F"
Up	"D"-"E"; "C"-"G"
Down	"C"-"D"; "G"-"H"
Vigor	
Off	"D"-"E"
Up	"A"-"B"
Down	"A"-"C"; "B"-"D"

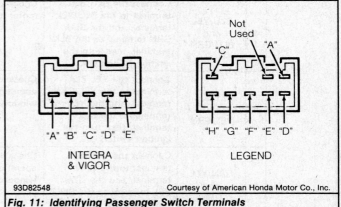

Fig. 11: Identifying Passenger Switch Terminals

REMOVAL & INSTALLATION

WINDOW MOTOR

Removal & Installation – Information is not available from manufacturer.

WINDOW SWITCH

Removal & Installation – Remove door panel. Unplug connectors. Remove mounting screws. To install, reverse removal procedure.

WIRING DIAGRAMS

See appropriate chassis wiring diagram in WIRING DIAGRAMS.

Integra, Legend, Vigor

CAUTION: *Legend and Vigor are equipped with Supplemental Restraint System (SRS). SRS wiring harness is routed close to instrument cluster, steering wheel, and related components. All SRS wiring harnesses are covered by Yellow outer insulation. DO NOT use electrical test equipment on these circuits. Before working on steering column components, disable air bag system. See AIR BAG RESTRAINT SYSTEM article in ACCESSORIES & EQUIPMENT.*

WARNING: *Wait about 3 minutes after disabling air bag system. Back-up power circuit, capacitor internal to SRS unit, maintains system voltage for about 3 minutes after battery is disconnected. Servicing air bag system before 3 minutes may cause accidental air bag deployment and possible personal injury.*

NOTE: *Radio/cassette or radio/CD player contains an anti-theft protection circuit. Whenever battery is disconnected, radio will go into anti-theft mode. When battery is reconnected, radio will display CODE and will be inoperative until proper code number is entered by vehicle owner.*

TESTING

COMBINATION SWITCH (TURN SIGNAL/HEADLIGHT)

Integra – Remove steering column upper and lower covers. Unplug electrical connectors from switch. Check for continuity between specified terminals in each switch position. *See Fig. 1.* Replace switch if continuity is not as specified.

HEADLIGHT/DIMMER/PASSING SWITCH

Position		D	E	F	G	I	J
Lighting switch	OFF						
	● LOW	o———	———o				
	● HIGH	o———	———o		o———	———o	———o
Passing switch	OFF						
	ON					o———	———o

(CANADA)

TURN SIGNAL SWITCH

Position	A	B	C
R			
NEUTRAL			
L			

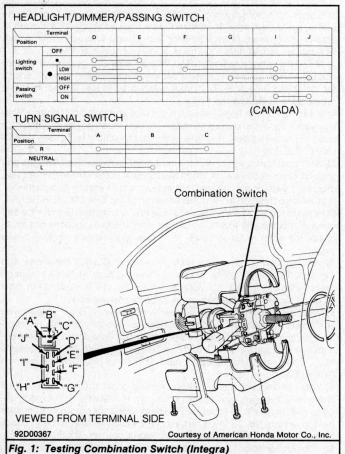

Combination Switch

VIEWED FROM TERMINAL SIDE

92D00367   Courtesy of American Honda Motor Co., Inc.

Fig. 1: Testing Combination Switch (Integra)

HEADLIGHT/DIMMER/PASSING SWITCH

Position		2	3	11	12
Lighting Switch	OFF				
	●		o———	———o	
	●		o———	———o	———o
Dimmer Switch	LOW				
	HIGH	o———		———o	
Passing Switch	OFF				
	ON	o———		———o	

TURN SIGNAL SWITCH

Position	4	5	6
R	o———		———◄
NEUTRAL			
L		o———	———◄

VIEWED FROM TERMINAL SIDE

14-Pin Connector

92E00368   Courtesy of American Honda Motor Co., Inc.

Fig. 2: Testing Combination Switch (Legend)

Legend – Remove instrument panel lower cover. Unplug 10-pin and 4-pin connectors. Check for continuity between specified terminals in each switch position. *See Fig. 2.* Replace switch if continuity is not as specified.

Vigor – Remove instrument panel lower cover. Remove knee bolster and instrument panel lower frame. Unplug 12-pin connector. Check for continuity between specified terminals in each switch position. *See Fig. 3.* Replace switch if continuity is not as specified.

DAYTIME RUNNING LIGHT CIRCUIT (CANADA)

Integra – **1)** Remove right kick panel. Unplug 8-pin and 4-pin connectors from daytime running light relay. *See Fig. 4.* Perform circuit test at daytime running light relay harness connectors.

2) Check for continuity between Black wire and ground. If continuity exists, go to next step. If continuity does not exist, check for poor ground connections at left front of engine compartment (next to washer reservoir) and behind left kick panel.

3) With ignition on, measure voltage between Yellow/Black wire and ground. If battery voltage exists, go to next step. If battery voltage does not exist, check for defective fuse No. 33 in main fuse block. If fuse is okay, check for open in Yellow/Black wire. If Yellow/Black wire is okay, test headlight switch. See COMBINATION SWITCH (TURN SIGNAL/HEADLIGHT) under TESTING.

4) Measure voltage between White wire and ground. If battery voltage exists, go to next step. If battery voltage does not exist, check for defective fuse No. 26 in auxiliary fuse block. If fuse is okay, repair open in White wire.

5) With headlight switch in ON position and dimmer switch in HI position, measure voltage between Red wire and ground. If battery voltage exists, go to next step. If battery voltage does not exist, repair open in Red wire.

6) Connect a jumper wire between Yellow/Black and White/Red wires. With ignition on, right headlight (high beam) and high beam indicator should be on. If operation is as specified, go to next step. If operation is not as specified, check for open in Yellow/Black and/or White/Red wires. If wires are okay, test headlight switch. See COMBINATION SWITCH (TURN SIGNAL/HEADLIGHT).

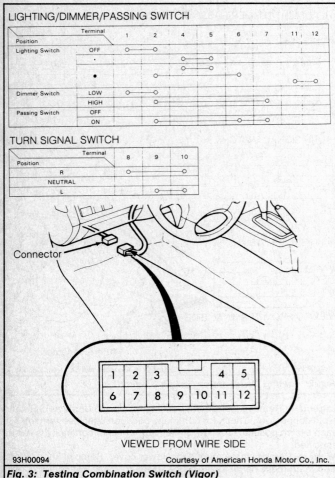

LIGHTING/DIMMER/PASSING SWITCH

Position	Terminal	1	2	4	5	6	7	11	12
Lighting Switch	OFF	O—O							
	•			O—O					
	●		O—	—O	—O				
								O—O	
Dimmer Switch	LOW	O—		—O					
	HIGH		O—				—O		
Passing Switch	OFF								
	ON	O—				—O			

TURN SIGNAL SWITCH

Position	Terminal	8	9	10
R		O—	—O	
NEUTRAL				
L			O—	—O

Connector

```
 _____
|  1 | 2 | 3 |     |  4 | 5  |
|  6 | 7 | 8 | 9 |10 |11 |12 |
 _____
```

VIEWED FROM WIRE SIDE

93H00094   Courtesy of American Honda Motor Co., Inc.

Fig. 3: Testing Combination Switch (Vigor)

7) With ignition on, connect a jumper wire between Green/Red wire and ground. Brake warning light indicator should come on. If indicator light comes on, go to next step. If indicator light does not come on, check for bad indicator bulb. If bulb is okay, repair open in Green/Red wire.

8) With parking brake on, check for continuity between Red/Green wire and ground. If continuity exists, go to next step. If continuity does not exist, check parking brake switch. If switch is okay, repair open in Red/Green wire.

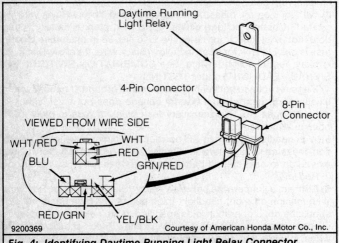

Daytime Running Light Relay

4-Pin Connector

8-Pin Connector

VIEWED FROM WIRE SIDE

WHT/RED   WHT
BLU   RED
             GRN/RED

RED/GRN   YEL/BLK

9200369   Courtesy of American Honda Motor Co., Inc.

Fig. 4: Identifying Daytime Running Light Relay Connector Terminals (Integra – Canada)

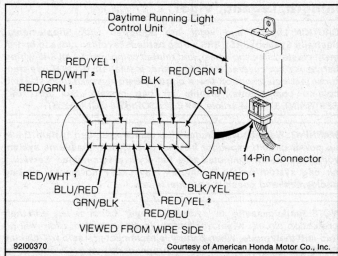

Daytime Running Light Control Unit

RED/YEL ¹
RED/WHT ²
RED/GRN ¹   BLK   RED/GRN ²
                            GRN

14-Pin Connector

RED/WHT ¹
BLU/RED
GRN/BLK   GRN/RED ¹
                 BLK/YEL
            RED/YEL ²
       RED/BLU

VIEWED FROM WIRE SIDE

92I00370   Courtesy of American Honda Motor Co., Inc.

Fig. 5: Identifying Daytime Running Light Control Unit Connector Terminals (Legend – Canada)

9) If all test results are okay and system still does not work, replace daytime running light relay.

Legend – 1) Remove lower dash panel. Unplug 14-pin connector from daytime running light control unit. Perform circuit test at control unit relay connector.

NOTE: For testing purposes, wires of same color have been given superscript numbers for identification. See Fig. 5.

---

2) Check for continuity between Black wire and ground. If continuity exists, go to next step. If continuity does not exist, check for open in Black wire. If wire is okay, check for bad ground connection behind left kick panel, behind right kick panel and at right shock tower.

3) Measure voltage between Red/White ² wire and ground. If battery voltage exists, go to next step. If battery voltage does not exist, check for defective fuse No. 16 in underdash fuse block. If fuse is okay, repair open in Red/White ² wire.

4) Measure voltage between Blue/Red wire and ground. If battery voltage exists, go to next step. If battery voltage does not exist, check for open in Blue/Red wire. If wire is okay, test headlight relay. See HEADLIGHT RELAY.

5) With headlights off, check for continuity between Red/White ² and ground. If continuity exists, go to next step. If continuity does not exist, check for bad ground connection at left front of engine compartment. If ground connection is okay, test dimmer relay. See DIMMER RELAY.

6) With parking brake on, check for continuity between Green wire and ground. If continuity exists, go to next step. If continuity does not exist, check for open in Green wire. If wire is okay, check parking brake switch.

7) With ignition on, measure voltage between Black/Yellow wire and ground. If battery voltage exists, go to next step. If battery voltage does not exist, check for defective fuse No. 12 in underdash fuse block. If fuse is okay, repair open in Black/Yellow wire.

8) With ignition on, connect jumper wire between Green/Black wire and ground. Daytime running light indicator should come on. If indicator light comes on, go to next step. If indicator light does not come on, check for defective fuse No. 13 in underdash fuse block. If fuse is okay, check for bad indicator bulb. If bulb is okay, repair open in Green/Black wire.

9) With ignition on, use a jumper wire to ground Green/Red ¹ wire. Brake warning indicator should come on. If indicator light comes on, go to next step. If brake warning indicator does not come on, check for defective fuse No. 13 in underdash fuse block. If fuse is okay, check for bad indicator bulb. If bulb is okay, repair open in Green/Red ¹ wire.

10) Check for continuity between Red/Green ², Red/Blue, and Red/Yellow ² wires. If continuity exists between all 3 wires, go to next step. If continuity does not exist between any of these wires, repair open in suspect wire.

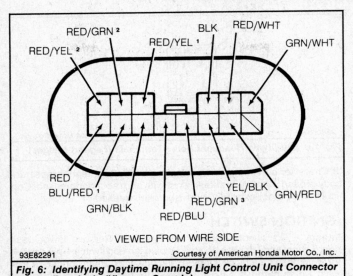

RED/GRN [2]
RED/YEL [2]
RED/YEL [1]
BLK
RED/WHT
GRN/WHT

RED
BLU/RED [1]
GRN/BLK
RED/BLU
RED/GRN [3]
YEL/BLK
GRN/RED

VIEWED FROM WIRE SIDE

93E82291

Courtesy of American Honda Motor Co., Inc.

Fig. 6: Identifying Daytime Running Light Control Unit Connector Terminals (Vigor – Canada)

11) With headlight switch in ON position, measure voltage between Red/Yellow [1] wire and ground. If battery voltage exists, go to next step. If battery voltage does not exist, check for defective fuse No. 46 in underhood relay/fuse block. If fuse is okay, repair open in Red/Yellow [1] wire.

12) With headlight switch still in ON position, measure voltage between Red/Green [1] wire and ground. If battery voltage exists, go to next step. If battery voltage does not exist, repair open in Red/Green [1] wire.

13) If all test results are okay but system still does not work, replace daytime running light control unit.

Vigor – 1) Remove glove box and right kick panel. Unplug 14-pin connector from daytime running light control unit, located behind glove box. Perform circuit tests at control unit relay connector.

NOTE: *For testing purposes, wires of same color have been given superscript numbers for identification. See Fig. 6.*

2) Check for continuity between Black wire and ground. If continuity exists, go to next step. If continuity does not exist, repair open in Black wire.

3) Measure voltage between Red/Green [2] wire and ground. If battery voltage exists, go to next step. If battery voltage does not exist, check for defective fuse No. 21 in underdash fuse block. If fuse is okay, repair open in Red/Green [2] wire.

4) Measure voltage between Blue/Red wire and ground. If battery voltage exists, go to next step. If battery voltage does not exist, check for open in Blue/Red wire. If wire is okay, test dimmer relay. See DIMMER RELAY.

5) With headlights off, check for continuity between Red wire and ground. If continuity exists, go to next step. If continuity does not exist, check for open in Red wire. If wire is okay, check for bad ground connection, located at right side of engine compartment. If ground connection is okay, test dimmer relay. See DIMMER RELAY.

6) With parking brake on, measure voltage between Green/White wire and ground. If voltage is one volt or less, go to next step. If voltage is more than one volt, check for open in Green wire. If wire is okay, check parking brake switch.

7) With ignition on, measure voltage between Yellow/Black wire and ground. If battery voltage exists, go to next step. If battery voltage does not exist, check for defective fuse No. 10 in underdash fuse block. If fuse is okay, repair open in Yellow/Black wire.

8) With ignition on, connect jumper wire between Green/Black wire and ground. Daytime running light indicator should come on. If indicator light comes on, go to next step. If indicator light does not come on,

check for defective fuse No. 1 in underdash fuse block. If fuse is okay, check for bad indicator bulb. If bulb is okay, repair open in Green/Black wire.

9) With ignition on, use a jumper wire to ground Green/Red wire. Brake warning indicator should come on. If indicator light comes on, go to next step. If brake warning indicator does not come on, check for defective fuse No. 1 in underdash fuse block. If fuse is okay, check for bad indicator bulb. If bulb is okay, repair open in Green/Red wire.

10) Check for continuity between Red/Yellow [2], Red/Green [3], and Red/Blue [1] wires. If continuity exists between all 3 wires, go to next step. If continuity does not exist for any of these wires, repair open in suspect wire.

11) With headlight switch in ON position, measure voltage between Red/Yellow [1] wire and ground. If battery voltage exists, go to next step. If battery voltage does not exist, check for defective fuse No. 19 in underdash fuse block. If fuse is okay, repair open in Red/Yellow wire [1].

12) With headlight switch still in ON position, measure voltage between Red/White wire and ground. If battery voltage exists, go to next step. If battery voltage does not exist, check for defective fuse No. 20 in underdash fuse block. If fuse is okay, repair open in Red/White wire.

13) If all test results are okay but system still does not work, replace daytime running light control unit.

DAYTIME RUNNING LIGHT RESISTOR (CANADA)

Integra – Unplug 3-pin connector from resistor. Resistor is located on left front of engine compartment. Measure resistance between terminals "A" and "B" and between terminals "C" and "B". See Fig. 7. Resistance should be 0.5-1.5 ohms . If resistance is not as specified, replace resistor.

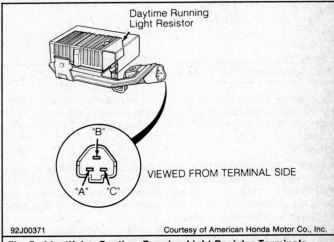

Daytime Running Light Resistor

"B"

"A"   "C"

VIEWED FROM TERMINAL SIDE

92J00371

Courtesy of American Honda Motor Co., Inc.

Fig. 7: Identifying Daytime Running Light Resistor Terminals (Integra – Canada)

DIMMER RELAY

Legend & Vigor – On Legend, relay is located in underhood relay/fuse block, on left side. See Fig. 8. On Vigor, relay is located in underhood relay/fuse block, on right side. On all models, unplug relay wiring connector. Check for continuity between terminals "B" and "C". See Fig. 9. Continuity should exist. With battery voltage applied between terminals "D" and "E", continuity should exist between terminals "A" and "C". If relay does not function as specified, replace relay.

HEADLIGHT RELAY

Legend & Vigor – On Legend, relay is located in underhood relay/fuse block, on left side. See Fig. 8. On Vigor, relay is located in underhood relay/fuse block, on right side. On all models, unplug relay wiring harness connector. Check for continuity between terminals "C" and

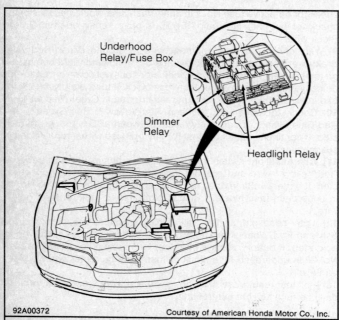

Underhood Relay/Fuse Box

Dimmer Relay

Headlight Relay

92A00372   Courtesy of American Honda Motor Co., Inc.

Fig. 8: Locating Headlight & Dimmer Relays (Legend)

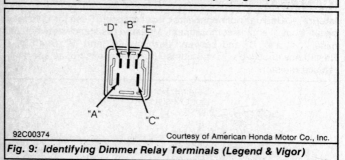

92C00374   Courtesy of American Honda Motor Co., Inc.

Fig. 9: Identifying Dimmer Relay Terminals (Legend & Vigor)

"D". See Fig. 10. Continuity should exist. With battery voltage applied between terminals "C" and "D", continuity should exist between terminals "A" and "B". If relay does not function as specified, replace relay.

HORN

Integra – Remove steering wheel. See STEERING WHEEL & HORN PAD under REMOVAL & INSTALLATION. On models with cruise control, check for continuity between hub core and Blue/Red wire. Continuity should exist with horn sounder pressed. Continuity should not exist with horn sounder released.

Legend – 1) Obtain radio anti-theft code. Position front wheels in straight-ahead position. Disconnect negative and positive battery cables. Remove lower instrument panel cover.

2) Disable air bag system. See AIR BAG RESTRAINT SYSTEM article in ACCESSORIES & EQUIPMENT. Unplug air bag connector from clockspring. Install shorting connector. Unplug 7-pin connector from vehicle harness. Install Test Harness (07MAZ-SP00600).

3) Check for continuity between terminal No. 3 on test harness and body ground. Continuity should exist with horn sounder pressed. Continuity should not exist with horn sounder released.

Vigor – 1) Obtain radio anti-theft code. Position front wheels in straight-ahead position. Disconnect negative and positive battery cables. Remove lower instrument panel cover.

2) Disable air bag system. See AIR BAG RESTRAINT SYSTEM article in ACCESSORIES & EQUIPMENT. Unplug air bag connector from clockspring. Install shorting connector. Unplug 6-pin connector from vehicle harness. Install Test Harness (07LAZ-SL40300).

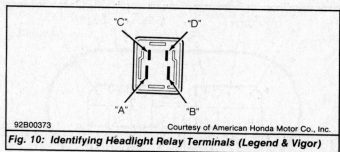

92B00373   Courtesy of American Honda Motor Co., Inc.

Fig. 10: Identifying Headlight Relay Terminals (Legend & Vigor)

3) Check for continuity between terminal No. 3 on test harness and body ground. Continuity should exist with horn sounder pressed. Continuity should not exist with horn sounder released.

IGNITION SWITCH

Integra – Disconnect negative battery cable. Remove lower dashboard panel and left knee bolster. Unplug ignition switch 4-pin connector from dash fuse block. Unplug ignition switch 5-pin connector from main wiring harness. Check continuity at each switch position. See Fig. 11. Replace switch if continuity is not as specified.

Legend – Disconnect negative battery cable. Remove lower dashboard panel. Unplug ignition switch 7-pin connector from underdash fuse block. Test for continuity at each switch position. See Fig. 12. Replace switch if continuity is not as specified.

Vigor – Remove lower instrument panel cover, left knee bolster and left kick panel. Unplug 7-pin connector from underdash fuse block. Check switch continuity at each switch position. See Fig. 13. Replace switch if continuity is not as specified.

WINDSHIELD WIPER/WASHER SWITCH

For testing information, see WIPER/WASHER SYSTEMS article in ACCESSORIES & EQUIPMENT.

Terminal Position	WHT/ RED (ACC)	WHT/ BLK (BAT -B)	BLU/ WHT (IG2 -B)	WHT (BAT -A)	BLK/ YEL (IG1)	YEL (IG2 -A)	BLK/ WHT (ST)
0							
I	o	o					
II	o	o	o	o	o	o	
III					o	o	o

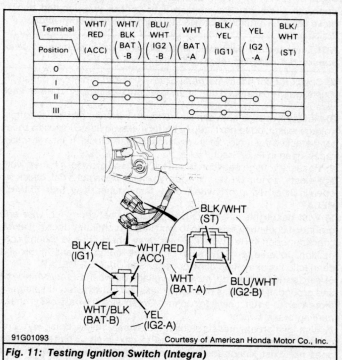

BLK/WHT (ST)

BLK/YEL (IG1)   WHT/RED (ACC)

WHT (BAT-A)   BLU/WHT (IG2-B)

WHT/BLK (BAT-B)   YEL (IG2-A)

91G01093   Courtesy of American Honda Motor Co., Inc.

Fig. 11: Testing Ignition Switch (Integra)

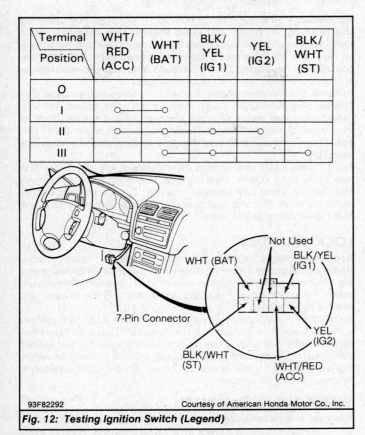

Terminal / Position	WHT/RED (ACC)	WHT (BAT)	BLK/YEL (IG1)	YEL (IG2)	BLK/WHT (ST)
O					
I	O——————O				
II	O————O————O————O			
III		O————O————————O			O

Fig. 12: Testing Ignition Switch (Legend)

93F82292 — Courtesy of American Honda Motor Co., Inc.

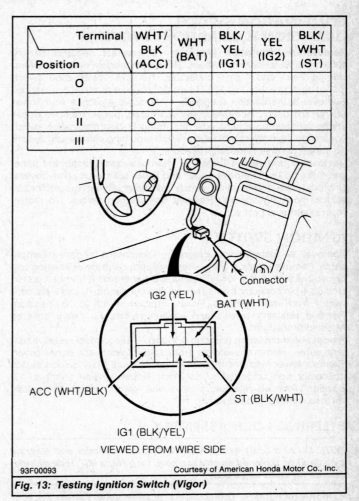

Terminal / Position	WHT/BLK (ACC)	WHT (BAT)	BLK/YEL (IG1)	YEL (IG2)	BLK/WHT (ST)
O					
I	O——————O				
II	O————O————O————O			
III	O————O————O———————————O

Fig. 13: Testing Ignition Switch (Vigor)

VIEWED FROM WIRE SIDE

93F00093 — Courtesy of American Honda Motor Co., Inc.

REMOVAL & INSTALLATION

STEERING WHEEL & HORN PAD

CAUTION: Legend and Vigor are equipped with Supplemental Restraint System (SRS). SRS wiring harness is routed close to instrument cluster, steering wheel, and related components. All SRS wiring harnesses are covered by Yellow outer insulation. DO NOT use electrical test equipment on these circuits. Before working on steering column components, disable air bag system. See AIR BAG RESTRAINT SYSTEM article in ACCESSORIES & EQUIPMENT.

Removal & Installation (Integra) – Carefully pry out center pad. Remove steering wheel retaining nut. Apply steady upward pull while rocking steering wheel from side to side. To install, reverse removal procedure. Install NEW steering wheel retaining nut.

Removal (Legend) – 1) Obtain anti-theft code. Disconnect negative and positive battery cables. Disable air bag system. See AIR BAG RESTRAINT SYSTEM article in ACCESSORIES & EQUIPMENT. Remove access panel from steering wheel lower cover. Remove Red shorting connector. Unplug connector between air bag and clockspring.

2) Plug air bag harness connector into shorting connector. On "L" and "LS" models, plug clockspring connector into Shorting Connector (07MAZ-SP00100). On all models, remove switch assembly covers. Remove Torx bolts and air bag module.

WARNING: Place air bag module on bench only with pad surface up.

3) Unplug connectors from horn, remote audio, and SET/RESUME switches. Remove steering wheel retaining nut. Remove steering wheel by applying steady upward pull while rocking steering wheel from side to side.

Installation – 1) Position front wheels face straight ahead. Rotate clockspring clockwise until it stops. Rotate clockspring about 2 turns counterclockwise until Yellow gear tooth aligns with mark on cover, and arrow on clockspring points straight upward.

2) Install steering wheel. Install NEW steering wheel retaining nut. Ensure steering wheel shaft engages clockspring. Install NEW Torx bolts. To complete installation, reverse removal procedure. Verify proper air bag system operation. See AIR BAG RESTRAINT SYSTEM article in ACCESSORIES & EQUIPMENT. Enter anti-theft code into radio.

Removal (Vigor) – 1) Obtain anti-theft code. Position front wheels in straight-ahead position. Disable air bag system. See AIR BAG RESTRAINT SYSTEM article in ACCESSORIES & EQUIPMENT. Disconnect negative and positive battery cables. Remove access panel from steering wheel lower cover. Remove Red shorting connector. Unplug connector between air bag and clockspring. Plug air bag harness connector into shorting connector.

2) Remove air bag retaining bolt cover. Remove SET/RESUME switch cover. Remove Torx bolts and air bag module.

WARNING: Place air bag module on bench only with pad surface up.

3) Unplug connectors from horn and SET/RESUME switches. Remove steering wheel retaining nut. Apply steady upward pull while rocking steering wheel from side to side.

Installation – 1) Position front wheels straight ahead. Rotate clockspring clockwise until it stops. Rotate clockspring about 2 turns counterclockwise until Yellow gear tooth aligns with mark on cover, and arrow on clockspring points straight upward.

2) Install steering wheel. Install NEW steering wheel retaining nut. Ensure steering wheel shaft engages clockspring. Install NEW Torx bolts. To complete installation, reverse removal procedure. Verify proper air bag system operation. See AIR BAG RESTRAINT SYSTEM article in ACCESSORIES & EQUIPMENT. Enter anti-theft code into radio.

COMBINATION SWITCH
(TURN SIGNAL/HEADLIGHT SWITCH)

Removal & Installation (Integra) – Disconnect negative battery cable. Remove steering wheel. Remove steering column covers. Unplug 7-pin and 4-pin connectors. Remove combination switch mounting screws and switch. To install, reverse removal procedure.

Removal & Installation (Legend) – Remove switches from lower dashboard panel. Remove lower dashboard panel. Remove upper and lower steering column covers. Unplug 14-pin combination switch connector. Remove combination switch mounting screws and switch. To install, reverse removal procedure.

Removal & Installation (Vigor) – Remove lower dashboard panel and knee bolster. Remove upper and lower steering column covers. Unplug 12-pin combination switch connector. Remove combination switch mounting screws. Remove combination switch. To install, reverse removal procedure.

IGNITION SWITCH

Removal & Installation (Integra) – Disconnect negative battery cable. Remove steering wheel. Remove upper and lower steering column covers. Remove lower dashboard panel and left knee bolster. Unplug 4-pin conector from fuse/relay box under dash, and 5-pin connector from main harness. Rotate ignition switch to "O" position. Remove retaining screws and ignition switch. To install, reverse removal procedure.

Removal & Installation (Legend & Vigor) – Disconnect negative battery cable. Remove switches from lower instrument panel cover. Remove lower instrument panel cover. Unplug 7-pin ignition switch connector from underdash fuse block. Rotate ignition switch to "O" position. Remove retaining screws and ignition switch. To install, reverse removal procedure.

STEERING LOCK ASSEMBLY

NOTE: On all models except Integra M/T, lock cylinder and steering lock must be replaced as an assembly. On Integra M/T, lock cylinder may be removed separately.

Removal (Integra) – **1)** Disconnect negative battery cable. Remove horn pad and steering wheel. Remove upper and lower steering column covers. Remove lower dashboard panel and left knee bolster. Unplug 7-pin ignition switch connector from main wiring harness.
2) Remove steering column mounting bolts/nuts. Lower steering column assembly. Center-punch both shear bolts. Using a 3/16" bit, drill heads from bolts. Remove shear bolts and ignition lock assembly.

Installation – To install, reverse removal procedure. Tighten new shear bolts until heads twist off. Check for proper ignition switch steering lock operation.

Removal (Legend) – **1)** Obtain radio anti-theft code. Disconnect negative battery cable. Remove switches from lower dashboard panel. Remove lower dashboard panel. Unplug wiring harness connectors as necessary. Remove steering column mounting bolts/nuts. Lower steering column assembly.
2) Grind slot into shear bolt. Using a screwdriver, remove shear bolt. Rotatet ignition switch to "1" position. Push steering lock retaining pin inward. Remove steering lock assembly.

Installation – Rotate ignition switch to "1" position. Push steering lock retaining pin inward and insert steering lock assembly until it clicks into place. Install and loosely tighten new shear bolt. Insert ignition key, and check for proper steering lock operation. Tighten shear bolt until hex head twists off. To complete installation, reverse removal procedure. Enter anti-theft code into radio.

Removal & Installation (Vigor) – **1)** Obtain radio anti-theft code. Disconnect negative battery cable. Remove left knee bolster, left kick panel, and lower panel. Remove steering column covers. Remove instrument cluster trim panel. Center-punch both shear bolts. Drill heads from bolts with a 3/16" bit. Remove shear bolts and ignition lock assembly.
2) To install, install new ignition switch without key inserted. Install new shear bolts loosely. Insert ignition key. Ensure key turns freely and steering wheel lock operates properly. Tighten shear bolts until heads break off. To complete installation, reverse removal procedure. Enter anti-theft code into radio.

LOCK CYLINDER

Removal (Integra M/T) – Disconnect negative battery cable. Remove horn pad and steering wheel. Remove upper and lower steering column covers. Set ignition switch to "1" position. Remove set screw from lock body. Push lock body retaining pin inward, and remove lock cylinder.

Installation – Set ignition switch to "O" position. Align lock cylinder with lock body. Turn ignition switch halfway to "1" position. Insert lock cylinder until lock body retaining pin touches cylinder. Set ignition switch to "1" position and push lock body cylinder inward until retaining pin clicks into place. Install set screw. To complete installation, reverse removal procedure.

WIPER/WASHER SWITCH

Removal & Installation (Integra) – Remove horn pad and steering wheel. Remove upper and lower steering column covers. Unplug wiper/washer wiring harness connectors. Remove cruise control slip ring (if equipped). Remove 2 screws and wiper/washer switch. To install, reverse removal procedure.

Removal & Installation (Legend) – Remove switches from lower dashboard panel. Remove lower dashboard panel. Remove upper and lower steering column covers. Unplug wiper/washer connector. Remove wiper/washer switch. To install, reverse removal procedure.

Removal & Installation (Vigor) – Remove lower dashboard panel and knee bolster. Remove upper and lower steering column covers. Unplug 10-pin windshield wiper/washer switch connector. Remove wiper/washer switch. To install, reverse removal procedure.

TORQUE SPECIFICATIONS
TORQUE SPECIFICATIONS

Application	Ft. Lbs. (N.m)
Steering Wheel Nut [1]	37 (50)
	INCH Lbs. (N.m)
Air Bag Module Retaining Bolts	88 (10)

[1] – Always install NEW retaining nut.

Integra, Legend, Vigor

CAUTION: Legend and Vigor are equipped with Supplemental Restraint System (SRS). SRS wiring harness is routed close to instrument cluster, steering wheel, and related components. All SRS wiring harnesses are covered by Yellow outer insulation. DO NOT use electrical test equipment on these circuits. Before working on steering column components, disable air bag system. See AIR BAG RESTRAINT SYSTEM article in ACCESSORIES & EQUIPMENT.

WARNING: Wait about 3 minutes after disabling air bag system. An internal back-up power circuit maintains system voltage for about 3 minutes after battery is disconnected. Servicing air bag system before 3 minutes may cause accidental air bag deployment and possible personal injury.

NOTE: Radio/cassette or radio/CD player contains anti-theft protection circuit. Whenever battery is disconnected, radio enters anti-theft mode. When battery is reconnected, radio displays CODE and will be inoperative until proper code number is entered. Obtain radio code before disconnecting battery or radio fuse.

DESCRIPTION & OPERATION

All models are equipped with a 2-speed front wiper motor with intermittent feature. On some models, intermittent delay is adjustable. Integra 3-door is equipped with a rear wiper/washer system.

TESTING

FRONT WIPER MOTOR TEST

1) Remove wiper arms. To gain access to wiper motor connector, remove lower windshield molding, hood seal, and air scoop. Unplug wiper motor 5-pin connector.
2) To test low speed operation, connect battery voltage to Green/Black wire. Connect Blue wire to ground. Motor should run smoothly at low speed. If motor does not run smoothly, replace wiper motor.
3) To test high speed operation, connect battery voltage to Green/Black wire. Connect Blue/Yellow wire to ground. Motor should run smoothly at high speed. If motor does not run smoothly, replace wiper motor.

FRONT WIPER RELAY TEST

Intermittent Relay (Legend & Vigor) – **1)** On Legend, relay is located on underhood relay panel on left side, toward front. On Vigor, relay is located over radiator fan, on left side of vehicle. Unplug relay from socket.

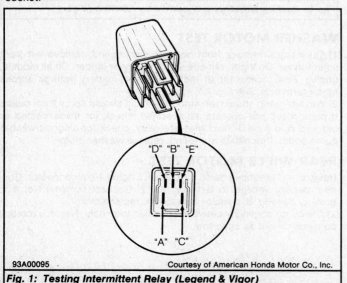

93A00095   Courtesy of American Honda Motor Co., Inc.

Fig. 1: Testing Intermittent Relay (Legend & Vigor)

2) Continuity should exist between terminals "B" and "C" with no power applied to relay coil. Continuity should not exist between terminals "A" and "C" with no power applied to relay coil. See Fig. 1.
3) Using fused jumper wires, apply battery voltage between coil terminals "D" and "E". Continuity should not exist between terminals "B" and "C". Continuity should exist between terminals "A" and "C". Replace relay if continuity is not as specified.

High-Speed Relay (Legend & Vigor) – **1)** On Legend, relay is located on underhood relay panel on left side, toward front. On Vigor, relay is located at relay panel under dash on right side. Unplug relay from socket.
2) Continuity should not exist between terminals "A" and "B" with no voltage applied to relay coil. See Fig. 2. Using fused jumper wires, apply battery voltage between coil terminals "C" and "D". Continuity should exist between terminals "A" and "B". Replace relay if continuity is not as specified.

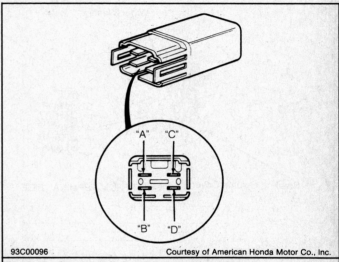

93C00096   Courtesy of American Honda Motor Co., Inc.

Fig. 2: Testing High-Speed Relay (Legend & Vigor)

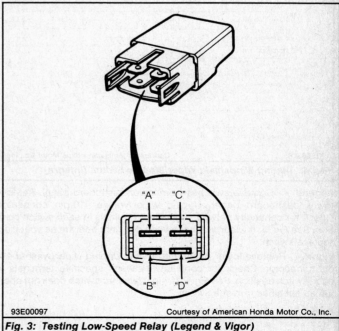

93E00097   Courtesy of American Honda Motor Co., Inc.

Fig. 3: Testing Low-Speed Relay (Legend & Vigor)

Low-Speed Relay (Legend & Vigor) – 1) On Legend, relay is located on underhood relay panel on left side, toward front. On Vigor, relay is located at relay panel under dash on right side. Unplug relay from socket.

2) Continuity should exist between terminals "A" and "B" with no voltage applied to relay coil. *See Fig. 3.* Using fused jumper wires, apply battery voltage between coil terminals "C" and "D". No continuity should exist between terminals "A" and "B". Replace relay if continuity is not as specified.

WIPER/WASHER SWITCH TEST

Integra – Remove horn pad and steering wheel. Remove upper and lower steering column covers. Unplug 6-pin and 8-pin connectors from wiper/washer switch. Check for continuity between specified terminals in each switch position. *See Fig. 4.* If wiper/washer switch does not operate as specified, replace switch.

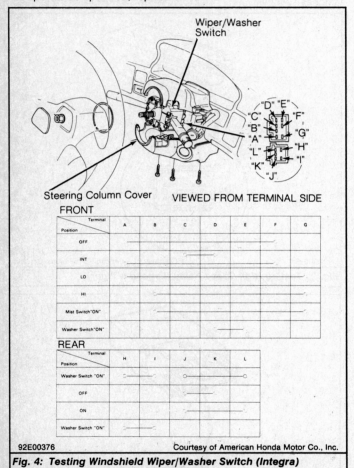

FRONT

Terminal Position	A	B	C	D	E	F	G
OFF							
INT							
LO							
HI							
Mist Switch "ON"							
Washer Switch "ON"							

REAR

Terminal Position	H	I	J	K	L
Washer Switch "ON"					
OFF					
ON					
Washer Switch "ON"					

92E00376   Courtesy of American Honda Motor Co., Inc.

Fig. 4: Testing Windshield Wiper/Washer Switch (Integra)

Legend – Remove switches from lower dashboard panel. Remove lower dashboard panel. Unplug wiper/washer 10-pin connector. Check for continuity between specified terminals in each switch position. *See Fig. 5.* If wiper/washer switch does not operate as specified, replace switch.

Vigor – Remove lower dashboard panel. Unplug wiper/washer 10-pin connector. Check for continuity between specified terminals in each switch position. *See Fig. 6.* If wiper/washer switch does not operate as specified, replace switch.

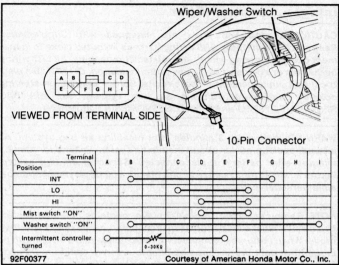

Terminal Position	A	B	C	D	E	F	G	H	I
INT		○					○		
LO			○			○			
HI				○		○			
Mist switch "ON"			○			○			
Washer switch "ON"		○							○
Intermittent controller turned	○	0-30KΩ			○				

92F00377   Courtesy of American Honda Motor Co., Inc.

Fig. 5: Testing Windshield Wiper/Washer Switch (Legend)

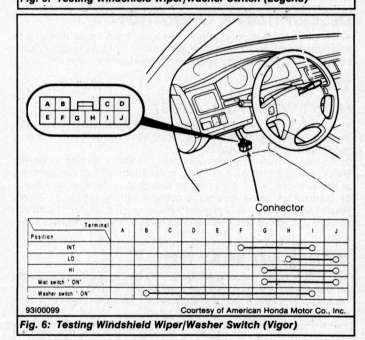

Terminal Position	A	B	C	D	E	F	G	H	I	J
INT						○	○		○	
LO							○		○	
HI							○	○	○	
Mist switch "ON"							○	○	○	
Washer switch "ON"		○				○				

93I00099   Courtesy of American Honda Motor Co., Inc.

Fig. 6: Testing Windshield Wiper/Washer Switch (Vigor)

WASHER MOTOR TEST

1) On Integra, remove front bumper. On Legend, remove left front inner fender. On Vigor, remove right front inner fender. On all models, unplug 2-pin connector at motor. Connect battery voltage across motor terminals. *See Fig. 7.*

2) Washer pump should run smoothly. Fluid should spray from outlet. If pump does not operate as specified, check for disconnected or blocked fluid lines. If fluid lines are okay, check for clogged washer pump outlet. If no faults are found, replace washer motor.

REAR WIPER MOTOR TEST

Integra – 1) Remove hatch trim panel. Unplug 4-pin connector. Connect battery voltage to terminal No. 2. Connect terminal No. 4 to ground. *See Fig. 8.* If motor fails to run, replace motor.

2) Check for continuity between specified terminals. Replace motor if continuity is not as specified.

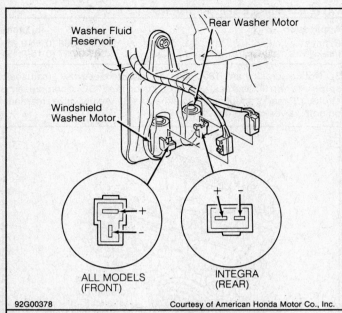

Fig. 7: Identifying Washer Motor Connector Terminals

92G00378   Courtesy of American Honda Motor Co., Inc.

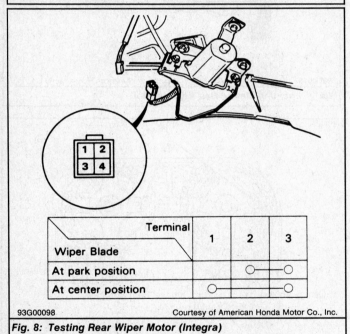

	Terminal	1	2	3
Wiper Blade				
At park position			○—	—○
At center position		○—		—○

93G00098   Courtesy of American Honda Motor Co., Inc.

Fig. 8: Testing Rear Wiper Motor (Integra)

REMOVAL & INSTALLATION

FRONT WIPER MOTOR

Removal & Installation – Remove wiper arms. Remove lower windshield molding, hood seal, and air scoop. Unplug wiper motor connector. Remove wiper linkage from wiper motor arm. Remove wiper motor mounting bolts and nuts. Remove wiper motor. To install, reverse removal procedure. Operate motor once, and allow it to park. Install wiper arms.

WIPER/WASHER SWITCH

Removal & Installation (Integra) – Remove horn pad and steering wheel. Remove upper and lower steering column covers. Unplug wiper/washer wiring harness connectors. Remove cruise control slip ring (if equipped). Remove retaining screws and wiper/washer switch. To install, reverse removal procedure.

Removal & Installation (Legend) – Remove switches from lower dashboard panel. Remove lower instrument panel cover. Remove upper and lower steering column covers. Unplug wiper/washer connector. Remove wiper/washer switch. To install, reverse removal procedure.

Removal & Installation (Vigor) – Remove lower instrument panel cover and knee bolster. Remove upper and lower steering column covers. Unplug wiper/washer connector. Remove wiper/washer switch. To install, reverse removal procedure.

WASHER MOTOR

Removal & Installation – On Integra, remove front bumper. On Legend, remove left front inner fender. On Vigor, remove right front inner fender. On all models, disconnect washer hoses and wiring harness connectors from washer motor. Remove mounting bolts and washer motor. To install, reverse removal procedure.

REAR WIPER MOTOR

Removal & Installation (Integra) – Remove rear hatch trim panel. Remove nut cover, retaining nut, wiper arm, cap, nut, washer, and rubber cushion. Unplug wiper motor connector. Remove mounting bolts and wiper motor. To install, reverse removal procedure. *See Fig. 9.*

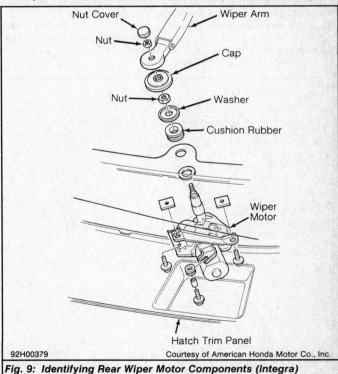

92H00379   Courtesy of American Honda Motor Co., Inc.

Fig. 9: Identifying Rear Wiper Motor Components (Integra)

WIRING DIAGRAMS

See appropriate wiring diagram in WIRING DIAGRAMS.

1993 ENGINES
1.7L 4-Cylinder

Integra

NOTE: For repair procedures not covered in this article, see ENGINE OVERHAUL PROCEDURES article in GENERAL INFORMATION.

ENGINE IDENTIFICATION

Engine identification code is stamped on right rear of cylinder block as viewed from flywheel, below cylinder head mating surface. First 5 numbers of code indicate engine type. Last 7 numbers of code indicate engine serial number. Engine serial number starting from 2000001 indicates a California vehicle. Engine serial number starting from 2300001 indicates a Federal vehicle.

ENGINE IDENTIFICATION CODE

Application	Code
1.7L	B17A1

ADJUSTMENTS

VALVE CLEARANCE

CAUTION: Always rotate engine only in direction of normal rotation (counterclockwise as viewed from front of engine). Backward rotation may cause timing belt to jump time.

1) Adjust valves when engine temperature is 100°F (38°C) or less. Remove valve cover. Rotate crankshaft counterclockwise until No. 1 piston is at TDC of compression stroke. Ensure UP marks on camshaft sprockets are at top and TDC grooves on pulleys are aligned with TDC groove on back cover. See Fig. 1.
2) Adjust valve clearance on both valves for No. 1 cylinder. Loosen lock nuts. Rotate adjuster screw until clearance is as specified. Tighten lock nut to 15 ft. lbs. (20 N.m). Recheck adjustment. See VALVE CLEARANCE SPECIFICATIONS table.

VALVE CLEARANCE SPECIFICATIONS

Application	In. (mm)
Exhaust	0.007-0.008 (0.17-0.21)
Intake	0.006-0.007 (0.15-0.19)

3) Rotate crankshaft 180 degrees counterclockwise (camshaft sprockets turn 90 degrees) until No. 3 piston is at TDC of compression stroke. UP marks should point to exhaust side. Adjust valve clearance on both valves for No. 3 cylinder.

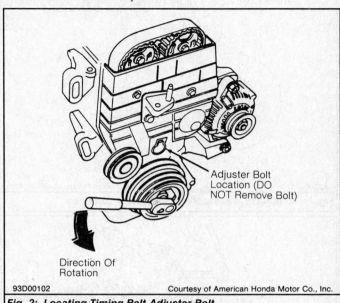

Adjuster Bolt Location (DO NOT Remove Bolt)

Direction Of Rotation

93D00102   Courtesy of American Honda Motor Co., Inc.

Fig. 2: Locating Timing Belt Adjuster Bolt

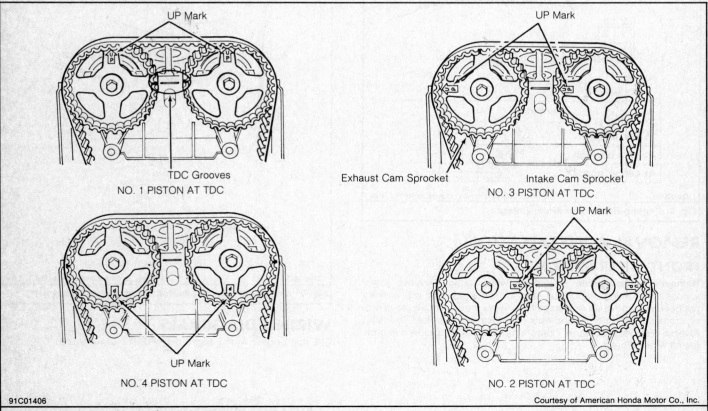

91C01406   Courtesy of American Honda Motor Co., Inc.

Fig. 1: Positioning Camshafts For Valve Clearance Adjustment

4) Rotate crankshaft 180 degrees counterclockwise until No. 4 piston is at TDC of compression stroke. Ensure UP marks are pointing down. Adjust valve clearance on both valves for No. 4 cylinder.

5) Rotate crankshaft 180 degrees counterclockwise until No. 2 piston is at TDC of compression stroke. Ensure UP marks are pointing to intake side. Adjust valve clearances on both valves for No. 2 cylinder. Install new valve cover gasket. Retighten crankshaft pulley bolt to 133 ft. lbs. (180 N.m).

TIMING BELT TENSION

CAUTION: Adjust timing belt with engine cold. DO NOT rotate crankshaft with timing belt tensioner adjuster bolt loose.

Remove valve cover. Rotate crankshaft counterclockwise until No. 1 piston is at TDC. Rotate crankshaft 3 teeth counterclockwise on camshaft sprocket to create tension on timing belt. Loosen tension adjuster bolt to create tension on belt. *See Fig. 2.* Tighten tension adjuster bolt to specification. See TORQUE SPECIFICATIONS. Install valve cover with new gaskets.

REMOVAL & INSTALLATION

NOTE: For reassembly reference, label all electrical connectors, vacuum hoses, and fuel lines before removal. Also place mating marks on engine hood and other major assemblies before removal.

NOTE: On some vehicles, radio/cassette or radio/CD player contains an anti-theft protection circuit. Whenever battery is disconnected, radio will go into anti-theft mode. When battery is reconnected, radio will display CODE and will be inoperative until proper code number is entered. Obtain code number before disconnecting battery.

CAUTION: Fuel system is under pressure. Release pressure before servicing fuel system components.

FUEL PRESSURE RELEASE

Disconnect negative battery cable. Remove fuel tank filler cap. Place a shop towel on top of fuel filter. Release fuel injection system pressure by slowly loosening fuel injection service bolt. *See Fig. 3.*

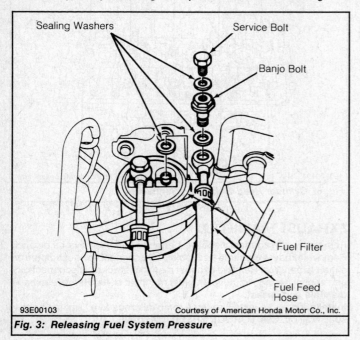

Sealing Washers

Service Bolt

Banjo Bolt

Fuel Filter

Fuel Feed Hose

93E00103   Courtesy of American Honda Motor Co., Inc.

Fig. 3: Releasing Fuel System Pressure

BLEEDING COOLING SYSTEM

1) To bleed air from cooling system, set heater controls to maximum temperature. Loosen bleed bolt located on thermostat housing. Fill cooling system with a 50/50 mixture of coolant and water to bottom of filler neck.

2) Tighten bleed bolt when coolant flows from bleed bolt in steady stream without bubbles. With radiator cap off, start and warm engine to normal operating temperature. Add coolant as necessary. Install radiator cap.

ENGINE

Removal – 1) Disconnect battery cables. Remove hood hinge stops. Secure hood in vertical position. DO NOT remove hood. Raise and support vehicle. Drain engine oil and transmission fluid. Remove front wheels and splash shield. Remove radiator cap to release system pressure. Drain cooling system. Remove battery and battery tray.

2) Release fuel pressure. See FUEL PRESSURE RELEASE. Remove fuel inlet hose. Unplug harness connectors from distributor. Remove distributor. Remove intake air duct and air cleaner housing. Unplug engine wiring harness connectors on left side of engine compartment. Disconnect throttle cable.

3) Unplug engine wiring harness connectors on right side of engine compartment. Disconnect power cables from underhood fuse/relay box. Disconnect brake booster vacuum hose from intake manifold. Disconnect fuel return hose. Disconnect ground cable at cylinder head. Remove power steering pump with hoses attached. Set power steering pump aside.

4) Remove A/C compressor with hoses attached, and set it aside. Remove alternator. Disconnect transmission cooler lines. Remove radiator and heater hoses. Remove speed sensor, leaving hoses attached. Unplug cooling fan connectors. Remove radiator.

5) Remove exhaust pipe. Disconnect drive shafts. See FWD AXLE SHAFTS article in DRIVE AXLES. On M/T models, disconnect clutch cable, shift rod, and shift lever torque rod. On A/T models, remove torque converter cover and disconnect shift control cable.

6) On all models, attach chain hoist to engine. Raise hoist to take all slack from chain. Remove rear transmission mount and rear transmission mounting bracket. Remove front transmission mount. Remove side transmission mount and side transmission mounting bracket. Remove side engine mount.

7) Slowly raise engine/transaxle about 6 inches. Ensure all hoses and wiring have been disconnected. Carefully remove engine and transaxle from vehicle.

Installation – 1) To install, reverse removal procedure. To prevent excessive engine vibration and premature engine mount wear, tighten engine/transaxle mounts in specified sequence. *See Fig. 4.*

2) When installing drive axles, use new spring clips. Insert drive axles until spring clips click into groove of differential side gear. Ensure harness connectors and hoses are connected properly.

3) Ensure control cables are not bent or pinched and are adjusted properly. On M/T models, adjust clutch pedal free play. Verify transaxle shifts smoothly.

4) On all models, adjust drive belt tension. Fill or top off all fluids. Fill and bleed air from cooling system. See BLEEDING COOLING SYSTEM. Start engine and check for leaks.

INTAKE MANIFOLD

Removal – 1) Disconnect negative battery cable. Release fuel system pressure. See FUEL PRESSURE RELEASE. Carefully remove radiator cap to release cooling system pressure. Drain cooling system. Remove upper and lower radiator hoses. Remove air intake duct and air cleaner assembly.

2) Disconnect fuel inlet and return hoses. Mark and disconnect vacuum hoses and wiring harness connectors. Remove fuel evaporation canister hose from throttle body.

3) Remove brake booster and PCV hoses from intake manifold. Disconnect throttle cable. Remove intake manifold nuts, intake manifold, and gasket.

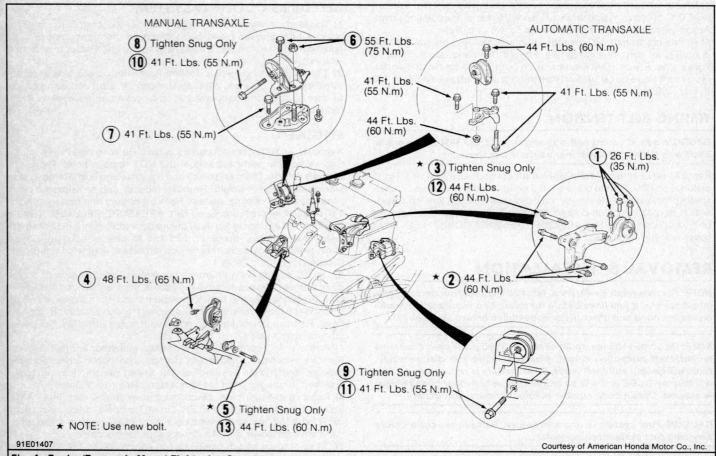

Fig. 4: Engine/Transaxle Mount Tightening Sequence

91E01407

Courtesy of American Honda Motor Co., Inc.

Installation – Clean gasket surfaces. Install intake manifold, using new intake manifold gasket. Tighten nuts to specification, using a crisscross pattern in 2-3 stages, beginning with inner nuts. See TORQUE SPECIFICATIONS. To complete installation, reverse removal procedure. Refill and bleed air from cooling system. See BLEEDING COOLING SYSTEM.

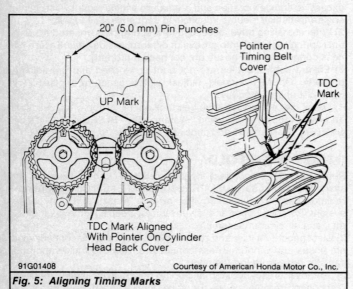

Fig. 5: Aligning Timing Marks

91G01408

Courtesy of American Honda Motor Co., Inc.

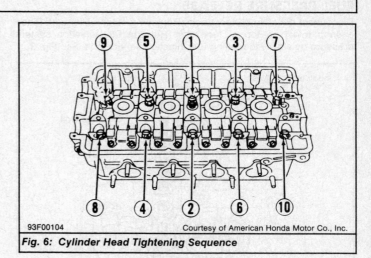

Fig. 6: Cylinder Head Tightening Sequence

93F00104

Courtesy of American Honda Motor Co., Inc.

EXHAUST MANIFOLD

Removal – Disconnect negative battery cable. Remove oil dipstick. Remove exhaust manifold heat shield. Disconnect exhaust pipe from exhaust manifold. Remove exhaust manifold bracket. Disconnect oxygen sensor wiring. Remove exhaust manifold bolts. Remove exhaust manifold and gasket.

Installation – To install, reverse removal procedure. Tighten bolts to specification. See TORQUE SPECIFICATIONS.

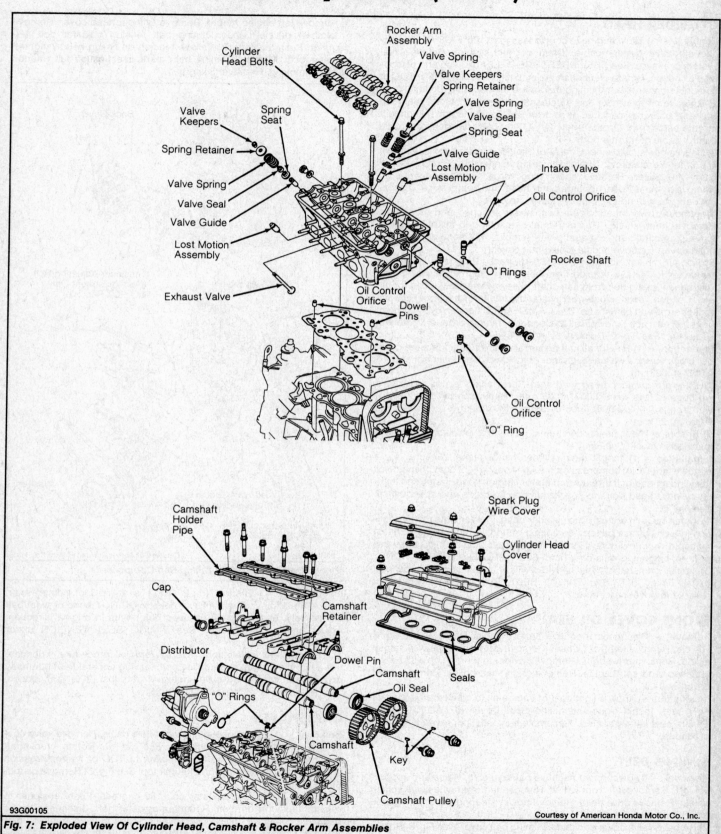

Fig. 7: Exploded View Of Cylinder Head, Camshaft & Rocker Arm Assemblies

93G00105

Courtesy of American Honda Motor Co., Inc.

CYLINDER HEAD

Removal – 1) Allow engine to cool to less than 100°F (38°C). Disconnect negative battery cable. Drain cooling system. Release fuel system pressure. See FUEL PRESSURE RELEASE. Tag and disconnect all hoses. Rotate crankshaft pulley until No. 1 piston is at TDC of compression stroke and timing marks are aligned. *See Fig. 5.*

2) Remove air inlet duct and air cleaner cover. Disconnect fuel feed line and charcoal canister hose from intake manifold. Disconnect throttle cable from throttle body. On A/T models, disconnect throttle control cable at throttle body.

3) On all models, disconnect fuel return line and brake booster vacuum line at intake manifold. Unplug all wiring connectors. Remove spark plug wire cover. Remove spark plug wires. Remove distributor. Remove by-pass hose, upper radiator hose, and heater hose. Disconnect engine ground cable at cylinder head cover.

4) Remove power steering pump with hoses attached, and set it aside. Remove heat shield. Remove intake manifold bracket. Remove exhaust manifold and exhaust pipe. Remove PCV hose and cylinder head cover. Remove middle timing belt cover.

5) Loosen timing adjuster bolt 180 degrees. Push on timing belt tensioner to release tension from belt, then retighten adjuster bolt. Disengage timing belt from camshaft pulleys. Remove camshaft pulleys. Loosen valve adjuster screws and camshaft retainers. Remove rocker arms and camshafts. See CAMSHAFTS. Loosen cylinder head bolts 1/3 turn at a time until all are loose, in reverse order of tightening sequence. *See Fig. 6.* Remove cylinder head.

Inspection – 1) Ensure all mating surfaces are clean. Measure cylinder block surface warpage. Cylinder block warpage must not exceed 0.003" (0.08 mm).

2) Measure cylinder head warpage. Resurfacing is not required if warpage is less than 0.002" (0.05 mm). Resurface cylinder head if warpage is 0.002-0.008" (0.05-0.20 mm). Maximum resurface limit is 0.008" (0.20 mm).

3) Ensure cylinder head dowel pins, oil control jet, and "O" ring are installed in block. *See Fig. 7*

Installation – 1) Install new cylinder head gasket. Ensure No. 1 piston is at TDC of compression stroke. Apply a light coat of engine oil to cylinder head bolt threads and bottom of bolt head. Install and tighten cylinder head bolts to specification in 2 stages and in sequence. *See Fig. 6.*

2) Install intake manifold onto cylinder head. Tighten nuts to specification in a crisscross pattern, beginning with inner nuts. Install exhaust manifold with new nuts. Tighten nuts to specification in a crisscross pattern, beginning with inner nuts. See TORQUE SPECIFICATIONS.

3) Install camshafts. See CAMSHAFTS. Install camshaft pulleys. Install timing belt. See TIMING BELT. To complete installation, reverse removal procedure.

FRONT COVER OIL SEAL

Removal – Disconnect negative battery cable. Raise and support vehicle. Remove left front wheel. Remove left front wheelwell splash shield. Remove drive belts. Remove power steering pump with hoses attached, and set it aside. Remove crankshaft pulley. Remove front cover oil seal.

Installation – Apply a light coat of engine oil to crankshaft and lip of new seal. Install front seal using Seal Driver (07LAD-PR4010A). Ensure seal is fully seated. To complete installation, reverse removal procedure.

TIMING BELT

Removal – 1) Disconnect negative battery cable. Raise and support vehicle. Remove left front wheel. Remove left front wheelwell splash shield. Remove drive belts. Remove power steering pump with hoses attached, and set it aside.

2) Remove valve cover and middle timing belt cover. *See Fig. 8.* Rotate crankshaft counterclockwise to bring No. 1 piston to TDC of its compression stroke. Position UP mark on sprockets at top. *See Fig. 5.* Align grooves on sprockets. Remove crankshaft pulley.

3) Remove left engine mount. Remove cylinder head cover. Remove crankshaft pulley. Loosen timing belt tension adjuster bolt 180 degrees. Push tensioner to relieve tension on timing belt. Retighten adjuster bolt. If reusing timing belt, mark direction of belt rotation before removing. Remove timing belt.

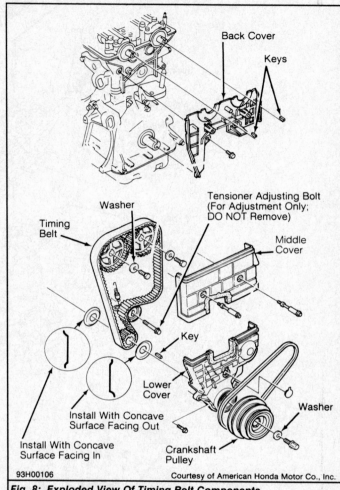

Fig. 8: Exploded View Of Timing Belt Components

Labels in figure: Back Cover, Keys, Tensioner Adjusting Bolt (For Adjustment Only; DO NOT Remove), Washer, Middle Cover, Timing Belt, Key, Lower Cover, Washer, Install With Concave Surface Facing Out, Install With Concave Surface Facing In, Crankshaft Pulley, 93H00106, Courtesy of American Honda Motor Co., Inc.

Installation – 1) Ensure No. 1 piston is at TDC of compression stroke. Install timing belt onto sprockets. DO NOT bend or twist belt excessively. Ensure arrow on used belt points in original direction. Adjust timing belt tension. See TIMING BELT TENSION under ADJUSTMENTS.

2) To complete installation, reverse removal procedure. Lubricate threads only of crankshaft pulley bolt, leaving underside of bolt head dry. Tighten crankshaft pulley bolt to 147 ft. lbs. (200 N.m), loosen, then retighten to 133 ft. lbs. (180 N.m).

CAMSHAFTS

Removal – 1) Disconnect negative battery cable. Remove valve cover and middle timing belt cover. *See Fig. 8.* Rotate crankshaft counterclockwise to bring No. 1 piston to TDC of its compression stroke, with UP mark on sprockets at top. *See Fig. 5.* Remove distributor.

2) Loosen timing belt adjuster bolt 180 degrees. Push tensioner to release tension from belt. Retighten adjuster bolt. Disengage timing belt from camshaft pulleys. Remove camshaft pulleys. Loosen valve adjuster screws and camshaft retainer bolts. Remove camshaft and rocker arms.

Installation – 1) Lubricate camshaft journals and bearings. Install rocker arms (if removed) into original positions. Install camshafts into cylinder head. Keyways must face upward. Apply sealant to mating surfaces of camshaft retainers at each end. Arrows on camshaft retainers must point toward timing belt. Temporarily tighten camshaft retainer bolts. Drive camshaft oil seals securely against bases of camshaft retainers.

2) Tighten camshaft bolts to specification in sequence. *See Fig. 9*. See TORQUE SPECIFICATIONS. To complete installation, reverse removal procedure. Adjust timing belt tension and valve clearance. See TIMING BELT TENSION and VALVE CLEARANCE under ADJUSTMENTS.

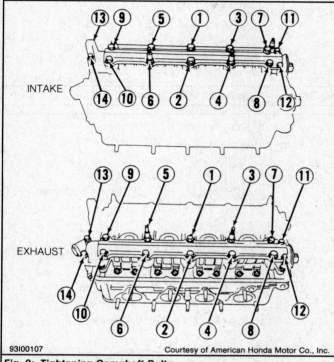

93I00107   Courtesy of American Honda Motor Co., Inc.

Fig. 9: Tightening Camshaft Bolts

REAR CRANKSHAFT OIL SEAL

Removal – 1) Disconnect negative battery cable. Remove transaxle assembly. See appropriate article in CLUTCHES (M/T models) or TRANSMISSION SERVICING (A/T models).

2) Place reference mark on clutch pressure plate (M/T models) and flywheel for reassembly reference. Remove pressure plate and clutch disc (if equipped). Remove flywheel. Pry seal from cover.

NOTE: *When installing new crankshaft oil seal, align hole in Driver Attachment (07948-SB00101) with pin on crankshaft.*

Installation – Apply a light coat of engine oil to crankshaft and lip of new seal. Using Seal Driver (07749-0010000) and Driver Attachment (07948-SB00101), install new seal. To complete installation, reverse removal procedure.

WATER PUMP

Removal – Disconnect negative battery cable. Drain cooling system. Remove timing belt. See TIMING BELT. Remove timing belt back cover. *See Fig. 8*. Remove retaining bolts, water pump, and "O" rings.

Installation – 1) Clean gasket surfaces. Install water pump. Install new "O" rings. To complete installation, reverse removal procedure. Tighten bolts to specifications. See TORQUE SPECIFICATIONS.

2) Adjust timing belt tension. See TIMING BELT TENSION under ADJUSTMENTS. Fill and bleed air from cooling system. See BLEEDING COOLING SYSTEM.

OIL PAN

Removal – 1) Drain engine oil. Rotate crankshaft counterclockwise to align crankshaft pulley timing marks. *See Fig. 5*. Remove valve cover and middle timing belt cover. *See Fig. 8*. Remove accessory drive belts.

2) Remove crankshaft pulley and timing belt lower cover. Mark timing belt for installation reference. Loosen belt tensioner. Remove timing belt and crankshaft sprocket. See TIMING BELT. Remove oil pan and gasket.

Installation – Clean gasket mating surfaces. Install new gasket and oil pan. Tighten bolts to specification. See TORQUE SPECIFICATIONS. To complete installation, reverse removal procedure.

OVERHAUL

CYLINDER HEAD

Cylinder Head – Ensure all mating surfaces are clean. Measure cylinder head warpage. If warpage is less than 0.002" (0.05 mm), resurfacing is not required. If warpage is 0.002-0.008" (0.05-0.20 mm), resurface cylinder head. Maximum resurface limit is 0.008" (0.20 mm).

Valve Springs – Measure free length of valve springs. If measurements are not within specifications, replace valve springs. See VALVES & VALVE SPRINGS table under ENGINE SPECIFICATIONS.

Valve Stem Oil Seals – Intake and exhaust valve stem seals are not interchangeable. Intake valve stem seals have a White spring around neck of seal. Oil seals for exhaust valves have a Black spring around neck of seal. Use Valve Stem Seal Installer (KD-2899) to install valve stem seals.

Valve Guide Inspection – Measure valve guide clearance using a dial indicator placed on valve head. Zero dial indicator. Rock valve stem from side to side. Valve guides can be replaced if valve stem oil clearance is not within specification. See CYLINDER HEAD table under ENGINE SPECIFICATIONS.

Valve Guide Removal – 1) Use a hot plate or oven to heat cylinder head to 300°F (150°C). Use Valve Guide Driver (07742-0010100), or fabricate valve guide remover from an air-impact chisel. *See Fig. 10*. Using an air hammer and valve guide remover, drive valve guide 0.079" (2.0 mm) toward combustion chamber.

CAUTION: *DO NOT heat cylinder head using a torch or heat cylinder head warmer than 300°F (150°C). Excessive heat may loosen valve seats.*

2) Turn head over. Working from combustion chamber side of head, drive valve guide out toward camshaft side of head. If valve guide does not move, drill valve guide with a 5/16" bit and try again to drive out guide.

CAUTION: *Drill guides in extreme cases only. Cylinder head damage can occur if valve guide breaks.*

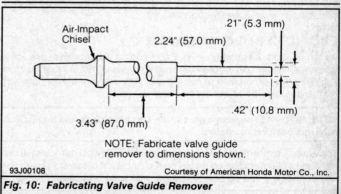

93J00108   Courtesy of American Honda Motor Co., Inc.

Fig. 10: Fabricating Valve Guide Remover

Valve Guide Installation – 1) Cool new valve guides in freezer for about one hour. Remove new valve guides from freezer as needed. Slip a 15/64" (6 mm) steel washer and appropriate driver attachment over Valve Guide Driver (07742-0010100).

2) Install new valve guides from camshaft side of cylinder head. Drive each guide into heated head until driver attachment bottoms on head. If replacing all valve guides, reheat cylinder head as necessary.
3) Valve guide installed height must be 0.4941-0.5138" (12.55-13.05 mm). Using cutting oil, ream new valve guides by rotating Valve Guide Reamer (07HAH-PJ7010A) clockwise full length of valve guide bore. Measure valve stem oil clearance. See CYLINDER HEAD table under ENGINE SPECIFICATIONS.

NOTE: Always reface valve seat after replacing valve guide.

Valve Seat – Valve seat replacement procedure is not available.
Valve Seat Correction Angles – If valve guides are to be replaced, perform guide replacement before refacing valve seats. If seat width is too wide, use 60-degree stone to raise seat, or 30-degree stone to lower seat. Ensure valve seat width is within specification. See CYLINDER HEAD table under ENGINE SPECIFICATIONS.
Valve Stem Installed Height – After servicing valves, measure valve stem installed height. *See Fig. 11.* If valve stem installed height exceeds 1.5033" (38.185 mm) for intake valve or 1.4915" (37.885 mm) for exhaust valves, replace valve. If valve stem installed height still exceeds limit, replace cylinder head.

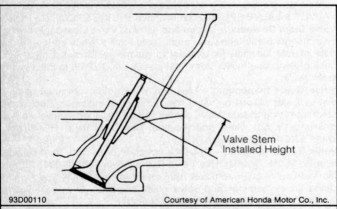

Fig. 11: **Measuring Valve Stem Installed Height**

VALVE TRAIN

Removal – Place a rubber band around each set of rocker arms to keep them together. Remove intake and exhaust rocker shaft oil control orifices. Thread a 12-mm bolt into end of rocker shaft. Pull bolt head to remove rocker shaft and rocker arms. Tag parts for installation reference as they are removed.
Installation – Lubricate all components before installation. Install all components into original locations. Back off valve adjuster screws before installation. If holes in cylinder head and rocker shafts are not in line, turn shaft with a 12-mm bolt threaded into end. To complete installation, reverse removal procedure.

CYLINDER BLOCK ASSEMBLY

Piston & Rod Assembly – 1) Each rod is sorted into one of 4 tolerance ranges. Size depends on crank journal bore. Number from 1 to 4 is stamped on side of rod big end. Any combination of numbers from 1 to 4 may be found on any engine.

NOTE: Reference numbers are for big end bore code and do not indicate rod position in engine.

2) Nominal connecting rod big bore size is 1.89" (48.0 mm). Install piston and connecting rod so arrow on top of piston is toward timing belt and connecting rod oil hole is toward intake manifold. *See Fig. 12.*

NOTE: All replacement piston pins are oversize.

Piston Pin Removal – 1) Install Piston Base Head (07HAF-PL20102) and Piston Pin Base Insert (07GAF-PH60300) into Base

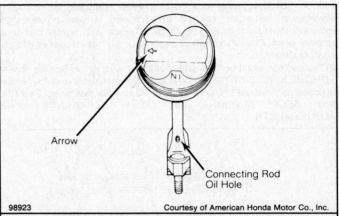

Fig. 12: **Positioning Piston Onto Connecting Rod**

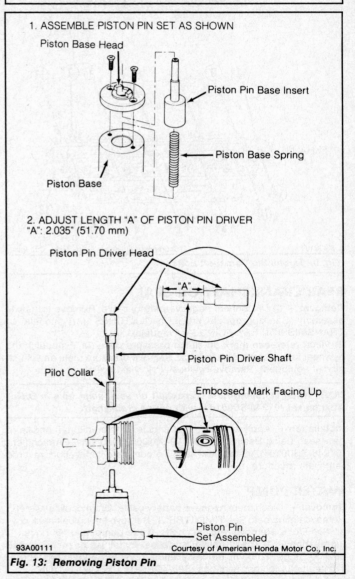

Fig. 13: **Removing Piston Pin**

(07973-6570500). Turn handle on Piston Pin Driver Head (07973-PE00320) so piston driver length is 2.035" (51.70 mm). *See Fig. 13.*
2) Insert Piston Driver Shaft (07973-PE00310) into Pilot Collar (07LAF-PR30100). Place piston onto base. Press out piston pin. When removing or installing piston pin, set piston in press with embossed side facing up. Align lugs on base insert with recessed part of piston.

Piston Pin Inspection – **1)** Measure diameter of piston pin. Zero dial indicator to piston pin diameter. Insert gauge into piston boss to measure piston pin-to-piston clearance.

2) Piston pin clearance must be 0.0004-0.0009" (0.010-0.022 mm). If piston pin clearance is greater than 0.0009" (0.022 mm), install an oversize piston pin and recheck clearance.

3) Determine difference between piston pin diameter and connecting rod small end diameter. Interference fit between piston and connecting rod must be 0.0005-0.0013" (0.013-0.032 mm).

Piston Pin Installation – **1)** Ensure piston and connecting rod are positioned as shown. *See Fig. 12.* Turn handle on Piston Pin Driver (07973-PE00320) so piston driver length is 2.035" (51.70 mm).

2) Install Pilot Collar (07LAF-PR30100) into piston and connecting rod. Lightly oil new piston pin. Place piston onto base. Press in piston pin.

Fitting Pistons – **1)** Using a feeler gauge, measure piston-to-cylinder bore clearance. If clearance is near or exceeds 0.002" (0.05 mm), measure each piston and cylinder. If piston clearance exceeds service limit, rebore cylinder and install oversize piston.

2) Measure piston diameter at a point 0.6" (15 mm) from bottom of piston skirt. If diameter is not within specification, replace piston. See PISTON DIAMETER table. See PISTONS, PINS & RINGS table under ENGINE SPECIFICATIONS.

PISTON DIAMETER

Application [1]	In. (mm)
Standard (New)	3.1882-3.1886 (80.980-80.990)
Service Limit	3.1878 (80.970)
Oversize 0.010" (0.25 mm)	3.1980-3.1984 (81.230-81.240)

[1] – Measured at 0.6" (15 mm) from bottom of piston skirt.

Piston Rings – **1)** Using inverted piston, push new piston ring into cylinder bore 0.6-0.8" (15-20 mm) from bottom. Measure piston ring end gap. Repeat for each ring. See PISTONS, PINS & RINGS table under ENGINE SPECIFICATIONS.

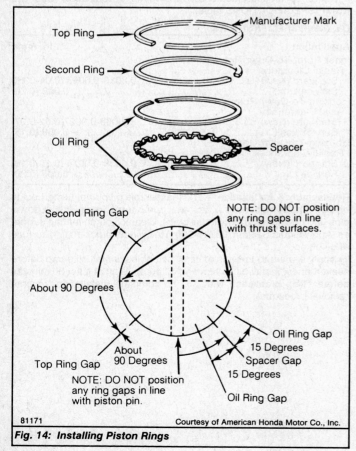

81171   Courtesy of American Honda Motor Co., Inc.

Fig. 14: Installing Piston Rings

2) Clean piston ring grooves thoroughly. Install piston rings with identification mark toward top of piston. Using a feeler gauge, measure piston ring side clearance between ring and ring land.

3) If ring lands are excessively worn, replace piston. See PISTONS, PINS & RINGS table. Align piston ring end gaps properly on piston. *See Fig. 14.*

Rod Bearings – **1)** Using Plastigage, measure rod bearing oil clearance. Tighten bearing cap to 24 ft. lbs. (32 N.m).

2) If oil clearance is not within specification, install a new bearing set (same color code) and recheck oil clearance. DO NOT shim or file cap to adjust oil clearance.

3) If oil clearance is still incorrect, try next larger or smaller bearing. Measure oil clearance once more. If proper oil clearance cannot be obtained by using larger or smaller bearings, replace crankshaft and repeat procedure.

NOTE: A number indicating connecting rod bore is stamped on side of each connecting rod and cap. Connecting rod journal diameter codes (letters) are stamped on crankshaft counterweight pads. See Fig. 15. Use both codes when ordering replacement bearings.

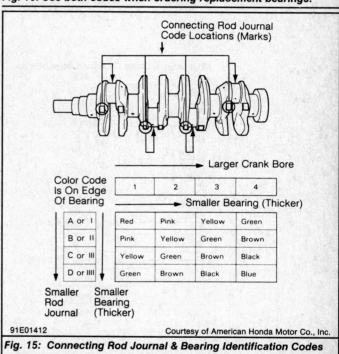

91E01412   Courtesy of American Honda Motor Co., Inc.

Fig. 15: Connecting Rod Journal & Bearing Identification Codes

Crankshaft & Main Bearings – **1)** Remove rear crankshaft oil seal cover, oil screen, oil pump, and baffle plate. Rotate crankshaft so No. 2 and No. 3 crankpins are at bottom. Remove all connecting rod caps and bearings.

2) Mark all main bearing caps for assembly reference. Remove main bearing caps and bearing halves. Lift crankshaft from block, being careful not to damage journals.

3) Using a lathe or "V" blocks to support crankshaft, measure crankshaft runout, out-of-round, and taper. If any measurement exceeds service limit, replace crankshaft. See CRANKSHAFT, MAIN & CONNECTING ROD BEARINGS table under ENGINE SPECIFICATIONS.

4) Install crankshaft into block. Measure oil clearance with Plastigage. Tighten main bearing caps to 58 ft. lbs. (78 N.m). If oil clearance is not within specification, install a new bearing set (same color code) and recheck oil clearance.

5) If oil clearance is still incorrect, try next larger or smaller bearing and measure oil clearance once more. If proper oil clearance cannot be obtained by using larger or smaller bearings, replace crankshaft and repeat procedure.

NOTE: *A letter indicating main journal bore diameters is stamped on cylinder block. See Fig. 16. Use these codes, together with crankshaft main journal diameter numbers, when ordering replacement bearings.*

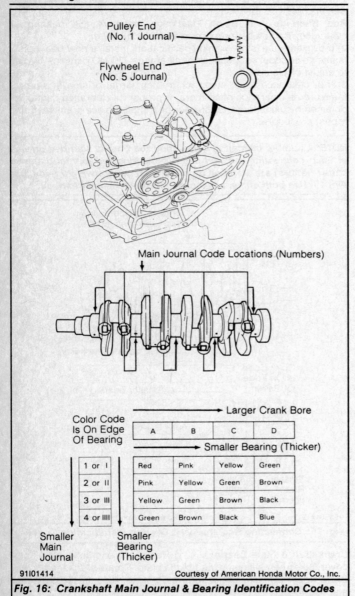

Fig. 16: Crankshaft Main Journal & Bearing Identification Codes

Thrust Bearing – 1) Measure crankshaft end play with a dial indicator. If end play exceeds specification, inspect thrust washers and thrust surface of crankshaft. See CRANKSHAFT, MAIN & CONNECTING ROD BEARINGS table under ENGINE SPECIFICATIONS.
2) Replace worn parts as necessary. Thrust washer thickness is fixed. DO NOT change thrust washer thickness by grinding or shimming. Install thrust washers with grooved side out.

Cylinder Block – 1) Measure cylinder bore out-of-round and taper. If either out-of-round or taper exceeds 0.002" (0.05 mm), rebore cylinder for oversize pistons. If any cylinder exceeds oversize bore service limit, replace cylinder block. See CYLINDER BLOCK table under ENGINE SPECIFICATIONS.
2) Using a feeler gauge and straightedge, measure cylinder block deck surface warpage. Service limit is 0.003" (0.08 mm). If cylinder bore is okay, hone cylinder to obtain a 60-degree crosshatch pattern. After honing, wash cylinder bore wish hot soapy water. Air-dry cylinder bore, and apply engine oil to prevent rusting.

ENGINE OILING

ENGINE LUBRICATION SYSTEM

A rotor-type oil pump draws oil from oil pan and delivers it under pressure to main and connecting rod bearings. An oil hole in each connecting rod lubricates thrust side of piston and cylinder wall. An oil passage carries oil to camshaft and rocker arms. Oil spray lubricates valve stems.
Crankcase Capacity – Crankcase capacity is 4.2 qts. (4.0L) including oil filter. Capacity is 5.1 qts. (4.8L) after engine overhaul.
Oil Pressure – Oil pressure should be at least 10 psi (0.7 kg/cm²) at idle and at least 50 psi (3.5 kg/cm²) at 3000 RPM.

OIL PUMP

Removal & Disassembly – Remove oil pan. See OIL PAN under REMOVAL & INSTALLATION. Remove oil screen and oil pump assembly. Remove screws from oil pump housing. Separate housing and cover.
Inspection – Measure radial clearance between rotors. Measure axial clearance between outer rotor and housing. Inspect both rotors and pump housing for scoring or other damage. Replace components if clearance measurements are not within specification. See OIL PUMP SPECIFICATIONS table.

OIL PUMP SPECIFICATIONS

Application	In. (mm)
Inner Rotor-To-Outer Rotor	
Radial Clearance	
Standard (New)	0.0016-0.0063 (0.04-0.16)
Service Limit	0.008 (0.20)
Housing-To-Outer Rotor	
Axial Clearance	
Standard (New)	0.0008-0.0027(0.02-0.07)
Service Limit	0.006 (0.15)
Housing-To-Outer Rotor	
Radial Clearance	
Standard (New)	0.0039-0.0074 (0.10-0.19)
Service Limit	0.008 (0.20)

Reassembly & Installation – 1) Reassemble oil pump, using Loctite on pump housing screws. Ensure oil pump turns freely. Install dowel pins and new "O" ring in cylinder block. Clean oil pump mating surfaces. Apply Liquid Sealant (08718-0001) to cylinder block mating surface of oil pump.
2) Apply sealant to threads of inner bolt holes. Install oil pump before sealant dries. Install oil screen and oil pump. Wait at least 30 minutes before filling crankcase with oil. To complete installation, reverse removal procedure.

TORQUE SPECIFICATIONS

TORQUE SPECIFICATIONS

Application	Ft. Lbs. (N.m)
A/C Compressor Bracket Bolts	17 (23)
Alternator Belt Adjustment Bolt	17 (23)
Alternator Mount Bolt	33 (45)
Camshaft Retaining Bolts	[1]
Camshaft Sprocket Bolts	27 (37)
Connecting Rod Nuts	[2] 24 (32)
Crankshaft Pulley Bolt	133 (180)
Cylinder Head Bolts	[3] 63 (85)
Distributor Mount Bolts	16 (22)
Engine Block-To-Transaxle Housing Bolts	47 (64)
Engine Mount Bolts	[4]
Exhaust Manifold Nuts	23 (31)
Exhaust Pipe Flange Nuts	40 (54)
Flexplate (A/T)	[5] 55 (75)
Flywheel Bolts (M/T)	[5] 77 (105)
Intake Manifold Nuts	17 (23)
Main Bearing Cap Bolts	[6] 57 (78)
Oil Pump Bolts	
6-mm Bolts	[7]
8-mm Bolts	17 (23)
Power Steering Mount Bolt	17 (23)
Rocker Arm Lock Nuts	18 (24)
Rocker Arm Pivot Bolt	46 (62)
Shift Lever Torque Rod Bolt	16 (22)
Timing Belt Tension Adjuster Bolt	40 (54)

Application	INCH Lbs. (N.m)
Camshaft Bearing Bolt	84 (10)
Crankshaft Rear Seal Cover Bolts	96 (11)
Fuel Service Bolt	108 (12)
Oil Pan Bolts	[5] 108 (12)
Oil Pump Screen Nuts	96 (11)
Timing Belt Cover Bolts	108 (12)
Valve Cover Nuts	84 (10)
Water Pump Bolt	108 (12)

[1] – Tighten 6-mm bolts to 96 INCH lbs. (11 N.m). Tighten 8-mm bolts to 16 ft. lbs. (22 N.m). Bolts must be tightened in sequence shown. *See Fig. 9.*
[2] – Tighten connecting rod nuts in 2 stages. First tighten nuts to 14 ft. lbs. (20 N.m), then tighten them to 24 ft. lbs. (32 N.m).
[3] – Tighten cylinder head bolts in 2 stages. First tighten bolts to 22 ft. lbs. (30 N.m) and then to 63 ft. lbs. (85 N.m). *See Fig. 6.*
[4] – *See Fig. 4.*
[5] – Tighten in a crisscross pattern.
[6] – Tighten main bearing bolts in 2 stages. First tighten bolts to 22 ft. lbs. (30 N.m), then tighten them to 57 ft. lbs. (78 N.m).
[7] – Tighten to 96 INCH lbs. (11 N.m).

ENGINE SPECIFICATIONS

GENERAL SPECIFICATIONS

Application	Specification
Displacement	104 Cu. In. (1.7L)
Bore	3.19" (81.0 mm)
Stroke	3.20" (81.4 mm)
Compression Ratio	9.7:1
Fuel System	SFI
Horsepower @ RPM	160 @ 7600
Torque Ft. Lbs. @ RPM	117 @ 7000

CONNECTING RODS

Application	In. (mm)
Bore Diameter	
Crankpin Bore	1.89 (48.0)
Pin Bore	0.8255-0.8260 (20.968-20.981)
Side Play	
Standard	0.006-0.012 (0.15-0.30)
Service Limit	0.016 (0.40)

CRANKSHAFT, MAIN & CONNECTING ROD BEARINGS

Application	In. (mm)
Crankshaft	
End Play	
Standard	0.004-0.014 (0.10-0.35)
Service Limit	0.018 (0.45)
Runout	
Standard	0.0008 (0.020)
Service Limit	0.0012 (0.030)
Main Bearings	
Journal Diameter	
Except No. 3	2.1644-2.1654 (54.976-55.000)
No. 3	2.1642-2.1651 (54.970-54.994)
Journal Out-Of-Round	
Standard	0.00016 (0.0040)
Service Limit	0.00020 (0.0060)
Journal Taper	
Standard	0.0002 (0.005)
Service Limit	0.0002 (0.005)
Oil Clearance	
Except No. 3 Journal	
Standard	0.0009-0.0017 (0.024-0.042)
Service Limit	0.0020 (0.050)
No. 3 Journal	
Standard	0.0012-0.0019 (0.030-0.048)
Service Limit	0.0024 (0.060)
Connecting Rod Bearings	
Journal Diameter	1.7707-1.7717 (44.976-45.000)
Journal Out-Of-Round	
Standard	0.00016 (0.0040)
Service Limit	0.00020 (0.0060)
Journal Taper	
Service Limit	0.0002 (0.005)
Oil Clearance	
Standard	0.0013-0.0020 (0.032-0.050)
Service Limit	0.0024 (0.060)

PISTONS, PINS & RINGS

Application	In. (mm)
Pistons	
Clearance	
Standard	0.0004-0.0014 (0.010-0.035)
Service Limit	0.0020 (0.050)
Diameter [1]	
Standard	3.1882-3.1886 (80.980-80.990)
Service Limit	3.1878 (80.970)
Oversize 0.010" (0.25 mm)	3.1980-3.1984 (81.230-81.240)
Pins	
Diameter	0.8265-0.8268 (20.994-21.000)
Piston Fit	0.0004-0.0009 (0.010-0.022)
Rod Fit	0.0005-0.0013 (0.013-0.032)
Rings	
No. 1	
End Gap	0.008-0.014 (0.20-0.35)
Side Clearance	0.0018-0.0028 (0.045-0.070)
No. 2	
End Gap	0.016-0.022 (0.40-0.55)
Side Clearance	0.0018-0.0028 (0.045-0.070)
No. 3 (Oil)	
End Gap	0.008-0.020 (0.20-0.50)

[1] – Measure at 0.6" (15 mm) from bottom of skirt.

1993 ENGINES
1.7L 4-Cylinder (Cont.)

CYLINDER BLOCK

Application	In. (mm)
Cylinder Bore	
Standard Diameter	3.1890-3.1898 (81.000-81.020)
Service Limit	3.1917 (81.070)
Maximum Taper	0.002 (0.05)
Maximum Rebore Limit	.01 (0.25)
Maximum Deck Warpage	0.002 (0.05)

VALVES & VALVE SPRINGS

Application	Specification
Intake Valves	
Face Angle	45°
Head Diameter	1.295-1.303" (32.90-33.10 mm)
Margin	
Standard	0.041-0.053" (1.05-1.35 mm)
Service Limit	0.033" (0.85 mm)
Stem Diameter	
Standard	0.2156-0.2159" (5.475-5.485 mm)
Service Limit	0.2144" (5.445 mm)
Exhaust Valves	
Face Angle	45°
Head Diameter	1.098-1.106" (27.90-28.10 mm)
Margin	
Standard	0.065-0.077" (1.65-1.95 mm)
Service Limit	0.057" (1.45 mm)
Stem Diameter	
Standard	0.2146-0.2150" (5.450-5.460 mm)
Service Limit	0.2134" (5.420 mm)
Valve Springs Free Length	
Intake	1.611" (40.92 mm)
Exhaust	1.651" (41.94 mm)

VALVE STEM INSTALLED HEIGHT

Application [1]	In. (mm)
Intake	
Standard	1.4750-1.4935 (37.465-37.935)
Service Limit	1.5033 (38.185)
Exhaust	
Standard	1.4632-1.4817 (37.165-37.635)
Service Limit	1.4915 (37.885)

[1] – Measure from base of valve guide to tip of valve stem.

CYLINDER HEAD

Application	Specification
Cylinder Head	
Height	5.589-5.593" (141.95-142.05 mm)
Maximum Warpage	[1] 0.002" (0.05 mm)
Valve Seats (Exhaust & Intake)	
Seat Angle	45°
Seat Width	
Standard	0.049-0.061" (1.25-1.55 mm)
Service Limit	0.079" (2.00 mm)
Valve Guides	
Exhaust	
Valve Guide I.D.	
Standard	0.217-0.218" (5.51-5.53 mm)
Service Limit	0.219" (5.55 mm)
Valve Guide Installed Height	0.494-0.514" (12.55-13.05 mm)
Valve Stem-To-Guide Oil Clearance	
Standard	0.002-0.003" (0.05-0.08 mm)
Service Limit	0.004" (0.10 mm)
Intake	
Valve Guide I.D.	
Standard	0.217-0.218" (5.51-5.53 mm)
Service Limit	0.219" (5.55 mm)
Valve Guide Installed Height	0.494-0.514" (12.55-13.05 mm)
Valve Stem-To-Guide Oil Clearance	
Standard	0.0010-0.0022" (0.025-0.055 mm)
Service Limit	0.0030" (0.080 mm)

[1] – Maximum resurface limit is 0.008" (0.20 mm).

CAMSHAFT

Application	In. (mm)
End Play	
Standard	0.002-0.006 (0.05-0.15)
Service Limit	0.020 (0.50)
Journal Runout	
Standard	0.0012 (0.030)
Service Limit	0.002 (0.06)
Oil Clearance	
Standard	0.002-0.004 (0.05-0.09)
Service Limit	0.006 (0.15)

Integra

NOTE: For repair procedures not covered in this article, see ENGINE OVERHAUL PROCEDURES article in GENERAL INFORMATION.

ENGINE IDENTIFICATION

Engine identification code is stamped on right rear of cylinder block as viewed from flywheel, below cylinder head mating surface. The first 5 characters of the code indicate engine type. The last 7 numbers of the code indicate engine serial number. Engine serial numbers starting from 2000001 indicate California vehicle. Engine serial numbers starting from 2300001 indicate Federal vehicle.

ENGINE IDENTIFICATION CODE

Application	Code
1.8L	B18A1

ADJUSTMENTS

VALVE CLEARANCE ADJUSTMENT

CAUTION: Always rotate engine in direction of normal rotation (counterclockwise as viewed from front of engine). Backward rotation may cause timing belt to jump time.

1) Adjust valves when engine temperature is 100°F (38°C) or less. Remove valve cover. Rotate crankshaft counterclockwise until No. 1 piston is at TDC of compression stroke.
2) Ensure UP marks on camshaft sprockets are at top, and TDC grooves on pulleys are aligned with TDC groove on back cover. *See Fig. 1.* Adjust clearance on both valves for No. 1 cylinder. Loosen lock nuts, and turn adjustment screw until clearance is as specified. Tighten lock nut to 18 ft. lbs. (25 N.m). Recheck adjustment. See VALVE CLEARANCE SPECIFICATIONS table.

3) Rotate crankshaft 180 degrees counterclockwise (camshaft sprockets turn 90 degrees) so No. 3 piston is at TDC of compression stroke. UP marks should point to exhaust side. Adjust clearance on both valves for No. 3 cylinder.
4) Rotate crankshaft 180 degrees counterclockwise so No. 4 piston is at TDC of compression stroke. Ensure UP marks are pointing down. Adjust clearance on both valves for No. 4 cylinder.
5) Rotate crankshaft 180 degrees counterclockwise so No. 2 piston is at TDC of compression stroke. Ensure UP marks are pointing to intake side. Adjust clearances on both valves for No. 2 cylinder. Install new valve cover gasket. Install valve cover. Retighten crankshaft pulley bolt to 133 ft. lbs. (180 N.m).

VALVE CLEARANCE SPECIFICATIONS

Application	In. (mm)
Exhaust	0.006-0.008 (0.16-0.20)
Intake	0.003-0.005 (0.08-0.12)

TIMING BELT TENSION ADJUSTMENT

CAUTION: Adjust timing belt with engine cold. DO NOT rotate crankshaft with timing belt tensioner adjusting bolt loose.

Remove valve cover. Rotate crankshaft counterclockwise until No. 1 piston is at TDC. Rotate crankshaft 3 teeth counterclockwise on camshaft sprocket to create tension on timing belt. Loosen tension adjuster bolt to create tension on belt. *See Fig. 2.* Tighten tension adjuster bolt to specification. See TORQUE SPECIFICATIONS. Install valve cover using new gaskets.

REMOVAL & INSTALLATION

NOTE: For reassembly reference, label all electrical connectors, vacuum hoses, and fuel lines before removal. Place mating marks on engine hood and other major assemblies before removal.

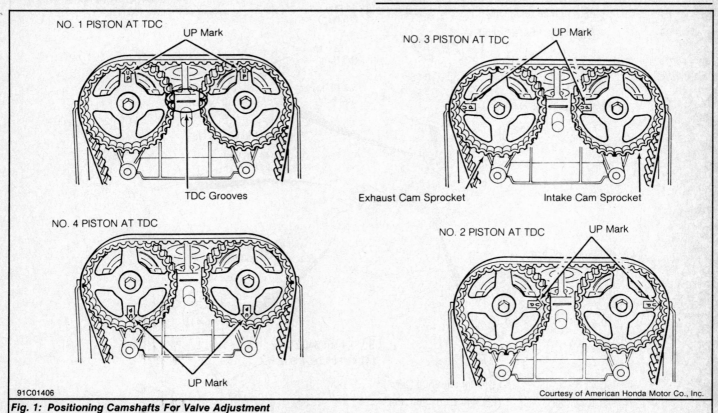

91C01406

Courtesy of American Honda Motor Co., Inc.

Fig. 1: Positioning Camshafts For Valve Adjustment

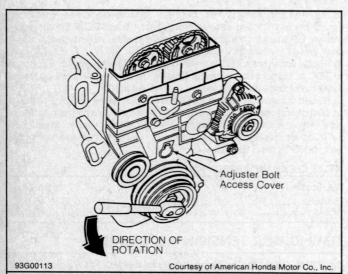

DIRECTION OF ROTATION

93G00113   Courtesy of American Honda Motor Co., Inc.

Fig. 2: Locating Timing Belt Adjuster Bolt

FUEL PRESSURE RELEASE

CAUTION: Fuel system is under pressure. Release pressure before servicing fuel system components.

Disconnect negative battery cable. Remove fuel tank filler cap. Place a shop towel on top of fuel filter to absorb any fuel spray. Release fuel injection system pressure by slowly loosening fuel injection service bolt. *See Fig. 3.*

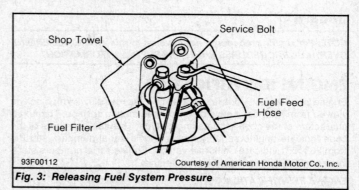

Shop Towel   Service Bolt

Fuel Feed Hose

Fuel Filter

93F00112   Courtesy of American Honda Motor Co., Inc.

Fig. 3: Releasing Fuel System Pressure

BLEEDING COOLING SYSTEM

1) To bleed air from cooling system, set heater controls to maximum temperature. Loosen bleed bolt located on thermostat housing. Fill cooling system with a 50/50 mixture of coolant and water to bottom of filler neck.

2) Tighten bleed bolt when coolant flows from bleed bolt in steady stream without bubbles. With radiator cap off, start and warm engine to normal operating temperature. Add coolant as necessary. Install radiator cap.

ENGINE

Removal – 1) Disconnect battery cables. Remove hood hinge stops. Secure hood in vertical position. DO NOT remove hood. Raise and support vehicle. Drain engine oil and transmission fluid. Remove front wheels and splash shield. Remove radiator cap to release system pressure. Drain cooling system. Remove battery and battery tray.

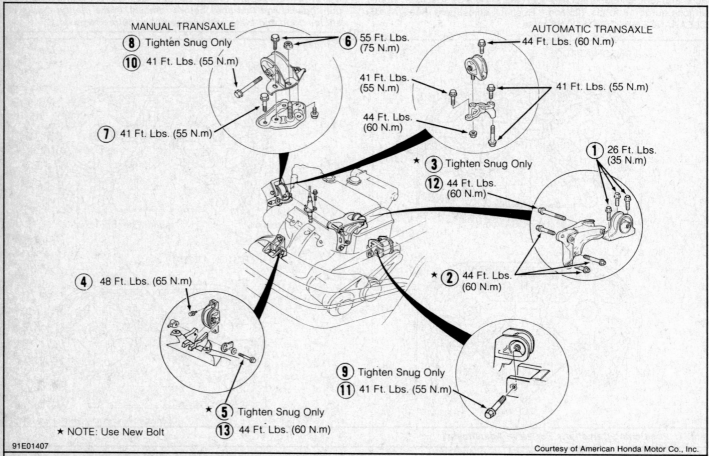

MANUAL TRANSAXLE   AUTOMATIC TRANSAXLE

⑧ Tighten Snug Only   ⑥ 55 Ft. Lbs. (75 N.m)   ④ 44 Ft. Lbs. (60 N.m)

⑩ 41 Ft. Lbs. (55 N.m)

41 Ft. Lbs. (55 N.m)   41 Ft. Lbs. (55 N.m)

44 Ft. Lbs. (60 N.m)

⑦ 41 Ft. Lbs. (55 N.m)

★ ③ Tighten Snug Only   ① 26 Ft. Lbs. (35 N.m)

⑫ 44 Ft. Lbs. (60 N.m)

④ 48 Ft. Lbs. (65 N.m)

★ ② 44 Ft. Lbs. (60 N.m)

⑨ Tighten Snug Only

⑪ 41 Ft. Lbs. (55 N.m)

★ ⑤ Tighten Snug Only

★ NOTE: Use New Bolt   ⑬ 44 Ft. Lbs. (60 N.m)

91E01407   Courtesy of American Honda Motor Co., Inc.

Fig. 4: Engine/Transaxle Mount Tightening Sequence

2) Release fuel pressure. See FUEL PRESSURE RELEASE. Remove fuel inlet hose. Unplug harness connectors from distributor. Remove distributor. Remove intake air duct and air cleaner housing. Unplug engine wiring harness connectors on left side of engine compartment. Disconnect throttle cable.

3) Unplug engine wiring harness connectors on right side of engine compartment. Disconnect power cables from underhood fuse/relay box. Disconnect brake booster vacuum hose from intake manifold. Disconnect fuel return hose. Disconnect ground cable at cylinder head. Remove power steering pump with hoses attached. Set power steering pump aside.

4) Remove A/C compressor with hoses attached, and set it aside. Remove alternator. Disconnect transmission cooler lines. Remove radiator and heater hoses. Remove speed sensor, leaving hoses attached. Unplug cooling fan connectors. Remove radiator.

5) Remove exhaust pipe. Disconnect drive shafts. See FWD AXLE SHAFTS article in DRIVE AXLES. On M/T models, disconnect clutch cable, shift rod, and shift lever torque rod. On A/T models, remove torque converter cover and disconnect shift control cable.

6) On all models, attach chain hoist to engine. Raise hoist to take all slack from chain. Remove rear transmission mount and rear transmission mounting bracket. Remove front transmission mount. Remove side transmission mount and side transmission mounting bracket. Remove side engine mount.

7) Slowly raise engine/transaxle about 6 inches. Ensure all hoses and wiring have been disconnected. Carefully remove engine and transaxle from vehicle.

Installation – 1) To install, reverse removal procedure. To prevent excessive engine vibration and premature engine mount wear, tighten engine/transaxle mounts in specified sequence. *See Fig. 4.*

2) When installing drive axles, use new spring clips. Insert drive axles until spring clips click into groove of differential side gear. Ensure harness connectors and hoses are connected properly.

3) Ensure control cables are not bent or pinched and are adjusted properly. On M/T models, adjust clutch pedal free play. Verify transaxle shifts smoothly.

4) On all models, adjust drive belt tension. Fill or top off all fluids. Fill and bleed air from cooling system. See BLEEDING COOLING SYSTEM. Start engine and check for leaks.

INTAKE MANIFOLD

Removal – 1) Allow engine to cool. Disconnect negative battery cable. Release fuel pressure. See FUEL PRESSURE RELEASE under REMOVAL & INSTALLATION. Carefully remove radiator cap to release system pressure. Drain cooling system. Remove upper and lower radiator hoses. Remove air intake duct and air cleaner assembly.

2) Disconnect fuel inlet and return hoses. Mark and disconnect vacuum hoses and wire harness connectors as necessary. Remove fuel evaporation canister hose from throttle body.

3) Remove brake booster and PCV vacuum hoses from intake manifold. Disconnect throttle cable. Remove intake manifold and gasket.

Installation – Clean gasket surfaces. Install intake manifold, using new intake manifold gasket. Tighten nuts, using a crisscross pattern in 2 or 3 stages, beginning with inner nuts. See TORQUE SPECIFICATIONS. To complete installation, reverse removal procedure. Fill and bleed air from cooling system. See BLEEDING COOLING SYSTEM under REMOVAL & INSTALLATION.

EXHAUST MANIFOLD

Removal – Disconnect negative battery cable. Remove oil dipstick. Remove exhaust manifold heat shield. Disconnect exhaust pipe from exhaust manifold. Remove exhaust manifold bracket. Disconnect oxygen sensor. Remove exhaust manifold bolts. Remove exhaust manifold and gasket.

Installation – To install, reverse removal procedure. Tighten bolts to specification. See TORQUE SPECIFICATIONS.

CYLINDER HEAD

Removal – 1) Disconnect negative battery cable. Rotate crankshaft counterclockwise until No. 1 piston is at TDC of compression stroke. Ensure timing marks are aligned. *See Fig. 5.* Drain cooling system. Release fuel pressure. See FUEL PRESSURE RELEASE under REMOVAL & INSTALLATION. Disconnect fuel inlet hose. Mark and disconnect vacuum hoses, breather hose, and air intake hose. Remove coolant by-pass hose from cylinder head.

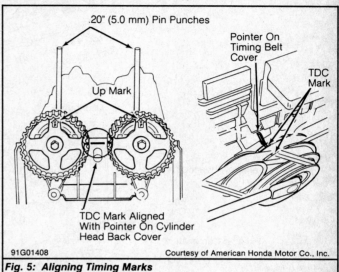

.20" (5.0 mm) Pin Punches

Up Mark

Pointer On Timing Belt Cover

TDC Mark

TDC Mark Aligned With Pointer On Cylinder Head Back Cover

91G01408   Courtesy of American Honda Motor Co., Inc.

Fig. 5: Aligning Timing Marks

2) Disconnect fuel evaporation canister hose from throttle body. Disconnect brake booster and PCV hoses from intake manifold. Disconnect fuel return hose. Disconnect throttle cable at throttle body.

3) Remove spark plug wires. Remove distributor. Disconnect any remaining hoses. Unplug engine harness connectors on left side of engine compartment. Disconnect engine wire harness clamps from cylinder head and intake manifold. Disconnect all remaining wiring from cylinder head.

4) Remove upper radiator hose, heater inlet hose, and by-pass hoses from intake manifold. Remove power steering pump, leaving hoses attached. Set power steering pump aside. Raise and support vehicle.

5) Remove left front wheel. Remove splash shield. Remove intake manifold bracket bolts. Remove exhaust manifold upper shroud and bracket. Remove exhaust pipe. Remove exhaust manifold. Remove cylinder head cover. Disconnect ground cable.

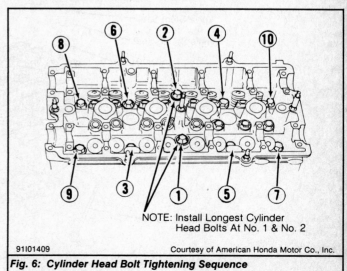

NOTE: Install Longest Cylinder Head Bolts At No. 1 & No. 2

91I01409   Courtesy of American Honda Motor Co., Inc.

Fig. 6: Cylinder Head Bolt Tightening Sequence

1993 ENGINES
1.8L 4-Cylinder (Cont.)

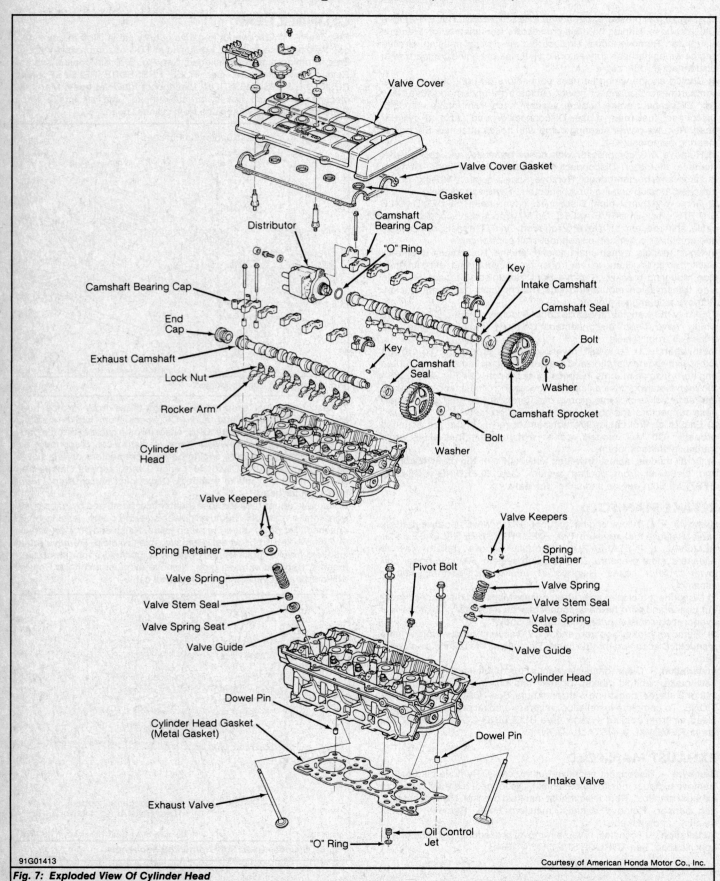

Valve Cover

Valve Cover Gasket

Gasket

Distributor

Camshaft Bearing Cap

"O" Ring

Key

Intake Camshaft

Camshaft Bearing Cap

Camshaft Seal

End Cap

Bolt

Exhaust Camshaft

Key

Washer

Lock Nut

Camshaft Seal

Rocker Arm

Camshaft Sprocket

Cylinder Head

Washer

Bolt

Valve Keepers

Valve Keepers

Spring Retainer

Spring Retainer

Valve Spring

Pivot Bolt

Valve Spring

Valve Stem Seal

Valve Stem Seal

Valve Spring Seat

Valve Spring Seat

Valve Guide

Valve Guide

Cylinder Head

Dowel Pin

Cylinder Head Gasket (Metal Gasket)

Dowel Pin

Intake Valve

Exhaust Valve

"O" Ring

Oil Control Jet

91G01413

Fig. 7: Exploded View Of Cylinder Head

6) Remove upper timing belt cover. Loosen timing belt adjuster bolt, push timing belt to relieve tension, and retighten adjuster bolt. If timing belt is to be reused, mark an arrow on belt to indicate direction of rotation. Remove timing belt from camshaft sprockets.

7) Remove camshafts. Mark all parts for installation reference. Remove cylinder head bolts, 1/3 turn at a time, in reverse order of tightening sequence. *See Fig. 6.* Remove cylinder head. Separate intake manifold from cylinder head.

Inspection – Ensure all mating surfaces are clean. Check cylinder block surface for warpage. Measure cylinder head for warpage. Resurfacing is not required if warpage is less than 0.002" (0.05 mm). Resurface cylinder head if warpage is 0.002-0.008" (0.05-0.20 mm). Maximum resurface limit is 0.008" (0.20 mm). Ensure cylinder head dowel pins, oil control jet, and "O" ring are installed. *See Fig. 7.*

Installation – 1) Install new intake manifold gasket. Install intake manifold onto cylinder head. Tighten nuts in a crisscross pattern, beginning with inner nuts. See TORQUE SPECIFICATIONS.

2) Ensure No. 1 piston is at TDC. Apply a light coat of engine oil to cylinder head bolts and washers. Install longer cylinder head bolts into positions 1 and 2. Install remaining bolts. Tighten cylinder head bolts to specification, in sequence, in 2 stages. *See Fig. 6.*

3) Reverse removal procedure to complete installation. If reusing timing belt, install belt with arrow mark (made in removal procedure) in direction of original rotation. Adjust timing belt tension. See TIMING BELT TENSION ADJUSTMENT under ADJUSTMENTS. Fill and bleed cooling system. See BLEEDING COOLING SYSTEM under REMOVAL & INSTALLATION.

FRONT COVER OIL SEAL

Removal – Disconnect negative battery cable. Raise and support vehicle. Remove left front wheel. Remove left front wheelwell splash shield. Remove drive belts. Remove and set aside power steering pump with hoses attached. Remove crankshaft pulley. Remove front cover oil seal.

Installation – Apply a light coat of engine oil to crankshaft and lip of new seal. Install front seal using Seal Driver (07LAD-PR4010A). Ensure seal is fully seated. To complete installation, reverse removal procedure.

TIMING BELT

Removal – 1) Disconnect negative battery cable. Raise and support vehicle. Remove left front wheel. Remove left front wheelwell splash shield. Remove all drive belts. Remove power steering pump with hoses attached. Set power steering pump aside.

2) Remove valve cover and upper timing belt cover. *See Fig. 8.* Turn crankshaft counterclockwise to bring No. 1 piston to TDC of its compression stroke. Position UP mark on sprockets at top. *See Fig. 5.* Align grooves on sprockets. Remove crankshaft pulley.

3) Remove left engine mount bolts and nut. Remove engine mount. Remove lower timing belt cover. Loosen timing belt tension adjuster bolt. Push tensioner to relieve tension on timing belt. Retighten adjuster bolt. If reusing timing belt, mark direction of belt rotation before removing. Remove timing belt.

Installation – Ensure No. 1 piston is at TDC. Install timing belt onto sprockets. DO NOT bend or twist belt excessively. Ensure arrow (made during removal procedure) on used belt points in original rotation direction. Adjust timing belt tension. See TIMING BELT TENSION ADJUSTMENT under ADJUSTMENTS. To complete installation, reverse removal procedure. Tighten crankshaft pulley bolt to 147 ft. lbs. (200 N.m), loosen, then retighten to 133 ft. lbs. (180 N.m).

CAMSHAFTS

Removal – 1) Ensure No. 1 piston is at TDC. Position UP mark on sprockets at top. *See Fig. 5.* Align grooves on sprockets. Remove timing belt. See TIMING BELT under REMOVAL & INSTALLATION.

2) Remove camshaft sprockets. Camshafts may be held in place by installing 5-mm pin punches in No. 1 cam bearing caps. Mark position of distributor. Remove distributor. Loosen rocker arm adjuster screws.

3) Measure camshaft end play by prying camshaft toward front of cylinder head. Attach dial indicator, and zero it against sprocket end of camshaft. Pry camshaft away from dial indicator. Read dial indicator. Desired end play is 0.002-0.006" (0.05-0.15 mm). Maximum allowable end play is 0.020" (0.50 mm). If end play exceeds limit, replace camshaft.

4) Remove camshaft bearing cap bolts by turning bolts 2 turns at a time in a crisscross pattern. Tag all parts for installation reference. Remove camshafts. Remove rocker arms if necessary.

Installation – 1) Lubricate camshaft journals and bearing surfaces in caps and cylinder head. Install rocker arms (if removed) in their original positions. Install camshafts with keyways pointing upward (No. 1 piston at TDC). Install camshaft bearing caps in original positions.

2) Starting with center caps and working outward, tighten camshaft bearing cap bolts to 88 INCH lbs. (10 N.m) in 2 stages.

3) Install new camshaft seals (if removed). To complete installation, reverse removal procedure. Adjust timing belt tension. See TIMING BELT TENSION ADJUSTMENT under ADJUSTMENTS. Adjust valve clearance. See VALVE CLEARANCE ADJUSTMENT under ADJUSTMENTS.

REAR CRANKSHAFT OIL SEAL

Removal – 1) Disconnect negative battery cable. Remove transaxle assembly. See appropriate article in CLUTCHES (manual transaxle) or TRANSMISSION SERVICING (automatic transaxle).

2) Place reference mark on clutch pressure plate (M/T) and flywheel for installation reference. Remove pressure plate and clutch disc (if equipped). Remove flywheel. Pry seal from cover.

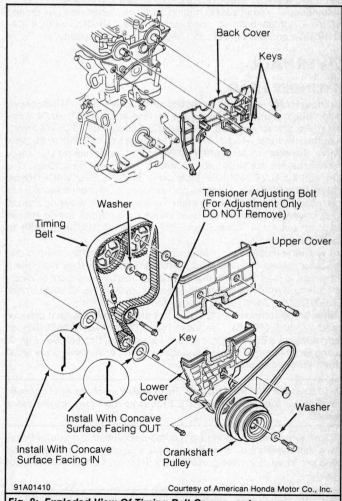

91A01410   Courtesy of American Honda Motor Co., Inc.

Fig. 8: Exploded View Of Timing Belt Components

Installation – Apply a light coat of engine oil to crankshaft and lip of new seal. Using Seal Driver (07749-0010000) and Driver Attachment (07948-SB00101), install new seal. To complete installation, reverse removal procedure.

NOTE: *When installing new crankshaft oil seal, align hole in Driver Attachment (07948-SB00101) with pin on crankshaft.*

WATER PUMP

Removal – Disconnect negative battery cable. Drain cooling system. Remove timing belt. See TIMING BELT under REMOVAL & INSTALLATION. Remove timing belt back cover. *See Fig. 8.* Remove bolts, water pump, and "O" rings.
Installation – 1) Clean gasket surfaces. Install water pump. Install new "O" rings. To complete installation, reverse removal procedure. Tighten bolts to specifications. See TORQUE SPECIFICATIONS.
2) Adjust timing belt tension. See TIMING BELT TENSION ADJUSTMENT under ADJUSTMENTS. Fill and bleed air from cooling system. See BLEEDING COOLING SYSTEM under REMOVAL & INSTALLATION.

OIL PAN

Removal – 1) Drain engine oil. Turn crankshaft counterclockwise to align crankshaft pulley timing marks. *See Fig. 5.* Remove valve cover and upper timing belt cover. *See Fig. 8.* Remove accessory drive belts.
2) Remove crankshaft pulley and timing belt lower cover. Mark timing belt for installation reference. Loosen belt tensioner. Remove timing belt and crankshaft sprocket. Remove oil pan and gasket.
Installation – Clean gasket mating surfaces. Install new gasket and oil pan. Tighten bolts to specification. See TORQUE SPECIFICATIONS. To complete installation, reverse removal procedure.

OVERHAUL

CYLINDER HEAD

Cylinder Head – Ensure all mating surfaces are clean. Measure cylinder head warpage. If warpage is less than 0.002" (0.05 mm), resurfacing is not required. If warpage is 0.002-0.008" (0.05-0.20 mm), resurface cylinder head. Maximum resurface limit is 0.008" (0.20 mm).
Valve Springs – Measure free length of valve springs. If measurements are not within specifications, replace valve springs. See VALVES & VALVE SPRINGS table under ENGINE SPECIFICATIONS.
Valve Stem Oil Seals – Intake and exhaust valve stem seals are not interchangeable. Intake valve stem seals have a White spring around neck of seal. Oil seals for exhaust valves have a Black spring around neck of seal. Use Valve Stem Seal Installer (07GAD-PH70100) to install valve stem seals.
Valve Guide Inspection – Measure valve guide clearance with a dial indicator placed on valve head. Zero dial indicator. Rock valve stem from side to side. Valve guides can be replaced if valve stem oil clearance is not within specification. See CYLINDER HEAD table under ENGINE SPECIFICATIONS at end of article.
Valve Guide Removal – 1) Use a hot plate or oven to heat cylinder head to 300°F (150°C). Use Valve Guide Driver (07942-6570100), or fabricate valve guide remover from an air impact chisel. *See Fig. 9.* Using an air hammer and valve guide remover, drive valve guide 5/64" (2 mm) toward combustion chamber.

CAUTION: *DO NOT heat cylinder head with a torch, or heat cylinder head hotter than 300°F (150°C). Excessive heat may loosen valve seats.*

2) Turn head over. Working from combustion chamber side of head, drive valve guide out toward camshaft side of head. If valve guide does not move, drill valve guide using a 5/16" bit, then try to drive it out again.

CAUTION: *Drill guides in extreme cases only. Cylinder head damage can occur if valve guide breaks.*

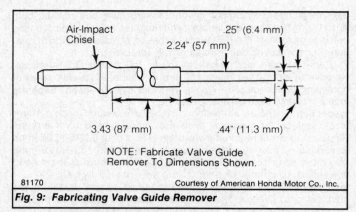
NOTE: Fabricate Valve Guide
Remover To Dimensions Shown.
81170   Courtesy of American Honda Motor Co., Inc.
Fig. 9: Fabricating Valve Guide Remover

Valve Guide Installation – 1) Cool new valve guides in freezer for about one hour. Remove new valve guides from freezer as needed. Install new valve guides from camshaft side of cylinder head.
2) Drive each guide into heated head until attachment bottoms against head. If replacing all valve guides, reheat cylinder head as necessary.
3) Intake valve guide installed height must be 0.55" (14 mm). Exhaust valve guide installed height must be 0.63" (16 mm). Using cutting oil, ream new valve guides by rotating Valve Guide Reamer (07984-657010C) clockwise the full length of valve guide bore. Measure valve stem oil clearance. See CYLINDER HEAD table under ENGINE SPECIFICATIONS.

NOTE: *Always reface valve seat after replacing valve guide.*

Valve Seat – Valve seat replacement procedure is not available from manufacturer.
Seat Correction Angles – If replacing valve guides, perform replacement before refacing valve seats. After refacing, if seat width is too wide, use 60-degree stone to raise seat, or 30-degree stone to lower seat. Ensure valve seat width is within specification. See CYLINDER HEAD table under ENGINE SPECIFICATIONS.
Valve Stem Installed Height – After servicing valves, measure valve stem installed height. *See Fig. 10.* If valve stem installed height exceeds 1.633" (41.485 mm) for intake valve, or 1.712" (43.485 mm) for exhaust valve, replace valve. If valve stem installed height still exceeds limit, replace cylinder head.

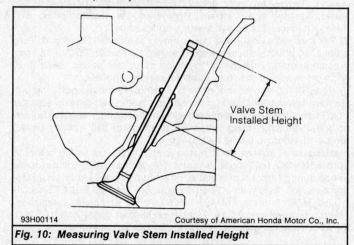
93H00114   Courtesy of American Honda Motor Co., Inc.
Fig. 10: Measuring Valve Stem Installed Height

CYLINDER BLOCK ASSEMBLY

Piston & Rod Assembly – 1) Each rod is sorted into one of 4 tolerance ranges. Size depends on crank journal bore. A number between 1 and 4 is stamped on split line of rod big end. Any combination of numbers between 1 and 4 may be found on any engine. See CONNECTING RODS under ENGINE SPECIFICATIONS.

NOTE: Reference numbers are for big end bore code, and do not indicate rod position in engine.

2) Connecting rod big end bore size range is 1.8898-1.8907" (48.000-48.024 mm). Install piston and connecting rod so arrow on top of piston is toward timing belt, and connecting rod oil hole is toward intake manifold side of engine. *See Fig. 11.*

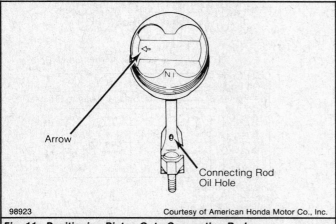

98923   Courtesy of American Honda Motor Co., Inc.

Fig. 11: Positioning Piston Onto Connecting Rod

Piston Pin Removal – 1) Install Piston Base Head (07HAF-PL20102) and Piston Pin Base Insert (07GAF-PH60300) into Base (07973-6570500). Turn handle on Piston Pin Driver Head (07973-PE00320) so piston driver length is 1.957" (49.70 mm). *See Fig. 12.*
2) Insert Piston Driver Shaft (07973-PE00310) into Pilot Collar (07LAF-PR30100). Place piston onto base. Press out piston pin. When removing or installing piston pin, place piston into press with embossed side facing up. Align recessed part of piston with lugs on base insert.

NOTE: Piston pins are available in oversize.

Piston Pin Inspection – 1) Measure diameter of piston pin. Measure diameter of piston pin bore in piston. Piston pin clearance is difference between the two measurements.
2) Piston pin clearance must be 0.0004-0.0009" (0.010-0.022 mm). If piston pin clearance is greater than 0.0009" (0.022 mm), install an oversize piston pin and recheck clearance. Oversize pin diameter is .8267-.8269" (20.997-21.003 mm).
3) Determine difference between piston pin diameter and connecting rod small end bore. Interference fit between piston pin and connecting rod must be 0.0005-0.0013" (0.013-0.032 mm).
Piston Pin Installation – 1) Ensure piston and connecting rod are positioned as shown. *See Fig. 12.* Turn handle on Piston Pin Driver (07973-PE00320) so piston driver length is 1.957" (49.70 mm).
2) Install Pilot Collar (07LAF-PR30100) into piston and connecting rod. Lubricate new piston pin lightly. Place piston onto base. Press in piston pin.
Fitting Pistons – 1) Using a feeler gauge, measure clearance between piston and cylinder bore. If clearance is near or exceeds 0.002" (0.05 mm), measure each piston and cylinder. Piston clearance is difference between cylinder bore and piston diameter. If piston clearance exceeds service limit, rebore cylinder and install oversize piston. New piston-to-bore clearance is .0004-.0014" (.010-.035 mm).
2) Remove all rings from piston. Clean piston thoroughly. Inspect piston for damage. Measure piston diameter at a point 0.6" (15 mm) from bottom of piston skirt. If diameter is not within specification, replace piston. See PISTON DIAMETERS table. See PISTONS, PINS & RINGS table under ENGINE SPECIFICATIONS.

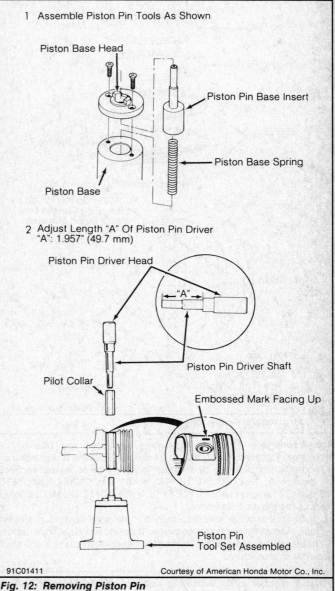

1   Assemble Piston Pin Tools As Shown

2   Adjust Length "A" Of Piston Pin Driver
    "A": 1.957" (49.7 mm)

91C01411   Courtesy of American Honda Motor Co., Inc.

Fig. 12: Removing Piston Pin

PISTON DIAMETERS [1]

Application	In. (mm)
Standard (New)	3.1882-3.1886 (80.98-80.99)
Service Limit	3.1878 (80.97)
Oversize 0.010" (0.25 mm)	3.1980-3.1984 (81.23-81.24)

[1] – Measured at 0.6" (15 mm) from bottom of piston skirt.

Piston Rings – 1) Using inverted piston, push new piston ring into cylinder bore 0.6-0.8" (15-20 mm) from bottom. Measure piston ring end gap using a feeler gauge. Repeat for each ring. See PISTONS, PINS & RINGS table under ENGINE SPECIFICATIONS.
2) Clean piston ring grooves thoroughly. Install piston rings with identification mark toward top of piston. Using a feeler gauge, measure piston ring side clearance between ring and ring land.
3) If ring lands are excessively worn, replace piston. See PISTONS, PINS & RINGS table. Align piston ring end gaps properly on piston. *See Fig. 13.*

1993 ENGINES
1.8L 4-Cylinder (Cont.)

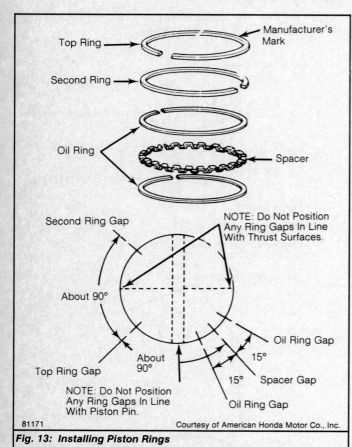

81171   Courtesy of American Honda Motor Co., Inc.

Fig. 13: Installing Piston Rings

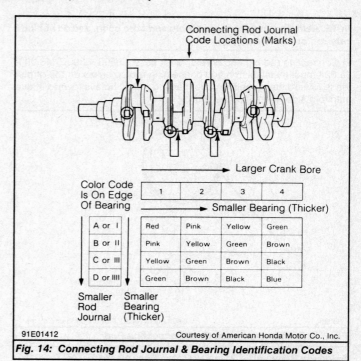

91E01412   Courtesy of American Honda Motor Co., Inc.

Fig. 14: Connecting Rod Journal & Bearing Identification Codes

Rod Bearings – 1) Using Plastigage, measure rod bearing oil clearance. Tighten bearing cap to 24 ft. lbs. (32 N.m). If oil clearance is incorrect, install a new bearing set (same color code) and recheck oil clearance. See CRANKSHAFT, MAIN & CONNECTING ROD BEARINGS table under ENGINE SPECIFICATIONS. DO NOT shim or file cap to adjust oil clearance.
2) If oil clearance is still incorrect, try the next larger or smaller bearing. Measure oil clearance again. If correct oil clearance cannot be obtained by using larger or smaller bearings, replace crankshaft and repeat procedure.

NOTE: A number code indicating connecting rod big end bore is stamped on side of each connecting rod and cap. Connecting rod journal diameter codes (letters) are stamped on crankshaft counterweight pads. See Fig. 14. Use both codes when ordering replacement bearings.

Crankshaft & Main Bearings – 1) Remove rear crankshaft oil seal cover, oil screen, oil pump, and baffle plate. Rotate crankshaft so No. 2 and No. 3 crankpins are at bottom. Remove all connecting rod caps and bearings.
2) Mark all main bearing caps for assembly reference. Remove main bearing caps and bearing halves. Lift crankshaft from block, being careful not to damage journals.
3) Using a lathe or "V" blocks to support crankshaft, measure crankshaft runout, out-of-round, and taper. If any measurement exceeds service limit, replace crankshaft. See CRANKSHAFT, MAIN & CONNECTING ROD BEARINGS table under ENGINE SPECIFICATIONS.
4) Install crankshaft into block. Measure main bearing oil clearance, using Plastigage. If engine is in vehicle, support counterweights, and measure only one bearing at a time. Tighten main bearing caps to 58 ft. lbs. (78 N.m).
5) If oil clearance is incorrect, install a new bearing set (same color code) and recheck oil clearance. See CRANKSHAFT, MAIN &

CONNECTING ROD BEARINGS table under ENGINE SPECIFICATIONS. If oil clearance is still incorrect, try next larger or smaller bearing and measure oil clearance once more.
6) If correct oil clearance cannot be obtained by using larger or smaller bearings, replace crankshaft and repeat procedure.

NOTE: A letter code indicating main journal bore diameters is stamped on cylinder block. See Fig. 15. Use these codes, together with crankshaft main journal diameter numbers, when ordering replacement bearings.

Thrust Bearing – 1) Measure crankshaft end play, using a dial indicator. If end play exceeds specification, inspect thrust washers and thrust surface of crankshaft. See CRANKSHAFT, MAIN & CONNECTING ROD BEARINGS table under ENGINE SPECIFICATIONS.
2) Replace worn parts as necessary. Thrust washer thickness is fixed. DO NOT change thrust washer thickness by grinding or shimming. Install thrust washers with grooved side out.
Cylinder Block – 1) Measure cylinder bore out-of-round and taper. If either out-of-round or taper exceeds 0.002" (0.05 mm), rebore cylinder for oversize pistons. If any cylinder exceeds oversize bore service limit, replace cylinder block. See CYLINDER BLOCK table under ENGINE SPECIFICATIONS at end of article.
2) Service limit is 0.004" (0.10 mm). If cylinder bore is okay, hone cylinder to obtain a 60-degree crosshatch pattern. After honing, wash cylinder bore with hot soapy water. Air-dry cylinder bore, and apply engine oil to prevent rusting. Using a feeler gauge and straightedge, measure cylinder block deck surface warpage.

ENGINE OILING

ENGINE LUBRICATION SYSTEM

A rotor-type oil pump draws oil from oil pan and delivers it under pressure to main and connecting rod bearings. An oil hole in each connecting rod lubricates thrust side of piston and cylinder wall. An oil passage carries oil to camshaft and rocker arms. Oil spray lubricates valve stems.
Crankcase Capacity – Crankcase capacity is 4.0 qts. (3.8L) including oil filter.
Oil Pressure – Oil pressure at idle should be 10 psi (0.7 kg/cm²) minimum. Oil pressure at 3000 RPM should be 50 psi (3.5 kg/cm²) minimum.

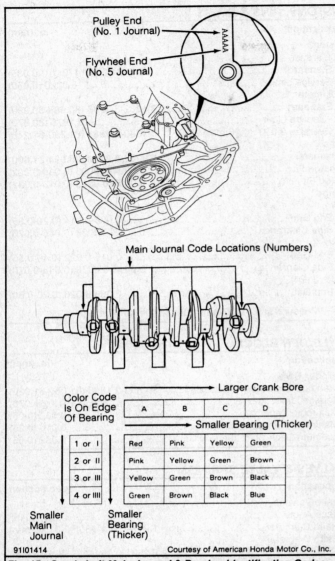

Fig. 15: Crankshaft Main Journal & Bearing Identification Codes

OIL PUMP

Removal & Disassembly – Remove oil pan. See OIL PAN under REMOVAL & INSTALLATION. Remove oil screen and oil pump assembly. Remove screws from oil pump housing. Separate housing and cover.

Inspection – Measure radial clearance between inner and outer rotors. Measure axial clearance between housing and outer rotor. Inspect both rotors and pump housing for scoring or other damage. Replace components if clearance measurements are not within specification. See OIL PUMP SPECIFICATIONS table.

OIL PUMP SPECIFICATIONS

Application	In. (mm)
Inner Rotor-To-Outer Rotor	
Radial Clearance	
Standard (New)	0.002-0.006 (0.05-0.15)
Service Limit	0.008 (0.20)
Housing-To-Outer Rotor	
Axial Clearance	
Standard (New)	0.001-0.003 (0.03-0.08)
Service Limit	0.006 (0.15)
Housing-To-Outer Rotor	
Radial Clearance	
Standard (New)	0.004-0.007 (0.10-0.18)
Service Limit	0.008 (0.20)

Reassembly & Installation – **1)** Reassemble oil pump, using Loctite on pump housing screws. Ensure oil pump turns freely. Install dowel pins and new "O" ring into cylinder block. Clean oil pump mating surfaces. Apply Liquid Sealant (08718-0001) to cylinder block mating surface of oil pump.

2) Apply sealant to threads of inner bolt holes. Install oil pump before sealant dries. Install oil screen and oil pump. Wait at least 30 minutes before filling crankcase with oil. To complete installation, reverse removal procedure.

TORQUE SPECIFICATIONS
TORQUE SPECIFICATIONS

Application	Ft. Lbs. (N.m)
A/C Compressor Bracket Bolts	17 (23)
Alternator Belt Adjustment Bolt	17 (23)
Alternator Mount Bolt	33 (45)
Camshaft Sprocket Bolts	27 (37)
Connecting Rod Nuts	[1] 24 (32)
Crankshaft Pulley Bolt	133 (180)
Cylinder Head Bolts	[2] 63 (85)
Distributor Mount Bolts	16 (22)
Engine Block-To-Transaxle Housing Bolts	47 (64)
Engine Mount Bolts	[3]
Exhaust Manifold Nuts	23 (31)
Exhaust Pipe Flange Nuts	40 (54)
Flexplate (A/T)	55 (75)
Flywheel Bolts (M/T)	[4] 77 (105)
Intake Manifold Nuts	17 (23)
Main Bearing Cap Bolts	[5] 58 (78)
Oil Pump Bolts	
6-mm Bolts	[6]
8-mm Bolts	17 (23)
Power Steering Mount Bolt	17 (23)
Rocker Arm Lock Nuts	18 (24)
Rocker Arm Pivot Bolt	46 (62)
Shift Lever Torque Rod Bolt	16 (22)
Timing Belt Tension Adjuster Bolt	40 (54)

	INCH Lbs. (N.m)
Camshaft Bearing Bolt	88 (10)
Crankshaft Rear Seal Cover Bolts	98 (11)
Fuel Service Bolt	106 (12)
Oil Pan Bolts	106 (12)
Oil Pump Screen Nuts	98 (11)
Timing Belt Cover Bolts	106 (12)
Valve Cover Nuts	88 (10)
Water Pump Bolt	106 (12)

[1] – Tighten connecting rod nuts in 2 stages. First tighten nuts to 15 ft. lbs. (20 N.m), then tighten them to 24 ft. lbs. (32 N.m).
[2] – Tighten cylinder head bolts in 2 stages. First tighten bolts to 22 ft. lbs. (30 N.m) and then to 63 ft. lbs. (85 N.m). See Fig. 6.
[3] – See Fig. 4.
[4] – Tighten in a crisscross pattern.
[5] – Tighten main bearing bolts in 2 stages. First tighten bolts to 22 ft. lbs. (30 N.m), then tighten them to 58 ft. lbs. (78 N.m).
[6] – Tighten to 96 INCH lbs. (11 N.m).

ENGINE SPECIFICATIONS
GENERAL SPECIFICATIONS

Application	Specification
Displacement	112 Cu. In. (1.8L)
Bore	3.19" (81 mm)
Stroke	3.50" (89 mm)
Compression Ratio	9.2:1
Fuel System	SFI
Horsepower @ RPM	140 @ 6000
Torque Ft. Lbs. @ RPM	126 @ 5000

CRANKSHAFT, MAIN & CONNECTING ROD BEARINGS

Application	In. (mm)
Crankshaft	
End Play	
Standard	0.004-0.014 (0.10-0.35)
Service Limit	0.018 (0.45)
Runout	
Standard	0.0008 (0.020)
Service Limit	0.0012 (0.030)
Main Bearings	
Journal Diameter	
Except No. 3	2.1644-2.1654 (54.976-55.000)
No. 3	2.1642-2.1651 (54.970-54.994)
Journal Out-Of-Round	
Standard	0.00016 (0.0040)
Service Limit	0.00020 (0.0060)
Journal Taper	
Standard	0.0002 (0.005)
Service Limit	0.0002 (0.005)
Oil Clearance	
Except No. 3 Journal	
Standard	0.0009-0.0017 (0.024-0.042)
Service Limit	0.0020 (0.050)
No. 3 Journal	
Standard	0.0012-0.0019 (0.030-0.048)
Service Limit	0.0024 (0.060)
Connecting Rod Bearings	
Journal Diameter	1.7707-1.7717 (44.976-45.000)
Journal Out-Of-Round	
Standard	0.00016 (0.0040)
Service Limit	0.00020 (0.0060)
Journal Taper	
Service Limit	0.0002 (0.005)
Oil Clearance	
Standard	0.0013-0.0020 (0.032-0.050)
Service Limit	0.0024 (0.060)

CONNECTING RODS

Application	In. (mm)
Bore Diameter	
Crankpin Bore [1]	
1	1.8898-1.8900 (48.000-48.006)
2	1.8900-1.8902 (48.006-48.012)
3	1.8902-1.8905 (48.012-48.018)
4	1.8905-1.8907 (48.018-48.024)
Pin Bore	0.8255-0.8260 (20.968-20.981)
Side Play	
Standard	0.006-0.012 (0.15-0.30)
Service Limit	0.016 (0.40)

[1] – Big end bore reference number is stamped on side of rod big end split line. Number is size reference and DOES NOT indicate position in engine or cylinder location.

PISTONS, PINS & RINGS

Application	In. (mm)
Pistons	
Clearance	
Standard	0.0004-0.0014 (0.010-0.035)
Service Limit	0.0020 (0.050)
Diameter [1]	
Standard	3.1882-3.1886 (80.980-80.990)
Service Limit	3.1878 (80.970)
Oversize 0.010" (0.25 mm)	3.1980-3.1984 (81.230-81.240)
Pins	
Diameter	0.8265-0.8268 (20.994-21.000)
Piston Fit	0.0004-0.0009 (0.010-0.022)
Rod Fit	0.0005-0.0013 (0.013-0.032)
Rings	
No. 1	
End Gap	0.008-0.014 (0.20-0.35)
Side Clearance	0.0018-0.0028 (0.045-0.070)
No. 2	
End Gap	0.016-0.022 (0.40-0.55)
Side Clearance	0.0018-0.0028 (0.045-0.070)
No. 3 (Oil)	
End Gap	0.008-0.020 (0.20-0.50)

[1] – Measure at 0.6" (15 mm) from bottom of skirt.

CYLINDER BLOCK

Application	In. (mm)
Cylinder Bore	
Standard Diameter	3.1890-3.1898 (81.000-81.020)
Service Limit	3.1917 (81.070)
Maximum Taper	0.002 (0.05)
Maximum Rebore Limit	0.010 (0.25)
Maximum Deck Warpage	0.002 (0.05)

VALVES & VALVE SPRINGS

Application	Specification
Intake Valves	
Face Angle	45°
Head Diameter	1.217-1.224" (30.90-31.10 mm)
Stem Diameter	
Standard	0.2591-0.2594" (6.58-6.59 mm)
Service Limit	0.258" (6.55 mm)
Minimum Margin	0.045" (1.15 mm)
Exhaust Valves	
Face Angle	45°
Head Diameter	1.098-1.106" (27.90-28.10 mm)
Stem Diameter	
Standard	0.2579-0.2583" (6.55-6.56 mm)
Service Limit	0.257" (6.52 mm)
Minimum Margin	0.057" (1.45 mm)
Valve Springs Free Length	
Intake	1.668" (42.36 mm)
Exhaust	1.578" (40.09 mm)

CYLINDER HEAD

Application	Specification
Cylinder Head	
Height	5.195-5.199" (131.95-132.05 mm)
Maximum Warpage	[1] 0.002-0.008" (0.05-0.20 mm)
Valve Seats	
Intake Valve	
Seat Angle	45°
Seat Width	
Standard	0.049-0.061" (1.25-1.55 mm)
Service Limit	0.079" (2.00 mm)
Exhaust Valve	
Seat Angle	45°
Seat Width	
Standard	0.049-0.061" (1.25-1.55 mm)
Service Limit	0.079" (2.00 mm)
Valve Guides	
Intake	
Valve Guide I.D.	
Standard	0.260-0.261" (6.61-6.63 mm)
Service Limit	0.262" (6.65 mm)
Valve Guide Installed Height	0.55" (14 mm)
Valve Stem-To-Guide Oil Clearance	
Standard	0.001-0.002" (0.02-0.05 mm)
Service Limit	0.003" (0.08 mm)
Exhaust Valve	
Valve Guide I.D.	
Standard	0.260-0.261" (6.61-6.63 mm)
Service Limit	0.262" (6.65 mm)
Valve Guide Installed Height	0.63" (16 mm)
Valve Stem-To-Guide Oil Clearance	
Standard	0.002-0.003" (0.05-0.08 mm)
Service Limit	0.004" (0.10 mm)

[1] – Maximum resurface limit is 0.008" (0.20 mm).

CAMSHAFT

Application	In. (mm)
End Play	
Standard	0.002-0.006 (0.05-0.15)
Service Limit	0.020 (0.50)
Journal Runout	
Standard	0.001 (0.03)
Service Limit	0.002 (0.06)
Oil Clearance	
Standard	0.002-0.004 (0.05-0.10)
Service Limit	0.006 (0.15)

VALVE STEM INSTALLED HEIGHT [1]

Application	In. (mm)
Intake	
Standard	1.605-1.623 (40.765-41.235)
Service Limit	1.633 (41.485)
Exhaust	
Standard	1.684-1.702 (42.765-43.235)
Service Limit	1.712 (43.485)

[1] – Measure from base of valve guide to tip of valve stem.

1993 ENGINES
2.5L 5-Cylinder

Vigor

NOTE: For repair procedures not covered in this article, see ENGINE OVERHAUL PROCEDURES article in GENERAL INFORMATION.

ENGINE IDENTIFICATION

Engine identification code is stamped on block on left side, below cylinder head mating surface. The first 5 characters of the code indicate engine type. The last 7 characters of the code indicate engine serial number. Engine serial numbers starting from 2000001 indicate California vehicle. Engine serial numbers starting from 2300001 indicate Federal vehicle.

ENGINE IDENTIFICATION CODE

Application	Code
2.5L	G25A1

ADJUSTMENTS

VALVE CLEARANCE ADJUSTMENT

CAUTION: Always rotate engine in direction of normal rotation (counterclockwise as viewed from front of engine). Backward rotation may cause timing belt to jump time.

1) Adjust valves when engine temperature is 100°F (38°C) or less. Remove valve cover. Rotate crankshaft counterclockwise until No. 1 piston is at TDC of compression stroke.
2) Ensure No. 1 mark on camshaft pulley aligns with TDC groove on cam holder. *See Fig. 1.* Adjust clearance on valves for No. 1 cylinder. Slide feeler gauge between camshaft lobe and rocker arm. Loosen lock nuts, and turn adjustment screw until clearance is correct. Tighten lock nuts. See VALVE CLEARANCE SPECIFICATIONS table.
3) Rotate crankshaft 144 degrees counterclockwise (camshaft pulley turns 72 degrees) so No. 2 piston is at TDC of compression stroke. Ensure No. 2 mark on camshaft pulley aligns with TDC groove on cam holder. Adjust clearance on valves for No. 2 cylinder.
4) Rotate crankshaft 144 degrees counterclockwise (camshaft pulley turns 72 degrees) so No. 4 piston is at TDC of compression stroke. Ensure No. 4 mark on camshaft pulley aligns with TDC groove on cam holder. Adjust clearance on valves for No. 4 cylinder.
5) Rotate crankshaft 144 degrees counterclockwise (camshaft pulley turns 72 degrees) so No. 5 piston is at TDC of compression stroke. Ensure No. 5 mark on camshaft pulley aligns with TDC groove on cam holder. Adjust clearance on valves for No. 5 cylinder.

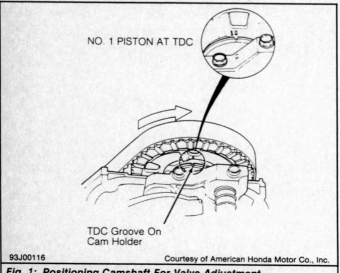

NO. 1 PISTON AT TDC

TDC Groove On Cam Holder

93J00116   Courtesy of American Honda Motor Co., Inc.

Fig. 1: Positioning Camshaft For Valve Adjustment (No. 1 Cylinder Shown; Others Are Similar)

6) Rotate crankshaft 144 degrees counterclockwise (camshaft pulley turns 72 degrees) so No. 3 piston is at TDC of compression stroke. Ensure No. 3 mark on camshaft pulley aligns with TDC groove on cam holder. Adjust clearance on valves for No. 3 cylinder. Retighten crankshaft pulley bolt to 184 ft. lbs. (250 N.m).

VALVE CLEARANCE SPECIFICATIONS

Application	In. (mm)
Exhaust	0.009-0.011 (0.24-0.28)
Intake	0.011-0.013 (0.28-0.32)

TIMING BELT TENSION ADJUSTMENT

CAUTION: Adjust timing belt with engine cold. DO NOT rotate crankshaft with timing belt tension adjuster bolt loose.

Remove valve cover. Rotate crankshaft counterclockwise until No. 1 piston is at TDC. Loosen adjuster bolt 180 degrees. *See Fig. 2.* Rotate crankshaft 3 teeth counterclockwise on camshaft pulley to create tension on timing belt. Tighten tension adjuster bolt to specification. See TORQUE SPECIFICATIONS. Install valve cover, using new gaskets.

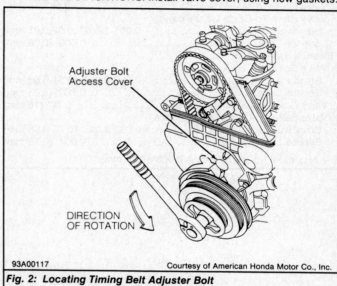

Adjuster Bolt Access Cover

DIRECTION OF ROTATION

93A00117   Courtesy of American Honda Motor Co., Inc.

Fig. 2: Locating Timing Belt Adjuster Bolt

REMOVAL & INSTALLATION

NOTE: For reassembly reference, label all electrical connectors, vacuum hoses, and fuel lines before removal. Also place mating marks on major assemblies before removal.

NOTE: Radio/cassette or radio/CD player is equipped with an anti-theft protection circuit. Whenever battery is disconnected, radio will go into anti-theft mode. When battery is reconnected, radio will display CODE, and will be inoperative until proper code number is entered. Obtain code number before disconnecting battery.

FUEL PRESSURE RELEASE

CAUTION: Fuel system is under pressure. Release pressure before servicing fuel system components.

Disconnect negative battery cable. Remove fuel tank filler cap. Place shop towel on top of fuel filter to absorb any fuel spray. Release fuel injection system pressure by slowly loosening fuel injection service bolt. *See Fig. 3.*

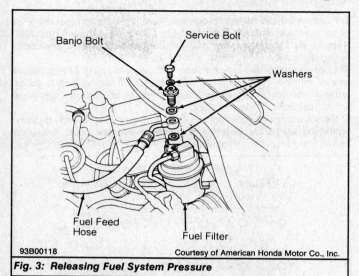

93B00118   Courtesy of American Honda Motor Co., Inc.

Fig. 3: Releasing Fuel System Pressure

BLEEDING COOLING SYSTEM

1) Set heater controls for maximum heat. Fill cooling system with a 50/50 mixture of coolant and water to bottom of filler neck. Loosen bleed bolt, located on thermostat housing.

2) Tighten bleed bolt when coolant flows from bleed bolt in steady stream without bubbles. With radiator cap off, start and operate engine to normal operating temperature. Add coolant as necessary. Install radiator cap.

ENGINE

Removal – **1)** Disconnect battery cables. Secure hood as far open as possible. Raise and support vehicle. Drain engine oil and transmission fluid. Remove splash shield. Remove radiator cap to release system pressure. Drain cooling system. Lower vehicle. Disconnect coil wire, condenser, and engine ground wire.

2) Remove ABS relay box, battery heat shield, and battery. Remove air inlet duct and air cleaner housing. Release fuel pressure. See FUEL PRESSURE RELEASE under REMOVAL & INSTALLATION. Disconnect fuel inlet and return hoses. Disconnect throttle cable. Remove throttle cable clamp. Unplug fuel injector resistor connector.

3) Unplug engine wire harness connectors and remove harness clamps. Disconnect hoses from intake manifold. Disconnect heater hoses. Unplug connectors at transmission. Remove distributor. Disconnect power cables from underhood fuse/relay box. Disconnect ground cables at cylinder head and transmission. Remove power steering pump with hoses attached. Set power steering pump aside.

4) Remove A/C compressor with hoses attached. Set A/C compressor aside. Remove alternator. Disconnect transmission cooler lines. Remove radiator and fans as an assembly. Remove speed sensor with hoses still attached.

5) On models with A/T, remove torque converter cover. Rotate crankshaft pulley as necessary to remove drive plate bolts. On vehicles with M/T, remove transmission housing bolts and 26-mm shim. On all models, unplug wiring at transmission. Remove drive shafts. See FWD AXLE SHAFTS article in DRIVE AXLES.

6) Remove O_2 sensor. Remove exhaust pipe. Remove transmission mount and mounting bracket. Shift transmission into Park (A/T), or first gear (M/T). Remove secondary cover and sealing bolt. Using Extension Shaft Puller (07LAC-PW50101), remove extension shaft from differential.

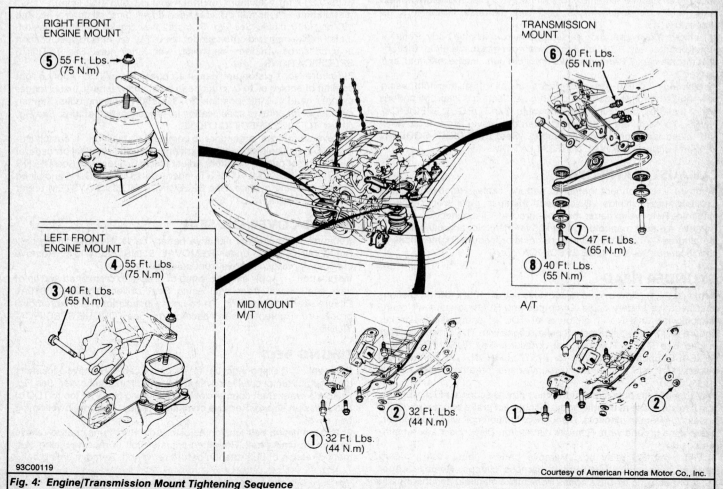

93C00119   Courtesy of American Honda Motor Co., Inc.

Fig. 4: Engine/Transmission Mount Tightening Sequence

7) Attach chain hoist to engine. Remove left front engine mount and engine mount damper bolt. Remove right front engine mount nut. Remove middle engine mounts. Remove transmission housing mount bolts and side transmission mounting bracket. Remove side engine mount. Remove transmission housing mount bolts.

8) Remove clutch cover (M/T) or torque converter cover (A/T). Separate engine and transmission. Reinstall and tighten transmission mount bolts. See TORQUE SPECIFICATIONS. Raise chain hoist to take all slack from cable.

9) Slowly raise engine/transmission about 6 inches. Ensure that all hoses and wiring have been disconnected. Carefully remove engine and transmission from vehicle.

Installation – 1) To install, reverse removal procedure. To prevent excessive engine vibration and premature engine mount wear, tighten engine/transmission mounts in specified sequence. *See Fig. 4.*

2) When installing drive axles, use new spring clips. Insert drive axles until spring clips click into grooves of differential side gears. Ensure harness connectors and hoses are connected properly.

3) Check that control cables are not bent or pinched, and are adjusted properly. On M/T vehicles, adjust clutch pedal free play. Verify transmission shifts smoothly.

4) On all models, adjust drive belt tension. Fill or top off all fluids. Fill and bleed air from cooling system. See BLEEDING COOLING SYSTEM under REMOVAL & INSTALLATION. Start engine and check for leaks.

INTAKE MANIFOLD

Removal – 1) Allow engine to cool. Drain cooling system. Disconnect battery negative cable. Release fuel pressure. See FUEL PRESSURE RELEASE under REMOVAL & INSTALLATION. Remove air intake duct and air cleaner assembly. Disconnect fuel inlet and return hoses. Mark and disconnect hoses and wire harness connectors as necessary.

2) Remove fuel evaporation canister hose from throttle body. Remove brake booster and PCV vacuum hoses from intake manifold. Disconnect throttle cable. Remove intake manifold nuts, intake manifold, and gasket.

Installation – Clean gasket surfaces. Install intake manifold, using new intake manifold gasket. Tighten nuts, using a crisscross pattern in 2 or 3 stages, beginning with inner nuts. See TORQUE SPECIFICATIONS. To complete installation, reverse removal procedure. Refill and bleed air from cooling system. See BLEEDING COOLING SYSTEM under REMOVAL & INSTALLATION.

EXHAUST MANIFOLD

Removal – Disconnect negative battery cable. Remove exhaust manifold heat shields. Disconnect exhaust pipe from exhaust manifold. Remove exhaust manifold bracket. Disconnect O₂ sensor. Remove exhaust manifold bolts, exhaust manifold, and gasket.

Installation – To install, reverse removal procedure. Tighten bolts to specification. See TORQUE SPECIFICATIONS.

CYLINDER HEAD

Removal – 1) Allow engine to cool to less than 100°F (38°C). Disconnect negative battery cable. Drain coolant. Rotate crankshaft counterclockwise until No. 1 piston is at TDC of compression stroke. Ensure No. 1 mark on camshaft pulley aligns with TDC groove on cam holder. *See Fig. 1.* Release fuel pressure. See FUEL PRESSURE RELEASE under REMOVAL & INSTALLATION. Disconnect fuel hoses. Mark and disconnect vacuum hoses, breather hose, and air intake duct.

2) Disconnect throttle cable at throttle body. Disconnect fuel evaporation canister hose at throttle body. Disconnect brake booster and PCV hoses from intake manifold. Disconnect ignition coil wire, condenser, and engine ground wire. Remove distributor. Disconnect any remaining hoses.

3) Remove ABS relay box. Remove battery heat shield. Unplug harness connectors and remove harness clamps. Remove upper radiator hose and by-pass hoses from intake manifold and thermostat housing. Remove intake manifold bracket bolts.

4) Remove exhaust manifold bracket. Remove exhaust pipe. Remove upper exhaust manifold heat shield. Remove exhaust manifold. Remove insulator plate. Remove cylinder head cover. Remove upper timing belt cover.

5) Loosen timing belt adjuster bolt 180 degrees, push timing belt to relieve tension, and retighten adjuster bolt. If timing belt is to be reused, mark arrow on belt to indicate direction of rotation. Disengage timing belt from camshaft pulley.

6) Remove cylinder head bolts, 1/3 turn at a time, in reverse order of tightening sequence. *See Fig. 5.* Remove cylinder head. Separate intake manifold from cylinder head.

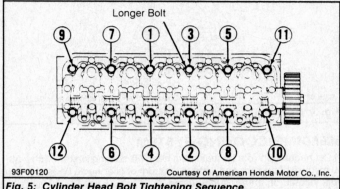

93F00120   Courtesy of American Honda Motor Co., Inc.

Fig. 5: Cylinder Head Bolt Tightening Sequence

Inspection – Ensure all mating surfaces are clean. Measure cylinder head for warpage. Resurfacing is not required if warpage is less than 0.002" (0.05 mm). Resurface cylinder head if warpage is 0.002-0.008" (0.05-0.20 mm). Maximum resurface limit is 0.008" (0.20 mm).

Installation – 1) Install cylinder head dowel pins, oil control jet, and "O" ring into block. *See Fig. 6.* Install new intake manifold gasket. Install intake manifold onto cylinder head. Tighten nuts to specification in a crisscross pattern, beginning with inner nuts. See TORQUE SPECIFICATIONS.

2) Ensure No. 1 piston and camshaft pulley are at TDC. Apply a light coating of engine oil to cylinder head bolts and washers. Install longer cylinder head bolt into position No. 3. Install remaining bolts. Tighten cylinder head bolts to specification in sequence, in 2 stages. *See Fig. 5.* See TORQUE SPECIFICATIONS.

3) Reverse removal procedure to complete installation. If reusing timing belt, install belt with arrow mark (made during removal procedure) in direction of original rotation. Adjust timing belt tension. See TIMING BELT TENSION ADJUSTMENT under ADJUSTMENTS. Fill and bleed air from cooling system. See BLEEDING COOLING SYSTEM under REMOVAL & INSTALLATION.

FRONT COVER OIL SEAL

Removal – Disconnect negative battery cable. Remove timing belt. See TIMING BELT under REMOVAL & INSTALLATION. Remove crankshaft pulley. Remove front cover oil seal.

Installation – Apply a light coating of grease to crankshaft and lip of new seal. Install front seal using Seal Driver (07LAD-PT3010A). Ensure seal is fully seated. To complete installation, reverse removal procedure. Tighten bolts to specification. See TORQUE SPECIFICATIONS.

TIMING BELT

Removal – 1) Disconnect battery negative cable. Remove accessory drive belts. Remove valve cover and upper timing belt cover. *See Fig. 7.* Rotate crankshaft counterclockwise to bring No. 1 piston to TDC of compression stroke. Remove crankshaft pulley. Remove lower timing belt cover.

2) Loosen timing belt tension adjuster bolt. Push tensioner to relieve tension on timing belt. Retighten adjuster bolt. If reusing timing belt, mark direction of belt rotation before removing. Remove timing belt.

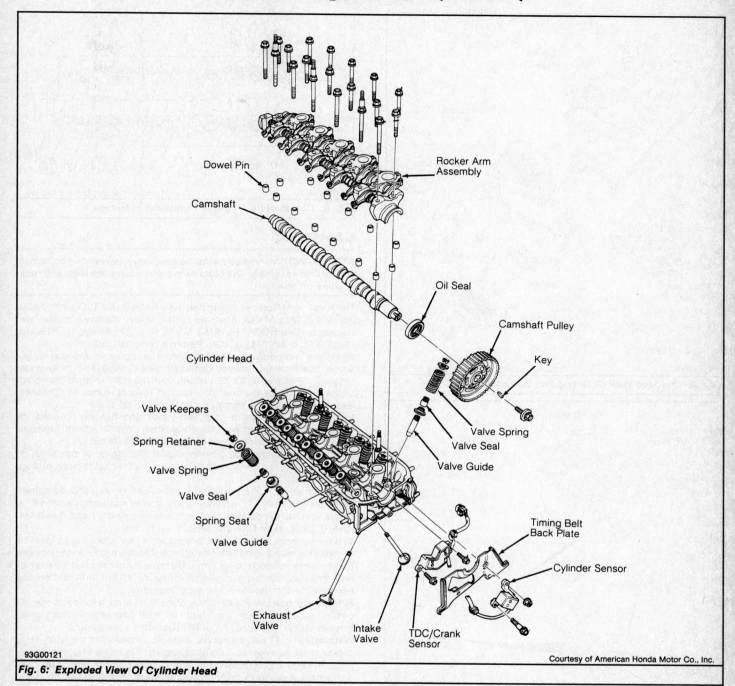

Fig. 6: Exploded View Of Cylinder Head

93G00121

Courtesy of American Honda Motor Co., Inc.

Installation – Ensure No. 1 piston is at TDC. Position timing marks on camshaft pulley as shown. *See Fig. 8.* Install timing belt onto crankshaft pulley, tension adjuster pulley, water pump pulley, and camshaft pulley. DO NOT bend or twist belt excessively. Ensure arrow on used belt points in original rotation direction. Adjust timing belt tension. See TIMING BELT TENSION ADJUSTMENT under ADJUSTMENTS. To complete installation, reverse removal procedure. Tighten bolts to specification. See TORQUE SPECIFICATIONS.

ROCKER ARMS & VALVE LASH ADJUSTERS

NOTE: DO NOT remove camshaft bearing cap (cam holder) bolts from rocker arm assembly. The bolts keep cam holders, springs, and rocker arms on shaft.

Removal – Loosen all valve adjuster screws. Loosen, but DO NOT remove, camshaft bearing cap bolts 2 turns at a time in reverse order of tightening sequence. Remove bolts, rocker arms, and rocker shaft as an assembly. If rocker shafts and arms are to be disassembled, tag all parts for reassembly reference, and carefully remove cam holder bolts one at a time.

Installation – To install, reverse removal procedure. Clean all parts in solvent. Lubricate all moving parts. All parts must be installed into their original positions. Tighten bolts in sequence, 2 turns at a time. *See Fig. 9.* See TORQUE SPECIFICATIONS. Adjust valve clearance. See VALVE CLEARANCE ADJUSTMENT under ADJUSTMENTS.

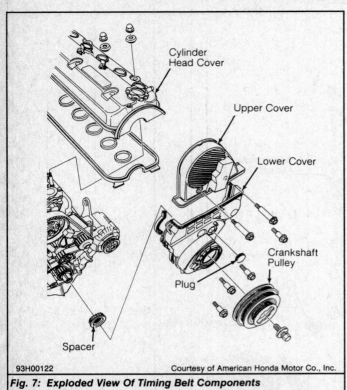

93H00122   Courtesy of American Honda Motor Co., Inc.

Fig. 7: Exploded View Of Timing Belt Components

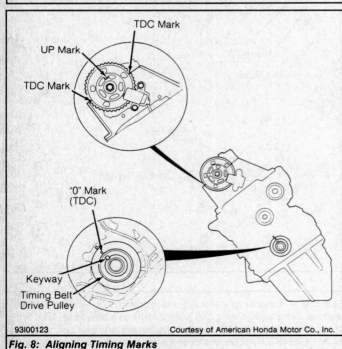

93I00123   Courtesy of American Honda Motor Co., Inc.

Fig. 8: Aligning Timing Marks

93J00124   Courtesy of American Honda Motor Co., Inc.

Fig. 9: Camshaft Bearing Cap Tightening Sequence

CAMSHAFT

NOTE: DO NOT remove camshaft bearing cap (cam holder) bolts from rocker arm assembly. The bolts keep cam holders, springs, and rocker arms on shaft.

Removal – 1) Remove timing belt. See TIMING BELT under REMOVAL & INSTALLATION. Remove valve cover. Remove rocker arm assembly. See ROCKER ARMS & VALVE LASH ADJUSTERS under REMOVAL & INSTALLATION. Remove camshaft pulley.

2) Before removing camshaft, measure end play. If end play is not within specification, replace camshaft. See CAMSHAFT table under ENGINE SPECIFICATIONS. Loosen, but DO NOT remove, camshaft bearing cap bolts 2 turns at a time in reverse order of tightening sequence. *See Fig. 9.* Remove camshaft and oil seal.

Inspection – 1) Inspect camshaft lobes and bearing journals for excessive wear or damage. Place camshaft onto "V" blocks. Measure runout. Total runout must not exceed 0.001" (0.03 mm).

2) Measure camshaft oil clearance with Plastigage. If camshaft oil clearance exceeds specification, but camshaft runout is okay, replace cylinder head.

3) If camshaft runout exceeds specification, replace camshaft. Measure camshaft oil clearance again. If after replacing camshaft, oil clearances still exceed specification, replace cylinder head. See CAMSHAFT table under ENGINE SPECIFICATIONS.

4) If rocker arms are to be removed from rocker shafts, note location of rocker arms for installation reference. Measure clearance between rocker arm shaft and rocker arms. Measure rocker shaft at first rocker arm location. Measure inside diameter of rocker arm. Difference between the 2 measurements is oil clearance.

5) Repeat procedure for all rocker arms. If clearance exceeds specification, replace rocker shaft and all over-tolerance rocker arms. Inspect rocker arm faces for wear. Replace as necessary.

Installation – 1) Ensure rocker arms are assembled correctly onto rocker shaft. *See Fig. 10.* Lubricate camshaft journals and journal surfaces in caps and cylinder head. Install camshaft and camshaft seal. Apply gasket sealer to cylinder head mating surfaces of No. 1 and No. 7 cam holders.

2) Install rocker arm assembly, and tighten bolts finger tight. Ensure rocker arms are properly positioned onto valve stems. Tighten camshaft bearing cap bolts in sequence to specification 2 turns at a time. *See Fig. 9.* See TORQUE SPECIFICATIONS. To complete installation, reverse removal procedure.

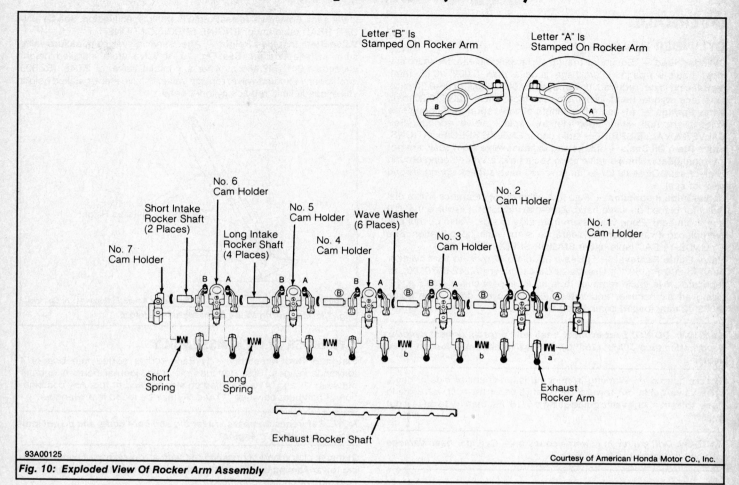

Fig. 10: Exploded View Of Rocker Arm Assembly

93A00125

Courtesy of American Honda Motor Co., Inc.

REAR CRANKSHAFT OIL SEAL

Removal & Installation – 1) Disconnect negative battery cable. Remove transmission. See FWD article in CLUTCHES (manual transmission) or AUTOMATIC TRANSMISSION article in TRANSMISSION SERVICING (automatic transmission). On models with manual transmission, place reference marks on clutch pressure plate and flywheel for installation reference.

2) Remove pressure plate and clutch disc (if equipped). On all models, remove flywheel or flexplate. Remove rear crankshaft oil seal. Install new seal with part number facing out.

3) Apply light coating of grease to seal lip and crankshaft. Using Seal Driver Attachment (07948-SB00101) and Driver (07749-0010000), drive in new oil seal. Align hole in seal driver with pin on crankshaft. Drive in oil seal until driver bottoms against cylinder block. To complete installation, reverse removal procedure.

WATER PUMP

Removal & Installation – Drain cooling system. Remove timing belt. See TIMING BELT under REMOVAL & INSTALLATION. Remove thermostat housing bolts. Remove water pump and "O" ring. To install, reverse removal procedure. Fill and bleed air from cooling system. Adjust timing belt tension. See TIMING BELT TENSION ADJUSTMENT under ADJUSTMENTS. See BLEEDING COOLING SYSTEM under REMOVAL & INSTALLATION.

OIL PAN

Removal – 1) Disconnect battery cables. Remove battery. Raise and support vehicle. Remove front wheels. Remove drive shafts. See FWD AXLE SHAFTS article in DRIVE AXLES. Remove differential. See DIFFERENTIALS article in DRIVE AXLES.

2) Remove A/C bracket. Remove setting plate and oil pan inner pipe. Remove oil pan and "O" rings. Clean oil pan and cylinder block mating surfaces.

Installation – 1) Install new oil pan "O" rings and seal. Apply a continuous bead of Liquid Gasket Sealer (08718-0001) to oil pan, inside of bolt holes. Apply liquid gasket sealer to bolt threads.

2) Install oil pan. Tighten bolts in sequence to specification. *See Fig. 11.* See TORQUE SPECIFICATIONS. Install differential. See DIFFERENTIALS article in DRIVE AXLES.

3) Fill or top off all fluids. Wait a minimum of 30 minutes before filling crankcase with engine oil. Fill and bleed air from cooling system. See BLEEDING COOLING SYSTEM under REMOVAL & INSTALLATION.

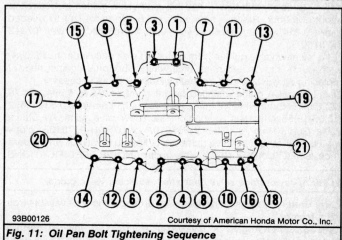

93B00126

Courtesy of American Honda Motor Co., Inc.

Fig. 11: Oil Pan Bolt Tightening Sequence

OVERHAUL

CYLINDER HEAD

Cylinder Head – Ensure all mating surfaces are clean. Measure cylinder head warpage. If warpage is less than 0.002" (0.05 mm), resurfacing is not required. If warpage is 0.002-0.008" (0.05-0.20 mm), resurface cylinder head. Maximum resurface limit is 0.008" (0.20 mm).

Valve Springs – Measure free length of valve springs. If spring free lengths are not within specification, replace valve springs. See VALVES & VALVE SPRINGS table under ENGINE SPECIFICATIONS.

Valve Stem Oil Seals – Intake and exhaust valve stem seals are not interchangeable. Intake valve stem seals have a White spring around neck of seal. Oil seals for exhaust valves have a Black spring around neck of seal.

Valve Guide Inspection – Measure valve guide clearance with a dial indicator placed on valve head. Zero dial indicator. Lift valve 0.4" (10 mm) from seat. Rock valve stem from side to side. Valve guides can be replaced if valve stem oil clearance is not within specification. See CYLINDER HEAD table under ENGINE SPECIFICATIONS.

Valve Guide Removal – 1) Use a hot plate or oven to heat cylinder head to 300°F (150°C). Use Valve Guide Driver (07742-6570100), or fabricate valve guide remover from an air impact chisel. *See Fig. 12.* Using an air hammer and valve guide remover, drive valve guide 0.078" (2 mm) toward combustion chamber.

CAUTION: DO NOT heat cylinder head with a torch, or heat cylinder head hotter than 300°F (150°C). Excessive heat may loosen valve seats.

2) Turn head over. Working from combustion chamber side of head, drive valve guide out toward camshaft side of head. If valve guide does not move, drill valve guide using a 5/16" bit, then try to drive it out again.

CAUTION: Drill guides in extreme cases only. Cylinder head damage can occur if valve guide breaks.

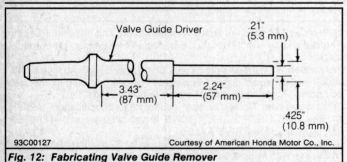

93C00127   Courtesy of American Honda Motor Co., Inc.

Fig. 12: Fabricating Valve Guide Remover

Valve Guide Installation – 1) Chill new valve guides in freezer for about one hour. Remove new valve guides from freezer as needed. Slip a 0.234" (6 mm) steel washer over Valve Guide Driver (07742-6570100).

2) Install new valve guides from camshaft side of cylinder head. Drive each guide into heated head until washer bottoms against head. If replacing all valve guides, reheat cylinder head as necessary.

3) Intake valve guide installed height must be 0.974-0.994" (24.75-25.25 mm). Exhaust valve guide installed height must be 0.632-0.652" (16.05-16.55 mm). Using cutting oil, ream new valve guides by rotating Valve Guide Reamer (07HAH-PJ7010A or 07HAH-PJ7010B) clockwise the full length of valve guide bore. Measure valve stem oil clearance. See CYLINDER HEAD table under ENGINE SPECIFICATIONS.

NOTE: Always reface valve seat after replacing valve guide.

Valve Seat – Valve seat replacement procedure is not available from manufacturer.

Seat Correction Angles – If valve guides are to be replaced, perform replacement before refacing valve seats. After refacing, if seat width is too wide, use 60-degree stone to raise seat, or 30-degree stone to

lower seat. Ensure valve seat width is within specification. See CYLINDER HEAD table under ENGINE SPECIFICATIONS.

Valve Stem Installed Height – After servicing valves, measure valve stem installed height. *See Fig. 13.* If valve stem installed height exceeds 1.947" (49.465 mm) for any intake valve, or 2.048" (52.035 mm) for any exhaust valve, replace valve. If valve stem installed height still exceeds limit, replace cylinder head.

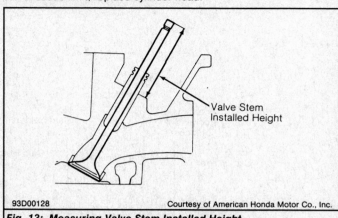

93D00128   Courtesy of American Honda Motor Co., Inc.

Fig. 13: Measuring Valve Stem Installed Height

CYLINDER BLOCK ASSEMBLY

Piston & Rod Assembly – 1) Each rod is sorted into one of 4 tolerance ranges. Size depends on crank journal bore. A number between "1" and "4" is stamped on side big end of rod. Any combination of numbers between "1" and "4" may be found in any engine.

NOTE: Reference numbers are for big end bore code, and do not indicate rod position in engine.

2) Install piston and connecting rod with arrow on top of piston pointing toward timing belt, and connecting rod oil hole toward intake manifold side of engine. *See Fig. 14.*

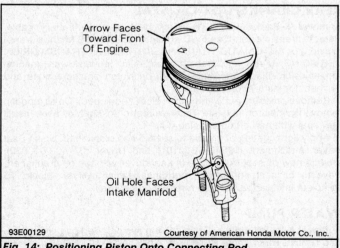

93E00129   Courtesy of American Honda Motor Co., Inc.

Fig. 14: Positioning Piston Onto Connecting Rod

Piston Pin Removal – 1) Install Piston Base Head (07HAF-PL20102) and Piston Pin Base Insert (07GAF-PH60300) into Base (07973-6570500). Turn handle on Piston Pin Driver (07973-PE00320) so piston driver length is 2.03" (51.5 mm). *See Fig. 15.*

2) Insert Piston Driver Shaft (07973-PE00310) into Pilot Collar (07GAF-PH60300). Place piston onto base with embossed side facing up. Press out piston pin. Align recessed part of piston with lugs on base insert.

NOTE: All replacement piston pins are oversize.

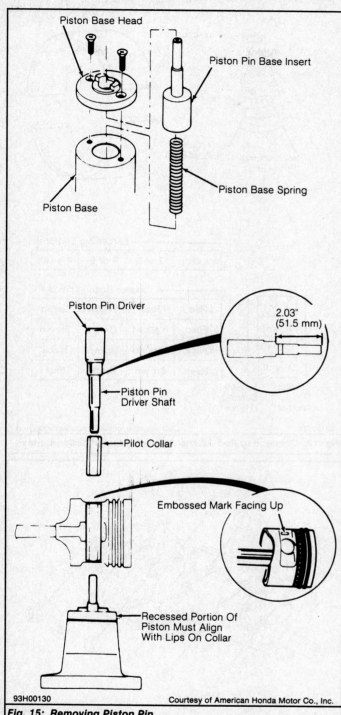

Piston Base Head

Piston Pin Base Insert

Piston Base

Piston Base Spring

Piston Pin Driver

2.03"
(51.5 mm)

Piston Pin
Driver Shaft

Pilot Collar

Embossed Mark Facing Up

Recessed Portion Of
Piston Must Align
With Lips On Collar

93H00130

Courtesy of American Honda Motor Co., Inc.

Fig. 15: Removing Piston Pin

Piston Pin Inspection – 1) Measure diameter of piston pin. Measure diameter of piston pin bore in piston. Piston pin clearance is difference between the 2 measurements.

2) Piston pin clearance must be 0.0005-0.0009" (0.013-0.024 mm). If piston pin clearance is greater than 0.0009" (0.024 mm), install an oversize piston pin and recheck clearance.

3) Determine difference between piston pin diameter and connecting rod small end bore. Interference fit between piston pin and connecting rod must be 0.0005-0.0013" (0.013-0.032 mm).

Piston Pin Installation – 1) Position piston and connecting rod as shown. See Fig. 14. Turn handle on Piston Pin Driver (07973-PE00320) so piston driver length is 2.03" (51.5 mm).

2) Install Pilot Collar (07LAF-PR30100) into piston and connecting rod. Lubricate new piston pin lightly. Place piston onto base with embossed side facing up. Press in piston pin.

Fitting Pistons – 1) Using a feeler gauge, measure clearance between piston and cylinder bore. If clearance is near or exceeds 0.002" (0.05 mm), measure each piston and cylinder. Piston clearance is difference between cylinder bore and piston diameter. If piston clearance exceeds service limit, rebore cylinder and install oversize piston.

2) Standard size pistons are marked with "A" or "B" on top of piston. Pistons are also available in 0.010" (0.25 mm) and 0.020" (0.50 mm) oversize. Standard cylinder block bore size is identified by letters "A" or "B" stamped on cylinder block.

3) Remove all rings from piston. Clean piston thoroughly. Inspect piston for distortion and cracks. Measure piston diameter at a point 0.83" (21 mm) from bottom of piston skirt. If diameter is not within specification, replace piston. See PISTON DIAMETERS table. See PISTONS, PINS & RINGS table under ENGINE SPECIFICATIONS.

PISTON DIAMETERS [1]

Application	In. (mm)
"A" Pistons	
Standard	3.3457-3.3461 (84.98-84.99)
Service Limit	3.3453 (84.97)
"B" Pistons	
Standard	3.3453-3.3457 (84.97-84.98)
Service Limit	3.3449 (84.96)

[1] – Measured at 0.83" (21 mm) from bottom of piston skirt.

Piston Rings – 1) Using inverted piston, push new piston ring into cylinder bore 0.6-0.8" (15-20 mm) from bottom. Measure piston ring end gap, using a feeler gauge. Repeat for each ring. See PISTONS, PINS & RINGS table under ENGINE SPECIFICATIONS.

2) Clean piston ring grooves thoroughly. Install piston rings with identification mark toward top of piston. Using a feeler gauge, measure piston ring side clearance between ring and ring land.

3) If ring lands are excessively worn, replace piston. See PISTONS, PINS & RINGS table. Align piston ring end gaps properly on piston. See Fig. 16.

Rod Bearings – 1) Using Plastigage, measure rod bearing oil clearance. Tighten bearing cap to 24 ft. lbs. (32 N.m).

2) If oil clearance is incorrect, install a new bearing set (same color code) and recheck oil clearance. DO NOT shim or file cap to adjust oil clearance.

3) If oil clearance is still incorrect, try the next larger or smaller bearing. Measure oil clearance again. If proper oil clearance cannot be obtained by using larger or smaller bearings, replace crankshaft and repeat procedure.

NOTE: A number code indicating connecting rod bore is stamped on side of each connecting rod and cap. Connecting rod journal diameter codes (letters) are stamped on crankshaft counterweight pad, at pulley end. See Fig. 17. Use both codes when ordering replacement bearings.

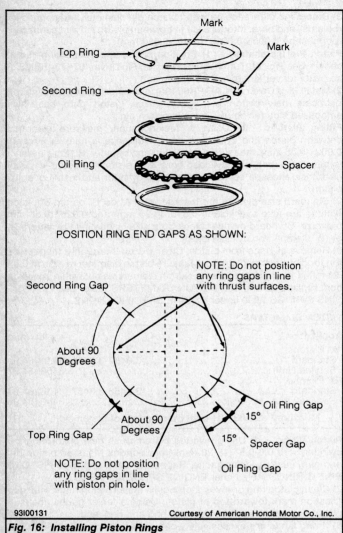

POSITION RING END GAPS AS SHOWN:

NOTE: Do not position any ring gaps in line with thrust surfaces.

NOTE: Do not position any ring gaps in line with piston pin hole.

93I00131   Courtesy of American Honda Motor Co., Inc.

Fig. 16: Installing Piston Rings

Crankshaft & Main Bearings – 1) Remove all connecting rod and main bearing caps in reverse order of sequence shown. *See Fig. 18*. Mark all bearing caps for reassembly reference. Lift crankshaft from block, being careful not to damage journals.

2) Using a lathe or "V" blocks to support crankshaft, measure crankshaft runout, out-of-round, and taper. If any measurement exceeds service limit, replace crankshaft. See CRANKSHAFT, MAIN & CONNECTING ROD BEARINGS table under ENGINE SPECIFICATIONS.

3) Install crankshaft into block. Measure main bearing oil clearance with Plastigage. If engine is in vehicle, support counterweights, and measure only one bearing at a time. Tighten main bearing caps, in sequence, in 2 stages, first to 22 ft. lbs. (30 N.m), then to 50 ft. lbs. (68 N.m). *See Fig. 18*.

4) If oil clearance is not within specification, install a new bearing set (same color code) and recheck oil clearance. If oil clearance is still incorrect, try next larger or smaller bearing and measure oil clearance once more.

5) If proper oil clearance cannot be obtained by using larger or smaller bearings, replace crankshaft and repeat procedure.

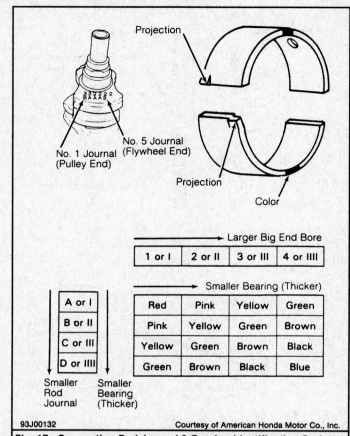

	Larger Big End Bore		
1 or I	2 or II	3 or III	4 or IIII

Smaller Bearing (Thicker)

Red	Pink	Yellow	Green
Pink	Yellow	Green	Brown
Yellow	Green	Brown	Black
Green	Brown	Black	Blue

A or I
B or II
C or III
D or IIII

Smaller Rod Journal

Smaller Bearing (Thicker)

93J00132   Courtesy of American Honda Motor Co., Inc.

Fig. 17: Connecting Rod Journal & Bearing Identification Codes

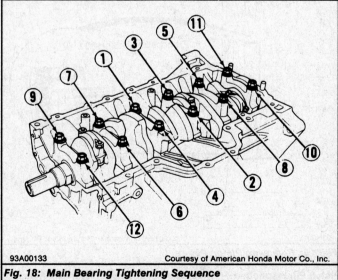

93A00133   Courtesy of American Honda Motor Co., Inc.

Fig. 18: Main Bearing Tightening Sequence

NOTE: A letter code indicating main journal bore diameters is stamped on cylinder block, on oil pan mating surface. See Fig. 19. Use these codes, together with crankshaft main journal diameter numbers, when ordering replacement bearings.

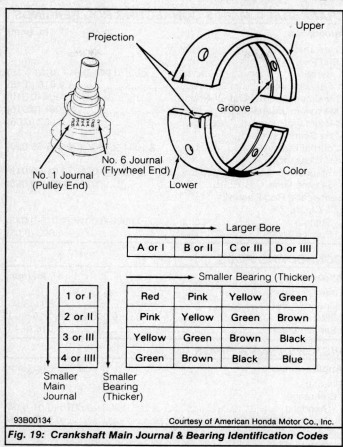

Fig. 19: Crankshaft Main Journal & Bearing Identification Codes

93B00134 — Courtesy of American Honda Motor Co., Inc.

Thrust Bearing – 1) Measure crankshaft end play, using a dial indicator. If end play exceeds specification, inspect thrust washers and thrust surface of crankshaft. See CRANKSHAFT, MAIN & CONNECTING ROD BEARINGS table under ENGINE SPECIFICATIONS.
2) Replace worn parts as necessary. Thrust washer thickness is fixed. DO NOT change thrust washer thickness by grinding or shimming. Install thrust washers with grooved side out.

Cylinder Block – 1) Measure cylinder bore out-of-round and taper. If either out-of-round or taper exceeds 0.002" (0.05 mm), rebore cylinder for oversize pistons. If any cylinder exceed oversize bore service limit, replace cylinder block. See CYLINDER BLOCK table under ENGINE SPECIFICATIONS.
2) Using a feeler gauge and straightedge, measure cylinder block deck surface warpage. Service limit is 0.003" (0.07 mm). If cylinder bore is okay, hone cylinder to obtain a 60-degree crosshatch pattern. After honing, wash cylinder bore with hot soapy water. Air-dry cylinder bore, and apply engine oil to prevent rusting.

ENGINE OILING

ENGINE LUBRICATION SYSTEM

A rotor-type oil pump draws oil from the oil pan and delivers it under pressure to main and connecting rod bearings. An oil hole in each connecting rod supplies oil to thrust side of piston and cylinder wall. An oil passage carries oil to camshaft and rocker arms. Oil spray lubricates valve stems.

Oil Pressure – Minimum oil pressure with engine at idle should be 10 psi (0.7 kg/cm²). Minimum oil pressure at 3000 RPM should be 50 psi (3.5 kg/cm²).

OIL PUMP

Removal & Disassembly – 1) Raise and support vehicle. Drain engine oil and differential oil. Remove spark plugs. Rotate crankshaft clockwise until No. 1 piston is at TDC of compression stroke. Remove timing belt. See TIMING BELT under REMOVAL & INSTALLATION. Remove oil pan. See OIL PAN under REMOVAL & INSTALLATION.
2) Remove oil pump screen. Remove oil pump assembly. Separate pump cover from pump housing. Using a screwdriver, pry oil seal from oil pump housing.

Inspection – Measure radial clearance between inner and outer rotors. Measure axial clearance between housing and outer rotor. Inspect rotors and pump housing for scoring or other defects. Replace components if not within specification or defective. See OIL PUMP SPECIFICATIONS table.

OIL PUMP SPECIFICATIONS

Application	In. (mm)
Inner Rotor-To-Outer Rotor	
Radial Clearance	
Standard	0.002-0.006 (0.04-0.16)
Service Limit	0.008 (0.20)
Housing-To-Outer Rotor	
Axial Clearance	
Standard	0.001-0.003 (0.02-0.07)
Service Limit	0.005 (0.13)
Housing-To-Outer Rotor	
Radial Clearance	
Standard	0.004-0.007 (0.10-0.18)
Service Limit	0.008 (0.20)

Reassembly & Installation – 1) Apply light coating of grease to crankshaft and lip of new seal. Using Seal Driver (07749-0010000) and Attachment (07746-0010500), install oil seal. Ensure seal is fully seated into oil pump housing. Install dowel pins and "O" ring into cylinder block. Clean oil pump and engine mating surfaces.
2) Apply Liquid Sealant (08718-0001) to cylinder block mating surface of oil pump. Apply sealant to threads of inner bolt holes. Install oil pump before sealant dries. Wait at least 30 minutes before filling crankcase with oil. To complete installation, reverse removal procedure.

1993 ENGINES
2.5L 5-Cylinder (Cont.)

TORQUE SPECIFICATIONS

TORQUE SPECIFICATIONS

Application	Ft. Lbs. (N.m)
A/C Compressor Bolts	16 (22)
A/C Compressor Bracket Bolts	33 (45)
Alternator Bracket Bolts	33 (45)
Camshaft Bearing Cap Bolts [1]	
6-mm Bolts	[2]
8-mm Bolts	16 (22)
Camshaft Pulley Bolts	55 (75)
Clutch Slave Cylinder Bolts	16 (22)
Connecting Rod Nuts	24 (33)
Crankshaft Pulley Bolt	184 (250)
Cylinder Head Bolts [3]	
Stage 1	55 (75)
Stage 2	74 (100)
Engine Mounts	[4]
Engine Block-To-Transaxle	
Housing Bolts	55 (75)
Exhaust Manifold	
Shroud Bolts	16 (22)
Nuts	22 (30)
Exhaust Pipe Flange Nuts	40 (54)
Flywheel Bolts [5]	77 (105)
Intake Manifold Bolts/Nuts	16 (22)
Main Bearing Cap Bolts [6]	
Stage 1	22 (30)
Stage 2	50 (68)
Oil Pan Bolts [7]	18 (24)
Oil Pump Housing Bolts	
6-mm Bolts	[2]
8-mm Bolts	16 (22)
Power Steering Pump Mount Bolt	33 (45)
Timing Belt Tension Adjuster Bolt	33 (45)
Torque Converter Drive Plate Bolts [5]	55 (75)

	INCH Lbs. (N.m)
Fuel Service Bolt	106 (12)
Oil Pump Screen Bolts	106 (12)
Speed Sensor Bolt	106 (12)
Timing Belt Cover Bolts	106 (12)
Valve Cover Bolts	106 (12)
Water Pump Bolts	106 (12)

[1] – Tighten bolts 2 turns at a time in sequence. *See Fig. 9.*
[2] – Tighten to 106 INCH lbs. (12 N.m).
[3] – Tighten in sequence. *See Fig. 5.*
[4] – Tighten in sequence to specification. *See Fig. 4.*
[5] – Tighten in a crisscross pattern.
[6] – Tighten in sequence. *See Fig. 18.*
[7] – Tighten in sequence. *See Fig. 11.*

ENGINE SPECIFICATIONS

GENERAL SPECIFICATIONS

Application	Specification
Displacement	150 Cu. In. (2.5L)
Bore	3.35" (85 mm)
Stroke	3.40" (86.4 mm)
Compression Ratio	9.0:1
Fuel System	SFI
Horsepower @ RPM	176 @ 6300
Torque Ft. Lbs. @ RPM	170 @ 3900

CRANKSHAFT, MAIN & CONNECTING ROD BEARINGS

Application	In. (mm)
Crankshaft	
End Play	
Standard	0.004-0.014 (0.10-0.35)
Service Limit	0.018 (0.45)
Maximum Journal Out-Of-Round	0.0004 (0.010)
Maximum Journal Taper	0.0004 (0.010)
Maximum Runout	0.002 (0.06)
Main Bearings	
Journal Diameter	2.1644-2.1654 (54.976-55.000)
Oil Clearance	
Standard	0.0007-0.0019 (0.018-0.048)
Service Limit	0.002 (0.053)
Connecting Rod Bearings	
Oil Clearance	
Standard	0.0006-0.0017 (0.015-0.043)
Service Limit	0.002 (0.05)

CONNECTING RODS

Application	In. (mm)
Bore Diameter	
Crankpin Bore	1.89 (48.00)
Side Play	0.006-0.012 (0.15-0.30)
Service Limit	0.016 (0.40)

PISTONS, PINS & RINGS

Application	In. (mm)
Pistons	
Clearance	
Standard	0.0004-0.0016 (0.01-0.04)
Service Limit	0.002 (0.05)
Diameter	
Standard [1]	
"A" Piston	3.3457-3.3461 (84.98-84.99)
"B" Piston	3.3453-3.3457 (84.97-84.98)
Piston Pins	
Diameter	0.8659-0.8661 (21.994-22.000)
Piston Fit	0.0005-0.0009 (0.012-0.024)
Rod Interference Fit	0.0005-0.0013 (0.013-0.032)
Rings	
No. 1	
End Gap	
Standard	0.008-0.014 (0.20-0.35)
Service Limit	0.024 (0.60)
Side Clearance	0.0014-0.0024 (0.035-0.060)
No. 2	
End Gap	
Standard	0.016-0.022 (0.40-0.55)
Service Limit	0.028 (0.70)
Side Clearance	0.0012-0.0022 (0.030-0.055)
No. 3 (Oil)	
End Gap	
Standard	0.008-0.028 (0.20-0.70)
Service Limit	0.032 (0.80)

[1] – Piston identification letter is located on top of piston.

CYLINDER BLOCK

Application	In. (mm)
Cylinder Bore	
Diameter	
Standard [1]	3.3465-3.3472 (85.000-85.020)
Service Limit	3.3492 (85.070)
Maximum Taper	0.002 (0.05)
Maximum Deck Warpage	0.004 (0.10)

[1] – Standard bore size is identified by "A" or "B" stamped on cylinder block deck surface.

VALVES & VALVE SPRINGS

Application	Specification
Intake Valves	
Face Angle	45°
Head Diameter	1.33-1.34" (33.9-34.1 mm)
Margin	
Standard	0.033-045" (0.85-1.15 mm)
Service Limit	0.026" (0.65 mm)
Stem Diameter	
Standard	0.2156-0.2159" (5.475-5.485 mm)
Service Limit	0.2144" (5.445 mm)
Valve Length	4.365-4.377" (110.88-111.18 mm)
Valve Stem Installed Height	
Standard	1.9191-1.9376" (48.745-49.215 mm)
Service Limit	1.9474" (49.465 mm)
Exhaust Valves	
Face Angle	45°
Head Diameter	1.14-1.15" (28.9-29.1 mm)
Margin	
Standard	0.061-073" (1.55-1.85 mm)
Service Limit	0.053" (1.36 mm)
Valve Length	4.848-4.860" (123.15-123.45 mm)
Stem Diameter	
Standard	0.2146-0.2150" (5.450-5.460 mm)
Service Limit	0.2134" (5.420 mm)
Valve Stem Installed Height	
Standard	2.0203-2.0239" (51.315-51.785 mm)
Service Limit	2.049" (52.035 mm)
Valve Springs	
Free Length	
Intake	2.052" (52.12 mm)
Exhaust	2.208" (56.08 mm)

CYLINDER HEAD

Application	Specification
Cylinder Head Height	3.935-3.939" (99.95-100.05 mm)
Maximum Warpage [1]	0.002" (0.05 mm)
Valve Seats	
Intake & Exhaust	
Seat Angle	45°
Seat Width	
Standard	0.049-0.061" (1.25-1.55 mm)
Service Limit	0.079 (2.00)
Valve Guides	
Intake	
Valve Guide I.D.	0.2167-0.2173" (5.505-5.520 mm)
Valve Guide Installed Height	0.974-0.994" (24.75-25.25 mm)
Exhaust	
Valve Guide I.D.	0.2167-0.2173" (5.505-5.520 mm)
Valve Guide Installed Height	0.632-0.652" (16.05-16.55 mm)
Valve Stem-To-Guide Oil Clearance	
Intake	
Standard	0.0008-0.0018 (0.02-0.045 mm)
Service Limit	0.003 (0.075)
Exhaust	
Standard	0.002-0.003" (0.05-0.08 mm)
Service Limit	0.005 (0.12)

[1] - Maximum resurface limit is 0.008" (0.20 mm)

CAMSHAFT

Application	In. (mm)
End Play	0.002-0.006 (0.05-0.15)
Journal Runout	0.001 (0.03)
Lobe Height	
Intake	1.5434 (39.203)
Exhaust	1.5305 (38.875)
Oil Clearance	0.002-0.004 (0.05-0.09)

Legend

NOTE: For repair procedures not covered in this article, see ENGINE OVERHAUL PROCEDURES article in GENERAL INFORMATION.

ENGINE IDENTIFICATION

Engine identification code is located on left front side of engine block, below cylinder head mating surface. First 5 characters of code indicate engine type. California models have number 30 as sixth and seventh characters. Federal models have number 33 as sixth and seventh characters. Last 5 digits of engine code indicate engine serial number.

ENGINE IDENTIFICATION CODES

Application	Code
3.2L	C32A1

ADJUSTMENTS

VALVE CLEARANCE ADJUSTMENT

NOTE: The 3.2L engine uses hydraulic valve lifters. Valve clearance adjustment is not necessary.

THROTTLE CABLE ADJUSTMENT

1) With engine at normal operating temperature, check throttle cable for binding and sticking. Repair as necessary. Check cable free play at throttle linkage.
2) Cable deflection should be 0.39-0.47" (10-12 mm). *See Fig. 1.* If deflection is not within specification, loosen lock nut and turn adjuster nut until deflection is within specification. With throttle cable properly adjusted, recheck throttle operation.

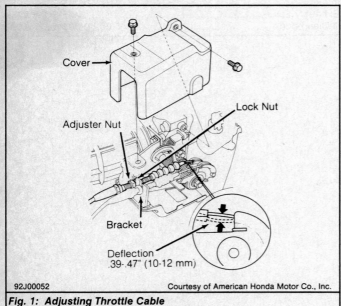

92J00052   Courtesy of American Honda Motor Co., Inc.

Fig. 1: Adjusting Throttle Cable

TIMING BELT TENSION ADJUSTMENT

CAUTION: Adjust timing belt with engine cold. DO NOT rotate crankshaft while belt tension adjuster bolt is loose.

Remove upper left camshaft cover. Rotate crankshaft clockwise until No. 1 piston is at TDC of compression stroke. Rotate crankshaft clockwise 9 teeth on crankshaft pulley. Align Blue mark on crankshaft pulley with pointer on lower cover. *See Fig. 2.* Loosen tensioner adjusting bolt 1/2 turn, and then tighten bolt to 31 ft. lbs. (42 N.m). Install upper camshaft cover.

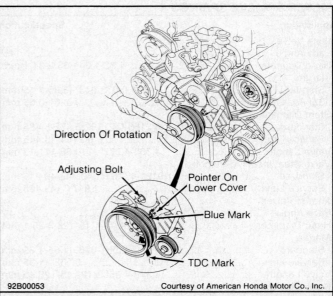

92B00053   Courtesy of American Honda Motor Co., Inc.

Fig. 2: Aligning Timing Marks For Timing Belt Tension Adjustment

REMOVAL & INSTALLATION

NOTE: For reassembly reference, label all electrical connectors, vacuum hoses, and fuel lines before removal. Also place mating marks on other major assemblies before removal.

NOTE: Radio/cassette or radio/CD player is equipped with an anti-theft protection circuit. Whenever battery is disconnected, radio will go into anti-theft mode. When battery is reconnected, radio will display CODE, and will be inoperative until proper code number is entered. Obtain code number before disconnecting battery.

FUEL PRESSURE RELEASE

CAUTION: Fuel system is under pressure. Pressure must be released before servicing fuel system components.

Remove fuel tank filler cap. Disconnect negative battery cable. Place shop towel over fuel filter to absorb excess fuel. Loosen fuel injection service bolt while holding banjo bolt. *See Fig. 3.* Fuel filter is located next to brake booster.

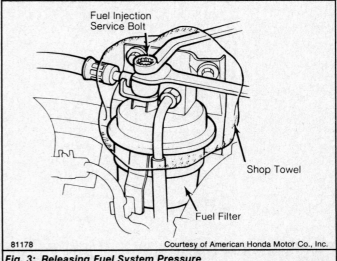

81178   Courtesy of American Honda Motor Co., Inc.

Fig. 3: Releasing Fuel System Pressure

BLEEDING COOLING SYSTEM

Set heater controls for maximum heat. Loosen bleed bolt, located next to engine end of upper radiator hose. Fill cooling system with a 50/50 mixture of coolant/water to bottom of filler neck. Tighten bleed bolt when coolant from bleed bolt runs in a steady stream without air bubbles. With radiator cap off, start and run engine until coolant reaches normal operating temperature. Add coolant as necessary. Install radiator cap.

ENGINE

NOTE: Engine and transaxle are removed as an assembly.

Removal – 1) Disconnect battery cables. Remove battery and battery tray. Remove radiator cap. Raise and support vehicle. Remove engine splash shield. Drain engine oil, transaxle oil, and coolant. Disconnect exhaust pipe.

2) Lower vehicle. Disconnect hood stay. Support hood in a vertical position. Remove engine compartment strut bar and bracket. Unplug engine wiring harness connectors as necessary. Disconnect battery cable at starter. Remove relay box bolts, and set relay box aside. Remove throttle cover. Disconnect throttle cable.

3) Remove air cleaner and air duct. Unplug ignitor connector. Disconnect engine ground cable. Remove emission control box from firewall, leaving hoses connected. Release fuel pressure. See FUEL PRESSURE RELEASE under REMOVAL & INSTALLATION. Disconnect fuel inlet and return hoses. Disconnect brake booster vacuum hose. Disconnect fuel vapor purge hose.

4) Unplug wiring harness connector at left rear of engine compartment. Remove coolant hoses as necessary. Remove radiator, shroud, and fans as an assembly. Remove air suction control solenoid valve and vacuum tank from right front of engine compartment. Remove accessory drive belts. Remove power steering pump, leaving hoses attached. Set power steering pump aside.

5) Raise and support vehicle. Remove front wheels. Remove axle shafts. See FWD AXLE SHAFTS article in DRIVE AXLES. Remove lower plate from rear crossmember, then retighten steering gear bolts. Remove power steering speed sensor, leaving hoses attached. Remove catalytic converter and heat shields.

6) Remove A/C compressor, leaving hoses attached. Remove exhaust pipe. On automatic transaxle, disconnect shift control cable from transaxle. Remove rear transaxle mounting bracket. On manual transaxle, remove clutch slave cylinder. Slide pin retainer back, and use a 5/16" pin punch to disconnect transaxle shift rod. Disconnect shift lever torque rod from rear of engine.

7) On all models, remove nuts and bolts from middle engine mounts. Lower hoist. Remove rear transaxle mount bracket. Remove front engine mount nuts. Install decking hook onto EGR valve through-bolt. Attach hoist to engine, and remove slack from chain.

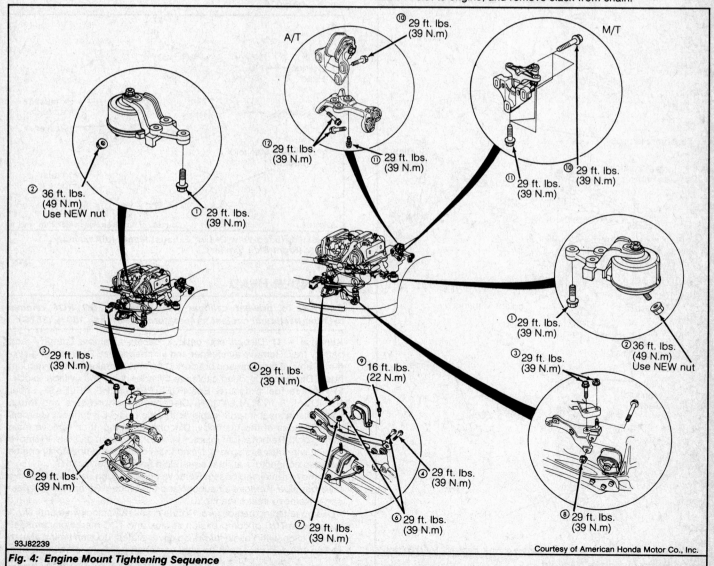

93J82239

Courtesy of American Honda Motor Co., Inc.

Fig. 4: Engine Mount Tightening Sequence

8) Ensure all wiring harness connectors, vacuum, fuel, and coolant hoses affecting engine removal are disconnected. Slowly raise engine. Remove engine and transaxle assembly.

Installation – 1) To install, reverse removal procedure. Tighten engine mounts in specified sequence. See Fig. 4. Improper engine mount tightening will result in excessive engine vibration and premature engine mount wear.

2) When installing drive axles, use new spring clips. Insert each drive axle until spring clip clicks into groove of differential side gear. Ensure all wire harness connectors and hoses are connected properly. Check throttle cable adjustment. See THROTTLE CABLE ADJUSTMENT under ADJUSTMENTS.

3) On manual transaxle, adjust clutch pedal free play. Verify transaxle shifts smoothly. On automatic transaxle, adjust transaxle range indicator to agree with actual drive range.

4) On all models, adjust accessory drive belt tension. Fill all fluids to proper level. Bleed air from cooling system. See COOLING SYSTEM BLEEDING under REMOVAL & INSTALLATION.

INTAKE MANIFOLD

Removal – 1) Disconnect battery cables. Remove battery and battery tray. Remove air cleaner and air duct hose. Drain cooling system. Disconnect power brake booster vacuum hose.

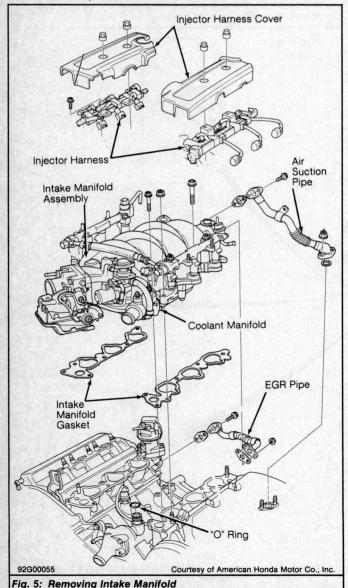

Fig. 5: Removing Intake Manifold

92G00055   Courtesy of American Honda Motor Co., Inc.

2) Disconnect engine ground straps from cylinder head and cylinder block. Release fuel pressure. See FUEL PRESSURE RELEASE under REMOVAL & INSTALLATION. Disconnect fuel inlet and return hoses. Disconnect throttle cable at throttle body.

3) Disconnect charcoal canister hose from throttle body. Unplug wiring harness connectors from main fuse block. Remove fuse block. Remove ignition coils. Remove injector harness covers. See Fig. 5. Unplug wiring harness connectors as necessary.

4) Mark and remove vacuum hoses as necessary. Unplug and remove fuel injector wiring harness connectors. Remove air suction pipe and EGR pipe. Remove intake manifold, throttle body, fuel injectors, and coolant manifold as an assembly.

Installation – 1) To install, reverse removal procedure. Clean intake manifold gasket mating surfaces. Install new gaskets and intake manifold. Install and tighten manifold bolts to specification. See TORQUE SPECIFICATIONS.

2) Check throttle cable adjustment. See THROTTLE CABLE ADJUSTMENT under ADJUSTMENTS. Fill and bleed air from cooling system. See COOLING SYSTEM BLEEDING under REMOVAL & INSTALLATION.

EXHAUST MANIFOLD

Removal & Installation – Exhaust manifold removal and installation procedures are not available from manufacturer. Use illustration as a guide. See Fig. 6.

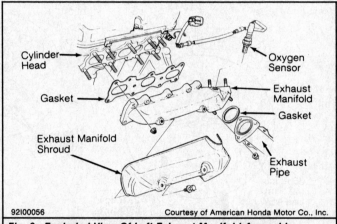

92I00056   Courtesy of American Honda Motor Co., Inc.

Fig. 6: Exploded View Of Left Exhaust Manifold Assembly (Right Side Similar)

CYLINDER HEAD

CAUTION: To prevent cylinder head damage, DO NOT remove cylinder head until coolant temperature is less than 100°F (38°C).

Removal – 1) Disconnect battery cables. Remove battery and battery tray. Remove air cleaner and air intake duct. Drain cooling system. Remove strut bar and bracket. Disconnect brake booster vacuum hose. Disconnect ground cables at cylinder head and cylinder block.

2) Release fuel pressure. See FUEL PRESSURE RELEASE under REMOVAL & INSTALLATION. Disconnect fuel pressure and return lines. Disconnect throttle cable at throttle body. Disconnect charcoal canister hose at throttle body. Disconnect wiring, then remove main fuse block. Remove fuel injector resistor and ignition coils. Remove engine wire harness covers. Disconnect clamps and unplug all engine harness connectors at intake manifold and cylinder heads.

3) Remove remaining hoses. Remove engine wiring harness. Remove breather pipe. Remove air suction and EGR tubes. Remove water passage. Remove intake manifold.

4) Remove timing belt covers. Rotate crankshaft clockwise until No. 1 piston is at TDC of compression stroke, and TDC marks on camshaft pulleys align with Yellow marks on cover plates. Loosen timing adjuster bolt 180 degrees, push on right camshaft pulley to release tension, then retighten bolt. Disengage timing belt from camshaft pulleys. Remove camshaft pulleys. Remove timing belt cover plates.

5) If reusing timing belt, mark belt with an arrow to indicate direction of rotation for installation reference. Remove crank/cylinder sensor from left cylinder head. Remove valve covers. Remove 3 bolts from alternator bracket. Remove 2 bolts from power steering bracket. Disconnect exhaust pipes from exhaust manifold.

6) Loosen cylinder head bolts 1/3 turn at a time in reverse order of tightening sequence. See Fig. 7. Remove cylinder head and gaskets. Remove exhaust manifold covers and exhaust manifolds.

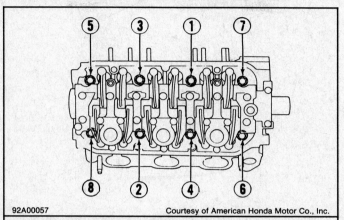

92A00057   Courtesy of American Honda Motor Co., Inc.

Fig. 7: Cylinder Head Tightening Sequence

Inspection – Clean gasket mating surfaces. Measure cylinder head for warpage. If warpage is less than 0.002" (0.05 mm), resurfacing is not required. If warpage is between 0.002-0.008" (0.05-0.20 mm), resurface cylinder head. Maximum resurface limit is 0.008" (0.20 mm). Remove and clean oil control orifices. See Fig. 8.

Installation – **1)** Install cylinder head dowel pins and oil control orifices with new "O" rings. Install exhaust manifolds, using new gaskets. Using a crisscross pattern, tighten exhaust manifold nuts to specification. See TORQUE SPECIFICATIONS.

2) Install cylinder head. Tighten cylinder head bolts in 2 or 3 stages to specification, in sequence. See Fig. 7. See TORQUE SPECIFICATIONS. Install new valve cover gaskets and seals. Apply gasket sealer to areas indicated. See Fig. 9.

3) Install timing belt cover plates and seals. Install camshaft pulleys. Tighten camshaft pulley bolts to specification. See TORQUE SPECIFICATIONS. Install timing belt. See TIMING BELT under REMOVAL & INSTALLATION.

4) Adjust timing belt tension. See TIMING BELT TENSION ADJUSTMENT under ADJUSTMENTS. To complete installation, reverse removal procedure. Fill and bleed cooling system. See BLEEDING COOLING SYSTEM under REMOVAL & INSTALLATION.

FRONT COVER OIL SEAL

Removal & Installation – Remove crankshaft pulley and timing belt. See TIMING BELT under REMOVAL & INSTALLATION. Pry oil seal from oil pump housing. Apply light coating of grease to crankshaft and lip on new seal. Using Seal Driver (07GAD-PH70201), install oil seal. Ensure seal is fully seated into housing. To complete installation, reverse removal procedure.

TIMING BELT

Removal – **1)** Remove negative battery cable. Remove injector harness covers. See Fig. 5. Remove engine wiring harness. Disconnect breather pipe. Remove vacuum line "A" bracket. Remove accessory drive belts. Remove spark plugs.

2) Remove timing belt upper covers. See Fig. 10. Rotate crankshaft clockwise until No. 1 piston is at TDC of compression stroke. Align timing marks. See Fig. 11. Remove A/C belt tensioner pulley. Remove crankshaft pulley. Remove engine oil dipstick tube.

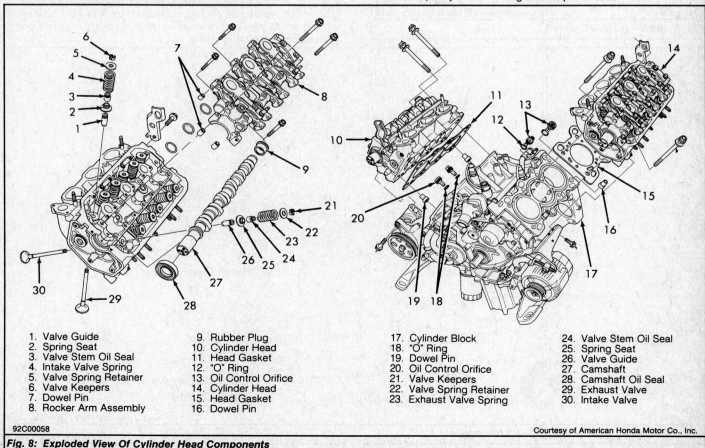

1. Valve Guide	9. Rubber Plug
2. Spring Seat	10. Cylinder Head
3. Valve Stem Oil Seal	11. Head Gasket
4. Intake Valve Spring	12. "O" Ring
5. Valve Spring Retainer	13. Oil Control Orifice
6. Valve Keepers	14. Cylinder Head
7. Dowel Pin	15. Head Gasket
8. Rocker Arm Assembly	16. Dowel Pin
17. Cylinder Block	24. Valve Stem Oil Seal
18. "O" Ring	25. Spring Seat
19. Dowel Pin	26. Valve Guide
20. Oil Control Orifice	27. Camshaft
21. Valve Keepers	28. Camshaft Oil Seal
22. Valve Spring Retainer	29. Exhaust Valve
23. Exhaust Valve Spring	30. Intake Valve

92C00058   Courtesy of American Honda Motor Co., Inc.

Fig. 8: Exploded View Of Cylinder Head Components

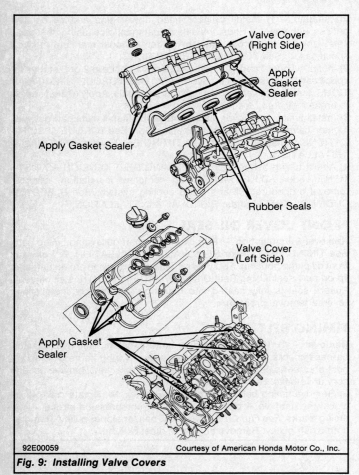

Fig. 9: Installing Valve Covers

92E00059   Courtesy of American Honda Motor Co., Inc.

3) Remove timing belt lower cover. If timing belt is to be reused, mark belt with an arrow to indicate direction of rotation for installation reference. Loosen timing belt tensioner adjusting bolt 1/2 turn. Push tensioner to release belt tension, then retighten bolt. Remove timing belt.

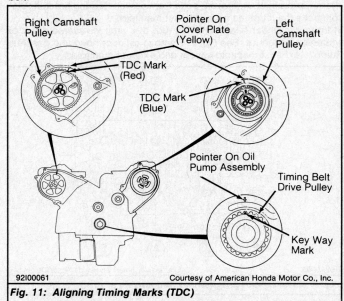

92I00061   Courtesy of American Honda Motor Co., Inc.

Fig. 11: Aligning Timing Marks (TDC)

Installation – 1) Ensure No. 1 piston is at TDC of compression stroke. Verify camshafts are at TDC. *See Fig. 11*. If camshafts are not at TDC and No. 1 piston is at TDC of compression stroke, advance crankshaft clockwise an additional 15 degrees from TDC position.

2) Adjust camshaft pulley(s) until TDC mark on pulley and pointer on cover plate are aligned. Rotate crankshaft back to TDC position. If reusing timing belt, ensure arrow made in removal procedure points in direction of original rotation.

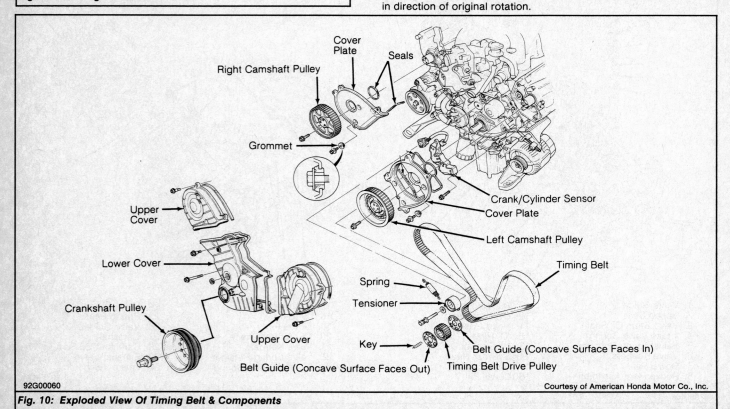

92G00060   Courtesy of American Honda Motor Co., Inc.

Fig. 10: Exploded View Of Timing Belt & Components

3) To aid in belt installation, advance right camshaft pulley about 1/2 tooth from TDC position. Install timing belt around timing belt drive pulley, over tensioner pulley, around left camshaft pulley, under water pump pulley, and around right camshaft pulley.

4) Loosen and tighten tensioner adjuster bolt to remove slack in belt. Rotate crankshaft clockwise about 5 revolutions to seat timing belt. Adjust timing belt tension. See TIMING BELT TENSION ADJUSTMENT under ADJUSTMENTS.

5) Rotate crankshaft clockwise until No. 1 piston is at TDC of compression stroke. Verify timing marks are aligned. If timing marks are not aligned, repeat timing belt installation procedure. To complete installation, reverse removal procedure.

NOTE: After installing timing belt, rotate engine clockwise several times to be sure valves do not contact pistons.

CAMSHAFTS, ROCKER ARMS & HYDRAULIC LIFTERS

Removal – 1) Remove timing belt. See TIMING BELT under REMOVAL & INSTALLATION. Remove camshaft pulleys. Remove upper cover plates. Remove valve covers. Before removing camshaft, measure end play. If end play is not within specification, replace camshaft. See CAMSHAFT table under ENGINE SPECIFICATIONS.

2) Remove camshaft bearing cap bolts 2 turns at a time in reverse order of tightening sequence. *See Fig. 13.* Remove rocker shaft assembly. DO NOT remove lifters from rocker arms unless lifter replacement is necessary. Remove camshaft and oil seal.

Inspection – 1) Inspect camshaft lobes and bearing journals for excessive wear or damage. Place camshaft onto "V" blocks. Measure runout. Total runout must not exceed 0.001" (0.03 mm).

2) Measure camshaft oil clearance with Plastigage. If camshaft oil clearance exceeds specification, but camshaft runout is okay, replace cylinder head. See CAMSHAFT table under ENGINE SPECIFICATIONS.

3) If camshaft runout exceeds specification, replace camshaft. Measure camshaft oil clearance again. If after replacing camshaft, oil clearances still exceed specification, replace cylinder head.

4) If rocker arms must be removed from rocker shafts, note location of rocker arms for installation reference. Measure clearance between rocker arm shaft and rocker arms. Measure rocker shaft at first rocker arm location. Measure inside diameter of rocker arm. Difference between the 2 measurements is oil clearance.

5) Repeat procedure for all rocker arms. If clearance exceeds specification, replace rocker shaft and all over-tolerance rocker arms. Inspect rocker arm faces for wear. Replace as necessary.

Installation – 1) Ensure rocker arms are assembled correctly onto rocker shaft. *See Fig. 12.* If lifters were replaced or removed from rocker arms, bleed air from lifters. Fill container with 10W-30 oil. Place lifter into container. Using a thin wire and a vertical motion, pump lifter plunger until no air bubbles emerge from lifter.

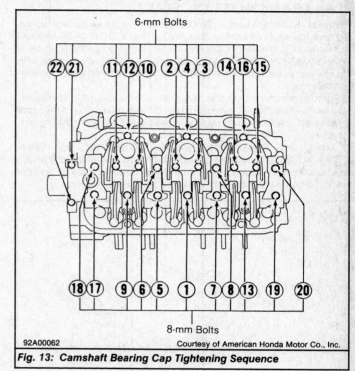

92A00062　　　　Courtesy of American Honda Motor Co., Inc.

Fig. 13: Camshaft Bearing Cap Tightening Sequence

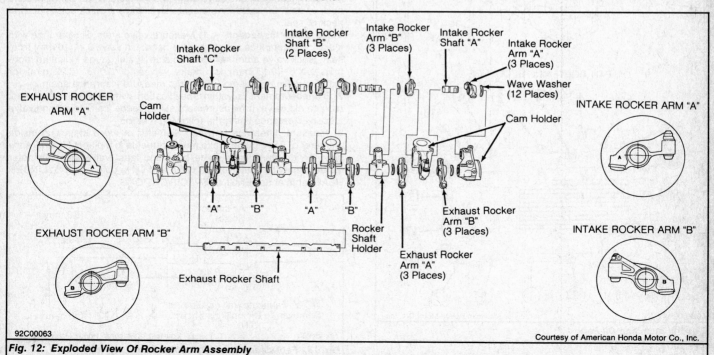

92C00063　　　　Courtesy of American Honda Motor Co., Inc.

Fig. 12: Exploded View Of Rocker Arm Assembly

2) Install new "O" ring onto lifter. Install lifter into rocker arm. Lubricate camshaft journals and journal surfaces in caps and cylinder head. Install camshaft and camshaft seal. Apply gasket sealer to cylinder head mating surfaces of No. 1 and No. 7 camshaft holders.

3) Install rocker arm assembly, and tighten bolts finger tight. Ensure rocker arms are properly positioned onto valve stems. Tighten camshaft bearing cap bolts to specification 2 turns at a time and in sequence. See Fig. 13. See TORQUE SPECIFICATIONS. To complete installation, reverse removal procedure.

REAR CRANKSHAFT OIL SEAL

Removal & Installation – 1) Disconnect negative battery cable. Remove transaxle assembly. See FWD article in CLUTCHES (manual transaxle) or TRANSMISSION REMOVAL & INSTALLATION article in TRANSMISSION SERVICING (automatic transaxle). On models with manual transaxle, mark clutch pressure plate and flywheel for installation reference.

2) Remove pressure plate and clutch disc (if equipped). On all models, remove flywheel. Pry oil seal from rear oil seal cover. If oil seal cover is removed, use nonhardening liquid gasket to seal block mating surface.

3) Using Seal Driver Attachment (07748-SB00101) and Driver (07749-0010000), install new oil seal. Align hole in seal driver with pin on crankshaft. Drive in oil seal until driver bottoms against cylinder block. To complete installation, reverse removal procedure.

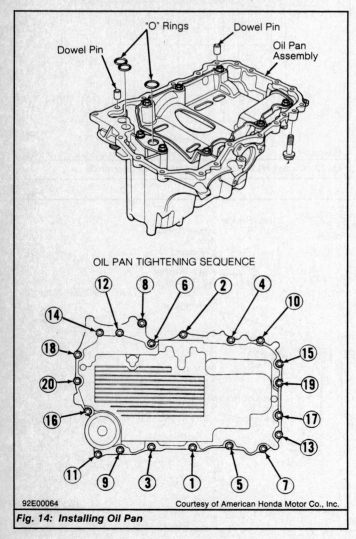

OIL PAN TIGHTENING SEQUENCE

92E00064   Courtesy of American Honda Motor Co., Inc.

Fig. 14: Installing Oil Pan

WATER PUMP

Removal & Installation – Drain cooling system. Remove timing belt. See TIMING BELT under REMOVAL & INSTALLATION. Remove thermostat housing bolts. Remove water pump and "O" ring. To install, reverse removal procedure. Fill and bleed air from cooling system. See BLEEDING COOLING SYSTEM under REMOVAL & INSTALLATION.

OIL PAN

Removal – 1) Disconnect battery cables. Remove battery. Raise and support vehicle. Remove front wheels. Remove differential. See DIFFERENTIALS article in DRIVE AXLES.

2) Remove A/C compressor. Remove engine stiffener (bracket). Remove intermediate shaft. Remove flywheel inspection and drive plate covers. Remove oil pan and "O" rings. Clean oil pan and cylinder block mating surfaces.

Installation – 1) Install new oil pan "O" rings. See Fig. 14. Apply a continuous bead of Liquid Gasket Sealer (08718-0001) to oil pan, inside of bolt holes. Apply liquid gasket sealer to bolt threads.

2) Install oil pan. Tighten bolts in sequence to specification. See Fig. 14. See TORQUE SPECIFICATIONS. Install differential. See DIFFERENTIALS article in DRIVE AXLES.

3) Fill or top off all fluids. Wait a minimum of 30 minutes before filling crankcase with engine oil. Fill and bleed air from cooling system. See BLEEDING COOLING SYSTEM under REMOVAL & INSTALLATION.

OVERHAUL

CYLINDER HEAD

Cylinder Head – After cylinder head has been disassembled, clean mating surfaces. Measure cylinder head for warpage. If warpage is less than 0.002" (0.05 mm), resurfacing is not required. If warpage is between 0.002-0.008" (0.05-0.20 mm), resurface cylinder head. Maximum resurface limit is 0.008" (0.20 mm).

Valve Springs – Measure free length of valve springs. If spring free length is not within specification, replace valve springs. See VALVES & VALVE SPRINGS table under ENGINE SPECIFICATIONS. Install springs with closer coils toward cylinder head.

Valve Stem Oil Seals – Intake and exhaust valve stem seals are not interchangeable. Intake valve stem seals have a White spring around neck of seal. Oil seals for exhaust valves have a Black spring around neck of seal.

Valve Guide Inspection – 1) Measure valve stem oil clearance with a dial indicator placed against valve head. Lift valve 0.4" (10 mm) from seat. Rock valve stem from side to side. If dial gauge indicates more than 0.006" (0.16 mm) for intake valves, or 0.009" (0.22 mm) for exhaust valve, install new valve and measure clearance again.

2) If measurement is within specification with new valve installed, replace old valve. If measurement still exceeds limit, determine valve stem oil clearance using the following method.

3) Measure difference between diameter of valve stem and inside diameter of valve guide. Take measurements in 3 places. If difference between greatest valve guide bore and least valve stem diameter exceeds service limit, replace valve and valve guide. See CYLINDER HEAD table under ENGINE SPECIFICATIONS.

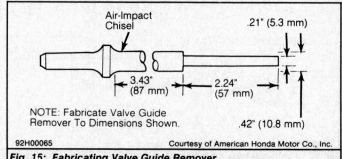

NOTE: Fabricate Valve Guide Remover To Dimensions Shown.

92H00065   Courtesy of American Honda Motor Co., Inc.

Fig. 15: Fabricating Valve Guide Remover

CAUTION: *DO NOT use a torch to heat cylinder head, as it could cause warpage. DO NOT heat cylinder head warmer than 300°F (150°C); this may loosen valve seats.*

Valve Guide Replacement – 1) Use a modified air impact chisel or Valve Guide Driver (07742-0010100) to remove and install valve guides. *See Fig. 15.* Chill replacement guides in a freezer for about an hour. Use a hot plate or oven to heat cylinder head evenly to 300°F (150°C).
2) Working from camshaft side, drive valve guide about 5/64" (2 mm) toward combustion chamber to dislodge carbon and make removal easier. Turn cylinder head over. Drive valve guide out toward camshaft side. If guide does not move, drill out with 5/16" drill and try again.

CAUTION: *Drill guides only in extreme cases. Cylinder head damage can occur if valve guide breaks.*

3) Remove new guides from freezer individually as necessary. Slip a 15/64" (6 mm) steel washer over end of driver. Install new guides from camshaft side of head. Drive guides in until driver bottoms on head. If all guides are being replaced, cylinder head may have to be reheated once or twice.
4) Ensure valve guide height is within specification. See CYLINDER HEAD table under ENGINE SPECIFICATIONS. Using cutting oil, ream new valve guides by rotating Valve Guide Reamer (07HAH-PJ70110A or 07HAH-PJ70110B) clockwise full length of valve guide bore. Measure oil clearance between valve stem and valve guide. See CYLINDER HEAD table under ENGINE SPECIFICATIONS.

NOTE: *Always reface valve seat after replacing valve guide.*

Valve Seat – Valve seat replacement procedure is not available from manufacturer.
Valves – Measure valve stem diameter and margin. Replace any valve that does not meet specifications. See VALVES & VALVE SPRINGS table under ENGINE SPECIFICATIONS.
Valve Stem Installed Height – 1) Insert valve into cylinder head. Holding valve closed, measure valve stem installed height from base of valve guide to tip of valve stem. *See Fig. 16.*

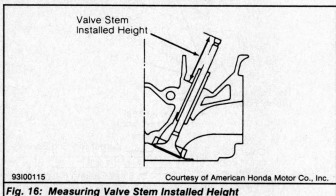

93I00115   Courtesy of American Honda Motor Co., Inc.

Fig. 16: Measuring Valve Stem Installed Height

2) If valve stem installed height is not within specification, replace valve and remeasure. If installed height is still not within specification, valve seat is too deep. Replace cylinder head. See VALVES & VALVE SPRINGS table under ENGINE SPECIFICATIONS.
Valve Seat Correction Angles – If valve guides are to be replaced, perform replacement before refacing valve seats. If seat width is too wide after refacing, use 60-degree stone to raise seat, or 30-degree stone to lower seat. Ensure valve seat width is within specification. See CYLINDER HEAD table under ENGINE SPECIFICATIONS.

CYLINDER BLOCK ASSEMBLY

Piston & Rod Assembly – 1) Each rod is sorted into one of 4 tolerance ranges. Size depends on crank journal bore. A number

between 1 and 4 is stamped on side of rod big end. Any combination of numbers may be found in engine.

NOTE: *Reference numbers are for big end bore code, and do not indicate rod position in engine.*

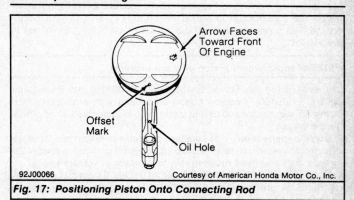

Arrow Faces Toward Front Of Engine

Offset Mark

Oil Hole

92J00066   Courtesy of American Honda Motor Co., Inc.

Fig. 17: Positioning Piston Onto Connecting Rod

1. Assemble Special Tool As Shown

Piston Base Head

Piston Pin Base Insert

Piston Base Spring

Piston Base

2. Adjust The Length Of Piston Pin Driver To 2.07" (52.5 mm) as shown.

Piston Pin Driver Head

2.07" (52.5 mm)

Piston Pin Driver Shaft

Pilot Collar

Embossed Mark Facing Up

Ensure Recessed Portion Of Piston Aligns With Lugs On Base.

3. Place Piston On Piston Pin Base And Press Out Pin Using Hydraulic Press.

93C82240   Courtesy of American Honda Motor Co., Inc.

Fig. 18: Removing Piston Pin

1993 ENGINES
3.2L V6 (Cont.)

Piston Pin Removal – **1)** Install Piston Base Head (07HAF-PL20102 or 07HAF-PL20101), Piston Base Spring (07973-6570600), and Piston Pin Base Insert (07GAF-PH60300) into Piston Base (07973-6570500). Adjust Piston Pin Driver Head (07973-PE00320) so piston driver length is 2.07" (52.5 mm). *See Fig. 18.*
2) Nominal connecting rod large end bore size is 2.24" (57 mm). Install piston and connecting rod with arrow on top of piston toward front of engine, and connecting rod oil hole toward offset mark in top of piston. *See Fig. 17.*

NOTE: All replacement piston pins are oversize.

---

2) Insert Piston Pin Driver Shaft (07973-PE00310) into Pilot Collar (07GAF-PH70100). Position piston onto base with embossed mark facing up. Align recessed part of piston with lugs on base insert. Press out piston pin.
Piston Pin Inspection – **1)** Measure diameter of piston pin. Zero dial indicator to piston pin diameter. Measure piston pin bore in piston. Difference between the 2 measurements is piston pin clearance.
2) Clearance must be 0.0005-0.0009" (0.012-0.024 mm). If piston pin clearance is greater than 0.0009" (0.024 mm), install an oversize piston pin and remeasure clearance.
3) Measure difference between piston pin diameter and connecting rod small end bore. Interference fit between piston pin and connecting rod must be 0.0005-0.0013" (0.013-0.032 mm).
Piston Pin Installation – **1)** Position piston and connecting rod as shown. *See Fig. 17.* Adjust Piston Pin Driver Head (07973-PE00320) so piston driver length is 2.07" (52.5 mm).
2) Install Pilot Collar (07GAF-PH70100) into piston and connecting rod. Lubricate new piston pin lightly. Position piston onto base with embossed mark facing up. Press in piston pin.
Fitting Pistons – **1)** Using a feeler gauge, measure clearance between piston and cylinder bore. If clearance is near or exceeds 0.002" (0.05 mm), measure cylinder bore and piston diameter. Piston clearance is difference between the 2 measurements.
2) If clearance exceeds service limit, rebore cylinder and install oversize piston. See PISTONS, PINS & RINGS table under ENGINE SPECIFICATIONS.

3) Remove all rings from piston. Ensure piston is clean. Inspect piston for distortion or cracks. Measure piston diameter at a point 0.7" (17 mm) from bottom of piston skirt.
4) Standard size pistons are marked with "A" or "B" on top of piston. Pistons are also available in 0.010" (0.25 mm) and 0.020" (0.50 mm) oversize. Standard bore size is identified by "A" or "B" stamped on cylinder block deck surface (right front).
5) Identification letters on block read from front cylinder to rear cylinder. Letters for No. 1 through No. 3 cylinders are on first line, and letters for No. 4 through No. 6 cylinders are on second line. Identification letters are also stamped on cylinder block deck surface. If piston diameter is not within specification, replace piston. See PISTONS, PINS & RINGS table under ENGINE SPECIFICATIONS.
Piston Rings – **1)** Using inverted piston, push new piston ring into cylinder bore 0.6-0.8" (15-20 mm) from bottom. Using a feeler gauge, measure ring end gap. See PISTONS, PINS & RINGS table under ENGINE SPECIFICATIONS.
2) Clean piston ring grooves thoroughly. Install rings onto piston with identification mark toward top of piston. Using a feeler gauge, measure side clearance between ring and ring land.
3) If ring lands are excessively worn, replace piston. See PISTONS, PINS & RINGS table under ENGINE SPECIFICATIONS. Space piston ring end gaps properly around piston. *See Fig. 19.*
Rod Bearings – **1)** Measure oil clearance with Plastigage. Tighten bearing cap to 33 ft. lbs. (45 N.m). If oil clearance is not within specification, install a new bearing set (same color code) and recheck oil clearance. See CRANKSHAFT, MAIN & CONNECTING ROD BEARINGS table under ENGINE SPECIFICATIONS. DO NOT shim or file cap to adjust oil clearance.
2) If oil clearance is still incorrect, try next larger or smaller bearing and measure oil clearance again. If proper oil clearance cannot be obtained by using larger or smaller bearings, replace crankshaft and repeat procedure.

NOTE: A number code indicating connecting bore is stamped on side of each connecting rod and cap. Connecting rod journal diameter codes (letters) are stamped on front crankshaft counterweight pad. See Fig. 20. Use both codes when ordering replacement bearings.

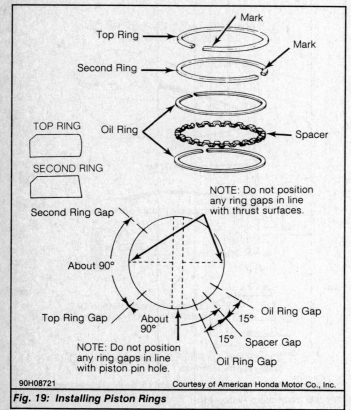

90H08721 — Courtesy of American Honda Motor Co., Inc.

Fig. 19: Installing Piston Rings

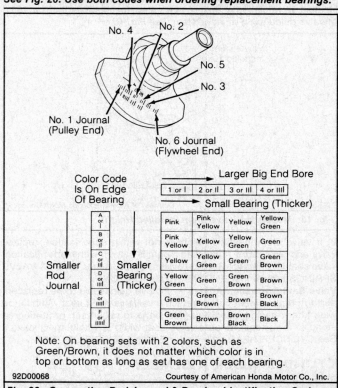

Note: On bearing sets with 2 colors, such as Green/Brown, it does not matter which color is in top or bottom as long as set has one of each bearing.

92D00068 — Courtesy of American Honda Motor Co., Inc.

Fig. 20: Connecting Rod Journal & Bearing Identification Codes

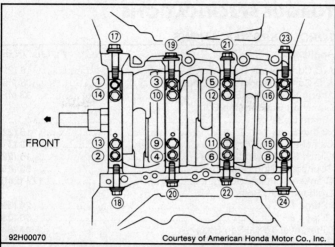

92H00070   Courtesy of American Honda Motor Co., Inc.

Fig. 21: Crankshaft Main Bearing Cap Bolt Tightening Sequence

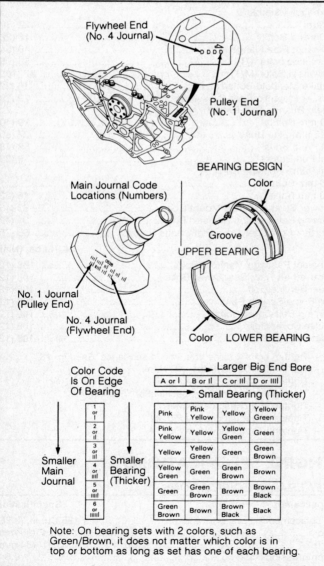

92F00069   Courtesy of American Honda Motor Co., Inc.

Fig. 22: Crankshaft Main Journal & Bearing Identification Codes

Crankshaft & Main Bearings – **1)** Mark rod and main bearing caps for identification. Remove all connecting rod caps and bearings. Remove main bearing caps and bearing halves. Lift crankshaft from block, being careful not to damage journals.

2) Using a lathe or "V" blocks to support crankshaft, measure crankshaft runout, out-of-round, and taper. If any measurement exceeds service limit, replace crankshaft. See CRANKSHAFT, MAIN & CONNECTING ROD BEARINGS table under ENGINE SPECIFICATIONS.

3) Install crankshaft into block. Measure main bearing oil clearance with Plastigage. If engine is in vehicle, support counterweights and measure only one bearing at a time. Tighten main bearing cap bolts in sequence to specification. *See Fig. 21*. See TORQUE SPECIFICATIONS.

4) If oil clearance is not within specification, install a new bearing set (same color code) and remeasure oil clearance. If oil clearance is still incorrect, try next larger or smaller bearing. If specified oil clearance cannot be obtained by using larger or smaller bearings, replace crankshaft and repeat procedure.

NOTE: A letter code indicating main journal bore diameters is stamped on cylinder block. Main journal diameter codes (numbers) are stamped on front crankshaft counterweight pad. See Fig. 22. Use both codes when ordering replacement bearings.

Thrust Bearing – **1)** Measure crankshaft end play with a dial indicator. See CRANKSHAFT, MAIN & CONNECTING ROD BEARINGS table under ENGINE SPECIFICATIONS. If end play exceeds specification, inspect thrust washers and thrust surface of crankshaft. Crankshaft thrust washers are located at No. 4 main bearing journal.

2) Replace worn parts as necessary. Thrust washer thickness is fixed. DO NOT change thrust washer thickness by grinding or shimming. Install thrust washers with grooved side facing out.

Cylinder Block – **1)** Measure cylinder bore taper. If taper exceeds 0.002" (0.05 mm), rebore cylinder for oversize pistons. If measurements in any cylinder exceed oversize bore service limit, replace cylinder block. See CYLINDER BLOCK table under ENGINE SPECIFICATIONS.

2) Using a feeler gauge and straightedge, measure cylinder block deck surface for warpage. Service limit is 0.004" (0.10 mm). If cylinder bore is okay, hone cylinder to obtain a 60-degree crosshatch pattern. After honing, wash cylinder bore with hot soapy water. Air-dry cylinder bore, and apply engine oil to prevent rusting.

ENGINE OILING

ENGINE LUBRICATION SYSTEM

A rotor-type oil pump draws oil from the oil pan, and delivers it under pressure to main and connecting rod bearings. An oil hole in each connecting rod supplies oil to thrust side of piston and cylinder wall. An oil passage carries oil to camshaft and rocker arms. Oil spray lubricates valve stems.

Oil Pressure – Minimum oil pressure with engine at idle should be 10 psi (0.7 kg/cm²). Minimum oil pressure at 3000 RPM should be 50 psi (3.5 kg/cm²).

OIL PUMP

Removal & Disassembly – **1)** Raise and support vehicle. Drain engine oil and differential oil. Remove spark plugs. Rotate crankshaft clockwise until No. 1 piston is at TDC of compression stroke.

2) Align TDC mark on crankshaft pulley with pointer on lower cover. Remove timing belt. See TIMING BELT under REMOVAL & INSTALLATION. Remove oil pan. See OIL PAN under REMOVAL & INSTALLATION.

3) Disconnect engine oil cooler hoses. Remove oil pump assembly. *See Fig. 23.* Remove screen from oil pump. Separate pump cover from pump housing. Using a screwdriver, pry oil seal from oil pump housing.

1993 ENGINES
3.2L V6 (Cont.)

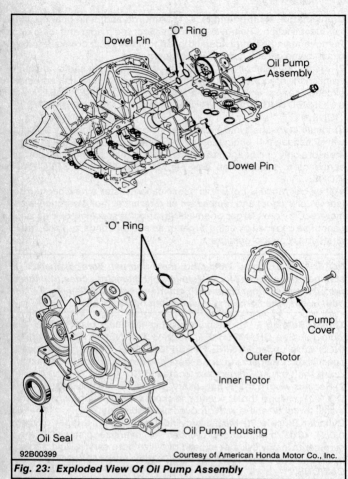

92B00399   Courtesy of American Honda Motor Co., Inc.

Fig. 23: Exploded View Of Oil Pump Assembly

Inspection – Measure radial clearance between inner and outer rotors. Measure axial clearance and radial clearance between housing and outer rotor. Inspect both rotors and pump housing for scoring or other damage. Replace components if not within specification. See OIL PUMP SPECIFICATIONS table.

OIL PUMP SPECIFICATIONS

Application	In. (mm)
Inner Rotor-To-Outer Rotor	
Radial Clearance	
Standard (New)	0.002-0.006 (0.04-0.16)
Service Limit	0.008 (0.20)
Housing-To-Outer Rotor	
Axial Clearance	
Standard (New)	0.001-0.003 (0.02-0.07)
Service Limit	0.005 (0.13)
Housing-To-Outer Rotor	
Radial Clearance	
Standard (New)	0.004-0.007 (0.10-0.18)
Service Limit	0.008 (0.20)

Reassembly & Installation – 1) Apply light coating of grease to crankshaft and lip of new seal. Using Seal Driver (07749-0010000) and Attachment (07746-0010500), install oil seal. Ensure seal is fully seated into oil pump housing. Install dowel pins and "O" ring into cylinder block. Clean oil pump and engine mating surfaces.
2) Apply Liquid Sealant (08718-0001) to cylinder block mating surface of oil pump. Apply sealant to threads of inner bolt holes. Install oil pump before sealant dries. Wait at least 30 minutes before filling crankcase with oil. To complete installation, reverse removal procedure.

TORQUE SPECIFICATIONS

TORQUE SPECIFICATIONS

Application	Ft. Lbs. (N.m)
A/C Compressor Bolts	16 (22)
A/C Compressor Bracket Bolts	33 (45)
Alternator Bracket Bolts	33 (45)
Camshaft Bearing Cap Bolts [1]	
6 mm Bolts	[2]
8 mm Bolts	16 (22)
Camshaft Pulley Bolts	23 (31)
Clutch Slave Cylinder Bolts	16 (22)
Connecting Rod Nuts	33 (45)
Crankshaft Pulley Bolt	177 (240)
Cylinder Head Bolts [3]	
Stage 1	29 (39)
Stage 2	58 (78)
Differential-To-Oil Pan Bolts	47 (64)
Engine Block-To-Transaxle	
Housing Bolts	54 (73)
Engine Mounts	[4]
Exhaust Manifold	
Nuts	22 (30)
Shroud Bolts	16 (22)
Exhaust Pipe Flange Nuts	40 (54)
Flexplate bolts A/T [5]	55 (75)
Flywheel Bolts (M/T) [5]	77 (105)
Intake Manifold Bolts/Nuts	16 (22)
Lower Plate-To-Rear Crossmember Bolts	29 (39)
Main Bearing Cap Bolts [6]	
9 mm Bolts	29 (40)
10 mm Side Bolts	37 (50)
11 mm Bolts	58 (78)
Oil Pan Bolts [7]	16 (22)
Oil Pump Housing Bolts	
6 mm Bolts	[2]
8 mm Bolts	16 (22)
Power Steering Pump Mount Bolt	33 (45)
Timing Belt Tension Adjuster Bolt	31 (42)
Torque Converter Drive Plate Bolts [5]	55 (75)

	INCH Lbs. (N.m)
Coolant Passage Manifold Bolts	106 (12)
Crankshaft Rear Seal Cover Bolts	106 (12)
Fuel Service Bolt	106 (12)
Oil Pump Screen Bolts	106 (12)
Timing Belt Cover Bolts	106 (12)
Valve Cover Bolts	106 (12)
Water Pump Bolts	106 (12)

[1] – Tighten bolts 2 turns at a time in sequence. *See Fig. 13.*
[2] – Tighten to 106 INCH lbs. (12 N.m).
[3] – Tighten in sequence. *See Fig. 7.*
[4] – Tighten in sequence to specification. *See Fig. 4.*
[5] – Tighten in a crisscross pattern.
[6] – Tighten in sequence. *See Fig. 21.*
[7] – Tighten in sequence. *See Fig. 14.*

ENGINE SPECIFICATIONS

GENERAL SPECIFICATIONS

Application	Specification
Displacement	196 Cu. In. (3.2L)
Bore	3.54" (90 mm)
Stroke	3.31" (84 mm)
Compression Ratio	9.6:1
Fuel System	SFI
Horsepower @ RPM	200 @ 5500
Torque Ft. Lbs. @ RPM	210 @ 4500

CRANKSHAFT, MAIN & CONNECTING ROD BEARINGS

Application	In. (mm)
Crankshaft	
End Play	
Standard	0.004-0.011 (0.10-0.29)
Service Limit	0.018 (0.45)
Maximum Journal Out-Of-Round	0.0004 (0.010)
Maximum Journal Taper	0.0004 (0.010)
Maximum Runout	0.001 (0.030)
Main Bearings	
Journal Diameter	2.6762-2.6772 (67.976-68.000)
Oil Clearance	
Standard	0.0008-0.0016 (0.020-0.040)
Service Limit	0.002 (0.05)
Connecting Rod Bearings	
Journal Diameter	2.0866-2.1250 (53.000-53.975)
Oil Clearance	
Standard	0.0008-0.0018 (0.020-0.046)
Service Limit	0.002 (0.05)

CONNECTING RODS

Application	In. (mm)
Side Play	0.006-0.012 (0.15-0.30)

PISTONS, PINS & RINGS

Application	In. (mm)
Pistons	
Clearance	
Standard	0.001-0.002 (0.02-0.04)
Service Limit	0.003 (0.08)
Diameter	
Standard [1]	
"A" Piston	3.5425-3.5429 (89.98-89.99)
"B" Piston	3.5421-3.5425 (89.97-89.98)
Oversize	
.010" (0.25 mm)	3.5520-3.5524 (90.22-90.23)
.020" (0.50 mm)	3.5618-3.5622 (90.47-90.48)
Piston Pins	
Diameter	
Standard	0.8659-0.8661 (21.994-22.000)
Oversize	0.8660-0.8663 (21.997-22.003)
Piston Fit	0.0005-0.0009 (0.012-0.024)
Rod Interference Fit	0.0005-0.0013 (0.013-0.032)
Rings	
No. 1	
End Gap	
Standard	0.010-0.016 (0.25-0.40)
Service Limit	0.027 (0.70)
Side Clearance	0.0014-0.0024 (0.035-0.060)
No. 2	
End Gap	
Standard	0.016-0.022 (0.40-0.55)
Service Limit	0.033 (0.85)
Side Clearance	0.0012-0.0022 (0.030-0.055)
No. 3 (Oil)	
End Gap	
Standard	0.008-0.028 (0.20-0.70)
Service Limit	0.032 (0.80)

[1] – Piston identification letter is located on top of piston.

CYLINDER BLOCK

Application	In. (mm)
Cylinder Bore	
Standard Diameter	
"A" Piston [1]	3.5437-3.5441 (90.010-90.020)
"B" Piston [1]	3.5433-3.5437 (90.000-90.010)
Service Limit	3.546 (90.07)
Oversize	
.25 O/S	3.553-3.554 (90.25-90.27)
.50 O/S	3.563-3.564 (90.50-90.52)
Maximum Taper	0.002 (0.05)
Maximum Deck Warpage	0.004 (0.10)

[1] – Standard bore size is identified by "A" or "B" stamped on cylinder block deck surface (right front). Letters on block read from front cylinder to rear cylinder. Identification letters for No. 1 through No. 3 cylinders are on first line, and letters for No. 4 through No. 6 cylinders are on second line.

VALVES & VALVE SPRINGS

Application	Specification
Intake Valves	
Face Angle	45°
Head Diameter	1.295-1.303" (32.90-33.10 mm)
Margin	
Standard	0.033-0.045" (0.85-1.15 mm)
Service Limit	0.026" (0.65 mm)
Stem Diameter	
Standard	0.2157-0.2161" (5.480-5.490 mm)
Service Limit	0.2146" (5.450 mm)
Valve Length	4.472-4.483" (113.58-113.88 mm)
Valve Stem Installed Height	
Standard	1.8478-1.8651" (46.935-47.375 mm)
Service Limit	1.8750" (47.625 mm)
Exhaust Valves	
Face Angle	45°
Head Diameter	1.098-1.106" (27.90-28.10 mm)
Margin	
Standard	0.053-0.065" (1.35-1.65 mm)
Service Limit	0.045" (1.15 mm)
Stem Diameter	
Standard	0.2146-0.2150" (5.451-5.461 mm)
Service Limit	0.2134" (5.420 mm)
Valve Length	4.568-4.580" (116.03-116.33 mm)
Valve Stem Installed Height	
Standard	1.8852-1.9045" (47.885-48.375 mm)
Service Limit	1.9124" (48.575 mm)
Valve Springs	
Free Length	
Intake	
Standard	1.975" (50.17 mm)
Exhaust	
Standard	1.983" (50.36 mm)

1993 ENGINES
3.2L V6 (Cont.)

CYLINDER HEAD

Application	Specification
Cylinder Head Height	3.935-3.939" (99.95-100.05 mm)
Maximum Warpage ¹	0.002" (0.05-0.20 mm)
Valve Seats	
Intake & Exhaust	
Seat Angle	45°
Seat Width	
Standard	0.049-0.061" (1.25-1.55 mm)
Service Limit	0.079" (2.00 mm)
Valve Guides	
Intake & Exhaust	
Valve Guide I.D.	0.2188-0.2192" (5.558-5.568 mm)
Valve Guide Installed Height	0.620-0.640" (15.75-16.25 mm)
Valve Stem-To-Guide Oil Clearance	
Intake	
Standard	0.001-0.002" (0.02-0.05 mm)
Service Limit	0.003" (0.08 mm)
Exhaust	
Standard	0.002-0.003" (0.05-0.08 mm)
Service Limit	0.004" (0.11 mm)

¹ - Maximum resurface limit is 0.008" (0.20 mm).

CAMSHAFT

Application	In. (mm)
End Play	
Standard	0.002-0.006 (0.05-0.15)
Service Limit	0.006 ().15)
Maximum Journal Runout	0.0006 (0.015)
Lobe Height	
Intake	1.4872 (37.766)
Exhaust	1.4975 (38.037)
Oil Clearance	0.002-0.004 (0.05-0.09)

Integra, Legend, Vigor

SPECIFICATIONS

BELT ADJUSTMENT

BELT ADJUSTMENT

Application	[1] Deflection – In. (mm)
A/C Compressor	
Integra	9/32-11/32 (7.0-9.0)
Legend	5/16-3/8 (8.0-10.0)
Vigor	1/4-3/8 (6.0-9.0)
Alternator	
Integra	9/32-13/32 (7.0-10.5)
Legend	11/32-13/32 (9.0-10.5)
Vigor	5/16-3/8 (7.5-9.5)
Power Steering	
Integra	3/8-15/32 (9.5-11.5)
Legend	7/16-1/2 (11.0-13.5)
Vigor	1/4-11/32 (6.5-9.0)

[1] – Deflection is with 22 lbs. (10 kg) pressure applied midway on longest belt run, after belt has run at least 5 minutes.

COOLING SYSTEM SPECIFICATIONS

COOLING SYSTEM SPECIFICATIONS

Model	Specification
Coolant Replacement Interval	[1] 45,000 Miles
Coolant Capacity	
Integra	
Automatic Transaxle	6.3 qts. (6.0L)
Manual Transaxle	6.15 qts. (5.8L)
Legend	9.2 qts. (8.7L)
Vigor	7.9 qts. (7.5L)
Pressure Cap	
Integra	11-15 psi
Legend	14-16 psi
Vigor	14-18 psi
Thermostat Opens	
Integra & Legend	
Starts	169-176°F (76-80°C)
Fully Open	194°F (90°C)
Vigor	
Primary	
Starts	176-183°F (80-84°C)
Fully Open	203°F (95°C)
Secondary	
Starts	181-189°F (83-87°C)
Fully Open	203°F (95°C)

[1] – Replace every 2 years or 30,000 miles thereafter.

BLEEDING COOLING SYSTEM

Always bleed air from cooling system after replacing coolant. Open bleed bolt on coolant outlet. Fill system. Close bleed bolt when coolant starts to run out without bubbles. Tighten bleed bolt to 88 INCH lbs. (10 N.m). With radiator cap removed, start and run engine until normal operating temperature is reached. Top off coolant and install radiator cap.

ELECTRIC COOLING FANS

DESCRIPTION

All models use electric cooling fans. Integra models not equipped with A/C use one cooling fan. A/C-equipped Integra and all Legend models use 2 cooling fans. Legend has a 2-speed cooling fan and a condenser fan. Vigor has a radiator fan and a condenser fan.

OPERATION

Integra – Integra cooling fan is controlled by a coolant temperature switch and relay. The fan on A/C-equipped models is controlled by a radiator fan control module, through a condenser fan relay. If engine oil temperature is greater than 226°F (108°C) when ignition switch is off, the radiator fan control module supplies power to the fan for up to 15 minutes after engine is shut off. Radiator fan control module is located under dash, on right side of heater unit.

Legend – A Fan Control Unit (FCU) controls the radiator and condenser fans. Both fans run whenever the engine is running. The fans run at either low or high speed, depending on engine temperature. If A/C system pressure is higher than normal, both fans run at high speed regardless of engine temperature. The FCU is located underneath a cover at passenger's front floor area. The FCU receives input from a radiator fan control sensor, the ECM, a radiator fan control module, and A/C pressure switches.

An engine oil temperature sensor sends a signal to the radiator fan control module, which then operates the condenser fan for up to 15 minutes after the engine is shut off, depending on engine temperature. This module is located below then dash, behind the right side kick panel.

Vigor – Vigor cooling fan is controlled by a coolant temperature switch and relay. If engine coolant temperature is higher than 226°F (108°C) when ignition switch is off, a radiator fan control module supplies power the fan for up to 15 minutes after engine is shut off. This module is located under dash, behind glove box.

TROUBLE SHOOTING & TESTING

To trouble shoot cooling fans, use appropriate cooling fan wiring diagrams. See WIRING DIAGRAMS.

COMPONENT TESTING

Cooling Fan Motor – Unplug connector at fan motor. Using jumper wires, apply battery voltage to terminal "A" of fan motor connector. Ground terminal "B." *See Fig. 1.* Fan motor should operate. If fan motor fails to operate, replace it. If fan motor operates, check related components and wiring. See COOLANT TEMPERATURE SENSOR/SWITCH and RADIATOR FAN CONTROL MODULE & FAN CONTROL UNIT.

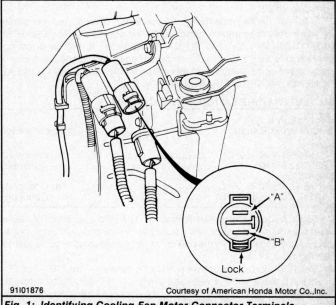

91I01876   Courtesy of American Honda Motor Co.,Inc.

Fig. 1: Identifying Cooling Fan Motor Connector Terminals

Coolant Temperature Sensor/Switch (Integra & Vigor) – 1) Remove coolant temperature switch or sensor. On Integra, switches are located on rear of engine cylinder block. On Vigor, one sensor is located on thermostat housing, the other is threaded into the lower radiator tank, on the driver's side.

2) Suspend switch and a thermometer in a container partially filled with coolant. Heat coolant while monitoring temperature. Measure sensor resistance or check for continuity at temperatures specified. See TEMPERATURE SENSOR/SWITCH SPECIFICATIONS table.

3) If continuity or resistance is not as specified, replace sensor or switch. If continuity or resistance is as specified, check relay and all related wiring. See RADIATOR FAN CONTROL MODULE & FAN CONTROL UNIT.

Radiator Fan Control Sensor (Legend) – **1)** Sensor is threaded into lower radiator tank, on rear side. Remove sensor.

2) Suspend switch and a thermometer in a container partially filled with coolant. Heat coolant while monitoring temperature. Measure sensor resistance temperatures specified. See TEMPERATURE SENSOR/SWITCH SPECIFICATIONS table.

3) If continuity or resistance is not as specified, replace sensor or switch. If continuity or resistance is as specified, check relay and all related wiring. See RADIATOR FAN CONTROL MODULE & FAN CONTROL UNIT.

TEMPERATURE SENSOR/SWITCH SPECIFICATIONS

Application & Temperature	Specification
Integra	
Less Than 181-187°F (83-87°C)	No Continuity
Greater Than 196-203°F (91-95°C)	Continuity
Legend	
183°F (84°C)	1047-1255 Ohms
194°F (90°C)	872-1024 Ohms
230°F (110°C)	489-541 Ohms
Vigor	
Less Than 190°F (88°C)	No Continuity
Greater Than 191°F (89°C)	Continuity

WARNING: DO NOT heat oil hotter than is necessary to test switch.

Oil Temperature Switch (Integra With A/C & Legend) – **1)** Remove oil temperature switch. Switch is located on cylinder head at rear of engine, on passenger side. Suspend switch and a thermometer in a container of oil.

2) Heat oil while monitoring temperature. Check for continuity between switch terminals at specified temperatures. See OIL TEMPERATURE SWITCH SPECIFICATIONS table. If switch does not operate as specified, replace it. If switch operates as specified, check relay, other components, and all related wiring. See RADIATOR FAN CONTROL MODULE & FAN CONTROL UNIT.

OIL TEMPERATURE SWITCH SPECIFICATIONS

Application & Temperature Range	Specification
Integra	
208-228°F (98-109°C)	No Continuity
221-232°F (105-111°C)	Continuity
Legend	
At 156-185°F (69-85°C)	No Continuity
At 192-203°F (89-95°C)	Continuity

Radiator & Condenser Fan Relays – **1)** Basic operation of relays used for A/C compressor and cooling fans is similar, although physical appearance of relays may be different. Remove relay to be tested. See Fig. 2, 3, or 4.

2) Check for continuity between relay terminals "A" and "B". See Fig. 5. Apply battery voltage between terminals "C" and "D". Continuity between terminals "A" and "B" should exist only when battery voltage is applied to terminals "C" and "D".

3) If relay does not operate as specified, replace relay. If relay operates as specified, check related wiring. See RADIATOR FAN CONTROL MODULE & FAN CONTROL UNIT.

Radiator Fan Main Relay (Legend) – Remove radiator fan main relay. Relay is located in underhood relay box "A". See Fig. 3. Continuity should exist between terminals "D" and "E". See Fig. 6. With battery voltage disconnected, continuity should exist between terminals "B" and "C". If relay does not operate as specified, replace relay.

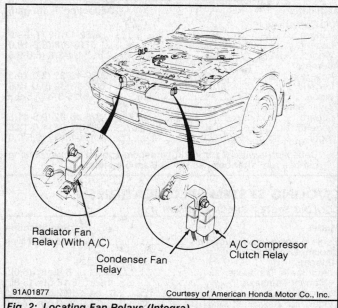

91A01877   Courtesy of American Honda Motor Co., Inc.

Fig. 2: Locating Fan Relays (Integra)

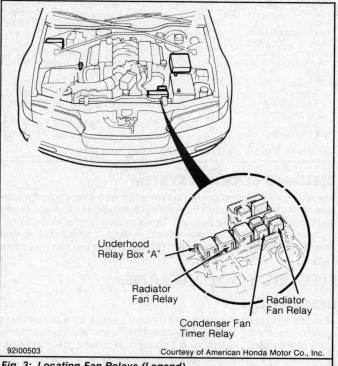

92I00503   Courtesy of American Honda Motor Co., Inc.

Fig. 3: Locating Fan Relays (Legend)

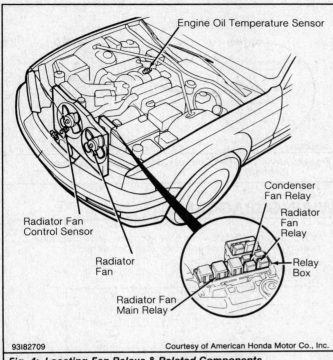

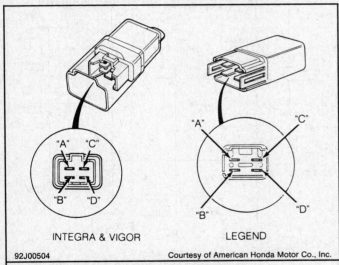

93182709   Courtesy of American Honda Motor Co., Inc.

Fig. 4: Locating Fan Relays & Related Components (Vigor)

INTEGRA & VIGOR   LEGEND

92J00504   Courtesy of American Honda Motor Co., Inc.

Fig. 5: Identifying Cooling Fan Relay Terminals

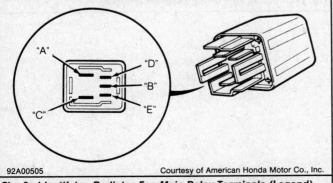

92A00505   Courtesy of American Honda Motor Co., Inc.

Fig. 6: Identifying Radiator Fan Main Relay Terminals (Legend)

Radiator Fan Control Module & Fan Control Unit – If fan does not operate, check for open or short circuits in wiring between components and radiator fan control module or fan control unit. See appropriate RADIATOR FAN CONTROL MODULE TERMINAL IDENTIFICATION table or FAN CONTROL UNIT TERMINAL IDENTIFICATION table. See Fig. 7, 8, 9, or 10. Also see appropriate wiring diagram. See Fig. 11, 12, or 13. If all wiring and other components are okay, replace fan control unit or radiator fan control module .

RADIATOR FAN CONTROL MODULE TERMINAL IDENTIFICATION (INTEGRA WITH A/C)

Terminal [1]	Wire Color	Circuit
1	Yellow/White	Condenser Fan Relay
2	Yellow/Black	Ignition Voltage
3		Not Used
4	Black	Ground
5	White/Green	Oil Temperature Switch
6	White	Battery Voltage
7	Black/Yellow	Ignition Voltage
8	Blue/Red	Condenser Fan Relay

[1] – See Fig. 7.

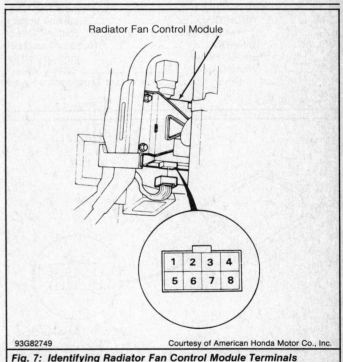

93G82749   Courtesy of American Honda Motor Co., Inc.

Fig. 7: Identifying Radiator Fan Control Module Terminals (Integra)

RADIATOR FAN CONTROL MODULE TERMINAL IDENTIFICATION (LEGEND)

Terminal [1]	Wire Color	Circuit
B1	Black	Ground
B2	Blue/Yellow	Fan Control Unit
B3	Blue/Red	Condenser Fan Relay
B4	Yellow/Blue	Ignition Voltage
B5	Green	Condenser Fan Relay
B6	Black/Red	Battery Voltage
B7		Not Used
B8	Orange	Oil Temperature Switch

[1] – See Fig. 8.

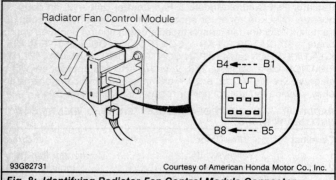

93G82731   Courtesy of American Honda Motor Co., Inc.

Fig. 8: Identifying Radiator Fan Control Module Connector Terminals (Legend)

RADIATOR FAN CONTROL MODULE TERMINAL IDENTIFICATION (VIGOR)

Terminal [1]	Wire Color	Circuit
A	Black	Ground
B	Yellow/White	Condenser Fan Relay
C	Yellow/Black	Ignition Voltage
D	Yellow	Battery Voltage
E	Green/Yellow	Radiator Fan Relay
F	Black/Yellow	Ignition Voltage
G	White/Green	Battery Voltage
H	Green	Coolant Temperature Switch

[1] – See Fig. 9.

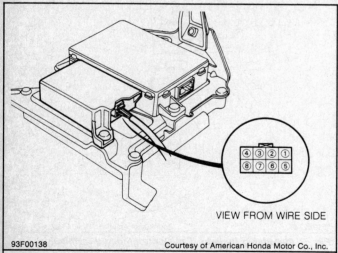

VIEW FROM WIRE SIDE

93F00138   Courtesy of American Honda Motor Co., Inc.

Fig. 9: Identifying Radiator Fan Control Module Connector Terminals (Vigor)

FAN CONTROL UNIT TERMINAL IDENTIFICATION (LEGEND)

Terminal [1]	Wire Color	Circuit
A1	Blue/Green	Coolant Temp. Switch
A2	Blue	Radiator Fan Relay
A3	Light Blue	A/C Pressure Switch
A4	Black	Ground
A5	Green	ECU
A6	Red/Blue	A/C Pressure Switch
A7	Blue/White	Coolant Temp. Switch
A8		Not Used
A9	Blue/Yellow	Fan Control Module
A10		Not Used
A11	Blue/Black	ECU
A12	Yellow/Black	Ignition Voltage

[1] – See Fig. 10.

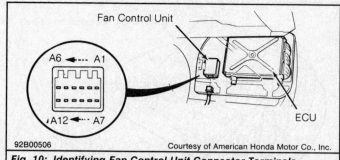

92B00506   Courtesy of American Honda Motor Co., Inc.

Fig. 10: Identifying Fan Control Unit Connector Terminals (Legend)

WIRING DIAGRAMS

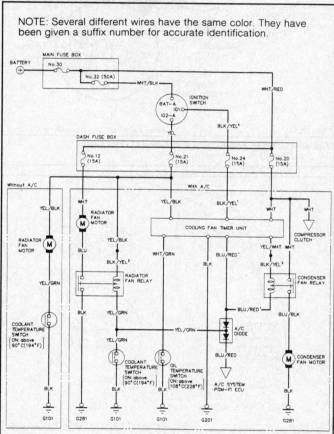

NOTE: Several different wires have the same color. They have been given a suffix number for accurate identification.

91D01874   Courtesy of American Honda Motor Co., Inc.

Fig. 11: Cooling Fan Wiring Diagram (Integra)

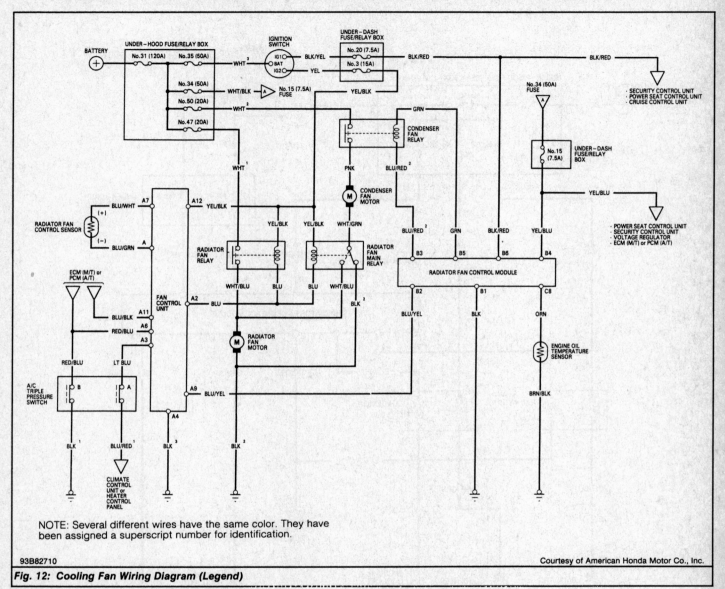

NOTE: Several different wires have the same color. They have
been assigned a superscript number for identification.

93B82710

Courtesy of American Honda Motor Co., Inc.

Fig. 12: Cooling Fan Wiring Diagram (Legend)

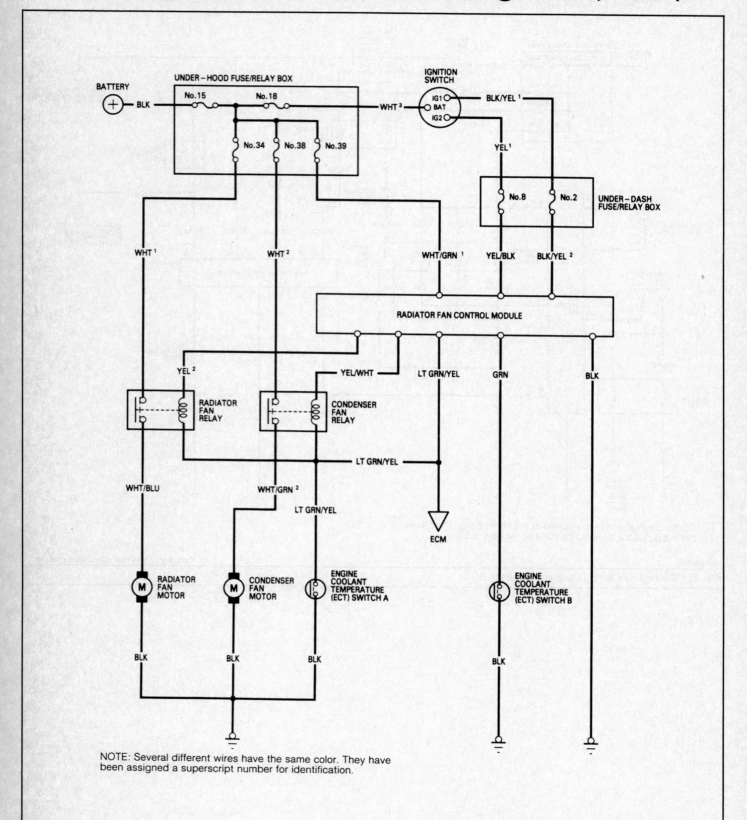

93C82711

Fig. 13: Cooling Fan Wiring Diagram (Vigor)

Integra, Legend, Vigor

DESCRIPTION

On all models, the clutch uses a diaphragm spring to engage the pressure plate. Integra uses a cable-operated release system. Legend and Vigor use a hydraulic release system.

ADJUSTMENTS

NOTE: Hydraulic clutches on Legend and Vigor do not require periodic adjustment for free play. See Fig. 2 or 3.

CLUTCH PEDAL FREE PLAY

Integra – Adjust clutch pedal free play by turning adjuster nut at clutch release arm to obtain 0.6-0.8" (15-20 mm) free play at clutch pedal, with 0.6" (15 mm) preferred. When adjustment is correct, there should be 0.16-0.20" (4.0-5.0 mm) free play at tip of release arm.

CLUTCH PEDAL TRAVEL & HEIGHT

Integra – Check clutch pedal travel. Pedal travel should be 5.6-5.8" (142-147 mm). If pedal travel is not within specification, loosen clutch pedal stop lock nut "A". *See Fig. 1.* Turn pedal stop bolt (without cruise control) or clutch switch (with cruise control) in or out to obtain specified pedal travel. Tighten lock nut.

Legend – Loosen lock nut "A". *See Fig. 2.* Loosen clutch switch until plunger no longer touches clutch pedal. Loosen lock nut "C". Rotate clutch pedal push rod to obtain specified pedal travel and height. Tighten lock nut "C". Turn clutch switch inward until it contacts clutch pedal, then turn it in another 1/4 - 1/2 turn. Tighten lock nut "A".

Vigor – 1) Loosen lock nut "A". *See Fig. 3.* Back out pedal switch "A" until it does not touch pedal. Loosen lock nut "C". Turn push rod until pedal stroke is 5.5-5.9" (140-150 mm). Turn in pedal switch "A" until it contacts pedal. Tighten lock nut "A".

2) Loosen lock nut "B" and pedal switch "B". Measure clearance between floor panel and clutch pedal when pedal is fully pressed, and then allow pedal to come up 0.6-0.8" (15-20 mm). With pedal in this position, adjust position of switch "B" so engine will start. Turn switch "B" inward an additional 1/4 - 1/2 turn. Tighten lock nut "B".

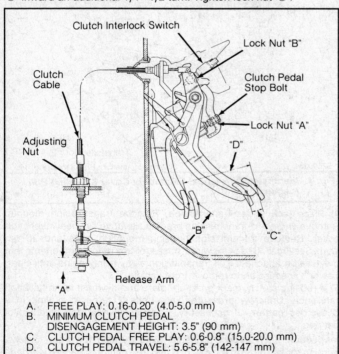

A. FREE PLAY: 0.16-0.20" (4.0-5.0 mm)
B. MINIMUM CLUTCH PEDAL DISENGAGEMENT HEIGHT: 3.5" (90 mm)
C. CLUTCH PEDAL FREE PLAY: 0.6-0.8" (15.0-20.0 mm)
D. CLUTCH PEDAL TRAVEL: 5.6-5.8" (142-147 mm)

93E82903   Courtesy of American Honda Motor Co., Inc.

Fig. 1: Adjusting Clutch (Integra)

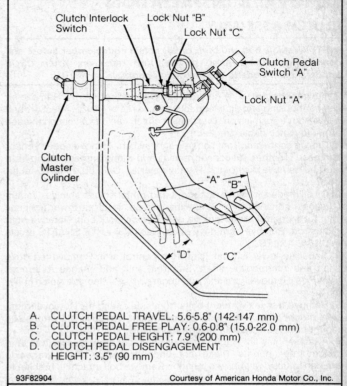

A. CLUTCH PEDAL TRAVEL: 5.6-5.8" (142-147 mm)
B. CLUTCH PEDAL FREE PLAY: 0.6-0.8" (15.0-22.0 mm)
C. CLUTCH PEDAL HEIGHT: 7.9" (200 mm)
D. CLUTCH PEDAL DISENGAGEMENT HEIGHT: 3.5" (90 mm)

93F82904   Courtesy of American Honda Motor Co., Inc.

Fig. 2: Adjusting Clutch (Legend)

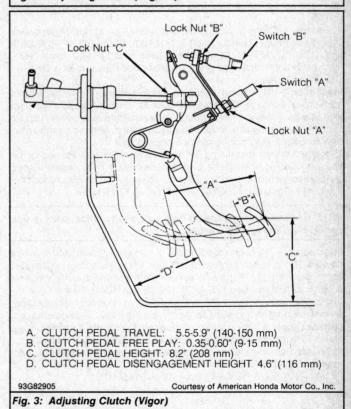

A. CLUTCH PEDAL TRAVEL: 5.5-5.9" (140-150 mm)
B. CLUTCH PEDAL FREE PLAY: 0.35-0.60" (9-15 mm)
C. CLUTCH PEDAL HEIGHT: 8.2" (208 mm)
D. CLUTCH PEDAL DISENGAGEMENT HEIGHT 4.6" (116 mm)

93G82905   Courtesy of American Honda Motor Co., Inc.

Fig. 3: Adjusting Clutch (Vigor)

REMOVAL & INSTALLATION

CLUTCH ASSEMBLY

NOTE: If vehicle has anti-theft radio, obtain code number before disconnecting battery. After service, turn radio on. When CODE appears, enter code to restore radio operation.

Removal (Integra) – 1) Remove battery and battery tray. Remove air cleaner housing and air inlet duct as an assembly. Disconnect ground cable from transmission. Disconnect clutch cable from clutch release arm and clutch cable bracket.

2) Unplug connector from back-up light switch. Remove speed sensor and hose together. Disconnect cables and wiring harness clamp from starter. Remove distributor. Remove starter. On 1.8L, remove center beam.

3) On all models, remove right front and center splash shields. Unplug O$_2$ sensor connector. Remove exhaust pipe. Separate lower right ball joint from control arm. Remove right damper fork bolt. Remove right radius rod. Remove right drive shaft. See FWD AXLE SHAFTS article in DRIVE AXLES.

4) Separate lower left ball joint from control arm. Remove left drive shaft and intermediate shaft. Separate shift and change rods from transaxle. Remove front and rear engine braces. Remove clutch housing cover.

5) Remove transaxle mount bolts from side of engine. Remove transaxle mount bolts from rear engine mount. Remove side transaxle mount bolt. Remove front transaxle mount.

6) Attach engine lift sling to cylinder head. Lift engine enough to take weight from mounts. Place jack under transaxle. Raise transaxle enough to take weight from mounts. Remove bolt attaching bracket to side transaxle mount.

7) Remove mount bolts from side of transaxle. Move transaxle away from engine until shaft clears clutch. Lower transaxle to remove from vehicle.

8) Before removing clutch, measure diaphragm spring fingers wear with feeler gauge, Handle (07936-3710100), Shaft (07LAF-PR30210), and Disc (07JAF-PM7011A). Wear limit is 0.04" (1.0 mm). Install flywheel holder. Unscrew pressure plate bolts 2 turns at a time in a crisscross pattern.

Inspection – 1) Inspect pressure plate surface for wear, cracks, burning, or warpage in excess of 0.006" (0.15 mm). Measure warpage with straightedge and feeler gauge at several different points. Inspect clutch pilot bearing for smooth operation. Clutch release bearing must turn smoothly. Replace bearings if necessary.

2) Inspect clutch disc lining for excessive wear and burned or oil-soaked condition. Measure disc thickness and rivet depth. Inspect clutch disc for loose torsion dampers. Measure clutch disc runout and flywheel runout. See CLUTCH SPECIFICATIONS table.

NOTE: Use new spring clips on both axle shafts. Slide axles in until spring clips engage differential.

Installation – 1) Align dowel holes in pressure plate with flywheel dowels. Using clutch alignment tool and ring gear holder, install disc and pressure plate. Tighten pressure plate bolts to specification in a crisscross pattern. See TORQUE SPECIFICATIONS.

2) Ensure both dowel pins are installed in clutch housing. Clean release bearing sliding surface. Apply molybdenum disulfide grease to surface. Apply a light coating of grease to input shaft splines. Keep clutch disc and pressure plate surfaces free of grease and dirt.

3) To complete installation, reverse removal procedure. Refill all fluids to proper level. Adjust clutch pedal height and free play. See CLUTCH PEDAL TRAVEL & HEIGHT under ADJUSTMENTS.

CLUTCH SPECIFICATIONS

Application	In. (mm)
Disc Thickness	
Standard (New)	0.33-0.36 (8.4-9.1)
Service Limit	0.24 (6.0)
Disc Runout	0.04 (1.0)
Maximum Flywheel Runout	
Standard (New)	0.002 (0.05)
Service Limit	0.006 (0.15)
Rivet Depth	
Standard (New)	0.05 (1.30)
Service Limit	0.008 (0.20)

NOTE: Obtain radio anti-theft code number before disconnecting battery. After service, turn radio on. When CODE appears, enter code to restore radio operation.

Removal (Legend) – 1) Disconnect battery cables. Remove strut bar. Drain transaxle fluid. Without removing vacuum lines, remove emission control box and set it aside. Unplug harness connectors (if necessary). Remove transmission housing bolts.

2) Remove release cylinder hose bracket from rear engine hanger. Remove exhaust pipe and catalytic converter. Remove secondary cover and 36-mm sealing bolt. *See Fig. 4.* Remove heat shield and bracket. Shift transmission into first gear to lock secondary gear. Using Puller (07LAC-PW50100), separate extension shaft from differential. *See Fig. 5.* Disconnect shift rod and torque rod from transmission. Remove clutch release fork cover. Remove clutch release cylinder. Disconnect oil cooler hoses from oil pump pipes.

3) Remove lower engine shield. Temporarily reinstall steering gear bolts. Remove exhaust pipe bracket, transmission mount, and transmission bracket. Pull out release fork to disengage it from pivot and release bearing. Let fork hang from housing.

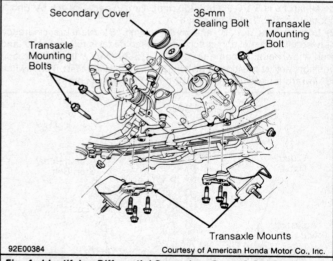

Secondary Cover — 36-mm Sealing Bolt — Transaxle Mounting Bolt — Transaxle Mounting Bolts — Transaxle Mounts

92E00384   Courtesy of American Honda Motor Co., Inc.

Fig. 4: Identifying Differential Secondary Cover & Sealing Bolt (Legend)

4) Place jack under transmission. Remove transmission mounts. Remove engine-to-transmission bracket. Remove flywheel inspection cover. Remove transmission housing mounting bolts and 26-mm shim. *See Fig. 6.* Check for wires, hoses, or any other components that may still be attached. Pull transmission away from engine until clear. Lower transmission to remove from vehicle.

5) If reusing clutch, mark pressure plate and flywheel for installation reference. Unscrew pressure plate bolts 2 turns at a time in a crisscross pattern. If necessary, remove flywheel and clutch pilot bearing.

Inspection – 1) Inspect pressure plate surface for wear, cracks, burning, or warpage in excess of 0.006" (0.15 mm). Measure warpage with straightedge and feeler gauge at several different points. Inspect clutch pilot bearing for smooth operation. Clutch release bearing must turn smoothly. Replace bearings if necessary.

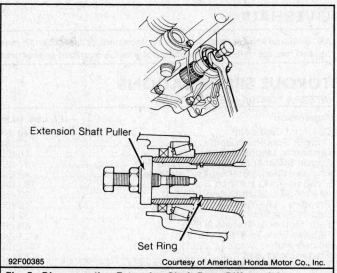

Fig. 5: Disconnecting Extension Shaft From Differential (Legend Shown; Vigor Is Similar)

92F00385   Courtesy of American Honda Motor Co., Inc.

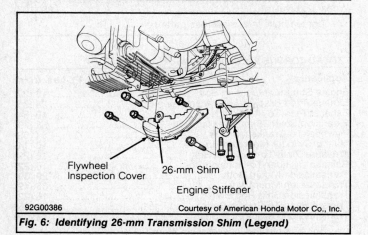

Fig. 6: Identifying 26-mm Transmission Shim (Legend)

92G00386   Courtesy of American Honda Motor Co., Inc.

2) Inspect clutch disc lining for excessive wear and burned or oil-soaked condition. Measure disc thickness and rivet depth. Inspect clutch disc for loose torsion dampers. Measure clutch disc and flywheel runout. Replace clutch disc if it is not within specifications. See CLUTCH SPECIFICATIONS table.

Installation – 1) Using Driver (07749-0010000) and Attachment (07746-0010200), install new pilot bearing into flywheel. Align hole in flywheel with crankshaft dowel pin. Install flywheel.

2) Tighten flywheel bolts to specification in a crisscross pattern. Align clutch cover dowel holes with dowels in flywheel. Using clutch alignment tool and ring gear holder, install clutch disc and pressure plate. Tighten bolts to specification in a crisscross pattern. See TORQUE SPECIFICATIONS.

3) Ensure both dowel pins are installed in clutch housing. Clean release bearing sliding surface. Apply molybdenum disulfide grease to contact surface. Apply a light coating of molybdenum disulfide grease to input shaft splines.

4) Keep clutch disc and pressure plate surfaces free of grease and dirt. Apply High Temp Urea Grease (08798-9002) to extension shaft splines. Install new extension shaft set ring. Ensure open slot in set ring is facing upward.

5) Using Extension Shaft Installer (07MAF-PY40100), install extension shaft. Ensure set ring locks into extension shaft groove. Install 36-mm sealing bolt and tighten it to specification. See TORQUE SPECIFICATIONS.

6) To complete installation, reverse removal procedure. Refill all fluids to proper level. Adjust clutch pedal travel and height. See CLUTCH PEDAL TRAVEL & HEIGHT under ADJUSTMENTS.

NOTE: Obtain radio anti-theft code number before disconnecting battery. After service, turn radio on. When CODE appears, enter code to restore radio operation.

Removal (Vigor) – 1) Remove battery and battery tray. Remove ABS relay box, located near corner of battery. Leave wiring harness connected to relay box. Remove heat shield. Remove distributor, leaving wiring connected. Remove control box, leaving vacuum hoses connected.

2) Unplug back-up switch connector. Disconnect transmission ground wire. Remove clutch release cylinder. Remove transmission housing bolts and 26-mm shim. Remove transmission mount beam and transmission mount bracket. Remove secondary cover and 33-mm sealing bolt.

3) Shift transmission into low gear. Using Extension Shaft Puller (07LAC-PW50100), disengage extension shaft from differential. See Fig. 5. Remove exhaust pipe and exhaust pipe brace. Remove shift rod and extension rod. See Fig. 7. Remove transmission mount nuts. Place jack under transmission. Remove transmission mounts. See Fig. 8.

4) Remove clutch housing cover. Remove transmission housing bolt. Pull transmission away from engine until clear. Lower transmission from vehicle to remove.

5) If reusing clutch, mark pressure plate and flywheel for installation reference. Install flywheel holder. Unscrew pressure plate bolts 2 turns at a time in a crisscross pattern.

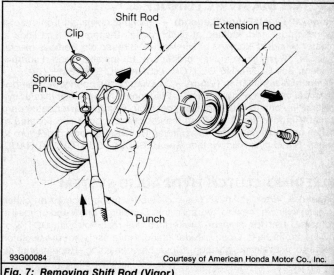

93G00084   Courtesy of American Honda Motor Co., Inc.

Fig. 7: Removing Shift Rod (Vigor)

Inspection – 1) Inspect pressure plate surface for wear, cracks, burning and warpage in excess of 0.006" (0.15 mm). Measure warpage with straightedge and feeler gauge at several different points. Check clutch pilot bearing for smooth operation. Clutch release bearing must turn smoothly. Replace bearings if necessary.

2) Inspect clutch disc lining for excessive wear and burned or oil-soaked condition. Measure disc thickness and rivet depth. Inspect clutch disc for loose torsion dampers. Measure disc runout and flywheel runout. Replace clutch disc if it does not meet specifications. See CLUTCH SPECIFICATIONS table.

Installation – 1) Ensure both locating dowels are in place. Pack clutch release bearing, release fork, and release guide with molybdenum disulfide grease. Apply high temperature molybdenum disulfide grease to extension shaft splines. Pack secondary gear and extension shaft cavity with high temperature molybdenum disulfide grease.

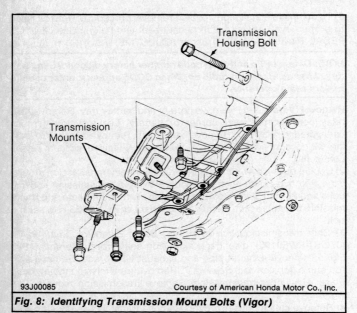

Fig. 8: Identifying Transmission Mount Bolts (Vigor)

Transmission Housing Bolt

Transmission Mounts

93J00085

Courtesy of American Honda Motor Co., Inc.

2) Install new shift rod retainer pin and extension shaft retaining ring. Turn release fork upward, then guide it into groove on release bearing. To complete installation, reverse removal procedure. Tighten bolts to specification. See TORQUE SPECIFICATIONS.

CLUTCH MASTER CYLINDER

Removal & Installation (Legend) – Remove clevis pin from master cylinder push rod, located at clutch pedal. Disconnect fluid lines at master cylinder. Plug end of line from fluid reservoir. Remove master cylinder. Reverse removal procedure to install. Bleed hydraulic system. See BLEEDING CLUTCH HYDRAULIC SYSTEM.

Removal & Installation (Vigor) – Leaving hoses connected, remove charcoal canister and set it aside. Disconnect fluid lines at master cylinder. Plug end of line from fluid reservoir. Remove lower dashboard panel. Remove clevis pin from master cylinder push rod, located at clutch pedal. Remove master cylinder. Reverse removal procedure to install. Bleed hydraulic system. See BLEEDING CLUTCH HYDRAULIC SYSTEM.

BLEEDING CLUTCH HYDRAULIC SYSTEM

Legend & Vigor – Attach hose to bleeder fitting, located on clutch release cylinder, next to hydraulic line. Submerge other end of hose in container half full of clean brake fluid. Fill reservoir with DOT 3 or DOT 4 brake fluid. Open bleeder fitting. Have assistant press clutch pedal to full release position. Close bleeder fitting. Repeat until air bubbles no longer emerge from hose. Refill reservoir

OVERHAUL

NOTE: Manufacturer recommends replacement of faulty clutch master and release cylinders and does not provide overhaul procedures.

TORQUE SPECIFICATIONS
INTEGRA TORQUE SPECIFICATIONS

Application	Ft. Lbs. (N.m)
Ball Joint Castle Nut	40 (54)
Damper Fork Pinch Bolt	47 (64)
Distributor Mounting Bolt	16 (22)
Engine Stiffener Bracket-To-Engine Bolt	17 (23)
Engine Stiffener Bracket-To-Transaxle Bolt	42 (57)
Flywheel-To-Crankshaft Bolt [1]	76 (103)
Intermediate Shaft Support Bolt	29 (39)
Pressure Plate-To-Flywheel Bolt [1]	19 (26)
Radius Arm Nut	32 (43)
Rear Mount-To-Transaxle Bolt	43 (58)
Release Fork-To-Transaxle Bolt	21 (28)
Spindle Nut	134 (182)
Starter Motor Bolt	32 (43)
Transaxle Mounting Bolt/Nut (Firewall Side)	54 (73)
Transaxle Mounting Bolt/Nut (Front)	47 (64)
Transaxle-To-Engine Mounting Bolt	42 (57)
Transaxle Torque Rod Bolt	16 (22)
Wheel Lug Nut	80 (108)

[1] – Tighten bolts in a crisscross pattern.

LEGEND TORQUE SPECIFICATIONS

Application	Ft. Lbs. (N.m)
Engine Stiffener Mounting Bolt	16 (22)
Exhaust Pipe Bracket-To-Transmission Bolt	26 (35)
Exhaust Pipe-To-Manifold Nut	40 (54)
Extension Shaft 36-mm Sealing Bolt	58 (79)
Flywheel-To-Crankshaft Bolt [1]	76 (103)
Master Cylinder Mounting Bolt	10 (14)
Pressure Plate-To-Flywheel Bolt [1]	16 (22)
Release Cylinder-To-Housing Bolt	16 (22)
Transmission Mount Bolt	29 (39)
Transmission Mount Nut	36 (49)
Transmission Shift Rod Bolt	16 (22)
Transmission-To-Engine Bolt	55 (75)
Transmission Torque Rod Bolt	16 (22)

[1] – Tighten bolts in a crisscross pattern.

VIGOR TORQUE SPECIFICATIONS

Application	Ft. Lbs. (N.m)
Exhaust Pipe Bracket Bolt	16 (22)
Exhaust Manifold Nut	40 (54)
Extension Shaft Sealing Bolt	58 (79)
Flywheel-To-Crankshaft Bolt [1]	76 (103)
Pressure Plate-To-Flywheel Bolt [1]	19 (26)
Release Cylinder Bolt	16 (22)
Torque Rod Bolt	16 (22)
Transmission Mount Nut	36 (49)
Transmission Shift Rod Bolt	16 (22)
Transmission-To-Engine Bolt	55 (75)

[1] – Tighten bolts in a crisscross pattern.

Integra, Legend, Vigor

DESCRIPTION & OPERATION

Each axle shaft consists of a shaft and a Constant Velocity (CV) joint at each end. Inner CV joint is splined to transaxle. Outer CV joint is splined to hub assembly and secured by a spindle nut. Inner and outer CV joints are enclosed by boots. Inner CV joints can be repaired; outer CV joints can be serviced only as an assembly.

TROUBLE SHOOTING

NOTE: See TROUBLE SHOOTING article in GENERAL INFORMATION.

REMOVAL, DISASSEMBLY, REASSEMBLY & INSTALLATION

FWD AXLE SHAFTS

Removal – **1)** Pry lock tab away from spindle nut. Loosen spindle nut and wheel lug nuts. Raise and support vehicle. Drain transaxle fluid. On Integra and Legend, draining transaxle fluid is not necessary if removing only left axle shaft. On Vigor, draining transaxle fluid is not necessary if removing only right axle shaft. On all models, remove front wheels and spindle nut. Remove damper pinch bolt and damper fork bolt. Remove damper fork. See Fig. 1.

2) Remove lower ball joint cotter pin. Back off castle nut until outer surface is flush with end of stud. Using ball joint puller, separate ball joint from lower control arm. Remove ball joint castle nut and ball joint from lower control arm. Pull steering knuckle outward. Remove axle shaft from hub assembly. If necessary, use plastic mallet to drive axle from hub.

NOTE: DO NOT pull on inner CV joint; it may come apart. Be careful not to damage seals.

---

3) Using a large screwdriver, carefully pry inner CV joint and shaft assembly outward to disengage retaining ring from groove at end of inner drive axle. Grip both sides of inner CV joint, and remove axle shaft and CV joint from vehicle.

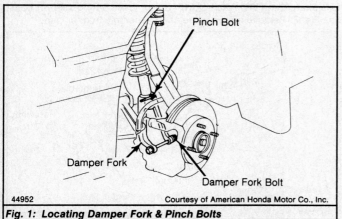

44952   Courtesy of American Honda Motor Co., Inc.

Fig. 1: Locating Damper Fork & Pinch Bolts

NOTE: DO NOT disassemble outer CV joint. If service is necessary, replace it as an assembly. On inner CV joint, mark rollers and roller grooves for reassembly reference.

Disassembly – **1)** Remove axle shaft from vehicle, and place on work bench. Remove and discard inner CV joint boot clamps. Slide boot toward outer CV joint for access to inner CV joint. See Fig. 2.

2) Mark axle shaft, inner CV joint housing, and spider roller for reassembly reference. Remove housing from spider assembly. Mark rollers and spider for reassembly reference. Remove rollers from spider.

3) Remove snap ring retaining spider to axle shaft. Remove spider. Remove stopper ring. Slide boot from axle shaft. Remove outer CV joint boot clamps. Slide boot from axle shaft inner CV joint end.

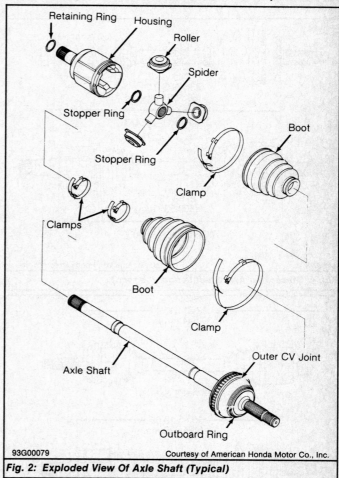

93G00079   Courtesy of American Honda Motor Co., Inc.

Fig. 2: Exploded View Of Axle Shaft (Typical)

Reassembly – **1)** Thoroughly clean axle shaft, and inspect for wear. Replace all defective parts. Wrap axle shaft splines with vinyl tape to prevent damage to CV joint boots.

2) Install inner and outer CV joint boots. Remove vinyl tape from axle shaft. DO NOT install CV joint boot clamps yet.

3) Install stopper ring into groove on axle shaft. Install spider onto axle shaft with reference marks aligned. Install snap ring into groove. Pack outer CV joint boot with grease supplied with joint kit. Lubricate spider and inner bore of rollers.

4) Align rollers with marks made at disassembly. Ensure high sides of rollers face outward. Install rollers. Pack inner CV joint and boot with grease. Install housing onto spider assembly. Align reference marks made at disassembly while installing housing onto spider assembly. Adjust length of axle shaft. See Fig. 3, 4 or 5.

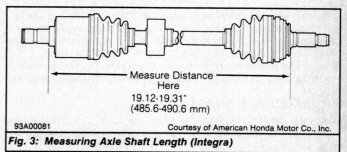

93A00081   Courtesy of American Honda Motor Co., Inc.

Fig. 3: Measuring Axle Shaft Length (Integra)

5) Position boots halfway between full compression and full extension. Install new boot clamps. Lightly tap boot clamp to reduce clamp height. Install new retaining ring onto end of inner CV joint. Install axle shaft.

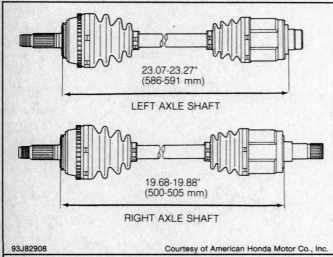

93J82908   Courtesy of American Honda Motor Co., Inc.
Fig. 4: Measuring Axle Shaft Length (Legend)

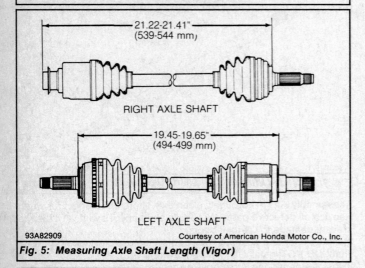

93A82909   Courtesy of American Honda Motor Co., Inc.
Fig. 5: Measuring Axle Shaft Length (Vigor)

CAUTION: Always use a NEW retaining ring when installing axle shaft.

Installation – 1) Ensure length of assembled axle shaft is within specification. See Fig. 3, 4 or 5. Install new retaining ring into groove at end of axle shaft. Install new clamps onto boots.
2) Slide axle into transaxle or intermediate shaft. Seat retaining ring fully into groove. Check by attempting to pull axle out of installed position.
3) Pull hub assembly away from axle shaft. Slide axle into hub assembly. Install and lightly tighten spindle nut. Position ball joint into hub. Raise lower control arm with floor jack. Install ball joint nut. Tighten ball joint nut to specification. See TORQUE SPECIFICATIONS.
4) Install and secure cotter pin. Remove floor jack. Tighten spindle nut to specification. To complete installation, reverse removal procedure.

INTERMEDIATE SHAFT

Removal (Integra) – 1) Drain fluid from transaxle. Remove left axle shaft. See FWD AXLE SHAFTS. Remove bearing support bolts. See Fig. 6.

CAUTION: To prevent damaging oil seal when removing intermediate shaft, hold shaft in horizontal position until shaft is clear of seal.

2) Lower bearing support. Remove intermediate shaft from differential. To prevent damage to seal, hold intermediate shaft in horizontal position when removing.

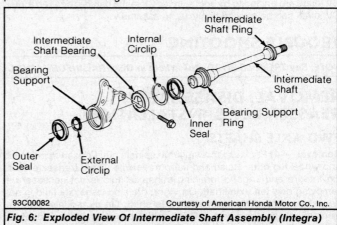

93C00082   Courtesy of American Honda Motor Co., Inc.
Fig. 6: Exploded View Of Intermediate Shaft Assembly (Integra)

Disassembly – Remove intermediate shaft outer seal. Remove external circlip. Press intermediate shaft from shaft bearing. Remove intermediate shaft inner seal. Remove internal circlip. Press intermediate shaft bearing from bearing support. Inspect all components for wear or damage. Replace as necessary.
Reassembly – 1) Press intermediate shaft bearing into bearing support. Seat internal circlip into groove of bearing support. Install circlip so tapered end faces outward.
2) Press intermediate shaft inner seal into bearing support. Press intermediate shaft into shaft bearing. Install external circlip into intermediate shaft groove so tapered end faces outward. Press outer seal into bearing support.
Installation – To install, reverse removal procedure. Refill transaxle.
Removal (Legend & Vigor) – Drain fluid from transaxle. Remove left axle shaft. See FWD AXLE SHAFTS. Remove bearing support bolts. See Fig. 7. Remove intermediate shaft assembly from oil pan.

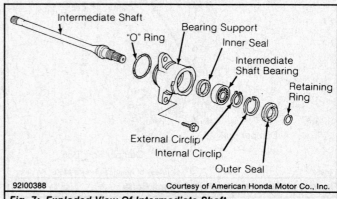

92I00388   Courtesy of American Honda Motor Co., Inc.
Fig. 7: Exploded View Of Intermediate Shaft (Legend Shown; Vigor Is Similar)

CAUTION: Bearing support is made of aluminum. DO NOT overstess when servicing intermediate shaft.

Disassembly – Remove intermediate shaft outer seal from bearing support. Remove external and internal circlips. Press intermediate shaft from shaft bearing. Press intermediate shaft bearing from bearing support. Remove intermediate shaft inner seal from bearing support. Remove "O" ring. Inspect all components for wear or damage. Replace as necessary.

Reassembly – 1) Press intermediate shaft inner seal into bearing support. Seat internal circlip into bearing support groove so tapered end faces outward.

2) Press intermediate shaft into shaft bearing. Install external circlip into intermediate shaft groove so tapered end faces outward. On Legend, press in seal until it is flush with bearing support. On Vigor, press seal into bearing support until seal is 0.28" (7 mm) from end of bearing support.

Installation – To install, reverse removal procedure. Refill transaxle.

TORQUE SPECIFICATIONS
TORQUE SPECIFICATIONS

Application	Ft. Lbs. (N.m)
Integra	
Ball Joint Nut	41 (55)
Damper Fork Bolt	48 (65)
Damper Pinch Bolt	32 (44)
Intermediate Shaft Bearing Support Bolts	29 (40)
Spindle Nut	136 (185)
Wheel Lug Nut	81 (110)
Legend	
Ball Joint Nut	52-59 (70-80)
Damper Fork Bolt	52 (70)
Damper Pinch Bolt	37 (50)
Intermediate Shaft Bearing Support Bolts	16 (22)
Spindle Nut	240 (325)
Wheel Lug Nut	81 (110)
Vigor	
Ball Joint Nuts	37-44 (50-60)
Damper Fork Bolt	48 (65)
Damper Fork Pinch Bolt	32 (44)
Intermediate Shaft Bearing Support Bolts	16 (22)
Spindle Nut	184 (250)
Wheel Lug Nut	81 (110)

Legend

DESCRIPTION

Although Legend has FWD, it is equipped with a separate differential assembly that is bolted to right side of engine oil pan and to transaxle. Differential assembly is linked internally to transaxle by an extension shaft.

AXLE RATIO

Axle ratio is determined by dividing number of ring gear teeth by number of drive pinion teeth.

AXLE RATIO SPECIFICATIONS

Application	Ratio
Automatic Transaxle (A/T)	4.35:1
Manual Transaxle (M/T)	4.48:1

LUBRICATION

CAPACITY

DIFFERENTIAL OIL CAPACITY & TYPE

Qt. (L)	Type
1.11 (1.05) After Drain	[1] API GL-4 Or GL-5 SAE 90
1.16 (1.10) After Overhaul	[1] API GL-4 Or GL-5 SAE 90

[1] – Below 0°F (–18°C), use API GL-4 or GL-5 SAE 80 or SAE 80W 90.

TROUBLE SHOOTING

NOTE: See TROUBLE SHOOTING article in GENERAL INFORMATION.

REMOVAL & INSTALLATION

DIFFERENTIAL CARRIER

Removal – 1) Disconnect negative battery cable. Raise and support vehicle. Drain cooling system. Drain differential fluid. Remove drive axles and intermediate shaft. See FWD AXLE SHAFTS article in DRIVE AXLES. Remove lower engine splash shield.

NOTE: Reinstall steering gearbox mounting bolts after removing engine splash shield.

2) Disconnect differential cooler hoses at joint pipes. Remove speed sensor without removing hydraulic lines and set aside. Remove secondary cover 36-mm sealing bolt from transaxle. *See Fig. 1.* Shift transaxle into 1st gear or Park to lock secondary gear.
3) Using Extension Shaft Puller (07LAC-PW50100), disconnect extension shaft from differential. Remove and discard set ring. Note location of 26-mm shim. *See Fig. 2.* Remove differential carrier mounting bolts, shim, and carrier.
Installation – 1) To install, reverse removal procedure. Install new oil pan-to-differential "O" ring. Install differential carrier. Using a feeler gauge, measure clearance between differential and transaxle. *See Fig. 3.* Use clearance measurement to determine appropriate shim to be installed.
2) Shims are available in 0.004" (0.10 mm) increments, ranging from 0.0748" (1.900 mm) to 0.1181" (3.000 mm). Tighten bolt retaining shim first, then tighten remaining carrier bolts. Apply High Temp Urea Grease (08798-9002) to extension shaft splines. Install new extension shaft set ring.
3) Ensure open slot of set ring faces up. Using Installer (07MAF-PY40100), install extension shaft. Ensure set ring locks into extension shaft groove. Apply high temperature urea grease around end of extension shaft.
4) Coat threads with Loctite and install 36-mm sealing bolt. Tighten bolt to specification. See TORQUE SPECIFICATIONS. Replenish all fluids.

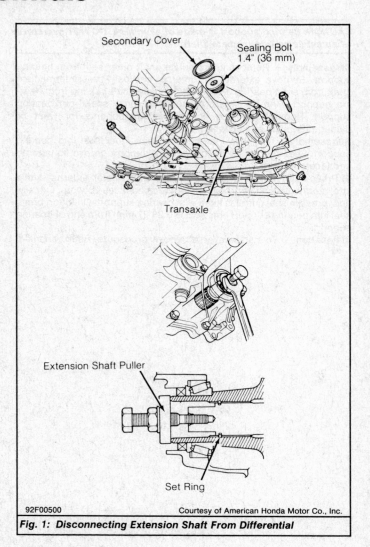

92F00500   Courtesy of American Honda Motor Co., Inc.

Fig. 1: Disconnecting Extension Shaft From Differential

OVERHAUL

DISASSEMBLY & INSPECTION

CAUTION: Mark thrust shims for reassembly reference. Shims must be installed in original location.

NOTE: To establish a starting point before disassembly, measure backlash and preload, and check gear contact.

Differential Assembly – 1) With differential assembly removed from vehicle, remove oil filler plug and differential cover oil seal. Place differential carrier into soft-jawed vise. Align differential gear inspection hole with oil filler plug hole. Using dial indicator, Lock Nut Wrench (07LAA-SM40200), and ratchet, measure and record ring gear backlash. *See Fig. 4.*
2) Rotate drive pinion with torque wrench to measure total preload. Preload should be 12.1-17.7 INCH lbs. (1.37-2.00 N.m) for manual transmission, or 21.3-26.9 INCH lbs. (2.41-3.04 N.m) for automatic transmission.
3) Loosen differential case cover in a crisscross pattern. Remove differential case cover. Clean gear teeth, then coat lightly with Prussian Blue dye on both sides of each gear tooth. Reinstall cover. Tighten bolts in a crisscross pattern to 33 ft. lbs. (45 N.m). Using Locknut

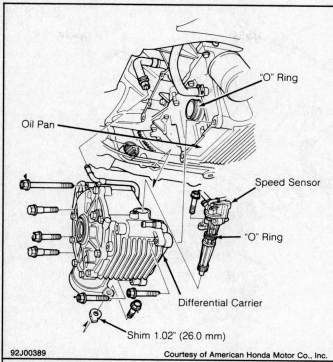

Fig. 2: Removing Differential Carrier

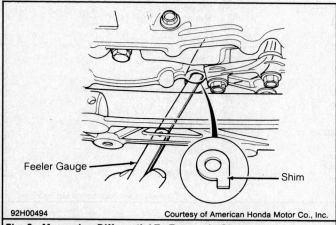

Fig. 3: Measuring Differential-To-Transaxle Clearance

Wrench (07HAA-SF10100), rotate ring gear one full turn while applying resistance to drive pinion. Remove differential case cover and check tooth contact pattern. See GEAR TOOTH CONTACT PATTERNS article in GENERAL INFORMATION.

4) On M/T vehicles, use Attachment (07GAD-PG40100) and Driver (07749-0010000) to remove outer bearing race and 79.5-mm shims from differential cover. On A/T vehicles, pry up on bearing race, or heat differential housing to maximum of 212°F (100°C) to remove race.

CAUTION: On A/T vehicles, DO NOT reuse thrust shim(s) if prying method was used to remove bearing race.

---

5) On all vehicles, remove breather plate from differential cover. *See Fig. 5.* Remove differential case assembly from carrier. Invert carrier and remove oil cooler lines from carrier. Remove nuts securing oil cooler. Remove oil cooler, "O" rings, and oil guide pipe.

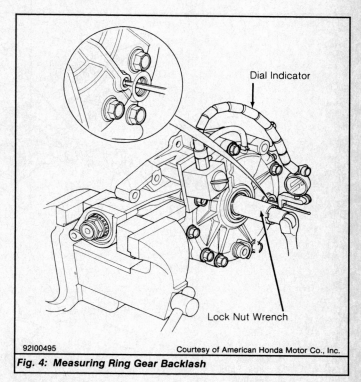

Fig. 4: Measuring Ring Gear Backlash

6) Hold drive pinion with 17-mm hex wrench and vise. *See Fig. 6.* Raise pinion shaft lock nut tab from groove on pinion drive gear. Remove lock nut, thrust washer, and pinion hub. Remove drive pinion oil seal, thrust washer, and bearing.

7) Remove drive pinion, pinion spacer, and thrust washer. On M/T vehicles, use a punch to remove inner and outer bearing races from carrier. On A/T vehicles, pry out bearing race, or heat differential housing to maximum of 212°F (100°C) to remove outer and inner bearing races.

CAUTION: On A/T vehicles, DO NOT reuse thrust shim(s) if bearing race was removed by prying.

---

8) On all vehicles, use bearing separator and hydraulic press to remove differential case bearings. Install left axle shaft and intermediate shaft into differential case. Set differential case onto "V" blocks. Measure backlash at both pinion gears. If pinion backlash exceeds 0.012" (0.30 mm), replace differential assembly.

9) Remove ring gear from differential case. Remove roll pin from pinion shaft. Keeping in order of removal, remove pinion shaft, pinion gears, side gears, thrust washers, and thrust shims. Clean all parts thoroughly in solvent. Blow dry with compressed air. Inspect parts for wear or damage. Replace if necessary.

NOTE: If replacement of ring gear or pinion is necessary, replace drive pinion and ring gear as a set.

REASSEMBLY

Differential Case – 1) Coat differential side gears on both sides with molybdenum disulfide grease. Install gears and thrust shims into differential case. Coat pinion gears with grease. Install gears and thrust washers into differential case. Pinion thrust washers must be of equal thickness.

2) Rotate gears until shaft holes in pinion gears align with shaft holes in differential case. Install pinion shaft, and align roll pin holes in shaft with hole in case. Install new roll pin into pinion shaft.

3) Measure pinion gear backlash. See step **1)** under DISASSEMBLY & INSPECTION. Install ring gear. Tighten bolts to specification. See TORQUE SPECIFICATIONS. Using hydraulic press and Attachment (07MAD-PR90100), install side bearings into differential case.

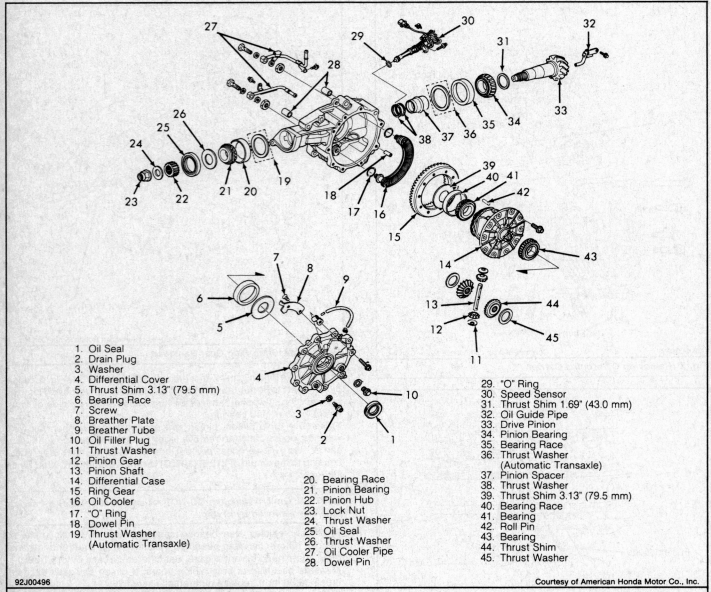

1. Oil Seal
2. Drain Plug
3. Washer
4. Differential Cover
5. Thrust Shim 3.13" (79.5 mm)
6. Bearing Race
7. Screw
8. Breather Plate
9. Breather Tube
10. Oil Filler Plug
11. Thrust Washer
12. Pinion Gear
13. Pinion Shaft
14. Differential Case
15. Ring Gear
16. Oil Cooler
17. "O" Ring
18. Dowel Pin
19. Thrust Washer
   (Automatic Transaxle)

20. Bearing Race
21. Pinion Bearing
22. Pinion Hub
23. Lock Nut
24. Thrust Washer
25. Oil Seal
26. Thrust Washer
27. Oil Cooler Pipe
28. Dowel Pin

29. "O" Ring
30. Speed Sensor
31. Thrust Shim 1.69" (43.0 mm)
32. Oil Guide Pipe
33. Drive Pinion
34. Pinion Bearing
35. Bearing Race
36. Thrust Washer
   (Automatic Transaxle)
37. Pinion Spacer
38. Thrust Washer
39. Thrust Shim 3.13" (79.5 mm)
40. Bearing Race
41. Bearing
42. Roll Pin
43. Bearing
44. Thrust Shim
45. Thrust Washer

92J00496   Courtesy of American Honda Motor Co., Inc.

Fig. 5: Exploded View Of Differential Assembly

NOTE: Manufacturer recommends measuring drive pinion depth only when installing new drive pinion and ring gear.

Drive Pinion Inner Bearing – If installing new drive pinion and ring gear, measure drive pinion depth before installing inner bearing. See DRIVE PINION DEPTH under ADJUSTMENTS. Install 43-mm thrust shim and roller bearing onto drive pinion. Using used pinion spacer, Attachment (07746-0030400), Driver (07746-0030100), and hydraulic press, install bearing. *See Fig. 7.* Discard used spacer after installing bearing.

Differential Carrier – 1) To install pinion bearing races, assemble thrust washers (A/T), thrust shim, bearing races, Bearing Race Installers (07MAF-SP00110 and 07MAF-SP00120), Shaft (07JAF-SJ80110), and Nut (07JAF-SJ80120). Install races. *See Fig. 8.*
2) Using Attachment (07GAD-SD40101) and Driver (07749-0010000), drive side bearing race into differential carrier. Lubricate drive pinion inner bearing. Assemble new pinion spacer and thrust washers onto drive pinion. Install drive pinion into differential carrier.

3) Install outer drive pinion bearing, pinion hub, and thrust washer. Tighten drive pinion nut to 162 ft. lbs. (220 N.m). Measure torque necessary to rotate drive pinion. Tighten drive pinion nut a little at a time until torque necessary to rotate drive pinion is as specified. See DRIVE PINION BEARING PRELOAD SPECIFICATIONS table. Pinion nut torque should be between 162-236 ft. lbs. (220-320 N.m).
4) If preload exceeds specification, replace drive pinion spacer, and remeasure preload. With preload properly adjusted, record pinion nut torque obtained during preload adjustment.

DRIVE PINION BEARING PRELOAD SPECIFICATIONS [1]

Application	INCH Lbs. (N.m)
Manual Transmission	
New Bearings	8.2-13.9 (0.93-1.57)
Old Bearings	6.4-10.7 (0.72-1.21)
Automatic Transmission	
New Bearings	16.5-22.5 (1.86-2.54)
Old Bearings	12.8-17.3 (1.45-1.95)

[1] – Specification is with differential case removed from carrier.

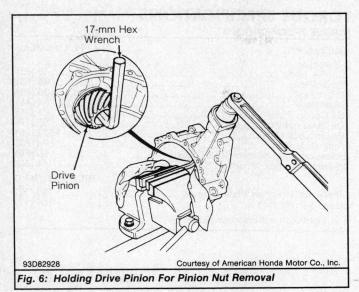

Fig. 6: Holding Drive Pinion For Pinion Nut Removal

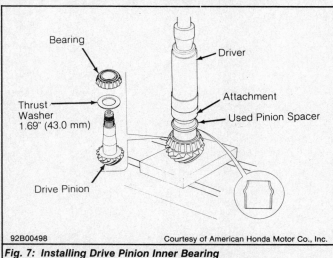

Fig. 7: Installing Drive Pinion Inner Bearing

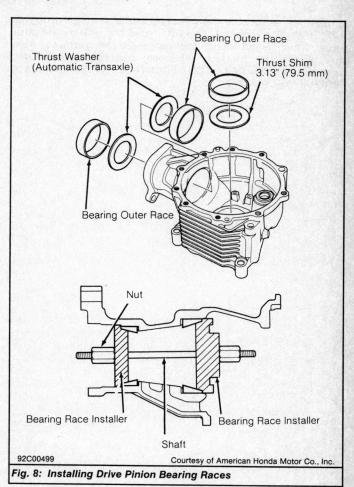

Fig. 8: Installing Drive Pinion Bearing Races

5) Clean gear teeth, then coat lightly with Prussian Blue dye on both sides of each gear tooth. Reinstall cover. Tighten bolts in a crisscross pattern to 33 ft. lbs. (45 N.m). Using Locknut Wrench (07HAA-SF10100), rotate ring gear one full turn in each direction while applying resistance to drive pinion. Remove differential case cover and check tooth contact pattern. See GEAR TOOTH CONTACT PATTERNS article in GENERAL INFORMATION.

6) Mark pinion lock nut-to-drive pinion location. Remove pinion lock nut, thrust washer, and pinion hub. Using Attachment (07MAD-SP00200) and Driver (07749-0010000), install pinion oil seal.

7) Drive seal into carrier until distance between top of seal and face of differential carrier is 0.61-.63" (15.5-16.0 mm) on A/T vehicles or 0.22-0.24" (5.5-6.0 mm) on M/T vehicles.

8) Install pinion hub, thrust washer, and pinion lock nut. Tighten lock nut to torque value recorded in step **4)**. Ensure pinion lock nut-to-drive pinion marks align. Install new "O" rings onto oil cooler, and install cooler and oil guide pipe into differential carrier.

9) Tighten oil cooler retaining nuts to specification. See TORQUE SPECIFICATIONS. Using new washers, install oil cooler lines. Install differential case into carrier. Install breather plate in differential cover. Stake retaining screws.

10 Install original side bearing thrust shim into differential cover. Using Attachment (07GAD-SD40101) and Driver (07749-0010000), install side bearing race. Install differential cover. Tighten cover bolts in a crisscross pattern to specification. See TORQUE SPECIFICATIONS.

11) Mount differential assembly in soft-jawed vise. Measure ring gear backlash. *See Fig. 4.* If ring gear backlash is not 0.0024-0.0055" (0.061-0.140 mm), adjust backlash. See RING GEAR BACKLASH under ADJUSTMENTS.

12) With backlash adjustment completed, check tooth contact pattern. See GEAR TOOTH CONTACT PATTERNS article in GENERAL INFORMATION. Using Attachment (07965-SA00600) and Driver (07749-0010000), install oil seal into differential cover.

ADJUSTMENTS

DRIVE PINION DEPTH

1) To select proper drive pinion shim, calculate the difference in size between old shim and new drive pinion. A number with a plus (+) or a minus (–) is located on the drive pinion. If number on old drive pinion is a (+), add that number to old shim thickness and record number. If number on old drive pinion is a (–), subtract that number from old shim thickness and record number.

2) If number on new drive pinion is a (+), subtract that number from number recorded in step **1)**. If number on new drive pinion is a (–), add that number to number recorded in step **1)**.

3) Select a shim that is closest, but not more than, the final number recorded in step **2)**. Shim sizes are available in 0.001" (0.03 mm) increments, ranging from 0.0646" (1.641 mm) to 0.0894" (2.271 mm).

RING GEAR BACKLASH

1) If backlash exceeds 0.0024-0.0055" (0.061-0.140 mm), correct backlash by decreasing shim thickness on one side and increasing shim thickness on other side by the same amount. Shims are located behind side bearing races.

2) Total thickness of both shims must equal total thickness of original shims. If there is too much backlash, move ring gear toward drive pinion. If there is not enough backlash, move ring gear away from drive pinion. With backlash adjustment completed, check tooth contact pattern. See GEAR TOOTH CONTACT PATTERNS article in GENERAL INFORMATION.

TORQUE SPECIFICATIONS
TORQUE SPECIFICATIONS

Application	Ft. Lbs. (N.m)
Differential	
Carrier Bolts	48 (65)
Cover Bolts [1]	48 (65)
Drain Plug	30 (40)
Filler Plug	33 (45)
Oil Cooler Bolts	21 (29)
Oil Cooler Nuts	55 (75)
Pinion Lock Nut	162 (220)
Ring Gear Bolt	89 (120)
Extension Shaft 36-mm Sealing Bolt	59 (80)
Steering Gearbox Mounting Bolts	44 (60)
	INCH Lbs. (N.m)
Differential Breather Plate Screws	106 (12)
Speed Sensor Bolt	106 (12)

[1] – Tighten in a crisscross pattern.

Integra, Legend, Vigor

DESCRIPTION

Integra, Legend, and Vigor are equipped with front and rear disc brakes. A cable operates parking brake at rear wheels.

WARNING: DO NOT use air pressure or a dry brush to clean brake assemblies. Avoid breathing brake dust. Use OSHA-approved vacuum cleaner for cleaning and dust collection. Avoid contaminating brake pads and discs with brake fluid or grease.

BLEEDING BRAKE SYSTEM

BLEEDING PROCEDURES

CAUTION: Use only clean brake fluid. Ensure no dirt or other foreign matter contaminates brake fluid. DO NOT mix different brands of brake fluid as they may not be compatible. Avoid spilling brake fluid on car, as it will damage paint. If brake fluid contacts paint, immediately flush with water.

1) Reservoir on master cylinder must be full at start of bleeding procedure. Refill reservoir after bleeding each wheel. With aid of assistant, slowly pump brake pedal several times; then apply steady pressure. Loosen brake bleed screw to allow air to escape from system.
2) Tighten bleed screw securely. Repeat procedure for each wheel in the following sequence:
- Right Rear
- Left Front
- Left Rear
- Right Front
3) Road test vehicle and check brake performance.

ADJUSTMENTS

PEDAL PLAY & HEIGHT

1) Measure pedal height from center of pedal pad to floorboard, with carpet removed. To adjust pedal height, loosen stoplight switch lock nut and back switch away from brake pedal arm.
2) Loosen power brake unit push rod lock nut, and rotate push rod to adjust pedal height. See BRAKE PEDAL HEIGHT table.
3) Tighten lock nut. Adjust stoplight switch. After adjustment, brake pedal free play should be 0.04-0.20" (1.0-5.0 mm).

BRAKE PEDAL HEIGHT

Application	In. (mm)
Integra	
Automatic Transaxle	6.3 (160)
Manual Transaxle	6.1 (155)
Legend	8.4 (213)
Vigor	
Automatic Transaxle	7.6 (194)
Manual Transaxle	7.8 (199)

STOPLIGHT SWITCH

Stoplight switch is located under dash, above brake pedal. To adjust switch, loosen lock nuts, then turn switch until plunger is fully inward, with threaded end touching pedal arm pad. Back off switch 1/2 turn, then tighten lock nuts. Check that brakelights go off when pedal is released.

PARKING BRAKE

Integra & Vigor – 1) Raise and support rear of vehicle. Ensure rear brake caliper lever contacts brake caliper pin. *See Fig. 1.* Pull parking brake lever up one notch.
2) Remove end panel from rear of parking brake lever cover. Tighten equalizer nut until rear wheels drag slightly when turned. Release brake lever. Rear wheels should rotate freely. Rear wheels should lock when lever is pulled up 6-10 clicks.

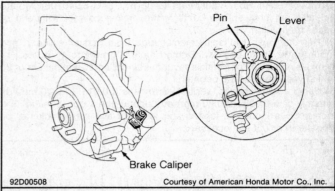

92D00508   Courtesy of American Honda Motor Co., Inc.

Fig. 1: Checking Brake Caliper Lever Position (Integra Shown; Vigor Is Similar)

Legend – 1) Parking brake shoes are located inside of rear brake disc. Parking brake should hold when parking brake lever is pulled up 8-12 clicks. If number of clicks to fully set brake is excessive, minor adjustments (1-2 clicks) can be made by adjusting equalizer. For minor adjustment, go to next step. For major adjustment, see step 3).
2) Remove end cover from parking brake console. Pull parking brake lever up one click. Raise and support rear of vehicle. Tighten equalizer adjusting nut until slight drag is felt when wheels are turned. Release parking brake lever. Wheels should not drag. Readjust if necessary. With equalizer properly adjusted, parking brake should be fully applied when parking brake lever is pulled 8-12 clicks.
3) Release parking brake lever. Remove end cover from parking brake console. Back off equalizer adjusting nut. Raise and support rear of vehicle. Remove rear wheels. Using brake spoon, turn adjuster up until brake shoes lock, and then back off 8 stops.
4) Tighten equalizer adjusting nut so parking brake is fully applied when parking brake lever is pulled up 8 to 12 clicks. Install rear wheels. Rear wheels should not drag when parking brake lever is released. Readjust if necessary. Install console rear cover.

BRAKE WARNING LIGHT

Brake warning light indicates parking brake is engaged and/or warns of low brake fluid level. To adjust parking brake light operation, remove center console. Turn ignition on. Bend switch plate downward until light comes on when parking brake lever is pulled one notch and goes out when lever is released.

MASTER CYLINDER PUSH ROD

NOTE: Master cylinder push rod-to-piston clearance must be checked and adjusted before installing master cylinder.

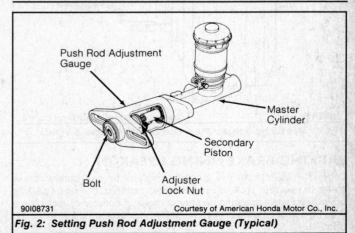

90I08731   Courtesy of American Honda Motor Co., Inc.

Fig. 2: Setting Push Rod Adjustment Gauge (Typical)

1) Mount Push Rod Adjustment Gauge (07JAG-SD40100). Rotate adjuster nut until end of center shaft makes contact with end of secondary piston. *See Fig. 2.*

2) Remove push rod adjustment gauge from master cylinder, and mount onto brake booster. Tighten mounting nuts to 11 ft. lbs. (15 N.m) Using engine or outside vacuum source, apply a minimum of 20 in. Hg vacuum to brake booster.

3) Using a feeler gauge, verify clearance is 0-0.016" (0-0.40 mm) on Integra, or 0-0.008" (0-0.20 mm) on Legend and Vigor. *See Fig. 3.* If clearance is incorrect, loosen star lock nut and rotate adjuster on booster in or out as necessary.

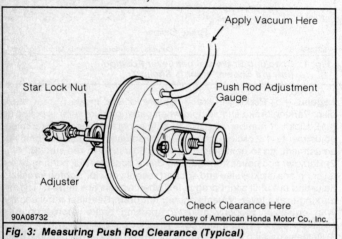

Fig. 3: Measuring Push Rod Clearance (Typical)

BRAKE BOOSTER PUSH ROD

Brake booster push rod length should be 4.58-4.62" (115.5-116.5 mm) on Integra and 4.78-4.82" (121.5-122.5 mm) on Vigor. *See Fig. 4.* On Legend, the booster push rod length is governed by pedal height adjustment.

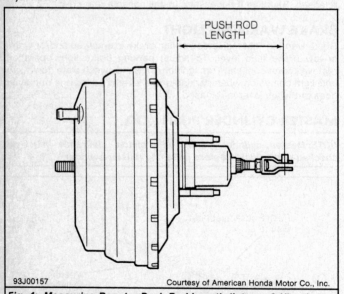

Fig. 4: Measuring Booster Push Rod Length (Integra & Vigor)

PARKING BRAKE LINING BREAK-IN

Legend – 1) Perform this procedure only when new parking brake shoes or new rear brake discs have been installed. Pull up on parking brake lever while counting number of clicks. If number of clicks is not 8 to 12, adjust parking brake. See PARKING BRAKE under ADJUSTMENTS.

2) With parking brake adjusted correctly, park car on firm, level surface. Tape end of parking brake release lever so release button is

held in. With help of an assistant, drive vehicle about 30 MPH for 1/4 mile while assistant pulls up on parking brake lever with a force of 20 lbs. (9 kg). Release parking brake lever. Park vehicle 5 to 10 minutes to allow brake discs to cool.

3) After cooling period, repeat step **2)**. Remove tape from parking brake lever. Check and adjust parking brake as necessary. See PARKING BRAKE under ADJUSTMENTS.

TESTING

POWER BRAKE UNIT

Functional Test – 1) Start engine. Turn ignition off. Press brake pedal several times. Press and hold pedal firmly for 15 seconds. If pedal sinks, master cylinder, brake line, or caliper piston is faulty.

2) Start engine with pedal pressed. If pedal sinks slightly, vacuum unit is working properly. If pedal height does not change, booster or check valve is faulty.

Leak Test – 1) Press brake pedal with engine running. Turn ignition off. If pedal height does not change while pressed for 30 seconds, vacuum booster is okay. If pedal rises, vacuum booster is leaking.

2) With engine stopped, press brake pedal several times with normal pressure. Pedal should be low when first pressed. On consecutive applications, pedal height should gradually increase. If pedal height does not change, check power brake booster check valve.

Check Valve Test – Disconnect power brake unit vacuum hose at booster. Start and idle engine. Check for vacuum at booster end of hose. If vacuum is not available, vacuum source or check valve is faulty. Repair vacuum source or replace check valve, and retest.

REMOVAL & INSTALLATION

FRONT DISC BRAKE PADS

Removal – 1) Raise and support front of vehicle. Remove wheels. Remove lower caliper guide pin. Pivot caliper body out of way, or remove caliper bolts.

2) Remove pads, pad shims, and pad retainers. Measure brake friction pad thickness. Minimum brake pad thickness is 0.063" (1.60 mm).

NOTE: Replace brake pads in axle sets. Do not allow grease, brake fluid, or other contaminants to contact lining surface. Inspect, clean, and resurface rotor as necessary.

Installation – 1) Lubricate shim and sliding surfaces with high-temperature silicone grease. Install pad retainers. Apply Molykote M77 compound to both sides of pad shims and back of pads.

2) Install inner and outer pad shims. Install brake pads. Install brake pad with pad wear indicator on the inside. Loosen bleeder screw. Install piston into caliper bore with finger pressure.

3) Tighten bleeder screw. Position caliper and install lower guide pin or caliper bolts. Press brake pedal several times to seat pads. Bleed brakes as necessary. See BLEEDING PROCEDURES under BLEEDING BRAKE SYSTEM.

REAR DISC BRAKE PADS

Removal (Integra & Vigor) – 1) Raise and support rear of vehicle. Remove wheels. Remove caliper shield. Disconnect parking brake cable by removing clip mounting cable to caliper (if necessary).

2) Pull out lock pin from caliper to cable attachment. Remove pin from caliper. Remove caliper mounting bolts. Remove caliper from bracket. Remove shims, brake pads, and retainers. Measure friction pad thickness. Service limit is 0.063" (1.6 mm).

Installation – 1) Apply Molykote M77 compound to both sides of inner and outer pad shims. Install brake pads and shims. Rotate caliper piston clockwise in caliper (if necessary). Align cut-out in piston with tab on inner pad.

2) Avoid twisting piston boot. Install brake caliper and parking brake cable. Pump brake pedal several times to seat pads. Bleed brakes as necessary. See BLEEDING PROCEDURES under BLEEDING BRAKE SYSTEM. Adjust parking brake if necessary.

Removal (Legend) – Raise and support rear of vehicle. Remove wheels. Loosen upper caliper mounting bolt. Remove lower caliper mounting bolt. Pivot caliper up out of way. Remove shims, pads, and retainers. Measure friction pad thickness. Service limit is 0.063" (1.6 mm).

Installation – Apply Molykote M77 compound to both sides of inner and outer pad shims. Install brake pads and shims. Push in piston so caliper will fit over rotor. Pivot brake caliper down into position. Install lower caliper mounting bolt. Tighten caliper mounting bolts to specification. See TORQUE SPECIFICATIONS. Pump brake pedal several times to seat pads.

FRONT DISC BRAKE CALIPER

Removal – Raise and support front of vehicle. Remove wheels. Disconnect brake line from caliper. Plug hydraulic line and caliper. Remove caliper mounting bolts and caliper. Remove pads, pad shims, and pad retainers.

Installation – To install, reverse removal procedure. Replace copper banjo bolt washers when connecting brake hose. Install brake pads. See FRONT DISC BRAKE PADS under REMOVAL & INSTALLATION. Bleed brake system. See BLEEDING PROCEDURES under BLEEDING BRAKE SYSTEM.

REAR DISC BRAKE CALIPER

Removal – Raise and support rear of vehicle. Remove wheels. Remove caliper shield (if equipped). On Integra, disconnect parking brake cable from caliper. On all models, disconnect brake hose from caliper. Plug hydraulic line and caliper. Remove caliper mounting bolts and caliper.

Installation – To install, reverse removal procedure. Replace copper banjo bolt washers when connecting brake hose. Install brake pads. See REAR DISC BRAKE PADS under REMOVAL & INSTALLATION. Bleed brake system. See BLEEDING PROCEDURES under BLEEDING BRAKE SYSTEM.

DISC BRAKE ROTOR

Removal (Front & Rear) – 1) Raise and support vehicle. Remove wheels. Remove caliper assembly, and wire aside. See FRONT DISC BRAKE CALIPER or REAR DISC BRAKE CALIPER under REMOVAL & INSTALLATION. Measure rotor runout before removal. Remove rotor retaining screws.

2) Install two 8 x 1.25 x 12 mm bolts into existing holes. To prevent warpage, turn bolts alternately 2 turns at a time until rotor can be removed from hub. Clean rust from rotor. Inspect rotor surfaces for cracks or grooves. Resurface or replace rotor as necessary.

Installation – To install, reverse removal procedure. Tighten retaining screws. Bleed hydraulic system (if necessary). See BLEEDING PROCEDURES under BLEEDING BRAKE SYSTEM.

MASTER CYLINDER & BOOSTER

CAUTION: DO NOT disassemble master cylinder or booster. Service these components as complete assemblies.

Removal & Installation (Integra) – 1) Empty brake fluid from master cylinder. Unplug brake fluid level switch connectors. Disconnect brake lines from master cylinder. Remove master cylinder mounting nuts and master cylinder. *See Fig. 5.* Disconnect vacuum hose from brake booster. Remove vacuum hose bracket.

2) On GSR models, loosen alternator belt adjuster nut and alternator nut. Move alternator toward engine, and temporarily tighten nuts. Remove bolts attaching power steering lines to left side of frame.

3) On all models, remove clevis pin from booster push rod. Remove booster mounting nuts and booster. To install, reverse removal procedure after checking push rod clearance and length. After installation, check and adjust pedal height. Fill and bleed brake system.

Removal & Installation (Legend) – *See Fig. 6.*

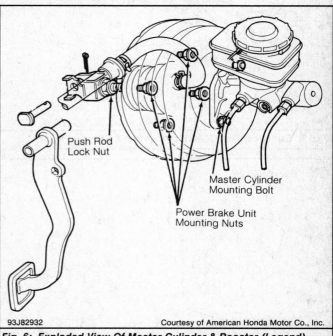

Push Rod
Lock Nut

Master Cylinder
Mounting Bolt

Power Brake Unit
Mounting Nuts

93J82932   Courtesy of American Honda Motor Co., Inc.

Fig. 6: Exploded View Of Master Cylinder & Booster (Legend)

Removal & Installation (Vigor) – 1) Empty master cylinder reservoir. Remove 4-way joint mounting bolt. *See Fig. 7.* Disconnect check valve and throttle cable from 4-way joint bracket. Remove master cylinder mounting nuts, washers, and 4-way joint bracket. Remove master cylinder from brake booster.

2) Remove throttle cable clamp bolt. Disconnect vacuum tube from brake booster. Remove clevis pin from booster push rod. Remove brake booster mounting nuts and brake booster. To install, reverse removal procedure after measuring push rod clearance and length. See MASTER CYLINDER PUSH ROD. After installation, check and adjust pedal height. See PEDAL PLAY & HEIGHT under ADJUSTMENTS. Fill and bleed brake system.

PARKING BRAKE SHOES

Removal (Legend) – 1) Raise and support rear of vehicle. Remove rear wheels. Remove rear brake rotor. See DISC BRAKE ROTOR under REMOVAL & INSTALLATION. Turn and push in on retainer spring to remove tension pins. *See Fig. 8.*

2) Remove rear hub assembly. See REAR AXLE BEARINGS & OIL SEAL under REMOVAL & INSTALLATION. Remove brake shoe assembly. Disconnect parking brake cable from parking brake arm. Remove adjuster and springs from brake shoes. Remove wave washer, parking brake lever, and pivot pin from brake shoes.

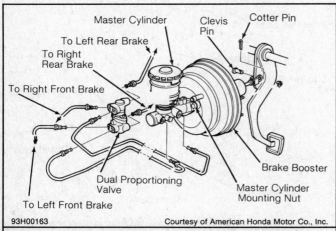

Master Cylinder

Clevis Pin

Cotter Pin

To Left Rear Brake

To Right Rear Brake

To Right Front Brake

Dual Proportioning Valve

To Left Front Brake

Brake Booster

Master Cylinder Mounting Nut

93H00163   Courtesy of American Honda Motor Co., Inc.

Fig. 5: Exploded View Of Master Cylinder & Booster (Integra)

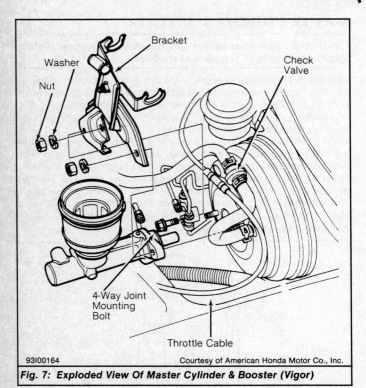

Fig. 7: **Exploded View Of Master Cylinder & Booster (Vigor)**

- Bracket
- Washer
- Nut
- Check Valve
- 4-Way Joint Mounting Bolt
- Throttle Cable

93I00164   Courtesy of American Honda Motor Co., Inc.

Fig. 8: **Exploded View Of Parking Brake Assembly (Legend)**

- Backing Plate
- "U" Clip
- Wave Washer
- Brake Shoe
- Return Spring
- Connecting Rod
- Tension Pin
- Parking Brake Lever
- Rod Spring
- Adjuster
- Return Spring
- Hub Assembly
- Rear Brake Disc
- Spindle Nut

92I00511   Courtesy of American Honda Motor Co., Inc.

Inspection – Inspect brake shoe linings for cracking, glazing, or wear. Measure brake lining thickness. If measurement is less than 0.04" (1 mm), replace brake shoes. Inspect inside of disc for scoring, grooves, or cracks. Measure inside diameter of brake disc. If diameter exceeds 6.73" (171 mm), replace brake disc.

NOTE: If refinish limit stamped on brake disc is not 6.73" (171 mm), use limit marked on brake disc.

Installation – **1)** Apply brake cylinder grease to sliding surface of pivot pin. Install pivot pin into brake shoe. Install parking brake lever and wave washer onto pivot pin. Secure with new "U" clip. Apply brake cylinder grease to brake shoe contact points.
2) To complete installation, reverse removal procedure. Bleed hydraulic system if necessary. See BLEEDING PROCEDURES under BLEEDING BRAKE SYSTEM. If new parking brake shoes or new brake discs have been installed, perform brake shoe lining break-in procedure. See PARKING BRAKE LINING BREAK-IN under ADJUSTMENTS.

REAR AXLE BEARINGS & OIL SEAL

NOTE: Rear axle bearing and hub are replaced as an assembly.

Removal & Installation – Raise rear of vehicle and support with safety stands. Remove wheel assembly. Remove caliper and wire aside. Remove brake disc. Remove hub cap. Pry spindle nut lock tab away from spindle and loosen nut. Remove hub/bearing assembly. To install, reverse removal procedure. Tighten spindle nut to specification. See TORQUE SPECIFICATIONS.

OVERHAUL

FRONT DISC BRAKE CALIPER

Disassembly – **1)** Disconnect brake hose from caliper. Remove pad spring from caliper. See Fig. 9. Install wooden block or shop towel in caliper, opposite piston.
2) Slowly apply 30 psi (2.1 kg/cm²) air pressure to brake fluid inlet port to force piston from caliper bore. Remove piston square ring seal.

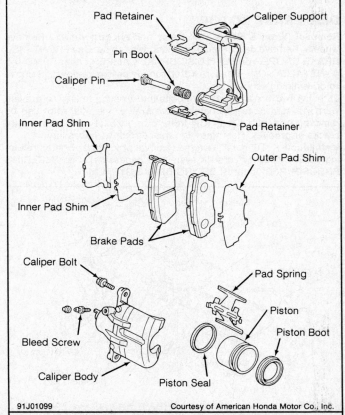

- Pad Retainer
- Caliper Support
- Pin Boot
- Caliper Pin
- Pad Retainer
- Inner Pad Shim
- Outer Pad Shim
- Inner Pad Shim
- Brake Pads
- Caliper Bolt
- Pad Spring
- Piston
- Piston Boot
- Bleed Screw
- Caliper Body
- Piston Seal

91J01099   Courtesy of American Honda Motor Co., Inc.

Fig. 9: **Exploded View Of Front Brake Caliper Assembly (Integra Shown; Legend & Vigor Are Similar)**

Take care that caliper bore is not scored or damaged during removal of seal. Discard rubber components.

CAUTION: DO NOT put hand inside caliper when using air pressure to remove piston.

NOTE: Take care that brake fluid does not spill on painted surfaces or damage to finish will result. DO NOT place fingers in front of piston when air pressure is used for removal.

Reassembly – **1)** Clean piston and caliper bore with clean brake fluid. Inspect for wear or damage. Apply silicone grease to piston seal. Install piston seal into cylinder groove. Install piston boot.

2) Lubricate caliper cylinder and piston with clean brake fluid. Install piston into cylinder with dished end facing inward. To complete reassembly, reverse removal procedure. Replace washers when installing brake line. Bleed system after installation. See BLEEDING PROCEDURES under BLEEDING BRAKE SYSTEM.

REAR DISC BRAKE CALIPER

Disassembly (Integra & Vigor) – **1)** Remove brake caliper. See REAR DISC BRAKE CALIPER under REMOVAL & INSTALLATION. Remove pad spring from caliper. Rotate piston counterclockwise with Wrench (07916-63900010) to remove. *See Fig. 10.* Remove boot. Remove piston seal from caliper bore. Take care that caliper bore or piston components are not damaged.

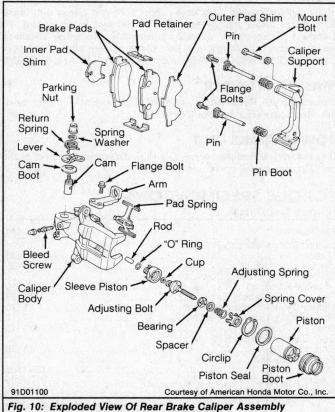

91D01100   Courtesy of American Honda Motor Co., Inc.

Fig. 10: Exploded View Of Rear Brake Caliper Assembly (Integra Shown; Vigor Is Similar)

2) Install Brake Spring Compressor (07HAE-SG00100) between caliper body and spring cover. Position lock nuts as shown, then rotate shaft until plate just contacts caliper body. *See Fig. 11.* Rotate shaft clockwise 1/4 – 1/2 turn to compress spring. Lower lock nuts to plate, then tighten securely. Remove retaining ring. Relax spring compressor before removing it.

3) Remove spring cover, adjuster spring, adjuster bolt, and cup. Remove sleeve piston and "O" ring. Remove pin from cam. Remove return spring, parking nut, spring washer, lever, cam, and cam boot.

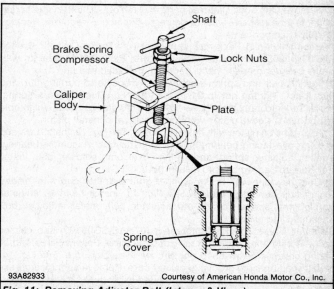

93A82933   Courtesy of American Honda Motor Co., Inc.

Fig. 11: Removing Adjuster Bolt (Integra & Vigor)

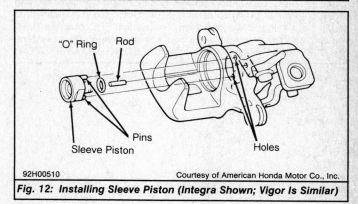

92H00510   Courtesy of American Honda Motor Co., Inc.

Fig. 12: Installing Sleeve Piston (Integra Shown; Vigor Is Similar)

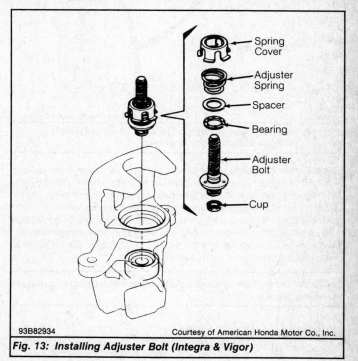

93B82934   Courtesy of American Honda Motor Co., Inc.

Fig. 13: Installing Adjuster Bolt (Integra & Vigor)

4) Remove cam boot. Clean all parts in clean brake fluid. Inspect components for excessive wear or damage. Replace as required. Replace all rubber components.

Reassembly – 1) Pack new cam boot with Brake Cylinder Grease (08733-B020E) and install into cam bore. Pack needle bearing with brake cylinder grease. Install cam with threaded end up.

2) Install lever and spring washer. Apply Loctite to parking nut, and install nut. Tighten nut to 21 ft. lbs. (28 N.m). Install return spring. Install rod into cam. Install new "O" ring onto sleeve piston. Align hole in bottom of sleeve piston with rod in cam, and install piston.

3) Align pins on piston with holes in caliper. *See Fig. 12.* Install new cup with groove facing bearing side of adjuster bolt. Assemble bearing, spacer, adjuster spring, and spring cover onto adjuster bolt. Install adjuster bolt assembly into caliper bore.

4) Coat new cup with brake cylinder grease. Install cup with groove facing adjuster bolt bearing. *See Fig. 13.* Install bearing, adjuster spring, and spring cover onto adjuster bolt. Install adjuster bolt assembly into caliper.

5) Install Brake Spring Compressor (07HAE-SG00100) into caliper body. Rotate shaft until lock nut contacts plate. Ensure flared end of spring cover is below snap ring groove in caliper bore. *See Fig. 14.* Install snap ring into groove of caliper bore. Remove spring compressor. Ensure snap ring is properly seated in groove.

6) Coat new piston seal and piston boot with silicone grease, and install in caliper bore. Apply grease to piston outside diameter, and install onto push rod while turning piston clockwise. Take care that piston boot is not damaged during installation. To complete reassembly, reverse disassembly procedure. Install caliper. Bleed system. See BLEEDING PROCEDURES under BLEEDING BRAKE SYSTEM.

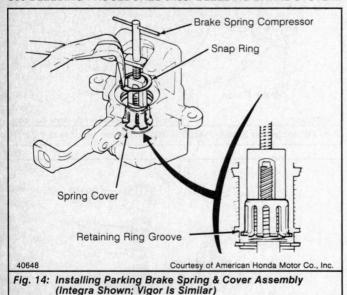

Fig. 14: Installing Parking Brake Spring & Cover Assembly (Integra Shown; Vigor Is Similar)

Disassembly (Legend) – 1) Disconnect brake hose from caliper. Plug end of brake hose. Remove caliper mounting bolts. Remove caliper from bracket. *See Fig. 15.* Remove pad spring from caliper. Install wooden block or shop towel into caliper, opposite piston.

2) Slowly apply 30 psi (2.1 kg/cm²) air pressure to brake fluid inlet port to force piston from caliper bore. Remove piston boot and piston seal. Take care that caliper bore is not scored or damaged during removal of seal. Discard rubber components.

CAUTION: DO NOT allow hand inside caliper when using air pressure to remove piston.

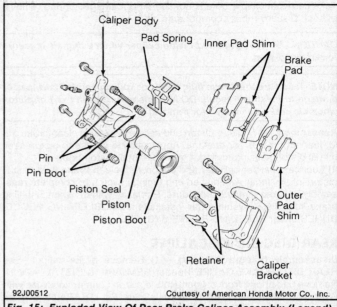

Fig. 15: Exploded View Of Rear Brake Caliper Assembly (Legend)

Reassembly – Coat new piston seal and boot with silicone grease, and install into caliper. Lubricate caliper bore and piston with brake fluid. Install piston into cylinder with dished end facing inward. To complete reassembly, reverse disassembly procedure. Replace washers when installing brake line. Bleed system after installation. See BLEEDING PROCEDURES under BLEEDING BRAKE SYSTEM.

MASTER CYLINDER

Disassembly & Reassembly – DO NOT disassemble master cylinder. Replace master cylinder if defective.

POWER BRAKE UNIT

Disassembly & Reassembly – DO NOT disassemble power brake unit. Replace power brake unit if defective.

TORQUE SPECIFICATIONS
TORQUE SPECIFICATIONS

Application	Ft. Lbs. (N.m)
Caliper Body Mounting Bolt	
Front	24 (33)
Rear	29 (39)
Caliper Mount Bracket Bolt	
Integra & Legend	81 (110)
Flex Hose-To-Caliper Banjo Bolt	25 (34)
Master Cylinder Mounting Bolt	11 (15)
Power Brake Unit Mounting Nut	10 (13)
Push Rod Lock Nut	11 (15)
Rear Caliper Parking Nut	
Integra & Vigor	21 (28)
Rear Spindle Nut	
Integra	136 (185)
Legend & Vigor	210 (285)
Wheel Lug Nut	81 (110)
	INCH Lbs. (N.m)
Brake Bleed Screw	80 (9)

DISC BRAKE SPECIFICATIONS

DISC BRAKE SPECIFICATIONS

Application	In. (mm)
Integra	
Disc Diameter	
Front	10.3 (262)
Rear	9.4 (239)
Parallelism	0.0006 (0.015)
Maximum Runout	
Front	0.004 (0.10)
Rear	0.006 (0.15)
Original Thickness	
Front	0.83 (21)
Rear	0.39 (9.9)
Minimum Refinish Thickness	
Front	0.75 (19.0)
Rear	0.315 (8)
Discard Thickness	
Front & Rear	[1]
Legend	
Disc Diameter	
Front	11 (280)
Rear	11 (280)
Parallelism	0.0006 (0.015)
Maximum Runout	
Front & Rear	0.004 (0.10)
Original Thickness	
Front	0.91 (23)
Rear	0.35 (8.9)
Minimum Refinish Thickness	
Front	0.83 (21)
Rear	0.30 (7.6)
Discard Thickness	
Front & Rear	[1]
Vigor	
Disc Diameter	
Front	11.1 (282)
Rear	10.2 (260)
Parallelism	0.0006 (0.015)
Maximum Runout	
Front & Rear	0.004 (0.10)
Original Thickness	
Front	0.91 (23)
Rear	0.4 (10)
Minimum Refinish Thickness	
Front	0.83 (21)
Rear	0.315 (8)
Discard Thickness	
Front & Rear	[1]

[1] – Use discard thickness stamped on rotor if different from minimum refinish thickness shown in table.

1993 BRAKES
Anti-Lock

Integra, Legend, Vigor

DESCRIPTION

The Anti-Lock Brake System (ABS) is designed to prevent wheel lock-up during hard braking. This effect allows driver to maintain control of vehicle under severe braking conditions. System consists of control unit, accumulator, power unit, 4 wheel sensors, 4 gear pulsers, modulator, warning light, master cylinder, power booster assembly, motor and fail-safe relays and connecting wiring. *See Fig. 1, 2 or 3.*

NOTE: For more information on brake system, see appropriate DISC article.

OPERATION

The control unit receives an AC signal (wheel speed) from each wheel sensor. With this information, control unit electronically opens or closes the solenoids, located inside modulator, to prevent wheel lock-up.

CAUTION: See ANTI-LOCK BRAKE SAFETY PRECAUTIONS article in GENERAL INFORMATION.

SERVICING

Replace brake fluid every 30,000 miles. Replace ABS high-pressure hose every 60,000 miles.

BLEEDING BRAKE SYSTEM

RELIEVING ACCUMULATOR/LINE PRESSURE

Drain brake fluid from master cylinder and modulator reservoir. Remove red cap from maintenance bleeder screw. *See Fig. 4 or 5.* Using ABS "T" Wrench (07HAA-SG00100), loosen maintenance bleeder screw 1/4 turn to release high pressure fluid into reservoir. Turn "T" wrench one complete turn to relieve remaining accumulator line pressure. Tighten bleeder screw.

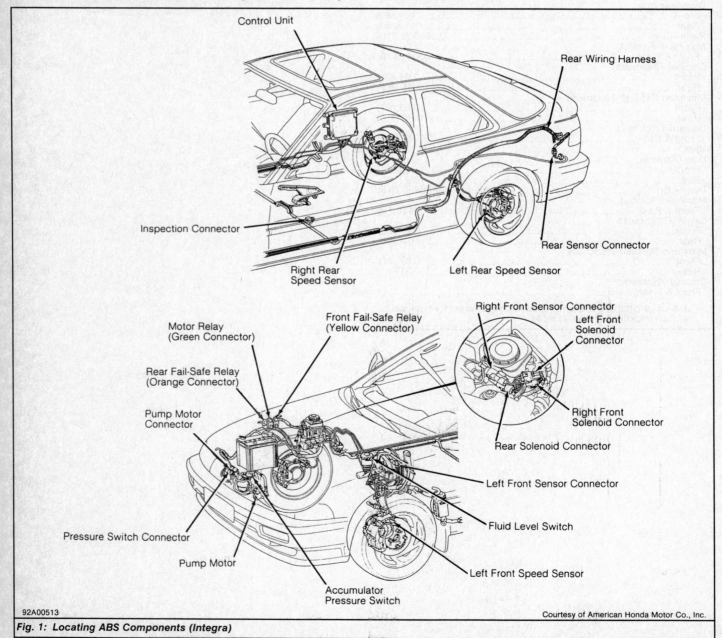

92A00513

Courtesy of American Honda Motor Co., Inc.

Fig. 1: Locating ABS Components (Integra)

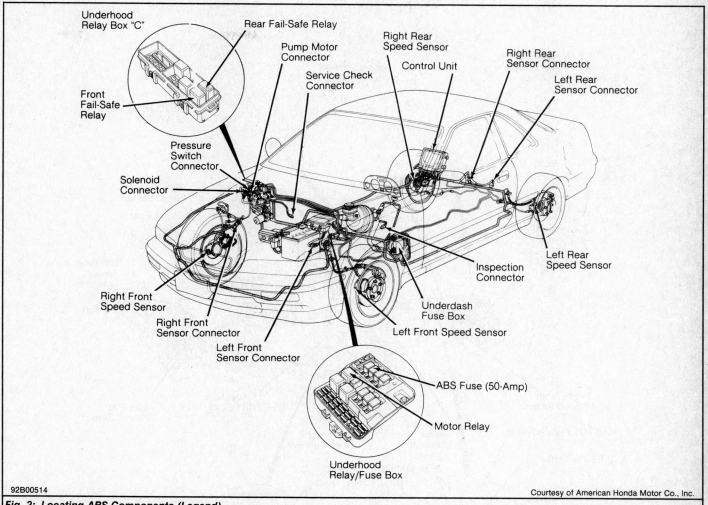

92B00514

Courtesy of American Honda Motor Co., Inc.

Fig. 2: Locating ABS Components (Legend)

AIR BLEEDING

Using ABS Tester – 1) Ensure ignition is off. Block wheels, and set parking brake. Connect ABS Tester (07HAJ-SG0010B) to 6-pin inspection connector. *See Fig. 1, 2 or 3.* Ensure vehicle is on level ground and automatic transmission is in Park or manual transmission is in Neutral.

2) Fill modulator reservoir to MAX level. Bleed high-pressure fluid from maintenance bleeder screw. *See Fig. 4 or 5.* Start engine, and release parking brake. Turn ABS tester mode selector to "2" position. Depress brake pedal firmly and press START TEST button.

3) At least 2 strong kickbacks should be felt from brake pedal. Repeat procedure in ABS tester mode selector positions "3", "4" and "5". If kickbacks are not felt, repeat step **2)**.

4) Fill modulator reservoir to MAX level. Perform system function test. See ABS FUNCTION TEST under DIAGNOSIS & TESTING.

TROUBLE SHOOTING

ANTI-LOCK WARNING LIGHT

ANTI-LOCK warning light will come on for any of following reasons:
- Brake fluid pump runs longer 2 minutes.
- Vehicle driven longer than 30 seconds with parking brake applied.
- Rear wheels locked longer than specified time.
- Wheel speed sensor not transmitting a signal.
- Operation time of solenoid valves exceeds a specified value and control unit finds an open circuit in solenoid circuit.
- Output signals from control unit are not transmitted to solenoid valves.

- Temporary loss of traction due to excessive cornering speed or starting from stuck condition (mud, snow or sand).
- Vehicle driven on extremely rough road.
- Low battery voltage.

If low battery voltage caused problem, recharge battery. Remove ABS fuse No. 2 for 3 seconds. Reinstall fuse, and check light. To reset light for any other condition, turn ignition off. ABS system should reset automatically.

ANTI-LOCK WARNING LIGHT DOES NOT COME ON

If light does not come on when ignition is on, check bulb. On Integra, check Yellow wire between fuse No. 23 (7.5-amp) and instrument panel. On Legend, check Yellow wire between fuse No. 13 (7.5-amp) and instrument panel. On Vigor, check Yellow wire between fuse No. 1 (10-amp) and instrument panel. On all models, check Blue/Red wire from instrument panel to control unit. Check control unit ground circuit. If circuits are okay, check control unit connectors. If connectors are okay, install new control unit and recheck.

DIAGNOSIS & TESTING

ABS FUNCTION TEST

ABS function test should be performed after any ABS component repair or replacement, system bleeding or any repair affecting sensors or wiring.

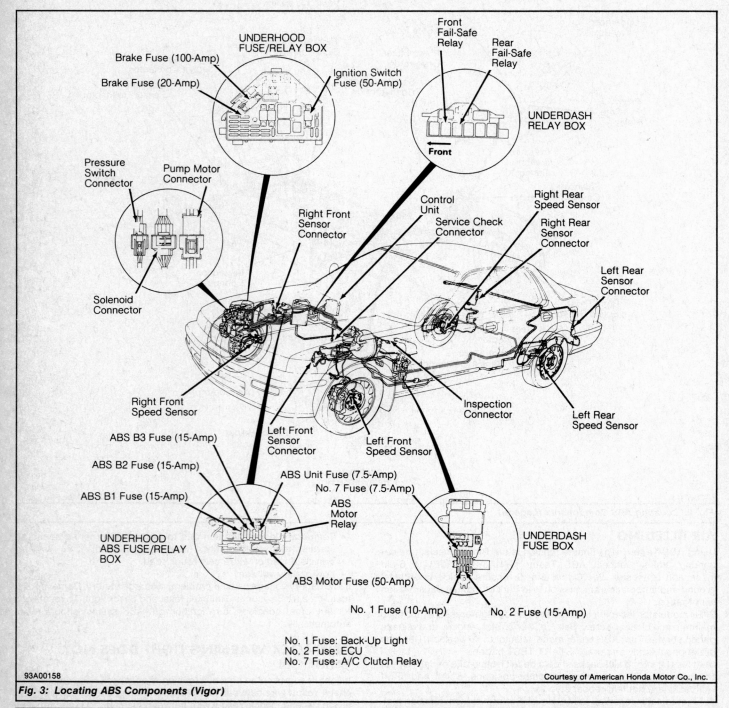

Fig. 3: Locating ABS Components (Vigor)

93A00158

Courtesy of American Honda Motor Co., Inc.

WARNING: DO NOT drive vehicle with ABS tester connected to vehicle. Loss of braking can occur.

Preliminary Procedure – Confirm ANTI-LOCK warning light is not indicating a malfunction with system. If malfunction is indicated, see RETRIEVING CODES. If anti-lock light stays on, see ANTI-LOCK WARNING LIGHT STAYS ON. Place vehicle on level surface. Block wheels, and place automatic transmission in Park or manual transmission in Neutral.

Testing – **1)** Turn ignition switch to OFF position. Connect ABS Tester (07HAJ-SG0010B) to 6-pin inspection connector. *See Fig. 1, 2 or 3.* Start engine. Release parking brake. Place mode selector to "1" position. Push START TEST button. TEST-IN-PROGRESS light should

come on. Within 1-2 seconds, 4 monitor lights should come on. If tester lights do not come on, ABS tester is faulty.

2) If ANTI-LOCK light comes on, ABS tester harness is faulty. Turn mode selector to "2" position. Depress brake pedal. Push START TEST button. ANTI-LOCK warning light should not come on and kickback should be felt in brake pedal.

3) If light comes on or kickback is not felt, see ANTI-LOCK WARNING LIGHT under TROUBLE SHOOTING. Place mode selector in "3", "4" and "5" positions. Repeat step **2)** for each test mode. Results should be as in test mode "2". If results differ, see ANTI-LOCK WARNING LIGHT. Breakdown of modes is as follows:

Mode 1 – Sends simulated driving signal of each wheel to control unit to check self-diagnostic circuit. No kickback should be felt in brake pedal.

Mode 2 – Sends driving signal of each wheel and then sends lock signal of left rear wheel to control unit. A kickback should be felt in brake pedal.

Mode 3 – Sends driving signal of each wheel and then sends lock signal of right rear wheel to control unit. A kickback should be felt in brake pedal.

Mode 4 – Sends driving signal of each wheel and then sends lock signal of left front wheel to control unit. A kickback should be felt in brake pedal.

Mode 5 – Sends driving signal of each wheel and then sends lock signal of right front wheel to control unit. A kickback should be felt in brake pedal.

Mode 6 – Not used.

If brake pedal does not kickback in modes 2-5 as indicated, perform test several times before trouble shooting other parts of system.

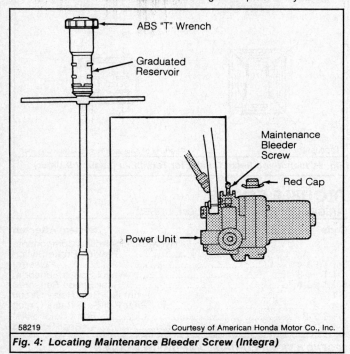

Fig. 4: Locating Maintenance Bleeder Screw (Integra)

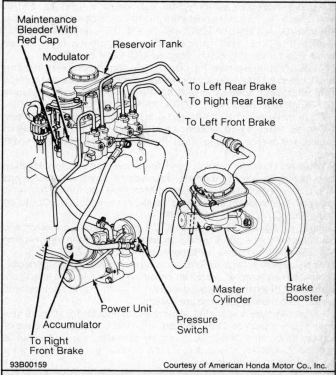

Fig. 5: Locating Maintenance Bleeder Screw (Legend & Vigor)

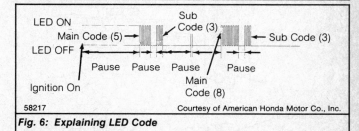

Fig. 6: Explaining LED Code

RETRIEVING CODES

1) Turn engine off. Turn ignition on. Ensure ANTI-LOCK warning light comes on. Start engine and check ANTI-LOCK warning light. If warning light goes out, no fault codes exist.

2) If warning light stays on, turn engine off. Turn ignition on, but DO NOT start engine. Record LED blinking sequence on control unit.

3) First number of code indicates main code. *See Fig. 6.* Second number indicates sub code. An approximate 10-second delay should occur before LED starts blinking after ignition is turned on. Total of 3 codes can be set at one time. To recheck sequence, turn ignition off for a few seconds and then turn ignition back on.

CLEARING CODES

Codes can be cleared by removing ABS fuse No. 2 for at least 3 seconds or disconnecting control unit connector.

WHEEL SENSOR CHECK

1) Place ABS tester mode selector to "0" position. Raise and support vehicle so wheels can be rotated. Turn ignition on. Place transmission in Neutral. Rotate wheels by hand (one revolution per second). Appropriate monitor light should blink each time wheel is rotated.

2) In some instances, front wheels may not rotate fast enough to make tester light blink. If this happens, start engine. Slowly accelerate and decelerate front wheels. If light does not blink, check suspect wheel sensor, sensor air gap and wiring.

ANTI-LOCK WARNING LIGHT STAYS ON

1) If warning light stays on after 3 seconds, ensure LED on control unit is blinking. If LED is not blinking, see ANTI-LOCK WARNING LIGHT under TROUBLE SHOOTING. If warning light is still on after going through checks in ANTI-LOCK WARNING LIGHT, check control unit connector.

2) If connector is okay, check ABS fuse No. 2. Check for open in White wire between ABS fuse No. 2 and control unit.

3) On Integra, check Black/Yellow wire between fuse No. 17 and fail-safe relays. Check Green wire between fail safe relays.

4) On Legend, check Yellow/Black wire between ABS fuse No. 3 and fail-safe relays. Check Yellow/Green wire between fail-safe relays.

5) On Vigor, check Black/Yellow wire between ABS fuse No. 7 and fail-safe relays. Check Yellow/Green wire between fail-safe relays.

6) On all models, check for short in Blue/Red wire between instrument panel and control unit. Check for open in White/Blue wire between alternator and control unit. If problem cannot be found, install a known good control unit and retest.

SOLENOID LEAK TEST

NOTE: If solenoid leaks excessively, brake fluid in modulator reservoir will rise when ABS power unit is operated.

Integra – **1)** Turn ignition off. Connect ABS Tester (07HAJ-SG0010B) to 6-pin inspection connector. *See Fig. 1* for connector location. Ensure vehicle is on level ground and automatic transmission is in Park or manual transmission is in Neutral.

2) Remove modulator reservoir filter. Fill modulator reservoir to MAX level. Bleed high pressure fluid from maintenance bleeder screw. See RELIEVING ACCUMULATOR/LINE PRESSURE under BLEEDING BRAKE SYSTEM. Start engine, and release parking brake. Place mode selector to "1" position. Push START TEST button.

3) While ABS pump is running, place finger over top of solenoid return tube located inside of modulator reservoir. If brake fluid is felt coming from return line, solenoid is leaking. Relieve accumulator pressure. See RELIEVING ACCUMULATOR/LINE PRESSURE.

4) Place mode selector of ABS tester in position "3" and "6". Run test 3-4 times. Place mode selector of ABS tester to "1" position. Start engine, and release parking brake. Push START TEST button on ABS tester.

5) While ABS pump is running, place finger over top of solenoid return tube located inside of modulator reservoir. If solenoid leakage has stopped, refill modulator reservoir to MAX level. No further testing is required. If solenoid is still leaking, replace solenoid. See SOLENOID under REMOVAL & INSTALLATION.

Legend & Vigor – 1) Disconnect pressure switch connector and pump motor connector. Connect an ohmmeter between Yellow wires of accumulator pressure switch connector. *See Fig. 7.*

2) Apply battery voltage to Red/White wire on pump motor connector. Ground Green terminal. Install an on/off switch in negative lead. Turn switch to ON position. Allow pressure to build inside accumulator. Check for continuity at pressure switch.

3) Once continuity is indicated, allow pump to operate for 10 more seconds. Turn switch to OFF position. If solenoid hisses or squeaks, replace modulator. Check for continuity at pressure switch within 30 minutes. Continuity should exist. If no continuity exists, solenoid is faulty. Replace modulator.

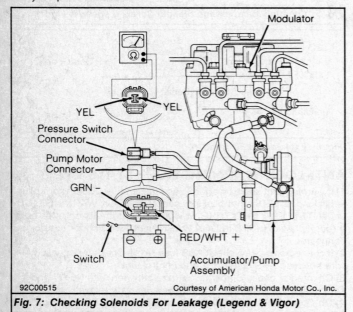

Fig. 7: Checking Solenoids For Leakage (Legend & Vigor)

RELAY TEST

Integra – Remove relay to be tested. *See Fig. 1.* Using an ohmmeter, check for continuity between relay terminals No. 3 and 4. *See Fig. 8.* Continuity should not exist. Apply battery voltage between terminals No. 1 and 2. Continuity should exist between terminals No. 3 and 4. If relay fails any of these tests, replace relay.

Legend & Vigor – Remove relay to be tested. *See Fig. 2 or 3.* Using an ohmmeter, check for continuity between terminals "C" and "D". *See Fig. 9.* Continuity should exist. Apply battery voltage between terminals "C" and "D". Continuity should exist between terminals "A" and "B". If relay fails any of these tests, replace relay.

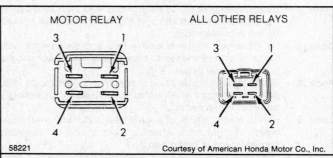

Fig. 8: Identifying Relay Connector Terminals (Integra)

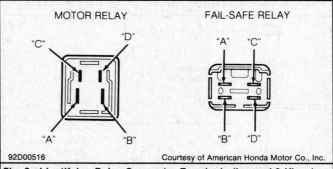

Fig. 9: Identifying Relay Connector Terminals (Legend & Vigor)

TROUBLE CODES

INTEGRA CONTROL UNIT TROUBLE CODES

Code	System Affected
1	Hydraulic Controlled Components
2	Parking Brake Switch
3-1 To 3-4	Pulser(s)
4-1 To 4-8	Wheel Speed Sensor(s)
5-4 To 5-8	Rear Speed Sensor(s)
6-1	Front Fail-Safe Relay Circuit
6-4	Rear Fail-Safe Relay Circuit
7-1 & 7-2	Front Solenoid(s)
7-4	Rear Solenoid

LEGEND & VIGOR CONTROL UNIT TROUBLE CODES

Code	System Affected
1	Pump Motor
1-2	Pump Motor Circuit
1-3	High Pressure Leakage
1-4	Pressure Switch
1-8	Accumulator Gas Leakage
2-1	Parking Brake Switch
3-1 To 3-8	Pulser(s)
4-1 To 4-8	Wheel Speed Sensor(s)
5-4 To 5-8	Rear Speed Sensor(s)
6-1	Front Fail-Safe Relay
6-4	Rear Fail-Safe Relay
7-1 & 7-2	Front Solenoid(s) Circuit
7-4	Rear Solenoid Circuit

NOTE: Use only high impedance Digital Volt-Ohmmeter (DVOM) for testing.

INTEGRA

Code 1, Hydraulic Controlled Components – 1) Check ABS fuses. Ensure brake lines are not kinked or leaking and brake fluid level is filled to maximum. Disconnect pressure switch connector. Using an ohmmeter, check for continuity between Black and Yellow wires. If continuity exists, go to next step. If no continuity exists, go to step 3).
2) Using ABS "T" Wrench (07HAA-SG00100), bleed high pressure fluid from maintenance bleeder screw. See RELIEVING ACCUMULATOR/

LINE PRESSURE under BLEEDING BRAKE SYSTEM. Recheck pressure switch for continuity. If no continuity exists, go to next step. If continuity exists, replace defective pressure switch.

3) Reconnect pressure switch connector. Using ABS "T" wrench, loosen maintenance bleeder screw to relieve accumulator line pressure. See RELIEVING ACCUMULATOR/LINE PRESSURE under BLEEDING BRAKE SYSTEM. Go to next step.

4) Raise and support vehicle. Start engine, and place transmission into gear. With vehicle running at a minimum of 6 MPH, check pump motor operation. If pump motor operates, go to step **7)**. If pump motor does not operate, disconnect 18-pin connector from control unit. Check for continuity between Yellow wire and ground. If no continuity exists, go to next step. If continuity exists, repair Yellow wire between control unit and pressure switch.

5) Using a jumper wire, connect Yellow/Red wire to ground. Turn ignition on. If pump motor runs, replace faulty control unit. If pump motor does not run, remove and test pump motor relay. See RELAY TEST under DIAGNOSIS & TESTING. Replace relay if it is defective. If pump motor relay is okay, use a jumper wire to connect White/Red and White/Blue wires together.

6) If pump motor does not run, go to step **10)**. If pump motor runs, check for battery voltage between Black/Yellow wire and ground. If battery voltage is not present, repair Black/Yellow wire between fuse No. 17 and pump motor relay. If battery voltage is present, repair Yellow/Red wire between control unit and pump motor relay.

7) If pump motor operated in step **4)**, check if pump motor operates with an increasingly loud, raspy noise. If noise is not present, bleed system. See AIR BLEEDING under BLEEDING BRAKE SYSTEM. If noise exists, motor should stop after one minute. If motor stops after about one minute, go to next step. If motor stops after about 2 minutes, replace pressure switch.

8) Ensure fluid level in reservoir drops and contains no air. Allow fluid to stabilize before checking. If fluid level responds correctly, system is okay. Recheck pump motor to ensure problem is not intermittent. If fluid level remains unchanged and air bubbles are present in reservoir tank, go to next step.

9) Using ABS "T" wrench, bleed accumulator line pressure and check modulator fluid level. See RELIEVING ACCUMULATOR/LINE PRESSURE. See Fig. 10. Replace accumulator if fluid quantity in graduated reservoir is more than 160 cc. If fluid quantity is less than 100 cc, check for modulator inlet solenoid leak and accumulator leak. If fluid level rises, replace modulator.

10) Using a DVOM, check for battery voltage between White/Red wire and ground. If battery voltage is present, go to next step. If battery voltage is not present, repair open in White/Red wire between fuse and pump motor relay.

11) Check for battery voltage between pump motor White/Blue wire and ground. If battery voltage is present, replace faulty pump motor. If battery voltage is not present, repair open in White/Blue wire between motor relay and pump motor or open in Black wire between pump motor and ground. Also check for poor ground connection at right front of engine compartment.

Code 2, Parking Brake Switch – 1) Remove ABS fuse No. 2 for 3 seconds to clear trouble code. Test drive vehicle. If ANTI-LOCK warning light and control unit LED are off (no code), vehicle was probably driven with parking brake applied.

2) If parking brake was not applied, check for low brake fluid level in master cylinder reservoir. Refill if necessary. Check for short circuit in Green/Red wire between BRAKE warning light and parking brake switch. Check for short circuit in Green/Red wire between BRAKE warning light and brake fluid level switch.

3) Also check for blown bulb in BRAKE warning light. Check for open circuit in Green/Red wire between BRAKE warning light and parking brake switch. Check for open circuit in Green/Red wire between parking brake switch and control unit. If all items are okay, check for loose or damaged control unit connectors. If connectors are okay, install a known good control unit and retest.

Codes 3-1 To 3-4 – No testing is available from manufacturer.

Codes 4-1 To 4-8 & 5-4 To 5-8, Speed Sensor(s) – 1) Disconnect speed sensor connector. See Fig. 1. Using a DVOM, check resistance between speed sensor terminals. If resistance is not 500-1000 ohms (front sensor) or 700-1200 (rear sensor), replace speed sensor. If resistance is okay, disconnect 18-pin connector from control unit. Using a DVOM, check for continuity between control unit connector and each speed sensor. If no continuity exists in any circuit, repair open circuit. If continuity exists, go to next step.

2) Reconnect 18-pin connector and wheel sensor connectors. Connect ABS tester to system. Check ABS function in modes "2" and "3". Refer to ABS FUNCTION TEST under DIAGNOSIS & TESTING. If ABS system functions properly, replace faulty control unit. If ABS system does not function properly, replace faulty modulator.

Code 6-1, Front Fail-Safe Relay Circuit – 1) Remove and test front fail-safe relay. See RELAY TEST under DIAGNOSIS & TESTING. Replace relay if it is defective. If relay is okay, disconnect 3-pin connectors from front solenoids. Using a DVOM, check continuity between Brown/Black wire and ground. If no continuity exists, go to next step. If continuity exists, repair short in Brown/Black wire between solenoids and fail-safe relay.

2) Check for continuity between Black wire and ground. If continuity exists, replace defective solenoid. If no continuity exists, disconnect 18-pin and 12-pin connectors from control unit. Using a DVOM, check for continuity between control unit connector and each speed sensor. If no continuity exists, go to next step. If continuity exists in any circuit, repair short in suspect wire between solenoid and control unit connector.

3) Check for continuity between Yellow/Green wire and ground. If continuity exists, repair short in Yellow/Green wire. If no continuity exists, check for loose control unit connectors. If connectors are okay, install a known good control unit and retest.

Code 6-4, Rear Fail-Safe Relay Circuit – 1) Remove and test rear fail-safe relay. See RELAY TEST under DIAGNOSIS & TESTING. Replace relay if it is defective. If relay is okay, disconnect 3-pin connector (Pink) from rear solenoid. Using a DVOM, check for continuity between Blue/Black wire and ground. If continuity does not exist, go to next step. If continuity exists, repair short in Blue/Black wire between relay and solenoid.

2) Check for continuity between Black wire and ground. If continuity exists, replace defective solenoid. If no continuity exists, disconnect 18-pin and 12-pin connectors from control unit. Check for continuity between Red/White wire and ground and between Yellow/White wire and ground. If continuity does not exist, go to next step. If continuity exists in any wire, repair short in wire between solenoid and control unit connector having continuity.

3) Check for continuity between Yellow/Green wire and ground. If continuity exists, repair short in Yellow/Green wire between rear fail-safe relay and ground. If no continuity exists, check for loose control unit connectors. If connectors are okay, install a known good control unit and retest.

Codes 7-1 & 7-2, Front Solenoid(s) – 1) Disconnect 3-pin connectors from front solenoids. Using a DVOM, check resistance between Red and Black wires on front solenoid. If resistance is 1-3 ohms, go to next step. If resistance is not 1-3 ohms, replace front solenoid.

2) Disconnect 12-pin connector from control unit. Check for continuity between control unit connector and front solenoids. If continuity exists

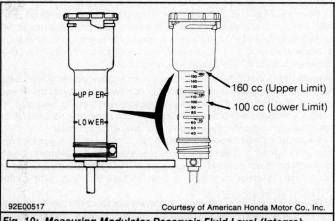

92E00517   Courtesy of American Honda Motor Co., Inc.

160 cc (Upper Limit)
100 cc (Lower Limit)

Fig. 10: Measuring Modulator Reservoir Fluid Level (Integra)

in all wires, go to next step. If continuity does not exist in any wire, repair open in wire.

3) Check for continuity at control unit connector between ground and Red/Black, Yellow/Black, Red/Blue and Yellow/Blue wires. If continuity does not exist in any wire, go to next step. If continuity exists in any wire, repair short in wire having continuity.

4) Remove and test front fail-safe relay. See RELAY TEST under DIAGNOSIS & TESTING. Replace relay if it is defective. If relay is okay, check for continuity between Black wire and ground. If continuity exists, go to next step. If no continuity exists, check for bad ground at right front of engine compartment. If ground is okay, repair open in Black wire.

5) Check Brown/Black wire for continuity between solenoids and front fail-safe relay. If no continuity exists, repair open in Brown/Black wire between solenoids and fail-safe relay. If continuity exists, check for loose control unit connectors. If connectors are okay, install a known good control unit and retest.

Code 7-4, Rear Solenoid – 1) Disconnect 3-pin connector from rear solenoid connector. Using a DVOM, measure resistance between Red and Black wires and between Yellow and Black wires of rear solenoid. If resistance is 1-3 ohms, go to next step. If resistance is not 1-3 ohms, replace faulty solenoid.

2) Disconnect 12-pin connector from control unit. Check for continuity of Red/White wire between control unit connector and rear solenoid. If continuity exists, go to next step. If no continuity exists, repair open in Red/White wire.

3) Check for continuity between Yellow/White wire of control unit connector and rear solenoid. If continuity exists, go to next step. If no continuity exists, repair open in Yellow/White wire.

4) Check for continuity between Red/White wire of control unit connector and ground. If no continuity exists, go to next step. If continuity exists, repair short in Red/White wire.

5) Check for continuity between Yellow/White wire of control unit connector and ground. If no continuity exists, go to next step. If continuity exists, repair short in Yellow/White wire.

6) Remove and test rear fail-safe relay. See RELAY TEST under DIAGNOSIS & TESTING. Replace relay if it is defective. If relay is okay, check for continuity between Black wire and ground. If continuity exists, go to next step. If no continuity exists, check for bad ground at right front of engine compartment. If ground is okay, repair open in Black wire between fail-safe relay and ground.

7) Check Blue/Black wire for continuity between rear solenoid and rear fail-safe relay. If no continuity exists, repair open in Blue/Black wire between solenoid and fail-safe relay. If continuity exists, check for loose control unit connectors. If necessary, install a known good control unit and retest.

LEGEND

NOTE: Manufacturer recommends replacing accumulator, power unit and pressure switch as an assembly

Code 1, Pump Motor Overrun – 1) Bleed high-pressure fluid from maintenance bleeder using ABS "T" Wrench (07HAA-SG00100). See RELIEVING ACCUMULATOR/LINE PRESSURE under BLEEDING BRAKE SYSTEM. Disconnect pump motor relay connector, and remove relay. *See Fig. 2.* Connect terminals No. 1 and 2 together for about 8 seconds using a jumper wire. *See Fig. 11.*

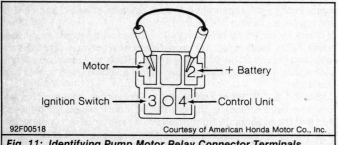

92F00518   Courtesy of American Honda Motor Co., Inc.

Fig. 11: Identifying Pump Motor Relay Connector Terminals (Legend)

2) If pump motor runs with a constant soft sound, use ABS "T" wrench to bleed air from brake system at maintenance bleeder and recheck pump sound. If pump motor runs with an increasingly loud, raspy sound, bleed high pressure fluid from maintenance bleeder using bleeder "T" wrench. Check modulator reservoir fluid level. *See Fig. 12.*

3) If 40-70 cc of fluid exists in reservoir, go to next step. If 40-70 cc of fluid does not exist in reservoir, use a jumper wire to connect terminals No. 1 and 2 of pump motor relay together for about 10 seconds. *See Fig. 11.* Check fluid reservoir level. If fluid level does not change, relief valve in pump motor is defective. If fluid level changes, solenoid is defective (leaking).

4) Using a jumper wire, connect terminals No. 1 and 2 together for about 10 seconds. *See Fig. 11.* Disconnect pressure switch 2-pin connector. Check for continuity between pressure switch terminals. If no continuity exists, replace defective pressure switch. If continuity exists, accumulator is defective.

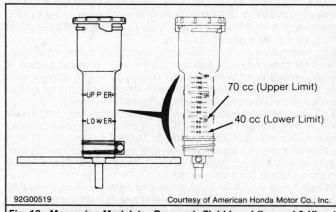

92G00519   Courtesy of American Honda Motor Co., Inc.

Fig. 12: Measuring Modulator Reservoir Fluid Level (Legend & Vigor)

Code 1-2, Pump Motor Circuit – 1) Check ABS fuses. Remove and check pump motor relay. See RELAY TEST under DIAGNOSIS & TESTING. Replace relay if it is defective. If relay is okay, use a jumper wire to connect terminals No. 1 and 2 of pump motor relay connector together. If pump motor does not run, go to next step. If pump motor runs, go to step **5)**.

2) Using DVOM, measure voltage between terminal No. 2 of pump motor relay connector and ground. If battery voltage is present, go to next step. If battery voltage is not present, relay/fuse box connections are bad or relay/fuse box is defective. Repair or replace as necessary.

3) Disconnect 2-pin connector from pump motor. Measure voltage between White/Blue wire and ground. If battery voltage is present, go to next step. If battery voltage is not present, repair open in White/Blue wire.

4) Measure voltage between White/Blue wire and Black wire of pump motor connector. If battery voltage is present, pump motor is defective. If battery voltage is not present, check ground connection. *See Fig. 13.* If ground connection is okay, repair open in Black wire.

5) Remove ABS unit 7.5-amp fuse from underhood relay/fuse box. With ignition on, measure voltage between fuse holder terminal "A" and ground. *See Fig. 14.* If battery voltage is present, go to next step. If battery voltage is not present, repair open in White/Blue wire between ABS unit fuse holder and control unit.

6) Install ABS unit 7.5-amp fuse back into underhood relay/fuse box. Measure voltage between pump relay connector terminal No. 1 and ground. *See Fig. 11.* If battery voltage is present, go to next step. If battery voltage is not present, relay/fuse box connections are bad or relay/fuse box is defective. Repair or replace as necessary.

7) Measure voltage between terminal No. 3 of pump motor relay connector and ground. If battery voltage is present, go to next step. If battery voltage is not present, repair open in Yellow/Black wire between No. 3 fuse (15-amp), located in underdash fuse box, and pump motor relay connector.

8) Reinstall pump motor relay. Disconnect 18-pin connector from control unit. Measure voltage between Yellow/Red wire and ground. If

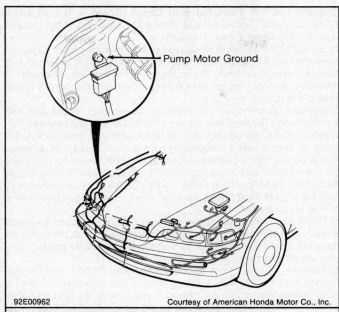

92E00962   Courtesy of American Honda Motor Co., Inc.

Fig. 13: Locating Pump Motor Ground (Legend)

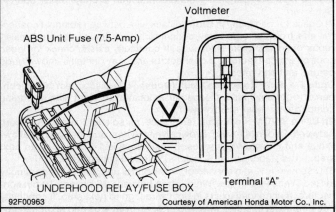

92F00963   Courtesy of American Honda Motor Co., Inc.

Fig. 14: Identifying ABS Unit Fuse Holder Terminal (Legend)

battery voltage is not present, repair open in Yellow/Red wire. If battery voltage is present, check for loose control unit connectors. If connectors are okay, install a known good control unit and retest.

Code 1-3, High Pressure Leakage – 1) Check for external fluid leakage at modulator, power unit and high pressure hoses. Replace as necessary. Using ABS "T" Wrench (07HAA-SG00100), bleed high pressure fluid from maintenance bleeder screw. See RELIEVING ACCUMULATOR/LINE PRESSURE under BLEEDING BRAKE SYSTEM. Remove pump motor relay. See Fig. 2.

2) Using jumper wire, connect terminals No. 1 and 2 of pump motor relay connector for about 10 seconds. See Fig. 11. Disconnect 2-pin connector from pressure switch. After a 30-minute waiting period, check for continuity across pressure switch terminals. If continuity exists, system is okay. If no continuity exists, solenoid is leaking and defective.

Code 1-4, Pressure Switch Circuit – 1) Using ABS "T" Wrench (07HAA-SG00100), bleed high pressure fluid from maintenance bleeder screw. See RELIEVING ACCUMULATOR/LINE PRESSURE under BLEEDING BRAKE SYSTEM. Disconnect 2-pin connector from pressure switch. Check for continuity between pressure switch terminals. If no continuity exists, go to next step. If continuity exists, pressure switch is defective.

2) Check for continuity between Yellow wire of pressure switch connector and ground. If continuity exists, repair short in Yellow wire between pressure switch and control unit. If no continuity exists,

check for loose control unit connectors. If connectors are okay, install a known good control unit and retest.

Code 1-8, Accumulator Gas Leakage – Ensure relief plug on accumulator is tight. Ensure relief plug "O" ring is not out of place or defective. Using ABS "T" Wrench (07HAA-SG00100), bleed high pressure fluid from maintenance bleeder screw. See RELIEVING ACCUMULATOR/LINE PRESSURE under BLEEDING BRAKE SYSTEM. If no fluid bleeds from accumulator, all nitrogen gas has likely leaked out of accumulator.

Code 2-1, Parking Brake Switch – 1) Clear trouble code by removing ABS fuse No. 2 (15-amp) for at least 3 seconds. Test drive vehicle. If ANTI-LOCK warning light and control unit LED are off (no code), vehicle was probably driven with parking brake applied.

2) If parking brake was not applied, check for low brake fluid level in master cylinder reservoir. Refill if necessary. Check for short circuit in Green/Red wire between BRAKE warning light and parking brake switch. Check for short circuit in Green/Red wire between BRAKE warning light and brake fluid level switch.

3) Also check for blown bulb in BRAKE warning light. Check for open circuit in Green/Red wire between BRAKE warning light and parking brake switch. Check for open circuit in Green/Red wire between parking brake switch and control unit. If all items are okay, check for loose or damaged control unit connectors. If connectors are okay, install a known good control unit and retest.

Codes 3-1 To 3-8 – No testing is available from manufacturer.

Codes 4-1 To 4-8, Front & Rear Speed Sensor(s) – 1) Disconnect 18-pin connector from control unit. Use DVOM to measure resistance between Green/Black and Green wires (right front sensor) and between Green/Blue and Brown wires (left front sensor). Measure resistance between Green/Yellow and Blue/Yellow wires (right rear sensor) and between Light Blue and Gray wires (left rear sensor).

2) Resistance for front speed sensors should be 500-1000 ohms. Resistance for rear speed sensors should be 1000-1500 ohms. If resistance is as specified in all wires, go to next step. If resistance is not as specified, go to step **4)**.

3) Check for continuity between ground and each speed sensor wire in step **1)**. If no continuity exists in all wires, check for loose control unit connectors. If connectors are okay, install a known good control unit and retest. If continuity exists in any wire, repair short in sensor wire with continuity or replace faulty speed sensor.

4) Disconnect connector at speed sensor not having correct resistance in step **2)**. Measure resistance between speed sensor terminals. If resistance is 500-1000 ohms for front sensors or 1000-1500 for rear sensors, go to next step. If resistance is not as specified, replace defective speed sensor.

5) Reconnect 18-pin connector at control unit. Check continuity between each wire at speed sensor connector and ground. If no continuity exists, repair open in sensor wire. If continuity exists, check for loose control unit connectors. If connectors are okay, install a known good control unit and retest.

Codes 5-4 To 5-8, Rear Speed Sensor(s) – 1) Disconnect 18-pin connector from control unit. Using DVOM, measure resistance between Green/Yellow and Blue/Yellow wires (right rear sensor) and between Light Blue and Gray wires (left rear sensor). If resistance is 1000-1500 ohms, go to step **4)**. If resistance is not 1000-1500 ohms, go to step **4)**.

2) Check for continuity between ground and each speed sensor wire in step **1)**. If continuity does not exist in all wires, go to next step. If continuity exists in any wire, repair short in sensor wire or replace faulty speed sensor.

3) Reconnect 18-pin connector to control unit. Connect ABS Tester (07HAJ-SG0010B) to inspection connector. See Fig. 2. Check ABS function in modes "2" and "3". If ABS system does not function properly, modulator is defective. If ABS system functions properly, check for rear brake drag. If brake drag is okay, install a known good control unit and retest.

4) Disconnect speed sensor wiring harness connector. Measure resistance between sensor terminals. If resistance is not 1000-1500 ohms, replace defective speed sensor. If resistance is 1000-1500 ohms, go to next step.

5) Reconnect 18-pin connector at control unit. Check continuity between each wire at speed sensor connector and ground. If no continuity exists, repair open in sensor wire. If continuity exists, check for loose control unit connectors. If connectors are okay, install a known good control unit, and retest.

Code 6-1, Front Fail-Safe Relay Circuit – 1) Remove and test front fail-safe relay. See RELAY TEST under DIAGNOSIS & TESTING. Replace relay if it is defective. If relay is okay, turn ignition on. Measure voltage between Yellow/Black wire of fail-safe relay and ground.

2) If no battery voltage exists, repair open Yellow/Black wire between fuse No. 3 and front fail-safe relay. If battery voltage is present, turn ignition off and disconnect 10-pin connector from solenoids. Connector is located on right side of engine compartment, near shock tower.

3) Using DVOM, check for continuity between Brown/Black wire of fail-safe relay and ground. If no continuity exists, go to next step. If continuity exists, repair short in Brown/Black wire between solenoid and front fail-safe relay.

4) Check for continuity at solenoid connector (solenoid side) between Brown/Black wire and ground and between Brown/Blue wire and ground. If no continuity exists, go to next step. If continuity exists, solenoid is defective.

5) Disconnect 18-pin and 12-pin connectors from control unit. Check for continuity at 12-pin connector between ground and Red/Black, Yellow/Black, Red/Blue and Yellow/Blue wires. If continuity does not exist, go to next step. If continuity exists in any wire, repair short in wire having continuity between solenoid and control unit connector.

6) Remove rear fail-safe relay. Check for continuity at 18-pin connector between Yellow/Green wire and ground. If continuity exists, repair short in Yellow/Green wire control unit connector and front fail-safe relay. If no continuity exists, reinstall front fail-safe relay and turn ignition on.

7) Measure voltage at 18-pin connector between Yellow/Black wire and ground. If no battery voltage exists, repair open Yellow/Black wire between ABS control unit and front fail-safe relay. If battery voltage is present, check for loose control unit connectors. If connectors are okay, install a known good control unit and retest.

Code 6-4, Rear Fail-Safe Relay Circuit – 1) Remove and test rear fail-safe relay. See RELAY TEST under DIAGNOSIS & TESTING. Replace relay if it is defective. If relay is okay, turn ignition on. Measure voltage between Yellow/Black wire of fail-safe relay and ground.

2) If no battery voltage exists, repair open Yellow/Black wire between fuse No. 1 and rear fail-safe relay. If battery voltage is present, turn ignition off and disconnect 10-pin connector from solenoids. Connector is located on right side of engine compartment, near shock tower.

3) Using DVOM, check for continuity between Blue/Black wire of fail-safe relay and ground. If continuity does not exist, go to next step. If continuity exists, repair short in Blue/Black wire between solenoid and rear fail-safe relay.

4) Check for continuity at solenoid connector (solenoid side) between Brown/White wire and ground. If continuity does not exist, go to next step. If continuity exists, solenoid is defective.

5) Disconnect 18-pin and 12-pin connectors from control unit. Check for continuity at 12-pin connector between Red/White wire and ground and between Yellow/White wire and ground. If continuity does not exist in both wires, go to next step. If continuity exists in either wire, repair short in wire having continuity between solenoid and control unit connector.

6) Remove front fail-safe relay. Check for continuity at 18-pin connector between Yellow/Green wire and ground. If continuity exists, repair short in Yellow/Green wire between control unit connector and front fail-safe relay. If continuity does not exist, reinstall rear fail-safe relay and turn ignition on.

7) Measure voltage at 18-pin connector between Yellow/Black wire and ground. If no battery voltage exists, repair open Yellow/Black wire between ABS control unit and rear fail-safe relay. If battery voltage is present, check for loose control unit connectors. If connectors are okay, install a known good control unit and retest.

Codes 7-1 & 7-2, Front Solenoid Circuit (Open) – 1) Disconnect 10-pin connector from solenoids. Connector is located on right side of engine compartment, near shock tower.

2) Using DVOM, measure resistance of solenoid inlet wires. Measure between Red/Black and Brown/Black wires for right solenoid and between Red/Blue and Brown/Blue wires for left solenoid. If resistance is 1-3 ohms, go to next step. If resistance is not 1-3 ohms, solenoid is defective.

3) Measure resistance of solenoid outlet wires. Measure between Yellow/Black and Brown/Black wires for right solenoid and between Yellow/Blue and Brown/Blue wires for left solenoid. If resistance is 1-3 ohms, go to next step. If resistance is not 1-3 ohms, solenoid is defective.

4) Disconnect 12-pin connector from control unit. Check for continuity between 12-pin and 10-pin connectors at Red/Black, Yellow/Black, Red/Blue and Yellow/Blue wires. If continuity exists in all wires, go to next step. If continuity does not exist in any wire, repair open in wire having no continuity.

5) Check for continuity at 12-pin connector between ground and Red/Black, Yellow/Black, Red/Blue and Yellow/Blue wires. If continuity does not exist in all wires, go to next step. If continuity exists in any wire, repair short in wire having continuity.

6) Remove and test front fail-safe relay. See RELAY TEST under DIAGNOSIS & TESTING. Replace relay if it is defective. If relay is okay, check for continuity between Black wire of fail-safe relay connector and ground. If continuity exists, go to next step. If continuity does not exist, check fail-safe relay ground connection, located behind right kick panel. If ground connection is okay, repair open in Black wire.

7) Check for continuity in Brown/Black wire between solenoid connector and front fail-safe relay connector. If continuity does not exist, repair open in Brown/Black wire. If continuity exists, check for loose control unit connectors. If connectors are okay, install a known good control unit and retest.

Code 7-4, Rear Solenoid Circuit (Open) – 1) Disconnect 10-pin connector from solenoids. Connector is located on right side of engine compartment, near shock tower.

2) Using DVOM, measure resistance of solenoid wires. Measure between Red/White and Brown/White wires and between Yellow/White and Brown/White wires. If resistance is 1-3 ohms, go to next step. If resistance is not 1-3 ohms, solenoid is defective.

3) Disconnect 12-pin connector from control unit. Check for continuity in Red/White and Yellow/White wires between 12-pin and 10-pin connectors. If continuity exists in both wires, go to next step. If continuity does not exist in either wire, repair open in wire having no continuity.

4) Check for continuity in Red/White and Yellow/White wires between 12-pin connector and ground. If continuity does not exist in both wires, go to next step. If continuity exists in either wire, repair short in wire having continuity.

5) Remove and test rear fail-safe relay. See RELAY TEST under DIAGNOSIS & TESTING. Replace relay if it is defective. If relay is okay, check for continuity between Black wire of fail-safe relay connector and ground. If continuity exists, go to next step. If continuity does not exist, check fail-safe relay ground connection, located behind right kick panel. If ground connection is okay, repair open in Black wire.

6) Check for continuity in Blue/Black wire between solenoid connector and rear fail-safe relay connector. If continuity does not exist, repair open in Blue/Black wire. If continuity exists, check for loose control unit connectors. If connectors are okay, install a known good control unit and retest.

VIGOR

NOTE: Manufacturer recommends replacing accumulator, power unit and pressure switch as an assembly

Code 1, Pump Motor Overrun – 1) Bleed high-pressure fluid from maintenance bleeder using ABS "T" Wrench (07HAA-SG00100). See RELIEVING ACCUMULATOR/LINE PRESSURE under BLEEDING BRAKE SYSTEM. Disconnect pump motor relay connector, and remove relay. *See Fig. 3.* Connect terminals No. 3 and 8 together for about 8 seconds using a jumper wire. *See Fig. 15.*

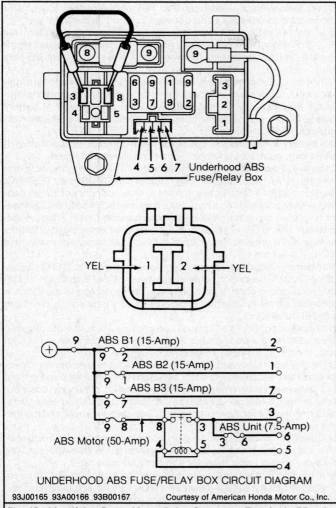

UNDERHOOD ABS FUSE/RELAY BOX CIRCUIT DIAGRAM

93J00165 93A00166 93B00167   Courtesy of American Honda Motor Co., Inc.

Fig. 15: Identifying Pump Motor Relay Connector Terminals (Vigor)

2) If pump motor runs with a constant soft sound, use ABS "T" wrench to bleed air from brake system at maintenance bleeder. Recheck pump sound. If pump motor runs with an increasingly loud, raspy sound, bleed high pressure fluid from maintenance bleeder using bleeder "T" wrench. Check modulator reservoir fluid level. *See Fig. 12.*
3) If 40-70 cc of fluid exists in reservoir, go to next step. If 40-70 cc of fluid does not exist in reservoir, use a jumper wire to connect terminals No. 3 and 8 of pump motor relay together for about 10 seconds. *See Fig. 15.* Check fluid reservoir level. If fluid level does not change, relief valve in pump motor is defective. If fluid level changes, solenoid is defective (leaking).
4) Using a jumper wire, connect terminals No. 3 and 8 together for about 10 seconds. *See Fig. 15.* Disconnect pressure switch 2-pin connector. Check for continuity between pressure switch terminals. If continuity does not exist, replace defective pressure switch. If continuity exists, vehicle is okay at this time.
Code 1-2, Pump Motor Circuit – 1) Check ABS fuses. Remove and check pump motor relay. See RELAY TEST under DIAGNOSIS & TESTING. Replace relay if it is defective. If relay is okay, use a jumper wire to connect terminals No. 3 and 8 of pump motor relay connector together. If pump motor does not run, go to next step. If pump motor runs, go to step 5).
2) Using DVOM, measure voltage between terminal No. 8 of pump motor relay connector and ground. If battery voltage is present, go to next step. If battery voltage is not present, relay/fuse box connections are bad or relay/fuse box is defective. Repair or replace as necessary.
3) Disconnect 2-pin connector from pump motor. Measure voltage between White/Blue wire and ground. If battery voltage is present, go

to next step. If battery voltage is not present, repair open in White/Blue wire.
4) Measure voltage between White/Blue wire and Black wire of pump motor connector. If battery voltage is present, pump motor is defective. If battery voltage is not present, check ground connection. If ground connection is okay, repair open in Black wire.
5) Remove ABS unit 7.5-amp fuse from underhood relay/fuse box. With ignition on, measure voltage between fuse holder No. 6 terminal and ground. If battery voltage is present, go to next step. If battery voltage is not present, repair open in White/Red wire between ABS unit fuse holder and control unit.
6) Install ABS unit 7.5-amp fuse back into underhood relay/fuse box. Disconnect 2-pin connector. Measure voltage between pump relay connector terminal No. 3 and ground. *See Fig. 15.* If battery voltage is present, go to next step. If battery voltage is not present, relay/fuse box connections are bad or relay/fuse box is defective. Repair or replace as necessary.
7) Measure voltage between terminal No. 4 of pump motor relay connector and ground. If battery voltage is present, go to next step. If battery voltage is not present, repair open in Black/Yellow wire between No. 3 fuse (15-amp), located in underdash fuse box, and pump motor relay connector.
8) Reinstall pump motor relay. Disconnect 18-pin connector from control unit. Measure voltage between Yellow/Red wire and ground. If battery voltage is not present, repair open in Yellow/Red wire. If battery voltage is present, check for loose control unit connectors. If connectors are okay, install a known good control unit and retest.
Code 1-3, High Pressure Leakage – 1) Check for external fluid leakage at modulator, power unit and high pressure hoses. Replace as necessary. Using ABS "T" Wrench (07HAA-SG00100), bleed high-pressure fluid from maintenance bleeder screw. See RELIEVING ACCUMULATOR/LINE PRESSURE under BLEEDING BRAKE SYSTEM. Remove pump motor relay. *See Fig. 3.*
2) Using jumper wire, connect terminals No. 3 and 8 of pump motor relay connector for about 10 seconds. *See Fig. 15.* Disconnect 2-pin connector from pressure switch. After 30 minutes, check for continuity across pressure switch terminals. If continuity exists, system is okay at this time.. If continuity does not exist, solenoid is leaking and defective.
Code 1-4, Pressure Switch Circuit – 1) Using ABS "T" Wrench (07HAA-SG00100), bleed high pressure fluid from maintenance bleeder screw. See RELIEVING ACCUMULATOR/LINE PRESSURE under BLEEDING BRAKE SYSTEM. Disconnect 2-pin connector from pressure switch. Check for continuity between pressure switch terminals. If continuity does not exist, go to next step. If continuity exists, pressure switch is defective.
2) Check for continuity between Yellow wire of pressure switch connector and ground. If continuity exists, repair short in Yellow wire between pressure switch and control unit. If continuity does not exist, check for loose control unit connectors. If connectors are okay, install a known good control unit and retest.
Code 1-8, Accumulator Gas Leakage – Ensure relief plug on accumulator is tight. Ensure relief plug "O" ring is not out of place or defective. Using ABS "T" Wrench (07HAA-SG00100), bleed high pressure fluid from maintenance bleeder screw. See RELIEVING ACCUMULATOR/LINE PRESSURE under BLEEDING BRAKE SYSTEM. If little or no fluid bleeds from accumulator, accumulator has likely leaked out all nitrogen gas.
Code 2-1, Parking Brake Switch – 1) Clear trouble code by removing ABS fuse No. 2 (15-amp) for at least 3 seconds. Test drive vehicle. If ANTI-LOCK warning light and control unit LED are off (no code), vehicle was probably driven with parking brake applied.
2) If parking brake was not applied, check for low brake fluid level in master cylinder reservoir. Refill if necessary. Check for short circuit in Green/Red wire between BRAKE warning light and parking brake switch. Check for short circuit in Green/Red wire between BRAKE warning light and brake fluid level switch.
3) Also check for blown bulb in BRAKE warning light. Check for open circuit in Green/Red wire between BRAKE warning light and parking brake switch. Check for open circuit in Green/Red wire between parking brake switch and control unit. If all items are okay, check for loose

or damaged control unit connectors. If connectors are okay, install a known good control unit and retest.

Codes 3-1 To 3-8 – No testing is available from manufacturer.

Codes 4-1 To 4-8, Front & Rear Speed Sensor(s) – **1)** Disconnect 18-pin connector from control unit. Use DVOM to measure resistance between Green/Black and Green wires (right front sensor) and between Green/Blue and Brown wires (left front sensor). Measure resistance between Green/Yellow and Blue/Yellow wires (right rear sensor) and between Light Blue and Gray wires (left rear sensor).

2) Resistance for front speed sensors should be 750-1200 ohms. Resistance for rear speed sensors should be 1100-1600 ohms. If resistance is as specified in all wires, go to next step. If resistance is not as specified, go to step **4)**.

3) Check for continuity between ground and each speed sensor wire in step **1)**. If continuity does not exist in all wires, check for loose control unit connectors. If connectors are okay, install a known good control unit and retest. If continuity exists in any wire, repair short in sensor wire with continuity or replace faulty speed sensor.

4) Disconnect connector at speed sensor not having correct resistance in step **2)**. Measure resistance between speed sensor terminals. If resistance is 750-1200 ohms for front sensors or 1100-1600 ohms for rear sensors, go to next step. If resistance is not as specified, replace defective speed sensor.

5) Reconnect 18-pin connector at control unit. Check continuity between each wire at speed sensor connector and ground. If continuity does not exist, repair open in sensor wire. If continuity exists, check for loose control unit connectors. If connectors are okay, install a known good control unit and retest.

Codes 5-4 To 5-8, Rear Speed Sensor(s) – **1)** Disconnect 18-pin connector from control unit. Using DVOM, measure resistance between Green/Yellow and Blue/Yellow wires (right rear sensor) and between Light Blue and Gray wires (left rear sensor). If resistance is 1100-1600 ohms, go to next step. If resistance is not 1100-1600 ohms, go to step **4)**.

2) Check for continuity between ground and each speed sensor wire in step **1)**. If continuity does not exist in all wires, go to next step. If continuity exists in any wire, repair short in sensor wire or replace faulty speed sensor.

3) Reconnect 18-pin connector to control unit. Connect ABS Tester (07HAJ-SG0010B) to inspection connector. *See Fig. 3.* Check ABS function in modes "2" and "3". If ABS system does not function properly, modulator is defective. If ABS system functions properly, check for rear brake drag. If brake drag is okay, install a known good control unit and retest.

4) Disconnect speed sensor wiring harness connector. Measure resistance between sensor terminals. If resistance is not 1100-1600 ohms, replace defective speed sensor. If resistance is 1100-1600 ohms, go to next step.

5) Reconnect 18-pin connector at control unit. Check continuity between each wire at speed sensor connector and ground. If continuity does not exist, repair open in sensor wire. If continuity exists, check for loose control unit connectors. If connectors are okay, install a known good control unit and retest.

Code 6-1, Front Fail-Safe Relay Circuit – **1)** Remove and test front fail-safe relay and ABS fuses. See RELAY TEST under DIAGNOSIS & TESTING. Replace relay if it is defective. If relay is okay, disconnect 10-pin connector from solenoids. Connector is located on right side of engine compartment, near shock tower.

2) With front fail-safe relay removed, turn ignition switch to ON position. Using DVOM, check for voltage between Black/Yellow wire of fail-safe relay and ground. If battery voltage is not present, repair open in Black/Yellow wire.

3) If battery voltage is present, turn ignition switch to OFF position. Check for continuity between Brown/Black wire of fail-safe relay and ground. If continuity exists, repair short in Brown/Black wire.

4) Reinstall front fail-safe relay. Check for continuity between ground and Brown/Black and Brown/Blue solenoid terminals. If continuity exists, replace shorted solenoid.

5) If continuity does not exist, disconnect 18-pin and 12-pin connectors from control unit. Check continuity from ground to Red/

Black, Yellow/Black, Red/Blue and Yellow/Blue wires. If any wire shows continuity, repair short between solenoid and control unit.

6) If continuity does not exist, check for continuity between terminal No. 17 (Yellow/Green wire) and ground. If continuity exists, repair short in Yellow/Green wire between control unit and front fail-safe relay.

7) If continuity does not exist, remove rear fail-safe relay and turn ignition switch to ON position. Check for voltage between control unit connector terminal No. 17 (Yellow/Green wire) and ground. If battery voltage is not present, repair open in Yellow/Green wire between fail-safe relay and control unit.

8) If battery voltage exists, check for loose control unit connectors. If necessary, substitute a known-good control unit and retest.

Code 6-4, Rear Fail-Safe Relay Circuit – **1)** Remove and test rear fail-safe relay. See RELAY TEST under DIAGNOSIS & TESTING. Replace relay if it is defective. If relay is okay, disconnect 10-pin connector from solenoids and turn ignition switch to ON position. Connector is located on right side of engine compartment, near shock tower.

2) Check Black/Yellow terminal of fail-safe relay and ground. If battery voltage is not present, repair open in Black/Yellow wire between fuse and fail-safe relay.

3) If battery voltage is present, turn ignition switch to OFF position. Using DVOM, check for continuity between Blue/Black wire of fail-safe relay and ground. If continuity does not exist, go to next step. If continuity exists, repair short in Blue/Black wire between solenoid and rear fail-safe relay.

4) Check for continuity at solenoid connector (solenoid side) between Brown/White wire and ground. If continuity does not exist, go to next step. If continuity exists, solenoid is defective.

5) Disconnect 18-pin and 12-pin connectors from control unit. Check for continuity at 12-pin connector between Red/White wire and ground and between Yellow/White wire and ground. If continuity does not exist in both wires, go to next step. If continuity exists in either wire, repair short in wire having continuity between solenoid and control unit connector.

6) Check for continuity at 18-pin connector between Yellow/Green wire and ground. If continuity exists, repair short in Yellow/Green wire between control unit and front fail-safe relay.

7) If continuity does not exist, turn ignition switch to ON position. Check for battery voltage between Yellow/Green wire in control unit connector and ground. If battery voltage is not present, repair Yellow/Green wire between rear fail-safe relay and control unit. If battery voltage exists, check for loose control unit connectors. If connectors are okay, install a known good control unit and retest.

Codes 7-1 & 7-2, Front Solenoid Circuit (Open) – **1)** Disconnect 10-pin connector from solenoids. Connector is located on right side of engine compartment, near shock tower.

2) Using DVOM, measure resistance of solenoid inlet wires. Measure between Red/Black and Brown/Black wires for right solenoid and between Red/Blue and Brown/Blue wires for left solenoid. If resistance is 1-3 ohms, go to next step. If resistance is not 1-3 ohms, solenoid is defective.

3) Measure resistance of solenoid outlet wires. Measure between Yellow/Black and Brown/Black wires for right solenoid and between Yellow/Blue and Brown/Blue wires for left solenoid. If resistance is 1-3 ohms, go to next step. If resistance is not 1-3 ohms, solenoid is defective.

4) Disconnect 12-pin connector from control unit. Check for continuity between 12-pin and 10-pin connectors at Red/Black, Yellow/Black, Red/Blue and Yellow/Blue wires. If continuity exists in all wires, go to next step. If continuity does not exist in any wire, repair open in wire having no continuity.

5) Check for continuity at 12-pin connector between ground and Red/Black, Yellow/Black, Red/Blue and Yellow/Blue wires. If continuity does not exist in all wires, go to next step. If continuity exists in any wire, repair short in wire having continuity.

6) Remove and test front fail-safe relay. See RELAY TEST under DIAGNOSIS & TESTING. Replace relay if it is defective. If relay is okay, check for continuity between Black wire of fail-safe relay connector and ground. If continuity exists, go to next step. If continuity does not exist, check fail-safe relay ground connection, located behind right kick panel. If ground connection is okay, repair open in Black wire.

7) Check for continuity in Brown/Black wire between solenoid connector and front fail-safe relay connector. If continuity does not exist, repair open in Brown/Black wire. If continuity exists, check for loose control unit connectors. If connectors are okay, install a known good control unit and retest.

Code 7-4, Rear Solenoid Circuit (Open) – 1) Disconnect 10-pin connector from solenoids. Connector is located on right side of engine compartment, near shock tower.

2) Using DVOM, measure resistance of solenoid wires. Measure between Red/White and Brown/White wires and between Yellow/White and Brown/White wires. If resistance is 1-3 ohms, go to next step. If resistance is not 1-3 ohms, solenoid is defective.

3) Disconnect 12-pin connector from control unit. Check for continuity in Red/White and Yellow/White wires between 12-pin and 10-pin connectors. If continuity exists in both wires, go to next step. If continuity does not exist in either wire, repair open in wire having no continuity.

4) Check for continuity in Red/White and Yellow/White wires between 12-pin connector and ground. If continuity does not exist in both wires, go to next step. If continuity exists in either wire, repair short in wire having continuity.

5) Remove and test rear fail-safe relay. See RELAY TEST under DIAGNOSIS & TESTING. Replace relay if it is defective. If relay is okay, check for continuity between Black wire of fail-safe relay connector and ground. If continuity exists, go to next step. If no continuity exists, check fail-safe relay ground connection, located behind right kick panel. If ground connection is okay, repair open in Black wire.

6) Check for continuity in Blue/Black wire between solenoid connector and rear fail-safe relay connector. If continuity does not exist, repair open in Blue/Black wire. If continuity exists, check for loose control unit connectors. If connectors are okay, install a known good control unit and retest.

REMOVAL & INSTALLATION

ACCUMULATOR/PRESSURE SWITCH

WARNING: Accumulator contains high-pressure nitrogen gas. DO NOT puncture, expose to flame or attempt to disassemble accumulator. It could explode and cause severe injury.

Removal & Installation (Integra) – 1) Using ABS "T" Wrench (07HAA-SG00100), bleed high-pressure fluid from maintenance bleeder screw. See RELIEVING ACCUMULATOR/LINE PRESSURE under BLEEDING BRAKE SYSTEM. Remove flange bolts. Remove accumulator from bracket. *See Fig. 16.*

2) To dispose of accumulator, secure accumulator in vice with relief plug pointing straight up. *See Fig. 16.* DO NOT tighten accumulator body in vise. Slowly turn relief plug 3 1/2 turns, and wait at least 3 minutes for all pressure to escape. Remove relief plug, and dispose of accumulator.

3) To install new accumulator, reverse removal procedure. If necessary, bleed system. See AIR BLEEDING under BLEEDING BRAKE SYSTEM.

Removal & Installation (Legend & Vigor) – 1) Using ABS "T" Wrench (07HAA-SG00100), bleed high pressure fluid from maintenance bleeder screw. See RELIEVING ACCUMULATOR/LINE PRESSURE under BLEEDING BRAKE SYSTEM. Remove accumulator and "O" ring from power unit. *See Fig. 17.*

2) To dispose of accumulator, secure accumulator in vice with relief plug pointing straight up. *See Fig. 17.* DO NOT tighten accumulator body in vise. Slowly turn relief plug 3 1/2 turns, and wait at least 3 minutes for all pressure to escape. Remove relief plug, and dispose of accumulator.

3) To install new accumulator, reverse removal procedure. Use new "O" ring when installing accumulator. If necessary, bleed system. See AIR BLEEDING under BLEEDING BRAKE SYSTEM.

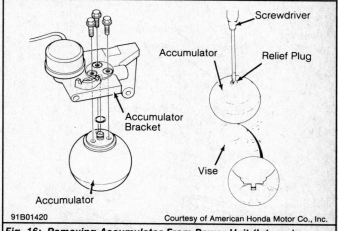

91B01420   Courtesy of American Honda Motor Co., Inc.
Fig. 16: Removing Accumulator From Power Unit (Integra)

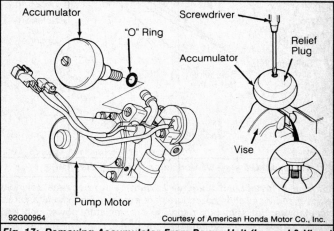

92G00964   Courtesy of American Honda Motor Co., Inc.
Fig. 17: Removing Accumulator From Power Unit (Legend & Vigor)

SOLENOID

Removal (Integra) – 1) Bleed high pressure from maintenance bleeder screw. See RELIEVING ACCUMULATOR/LINE PRESSURE under BLEEDING BRAKE SYSTEM. Without removing pump inlet line, remove brake fluid from modulator reservoir. Remove reservoir strainer. *See Fig. 18.*

2) Remove 2 screws from inside of modulator reservoir, and remove reservoir. Screw 6-mm bolt into center of solenoid head. Tighten bolt until solenoid head can be lifted off solenoids. Lift solenoid head, and set it aside without disconnecting pump inlet line.

3) Remove solenoid set plate bolts and loosen solenoid set plate. Turn solenoid valves several times, freeing valves in bore. Turn solenoids 1/2 turn to align solenoid tab with cutout in set plate. Remove solenoid valves as an assembly with set plate.

4) Each solenoid is marked to match mark on solenoid set plate. Solenoids are not interchangeable. If solenoid is being replaced, ensure new solenoid has same marking as solenoid being replaced.

Installation – 1) Fill modulator body with clean brake fluid up to step in solenoid mounting hole. Coat new solenoid "O" rings with clean brake fluid, and install "O" rings on solenoid. Apply thin film of clean brake fluid to solenoid body and "O" rings. Position solenoid on set plate.

2) Ensure mark on set plate matches mark on solenoid. Align solenoid projection with cutout in set plate and turn valves 1/2 turn. Install solenoid adjust springs in modulator body. Install set plate bolt removed in step **3)** of REMOVAL procedure. Tighten all set plate bolts to 11 ft. lbs. (15 N.m). Install reservoir and filter.

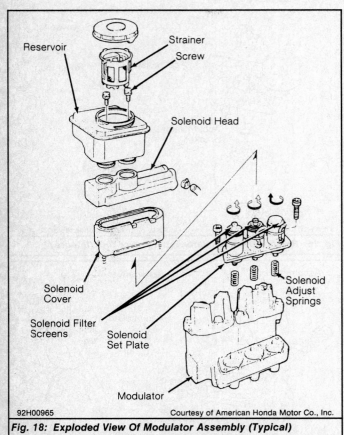

92H00965   Courtesy of American Honda Motor Co., Inc.

Fig. 18: Exploded View Of Modulator Assembly (Typical)

Removal & Installation (Legend & Vigor) – No separate solenoid removal and installation procedures are available from manufacturer. Manufacturer recommends replacing accumulator, power unit and pressure switch as an assembly.

WHEEL SENSOR

Removal & Installation – Unplug wheel sensor connector. Remove wheel sensor from vehicle. To install, reverse removal procedure. Ensure wheel sensor-to-pulser air gap is within specification. See WHEEL SENSOR AIR GAP SPECIFICATIONS table.

WHEEL SENSOR AIR GAP SPECIFICATIONS

Application	In. (mm)
Integra	.016-.039 (.40-1.00)
Legend	
Front	.024-.047 (.60-1.20)
Rear	.012-.051 (.30-1.30)
Vigor	
Front	.024-.035 (.60-.90)
Rear	.020-.035 (.50-.90)

TORQUE SPECIFICATIONS
TORQUE SPECIFICATIONS

Application	Ft. Lbs. (N.m)
Caliper Body Mounting Bolt	
Front	24 (33)
Rear	28 (39)
Caliper Mounting Bracket Bolt (Integra & Legend)	81 (110)
Flex Hose-To-Caliper Banjo Bolt	25 (34)
Master Cylinder Mounting Bolt	11 (15)
Modulator Set Plate Bolts	11 (15)
Push Rod Lock Nut	11 (15)
Rear Caliper Parking Nut (Integra)	21 (28)
Rear Spindle Nut	
Integra	136 (185)
Legend & Vigor	210 (285)
Speed Sensor Mounting Bolts	
Integra	[1]
Legend	
Front	16 (22)
Rear	[1]
Wheel Lug Nut	81 (110)
	INCH Lbs. (N.m)
Accumulator Mounting Bolts (Integra)	84 (9.5)
Brake Bleed Screw	80 (9.0)
Control Unit Mounting Screws	84 (9.5)
Maintenance Bleeder Screw	48 (5.4)
Power Brake Unit Mounting Nut	9 (1.2)

[1] – Tighten bolts to 84 INCH lbs. (9.5 N.m).

WIRING DIAGRAMS

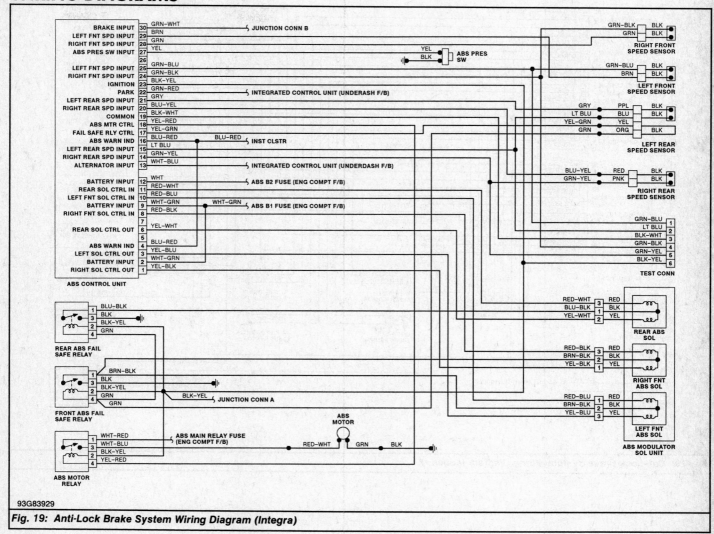

Fig. 19: *Anti-Lock Brake System Wiring Diagram (Integra)*

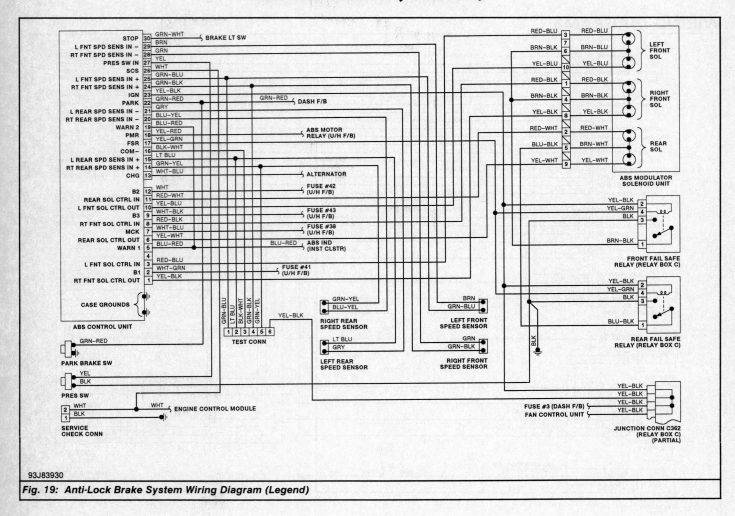

Fig. 19: Anti-Lock Brake System Wiring Diagram (Legend)

93J83930

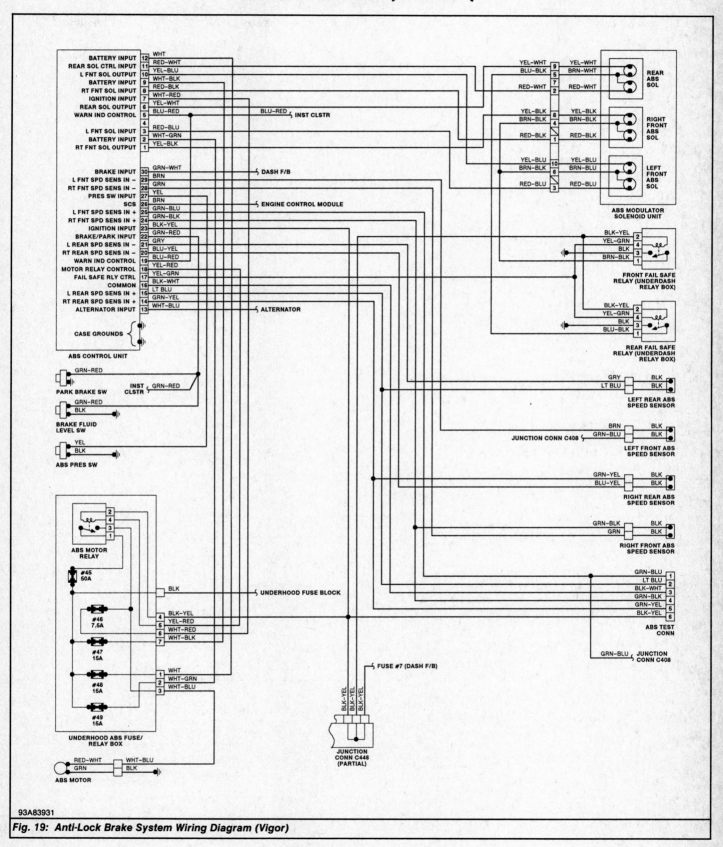

Fig. 19: Anti-Lock Brake System Wiring Diagram (Vigor)

93A83931

Integra, Legend, Vigor

NOTE: Prior to performing wheel alignment, perform preliminary visual and mechanical inspection of wheels, tires, and suspension components. See PRE-ALIGNMENT INSTRUCTIONS in WHEEL ALIGNMENT THEORY & OPERATION article in GENERAL INFORMATION.

RIDING HEIGHT ADJUSTMENT

NOTE: Riding height specification is not available from manufacturer. Ensure riding height between left and right side of vehicle does not differ by more than 1" (25 mm).

JACKING & HOISTING

WARNING: Never use a bumper jack for lifting or supporting vehicle.

LIFTING USING FLOOR JACK

Set parking brake. Block wheels not being lifted. When lifting rear of vehicle, set manual transmission into Reverse, or automatic transmission into Park. Lift vehicle at indicated points. *See Fig. 1.*

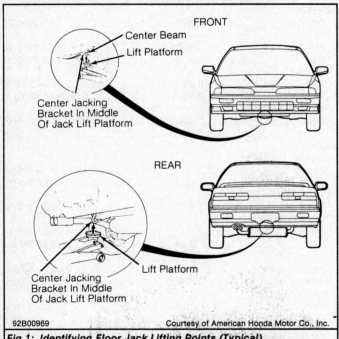

92B00969   Courtesy of American Honda Motor Co., Inc.

Fig 1: Identifying Floor Jack Lifting Points (Typical)

LIFTING USING HOIST

Position lift blocks as shown. *See Fig. 2.*

WHEEL ALIGNMENT PROCEDURES

CAMBER INSPECTION

1) Ensure tire pressure is correct. With wheels facing straight ahead, install camber/caster gauge parallel to front hub. On Integra, use Gauge Attachment (07HGK-0010100). On Legend and Vigor, use Gauge Attachment (07MGK-0010100).

2) On all models, read camber on gauge with bubble at center of gauge. If camber is not within specification, check for bent or damaged suspension components. See WHEEL ALIGNMENT SPECIFICATIONS table.

CASTER INSPECTION

Integra – 1) Ensure tire pressure is correct. Position wheels in straight-ahead position. Install camber/caster gauge and Gauge

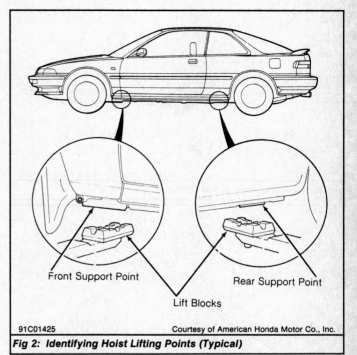

91C01425   Courtesy of American Honda Motor Co., Inc.

Fig 2: Identifying Hoist Lifting Points (Typical)

Attachment (07HGK-0010100). Apply front brake. Turn front wheel 20 degrees inward. Turn adjuster screw on caster gauge to position bubble at zero degrees.

2) Turn wheel outward 20 degrees. Read caster on gauge with bubble at center of gauge. If readings are not within specification, check for bent or damaged suspension components. See WHEEL ALIGNMENT SPECIFICATIONS table.

Legend & Vigor – 1) Ensure tire pressure is correct. Lift front of vehicle, and place turning radius gauges beneath front wheels. Lower vehicle. Raise rear of vehicle, and place boards of same thickness as turning radius gauges under rear wheels.

2) Lower vehicle. Install Camber/Caster Gauge and Gauge Attachment (07MGK-0010100). Apply front brake. Turn front wheel 20 degrees inward. Turn adjuster screw on caster gauge to position bubble at zero degrees.

3) Turn wheel outward 20 degrees. Read caster on gauge with bubble at center of gauge. If readings are not within specification, check for bent or damaged suspension components. See WHEEL ALIGNMENT SPECIFICATIONS table.

TOE-IN ADJUSTMENT

NOTE: Measure toe-in with wheels facing straight ahead.

Front – 1) Center steering wheel. Measure toe-in. If toe-in is not within specification, adjustment is required. See WHEEL ALIGNMENT SPECIFICATIONS table. If adjustment is necessary, go to next step.

2) Loosen tie rod lock nuts. Turn both tie rods in same direction until wheels are straight. Turn both tie rods equally until toe-in is as specified. Tighten tie rod lock nuts. See TORQUE SPECIFICATIONS. Reposition tie rod boot if necessary.

Rear (Integra) – Release parking brake. If parking brake is engaged, toe reading may be incorrect. Note locations of right and left compensator arm adjusting bolts. *See Fig. 3.* Loosen adjuster bolt. Slide compensator arm in or out to adjust toe-in. See WHEEL ALIGNMENT SPECIFICATIONS table. Tighten adjuster bolt. See TORQUE SPECIFICATIONS.

Rear (Legend & Vigor) – Release parking brake. If parking brake is engaged, toe-in measurement may be incorrect. Hold adjuster bolt on lower control arm, and loosen lock nut. *See Fig. 4.* Turn adjuster bolt until toe-in is as specified. See WHEEL ALIGNMENT SPECIFICATIONS table. Install new lock nut, and tighten to specification. See TORQUE SPECIFICATIONS.

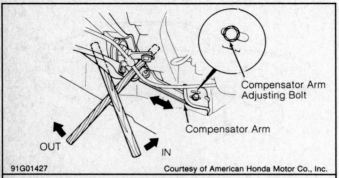

Fig 3: Adjusting Rear Toe-In (Integra)

91G01427   Courtesy of American Honda Motor Co., Inc.

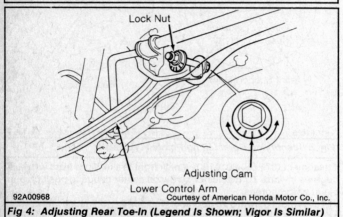

Fig 4: Adjusting Rear Toe-In (Legend Is Shown; Vigor Is Similar)

92A00968   Courtesy of American Honda Motor Co., Inc.

TORQUE SPECIFICATIONS

TORQUE SPECIFICATIONS

Application	Ft. Lbs. (N.m)
Integra	
Compensator Arm Adjusting Bolt	48 (65)
Spindle Nut	
Front	136 (185)
Rear	136 (185)
Tie Rod Lock Nut	41 (55)
Wheel Lug Nut	81 (110)
Legend	
Radius Rod	63 (85)
Rear Control Arm Lock Nut	41 (55)
Spindle Nut	
Front	247 (335)
Rear	210 (285)
Tie Rod Lock Nut	33 (45)
Wheel Lug Nut	81 (110)
Vigor	
Radius Rod Lock Nut	32 (44)
Rear Control Arm	41 (55)
Spindle Nut	
Front	184 (250)
Rear	100 (134)
Tie Rod Lock Nut	33 (45)
Wheel Lug Nut	81 (110)

WHEEL ALIGNMENT SPECIFICATIONS

WHEEL ALIGNMENT SPECIFICATIONS

Application	Preferred	Range
Integra		
Camber [1]		
Front	0	– 1 To 1
Rear	– 0.67	– 1.67 To 0.33
Caster [1]		
Front	1.5	0.5 To 2.5
Toe-In [1]		
Front	0	– 0.16 To 0.16
Rear	0.16	0 To 0.24
Toe-In [2]		
Front	0 (0)	– 0.08 To 0.08 (– 2 To 2)
Rear	0.08 (2)	0 To 0.12 (0 To 3)
Toe-Out On Turns [1]		
Inner	40.5	N/A
Outer	32	N/A
Legend		
Camber [1]		
Front	0	– 1 To 1
Rear	– 0.33	1.33 To 0.67
Caster [1]		
Front	3.75	2.75 To 4.75
Toe-In [1]		
Front	– 0.08	– 0.24 To 0.08
Rear	0.16	0 To 0.32
Toe-In [2]		
Front	– 0.04 (– 1)	– 0.12 To 0.04 (– 3 To 1)
Rear	0.08 (2)	0 To 0.16 (0 To 4)
Toe-Out On Turns [1]		
Inner	44	N/A
Outer	35	N/A
Vigor		
Camber [1]		
Front	0	– 1 To 1
Rear	– 0.5	– 1.5 To 0.5
Caster [1]		
Front	1.63	0.63 To 2.63
Toe-In [1]		
Front	0	– 0.16 To 0.16
Rear	0.24	0.06 To 0.4
Toe-In [2]		
Front	0 (0)	– 0.08 To 0.08 (– 2 To 2)
Rear	0.12 (3)	0.04 To 0.2 (1 To 5)
Toe-Out On Turns [1]		
Inner	39.4	N/A
Outer	33.6	N/A

[1] – Measurements are in degrees.

[2] – Measurements are in inches (mm).

1993 SUSPENSION
Front

Integra, Legend, Vigor

CAUTION: Use extreme care when working around Supplemental Restraint System (SRS) wiring and components at front fenderwells. All SRS wiring harnesses and connectors are color-coded Yellow. DO NOT damage this wiring.

DESCRIPTION

Integra, Legend, and Vigor use independent wishbone MacPherson strut front suspension. Vertically mounted strut assembly is attached to lower control arm by a fork assembly. *See Fig. 1, 2, or 3.* Steering knuckle is attached to upper and lower control arms by ball joints. A stabilizer bar and radius rod are attached to the lower control arm.

ADJUSTMENTS & INSPECTION

WHEEL ALIGNMENT
SPECIFICATIONS & PROCEDURES

NOTE: See SPECIFICATIONS & PROCEDURES article in WHEEL ALIGNMENT.

WHEEL BEARINGS

Wheel bearings are not adjustable.

BALL JOINT CHECKING

Information is not available from manufacturer.

REMOVAL & INSTALLATION

NOTE: Always grease new bushings with silicone grease before installation.

HUB & KNUCKLE ASSEMBLY

Removal (Integra) – **1)** Raise and support front of vehicle. Allow suspension to hang freely. Remove wheel assembly and spindle nut. Remove brake caliper mounting bolts, and wire caliper aside.
2) Remove brake disc retaining screws. Screw two 8 x 10-mm bolts into disc to push disc away from hub. Turn each screw alternately, 2 turns at a time, to prevent disc from cocking.
3) Remove cotter pin from lower control arm ball joint. *See Fig. 4.* Loosen castle nut half length of joint threads. Using bearing puller, break lower control arm ball joint loose.
4) Remove cotter pin from upper ball joint. Loosen castle nut half length of joint threads. Using ball joint remover, break upper ball joint loose. Remove castle nut, and pull hub/knuckle assembly from axle.
Installation – To install, reverse removal procedure. Tighten bolts and nuts to specification. Use new spindle nut, and stake it after tightening. See TORQUE SPECIFICATIONS.

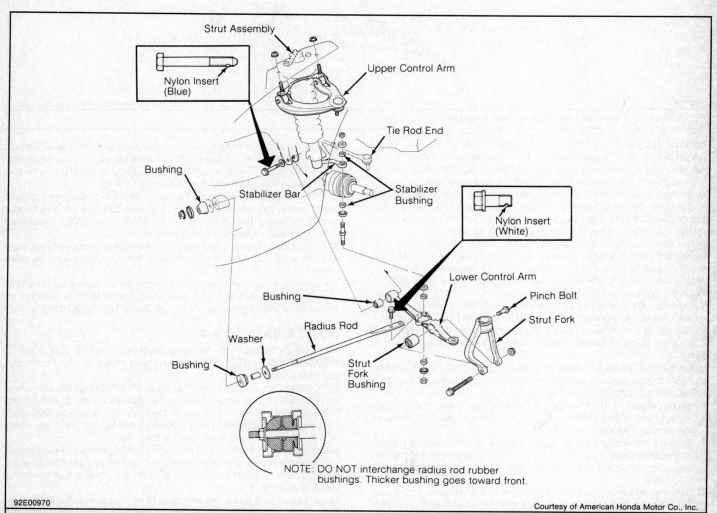

NOTE: DO NOT interchange radius rod rubber bushings. Thicker bushing goes toward front.

92E00970

Courtesy of American Honda Motor Co., Inc.

Fig. 1: Exploded View Of Front Suspension (Integra)

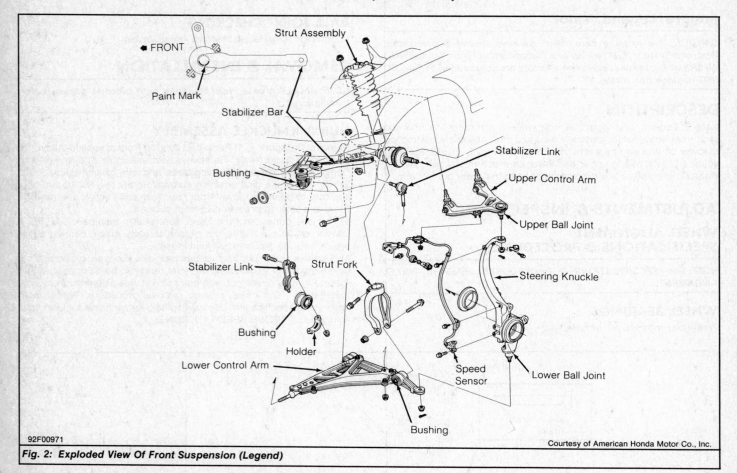

FRONT
Strut Assembly
Paint Mark
Stabilizer Bar
Stabilizer Link
Upper Control Arm
Bushing
Upper Ball Joint
Stabilizer Link
Strut Fork
Steering Knuckle
Bushing
Holder
Speed Sensor
Lower Control Arm
Lower Ball Joint
Bushing

92F00971

Courtesy of American Honda Motor Co., Inc.

Fig. 2: Exploded View Of Front Suspension (Legend)

Removal (Legend) – 1) Raise and support front of vehicle. Allow suspension to hang freely. Remove wheel assembly and spindle nut. Remove brake hose mounting bolts. Without disconnecting wiring, remove speed sensor from knuckle and lower control arm.

2) Without disconnecting hydraulic hose, remove brake caliper and wire it aside. Remove brake disc retaining screws. Screw two 8 x 12-mm bolts into disc to push disc away from hub. Turn each screw alternately, 2 turns at a time, to prevent disc from cocking.

3) Remove cotter pin from tie rod ball joint, and remove castle nut. Using Ball Joint Remover (07MAC-SL00200), break tie rod ball joint loose. Separate tie rod from knuckle. Remove cotter pin from lower control arm ball joint, and loosen castle nut half length of joint threads.

4) Using bearing puller, break lower control arm ball joint loose. Remove castle nut, and pull arm down until ball joint is clear of knuckle. Remove cotter pin from upper ball joint, and loosen castle nut half length of joint threads. Using ball joint remover, break upper ball joint loose. Remove castle nut, and pull hub/knuckle assembly from axle.

Installation – To install, reverse removal procedure. Tighten bolts and nuts to specification. Use NEW spindle nut, and stake it after tightening. See TORQUE SPECIFICATIONS.

Removal (Vigor) – 1) Lift spindle nut locking tab. Remove nut. Loosen wheel nuts slightly. Raise and support front of vehicle. Remove wheel nuts and wheel.

2) Remove mounting bolt for brake hose bracket. Remove caliper mounting bolts, and wire caliper aside. Without disconnecting speed sensor wire, remove speed sensor wire bracket and speed sensor from knuckle.

3) Remove cotter pin from tie rod ball joint, and remove castle nut. Install a 12-mm hex nut flush with ball joint pin as a thread protector. Using Ball Joint Remover (07MAC-SL00200), break tie rod ball joint loose. Separate tie rod from knuckle.

4) Remove cotter pin from lower arm ball joint, and remove castle nut. Install a 14-mm hex nut flush with ball joint pin as a thread protector. Using Ball Joint Remover (07MAC-SL00100), break lower arm ball joint loose and separate ball joint and lower arm.

5) Remove knuckle protector. Remove cotter pin and upper ball joint castle nut. Install a 10-mm hex nut flush with ball joint pin as a thread protector. Using Ball Joint Remover (07MAC-SL00200), break ball joint loose and separate it from knuckle.

6) Pull knuckle outward, and separate drive shaft outboard joint from knuckle with a plastic mallet. Remove hub/knuckle assembly from vehicle.

Installation – To install hub/knuckle assembly, reverse removal procedure. Tighten bolts and nuts to specification. Use NEW spindle nut, and stake it after tightening. See TORQUE SPECIFICATIONS.

LOWER BALL JOINT

Removal (Integra) – 1) Remove steering knuckle. See HUB & KNUCKLE ASSEMBLY. Remove dust boot snap ring, dust boot, and ball joint snap ring.

2) Position Ball Joint Installer/Remover (07965-SB00100) so narrow end of tool fits over tapered end of ball joint shaft. Install and tighten ball joint nut. Position Ball Joint Removal Base (07965-SB00300) between ball joint housing and steering knuckle, and place assembly in vise. Press ball joint from knuckle. *See Fig. 5.*

Installation – 1) Position ball joint into steering knuckle. Position ball joint installer wide end on ball joint shaft. Position Ball Joint Installation Base (07965-SB00300) over end of ball joint. Press ball joint into knuckle. *See Fig. 5.*

2) Install ball joint snap ring and dust boot. Install dust boot clip with Boot Clip Guide (07974-SA50700). To complete installation, reverse removal procedure.

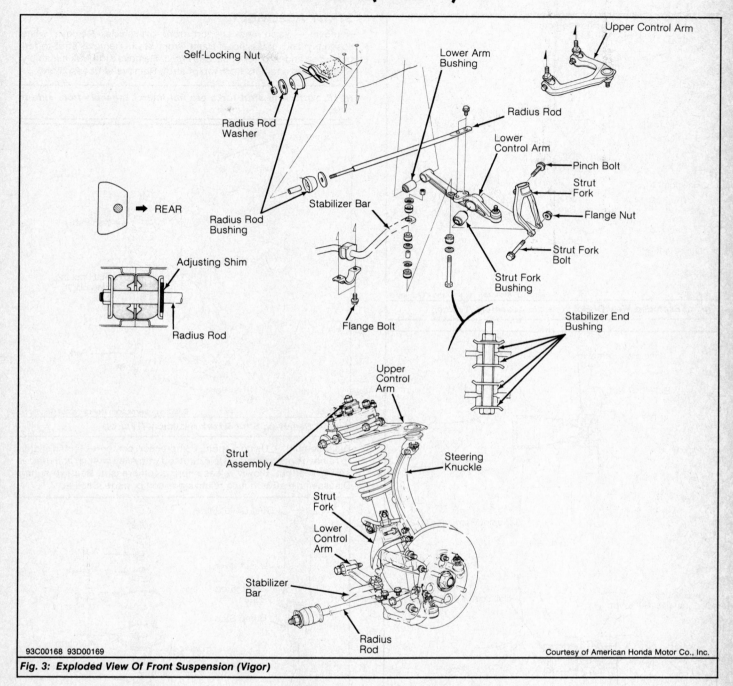

93C00168 93D00169

Courtesy of American Honda Motor Co., Inc.

Fig. 3: Exploded View Of Front Suspension (Vigor)

Removal & Installation (Legend) – Remove steering knuckle. See HUB & KNUCKLE ASSEMBLY. Remove cotter pin and lower ball joint nut. Using Balll Joint Remover (07MAC-SL00200), separate ball joint from lower arm.

Removal (Vigor) – **1)** Remove steering knuckle. See HUB & KNUCKLE ASSEMBLY. Remove dust boot snap ring, dust boot, and ball joint snap ring.

2) Position Ball Joint Installer/Remover (07GAF-SD40330) so narrow end of tool fits over tapered end of ball joint shaft. Install and tighten ball joint nut. Position Ball Joint Removal Base (07GAF-SD40310) between ball joint housing and steering knuckle, and place assembly in vise. Press ball joint from knuckle. *See Fig. 5.*

Installation – **1)** Position ball joint into steering knuckle. Position ball joint installer wide end on ball joint shaft. Position Ball Joint Installation Base (07GAF-SD40320) over end of ball joint. Press ball joint into knuckle. *See Fig. 5.*

2) Install ball joint snap ring and dust boot. Install dust boot clip with Boot Clip Guide (07GOG-SD40700). To complete installation, reverse removal procedure.

LOWER CONTROL ARM

Removal (Integra) – **1)** Raise and support front of vehicle. Remove wheel assembly. Remove strut fork and strut rod (radius arm) bolts. Remove nut, bolt, and bushings from stabilizer bar.

2) Remove cotter pin from lower control arm ball joint, and remove castle nut. Break lower control arm ball joint loose, and pull arm down until ball joint is clear of knuckle. Remove lower control arm pivot bolt. Remove control arm.

Installation – Inspect parts for deterioration and damage. Replace worn or damaged parts. Reverse removal procedure to install control arm.

Removal & Installation (Legend & Vigor) – *See Fig. 2 or 3.*

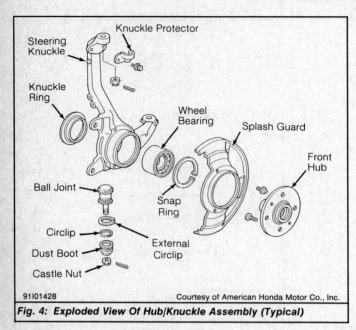

Fig. 4: Exploded View Of Hub/Knuckle Assembly (Typical)

Steering Knuckle

Knuckle Protector

Knuckle Ring

Wheel Bearing

Splash Guard

Front Hub

Ball Joint

Circlip

External Circlip

Snap Ring

Dust Boot

Castle Nut

91I01428   Courtesy of American Honda Motor Co., Inc.

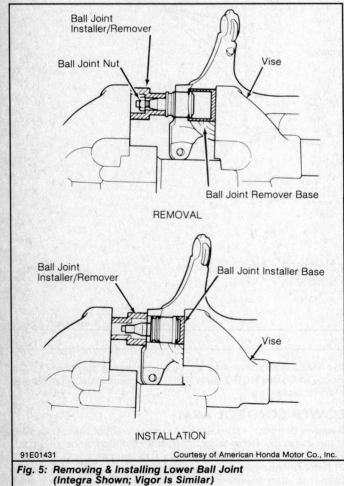

Ball Joint Installer/Remover

Ball Joint Nut

Vise

Ball Joint Remover Base

REMOVAL

Ball Joint Installer/Remover

Ball Joint Installer Base

Vise

INSTALLATION

91E01431   Courtesy of American Honda Motor Co., Inc.

Fig. 5: Removing & Installing Lower Ball Joint (Integra Shown; Vigor Is Similar)

STABILIZER BAR

Removal & Installation – *See Fig. 1, 2, or 3.*

STRUT ASSEMBLY

Removal – Raise and support front of vehicle. Remove wheel assembly and brake hose clamp from strut. Remove strut-to-fork pinch bolt and strut fork bolt. *See Fig. 6.* Remove strut fork assembly. Remove cap and nuts from top of strut. Remove strut assembly.

NOTE: Struts and strut forks are not interchangeable from side to side.

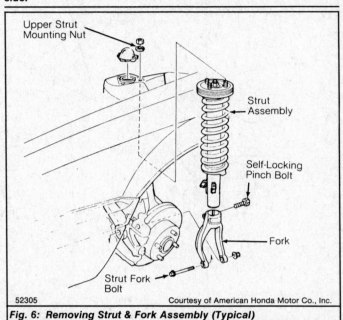

Upper Strut Mounting Nut

Strut Assembly

Self-Locking Pinch Bolt

Fork

Strut Fork Bolt

52305   Courtesy of American Honda Motor Co., Inc.

Fig. 6: Removing Strut & Fork Assembly (Typical)

Disassembly – Using a spring compressor, compress spring slightly to remove spring tension. Hold strut rod with Allen wrench and remove spring seat nut. Slowly release spring compressor. Remove spring. Disassemble strut, noting relative position of parts. *See Fig. 7.*

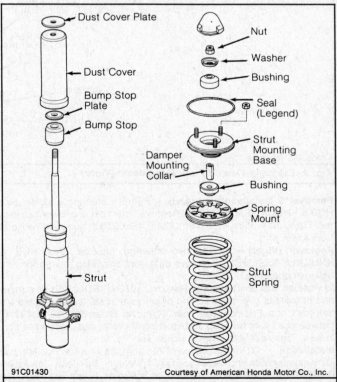

Dust Cover Plate

Dust Cover

Bump Stop Plate

Bump Stop

Strut

Nut

Washer

Bushing

Seal (Legend)

Strut Mounting Base

Damper Mounting Collar

Bushing

Spring Mount

Strut Spring

91C01430   Courtesy of American Honda Motor Co., Inc.

Fig. 7: Exploded View Of Strut Assembly (Typical)

Reassembly – Inspect parts for cracks, deterioration, or damage. Check shock absorber for leaks and improper operation. Replace strut if resistance is weak, uneven, or jerky when strut is compressed. Replace worn or damaged parts. Position mounting base with one stud aligned with tab on strut housing. To complete reassembly, reverse disassembly procedure.

Installation – 1) Install strut fork onto lower control arm. Position strut assembly so tab on strut housing aligns with slot in fork. Align upper strut studs with strut tower holes. Place jack under knuckle, and raise it until vehicle just lifts from safety stand.

NOTE: *Strut mount base nuts must be tightened with strut under vehicle weight.*

---

2) Install upper strut mount nuts. Tighten strut assembly while strut is under load. Reverse removal procedure to complete installation. Tighten nuts and bolts to specification. See TORQUE SPECIFICATIONS.

UPPER CONTROL ARM

Inspection – Raise and support front of vehicle. Remove wheel assembly. Rock upper ball joint front to back. Replace upper arm bushings if any play exists.

Removal (Integra) – 1) Raise and support front of vehicle. Remove wheel assembly. Remove cotter pin from upper ball joint, and remove castle nut.

2) Break upper control arm ball joint loose, and push arm up until ball joint is clear of knuckle. Remove anchor bolt nuts. Remove bolts and upper control arm. Clamp each upper arm anchor bolt in a vise. Remove upper arm bushings.

Installation – Coat new upper arm bushings with grease. Install upper arm bushings into upper arm anchor bolts. Center bushing so that 0.4" (10 mm) protrudes from each side of anchor bolt. Install and tighten upper arm bolts/nuts. See TORQUE SPECIFICATIONS. To complete installation, reverse removal procedure. Check camber, and adjust if necessary.

Removal & Installation (Legend & Vigor) – See Fig. 2 or 3.

UPPER BALL JOINT

Removal & Installation (Legend) – Upper ball joint is not replaceable as a separate component. If ball joint is worn excessively, replace upper control arm.

WHEEL BEARING

Removal (Integra) – 1) Remove steering knuckle. See HUB & KNUCKLE ASSEMBLY. Remove splash guard screws and splash guard. Using Front Hub Remover/Installer (07GAF-SE00100) and hydraulic press, press hub from steering knuckle. Remove bearing retaining snap ring and knuckle ring from knuckle.

2) Press bearing from knuckle. Using bearing puller, remove outboard bearing from hub. Clean knuckle and hub thoroughly before reassembly.

Installation – Press new bearing into knuckle. Install snap ring into knuckle groove. Install splash guard. Invert knuckle. Press new bearing into hub. Press hub into knuckle. To complete installation, reverse removal procedure.

Removal & Installation (Legend) – 1) Remove steering knuckle. See HUB & KNUCKLE ASSEMBLY. Clamp steering knuckle into soft-jawed vise. Using universal hub puller, separate hub from knuckle. Remove splash guard screws and splash guard.

2) Remove circlip from knuckle. Press inner and outer bearings from hub. Clean knuckle and hub thoroughly before reassembly. To install, reverse removal procedure.

Removal & Installation (Vigor) – 1) Remove steering knuckle. See HUB & KNUCKLE ASSEMBLY. Remove knuckle from hub unit. Separate hub unit from brake disk. Using Hub Disassembly Driver (07GAF-SE00100) and Hub Disassembly Base (07GAF-SD40700), press front hub from wheel bearing.

2) Using bearing separator, Hub Disassembly Driver (07GAF-SE00100), and Support Base (07965-SD90100), press out bearing race. Clean knuckle and hub thoroughly before reassembly. To install, reverse removal procedure, using Driver (07749-0010000), Hub Assembly Guide (07GAF-0SE00200), Hub Driver (07GAF-SE00100), Support Base (07965-SD90100), and a hydraulic press.

TORQUE SPECIFICATIONS

TORQUE SPECIFICATIONS

Application	Ft. Lbs. (N.m)
Integra	
Brake Caliper Bolt	81 (110)
Lower Ball Joint-To-Knuckle Nut	41 (55)
Radius Arm Nut	32 (44)
Radius Arm-To-Control Arm Bolt	77 (105)
Spindle Nut	136 (185)
Splash Guard Bolt	[1]
Stabilizer Bar-To-Control Arm Nut	16 (22)
Steering Knuckle Protector Bolt	[2]
Strut Fork Pinch Bolt	32 (44)
Strut Fork-To-Control Arm Nut	48 (65)
Strut Mounting Base Nut	37 (50)
Strut Mounting Nut	30 (40)
Tie Rod End-To-Knuckle Nut	77 (105)
Upper Ball Joint-To-Knuckle Nut	30-35 (40-48)
Upper Control Arm Anchor Bolt Nut	48 (65)
Upper Control Arm Nut	22 (30)
Wheel Lug Nut	81 (110)
Legend	
Brake Caliper Mounting Bolt	81 (110)
Lower Ball Joint-To-Knuckle Nut	59 (80)
Radius Rod-To-Knuckle Bolt	77 (105)
Spindle Nut	247 (335)
Strut Fork Pinch Bolt	38 (51)
Strut Mounting Base Nut	37 (50)
Strut Mounting Nut	30 (40)
Tie Rod Lock Nut	33 (45)
Upper Ball Joint-To-Knuckle Nut	30-35 (40-48)
Upper Control Arm Anchor Bolt Nut	48 (65)
Upper Strut Mounting Nut	29 (39)
Wheel Lug Nut	81 (110)
Vigor	
Brake Caliper Bolt	81 (110)
Lower Ball Joint-To-Knuckle Nut	37-44 (50-60)
Radius Arm Nut	32 (44)
Radius Arm-To-Control Arm Bolt	77 (105)
Spindle Nut	184 (250)
Splash Guard Bolt	[1]
Stabilizer Bar-To-Control Arm Nut	14 (19)
Steering Knuckle Protector Bolt	[2]
Strut Fork Pinch Bolt	32 (44)
Strut Fork-To-Control Arm Nut	48 (65)
Strut Mounting Base Nut	29 (39)
Strut Mounting Nut	29 (39)
Tie Rod End-To-Knuckle Nut	37-44 (50-60)
Upper Ball Joint-To-Knuckle Nut	30-35 (40-48)
Upper Control Arm Anchor Bolt Nut	48 (65)
Upper Control Arm Nut	22 (30)
Wheel Lug Nut	81 (110)

[1] – Tighten to 44 INCH lbs. (5 N.m).
[2] – Tighten to 88 INCH lbs. (10 N.m).

Integra, Legend, Vigor

DESCRIPTION

Integra, Legend, and Vigor use an independent control arm suspension system. Suspension consists of a vertically mounted strut with coil spring connected to a knuckle/spindle assembly, upper control arm, one or 2 lower control arms, trailing arm (Integra and Vigor), and a stabilizer bar. *See Figs. 1, 2, and 3.*

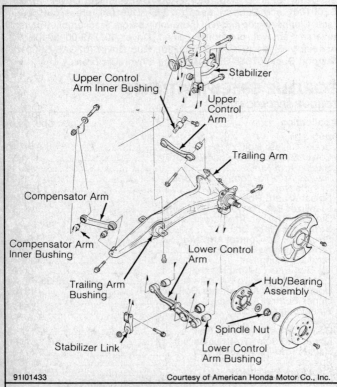

91I01433   Courtesy of American Honda Motor Co., Inc.

Fig. 1: Exploded View Of Rear Suspension (Integra)

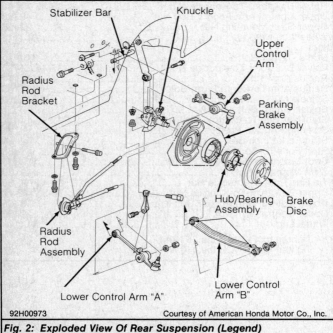

92H00973   Courtesy of American Honda Motor Co., Inc.

Fig. 2: Exploded View Of Rear Suspension (Legend)

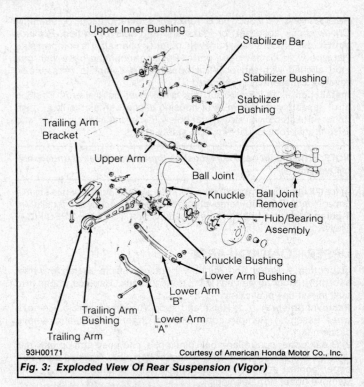

93H00171   Courtesy of American Honda Motor Co., Inc.

Fig. 3: Exploded View Of Rear Suspension (Vigor)

ADJUSTMENTS & INSPECTION

WHEEL ALIGNMENT
SPECIFICATIONS & PROCEDURES

NOTE: See SPECIFICATIONS & PROCEDURES article in WHEEL ALIGNMENT.

WHEEL BEARING

Wheel bearings are not adjustable.

REMOVAL & INSTALLATION

HUB/BEARING ASSEMBLY

Removal & Installation – Raise and support rear of vehicle. Remove wheel assembly. Remove caliper, and wire it aside. Remove brake disc. Remove hub cap. Pry spindle nut lock tab away from spindle, and remove nut. Remove hub/bearing assembly. *See Fig. 1, 2, or 3.* To install, reverse removal procedure.

UPPER & LOWER CONTROL ARMS

Removal & Installation (Integra) – *See Fig. 1.*
Removal & Installation (Legend) – **1)** Remove hub/bearing assembly. See HUB/BEARING ASSEMBLY. Without disconnecting wiring, remove speed sensor from knuckle and lower control arm. Remove parking brake cable retaining brackets.
2) Remove parking brake assembly. Separate strut from knuckle by removing strut mounting bolt. Remove cotter pin from lower control arm ball joint, and loosen castle nut half length of joint threads.
3) Using Ball Joint Remover (07MAC-SL00200), break lower ball joint loose from knuckle. Remove castle nut. Remove cotter pin from upper control arm ball joint, and loosen castle nut half length of joint threads. Using ball joint remover, break upper control arm ball joint loose. Remove castle nut.
4) Remove lower control arm "B". *See Fig. 2.* Remove knuckle. Remove upper radius rod nut. Remove upper control arm. Remove stabilizer link from lower control arm "A". Remove lower radius rod nut. Remove lower control arm "A". Remove radius rod assembly. To install, reverse removal procedure.

NOTE: *Control arms are not interchangeable. Painted identification mark is SPO-L-UP for left lower control arm or SPO-R-UP for right control arm. Install control arm so painted identification mark faces toward front. Upper control arms are marked POL for left upper control arm, or POR for right upper control arm.*

Removal & Installation (Vigor) – *See Fig. 3.*

UPPER ARM BUSHING

Removal & Installation (Integra) – Drive out upper arm inner bushing and upper arm bushing. *See Fig. 4.* Scribe a line on upper arm inner bushing in line with bolt mounting surface. Mark upper arm at 2 points so they are in line and make a right angle with arm. *See Fig. 4.* Drive in upper arm inner bushing with marks aligned. Drive upper arm bushing into upper arm until their leading edges are flush with upper arm. *See Fig. 4.*

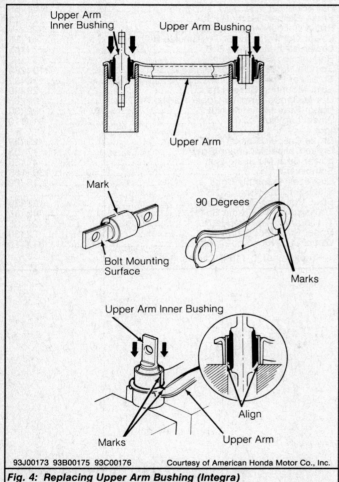

Fig. 4: **Replacing Upper Arm Bushing (Integra)**

93J00173 93B00175 93C00176   Courtesy of American Honda Motor Co., Inc.

COMPENSATOR ARM BUSHING

Removal & Installation (Integra) – Drive compensator arm bushing out of compensator arm in appropriate direction. *See Fig. 5.* Drive bushings in from indicated direction, with leading edges flush with compensator arm. *See Fig. 5.*

TRAILING ARM

Removal & Installation (Integra & Vigor) – *See Fig. 1 or 3.*

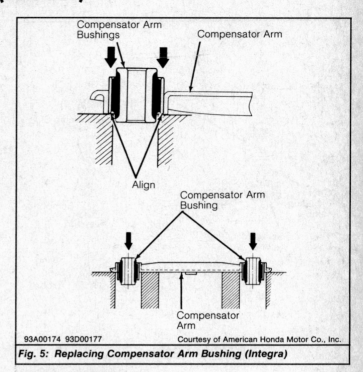

93A00174 93D00177   Courtesy of American Honda Motor Co., Inc.

Fig. 5: **Replacing Compensator Arm Bushing (Integra)**

STRUT ASSEMBLY

WARNING: *Strut contains pressurized nitrogen gas. To dispose of properly, drill a 5/64" (2.0 mm) hole at base of strut. Always wear eye protection when drilling.*

Removal – **1)** Lift and support vehicle. Remove wheel assembly. On Integra, remove strut cover behind rear seat trim panel. On Legend, remove rear speaker. On Vigor, remove rear seat. On all models, remove strut mounting base nuts. *See Fig. 6 or 7.*
2) Place floor jack under lower control arm. Compress strut slightly. Remove strut lower mounting nut. Lower rear suspension. Remove strut assembly.

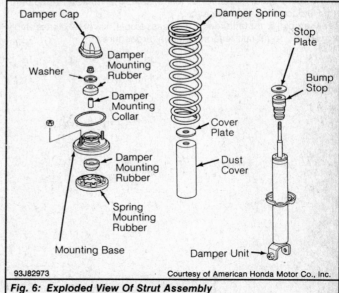

93J82973   Courtesy of American Honda Motor Co., Inc.

Fig. 6: **Exploded View Of Strut Assembly (Integra Shown; Legend Is Similar)**

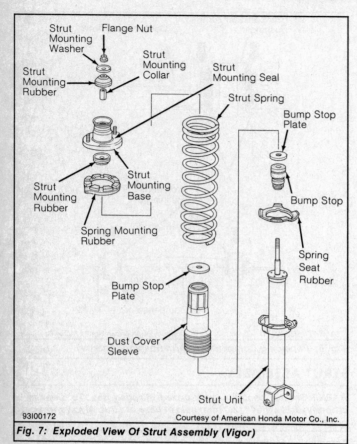

Fig. 7: Exploded View Of Strut Assembly (Vigor)

93I00172   Courtesy of American Honda Motor Co., Inc.

Disassembly – 1) Compress strut spring with spring compressor. DO NOT compress spring more than necessary to remove 10-mm self-locking nut. Remove 10-mm self-locking nut from strut assembly. **2)** Remove spring compressor. Note component locations, and complete disassembly by removing components.

Inspection – Check for smooth operation in both compression and extension strokes. Check for oil leaks, abnormal noises, or and binding. Replace strut as necessary.

Reassembly & Installation – To reassemble, reverse disassembly procedure. To install, reverse removal procedure.

TORQUE SPECIFICATIONS

TORQUE SPECIFICATIONS

Application	Ft. Lbs. (N.m)
Integra	
Brake Caliper Bolt	17 (23)
Brake Caliper Bracket Bolt	29 (40)
Compensator Arm Adjusting Bolt	29 (40)
Compensator-To-Frame Bolt	29 (40)
Lower Strut Mounting Bolt	41 (55)
Spindle Nut	136 (185)
Stabilizer Assembly Bolts	16 (22)
Stabilizer Link Nut	30 (40)
Strut Mounting Base Nuts	30 (40)
Trailing Arm-To-Compensator Arm Bolt	30 (40)
Trailing Arm-To-Upper Arm	41 (55)
Upper Strut Mounting Nut	22 (30)
Wheel Lug Nut	81 (110)
Legend	
Ball Joint Nut	41 (55)
Brake Caliper Bracket Bolt	29 (39)
Brake Caliper Mounting Bolt	29 (39)
Lower Control Arm "B"-To-Knuckle Bolt	41 (55)
Lower Strut Mounting Bolt	77 (105)
Radius Rod Bracket Bolt	77 (105)
Spindle Nut	210 (285)
Stabilizer Link Bolt	16 (22)
Strut Mounting Base Nuts	29 (39)
Upper Control Arm-To-Upper Radius Rod Nut	62 (85)
Upper Strut Mounting Nut	22 (30)
Wheel Lug Nut	81 (110)
Vigor	
Brake Caliper Bracket Bolt	29 (39)
Brake Caliper Mounting Bolt	17 (23)
Lower Strut Mounting Bolt	41 (55)
Spindle Nut	136 (185)
Stabilizer Assembly Bolts	16 (22)
Stabilizer Link Nut	[1]
Strut Mounting Base Nuts	29 (39)
Trailing Arm-To-Frame Bolt	48 (65)
Trailing Arm-To-Knuckle Nut	27 (36)
Upper Strut Mounting Nut	22 (30)
Wheel Lug Nut	81 (110)

[1] – Tighten nut to 115 INCH lbs. (13 N.m).

Integra, Legend, Vigor

DESCRIPTION

All models use a 2-piece safety steering column with a slip joint flange connection. The steering column is supported by a column tube.

WARNING: Legend and Vigor are equipped with Supplemental Restraint System (SRS). All SRS wiring is color coded Yellow. Before performing any repairs on steering column, disable air bag system. See DISABLING SYSTEM under DISABLING & ACTIVATING AIR BAG SYSTEM.

DISABLING & ACTIVATING AIR BAG SYSTEM

DISABLING SYSTEM

WARNING: Wait at least 3 minutes after deactivating air bag system. System maintains voltage for about 3 minutes after battery is disconnected. Servicing air bag system before 3 minutes may cause accidental air bag deployment and possible personal injury.

CAUTION: Radio has a coded theft protection circuit. Before disconnecting battery cables, obtain radio anti-theft code number from customer. After reconnecting power, turn radio on. Word CODE will be displayed. Enter customer 5-digit code to restore radio operation.

1) To disable SRS, turn ignition off. Wait at least 3 minutes to allow capacitor in back-up circuit to discharge, preventing a malfunction of seat belt pretensioner or accidental deployment of air bag.
2) Disconnect battery cables. Remove maintenance lid below driver-side air bag. *See Fig. 1.* Remove Red short connector. Unplug 3-pin connector between air bag and cable reel. Connect Red short connector to air bag side of connector. On models equipped with anti-theft circuit, connect SRS Short Connector "A" (07MAZ-SP00200 on Legend or 07MAZ-SP00100 on Vigor) to cable reel side of connector. *See Fig. 2.*
3) On Vigor, go to step **4)**. Remove glove box. Unplug connector between passenger-side air bag and SRS harness. Plug Red short connector into air bag side of connector. Install SRS Short Connector (07MAZ-SP0020A) into SRS wiring harness. *See Figs. 3 and 4.*
4) Remove glove box. Remove Red short connector from holder. Unplug connector between passenger-side air bag and SRS harness. Install SRS short connector into SRS wiring harness. *See Fig. 5.*

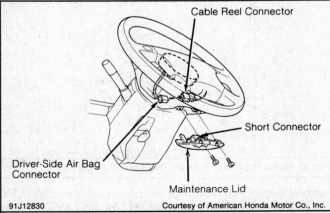

91J12830   Courtesy of American Honda Motor Co., Inc.

Fig. 1: Locating SRS Maintenance Lid & Short Connector (Legend Shown; Vigor Is Similar)

ACTIVATING SYSTEM

1) Unplug Red short connector from connector(s) and SRS short connector "A" from cable reel connector (if equipped). On all models,

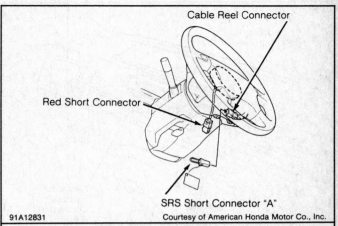

91A12831   Courtesy of American Honda Motor Co., Inc.

Fig. 2: Installing SRS Short Connector "A" Onto Cable Reel Connector (Legend Coupe Shown; Others Are Similar)

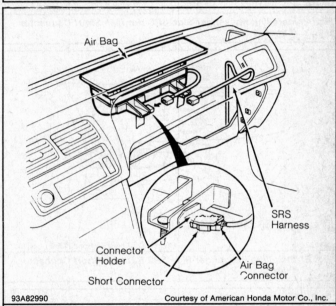

93A82990   Courtesy of American Honda Motor Co., Inc.

Fig. 3: Installing Passenger-Side Air Bag Short Connector (Legend)

reconnect driver-side air bag connector to cable reel connector.
2) Install short connectors into their holders. Reinstall lid on steering wheel. On Legend and Vigor, install glove box. On all models, reconnect battery. Turn ignition on. Observe SRS indicator light to verify system is functioning properly. SRS light should come on for about 6 seconds and then go off.

REMOVAL & INSTALLATION

STEERING WHEEL & HORN PAD

WARNING: Never store air bag upside down. Accidental deployment could cause serious injury. Store air bag with pad surface up and away from work area. DO NOT disassemble or tamper with air bag assembly.

Removal & Installation (Integra) – 1) Disconnect battery ground cable. Position front wheels straight ahead. Remove horn button center pad. Mark steering wheel and steering shaft for installation reference. Remove steering wheel shaft nut.
2) Remove steering wheel by rocking slightly while pulling steadily with both hands. To install, reverse removal procedure. Align marks properly upon assembly.

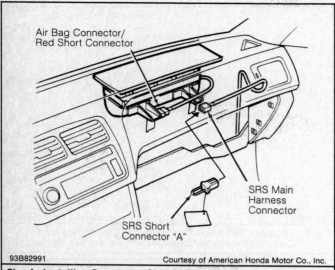

93B82991   Courtesy of American Honda Motor Co., Inc.

Fig. 4: Installing Passenger-Side SRS Harness Short Connector (Legend)

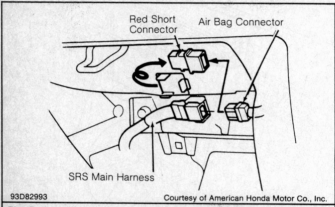

93D82993   Courtesy of American Honda Motor Co., Inc.

Fig. 5: Installing Passenger-Side SRS Harness Short Connector (Vigor)

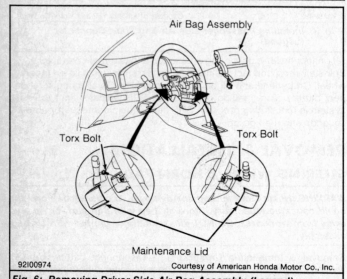

92I00974   Courtesy of American Honda Motor Co., Inc.

Fig. 6: Removing Driver-Side Air Bag Assembly (Legend)

Removal (Legend) – 1) Deactivate air bag system. See DISABLING SYSTEM under DISABLING & ACTIVATING AIR BAG SYSTEM. Position front wheels straight ahead. Remove maintenance lids from headlight/turn signal switch and wiper/washer switch. *See Fig. 6.* Remove and discard Torx bolts. Remove air bag assembly.

2) Mark steering wheel and shaft for installation reference. Note position of all connectors, and unplug as necessary. Remove steering wheel nut. Remove steering wheel by rocking slightly while pulling steadily with both hands.

Installation – 1) Align reference marks. Center cable reel by rotating cable reel clockwise until it stops. Rotate cable reel counterclockwise about 2 turns.

2) Yellow gear tooth should line up with alignment mark on cover, and arrow mark on cable reel should point straight up. *See Fig. 7.* Install steering wheel.

3) To complete installation, reverse removal procedure. Install air bag. Install new Torx bolts, and tighten bolts to 88 INCH lbs. (10 N.m). Reactivate air bag system. See ACTIVATING SYSTEM under DISABLING & ACTIVATING AIR BAG SYSTEM.

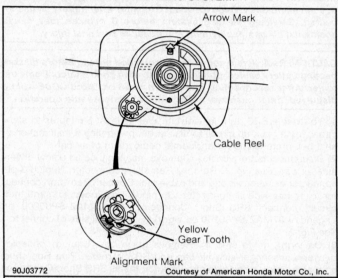

90J03772   Courtesy of American Honda Motor Co., Inc.

Fig. 7: Centering Cable Reel (Legend Shown; Vigor Is Similar)

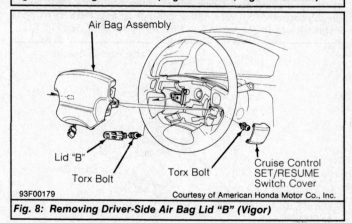

93F00179   Courtesy of American Honda Motor Co., Inc.

Fig. 8: Removing Driver-Side Air Bag Lid "B" (Vigor)

Removal (Vigor) – 1) Deactivate air bag system. See DISABLING SYSTEM under DISABLING & ACTIVATING AIR BAG SYSTEM. Position front wheels straight ahead.

2) Remove access panel from steering wheel lower cover. Remove short connector. Unplug connector between air bag and cable reel. Connect short connector to air bag side of connector. *See Fig. 1.*

3) Remove lid "B" and cruise control SET/RESUME switch cover. *See Fig. 8.* Remove and discard Torx bolts. Remove air bag assembly.

4) Unplug connectors from horn and cruise control SET/RESUME switches. Remove steering wheel nut. Mark steering wheel and shaft for reassembly. Remove steering wheel by rocking slightly while pulling steadily with both hands.

Installation – **1)** Align reference marks. Center cable reel by rotating clockwise until it stops. Rotate cable reel counterclockwise about 2 turns.

2) Yellow gear tooth should align up with mark on cover, and arrow mark on cable reel should point straight up. *See Fig. 7.* Install steering wheel.

3) To complete installation, reverse removal procedure. Install air bag. Install new Torx bolts, and tighten to 88 INCH lbs. (10 N.m). Reactivate air bag system. See ACTIVATING SYSTEM under DISABLING & ACTIVATING AIR BAG SYSTEM.

COMBINATION SWITCH (TURN SIGNAL/HEADLIGHT SWITCH)

Removal & Installation (Integra) – Disconnect negative battery cable. Remove steering wheel. Remove steering column covers. Unplug connectors from switch. Remove turn signal canceling sleeve. Remove combination switch mounting screws and switch. To install, reverse removal procedure.

NOTE: On Legend, removing steering wheel or air bag assembly is not necessary to remove combination switch.

Removal & Installation (Legend) – Disable air bag system. See DISABLING SYSTEM under DISABLING & ACTIVATING AIR BAG SYSTEM. Remove switches from lower dashboard panel. Remove lower dashboard panel. Remove upper and lower steering column covers. Unplug combination switch 14-pin connector. Remove combination switch mounting screws and switch. To install, reverse removal procedure.

Removal & Installation (Vigor) – Disable air bag system. See DISABLING SYSTEM under DISABLING & ACTIVATING AIR BAG SYSTEM. Remove steering wheel. Remove steering column covers. Unplug 10-pin and 12-pin connectors. Remove turn signal canceling sleeve. Remove combination switch mounting screws and switch. To install, reverse removal procedure.

WIPER/WASHER SWITCH

Removal & Installation (Integra) – Disable air bag system. See DISABLING SYSTEM under DISABLING & ACTIVATING AIR BAG SYSTEM. Remove horn pad and steering wheel. Remove upper and lower steering column covers. Unplug wiper/washer wiring harness connectors. Remove cruise control slip ring (if equipped). Remove 2 screws and wiper/washer switch. To install, reverse removal procedure.

Removal & Installation (Legend) – Disable air bag system. See DISABLING SYSTEM under DISABLING & ACTIVATING AIR BAG SYSTEM. Remove switches from lower dashboard panel. Remove lower dashboard panel. Remove upper and lower steering column covers. Unplug wiper/washer connector. Remove wiper/washer switch. To install, reverse removal procedure.

Removal & Installation (Vigor) – Disable air bag system. See DISABLING SYSTEM under DISABLING & ACTIVATING AIR BAG SYSTEM. Remove dashboard lower panel and knee bolster. Remove steering column covers. Unplug 10-pin connector. Remove mounting screws and washer/wiper switch. To install, reverse removal procedure.

IGNITION SWITCH

Removal & Installation (Integra) – Disconnect negative battery cable. Remove steering wheel. Remove upper and lower steering column covers. Remove lower dashboard panel and left knee bolster. Unplug 4-pin connector from underdash fuse block. Unplug 5-pin connector from main wire harness. Set ignition switch to "O" position. Remove 2 screws and ignition switch. To install, reverse removal procedure.

Removal & Installation (Legend) – Disable air bag system. See DISABLING SYSTEM under DISABLING & ACTIVATING AIR BAG SYSTEM. Remove switches from lower dashboard panel. Remove lower dashboard panel. Unplug ignition switch 7-pin connector from underdash fuse box. Set ignition switch to "O" position. Remove 2 screws and ignition switch. To install, reverse removal procedure.

Removal & Installation (Vigor) – Disable air bag system. See DISABLING SYSTEM under DISABLING & ACTIVATING AIR BAG SYSTEM. Remove dashboard lower cover and knee bolster. Unplug 7-pin connector from underdash fuse block. Remove steering column covers. Set ignition switch to "O" position. Remove 2 screws and ignition switch. To install, reverse removal procedure.

STEERING LOCK ASSEMBLY

Removal (Integra) – **1)** Disconnect negative battery cable. Remove steering wheel. Remove upper and lower steering column covers. Remove lower dashboard panel and left knee bolster. Unplug ignition switch 7-pin connector from main wiring harness.

2) Remove steering column mounting bolts/nuts. Lower steering column. Center-punch both shear bolts. Using a 3/16" bit, drill heads from bolts. Remove shear bolts and ignition lock assembly.

Installation – To install, reverse removal procedure. Tighten new shear bolts until heads twist off. Check for proper ignition switch steering lock operation.

Removal (Legend) – **1)** Remove switches from lower dashboard panel. Remove lower dashboard panel. Unplug wiring harness connectors as necessary. Remove steering column mounting bolts/nuts. Lower steering column assembly.

2) Grind slot into shear bolt. Using a screwdriver, remove shear bolt. Set ignition switch to "I" position. Push in on steering lock retaining pin. Remove steering lock assembly.

Installation – Set ignition switch to "I" position. Push in on steering lock retaining pin and insert steering lock assembly until assembly clicks into place. Loosely install new shear bolt. Insert ignition key and check for proper steering lock operation. Tighten shear bolt until hex head twists off. To complete installation, reverse removal procedure.

Removal (Vigor) – **1)** Disable air bag system. See DISABLING SYSTEM under DISABLING & ACTIVATING AIR BAG SYSTEM. Remove lower dashboard panel and left knee bolster. Unplug ignition switch 7-pin connector from main wiring harness. On models with A/T, unplug 8-pin connector from main wiring harness.

2) On all models, remove upper and lower steering column covers. Remove instrument panel trim panel. Center-punch both shear bolts. Using a 3/16" bit, drill heads from bolts. Remove shear bolts and lock assembly.

Installation – Install new switch without key inserted. Finger-tighten new shear bolts. Insert key. Check for proper operation. Tighten shear bolts until heads break off. To complete installation, reverse removal procedure.

LOCK CYLINDER

Removal (Integra M/T) – Disconnect negative battery cable. Remove horn pad and steering wheel. Remove upper and lower steering column covers. Set ignition switch to "I" position. Remove set screw from lock body. Push lock body retaining pin inward and remove lock cylinder.

Installation – Set ignition switch to "O" position. Align lock cylinder with lock body. Rotate ignition switch halfway to "I" position and insert lock cylinder until lock body retaining pin touches cylinder. Set ignition switch to "I" position and push lock body cylinder in until retaining pin clicks into place. Install set screw. To complete installation, reverse removal procedure.

Removal (Vigor) – **1)** Disconnect battery ground cable. Remove steering column covers. Remove bulb/socket from key light case by turning socket 45 degrees. Remove screw and key light case from lock body.

2) Set ignition switch to "I" position. Push pin in and remove lock cylinder from lock body. *See Fig. 9.*

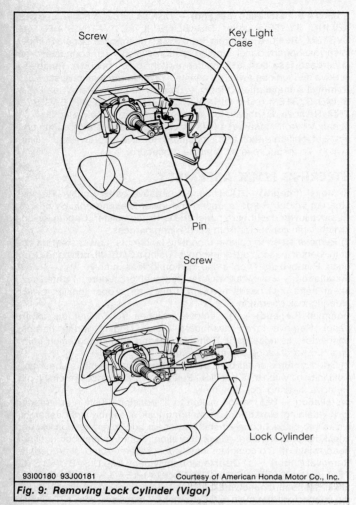

93I00180 93J00181   Courtesy of American Honda Motor Co., Inc.

Fig. 9: Removing Lock Cylinder (Vigor)

Installation – Set ignition switch to "O" position, and align lock cylinder with lock body. Rotate switch almost to "I" position, and insert lock cylinder until pin touches body. Set switch to "I" position , push pin, and insert lock cylinder into lock body until pin clicks into place. To complete installation, reverse removal procedure.

STEERING COLUMN ASSEMBLY

Removal (Integra) – 1) Remove steering wheel. See STEERING WHEEL & HORN PAD. Remove left and right lower covers from instrument panel. Remove front console. Remove left knee bolster from steering hanger.
2) Remove steering joint cover. Remove steering shaft joint pinch bolts. Mark steering joint and pinion shaft for installation reference. Remove steering joint.
3) Remove upper and lower steering column covers. Remove turn signal canceling sleeve and combination switch. Unplug all wiring harness connectors. Remove steering column assembly.
Installation – Position steering column assembly into hole in floorboard. Align reference marks, and install steering joint onto pinion shaft. Install and tighten steering joint pinch bolts. See TORQUE SPECIFICATIONS. Install steering joint cover. Install steering column to underside of dashboard. To complete installation, reverse removal procedure.
Removal (Legend) – 1) Deactivate air bag system. See DISABLING SYSTEM under DISABLING & ACTIVATING AIR BAG SYSTEM. Remove steering wheel. See STEERING WHEEL & HORN PAD.
2) Remove pinch bolt from lower steering joint in engine compartment. Remove courtesy light control switch from lower dashboard panel. Remove lower dashboard panel. Remove upper and lower steering column covers.

CAUTION: DO NOT disconnect cable reel connector and SRS wiring harness.

3) Remove steering joint cover. Without unplugging connector, remove cable reel box from underneath steering column, and place it aside on floor. *See Fig. 10*. Remove clip. Remove cable reel, turn signal canceling sleeve, and combination switch from column assembly, and place them aside on floor.
4) Unplug ignition switch connector from underdash fuse box. Remove steering column mounting bolts/nuts. Carefully remove steering column assembly.

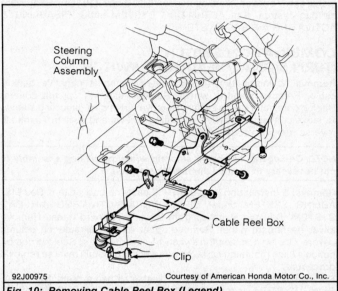

92J00975   Courtesy of American Honda Motor Co., Inc.

Fig. 10: Removing Cable Reel Box (Legend)

Installation – 1) Position steering column assembly into hole on floorboard. Align bolt hole in steering joint with slot in steering shaft. Insert shaft into steering joint.
2) Install steering column mounting bolts/nuts, and tighten them to specification. See TORQUE SPECIFICATIONS. Install and tighten lower steering joint pinch bolt. To complete installation, reverse removal procedure.
Removal (Vigor) – 1) Deactivate air bag system. See DISABLING SYSTEM under DISABLING & ACTIVATING AIR BAG SYSTEM. Remove steering wheel. See STEERING WHEEL & HORN PAD.
2) Remove pinch bolt from lower steering joint in engine compartment. Remove lower cover and driver-side knee bolster. Remove upper and lower steering column covers.
3) Remove steering joint cover. Remove SRS wiring harness from underside of column bracket by removing clip. Remove cable reel assembly and turn signal canceling sleeve from combination switch assembly. Remove combination switch assembly.

NOTE: Place combination switch assembly aside on floor gently. DO NOT disconnect cables from combination switch assembly.

4) Disconnect wire coupler of ignition switch. Remove steering column assembly attaching nuts and bolts. Remove steering column.
Installation – 1) Guide steering shaft through engine bulkhead. Align bolt hole in steering joint with slot in steering shaft, insert shaft into steering joint, and install bolt.
2) Install steering column assembly and nuts and steering column holder. Connect ignition switch wiring. Install combination switch.

NOTE: Ensure wires are not caught or pinched by any parts when connecting combination switch and cable reel.

3) Install turn signal switch canceling sleeve and cable reel onto steering column. Align slot in canceling sleeve with projection on cable reel.

4) Install SRS wiring harness onto underside of column bracket with clip. Install steering joint cover. Install upper and lower column covers. Install knee bolster and lower cover. Install steering wheel and air bag assembly.

OVERHAUL

NOTE: For exploded view of steering column, see Fig. 11, 12, or 13.

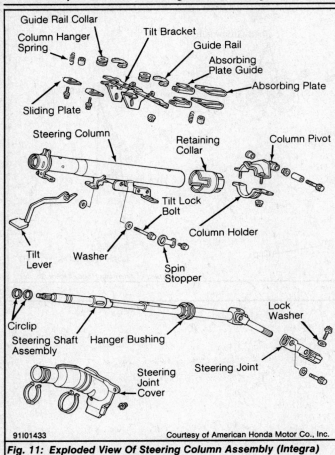

Fig. 11: Exploded View Of Steering Column Assembly (Integra)

91I01433   Courtesy of American Honda Motor Co., Inc.

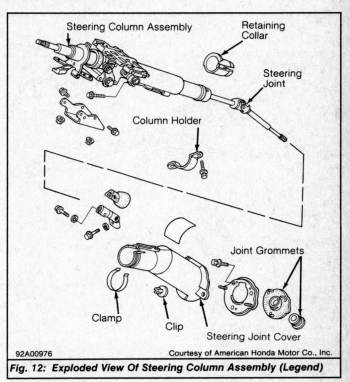

92A00976   Courtesy of American Honda Motor Co., Inc.

Fig. 12: Exploded View Of Steering Column Assembly (Legend)

TORQUE SPECIFICATIONS

TORQUE SPECIFICATIONS

Application	Ft. Lbs. (N.m)
Air Bag Torx Bolts (Legend & Vigor)	[1]
Column Holder Bolts/Nuts	
Integra & Legend	16 (22)
Vigor	29 (39)
Steering Joint Pinch Bolt	16 (22)
Steering Wheel Nut	37 (50)
Upper Column Mounting Bolts/Nuts	
Integra	[2]
Legend & Vigor	12 (16)

[1] – Tighten to 88 INCH lbs. (10 N.m).
[2] – Tighten to 115 INCH lbs. (13 N.m).

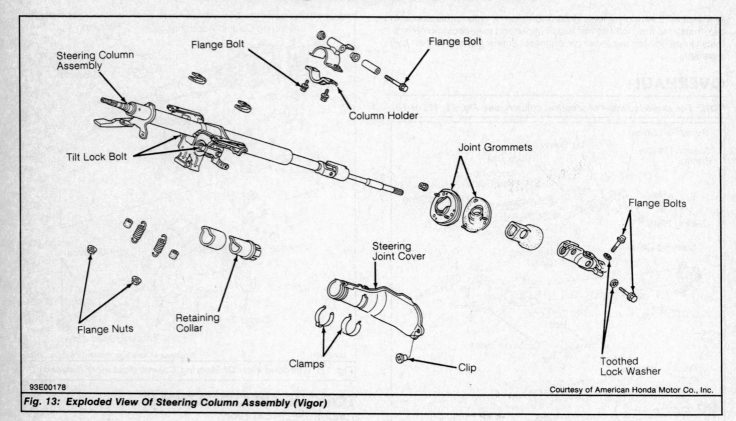

93E00178

Courtesy of American Honda Motor Co., Inc.

Fig. 13: Exploded View Of Steering Column Assembly (Vigor)

Integra, Legend, Vigor

DESCRIPTION

The power steering system is rack and pinion type. Power assistance is variable according to vehicle speed and steering load. Power assist is high at low vehicle speeds and low at high vehicle speeds.

The speed sensor is a pump driven by a speedometer gear shaft, driven by a gear in the differential. When the vehicle is in motion, the speed sensor pump relieves a portion of the hydraulic pressure, reducing power assist. System consists of a power rack and pinion steering gear, steering pump, fluid filter/reservoir, control unit, speed sensor, cooler lines, and hoses.

LUBRICATION

CAPACITY

SYSTEM CAPACITY

Application	Qts. (L)
Integra	
Reservoir	0.53 (0.5)
System	1.50 (1.4)
Legend	
Reservoir	0.53 (0.5)
System	1.80 (1.7)
Vigor	
Reservoir	0.53 (0.5)
System	1.90 (1.8)

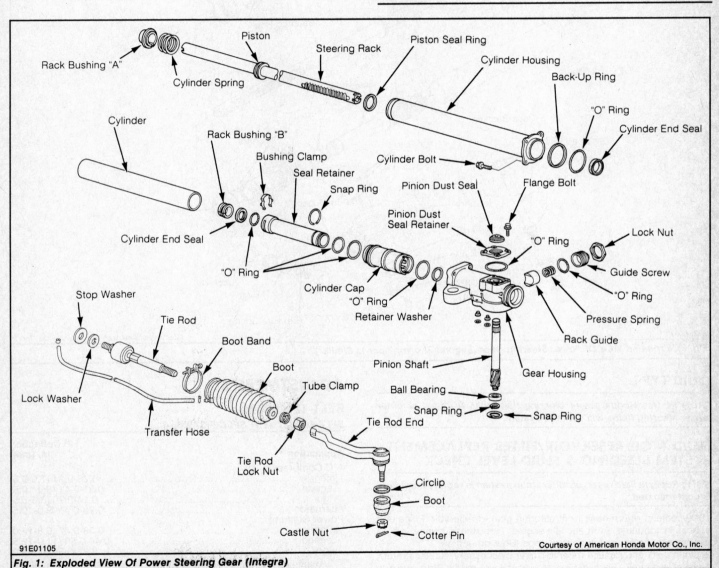

91E01105

Courtesy of American Honda Motor Co., Inc.

Fig. 1: Exploded View Of Power Steering Gear (Integra)

1993 STEERING
Power Rack & Pinion (Cont.)

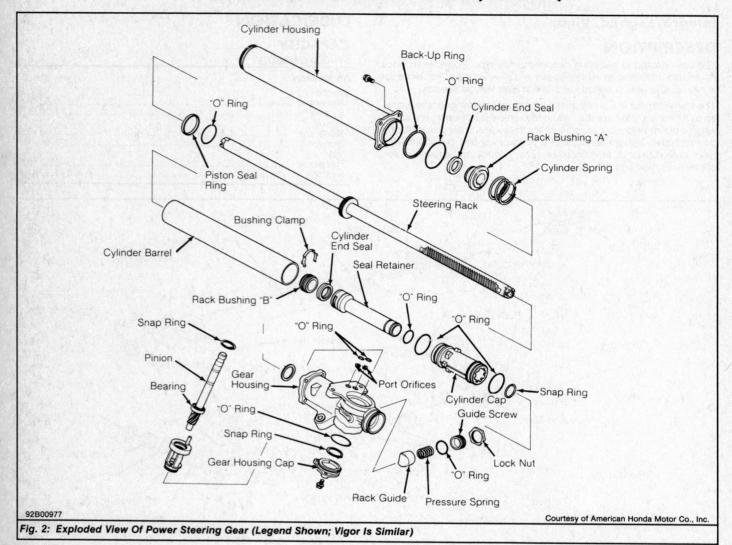

Fig. 2: Exploded View Of Power Steering Gear (Legend Shown; Vigor Is Similar)

92B00977   Courtesy of American Honda Motor Co., Inc.

FLUID TYPE

CAUTION: Use Honda power steering fluid only. A/T fluid or other power steering fluids will damage system.

FLUID & OIL RESERVOIR/FILTER REPLACEMENT, SYSTEM BLEEDING & FLUID LEVEL CHECK

NOTE: Replace fluid reservoir/filter when system is repaired or if fluid is contaminated.

1) Disconnect return hose from steering gear at reservoir. Place end of hose in container. Start and idle engine. Turn steering wheel lock to lock several times until fluid flow stops. Shut off engine.
2) Drain fluid, and replace reservoir/filter if necessary. Replace return hose at reservoir. Fill reservoir to upper level mark. Start and run engine at fast idle. Turn steering wheel lock to lock several times to bleed trapped air. Recheck fluid level in reservoir.

ADJUSTMENTS

BELT TENSION
BELT ADJUSTMENT SPECIFICATIONS

Application	[1] Deflection In. (mm)
A/C Compressor	
Integra	0.28-0.34 (7.0-9.0)
Legend	0.31-0.41 (8.0-10.5)
Vigor	0.14-0.20 (3.5-5.5)
Alternator	0.28-0.41 (9.0-10.5)
Power Steering	
Integra	0.38-0.47 (9.5-12.0)
Legend	0.44-0.50 (11.0-12.5)
Vigor	0.27-0.34 (6.5-9.0)

[1] – With 22 lbs. (10 kg) pressure applied midway on longest belt run.

PUMP PRELOAD

Integra & Vigor – Measure power steering pump preload with torque wrench after overhauling pump or installing replacement pump. Check preload with pump mounted in a vise. Maximum preload should be 36 INCH lbs. (4 N.m) for Integra and 71 INCH lbs. (8 N.m) for Vigor. If preload is higher than specification, disassemble and inspect pump.
Legend – Information is not available from manufacturer.

RACK GUIDE

1) Using Lock Nut Wrench (07916-SA50001), loosen rack guide screw lock nut. *See Fig. 1 or 2.* Tighten rack guide screw until spring is compressed against guide.

2) Loosen rack guide screw, and retighten it to 36 INCH lbs. (4 N.m). Back off rack guide screw about 25 degrees. Holding rack guide screw in place, tighten lock nut to 18 ft. lbs. (24 N.m). Measure steering effort. See STEERING WHEEL TURNING FORCE under TESTING.

TESTING

PUMP PRESSURE CHECK

1) Check fluid level and belt tension. Adjust as necessary. Disconnect outlet hose from pump. Install Pump Joint Adapter (07GAK-SE00110 on Integra and Vigor, or 07GAD-SE00112 on Legend) onto pump outlet fitting. *See Fig. 3.*

2) Install Hose Joint Adapter (07GAK-SE00120) onto outlet hose. Install Pressure Gauge Set (07406-0010000) between pump and hose joint adapters. Fully open shutoff and pressure control valves.

3) Start and idle engine. Turn steering wheel lock to lock several times to warm fluid. Completely close shutoff valve.

4) Gradually close pressure control valve until pressure gauge needle stabilizes. Read pressure. Immediately open shutoff valve. Pump pressure should be at least 1140 psi (80 kg/cm²). Repair or replace pump if pressure is not within specification.

CAUTION: To prevent damage to pump, DO NOT keep shutoff valve closed for longer than 5 seconds.

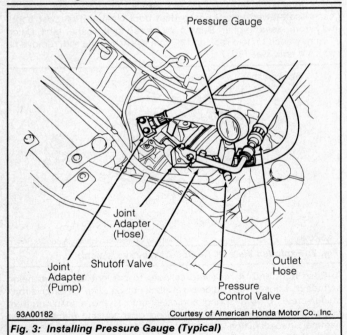

Pressure Gauge

Joint Adapter (Hose)

Joint Adapter (Pump)

Shutoff Valve

Outlet Hose

Pressure Control Valve

93A00182 Courtesy of American Honda Motor Co., Inc.

Fig. 3: Installing Pressure Gauge (Typical)

STEERING WHEEL TURNING FORCE

Low-Speed Assist – 1) Check fluid level and belt tension. Start and idle engine. Turn steering wheel lock to lock several times to warm fluid. Attach a spring tension scale to steering wheel at outer end of spoke.

2) Ensure vehicle is on a clean, dry surface. With engine at idle, pull tension scale. Read scale as soon as wheels begin to move. Reading should be a maximum of 7.1 lbs. (3.2 kg) for Integra and Vigor, or 6.6 lbs. (3.0 kg) for Legend.

3) If reading does not meet specification, stop engine and disconnect hose between control unit and speed sensor at sensor. Plug hose and sensor fitting.

4) Start and idle engine. Measure pull as described in steps **1)** and **2)**. If scale reading is 7.1 lbs. (3.2 kg) or less for Integra and Vigor, or 6.6 lbs. (3.0 kg) or less for Legend, replace speed sensor. If scale reading is higher, check steering rack and power steering pump.

Simulated High-Speed Assist – 1) Check fluid level and belt tension. Start and idle engine. Turn steering wheel lock to lock several times to warm fluid. Stop engine. To simulate speeds greater than 30 MPH, disconnect hoses at speed sensor and connect By-Pass Tube Connector (07406-0010101) to speed sensor hoses. *See Fig. 4.*

2) Attach spring tension scale to outer end of steering wheel spoke. With vehicle on clean, dry floor, start and idle engine. Pull on tension scale until wheels begin to move.

3) If turning force is less than 11 lbs. (5.0 kg) on Integra and Vigor, or less than 9 lbs. (4.0 kg) on Legend, speed sensor is okay. Check for pinched or bent sensor feed. If feed line is okay, problem is in pump or control unit. If turning force is 11 lbs. (5.0 kg) or more on Integra and Vigor, or 9 lbs. (4.0 kg) or more on Legend, replace faulty speed sensor.

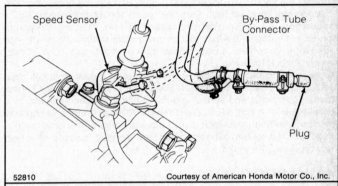

Speed Sensor

By-Pass Tube Connector

Plug

52810 Courtesy of American Honda Motor Co., Inc.

Fig. 4: Simulating High Speed Assist (Integra Shown; Legend & Vigor Are Similar)

REMOVAL & INSTALLATION

POWER RACK & PINION

Removal (Integra) – 1) Remove steering joint cover. Remove steering shaft joint pinch bolt. Disconnect steering shaft from steering gear. Drain power steering fluid. Remove steering gear shield.

2) Thoroughly clean area around valve body. Raise and support front of vehicle. Remove front wheels. Separate tie rod ends from steering knuckles. On M/T models, remove shift rod from transaxle case. Slide shift retaining pin cover back away from transaxle. Using a drift, drive shift rod retaining pin from shift rod. Disconnect shift rod from transaxle.

3) On A/T models, remove shift cable holder and cable clamp. Remove shift cable from transaxle.

4) On all models, remove exhaust pipe between exhaust header pipe and converter. Remove steering fluid tubes from valve body. Remove crossmember from below steering gear. Remove steering gear mounting bolts. Slide assembly to right until left tie rod clears frame. Lower steering gear, and remove it through left side.

Installation – To install, reverse removal procedure. Tighten steering gear mounting bolts to specification. See TORQUE SPECIFICATIONS. Use new self-locking nuts on exhaust pipe bolts. Use new exhaust gaskets. Fill reservoir with power steering fluid, and check for leaks.

Removal (Legend & Vigor) – 1) Ensure wheels are pointing straight ahead. Disconnect battery cables. Drain power steering fluid. Raise and support front of vehicle. Remove front wheels. Separate tie rod ends from steering knuckles.

2) Loosen steering shaft joint pinch bolt. DO NOT remove bolt yet. Remove engine splash guard. Thoroughly clean area around valve body and lines. Remove hose clamp from right side of steering gear. Disconnect lines from valve body. Remove hydraulic line clamps. Disconnect speed sensor line. Plug all hydraulic lines to exclude foreign matter.

3) Remove steering joint bolt. Disconnect steering shaft from steering gear. Support steering gear. Remove steering gear mounting bolts and steering gear.

Installation – To install, reverse removal procedure. Fill reservoir with power steering fluid, and check for leaks. Tighten splash guard and steering gear mounting bolts to specification. See TORQUE SPECIFICATIONS.

POWER STEERING PUMP

Removal & Installation – Drain fluid. Disconnect inlet and outlet hoses at pump. On Legend, remove air cleaner cover and duct. On all models, remove power steering belt. Remove pump retaining bolts. Remove pump. To install, reverse removal procedure. Adjust belt tension. Fill reservoir with new fluid. Check for leaks.

SPEED SENSOR

Removal (Integra) – Lift speedometer cable boot. Remove retaining clip. Pull out cable. Disconnect and plug speed sensor hoses. Loosen speedometer gear set bolt. Remove speed sensor from transaxle .

Installation – Install new speed sensor "O" ring. After replacing sensor, turn steering wheel lock to lock several times with engine idling to bleed air from system. Check power steering fluid, and top off if necessary. Check for leaks.

Removal (Legend & Vigor) – Remove rear mount bracket stay. Unplug speed sensor connector. Disconnect and plug speed sensor hoses. Remove speed sensor mounting bolt and speed sensor.

Installation – Install NEW speed sensor "O" ring. After replacing sensor, turn steering wheel lock to lock several times with engine idling to bleed air from system. Check power steering fluid, and top off if necessary. Check for leaks.

VALVE BODY

Removal & Installation (Integra) – Drain power steering fluid. Remove gear box shield. Thoroughly clean area around valve body. Disconnect fluid lines from valve body, and remove flange bolts. *See Fig. 5*. Remove valve body from gear box. To install, reverse removal procedure. Check for leaks.

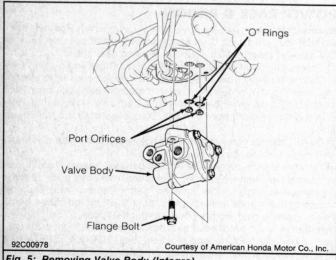

92C00978   Courtesy of American Honda Motor Co., Inc.

Fig. 5: Removing Valve Body (Integra)

Removal & Installation (Legend & Vigor) – Remove steering gear. See POWER RACK & PINION under REMOVAL & INSTALLATION. Remove pinion dust cover. *See Fig. 6*. Thoroughly clean area around valve body. Remove flange bolts and valve body from gear box. To install, reverse removal procedure. Check for leaks.

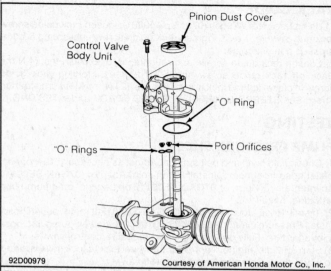

92D00979   Courtesy of American Honda Motor Co., Inc.

Fig. 6: Removing Valve Body (Legend Shown; Vigor Is Similar)

OVERHAUL

POWER RACK & PINION (INTEGRA)

Disassembly – **1)** Remove valve body from housing. See VALVE BODY under REMOVAL & INSTALLATION. Carefully clamp steering gear in soft-jawed vise. Loosen dust boot clamps. Pull dust boots away from steering gear. Bend back tie rod lock washer tabs. Using 22-mm wrench to hold rack and 17-mm wrench on tie rod, remove tie rod from rack. *See Fig. 7*.

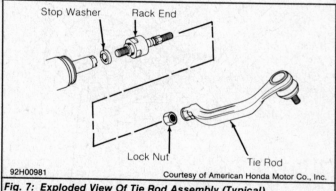

92H00981   Courtesy of American Honda Motor Co., Inc.

Fig. 7: Exploded View Of Tie Rod Assembly (Typical)

2) Push right end of rack into cylinder to prevent rack from being scratched. Loosen rack guide screw lock nut. *See Fig. 1*. Remove rack guide screw, "O" ring, spring, and rack guide. Remove snap ring from bottom of gear housing. Tap pinion from gear housing with soft-faced hammer. Inspect pinion lower ball bearing for excessive play. Replace as necessary.

3) Remove 4 bolts at end of cylinder housing. Separate rack from cylinder housing. Remove "O" ring, back-up ring, rack bushing "A", and cylinder spring. To avoid damaging cylinder housing, use a plastic or wooden tool to remove end seal from housing. Remove cylinder, seal retainer, cylinder cap, and rack from gear housing. Remove retainer washer.

4) Remove housing cap retaining bolts. Remove pinion dust seal retainer and "O" ring from gear housing. Remove pinion seal from pinion dust seal retainer. Inspect pinion upper bearing for excessive play. If pinion bearing is okay, go to step **7)**. If pinion bearing is to be replaced, go to next step.

5) Remove 30-mm snap ring from pinion holder. *See Fig. 8.* Remove pinion holder and pinion upper bearing from gear housing. Inspect needle bearings in pinion holder and gear housing. Replace as necessary. Replace needle bearings as a set. If needle bearings are okay, pack with grease and reuse.

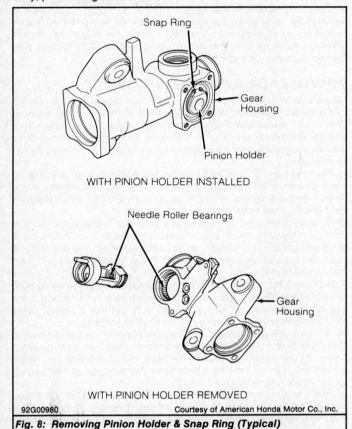

Snap Ring

Gear Housing

Pinion Holder

WITH PINION HOLDER INSTALLED

Needle Roller Bearings

Gear Housing

WITH PINION HOLDER REMOVED

92G00980   Courtesy of American Honda Motor Co., Inc.

Fig. 8: Removing Pinion Holder & Snap Ring (Typical)

6) Pack a new pinion upper bearing with grease. Drive bearing into gear housing with sealed side facing out, using Driver (07749-0010000) and Attachment (07746-0010300). Install pinion holder into gear housing. Install snap ring with tapered side facing away from housing. Align snap ring ends with flat part of pinion holder.

7) Remove cylinder and seal retainer from rack. Remove "O" rings and snap ring from seal retainer. Remove cylinder cap from seal retainer. Remove "O" rings from cylinder cap. Remove bushing clamp from seal retainer. Remove rack bushing "B" and cylinder end seal with back-up ring.

8) Carefully pry piston seal ring and "O" ring from rack. Clean all parts, and inspect them for wear or damage. In addition to standard overhaul kit replacement parts, replace any other parts showing excessive wear or damage.

Reassembly – 1) Install new "O" ring onto rack, with narrow edge facing out. Coat Pinion Seal Ring Guide (07GAG-SD40100) with power steering fluid, and slide it onto rack, big end first. Position new piston seal ring on seal ring guide big end. Push new seal into piston seal ring guide groove so it sits on top of "O" ring.

2) Coat piston seal ring and Piston Seal Ring Sizer (07GAG-SD40200) with power steering fluid. Slide ring sizer onto rack and over piston seal ring. Rotate ring sizer while moving it up and down to seat piston seal ring. Coat new "O" rings with grease, and install onto cylinder cap.

3) Slide cylinder cap onto seal retainer. Install snap ring and "O" ring onto seal retainer. Grease sliding surface of steering rack bushing "B", and install onto steering rack with groove in bushing facing steering rack piston. Grease sliding surfaces of new cylinder end seal and Cylinder End Seal Slider (07GAG-SD40300).

4) Put seal onto seal slider with groove facing opposite slider. Grease rack, and slide seal slider onto rack past gear tooth section. Remove seal slider from cylinder end seal. Separate seal slider and remove it from rack. Fit seal retainer onto rack.

5) Push rack bushing "B" toward seal retainer by hand until cylinder end seal is seated in retainer. Fit bushing clamp into groove of seal retainer. Install retainer washer into gear housing. Insert seal retainer and rack into gear housing. Coat inside of cylinder with power steering fluid.

6) Slide cylinder over rack and into gear housing. Press cylinder into gear housing until it seats. Install cylinder spring over rack. Coat rack bushing "A" with power steering fluid, and install onto spring. Grease End Seal Guide (07GAG-SD40400), and slip guide onto end of rack.

7) Coat inside of cylinder housing with power steering fluid, and install cylinder end seal with grooved side facing inside of cylinder. Install "O" ring and back-up ring onto gear housing. Carefully position cylinder onto gear housing, and loosely install bolts. Remove cylinder end seal guide.

8) Carefully insert rack into cylinder housing without damaging rack sliding surface. Tighten cylinder housing bolts to specification. See TORQUE SPECIFICATIONS. Using a press and Bearing Attachment (07746-0010300), install pinion lower bearing onto pinion shaft with shielded side facing down.

9) Apply grease to pinion lower bearing, and check for smooth operation. Install lower bearing snap ring. Install pinion shaft into pinion holder. Install 28-mm snap ring into pinion holder groove. Grease pinion seal, and install into gear housing with Driver (07749-0010000) and Driver Attachment (07947-6340300). Grease new "O" ring, and install into groove in pinion seal retainer.

10) Use Pinion Seal Guide (07974-SA50600) to cover pinion shaft. If seal guide is not available, use vinyl tape covered with grease. Carefully slide cap over pinion shaft. Remove special tool or tape. Install and tighten flange bolts. Install valve body.

11) Install "O" ring onto rack guide screw. Coat rack guide with grease. Install rack guide, spring, and rack guide screw onto gear housing. Tighten rack guide screw until it compresses spring and seats against rack guide, then loosen screw.

12) Retighten rack guide screw to 36 INCH lbs. (4 N.m), then loosen it about 25 degrees. Install lock nut onto rack guide screw. Tighten lock nut while holding rack guide screw with Lock Nut Wrench (07916-SA50001). Screw each tie rod into rack while holding lock washer to ensure washer tabs are in slots at end of rack.

13) Install stopper washer with chamfered side facing out. Tighten tie rod securely onto rack, and bend lock washer back to secure. Install tie rod boots and clamps. Install air transfer hose. To complete reassembly, reverse disassembly procedure.

14) Fill pump reservoir with Honda power steering fluid. Start and run engine at fast idle. Rotate steering wheel lock to lock several times to bleed air from system. Add fluid as necessary. Check for leaks.

POWER RACK & PINION (LEGEND)

Disassembly – 1) Remove valve body from housing. See VALVE BODY under REMOVAL & INSTALLATION. Carefully clamp steering gear in soft-jawed vise. Remove tie rod assembly. Loosen dust boot clamps. Pull dust boots away from steering gear. Using a wrench, hold steering rack. Unscrew and remove tie rod end. Remove stop washer. *See Fig. 7.*

2) Push right end of rack into cylinder to prevent rack from being scratched. Loosen rack guide screw lock nut. *See Fig. 2.* Remove rack guide screw, "O" ring, spring, and rack guide. Remove gear housing cap. Remove snap ring from bottom of gear housing. Tap pinion from gear housing with soft hammer. Inspect upper pinion bearing for excessive play. If bearing is defective, replace pinion assembly.

3) Remove bolts at end of cylinder housing. Separate rack from cylinder housing. Remove "O" ring, back-up ring, rack bushing "A", and cylinder spring. To avoid damaging cylinder housing, use a plastic or wooden tool to remove end seal from housing.

4) Remove cylinder, seal retainer, cylinder cap, and rack from gear housing. Remove retainer washer from gear housing. Inspect pinion lower bearing for excessive play. If pinion bearing needs to be replaced, go to next step. If lower pinion bearing is okay, go to step **7)**.

5) Remove snap ring from pinion holder. See Fig. 8. Remove pinion holder and pinion bearing from gear housing. Inspect needle bearings in pinion holder and gear housing. Replace as necessary. Replace needle bearings as a set. If needle bearings are okay, pack with grease and reuse.

6) Pack a new lower pinion bearing with grease. Drive bearing into gear housing with sealed side facing out, using Driver (07749-0010000) and Attachment (07746-0010400). Install pinion holder into gear housing. Install snap ring with tapered side facing away from housing. Align snap ring ends with flat part of pinion holder.

7) Remove cylinder and seal retainer from rack. Remove "O" rings and snap ring from seal retainer. Remove cylinder cap from seal retainer. Remove "O" rings from cylinder cap. Remove bushing clamp from seal retainer. Remove rack bushing "B" and cylinder end seal with back-up ring.

8) Carefully pry piston seal ring and "O" ring from rack. Clean all parts, and inspect for wear or damage. In addition to standard overhaul kit replacement parts, replace any other parts showing excessive wear or damage.

Reassembly – 1) Install new "O" ring onto rack, with narrow edge facing out. Coat Pinion Seal Ring Guide (07MAG-SP00100) with power steering fluid, and slide it onto rack, big end first. Position new piston seal ring onto seal ring guide big end. Push new seal into piston seal ring guide groove so that it sits on top of "O" ring.

2) Coat piston seal ring and Piston Seal Ring Sizer (07LAG-SM40200) with power steering fluid. Slide ring sizer onto rack and over piston seal ring. Rotate ring sizer while moving it up and down to seat piston seal ring. Coat new "O" rings with grease, and install rings onto cylinder cap.

3) Slide cylinder cap onto seal retainer. Install snap ring and "O" ring onto seal retainer. Grease sliding surface of steering rack bushing "B". Install bushing onto steering rack with groove in bushing facing steering rack piston. Grease sliding surfaces of new cylinder end seal and Cylinder End Seal Slider (07GAG-SD40300).

4) Position seal and back-up ring onto seal slider, with groove facing opposite slider. Grease rack, and slide seal slider onto rack past gear tooth section. Remove seal slider from cylinder end seal, then separate seal slider and remove it from rack. Fit seal retainer onto rack.

5) Push rack bushing "B" toward seal retainer by hand until cylinder end seal is seated in retainer. Fit bushing clamp in groove of seal retainer. Grease steering rack. Install retainer washer into gear housing. Insert seal retainer and rack into gear housing. Coat inside of cylinder with power steering fluid.

6) Slide cylinder over rack and into gear housing. Press cylinder into gear housing until it seats. Install cylinder spring over rack. Coat rack bushing "A" with power steering fluid, and install it onto spring. Wrap end of steering rack with vinyl tape. Coat tape with grease.

7) Coat inside of cylinder housing with power steering fluid. Install cylinder end seal with lip of seal facing toward inside of cylinder. Install "O" ring and back-up ring onto gear housing. Carefully position cylinder onto gear housing, and loosely install bolts. Remove vinyl tape from steering rack.

8) Tighten cylinder housing bolts to specification. See TORQUE SPECIFICATIONS. Carefully insert rack into cylinder housing without damaging rack sliding surface. Install pinion shaft into pinion holder. Install snap ring into pinion holder groove, with tapered side facing out. Grease new "O" ring, and place it into groove in gear housing cap. Install gear housing cap.

9) Install new "O" ring onto rack guide screw. Coat rack guide with grease. Install rack guide, spring, and rack guide screw onto gear housing. Tighten rack guide screw until it compresses spring and seats against rack guide, then loosen screw.

10) Retighten rack guide screw to 36 INCH lbs. (4 N.m), then loosen it about 25 degrees. Install lock nut onto rack guide screw. Tighten lock nut while holding rack guide screw with Lock Nut Wrench (07916-SA50001). Grease and install new valve body "O" rings. Install valve body orifices. Use Pinion Seal Guide (07974-SA50600) to cover pinion shaft.

11) Coat pinion holder with grease, and install valve body unit. Remove seal guide. Install new stop washer into groove of steering rack end. See Fig. 7. Install and tighten steering rack end. Stake 2 sections of stop washer. Apply steering grease to outside rack end housing. Install tie rod dust boots and clamps. Position dust boot clamps so locking tab faces up and slightly forward.

12) Bend locking tabs on dust boot clamps, and lightly tap doubled portions to reduce clamp height. Install tie rods. To complete reassembly, reverse disassembly procedure. Fill pump reservoir with Honda power steering fluid. Start and run engine at fast idle. Rotate steering wheel lock to lock several times to bleed air from system. Add fluid as necessary. Check for leaks.

POWER RACK & PINION (VIGOR)

Disassembly – 1) Remove valve body from housing. See VALVE BODY under REMOVAL & INSTALLATION. Carefully clamp steering gear in soft-jawed vise. Remove tie rod assembly. Loosen dust boot clamps. Pull dust boots away from steering gear. Using a wrench, hold steering rack while unscrewing tie rod end. See Fig. 7. Remove tie rod lock washer.

2) Push right end of rack into cylinder housing to prevent damage to sealing surface. Loosen rack screw lock nut, and remove rack guide screw. Remove spring and rack guide from gear housing. Remove gear housing cap bolts and gear housing cap.

3) Remove circlip from bottom of gear housing. Tap pinion assembly from gear housing. Inspect lower pinion bearing for play. If bearing is good and grease in it is clean, go to next step. If bearing needs to be replaced, remove snap ring from shaft. Press bearing from shaft, then install new bearing.

4) Remove bolts from end of cylinder housing, and slide housing from rack. Remove "O" ring, back-up ring, steering rack bushing, and cylinder spring. Remove cylinder end seal from cylinder housing, using wooden stick or fingers to prevent damage to housing.

5) Remove cylinder, cylinder seal retainer, cylinder cap, and steering rack from gear housing. Remove retainer washer from gear housing. Check pinion holder for free movement, excessive play, or rough movement. If pinion bearing needs to be replaced, go to next step. If pinion bearing is okay, go to step 7).

6) Remove snap ring from pinion holder. See Fig. 8. Remove pinion holder and pinion upper bearing from gear housing. Inspect needle bearings in pinion holder and gear housing. If replacing needle bearings, replace them as a set. If needle bearings are okay, pack them with grease and reuse them. Replace damaged pinion bearings as necessary.

7) Remove cylinder and seal retainer from steering rack. Remove "O" ring and snap ring from seal retainer. Remove cylinder cap from seal retainer. Remove "O" rings from cylinder cap. Remove bushing stopper ring from seal retainer. Remove cylinder end seal and rack bushing. Carefully pry piston seal ring and "O" ring from rack.

Reassembly – 1) Install new "O" ring onto rack, with narrow edge facing out. Coat Pinion Seal Ring Guide (07HAG-SF10100) with power steering fluid, and slide it onto rack, big end first. Position new piston seal ring onto seal ring guide big end. Push new seal into piston seal ring guide groove so it sits on top of "O" ring.

2) Coat piston seal ring and Piston Seal Ring Sizer (07HAG-SF10200) with power steering fluid. Slide ring sizer onto rack and over piston seal ring. Rotate ring sizer while moving it up and down to seat piston seal ring. Coat new "O" rings with grease, and install onto cylinder cap.

3) Slide cylinder cap onto seal retainer. Install snap ring and "O" ring onto seal retainer. Grease sliding surface of steering rack bushing "B", and install bushing onto steering rack with groove in bushing facing steering rack piston. Grease sliding surfaces of new cylinder end seal and Cylinder End Seal Slider (07GAG-SD40300).

4) Position seal and back-up ring onto seal slider, with groove facing opposite slider. Grease rack, and position seal slider onto rack past gear tooth section. Remove seal slider from cylinder end seal. Separate seal slider and remove it from rack. Fit seal retainer onto rack.

5) Push rack bushing "B" toward seal retainer by hand until cylinder end seal is seated in retainer. Fit bushing clamp in groove of seal retainer. Grease steering rack. Install retainer washer into gear housing. Insert seal retainer and rack into gear housing. Coat inside of cylinder with power steering fluid.

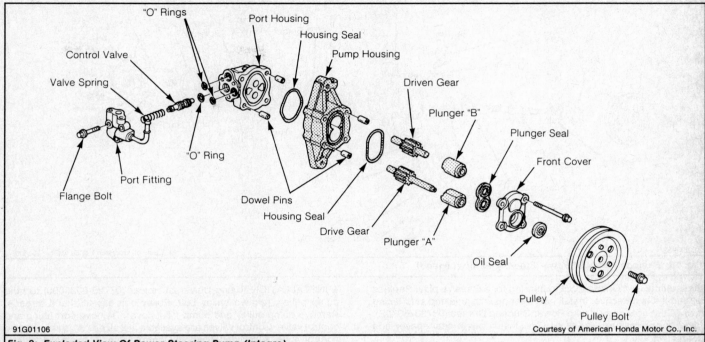

91G01106   Courtesy of American Honda Motor Co., Inc.

Fig. 9: Exploded View Of Power Steering Pump (Integra)

6) Slide cylinder over rack and into gear housing. Press cylinder into gear housing until it seats. Install cylinder spring over rack. Coat rack bushing "A" with power steering fluid, and install it onto spring. Wrap end of steering rack with vinyl tape. Coat tape with grease.

7) Coat inside of cylinder housing with power steering fluid. Install cylinder end seal with lip of seal facing toward inside of cylinder. Install "O" ring and back-up ring onto gear housing. Carefully position cylinder onto gear housing, and loosely install bolts. Remove vinyl tape from steering rack.

8) Tighten cylinder housing bolts to specification. See TORQUE SPECIFICATIONS. Carefully insert rack into cylinder housing without damaging rack sliding surface. Install pinion shaft into pinion holder. Install snap ring into pinion holder groove, with tapered side facing out. Grease new "O" ring, and place into groove in gear housing cap. Install gear housing cap.

9) Install new "O" ring onto rack guide screw. Coat rack guide with grease. Install rack guide, spring, and rack guide screw onto gear housing. Tighten rack guide screw until it compresses spring and seats against rack guide, then loosen screw.

10) Retighten rack guide screw to 36 INCH lbs. (4 N.m), then loosen it about 25 degrees. Install lock nut onto rack guide screw. Tighten lock nut while holding rack guide screw with Lock Nut Wrench (07916-SA50001). Grease and install new valve body "O" rings. Install valve body orifices. Use Pinion Seal Guide (07974-SA50600) to cover pinion shaft.

11) Coat pinion holder with grease. Install valve body unit. Remove seal guide. Install new stop washer into groove of steering rack end. See Fig. 7. Install and tighten steering rack end. Stake 2 sections of stop washer. Apply steering grease to outside rack end housing. Install tie rod dust boots and clamps. Position dust boot clamps so locking tab faces up and slightly forward.

12) Bend locking tabs on dust boot clamps, and lightly tap on doubled portions to reduce clamp height. Install tie rods. To complete reassembly, reverse disassembly procedure. Fill pump reservoir with Honda power steering fluid. Start and run engine at fast idle. Rotate steering wheel lock to lock several times to bleed air from system. Add fluid as necessary. Check for leaks.

POWER STEERING PUMP

Disassembly & Reassembly (Integra) – 1) Remove power steering pump from vehicle. See POWER STEERING PUMP under REMOVAL & INSTALLATION. Using Universal Holder (07725-0030000) to hold pump pulley, remove pulley bolt. Pulley bolt has left-hand threads. Remove pump pulley and pump front cover. Remove port fitting and control valve. Control valves are available in 2 sizes. "A" is stamped on control valve "A" for identification. Control valve "B" has no identification mark. Ensure same size control valve is returned to pump on reassembly. Remove "O" ring from control valve. See Fig. 9.

2) Remove dowel pins and housing seal from pump housing. Remove dowel pins, plunger seal, and "O" ring. Separate port housing from pump housing. Remove housing seal and dowel pins.

3) Remove dowel pins from pump housing. Remove housing seal and "O" ring from port housing. Remove pump drive and driven gears from housing. Remove plunger seal and plungers.

4) Pry out oil seal from front pump cover. Clean and inspect all parts, and replace as necessary. To reassemble, reverse disassembly procedure. Coat new oil seal with Power Steering Grease (08733-B070E) before assembly. Coat all other parts with power steering fluid. Use a 30-mm socket to install front pump cover seal.

Disassembly (Legend) – 1) Remove power steering pump from vehicle. See POWER STEERING PUMP under REMOVAL & INSTALLATION. Using Universal Holder (07725-0030000) to hold pump pulley, remove pulley bolt and pulley. Pulley bolt has right-hand threads.

2) Remove control valve cap. See Fig. 10. Remove control valve, spring, and "O" ring. Inspect control valve for wear and damage. Check that valve moves in and out of pump smoothly. Control valves are available in 2 sizes. "A" is stamped on control valve "A" for identification. Control valve "B" has no identification mark. Remove inlet joint and "O" ring. Remove pump front cover.

3) Remove pump cam ring from pump housing. Remove pump rotor and vanes. Remove rollers, side plate, and preload spring. Remove snap ring from drive shaft. Using a plastic mallet, remove drive shaft assembly from pump housing. Remove pump seal spacer and oil seal.

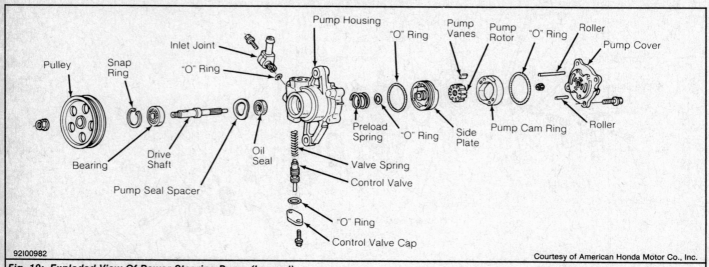

92I00982   Courtesy of American Honda Motor Co., Inc.

Fig. 10: Exploded View Of Power Steering Pump (Legend)

Reassembly – 1) Inspect pump bearing for excessive play. Replace bearing if it is defective. Install new bearing with shielded side facing down. Coat new oil seal with Power Steering Grease (08733-B070E). Using hand pressure, install oil seal. Install pump seal spacer and pump drive shaft.

2) Install drive shaft snap ring. Oil and install new "O" rings onto side plate. Install preload spring into pump housing. Install one roller into hole in pump housing. Align hole in side plate with roller, and install side plate. *See Fig. 10.* Install remaining roller into side plate.

3) Install pump cam ring with "0" (zero) mark on cam ring facing upward. Install pump rotor onto drive shaft with "0" (zero) mark on rotor facing upward. Install vanes into rotor grooves. Rounded ends of vanes face toward cam ring. To complete reassembly, reverse disassembly procedure. Ensure pump turns smoothly when rotating pump pulley.

Disassembly & Reassembly (Vigor) – 1) Remove power steering pump from vehicle. See POWER STEERING PUMP under REMOVAL

& INSTALLATION. Using Universal Holder (07725-0030000) to hold pump pulley, remove pulley bolt. Pulley bolt has left-hand threads. Remove pump pulley and pump front cover. Remove port fitting and control valve. Control valves are available in 2 sizes. "A" is stamped on control valve "A" for identification. Control valve "B" has no identification mark. Ensure same size control valve is returned to pump on reassembly. Remove "O" ring from control valve. *See Fig. 11.*

2) Remove dowel pins and housing seal from pump housing. Remove dowel pins, plunger seal, and "O" ring. Separate port housing from pump housing. Remove housing seal and dowel pins.

3) Remove dowel pins from pump housing. Remove housing seal and "O" ring from port housing. Remove pump drive and driven gears from housing. Remove plunger seal and plungers.

4) Pry oil seal from front pump cover. Clean and inspect all parts, and replace as necessary. To reassemble, reverse disassembly procedure. Coat new oil seal with Power Steering Grease (08733-B070E) before assembly. Coat all other parts with power steering fluid. Use a 30-mm socket to install front pump cover seal.

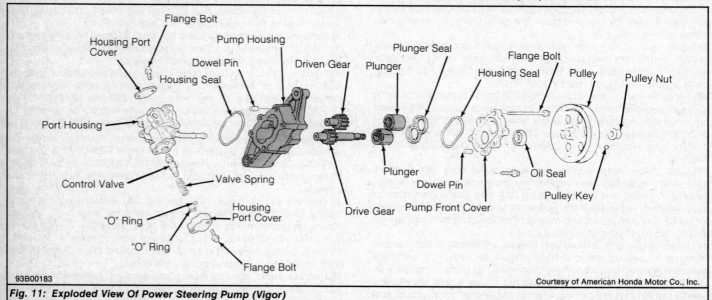

93B00183   Courtesy of American Honda Motor Co., Inc.

Fig. 11: Exploded View Of Power Steering Pump (Vigor)

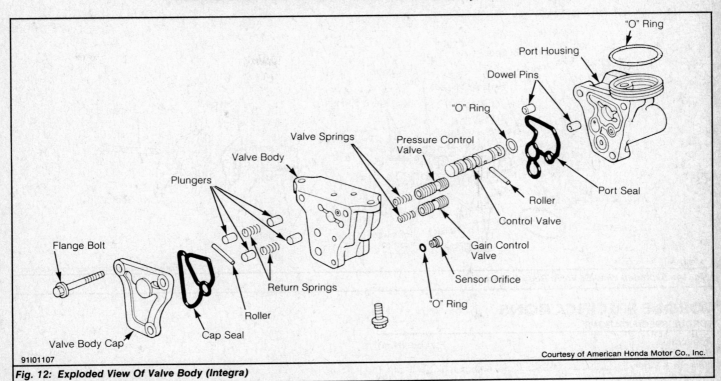

91I01107

Fig. 12: Exploded View Of Valve Body (Integra)

VALVE BODY

Disassembly & Reassembly – 1) On Legend, remove pinion dust seal. On all models, remove valve body housing bolts. Remove cap from valve body. *See Fig. 12, 13, or 14.* Remove cap seal from cap. Remove pressure control valve and spring from valve body. Inspect pressure control valve for wear or damage. Replace valve as necessary.

2) Remove gain control valve and spring from valve body. Inspect gain control valve for wear or damage. Replace as necessary. Separate valve body and port housing. Remove port seal and dowel from port housing. Remove rollers from control valve by pushing valve out one side and then the other.

3) Remove plungers, return springs, and control valve from valve body.

4) Inspect plungers and control valve for wear or damage. Using a 1/16" (1.5 mm) drill bit, remove sensor orifice and "O" ring. If valve body is damaged, replace it as an assembly. Inspect all parts for wear or damage, and replace as necessary. To reassemble, reverse disassembly procedure. Coat all parts with Power Steering Grease (08733-B070E) before assembly.

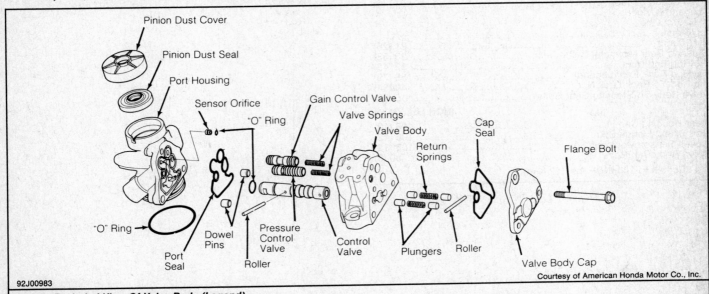

92J00983

Fig. 13: Exploded View Of Valve Body (Legend)

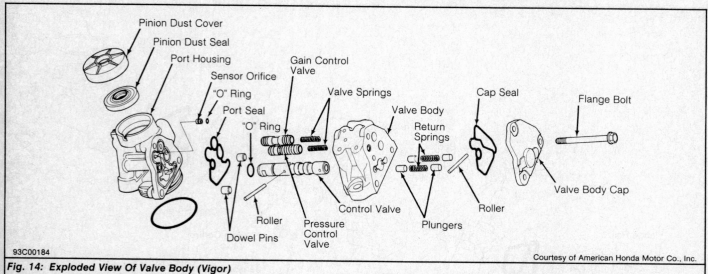

93C00184

Courtesy of American Honda Motor Co., Inc.

Fig. 14: Exploded View Of Valve Body (Vigor)

TORQUE SPECIFICATIONS

TORQUE SPECIFICATIONS

Application	Ft. Lbs. (N.m)
Pump Front Cover Bolts	
Integra & Vigor	1
Legend	14 (19)
Pump Pulley Nut	
Integra	24 (33)
Legend & Vigor	47 (64)
Pump-To-Bracket Bolt	
Integra	18 (24)
Legend & Vigor	33 (45)
Rack Cylinder-To-Gear Housing Bolt	16 (22)
Rack Guide Lock Nut	18 (24)
Shift Cable Holder (Legend)	20 (27)
Steering Gear Hydraulic Lines	
Integra	
From Pump	28 (38)
To Oil Cooler	20 (27)
To Reservoir	1
To Speed Sensor	1
Legend & Vigor	
Return Line	
6 mm	1
10 mm	21 (28)
Steering Gear Mounting Bolts	28 (38)
Tie Rod End Nuts	32 (43)
Tie Rod Rack End (Legend)	58 (79)
Tie Rod-To-Rack Lock Nut	40 (54)
Valve Body-To-Steering Gear Bolts	16 (22)
	INCH Lbs. (N.m)
Gear Housing Cap	106 (12)
Port Fitting Flange Bolt	106 (12)
Speed Sensor Mounting Bolt	106 (12)
Valve Body Cap Bolts	80 (9)

[1] – Tighten to 106 INCH lbs. (12 N.m).

Integra, Legend, Vigor

IDENTIFICATION

AUTOMATIC TRANSAXLE APPLICATIONS

Model	Transaxle
Integra	Model MPRA
Legend	Model MPYA
Vigor	Model MPWA

LUBRICATION

SERVICE INTERVALS

Change fluid every 30,000 miles. No filter service or band adjustment is required.

CHECKING FLUID LEVEL

Start and run engine until it reaches normal operating temperature. Turn ignition off. Check fluid level with vehicle on level floor. Fluid level should be between FULL and LOW marks. Add fluid if necessary. On Integra, DO NOT use a wrench to secure dipstick.

RECOMMENDED FLUID

Use Honda premium formula Automatic Transmission Fluid (ATF) or Dexron-II transmission fluid.

FLUID CAPACITIES

TRANSAXLE REFILL CAPACITIES

Application	Refill Qts. (L)	Dry Fill Qts. (L)
Integra	3.2 (3.0)	6.7 (6.3)
Legend	3.5 (3.3)	9.2 (8.7)
Vigor	2.6 (2.5)	7.6 (7.2)

DIFFERENTIAL REFILL CAPACITIES

Application	Refill Qts. (L)	Dry Fill Qts. (L)
Legend [1]	1.1 (1.00)	1.2 (1.10)
Vigor [1]	1.0 (0.95)	1.1 (1.00)

[1] – Use Hypoid SAE 90 fluid above 0°F (-18°C). Use SAE 80W-90 below 0°F (-18°C).

DRAINING & REFILLING

Warm transaxle to normal operating temperature. Remove transaxle drain plug. Using new gasket, replace drain plug when fluid is drained. Tighten drain plug to specification. See TORQUE SPECIFICATIONS. Refill transaxle to FULL mark on dipstick. See TRANSAXLE REFILL CAPACITIES table under FLUID CAPACITIES.

ADJUSTMENTS

WARNING: Legend and Vigor are equipped with Supplemental Restraint System (SRS). All SRS wiring is color-coded Yellow. DO NOT use electrical test equipment on these circuits. Disconnect negative and positive battery cables before removing console. Wait at least 3 minutes after deactivating air bag system. System maintains voltage for about 3 minutes after battery is disconnected. Servicing air bag system before 3 minutes may cause accidental air bag deployment and possible personal injury.

CAUTION: Radio has a coded theft protection circuit. Before disconnecting battery cables, obtain radio anti-theft code number from customer. After reconnecting power, turn radio on. Word CODE will be displayed. Enter customer 5-digit code to restore radio operation.

SHIFT CONTROL CABLE

Integra & Legend – 1) Start engine. Shift to Reverse. Verify transaxle engages in Reverse. With engine off, remove console. Shift gear selector into Neutral (Integra) or Reverse (Legend) position. Remove lock pin from cable adjuster. Align hole in adjuster with hole in shift cable. *See Fig. 1.*

2) Two holes in end of shift cable are positioned at 90 degrees to allow cable adjustments in 1/4-turn increments. Loosen lock nut on shift cable, and adjust if necessary. *See Fig. 1.* Tighten lock nut. Install lock pin.

3) Lock pin should not bind as it is installed. If it binds, cable is still out of adjustment. Repeat adjustment procedure. Start engine, and check shift lever selection of all gears.

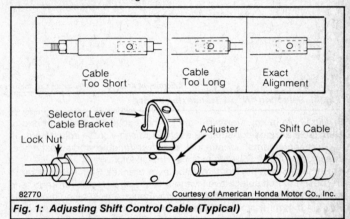

Fig. 1: Adjusting Shift Control Cable (Typical)

Vigor – 1) Start engine. Shift to Reverse. Verify transaxle engages in Reverse. With engine off, remove console. Shift gear selector into Neutral position. Remove lock pin from cable adjuster. Insert a 6-mm pin into selector lever bracket through lock pin sliding hole. *See Fig. 2.*

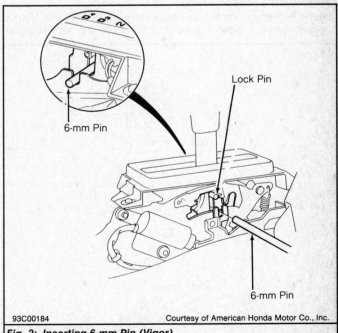

Fig. 2: Inserting 6-mm Pin (Vigor)

2) Verify shift position is in "N" position on transaxle. See Fig. 3. Mark on indicator should align with "N" mark at shift indicator panel. If marks are not aligned, loosen indicator panel mounting screws and adjust by moving panel. Set ignition switch to ON position, and verify "N" indicator light comes on.

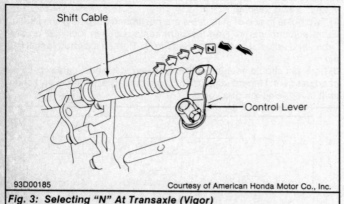

93D00185   Courtesy of American Honda Motor Co., Inc.

Fig. 3: Selecting "N" At Transaxle (Vigor)

3) Align hole in adjuster with hole in shift cable. Two holes in end of shift cable are positioned at 90 degrees to allow cable adjustments in 1/4-turn increments. Loosen lock nut on shift cable, and adjust if necessary. See Fig. 1. Tighten lock nut. Install lock pin.

4) Remove 6-mm pin from selector lever bracket. Shift select lever to "P" position. Pull select lever without pressing select lever knob, and measure movement from console. Movement should be no more than 0.16" (4.0 mm). If movement is greater than 0.16" (4.0 mm), readjust alignment holes in adjuster and shift cable.

5) Move select lever through all gears. Verify shift lever indicator agrees with shift position sensor. Start engine, and verify shift lever selection of all gears.

GEARSHIFT SELECTOR

Legend – Remove center console. Shift gear selector into Neutral position. Measure clearance between lock pin and lock pin gate.

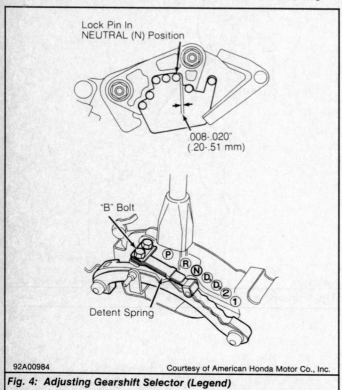

92A00984   Courtesy of American Honda Motor Co., Inc.

Fig. 4: Adjusting Gearshift Selector (Legend)

Clearance should be 0.008-0.020" (0.20-0.51 mm). See Fig. 4. If clearance is not within specification, loosen bolt "B" and adjust. After adjustment, verify gearshift selector movement.

SHIFT INDICATOR PANEL

Legend & Vigor – Shift gear selector into Neutral position. Index mark on shift indicator should align with "N" mark on shift indicator panel. See Fig. 5. If index mark is not aligned, remove center console. Remove shift indicator panel mounting screws, and adjust by moving panel.

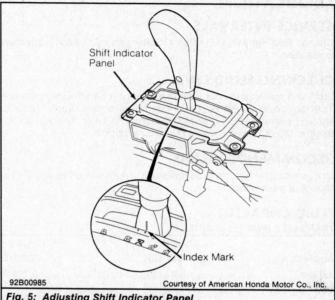

92B00985   Courtesy of American Honda Motor Co., Inc.

*Fig. 5: Adjusting Shift Indicator Panel
(Legend Shown; Vigor Is Similar)*

NEUTRAL SAFETY SWITCH

Neutral safety switch is located at bottom of shift lever, under console. Engine should start in Park and Neutral only. If vehicle does not operate as described, loosen 2 switch mounting screws and readjust.

VACUUM MODULATOR VALVE

Integra – **1)** Ensure atmospheric pressure tube is not restricted and vacuum hose is in good condition. With engine off, connect a hand vacuum pump to intake manifold fitting of vacuum modulator valve. See Fig. 6. Apply 19.7-23.6 in. Hg to valve.

2) If valve does not hold vacuum, replace modulator valve assembly. If valve holds vacuum, remove valve assembly. Apply 19.7-23.6 in. Hg to intake manifold fitting again to observe modulator valve movement.

3) Valve should move in opposite direction when vacuum is released. Repeat these steps 2-3 times. Valve movement can be seen through oil passage on valve. If valve binds or moves sluggishly, replace assembly.

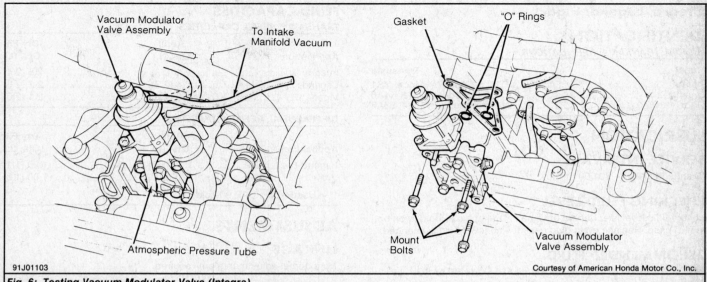

Fig. 6: Testing Vacuum Modulator Valve (Integra)

TORQUE SPECIFICATIONS

TORQUE SPECIFICATIONS

Application	Ft. Lbs. (N.m)
Differential Drain Plug	
Legend	33 (45)
Vigor	35 (48)
Transaxle Drain Plug	
Integra	29 (39)
Legend & Vigor	37 (50)
	INCH Lbs. (N.m)
Shift Cable Lock Nut	62 (7)
Vacuum Modulator Bolts (Integra)	106 (12)

1993 TRANSMISSION SERVICING
Manual Transaxle

Integra, Legend, Vigor

IDENTIFICATION

MANUAL TRANSAXLE APPLICATIONS

Model	Transaxle
Integra	5-Speed – Model YS1
Legend	5-Speed – Model K4A6
Vigor	5-Speed – Model L3A3

LUBRICATION

SERVICE INTERVALS

Change fluid every 30,000 miles.

CHECKING FLUID LEVEL

Ensure fluid level is at bottom of fill hole. Drain plug is located on bottom of case. Replace drain plug gasket whenever fluid is changed.

RECOMMENDED FLUID

Use SAE 10W-30 or 10W-40 engine oil API grade SF or SG.

FLUID CAPACITIES

TRANSAXLE REFILL CAPACITIES

Application	Refill Qts. (L)	Dry Fill Qts. (L)
Integra	2.4 (2.3)	2.5 (2.4)
Legend	2.4 (2.3)	2.7 (2.6)
Vigor	1.9 (1.8)	2.1 (2.0)

DIFFERENTIAL REFILL CAPACITIES

Application	Refill Qts. (L)	Dry Fill Qts. (L)
Legend [1]	1.10 (1.0)	1.20 (1.1)
Vigor [1]	0.95 (0.9)	1.06 (1.0)

[1] – Use Hypoid SAE 90 fluid.

ADJUSTMENTS

LINKAGE

No external adjustments are required.

Integra, Legend, Vigor

MANUAL

NOTE: For manual transaxle replacement procedures, see FWD article in CLUTCHES.

AUTOMATIC

WARNING: Legend and Vigor are equipped with Supplemental Restraint System (SRS). All SRS wiring is color-coded Yellow. Before performing any repairs, disable air bag system. See AIR BAG RESTRAINT SYSTEM article in SAFETY EQUIPMENT. Wait at least 3 minutes after deactivating air bag system. System maintains voltage for about 3 minutes after battery is disconnected. Servicing air bag system before 3 minutes may cause accidental air bag deployment and possible personal injury.

CAUTION: Radio has a coded theft protection circuit. Before disconnecting battery cables, obtain radio anti-theft code number from customer. After reconnecting power, turn radio on. Word CODE will be displayed. Enter customer 5-digit code to restore radio operation.

INTEGRA

Removal – 1) Disconnect negative and then positive battery cable. Remove battery. Remove air intake hose and battery base. Disconnect starter wiring. Remove starter retaining bolts and starter. Disconnect transaxle ground strap. Unplug speed sensor connector. Leaving hydraulic hose attached, remove speed sensor.
2) Unplug lock-up control solenoid valve connectors. Disconnect hose from vacuum modulator. Drain transaxle fluid. Disconnect and plug transaxle cooler lines. On all models except GSR, remove center crossmember. On all models, remove exhaust pipe. Turn ignition switch to release steering lock. Shift transaxle to Neutral.
3) Remove left and right axle shafts. See FWD AXLE SHAFTS article in DRIVE AXLES. Remove intermediate shaft. Remove engine and right wheelwell splash shields. Remove right damper bolt, and separate damper from damper fork.
4) Remove right radius rod. Remove front and rear engine stiffeners. Remove flywheel inspection cover and shift cable holder. Disconnect shift cable by removing cotter pin, control pin, and control lever roller. Remove shift cable guide. Remove drive plate bolts.
5) Remove bolt from front engine mount. Remove mounting bolts from rear engine mount bracket. Remove front and rear transaxle housing mounting bolts. Loosen differential housing mounting bolts. Attach a hoist to transaxle housing hoist bracket and differential housing-to-engine mounting bolt. Lift engine slightly to unload mounts.
6) Place a jack under transaxle, and raise transaxle just enough to take weight from mounts. Remove front engine mount. Remove transaxle mount and mount bracket bolts. Pull transaxle away from engine until it clears dowel pins. Lower transaxle and remove from vehicle.
Installation – To install transaxle, reverse removal procedure. Replace all exhaust system gaskets and self-locking bolts and nuts. Use new spring clips on ends of both axle shafts. Tighten bolts to specification. See TORQUE SPECIFICATIONS. Refill with A/T fluid.

LEGEND

Removal – 1) Disconnect negative and then positive battery cable. Remove strut bar. Drain transaxle fluid. Without removing vacuum lines, remove ignition timing control box and set it aside. Unplug wiring harness connectors as necessary. Remove fluid fill tube. Remove transaxle housing bolts.
2) Remove exhaust pipe from exhaust manifolds. Remove catalytic converter. Remove heat shield and bracket. Disconnect oil cooler hoses from joint pipes. *See Fig. 1.* Remove shift cable cover. Remove shift cable holder from shift cable holder base.

3) Remove control lever from control shaft. *See Fig. 1.* Remove lower plate, and reinstall steering gear assembly mounting bolts. *See Fig. 2.* Rotate control shaft and shift transaxle into "P" position (Park).

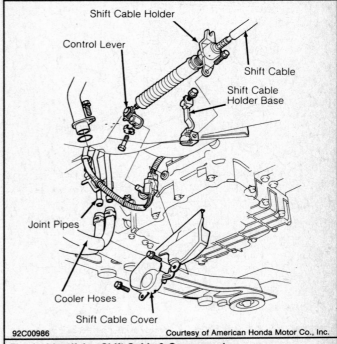

92C00986   Courtesy of American Honda Motor Co., Inc.

Fig. 1: Identifying Shift Cable & Components (Legend Shown; Vigor Is Similar)

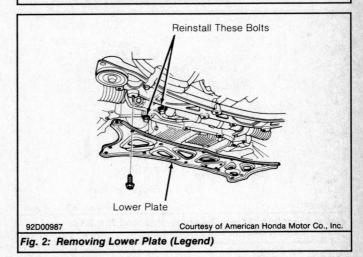

92D00987   Courtesy of American Honda Motor Co., Inc.

Fig. 2: Removing Lower Plate (Legend)

4) Remove secondary cover and 36-mm sealing bolt from transaxle. *See Fig. 3.* Using Extension Shaft Puller (07LAC-PW50100), disconnect extension shaft from differential. Remove and discard set ring. Place jack under transaxle.
5) Raise transaxle high enough to take weight from middle transaxle mounts. Remove middle transaxle mounts. Remove shift cable guide from transaxle. Remove rear transaxle mount/mount bracket and exhaust pipe bracket. Remove engine stiffener. Remove flywheel inspection cover.
6) Remove drive plate bolts. Remove transaxle housing mounting bolts and 26-mm shim. *See Fig. 4.* Check for wires, hoses, or other components that may still be attached. Pull transaxle away from engine until it clears dowel pins. Remove transaxle.

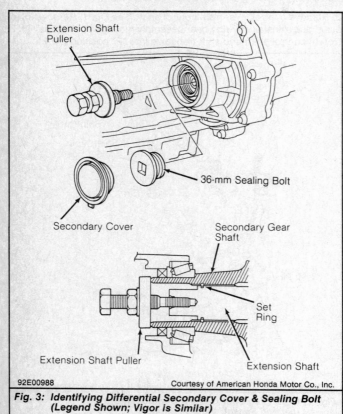

Fig. 3: Identifying Differential Secondary Cover & Sealing Bolt (Legend Shown; Vigor is Similar)

92E00988   Courtesy of American Honda Motor Co., Inc.

Extension Shaft Puller

Secondary Cover

36-mm Sealing Bolt

Secondary Gear Shaft

Set Ring

Extension Shaft Puller

Extension Shaft

Flywheel Inspection Cover

26-mm Shim

Engine Stiffener

92G00386   Courtesy of American Honda Motor Co., Inc.

Fig. 4: Identifying 26-mm Transaxle Mounting Bolt Shim (Legend Shown; Vigor Is Similar)

Installation – 1) Ensure both dowel pins are installed into torque converter housing. Apply Honda Grease (UM264) to extension shaft splines. Position secondary spring into differential side of extension housing. *See Fig. 5.*
2) Place transaxle on transmission jack, and raise it to engine level. Install 26-mm shim and transaxle housing mounting bolt. Install remaining transaxle housing bolts. Install drive plate bolts, and tighten to specification. See TORQUE SPECIFICATIONS.
3) Install flywheel inspection cover. Install engine stiffener. Install rear transaxle mount bracket and exhaust pipe bracket. Install shift cable guide. Install transaxle middle mounts. Install new extension shaft set ring, with open slot upward.

4) Using Extension Shaft Installer (07MAF-PY40100), install extension shaft. Ensure set ring locks into extension shaft groove. Apply Loctite to 36-mm sealing bolt threads, and install bolt. Tighten bolt to specification.
5) Remove steering gear mounting bolts, and install lower plate. Install steering gear mounting bolts. Replace all exhaust system gaskets and self-locking bolts and nuts. To complete installation, reverse removal procedure. Refill all fluids to proper level.

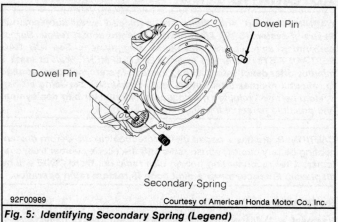

Dowel Pin

Dowel Pin

Secondary Spring

92F00989   Courtesy of American Honda Motor Co., Inc.

Fig. 5: Identifying Secondary Spring (Legend)

VIGOR

Removal – 1) Disconnect negative and then positive battery cable. Remove battery and battery box. Remove underhood ABS fuse/relay box. Remove ground cable. Remove heat shield. Remove distributor. Remove connector from control box. Without removing vacuum tubes, remove control box and lay it aside.
2) Remove torque converter cover. Remove plug, then remove drive plate bolts, one at a time, while rotating crankshaft pulley. Unplug transmission harness connector. Remove transmission ground cable. Remove transmission housing mounting bolts and 26-mm shim. *See Fig. 4.*
3) Remove transmission splash shield. Drain transaxle fluid. Reinstall drain plug using a new sealing washer. Remove transmission mount and mount bracket. Disconnect cooler hoses at joint pipes. Turn pipe ends up to avoid spilling fluid, then plug joint pipes. *See Fig. 1.*
4) Shift transaxle to "P" position (Park) by rotating control shaft. Remove secondary cover. Remove 33-mm sealing bolt. Remove extension shaft from differential with Puller (07LAC-PW50101). *See Fig. 3.* Remove bolts from exhaust pipe stay. Remove exhaust pipe. Remove exhaust manifold stay. Remove shift cable cover. Remove control lever from control shaft. Remove shift cable holder from transmission housing.

CAUTION: Take care not to bend shift cable.

5) Disconnect shift position sensor connector, and then remove harness stay. Remove transmission mid mount nuts. Using a transmission jack, raise transmission just enough to take weight from mounts. Remove mid mounts and mid mount spacer.

NOTE: DO NOT remove torque converter bolt on differential carrier side or torque converter cover.

6) Remove transmission housing mounting bolts. Remove torque converter cover mounting bolt on torque converter housing side.

7) Pull transmission away from engine until it clears dowel pins. Lower transmission from vehicle to remove.

Installation – 1) Install dowel pins into torque converter housing. Install extension shaft with Super High Temp Urea Grease (08798-9002) on shaft splines. Fill opening of drive pinion and extension shaft with urea grease. Place transmission on transmission jack, and raise it to engine level.

2) Install transmission housing mounting bolts. Install torque converter cover mounting bolt on torque converter housing side. Install mid mount spacer and mid mounts. Install mid mount nuts. Install transmission housing mounting bolts and 26-mm shim. *See Fig. 4.* Install new set ring into extension shaft groove. Fill opening of extension shaft and 33-mm sealing bolt with urea grease. Using Thread Sealant (08718-0001), install 33-mm sealing bolt.

3) To complete installation, reverse removal procedure. Replace all exhaust system gaskets and self-locking bolts and nuts. Tighten all bolts and nuts to specification. See TORQUE SPECIFICATIONS. Refill all fluids to proper level.

TORQUE SPECIFICATIONS
TORQUE SPECIFICATIONS

Application	Ft. Lbs (N.m)
Center Crossmember (Integra)	33 (45)
Drain Plug	
Integra	29 (40)
Legend & Vigor	37 (50)
Drive Plate-To-Crankshaft	55 (75)
Exhaust Header Pipe	41 (55)
Exhaust Pipe Bracket	29 (40)
Extension Shaft Sealing Bolt	59 (80)
Front Engine Mount Bolt	48 (65)
Intermediate Shaft Mount Bolt	29 (40)
Lower Plate Bolts	29 (39)
Rear Transaxle Mount Bolt	44 (60)
Rear Transaxle Mount Bracket	29 (40)
Shift Cable Guide Bolt	16 (22)
Starter-To-Housing Bolt	33 (45)
Top Transaxle Mount Bolt	41 (55)
Torque Converter Bolt	
Integra & Legend	[1]
Vigor	20 (27)
Transaxle Housing-To-Engine Bolt	
Integra	44-74 (60-100)
Legend	55 (75)
Vigor	59 (80)
Transaxle Middle Mount-To-Engine Bolt	28 (38)
	INCH Lbs. (N.m)
Flywheel Inspection Cover Bolt	106 (12)
Shift Cable Housing Bolt	88 (10)

[1] – Tighten bolt to 106 INCH lbs. (12 N.m).

1993 CHRYSLER CORP./MITSUBISHI
Contents

ENGINE PERFORMANCE

ENGINE PERFORMANCE (Cont.)

ACCESSORIES & EQUIPMENT (Cont.)

ACCESSORIES & EQUIPMENT (Cont.)

1993 CHRYSLER CORP./MITSUBISHI
Contents (Cont.)

1993 MODEL COVERAGE

MODEL	BODY CODE [1]	ENGINE [2]	ENGINE ID [3]	FUEL SYSTEM	IGNITION SYSTEM [4]
Colt	1, 6	1.5L 4-Cyl. (4G15) SOHC	A	MPI	Optical
		1.8L 4-Cyl. (4G93) SOHC	C	MPI	Optical
Colt Vista	0	1.8L 4-Cyl. (4G93) SOHC	C	MPI	Hall Effect
		2.4L 4-Cyl. (4G64) SOHC	G	MPI	Hall Effect
Colt 200 [5]	1, 6	1.5L 4-Cyl. (4G15) SOHC	A	MPI	Optical
Diamante	7	3.0L V6 (6G72) SOHC	H	MPI	Optical
		3.0L V6 (6G72) DOHC	J	MPI	DIS
Eclipse	4	1.8L 4-Cyl. (4G37) SOHC	B	MPI	Optical
		2.0L 4-Cyl. (4G63) DOHC	E	MPI	DIS
		2.0L 4-Cyl. (4G63) DOHC Turbo	F	MPI	DIS
Expo	0, 4, 9	1.8L 4-Cyl. (4G93) SOHC	C	MPI	Hall Effect
		2.4L 4-Cyl. (4G64) SOHC	G	MPI	Hall Effect
Galant	6	2.0L 4-Cyl. (4G63) SOHC	D	MPI	Optical
Mirage	1, 6	1.5L 4-Cyl. (4G15) SOHC	A	MPI	Optical
		1.8L 4-Cyl. (4G93) SOHC	C	MPI	Optical
Montero	1	3.0L V6 (6G72) SOHC	H	MPI	Optical
Pickup	4, 5, 9	2.4L 4-Cyl. (4G64) SOHC	G	MPI	Optical
		3.0L V6 (6G72) SOHC	H	MPI	Optical
Precis	A, D, F	1.5L 4-Cyl. (G4AJK) SOHC	J	MPI	Optical
Ram-50	1, 2	2.4L 4-Cyl. (4G64) SOHC	G	MPI	Optical
		3.0L V6 (6G72) SOHC	H	MPI	Optical
Stealth	4	3.0L V6 (6G72) SOHC	H	MPI	Optical
		3.0L V6 (6G72) DOHC	J	MPI	DIS
		3.0L V6 (6G72) DOHC Turbo	K	MPI	DIS
Summit	1, 6	1.5L 4-Cyl. (4G15) SOHC	A	MPI	Optical
		1.8L 4-Cyl. (4G93) SOHC	C	MPI	Optical
Summit Wagon	0	1.8L 4-Cyl. (4G93) SOHC	C	MPI	Hall Effect
		2.4L 4-Cyl. (4G64) SOHC	G	MPI	Hall Effect
3000GT	4	3.0L V6 (6G72) DOHC	J	MPI	DIS
		3.0L V6 (6G72) DOHC Turbo	K	MPI	DIS

[1] – Body code is seventh character (fifth character on Precis) of Vehicle Identification Number (VIN). VIN is located on upper left corner of instrument panel.

[2] – See ENGINE CODE LOCATION.

[3] – Engine ID is eighth character of VIN.

[4] – Ignition timing is computer-controlled. On all models with Distributorless Ignition System (DIS), crankshaft position sensor is mounted in place of distributor.

[5] – Canadian model.

VIN DEFINITION (EXCEPT PRECIS)

JB3CU14X1PU123456

① Indicates Nation of Origin.
② Indicates Manufacturer.
③ Indicates Vehicle Type.
④ Indicates Restraint System. [1]
⑤ Indicates Model.
⑥ Indicates Vehicle Series.
⑦ Indicates Body Type. [2]
⑧ **Indicates Engine Type and Make.**
⑨ Indicates Check Digit.
⑩ **Indicates Model Year.**
⑪ Indicates Assembly Plant.
⑫⑬⑭⑮⑯⑰ Indicates Plant Sequential Number.

[1] – On Pickup, Montero and Ram-50, fourth character of VIN indicates GVWR.

[2] – On Pickup, Montero and Ram-50, seventh character of VIN indicates restraint system.

VIN DEFINITION (PRECIS ONLY)

KPHVD32J0PK000047

① Indicates Nation of Origin.
② Indicates Manufacturer.
③ Indicates Vehicle Type.
④ Indicates Drive Line Type.
⑤ Indicates Body Type.
⑥ Indicates Vehicle Series.
⑦ Indicates Restraint Type.
⑧ **Indicates Engine Type and Make.**
⑨ Indicates Check Digit.
⑩ **Indicates Model Year.**
⑪ Indicates Assembly Plant.
⑫⑬⑭⑮⑯⑰ Indicates Plant Sequential Number.

MODEL YEAR VIN CODE APPLICATION

VIN Code	Model Year
M	1991
N	1992
P	1993

ENGINE CODE LOCATION

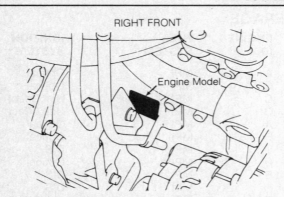

RIGHT FRONT

Engine Model

COLT, COLT 200, ECLIPSE, MIRAGE & SUMMIT
1.5L, 1.6L, 1.8L & 2.0L

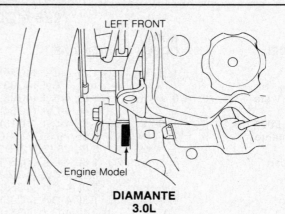

LEFT FRONT

Engine Model

DIAMANTE
3.0L

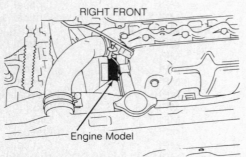

RIGHT FRONT

Engine Model

COLT VISTA, EXPO & SUMMIT WAGON
1.8L

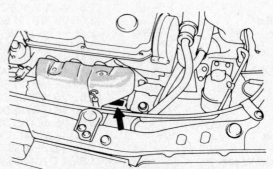

COLT VISTA, EXPO & SUMMIT WAGON
2.4L

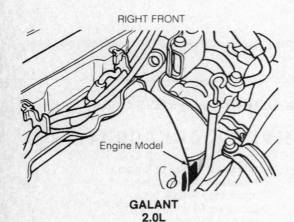

RIGHT FRONT

Engine Model

GALANT
2.0L

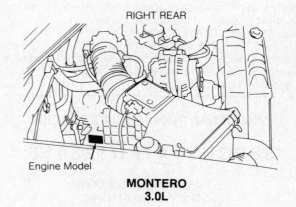

RIGHT REAR

Engine Model

MONTERO
3.0L

Courtesy of Chrysler Corp.

90I17341   92A25569   92D25570   93B78064   90C17345   92F25572

ENGINE CODE LOCATION (Cont.)

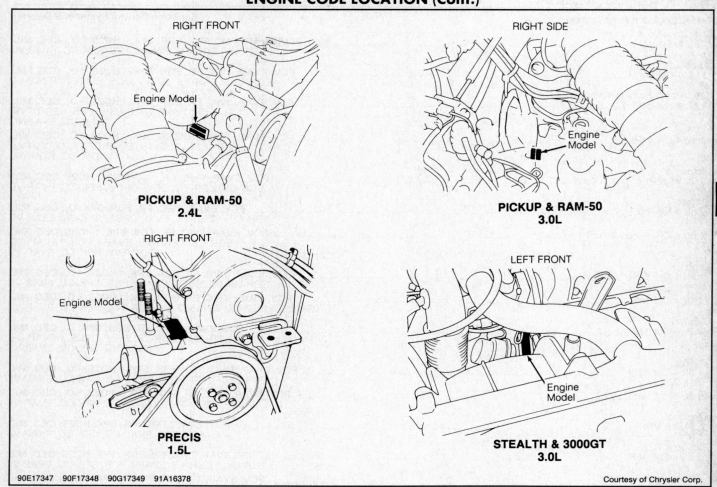

RIGHT FRONT

Engine Model

**PICKUP & RAM-50
2.4L**

RIGHT SIDE

Engine Model

**PICKUP & RAM-50
3.0L**

RIGHT FRONT

Engine Model

**PRECIS
1.5L**

LEFT FRONT

Engine Model

**STEALTH & 3000GT
3.0L**

90E17347   90F17348   90G17349   91A16378

Courtesy of Chrysler Corp.

1993 ENGINE PERFORMANCE
Emission Applications

1993 CHRYSLER CORP./MITSUBISHI

Model, Engine & Fuel System	Emission Control Systems & Devices
Colt, Colt 200 & Summit	
1.5L 4-Cyl. MPI	**PCV, EVAP, TWC, FR,** [1] **EGR, SPK,** [2] **HO2S,** [2] **O2, CEC, MIL,** [1] EGR-CS, [1] EGR-TS, EVAP-CPCS, SPK-CC, EVAP-VC
Colt & Summit	
1.8L 4-Cyl. MPI	**PCV, EVAP, TWC, FR, EGR, SPK,** [1] **HO2S,** [2] **O2, CEC, MIL,** [1] EGR-CS, [1] EGR-TS, EVAP-CPCS, SPK-CC, EVAP-VC
Colt Vista & Summit Wagon	
1.8L 4-Cyl. MPI	**PCV, EVAP, TWC, FR, EGR, SPK,** [1] **HO2S,** [2] **O2, CEC, MIL,** [1] EGR-CS, [1] EGR-TS, EVAP-CPCS, [2] EGR-TVV, SPK-CC, EVAP-VC
2.4L 4-Cyl. MPI	**PCV, EVAP, TWC, FR, EGR, SPK,** [1] **HO2S,** [2] **O2, CEC, MIL,** [1] EGR-CS, [1] EGR-TS, EVAP-CPCS, [2] EGR-TVV, SPK-CC, EVAP-VC
Diamante	
3.0L V6 MPI	**PCV, EVAP, TWC, FR,** [1] **EGR, SPK, HO2S, CEC, MIL,** EGR-CS, EGR-TS, EVAP-CPCS, SPK-CC, EVAP-VC
Eclipse	
1.8L 4-Cyl. MPI	**PCV, EVAP, TWC, FR, EGR, SPK, O2, CEC, MIL,** [1] EGR-CS, [1] EGR-TS, EVAP-CPCS, SPK-CC, EVAP-VC
2.0L 4-Cyl. Turbo & Non-Turbo MPI	**PCV, EVAP, TWC, FR, EGR, SPK,** [1] **HO2S, CEC, MIL,** [1] EGR-CS, [1] EGR-TS, EVAP-CPCS, [3] EVAP-CS, [2] EGR-TVV, SPK-CC, EVAP-VC
Expo	
1.8L 4-Cyl. MPI	**PCV, EVAP, TWC, FR, EGR, SPK,** [1] **HO2S,** [2] **O2, CEC, MIL,** [1] EGR-CS, [1] EGR-TS, EVAP-CPCS, [2] SPK-CC, EVAP-VC
2.4L 4-Cyl. MPI	**PCV, EVAP, TWC, FR, EGR, SPK,** [1] **HO2S,** [2] **O2, CEC, MIL,** EGR-CS, [1] EGR-TS, EVAP-CPCS, EGR-TVV, SPK-CC, EVAP-VC
Galant	
2.0L 4-Cyl. MPI	**PCV, EVAP, TWC, FR, EGR, SPK, O2, CEC, MIL,** [1] EGR-CS, [1] EGR-TS, EVAP-CPCS, [3] EVAP-CS, [2] EGR-TVV, SPK-CC, EVAP-VC
Mirage	
1.5L 4-Cyl. MPI	**PCV, EVAP, TWC, FR,** [1] **EGR, SPK,** [1] **HO2S,** [2] **O2, CEC, MIL,** [1] EGR-CS, [1] EGR-TS, EVAP-CPCS, SPK-CC, EVAP-VC
1.8L 4-Cyl. MPI	**PCV, EVAP, TWC, FR, EGR, SPK,** [1] **HO2S,** [2] **O2, CEC, MIL,** [1] EGR-CS, [1] EGR-TS, EVAP-CPCS, SPK-CC, EVAP-VC
Montero	
3.0L V6 MPI	**PCV, EVAP, TWC, FR, SPK, HO2S, CEC, MIL,** EVAP-CPCS, EVAP-CS, SPK-CC, EVAP-VC
Pickup & Ram-50	
2.4L 4-Cyl. MPI	**PCV, EVAP, TWC, FR, EGR, SPK, HO2S, CEC, MIL,** EGR-CS, [1] EGR-TS, EVAP-CPCS, SPK-CC, EVAP-VC
3.0L V6 MPI	**PCV, EVAP, TWC, FR,** [1] **EGR, SPK, HO2S, CEC, MIL,** EGR-CS, EGR-TS, EVAP-CPCS, SPK-CC, EVAP-VC
Precis	
1.5L 4-Cyl. MPI	**PCV, EVAP, TWC, FR, EGR, SPK, O2, CEC, MIL,** [1] EGR-CS, [1] EGR-TS, EVAP-CPCS, EGR-TVV, SPK-CC, EVAP-VC
Stealth & 3000GT	
3.0L V6 Turbo & Non-Turbo MPI	**PCV, EVAP, TWC, FR, EGR, SPK, HO2S, CEC, MIL,** [1] EGR-CS, [1] EGR-TS, EVAP-CPCS, [3] EVAP-CS, SPK-CC, EVAP-VC

[1] – Calif.
[2] – Federal.
[3] – Turbo.

NOTE: For quick reference, major emission control systems and devices are listed in bold type; components and other related devices are listed in light type.

CEC – Computerized Engine Control	**FR** – Fill Pipe Restrictor
EGR – Exhaust Gas Recirculation	**HO2S** – Heated Oxygen Sensor
EGR-CS – EGR Control Solenoid	**MIL** – Malfunction Indicator Light
EGR-TS – EGR Temperature Sensor	**MPI** – Multiport Fuel Injection
EGR-TVV – EGR Thermal Vacuum Valve	**O2** – Oxygen Sensor
EVAP – Fuel Evaporative System	**PCV** – Positive Crankcase Ventilation
EVAP-CS – EVAP Control Solenoid	**SPK** – Spark Controls
EVAP-CPCS – EVAP Canister Purge Control Solenoid	**SPK-CC** – SPK Computer Controlled
EVAP-VC – EVAP Vapor Canister	**TWC** – Three-Way Catalyst

Chrysler Corp.: Colt, Colt Vista, Colt 200, Ram-50, Stealth, Summit, Summit Wagon
Mitsubishi: Diamante, Eclipse, Expo, Galant, Mirage, Montero, Pickup, Precis, 3000GT

INTRODUCTION

Use this article to quickly find specifications related to servicing and on-vehicle adjustments. This is a quick reference article to use when you are familiar with an adjustment procedure and only need a specification.

CAPACITIES

BATTERY SPECIFICATIONS

Application	Group Size	CCA Rating
Colt, Colt 200, Mirage		
& Summit	24R	430
Diamante	26R	490
Eclipse	86	430
Colt Vista, Expo		
& Summit Wagon		
1.8L	26R	350
2.4L	26R	490
Galant	24R	430
Montero	26R	490
Pickup & Ram-50		
2.4L	24F	430
3.0L	26R	490
Precis	24	420
Stealth & 3000GT	26R	490

NOTE: *Refill capacities are approximate. Correct fluid level should be determined by mark on dipstick, if applicable.*

FLUID CAPACITIES

Application	Quantity
Automatic Transaxle (Mitsubishi Plus/Mopar Plus/Dexron-II)	
Colt, Colt 200, Mirage & Precis	6.3 Qts. (6.0L)
Colt Vista, Summit Wagon	
AWD	6.9 Qts. (6.5L)
FWD	6.3 Qts. (6.0L)
Diamante, Stealth & 3000GT	7.9 Qts. (7.5L)
Galant	
AWD	6.9 Qts. (6.5L)
Except AWD	6.3 Qts. (6.0L)
Eclipse	
Except Turbo	6.3 Qts. (6.0L)
Turbo	7.4 Qts. (7.0L)
Expo	
AWD	6.9 Qts. (6.5L)
FWD	6.3 Qts. (6.0L)
Summit	6.3 Qts. (6.0L)
Automatic Transmission (Mitsubishi Plus/Mopar Plus/Dexron II)	
Montero	7.7 Qts. (7.3L)
Pickup & Ram-50	7.4 Qts. (7.0L)
Cooling System (Includes Heater & Reserve Tank)	
Colt, Colt 200, Mirage & Summit	
1.5L	5.3 Qts. (5.0L)
1.8L	6.3 Qts. (6.0L)
Colt Vista & Summit Wagon	
1.8L	6.2 Qts. (5.9L)
2.4L	6.8 Qts. (6.4L)
Diamante	8.5 Qts. (8.0L)
Montero	10.0 Qts. (9.5L)
Eclipse	
1.8L	6.6 Qts. (6.2L)
2.0L	7.6 Qts. (7.2L)
Expo	
1.8L	6.2 Qts. (5.9L)
2.4L	6.8 Qts. (6.4L)
Galant	7.6 Qts. (7.2L)
Pickup, Ram-50	
2WD	
Auto. Trans.	6.3 Qts. (6.0L)
Man. Trans.	6.3 Qts. (6.0L)

FLUID CAPACITIES (Cont.)

Application	Quantity
4WD	8.9 Qts. (8.4L)
Precis	5.6 Qts. (5.3L)
Stealth & 3000GT	8.5 Qts. (8.0L)
Crankcase (Includes Filter)	
Colt, Colt 200 & Summit	
1.5L	3.5 Qts. (3.3L)
1.8L	4.0 Qts. (3.8L)
Colt Vista, Expo & Summit Wagon	
1.8L	4.0 Qts. (3.8L)
2.4L	4.5 Qts. (4.3L)
Diamante	4.4 Qts. (4.2L)
Eclipse	
1.8L	4.1 Qts. (3.9L)
2.0L Non-Turbo	4.6 Qts. (4.4L)
2.0 Turbo	4.8 Qts. (4.5L)
Galant	4.7 Qts. (4.4L)
Mirage	
1.5L	3.5 Qts. (3.3L)
1.8L	4.0 Qts. (3.8L)
Montero	5.5 Qts. (4.9L)
Pickup, Ram-50	
4 Cylinder	4.0 Qts. (3.8L)
V6	5.0 Qts. (4.6L)
Precis	3.6 Qts. (3.4L)
Stealth & 3000GT	
Non-Turbo	4.4 Qts. (4.2L)
Turbo	5.0 Qts. (4.6L)
Differential (SAE 80W-90/API GL-5)	
Eclipse & Galant	.75 Qts. (.7L)
Colt Vista, Expo, Stealth	
Summit Wagon & 3000GT	1.2 Qts. (1.1L)
Montero	
Front	1.3 Qts. (1.2L)
Rear	2.7 Qts. (2.6L)
Pickup & Ram-50	
2WD	1.6 Qts. (1.5L)
4WD	
Front	1.2 Qts. (1.1L)
Rear	2.7 Qts. (2.6L)
Manual Transaxle (SAE 75W-85/API GL-4)	
Colt, Colt 200, Mirage & Summit	
5-Speed	1.9 Qts. (1.8L)
Colt Vista & Summit Wagon	
FWD	
1.8L	1.9 Qts. (1.8L)
2.4L	2.4 Qts. (2.3L)
AWD	2.4 Qts. (2.3L)
Eclipse	
Non-Turbo	1.9 Qts. (1.8L)
Turbo	2.4 Qts. (2.3L)
Expo	
AWD	2.4 Qts. (2.3L)
FWD	
1.8L	1.9 Qts. (1.8L)
2.4L	2.4 Qts. (2.3L)
Galant	
F5M22	1.9 Qts. (1.8L)
F5M31	2.4 Qts. (2.3L)
Precis	
KM 201	1.9 Qts. (1.8L)
KM 200	1.8 Qts. (1.7L)
Stealth & 3000GT	
FWD	2.4 Qts. (2.3L)
AWD	2.5 Qts. (2.4L)
Manual Transmission (SAE 75W-85/API GL-4)	
Montero	2.6 Qts. (2.5L)
Pickup & Ram-50	
2WD	2.4 Qts. (2.3L)
4WD	2.6 Qts. (2.5L)
Power Steering (Dexron-II)	
Colt, Colt Vista, Colt 200, Eclipse, Expo	
Galant, Mirage, Pickup, Precis, Ram-50,	
Summit & Summit Wagon	1.9 Pts. (.9L)
Diamante, Stealth & 3000GT	
2-Wheel Steering	1.9 Pts. (.9L)
4-Wheel Steering	1.6 Pts. (1.5L)
Montero	2.1 Pts. (1.0L)
Transfer Case (SAE 75W-85/API GL-4)	
Eclipse, Expo & Galant	1.2 Pts. (.6L)
Montero, Pickup & Ram-50 ..	4.7 Pts. (2.2L)
Stealth & 3000GT	.7 Pt. (.3L)
Colt Vista & Summit Wagon .	1.2 Pts. (.6L)

1993 ENGINE PERFORMANCE
Service & Adjustment Specifications (Cont.)

QUICK-SERVICE

SERVICE INTERVALS & SPECIFICATIONS
REPLACEMENT INTERVALS

Component	Miles
Colt, Colt 200, Mirage & Summit	
Air Filter	30,000
Automatic Transaxle Fluid	30,000
Coolant	30,000
Oil	7500
Oil Filter	15,000
Spark Plugs	30,000
Timing Belt	60,000
Colt Vista, Expo & Summit Wagon	
Air Filter	30,000
Automatic Transaxle Fluid	30,000
Coolant	30,000
Oil	7500
Oil Filter	15,000
Rear Axle Fluid	30,000
Spark Plugs	30,000
Timing Belt	60,000
Diamante	
Air Filter	30,000
Automatic Transaxle Fluid	30,000
Coolant	30,000
Oil	7500
Oil Filter	15,000
Spark Plugs	
SOHC	30,000
DOHC	60,000
Timing Belt	60,000
Eclipse	
Air Filter	30,000
Automatic Transaxle Fluid	30,000
Coolant	30,000
Oil	
Non-Turbo	7500
Turbo	5000
Oil Filter	
Non-Turbo	15,000
Turbo	10,000
Spark Plugs	30,000
Timing Belt	60,000
Galant	
Air Filter	30,000
Automatic Transaxle Fluid	30,000
Coolant	30,000
Oil	7500
Oil Filter	15,000
Rear Axle Fluid	30,000
Spark Plugs	30,000
Timing & Balance Shaft Belts	60,000
Montero	
Air Filter	30,000
Automatic Transmission Fluid	30,000
Coolant	30,000
Front & Rear Axle Fluid	30,000
Oil	7500
Oil Filter	15,000
O$_2$ Sensor [1]	80,000
Spark Plugs	30,000
Spark Plug Wires [1]	60,000
Timing Belt	60,000
Transfer Case Fluid	30,000
Vapor Canister [1]	100,000
Pickup & Ram-50	
Air Filter	30,000
Automatic Transmission Fluid	30,000
Coolant	30,000
EGR Valve (2.4L) [1]	50,000
Front & Rear Axle Fluid	30,000
Oil	7500
Oil Filter	15,000
O$_2$ Sensor [1]	80,000
Spark Plugs	30,000
Spark Plug Wires [1]	60,000
Timing Belt	60,000
Transfer Case Fluid	30,000
Vapor Canister [1]	100,000

[1] – Federal models only.

REPLACEMENT INTERVALS (Cont.)

Component	Miles
Precis	
Air Filter	30,000
Automatic Transaxle Fluid	30,000
Brake Fluid	30,000
Coolant	30,000
Fuel Filter	60,000
Oil & Filter	7500
Spark Plugs	30,000
Timing Belt	60,000
Stealth	
Air Filter	30,000
Automatic Transaxle Fluid	30,000
Coolant	30,000
Rear Axle Fluid (AWD)	30,000
Fuel Filter	30,000
Oil	
Non-Turbo	7500
Turbo	5000
Oil Filter	
Non-Turbo	15,000
Turbo	10,000
Spark Plugs	
SOHC	30,000
DOHC	60,000
Timing Belt	60,000
3000GT	
Air Filter	30,000
Automatic Transaxle Fluid	30,000
Coolant	30,000
Rear Axle Fluid (AWD)	30,000
Fuel Filter	30,000
Oil	
Non-Turbo	7500
Turbo	5000
Oil Filter	
Non-Turbo	15,000
Turbo	10,000
Spark Plugs	60,000
Timing Belt	60,000

[1] – Federal models only.

BELT ADJUSTMENT

Application	[1] Deflection New Belt – In. (mm)	[1] Deflection Used Belt – In. (mm)
Colt, Colt 200, Mirage, Precis & Summit		
1.5L		
Alternator	.22-.28 (5.5-7.0)	.31 (7.8)
A/C	.20-.24 (5.0-6.0)	.24-.28 (6.0-7.0)
P/S	.16-.22 (4.0-5.5)	.22-.30 (5.5-7.6)
1.8L		
Alternator	.28-.34 (7.0-8.5)	.37 (9.5)
P/S (w/o A/C)	.22-.24 (5.5-6.0)	.27-.30 (6.8-7.6)
P/S (with A/C)	.30-.35 (7.6-9.0)	.37-.45 (9.5-11.5)
Diamante		
SOHC		
Alternator & P/S	.15-.19 (3.8-4.8)	.23-.31 (5.8-7.8)
A/C	.25-.27 (6.3-6.8)	.29-.33 (7.3-8.3)
DOHC		
Alternator & A/C	.13-.15 (3.3-3.8)	.15-.19 (3.8-4.8)
P/S	.30-.35 (7.6-9.0)	.41-.49 (10.5-12.5)
Eclipse		
1.8L		
Alternator	.31-.43 (7.8-10.9)	[2]
A/C	.16-.20 (4.1-5.1)	.22-.24 (5.5-6.0)
P/S	.23-.35 (5.8-8.8)	[2]
2.0L		
Alternator	.35-.45 (9.0-11.4)	[2]
A/C	.16-.20 (4.1-5.1)	.22-.24 (5.6-6.1)
P/S	.23-.35 (5.8-9.0)	[2]

[1] – With 22 lbs. (10 kg) pressure applied midway on belt run.
[2] – Information is not available from manufacturer.

BELT ADJUSTMENT (Cont.)

Application	[1] Deflection New Belt – In. (mm)	[1] Deflection Used Belt – In. (mm)
Expo		
1.8L		
Alternator	.28-.34 (7.1-8.5)	.37 (9.3)
P/S	.30-.35 (7.6-9.0)	.37-.45 (9.3-11.4)
A/C	.22-.24 (5.5-6.0)	.27-.30 (6.8-7.6)
2.4L		
Alternator	.30-.35 (7.6-8.8)	.40 (10.0)
P/S	.18-.26 (4.5-6.6)	.24-.35 (6.0-9.0)
A/C	.17-.19 (4.3-4.8)	.21-.24 (5.3-6.0)
Galant		
Alternator Belt	.29-.35 (7.3-8.8)	.39 (10.0)
A/C Belt	.19-.21 (4.8-5.5)	.23-.27 (5.8-6.8)
Montero		
Alternator	.25-.31 (6.3-7.8)	.35 (8.8)
P/S	.31 (7.8)	.39 (10.0)
A/C	.19-.23 (4.8-5.8)	.25-.29 (6.3-7.3)
Pickup & Ram-50		
2.4L		
Alternator	.27-.39 (6.8-10.0)	[2]
P/S	.23-.35 (5.8-8.8)	[2]
A/C	.33-.39 (8.3-10.0)	[2]
3.0L		
Alternator	.31-.39 (7.8-10.0)	[2]
P/S	.35-.47 (8.8-12.0)	[2]
A/C	.33-.39 (8.3-10.0)	[2]
Precis		
A/C	.34-.42 (8.6-10.6)	[2]
Alternator	.28-.32 (7.1-8.2)	[2]
P/S	.28-.39 (7.1-10.0)	[2]
Stealth		
SOHC		
Alternator & P/S	.15-.19 (3.8-4.8)	.23-.31 (5.8-7.8)
A/C	.25-.27 (6.3-6.8)	.29-.33 (7.3-8.3)
DOHC		
Alternator	.13-.15 (3.3-3.8)	.15-.19 (3.8-4.8)
P/S	.29-.35 (7.3-8.8)	.41-.49 (10.4-12.4)
Summit Wagon & Vista Wagon		
1.8L		
Alternator	.28-.34 (7.1-8.5)	.37 (9.3)
P/S	.30-.35 (7.5-8.9)	.37-.45 (9.3-11.4)
A/C	.22-.24 (5.5-6.0)	.27-.30 (6.8-7.6)
2.4L		
Alternator	.30-.35 (7.6-8.8)	.40 (10.0)
P/S	.18-.26 (4.5-6.6)	.24-.35 (6.0-8.8)
A/C	.17-.19 (4.3-4.8)	.21-.24 (5.3-6.0)
3000GT		
Alternator	.13-.15 (3.3-3.8)	.15-.19 (3.8-4.8)
P/S	.29-.35 (7.3-8.8)	.41-.49 (10.4-12.4)

[1] – With 22 lbs. (10 kg) pressure applied midway on belt run.
[2] – Information is not available from manufacturer.

MECHANICAL CHECKS

ENGINE COMPRESSION

Check engine compression with engine at normal operating temperature at specified cranking speed, all spark plugs removed and throttle wide open.

COMPRESSION SPECIFICATIONS

Application [1]	Specification
Compression Ratio	
1.5L (VIN A)	9.2:1
1.5L (VIN J)	9.4:1
1.8L (VIN C)	9.5:1
1.8L (VIN B)	9.0:1
2.0L (VIN D)	9.5:1
2.0L (VIN E)	9.0:1
2.0L (VIN F)	7.8:1
2.4L (VIN G)	8.5:1
3.0L (VIN J)	10.0:1
3.0L (VIN K)	8.0:1
3.0L (VIN H)	
Diamante & Stealth	10.0:1
Montero, Pickup & Ram-50	8.9:1
Compression Pressure	
1.5L (VIN A)	
Colt, Colt 200 & Summit	194 psi (13.6 kg/cm²)
Mirage	192 psi (13.4 kg/cm²)
1.5L (VIN J)	192 psi (13.4 kg/cm²)
1.8L (VIN C)	199 psi (13.9 kg/cm²)
1.8L (VIN B)	185 psi (13.0 kg/cm²)
2.0L (VIN D)	178 psi (12.5 kg/cm²)
2.0L (VIN E)	192 psi (13.4 kg/cm²)
2.0L (VIN F)	164 psi (11.5 kg/cm²)
2.4L (VIN G)	171 psi (12.0 kg/cm²)
3.0L (VIN J)	185 psi (13.0 kg/cm²)
3.0L (VIN K)	156 psi (10.9 kg/cm²)
3.0L (VIN H)	171 psi (12.0 kg/cm²)
Maximum Variation Between Cylinders	14 psi (1.0 kg/cm²)

[1] – See CHRYSLER MOTORS/MITSUBISHI INTRODUCTION article for VIN information.

VALVE CLEARANCE

NOTE: Valve adjustment is required on 1.5L and 1.8L engines only. Check adjustment at 15,000 mile intervals.

VALVE CLEARANCE SPECIFICATIONS

Application	[1] In. (mm)
1.5L (VIN A & J)	
Hot Engine	
Intake	.008 (.20)
Exhaust	.010 (.25)
1.8L (VIN C)	
Hot Engine	
Intake	.008 (.20)
Exhaust	.012 (.30)

[1] – Adjust valves with engine hot.

IGNITION SYSTEM

IGNITION COIL

IGNITION COIL RESISTANCE – Ohms @ 68°F (20°C)

Application	Primary	Secondary
1.5L (VIN A)	.9-1.2	20,000-29,000
1.5L (VIN J)	.72-.88	10,300-13,900
1.8L (VIN C)	.9-1.2	20,000-29,000
1.8L (VIN B)	.9-1.2	19,000-27,000
2.0L (VIN E & F)	.70-.86	11,300-15,300
2.0L (VIN D)	.72-.88	10,890-13,310
2.4L (VIN G)		
Pickup & Ram-50	.72-.88	10,300-13,900
All Others	.72-.88	10,900-13,300
3.0L (VIN J & K)	.67-.81	11,310-15,300
3.0L (VIN H)		
Diamante & Stealth	.72-.88	10,300-13,900

1993 ENGINE PERFORMANCE
Service & Adjustment Specifications (Cont.)

HIGH TENSION WIRE RESISTANCE

HIGH TENSION WIRE RESISTANCE

Application [1]	Ohms
1.5L (VIN A)	
Coil Wire	[2]
No. 1 Wire	11,500
No. 2 Wire	9100
No. 3 Wire	9000
No. 4 Wire	6600
1.5L (VIN J)	
Coil Wire	[2]
No. 1 Wire	10,100
No. 2 Wire	11,800
No. 3 Wire	11,800
No. 4 Wire	14,200
1.8L (VIN C)	
Coil Wire	[2]
No. 1 Wire	12,500
No. 2 Wire	11,700
No. 3 Wire	9300
No. 4 Wire	8500
1.8L (VIN B)	
Coil Wire	[2]
No. 1 Wire	10,100
No. 2 Wire	11,500
No. 3 Wire	12,000
No. 4 Wire	13,000
2.0L (VIN D)	
Galant	
Coil Wire	Not Used
No. 1 Wire	12,600
No. 2 Wire	11,700
No. 3 Wire	9400
No. 4 Wire	8500
2.0L (VIN E & F)	
Coil Wire	Not Used
No. 1 Wire	5800
No. 2 Wire	8400
No. 3 Wire	10,600
No. 4 Wire	9700
2.4L (VIN G)	
Pickup & Ram-50	
Coil Wire	3000
No. 1 Wire	10,000
No. 2 Wire	12,000
No. 3 Wire	12,000
No. 4 Wire	14,000
2.4L (VIN G)	
Expo	
Coil Wire	[2]
No. 1 Wire	12,500
No. 2 Wire	11,700
No. 3 Wire	9,300
No. 4 Wire	8,500
3.0L (VIN J & K)	
Coil Wire	Not Used
No. 1 Wire	8600
No. 2 Wire	13,900
No. 3 Wire	6400
No. 4 Wire	11,500
No. 5 Wire	4500
No. 6 Wire	11,780
3.0L (VIN H)	
Stealth	
Coil Wire	[2]
No. 1 Wire	7800
No. 2 Wire	6400
No. 3 Wire	9600
No. 4 Wire	7500
No. 5 Wire	10,400
No. 6 Wire	8600
Diamante	
Coil Wire	[2]
No. 1 Wire	7800
No. 2 Wire	6400
No. 3 Wire	9600
No. 4 Wire	7500
No. 5 Wire	10,400
No. 6 Wire	8600

[1] – See CHRYSLER MOTORS/MITSUBISHI INTRODUCTION article for VIN information.
[2] – Information IS not available from manufacturer.

HIGH TENSION WIRE RESISTANCE (Cont.)

Application	Ohms
Montero, Pickup & Ram-50	
Coil Wire	3000
No. 1 Wire	9000
No. 2 Wire	8500
No. 3 Wire	10,000
No. 4 Wire	9000
No. 5 Wire	12,000
No. 6 Wire	10,000

[1] – See CHRYSLER MOTORS/MITSUBISHI INTRODUCTION article for VIN information.
[2] – Information is not available from manufacturer.

SPARK PLUGS

SPARK PLUG TYPE

Application	Nippondenso No.
1.5L (VIN A)	
Mirage	W16EPR-11
Except Mirage	W20EPR-11
1.5L (VIN J)	[1] RN9YC4
1.8L (VIN C)	K16PR-U11
1.8L (VIN B)	W20EPR-11
2.0L (VIN D & E)	
Eclipse	W20EPR-11
Galant	K16PR-U11
2.0L (VIN F)	
Eclipse	W20EPR-11
2.4L (VIN G, 8 Valve)	W20EPR-11
2.4L (VIN G, 16 Valve)	K16EPR-11
3.0L (VIN J & K)	PK20PR-P11
3.0L (VIN H)	
Diamante & Stealth	W20EPR-11
Montero, Pickup & Ram-50	W16EPR-11

[1] – Champion spark plug.

SPARK PLUG SPECIFICATIONS

Application	Gap In. (mm)	Torque Ft. Lbs. (N.m)
Eclipse (2.0L Turbo)	.028-.031 (.7-.8)	15-21 (20-30)
All Others	.039-.043 (1.0-1.1)	15-21 (20-30)

FIRING ORDER & TIMING MARKS

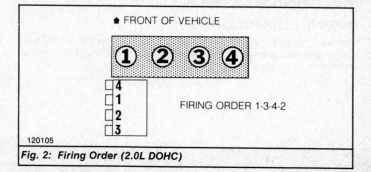

Fig. 1: Firing Order & Distributor Rotation (1.5L, 1.8L, 2.0L SOHC & 2.4L)

Fig. 2: Firing Order (2.0L DOHC)

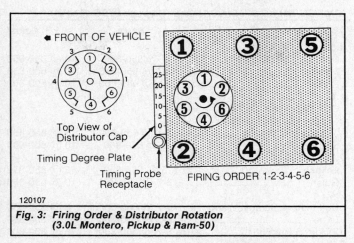

Fig. 3: Firing Order & Distributor Rotation
(3.0L Montero, Pickup & Ram-50)

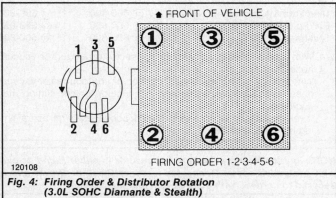

Fig. 4: Firing Order & Distributor Rotation
(3.0L SOHC Diamante & Stealth)

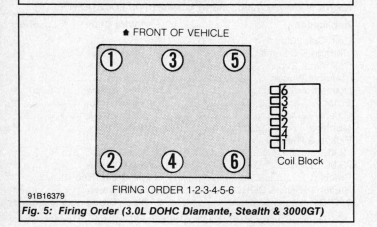

Fig. 5: Firing Order (3.0L DOHC Diamante, Stealth & 3000GT)

IGNITION TIMING

IGNITION TIMING (Degrees BTDC @ RPM)

Application	[1] Basic	[2] [3] Actual
1.5L		
Colt, Colt 200 & Summit	5 @ 650-850	10 @ 650-850
Mirage	3-7 @ 650-850	10 @ 650-850
Precis	3-7 @ 600-800	10 @ 600-800
1.8L		
Colt, Colt Vista, Colt 200, Expo, Mirage, Summit, & Summit Wagon	3-7 @ 650-850	5 @ 650-850
Eclipse	5 @ 600-800	10 @ 600-800
2.0L		
Eclipse	5 @ 650-850	8 @ 650-850
Galant	3-7 @ 650-850	10 @ 650-850
2.4L		
Colt Vista & Summit Wagon	3-7 @ 650-850	8 @ 650-850
Expo	3-7 @ 650-850	5 @ 650-850
Pickup & Ram-50	3-7 @ 600-800	8 @ 600-800
3.0L		
Diamante & Montero	3-7 @ 600-800	15 @ 600-800
Pickup & Ram-50	3-7 @ 650-850	15 @ 650-850
Stealth & 3000GT	2-8 @ 600-800	15 @ 600-800

[1] – With ignition timing adjustment connector grounded or vacuum hose (farthest from distributor) disconnected.

[2] – With ignition timing adjustment connector ungrounded or vacuum hose (farthest from distributor) connected. Ignition timing may fluctuate.

[3] – If vehicle altitude is more than 2300 ft. above sea level, actual timing may be advanced.

FUEL SYSTEM

FUEL PUMP

REGULATED FUEL PRESSURE

Application	At Idle w/Vacuum psi (kg/cm²)	At Idle w/o Vacuum psi (kg/cm²)
Eclipse (Turbo)		
Man. Trans.	27 (1.8)	36-38 (2.5-2.6)
Auto. Trans.	33 (2.3)	41-46 (2.8-3.2)
Stealth (Turbo) & 3000GT	34 (2.4)	43-45 (3.0-3.1)
All Others	38 (2.6)	47-50 (3.3-3.5)

INJECTOR RESISTANCE

INJECTOR RESISTANCE

Application	Ohms
Non-Turbo	13-16
Turbo	2-3

THROTTLE POSITION SENSOR (TPS)

TPS SPECIFICATIONS

Application	[1] Volts
Diamante (w/Traction Control)	.58-.69
Mirage, Pickup (2.4L), Ram-50 (2.4L) & Eclipse	.48-.52
All Others	.4-1.0

[1] – At idle.

1993 ENGINE PERFORMANCE
On-Vehicle Adjustments

Chrysler Corp: Colt, Colt Vista, Colt 200, Ram-50, Stealth, Summit, Summit Wagon, Mitsubishi: Diamante, Eclipse, Expo, Galant, Mirage, Montero, Pickup, Precis, 3000GT

ENGINE MECHANICAL

Before performing any on-vehicle adjustments to fuel or ignition system, ensure engine mechanical condition is okay.

VALVE CLEARANCE

NOTE: Valve adjustment is possible on 1.5L and 1.8L engines only. All other models use hydraulic lash adjusters.

VALVE ADJUSTMENT

CAUTION: DO NOT rotate crankshaft in opposite direction of normal engine rotation.

1.5L & 1.8L – 1) Ensure engine is at normal operating temperature. Remove all spark plugs and valve cover. Rotate crankshaft clockwise to position cylinder No. 1 at TDC of compression stroke. Adjust intake valves on cylinders No. 1 and 2, and exhaust valves on cylinders No. 1 and 3. See VALVE CLEARANCE SPECIFICATIONS table.
2) Rotate crankshaft 360 degrees to position cylinder No. 4 at TDC of compression stroke. Adjust intake valves on cylinders No. 3 and 4, and exhaust valves on cylinders No. 2 and 4. Install spark plugs and valve cover.

VALVE CLEARANCE SPECIFICATIONS

Application	¹ In. (mm)
1.5L (VIN A & J)	
Hot Engine	
Intake	.008 (.20)
Exhaust	.010 (.25)
1.8L (VIN C)	
Hot Engine	
Intake	.008 (.20)
Exhaust	.012 (.30)

¹ – Adjust valves with engine hot.

CHECKING HYDRAULIC VALVE LIFTERS

Except 1.5L & 1.8L – 1) Warm engine to normal operating temperature. Remove valve cover. Position cylinder No. 1 at TDC on compression stroke. Check intake rockers on cylinders No. 1 and 2. Check exhaust rockers on cylinders No. 1 and 3.
2) Push downward on end of rocker arm above lash adjuster. Rotate crankshaft 360 degrees and check intake rockers on cylinders No. 3 and 4. Check exhaust rockers on cylinders No. 2 and 4. If lash adjuster is normal, it will feel solid.
3) If lash adjuster moves downward easily when pushed, replace adjuster. If lash adjuster feels soft or spongy, air has probably entered lash adjuster. If this occurs, check engine oil level. If engine oil level is okay, check oil screen and oil screen gasket for damage.
4) After repairing cause of air leak, warm engine to operating temperature. Drive vehicle at low speed for approximately 5 minutes. Turn engine off for a few minutes.
5) Restart engine and drive at low speed for approximately 5 minutes. Repeat this step several times for about one hour. This helps remove air from engine oil.

IGNITION TIMING

NOTE: Perform all adjustments with engine at normal operating temperature, cooling fan and accessories off, transmission in Park or Neutral, and front wheels in straight-ahead position.

IGNITION TIMING SPECIFICATIONS (Degrees BTDC @ RPM)

Application	¹ Basic	² ³ Actual
1.5L		
Colt, Colt 200 & Summit	5 @ 650-850	10 @ 650-850
Mirage	3-7 @ 650-850	10 @ 650-850
Precis	3-7 @ 600-800	10 @ 600-800
1.8L		
Colt, Colt Vista, Colt 200, Expo, Mirage, Summit & Summit Wagon	3-7 @ 650-850	5 @ 650-850
Eclipse	5 @ 600-800	10 @ 600-800
2.0L		
Eclipse	5 @ 650-850	8 @ 650-850
Galant	3-7 @ 650-850	10 @ 650-850
2.4L		
Colt Vista & Summit Wagon	3-7 @ 650-850	8 @ 650-850
Expo	3-7 @ 650-850	5 @ 650-850
Pickup & Ram-50	3-7 @ 600-800	8 @ 600-800
3.0L		
Diamante & Montero	3-7 @ 600-800	15 @ 600-800
Pickup & Ram-50	3-7 @ 650-850	15 @ 650-850
Stealth & 3000GT	2-8 @ 600-800	15 @ 600-800

¹ – With ignition timing adjustment connector grounded or vacuum hose (farthest from distributor) disconnected.
² – With ignition timing adjustment connector ungrounded or vacuum hose (farthest from distributor) connected. Ignition timing may fluctuate.
³ – If vehicle altitude is more than 2300 ft. above sea level, actual timing may be advanced.

NOTE: Ignition timing adjustment connector is either round or oval with protective cover. Connector is either Black or Brown and is secured to harness with colored transparent tape.

IGNITION TIMING ADJUSTMENT CONNECTOR LOCATION

Application	¹ ² Wire Color	Location
Colt, Colt 200, Mirage & Summit	Black/Blue	³
Colt Vista, Expo Summit Wagon	Blue	⁵
Diamante	White/Yellow	³
Eclipse	Yellow/Red	⁴
Galant	Yellow/Red	⁵
Montero	White/Yellow	⁸
Pickup & Ram-50		
2.4L	Black/Blue	⁶
3.0L	White/Yellow	⁶
Precis	Light Green/Red	⁷
Stealth (SOHC & DOHC)	Black/Green	⁴
3000GT	Black/Green	⁴

¹ – Remove waterproof female connector (if equipped) for access to wire.
² – Ground connector at wire end for basic timing adjustment.
³ – On main wiring harness, near center of firewall.
⁴ – On main wiring harness, near wiper motor on firewall, behind battery.
⁵ – On main wiring harness, near master cylinder reservoir on firewall, near strut tower.
⁶ – Near left rear corner of engine compartment, below cruise control actuator (if equipped).
⁷ – Between air filter housing and upper radiator hose.
⁸ – On main wiring harness, near wiper motor on firewall.

NOTE: *Adjustment of ignition timing cannot be performed on vehicles equipped with Distributorless Ignition Systems (DIS). If ignition timing is not within specification, see CRANKSHAFT POSITION SENSOR in SYSTEM & COMPONENT TESTING article.*

1) Locate ignition timing adjustment connector. See IGNITION TIMING ADJUSTMENT CONNECTOR LOCATION table. Connect jumper wire between ignition timing adjustment connector and ground. Check ignition basic timing.
2) If ignition basic timing is not within specification, loosen distributor and rotate to adjust timing if necessary. See IGNITION TIMING SPECIFICATIONS table. Remove jumper wire from ignition timing adjustment connector.

IDLE SPEED & MIXTURE

NOTE: *Perform adjustments with engine at normal operating temperature, cooling fan and accessories off, transmission in Park or Neutral, and front wheels in straight-ahead position.*

CURB (SLOW) IDLE SPEED

NOTE: *Curb idle speed is controlled by Idle Air Control (IAC) motor. Adjustment is usually not necessary. For curb idle speed specifications, see IDLE SPEED SPECIFICATIONS table under BASIC IDLE SPEED.*

1) Check ignition timing and adjust if necessary. See IGNITION TIMING. Run engine at 2000-3000 RPM for more than 5 seconds. Allow engine to idle for 2 minutes. Check curb idle speed.
2) If curb idle speed is not within specification, check IAC system. See SYSTEM & COMPONENT TESTING article. If IAC system is okay, adjust basic idle speed. See BASIC IDLE SPEED.

BASIC IDLE SPEED

NOTE: *ALWAYS check TPS adjustment after adjusting basic idle speed. See THROTTLE POSITION SENSOR (TPS).*

NOTE: *For Data Link Connector (DLC) location, see SELF-DIAGNOSTICS article.*

NOTE: *Ensure vehicle is at normal operating temperature with all lights, cooling fan and accessories off. Shift transmission into Neutral or Park position.*

Colt, Colt Vista, Colt 200, Diamante, Expo, Galant, Mirage, Montero, Ram-50, Stealth, Summit, Summit Wagon, 3000GT & Pickup – 1) Insert paper clip or appropriate probe into tachometer connector. See TACHOMETER CONNECTOR LOCATION table. Connect a primary voltage detecting type tachometer to paper clip.
2) Connect a jumper wire between data link terminal No. 10 and vehicle ground. *See Fig. 1.* Connect a jumper wire between ignition timing adjustment connector and vehicle ground. See IGNITION TIMING ADJUSTMENT CONNECTOR LOCATION table under IGNITION TIMING.
3) Start and run engine at idle. Check basic idle speed. See IDLE SPEED SPECIFICATIONS table. If idle speed is not within specifications, turn engine speed adjusting screw until correct engine speed is obtained. *See Fig. 2.* Access to speed adjusting screw is obtained by removing rubber plug on throttle body.
4) If idle speed cannot be lowered by adjusting engine speed adjusting screw, determine if fixed speed adjusting screw (stop screw contacting throttle lever) has been adjusted. See FIXED SPEED ADJUSTING SCREW for procedure.
5) After all adjustments are verified correct, possible cause of incorrect idle speed is deterioration of fast idle air control motor. Throttle valve must be replaced to correct symptom. Disconnect jumper wires and recheck idle speed.

Eclipse (1.8L) & Precis – 1) Insert paper clip or appropriate probe into tachometer connector. See TACHOMETER CONNECTOR LOCATION table. Connect a primary voltage detecting type tachometer to paper clip. Run engine and read idle speed. See IDLE SPEED SPECIFICATIONS table.
2) If idle speed is not within specification, loosen accelerator cable adjusting bracket. Turn ignition switch to ON position with engine not running, (KOEO). Leave ignition on for 15 seconds to allow Idle Air Control (IAC) motor plunger to fully retract.
3) Turn ignition off and disconnect IAC motor connector. Loosen the Fixed Speed Adjusting Screw (FSAS). Start engine and adjust IAC adjusting screw to appropriate idle speed. *See Fig. 3.* Adjust FSAS until screw contacts throttle lever and then loosen 1/2 turn. Tighten lock nut. Connect IAC motor connector. Tighten accelerator cable adjusting bracket.

TACHOMETER CONNECTOR LOCATION

Application	Type	Location
Colt, Colt 200		
Mirage & Summit	1-Pin	1
Colt Vista, Expo &		
Summit Wagon	1-Pin	2
Diamante	1- Or 3-Pin	3
Eclipse (1.8L)	3-Pin	4
Eclipse (2.0L)	1-Pin	4
Montero, Ram-50 (3.0L)		
Pickup (3.0L)	1-Pin	6
Precis	1-Pin	7
Ram-50 (2.4L) & Pickup (2.4L)	1-Pin	8
Stealth, 3000GT	3-Pin	9 10

1 – Next to ignition timing adjustment connector.
2 – On main harness, on firewall below Vehicle Identification Plate.
3 – On SOHC & DOHC engine, 1-pin Blue connector is attached to main harness on center of firewall. 3-pin connector is mounted to ignition coil bracket and must be backprobed.
4 – Backprobe double wire side of noise filter connector located on right side of intake plenum above distributor.
5 – On main engine harness, on center of firewall next to cruise control actuator (if equipped).
6 – Backprobe connector to noise filter (White/Black wire) mounted on ignition coil bracket.
7 – Backprobe 1-pin connector to noise filter mounted on right front side of intake plenum.
8 – On main harness, on firewall to left of Vehicle Identification Plate.
9 – On SOHC, backprobe double wire portion of connector to noise filter (White/Black wire) behind intake plenum, near ignition coil.
10 – On DOHC, blue connector (Black/White wire) below wiper motor.

IDLE SPEED SPECIFICATIONS

Application	Curb Idle	Basic Idle
1.5L		
Colt, Colt 200, Mirage & Summit	650-850	650-850
Precis	600-800	600-800
1.8L		
Colt Vista, Expo &		
Summit Wagon	650-850	650-850
Eclipse	600-800	600-800
2.0L		
Eclipse, Galant	650-850	650-850
2.4L		
Colt Vista, Expo &		
Summit Wagon	650-850	650-850
Pickup & Ram-50	600-800	600-800
3.0L		
Diamante, Montero,		
Stealth & 3000GT	600-800	600-800
Pickup & Ram-50	650-850	650-850

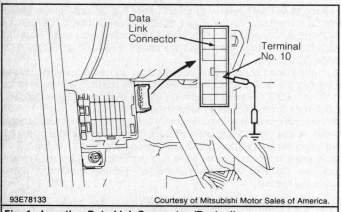

93E78133   Courtesy of Mitsubishi Motor Sales of America.

Fig. 1: Locating Data Link Connector (Typical)

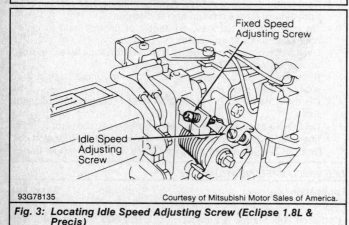

93F78134   Courtesy of Mitsubishi Motor Sales of America.

Fig. 2: Adjusting Idle Speed (Typical)

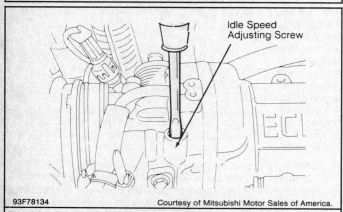

93G78135   Courtesy of Mitsubishi Motor Sales of America.

Fig. 3: Locating Idle Speed Adjusting Screw (Eclipse 1.8L & Precis)

FIXED SPEED ADJUSTING SCREW

NOTE: Fixed Speed Adjusting Screw (FSAS) is preset by manufacturer and usually does not require adjustment. Only adjust FSAS if other adjustment procedures require it, or if manufacturer's original setting has been changed.

Colt Vista, Expo, Diamante, Montero, Pickup (3.0L), Ram-50 (3.0L), Stealth, Summit Wagon & 3000GT – 1) Loosen throttle cable. Loosen FSAS lock nut. *See Fig. 4.* Turn FSAS counterclockwise until throttle valve is fully closed. Turn FSAS clockwise until throttle valve begins to open. Turn FSAS clockwise 1 1/4 turns after throttle valve begins to open.
2) Tighten lock nut while holding FSAS in position. Adjust throttle cable. Adjust basic idle speed. See BASIC IDLE SPEED under IDLE

SPEED & MIXTURE. Adjust throttle position sensor. See THROTTLE POSITION SENSOR (TPS).

NOTE: Eclipse 2.0L DOHC uses an idle position switch as the Fixed Speed Adjusting Screw (FSAS). For adjustment, see IDLE POSITION SWITCH under THROTTLE POSITION SENSOR (TPS).

All Other Models – To adjust Fixed Speed Adjusting Screw (FSAS), adjust basic idle speed. See BASIC IDLE SPEED under IDLE SPEED & MIXTURE.

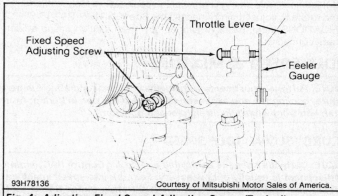

93H78136   Courtesy of Mitsubishi Motor Sales of America.

Fig. 4: Adjusting Fixed Speed Adjusting Screw (Typical)

IDLE MIXTURE

NOTE: Idle mixture is computer controlled on fuel injected engines and is nonadjustable. CO level specifications are not available from manufacturer.

THROTTLE POSITION SENSOR (TPS)

TPS ADJUSTMENT

NOTE: Ensure basic idle speed is set to specification before adjusting TPS. See BASIC IDLE SPEED under IDLE SPEED & MIXTURE. Perform all adjustments with engine at normal operating temperature, front wheels in straight-ahead position, cooling fan and all accessories off, and transmission in Park or Neutral.

TPS SPECIFICATIONS

Application	[1] Volts
Diamante (w/Traction Control)	.58-.69
Mirage, Pickup (3.0L), Ram-50 (2.4L), Eclipse	.48-.52
All Others	.4-1.0

[1] – At idle.

Colt Vista, Expo, Montero & Summit Wagon – 1) Disconnect TPS connector. Using external ohmmeter, measure resistance between TPS terminals No. 1 and 2. *See Fig. 5.* Insert .256" (.65 mm) feeler gauge between fixed speed adjusting screw and throttle lever.
2) Loosen TPS mounting screws and rotate TPS fully clockwise. Ensure there is continuity between terminals No. 1 and 2. Rotate TPS counterclockwise until there is no continuity and tighten screws. Install Test Harness (MB991348) between TPS and harness connector.
3) Turn ignition on. Using external voltmeter, measure TPS output voltage between terminals No. 1 and 3. See TPS SPECIFICATION table. If voltage is not within specifications, check harness and sensor. See SYSTEM & COMPONENT TESTING.
Colt, Colt 200, Diamante, Galant, Mirage, Pickup, Ram-50, Stealth, Summit & 3000GT – 1) Disconnect TPS connector. Using external ohmmeter, measure resistance between TPS terminals No. 3 and 4. *See Fig. 5.* Insert .256" (.65 mm) feeler gauge between fixed speed adjusting screw and throttle lever.
2) Loosen TPS mounting screws and rotate TPS fully clockwise. Ensure there is continuity between terminals No. 3 and 4. Rotate TPS

counterclockwise until there is no continuity and tighten screws. Install Test Harness (MB991348) between TPS and harness connector.

3) Turn ignition on. Using external voltmeter, measure TPS output voltage between terminals No. 2 and 4. See TPS SPECIFICATIONS table. If voltage is not within specification, check harness and sensor. See SYSTEM & COMPONENT TESTING article.

Precis – Disconnect TPS connector. Install Test Harness (MB991348) between TPS and harness connector. Turn ignition on. Using external voltmeter, measure TPS output voltage between terminals No. 3 and 4. See TPS SPECIFICATIONS table. If voltage is not within specification, check harness and sensor. See SYSTEM & COMPONENT TESTING article.

Eclipse – Disconnect TPS connector. Install Test Harness (MB991348) between TPS and harness connector. Turn ignition on. Using external voltmeter, measure TPS output voltage between terminals No. 2 and 4. See TPS SPECIFICATIONS table. If voltage is not within specifications, check harness and sensor. See SYSTEM & COMPONENT TESTING article.

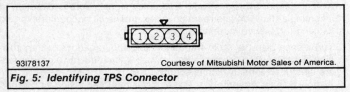

93I78137   Courtesy of Mitsubishi Motor Sales of America.

Fig. 5: Identifying TPS Connector

IDLE POSITION SWITCH

NOTE: Idle position switch is preset by manufacturer. Adjustment is usually not necessary. If other procedures require adjustment of idle position switch or if switch setting has been changed, adjust switch as follows.

2.0L Eclipse DOHC – **1)** Loosen throttle cable. Disconnect electrical connector from idle position switch. *See Fig. 6.* Loosen lock nut at base of switch. Turn switch counterclockwise until throttle valve is fully closed.

2) Connect ohmmeter between switch terminal and switch body (ground). Turn idle position switch clockwise until ohmmeter registers continuity. At this point, throttle valve should begin to open.

3) Turn switch 15/16 of a turn beyond contact point. Tighten lock nut at base of idle position switch, holding switch to prevent it from turning while tightening.

4) Adjust throttle cable. Adjust basic idle speed. See BASIC IDLE SPEED under IDLE SPEED & MIXTURE. Adjust TPS. See TPS ADJUSTMENT.

All Other Models – Idle position switch is incorporated into IAC motor and is automatically adjusted when TPS is adjusted. See TPS ADJUSTMENT.

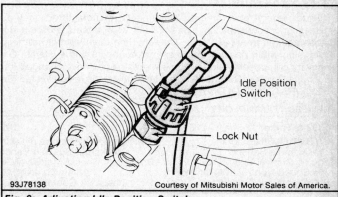

Idle Position Switch

Lock Nut

93J78138   Courtesy of Mitsubishi Motor Sales of America.

Fig. 6: Adjusting Idle Position Switch

1993 ENGINE PERFORMANCE
Theory & Operation

Chrysler Corp.: Colt, Colt Vista, Colt 200, Ram-50, Stealth, Summit, Summit Wagon
Mitsubishi: Diamante, Eclipse, Expo, Galant, Mirage, Montero, Pickup, Precis, 3000GT

INTRODUCTION

This article covers basic description and operation of engine performance-related systems and components. Read this article before diagnosing vehicles or systems with which you are not completely familiar.

1993 TERMINOLOGY

Due to Federal government requirements, manufacturers may use names and acronyms for systems and components different than those used in previous years. The following table will help eliminate confusion when dealing with these components and systems. Only relevant components and systems whose names have changed from previous Chrysler Corp./Mitsubishi terminology have been listed. See REVISED TERMINOLOGY table.

REVISED TERMINOLOGY

1992 & Earlier	1993
CHECK ENGINE Light	Malfunction Indicator Light (MIL)
Crank Angle Sensor	Crankshaft Position Sensor
Engine Control Unit (ECU)	Powertrain Control Module (PCM)
Idle Speed Control (ISC Or AIS)	Idle Air Control (IAC)
Self-Diagnostic Connector	Data Link Connector (DLC)

AIR INDUCTION SYSTEM

NON-TURBOCHARGED ENGINES

All Chrysler Corp./Mitsubishi engines with Multi-Point Injection (MPI) use same basic air induction system. Remote air filter (with airflow sensor) is ducted to a plenum-mounted throttle body.

TURBOCHARGED ENGINES

In addition to basic air induction system used on all other models, turbocharging system components include turbocharger(s), air-to-air intercooler(s), air by-pass valve(s), wastegate actuator(s), wastegate control solenoid valve(s) and intake duct.

Wastegate Control Solenoid Valve – Powertrain Control Module (PCM) energizes solenoid valve, controlling leakage rate of turbocharger pressure to wastegate actuator.

COMPUTERIZED ENGINE CONTROLS

Multi-Point Injection (MPI) is a computerized engine control system, which controls fuel injection, ignition timing, idle speed and emission control systems.

POWERTRAIN CONTROL MODULE (PCM)

PCM receives and processes signals from input devices. Operating conditions such as cold starting, altitude, acceleration and deceleration affect input device signals. Based on signals received, PCM sends signals to various components, which control fuel injection, ignition timing, idle speed and emission control systems. For PCM location, see PCM LOCATION table.

PCM LOCATION

Application	Location
Chrysler Corp.	Behind Right Side Of Instrument Panel, Next To Blower Motor
Mitsubishi Diamante, Expo, Galant, Mirage, Montero & Pickup	Behind Right Side Of Instrument Panel
Eclipse & 3000GT	Behind Radio Console
Precis	Behind Left Side Of Instrument Panel

NOTE: Components are grouped into 2 categories. The first category covers INPUT DEVICES, which control or produce voltage signals monitored by Powertrain Control Module (PCM). The second category covers OUTPUT SIGNALS, which are components controlled by PCM.

INPUT DEVICES

Vehicles are equipped with different combinations of input devices. Not all input devices are used on all models. To determine input device usage on specific models, see appropriate wiring diagram in WIRING DIAGRAMS article. The following are available input devices.

Air Conditioner Switch – When A/C is turned on, signal is sent to PCM. With engine at idle, PCM increases idle speed through Idle Air Control (IAC) motor.

Airflow Sensor – Incorporated in airflow sensor assembly, airflow sensor is a Karmen vortex-type sensor which measures intake airflow rate. Intake air flows through tunnel in airflow sensor assembly. Airflow sensor transmits radio frequency signals across direction of incoming airflow, downstream of vortex. Intake air encounters vortex, causing turbulence in tunnel.

Turbulence disrupts radio frequency, causing variations in transmission. Airflow sensor converts frequency transmitted into a proportionate electrical signal, which is sent to PCM.

Airflow Sensor Assembly – Assembly is mounted inside air cleaner, and incorporates airflow sensor, atmospheric pressure sensor and intake air temperature sensor.

Atmospheric (Barometric) Pressure Sensor – Sensor is incorporated in airflow sensor assembly. Sensor converts atmospheric pressure to electrical signal, which is sent to PCM. PCM adjusts air/fuel ratio and ignition timing according to altitude.

Closed Throttle Position Switch – Closed throttle position switch located in Throttle Position Sensor (TPS), senses whether accelerator pedal is depressed or not. High voltage (open) or low voltage (closed) signal is input to PCM, which then controls IAC motor based on input signal.

Coolant Temperature Sensor – Sensor converts coolant temperature to electrical signal for use by PCM. PCM uses coolant temperature information to control fuel enrichment when engine is cold.

Crankshaft Position & TDC Sensor Assembly – Assembly is located in distributor on SOHC engines. On DOHC engines, which use Direct (or Distributorless) Ignition System (DIS), assembly is a separate unit mounted in place of distributor. Assembly consists of triggering disc (mounted on shaft) and stationary optical sensing unit. Camshaft drives shaft, triggering optical sensing unit. PCM determines crankshaft position and TDC based on signals received from optical sensing unit.

Electrical Load Switch – Electrical load switch inputs on/off state of taillight relay, defogger relay and stoplight relay to PCM. PCM signals IAC to increase or decrease RPM depending on on/off state of relays.

Engine Speed (Tach Signal) – PCM uses ignition coil tach signal to determine engine speed.

Heated Oxygen Sensor (HO2S) – HO2S detects oxygen content in exhaust gas and sends this information to PCM. PCM uses input signals from sensor to vary duration of fuel injection. Oxygen sensor heater stabilizes sensor temperature regardless of exhaust gas temperature to allow for more accurate exhaust oxygen content readings.

Idle Position Switch – On all DOHC engines, idle position switch is a separate switch mounted on throttle body. On all other models, idle position switch is incorporated in IAC motor or throttle position sensor, depending on vehicle application. When throttle valve is closed, switch is activated. When throttle valve is at any other position, switch is deactivated. This input from idle position switch is used by PCM for controlling fuel delivery time during deceleration.

Ignition Timing Adjustment Terminal – Used for adjusting base ignition timing. When terminal is grounded, PCM timing control function is by-passed, allowing base timing to be adjusted.

Inhibitor Switch (Automatic Transmission) – Inhibitor switch senses position of transmission select lever, indicating engine load due to automatic transmission engagement. Based on this signal, PCM commands IAC motor to increase throttle angle, maintaining optimum idle speed.

Intake Air Temperature Sensor – Sensor is incorporated in airflow sensor assembly. This resistor-based sensor measures temperature of incoming air and supplies air density information to PCM.

Knock Sensor (Turbo) – Sensor is located in cylinder block and senses engine vibration during detonation (knock). Sensor converts vibration into electrical signal. PCM retards ignition timing based on this signal.

Motor Position Sensor (MPS) – Sensor is incorporated in IAC motor (or separate unit on some models). MPS senses IAC motor plunger position and sends electrical signal to PCM.

Oxygen (O_2) Sensor – O_2 sensor is located in exhaust system and generates an output voltage. Output voltage varies with oxygen content of exhaust gas stream. PCM adjusts air/fuel mixture based on signals from O_2 sensor.

Power Steering Oil Pressure Switch – Switch detects increase in power steering oil pressure. When power steering oil pressure increases, switch contacts close, signaling PCM. PCM commands IAC motor, raising idle speed to compensate for drop in engine RPM due to power steering load.

TDC Sensor – See CRANKSHAFT POSITION & TDC SENSOR ASSEMBLY under INPUT DEVICES.

Throttle Position Sensor (TPS) – TPS is a variable resistor mounted on throttle body. PCM uses voltage signal from TPS to determine throttle plate angle.

Vehicle Speed Sensor – Sensor is located in speedometer in instrument cluster, and uses a reed switch to sense speedometer gear revolutions. PCM uses gear revolutions to determine vehicle speed.

OUTPUT SIGNALS

NOTE: Vehicles are equipped with various combinations of computer-controlled components. Not all components listed below are used on every vehicle. For theory and operation on each output component, refer to system indicated after component.

Accelerator Pedal Position Sensor (APPS) – See MISCELLANEOUS CONTROLS.

Data Link Connector – See SELF-DIAGNOSTIC SYSTEM.

EGR Control Solenoid Valve – See EXHAUST GAS RECIRCULATION (EGR) CONTROL under EMISSION SYSTEMS.

Fuel Injectors – See FUEL CONTROL under FUEL SYSTEM.

Fuel Pressure Control Solenoid Valve (Turbo) – See FUEL DELIVERY under FUEL SYSTEM.

Fuel Pressure Regulator – See FUEL DELIVERY under FUEL SYSTEM.

Idle Speed Control Servo – See IDLE SPEED under FUEL SYSTEM.

Malfunction Indicator Light – See SELF-DIAGNOSTIC SYSTEM.

Power Transistor(s) & Ignition Coils – See IGNITION SYSTEMS.

Purge Control Solenoid Valve – See EVAPORATIVE CONTROL under EMISSION SYSTEMS.

Variable Induction Control (VIC) Motor Sensor – See MISCELLANEOUS CONTROLS.

Wastegate Control Solenoid Valve – See TURBOCHARGED ENGINES under AIR INDUCTION SYSTEM.

FUEL SYSTEM

FUEL DELIVERY

Electric fuel pump, located in gas tank, feeds fuel through in-tank fuel filter, external fuel filter (located in engine compartment) and fuel injector rail.

Fuel Pump – Fuel pump consists of a motor-driven impeller. Pump has an internal check valve to maintain system pressure, and a relief valve to protect fuel pressure circuit. Pump receives voltage supply from Multi-Point Injection (MPI) control relay.

Fuel Pressure Control Solenoid Valve (Turbo) – Valve prevents rough idle due to fuel percolation. On engine restart, if engine coolant or intake air temperature reaches a preset value, ECM applies voltage to fuel pressure control solenoid valve for 2 minutes after engine restart. Valve will open, allowing atmospheric pressure to be applied to fuel pressure regulator diaphragm. This allows maximum available fuel pressure at injectors, enriching fuel mixture and maintaining stable idle at high engine temperatures.

Fuel Pressure Regulator – Located on fuel injector rail, this diaphragm-operated relief valve adjusts fuel pressure according to engine manifold vacuum.

As engine manifold vacuum increases (closed throttle), fuel pressure regulator diaphragm opens relief valve, allowing pressure to bleed off through fuel return line, reducing fuel pressure.

As engine manifold vacuum decreases (open throttle), fuel pressure regulator diaphragm closes valve, preventing pressure from bleeding off through fuel return line, increasing fuel pressure.

FUEL CONTROL

Fuel Injectors – Fuel is supplied to engine through electronically pulsed (timed) injector valves located on fuel rail(s). PCM controls amount of fuel metered through injectors based on information received from sensors.

IDLE SPEED

Air Conditioner Relay – When A/C is turned on with engine at idle, PCM signals IAC motor to increase idle speed. To prevent A/C compressor from switching on before idle speed has increased, PCM momentarily opens A/C relay circuit.

Idle Air Control (IAC) Motor – Motor controls pintle-type air valve (DOHC engines) or throttle plate angle (SOHC engines) to regulate volume of intake air at idle.

During start mode, PCM controls idle intake air volume according to coolant temperature input. After starting, with idle position switch activated (throttle closed), fast idle speed is controlled by IAC motor and fast idle air control valve (if equipped).

When idle switch is deactivated (throttle open), IAC motor moves to a preset position in accordance with coolant temperature input.

PCM signals IAC motor to increase engine RPM in the following situations: A/T (if applicable) is shifted from Neutral to Drive, A/C is turned on, or power steering pressure reaches a preset value.

Fast Idle Air Control Valve – Some models use a coolant temperature-sensitive fast idle air control valve, located on throttle body, to admit additional intake air volume during engine warm-up. Control valve closes as temperature increases, restricting by-pass airflow rate. At engine warm-up, valve closes completely.

IGNITION SYSTEMS

DIRECT IGNITION SYSTEM (DOHC ENGINES)

Depending on number of cylinders, ignition system is a 2 or 3-coil distributorless ignition system. Crankshaft position and TDC sensor assembly, mounted in place of distributor, are optically controlled.

Power Transistors & Ignition Coils – Based on crankshaft position and TDC sensor inputs, PCM controls timing and directly activates each power transistor to fire coils. On 4-cylinder engines, power transistor "A" controls primary current of ignition coil "A" to fire spark plugs on cylinders No. 1 and No. 4 at the same time. Power transistor "B" controls primary current of ignition coil "B" to fire spark plugs on cylinders No. 2 and No. 3 at the same time. On V6 engines, companion cylinders No. 1 and 4, 2 and 5, and 3 and 6 are fired together.

On all models, although each coil fires 2 plugs at the same time, ignition takes place in only one cylinder, since the other cylinder is on its exhaust stroke when plug fires.

ELECTRONIC IGNITION SYSTEM (SOHC ENGINES)

Breakerless electronic ignition system uses a disc and optical sensing unit to trigger power transistor.

Power Transistor & Ignition Coil – Power transistor is mounted inside distributor with disc and optical sensing unit. When ignition is on, ignition coil primary circuit is energized. As distributor shaft rotates, disc rotates, triggering optical sensing unit. PCM receives signals from optical sensing unit. Signals are converted and sent to power transistor, interrupting primary current flow and inducing secondary voltage.

IGNITION TIMING CONTROL SYSTEM

Ignition timing is controlled by PCM. PCM adjusts timing based on various conditions such as engine temperature, altitude and detonation (turbo).

EMISSION SYSTEMS

EXHAUST GAS RECIRCULATION (EGR) CONTROL

Federal (Non-Turbo) – To lower oxides of nitrogen (NOx) exhaust emissions, a non-computer controlled exhaust gas recirculation system is used. EGR operation is controlled by throttle body ported vacuum. Vacuum is routed through thermovalve to prevent EGR operation at low engine temperatures.
Spring pressure holds EGR valve closed during low vacuum conditions (engine idling or wide open throttle). When vacuum pressure increases and overcomes EGR spring pressure, EGR valve is lifted to allow exhaust gases to flow into intake manifold for combustion.
California & Turbo – PCM controls EGR operation by activating EGR control solenoid valve according to engine load. When engine is cold, PCM signals EGR control solenoid valve to deactivate EGR.
California models are equipped with an EGR temperature sensor. When EGR malfunction occurs, EGR temperature decreases and PCM illuminates MIL (CHECK ENGINE light).
EGR Control Solenoid Valve – Valve denies or allows vacuum supply to EGR valve based on PCM commands.
Thermovalve – Thermovalve denies or allows vacuum supply to EGR valve based on coolant temperature.

EVAPORATIVE CONTROL

Fuel evaporation system prevents fuel vapor from entering atmosphere. System consists of the following: special fuel tank with vapor separator tanks (if equipped), vacuum relief filler cap, overfill limiter (2-way valve), fuel check valve, thermovalve (if equipped), charcoal canister, purge control valve, purge control solenoid valve, and connecting lines and hoses.
Purge Control Solenoid Valve – When engine is off, fuel vapors are vented into charcoal canister. When engine is warmed to normal operating temperature and running at speeds greater than idle, PCM energizes purge control solenoid valve, allowing vacuum to purge valve.
Canister vapors are then drawn through purge valve into intake manifold for burning. Purge control solenoid valve remains closed during idle and engine warm-up to reduce HC (hydrocarbons) and CO (carbon monoxide) emissions.

HIGH ALTITUDE CONTROL (HAC)

HAC system compensates for variations in altitude. When atmospheric (barometric) pressure sensor determines vehicle is at altitude greater than preset value, PCM compensates by adjusting air/fuel mixture and ignition timing. If HAC system is inoperative, there will be an increase in emissions.

POSITIVE CRANKCASE VENTILATION (PCV) VALVE

PCV valve operates in closed crankcase ventilation system. Closed crankcase ventilation system consists of PCV valve, oil separator, breather and ventilation hoses.

PCV valve is a one-way check valve located in valve cover. When engine is running, manifold vacuum pulls PCV valve open, allowing crankcase fumes to enter intake manifold. If engine backfires through intake manifold, PCV valve closes to prevent crankcase combustion.

MISCELLANEOUS CONTROLS

NOTE: Although not considered true engine performance-related systems, some controlled devices may affect driveability if they malfunction.

Accelerator Pedal Position Sensor (APPS) – PCM supplies one end of APPS resistor with a 5-volt signal. The other end of resistor is gounded at PCM. Accelerator pedal position sensor converts amount accelerator pedal is depressed into variable voltage input to traction control module for traction control.
Variable Induction Control (VIC) Motor Sensor – PCM controls VIC valve opening or closing. VIC valve controls length of intake air path to intake manifold. VIC valve closes at higher RPM to shorten intake air path and opens at lower RPM to lengthen intake air path. The result is more engine torque in a wider RPM range.

SELF-DIAGNOSTIC SYSTEM

NOTE: PCM diagnostic memory is retained by direct power supply from battery. Memory is not erased by turning off ignition, but it will be erased if battery or PCM is disconnected.

Self-diagnostic system monitors input and output signals through the data link connector. On all models, codes can be read using analog voltmeter. Scan tester can be used to read codes on some models. For additional information, see SELF-DIAGNOSTICS article.
Malfunction Indicator Light (MIL) – MIL (CHECK ENGINE light) comes on when ignition is turned on. MIL remains on for several seconds after engine has started. If an abnormal input signal occurs, MIL comes on and code is stored in memory. If an abnormal input signal returns to normal, PCM turns MIL off, but code remains stored in memory until it is cleared. If ignition is turned on again, MIL will not come on until PCM detects malfunction during system operation.

**Chrysler Corp.: Colt, Colt Vista, Colt 200, Ram-50, Stealth, Summit, Summit Wagon
Mitsubishi: Diamante, Eclipse, Expo, Galant Mirage, Montero, Pickup, Precis, 3000GT**

INTRODUCTION

The following diagnostic steps will help prevent overlooking a simple problem. This is also where to begin diagnosis for a no-start condition. The first step in diagnosing any driveability problem is verifying the customer's complaint with a test drive under the conditions the problem reportedly occurred.

Before entering self-diagnostics, perform a careful and complete visual inspection. Most engine control problems result from mechanical breakdowns, poor electrical connections or damaged/misrouted vacuum hoses. Before condemning the computerized system, perform each test listed in this article.

NOTE: *Perform all voltage tests with a Digital Volt-Ohmmeter (DVOM) with a minimum 10-megohm input impedance, unless stated otherwise in test procedure.*

PRELIMINARY INSPECTION & ADJUSTMENTS

VISUAL INSPECTION

Visually inspect all electrical wiring, looking for chafed, stretched, cut or pinched wiring. Ensure electrical connectors fit tightly and are not corroded. Ensure vacuum hoses are properly routed and are not pinched or cut. See VACUUM DIAGRAMS article to verify routing and connections (if necessary). Inspect air induction system for possible vacuum leaks.

MECHANICAL INSPECTION

Compression – Check engine mechanical condition with a compression gauge, vacuum gauge, or an engine analyzer. See engine analyzer manual for specific instructions.

WARNING: *DO NOT use ignition switch during compression tests on fuel injected vehicles. Use a remote starter to crank engine. Fuel injectors on many models are triggered by ignition switch during cranking mode, which can create a fire hazard or contaminate the engine's oiling system.*

COMPRESSION SPECIFICATIONS

Application [1]	psi (kg/cm²)
Compression Pressure	
1.5L (VIN A)	
Colt, Colt 200 & Summit	194 psi (13.6 kg/cm²)
Mirage	192 psi (13.4 kg/cm²)
1.5L (VIN J)	192 psi (13.4 kg/cm²)
1.8L (VIN C)	199 psi (13.9 kg/cm²)
1.8L (VIN B)	185 psi (13.0 kg/cm²)
2.0L (VIN D)	178 psi (12.5 kg/cm²)
2.0L (VIN E)	192 psi (13.4 kg/cm²)
2.0L (VIN F)	164 psi (11.5 kg/cm²)
2.4L (VIN G)	171 psi (12.0 kg/cm²)
3.0L (VIN J)	185 psi (13.0 kg/cm²)
3.0L (VIN K)	156 psi (10.9 kg/cm²)
3.0L (VIN H)	171 psi (12.0 kg/cm²)
Maximum Variation Between Cylinders	14 psi (1.0 kg/cm²)

[1] – See CHRYSLER CORP./MITSUBISHI INTRODUCTION article for VIN information.

Exhaust System Backpressure – Exhaust system can be checked with a vacuum or pressure gauge. Remove O_2 sensor or air injection check valve (if equipped). Connect a 0-5 psi pressure gauge and run engine at 2500 RPM. If exhaust system backpressure is greater than 1 3/4 - 2 psi, exhaust system or catalytic converter is plugged.

If using a vacuum gauge, connect vacuum gauge hose to intake manifold vacuum port and start engine. Observe vacuum gauge. Open throttle part way and hold steady. If vacuum gauge reading slowly drops after stabilizing, exhaust system should be checked for a restriction.

FUEL SYSTEM

WARNING: *ALWAYS relieve fuel pressure before disconnecting any fuel injection-related component. DO NOT allow fuel to contact engine or electrical components.*

FUEL PRESSURE

Relieving Fuel Pressure – 1) On all models except Colt, Colt 200, Colt Vista, Eclipse (AWD), Expo, Mirage, Montero, Stealth, Summit, Summit Wagon and 3000GT, disconnect fuel pump harness connector at fuel tank from underneath vehicle. On Colt, Colt 200, Colt Vista, Eclipse (AWD), Expo, Mirage, Montero, Stealth, Summit, Summit Wagon and 3000GT, remove rear seat cushion and remove access plate if required to disconnect fuel pump harness connector.
2) On all models, start engine. Let engine run until it stops. Turn ignition off. Disconnect negative battery terminal. Connect fuel pump harness connector. Reinstall rear seat (if necessary.)

WARNING: *Before disconnecting high pressure fuel hose at fuel delivery pipe, cover fuel hose connection with a rag. Some residual fuel pressure may still be in system.*

Pressure Testing – 1) Disconnect high pressure fuel hose at fuel delivery pipe. Remove throttle body bracket (if necessary). Connect fuel pressure gauge with adapter between fuel delivery pipe and high pressure hose. *See Fig. 1.*
2) Connect negative battery terminal. Operate fuel pump by connecting battery voltage to fuel pump test terminal. See FUEL PUMP TEST TERMINAL LOCATION table. Ensure no fuel leaks are present. Disconnect battery voltage to fuel pump test terminal.

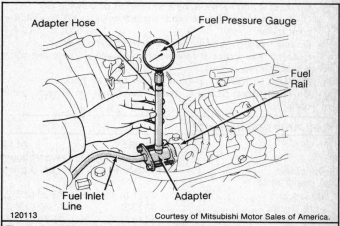

120113   Courtesy of Mitsubishi Motor Sales of America.

Fig. 1: Installing Fuel Pressure Tester (Typical)

3) Start engine and let idle. Measure fuel pressure with vacuum hose connected to fuel pressure regulator. Record fuel pressure reading. See FUEL PUMP PERFORMANCE table. Disconnect and plug vacuum hose from fuel pressure regulator. Record fuel pressure reading.
4) Check for fuel pressure in fuel return hose by gently pinching hose while increasing engine speed. If fuel volume is low, fuel pressure in return hose will not be felt. Increase engine speed to 2500-3000 RPM, 2-3 times. Return engine to idle. Fuel pressure should not drop when engine is returned to idle.
5) Turn ignition off. On all models except Precis, ensure fuel pressure reading does not decrease within 2 minutes. On Precis, fuel pressure

reading should not decrease within 5 minutes. On all models, if a decrease is noted, monitor speed of decrease.

6) If fuel pressure is lower than specification, fuel pressure drops at idle after increasing engine speed to 2500-3000 RPM, or no fuel pressure in fuel return hose can be felt, check for clogged fuel filter, or faulty fuel pressure regulator or fuel pump.

7) If fuel pressure is higher than specification, check for a faulty fuel pressure regulator or plugged fuel return line. If fuel pressure does not change when vacuum hose to regulator is connected or disconnected, check for a leaking or clogged vacuum hose to fuel pressure regulator or faulty fuel pressure regulator.

8) If fuel pressure decreases suddenly after engine is stopped, check valve in fuel pump is not seated. Replace fuel pump. If fuel pressure drops slowly, fuel injector is leaking or fuel pressure regulator valve seat is leaking. Check for faulty fuel injector or fuel pressure regulator. Repair as necessary.

9) When fuel pressure test is complete, repeat fuel pressure release procedure before disconnecting fuel pressure gauge. Install new "O" ring at end of high pressure hose. Check for fuel leaks.

FUEL PUMP TEST TERMINAL LOCATION

Application	Wire Color	Location
Colt, Colt 200		
Mirage & Summit	Black/Blue	1
Diamante	Black/Blue	1
Eclipse	Black/White	2
Colt Vista, Expo &		
Summit Wagon	Black/Blue	3
Galant	Yellow/Green	4
Montero	White	5
Ram-50 & Pickup	Blue	6
Precis	Yellow	7
Stealth & 3000GT	Black/Blue	8

1 – On main wiring harness, near center of firewall.
2 – On main wiring harness, near wiper motor on firewall, behind battery.
3 – On main wiring harness, near left center of firewall.
4 – On main wiring harness, near master cylinder on firewall, near strut tower.
5 – On main wiring harness, near wiper motor on firewall.
6 – Near left rear corner of engine compartment, below cruise control actuator (if equipped).
7 – Between air filter housing and upper radiator hose.
8 – On main wiring harness, near wiper motor on firewall, behind battery.

FUEL PUMP PERFORMANCE

Application	At Idle w/Vacuum [1] psi (kg/cm²)	At Idle w/o Vacuum [2] psi (kg/cm²)
Eclipse (Turbo)		
Man. Trans.	27 (1.8)	36-38 (2.5-2.6)
Auto. Trans.	33 (2.3)	41-46 (2.8-3.2)
Stealth (Turbo) & 3000GT	34 (2.4)	43-45 (3.0-3.1)
All Others	38 (2.6)	47-50 (3.3-3.5)

1 – With vacuum at pressure regulator.
2 – Without vacuum at pressure regulator.

MPI Control Relay – Multipurpose relay switches power to vehicle sensors and actuators including airflow sensor, crank angle sensor, idle speed control, injectors and fuel pump. When ignition switch is turned to ON position, ECM energizes coils controlling injectors, airflow sensor and idle speed control. When ignition switch is turned to START position, ECM energizes coils (through inhibitor switch on A/T models) to supply power to fuel pump. Relay failure will cause a no-start condition. For testing procedure, see SYSTEM & COMPONENT TESTING article.

IGNITION CHECKS

SPARK

Check for spark at coil wire (if applicable) and at each spark plug wire using a high output spark tester. Check spark plug wire resistance on suspect wires. For wire resistance specification, see SERVICE & ADJUSTMENT SPECIFICATIONS article.

CRANKSHAFT POSITION SENSOR

For crank position sensor testing procedure, see SYSTEM & COMPONENT TESTING article.

DISTRIBUTORLESS IGNITION SYSTEM (DIS) 4-CYLINDER

Ignition Coil Resistance – 1) Disconnect ignition coil connector. Using a Digital Volt-Ohmmeter (DVOM), measure primary coil resistance between ignition coil connector terminals No. 2 and 3 (coils for cylinders No. 1 and 4) and terminals No. 1 and 3 (coils for cylinders No. 2 and 3). See Fig. 2.

2) Remove ignition wires from coil. Measure secondary coil resistance between coil towers for cylinders No. 1 and 4 and between coil towers for cylinders No. 2 and 3. Primary and secondary coil resistance should be within specification. See IGNITION COIL RESISTANCE (4-CYLINDER) table. Connect coil harness connector. Connect ignition wires to coil.

IGNITION COIL RESISTANCE (4-CYLINDER) – Ohms @ 68°F (20°C)

Application	Primary	Secondary
Eclipse	.70-.86	11,300-15,300

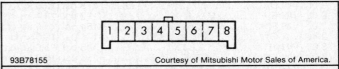

93A78154   Courtesy of Mitsubishi Motor Sales of America.

Fig. 2: Identifying Ignition Coil Connector (4-Cylinder)

Power Transistor – 1) To test the section of the power transistor that controls cylinders No. 1 and 4 of the ignition coil, disconnect power transistor connector. Using a 1.5-volt dry cell battery, connect negative end of battery to terminal No. 3 of power transistor and positive end to terminal No. 7. See Fig. 3.

2) Using an analog ohmmeter, check for continuity between terminals No. 3 and 8 of power transistor. Continuity should exist. With positive end of 1.5-volt battery disconnected, there should be no continuity. Replace power transistor if it fails test.

3) To test the section of the power transistor that controls cylinders No. 2 and 4 , connect negative end of 1.5-volt dry cell battery to terminal No. 3 of power transistor and positive end to terminal No. 2.

4) Using an analog ohmmeter, check for continuity between terminals No. 1 and 3 of power transistor. Continuity should exist. With positive end of 1.5-volt battery disconnected, there should be no continuity. Replace power transistor if it fails test.

93B78155   Courtesy of Mitsubishi Motor Sales of America.

Fig. 3: Identifying Power Transistor Connector (4-Cylinder)

DISTRIBUTORLESS IGNITION SYSTEM (DIS) V6

Ignition Coil Resistance – 1) Using a DVOM, measure primary coil resistance between terminal No. 3 (power terminal) and each individual coil terminal. See Fig. 4. To check secondary coil resistance, measure resistance between towers of each individual coil.

2) Replace coil if primary and secondary coil resistances are not within specification. See IGNITION COIL RESISTANCE (V6) table.

IGNITION COIL RESISTANCE (V6) – Ohms @ 68°F (20°C)

Application	Primary	Secondary
3.0L	.67-.81	11,300-15,300

93C78156   Courtesy of Mitsubishi Motor Sales of America.

Fig. 4: Identifying Ignition Coil Connector (V6)

Power Transistor – 1) To test section of power transistor that controls cylinders No. 1 and 4 of ignition coil, disconnect power transistor connector. Using a 1.5-volt dry cell battery, connect negative end of 1.5-volt battery to terminal No. 4 of power transistor and positive end to terminal No. 3. See Fig. 5.

2) Using an analog ohmmeter, check for continuity between terminals No. 4 and 13 of power transistor. Continuity should exist. With positive end of 1.5-volt battery disconnected, there should be no continuity. Replace power transistor if it fails test.

3) To test section of power transistor that controls cylinders No. 2 and 5 of ignition coil, connect negative end of 1.5-volt battery to terminal No. 4 of power transistor and positive end to terminal No. 2. See Fig. 5.

4) Using an analog ohmmeter, check for continuity between terminals No. 4 and 12 of power transistor. Continuity should exist. With positive end of 1.5-volt battery disconnected, there should be no continuity. Replace power transistor if it fails test.

5) To test section of power transistor that controls cylinders No. 3 and 6 of ignition coil, connect negative end of 1.5-volt battery to terminal No. 4 of power transistor and positive end to terminal No. 1. See Fig. 5.

6) Using an analog ohmmeter, check for continuity between terminals No. 4 and 11 of power transistor. Continuity should exist. With positive end of 1.5-volt battery disconnected, there should be no continuity. Replace power transistor if it fails test.

93D78157   Courtesy of Mitsubishi Motor Sales of America.

Fig. 5: Identifying Power Transistor Connector (V6)

HALL EFFECT & OPTICAL IGNITION

Ignition Coil Resistance – Using a DVOM, measure primary coil resistance between positive and negative terminals of coil. See Fig. 6. Measure secondary coil resistance between coil positive terminal and ignition coil tower. Primary and secondary coil resistance should be within specification. See IGNITION COIL RESISTANCE table.

IGNITION COIL RESISTANCE – Ohms @ 68°F (20°C)

Application	Primary	Secondary
1.5L (VIN A)	.9-1.2	20,000-29,000
1.5L (VIN J)	.72-.88	10,300-13,900
1.8L (VIN C)	.9-1.2	20,000-29,000
1.8L (VIN B)	.9-1.2	19,000-27,000
2.0L (VIN D)	.72-.88	10,890-13,310
2.4L (VIN G)		
Pickup & Ram-50	.72-.88	10,300-13,900
All Others	.72-.88	10,900-13,300
3.0L (VIN H)		
Diamante & Stealth	.72-.88	10,300-13,900

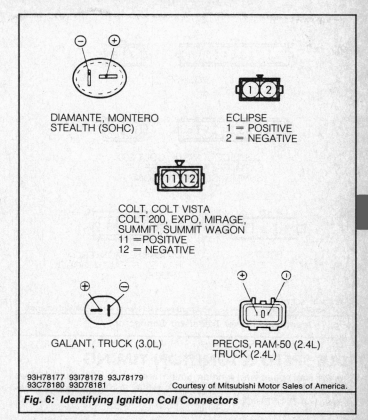

DIAMANTE, MONTERO
STEALTH (SOHC)

ECLIPSE
1 = POSITIVE
2 = NEGATIVE

COLT, COLT VISTA
COLT 200, EXPO, MIRAGE,
SUMMIT, SUMMIT WAGON
11 = POSITIVE
12 = NEGATIVE

GALANT, TRUCK (3.0L)

PRECIS, RAM-50 (2.4L)
TRUCK (2.4L)

93H78177 93I78178 93J78179
93C78180 93D78181   Courtesy of Mitsubishi Motor Sales of America.

Fig. 6: Identifying Ignition Coil Connectors

Power Transistor (Colt, Colt Vista 1.8L/2.4L, Colt 200, Expo 1.8L/2.4L, Galant, Mirage & Summit Wagon 1.8L/2.4L – 1) Disconnect power transistor connector. Using a 1.5-volt dry cell battery, connect negative end of 1.5-volt battery to terminal No. 5 of power transistor and positive end to terminal No. 6. See Fig. 7.

2) Using an analog ohmmeter, check for continuity between terminals No. 5 and 12 of power transistor. Continuity should exist. With positive end of 1.5-volt battery disconnected, there should be no continuity. Replace power transistor if it fails test.

Power Transistor (Eclipse) – 1) Disconnect power transistor connector. Using a 1.5-volt dry cell battery, connect negative end of 1.5-volt battery to terminal No. 5 of power transistor and positive end to terminal No. 6. See Fig. 7.

2) Using an analog ohmmeter, check for continuity between terminals No. 5 and 8 of power transistor. Continuity should exist. With positive end of 1.5-volt battery disconnected, there should be no continuity. Replace power transistor if it fails test.

Power Transistor (Precis) – 1) Disconnect power transistor connector. Using a 3.0-volt power source, connect negative end of power source to terminal No. 2 of power transistor and positive end to terminal No. 1. See Fig. 7.

2) Using an analog ohmmeter, check for continuity between terminals No. 1 and 2 of power transistor. Continuity should exist. With positive end of 3.0-volt power source disconnected, there should be no continuity. Replace power transistor if it fails test.

Power Transistor (All Others) – 1) Disconnect power transistor connector. Using a 1.5-volt dry cell battery, connect negative end of 1.5-volt battery to terminal No. 2 of power transistor and positive end to terminal No. 1. See Fig. 7.

2) Using an analog ohmmeter, check for continuity between terminals No. 2 and 3 of power transistor. Continuity should exist. With positive end of 1.5-volt battery disconnected, there should be no continuity. Replace power transistor if it fails test.

1993 ENGINE PERFORMANCE
Basic Diagnostic Procedures (Cont.)

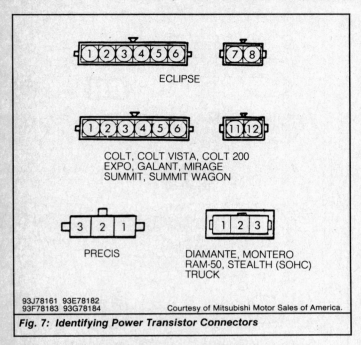

93J78161 93E78182
93F78183 93G78184

Courtesy of Mitsubishi Motor Sales of America.

Fig. 7: Identifying Power Transistor Connectors

IDLE SPEED & IGNITION TIMING

Ensure idle speed and ignition timing are set to specification. See IGNITION TIMING SPECIFICATIONS table. For adjustment procedures, see ON-VEHICLE ADJUSTMENTS article.

IGNITION TIMING (Degrees BTDC @ RPM)

Application	[1] Basic	[2] [3] Actual
1.5L		
Colt, Colt 200 & Summit	5 @ 650-850	10 @ 650-850
Mirage	3-7 @ 650-850	10 @ 650-850
Precis	3-7 @ 600-800	10 @ 600-800
1.8L		
Colt, Colt Vista, Colt 200 Expo, Mirage, Summit & Summit Wagon	3-7 @ 650-850	5 @ 650-850
Eclipse	5 @ 600-800	10 @ 600-800
2.0L		
Eclipse	5 @ 650-850	8 @ 650-850
Galant	3-7 @ 650-850	10 @ 650-850
2.4L		
Colt Vista & Summit Wagon	3-7 @ 650-850	8 @ 650-850
Expo	3-7 @ 650-850	5 @ 650-850
Pickup & Ram-50	3-7 @ 600-800	8 @ 600-800
3.0L		
Diamante & Montero	3-7 @ 600-800	15 @ 600-800
Pickup & Ram-50	3-7 @ 650-850	15 @ 650-850
Stealth & 3000GT	2-8 @ 600-800	15 @ 600-800

[1] – With ignition timing adjustment connector grounded or vacuum hose (farthest from distributor) disconnected.

[2] – With ignition timing adjustment connector ungrounded or vacuum hose (farthest from distributor) connected. Ignition timing may fluctuate.

[3] – If vehicle altitude is more than 2300 ft. above sea level, actual timing may be advanced.

SUMMARY

If no faults were found while performing BASIC DIAGNOSTIC PROCEDURES, proceed to SELF-DIAGNOSTICS article. If no hard codes are found in self-diagnostics, proceed to TROUBLE SHOOTING – NO CODES article for diagnosis by symptom (i.e., ROUGH IDLE, NO START, etc.) or intermittent diagnostic procedures.

Chrysler Corp.: Colt, Colt Vista, Colt 200, Ram-50, Stealth, Summit, Summit Wagon
Mitsubishi: Diamante, Eclipse, Expo, Galant, Mirage, Montero, Pickup, Precis, 3000GT

NOTE: For Precis self-diagnostics information, see appropriate Hyundai SELF-DIAGNOSTICS article.

INTRODUCTION

If no faults were found while performing BASIC DIAGNOSTIC PROCEDURES, proceed with self-diagnostics. If no fault codes or only pass codes are present after entering self-diagnostics, proceed to TROUBLE SHOOTING – NO CODES article for diagnosis by symptom (i.e., ROUGH IDLE, NO START, etc.).

SELF-DIAGNOSTIC SYSTEM

SYSTEM DIAGNOSIS

System diagnosis can be accomplished using a voltmeter or appropriate scan tester. See RETRIEVING CODES. Engine Control Module (ECM) monitors several different engine control system circuits. If an abnormal input signal occurs, a fault code is stored in ECM memory and assigned a fault code number. Each circuit has its own fault number and message. A specific fault code indicates a particular system failure, but it does not indicate that cause of failure is necessarily within system.

A fault code does not condemn any specific component; it simply points out a probable malfunctioning area. If a fault code is set, ECM will turn on Malfunction Indicator Light (MIL). Fault codes can be confirmed by using a voltmeter. System malfunctions encountered are identified as either hard failures or intermittent failures as determined by ECM.

Hard Failures – Hard failures cause Malfunction Indicator Light (MIL) to glow and remain on until malfunction is repaired. If MIL comes on and remains on (MIL may flash) during vehicle operation, cause of malfunction may be determined by using fault codes. See FAULT CODES. If a sensor fails, ECM will use a substitute value in its calculations to continue engine operation. In this condition, vehicle is functional, but loss of good driveability may result.

Intermittent Failures – Intermittent failures may cause Malfunction Indicator Light (MIL) to flicker or glow and go out after intermittent fault goes away. However, corresponding trouble code will be retained in ECM memory. If related fault does not reoccur within a certain time frame, related trouble code will be erased from ECM memory. Intermittent failures may be caused by a sensor, connector or wiring problems. See INTERMITTENTS in TROUBLE SHOOTING – NO CODES article.

SERVICE PRECAUTIONS

Before proceeding with diagnosis, following precautions must be observed:

- Ensure vehicle has a fully charged battery and functional charging system.
- Visually inspect connectors and circuit wiring being worked on.
- DO NOT disconnect battery or ECM. This will erase any fault codes stored in ECM.
- DO NOT cause short circuits when performing electrical tests. This will set additional fault codes, making diagnosis of original problem more difficult.
- DO NOT use a test light in place of a voltmeter.
- When checking for spark, ensure coil wire is NOT more than 1/4" from chassis ground. If coil wire is more than 1/4" from chassis ground, damage to vehicle electronics and/or ECM may result.
- DO NOT prolong testing of fuel injectors. Engine may hydrostatically (liquid) lock.
- When a vehicle has multiple fault codes, always repair lowest number fault code first.

RETRIEVING CODES

Using Scan Tester – 1) Refer to manufacturer's operation manual for instructions in use of scan tester. Before entering on-board diagnostics, see SERVICE PRECAUTIONS. Turn ignition switch to OFF position. Locate Data Link Connector (DLC), next to fuse block. Connect power source terminal of scan tester to cigarette lighter socket.

2) Connect scan tester to DLC. *See Fig. 1.* Turn ignition switch to ON position. Read and record scan tester self-diagnosis output. Perform necessary repair(s). See FAULT CODES.

Using Voltmeter – 1) Before entering on-board diagnostics, see SERVICE PRECAUTIONS. Turn ignition switch to OFF position. Locate Data Link Connector (DLC), next to fuse block. Connect voltmeter positive lead to DLC terminal No. 1 and negative lead to terminal No. 12 (ground). *See Fig. 1.*

2) Turn ignition switch to ON position. Disclosure of ECM memory will begin. If 2 or more systems are non-functional, they are indicated by order of increasing code number. Indication is made by 12-volt pulses of voltmeter pointer. A constant repetition of short 12-volt pulses indicates system is normal. If system is abnormal, voltmeter will pulse between zero and 12 volts.

3) Signals will appear on voltmeter as long and short 12-volt pulses. Long pulses represent tens; short pulses represent ones. For example, 4 long pulses and 3 short pulses indicate Code 43. After recording fault code(s), perform necessary repair(s) to indicated circuit(s). See FAULT CODES.

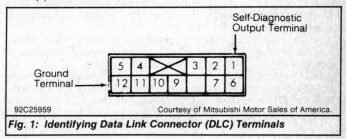

92C25959   Courtesy of Mitsubishi Motor Sales of America.

Fig. 1: Identifying Data Link Connector (DLC) Terminals

FAULT CODES

NOTE: Codes listed in FAULT CODES are not used on all vehicles.

MIL Stays On – ECM fault. Possible cause: faulty ECM.
Code 11 – Oxygen (O_2) sensor fault. Possible causes: faulty O_2 sensor, connector or harness, low or high fuel pressure, defective injector(s), intake air leaks.
Code 12 – Airflow sensor fault. Possible causes: faulty airflow sensor, connector or harness.
Code 13 – Intake air temperature sensor fault. Possible causes: faulty intake air temperature sensor, connector or harness.
Code 14 – Throttle Position Sensor (TPS) fault. Possible causes: faulty TPS, connector or harness, closed throttle position switch.
Code 15 – Idle Speed Control (ISC) motor position sensor fault. Possible causes: faulty ISC motor position sensor, faulty throttle position sensor, connector or harness.
Code 21 – Coolant temperature sensor fault. Possible causes: faulty coolant temperature sensor, connector or harness.
Code 22 – Crankshaft Position (CKP) sensor fault. Possible causes: faulty distributor assembly (if equipped), faulty CKP sensor, connector or harness.
Code 23 – Camshaft Position (CMP) sensor fault. Possible causes: faulty distributor assembly (if equipped), faulty CMP sensor, connector or harness.
Code 24 – Vehicle Speed Sensor (VSS) fault. Possible causes: faulty VSS, connector or harness.
Code 25 – Barometric (BARO) pressure sensor fault. Possible causes: faulty BARO pressure sensor, connector or harness.
Code 31 – Knock sensor fault. Possible causes: faulty knock sensor, connector or harness.
Code 32 – MAP sensor faulty. Possible causes: faulty MAP sensor, connector or harness.

Code 36 – Ignition timing adjustment signal fault. Possible causes: connector or harness.

Code 39 – Oxygen (O_2) sensor fault. Possible causes: faulty O_2 sensor, faulty O_2 sensor heater, connector or harness, low or high fuel pressure, defective injector(s), intake air leaks.

Code 41 – Injector(s) fault. Possible causes: low or high injector coil resistance, connector or harness.

Code 42 – Fuel pump fault. Possible causes: faulty ECM, faulty MPI relay, connector or harness.

Code 43 – EGR fault. Possible causes: faulty EGR valve, faulty EGR temperature sensor, faulty EGR solenoid, faulty EGR vacuum control, connector or harness.

Code 44 – Ignition coil (cylinders No. 1 and 4) fault. Possible causes: faulty ignition coil, faulty ignition power transistor unit, connector or harness.

Code 52 – Ignition coil (cylinders No. 2 and 5) fault. Possible causes: faulty ignition coil, faulty ignition power transistor unit, connector or harness.

Code 53 – Ignition coil (cylinders No. 3 and 6) fault. Possible causes: faulty ignition coil, faulty ignition power transistor unit, connector or harness.

Code 55 – Idle Air Control (IAC) valve position sensor fault. Possible causes: faulty IAC valve position sensor, faulty IAC motor assembly, faulty ECM, connector or harness.

Code 59 – Rear Oxygen (O_2) sensor fault. Possible causes: faulty O_2 sensor, faulty O_2 sensor heater, faulty ECM, connector or harness.

Code 61 – Transaxle control module torque reduction signal fault. Possible causes: faulty transaxle control module, connector or harness.

Code 62 – Variable Induction Control (VIC) Valve position sensor fault. Possible causes: faulty VIC valve position sensor, connector or harness.

Code 71 – Traction Control (TC) vacuum valve solenoid fault. Possible causes: faulty TC vacuum valve solenoid, connector or harness.

Code 72 – Traction Control (TC) vent valve solenoid fault. Possible causes: faulty TC vent valve solenoid, connector or harness.

CLEARING CODES

NOTE: To clear codes using a scan tester, refer to owners manual supplied with scan tester.

Fault codes may be cleared by disconnecting negative battery cable for at least 10 seconds, allowing ECM to clear fault codes. Reconnect negative battery cable and check for codes to confirm repair.

ECM LOCATION

ECM LOCATION

Application	Location
Eclipse, Stealth & 3000GT	Behind Radio Console
All Other Models	Behind Right Side Of Instrument Panel

SUMMARY

If no hard fault codes (or only pass codes) are present, driveability symptoms exist, or intermittent codes exist, proceed to TROUBLE SHOOTING – NO CODES article for diagnosis by symptom (i.e., ROUGH IDLE, NO START, etc.) or intermittent diagnostic procedures.

TERMINAL IDENTIFICATION

NOTE: The following terminals are shown as viewed from component side.

TERMINAL IDENTIFICATION DIRECTORY

Connector	See Fig.
Airflow Sensor	2
CKP/CMP Sensor	3
Coolant Temperature Sensor	4
ECM	5
EGR Temperature Sensor	6
Fuel Injector	7
Fuel Pump	8
Idle Air Control Valve Position Sensor	9
Idle Speed Control Motor & Position Sensor	10
Ignition Coil	11
Induction Control Valve Position Sensor	12
Knock Sensor	13
MAP Sensor	14
MPI Relay	15
Oxygen (O_2) Sensor	16
Throttle Position Sensor	17
Traction Control Vacuum Solenoid	18
Traction Control Vent Solenoid	19
Transaxle Control Module	20

(NON-TURBO)   ECLIPSE   (TURBO)

ALL OTHER MODELS

93F80254   Courtesy of Mitsubishi Motor Sales of America.

Fig. 2: Identifying Airflow Sensor Terminals

DIAMANTE (SOHC), ECLIPSE 2.0L, MONTERO, PICKUP & RAM-50 (3.0L), & STEALTH (SOHC)

DIAMANTE, STEALTH & 3000GT (DOHC)

PICKUP & RAM-50 (2.4L – 4WD)

ALL OTHER MODELS

93G80255   Courtesy of Mitsubishi Motor Sales of America.

Fig. 3: Identifying CKP/CMP Sensor Terminals

PICKUP & RAM-50 (2.4L – 4WD)   ALL OTHER MODELS

93H80256   Courtesy of Mitsubishi Motor Sales of America.

Fig. 4: Identifying Coolant Temperature Sensor Terminals

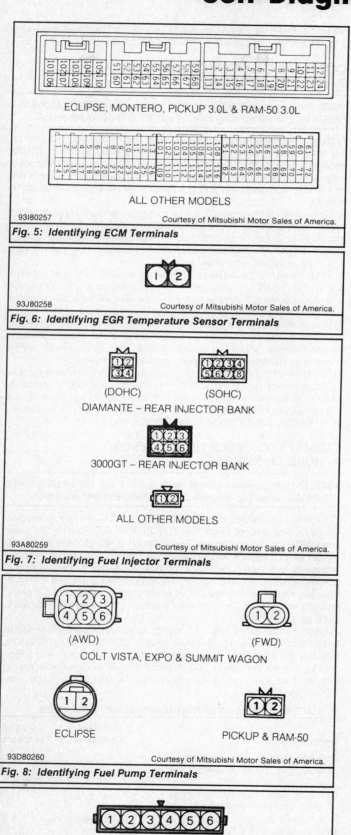

ECLIPSE, MONTERO, PICKUP 3.0L & RAM-50 3.0L

ALL OTHER MODELS

93I80257
Courtesy of Mitsubishi Motor Sales of America.

Fig. 5: Identifying ECM Terminals

93J80258
Courtesy of Mitsubishi Motor Sales of America.

Fig. 6: Identifying EGR Temperature Sensor Terminals

(DOHC)   **(SOHC)**
DIAMANTE – REAR INJECTOR BANK

3000GT – REAR INJECTOR BANK

ALL OTHER MODELS

93A80259
Courtesy of Mitsubishi Motor Sales of America.

Fig. 7: Identifying Fuel Injector Terminals

(AWD)   **(FWD)**
COLT VISTA, EXPO & SUMMIT WAGON

ECLIPSE   **PICKUP & RAM-50**

93D80260
Courtesy of Mitsubishi Motor Sales of America.

Fig. 8: Identifying Fuel Pump Terminals

93E80261
Courtesy of Mitsubishi Motor Sales of America.

Fig. 9: Identifying Idle Air Control Valve Position Sensor Terminals

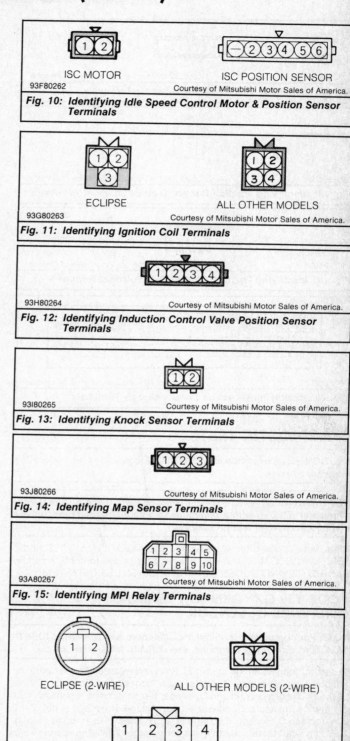

ISC MOTOR   **ISC POSITION SENSOR**
93F80262
Courtesy of Mitsubishi Motor Sales of America.

Fig. 10: Identifying Idle Speed Control Motor & Position Sensor Terminals

ECLIPSE   **ALL OTHER MODELS**
93G80263
Courtesy of Mitsubishi Motor Sales of America.

Fig. 11: Identifying Ignition Coil Terminals

93H80264
Courtesy of Mitsubishi Motor Sales of America.

Fig. 12: Identifying Induction Control Valve Position Sensor Terminals

93I80265
Courtesy of Mitsubishi Motor Sales of America.

Fig. 13: Identifying Knock Sensor Terminals

93J80266
Courtesy of Mitsubishi Motor Sales of America.

Fig. 14: Identifying Map Sensor Terminals

93A80267
Courtesy of Mitsubishi Motor Sales of America.

Fig. 15: Identifying MPI Relay Terminals

ECLIPSE (2-WIRE)   **ALL OTHER MODELS (2-WIRE)**

DIAMANTE, STEALTH & 3000GT (NON-TURBO)

ECLIPSE (4-WIRE)   **ALL OTHER MODELS**

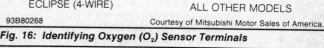

93B80268
Courtesy of Mitsubishi Motor Sales of America.

Fig. 16: Identifying Oxygen (O₂) Sensor Terminals

1993 ENGINE PERFORMANCE
Self-Diagnostics (Cont.)

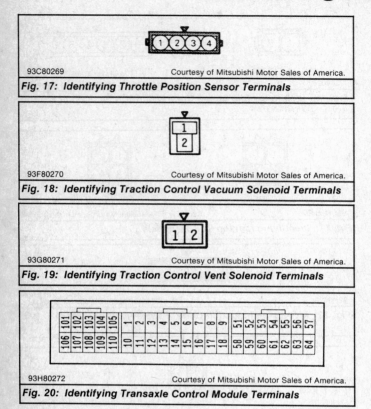

93C80269   Courtesy of Mitsubishi Motor Sales of America.

Fig. 17: Identifying Throttle Position Sensor Terminals

93F80270   Courtesy of Mitsubishi Motor Sales of America.

Fig. 18: Identifying Traction Control Vacuum Solenoid Terminals

93G80271   Courtesy of Mitsubishi Motor Sales of America.

Fig. 19: Identifying Traction Control Vent Solenoid Terminals

93H80272   Courtesy of Mitsubishi Motor Sales of America.

Fig. 20: Identifying Transaxle Control Module Terminals

DIAGNOSTIC TESTS

CAUTION: Ensure ignition switch is in OFF position when performing resistance tests.

NOTE: Perform all resistance and voltage tests using a Digital Volt-Ohmmeter (DVOM) with a minimum 10-megohm impedance, unless stated otherwise in test procedures.

Clear fault codes after each repair. See CLEARING CODES under SELF-DIAGNOSTIC SYSTEM. Recheck for codes to confirm repair. See RETRIEVING CODES under SELF-DIAGNOSTIC SYSTEM.

CODE 11: OXYGEN (O₂) SENSOR ONE-WIRE O₂ SENSOR

NOTE: For component terminal identification, see TERMINAL IDENTIFICATION. For wiring diagrams, see WIRING DIAGRAMS article.

1) If using scan tester, go to step **2)**. Start and warm engine to operating temperature. Disconnect O_2 sensor connector. Connect DVOM between chassis ground and O_2 sensor terminal. While repeatedly racing engine, measure O_2 sensor output voltage. If voltage is not .6-1.0 volt, replace O_2 sensor. If voltage is within specification, go to step **4)**.
2) Using scan tester, read O_2 sensor voltage. While monitoring scan tester, accelerate to 4000 RPM. Suddenly decelerate. Scan tester should read .3 volt or less. Suddenly accelerate. Scan tester should read .5-1.0 volt. If voltage is not as specified, replace O_2 sensor. If voltage is as specified, go to next step.
3) While monitoring scan tester, accelerate to 2000 RPM and decelerate to 700 RPM (idle). Scan tester should switch between .6-1.0 volt and .4 volt or less. If voltage is not as specified, replace O_2 sensor. If voltage is as specified, go to next step.
4) Disconnect O_2 sensor connector and ECM connector. Using DVOM, check for continuity between O_2 sensor terminal and ECM connector terminal No. 4. If continuity does not exist, repair wiring harness as necessary. If continuity exists, condition required to set fault is not

present at this time. Test is complete. Intermittent problem may exist. See TROUBLE SHOOTING – NO CODES article.

CODE 11: OXYGEN (O₂) SENSOR 2-WIRE O₂ SENSOR

NOTE: For component terminal identification, see TERMINAL IDENTIFICATION. For wiring diagrams, see WIRING DIAGRAMS article.

1) If using scan tester, go to step **2)**. Start and warm engine to operating temperature. Disconnect O_2 sensor connector. Connect DVOM between chassis ground and O_2 sensor terminal No. 1. While repeatedly racing engine, measure O_2 sensor output voltage. If voltage is not .6-1.0 volt, replace O_2 sensor. If voltage is within specification, go to step **4)**.
2) Using scan tester, read O_2 sensor voltage. While monitoring scan tester, accelerate to 4000 RPM. Suddenly decelerate. Scan tester should read .3 volt or less. Suddenly accelerate. Scan tester should read .5-1.0 volt. If voltage is not as specified, replace O_2 sensor. If voltage is as specified, go to next step.
3) While monitoring scan tester, accelerate to 2000 RPM and decelerate to 700 RPM (idle). Scan tester should switch between .6-1.0 volt and .4 volt or less. If voltage is not as specified, replace O_2 sensor. If voltage is as specified, go to next step.
4) Disconnect O_2 sensor connector and ECM connector. Using DVOM, check for continuity between O_2 sensor terminal No. 1 and ECM connector terminal No. 4. If continuity does not exist, repair wiring harness as necessary. If continuity exists, go to next step.
5) Using DVOM, check continuity between chassis ground and O_2 sensor connector terminal No. 2. If continuity does not exist, replace O_2 sensor. If continuity exists, condition required to set fault is not present at this time. Test is complete. Intermittent problem may exist. See TROUBLE SHOOTING – NO CODES article.

CODE 11: OXYGEN (O₂) SENSOR 4-WIRE O₂ SENSOR

NOTE: For component terminal identification, see TERMINAL IDENTIFICATION. For wiring diagrams, see WIRING DIAGRAMS article.

1) If using scan tester, go to step **3)**. Disconnect O_2 sensor connector. On all models except Diamante, Pickup, Ram-50, Stealth non-turbo and 3000GT non-turbo, install Test Harness (MB998464) between O_2 sensor and O_2 sensor connector. On all models, use DVOM to check resistance between specified O_2 sensor connector heater terminals. See O_2 SENSOR 4-WIRE CONNECTOR TERMINAL IDENTIFICATION table. O_2 sensor resistance should be 20 ohms at 68°F (20°C). If resistance is not as specified, replace O_2 sensor. If resistance is as specified, go to next step.
2) Using jumper wires, apply 12 volts to specified O_2 sensor connector heater terminals. See O_2 SENSOR 4-WIRE CONNECTOR TERMINAL IDENTIFICATION table. Using DVOM, check voltage between specified O_2 sensor connector output terminals, while repeatedly racing engine. If voltage is not .6-1.0 volt, replace O_2 sensor. If voltage is .6-1.0 volt, go to step **5)**.

O₂ SENSOR 4-WIRE CONNECTOR TERMINAL IDENTIFICATION

Application	[1] Heater Terminals	Output Terminals
Colt 1.5L, Mirage 1.5L, Montero, Stealth 3.0L Turbo, Summit 1.5L & 3000GT 3.0L Turbo	1 & 3	2 & 4
Colt 1.8L, Colt Vista, Expo, Mirage 1.8L, Pickup, Ram-50, Summit 1.8L & Summit Wagon	2 & 4	1 & 3
Diamante, Eclipse 2.0L, Stealth 3.0L Non-Turbo, & 3000GT 3.0L Non-Turbo	3 & 4	1 & 2

[1] – First terminal listed is positive. Second terminal listed is negative.

3) Start and warm engine to operating temperature. Using scan tester, read O_2 sensor voltage. While monitoring scan tester, accelerate to 4000 RPM. Suddenly decelerate. Scan tester should read .3 volt or less. Suddenly accelerate. Scan tester should read .5-1.0 volt. If voltage is not as specified, replace O_2 sensor. If voltage is as specified, go to next step.

4) While monitoring scan tester, accelerate to 2000 RPM and decelerate to 700 RPM (idle). Scan tester should switch between .6-1.0 volt and .4 volt or less. If voltage is not as specified, replace O_2 sensor. If voltage is as specified, go to next step.

5) Disconnect O_2 sensor connector. On Eclipse, Pickup 3.0L, Ram-50 3.0L, Stealth and 3000GT, go to next step. On all other models, disconnect MPI relay connector. Using DVOM, check for continuity between specified O_2 sensor connector terminals and MPI connector terminals. See O_2 SENSOR TO MPI WIRING HARNESS TERMINAL IDENTIFICATION table. If continuity does not exist, repair wiring harness as necessary. If continuity exists, go to step **7)**.

O_2 SENSOR TO MPI WIRING HARNESS TERMINAL IDENTIFICATION

Application	O_2 Sensor Terminals	MPI Terminals
All 1.5L Models	1	2
Diamante	3	5
Montero	1	5
All Other Models	2	2

6) Turn ignition switch to ON position. Using DVOM, check voltage between specified O_2 sensor connector terminal and chassis ground. See O_2 SENSOR CONNECTOR VOLTAGE CIRCUIT IDENTIFICATION table. If system voltage does not exist, repair wiring harness as necessary. If system voltage exists, go to next step.

O_2 SENSOR CONNECTOR VOLTAGE CIRCUIT IDENTIFICATION

Application	Terminal No.
Eclipse, Stealth & 3000GT (Non-Turbo)	3
Pickup 3.0L & Ram-50 3.0L	2
Stealth & 3000GT (Turbo)	1

7) Using DVOM, check for continuity between specified O_2 sensor connector terminals and ECM connector terminals. See O_2 SENSOR TO ECM WIRING HARNESS TERMINAL IDENTIFICATION table. If continuity does not exist on either circuit, repair appropriate circuit for open or short to ground as necessary. If continuity exists, go to next step.

O_2 SENSOR TO ECM WIRING HARNESS TERMINAL IDENTIFICATION

Application	O_2 Sensor Terminals	ECM Terminals
Colt, Colt Vista, Colt 200, Expo, Mirage, Pickup, Ram-50, Summit & Summit Wagon		
1.5L	3	56
	4	35
1.8L Except Summit Wagon	3	5
	4	35
2.4L & Summit Wagon	3	56
	4	105
3.0L	3	4
Diamante	1	56
Eclipse 2.0L	1	4
Montero	4	4
Stealth Non-Turbo & 3000GT Non-Turbo	1	56
Stealth Turbo & 3000GT Turbo	4	56

8) Disconnect O_2 sensor connector. Using DVOM, check for continuity between specified O_2 sensor connector terminal and chassis ground. See O_2 SENSOR CONNECTOR GROUND CIRCUIT IDENTIFICATION table. If continuity does not exist, repair wiring harness as necessary. If no system or component malfunctions occur in preceding tests, condition required to set fault is not present at this time. Test is complete. Intermittent problem may exist. See TROUBLE SHOOTING – NO CODES article.

O_2 SENSOR CONNECTOR GROUND CIRCUIT IDENTIFICATION

Application	Terminal No.
Colt 1.8L, Colt Vista, Expo, Mirage 1.8L, Pickup, Ram-50, Summit 1.8L & Summit Wagon	1
Eclipse	4
All Other Models	2

CODE 12: AIRFLOW SENSOR

NOTE: For component terminal identification, see TERMINAL IDENTIFICATION. For wiring diagrams, see WIRING DIAGRAMS article.

NOTE: Procedures are provided by manufacturer for component testing using an engine analyzer with oscilloscope capability. Refer to manufacturer's operation manual for instructions in use of oscilloscope. If using a scan tester, go to step 3).

1) If using scan tester, go to step **3)**. Disconnect Airflow Sensor (AFS) connector. Install Test Harness (MB991348) between AFS and AFS connector. Using engine analyzer with oscilloscope capability, connect special patterns probe to AFS connector terminal No. 3.

2) Start engine. Verify that wave form high frequency and low frequency patterns are of approximately the same length (time). *See Fig. 21.* Verify that wave length decreases and frequency increases as engine RPM increases. If conditions are not as specified, replace AFS. If conditions are as specified, go to step **4)**.

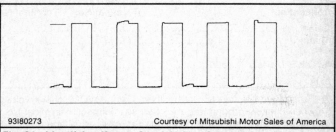

93180273   Courtesy of Mitsubishi Motor Sales of America

Fig. 21: Identifying Known-Good Airflow Sensor Wave Pattern

3) Warm vehicle to normal operating temperature. Ensure headlights and accessories are off. Ensure steering wheel is in straight-ahead position. Using scan tester, read Airflow Sensor (AFS) volume (frequency) value. See AIRFLOW SENSOR VALUES table. Frequency should increase when engine is raced. If values are not as specified, replace AFS. If values are as specified, go to next step.

AIRFLOW SENSOR VALUES

Application	Hz @ 700 RPM	Hz @ 2000 RPM
1.8L		
Colt, Colt Vista, Expo, Mirage, Summit & Summit Wagon	23-49	51-91
Eclipse	25-40	67-88
2.0L		
Eclipse		
Non-Turbo	25-50	70-90
Turbo	25-50	60-85
Galant	18-44	64-104
2.4L		
Colt Vista, Expo & Summit Wagon	18-44	43-83
Pickup & Ram-50	40-60	85-105
3.0L		
Diamante & Stealth SOHC	21-47	57-97
Montero	22-48	60-100
Pickup & Ram-50	25-45	70-90
Stealth & 3000GT		
DOHC Non-Turbo	22-48	50-90
DOHC Turbo	22-48	68-108

4) On Eclipse, Pickup 2.4L (4WD) and 3.0L, Ram-50 2.4L (4WD) and 3.0L, Stealth and 3000GT, go to step **8)**. On all other models, disconnect AFS connector and MPI relay connector. Using DVOM, check for continuity between specified AFS connector terminal and MPI relay connector terminal. See AFS TO MPI TERMINAL WIRING HARNESS IDENTIFICATION table. If continuity does not exist, repair wiring harness as necessary. If continuity exists, go to next step.

AFS TO MPI TERMINAL WIRING HARNESS IDENTIFICATION

Application	AFS Terminal No.	MPI Terminal No.
Diamante & Montero	4	4
Galant	2	3
All Other Models	4	3

5) Using DVOM, check for continuity between chassis ground and AFS connector terminal No. 5 (terminal No. 4 on Galant). If continuity does not exist, repair wiring harness as necessary. If continuity exists, go to next step.

6) Disconnect AFS connector and ECM connector. Using DVOM, check for continuity between specified AFS connector terminal and ECM connector terminal. See AFS TO ECM WIRING HARNESS TERMINAL IDENTIFICATION table. If continuity does not exist on specified circuit(s), repair appropriate circuit for open or short to ground as necessary. If continuity exists, go to next step.

AFS TO ECM WIRING HARNESS TERMINAL IDENTIFICATION

Application	AFS Terminal No.	ECM Terminal No.
Galant	1	70
Montero	3	70
	7	57
All Other Models	3	70
	7	19

7) Turn ignition switch to ON position. Using DVOM, check voltage between chassis ground and AFS harness connector terminal No. 1 on Galant or terminal No. 3 on all other models. If voltage is not 4.8-5.2 volts, replace ECM. If voltage is as specified, condition required to set fault is not present at this time. Test is complete. Intermittent problem may exist. See TROUBLE SHOOTING – NO CODES article.

8) Disconnect AFS connector. Turn ignition switch to ON position. Using DVOM, check voltage between specified terminal and chassis ground. See AFS CONNECTOR POWER SUPPLY CIRCUIT IDENTIFICATION table. If system voltage does not exist, repair wiring harness as necessary. If system voltage exists, go to next step.

AFS CONNECTOR POWER SUPPLY CIRCUIT IDENTIFICATION

Application	Terminal No.
Eclipse	
1.8L & 2.0L Turbo	2
2.0L Non-Turbo	1
Pickup 2.4L (4WD), Ram-50 2.4L (4WD), Stealth & 3000GT	4
Pickup 3.0L & Ram-50 3.0L	5

9) With ignition switch in ON position, use DVOM to check voltage between specified terminal and chassis ground. See AFS CONNECTOR VOLTAGE CIRCUIT IDENTIFICATION table. If voltage is not 4.8-5.2 volts, repair wiring harness as necessary. If voltage is as specified, go to next step.

AFS CONNECTOR VOLTAGE CIRCUIT IDENTIFICATION

Application	Terminal No.
Eclipse	
1.8L	1
2.0L Non-Turbo	2
All Other Models	3

10) Using DVOM, check for continuity between specified AFS connector terminal and chassis ground. See AFS CONNECTOR GROUND CIRCUIT IDENTIFICATION table. If continuity does not exist, repair wiring harness as necessary. If continuity exists on Eclipse 1.8L or 2.0L non-turbo, condition required to set fault is not present at this time. Test is complete. Intermittent problem may exist. See TROUBLE SHOOTING – NO CODES article. On all other models, go to next step.

AFS CONNECTOR GROUND CIRCUIT IDENTIFICATION

Application	Terminal No.
Eclipse	
1.8L & 2.0L Non-Turbo	4
2.0L Turbo	6
All Other Models	5

11) Disconnect AFS connector and ECM connector. Using DVOM, check for continuity between specified AFS connector terminal and ECM connector terminal. See ECM TO AFS WIRING HARNESS TERMINAL IDENTIFICATION table. If continuity does not exist on specified circuit(s), repair appropriate circuit for open or short to ground as necessary. If continuity exists, condition required to set fault is not present at this time. Test is complete. Intermittent problem may exist. See TROUBLE SHOOTING – NO CODES article.

ECM TO AFS WIRING HARNESS TERMINAL IDENTIFICATION

Application	ECM Terminal No.	AFS Terminal No.
Eclipse 2.0L Turbo	6	1
Stealth & 3000GT	19	7
All Other Models	57	7

CODE 13: INTAKE AIR TEMPERATURE SENSOR

NOTE: On all models except 1.5L engines, intake air temperature sensor is built into airflow sensor. For code 13 test purposes, the airflow sensor will be referred to as the intake air temperature sensor. For component terminal identification, see AIRFLOW SENSOR under TERMINAL IDENTIFICATION. For component terminal identification on 1.5L engines, see Fig. 22. For wiring diagrams, see WIRING DIAGRAMS article.

1) If using scan tester, go to step **3)**. Disconnect Intake Air Temperature (IAT) sensor connector. Using a thermometer, check engine compartment ambient temperature. Using DVOM, check resistance between specified IAT sensor terminals. See IAT SENSOR TERMINAL IDENTIFICATION table. Resistance should be 6000 ohms at 32°F (0°C), 2700 ohms at 68°F (20°C) or 400 ohms at 176°F (80°C). If resistance is not as specified, replace IAT sensor. If resistance is as specified, go to next step.

IAT SENSOR TERMINAL IDENTIFICATION

Application	Terminals No.
All 1.5L Models	1 & 2
Eclipse	
1.8L & 2.0L Non-Turbo	4 & 5
2.0L Turbo	6 & 8
Galant	4 & 6
All Other Models	5 & 6

93J80274   Courtesy of Mitsubishi Motor Sales of America

Fig. 22: Identifying IAT Component Terminals (1.5L)

2) Using a hair dryer, warm IAT sensor while monitoring DVOM. Resistance should decrease evenly as temperature rises. If resistance remains unchanged, replace IAT sensor. If resistance changes, go to step **4)**.

3) Turn ignition switch to ON or RUN position. Using a thermometer, check engine compartment ambient temperature. Using scan tester, read Intake Air Temperature (IAT) sensor temperature. See IAT SENSOR TEMPERATURE table. If temperatures are not as specified, replace IAT sensor. If temperatures are as specified, go to next step.

IAT SENSOR TEMPERATURE

Ambient Temperature	Standard Value
–4°F (–20°C)	–20°C
32°F (0°C)	0°C
68°F (20°C)	20°C
104°F (40°C)	40°C
176°F (80°C)	80°C

4) Disconnect IAT sensor connector. Using DVOM, check for continuity between chassis ground and specified IAT sensor connector terminal. See IAT SENSOR GROUND CIRCUIT TERMINAL IDENTIFICATION table. If continuity does not exist, repair wiring harness as necessary. If continuity exists, go to next step.

IAT SENSOR GROUND CIRCUIT TERMINAL IDENTIFICATION

Application	Terminal No.
All 1.5L Models	1
Eclipse	
1.8L	4
2.0L Non-Turbo	6
2.0L Turbo	8
Galant	4
All Other Models	5

5) On Eclipse 1.8L and 2.0L turbo, Pickup 2.4L (4WD) and 3.0L, Ram-50 2.4L (4WD) and 3.0L, Stealth and 3000GT, go to next step. On all other models, with IAT sensor connector and ECM connector disconnected, check for continuity between specified IAT sensor connector terminal and ECM connector terminal. See IAT TO ECM WIRING HARNESS TERMINAL IDENTIFICATION table. If continuity does not exist, repair wiring harness as necessary. If continuity exists, go to next step.

IAT TO ECM WIRING HARNESS TERMINAL IDENTIFICATION

Application	IAT Connector Terminal No.	ECM Connector Terminal No.
All 1.5L Models	2	52
Eclipse 2.0L Non-Turbo	5	16
Montero	6	8
All Other Models	6	52

6) Turn ignition switch to ON position. Check voltage between chassis ground and specified IAT sensor connector. See IAT SENSOR CONNECTOR VOLTAGE SUPPLY CIRCUIT TERMINAL IDENTIFICATION table. If voltage is not 4.5-4.9 volts, replace ECM. If voltage is as specified, replace IAT sensor.

IAT SENSOR CONNECTOR VOLTAGE SUPPLY CIRCUIT TERMINAL IDENTIFICATION

Application	Terminal No.
All 1.5L Models	2
Eclipse 2.0L	
Non-Turbo	3
Turbo	4
All Other Models	6

CODE 14: THROTTLE POSITION SENSOR

NOTE: For component terminal identification, see TERMINAL IDENTIFICATION. For wiring diagrams, see WIRING DIAGRAMS article.

1) If using scan tester, go to step 3). Disconnect Throttle Position Sensor (TPS) connector. Using DVOM, check resistance between TPS terminals No. 1 and 4. If resistance is not 3500-6500 ohms, replace TPS. If resistance is as specified, go to next step.
2) Check resistance between specified TPS terminals. See TPS TERMINAL IDENTIFICATION table. While monitoring DVOM, slowly open throttle from idle to fully open position. If resistance does not change smoothly, replace TPS. If resistance changes smoothly, go to step 4).

TPS TERMINAL IDENTIFICATION

Application	Terminals No.
Colt Vista, Expo, Montero, Pickup 3.0L, Ram-50 3.0L & Summit Wagon	1 & 3
All Other Models	2 & 4

3) Turn ignition switch to ON position. Using scan tester, read Throttle Position Sensor (TPS) voltage. With throttle at idle, voltage should read .3-1.0 volt. Voltage should increase while slowly opening throttle. At wide open throttle, voltage should read 4.5-5.5 volts. If voltage is not as specified, replace TPS. If voltage is as specified, go to next step.
4) On Eclipse, Pickup 2.4L (4WD) and 3.0L, Ram-50 2.4L (4WD) and 3.0L, Stealth and 3000GT, go to step 7). On all other models, disconnect TPS connector. Using DVOM, check continuity between chassis ground and specified TPS connector terminal. See TPS CONNECTOR GROUND CIRCUIT IDENTIFICATION table. If continuity does not exist, repair wiring harness as necessary. If continuity exists, go to next step.

TPS CONNECTOR GROUND CIRCUIT IDENTIFICATION

Application	Terminal No.
Colt Vista, Expo, Montero & Summit Wagon	1
All Other Models	4

5) Disconnect TPS connector and ECM connector. Check for continuity between specified TPS connector terminal and ECM connector terminal. See TPS TO ECM WIRING HARNESS TERMINAL IDENTIFICATION table. If continuity does not exist, repair wiring harness as necessary. If continuity exists, go to next step.

TPS TO ECM WIRING HARNESS TERMINAL IDENTIFICATION

Application	TPS Terminal No.	ECM Terminal No.
Colt, Colt 200, Diamante, Mirage & Summit	1	61
	2	64
Colt Vista, Expo & Summit Wagon	3	64
	4	61
Galant, Pickup 2.4L (RWD) & Ram-50 2.4L (RWD)	1	64
	2	61
Montero	3	19
	4	23

6) Check voltage between chassis ground and specified TPS connector terminal. See TPS VOLTAGE CIRCUIT IDENTIFICATION table. If voltage is not 4.8-5.2 volts, replace ECM. If voltage is as specified, condition required to set fault is not present at this time. Test is complete. Intermittent problem may exist. See TROUBLE SHOOTING – NO CODES article.

TPS VOLTAGE CIRCUIT IDENTIFICATION

Application	TPS Terminal No.
Colt, Colt 200, Diamante, Galant, Mirage Pickup 2.4L (RWD), Ram-50 2.4L (RWD) & Summit	1
Colt Vista, Expo, Montero & Summit Wagon	4

7) Disconnect TPS connector. Turn ignition switch to ON position. Using DVOM, check voltage between chassis ground and specified TPS connector terminal. See TPS VOLTAGE SUPPLY IDENTIFICATION table. If voltage is not 4.8-5.2 volts, repair wiring harness as necessary. If voltage is as specified, go to next step.

TPS VOLTAGE SUPPLY IDENTIFICATION

Application	TPS Terminal No.
Eclipse, Stealth & 3000GT	4
Pickup & Ram-50	
2.4L (4WD)	4
3.0L	1

8) Check continuity between chassis ground and specified TPS connector terminal. See TPS CONNECTOR GROUND CIRCUIT IDENTIFICATION table. If continuity does not exist, repair wiring harness as necessary. If continuity exists, go to next step.

TPS CONNECTOR GROUND CIRCUIT IDENTIFICATION

Application	Terminal No.
Pickup 3.0L	1
All Other Models	4

9) With TPS connector and ECM connector disconnected, check for continuity between specified TPS connector terminal and ECM connector terminal. See ECM TO TPS HARNESS IDENTIFICATION table. If continuity does not exist, repair wiring harness as necessary. If continuity exists, condition required to set fault is not present at this time. Test is complete. Intermittent problem may exist. See TROUBLE SHOOTING – NO CODES article.

ECM TO TPS HARNESS IDENTIFICATION

Application	ECM Terminal No.	TPS Terminal No.
Pickup 3.0L	19	3
Stealth & 3000GT	64	2
All Other Models	9	2

CODE 15: IDLE SPEED CONTROL POSITION SENSOR

NOTE: For component terminal identification, see TERMINAL IDENTIFICATION. For wiring diagrams, see WIRING DIAGRAMS article.

1) If using scan tester, go to step 3). Disconnect Idle Speed Control (ISC) motor position sensor connector. Using DVOM, check resistance between ISC motor position sensor terminals No. 2 and 3. If resistance is not 4000-6000 ohms, replace ISC motor position sensor. If resistance is as specified, go to next step.

CAUTION: Apply only 6 volts DC or less to ISC motor connector. Higher voltage could cause servo gears to lock up.

2) Disconnect ISC motor connector. Connect a 6-volt DC power supply between ISC motor connector terminals No. 1 and 2 to operate ISC motor. Check resistance between ISC motor position sensor terminals No. 3 and 5. Ensure ISC motor position sensor resistance changes smoothly as motor extends and retracts. If resistance does not change smoothly, replace ISC motor assembly. If resistance changes smoothly, go to step 4).

3) Ensure engine coolant temperature is 185-205°F (85-95°C). Place transmission in Park or Neutral. Turn off all accessories except A/C. Ensure A/C clutch is operating when A/C system is on. With engine at idle, use scan tester to read Idle Speed Control (ISC) motor position sensor voltage. See ISC VOLTAGE SPECIFICATIONS table. If voltage is not as specified, replace IAC motor position sensor. If voltage is as specified, go to next step.

ISC VOLTAGE SPECIFICATIONS

Application	A/C Switch Position	Standard Voltage
Eclipse	Off	.5-1.3
	On	.8-1.8
	[1]	.9-1.9
All Other Models	Off	.5-1.3
	On	.9-2.3
	[1]	.9-2.3

[1] – On A/T models only, apply brakes, place transmission selector in "D" position and A/C switch in ON position.

4) Disconnect ISC motor position sensor connector. Turn ignition switch to ON position. Using DVOM, check voltage between chassis ground and sensor connector terminal No. 2. Check voltage between chassis ground and sensor connector terminal No. 6. Voltage should be 4.8-5.2 volts on both circuits. If voltage is not as specified, repair appropriate wiring harness circuit(s) as necessary. If voltage is as specified, go to next step.

5) Check for continuity between chassis ground and sensor connector terminal No. 3. If continuity does not exist, repair wiring harness as necessary. If continuity exists, condition required to set fault is not present at this time. Test is complete. Intermittent problem may exist. See TROUBLE SHOOTING – NO CODES article.

CODE 21: COOLANT TEMPERATURE SENSOR

NOTE: For component terminal identification, see TERMINAL IDENTIFICATION. For wiring diagrams, see WIRING DIAGRAMS article.

1) If using scan tester, go to step 2). Remove Coolant Temperature Sensor (CTS) from intake manifold. Submerge temperature sensing portion of CTS in hot water. Using DVOM, check resistance across CTS terminals. See CTS RESISTANCE SPECIFICATIONS table. If resistance is not as specified, replace CTS. If resistance is as specified, go to step 3).

CTS RESISTANCE SPECIFICATIONS

Water Temperature	Approximate Ohms
32°F (0°C)	5800
68°F (20°C)	2400
104°F (40°C)	1100
176°F (80°C)	300

2) Turn ignition switch to ON or RUN position. Using a thermometer, check engine compartment ambient temperature. Using scan tester, read Coolant Temperature Sensor (CTS) voltage. See CTS VOLTAGE SPECIFICATIONS table. If voltage is not within specifications, replace CTS. If voltage is within specification, go to next step.

CTS VOLTAGE SPECIFICATIONS

Ambient Temperature	Standard Value °F (°C)
–4°F (–20°C)	–20°C
32°F (0°C)	0°C
68°F (20°C)	20°C
104°F (40°C)	40°C
176°F (80°C)	80°C

3) Disconnect CTS connector. Using DVOM, check continuity between chassis ground and specified connector terminal. See CTS GROUND CIRCUIT TERMINAL IDENTIFICATION table. If continuity does not exist, repair wiring harness as necessary. If continuity exists, go to next step.

CTS GROUND CIRCUIT TERMINAL IDENTIFICATION

Application	Terminal No.
All 1.5L Models, Eclipse 1.8L, Pickup 2.4L (4WD) & Ram-50 2.4L (4WD)	1
All Other Models	2

4) On Eclipse 2.0L, Pickup 2.4L (4WD) and 3.0L, Ram-50 2.4L (4WD) and 3.0L, Stealth, and 3000GT, go to next step. On all other models, Disconnect CTS connector and ECM connector. Check continuity between specified CTS connector terminals and ECM connector terminals. See CTS TO ECM WIRING HARNESS TERMINAL IDENTIFICATION table. If continuity does not exist, repair wiring harness as necessary. If continuity exists, go to next step.

CTS TO ECM WIRING HARNESS TERMINAL IDENTIFICATION

Application	CTS Terminal No.	ECM Terminal No.
All 1.5L Models	2	63
Montero	1	20
All Other Models	1	63

5) Turn ignition switch to ON position. Check voltage between chassis ground and specified CTS connector terminal. See CTS VOLTAGE CIRCUIT IDENTIFICATION table. If voltage is not 4.5-4.9 volts, replace ECM. If voltage is as specified, condition required to set fault is not present at this time. Test is complete. Intermittent problem may exist. See TROUBLE SHOOTING – NO CODES article.

CTS VOLTAGE CIRCUIT IDENTIFICATION

Application	Terminal No.
All 1.5L Models, Eclipse 1.8L, Pickup & Ram-50 (2.4L – 4WD)	1
All Other Models	2

CODE 22: CRANKSHAFT POSITION SENSOR

NOTE: For component terminal identification, see TERMINAL IDENTIFICATION. For wiring diagrams, see WIRING DIAGRAMS article.

NOTE: Procedures are provided by manufacturer for component testing using an engine analyzer with oscilloscope capability. Refer to manufacturer's operation manual for instructions in use of oscilloscope. If using a scan tester, go to step 3).

1) On all models except Eclipse, Galant, Pickup, Ram-50, Stealth, and 3000GT, disconnect Crankshaft/Camshaft Position (CKP/CMP) sensor connector. Install Test Harness (MB991348) between sensor and connector. On all models, using engine analyzer with oscilloscope capability, connect special patterns probe to specified connector terminal. See CKP PATTERN PICKUP TERMINAL IDENTIFICATION table.

CKP PATTERN PICKUP TERMINAL IDENTIFICATION

Application	Terminal No.
Diamante, Eclipse 2.0L, Montero, Pickup 3.0L, Ram-50 3.0L, Stealth & 3000GT	2
Pickup 2.4L & Ram-50 2.4L	1
All Other Models	3

2) Start engine. Compare oscilloscope wave pattern with known-good wave pattern. *See Fig. 23.* Verify that wave length (time) decreases as engine RPM increases. If a wave pattern is output and it fluctuates to left or right, check for loose timing belt or an abnormality in sensor pickup disc. If a rectangular wave pattern is output even when engine is not started, substitute known-good CKP sensor. Repeat test. If wave pattern is still abnormal, go to step 5).

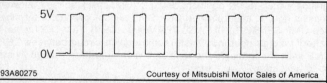

93A80275   Courtesy of Mitsubishi Motor Sales of America

Fig. 23: Identifying Known-Good CKP Sensor Wave Pattern

3) Connect an engine tachometer. Crank engine. Ensure ignition coil primary current toggles on and off. Using tachometer and scan tester, compare cranking speed and scan tester read out. If engine fails to start and tachometer reads zero RPM when engine is cranked, check for broken timing belt or faulty CKP sensor. If CKP sensor is suspected, substitute known-good CKP sensor. Repeat test procedure. If engine fails to start, tachometer reads zero RPM, and ignition coil primary current fails to toggle on and off, check for faulty ignition coil, ignition circuit or power transistor. If engine starts and readouts agree, go to next step.

4) Ensure A/C switch is in ON position to activate closed throttle position switch. Allow engine to idle. Check coolant temperature. Using scan tester, read idle speed. See IDLE RPM SPECIFICATIONS table. If RPM is not to specification, check for faulty coolant temperature sensor, basic idle speed adjustment, or idle air control motor. If RPM is within specifications, go to next step.

IDLE RPM SPECIFICATIONS

Coolant Temperature	Engine RPM
–4°F (–20°C)	
Colt, Colt Vista, Colt 200, Expo, Mirage, Pickup, Ram-50, Summit & Summit Wagon	
1.5L	1460-1660
1.8L	1380-1580
2.4L	1300-1500
3.0L	1500-1700
Diamante, Stealth & 3000GT	1300-1500
Eclipse & Montero	1500-1700
Galant	1275-1475
32°F (0°C)	
Colt, Colt Vista, Colt 200, Expo, Mirage, Pickup, Ram-50, Summit & Summit Wagon	
1.5L	1350-1550
1.8L	1330-1530
2.4L	1300-1500
3.0L	1250-1450
Diamante, Montero, Stealth & 3000GT	1250-1450
Eclipse	1350-1550
Galant	1220-1420
68°F (20°C)	
Colt, Colt Vista, Colt 200, Expo, Mirage, Pickup, Ram-50, Summit & Summit Wagon	
1.5L	1180-1380
1.8L	1250-1450
2.4L	1150-1350
Diamante DOHC, Galant, Stealth DOHC & 3000GT	1100-1300
Diamante SOHC, Montero, Pickup 3.0L, Ram-50 3.0L & Stealth SOHC	1050-1250
Eclipse	
1.8L	1150-1350
2.0L	1180-1380
104°F (40°C)	
Colt, Colt Vista, Colt 200, Expo, Mirage, Pickup, Ram-50, Summit & Summit Wagon	
1.5L	940-1140
1.8L	1000-1200
2.4L	950-1150
3.0L	850-1050
Diamante DOHC, Eclipse, Galant, Stealth DOHC & 3000GT	950-1150
Eclipse	
1.8L	950-1150
2.0L	1000-1200
Diamante SOHC, Montero & Stealth SOHC	850-1050
176°F (80°C)	
Colt, Colt Vista, Colt 200, Expo, Mirage, Pickup, Ram-50, Summit & Summit Wagon	
1.5L	650-850
1.8L	600-800
2.4L	650-850
3.0L	600-800
Diamante, Eclipse 1.8L, Galant, Montero, Stealth & 3000GT	600-800
Eclipse 2.0L	650-850

5) On all models except Colt, Colt 200, Mirage and Summit, go to next step. Disconnect CKP/CMP sensor connector and Ignition (IG) switch connector. Using DVOM, check for continuity between CKP/CMP sensor connector terminal No. 2 and IG switch connector terminal No. 3. *See Fig. 24.* If continuity does not exist, repair wiring harness as necessary. If continuity exists, go to step 8).

93B80276   Courtesy of Mitsubishi Motor Sales of America

Fig. 24: Identifying Ignition Switch Terminals

6) On all other models except Diamante and Montero, go to next step. Disconnect CKP/CMP connector and MPI relay connector. Using DVOM, check for continuity between CKP/CMP connector terminal No. 3 and MPI relay connector terminal No. 5. If continuity does not exist, repair wiring harness as necessary. If continuity exists, go to step 8).

7) On all other models, disconnect CKP/CMP sensor connector. Turn ignition switch to ON position. Using DVOM, check voltage between chassis ground and specified CKP/CMP sensor connector terminal. See CKP SENSOR VOLTAGE TERMINAL IDENTIFICATION table. If battery voltage does not exist, repair ignition circuit between CKP/CMP sensor connector and Ignition switch. If battery voltage exists, go to next step.

CKP SENSOR VOLTAGE TERMINAL IDENTIFICATION

Application	Terminal No.
Colt Vista, Eclipse 1.8L, Expo & Summit Wagon	2
All Other Models	3

8) With CKP/CMP sensor connector disconnected, check for continuity between chassis ground and specified CKP/CMP sensor connector terminal. See CKP SENSOR GROUND CIRCUIT TERMINAL IDENTIFICATION table. If continuity does not exist, repair wiring harness as necessary. If continuity exists, go to next step.

CKP SENSOR GROUND CIRCUIT TERMINAL IDENTIFICATION

Application	Terminal No.
Diamante SOHC, Eclipse 2.0L, Montero, Pickup 3.0L, Ram-50 3.0L & Stealth SOHC	4
Galant, Pickup 2.4L & Ram-50 2.4L	2
All Other Models	1

9) On Eclipse, Pickup 2.4L (4WD) and 3.0L, Ram-50 2.4L (4WD) and 3.0L, Stealth and 3000GT, go to next step. On all other models, with CKP/CMP sensor connector and ECM connector disconnected, check for continuity between specified CKP/CMP sensor connector terminal and ECM connector terminal. See CKP TO ECM CONNECTOR TERMINAL IDENTIFICATION table. If continuity does not exist, repair wiring harness as necessary. If continuity exists, go to next step.

CKP TO ECM CONNECTOR TERMINAL IDENTIFICATION

Application	CKP Terminal No.	ECM Terminal No.
Diamante	2	69
Montero	1	22
	2	21
Pickup 2.4L (RWD) & Ram-50 2.4L (RWD)	1	69
All Other Models	3	69

10) With ignition switch in ON position, check for voltage between chassis ground and specified CKP/CMP sensor connector terminal. See CKP SENSOR SUPPLY CIRCUIT IDENTIFICATION table. If 4.8-5.2 volts do not exist, replace ECM. If voltage is to specification and CKP sensor is suspected, replace CKP sensor.

CKP SENSOR SUPPLY CIRCUIT IDENTIFICATION

Application	Terminal No.
Diamante, Eclipse 2.0L, Montero, Pickup 3.0L, Ram-50 3.0L, Stealth & 3000GT	2
Galant, Pickup 2.4L & Ram-50 2.4L	1
All Other Models	3

CODE 23: CAMSHAFT POSITION SENSOR

NOTE: For component terminal identification, see TERMINAL IDENTIFICATION. For wiring diagrams, see WIRING DIAGRAMS article.

NOTE: Procedures are provided by manufacturer for component testing using an engine analyzer with oscilloscope capability. Refer to manufacturer's operation manual for instructions in use of oscilloscope. Manufacturer does not provide procedures for testing component using a scan tester.

1) On all models except Eclipse, Galant, Pickup, Ram-50, Stealth and 3000GT, disconnect Crankshaft/Camshaft Position (CKP/CMP) sensor connector. Install Test Harness (MB991348) between sensor and connector. On all models, using engine analyzer with oscilloscope capability, connect special patterns probe to specified connector terminal. See CMP PATTERN PICKUP TERMINAL IDENTIFICATION table.

CMP PATTERN PICKUP TERMINAL IDENTIFICATION

Application	Terminal No.
Diamante SOHC, Eclipse 2.0L, Montero, Pickup 3.0L, Ram-50 3.0L, Stealth & 3000GT	1
Diamante DOHC	2
All Other Models	4

2) Start engine. Compare oscilloscope wave pattern with known-good wave pattern. *See Fig. 25.* Verify that wave length (time) decreases as engine RPM increases. If a wave pattern is output and it fluctuates to left or right, check for loose timing belt or an abnormality in sensor pickup disc. If a rectangular wave pattern is output even when engine is not started, substitute known-good CMP sensor. Repeat test. If wave pattern is still abnormal, go to next step.

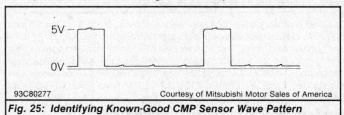

93C80277   Courtesy of Mitsubishi Motor Sales of America

Fig. 25: Identifying Known-Good CMP Sensor Wave Pattern

3) On all models except Colt, Colt 200, Mirage and Summit, go to step **4)**. Disconnect CKP/CMP sensor connector and Ignition (IG) switch connector. Using DVOM, check for continuity between CKP/CMP sensor connector terminal No. 2 and IG switch connector terminal No. 3. *See Fig. 24.* If continuity does not exist, repair wiring harness as necessary. If continuity exists, go to step **6)**.

4) On all other models except Diamante and Montero, go to next step. Disconnect CKP/CMP connector and MPI relay connector. Using DVOM, check for continuity between CKP/CMP connector terminal No. 3 and MPI relay connector terminal No. 5. If continuity does not exist, repair wiring harness as necessary. If continuity exists, go to step **6)**.

5) On all other models, disconnect CKP/CMP sensor connector. Turn ignition switch to ON position. Using DVOM, check voltage between chassis ground and specified CKP/CMP sensor connector terminal. See CMP SENSOR VOLTAGE TERMINAL IDENTIFICATION table. If battery voltage does not exist, repair ignition circuit between CKP/CMP sensor connector and Ignition switch. If battery voltage exists, go to next step.

CMP SENSOR VOLTAGE TERMINAL IDENTIFICATION

Application	Terminal No.
Colt Vista, Eclipse 1.8L, Expo, Galant, & Summit Wagon	2
All Other Models	3

6) With CKP/CMP sensor connector disconnected, check for continuity between chassis ground and specified CKP/CMP sensor connector terminal. See CMP SENSOR GROUND CIRCUIT TERMINAL IDENTIFICATION table. If continuity does not exist, repair wiring harness as necessary. If continuity exists, go to next step.

CMP SENSOR GROUND CIRCUIT TERMINAL IDENTIFICATION

Application	Terminal No.
Diamante SOHC, Eclipse 2.0L, Montero, Pickup 3.0L, Ram-50 3.0L & Stealth SOHC	4
Pickup 2.4L & Ram-50 2.4L	2
All Other Models	1

7) On Eclipse, Pickup 2.4L (4WD) and 3.0L, Ram-50 2.4L (4WD) and 3.0L, Stealth and 3000GT, go to next step. On all other models, with CKP/CMP sensor connector and ECM connector disconnected, check for continuity between specified CKP/CMP sensor connector terminal and ECM connector terminal. See CMP TO ECM CONNECTOR TERMINAL IDENTIFICATION table. If continuity does not exist, repair wiring harness as necessary. If continuity exists, go to next step.

CMP TO ECM CONNECTOR TERMINAL IDENTIFICATION

Application	CMP Terminal No.	ECM Terminal No.
Diamante		
SOHC	1	68
DOHC	2	68
Montero	1	22
	2	21
All Other Models	4	68

8) With ignition switch in ON position, check for voltage between chassis ground and specified CKP/CMP sensor connector terminal. See CMP SENSOR SUPPLY CIRCUIT IDENTIFICATION table. If 4.8-5.2 volts do not exist, replace ECM. If voltage is as specified, condition required to set fault is not present at this time. Test is complete. Intermittent problem may exist. See TROUBLE SHOOTING – NO CODES article.

CMP SENSOR SUPPLY CIRCUIT IDENTIFICATION

Application	Terminal No.
Diamante SOHC, Montero, Pickup 3.0L, Ram-50 3.0L & Stealth SOHC	1
Diamante DOHC, Stealth DOHC & 3000GT	2
All Other Models	4

CODE 24: VEHICLE SPEED SENSOR

NOTE: For component terminal identification, see TERMINAL IDENTIFICATION. For wiring diagrams, see WIRING DIAGRAMS article.

1) Manufacturer does not provide Vehicle Speed Sensor (VSS) testing procedures using scan tester. VSS is located in speedometer. VSS component testing procedures using DVOM require removal of instrument panel. Removal and installation of instrument panel is basically an unbolt and bolt-on procedure.

2) On Stealth turbo and 3000GT turbo, go to next step. On all other models, use DVOM to check continuity between indicated VSS terminals. *See Fig. 26.* Ensure continuity pulses on and off 4 times per speedometer shaft revolution. If continuity is not as specified, replace VSS. If continuity is as specified, go to step **4)**.

3) Remove VSS. Connect battery, resistor (3-10 ohms) and voltmeter to indicated terminals. *See Fig. 26.* Ensure voltage pulses 4 times per speedometer shaft revolution. If voltage is not as specified, replace VSS. If voltage is as specified, go to next step.

4) Disconnect ECM connector. Using DVOM, check continuity between chassis ground and specified ECM connector terminal. See VSS OUTPUT CIRCUIT IDENTIFICATION table. Move vehicle. Ensure continuity pulses on and off 4 times per tire revolution. If continuity is as specified: on Colt, Colt 200, Mirage and Summit, go to next step; on Eclipse, Stealth and 3000GT, conditions required to set code are not present at this time, test is complete; on all other models, go to step **7)**. If continuity is not as specified: on Colt, Colt 200, Mirage and Summit, go to step **7)**; on Eclipse, Pickup 2.4L (4WD) and 3.0L, Ram-50 2.4L (4WD) and 3.0L, Stealth and 3000GT, go to step **6)**; on all other models, go to next step.

VSS OUTPUT CIRCUIT IDENTIFICATION

Application	Terminal No.
Eclipse, Montero, Pickup & Ram-50	118
All Other Models	66

5) With ECM connector disconnected, disconnect VSS connector. Ground ECM connector VSS output terminal. See VSS OUTPUT CIRCUIT IDENTIFICATION table. Using DVOM, check for continuity between chassis ground and specified VSS connector terminal. See ECM TO VSS CIRCUIT IDENTIFICATION table. If continuity does not exist, repair wiring harness as necessary. If continuity exists, go to next step.

ECM TO VSS CIRCUIT IDENTIFICATION

Application	Terminal No.
Colt, Colt 200, Mirage & Summit	43
Montero, Pickup 2.4L (RWD) & Ram-50 2.4L (RWD)	1
All Other Models	9

6) With VSS connector disconnected, check for continuity between chassis ground and specified VSS connector terminal. See VSS GROUND CIRCUIT IDENTIFICATION table. If continuity does not exist, repair wiring harness as necessary. If continuity exists, go to next step.

VSS GROUND CIRCUIT IDENTIFICATION

Application	Terminal No.
Colt, Colt 200, Mirage & Summit	12
Colt Vista, Expo & Summit Wagon	5
Diamante & Montero	13
Eclipse	2
Galant	16
Pickup & Ram-50	10
Stealth & 3000GT	102

7) With VSS connector and ECM connector disconnected, turn ignition switch to ON position. Using DVOM, check for voltage between chassis ground and specified VSS connector terminal. See VSS VOLTAGE FEED CIRCUIT IDENTIFICATION table. If voltage is not 4.5-4.9 volts, replace ECM. If voltage is as specified, condition required to set fault is not present at this time. Test is complete. Intermittent problem may exist. See TROUBLE SHOOTING – NO CODES article.

VSS VOLTAGE FEED CIRCUIT IDENTIFICATION

Application	Terminal No.
Colt, Colt 200, Mirage & Summit	43
Eclipse	59
Montero, Pickup & Ram-50	1
Stealth & 3000GT	109
All Other Models	9

CODE 25: BAROMETRIC PRESSURE SENSOR

NOTE: Barometric (BARO) pressure sensor is built into airflow sensor. For code 25 test purposes, the airflow sensor will be referred to as the BARO pressure sensor. For component terminal identification, see AIRFLOW SENSOR under TERMINAL IDENTIFICATION. For wiring diagrams, see WIRING DIAGRAMS article.

1) Manufacturer does not provide component testing procedure without scan tester. Turn ignition switch to ON position. Using scan tester, read sensor pressure. See BARO PRESSURE SENSOR SPECIFICATIONS table. If pressure is not as specified, replace BARO pressure sensor. If pressure is as specified, go to next step.

BARO PRESSURE SENSOR SPECIFICATIONS

Altitude Ft. (M)	Pressure In. Hg
0 (0)	29.92
1969 (600)	27.95
3937 (1200)	25.98
5906 (1800)	24.02

2) Disconnect BARO pressure sensor connector. Using DVOM, check for continuity between chassis ground and specified BARO pressure sensor connector terminal. See BARO PRESSURE SENSOR GROUND CIRCUIT IDENTIFICATION table. If continuity does not exist, repair wiring harness as necessary. If continuity exists, go to next step.

1993 ENGINE PERFORMANCE
Self-Diagnostics (Cont.)

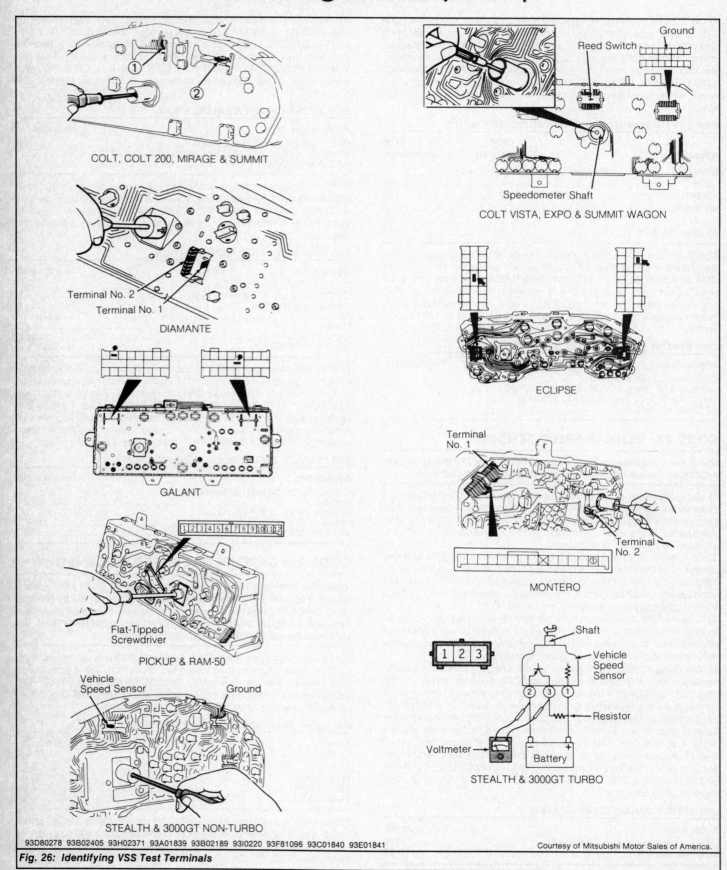

COLT, COLT 200, MIRAGE & SUMMIT

COLT VISTA, EXPO & SUMMIT WAGON

Terminal No. 2
Terminal No. 1
DIAMANTE

ECLIPSE

GALANT

MONTERO

Flat-Tipped
Screwdriver
PICKUP & RAM-50

Vehicle
Speed Sensor   Ground

STEALTH & 3000GT NON-TURBO

STEALTH & 3000GT TURBO

93D80278 93B02405 93H02371 93A01839 93B02189 93I0220 93F81096 93C01840 93E01841

Courtesy of Mitsubishi Motor Sales of America.

Fig. 26: Identifying VSS Test Terminals

BARO PRESSURE SENSOR GROUND CIRCUIT IDENTIFICATION

Application	Terminal No.
Eclipse	
Non-Turbo	4
Turbo	6
Galant	4
All Other Models	5

3) On Eclipse, Pickup 2.4L (4WD) and 3.0L, Ram-50 2.4L (4WD) and 3.0L, Stealth and 3000GT, go to step **5)**. On all other models, with BARO pressure sensor disconnected, disconnect ECM connector. Check for continuity between specified ECM connector terminal and BARO pressure sensor connector terminal. See BARO PRESSURE SENSOR TO ECM CIRCUIT IDENTIFICATION table. If continuity does not exist, repair wiring harness as necessary. If continuity exists, go to next step.

BARO PRESSURE SENSOR TO ECM CIRCUIT IDENTIFICATION

Application	BARO Terminal No.	ECM Terminal No.
Diamante	1	61
	2	65
Galant	5	65
Montero	1	23
	2	16
All Other Models	2	65

4) With BARO pressure sensor connector and ECM connector disconnected, turn ignition switch to ON position. Check for voltage between chassis ground and BARO pressure sensor connector terminal No. 1 (terminal No. 3 on Galant). If voltage is not 4.8-5.2 volts, replace ECM. If voltage is as specified, condition required to set code is not present at this time. Test is complete. Intermittent problem may exist. See TROUBLE SHOOTING – NO CODES article.

5) With BARO pressure sensor connector disconnected, turn ignition switch to ON position. Check for voltage between chassis ground and specified BARO pressure sensor connector terminal. See BARO PRESSURE SENSOR POWER SUPPLY CIRCUIT IDENTIFICATION table. If voltage is not 4.8-5.2 volts, repair wiring harness as necessary. If voltage is as specified, go to next step.

BARO PRESSURE SENSOR POWER SUPPLY CIRCUIT IDENTIFICATION

Application	Terminal No.
Eclipse	
Non-Turbo	3
Turbo	4
All Other Models	1

6) With BARO pressure sensor connector and ECM connector disconnected, ground ECM connector terminal No. 16 (terminal No. 65 on Stealth and 3000GT). Using DVOM, check for continuity between chassis ground and specified BARO pressure sensor connector terminal. See ECM TO BARO PRESSURE SENSOR GROUND CIRCUIT IDENTIFICATION table. If continuity does not exist, repair wiring harness as necessary. If continuity exists, condition required to set code is not present at this time. Test is complete. Intermittent problem may exist. See TROUBLE SHOOTING – NO CODES article.

ECM TO BARO PRESSURE SENSOR GROUND CIRCUIT IDENTIFICATION

Application	Terminal No.
Eclipse	
Non-Turbo	3
Turbo	4
Pickup, Ram-50, Stealth & 3000GT	1

CODE 31: KNOCK SENSOR

NOTE: For component terminal identification, see TERMINAL IDENTIFICATION. For wiring diagrams, see WIRING DIAGRAMS article.

1) Manufacturer does not provide component testing procedure using scan tester. On Diamante, Stealth and 3000GT, go to step **4)**. On Eclipse 2.0L turbo, manufacturer provides testing procedure using engine analyzer with oscilloscope capability. Refer to manufacturer's operation manual for instructions in use of oscilloscope. Go to next step.

2) Connect oscilloscope special patterns pickup between ECM and ECM connector at ECM terminal No. 9. Start engine. Accelerate engine to 5000 RPM. Compare oscilloscope wave pattern with known-good wave pattern. *See Fig. 27.* If wave pattern is abnormal, replace knock sensor. If wave pattern is normal, go to next step.

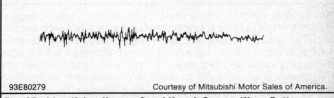

93E80279   Courtesy of Mitsubishi Motor Sales of America.

Fig. 27: Identifying Known-Good Knock Sensor Wave Pattern

3) Using DVOM, check voltage between chassis ground and knock sensor connector terminal No. 1. If voltage is not 8.0-11.0 volts, repair wiring harness as necessary. If voltage is as specified, go to step **5)**.

4) Disconnect knock sensor connector and ECM connector. Ground ECM connector terminal No. 58. Using DVOM, check continuity between chassis ground and knock sensor connector terminal No. 1. If continuity does not exist, repair wiring harness as necessary. If continuity exists, go to next step.

5) With knock sensor connector disconnected, check for continuity between chassis ground and knock sensor connector terminal No. 2. If continuity does not exist, repair wiring harness as necessary. If continuity exists, condition required to set code is not present at this time. Test is complete.

CODE 32: MAP SENSOR

NOTE: For component terminal identification, see TERMINAL IDENTIFICATION. For wiring diagrams, see WIRING DIAGRAMS article.

1) Manufacturer does not provide component testing procedure without scan tester. Ensure coolant temperature is 176-203°F (80-95°C). Ensure all accessories are off, transmission is in Neutral, and ignition switch is in ON position. Using scan tester, read intake manifold plenum pressure. See INTAKE MANIFOLD PLENUM PRESSURE SPECIFICATIONS table. If conditions are not as specified, replace Manifold Absolute Pressure (MAP) sensor. If conditions are as specified, go to next step.

INTAKE MANIFOLD PLENUM PRESSURE SPECIFICATIONS

Engine State	Altitude Ft. (M)	Pressure In. Hg
Off	0 (0)	29.92
	1969 (600)	27.95
	3937 (1200)	25.98
	5906 (1800)	24.02
Idle (750 RPM)		6.70-10.62
Suddenly Raced		[1]

[1] – Pressure should increase.

2) Disconnect MAP sensor connector. Using DVOM, check continuity between chassis ground and MAP sensor connector terminal No. 3. If continuity does not exist, repair wiring harness as necessary. If continuity exists, go to next step.

3) With MAP sensor connector disconnected, disconnect ECM connector. Ground ECM connector terminal No. 70. Using DVOM, check continuity between chassis ground and MAP sensor connector terminal No. 2. If continuity does not exist, repair wiring harness as necessary. If continuity exists, go to next step.

4) With MAP sensor connector and ECM connector disconnected, turn ignition switch to ON position. Check voltage between chassis ground and MAP sensor connector terminal No. 1. If 4.8-5.2 volts do not exist, replace ECM. If voltage is as specified, condition required to set code is not present at this time. Test is complete. Intermittent problem may exist. See TROUBLE SHOOTING – NO CODES article.

CODE 36: IGNITION TIMING ADJUSTMENT SIGNAL

NOTE: *For component terminal identification, see TERMINAL IDENTIFICATION. For wiring diagrams, see WIRING DIAGRAMS article.*

Turn ignition switch to ON position. Using DVOM, check voltage at ignition timing adjustment terminal (located at firewall) with terminal grounded and ungrounded. With terminal grounded, voltage should be 0-1.0 volt. With terminal ungrounded, voltage should be 4.0-5.5 volts. If voltage is not as specified, repair ignition timing adjustment terminal wiring harness or connector as necessary. If voltage is as specified, replace ECM.

CODE 39: OXYGEN (O_2) SENSOR

NOTE: *For component terminal identification, see TERMINAL IDENTIFICATION. For wiring diagrams, see WIRING DIAGRAMS article.*

1) If using scan tester, go to step **3)**. Disconnect O_2 sensor connector. Install Test Harness (MB998464) between O_2 sensor and O_2 sensor connector. Using DVOM, check resistance between O_2 sensor connector terminals No. 1 and 3. O_2 sensor resistance should be 20 ohms at 68°F (20°C). If resistance is not as specified, replace O_2 sensor. If resistance is as specified, go to next step.
2) Start and warm engine to operating temperature. Using jumper wires, ground O_2 sensor connector terminal No. 3 and apply 12 volts to O_2 sensor connector terminal No. 1. Using DVOM, check voltage between O_2 sensor connector terminals No. 2 and 4 while repeatedly racing engine. If voltage is not .6-1.0 volt, replace O_2 sensor. If voltage is as specified, go to step **5)**.
3) Start and warm engine to operating temperature. Using scan tester, read O_2 sensor voltage. While monitoring scan tester, accelerate to 4000 RPM. Suddenly decelerate. Scan tester should read .2 volt or less. Suddenly accelerate. Scan tester should read .6-1.0 volt. If voltage is not as specified, replace O_2 sensor. If voltage is as specified, go to next step.
4) While monitoring scan tester, accelerate to 2000 RPM and decelerate to 700 RPM (idle). Scan tester should switch between .6-1.0 volt and .4 volt or less. If voltage is not as specified, replace O_2 sensor. If voltage is as specified, go to next step.
5) With O_2 sensor connector disconnected, turn ignition switch to ON position. Using DVOM, check voltage between chassis ground and O_2 sensor connector terminal No. 1. If system voltage does not exist, repair wiring harness as necessary. If system voltage exists, go to next step.
6) Using DVOM, check for continuity between O_2 sensor connector terminal No. 4 and ECM connector terminal No. 56. If continuity does not exist, repair wiring harness as necessary. If continuity exists, go to next step.
7) With O_2 sensor connector disconnected, check for continuity between chassis ground O_2 sensor connector terminal No. 2. If continuity does not exist, repair wiring harness as necessary. If continuity exists, condition required to set fault is not present at this time. Test is complete. Intermittent problem may exist. See TROUBLE SHOOTING – NO CODES article.

CODE 41: FUEL INJECTOR

NOTE: *For component terminal identification, see TERMINAL IDENTIFICATION. For wiring diagrams, see WIRING DIAGRAMS article.*

1) Using a stethoscope or long-bladed screwdriver, listen for clicking sound from each injector while engine is running or being cranked. If no sound is heard from injector(s), check injector connections. If connections are not okay, repair connections as necessary. If connections are okay, go to next step.
2) Disconnect injector connector. Using DVOM, check resistance across injector terminals. If resistance is not 13-16 ohms, replace injector. If resistance is as specified, go to next step.
3) Using scan tester, read injector drive time while cranking engine. See INJECTOR CRANKING DRIVE TIME SPECIFICATIONS table. Go to next step.

INJECTOR CRANKING DRIVE TIME SPECIFICATIONS

Coolant Temperature	Drive Time
32°F (0°C)	
Colt, Colt Vista, Colt 200, Diamante DOHC, Eclipse Non-Turbo, Expo, Galant, Mirage, Pickup 2.4L, Ram-50 2.4L, Summit & Summit Wagon	17-20 ms
Diamante SOHC, Montero, Pickup 3.0L, Ram-50 3.0L, Stealth Non-Turbo & 3000GT Non-Turbo	14-16 ms
Eclipse Turbo	24 ms
Stealth Turbo & 3000GT Turbo	9 ms
68°F (20°C)	
Except 1.5L Models, Diamante DOHC, Eclipse Turbo, Stealth DOHC & 3000GT	38-41 ms
All 1.5L Models	35 ms
Diamante DOHC, Stealth DOHC Non-Turbo & 3000GT Non-Turbo	45-46 ms
Eclipse Turbo	12 ms
Stealth Turbo & 3000GT Turbo	28 ms
176°F (80°C)	
Except Diamante DOHC, Eclipse Turbo, Stealth SOHC & Turbo & 3000GT Turbo	9-10 ms
Diamante DOHC	11 ms
Eclipse Turbo	4-5 ms
Stealth SOHC	8 ms
Stealth Turbo & 3000GT Turbo	6 ms

4) Ensure coolant temperature is at 176-205°F (80-95°C), all accessories are off and transaxle is in Neutral position. Using scan tester, read injector drive time under specified engine conditions. See INJECTOR OPERATING DRIVE TIME SPECIFICATIONS table. Go to next step.

INJECTOR OPERATING DRIVE TIME SPECIFICATIONS

Engine State	Drive Time
750 RPM	
All 1.5L Models	1.7-2.9 ms
All 1.8L Models	2.5-3.7 ms
Colt Vista 2.4L, Expo 2.4L & Summit Wagon 2.4L	2.0-3.2 ms
Diamante, Stealth Non-Turbo & 3000GT Non-Turbo	2.3-3.5 ms
Eclipse 2.0L	[1]
Galant	2.2-3.4 ms
Montero	2.4-3.6
Pickup 2.4L & Ram-50 2.4L	[2]
Stealth Turbo	1.6-3.8 ms
2000 RPM	
All 1.5L Models	1.5-2.7 ms
Colt Vista 2.4L, Expo 2.4L & Summit Wagon 2.4L	1.8-3.0 ms
Eclipse	[3]
Galant	1.7-2.9 ms
Montero	2.3-3.5
Pickup 3.0L & Ram-50 3.0L	2.6-3.1 ms
Stealth Turbo & 3000GT Turbo	1.4-2.6 ms
All Other Models	2.0-3.3 ms
Suddenly Accelerated	
All Models	[4]

[1] – On non-turbo model, drive time is 2.4-3.2 ms. On turbo model, drive time is 1.6-2.2 ms.
[2] – On 2.4L, drive time is 3.0-4.0 ms. On 3.0L, drive time is 2.7-3.2 ms.
[3] – On 1.8L, drive time is 2.3-3.9 ms. On 2.0L non-turbo, drive time is 1.9-2.7 ms. On 2.0L turbo, drive time is 1.4-2.2 ms.
[4] – Drive time should increase.

5) Allow engine to idle after warm up. Using scan tester, shut off injectors in sequence. Idle should change when good injectors are shut off. If idle state does not change, check injector connection, spark plug and cable, and cylinder compression. If conditions are not as specified in preceding steps, go to next step.

6) On Eclipse, Pickup 2.4L (4WD) and 3.0L, Ram-50 2.4L (4WD) and 3.0L, Stealth and 3000GT, go to step 8). On all other models, disconnect MPI relay connector and injector connector at faulty injector. Using DVOM, check for continuity between specified MPI relay connector terminal and injector connector terminal. See MPI TO FUEL INJECTOR HARNESS TERMINAL IDENTIFICATION table. If continuity does not exist, repair wiring harness as necessary. If continuity exists, go to next step.

MPI TO FUEL INJECTOR HARNESS TERMINAL IDENTIFICATION

Application	MPI Terminal No.	Fuel Injector Terminal No.
Colt, Colt 200, Mirage & Summit	2	2
Diamante & Montero	5	1
All Other Models	2	1

7) Using a DVOM, check for continuity between injector connector terminal No. 2 (terminal No. 5 for No. 4 injector or terminal No. 6 for No. 6 injector on Diamante DOHC, or terminal No. 3 for No. 5 injector or terminal No. 4 for No. 6 injector on Diamante SOHC), and specified ECM connector terminal. See INJECTOR TO ECM CIRCUIT IDENTIFICATION table. If continuity does not exist, repair wiring harness as necessary. If continuity exists, condition required to set code is not present at this time. Intermittent problem may exist. See TROUBLE SHOOTING – NO CODES article.

INJECTOR TO ECM CIRCUIT IDENTIFICATION

Application	Injector No.	ECM Terminal No.
Diamante	1	1
	2	14
	3	2
	4	15
	5	3
	6	16
Montero	1	51
	2	52
	3	60
	4	61
	5	105
	6	109
All Other Models	1	1
	2	14
	3	2
	4	15

8) On Eclipse 2.0L, Stealth and 3000GT, go to step 10). Disconnect injector connector at faulty injector. Turn ignition switch to ON position. Using DVOM, check for voltage between chassis ground and injector connector terminal No. 1 (terminal No. 2 on Pickup 3.0L and Ram-50 3.0L). If battery voltage does not exist, repair wiring harness as necessary. If battery voltage exists, go to next step.

9) With injector connector disconnected, disconnect ECM connector. Check for continuity between injector connector terminal No. 2 and ECM connector terminal No. 51 for injector No. 1, No. 52 for injector No. 2, No. 60 for injector No. 3, or No. 61 for injector No. 4 (ECM connector terminal No. 105 for injector No. 5 or terminal No. 109 for injector No. 6 on Pickup 3.0L and Ram-50 3.0L). If continuity does not exist, repair wiring harness as necessary. If continuity exists, condition required to set code is not present at this time. Test is complete. Intermittent problem may exist. See TROUBLE SHOOTING – NO CODES article.

10) On Stealth and 3000GT, go to step 15). Turn ignition switch to ON position. With MPI relay connector connected, check for voltage between chassis ground and MPI relay connector terminals No. 4 and 5. If battery voltage does not exist, check MPI relay. If battery voltage exists: on turbo models, go to next step; on non-turbo models, go to step 13).

11) Disconnect MPI relay resistor connector. Turn ignition switch to ON position. Check for voltage between chassis ground and relay resistor connector terminal No. 3. If battery voltage does not exist,

repair wiring harness between MPI relay and relay resistor. If battery voltage exists, go to next step.

12) With relay resistor connector disconnected and injector connector connected, check resistance between relay resistor terminals No. 3 and 1 for injector No. 1, No. 3 and 4 for injector No. 2, No. 3 and 5 for injector No. 3, or No. 3 and 6 for injector No. 4. If resistance is not 5.5-6.5 ohms at 68°F (20°C), replace relay resistor. If resistance is as specified, go to next step.

13) On turbo and non-turbo models, disconnect injector connector at faulty injector. Using DVOM, check voltage between chassis ground and injector connector terminal No. 1 (non-turbo) or injector connector terminal No. 2 (turbo). If battery voltage does not exist, repair wiring harness as necessary. If battery voltage exists, go to next step.

14) With injector connector disconnected, disconnect ECM connector. Ground ECM connector terminal No. 51 for injector No.1, No. 52 for injector No. 2, No. 60 for injector No. 3, or No. 61 for injector No. 4. Check for continuity between chassis ground and injector connector terminal No. 1 (non-turbo) or No. 2 (turbo). If continuity does not exist, repair wiring harness as necessary. If continuity exists, condition required to set code is not present at this time. Test is complete. Intermittent problem may exist. See TROUBLE SHOOTING – NO CODES article.

15) Disconnect MPI relay resistor connector. Turn ignition switch to ON position. Using DVOM, check for voltage between chassis ground and resistor connector terminal No. 2. See Fig. 28. If battery voltage does not exist, repair wiring harness as necessary between MPI relay resistor connector and MPI relay. If battery voltage exists, reconnect MPI relay resistor connector. Go to next step.

VIEWED FROM HARNESS SIDE

93H80280   Courtesy of Mitsubishi Motor Sales of America

Fig. 28: Identifying MPI Relay Resistor Terminals

16) If faulty injector is on rear injector bank, go to next step. Disconnect injector connector at faulty front injector. Turn ignition switch to ON position. Using DVOM, check voltage between chassis ground and injector connector terminal No. 1. If battery voltage does not exist, repair wiring harness as necessary between injector connector and MPI relay. If voltage exists, go to step 18).

17) Disconnect rear bank injector connector. Using DVOM, check voltage between chassis ground and injector connector terminal No. 1. If battery voltage does not exist, repair wiring harness as necessary between injector connector and MPI relay. If voltage exists, go to step 19).

18) With injector connector disconnected, disconnect ECM connector. Ground ECM connector terminal No. 1 for injector No. 1, No. 2 for injector No. 3, or No. 3 for injector No. 5. Using DVOM, check for continuity between chassis ground and injector connector terminal No. 2. If continuity does not exist, repair wiring harness as necessary between appropriate injector connector and ECM connector terminal. If continuity exists, condition required to set code is not present at this time. Test is complete. Intermittent problem may exist. See TROUBLE SHOOTING – NO CODES article.

19) With rear bank injector connector disconnected, disconnect ECM connector. Ground ECM connector terminal No. 14 for injector No. 2, No. 15 for injector No. 4, or No. 16 for injector No. 6. Using DVOM, check for continuity between chassis ground and rear bank injector connector terminal No. 2 for injector No. 2, No. 3 for injector No. 4, or No. 4 for injector No. 6. If continuity does not exist, repair wiring harness between rear bank injector connector and ECM connector. If continuity exists, condition required to set code is not present at this time. Test is complete. Intermittent problem may exist. See TROUBLE SHOOTING – NO CODES article.

DETONATION OR KNOCKING

- Check airflow sensor.
- Check for cooling system problems.
- Check fuel quality.
- Check intake air temperature sensor.
- Check barometric pressure sensor.
- Check ignition coil.
- Check power transistor.
- Check for EGR system malfunction.

POOR FUEL MILEAGE

- Check intake air temperature sensor.
- Check engine coolant temperature sensor.
- Check barometric pressure sensor.
- Check ignition switch.
- Check idle position switch.
- Check throttle position sensor.
- Check TDC sensor.
- Check crankshaft position sensor.
- Check power steering oil pressure switch.
- Check A/C switch (if applicable).
- Check inhibitor switch (A/T).
- Check oxygen sensor.
- Check airflow sensor.
- Check motor position sensor (if applicable).
- Check fuel pressure.
- Check for MPI system malfunction.
- Check for stepper motor malfunction.
- Check for fuel injector malfunction.
- Check for power transistor malfunction.

INTERMITTENTS

INTERMITTENT PROBLEM DIAGNOSIS

Intermittent fault testing requires duplicating circuit or component failure to identify problem. These procedures may lead to computer setting a fault code (on some systems) which may help in diagnosis.

If problem vehicle does not produce fault codes, monitor voltage or resistance values using a DVOM while attempting to reproduce conditions causing intermittent fault. A status change on DVOM indicates a fault has been located.

Use a DVOM to pinpoint faults. When monitoring voltage, ensure ignition switch is in ON position or engine is running. Ensure ignition switch is in OFF position or negative battery cable is disconnected when monitoring circuit resistance. Status changes on DVOM during test procedures indicate area of fault.

TEST PROCEDURES

Intermittent Simulation – To reproduce conditions creating an intermittent fault, use following methods:
- Lightly vibrate component.
- Heat component.
- Wiggle or bend wiring harness.
- Spray component with water mist.
- Remove/apply vacuum source.

Monitor circuit/component voltage or resistance while simulating intermittent. If engine is running, monitor for self-diagnostic codes. Use test results to identify a faulty component or circuit.

Chrysler Corp.: Colt, Colt Vista, Colt 200, Ram-50, Stealth, Summit, Summit Wagon
Mitsubishi: Diamante, Eclipse, Expo, Galant, Mirage, Montero, Pickup, Precis, 3000GT

INTRODUCTION

NOTE: Testing individual components does not isolate shorts or opens. Perform all voltage tests using a Digital Volt-Ohmmeter (DVOM) with minimum 10-megohm input impedance, unless stated otherwise in test procedure. Use ohmmeter to isolate wiring harness shorts or opens.

Before testing separate components or systems, perform procedures in BASIC DIAGNOSTIC PROCEDURES article. Since many computer-controlled and monitored components set a trouble code if they malfunction, also perform procedures in SELF-DIAGNOSTICS article.

AIR INDUCTION SYSTEMS

TURBOCHARGED

Turbocharger Pressure Check – 1) Disconnect turbocharger pressure control hose at wastegate solenoid valve, and plug nipple. Attach pressure gauge to hose. Drive vehicle and accelerate engine, in 2nd gear, to 3500 RPM or greater. Measure turbocharger pressure when pressure gauge stabilizes. See TURBOCHARGER PRESSURE SPECIFICATIONS table.
2) If pressure gauge reading is more than specified, check wastegate actuator. See WASTEGATE ACTUATOR TEST. Replace wastegate actuator as required. If pressure gauge reading is less than specified, check for malfunctioning wastegate valve, turbocharger pressure leaks and faulty turbocharger.

TURBOCHARGER PRESSURE SPECIFICATIONS

Application	Pressure psi (kg/cm²)
Eclipse	
A/T	5.4-10.0 (37-68)
M/T	6.0-11.0 (41-78)
Stealth & 3000GT	2.9-8.7 (20-60)

Air By-Pass Valve – Remove air by-pass valve. Valve is mounted to intake air duct between air-to-air intercooler and intake plenum. Apply vacuum to diaphragm of vacuum valve. Valve should begin opening at approximately 7.7 in. Hg (Eclipse) or 16 in. Hg (Stealth and 3000GT). Observe operation of valve through by-pass opening.
Wastegate Actuator Test – Actuator is mounted on turbocharger. Apply vacuum to wastegate actuator to ensure actuator rod moves. Ensure diaphragm holds vacuum. DO NOT apply excessive vacuum to wastegate actuator or attempt to adjust wastegate valve.
Wastegate Control Solenoid Valve Test – 1) On Eclipse, valve is mounted to top back section of air cleaner. On Stealth and 3000GT, valve is mounted to firewall beside EGR solenoid. Disconnect White vacuum hose at valve, and connect vacuum pump. Apply vacuum to valve to check leakage. Disconnect harness connector at valve. Connect 12 volts across valve terminals. Valve should open and release vacuum.
2) Disconnect harness connector at valve. Using external ohmmeter, check resistance between valve terminals. Solenoid valve resistance should be 36-44 ohms.
3) Connect DVOM between Red wire terminal of valve harness connector and ground. Turn ignition on. Battery voltage should be present. If battery voltage is not present, check for open in Red wire. Repair as necessary. If Red wire is okay, replace control relay. Control relay is located near ECM, behind radio, under console.
4) If battery voltage is present, disconnect ECM connector. Connect DVOM between Orange wire terminal of wastegate control solenoid valve and ground.
5) Ground ECM harness connector terminal No. 105 (Orange wire). Check for continuity in circuit between ECM harness connector and

wastegate control solenoid valve harness connector. If continuity does not exist, check and repair circuit as necessary. If continuity exists, replace wastegate control solenoid valve.

NON-TURBOCHARGED

NOTE: For diagnosis and testing information concerning VIC motor position sensor, see SELF-DIAGNOSTICS article.

Variable Induction Control (Diamante, Stealth & 3000GT) –
1) Disconnect Variable Induction Control (VIC) valve position sensor connector. Connect test harness (MB991348) between connector and control valve. Measure voltage between terminals No. 2 (Red/White wire) and No. 3 (Black wire). Measure voltage between terminals No. 3 and 4 (Black/Blue wire). Voltage should be 0-1 or 4.5-5.5 volts.
2) Disconnect VIC servo connector. Connect DVOM between both servo connector terminals to check servo coil resistance. Resistance should be 5-35 ohms. Replace servo if resistance is not as specified.
3) Apply 6 volts between both servo connector terminals. Ensure variable induction control servo shaft turns smoothly. Reverse voltage to servo connector terminals. Servo shaft should turn smoothly in opposite direction. If servo shaft does not function properly, replace air intake plenum assembly.
4) Check for continuity in circuit between control motor connector and ECM. Disconnect VIC motor connector and ECM connector. Connect DVOM to Green/Black wire of VIC connector and vehicle ground. Ground terminal No. 109 (Green/Black wire) of ECM. Check circuit for continuity. If continuity does not exist, repair as needed.
5) Connect DVOM to Green/White wire of VIC connector and vehicle ground. Ground terminal No. 110 (Green/White wire) of ECM. Check circuit for continuity. If continuity does not exist, repair as needed.

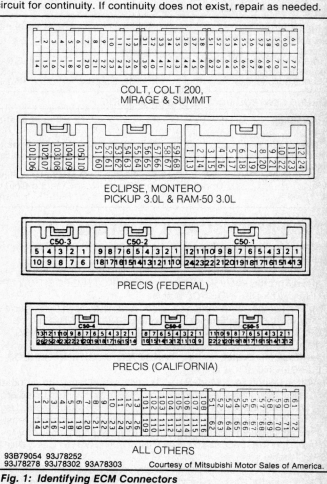

COLT, COLT 200,
MIRAGE & SUMMIT

ECLIPSE, MONTERO
PICKUP 3.0L & RAM-50 3.0L

PRECIS (FEDERAL)

PRECIS (CALIFORNIA)

ALL OTHERS

93B79054 93J78252
93J78278 93J78302 93A78303
Courtesy of Mitsubishi Motor Sales of America.

Fig. 1: Identifying ECM Connectors

COMPUTERIZED ENGINE CONTROLS

CONTROL UNIT

NOTE: For Engine Control Module (ECM) location, see ENGINE CONTROL MODULE (ECM) LOCATION table. To identify ECM power and ground circuits, see appropriate WIRING DIAGRAMS article.

Ground Circuits – 1) Turn ignition off. Using an ohmmeter, check continuity between chassis ground and ECM ground terminals. See GROUND TERMINAL IDENTIFICATION table. Ohmmeter should indicate zero ohms. If reading is not zero ohms, check and repair open circuit between ECM connector and ground.

2) Connect voltmeter negative lead to chassis ground. Connect positive lead to ECM ground terminals. See GROUND TERMINAL IDENTIFICATION table. *See Fig. 1.* With engine running, voltmeter should indicate less than one volt. If voltmeter reading is greater than one volt, check for open, corrosion or loose connection in ground circuit.

Power Circuits – Turn ignition on. Check for battery voltage on ECM power terminals. See POWER TERMINAL IDENTIFICATION table. If battery voltage is not present, check operation of MPI control relay. See RELAYS under MOTORS, RELAYS & SOLENOIDS.

GROUND TERMINAL IDENTIFICATION

Application	ECM Terminals
Eclipse, Montero, Pickup & Ram-50	101 & 106
Precis	
California (Connector C50-4)	1 & 14
Federal (Connector C50-3)	5 & 10
Except Eclipse, Montero, Pickup, Precis & Ram-50	13 & 26

POWER TERMINAL IDENTIFICATION

Application	ECM Terminals
Eclipse, Montero, Pickup & Ram-50	102 & 107
Precis	
California (Connector C50-4)	2 & 15
Federal (Connector C50-3)	4 & 9
Except Eclipse, Montero, Pickup, Precis & Ram-50	12 & 25

ENGINE CONTROL MODULE (ECM) LOCATION

Application	Location
Colt Vista, Expo & Summit Wagon	Under Right Side Of Dash, Near Speaker
Diamante	Behind Glove Box
Eclipse, Stealth & 3000GT	Forward Of Center Console Near Floor
Precis	Under Instrument Panel, Near Steering Column
All Others	Near Right Kick Panel

ENGINE SENSORS & SWITCHES

Barometric Pressure Sensor – Sensor is a part of airflow sensor assembly. See SELF-DIAGNOSTICS article.

Camshaft Position Sensor – See SELF-DIAGNOSTICS article.

Closed Throttle Position Switch – See THROTTLE POSITION SENSOR in SELF-DIAGNOSTICS article.

Coolant Temperature Sensor – See SELF-DIAGNOSTICS article.

Crankshaft Position Sensor – See SELF-DIAGNOSTICS article.

EGR Temperature Sensor (California) – See SELF-DIAGNOSTICS article.

Idle Position Switch – See THROTTLE POSITION SENSOR in SELF-DIAGNOSTICS article.

Inhibitor Switch (A/T Models) – 1) Switch is mounted to automatic transaxle, near shift lever mechanism. Ensure switch is adjusted properly. Switch output can be affected by improper adjustment. Using DVOM, measure resistance between selected terminals to ensure continuity between ignition switch and ECM when shift selector lever is in Park or Neutral position. See INHIBITOR SWITCH CONTINUITY CHECK table.

2) Using DVOM, measure power supply voltage of switch. Disconnect ECM connector. Disconnect inhibitor switch connector. Turn ignition switch to START position. Measure voltage between inhibitor switch

and vehicle ground. On Galant, Pickup 2.4L and Ram-50 2.4L, inhibitor switch wire color is Black/White; on all other models, inhibitor switch wire color is Black/Yellow. Supply voltage should be battery voltage. If voltage is within specification, go to step **3)**. If voltage is less than battery voltage, check and repair power supply circuit.

3) Using DVOM, measure inhibitor switch terminal input voltage. Connect ECM connector. Ensure inhibitor switch connector is disconnected. Turn ignition switch to ON position. Measure voltage between inhibitor switch and vehicle ground. Input voltage should be battery voltage. If voltage is within specification, go to step **4)**. If voltage is less than battery voltage, check and repair circuit.

4) Using DVOM, measure input voltage of ECM. Disconnect ECM connector. Connect inhibitor switch connector. Ensure shift selector lever is in "P" position. Turn ignition switch to ON position. Measure voltage between ECM connector and vehicle ground. See ECM TERMINAL IDENTIFICATION table. ECM input voltage should be 8 volts or greater. If voltage is within specification, system is okay. If voltage is less than 8 volts, replace ECM.

INHIBITOR SWITCH CONTINUITY CHECK

Application	[1] Wire Color	[2] Wire Color
Eclipse	Black/Yellow	Black/Yellow
Galant	Black/White	Black/Yellow
Montero, Pickup & Ram-50	Black/Yellow	Black/Blue
Precis	Black/Yellow	Black/Green
All Others	Black/Yellow	Black/Red

[1] – Ignition switch to inhibitor switch circuit.
[2] – Inhibitor switch to ECM circuit.

ECM TERMINAL IDENTIFICATION

Application	[1] Terminal Number
Eclipse, Montero, Ram-50 & Pickup	104
Precis	
California (Connector C50-5)	13
Federal (Connector C50-3)	2
Except Eclipse, Montero, Pickup, Precis & Ram-50	71

[1] – See Fig. 1.

Intake Air Temperature Sensor – See SELF-DIAGNOSTICS article.

Oxygen (O_2) Sensor – See SELF-DIAGNOSTICS article.

Power Steering Oil Pressure Switch – 1) Disconnect switch connector at pump. Using DVOM, check continuity between switch and vehicle ground. Continuity should not exist with wheels straight ahead and engine idling. Continuity should be present when wheels are turned.

2) Check continuity of circuit between switch and ECM. Disconnect power steering oil pressure switch connector and ECM connector. Connect jumper wire between ECM terminal and vehicle ground. See POWER STEERING PRESSURE SWITCH ECM TERMINAL NUMBER table. Using DVOM, check for continuity between switch harness connector and vehicle ground. Check and repair circuit if no continuity exists. Go to step **3)** if continuity exists.

3) Connect ECM connector. Turn ignition on. Using DVOM, measure voltage at switch harness connector. System is okay if battery voltage exists. Replace ECM if voltage does not exist.

POWER STEERING PRESSURE SWITCH ECM TERMINAL NUMBER

Application	[1] Terminal Number
Colt, Colt 200, Mirage & Summit	37
Colt Vista, Diamante, Expo, Galant, Stealth, Summit Wagon & 3000GT	107
Eclipse, Montero, Pickup & Ram-50	5
Precis	
California (Connector C50-6)	2
Federal (Connector C50-1)	8

[1] – See Fig. 1.

Throttle Position Sensor – See SELF-DIAGNOSTICS article.

Vehicle Speed Sensor – See SELF-DIAGNOSTICS article.

MOTORS, RELAYS & SOLENOIDS

MOTORS

IAC Motor – See IDLE CONTROL SYSTEM.

RELAYS

For MPI control relay location, see MPI CONTROL RELAY LOCATION table.

MPI CONTROL RELAY LOCATION

Application	Location
Colt Vista, Diamante, Expo, Galant & Summit Wagon	Behind glove box, next to ECM.
Montero	Under right corner of dash.
Pickup & Ram-50	Behind kick panel.
Precis	Behind glove box.
All Others	Behind center console.

MPI Control Relay (Colt, Colt Vista, Colt 200, Expo, Galant, Mirage, Pickup 2.4L, Ram-50 2.4L, Summit & Summit Wagon) – **1)** This step checks ignition switch supply voltage of control relay. Disconnect control relay connector. Turn ignition on. Using DVOM, measure voltage between terminal No. 8 of relay harness connector and vehicle ground. *See Fig. 2*. If voltage is battery voltage, go to step **2)**. If voltage is not battery voltage, check and repair circuit between ignition switch and control relay.

2) This step checks continuity of control relay ground circuit. Turn ignition off. Using DVOM, check continuity between control relay harness connector terminal No. 6 and vehicle ground. If continuity exists, go to step **3)**. If continuity does not exist, check and repair circuit between control relay and vehicle ground.

3) This step checks battery supply voltage of control relay. Using DVOM, measure voltage between terminal No. 4 of relay harness connector and vehicle ground. If voltage is battery voltage, go to step **4)**. If voltage is not battery voltage, check and repair circuit between battery and control relay.

4) This step checks continuity of circuit between control relay and ECM. Disconnect ECM connector. Using DVOM, check continuity between control relay harness connector terminal No. 3 and ECM connector terminals No. 12 and 25. *See Figs. 1 and 2*. If continuity exists, go to step **5)**. If continuity does not exist, check and repair circuits between control relay harness connector and ECM.

5) This step checks supply voltage to control relay actuator. Connect ECM and MPI control relay connectors. Using DVOM, backprobe control relay terminal No. 2. With engine cranking, voltage should be 8 volts or greater. Start engine and run at 2500 RPM or greater. If voltage is battery voltage, harness is okay. If voltage is not battery voltage, go to step **6)**.

6) If control relay tests okay in steps **6)** through **8)**, replace ECM. Removal of relay may assist in testing. Continuity should exist between terminals No. 5 and 7. Measure resistance between terminals No. 6 and 8. Continuity should exist in only one direction. Replace control relay if continuity is not as specified.

7) Connect 12-volt power source between relay terminals No. 5 and 7. Connect positive lead to terminal No. 7. With relay energized, battery voltage should exist between terminals No. 1 and 5. With power source removed, voltage should not exist.

8) Move 12-volt power source to relay terminals No. 6 and 8. Connect positive lead to terminal No. 8. With relay energized, continuity should exist between terminals No. 2 and 4 and between terminals No. 3 and 4. With power source removed, continuity should not exist. Replace control relay if measurements are not as specified.

MPI Control Relay (Diamante, Stealth & 3000GT) – **1)** This step checks ignition supply voltage to ECM. Disconnect ECM harness connector. Turn ignition on. Using DVOM, measure voltage between ECM harness connector terminal No. 62 and vehicle ground. *See Fig. 1*. If voltage measured is battery voltage, go to step **2)**. If voltage is not battery voltage, check and repair circuit between ignition switch and ECM harness connector.

COMPONENT CONNECTOR   HARNESS CONNECTOR

93C78453   Courtesy of Mitsubishi Motor Sales of America.

Fig. 2: Identifying MPI Control Relay Connectors (4-Cylinder Except Eclipse 2.0L & Precis)

2) This step checks battery supply voltage of control relay. Using DVOM, measure voltage between terminal No. 10 of relay harness connector and vehicle ground. *See Fig. 3*. If voltage measured is battery voltage, go to step **3)**. If voltage is not battery voltage, check and repair circuit between battery and control relay.

3) This step checks continuity of circuit between control relay and ECM. Disconnect ECM connector. Using DVOM, check continuity between control relay harness connector terminal No. 8 and ECM harness connector terminal No. 108. If continuity exists, go to step **4)**. If continuity does not exist, check and repair circuits between control relay harness connector and ECM.

4) This step checks continuity of circuit between control relay and ECM. Check continuity between control relay harness connector terminal No. 4 and ECM harness connector terminals No. 12 and 25. If continuity exists, go to step **5)**. If continuity does not exist, check and repair circuits between control relay harness connector and ECM.

5) This step checks supply voltage to control relay actuator. Connect ECM and MPI control relay connectors. Using DVOM, backprobe control relay terminal No. 5. With engine cranking, voltage should be 8 volts or greater. Start engine and run at 2500 RPM or greater. If voltage is battery voltage, harness is okay. If voltage is not battery voltage, go to step **6)**.

6) If control relay tests okay in steps **6)** through **8)**, replace ECM. Connect 12-volt power source between relay terminals No. 8 and 10. Connect positive lead to terminal No. 10. With relay energized, battery voltage should exist between terminals No. 4 and 8 and between terminals No. 5 and 8. With power source removed, voltage should not exist.

7) Move 12-volt power source to relay terminals No. 6 and 9. Connect positive lead to terminal No. 9. With relay energized, continuity should exist between terminals No. 2 and 3. With power source removed, continuity should not exist.

8) Move 12-volt power source to relay terminals No. 3 and 7. Connect positive lead to terminal No. 3. With relay energized, battery voltage should exist between terminals No. 2 and 7. With power source removed, voltage should not exist. Replace control relay if any measurements are not as specified.

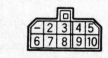

COMPONENT CONNECTOR   HARNESS CONNECTOR

93D78454   Courtesy of Mitsubishi Motor Sales of America.

Fig. 3: Identifying MPI Control Relay Connectors (All V6 Models & Eclipse 2.0L)

MPI Control Relay (Eclipse 1.8L) – **1)** This step checks ignition switch supply voltage of control relay. Disconnect control relay connector. Turn ignition on. Measure voltage between terminal No. 8 of relay harness connector and vehicle ground. *See Fig. 2*. If voltage is battery voltage, go to step **2)**. If voltage is not battery voltage, check and repair circuit between ignition switch and control relay.

2) This step checks continuity of control relay ground circuit. Turn ignition off. Using DVOM, check continuity between control relay harness connector terminal No. 6 and vehicle ground. If continuity exists, go to step **3)**. If continuity does not exist, check and repair circuit between control relay and vehicle ground.

3) This step checks battery supply voltage of control relay. Using DVOM, measure voltage between terminal No. 4 of relay harness connector and vehicle ground. If voltage is battery voltage, go to step **4)**. If voltage is not battery voltage, check and repair circuit between battery and control relay.

4) This step checks continuity of circuit between control relay and ECM. Disconnect ECM connector. Using DVOM, check continuity between control relay harness connector terminal No. 2 and ECM harness connector terminals No. 102 and 107. *See Figs. 1 and 2.*

5) If continuity exists, harness is okay. Go to step **6)**. If continuity does not exist, check and repair circuits between control relay harness connector and ECM.

6) Check continuity of control relay. Removal of relay may assist in testing. Measure resistance between terminals No. 2 and 5 and between terminals No. 3 and 5. Resistance should be about 95 ohms. Measure resistance between terminals No. 6 and 7. Resistance should be about 35 ohms. Measure resistance between terminals No. 6 and 8. Continuity should exist in only one direction. Replace control relay if measurements are not as specified.

7) Connect 12-volt power source between relay terminals No. 6 and 7. Connect positive lead to terminal No. 7. With relay energized, continuity should exist between terminals No. 1 and 4. With power source removed, continuity should not exist.

8) Move 12-volt power source to relay terminals No. 2 and 5. Connect positive lead to terminal No. 2. With relay energized, continuity should exist between terminals No. 1 and 4. With power source removed, continuity should not exist.

9) Move 12-volt power source to relay terminals No. 6 and 8. Connect positive lead to terminal No. 8. With relay energized, continuity should exist between terminals No. 2 and 4. With power source removed, continuity should not exist. Replace control relay if any measurements are not as specified.

MPI Control Relay (Eclipse 2.0L) – **1)** This step checks ignition supply voltage to ECM. Disconnect ECM harness connector. Turn ignition on. Using DVOM, measure voltage between ECM harness connector terminal No. 110 and vehicle ground. *See Fig. 1.* If voltage is battery voltage, go to step **2)**. If voltage is not battery voltage, check and repair circuit between ignition switch and ECM harness connector.

2) This step checks battery supply voltage of control relay. Using DVOM, measure voltage between terminal No. 10 of relay harness connector and vehicle ground. *See Fig. 3.* If voltage is battery voltage, go to step **3)**. If voltage is not battery voltage, check and repair circuit between battery and control relay.

3) This step checks continuity of circuit between control relay and ECM. Disconnect ECM connector. Using DVOM, check continuity between control relay harness connector terminal No. 8 and ECM connectors No. 63 and 66. If continuity exists, go to step **4)**. If continuity does not exist, check and repair circuits between control relay harness connector and ECM.

4) This step checks continuity of circuit between control relay and ECM. Check continuity between control relay harness connector terminal No. 4 and ECM harness connector terminals No. 102 and 107. If continuity exists, go to step **5)**. If continuity does not exist, check and repair circuits between control relay harness connector and ECM.

5) This step checks continuity of circuit between control relay and ECM. Disconnect ECM connector. Using DVOM, check continuity between control relay harness connector terminal No. 5 and ECM harness connector terminals No. 102 and 107. If continuity exists, harness is okay. Go to step **6)**. If continuity does not exist, check and repair circuits between control relay harness connector and ECM.

6) Connect 12-volt power source between relay terminals No. 8 and 10. Connect positive lead to terminal No. 10. With relay energized, battery voltage should exist between terminals No. 4 and 8 and between terminals No. 5 and 8. With power source removed, voltage should not exist.

7) Move 12-volt power source to relay terminals No. 6 and 9. Connect positive lead to terminal No. 9. With relay energized, continuity should exist between terminals No. 2 and 3. With power source removed, continuity should not exist.

8) Move 12-volt power source to relay terminals No. 3 and 7. Connect positive lead to terminal No. 3. With relay energized, battery voltage should exist between terminals No. 2 and 7. With power source removed, voltage should not exist. Replace control relay if any measurements are not as specified.

MPI Control Relay (Montero, Pickup 3.0L & Ram-50 3.0L) – **1)** This step checks ignition supply voltage to ECM. Disconnect ECM harness connector. Turn ignition on. Measure voltage between ECM harness connector terminal No. 110 and vehicle ground. *See Fig. 1.* If voltage is battery voltage, go to step **2)**. If voltage is not battery voltage, repair circuit between ignition switch and ECM harness connector.

2) This step checks battery supply voltage of control relay. Measure voltage between terminal No. 10 of relay harness connector and vehicle ground. *See Fig. 3.* If voltage is battery voltage, go to step **3)**. If voltage is not battery voltage, check and repair circuit between battery and control relay.

3) This step checks continuity of circuit between control relay and ECM. Disconnect ECM connector. Check continuity between control relay harness connector terminal No. 8 and ECM connectors No. 63 and 66. If continuity exists, go to step **4)**. If continuity does not exist, check and repair circuits between control relay harness connector and ECM.

4) This step checks continuity of circuit between control relay and ECM. Check continuity between control relay harness connector terminal No. 4 and ECM harness connector terminals No. 102 and 107. If continuity exists, go to step **5)**. If continuity does not exist, check and repair circuits between control relay harness connector and ECM.

5) Connect 12-volt power source between relay terminals No. 8 and 10. Connect positive lead to terminal No. 10. With relay energized, battery voltage should exist between terminals No. 4 and 8 and between terminals No. 5 and 8. With power source removed, voltage should not exist.

6) Move 12-volt power source to relay terminals No. 6 and 9. Connect positive lead to terminal No. 6. With relay energized, continuity should exist between terminals No. 2 and 3. With power source removed, continuity should not exist.

7) Move 12-volt power source to relay terminals No. 3 and 7. Connect positive lead to terminal No. 3. With relay energized, voltage should exist between terminals No. 2 and 7. With power source removed, voltage should not exist. Replace control relay if any measurements are not as specified.

MPI Control Relay (Precis) – **1)** This step checks ignition switch supply voltage of control relay. Disconnect control relay connector. Turn ignition on. Using DVOM, measure voltage between terminal No. 5 of relay harness connector and vehicle ground. *See Fig. 4.* If voltage is battery voltage, go to step **2)**. If voltage is not battery voltage, check and repair circuit between ignition switch and control relay.

2) This step checks continuity of control relay ground circuit. Turn ignition off. Using DVOM, check continuity between control relay harness connector terminal No. 7 and vehicle ground. If continuity exists, go to step **3)**. If continuity does not exist, check and repair circuit between control relay and vehicle ground.

3) This step checks battery supply voltage of control relay. Using DVOM, measure voltage between terminal No. 1 of relay harness connector and vehicle ground. If voltage is battery voltage, go to step **4)**. If voltage is not battery voltage, check and repair circuit between battery and control relay.

4) This step checks continuity of circuit between control relay and ECM. Disconnect ECM connector. Check continuity between control relay harness connector terminal No. 2 and ECM terminals No. 2 and 15 of connector C50-4 on California models or terminals No. 9 and 4 of connector C50-3 on Federal models. *See Figs. 1 and 4.*

5) If continuity exists, harness is okay. Go to step **6)**. If continuity does not exist, check and repair circuits between control relay harness connector and ECM.

6) This step checks continuity of control relay. Removal of relay may assist in testing. Measure resistance between terminals No. 2 and 8 and between terminals No. 3 and 8. Resistance should be about 95 ohms. Measure resistance between terminals No. 6 and 7. Resistance should be about 35 ohms. Measure resistance between terminals

No. 5 and 7. Continuity should exist in only one direction. Replace control relay if any measurements are not as specified.

7) Connect 12-volt power source between relay terminals No. 6 and 7. Connect positive lead to terminal No. 6. With relay energized, continuity should exist between terminals No. 1 and 4. With power source removed, continuity should not exist.

8) Move 12-volt power source to relay terminals No. 5 and 7. Connect positive lead to terminal No. 5. With relay energized, continuity should exist between terminals No. 1 and 3. With power source removed, continuity should not exist. Replace control relay if any measurements are not as specified.

 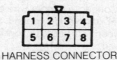

COMPONENT CONNECTOR   HARNESS CONNECTOR

93E78455   Courtesy of Mitsubishi Motor Sales of America.

Fig. 4: Identifying MPI Control Relay Connectors (Precis)

SOLENOIDS

Fuel Pressure Regulator Control Solenoid Valve (Turbo Models) – See FUEL DELIVERY under FUEL SYSTEM.

Wastegate Control Solenoid Valve – See TURBOCHARGED under AIR INDUCTION SYSTEMS.

FUEL SYSTEM

FUEL DELIVERY

NOTE: For fuel system pressure testing, see BASIC DIAGNOSTIC PROCEDURES article.

Fuel Pressure Regulator Control Solenoid Valve (Turbo Models) –
1) Label and remove vacuum hoses from solenoid valve. Disconnect wiring harness. Connect vacuum pump to nipple where Black vacuum hose was connected. Leave pump connected throughout procedure.
2) Apply vacuum and ensure valve leaks. Plug nipple where Blue-striped hose was connected. Apply vacuum and ensure vacuum holds. Remove plug from Blue-striped hose nipple. Apply battery voltage across valve terminals. Apply vacuum and ensure vacuum holds.
3) Using an ohmmeter, check resistance across terminals of solenoid. Resistance should be 36-46 ohms at 68°F (20°C). If resistance is not within specification, replace valve.
4) If resistance is within specification, disconnect solenoid connector. Turn ignition on. Using DVOM, measure voltage between harness connector terminal (Red wire) and vehicle ground. If voltage is battery voltage, go to step **5)**. If voltage is not battery voltage, check and repair circuit between MPI control relay and solenoid.
5) This step checks continuity of circuit between solenoid and ECM. Disconnect ECM connector. Connect jumper wire between ECM terminal No. 7 (No. 57 on Eclipse) and vehicle ground. *See Fig. 1.* Using DVOM, measure continuity between solenoid harness connector terminal Blue/Red wire (White wire on Eclipse) and vehicle ground. If continuity exists, system is okay. If continuity does not exist, check and repair circuit between solenoid and ECM.

FUEL CONTROL

Fuel Injectors – See SELF-DIAGNOSTICS article.

IDLE CONTROL SYSTEM

ELECTRICAL LOAD SWITCH

Diamante DOHC, Stealth DOHC & 3000GT DOHC – **1)** Disconnect ECM connector. Using DVOM, measure input voltage between terminal No. 24 (Red/Green wire) and vehicle ground. Turn headlights on. Measure voltage. Turn headlights off.

2) Turn defogger on. Measure voltage. Turn defogger off. Depress brake pedal. Measure voltage. Release brake pedal. If any measurement is less than battery voltage, check and repair malfunctioning circuit.

IDLE AIR CONTROL (IAC) MOTOR

CAUTION: DO NOT apply more than 6 volts to IAC motor.

NOTE: For diagnosis and testing information concerning IAC motor position sensor, see SELF-DIAGNOSTICS article.

Colt, Colt Vista, Colt 200, Eclipse 1.8L, Expo, Galant, Mirage, Pickup 2.4L, Ram-50 2.4L, Summit & Summit Wagon – **1)** Using a stethoscope, listen for operating sound of IAC motor when ignition switch is placed in ON position. If no operating sound can be heard, proceed with following tests.
2) This step checks for continuity between IAC motor and ECM. Disconnect IAC motor harness connector and ECM harness connector. Connect a jumper wire between ECM harness connector terminal No. 4 and vehicle ground. *See Fig. 1.* Using DVOM, check continuity between IAC motor connector terminal No. 5 and vehicle ground. *See Fig. 5.*
3) Move jumper wire to ECM harness connector terminal No. 17 and vehicle ground. Using DVOM, check continuity between IAC harness connector No. 6 and vehicle ground. If continuity does not exist, check and repair appropriate circuit. If continuity exists, go to step **4)**.
4) If preceding tests do not show any system or component malfunction and ECM is suspected, replace ECM and retest system.

COMPONENT CONNECTOR   HARNESS CONNECTOR

93G78473   Courtesy of Mitsubishi Motor Sales of America.

Fig. 5: Identifying IAC Motor Connectors (4-Cylinder Except Eclipse 2.0L)

NOTE: Procedures are provided by manufacturer for component testing using an engine analyzer with oscilloscope capability. Refer to manufacturer's operation manual for instructions in use of oscilloscope. Go to step 10) for test procedures using oscilloscope.

Diamante, Eclipse 2.0L, Montero, Pickup 3.0L, Ram-50 3.0L, Stealth & 3000GT – **1)** Using a stethoscope, listen for operating sound of IAC motor when ignition switch is placed in ON position. If no operating sound can be heard, proceed with following tests.
2) Disconnect IAC harness connector. Install Test Harness (MD998463-01) if necessary to aid testing. Using DVOM, measure resistance between IAC terminals No. 1 and 2 and between terminals No. 1 and 3. *See Fig. 6.* Resistance should be 28-33 ohms.

COMPONENT CONNECTOR   HARNESS CONNECTOR

93I78475   Courtesy of Mitsubishi Motor Sales of America.

Fig. 6: Identifying IAC Motor Connectors (All V6 Models & Eclipse 2.0L)

3) Measure resistance between terminals No. 4 and 5 and between terminals No. 5 and 6. Resistance should be 28-33 ohms. If resistance measurements are not within specification, replace IAC motor. Go to step **4)** if IAC motor is within specification.
4) Remove throttle body. See REMOVAL, OVERHAUL & INSTALLATION article. Remove stepper motor from throttle body. Connect Test Harness (MD998463-01) to IAC motor.

5) Hold IAC motor in hand. Place thumb on top of plunger. Connect positive lead of 6-volt power source to White and Green clips of test harness. Individually connect, then disconnect, negative lead of power source to Red and Black clips, Blue and Black clips, Blue and Yellow clips, and Red and Yellow clips. Finish by connecting negative lead to Red and Black clips again.

6) Connect negative lead to test leads in reverse sequence of step **5)**. Stepper motor should vibrate with each connection. Replace IAC motor if vibration is not felt with each connection.

7) Ensure MPI control relay is functioning properly. See RELAYS under MOTORS, RELAYS & SOLENOIDS. Disconnect IAC motor harness connector. Turn ignition on. Using DVOM, check for battery voltage between terminal No. 2 and vehicle ground and terminal No. 5 and vehicle ground. If voltage is not battery voltage, check and repair circuits between MPI control relay and IAC motor. If battery voltage exists, go to step **8)**.

8) This step checks for continuity between MPI control relay and IAC motor. Check for continuity between MPI control relay terminals No. 4 and 5 and IAC motor terminals No. 2 and 5. See Figs. 3 and 6. If continuity exists, go to step **9)**. If continuity does not exist, check and repair circuits.

9) This step checks for continuity between ECM and IAC motor. Disconnect ECM harness connector. Check continuity of specified circuits. See Figs. 1 and 6. See IAC TO ECM CIRCUIT CONTINUITY CHECK table. Check and repair any circuits without continuity.

IAC TO ECM CIRCUIT CONTINUITY CHECK

IAC Terminal Number	ECM Terminal Number
Eclipse 2.0L, Montero, Pickup & Ram-50	
1	58
3	59
4	68
6	67
Diamante, Stealth & 3000GT	
1	4
3	17
4	5
6	18

10) Connect ECM harness connector. Install harness connector and Test Harness (MB998463-01). Using engine analyzer with oscilloscope capability, connect special patterns probe to selected leads of test harness. Leads used are Red, Green, Black and Yellow clips.

11) Start engine, and allow it to idle. Connect special patterns probe to one test lead. Turn A/C on. When IAC motor operates to increase engine speed to compensate for A/C system, a waveform should be displayed. Conduct test with each remaining test lead and compare pattern to illustration. See Fig. 7.

12) If waveform is different, replace IAC motor. If all preceding tests do not show any system or component malfunction and ECM is suspected, replace ECM and retest system.

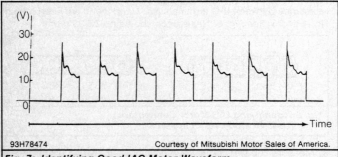

93H78474   Courtesy of Mitsubishi Motor Sales of America.

Fig. 7: Identifying Good IAC Motor Waveform

IDLE SPEED CONTROL MOTOR

NOTE: For diagnosis and testing information concerning ISC motor position sensor, see SELF-DIAGNOSTICS article.

Eclipse 1.8L – 1) Using a stethoscope, listen for operation of ISC motor when ignition switch is placed in ON position. If operation cannot be heard, proceed with following tests.

2) Disconnect ISC harness connector. Connect a 6-volt power source across ISC motor connectors. Check if motor operates. Reverse power source leads. Check if motor operates in opposite direction. Replace motor if it does not function properly.

3) Using DVOM, measure resistance between ISC motor connectors. Resistance should be 5-35 ohms. Replace motor if resistance is not within specification.

4) This step checks for continuity between ISC motor and ECM. Disconnect ISC motor harness connector and ECM harness connector. Connect a jumper wire between ECM harness connector terminal No. 58 and vehicle ground. See Fig. 1. Using DVOM, check continuity between ISC harness connector No. 1 (Blue/White wire) and vehicle ground.

5) Move jumper wire to ECM harness connector terminal No. 59 and vehicle ground. Using DVOM, check continuity between ISC harness connector No. 2 (Green/Black wire) and vehicle ground. If continuity does not exist, check and repair appropriate circuit. If continuity exists, go to step **6)**.

6) If preceding tests do not show any system or component malfunction and ECM is suspected, replace ECM and retest system.

Precis – 1) Using a stethoscope, listen for operation of ISC motor when ignition switch is placed in ON position. If operation cannot be heard, proceed with following tests.

2) Disconnect ISC harness connector. Connect a 6-volt power source across ISC motor connectors. Check if motor operates. Reverse power source leads and check if motor operates in opposite direction. Replace motor if does not function properly.

3) Using DVOM, measure resistance between ISC motor connectors. Resistance should be 5-70 ohms. Replace motor if resistance is not within specification.

4) This step checks for continuity between ISC motor and ECM. Disconnect ISC motor harness connector and ECM harness connector. Connect a jumper wire between selected ECM harness connector terminal and vehicle ground. See ECM TERMINAL SELECTION table. Using DVOM, check continuity between ISC harness connector No. 1 (Red wire) and vehicle ground.

5) Move jumper wire to selected ECM harness connector terminal and vehicle ground. See ECM TERMINAL SELECTION table. Using DVOM, check continuity between ISC harness connector No. 2 (Orange wire) and vehicle ground. If continuity does not exist, check and repair appropriate circuit. If continuity exists, go to step **6)**.

6) If preceding tests do not show any system or component malfunction and ECM is suspected, replace ECM and retest system.

ECM TERMINAL SELECTION

Terminal No. [1]	ISC Motor Terminal No.
California (Connector No. C50-4)	
23	1
10	2
Federal (Connector No. C50-2)	
1	1
2	2

[1] – See Fig. 1.

IGNITION SYSTEM

NOTE: For basic ignition checks, see BASIC DIAGNOSTIC PROCEDURES article.

TIMING CONTROL SYSTEMS

Camshaft Position Sensor – See SELF-DIAGNOSTICS article.
Crankshaft Position Sensor – See SELF-DIAGNOSTICS article.
Knock Sensor – See SELF-DIAGNOSTICS article.

EMISSION SYSTEMS & SUB-SYSTEMS

EXHAUST GAS RECIRCULATION (EGR)

See SELF-DIAGNOSTICS article.

FUEL EVAPORATION

Purge Control Solenoid Valve (Diamante, Montero, Pickup 3.0L, Ram-50 3.0L, Stealth & 3000GT) – **1)** Label and disconnect both vacuum hoses from solenoid valve. Disconnect electrical connector. Connect hand vacuum pump to solenoid valve nipple where Red-striped hose was connected. Apply vacuum to solenoid valve. Vacuum should hold.

2) Apply battery voltage to terminals of solenoid valve. Vacuum should bleed down when voltage is applied to terminals. Using an ohmmeter, check resistance across solenoid valve terminals. Reading should be 36-44 ohms at 68°F (20°C). If reading is not within specification, replace valve.

3) This step checks voltage at purge solenoid. Disconnect purge solenoid harness connector. Turn ignition on. Using DVOM, measure voltage at harness connector terminal No. 1 (horizontal terminal). If voltage is battery voltage, go to step **4)**. If voltage is not battery voltage, check and repair circuit between purge solenoid and MPI control relay.

4) This step checks continuity between ECM and purge solenoid. Disconnect ECM harness connector. Connect jumper wire between ECM terminal No. 9 (No. 62 on Montero, Pickup and Ram-50) and vehicle ground.

5) Using DVOM, check for continuity between purge solenoid harness connector terminal No. 2 (vertical terminal) and vehicle ground. If continuity exists, harness is good. If continuity does not exist, check and repair circuit.

6) If preceding tests do not show any system or component malfunction and ECM is suspected, replace ECM and retest system.

Purge Control Solenoid Valve (Except Diamante, Montero, Pickup 3.0L, Ram-50 3.0L, Stealth & 3000GT) – **1)** Label and disconnect both vacuum hoses from solenoid valve. Disconnect electrical connector. Connect hand vacuum pump to solenoid valve nipple where Red-striped hose was connected. Apply vacuum to solenoid valve. Vacuum should hold.

2) Apply battery voltage to terminals of solenoid valve. Vacuum should bleed down when voltage is applied to terminals. Using an ohmmeter, check resistance across solenoid valve terminals. Reading should be 36-44 ohms at 68°F (20°C). If reading is not within specification, replace valve.

3) This step checks voltage at purge solenoid. Disconnect purge solenoid harness connector. Turn ignition on. Using DVOM, measure voltage at harness connector terminal No. 2 (vertical terminal). If voltage is battery voltage, go to step **4)**. If voltage is not battery voltage, check and repair circuit between purge solenoid and MPI control relay.

4) This step checks continuity between ECM and purge solenoid. Disconnect ECM harness connector. Connect jumper wire between ECM terminal and vehicle ground. See ECM TERMINAL IDENTIFICATION table.

5) Using DVOM, check for continuity between purge solenoid harness connector terminal No. 1 (horizontal terminal) and vehicle ground. If continuity exists, harness is good. If continuity does not exist, check and repair circuit.

6) If preceding tests do not show any system or component malfunction and ECM is suspected, replace ECM and retest system.

ECM TERMINAL IDENTIFICATION

Application	Terminal Number
Eclipse	62
Precis	
California (Connector C50-4)	5
Federal (Connector C50-2)	16
Except Eclipse & Precis	9

POSITIVE CRANKCASE VENTILATION (PCV)

PCV Valve – Remove PCV valve. Shake valve by hand. Valve should rattle if moving freely. Apply air pressure to valve. Air should flow in one direction only. Connect PCV valve to vacuum hose and start engine. Ensure vacuum is flowing through valve.

MISCELLANEOUS CONTROLS

NOTE: Although some of the controlled devices listed here are not technically engine performance components, they can affect driveability if they malfunction.

Accelerator Pedal Position Sensor (Diamante With Traction Control) – **1)** Sensor is connected to throttle valve. Disconnect sensor connector. Measure resistance between terminals No. 1 (Black wire) and No. 4 (Green/Yellow wire). Resistance should be 3.5-6.5 ohms.

2) Using analog ohmmeter, measure resistance between terminals No. 1 (Black wire) and No. 3 (Yellow/Red wire). Monitor ohmmeter while slowly opening throttle from idle position to WOT. Resistance should change smoothly in proportion with throttle opening. Replace sensor if ohmmeter displays erratic changes in resistance when opening throttle.

3) Check for open or short in circuit between accelerator pedal position sensor and ECM. Disconnect sensor and ECM connectors. Connect ohmmeter between sensor connector terminal No. 4 (Green/Yellow wire) and vehicle ground. Ground ECM connector terminal No. 61 (Green/Yellow wire). Repair circuit as needed if continuity does not exist.

4) Check for continuity between sensor connector terminal No. 1 (Black wire) and vehicle ground. Repair circuit between sensor connector terminal No. 1 and ECM connector No. 72 as needed if continuity does not exist. Connect ECM connector. Turn ignition on. Using DVOM, measure voltage between sensor connector terminal No. 4 (Green/Yellow wire) and vehicle ground. Voltage should be 4.8-5.2 volts. Replace ECM is voltage is not within specification.

A/C Switch & Compressor Clutch Relay – Using DVOM, measure power supply voltage of ECM. Disconnect ECM connector. Turn A/C switch and ignition switch to ON positions. Measure voltage between specified ECM terminals and vehicle ground. See A/C POWER ECM TERMINAL LOCATION table. Voltage should be 6 volts or greater. If voltage is not battery voltage, check and repair circuit.

A/C POWER ECM TERMINAL LOCATION

Application	Wire Color	[1] Terminal No.
Colt, Colt 200,		
Mirage & Summit	Black/White	22
	Green/Yellow	45
Colt Vista, Expo &		
Summit Wagon	Black/White	22
	Green/Red	115
Diamante	Brown/Yellow	22
	Green/Red	115
Eclipse	Green/Yellow	7
	Red/Black	65
Galant	Black/White	22
	Green/Black	115
Montero	Green/Blue	7
	Green/White	65
Pickup & Ram-50	Green/Red	7
	Blue	65
Precis (California)	Black/White	[2] 6
	Black/Green	[3] 13
Precis (Federal)	Black/White	[4] 10
	Black/Green	[5] 18
Stealth & 3000GT	Green	22
	Blue/Red	115

[1] – *See Fig. 1.*
[2] – *ECM connector C50-1. See Fig. 1.*
[3] – *ECM connector C50-2. See Fig. 1.*
[4] – *ECM connector C50-6. See Fig. 1.*
[5] – *ECM connector C50-4. See Fig. 1.*

1993 ENGINE PERFORMANCE
Pin Voltage Charts

**Chrysler Corp.: Colt, Colt Vista, Colt 200, Ram-50, Stealth, Summit, Summit Wagon
Mitsubishi: Diamante, Eclipse, Expo, Galant, Mirage, Montero, Pickup, 3000GT**

INTRODUCTION

NOTE: Unless stated otherwise in testing procedures, perform all voltage tests using a Digital Volt-Ohmmeter (DVOM) with a minimum 10-megohm input impedance. Voltage readings may vary slightly due to battery condition or charging rate.

Pin voltage charts are supplied to reduce diagnostic time. Checking pin voltages at the ECM connector determines whether it is receiving and transmitting proper voltage signals. Diagnostic charts may also help determine if ECM harness is shorted or open.

TEST PROCEDURE

CAUTION: Shorting positive DVOM lead between connector terminal and ground could damage vehicle wiring, sensor and ECM.

1) If necessary, remove module to access harness connector. Using DVOM, backprobe terminals with positive lead. Connect negative lead to ECM ground terminal. See appropriate chart for identification of ground terminal. (ri)**See Figs. 1-19.**

2) All measurements are applicable to vehicle at normal operating temperature at sea level. Unless otherwise noted, engine is idling when specification requires engine running. If DVOM displays measurement that is not within specification, see SELF-DIAGNOSTICS or SYSTEM & COMPONENT TESTING article.

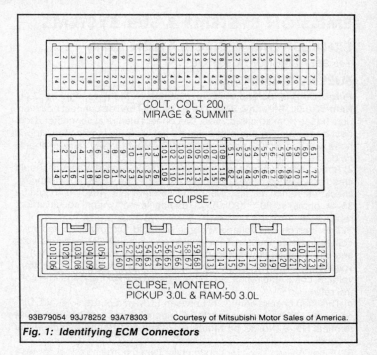

COLT, COLT 200,
MIRAGE & SUMMIT

ECLIPSE,

ECLIPSE, MONTERO,
PICKUP 3.0L & RAM-50 3.0L

93B79054 93J78252 93A78303   Courtesy of Mitsubishi Motor Sales of America.

Fig. 1: Identifying ECM Connectors

	Terminal ID.	Function/Description	Voltage Value (DC Volts Unless Otherwise Specified)
Yellow/Blue	1	Injector No. 1	Battery Voltage With KOER [1]
Blue/Green	2	Injector No. 3	Battery Voltage With KOER [1]
	3	BLANK	N/A
Blue/Yellow	4	Idle Air Control Motor	0-1 Volt With KOEO [2]
Red	5	Idle Air Control Motor Position Sensor	0-1 or 4.5-5.5 Volts With KOEO [2]
Brown/Red [3]	6	EGR Solenoid	Battery Voltage With KOEO [2]
White/Red	7	BLANK	N/A
Green/Red	8	Multiport Fuel Injection Relay	Battery Voltage With KOEO [2]
White	9	Purge Control Solenoid	Battery Voltage With KOEO [2]
	10	Ignition Power Transistor	0.3-3.0 Volts With Engine @ 3000 RPM
Red	11	BLANK	N/A
Black	12	Power Supply	Battery Voltage With KOEO [2]
Yellow/Black	13	System Ground	Not Applicable
Green/White	14	Injector No. 2	Battery Voltage With KOER [1]
	15	Injector No. 4	Battery Voltage With KOER [1]
Green/Black	16	BLANK	N/A
White	17	Idle Air Control Motor	0-1 Volt With KOEO [2]
Blue	18	Idle Air Control Motor Position Sensor	0-1 Or 4.5-5.5 Volts With KOEO [2]
	19	Airflow Sensor	0-1 Volt With KOER [1] (1.8L)
	20	BLANK	N/A
Black/White	21	BLANK	N/A
	22	Air Conditioning Clutch Relay	Battery Voltage With KOER [1]
Black/Blue	23	BLANK	N/A
Red	24	Electric Load Switch (1.8L)	0-3 Volts With KOEO [2] (Accessories Off)
Black	25	Power Supply	Battery Voltage With KOEO [2]
	26	System Ground	Not Applicable
Black/Yellow	31	BLANK	N/A
	32	Heated Oxygen Sensor	0-3 Volts With KOER [1]
Black/Blue	33	BLANK	N/A
Blue/Yellow	34	Ignition Timing Adjustment Terminal	4.0-5.5 Volts With KOEO [2]
Lt. Green/Red	35	Heated Oxygen Sensor	0-3 Volts With KOER [1]
Yellow	36	Malfunction Indicator Light	Battery Voltage With KOER [1]
	37	Power Steering Pressure Switch	Battery Voltage With KOER [1]

1 – KOER – Key On, Engine Running.
2 – KOEO – Key On, Engine Off.
3 – On 1.8L, wire color is Brown.

93H79068

Fig. 2: Pin Voltage Chart (Colt, Colt 200, Mirage & Summit – 1 Of 2)

1993 ENGINE PERFORMANCE
Pin Voltage Charts (Cont.)

Wire Color	Terminal ID.	Function/Description	Voltage Value (DC Volts Unless Otherwise Specified)
	38	BLANK	N/A
	39	BLANK	N/A
	40	BLANK	N/A
	41	BLANK	N/A
Yellow	42	Data Link Connector	Not Available
Green/White	43	Data Link Connector	Not Available
	44	BLANK	N/A
Green/Yellow	45	Air Conditioning Switch	Battery Voltage With KOER [1] (A/C On)
	46	BLANK	N/A
Black/Yellow [2]	51	Inhibitor Switch	8 Volts Or More (Engine Cranking)
Red/Black	52	Intake Air Temperature Sensor	0.4-1.0 Volt With KOEO [3]
Blue	53	EGR Temperature Sensor	2.2-3.0 Volts With KOEO [3] (Sensor @ 212°F)
	54	BLANK	N/A
White	55	Heated Oxygen Sensor (Rear)	0-.9 Volt With KOER [1] (WOT)
White	56	Heated Oxygen Sensor (Front)	0-.9 Volt With KOER [1] (2000 RPM)
	57	BLANK	N/A
	58	BLANK	N/A
	59	BLANK	N/A
Black/White [2]	60	Backup Power Supply	Battery Voltage With KOEO [3]
Green/Blue	61	Manifold Absolute Pressure Sensor [4]	4.5-5.5 Volts With KOEO [3]
	62	BLANK	N/A
Yellow/Green	63	Coolant Temperature Sensor	.3-.9 Volt With KOEO [3]
Green/White	64	Throttle Position Sensor	0.3-1.0 Volt With KOEO [3]
Pink	65	Barometric Pressure Sensor (1.8L)	3.7-4.3 Volts With KOEO [3]
Yellow/White	66	Vehicle Speed Sensor	0-5 Volts (Pulse) With KOEO [3] (Sensor Rotating)
Yellow/Red	67	Closed Throttle Position Switch	0-1 Volt With KOEO [3]
Brown/Red	68	Camshaft Position Sensor	0.5-2.0 Volts With KOER [1]
Brown/Green	69	Crankshaft Position Sensor	1.5-2.5 Volts With KOER [1]
White/Black	70	Manifold Absolute Pressure Sensor (1.5L)	0.9-1.5 Volts With KOER [1]
White/Black	70	Intake Airflow Sensor (1.8L)	2.2-3.2 Volts With KOER [1]
Black/Yellow [5]	71	Ignition Switch	Battery Voltage With KOEO [3]
Black	72	Coolant Temperature Switch	Not Available

[1] – KOER – Key On, Engine Running.
[2] – On M/T models, wire color is Black/Yellow.
[3] – KOEO – Key On, Engine Off.
[4] – Barometric sensor on 1.8L.
[5] – On M/T models, wire color is Black.

93I79069

Fig. 3: Pin Voltage Chart (Colt, Colt 200, Mirage & Summit – 2 Of 2)

	Terminal ID.	Function/Description	Voltage Value (DC Volts Unless Otherwise Specified)
Yellow/Blue ➡	1	Injector No. 1	Battery Voltage With KOER [1]
Blue/Green ➡	2	Injector No. 3	Battery Voltage With KOER [1]
	3	BLANK	N/A
Blue/Yellow ➡	4	Idle Air Control Motor	Battery Voltage/0-3 Volts (Load Controlled)
Green ➡	5	Idle Air Control Motor	Battery Voltage/0-3 Volts (Load Controlled)
Brown/Green ➡	6	EGR Solenoid	Battery Voltage With KOEO [2]
White/Red ➡	7	BLANK	N/A
Green/Red ➡	8	Multiport Fuel Injection Relay	Battery Voltage With KOEO [2]
White ➡	9	Purge Control Solenoid	Battery Voltage With KOEO [2]
	10	Ignition Power Transistor	0.3-3.0 Volts With Engine @ 3000 RPM
Red ➡	11	BLANK	N/A
Black ➡	12	Power Supply	Battery Voltage With KOEO [2]
Yellow/Black ➡	13	Ground Circuit	Not Applicable
Lt. Green/White ➡	14	Injector No. 2	Battery Voltage With KOER [1]
	15	Injector No. 4	Battery Voltage With KOER [1]
Green/Black ➡	16	BLANK	N/A
White ➡	17	Idle Air Control Motor	Battery Voltage/0-3 Volts (Load Controlled)
Yellow/White ➡	18	Idle Air Control Motor	Battery Voltage/0-3 Volts (Load Controlled)
	19	Airflow Sensor Reset Signal	0-1 Volt With KOER [1]
	20	BLANK	N/A
Black/White ➡	21	BLANK	N/A
	22	Air Conditioning Clutch Relay	Battery Voltage With KOER [1] (A/C Off)
Red/Green ➡	23	BLANK	N/A
Red ➡	24	Electrical Load Switch	0-3 Volts With KOER [1] (Accessories Off)
Black ➡	25	Power Supply	Battery Voltage With KOEO [2]
Black/Yellow [3] ➡	26	Ground Circuit	Not Applicable
Red/Black ➡	51	Ignition Switch	8 Volts Or More With Engine Cranking
Brown/White ➡	52	Intake Air Temperature Sensor	0.4-1.0 Volt With KOEO [2]
	53	EGR Temperature Sensor	2.2-3.0 Volts With KOEO [2] (Sensor @ 212°F)
White ➡	54	BLANK	N/A
White ➡	55	Heated Oxygen Sensor (Turbo)	0-.8 Volt (Pulse) With KOER [1]
	56	Heated Oxygen Sensor (All)	0.6-1.0 Volt With Engine @ 3000 RPM

[1] – KOER – Key On, Engine Running.
[2] – KOEO – Key On, Engine Off.
[3] – On A/T models, wire color is Black/Red.

93B79070

Fig. 4: Pin Voltage Chart (Colt Vista, Expo & Summit Wagon – 1 Of 2)

1993 ENGINE PERFORMANCE
Pin Voltage Charts (Cont.)

	Terminal ID.	Function/Description	Voltage Value (DC Volts Unless Otherwise Specified)
	57	BLANK	N/A
	58	BLANK	N/A
	59	BLANK	N/A
Black/Yellow →	60	Backup Power Supply	Battery Voltage With Ignition Off
Green/Red →	61	Throttle Position Sensor	4.5-5.5 Volts With KOEO [1]
	62	BLANK	N/A
Yellow/Green →	63	Coolant Temperature Sensor	.3-.9 Volt With KOEO [1]
Green/White →	64	Throttle Position Sensor	0.3-1.0 Volt With KOEO [1]
Pink →	65	Barometric Pressure Sensor	3.7-4.3 Volts With KOER [2]
Yellow/White →	66	Vehicle Speed Sensor	0-5 Volts (Pulse) With KOEO [1] (Sensor Rotating)
Yellow/Red →	67	Closed Throttle Position Switch	0-1 Volt With KOEO [1]
Brown/Red →	68	Camshaft Position Sensor	0.2-3.0 Volts With KOER [2]
Brown/Green →	69	Crankshaft Position Sensor	0.2-3.0 Volts With KOER [2]
White/Black →	70	Airflow Sensor	2.2-3.2 Volts With KOER [2]
Black [3] →	71	Inhibitor Switch	0-3 Volts With KOEO [1] In Park
Black →	72	Throttle Position Sensor	Not Available
	101	BLANK	N/A
	102	BLANK	N/A
	103	BLANK	N/A
Black/Blue →	104	Ignition Timing Adjustment Terminal	4.0-5.5 Volts With KOEO [1]
Black →	105	Oxygen Sensor Heater	0-3 Volts With KOER [2]
Lt. Green/Red →	106	Malfunction Indicator Light	0-3 Volts With KOEO [1] (Initially)
Yellow →	107	Power Steering Pressure Switch	Battery Voltage With KOER [2]
	108	BLANK	N/A
	109	BLANK	N/A
	110	BLANK	N/A
	111	BLANK	N/A
Yellow →	112	Data Link Connector	Not Available
Gray/White →	113	Data Link Connector	Not Available
	114	BLANK	N/A
Green/Red →	115	Air Conditioning Switch	0-3 Volts With KOER [2] (A/C Off)
	116	BLANK	N/A

[1] – KOEO – Key On, Engine Off.
[2] – KOER – Key On, Engine Running.
[3] – On A/T models, wire color is Black/Yellow.

93C79071

Fig. 5: Pin Voltage Chart (Colt Vista, Expo & Summit Wagon – 2 Of 2)

Blue/Yellow
Yellow/Red
Yellow
Green/Black
Gray/Blue
White
Brown/Red
White/Red
Brown/Green
White/Green [3]
Brown
Black/Red
Black
Yellow/Black
Lt. Green/White
Yellow/Green
Green/Red
Green/Blue
Green/White
Black
Brown/Red
Brown/Yellow
Black
Red/Green
Black/Red
Black
Black/Blue
Red/Blue
Blue/Black [4]

White

Terminal ID.	Function/Description	Voltage Value (DC Volts Unless Otherwise Specified)
1	Injector No. 1	Battery Voltage With KOER [1]
2	Injector No. 3	Battery Voltage With KOER [1]
3	Injector No. 5	Battery Voltage With KOER [1]
4	Idle Air Control Motor	Battery Voltage/0-3 Volts (Load Controlled)
5	Idle Air Control Motor	Battery Voltage/0-3 Volts (Load Controlled)
6	EGR Solenoid	Battery Voltage With KOEO [2]
7	Traction Control Signal	1-4 Volts With KOER [1]
8	Multiport Fuel Injection Relay	Battery Voltage With KOEO [2]
9	Purge Control Solenoid	Battery Voltage With KOEO [2]
10	Ignition Power Transistor	0.3-3.0 Volts With Engine @ 3000 RPM
11	Ignition Power Transistor (DOHC)	0.3-3.0 Volts With Engine @ 3000 RPM
12	Power Supply	Battery Voltage With KOEO [2]
13	Ground Circuit	Not Applicable
14	Injector No. 2	Battery Voltage With KOER [1]
15	Injector No. 4	Battery Voltage With KOER [1]
16	Injector No. 6	Battery Voltage With KOER [1]
17	Idle Air Control Motor	Battery Voltage/0-3 Volts (Load Controlled)
18	Idle Air Control Motor	Battery Voltage/0-3 Volts (Load Controlled)
19	Airflow Sensor Reset Signal	0-1 Volt With KOER [1]
20	Traction Control Module (DOHC)	Not Available
21	Traction Control Module (DOHC)	Not Available
22	Air Conditioning Clutch Relay	Battery Voltage With KOER [1]
23	Ignition Power Transistor (DOHC)	0.3-3.0 Volts With Engine @ 3000 RPM
24	Electrical Load Switch	0-3 Volts With KOER [1] (Accessories Off)
25	Power Supply	Battery Voltage With KOEO [2]
26	Ground Circuit	Not Applicable
51	Ignition Switch	8 Volts Or More With Engine Cranking
52	Intake Air Temperature Sensor	0.4-1.0 Volt With KOEO [2]
53	EGR Temperature Sensor	2.2-3.0 Volts With KOEO [2] (Sensor @ 212°F)
54	BLANK	N/A
55	BLANK	N/A
56	Heated Oxygen Sensor	0-.8 Volt (Pulse) With KOER [1]
57	BLANK	N/A

[1] – KOER – Key On, Engine Running.
[2] – KOEO – Key On, Engine Off.
[3] – On DOHC models, wire color is Black/Blue.
[4] – On DOHC models, wire color is Yellow.

93D79072

Fig. 6: Pin Voltage Chart (Diamante – 1 Of 2)

1993 ENGINE PERFORMANCE
Pin Voltage Charts (Cont.)

	Terminal ID.	Function/Description	Voltage Value (DC Volts Unless Otherwise Specified)
Black [1]	58	Knock Sensor	Not Available
White	59	Traction Control Signal (DOHC)	0-1 Volt With KOER [2]
Red/Yellow [3]	60	Backup Power Supply	Battery Voltage With Ignition Off
Green/Yellow	61	Accelerator Position Sensor	4.5-5.5 Volts With KOEO [4]
Black/White	62	Ignition Supply Voltage	Battery Voltage With KOEO [4]
Yellow/Green	63	Coolant Temperature Sensor	.3-.9 Volt With KOEO [4]
Brown/Red	64	Throttle Position Sensor	0.3-1.0 Volt With KOEO [4]
Pink	65	Barometric Pressure Sensor	Battery Voltage With KOER [2]
Yellow/White	66	Vehicle Speed Sensor	0-5 Volts (Pulse) With KOEO [4], Sensor Rotating
Yellow/Red	67	Closed Throttle Position Switch	0-1 Volt With KOEO [4]
Red/Black [5]	68	Camshaft Position Sensor	0.2-3.0 Volts With KOER [2]
Black/White [6]	69	Crankshaft Position Sensor	0.2-3.0 Volts With KOER [2]
White/Black	70	Airflow Sensor	2.2-3.2 Volts With KOER [2]
Black/Yellow	71	Inhibitor Switch	0-3 Volts With KOEO [4] In Park
Black	72	Coolant Temperature Sensor	Not Applicable
White	101	Ignition Signal (DOHC)	0.3-3.0 Volts With Engine @ 3000 RPM
	102	BLANK	N/A
Black/Blue	103	Variable Induction Control Position Sensor	0-1 Volt Or 4.5-5.5 Volts With KOEO [4]
White/Yellow	104	Ignition Timing Adjustment Terminal	4.0-5.5 Volts With KOEO [4]
	105	BLANK	N/A
Green/Yellow	106	Engine Alarm Light	0-3 Volts With KOEO [4] (Initially)
Blue/White	107	Power Steering Pressure Switch	Battery Voltage With KOER [2]
Blue/Green	108	MPI Relay Supply Voltage	Battery Voltage With Ignition Off
Green/Black	109	Variable Induction Control Motor	0-1 Volt With KOER [2]
Green/Red	110	Variable Induction Control Motor	0-1 Volt With KOER [2]
Green/White	111	Variable Induction Control Position Sensor	0-1 Volt Or 4.5-5.5 Volts With KOEO [4]
Yellow	112	Data Link Connector	Not Available
Gray/Red	113	Data Link Connector	Not Available
	114	BLANK	N/A
Green/White	115	Air Conditioning Switch	0-3 Volts With KOER [2] (A/C Off)
Yellow/Green	116	Traction Control Sensor	4.5-5.5 Volts With KOER [2] (DOHC)

[1] – On DOHC models, wire color is White.
[2] – KOER – Key On, Engine Running.
[3] – On DOHC models, wire color is Red/Black.
[4] – KOEO – Key On, Engine Off.
[5] – On DOHC models, wire color is Black.
[6] – On DOHC models, wire color is Blue/Yellow.

93E79073

Fig. 7: Pin Voltage Chart (Diamante – 2 Of 2)

	Terminal ID.	Function/Description	Voltage Value (DC Volts Unless Otherwise Specified)
Yellow	1	Data Link Connector	Not Available
White	2	Data Link Connector	Not Available
Black/Red	3	Boost Meter (Turbo)	4-13 Volts With KOEO [1]
White	4	Heated Oxygen Sensor	0-.8 Volt With KOER [2] (Fluctuating)
Yellow/Black	5	Power Steering Pressure Switch	Battery Voltage With KOER [2]
Green	6	Closed Throttle Position Switch (1.8L)	0-1 Volt With KOEO [1]
Green/White	6	Intake Airflow Sensor Reset Signal (2.0L)	0-1 Volt With KOER [2]
Black/Green	7	Air Conditioning Switch	Battery Voltage With KOER [2] (A/C On)
Green/Orange	8	Intake Air Temperature Sensor	0.4-1.0 Volt With KOEO [1]
White	9	Knock Sensor	Not Available
Green/Blue	10	Intake Airflow Sensor	2.2-3.2 Volts With KOER [2]
Red/Blue	11	Anti-Lock Braking Signal	Battery Voltage With KOER [2]
Yellow/Red	12	Ignition Timing Adjustment Terminal	4.0-5.5 Volts With KOEO [1]
Green/Red	13	Idle Speed Control Motor Position Sensor	Not Available
Black/White	13	Fuel Pump Drive Signal (2.0L)	Battery Voltage With KOER [2]
Green/Black	14	Closed Throttle Position Switch (2.0L)	0-1 Volt With KOEO [1]
Blue/Yellow	15	EGR Temperature Sensor	2.2-3.0 Volts With KOEO [1] (Sensor @ 212°F)
Green/Yellow	16	Barometric Pressure Sensor	3.7-4.3 Volts With KOEO [1]
Brown	17	Idle Speed Control Motor Position Sensor (1.8L)	0.7-1.1 Volts With KOEO [1]
Green/Black	17	Coolant Temperature Sensor (2.0L)	Not Available
Yellow/White	18	Vehicle Speed Sensor	0-5 Volts With KOEO [1] (Sensor Rotating)
Green/White	19	Throttle Position Sensor	0.3-1.0 Volt With KOEO [1]
Yellow/Green	20	Coolant Temperature Sensor	.3-.9 Volt With KOEO [1]
Brown/Yellow [3]	21	Crankshaft Position Sensor	0.2-3.0 Volts With KOER [2]
Black/Blue [4]	22	Camshaft Position Sensor	0.2-3.0 Volts With KOER [2]
Green/Red	23	Throttle Position Sensor	4.5-5.5 Volts With KOEO [1]
Green/Black	24	Sensor Ground	Not Applicable
Yellow/Blue	51	Injector No. 1	Battery Voltage With KOER [2]
Yellow/Black	52	Injector No. 2	Battery Voltage With KOER [2]
Brown/White [5]	53	EGR Solenoid	Battery Voltage With KOEO [1]
Green/Yellow [6]	54	Ignition Power Transistor	0.3-3.0 Volts With Engine @ 3000 RPM

[1] – KOEO – Key On, Engine Off.
[2] – KOER – Key On, Engine Running.
[3] – On A/T models, wire color is Black.
[4] – On A/T models, wire color is White.
[5] – On 2.0L, wire color is Black/Yellow.
[6] – On 2.0L, wire color is Yellow.

93F79074

Fig. 8: Pin Voltage Chart (Eclipse – 1 Of 2)

	Terminal ID.	Function/Description	Voltage Value (DC Volts Unless Otherwise Specified)
Yellow/Red	55	Ignition Power Transistor Unit "B"	0.3-3.0 Volts With Engine @ 3000 RPM
White/Red	56	Multiport Fuel Injection Relay	Battery Voltage With KOEO [1]
White	57	Fuel Pressure Solenoid	Battery Voltage With KOEO [1]
Blue/White [2]	58	Idle Air Control Motor	0-1 Volt With KOEO [1]
Green/Black [3]	59	Idle Air Control Motor	0-1 Volt With KOEO [1]
Lt. Green	60	Injector No. 3	Battery Voltage With KOEO [1]
Lt. Green/White	61	Injector No. 4	Battery Voltage With KOEO [1]
Black/White	62	Purge Control Solenoid	Battery Voltage With KOEO [1]
Black/Blue	63	Multiport Fuel Injection Relay	Battery Voltage With KOEO [1]
Red/Green	64	Malfunction Indicator Light	0-3 Volts With KOEO [1] (Initially)
Red/Black	65	Air Conditioning Clutch Relay	Battery Voltage With KOER [4] (A/C Off)
Black/Blue	66	Multiport Fuel Injection Relay	Battery Voltage With KOEO [1]
White	67	Idle Air Control Motor	Battery Voltage/0-3 Volts (Fluctuating)
Black	68	Idle Air Control Motor	Battery Voltage/0-3 Volts (Fluctuating)
Black	101	System Ground	Not Applicable
Red	102	Power Supply	Battery Voltage With KOEO [1]
Red/Black	103	Backup Power Supply	Battery Voltage With KOEO [1]
Black [5]	104	Ignition Switch	Battery Voltage (Engine Cranking)
Orange	105	Turbocharger Wastegate Solenoid	Battery Voltage With KOEO [1]
Black	106	System Ground	Not Applicable
Red	107	Power Supply	Battery Voltage With KOEO [1]
Black/Yellow	108	Inhibitor Switch	0-3 Volts With KOEO [1] (Park Or Neutral)
Black/White	109	Fuel Pump Drive Signal (1.8L)	Battery Voltage With KOER [4]
White	109	Ignition Power Transistor (2.0L)	Not Available
Black/White	110	Ignition Switch	Battery Voltage With KOEO [1]

[1] – KOEO – Key On, Engine Off.
[2] – On 2.0L, wire color is Blue.
[3] – On 2.0L, wire color is Yellow.
[4] – KOER – Key On, Engine Running.
[5] – On A/T models, wire color is Black/Yellow.

93G79075

Fig. 9: Pin Voltage Chart (Eclipse – 2 Of 2)

	Terminal ID.	Function/Description	Voltage Value (DC Volts Unless Otherwise Specified)
Yellow/Blue	1	Injector No. 1	Battery Voltage With KOER [1]
Blue/Green	2	Injector No. 3	Battery Voltage With KOER [1]
	3	BLANK	N/A
Blue/White	4	Idle Air Control Motor	Battery Voltage/0-3 Volts (Load Controlled)
White	5	Idle Air Control Motor	Battery Voltage/0-3 Volts (Load Controlled)
Lt. Green/Blue	6	EGR Solenoid	Battery Voltage With KOEO [2]
	7	BLANK	N/A
White/Red	8	Multiport Fuel Injection Relay	Battery Voltage With KOEO [2]
Yellow/Red	9	Purge Control Solenoid	Battery Voltage With KOEO [2]
Green/Yellow	10	Ignition Power Transistor	0.3-3.0 Volts With Engine @ 3000 RPM
	11	BLANK	N/A
Red	12	Power Supply	Battery Voltage With KOEO [2]
Black	13	Ground Circuit	Not Applicable
Yellow/Black	14	Injector No. 2	Battery Voltage With KOER [1]
Lt. Green/White	15	Injector No. 4	Battery Voltage With KOER [1]
	16	BLANK	N/A
Green/Black	17	Idle Air Control Motor	Battery Voltage/0-3 Volts (Load Controlled)
Green/Yellow	18	Idle Air Control Motor	Battery Voltage/0-3 Volts (Load Controlled)
N/A [3]	19	Airflow Sensor Reset Signal	0-1 Volt With KOER [1]
	20	BLANK	N/A
	21	BLANK	N/A
Black/White	22	Air Conditioning Clutch Relay	Battery Voltage With KOER [1] (A/C Off)
	23	BLANK	N/A
	24	BLANK	N/A
Red	25	Power Supply	Battery Voltage With KOEO [2]
Black	26	Ground Circuit	Not Applicable
Black/Yellow	51	Ignition Switch	8 Volts Or More With Engine Cranking
Green/Orange	52	Intake Air Temperature Sensor	0.4-1.0 Volt With KOEO [2]
Green/Red	53	EGR Temperature Sensor	2.2-3.0 Volts With KOEO [2] (Sensor @ 212°F)
	54	BLANK	N/A
	55	BLANK	N/A

[1] – KOER – Key On, Engine Running.
[2] – KOEO – Key On, Engine Off.
[3] – Wire color is not available from manufacturer.

93H79076

Fig. 10: Pin Voltage Chart (Galant – 1 Of 2)

1993 ENGINE PERFORMANCE
Pin Voltage Charts (Cont.)

Terminal ID.	Function/Description	Voltage Value (DC Volts Unless Otherwise Specified)
56	Heated Oxygen Sensor	0-.8 Volt With Engine at 2000 RPM
57	BLANK	N/A
58	BLANK	N/A
59	BLANK	N/A
60	Backup Power Supply	Battery Voltage With Ignition Off
61	Throttle Position Sensor	4.5-5.5 Volts With KOEO [1]
62	BLANK	N/A
63	Coolant Temperature Sensor	.3-.9 Volt With KOEO [1]
64	Throttle Position Sensor	0.3-1.0 Volt With KOEO [1]
65	Barometric Pressure Sensor	3.7-4.3 Volts With KOER [2]
66	Vehicle Speed Sensor	0-5 Volts (Pulse) With KOEO [1] (Sensor Rotating)
67	Closed Throttle Position Switch	0-1 Volt With KOEO [1]
68	Camshaft Position Sensor	0.2-3.0 Volts With KOER [2]
69	Crankshaft Position Sensor	0.2-3.0 Volts With KOER [2]
70	Airflow Sensor	2.2-3.2 Volts With KOER [2]
71	Inhibitor Switch	0-3 Volts With KOEO [1] In Park
72	Throttle Position Sensor	Not Available
101	BLANK	N/A
102	BLANK	N/A
103	BLANK	N/A
104	Ignition Timing Adjustment Terminal	4.0-5.5 Volts With KOEO [1]
105	BLANK	N/A
106	Malfunction Indicator Light	0-3 Volts With KOEO [1] (Initially)
107	Power Steering Pressure Switch	Battery Voltage With KOER [2]
108	BLANK	N/A
109	BLANK	N/A
110	BLANK	N/A
111	BLANK	N/A
112	Data Link Connector	Not Available
113	Data Link Connector	Not Available
114	BLANK	N/A
115	Air Conditioning Switch	0-3 Volts With KOER [2] (A/C Off)
116	BLANK	N/A

Wire colors (left margin, top to bottom):
White → 56
Red/Black → 60
Green/Red → 61
Yellow/Green → 63
Green/White → 64
Green/Yellow → 65
Yellow/White → 66
Green → 67
Black/Blue → 68
Blue/Yellow → 69
Green/Blue → 70
Black → 71
Green/Black → 72
Yellow/Red → 104
Blue/Yellow → 106
Yellow → 107
Yellow → 112
White → 113
Green/Black → 115

[1] – KOEO – Key On, Engine Off.
[2] – KOER – Key On, Engine Running.

93A79079

Fig. 11: Pin Voltage Chart (Galant – 2 Of 2)

	Terminal ID.	Function/Description	Voltage Value (DC Volts Unless Otherwise Specified)
Yellow	1	Data Link Connector	Not Available
Green/Red	2	Data Link Connector	Not Available
White	3	BLANK	N/A
Blue/White	4	Heated Oxygen Sensor	0-.8 Volt With KOER [1] (Fluctuating)
	5	Power Steering Pressure Switch	Battery Voltage With KOER [1]
Green/Blue	6	BLANK	N/A
Red/Black	7	Air Conditioning Switch	Battery Voltage With KOER [1] (A/C On)
Green/Black	8	Intake Air Temperature Sensor	0.4-1.0 Volt With KOEO [2]
White/Black	9	Anti-Lock Braking Signal	Battery Voltage With KOER [1]
	10	Intake Airflow Sensor	2.2-3.2 Volts With KOER [1]
White/Yellow	11	BLANK	N/A
	12	Ignition Timing Adjustment Terminal	4.0-5.5 Volts With KOEO [2]
Yellow/Red	13	BLANK	N/A
	14	Closed Throttle Position Switch	0-1 Volt With KOEO [2]
Pink	15	BLANK	N/A
Black	16	Barometric Pressure Sensor	3.7-4.3 Volts With KOEO [2]
Yellow/White	17	Sensor Ground	Not Applicable
Green/White	18	Vehicle Speed Sensor	0-5 Volts With KOEO [2] (Sensor Rotating)
Yellow/Green	19	Throttle Position Sensor	0.3-1.0 Volt With KOEO [2]
Green	20	Coolant Temperature Sensor	.3-.9 Volt With KOEO [2]
White	21	Crankshaft Position Sensor	0.2-3.0 Volts With KOER [1]
Green/Yellow	22	Camshaft Position Sensor	0.2-3.0 Volts With KOER [1]
Black	23	Throttle Position Sensor	4.5-5.5 Volts With KOEO [2]
Yellow/Blue	24	Throttle Position Sensor	Not Applicable
Yellow/Black	51	Injector No. 1	Battery Voltage With KOER [1]
	52	Injector No. 2	Battery Voltage With KOER [1]
	53	BLANK	N/A

[1] – KOER – Key On, Engine Running.
[2] – KOEO – Key On, Engine Off.

93D79080

Fig. 12: Pin Voltage Chart (Montero – 1 Of 2)

1993 ENGINE PERFORMANCE
Pin Voltage Charts (Cont.)

	Terminal ID.	Function/Description	Voltage Value (DC Volts Unless Otherwise Specified)
White	54	Ignition Power Transistor	0.3-3.0 Volts With Engine @ 3000 RPM
	55	BLANK	N/A
White/Red	56	Multiport Fuel Injection Relay	Battery Voltage With KOEO [1]
Blue/Black	57	Intake Airflow Sensor Reset Signal	0-1 Volt With KOEO [1]
Green/Red	58	Idle Air Control Motor	Battery Voltage/0-3 Volts (Fluctuating)
Green/Black	59	Idle Air Control Motor	Battery Voltage/0-3 Volts (Fluctuating)
Blue/Green	60	Injector No. 3	Battery Voltage With KOEO [1]
Lt. Green/White	61	Injector No. 4	Battery Voltage With KOEO [1]
Black/Red	62	Purge Control Solenoid	Not Available
Blue/Green	63	Multiport Fuel Injection Relay	Battery Voltage With KOEO [1]
Green/White	64	Malfunction Indicator Light	Battery Voltage With KOEO [1]
Green/White	65	Air Conditioning Clutch Relay	Battery Voltage With KOER [2] (A/C Off)
Blue/Green	66	Multiport Fuel Injection Relay	Battery Voltage With KOEO [1]
Gray/Blue	67	Idle Air Control Motor	Battery Voltage/0-3 Volts (Fluctuating)
Green/Blue	68	Idle Air Control Motor	Battery Voltage/0-3 Volts (Fluctuating)
Black	101	System Ground	Not Applicable
Black/Red	102	Power Supply	Battery Voltage With KOEO [1]
Black/Green	103	Backup Power Supply	Battery Voltage With KOEO [1]
Black/Yellow	104	Ignition Switch	Battery Voltage (Engine Cranking)
Yellow/White	105	Injector No. 5	Battery Voltage With KOER [2]
Black	106	System Ground	Not Applicable
Black/Red	107	Power Supply	Battery Voltage With KOEO [1]
Black/Blue	108	Inhibitor Switch	0-3 Volts With KOEO [1] (Park Or Neutral)
Yellow/Green	109	Injector No. 6	Battery Voltage With KOER [2]
Black/White	110	Ignition Switch	Battery Voltage With KOEO [1]

[1] – KOEO – Key On, Engine Off.
[2] – KOER – Key On, Engine Running.

93E79081

Fig. 13: Pin Voltage Chart (Montero – 2 Of 2)

Terminal ID.	Function/Description	Voltage Value (DC Volts Unless Otherwise Specified)
1	Injector No. 1	Battery Voltage With KOER [1]
2	Injector No. 3	Battery Voltage With KOER [1]
3	BLANK	N/A
4	Idle Air Control Motor	Battery Voltage/0-3 Volts (Load Controlled)
5	Idle Air Control Motor	Battery Voltage/0-3 Volts (Load Controlled)
6	EGR Solenoid	Battery Voltage With KOEO [2]
7	BLANK	N/A
8	Multiport Fuel Injection Relay	Battery Voltage With KOEO [2]
9	Purge Control Solenoid	Battery Voltage With KOEO [2]
10	Ignition Power Transistor	0.3-3.0 Volts With Engine @ 3000 RPM
11	BLANK	N/A
12	Power Supply	Battery Voltage With KOEO [2]
13	Ground Circuit	Not Applicable
14	Injector No. 2	Battery Voltage With KOER [1]
15	Injector No. 4	Battery Voltage With KOER [1]
16	BLANK	N/A
17	Idle Air Control Motor	Battery Voltage/0-3 Volts (Load Controlled)
18	Idle Air Control Motor	Battery Voltage/0-3 Volts (Load Controlled)
19	Airflow Sensor Reset Signal	0-1 Volt With KOER [1]
20	BLANK	N/A
21	BLANK	N/A
22	Air Conditioning Clutch Relay	Battery Voltage With KOER [1] (A/C Off)
23	BLANK	N/A
24	BLANK	N/A
25	Power Supply	Battery Voltage With KOEO [2]
26	Ground Circuit	Not Applicable
51	Ignition Switch	8 Volts Or More With Engine Cranking
52	Intake Air Temperature Sensor	0.4-1.0 Volt With KOEO [2]
53	EGR Temperature Sensor	2.2-3.0 Volts With KOEO [2] (Sensor @ 212°F)
54	BLANK	N/A

Left wire labels: Yellow/Blue, Blue/Green, Blue/Yellow, White, Brown, Black/Blue, Brown/Yellow, White, Red, Black, Yellow/Blue, Lt. Green/White, Green/Black, Green, Blue, Blue, Red, Black, Black/Yellow, Red/Black, Black/Blue

[1] – KOER – Key On, Engine Running.
[2] – KOEO – Key On, Engine Off.

93F79082

Fig. 14: Pin Voltage Chart (Pickup 2.4L & Ram-50 2.4L – 1 Of 2)

1993 ENGINE PERFORMANCE
Pin Voltage Charts (Cont.)

	Terminal ID.	Function/Description	Voltage Value (DC Volts Unless Otherwise Specified)
White	55	Heated Oxygen Sensor (Rear)	0-.8 Volt (Pulse) With KOER [1]
White	56	Heated Oxygen Sensor (Front)	0.6-1.0 Volt With Engine @ 3000 RPM
	57	BLANK	N/A
	58	BLANK	N/A
	59	BLANK	N/A
Black/Yellow	60	Backup Power Supply	Battery Voltage With Ignition Off
Green/Blue	61	Throttle Position Sensor	4.5-5.5 Volts With KOEO [2]
	62	BLANK	N/A
Yellow/Green	63	Coolant Temperature Sensor	.3-.9 Volt With KOEO [2]
Green/White	64	Throttle Position Sensor	0.3-1.0 Volt With KOEO [2]
Pink	65	Barometric Pressure Sensor	3.7-4.3 Volts With KOER [1]
Yellow/White	66	Vehicle Speed Sensor	0-5 Volts (Pulse) With KOEO [2] (Sensor Rotating)
Yellow/Red	67	Closed Throttle Position Switch	0-1 Volt With KOEO [2]
Brown/Red	68	Camshaft Position Sensor	0.2-3.0 Volts With KOER [1]
Brown/Green	69	Crankshaft Position Sensor	0.2-3.0 Volts With KOER [1]
White/Black	70	Airflow Sensor	2.2-3.2 Volts With KOER [1]
Black/Yellow	71	Inhibitor Switch	0-3 Volts With KOEO [2] (In Park)
Black	72	Throttle Position Sensor	Not Available
	101	BLANK	N/A
	102	BLANK	N/A
	103	BLANK	N/A
Black/Blue	104	Ignition Timing Adjustment Terminal	4.0-5.5 Volts With KOEO [2]
Black	105	Oxygen Sensor Heater	0-3 Volts With KOER [1]
Lt. Green/Red	106	Malfunction Indicator Light	0-3 Volts With KOEO [2] (Initially)
	107	BLANK	N/A
	108	BLANK	N/A
	109	BLANK	N/A
	110	BLANK	N/A
	111	BLANK	N/A
Yellow	112	Data Link Connector	Not Available
Green/White	113	Data Link Connector	Not Available
	114	BLANK	N/A
Green/Red	115	Air Conditioning Switch	0-3 Volts With KOER [1] (A/C Off)
	116	BLANK	N/A

[1] – KOER – Key On, Engine Running.
[2] – KOEO – Key On, Engine Off.

93G79083

Fig. 15: Pin Voltage Chart (Pickup 2.4L & Ram-50 2.4L – 2 Of 2)

	Terminal ID.	Function/Description	Voltage Value (DC Volts Unless Otherwise Specified)
Yellow	1	Data Link Connector	Not Available
Green/White	2	Data Link Connector	Not Available
	3	BLANK	N/A
White	4	Heated Oxygen Sensor	0-.8 Volt With KOER [1] (Fluctuating)
	5	BLANK	N/A
	6	BLANK	N/A
Green/Red	7	Air Conditioning Switch	Battery Voltage With KOER [1] (A/C On)
Red/Blue	8	Intake Air Temperature Sensor	0.4-1.0 Volt With KOEO [2]
	9	BLANK	N/A
White/Black	10	Intake Airflow Sensor	2.2-3.2 Volts With KOER [1]
	11	BLANK	N/A
White/Yellow	12	Ignition Timing Adjustment Terminal	4.0-5.5 Volts With KOEO [2]
	13	BLANK	N/A
Yellow/Red	14	Closed Throttle Position Switch	0-1 Volt With KOEO [2]
Lt. Green/Blue	15	EGR Temperature Sensor	2.2-3.0 Volts With KOER [1] (Sensor @ 212°F)
Pink	16	Barometric Pressure Sensor	3.7-4.3 Volts With KOEO [2]
Black	17	Sensor Ground	Not Applicable
Yellow/White	18	Vehicle Speed Sensor	0-5 Volts With KOEO [2] (Sensor Rotating)
Green/White	19	Throttle Position Sensor	0.3-1.0 Volt With KOEO [2]
Yellow/Green	20	Coolant Temperature Sensor	.3-.9 Volt With KOEO [2]
Blue/White	21	Crankshaft Position Sensor	0.2-3.0 Volts With KOER [1]
Blue/Red	22	Camshaft Position Sensor	0.2-3.0 Volts With KOER [1]
Green/Yellow	23	Throttle Position Sensor	4.5-5.5 Volts With KOEO [2]
Black	24	Throttle Position Sensor	Not Applicable
Yellow	51	Injector No. 1	Battery Voltage With KOER [1]
Yellow/Blue	52	Injector No. 2	Battery Voltage With KOER [1]
Lt. Green/Yellow	53	EGR Solenoid	Battery Voltage With KOEO [2]
White	54	Ignition Power Transistor	0.3-3.0 Volts With Engine @ 3000 RPM
	55	BLANK	N/A

[1] – KOER – Key On, Engine Running.
[2] – KOEO – Key On, Engine Off.

93H79084

Fig. 16: Pin Voltage Chart (Pickup 3.0L & Ram-50 3.0L – 1 Of 2)

1993 ENGINE PERFORMANCE
Pin Voltage Charts (Cont.)

White/Red
Red/Green
Green/Yellow
Green/Black
Blue/Green
Lt. Green/White
Brown/Blue
Blue/Green
Lt. Green/Red
Blue
Blue/Green
Green/Red
Green/Blue
Black
Red
Black/Yellow
Black/Yellow
Yellow/White
Black
Red
Black/Red
Yellow/Green
Black/White

Terminal ID.	Function/Description	Voltage Value (DC Volts Unless Otherwise Specified)
56	Multiport Fuel Injection Relay	Battery Voltage With KOEO [1]
57	Intake Airflow Sensor Reset Signal	0-1 Volt With KOEO [1]
58	Idle Air Control Motor	Battery Voltage/0-3 Volts (Fluctuating)
59	Idle Air Control Motor	Battery Voltage/0-3 Volts (Fluctuating)
60	Injector No. 3	Battery Voltage With KOEO [1]
61	Injector No. 4	Battery Voltage With KOEO [1]
62	Purge Control Solenoid	Not Available
63	Multiport Fuel Injection Relay	Battery Voltage With KOEO [1]
64	Malfunction Indicator Light	Battery Voltage With KOEO [1]
65	Air Conditioning Clutch Relay	Battery Voltage With KOER [2] (A/C Off)
66	Multiport Fuel Injection Relay	Battery Voltage With KOEO [1]
67	Idle Air Control Motor	Battery Voltage/0-3 Volts (Fluctuating)
68	Idle Air Control Motor	Battery Voltage/0-3 Volts (Fluctuating)
101	System Ground	Not Applicable
102	Power Supply	Battery Voltage With KOEO [1]
103	Backup Power Supply	Battery Voltage With KOEO [1]
104	Ignition Switch	Battery Voltage (Engine Cranking)
105	Injector No. 5	Battery Voltage With KOER [2]
106	System Ground	Not Applicable
107	Power Supply	Battery Voltage With KOEO [1]
108	Inhibitor Switch	0-3 Volts With KOEO [1] (Park Or Neutral)
109	Injector No. 6	Battery Voltage With KOER [2]
110	Ignition Switch	Battery Voltage With KOEO [1]

[1] – KOEO – Key On, Engine Off.
[2] – KOER – Key On, Engine Running.

93I79085

Fig. 17: Pin Voltage Chart (Pickup 3.0L & Ram-50 3.0L – 2 Of 2)

Wire Color	Terminal ID.	Function/Description	Voltage Value (DC Volts Unless Otherwise Specified)
Green	1	Injector No. 1	Battery Voltage With KOER [1]
Green/Yellow	2	Injector No. 3	Battery Voltage With KOER [1]
Green/Black	3	Injector No. 5	Battery Voltage With KOER [1]
Green/Black [2]	4	Idle Air Control Motor	Battery Voltage/0-3 Volts (Load Controlled)
Gray/Blue	5	Idle Air Control Motor	Battery Voltage/0-3 Volts (Load Controlled)
Lt. Green/Red	6	EGR Solenoid	Battery Voltage With KOEO [3]
Blue/White	7	Fuel Pressure Solenoid (Turbo)	Battery Voltage With KOEO [3]
White/Red	8	Multiport Fuel Injection Relay	Battery Voltage With KOEO [3]
Brown/Blue [4]	9	Purge Control Solenoid	Battery Voltage With KOEO [3]
Black/Blue	10	Ignition Power Transistor	0.3-3.0 Volts With Engine @ 3000 RPM
Brown/Red	11	Ignition Power Transistor (DOHC)	0.3-3.0 Volts With Engine @ 3000 RPM
Black/Red	12	Power Supply	Battery Voltage With KOEO [3]
Black	13	Ground Circuit	Not Applicable
Yellow/Black	14	Injector No. 2	Battery Voltage With KOER [1]
Green/Red	15	Injector No. 4	Battery Voltage With KOER [1]
Green/White	16	Injector No. 6	Battery Voltage With KOER [1]
Green/Black	17	Idle Air Control Motor	Battery Voltage/0-3 Volts (Load Controlled)
Green/Yellow	18	Idle Air Control Motor	Battery Voltage/0-3 Volts (Load Controlled)
Red/White	19	Airflow Sensor Reset Signal	0-1 Volt With KOER [1]
Blue/Orange	20	Air Conditioning Switch No. 2	0-3 Volts (A/C Off)
Brown/Red	21	Fuel Pump Relay (Turbo)	0-3 Volts (Snap Throttle)
Green	22	Air Conditioning Clutch Relay	Battery Voltage With KOER [1] (A/C Off)
Black/White	23	Ignition Power Transistor (DOHC)	0.3-3.0 Volts With Engine @ 3000 RPM
Red/Green	24	Electrical Load Switch	0-3 Volts With KOER [1] (Accessories Off)
Black/Red	25	Power Supply	Battery Voltage With KOEO [3]
Black	26	Ground Circuit	Not Applicable
Black/White [5]	51	Ignition Switch	8 Volts Or More With Engine Cranking
Red/Blue	52	Intake Air Temperature Sensor	0.4-1.0 Volt With KOEO [3]
Lt. Green/Blue [6]	53	EGR Temperature Sensor	2.2-3.0 Volts With KOEO [3] (Sensor @ 212°F)
	54	BLANK	N/A

[1] – KOER – Key On, Engine Running.
[2] – On turbo models, wire color is Gray.
[3] – KOEO – Key On, Engine Off.
[4] – On turbo models, wire color is Light Green/Blue.
[5] – On M/T models, wire color is Black/Yellow.
[6] – Non-turbo models.

93J79086

Fig. 18: Pin Voltage Chart (Stealth & 3000GT – 1 Of 2)

1993 ENGINE PERFORMANCE
Pin Voltage Charts (Cont.)

White		
White		
White		
White/Red		
Red/Black		
Green/Yellow		
Black/White		
Black/White		
Brown/Red		
Orange		
Yellow/White		
Yellow/Red		
Blue/Red		
Blue/Red		
Blue/Yellow		
Black/Yellow		
Black		
White		
Red/White		
Black/Blue		
Black/Green		
Red/Yellow		
Green/Red		
Blue/White		
Blue/Green		
Green/Black		
Green/White		
Red/White		
Red/Black		
Yellow		
Pink		
Red/Blue		
Blue/Red		
White/Blue		

Terminal ID.	Function/Description	Voltage Value (DC Volts Unless Otherwise Specified)
55	Heated Oxygen Sensor (Turbo)	0-.8 Volt (Pulse) With KOER [1]
56	Heated Oxygen Sensor (All)	0-.8 Volt (Pulse) With KOER [1]
57	BLANK	N/A
58	Knock Sensor	Not Available
59	Transaxle Control Module (Non-Turbo)	0-1 Volt With KOER [1]
60	Backup Power Supply	Battery Voltage With Ignition Off
61	Throttle Position Sensor	4.5-5.5 Volts With KOEO [2]
62	Ignition Supply Voltage	Battery Voltage With KOEO [2]
63	Coolant Temperature Sensor	.3-.9 Volt With KOEO [2]
64	Throttle Position Sensor	0.3-1.0 Volt With KOEO [2]
65	Barometric Pressure Sensor	3.7-4.3 Volts With KOER [1]
66	Vehicle Speed Sensor	0-5 Volts (Pulse) With KOEO [1] (Sensor Rotating)
67	Closed Throttle Position Switch	0-1 Volt With KOEO [2]
68	Camshaft Position Sensor	0.2-3.0 Volts With KOER [1]
69	Crankshaft Position Sensor	0.2-3.0 Volts With KOER [1]
70	Airflow Sensor	2.2-3.2 Volts With KOER [1]
71	Inhibitor Switch	0-3 Volts With KOEO [2] In Park
72	Throttle Position Sensor	Not Available
101	Ignition Signal (DOHC)	0.3-3.0 Volts With Engine @ 3000 RPM
102	Muffler Mode Changeover Switch (Turbo)	0-3 Volts With KOER [1]
103	Muffler Mode Changeover Switch (Turbo)	0-3 Volts (Sw. On), Battery Voltage (Sw. Off)
104	Ignition Timing Adjustment Terminal	4.0-5.5 Volts With KOEO [2]
105	Turbo Wastegate Solenoid	Battery Voltage With KOEO [2]
106	Malfunction Indicator Light	0-3 Volts With KOEO [2] (Initially)
107	Power Steering Pressure Switch	Battery Voltage With KOER [1]
108	MPI Relay Supply Voltage	Battery Voltage With Ignition Off
109	Variable Induction Control Motor	0-1 Volt With KOER [1]
110	Variable Induction Control Motor	0-1 Volt With KOER [1]
111	Variable Induction Control Position Sensor [3]	0-1 Volt Or 4.5-5.5 Volts With KOEO [2]
111	Turbo Boost Meter [4]	0-1 Volt Or 4.5-5.5 Volts With KOEO [2]
112	Data Link Connector	Not Available
113	Data Link Connector	Not Available
114	Anti-Lock Braking Signal (Turbo)	Battery Voltage With KOER [1]
115	Air Conditioning Switch	0-3 Volts With KOER [1] (A/C Off)
116	Transaxle Control Module (Non-Turbo)	4.5-5.5 Volts With KOER [1] (DOHC)

[1] – KOER – Key On, Engine Running.
[2] – KOEO – Key On, Engine Off.
[3] – Non-turbo models.
[4] – Turbo models.

93A79087

Fig. 19: Pin Voltage Chart (Stealth & 3000GT – 2 OF 2)

Chrysler Corp.: Colt, Colt Vista, Colt 200, Ram-50, Stealth, Summit, Summit Wagon
Mitsubishi: Diamante, Eclipse, Expo, Galant, Mirage, Montero, Pickup, Precis, 3000GT

INTRODUCTION

Sensor operating range information can help determine if a sensor is out of calibration. An out-of-calibration sensor may not set a trouble code, but it may cause driveability problems.

NOTE: *Unless stated otherwise in test procedure, perform all voltage tests using a Digital Volt-Ohmmeter (DVOM) with a minimum 10-megohm input impedance. For connector and terminal identification, see WIRING DIAGRAMS article.*

AIRFLOW METER HERTZ TEST [1]

Condition	Hz
Colt, Colt 200, Mirage & Summit	
1.8L	
700 RPM	23-49
2000 RPM	51-91
Diamante	
700 RPM	21-47
2000 RPM	51-97
Eclipse	
1.8L	
700 RPM	25-40
2000 RPM	67-88
2.0L	
750 RPM	25-50
2000 RPM	
Non-Turbo	70-90
Turbo	60-85
Colt Vista, Expo & Summit Wagon	
1.8L	
750 RPM	23-49
2000 RPM	51-91
2.4L	
750 RPM	18-44
2000 RPM	43-83
Galant	
SOHC	
750 RPM	18-44
2000 RPM	64-104
Montero	
700 RPM	22-48
2000 RPM	60-100
Pickup & Ram-50	
2.4L	
750 RPM	40-60
2000 RPM	85-105
3.0L	
700 RPM	25-45
2000 RPM	70-90
Precis	
750 RPM	27-33
2000 RPM	60-80
Stealth & 3000GT	
700 RPM	25-50
2000 RPM	70-100

[1] – Measure hertz frequency with Multi-Use Tester (MUT).

COOLANT TEMPERATURE SENSOR RESISTANCE

Temperature °F (°C)	Ohms
Eclipse	
68 (20)	2200-2600
176 (80)	264-328
Pickup 2.4L & Ram-50 2.4L	
32 (0)	5900
68 (20)	2500
104 (40)	1100
176 (80)	300
All Others	
32 (0)	5800
68 (20)	2400
104 (40)	1100
176 (80)	300

EGR TEMPERATURE SENSOR RESISTANCE TEST [1] [2]

Temperature °F (°C)	Ohms
122 (50)	60-83
212 (100)	11-14

[1] – Measure resistance across disconnected sensor terminals.
[2] – Specifications apply to all models except Montero.

INTAKE AIR TEMPERATURE SENSOR RESISTANCE

Temperature °F (°C)	Ohms
Precis	
32 (0)	5400-6600
68 (20)	2300-2970
176 (80)	310-430
All Others	
32 (0)	6000
68 (20)	2700
176 (80)	400

OXYGEN SENSOR VOLTAGE TEST [1] [2]

Application	Volts
All Models	
Lean	0.1
Rich	1.0

[1] – Measure between sensor terminal No. 1 and ground.
[2] – Test at normal operating temperature.

Throttle Position Sensor (TPS) – Measure total and variable resistance between specified TPS connector terminals. See TPS TEST TERMINALS table. Total resistance should be 3500-6500 ohms. Variable resistance should change smoothly between 3500 and 6500 ohms as throttle valve is moved from closed to wide open throttle.

TPS TEST TERMINALS

Application	Terminals No.
Total Resistance	
Eclipse 1.8L	1 & 2
Eclipse 2.0L	2 & 3
All Others	1 & 4
Variable Resistance	
Colt Vista, Expo, Montero, Pickup 3.0L, Precis, Ram-50 3.0L & Summit Wagon	1 & 3
Eclipse 1.8L	2 & 3
Eclipse 2.0L	3 & 4
All Others	2 & 4

VEHICLE SPEED SENSOR CONTINUITY TEST [1]

Application	[2] Continuity
All Models	4 Changes Per Revolution

[1] – Measure continuity at back of speedometer. See appropriate wiring diagram in WIRING DIAGRAMS article.
[2] – With ECM connector disconnected, turn speedometer cable to cycle reed switch on and off.

VEHICLE SPEED SENSOR VOLTAGE TEST [1]

Application	[2] Volts
All Models	
Ignition Switch Off	1 Or Less
Ignition Switch On	4.5-4.9

[1] – Measure voltage at back of speedometer. See appropriate wiring diagram in WIRING DIAGRAMS article.
[2] – With ECM connector disconnected, turn speedometer cable to cycle reed switch on and off.

1993 ENGINE PERFORMANCE
Vacuum Diagrams

Chrysler Corp.: Colt, Colt Vista, Colt 200, Ram-50, Stealth, Summit, Summit Wagon Mitsubishi: Diamante, Eclipse, Expo, Galant Mirage, Montero, Pickup, Precis, 3000GT

INTRODUCTION

This article contains underhood views or schematics of vacuum hose routing. Use these vacuum diagrams during the visual inspection in BASIC DIAGNOSTIC PROCEDURES article. This will assist in identifying improperly routed vacuum hoses, which cause driveability and/or computer-indicated malfunctions.

NOTE: Always refer to Emission Control label in engine compartment before attempting service. If manual and label differ, always use emission label specifications.

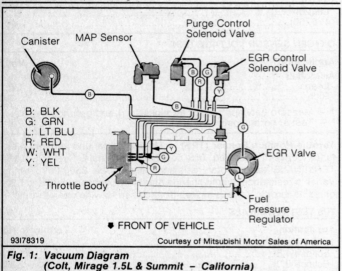

93I78319   Courtesy of Mitsubishi Motor Sales of America

Fig. 1: Vacuum Diagram (Colt, Mirage 1.5L & Summit – California)

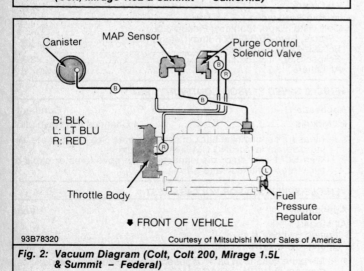

93B78320   Courtesy of Mitsubishi Motor Sales of America

Fig. 2: Vacuum Diagram (Colt, Colt 200, Mirage 1.5L & Summit – Federal)

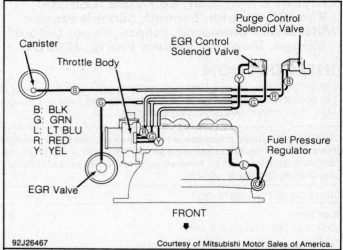

92J26467   Courtesy of Mitsubishi Motor Sales of America.

Fig. 3: Vacuum Diagram (Colt Vista, Expo, Mirage 1.8L & Summit Wagon – California)

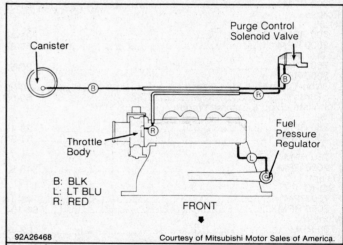

92A26468   Courtesy of Mitsubishi Motor Sales of America.

Fig. 4: Vacuum Diagram (Colt Vista 1.8L, Expo 1.8L, Mirage 1.8L & Summit Wagon 1.8L – Federal)

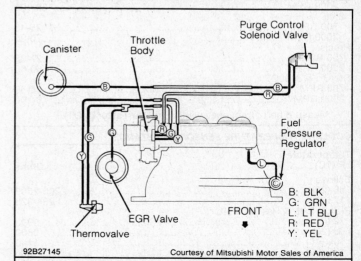

92B27145   Courtesy of Mitsubishi Motor Sales of America.

Fig. 5: Vacuum Diagram (Colt Vista 2.4L, Expo 2.4L & Summit Wagon 2.4L – Federal)

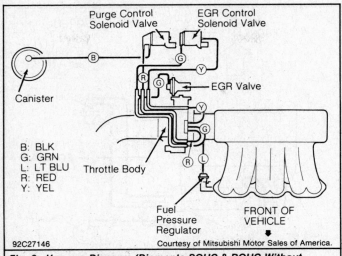

Fig. 6: Vacuum Diagram (Diamante SOHC & DOHC Without Traction Control – California)

92C27146 — Courtesy of Mitsubishi Motor Sales of America.

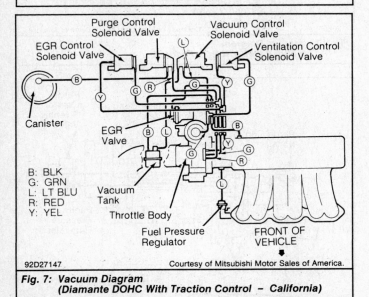

Fig. 7: Vacuum Diagram (Diamante DOHC With Traction Control – California)

92D27147 — Courtesy of Mitsubishi Motor Sales of America.

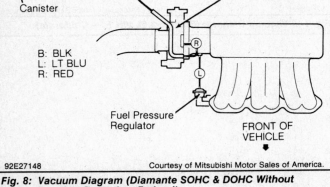

Fig. 8: Vacuum Diagram (Diamante SOHC & DOHC Without Traction Control – Federal)

92E27148 — Courtesy of Mitsubishi Motor Sales of America.

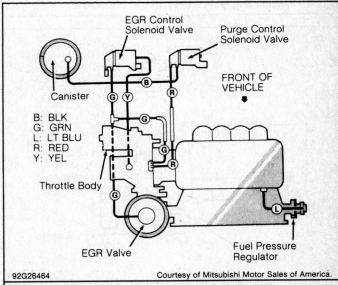

Fig. 9: Vacuum Diagram (Diamante DOHC With Traction Control – Federal)

92F27149 — Courtesy of Mitsubishi Motor Sales of America.

Fig. 10: Vacuum Diagram (Eclipse 1.8L – California)

92G26464 — Courtesy of Mitsubishi Motor Sales of America.

1993 ENGINE PERFORMANCE
Vacuum Diagrams (Cont.)

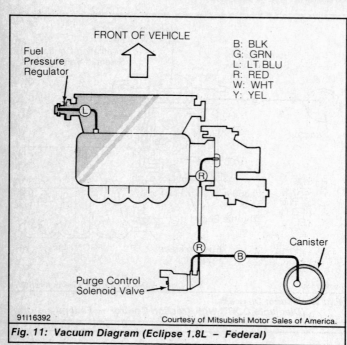

Fig. 11: Vacuum Diagram (Eclipse 1.8L – Federal)

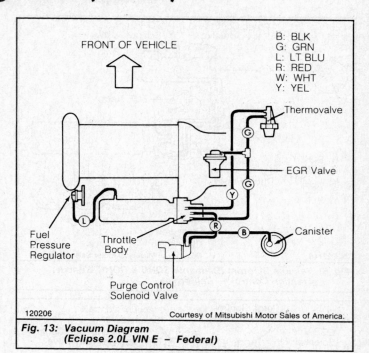

Fig. 13: Vacuum Diagram
(Eclipse 2.0L VIN E – Federal)

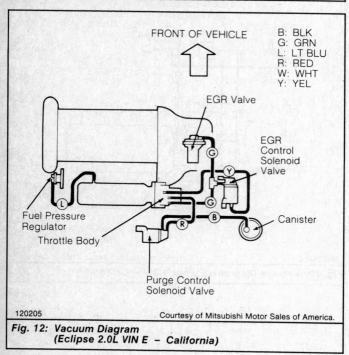

Fig. 12: Vacuum Diagram
(Eclipse 2.0L VIN E – California)

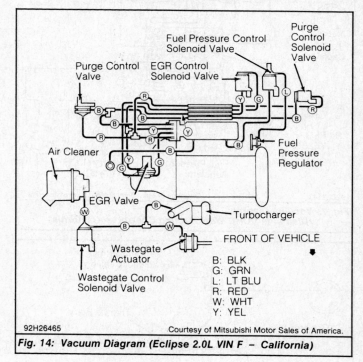

Fig. 14: Vacuum Diagram (Eclipse 2.0L VIN F – California)

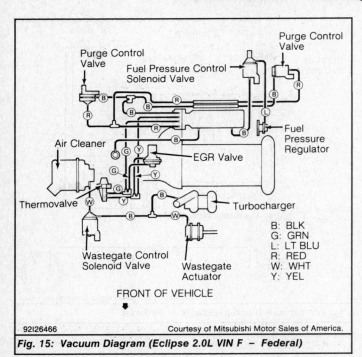

Fig. 15: Vacuum Diagram (Eclipse 2.0L VIN F – Federal)

Purge Control Valve
Purge Control Valve
Fuel Pressure Control Solenoid Valve
Air Cleaner
Thermovalve
EGR Valve
Fuel Pressure Regulator
Turbocharger
Wastegate Control Solenoid Valve
Wastegate Actuator
FRONT OF VEHICLE

B: BLK
G: GRN
L: LT BLU
R: RED
W: WHT
Y: YEL

92126466
Courtesy of Mitsubishi Motor Sales of America.

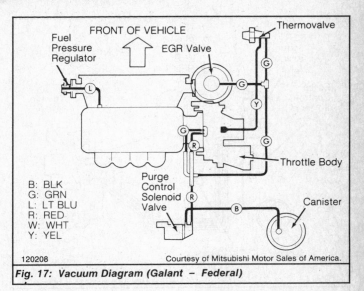

Fig. 17: Vacuum Diagram (Galant – Federal)

FRONT OF VEHICLE
Fuel Pressure Regulator
EGR Valve
Thermovalve
Purge Control Solenoid Valve
Throttle Body
Canister

B: BLK
G: GRN
L: LT BLU
R: RED
W: WHT
Y: YEL

120208
Courtesy of Mitsubishi Motor Sales of America.

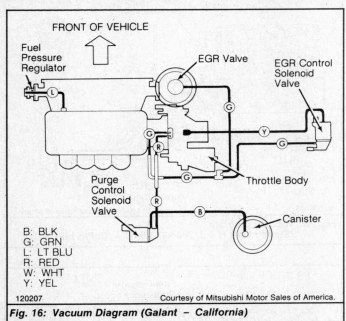

Fig. 16: Vacuum Diagram (Galant – California)

FRONT OF VEHICLE
Fuel Pressure Regulator
EGR Valve
EGR Control Solenoid Valve
Purge Control Solenoid Valve
Throttle Body
Canister

B: BLK
G: GRN
L: LT BLU
R: RED
W: WHT
Y: YEL

120207
Courtesy of Mitsubishi Motor Sales of America.

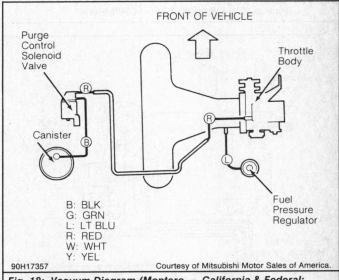

Fig. 18: Vacuum Diagram (Montero – California & Federal; Pickup 3.0L & Ram-50 3.0L – Federal)

FRONT OF VEHICLE
Purge Control Solenoid Valve
Throttle Body
Canister
Fuel Pressure Regulator

B: BLK
G: GRN
L: LT BLU
R: RED
W: WHT
Y: YEL

90H17357
Courtesy of Mitsubishi Motor Sales of America.

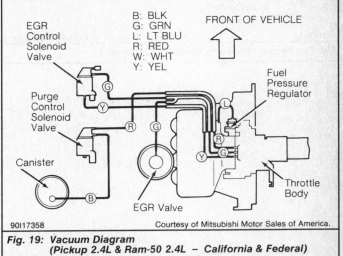

Fig. 19: Vacuum Diagram (Pickup 2.4L & Ram-50 2.4L – California & Federal)

EGR Control Solenoid Valve
Purge Control Solenoid Valve
Canister
EGR Valve
FRONT OF VEHICLE
Fuel Pressure Regulator
Throttle Body

B: BLK
G: GRN
L: LT BLU
R: RED
W: WHT
Y: YEL

90I17358
Courtesy of Mitsubishi Motor Sales of America.

1993 ENGINE PERFORMANCE
Vacuum Diagrams (Cont.)

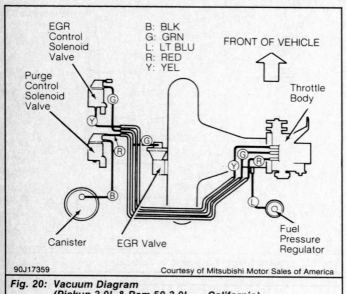

90J17359   Courtesy of Mitsubishi Motor Sales of America

Fig. 20: Vacuum Diagram
(Pickup 3.0L & Ram-50 3.0L – California)

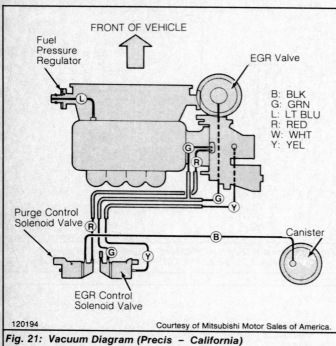
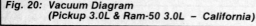

120194   Courtesy of Mitsubishi Motor Sales of America.

Fig. 21: Vacuum Diagram (Precis – California)

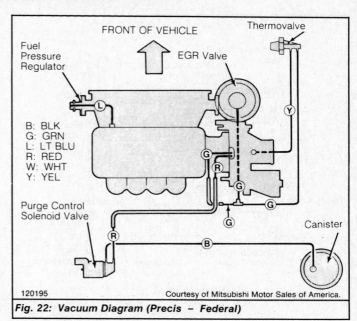

120195   Courtesy of Mitsubishi Motor Sales of America.

Fig. 22: Vacuum Diagram (Precis – Federal)

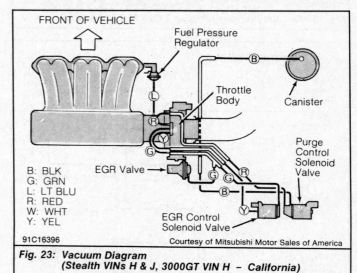

91C16396   Courtesy of Mitsubishi Motor Sales of America

Fig. 23: Vacuum Diagram
(Stealth VINs H & J, 3000GT VIN H – California)

91B16395   Courtesy of Mitsubishi Motor Sales of America

Fig. 24: Vacuum Diagram
(Stealth VINs H & J, & 3000GT VIN H – Federal)

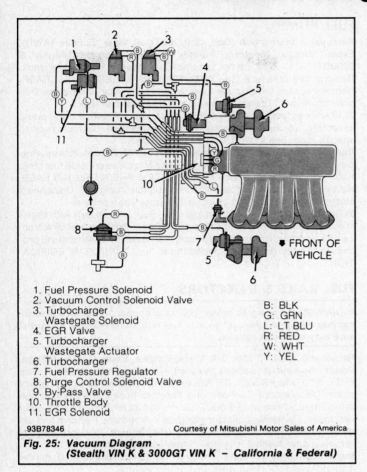

1. Fuel Pressure Solenoid
2. Vacuum Control Solenoid Valve
3. Turbocharger
   Wastegate Solenoid
4. EGR Valve
5. Turbocharger
   Wastegate Actuator
6. Turbocharger
7. Fuel Pressure Regulator
8. Purge Control Solenoid Valve
9. By-Pass Valve
10. Throttle Body
11. EGR Solenoid

B: BLK
G: GRN
L: LT BLU
R: RED
W: WHT
Y: YEL

◆ FRONT OF
VEHICLE

93B78346

Courtesy of Mitsubishi Motor Sales of America

Fig. 25: Vacuum Diagram
(Stealth VIN K & 3000GT VIN K – California & Federal)

1993 ENGINE PERFORMANCE
Removal, Overhaul & Installation

Chrysler Corp.: Colt, Colt Vista, Colt 200, Ram-50, Stealth, Summit, Summit Wagon
Mitsubishi: Diamante, Eclipse, Expo, Galant, Mirage, Montero, Pickup, Precis, 3000GT

INTRODUCTION

Removal, overhaul and installation procedures are covered in this article. If component removal and installation is primarily an unbolt and bolt-on procedure, only a torque specification may be furnished.

IGNITION SYSTEM

DISTRIBUTOR

NOTE: *Diamante 3.0L DOHC, Eclipse 2.0L, Stealth 3.0L DOHC & 3000GT use Distributorless Ignition System (DIS). All models (except Precis) with distributor type ignition systems have non-serviceable distributors. See Fig. 1 for exploded view of Precis distributor.*

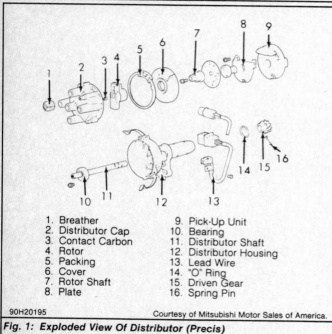

1. Breather
2. Distributor Cap
3. Contact Carbon
4. Rotor
5. Packing
6. Cover
7. Rotor Shaft
8. Plate
9. Pick-Up Unit
10. Bearing
11. Distributor Shaft
12. Distributor Housing
13. Lead Wire
14. "O" Ring
15. Driven Gear
16. Spring Pin

90H20195   Courtesy of Mitsubishi Motor Sales of America.

Fig. 1: Exploded View Of Distributor (Precis)

FUEL SYSTEM

WARNING: *Always relieve fuel pressure before disconnecting any fuel injection-related component. DO NOT allow fuel to contact engine or electrical components.*

FUEL SYSTEM PRESSURE RELEASE

Relieving Fuel Pressure – 1) On Diamante, Eclipse 2WD, Galant, Pickup, Precis and Ram-50, disconnect fuel pump harness connector at fuel tank from underneath vehicle. On Colt, Colt 200, Colt Vista, Eclipse (AWD), Expo, Mirage, Montero, Stealth, Summit, Summit Wagon and 3000GT, remove access panel under seat, in trunk or in rear cargo area to disconnect fuel pump harness connector.

2) On all models, start engine. Let engine run until it stops. Turn ignition off. Disconnect negative battery terminal. Connect fuel pump harness connector. Reinstall rear seat (if necessary.)

WARNING: *Before disconnecting high pressure fuel hose at fuel delivery pipe, cover fuel hose connection with a rag. Some residual fuel pressure may still be in system.*

FUEL PUMP

Removal & Installation (Colt, Colt 200, Colt Vista, Eclipse (AWD), Expo, Mirage, Montero, Stealth, Summit, Summit Wagon & 3000GT) – 1) Fuel pump assembly is located inside fuel tank. Release fuel pressure. See FUEL SYSTEM PRESSURE RELEASE. Remove access panel under seat, in trunk or in rear cargo area. Disconnect electrical connectors and fuel hoses at fuel tank.

2) Remove fuel filler hose from fuel tank. Remove fuel pump assembly. To install, reverse removal procedure. Tighten nuts to specification. See TORQUE SPECIFICATIONS.

Removal & Installation (Diamante, Eclipse 2WD, Galant, Pickup, Precis and Ram-50) – 1) Fuel pump assembly is located inside fuel tank. Release fuel pressure. See FUEL SYSTEM PRESSURE RELEASE. Raise vehicle on hoist. Drain fuel into suitable container. Disconnect electrical connectors and breather/fuel hoses at fuel tank.

2) Remove fuel filler hose from fuel tank. Support fuel tank with transmission jack. Remove nuts securing fuel tank. Remove fuel tank from vehicle. Remove fuel pump assembly. To install, reverse removal procedure. Tighten nuts to specification. See TORQUE SPECIFICATIONS.

FUEL RAILS & INJECTORS

WARNING: *Use a rag to cover fuel hose connection before disconnecting high pressure fuel hose at fuel rail. Some residual fuel pressure may still be in system.*

Removal (Colt, Colt 200, Colt Vista, Eclipse, Expo, Galant, Mirage, Precis, Summit & Summit Wagon) – Relieve fuel pressure. See FUEL SYSTEM PRESSURE RELEASE. Disconnect negative battery cable. Disconnect PCV hose and breather hoses. Disconnect high pressure fuel hose at fuel rail. Disconnect fuel return hose and vacuum hoses. Disconnect injector electrical connectors. Remove fuel rail bolts, and lift fuel rail and injectors from engine. Injectors may be removed after fuel rail is removed from intake manifold.

Installation – 1) To install, reverse removal procedure. Use new insulators and "O" rings when installing injectors.

2) Use lubricant on "O" rings. Install injectors into fuel rail with a twisting motion. Ensure injectors rotate smoothly when installing. DO NOT drop injectors while removing or installing fuel rail.

Removal (Pickup 2.4L & Ram-50 2.4L) – 1) Relieve fuel pressure. See FUEL SYSTEM PRESSURE RELEASE. Drain enough coolant to ensure coolant level is below throttle body. Disconnect negative battery cable. Remove air intake and breather hoses. Disconnect throttle body wiring harness connectors. Disconnect accelerator cable.

2) On A/T models, disconnect kickdown cable. Disconnect coolant hoses from throttle body. Label and disconnect vacuum hoses as necessary. Remove throttle body and gasket. Disconnect fuel injector wiring harness connectors.

3) Disconnect high pressure fuel hose at fuel rail. Disconnect fuel return hose. Disconnect vacuum hoses. Disconnect injector electrical connectors. Remove fuel rail bolts and lift fuel rail and injectors from engine. Injectors may be removed after fuel rail is removed from intake manifold.

Installation – 1) To install, reverse removal procedure. Use new insulators and "O" rings when installing injectors.

2) Use lubricant on "O" rings. Install injectors into fuel rail using a twisting motion. Ensure injectors rotate smoothly when installing. Adjust throttle and kickdown cable (if necessary). DO NOT drop injectors while removing or installing fuel rail.

Removal (Pickup 3.0L, Montero & Ram-50 3.0L) – 1) Relieve fuel pressure. See FUEL SYSTEM PRESSURE RELEASE. Disconnect negative battery cable. Remove air intake hose. Remove accelerator cable adjusting bolts. On A/T models, remove throttle control cable. On all models, remove accelerator cable. Label and disconnect all vacuum hoses from throttle body and upper intake manifold (air intake plenum).

2) Remove EGR pipe and gasket. Remove ignition coil (if necessary). Remove engine oil filler neck bracket. Disconnect PCV hose. Remove throttle body leaving coolant hoses connected. Remove throttle body gasket. Remove front and rear intake plenum brackets. Remove intake plenum mounting bolts. Remove intake plenum and gasket.

3) Disconnect high pressure fuel hose at fuel rail. Disconnect fuel return hose. Disconnect vacuum hoses. Disconnect injector electrical connectors. Remove fuel rail bolts and lift fuel rail and injectors from engine. Injectors may be removed after fuel rail is removed from intake manifold.

Installation – **1)** To install, reverse removal procedure. Use new insulators and "O" rings when installing injectors.

2) Use lubricant on "O" rings. Install injectors into fuel rail using a twisting motion. Ensure injectors rotate smoothly when installing. DO NOT drop injectors while removing or installing fuel rail. Adjust throttle control and accelerator cables (if necessary). Refill cooling system.

Removal (Diamante, Stealth & 3000GT) – **1)** Relieve fuel pressure. See FUEL SYSTEM PRESSURE RELEASE. Disconnect negative battery cable. Drain coolant. Remove air intake hose. Remove throttle body and gasket with control cables and vacuum hoses attached.

2) Remove EGR pipe (if equipped). Disconnect power brake hose. Label and disconnect vacuum hoses and wiring harness connectors as necessary. Remove intake plenum brackets and mounting bolts. Remove intake plenum and gasket.

3) Disconnect high pressure fuel hose at fuel rail. Disconnect fuel return hose. Disconnect vacuum hoses. Disconnect injector electrical connectors. Remove fuel rail bolts, and lift fuel rail and injectors from engine. Injectors may be removed after fuel rail is removed from intake manifold.

Installation – **1)** To install, reverse removal procedure. Use new insulators and "O" rings when installing injectors.

2) Use on "O" rings. Install injectors into fuel rail with a twisting motion. Ensure injectors rotate smoothly when installing. DO NOT drop injectors while removing or installing fuel rail. Refill cooling system.

OXYGEN (O₂) SENSOR

Removal & Installation – **1)** O₂ sensor is mounted in exhaust pipe below exhaust header. It is equipped with a permanent pigtail which must be protected from damage when sensor is removed. Ensure sensor is free of contaminants. Avoid using cleaning solvents of any type.

2) Sensor may be difficult to remove when engine temperature is less than 120°F (48°C). Always use anti-seize compound on threads before installation. Tighten O₂ sensor to specification. See TORQUE SPECIFICATIONS.

THROTTLE BODY

Removal – Disconnect air intake hose. Remove accelerator, cruise control and A/T throttle valve cables (if equipped). Disconnect fuel vapor hose, electrical harness connector, vacuum hose and coolant hoses. Remove throttle body retaining bolts.

Disassembly – Remove throttle position sensor. Remove idle speed control motor. Remove throttle bracket and connector bracket (if equipped). Remove idle position switch and adjusting nut (if equipped).

NOTE: *DO NOT remove throttle valve. DO NOT use cleaning solvents on throttle position sensor, idle speed control motor or idle position switch.*

Cleaning – Clean all parts except throttle position sensor, idle speed control motor and idle position switch in solvent. Check vacuum port and passage for clogging. Clean vacuum, vapor and fuel passages using compressed air.

Reassembly – To reassemble, reverse disassembly procedure.

Installation – To install, reverse removal procedure.

THROTTLE POSITION SENSOR

Removal & Installation – Throttle Position Sensor (TPS) is located on throttle body. Disconnect TPS electrical connector. Remove TPS screws and TPS. To install, reverse removal procedure. Tighten TPS screws to specification. See TORQUE SPECIFICATIONS. For TPS adjustment procedure, see ON-VEHICLE ADJUSTMENTS article.

TURBOCHARGERS

Removal (Eclipse) – **1)** Disconnect negative battery cable. Drain engine coolant and oil. On models with equipped A/C, remove condenser fan motor assembly. Remove O₂ sensor. Remove oil dipstick guide and "O" ring.

2) Disconnect air intake hose and vacuum hoses. Remove air hose and air outlet housing. Remove heat protectors. Disconnect exhaust pipe. Remove power steering oil pump and bracket. Remove engine hanger bracket. Disconnect oil inlet pipe.

3) Disconnect coolant hose and tubes. Remove nuts and bolts securing exhaust manifold. Remove exhaust manifold and gaskets. Disconnect oil return pipe. Remove turbocharger assembly.

Removal (Stealth & 3000GT – Front) – **1)** Disconnect negative battery cable. Drain engine oil and coolant. Remove radiator. Disconnect exhaust pipe. Remove air intake hose, air hoses and air pipe. Remove alternator and belt. Remove oil dipstick guide.

2) Remove heat protector. Disconnect oxygen sensor electrical connector. Remove oil return pipe. Remove turbocharger support bracket, and remove turbocharger from exhaust manifold.

Removal (Stealth & 3000GT – Rear) – **1)** Disconnect battery cables, and remove battery. Drain engine oil and drain cooling system. Remove accelerator cable. Remove air hose, air pipe and heat protectors. Disconnect clutch booster vacuum hose. Remove air intake hoses and EGR pipe. Disconnect O₂ sensor electrical connector.

2) Remove oil pipe and EGR valve. Disconnect exhaust fitting, and remove rear heat protector. Remove oil return pipe. Remove turbocharger assembly.

Inspection (All Models) – Check turbine and compressor wheels for cracking and other damage. Ensure turbine and compressor wheels turn smoothly. Check for oil leakage from turbocharger assembly. Check for proper wastegate valve operation. See SYSTEM & COMPONENT TESTING article.

Installation (All Models) – **1)** To install, reverse removal procedure. Before oil pipe flare nut (above turbocharger) is installed, pour clean engine oil into oil pipe installation hole of turbocharger. Ensure oil and air hoses are properly installed and securely clamped.

2) Use new gaskets. Adjust accelerator cable (if necessary). Refill engine oil and coolant. Check for oil and coolant leaks. Tighten all bolts to specification. See TORQUE SPECIFICATIONS table.

TORQUE SPECIFICATIONS
TORQUE SPECIFICATIONS

Applications	Ft. Lbs. (N.m)
Exhaust Manifold-To-Engine Nuts	18-22 (24-30)
Exhaust Manifold-To-Turbocharger Bolts	40-47 (54-64)
Exhaust Pipe Bolts	22-29 (30-39)
Fuel Tank Drain Plug	11-18 (15-24)
Fuel Tank Nuts	15-22 (20-30)
Oil Pipe-To-Engine	10-14 (14-19)
Oxygen (O₂) Sensor	29-36 (39-49)
Plenum-To-Intake Manifold Bolts	11-15 (15-20)
Water Pipe-To-Turbocharger	
Except Stealth & 3000GT	25-36 (34-49)
Stealth & 3000GT	22 (30)

	INCH Lbs. (N.m)
Fuel Rail Bolts	84-108 (9.0-12.0)
Heat Protector Bolts	108-132 (12.0-15.0)
ISC Switch Screws	20-54 (2.5-4.5)
TPS Switch Screws	13-20 (1.5-2.5)
Wastegate Actuator Bolts	84-108 (9.0-12.0)

1993 ENGINE PERFORMANCE
Wiring Diagrams

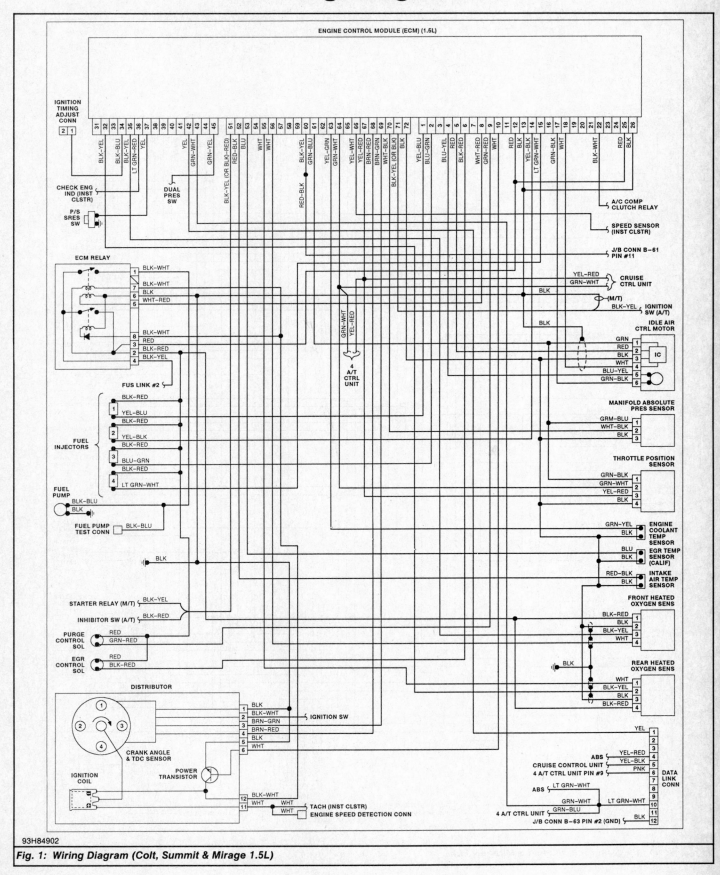

Fig. 1: Wiring Diagram (Colt, Summit & Mirage 1.5L)

93H84902

1993 ENGINE PERFORMANCE
Wiring Diagrams (Cont.)

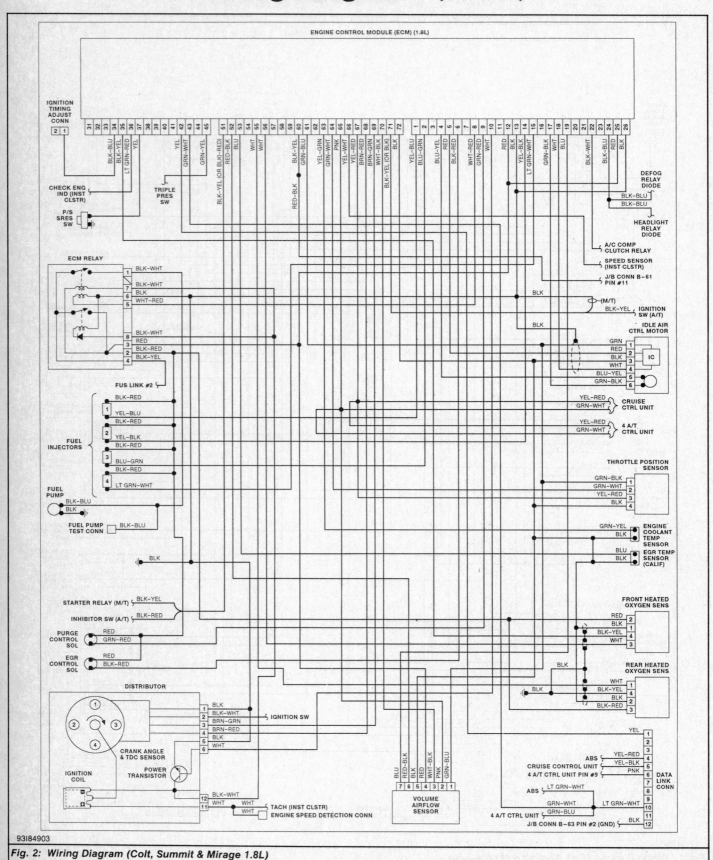

Fig. 2: *Wiring Diagram (Colt, Summit & Mirage 1.8L)*

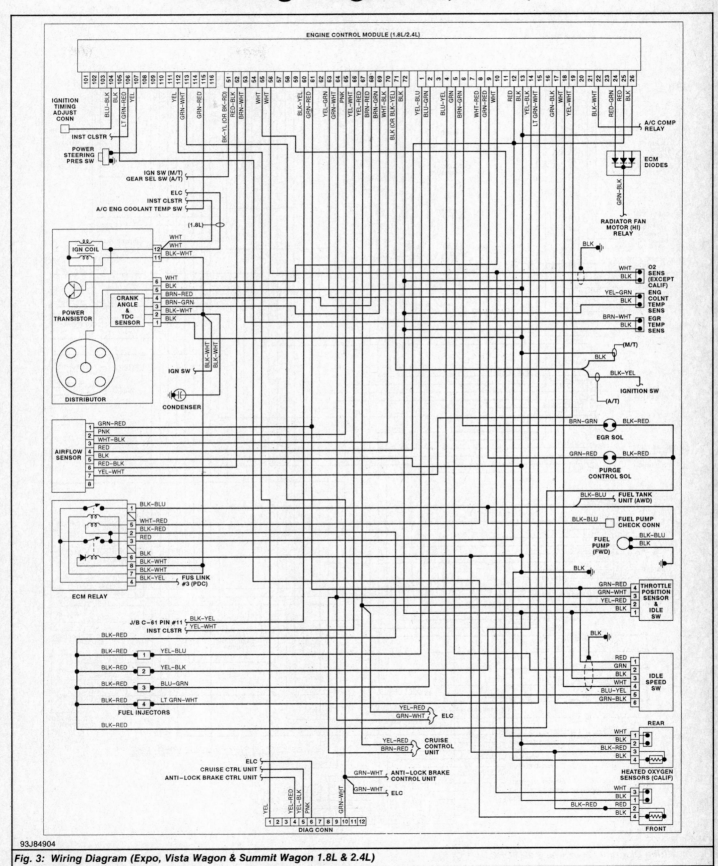

Fig. 3: Wiring Diagram (Expo, Vista Wagon & Summit Wagon 1.8L & 2.4L)

93J84904

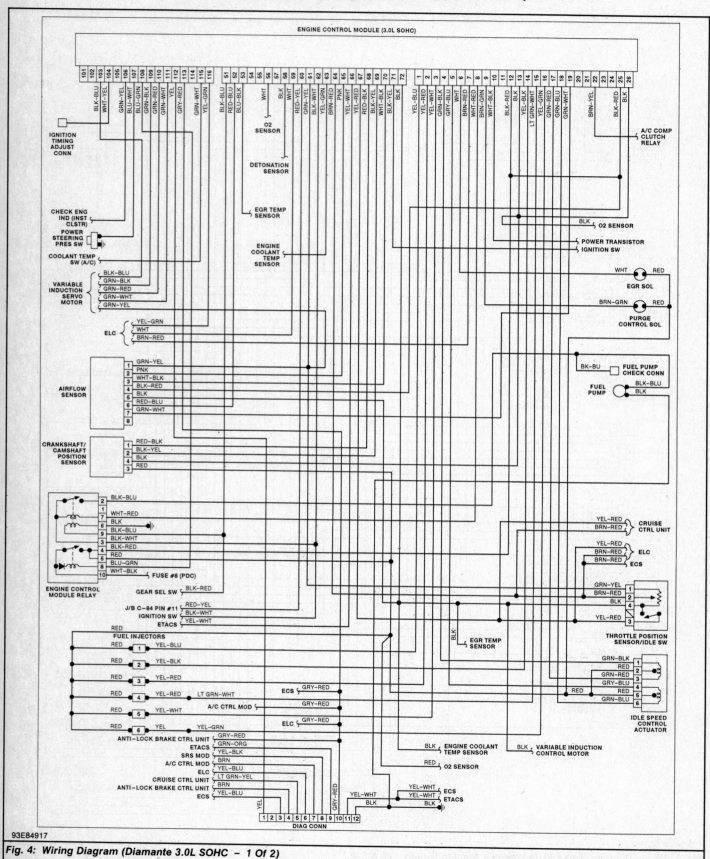

Fig. 4: Wiring Diagram (Diamante 3.0L SOHC - 1 Of 2)

93E84917

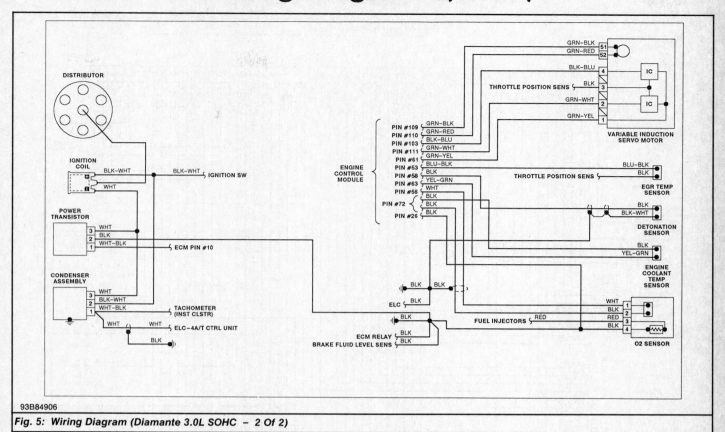

Fig. 5: *Wiring Diagram (Diamante 3.0L SOHC – 2 Of 2)*

93B84906

1993 ENGINE PERFORMANCE
Wiring Diagrams (Cont.)

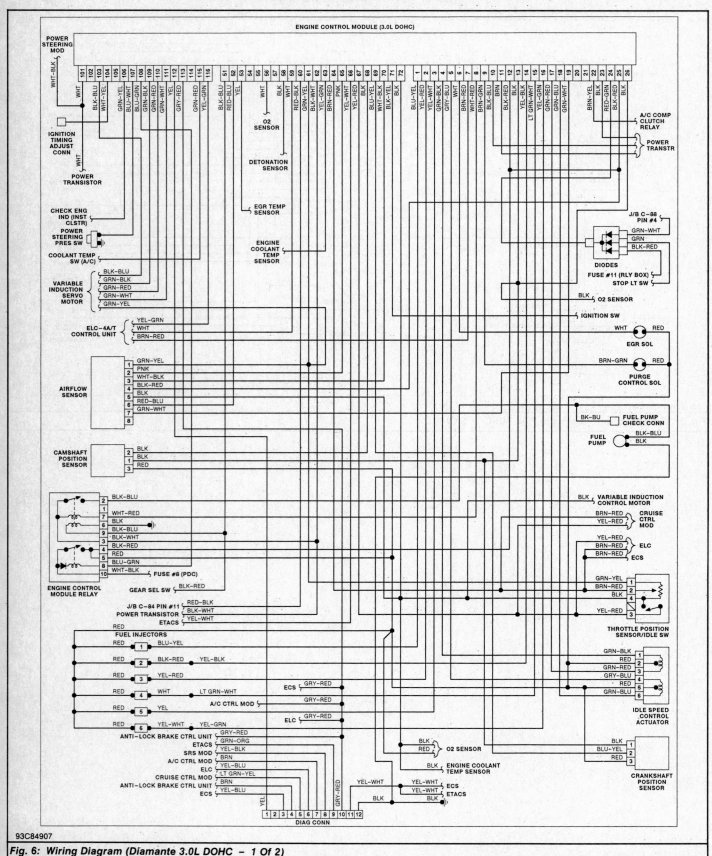

Fig. 6: Wiring Diagram (Diamante 3.0L DOHC – 1 Of 2)

93C84907

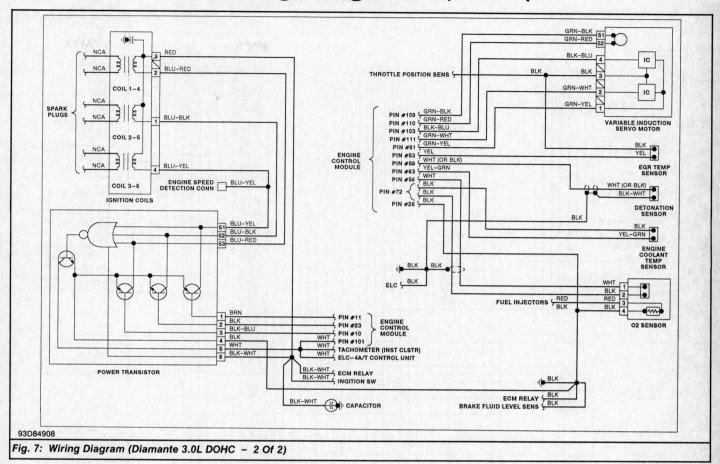

Fig. 7: Wiring Diagram (Diamante 3.0L DOHC – 2 Of 2)

93D84908

1993 ENGINE PERFORMANCE
Wiring Diagrams (Cont.)

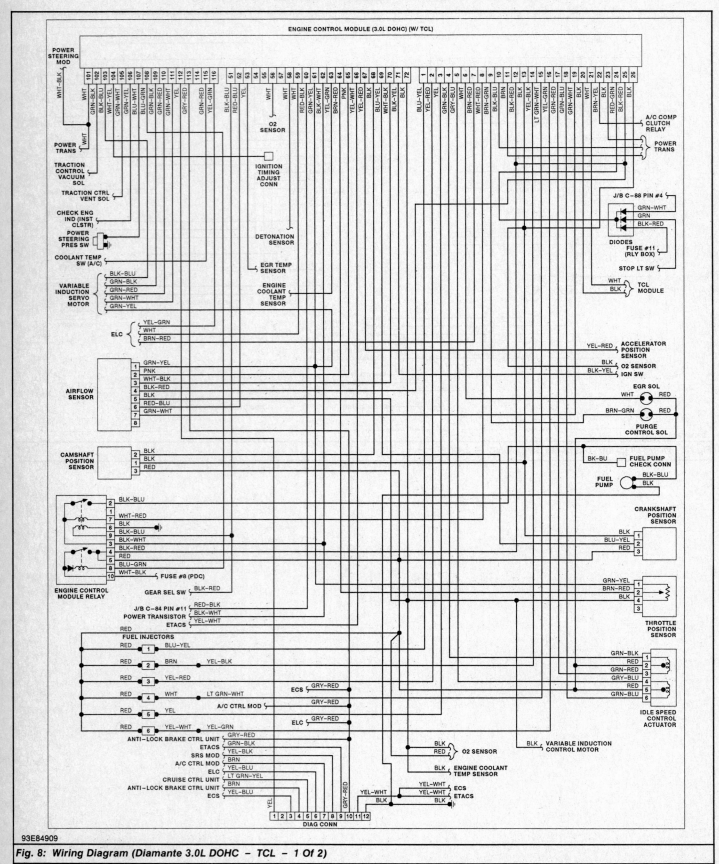

Fig. 8: Wiring Diagram (Diamante 3.0L DOHC – TCL – 1 Of 2)

93E84909

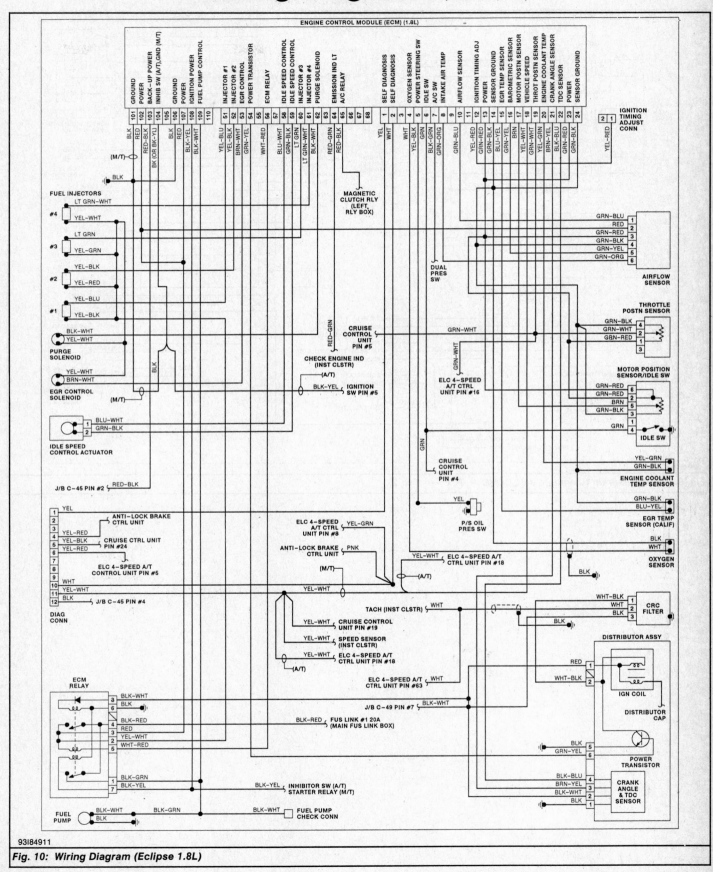

Fig. 10: *Wiring Diagram (Eclipse 1.8L)*

93I84911

1993 ENGINE PERFORMANCE
Wiring Diagrams (Cont.)

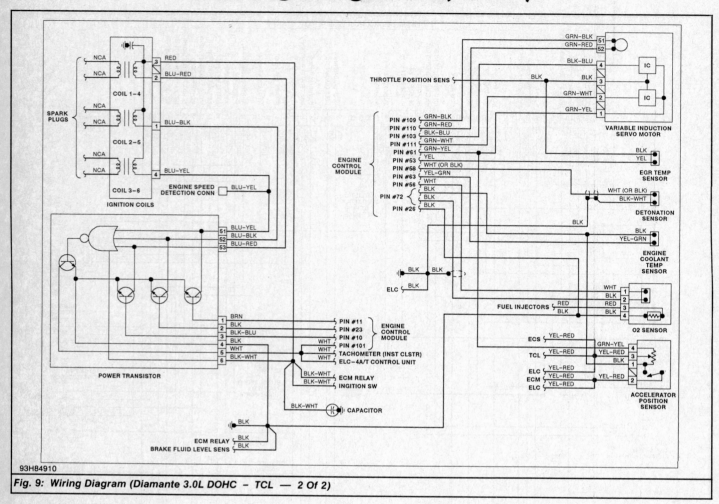

93H84910

Fig. 9: Wiring Diagram (Diamante 3.0L DOHC – TCL — 2 Of 2)

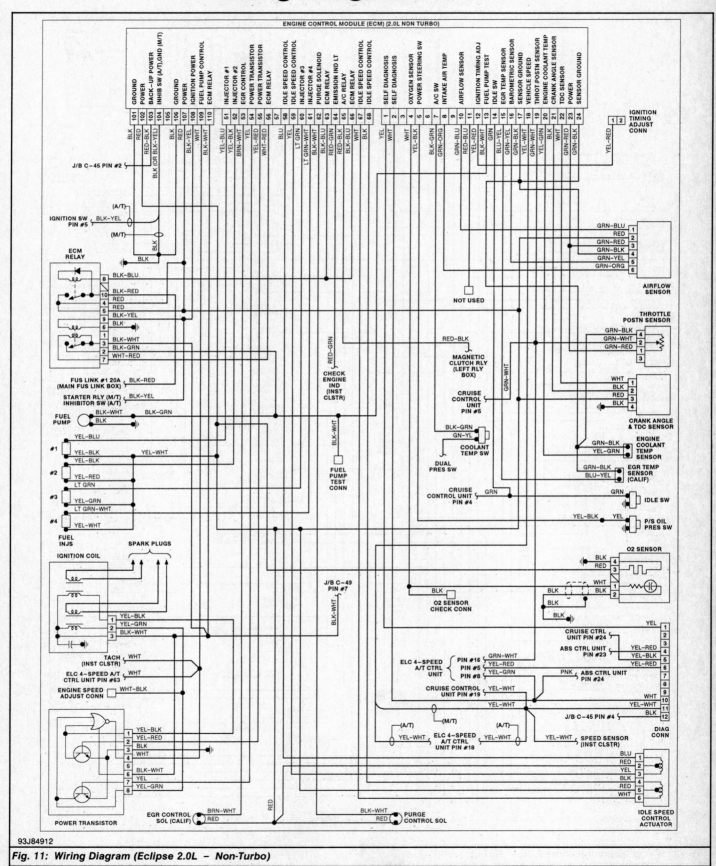

Fig. 11: Wiring Diagram (Eclipse 2.0L – Non-Turbo)

93J84912

1993 ENGINE PERFORMANCE
Wiring Diagrams (Cont.)

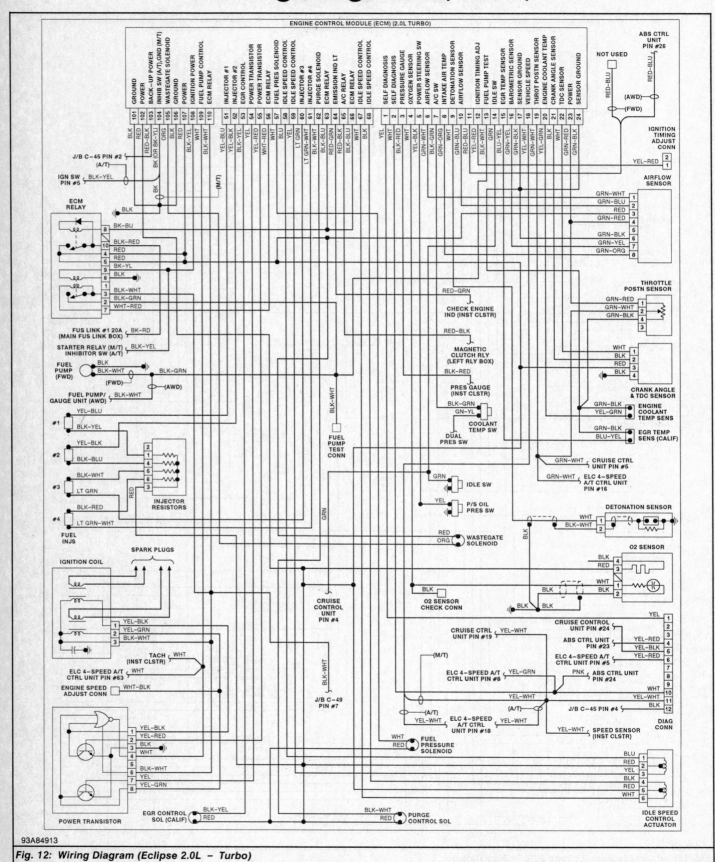

Fig. 12: Wiring Diagram (Eclipse 2.0L - Turbo)

93A84913

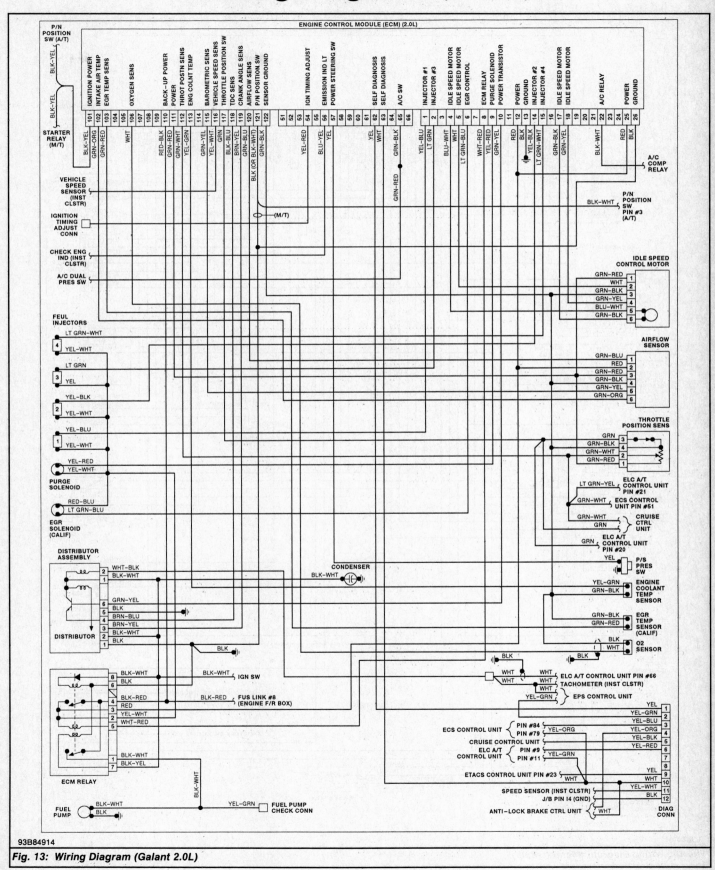

Fig. 13: Wiring Diagram (Galant 2.0L)

93B84914

1993 ENGINE PERFORMANCE
Wiring Diagrams (Cont.)

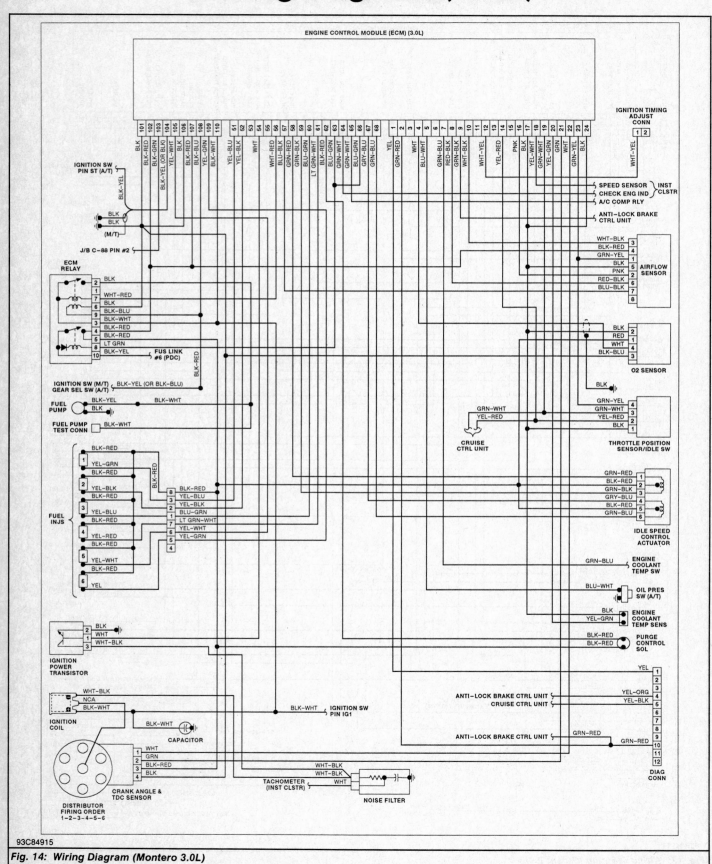

93C84915

Fig. 14: Wiring Diagram (Montero 3.0L)

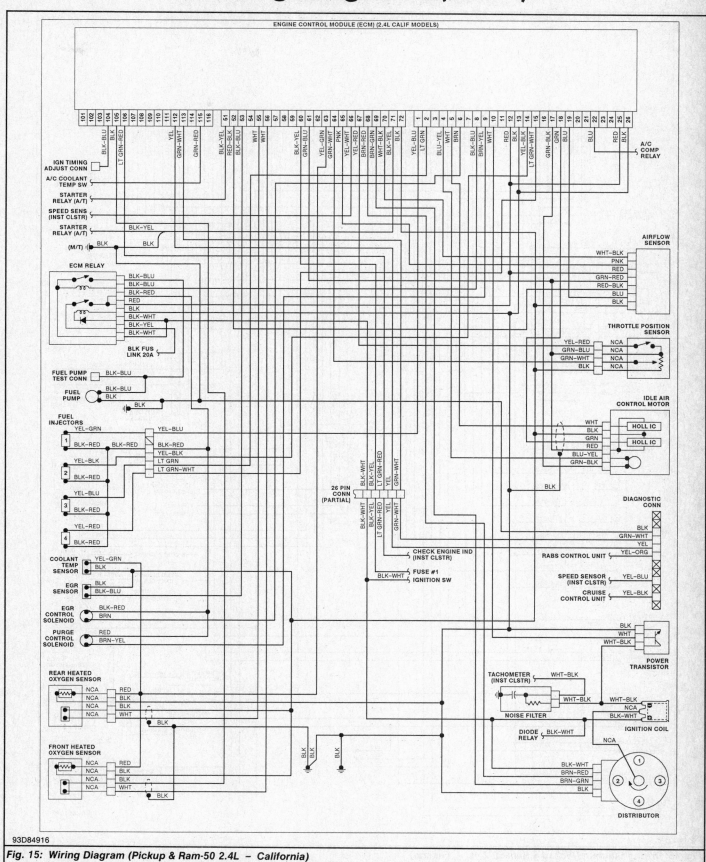

Fig. 15: *Wiring Diagram (Pickup & Ram-50 2.4L – California)*

93D84916

1993 ENGINE PERFORMANCE
Wiring Diagrams (Cont.)

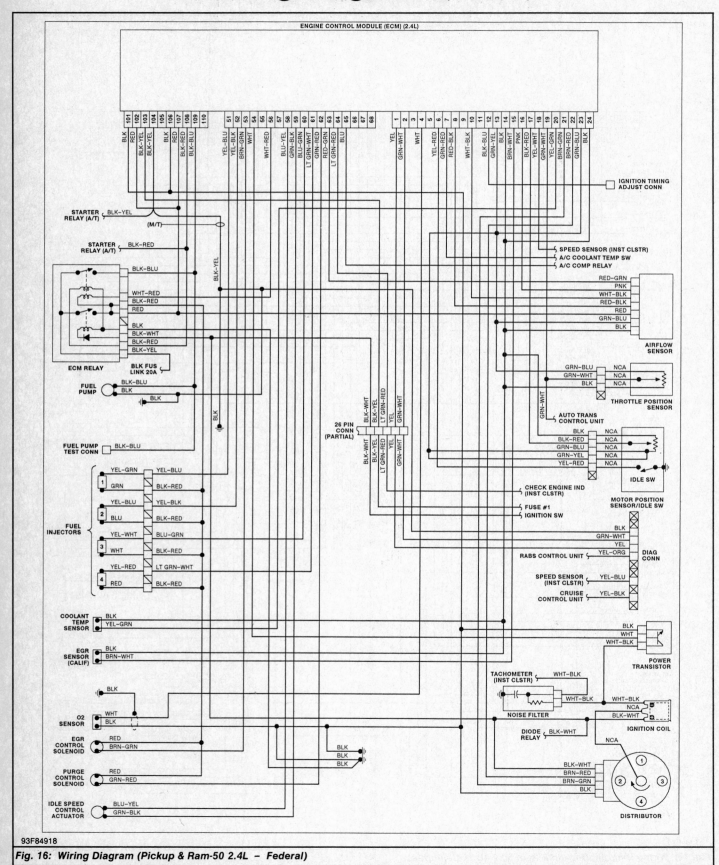

Fig. 16: Wiring Diagram (Pickup & Ram-50 2.4L – Federal)

93F84918

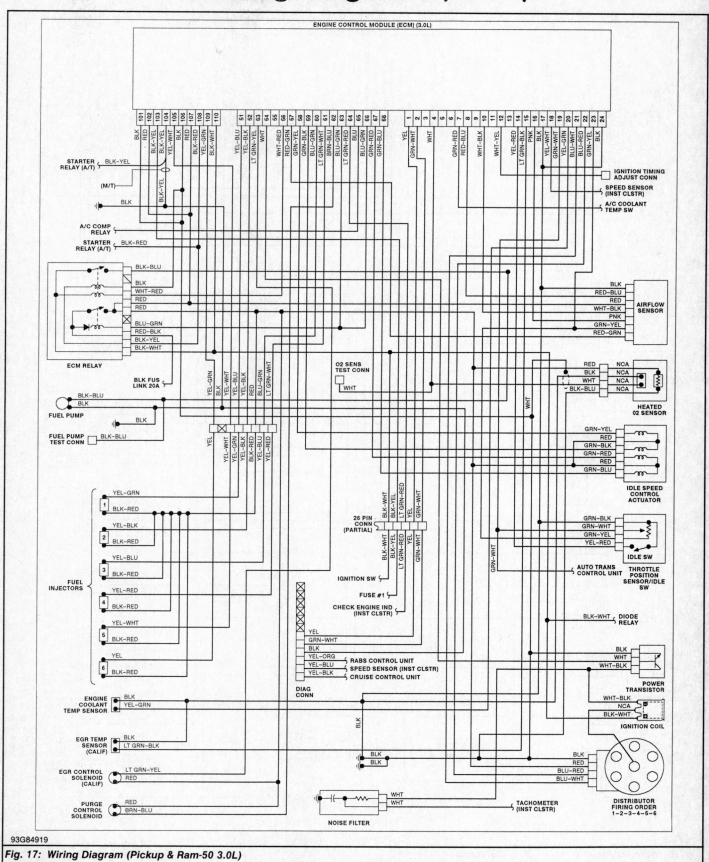

Fig. 17: Wiring Diagram (Pickup & Ram-50 3.0L)

1993 ENGINE PERFORMANCE
Wiring Diagrams (Cont.)

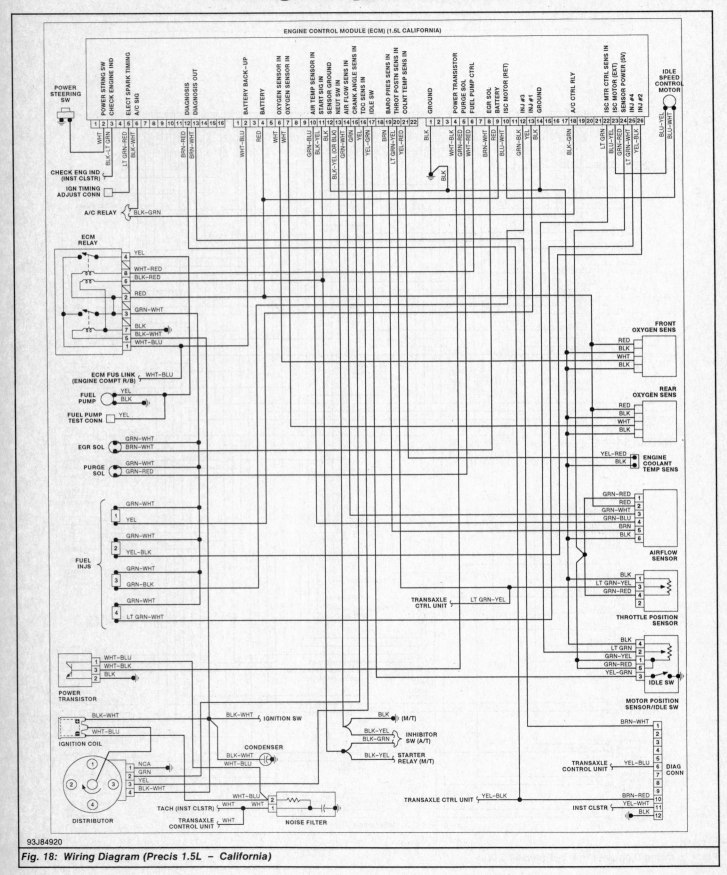

Fig. 18: Wiring Diagram (Precis 1.5L – California)

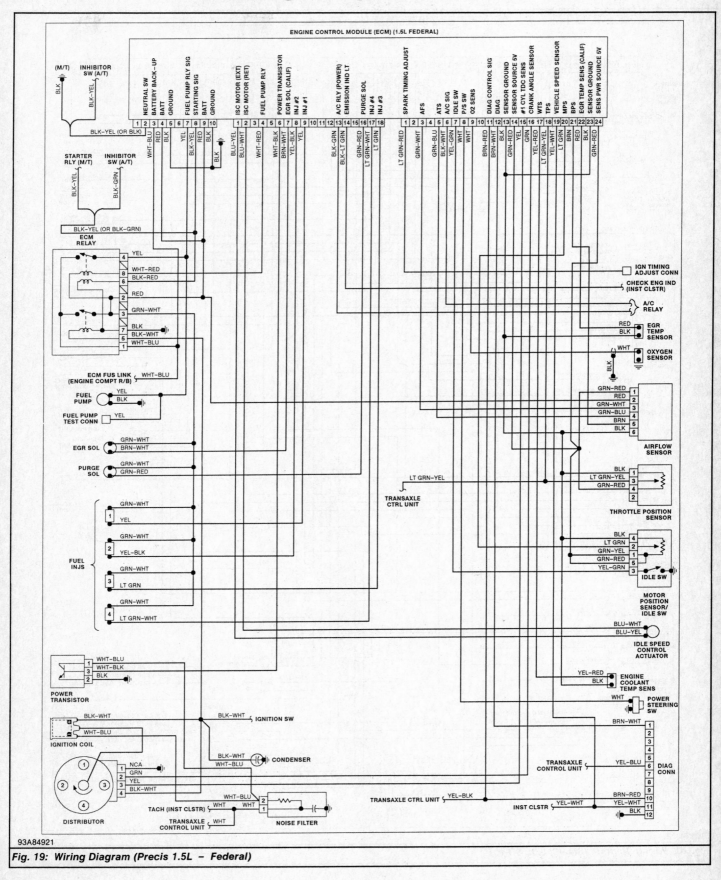

Fig. 19: Wiring Diagram (Precis 1.5L – Federal)

93A84921

1993 ENGINE PERFORMANCE
Wiring Diagrams (Cont.)

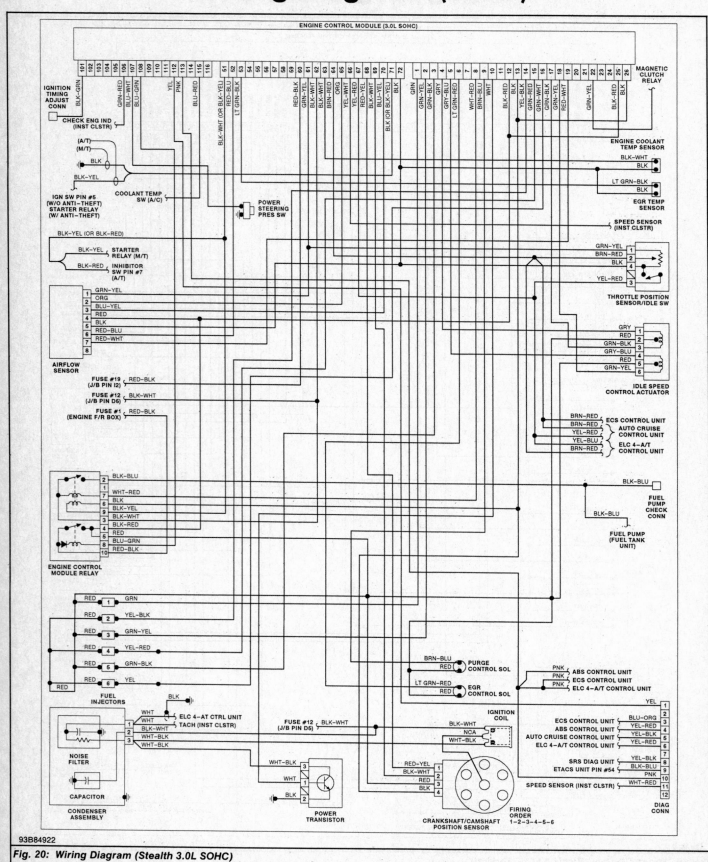

Fig. 20: Wiring Diagram (Stealth 3.0L SOHC)

93B84922

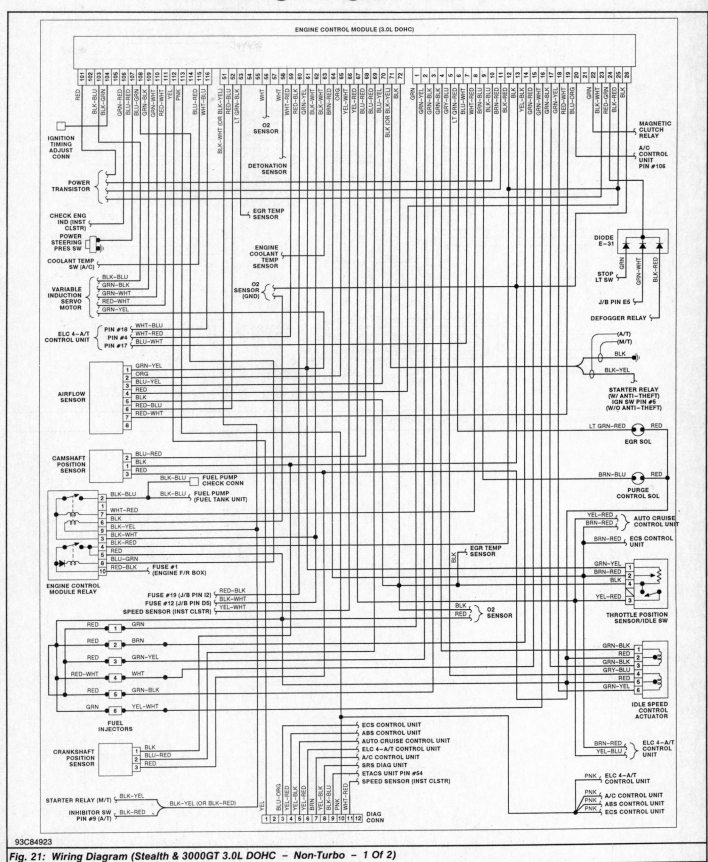

Fig. 21: Wiring Diagram (Stealth & 3000GT 3.0L DOHC – Non-Turbo – 1 Of 2)

93C84923

1993 ENGINE PERFORMANCE
Wiring Diagrams (Cont.)

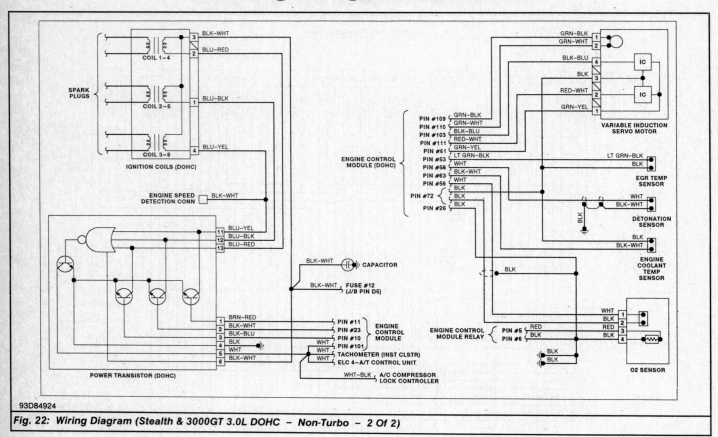

93D84924

Fig. 22: Wiring Diagram (Stealth & 3000GT 3.0L DOHC – Non-Turbo – 2 Of 2)

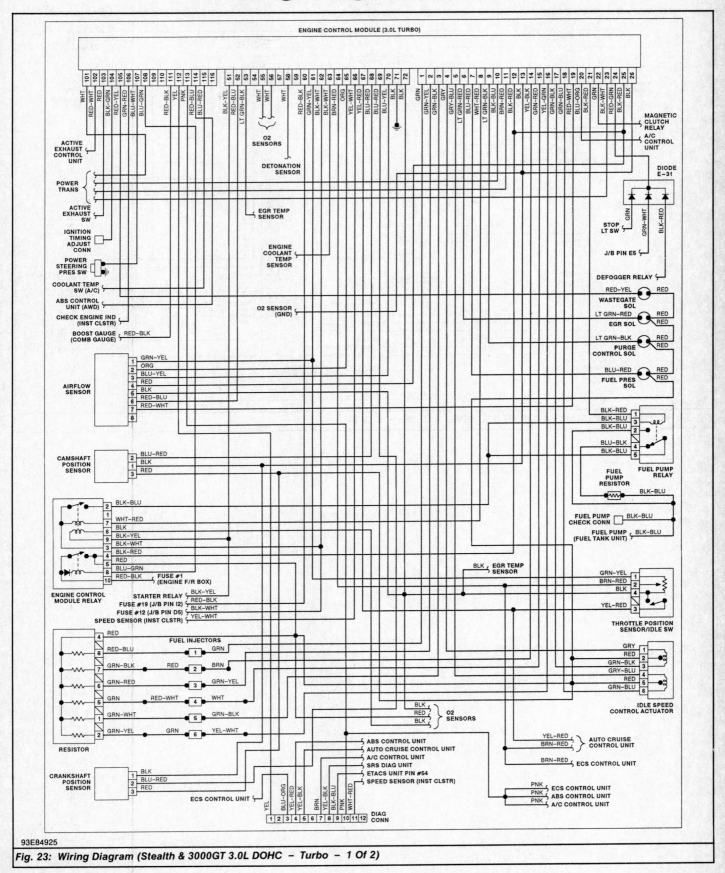

Fig. 23: Wiring Diagram (Stealth & 3000GT 3.0L DOHC – Turbo – 1 Of 2)

93E84925

1993 ENGINE PERFORMANCE
Wiring Diagrams (Cont.)

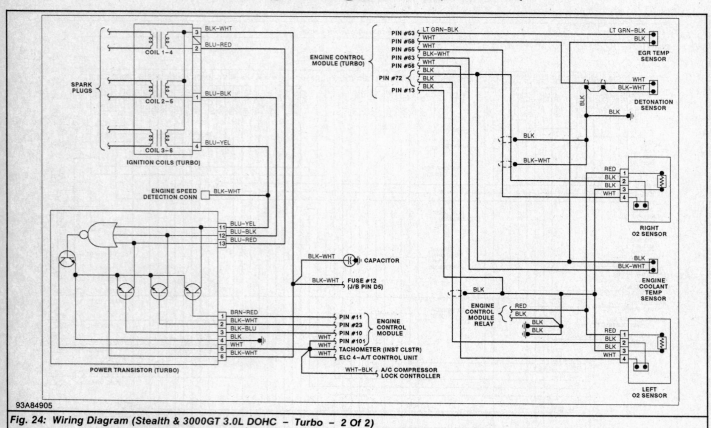

93A84905

Fig. 24: Wiring Diagram (Stealth & 3000GT 3.0L DOHC – Turbo – 2 Of 2)

**Chrysler Corp.: Colt, Colt Vista, Colt 200, Ram-50, Stealth, Summit, Summit Wagon
Mitsubishi: Diamante, Eclipse, Expo, Galant, Mirage, Montero, Pickup, Precis, 3000GT**

DESCRIPTION

Mitsubishi alternators are conventional 3-phase, self-rectifying type units containing 6 diodes (3 positive and 3 negative) which are used to rectify current. All models use a case-mounted Integrated Circuit (IC) voltage regulator.

Alternator relay or resistor with diode is used to ensure charging of battery even if charging indicator light is defective.

ADJUSTMENTS
ALTERNATOR BELT ADJUSTMENT

Application	Deflection [1] New Belt In. (mm)	Deflection [1] Used Belt In. (mm)
Colt, Colt 200, Mirage, & Summit		
1.5L	.22-.28 (5.6-7.1)	.31 (7.9)
1.8L	.28-.34 (7.1-8.6)	.37 (9.4)
Diamante		
SOHC	.15-.19 (3.8-4.8)	.23-.31 (5.8-7.9)
DOHC	.13-.15 (3.3-3.8)	.15-.19 (3.8-4.8)
Eclipse		
1.8L	.31-.43 (7.9-10.9)	[2]
2.0L	.35-.43 (8.9-10.9)	[2]
Colt Vista, Expo, & Summit Wagon		
1.8L	.28-.34 (7.1-8.6)	.37 (9.4)
2.4L	.30-.35 (7.6-8.9)	.40 (10.2)
Galant	.29-.35 (7.4-8.9)	.39 (9.9)
Montero	.25-.31 (6.4-7.9)	.35 (8.9)
Pickup & Ram-50		
2.4L	.27-.39 (6.9-9.9)	[2]
3.0L	.31-.39 (7.9-9.9)	[2]
Precis	.28-.32 (7.1-8.1)	[2]
Stealth		
SOHC	.15-.19 (3.8-4.8)	.23-.31 (5.8-7.9)
DOHC	.13-.15 (3.3-3.8)	.15-.19 (3.8-4.8)
3000GT	.13-.15 (3.3-3.8)	.15-.19 (3.8-4.8)

[1] – With 22 lbs. (10 kg) pressure applied midway on belt run.
[2] – Information is not available from manufacturer.

TROUBLE SHOOTING

NOTE: See TROUBLE SHOOTING article in GENERAL INFORMATION.

ON-VEHICLE TESTING
ALTERNATOR TO BATTERY CONTINUITY TEST

NOTE: Check alternator wiring harness connections and drive belt tension and ensure battery is fully charged before performing test.

1) Turn ignition switch to OFF position. Disconnect negative battery cable. Remove output lead from alternator terminal "B". *See Fig. 1.* Install a 100-amp ammeter in series with terminal "B" and disconnected output lead. Install positive lead of ammeter to terminal "B" and negative lead to disconnected output wire.

2) Install a digital voltmeter between alternator terminal "B" and positive battery terminal. Install positive voltmeter lead to terminal "B" and negative lead to positive battery terminal. Reconnect negative battery cable.

3) Start engine. Turn accessories on and adjust engine speed until ammeter indicates 20 amps, and note voltmeter reading. If voltmeter indicates .2 volt or less, system is okay.

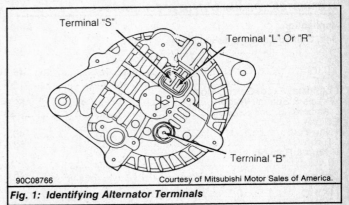

Fig. 1: Identifying Alternator Terminals

4) If voltage is greater than .2 volt, wiring is defective between alternator terminal "B", fusible link and positive battery terminal. Disconnect negative battery cable, and remove test equipment.

ALTERNATOR OUTPUT TEST

NOTE: During alternator output test, a slightly discharged battery should be used as a fully charged battery may not allow full alternator output.

1) Turn ignition switch to OFF position. Disconnect negative battery cable. Disconnect alternator output wire from terminal "B". Install positive lead of 100-amp ammeter to terminal "B" and negative lead to disconnected output lead.

CAUTION: Tighten each connection securely as heavy current flow will exist. DO NOT use clips on ammeter.

2) Connect positive voltmeter lead (0-20 volts) to alternator terminal "B" and negative lead to ground. Install tachometer, and reconnect negative battery cable.
3) Ensure voltmeter indicates battery voltage. If no voltage exists, an open circuit is present in wire between alternator terminal "B" and negative battery terminal. Check grounds and fusible link.
4) Turn headlights on, and start engine. Set headlights at high beam and heater switch on HIGH. Quickly accelerate engine speed to 2500 RPM and note alternator output current on ammeter. Minimum output should be within specification. See ALTERNATOR MINIMUM OUTPUT SPECIFICATIONS table.

NOTE: Output voltage changes with electrical load and temperature. Ensure proper electrical load is applied while checking output. Nominal output may not be obtained if alternator or ambient temperature is excessive. Allow alternator or temperature to cool, and recheck output. Alternator output is stamped on metal plate attached to alternator case.

5) If minimum output is not obtained and alternator wiring is okay, repair alternator. Disconnect negative battery cable, and remove test equipment.

REGULATED VOLTAGE TEST

NOTE: Ensure battery is fully charged and proper drive belt tension exists.

1) Turn ignition switch to OFF position. Disconnect negative battery cable. Connect positive voltmeter lead to terminal "S" of alternator. *See Fig. 1.* Connect negative voltmeter lead to ground.
2) Disconnect alternator output wire from terminal "B". Install a 100-amp ammeter in series with terminal "B" and disconnected output lead. Install positive lead of ammeter to terminal "B" and negative lead to disconnected output wire. Install a tachometer, and reconnect negative battery cable.

ALTERNATOR MINIMUM OUTPUT SPECIFICATIONS

Application	Amps
Colt, Colt 200, Mirage & Summit	
1.5L	52.5
1.8L	
M/T	45.5
A/T	49
Colt Vista, Expo, Galant, Montero,	
Precis & Summit Wagon	52.5
Diamante	63
Eclipse	
Non-Turbo	45.5
Turbo	52.5
Pickup & Ram-50	
2.4L	28
3.0L	45.5
Stealth	
DOHC	77
SOHC	63
3000GT	77

3) Turn ignition switch to ON position and ensure voltmeter indicates battery voltage. If no voltage exists, there is an open in wire between alternator terminal "S" and positive battery terminal or fusible link is blown.

4) Start engine. Ensure all lights and accessories are off. Operate engine at 2500 RPM and read voltmeter when alternator output current drops to 10 amps or less. Voltage regulator is okay if voltage output is within specification. See REGULATOR VOLTAGE SPECIFICATIONS table.

REGULATOR VOLTAGE SPECIFICATIONS

Ambient Temperature	Voltage
-4°F (-20°C)	14.2-15.4
68°F (20°C)	13.9-14.9
140°F (60°C)	13.4-14.6
176°F (80°C)	13.1-14.5

BENCH TESTING

RECTIFIER ASSEMBLY

1) Using ohmmeter, check for continuity between diodes and stator coil lead connection. *See Fig. 2.* Reverse leads. If continuity exists in both directions, diode is shorted. Replace rectifier assembly.

2) To check entire diode assembly, use an ohmmeter to check for continuity between both ends of each diode. *See Fig. 2.* Switch ohmmeter leads. Continuity should exist in one direction only. If no continuity exists or continuity exists in both directions, diode is defective. Replace rectifier assembly.

ROTOR

1) Check continuity across rotor slip rings. Resistance should be 3-5 ohms (3.1 ohms on Precis). Replace rotor if no continuity exists or resistance is not within specification.

2) Check continuity between individual slip rings and rotor shaft. If continuity exists, rotor coil or slip ring is grounded. Replace rotor.

STATOR

Ensure no continuity exists between stator coil leads and stator core. Check continuity between leads of stator coil. If no continuity exists between coil leads, replace stator.

OVERHAUL

Replace brushes if worn to limit line. Limit line is line closest to rotor contact end of brush. Brushes can be retained in brush holder while installing rotor by inserting wire into back of rear housing. *See Fig. 3.*

WIRING DIAGRAMS

See appropriate chassis wiring diagram in WIRING DIAGRAMS.

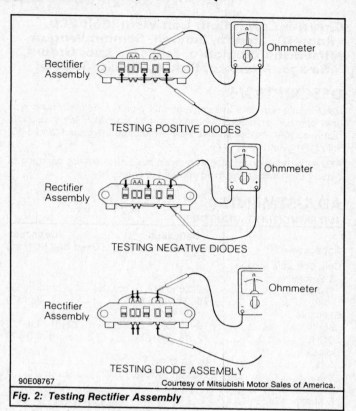

TESTING POSITIVE DIODES

TESTING NEGATIVE DIODES

TESTING DIODE ASSEMBLY

90E08767   Courtesy of Mitsubishi Motor Sales of America.

Fig. 2: Testing Rectifier Assembly

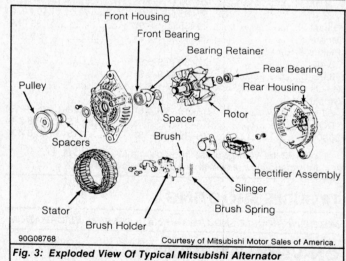

90G08768   Courtesy of Mitsubishi Motor Sales of America.

Fig. 3: Exploded View Of Typical Mitsubishi Alternator

Chrysler Corp.: Colt, Colt Vista, Colt 200, Ram-50, Stealth, Summit, Summit Wagon
Mitsubishi: Diamante, Eclipse, Expo, Galant, Mirage, Montero, Pickup, Precis, 3000GT

DESCRIPTION

The starter is a conventional 12-volt, 4-pole brush-type motor, with direct or gear reduction drive. The starter-mounted solenoid shifts overrunning clutch and pinion into flywheel when starter is energized.

BENCH TESTING

STARTER NO-LOAD TEST

CAUTION: Perform tests in less than 10 seconds to prevent coil damage.

1) Install starter in soft-jawed vise. Connect starter in series with a fully-charged 12-volt battery. Connect a 100-amp ammeter and carbon pile rheostat in series with positive battery post and starter motor terminal. *See Fig. 1.*
2) Install voltmeter across starter motor. Adjust carbon pile rheostat to full resistance. Connect cable from starter motor body to negative battery terminal. Adjust carbon pile rheostat to proper test voltage. See STARTER NO-LOAD TEST SPECIFICATIONS table.
3) Ensure maximum amperage is as specified and starter rotates smoothly. See STARTER NO-LOAD TEST SPECIFICATIONS table.

STARTER NO-LOAD TEST SPECIFICATIONS

Application	[1] Starter Type	Test Voltage	Maximum Amps @ Minimum RPM
Colt, Colt 200, Mirage & Summit			
1.5L			
A/T	GR	11	90 @ 3000
M/T	DD	11.5	60 @ 6600
1.8L			
A/T	GR	11	90 @ 3000
M/T	DD	11.5	53 @ 6000
Colt Vista, Expo & Summit			
1.8L			
A/T	GR	11	90 @ 3000
M/T	DD	11.5	53 @ 6000
2.4L			
A/T	GR	11	90 @ 3000
M/T	DD	11.5	60 @ 6600
Diamante, Galant, Montero, Stealth & 3000GT	GR	11	90 @ 3000
Eclipse			
1.8L	DD	11.5	60 @ 6600
2.0L	GR	11	90 @ 3000
Pickup & Ram-50			
2.4L			
A/T	GR	11	90 @ 3000
M/T	DD	11.5	60 @ 6600
3.0L	GR	11	90 @ 3000
Precis	DD	11.5	60 @ [2]

[1] – DD indicates direct drive. GR indicates gear reduction.
[2] – Minimum RPM information is not available for Precis.

PULL-IN COIL TEST

1) Disconnect field coil wire from terminal "M" at starter solenoid. *See Fig. 2.* Connect jumper wire between positive battery terminal of 12-volt battery and terminal "S" of solenoid.

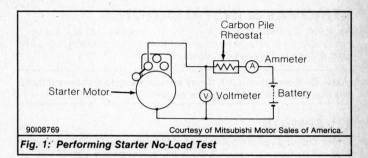

Fig. 1: Performing Starter No-Load Test

2) Connect a second jumper wire from negative battery terminal and touch terminal "M" of starter solenoid. If solenoid plunger moves inward, solenoid is good. If solenoid plunger does not move inward, replace solenoid.

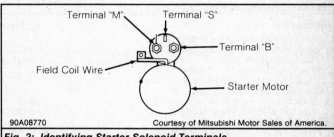

Fig. 2: Identifying Starter Solenoid Terminals

HOLD-IN COIL TEST

1) Disconnect field coil wire from terminal "M" at starter solenoid. *See Fig. 2.* Connect jumper wire between positive battery terminal of 12-volt battery and terminal "S" of starter solenoid.
2) Connect a second jumper wire from negative battery terminal and touch starter case. If solenoid plunger is pulled in, hold-in coil is good. If solenoid plunger is not pulled in, replace solenoid.

RETURN TEST

1) Disconnect field coil wire from terminal "M" at starter solenoid. *See Fig. 2.* Connect jumper wire between positive battery terminal of 12-volt battery and terminal "M" of starter solenoid.
2) Connect a second jumper wire from negative battery terminal and touch starter case. Pull pinion outward and release it. Replace solenoid if pinion remains out.

PINION GAP MEASUREMENT

1) Disconnect field coil wire from terminal "M" at starter solenoid. *See Fig. 2.* Connect jumper wire between positive battery terminal of 12-volt battery and terminal "S" of starter solenoid.
2) Connect a second jumper wire from negative battery terminal and touch terminal "M" of starter solenoid. Measure clearance between pinion and stopper. *See Fig. 3.*
3) Clearance should be within specification. See STARTER SPECIFICATIONS table. Adjust clearance by adding or removing gaskets between solenoid and front housing.

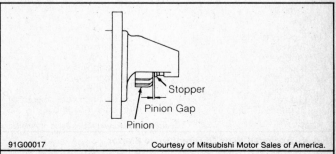

Fig. 3: Measuring Pinion Gap

REMOVAL & INSTALLATION

Removal & Installation – Disconnect negative battery cable. If necessary, raise vehicle on hoist. Remove starter mounting bolts and starter. To install, reverse removal procedure.

NOTE: On Montero with A/T, it may be necessary to disconnect transmission oil cooler line for starter removal.

OVERHAUL

Check commutator for out-of-round and proper amount of undercut. Replace or repair armature if not within specification. See STARTER SPECIFICATIONS table. Ensure brushes are not worn beyond wear line (outer line closest to commutator contact surface). Check pinion gap. See PINION GAP MEASUREMENT under BENCH TESTING. *See Figs. 4 and 5.*

STARTER SPECIFICATIONS

Application	In. (mm)
Commutator Maximum Runout [1]	
Except Pickup, Stealth & 3000GT	.002 (.05)
Pickup, Stealth & 3000GT	.004 (1.0)
Commutator Minimum Diameter [1]	
Colt, Colt Vista, Expo, Mirage	
Summit & Summit Wagon	
Direct Drive Type Starter	1.26 (32.0)
Gear Reduction Type Starter	1.16 (29.4)
Pickup & Ram-50	
2.4L	
A/T	1.16 (29.4)
M/T	1.26 (32.0)
Stealth & 3000GT	1.12 (28.4)
All Other Models	1.16 (29.4)
Commutator Undercut Depth [1]	.020 (.51)
Pinion Gap	.020-.079 (.51-2.01)

[1] – Information is not available for Precis.

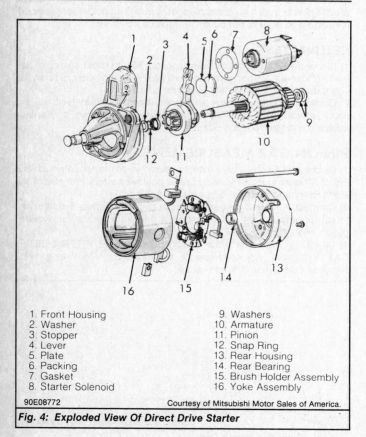

1. Front Housing
2. Washer
3. Stopper
4. Lever
5. Plate
6. Packing
7. Gasket
8. Starter Solenoid
9. Washers
10. Armature
11. Pinion
12. Snap Ring
13. Rear Housing
14. Rear Bearing
15. Brush Holder Assembly
16. Yoke Assembly

90E08772   Courtesy of Mitsubishi Motor Sales of America.

Fig. 4: Exploded View Of Direct Drive Starter

1. Packing
2. Ball
3. Starter Solenoid
4. Gasket
5. Packing
6. Plate
7. Lever
8. Front Housing
9. Snap Ring
10. Stopper
11. Pinion
12. Internal Gear
13. Planetary Gear Holder
14. Planetary Gear
15. Rear Housing
16. Brush Holder
17. Brush
18. Rear Bearing
19. Armature
20. Yoke Assembly

90I08774   Courtesy of Mitsubishi Motor Sales of America.

Fig. 5: Exploded View Of Gear Reduction Starter

WIRING DIAGRAMS

See appropriate chassis wiring diagram in WIRING DIAGRAMS.

1993 WIRING DIAGRAMS
Colt, Colt 200, Mirage & Summit

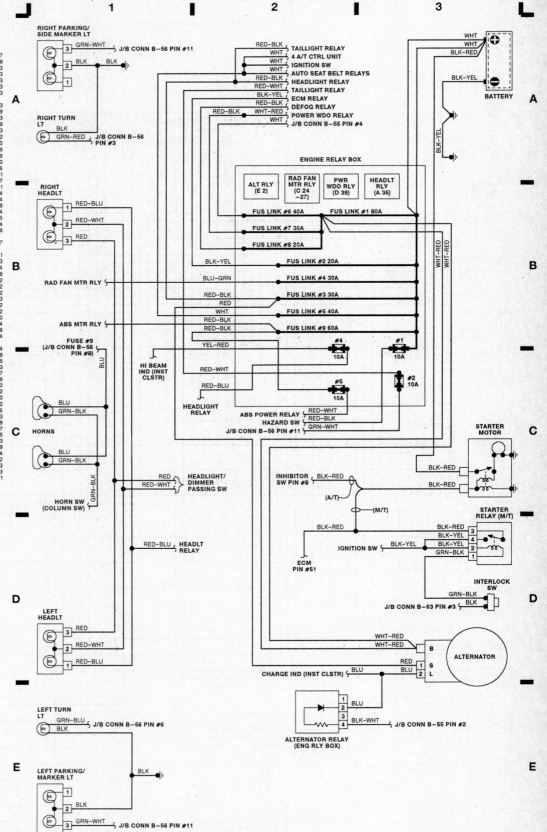

COMPONENT LOCATOR:

A/C–HEATER SYSTEM .... A–E 24–27
A/T SELECTOR LEVER ILLUM LT ..... B 28
ABS DIODE .... B 23
ABS MOTOR RELAY .... B 23
ABS POWER RELAY .... B 23
ALTERNATOR .... D 3
ALTERNATOR RELAY .... E 2–3
ANTI-LOCK BRAKE
  CTRL MODULE (ABS) .... A 20–23
ASHTRAY ILLUM LT .... E 39
AUTO SEAT BELT CTRL SYSTEM .. C–D 40–43
BACK-UP LT SWS .... B 28–29
BATTERY........................... A 3
BRAKE FLUID LEVEL SW .... E 32
BUZZER............................. E 40
CIG LTR/ILLUM LT .... E 39
CLOCK.............................. D 39
CLUTCH SW......................... C 30
CONN B–45 X (GROUND) .... A 36
CRUISE CTRL SYSTEM .... D–E 28–31
DATA LINK CONN (1.5L) .... E 7
DATA LINK CONN(1.8L) .... E 11
DEFOG SYSTEM................. D–E 44
DISTRIBUTOR (1.5L) .... E 4
DISTRIBUTOR (1.8L) .... E 8
DOME LT .... A 34
DOOR SWS........................ A 35
ECM RELAY (1.5L) .... B 4
ECM RELAY (1.8L) .... B 8
ENGINE CTRL MODULE
  (ECM) (1.5L) .... A–E 4–7
ENGINE CTRL MODULE
  (ECM) (1.8L) .... A 8–11
ENGINE RELAY BOX .... A–C 2–3
FUEL PUMP (1.5L) .... C 4
FUEL PUMP (1.8L) .... C 8
FUEL TANK UNIT .... E 32
FUS LINKS .... B–C 2
HAZARD SW....................... A 32
HEADLIGHT DIODE .... C 32–33
HEADLIGHT RELAY .... C 32
HEADLIGHT/DIMMER PASSING SW .. A–C 32
HORN SW.......................... E 20
IGNITION COIL (1.5L) .... E 4
IGNITION COIL (1.8L) .... E 8
IGNITION SW...................... E 14
IGNITION TIMING ADJUST
  CONN (1.5L) .... A 4
INHIBITOR SW .... A–B 28
INSTRUMENT CLUSTER .... B–E 35
INTERLOCK SW .... D 3
IOD OR STORAGE CONN .... D 3
JUNCTION BLOCK (J/B) ...... A–E 12–19
LUGGAGE COMPARTMENT LT/SW .. E 40
OIL PRES SW .... E 32
OVERDRIVE SW .... D 30
PARKING BRAKE SW .... E 32
POWER DOOR LOCK RELAY ...... C–D 36
POWER MIRROR SYSTEM ...... A–B 40–43
POWER WINDOW SYSTEM ..... A–D 37–39
RADIATOR FAN SYSTEM .... B–E 24–27
RHEOSTATS .... A–B 35
STARTER MOTOR/RELAY .... C–D 3
STOP LT SWS .... C–D 28–29
TAILLIGHT RELAY .... B 44
TURN SIGNAL SW .... D 32
WIPER MOTOR .... C 23
WIPER/WASHER SWS .... C–E 20–23
4 A/T CTRL UNIT .... A–D 31

1993 WIRING DIAGRAMS
Colt, Colt 200, Mirage & Summit (Cont.)

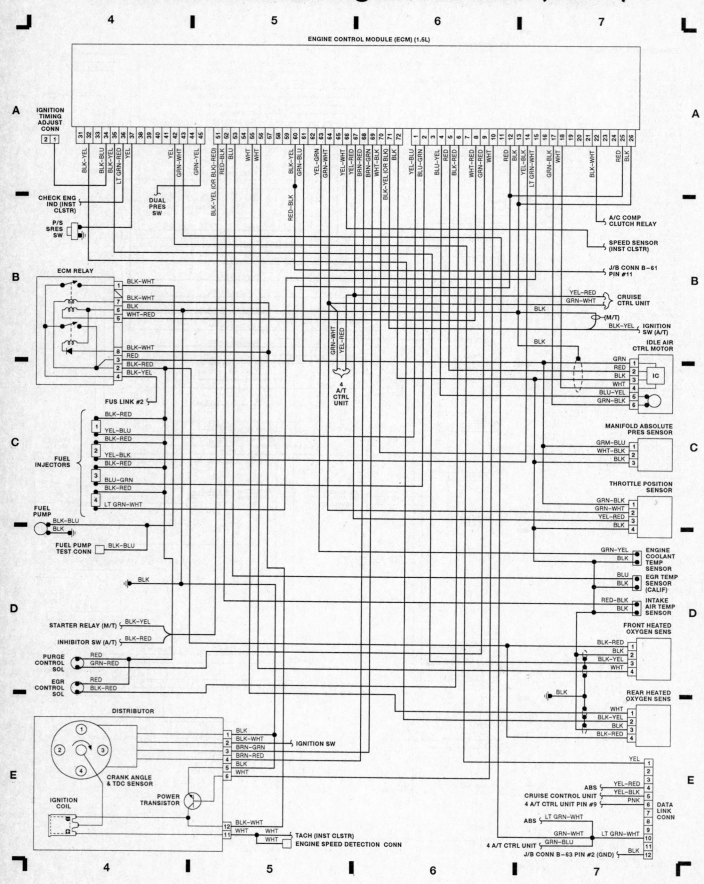

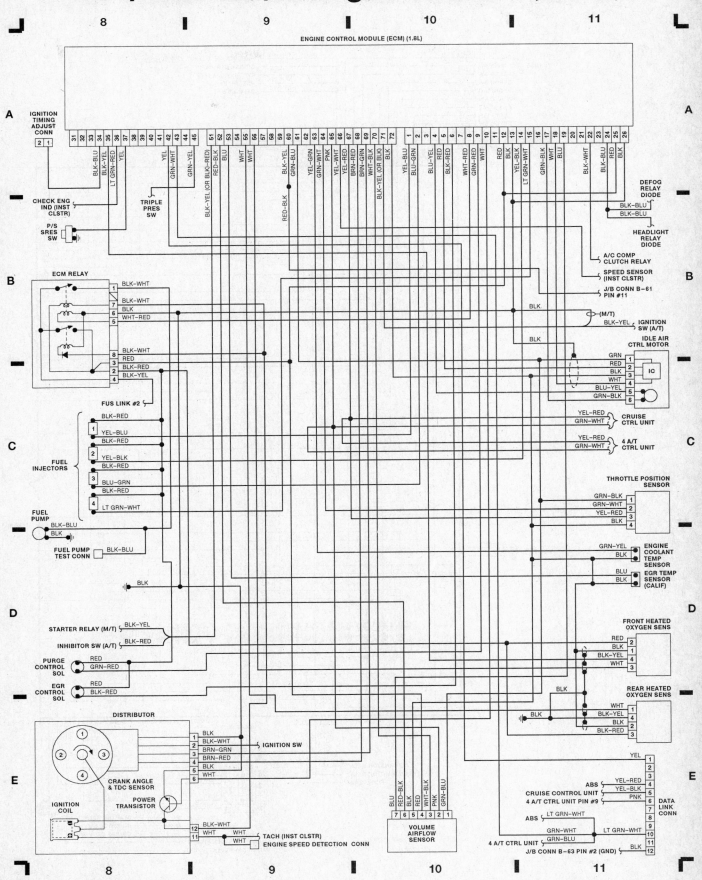

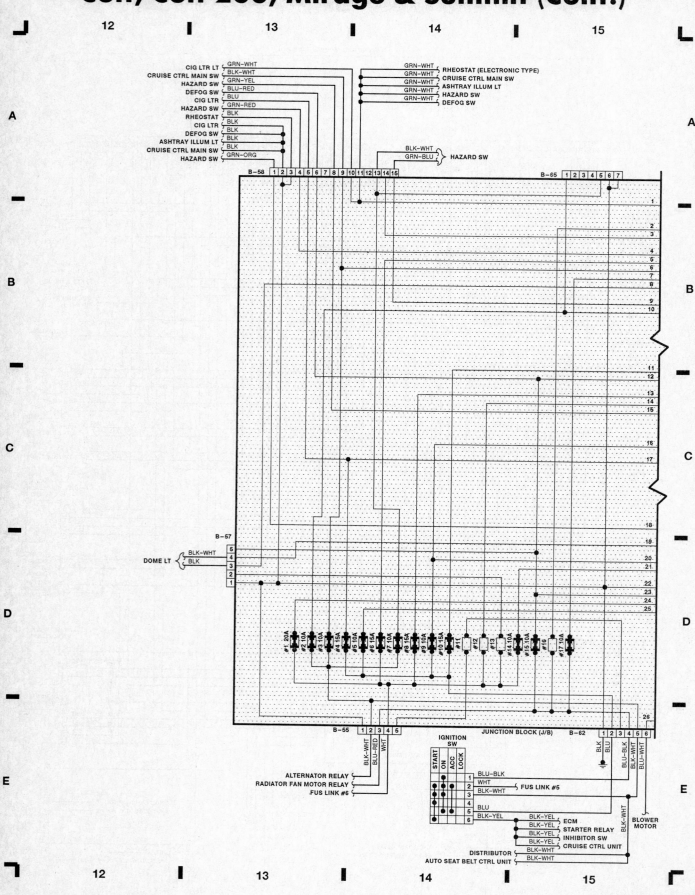

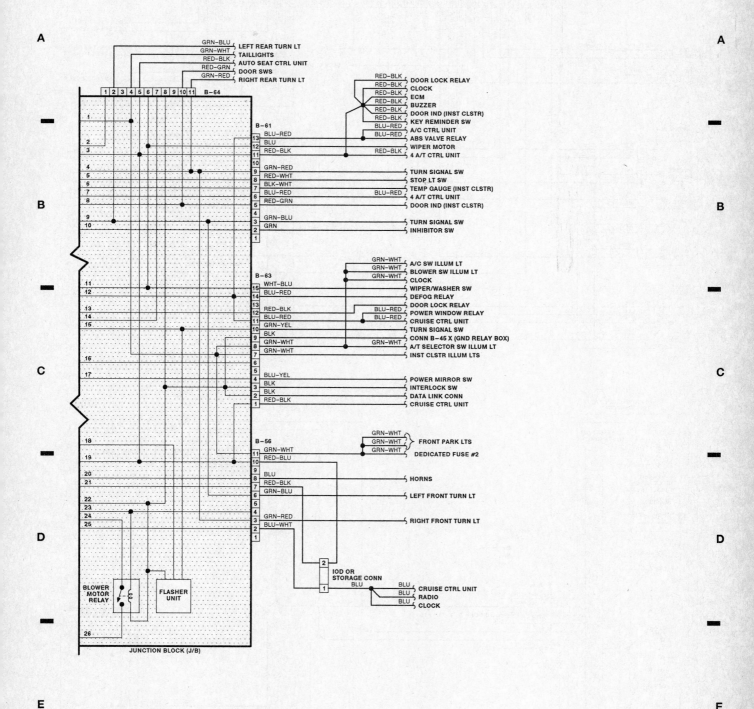

1993 WIRING DIAGRAMS
Colt, Colt 200, Mirage & Summit (Cont.)

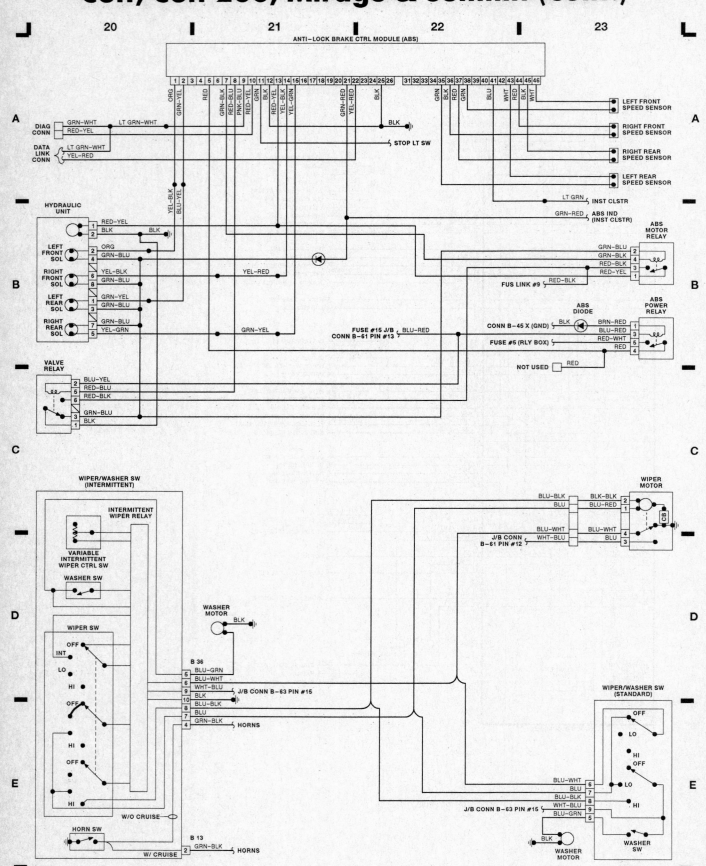

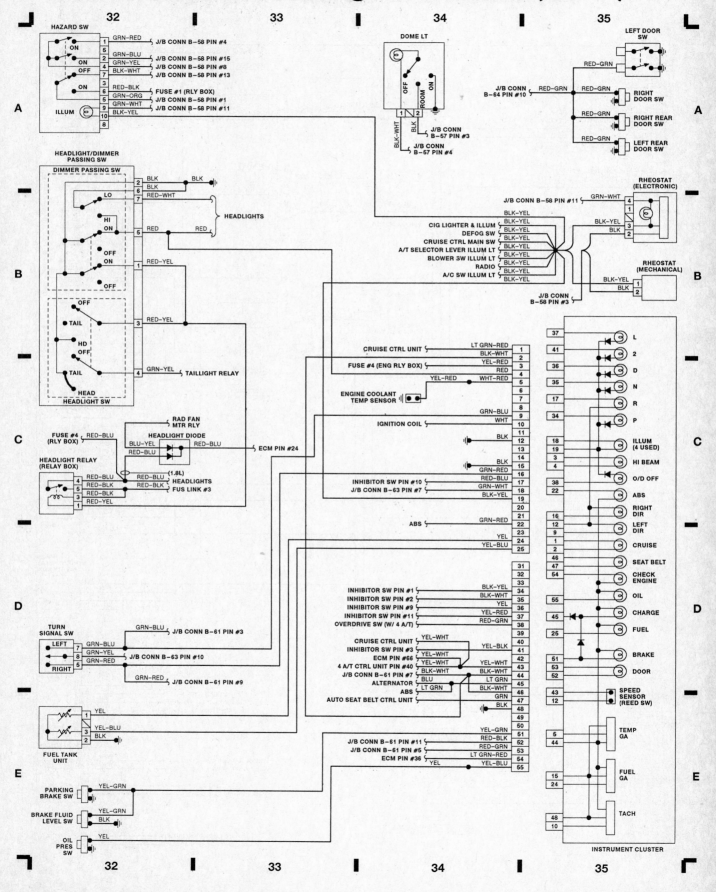

1993 WIRING DIAGRAMS
Colt, Colt 200, Mirage & Summit (Cont.)

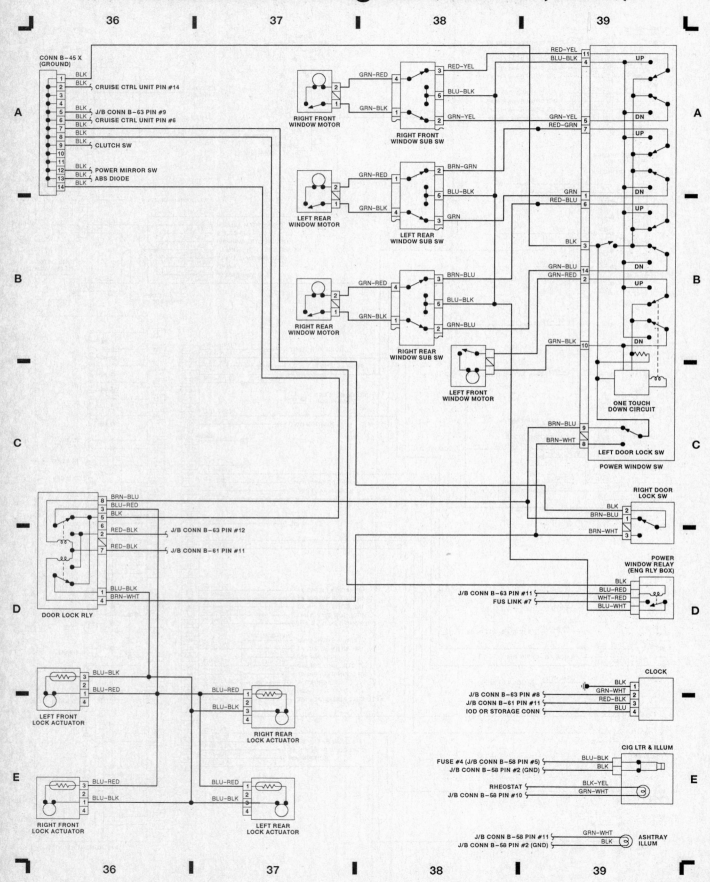

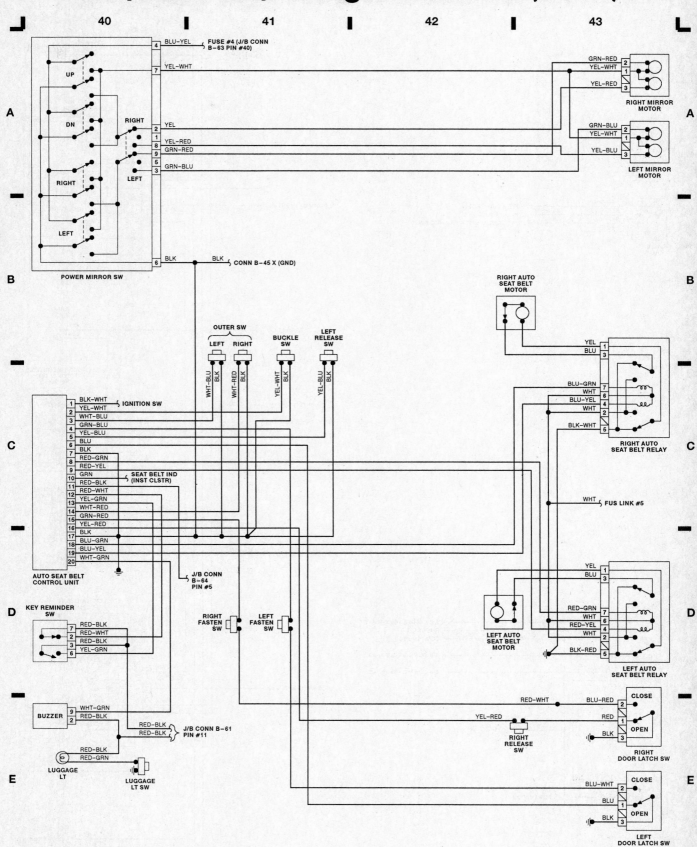

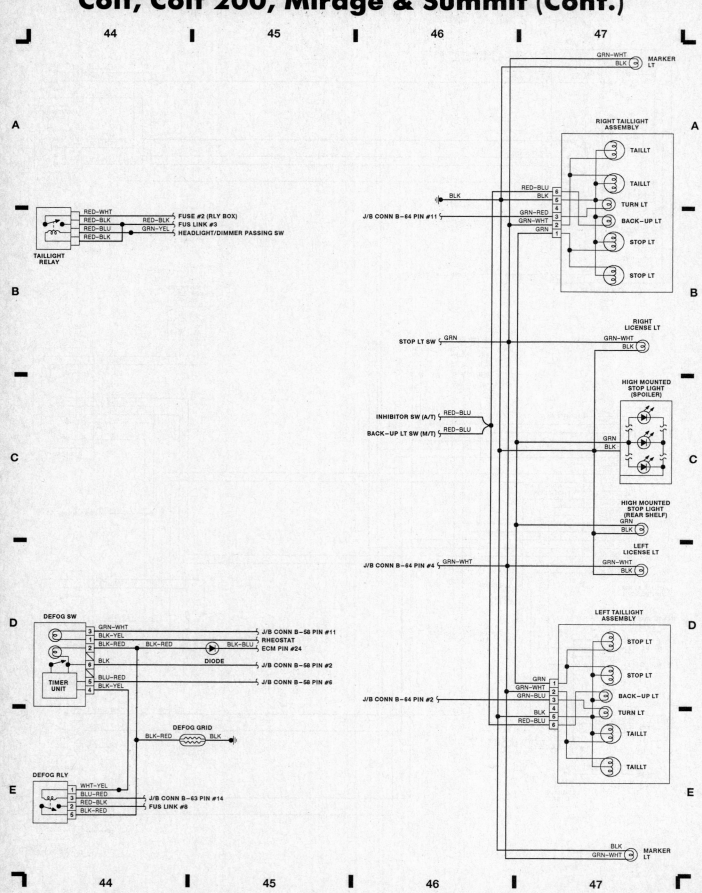

COMPONENT LOCATOR:

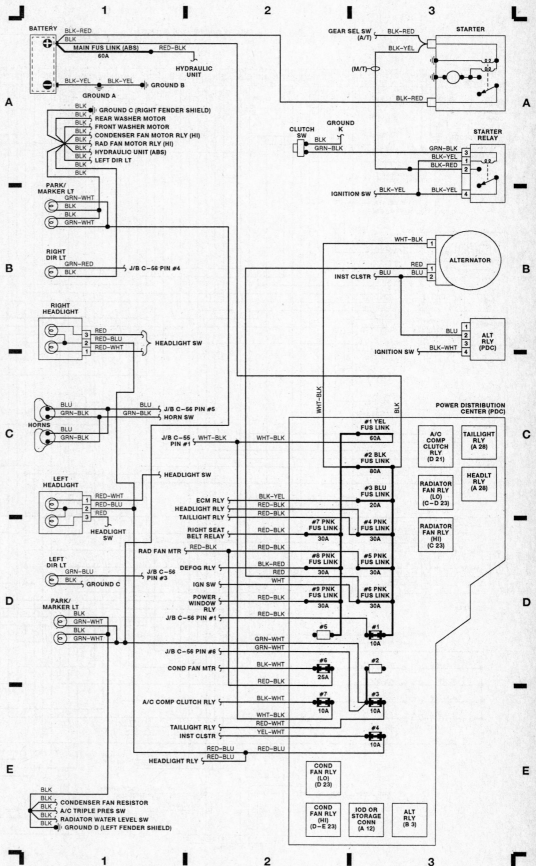

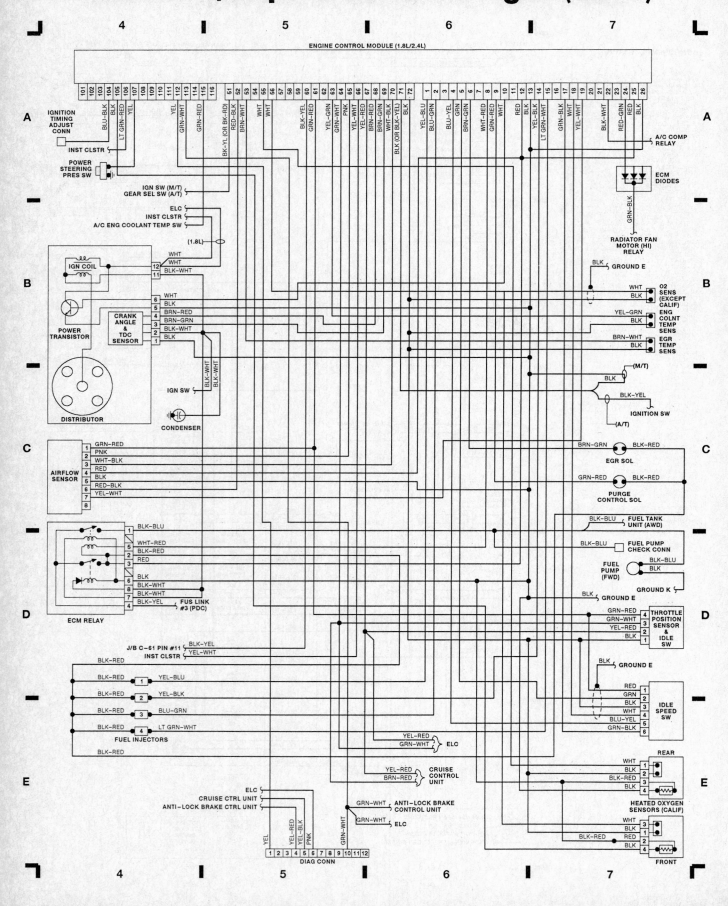

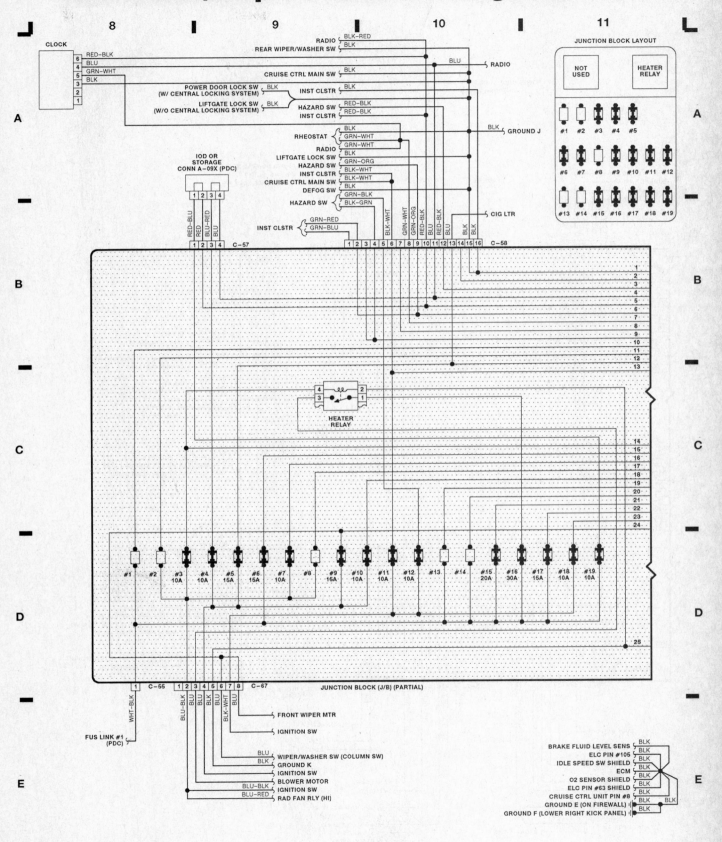

1993 WIRING DIAGRAMS
Colt Vista, Expo & Summit Wagon (Cont.)

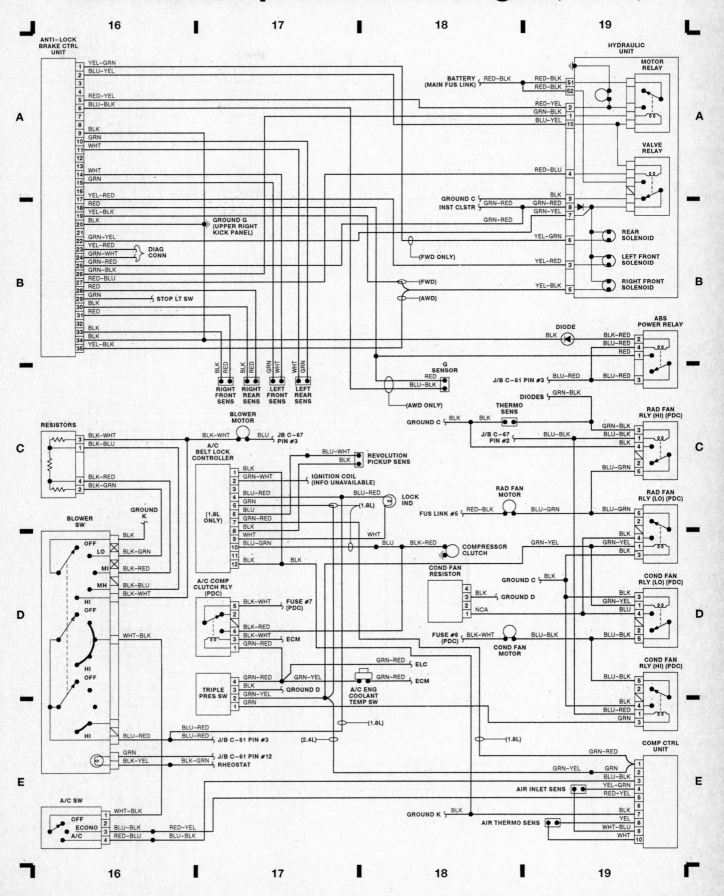

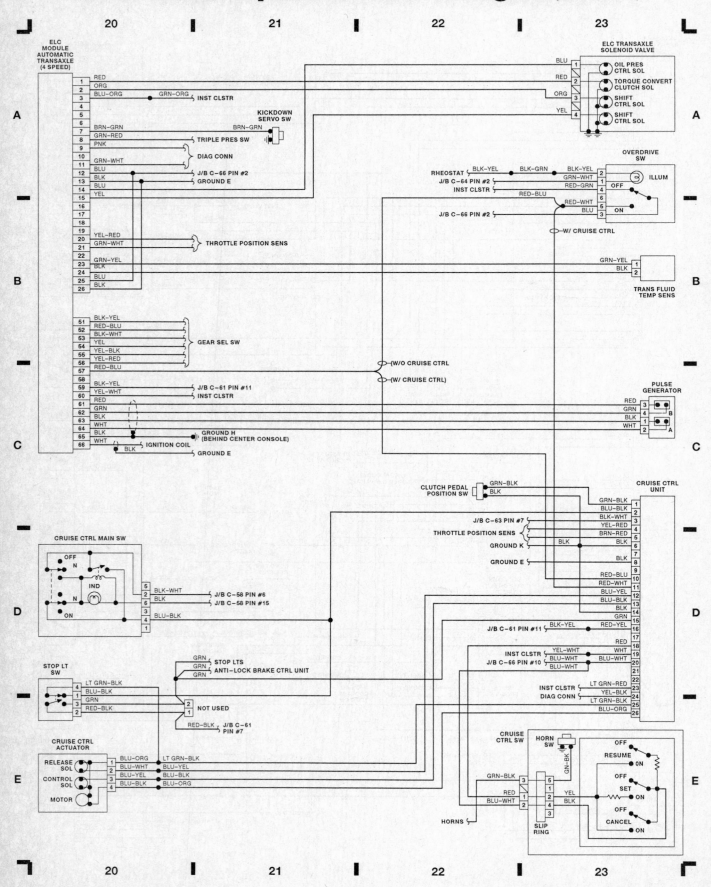

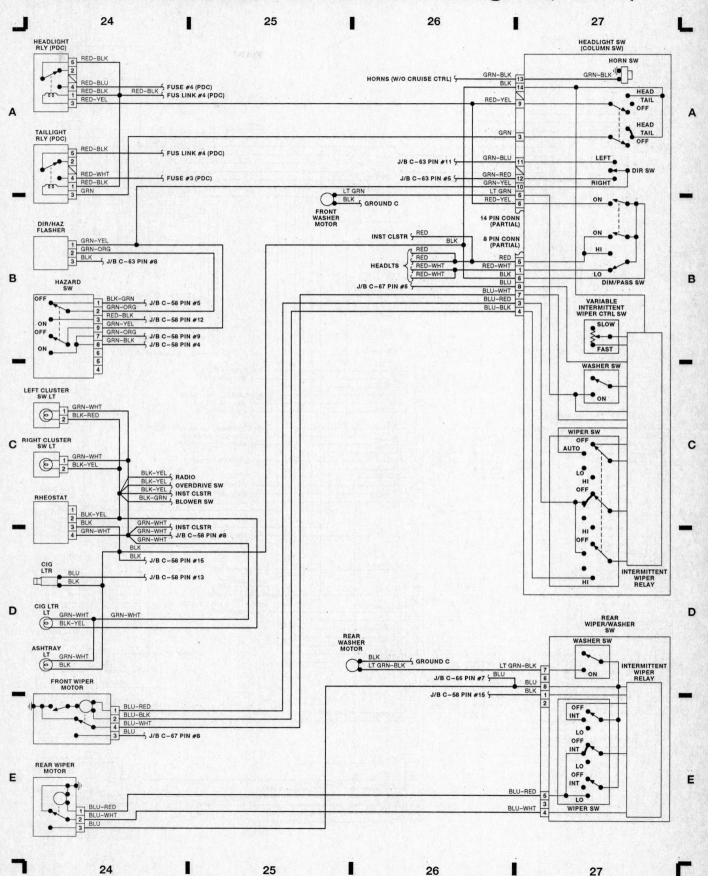

1993 WIRING DIAGRAMS
Colt Vista, Expo & Summit Wagon (Cont.)

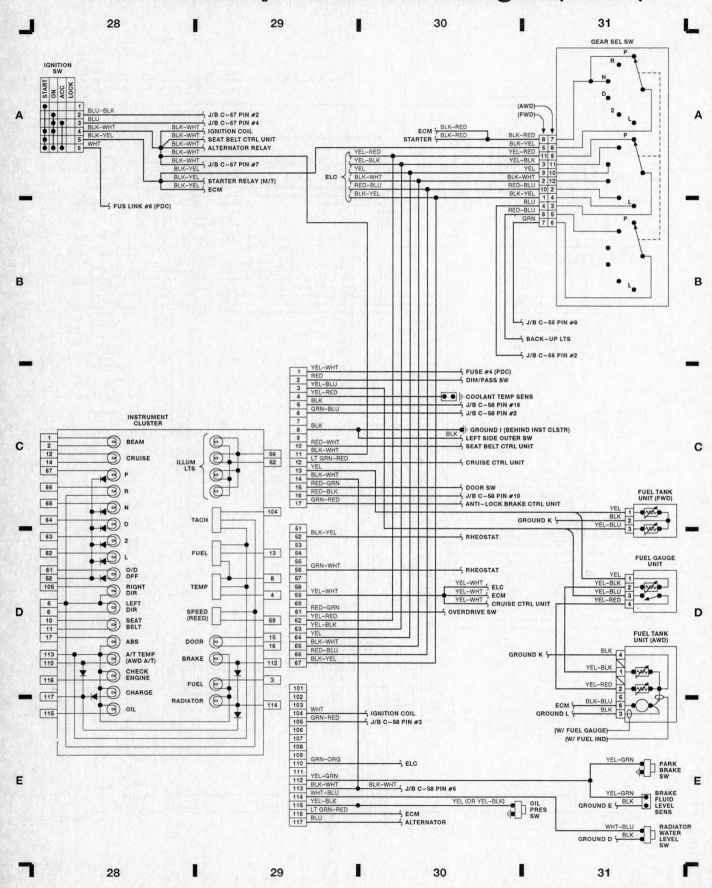

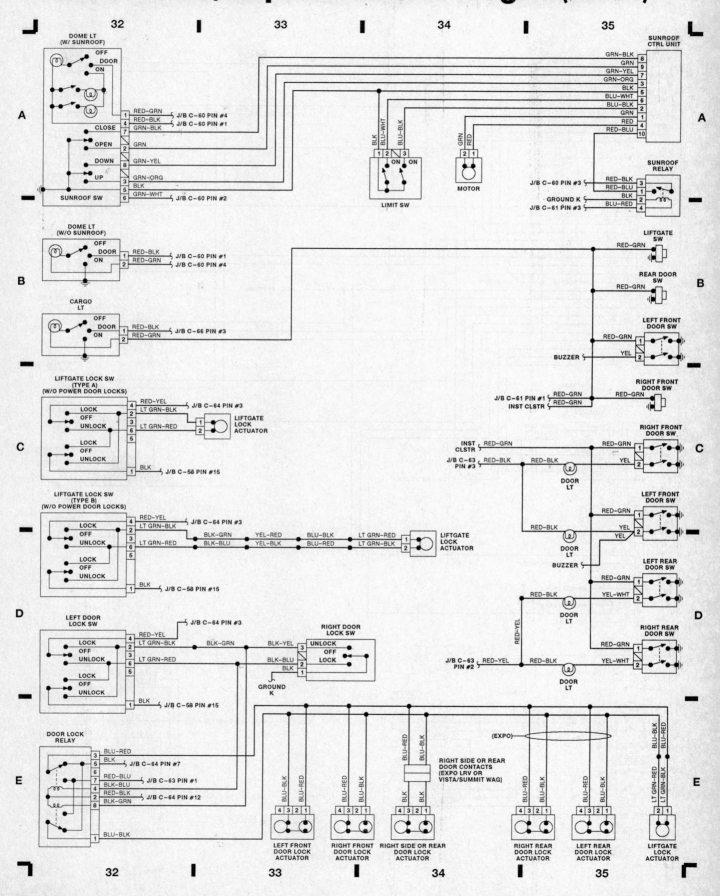

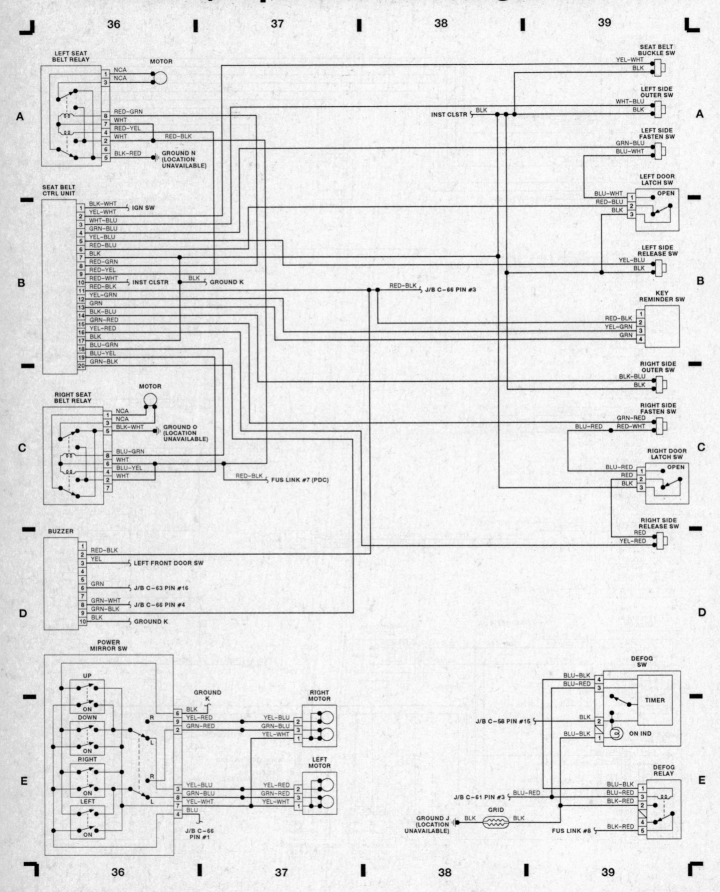

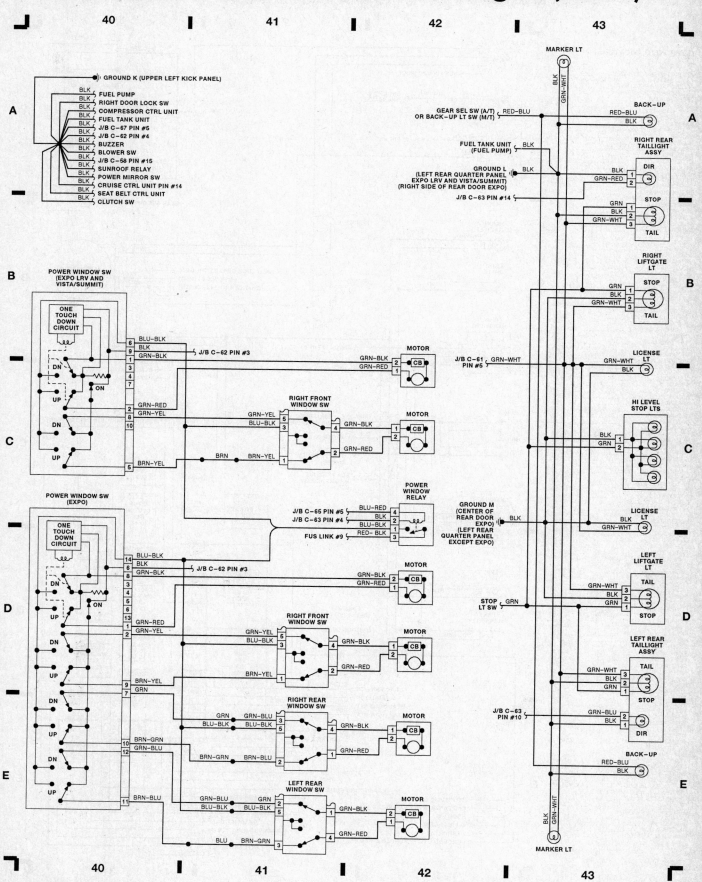

1993 WIRING DIAGRAMS
Diamante

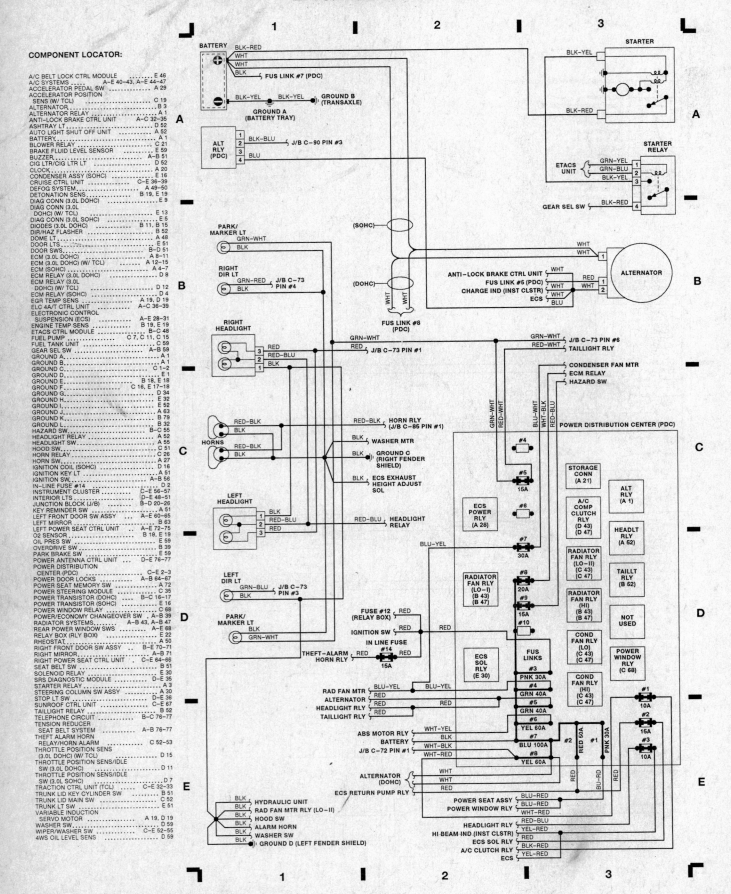

COMPONENT LOCATOR:

A/C BELT LOCK CTRL MODULE .... E 46
A/C SYSTEMS ...... A–E 40–43, A–E 44–47
ACCELERATOR PEDAL SW .... A 29
ACCELERATOR POSITION
  SENS (W/ TCL) .... C 19
ALTERNATOR .... B 3
ALTERNATOR RELAY .... A 1
ANTI-LOCK BRAKE CTRL UNIT .... A–C 32–35
ASHTRAY LT .... D 52
AUTO LIGHT SHUT OFF UNIT ..... A 52
BATTERY .... A 1
BLOWER RELAY .... C 21
BRAKE FLUID LEVEL SENSOR ..... E 59
BUZZER .... A–B 51
CIG LTR/CIG LTR LT .... D 52
CLOCK .... A 20
CONDENSER ASSY (SOHC) ...... E 16
CRUISE CTRL UNIT .... C–E 36–39
DEFOG SYSTEM .... A 49–50
DETONATION SENS .... B 19, E 19
DIAG CONN (3.0L DOHC) .... E 9
DIAG CONN (3.0L
  DOHC) (W/ TCL) .... E 13
DIAG CONN (3.0L SOHC) .... E 5
DIODES (3.0L DOHC) .... B 11, B 15
DIR/HAZ FLASHER .... B 52
DOME LT .... A 48
DOOR LTS .... E 51
DOOR SWS .... B–D 51
ECM (3.0L DOHC) .... A 8–11
ECM (3.0L DOHC) (W/ TCL) ..... A 12–15
ECM (SOHC) .... A 4–7
ECM RELAY (3.0L DOHC) .... D 8
ECM RELAY (3.0L
  DOHC) (W/ TCL) .... D 12
ECM RELAY (SOHC) .... A 19, D 19
EGR TEMP SENS .... D 4
ELC 4A/T CTRL UNIT .... A–C 36–39
ELECTRONIC CONTROL
  SUSPENSION (ECS) .... A–E 28–31
ENGINE TEMP SENS .... B 19, E 19
ETACS CTRL MODULE .... B–C 48
FUEL PUMP .... C 7, C 11, C 15
FUEL TANK UNIT .... C 59
GEAR SEL SW .... A–B 59
GROUND A .... A 1
GROUND B .... A 1
GROUND C .... C 1–2
GROUND D .... E 1
GROUND E .... B 18, E 18
GROUND F .... C 16, E 17–18
GROUND G .... D 34
GROUND H .... E 52
GROUND I .... E 52
GROUND J .... A 63
GROUND K .... B 79
GROUND L .... B 32
HAZARD SW .... B–C 55
HEADLIGHT RELAY .... A 52
HEADLIGHT SW .... A 55
HOOD SW .... C 51
HORN RELAY .... C 26
HORN SW .... A 27
IGNITION COIL (SOHC) .... D 16
IGNITION KEY LT .... A 51
IGNITION SW .... A–B 56
IN-LINE FUSE #14 .... D 2
INSTRUMENT CLUSTER .... C–E 56–57
INTERIOR LTS .... D–E 48–51
JUNCTION BLOCK (J/B) .... B–D 20–26
KEY REMINDER SW .... A 51
LEFT FRONT DOOR SW ASSY .... A–E 60–65
LEFT MIRROR .... B 63
LEFT POWER SEAT CTRL UNIT ... A–E 72–75
O2 SENSOR .... B 19, E 19
OIL PRES SW .... E 59
OVERDRIVE SW .... B 39
PARK BRAKE SW .... E 59
POWER ANTENNA CTRL UNIT .... D–E 76–77
POWER DISTRIBUTION
  CENTER (PDC) .... C–E 2–3
POWER DOOR LOCKS .... A–B 64–67
POWER SEAT MEMORY SW ..... A 72
POWER STEERING MODULE ..... C 35
POWER TRANSISTOR (DOHC) .... B–C 16–17
POWER TRANSISTOR (SOHC) .... E 16
POWER WINDOW RELAY .... C 68
POWER/ECONOMY CHANGEOVER SW .. A–B 39
RADIATOR SYSTEMS .... A–B 43, A–B 47
REAR POWER WINDOW SWS ..... A 62
RELAY BOX (RLY BOX) .... E 22
RHEOSTAT .... A 50
RIGHT FRONT DOOR SW ASSY ... B–E 70–71
RIGHT MIRROR .... A–B 71
RIGHT POWER SEAT CTRL UNIT .. C–E 64–66
SEAT BELT SW .... B 51
SOLENOID RELAY .... E 30
SRS DIAGNOSTIC MODULE ..... D–E 35
STARTER RELAY .... A 30
STEERING COLUMN SW ASSY ... A 30
STOP LT SW .... D–E 36
SUNROOF CTRL UNIT .... C–E 67
TAILLIGHT RELAY .... B 52
TELEPHONE CIRCUIT .... B–C 76–77
TENSION REDUCER
  SEAT BELT SYSTEM .... A–B 76–77
THEFT ALARM HORN
  RELAY/HORN ALARM ...... C 52–53
THROTTLE POSITION SENS
  (3.0L DOHC) (W/ TCL) ..... D 15
THROTTLE POSITION SENS/IDLE
  SW (3.0L DOHC) .... D 11
THROTTLE POSITION SENS/IDLE
  SW (3.0L SOHC) .... D 7
TRACTION CTRL UNIT (TCL) ... C–E 32–33
TRUNK LID KEY CYLINDER SW .. B 51
TRUNK LID MAIN SW .... C 52
TRUNK LT SW .... E 51
VARIABLE INDUCTION
  SERVO MOTOR .... A 19, D 19
WASHER SW .... D 59
WIPER/WASHER SW .... C–E 52–55
4WS OIL LEVEL SENS .... D 59

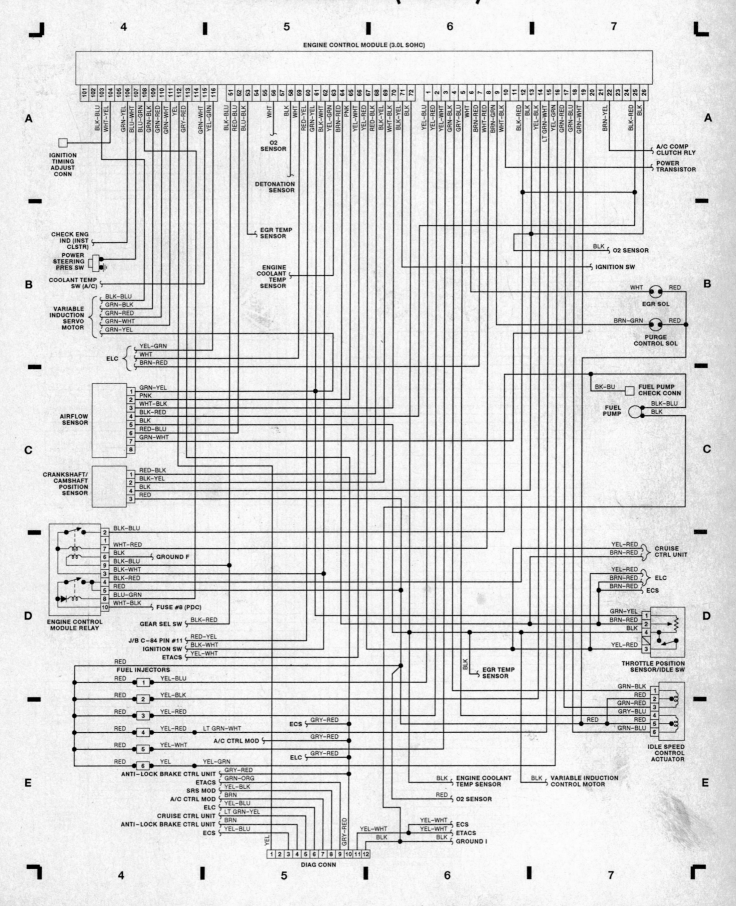

1993 WIRING DIAGRAMS
Diamante (Cont.)

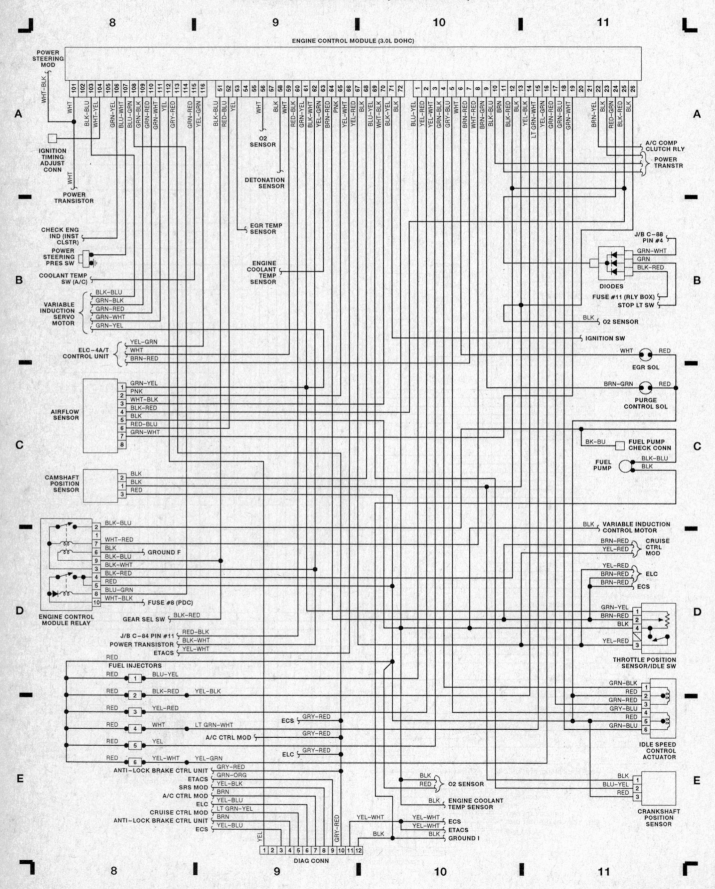

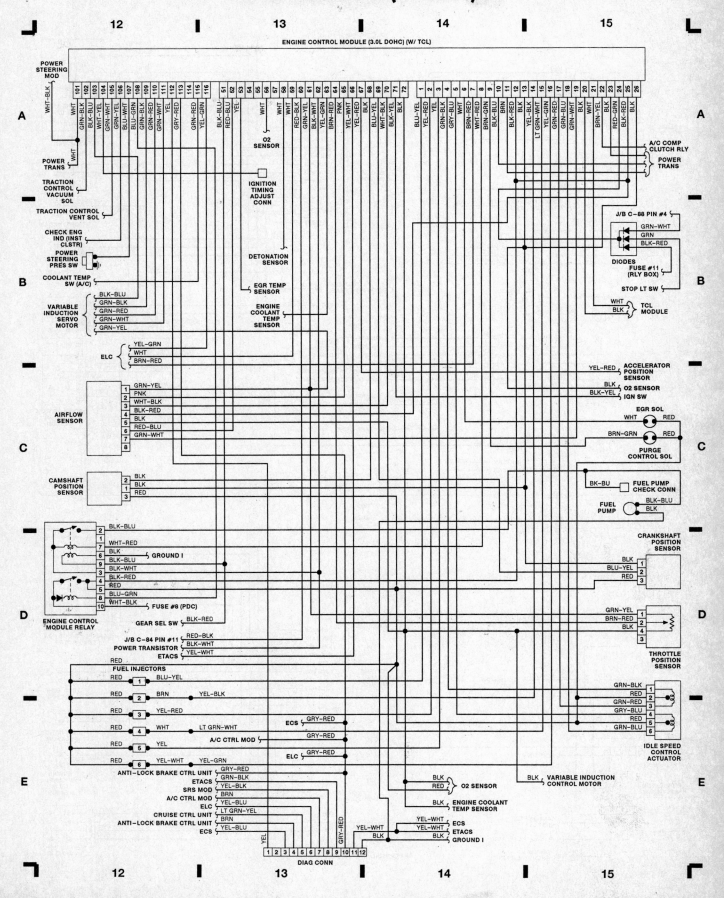

1993 WIRING DIAGRAMS
Diamante (Cont.)

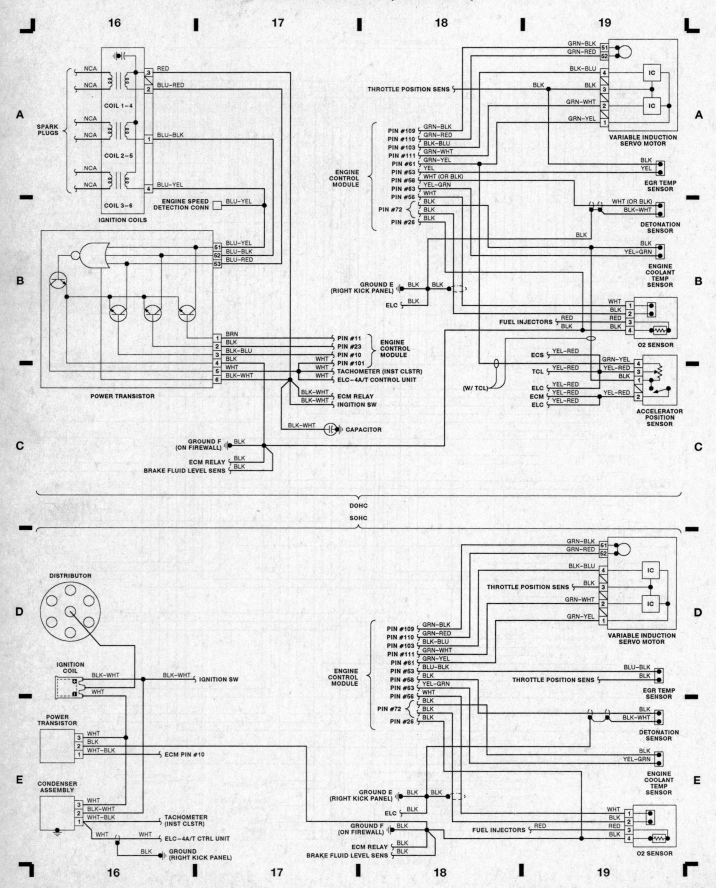

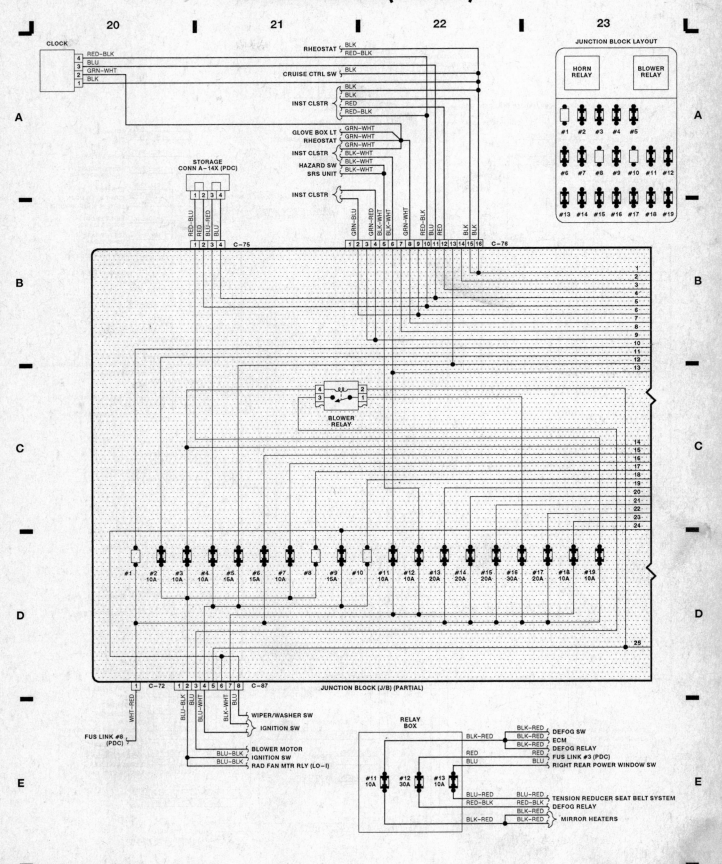

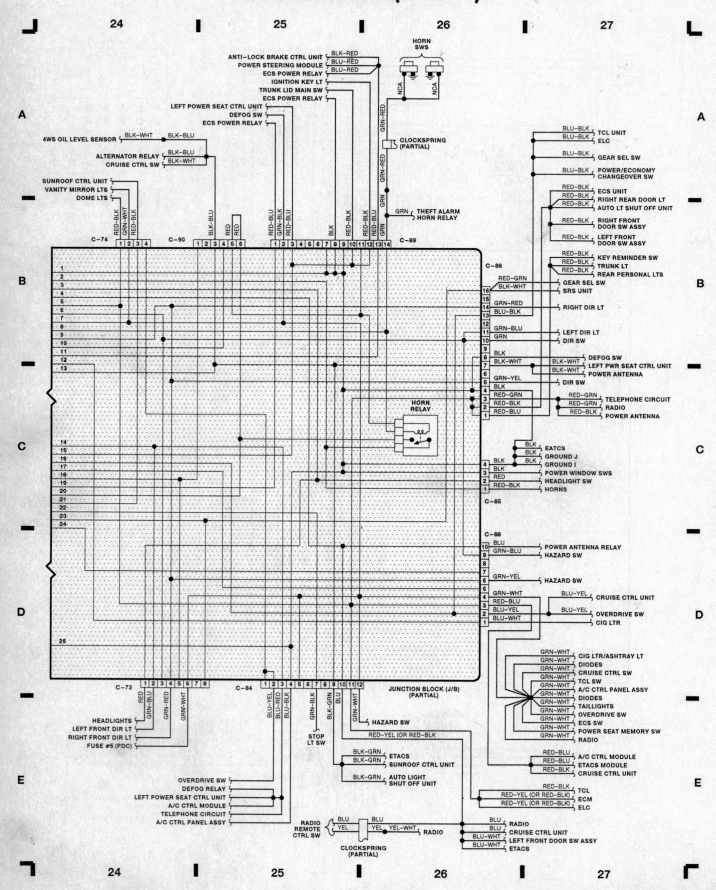

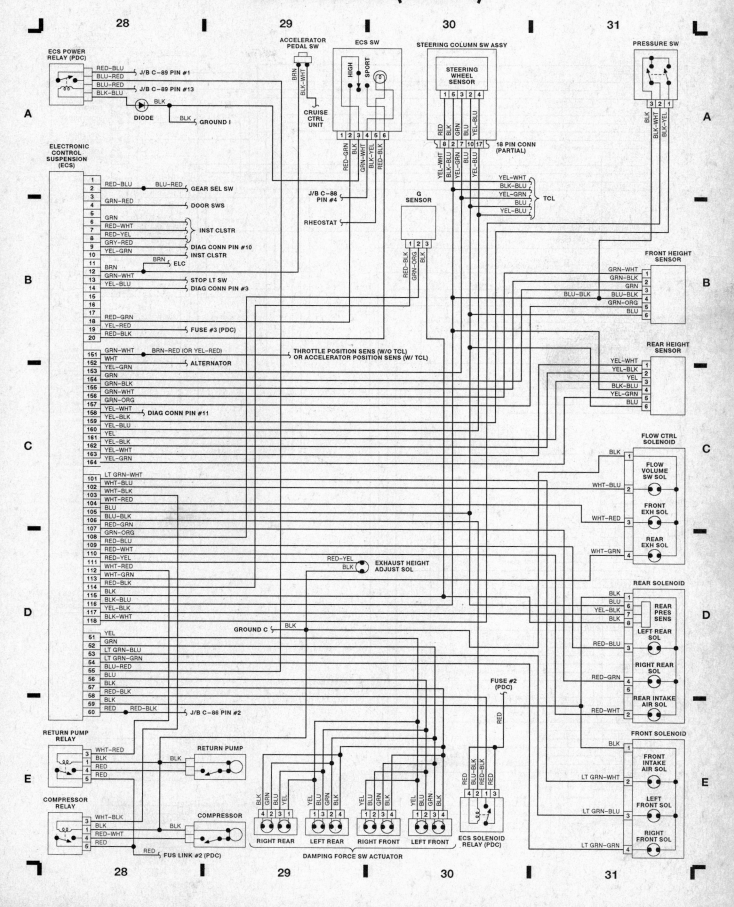

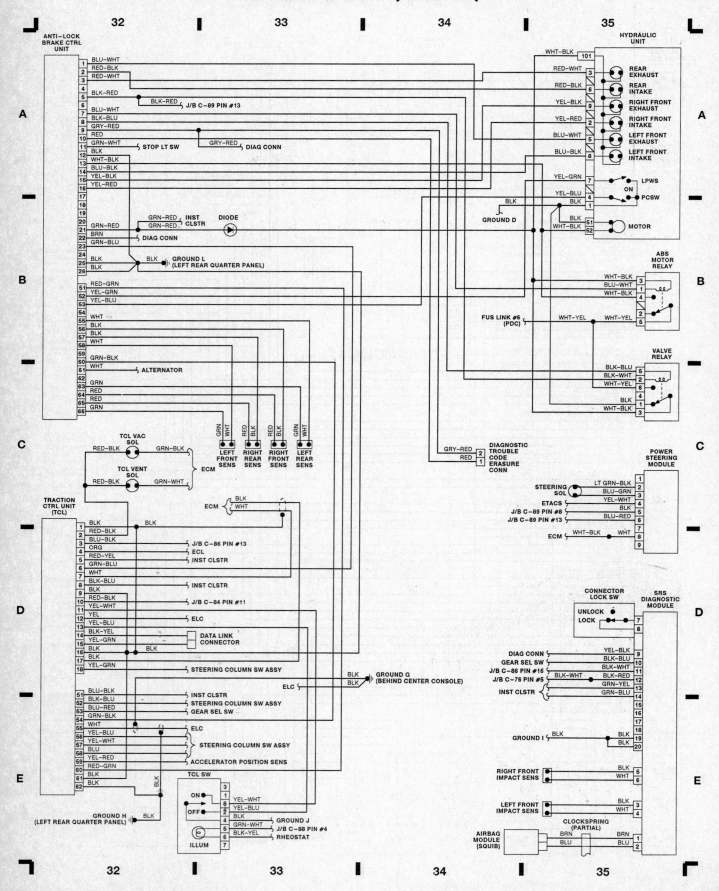

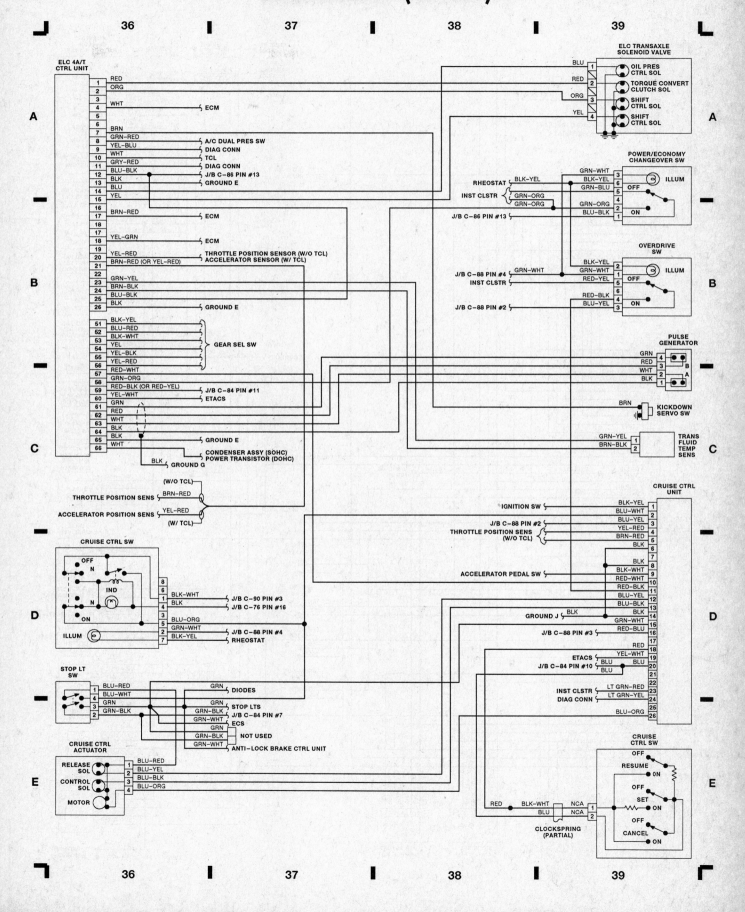

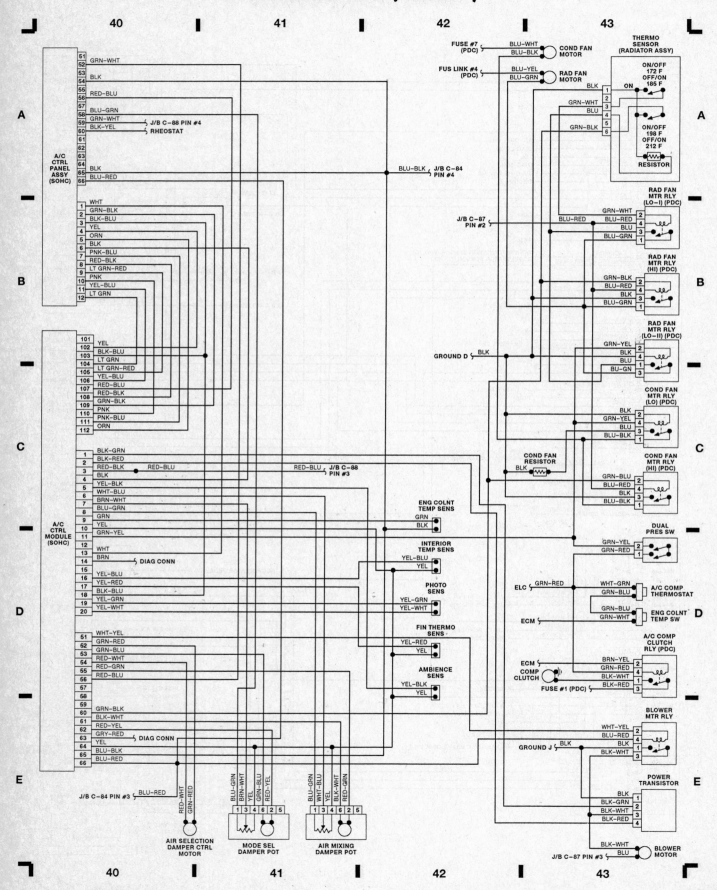

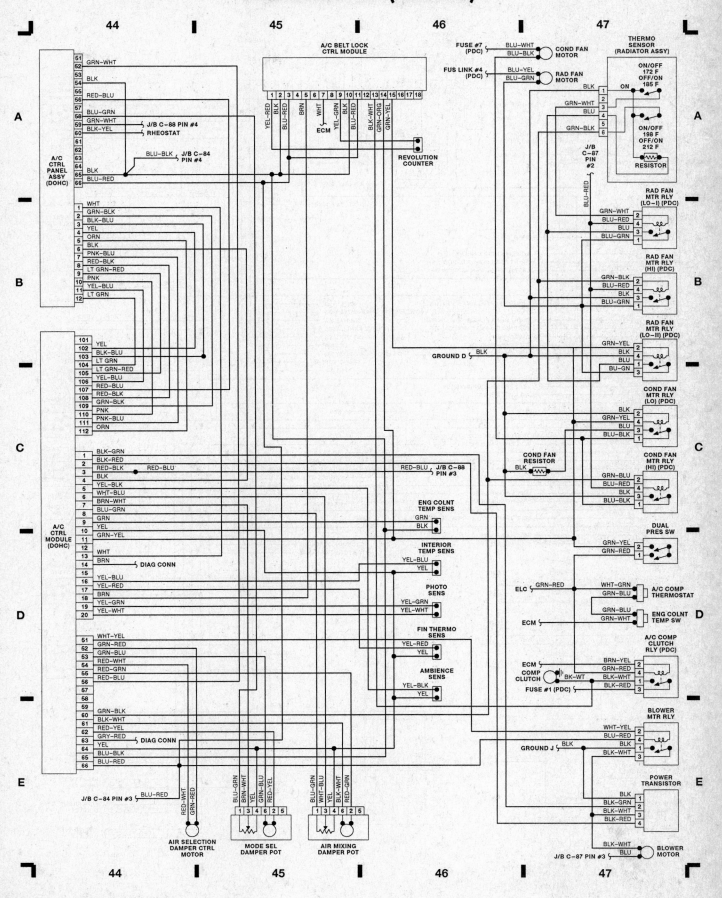

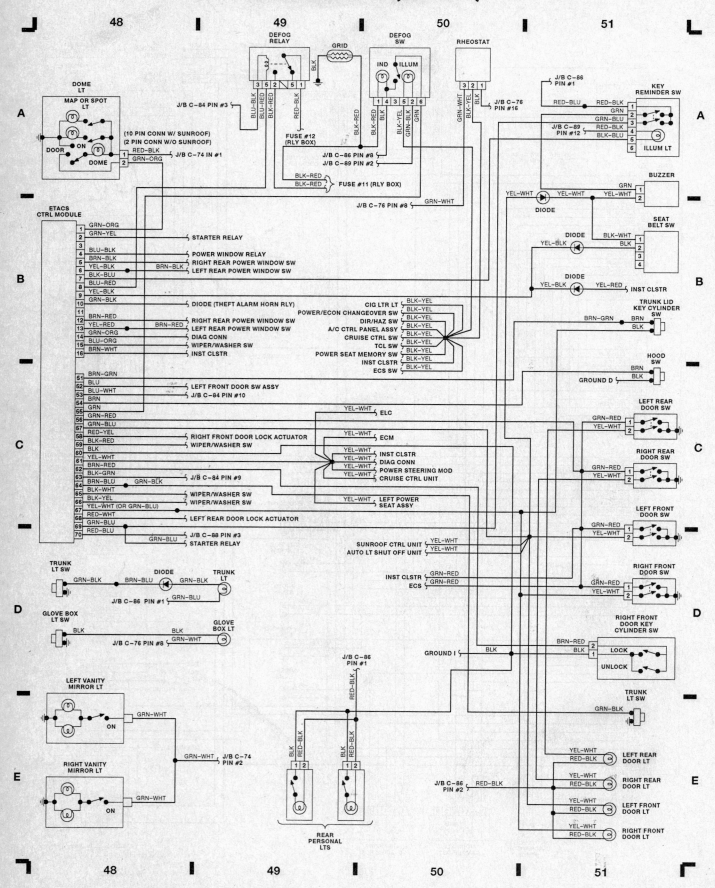

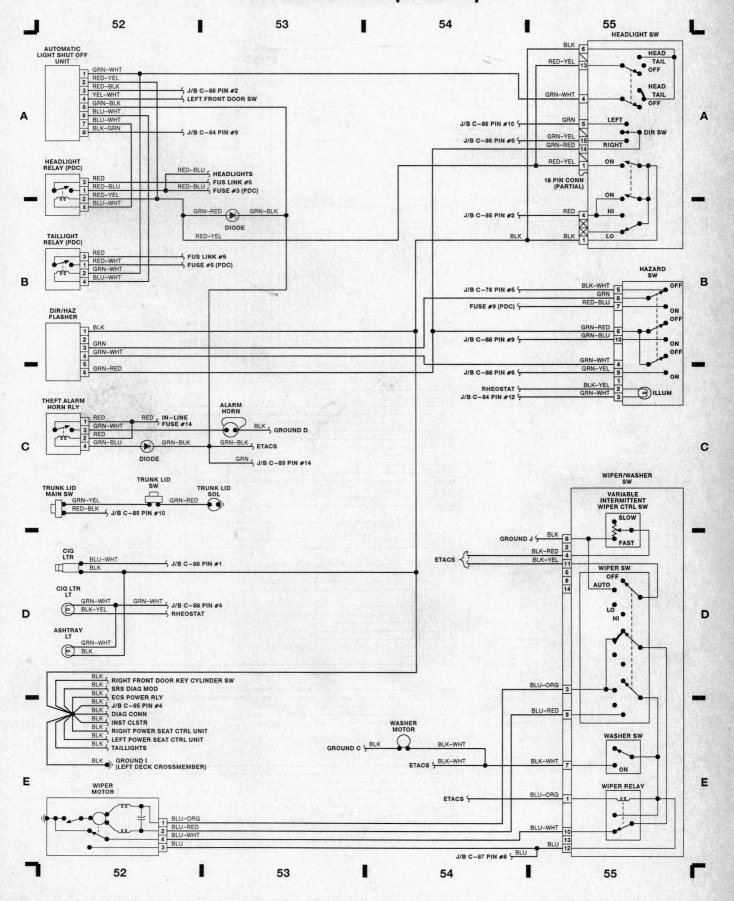

1993 WIRING DIAGRAMS
Diamante (Cont.)

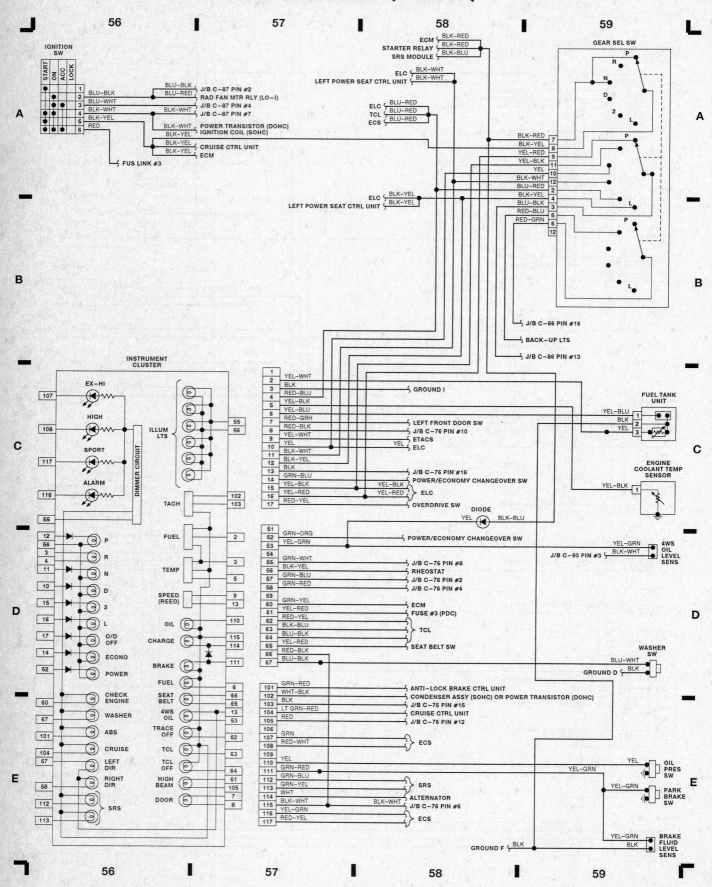

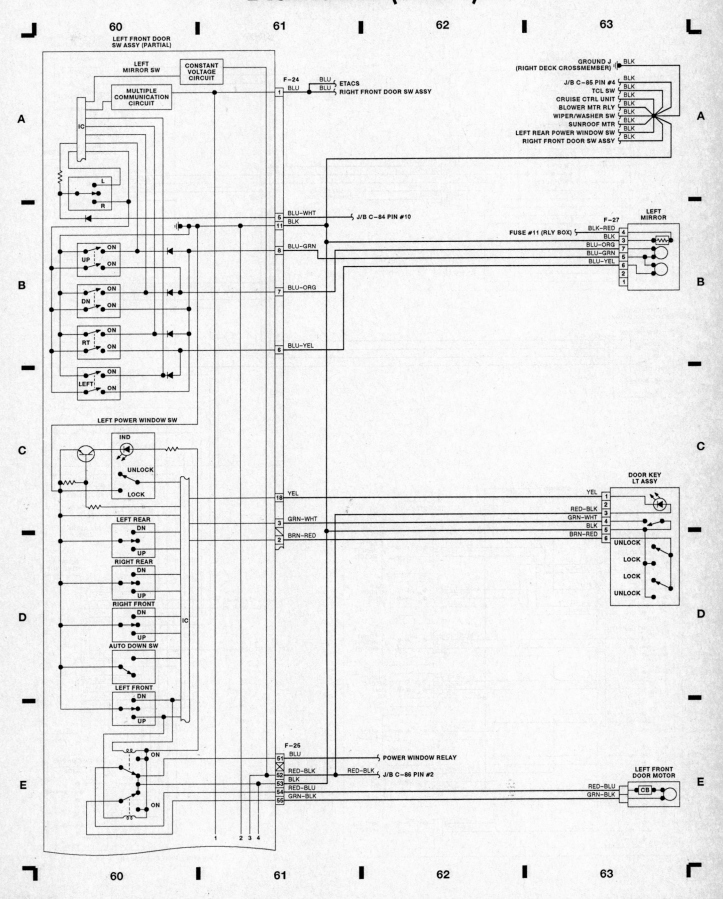

1993 WIRING DIAGRAMS
Diamante (Cont.)

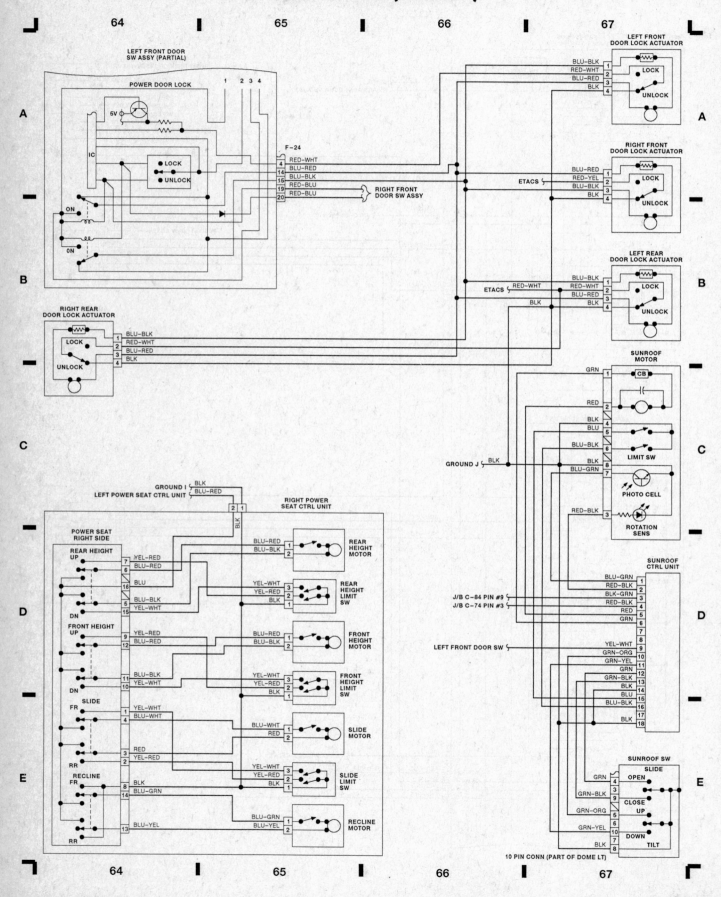

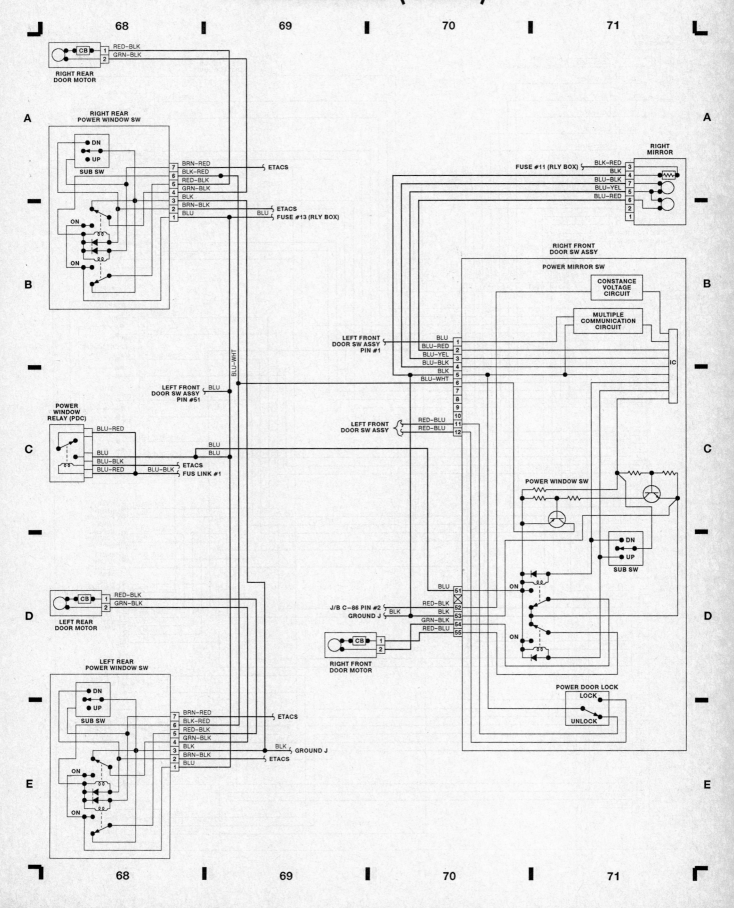

1993 WIRING DIAGRAMS
Diamante (Cont.)

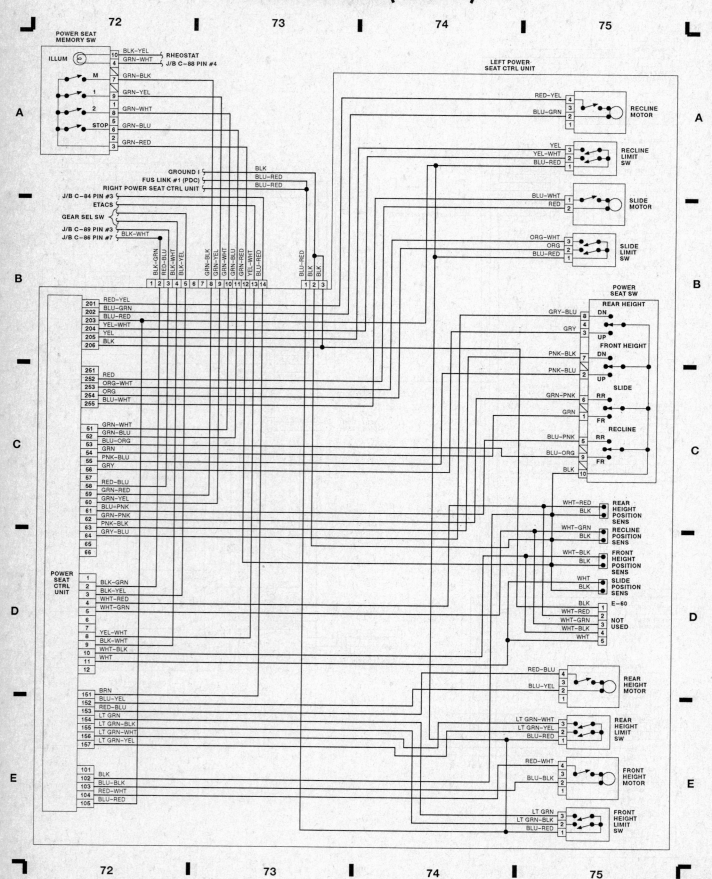

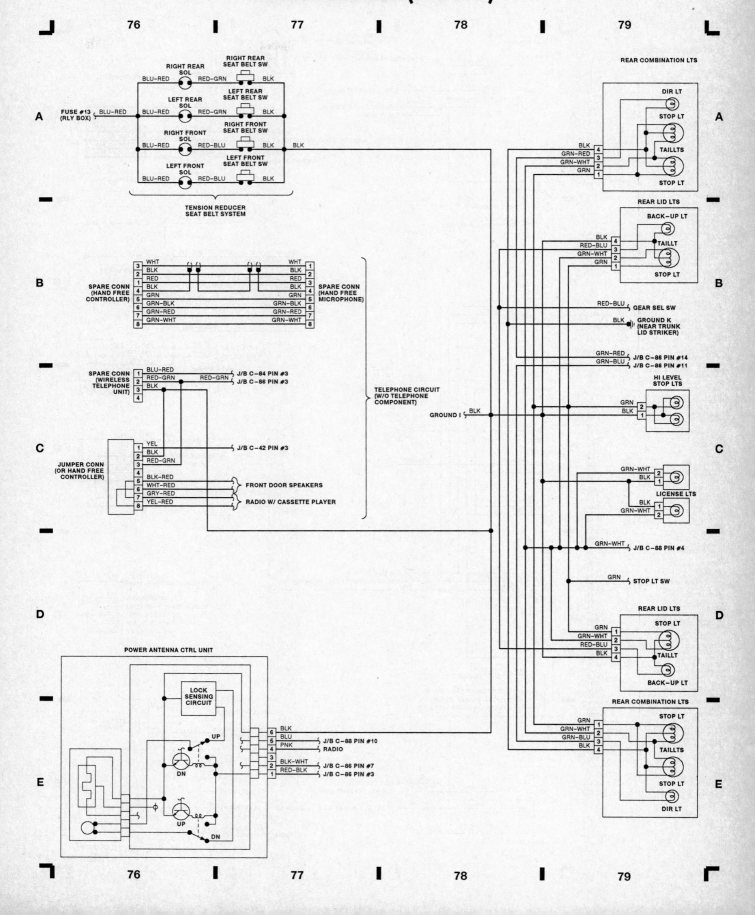

1993 WIRING DIAGRAMS
Eclipse

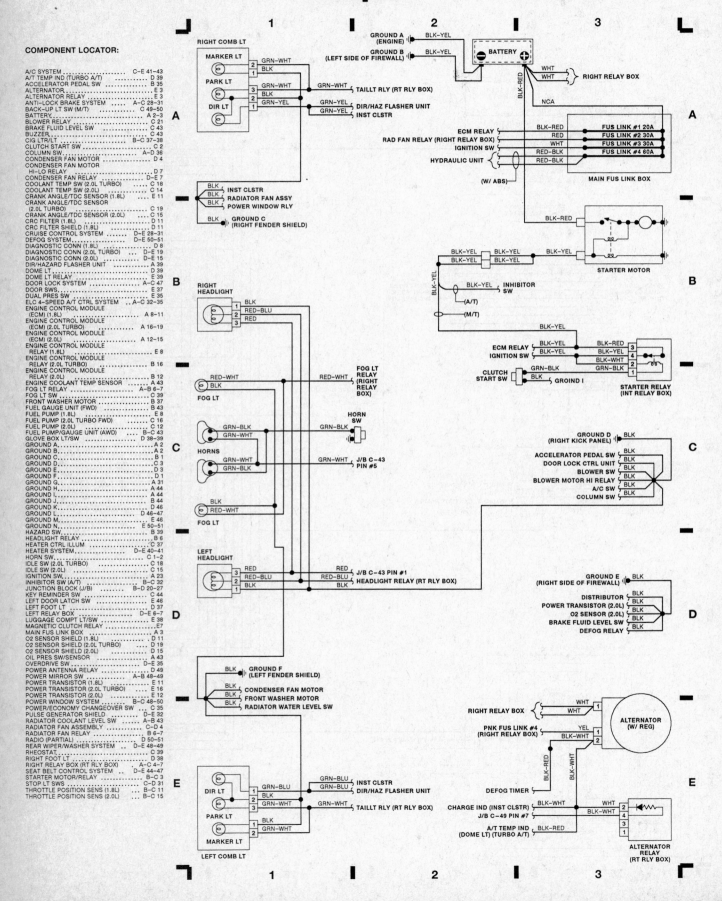

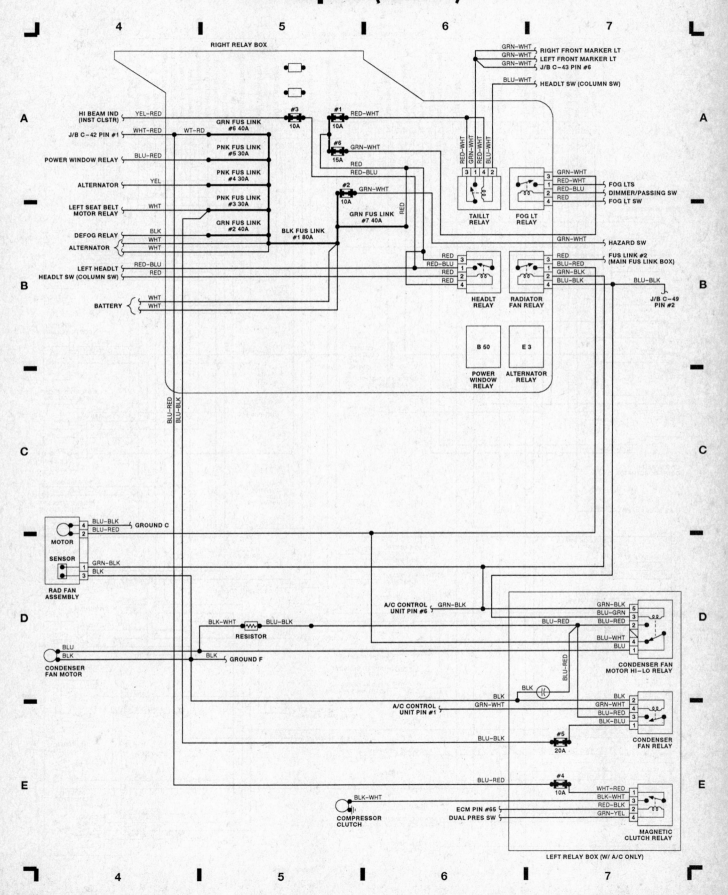

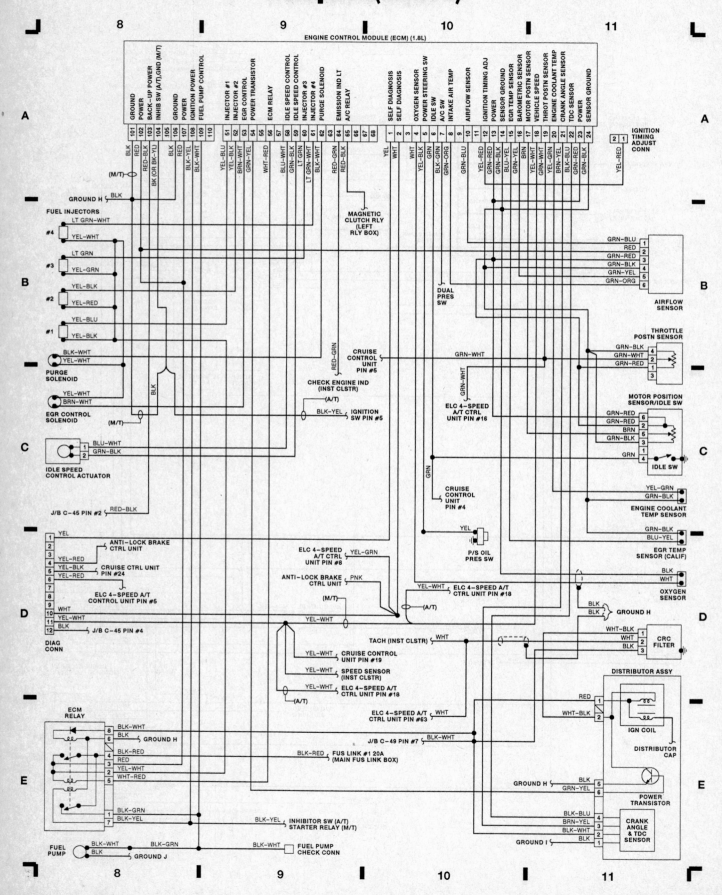

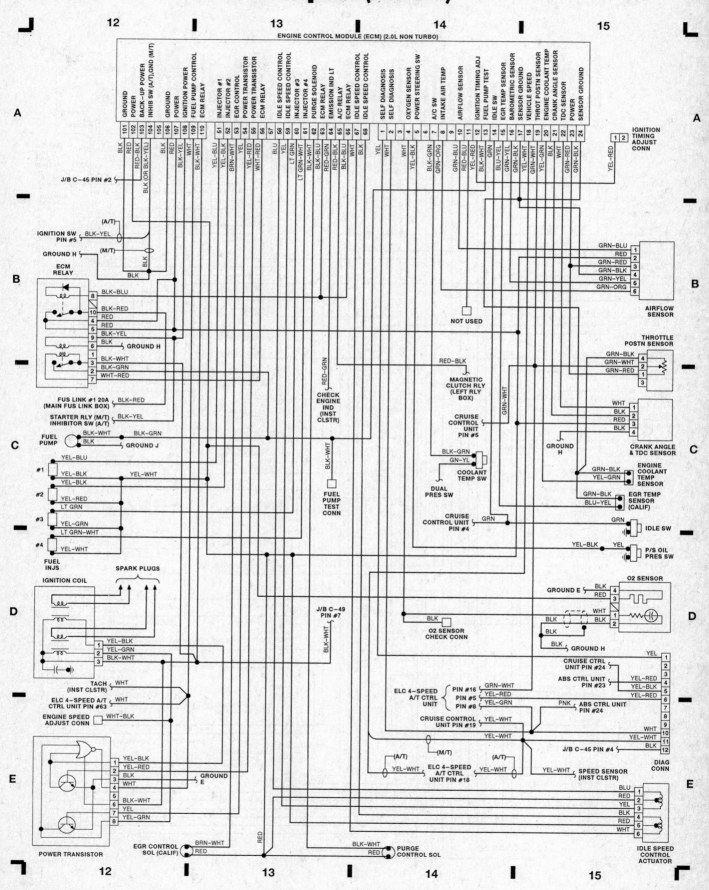

1993 WIRING DIAGRAMS
Eclipse (Cont.)

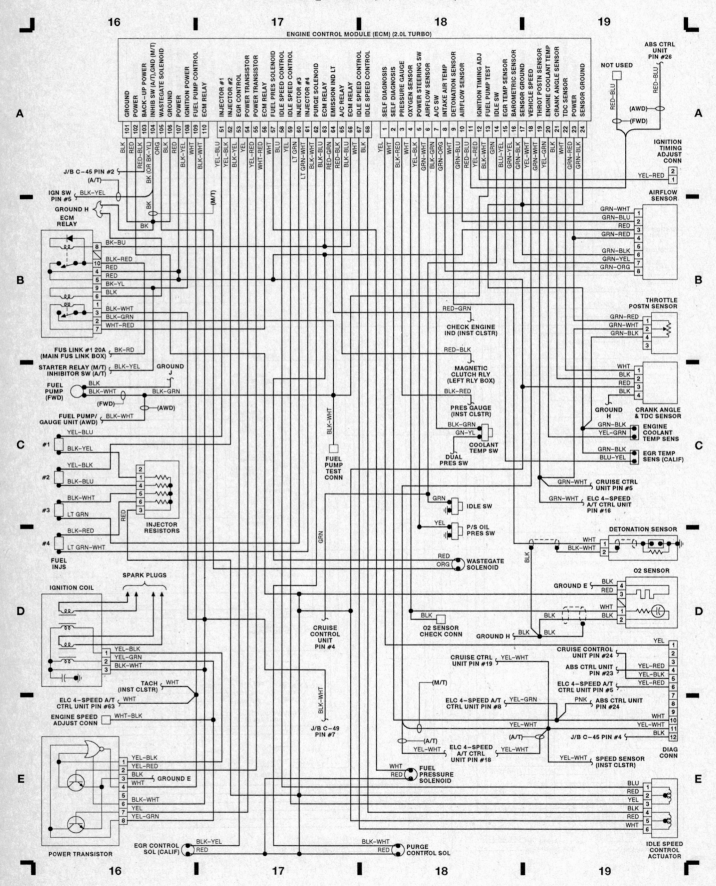

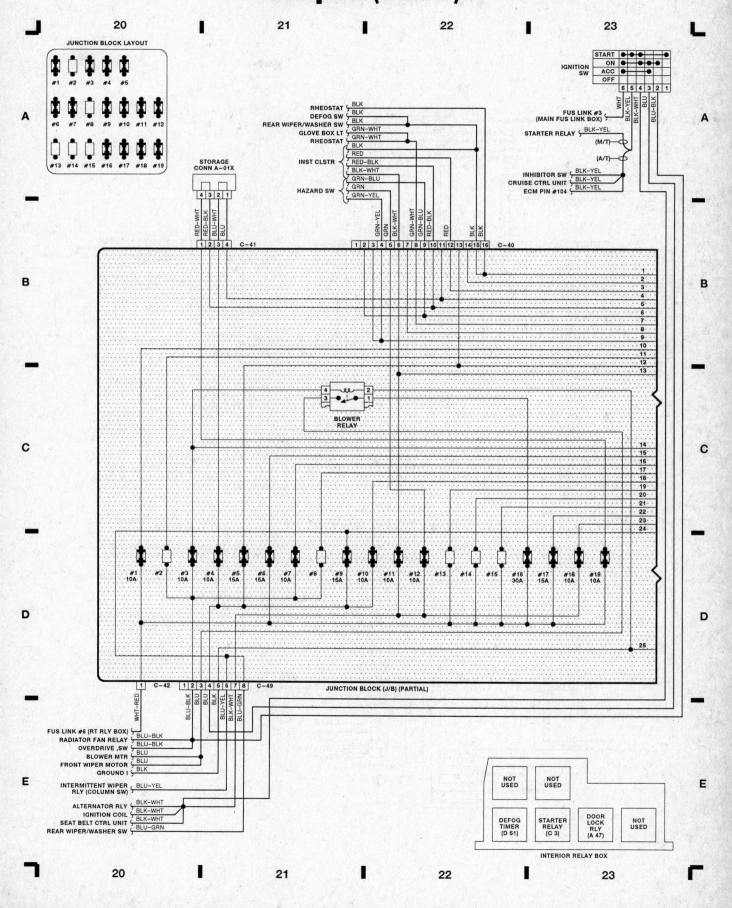

DOOR LOCK CTRL UNIT — RED-YEL
— RED-YEL
DEFOG TIMER — BLK
POWER MIRROR SW — BLK
LEFT DOOR LOCK ACTUATOR — BLK
LEFT DOOR LATCH SW — BLK
CIG LTR LT

HEADLIGHT SW (COLUMN SW) — RED-BLK
BUZZER — RED-BLK
POWER ANTENNA RLY — BLK-WHT
CRUISE CTRL SW — BLK-WHT

BLK-BLU
RED-BLK

GRN-BLK
BLK
BLK
RED-YEL
RED-YEL

| 1 2 3 4 | C-47 | 1 2 3 4 5 6 | 1 2 3 4 5 6 7 8 9 10 11 12 13 14 | C-46 |

BLU-BLK — A/T TEMP IND
BLU-RED — CRUISE CTRL UNIT
RED-BLK — ELC 4-SPEED A/T CTRL UNIT
RED-BLK — ECM PIN #103

C-45

RED — 16 — BACK-UP LT SW (M/T)
RED — 15 — INHIBITOR SW (A/T)
— 14 — DOME LT RLY
BLU-BLK — 13
— 12
— 11
GRN-BLU — 10 — DIR SW (COLUMN SW)
— 9
BLK — 8 — DIR/HAZ FLASHER UNIT
— 7
GRN-YEL — 6 — DIR SW (COLUMN SW)
BLK — 5 — DIAG CONN
RED-BLK — 4 — RADIO
RED-BLK — 3
RED-BLK — 2
RED-BLK — 1 — RED-BLK — ABS POWER RLY
RED-BLK — RIGHT FOOT LT
RED-BLK — DOOR CTRL UNIT

B   B

C-44
BLK — GROUND I
4 — BLK — BLK — GROUND J
3 — BLK — POWER WINDOW SWS
2 — RED — DIM/PASS SW (COLUMN SW)
1

NOT USED

C   C

GRN-WHT — BUZZER
GRN-WHT — TAILLIGHTS

C-48
10 — BLU — POWER ANTENNA RLY
9 — GRN-BLU — DIR/HAZ FLASHER UNIT
8
7 — BLU — REAR WIPER MTR
6 — GRN-YEL — DIR/HAZ FLASHER UNIT
5
4 — GRN-WHT
3 — RED-BLK
2 — BLU-BLK — OVERDRIVE SW
1 — BLU-WHT — BLU-WHT — POWER MIRROR SW
BLU-WHT — CIG LTR

D   D

RED-BLK — DOME LT
RED-BLK — SEAT BELT CTRL UNIT
RED-BLK — POWER ANTENNA RLY

25

| C-43 | 1 2 3 4 5 6 7 8 | C-50 | 1 2 3 4 5 6 7 8 9 10 11 12 |

JUNCTION BLOCK (J/B)
(PARTIAL)

HEADLIGHTS — RED
GRN-WHT
GRN-WHT
BLU
BLK
GRN-WHT
GRN-WHT
BLK-WHT
BLU
RED-BLK
GRN-WHT

RADIO
LEFT FOOT LT
RADIO
INST CLSTR
BUZZER

HORNS — GRN-WHT
TAILLIGHT RLY — GRN-WHT

DEFOG SW — GRN-RED
DEFOG TIMER — BLK-WHT
ABS POWER RLY — BLU-RED
BLOWER SW — BLU
POWER WINDOW RLY — BLU
CRUISE CTRL UNIT — BLK
DOOR LOCK RLY — BLK
A/C SW — GRN-WHT

BLK-WHT
BLK-WHT

STOP LT SW

E   E

24   25   26   27

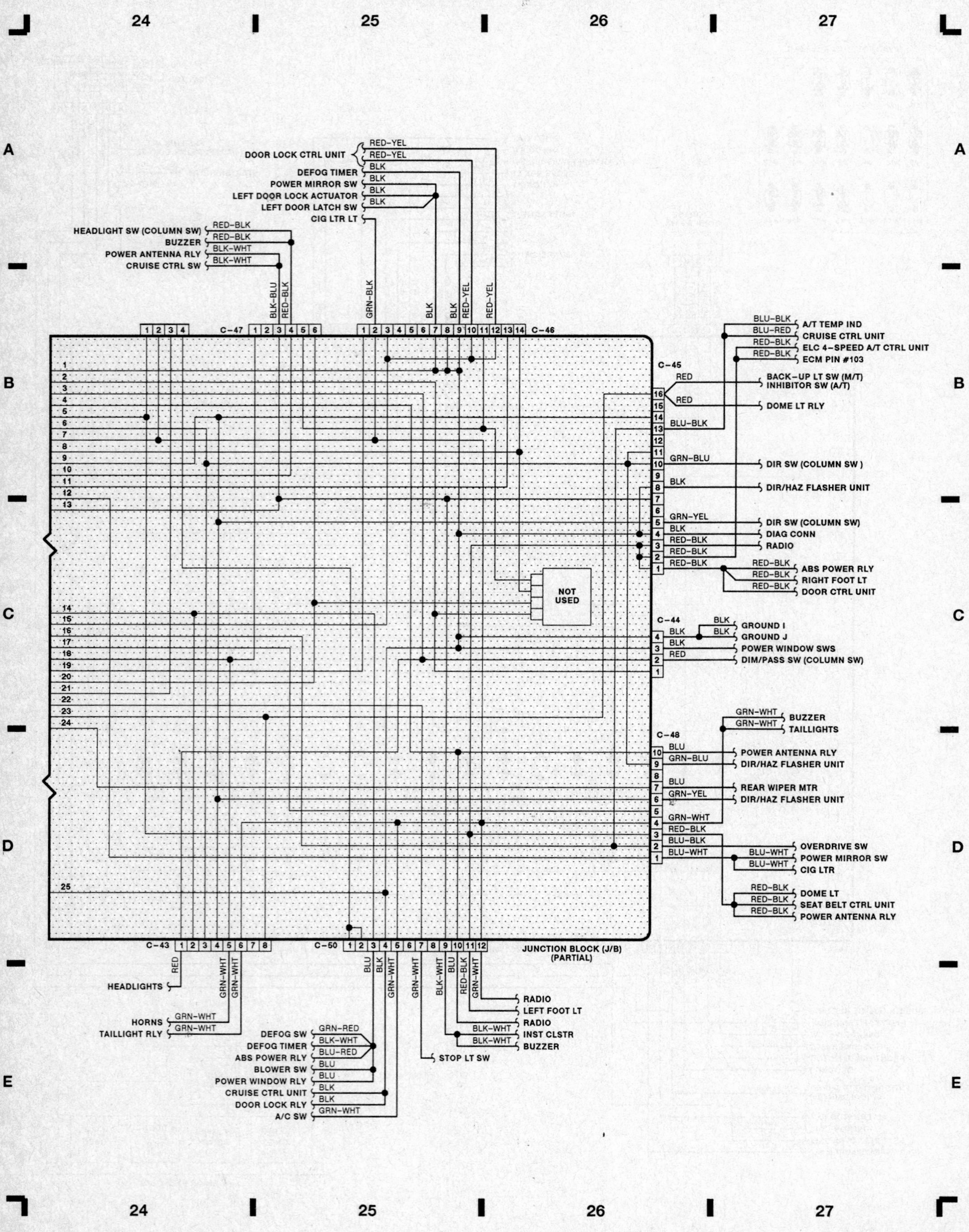

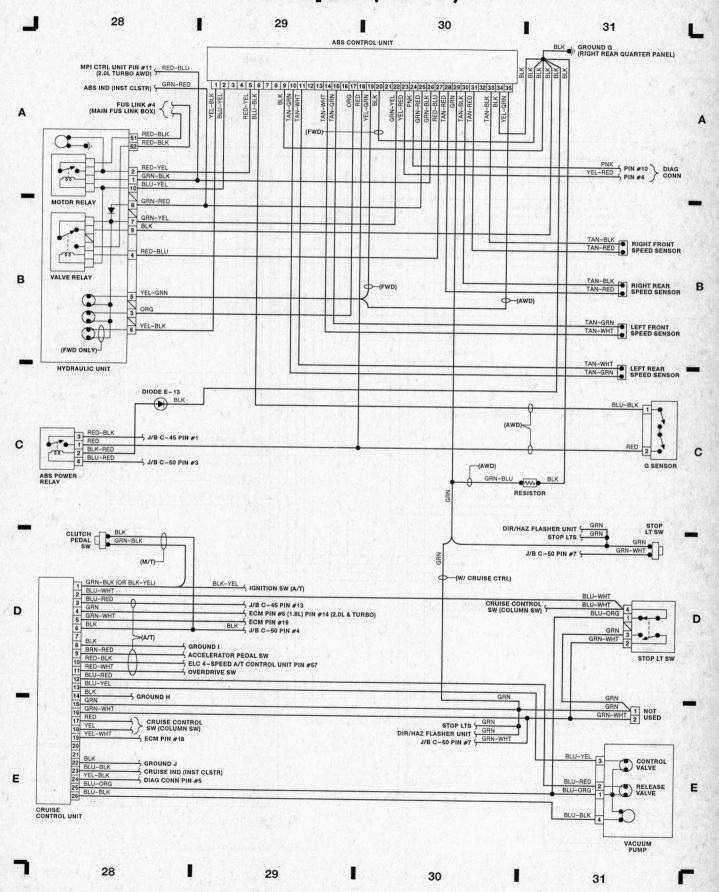

1993 WIRING DIAGRAMS
Eclipse (Cont.)

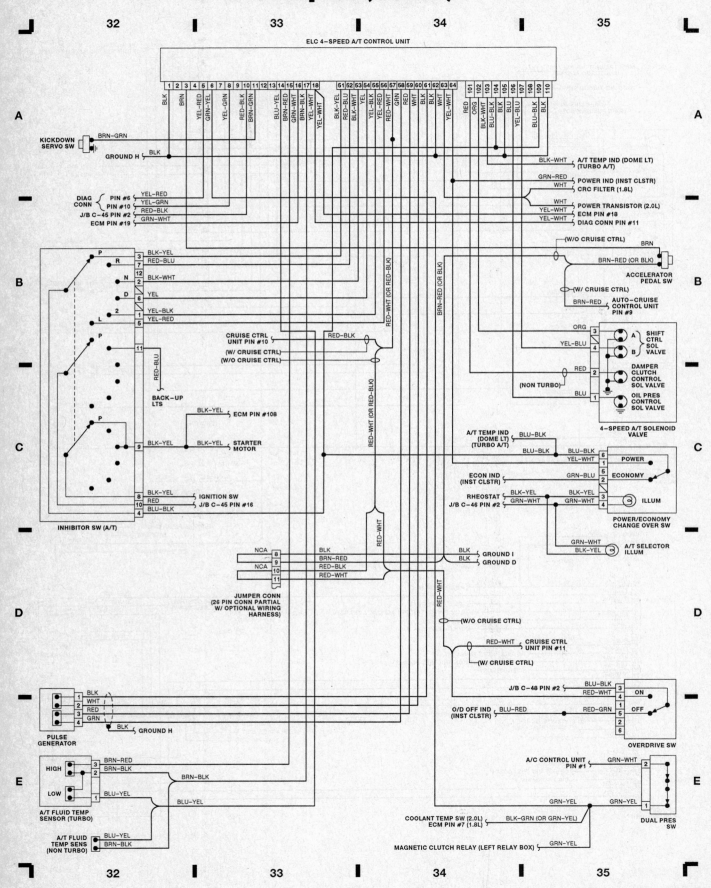

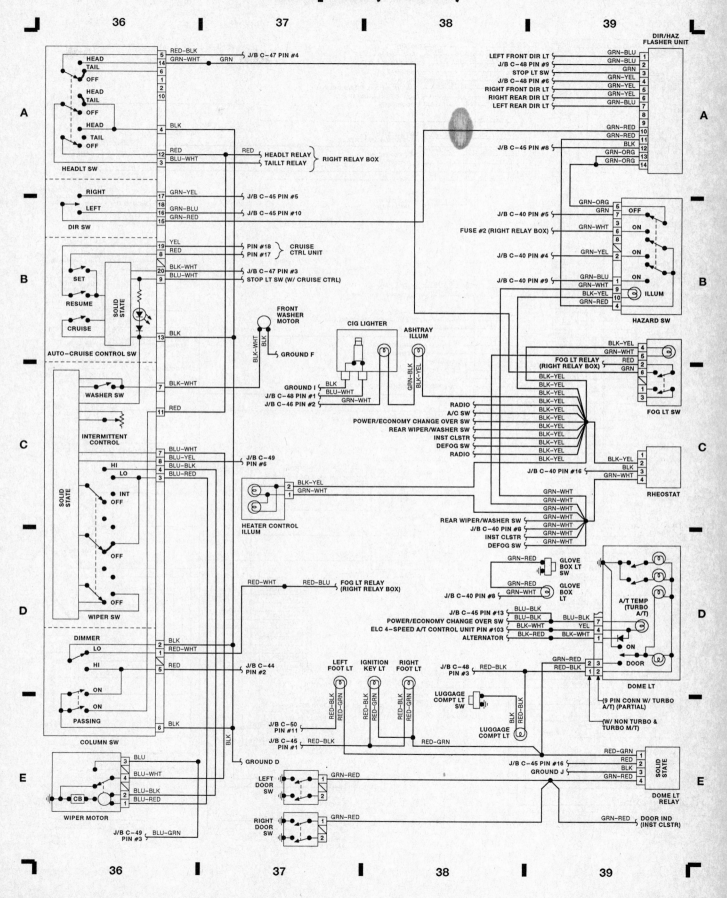

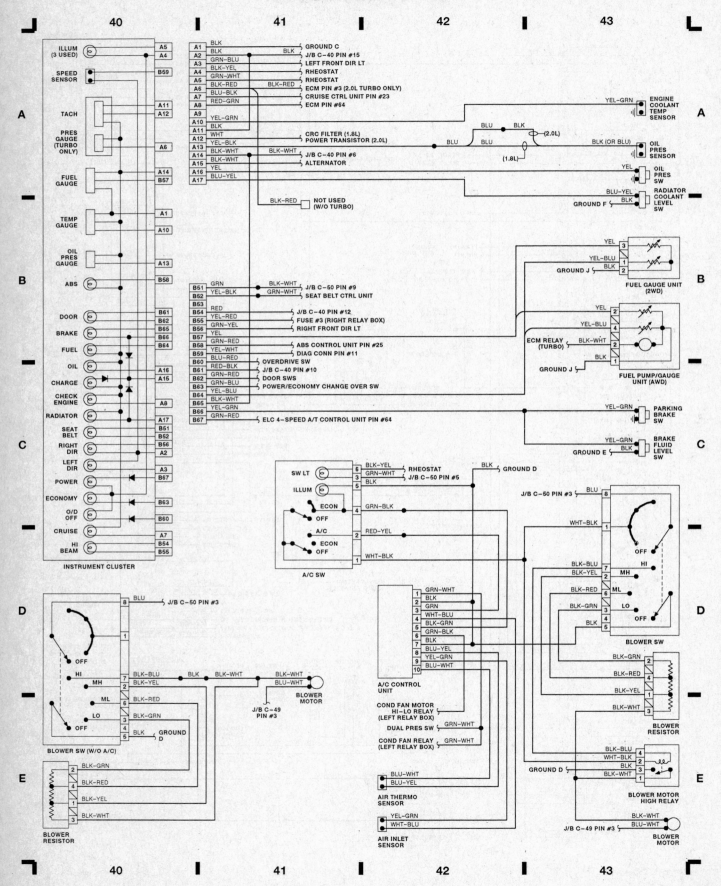

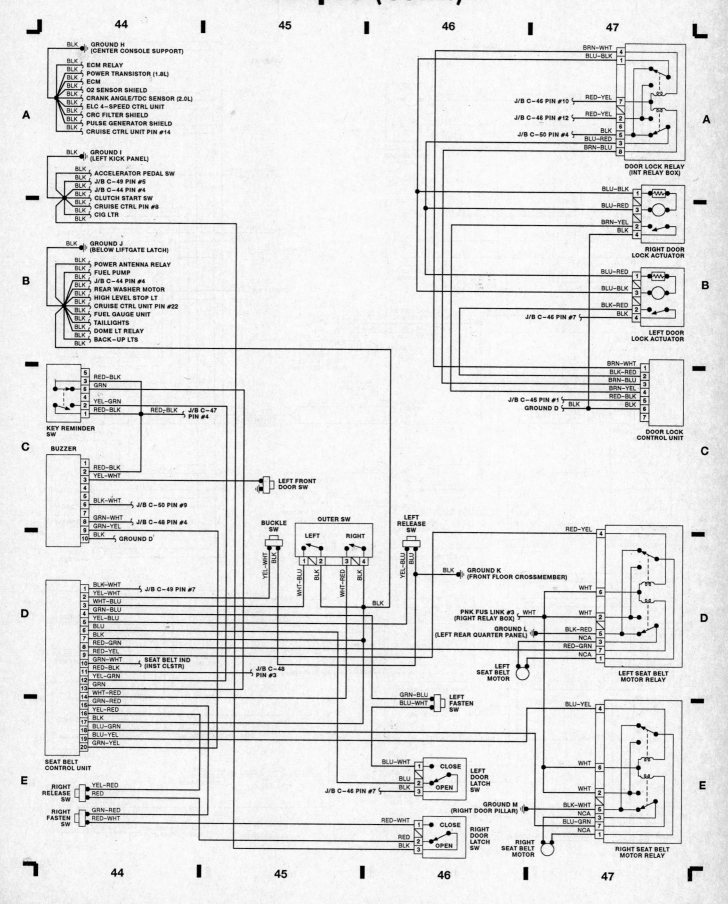

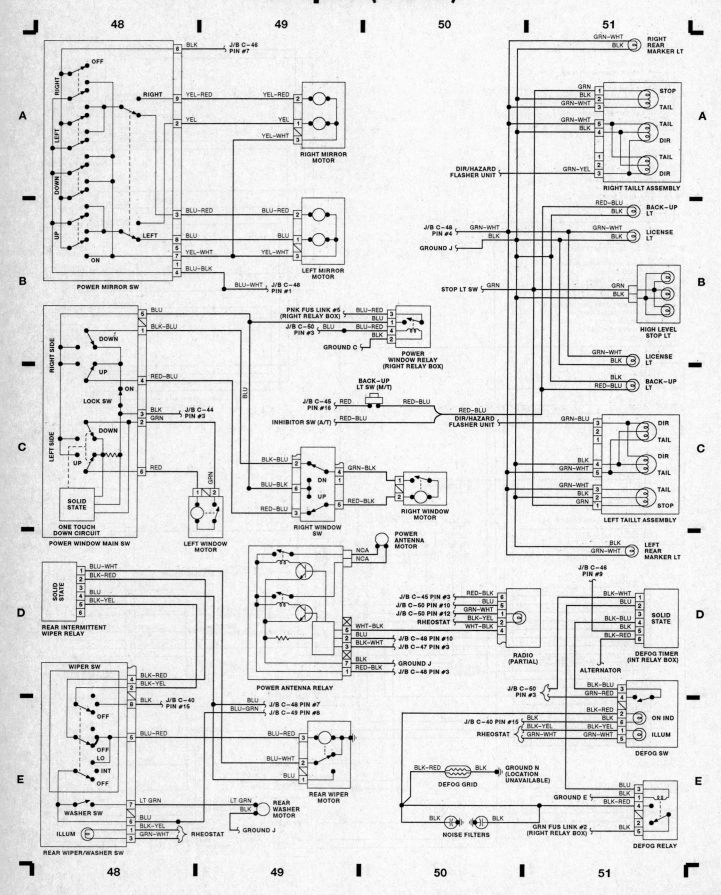

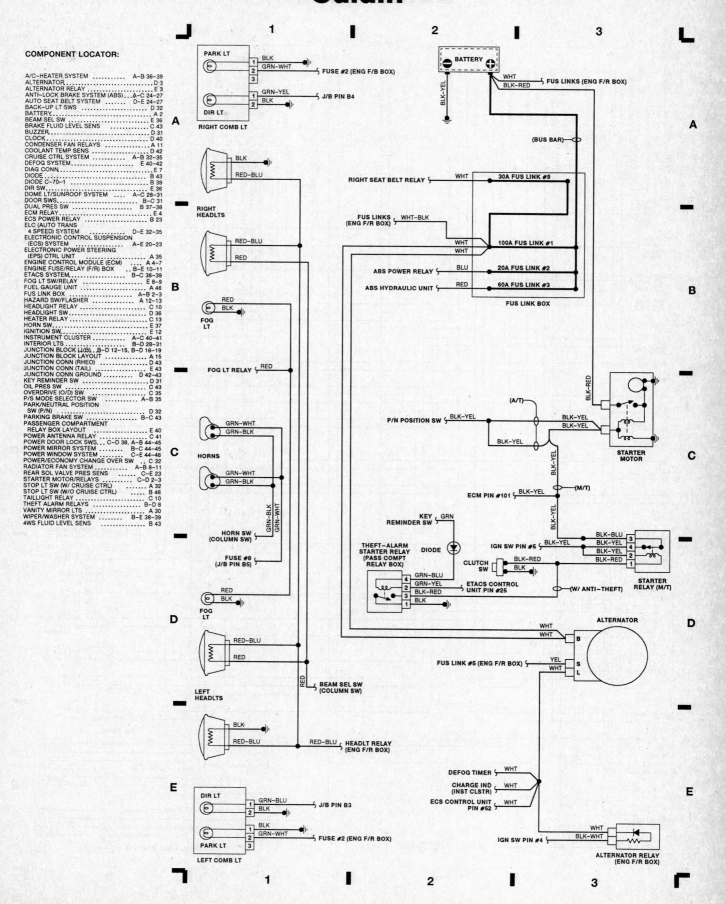

COMPONENT LOCATOR:

A/C–HEATER SYSTEM .... A–B 36–39
ALTERNATOR D–3
ALTERNATOR RELAY .... E 3
ANTI–LOCK BRAKE SYSTEM (ABS)... A–C 24–27
AUTO SEAT BELT SYSTEM .... D–E 24–27
BACK–UP LT SWS .... D 32
BATTERY.............................. A 2
BEAM SEL SW .... E 36
BRAKE FLUID LEVEL SENS .... C 43
BUZZER.............................. D 31
CLOCK .... D 40
CONDENSER FAN RELAYS .... A 11
COOLANT TEMP SENS .... D 42
CRUISE CTRL SYSTEM .... A–B 32–35
DEFOG SYSTEM..................... E 40–42
DIAG CONN........................... E 7
DIODE.............................. B 43
DIODE C–70–1 .... B 38
DIR SW.............................. E 36
DOME LT/SUNROOF SYSTEM .... A–C 28–31
DOOR SWS .... B–C 31
DUAL PRES SW .... B 37–38
ECM RELAY........................... E 4
ECS POWER RELAY .... B 23
ELC (AUTO TRANS
  4 SPEED) SYSTEM .... D–E 32–35
ELECTRONIC CONTROL SUSPENSION
  (ECS) SYSTEM .... A–E 20–23
ELECTRONIC POWER STEERING
  (EPS) CTRL UNIT .... A 35
ENGINE CONTROL MODULE (ECM) .... A 4–7
ENGINE FUSE/RELAY (F/R) BOX ... B–E 10–11
ETACS SYSTEM..................... B–C 36–39
FOG LT SW/RELAY .... E 8–9
FUEL GAUGE UNIT .... A 46
FUS LINK BOX .... A–B 2–3
HAZARD SW/FLASHER .... A 12–13
HEADLIGHT RELAY .... C 10
HEADLIGHT SW .... D 36
HEATER RELAY .... C 13
HORN SW .... E 37
IGNITION SW........................ E 12
INSTRUMENT CLUSTER .... A–C 40–41
INTERIOR LTS .... B–D 28–31
JUNCTION BLOCK (J/B)..B–D 12–15, B–D 16–19
JUNCTION BLOCK LAYOUT .... A 15
JUNCTION CONN (RHEO) .... D 43
JUNCTION CONN (TAIL) .... E 43
JUNCTION CONN GROUND .... D 42–43
KEY REMINDER SW .... D 31
OIL PRES SW .... C 43
OVERDRIVE (O/D) SW .... C 35
P/S MODE SELECTOR SW .... A–B 35
PARK/NEUTRAL POSITION
  SW (P/N) .... D 32
PARKING BRAKE SW .... B–C 43
PASSENGER COMPARTMENT
  RELAY BOX LAYOUT .... E 40
POWER ANTENNA RELAY .... C 41
POWER DOOR LOCK SWS... C–D 38, A–B 44–45
POWER MIRROR SYSTEM .... B–C 44–45
POWER WINDOW SYSTEM .... C–E 44–46
POWER/ECONOMY CHANGE OVER SW .. C 32
RADIATOR FAN SYSTEM .... A–B 8–11
REAR SOL VALVE PRES SENS .... C–E 23
STARTER MOTOR/RELAYS .... C–D 2–3
STOP LT SW (W/ CRUISE CTRL) ...... A 32
STOP LT SW (W/O CRUISE CTRL) ..... B 46
TAILLIGHT RELAY .... C 10
THEFT ALARM RELAYS .... B–D 8
VANITY MIRROR LTS .... A 30
WIPER/WASHER SYSTEM .... B–E 38–39
4WS FLUID LEVEL SENS .... B 43

1993 WIRING DIAGRAMS
Galant (Cont.)

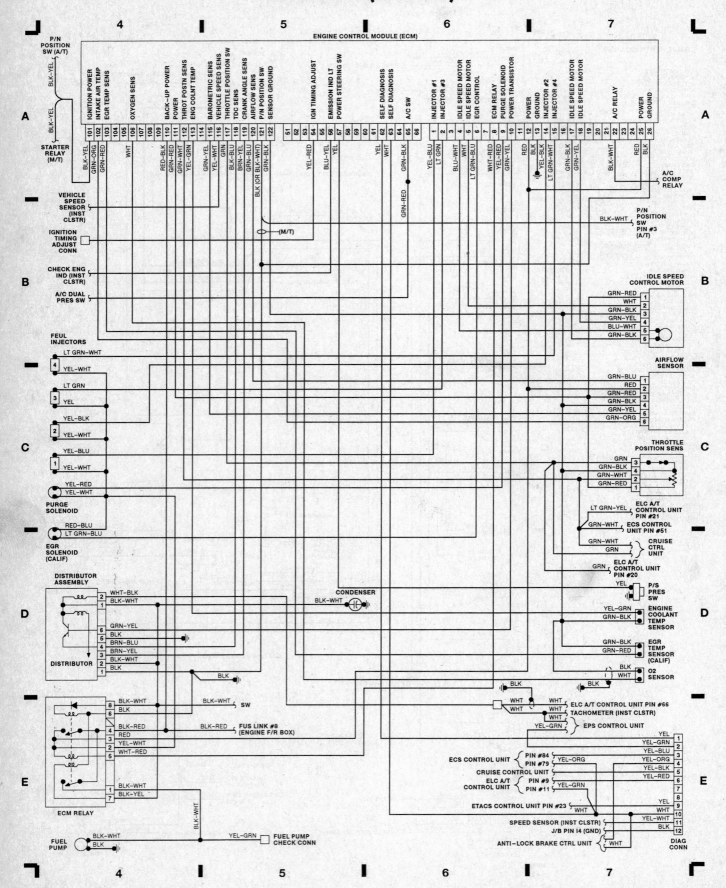

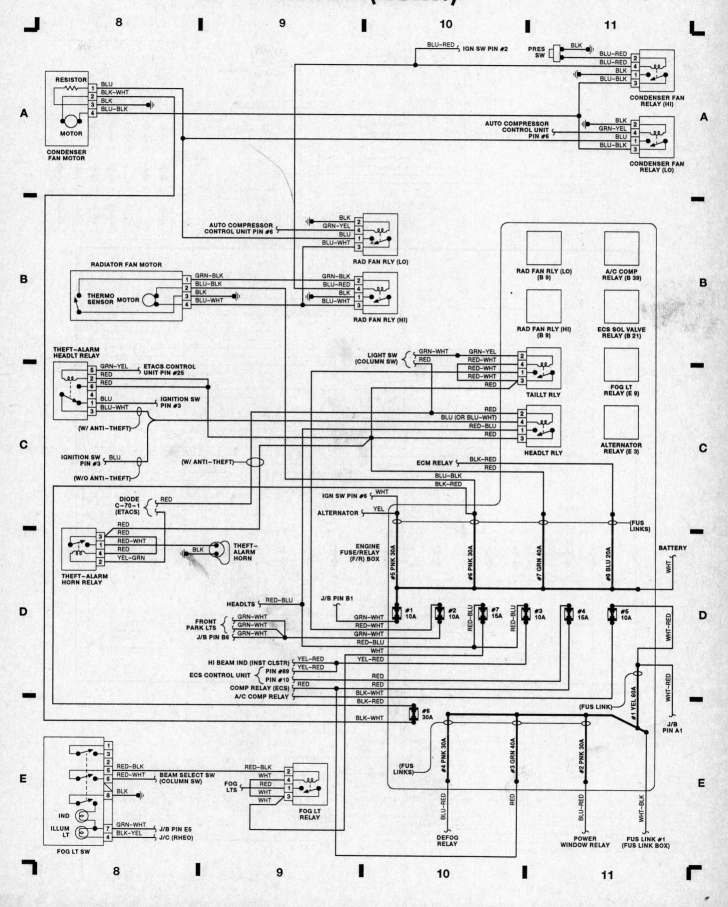

1993 WIRING DIAGRAMS
Galant (Cont.)

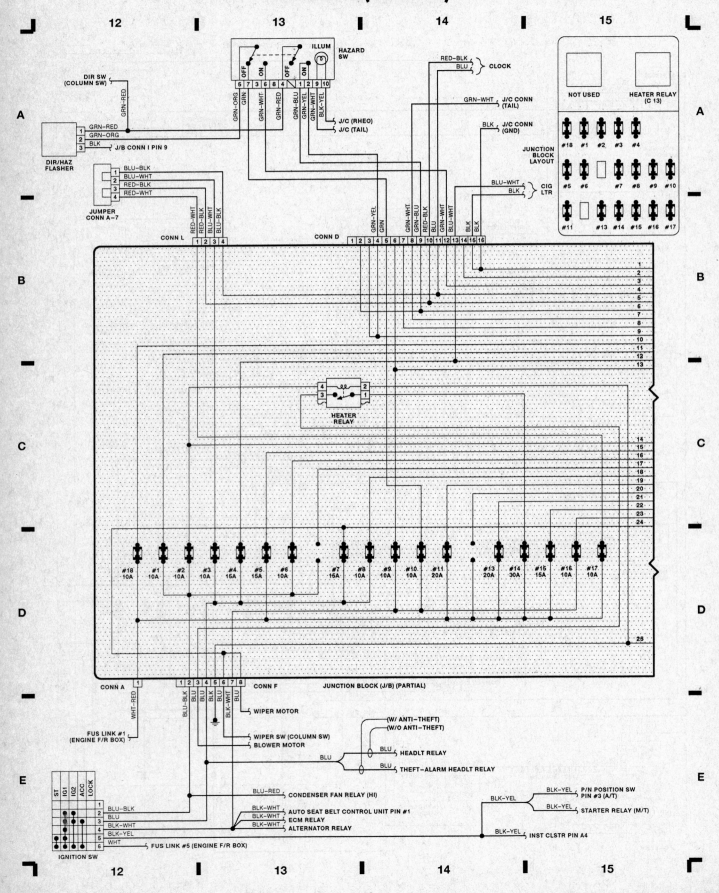

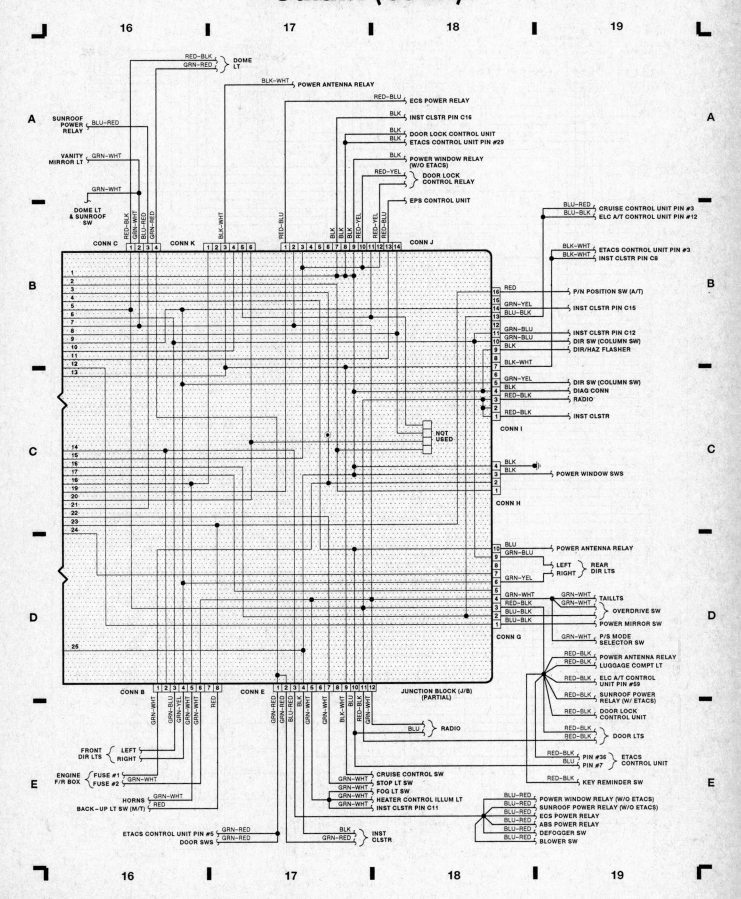

1993 WIRING DIAGRAMS
Galant (Cont.)

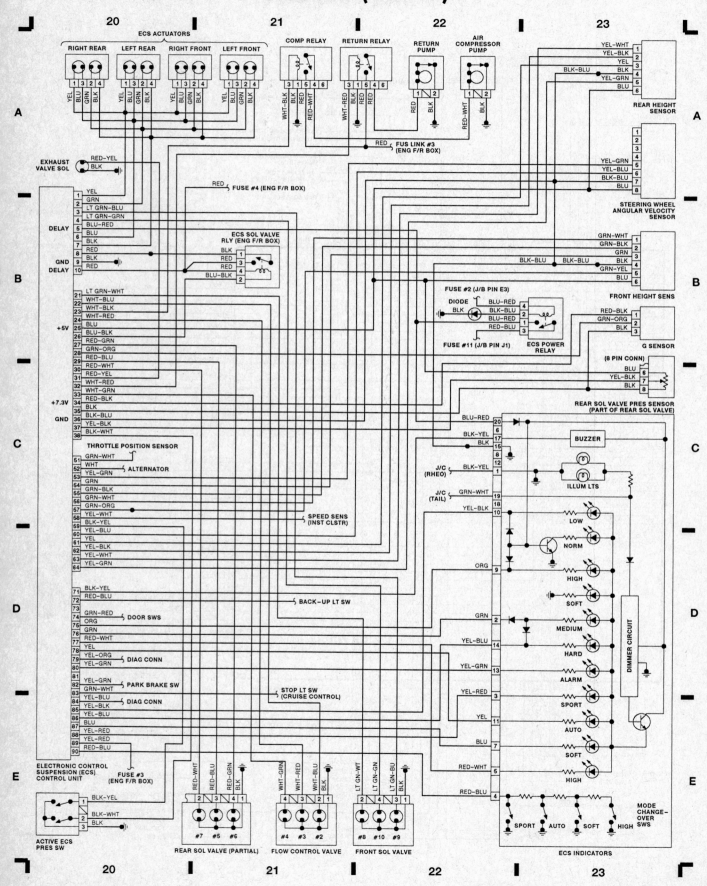

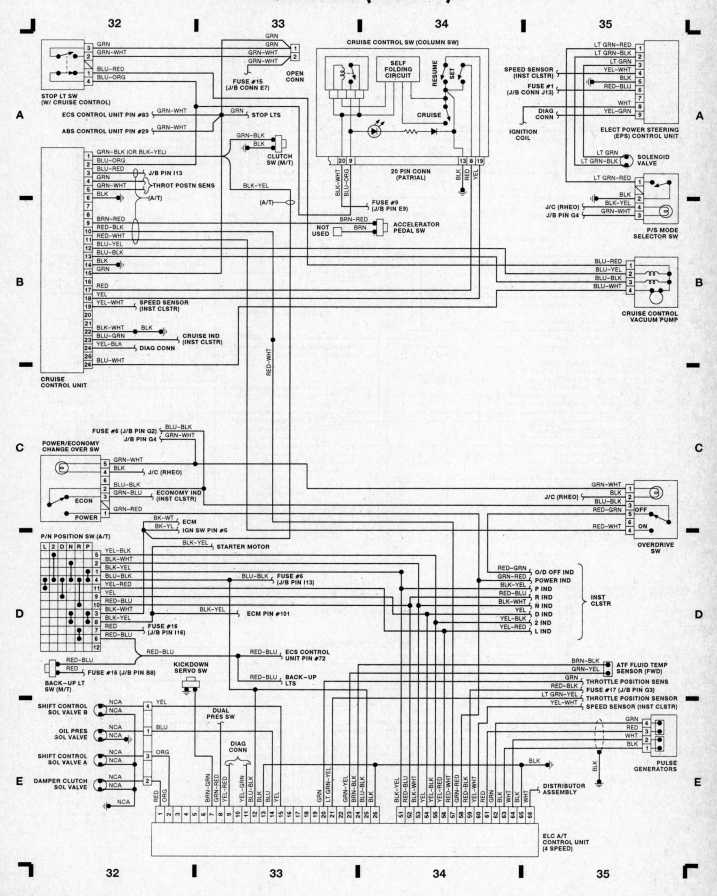

1993 WIRING DIAGRAMS
Galant (Cont.)

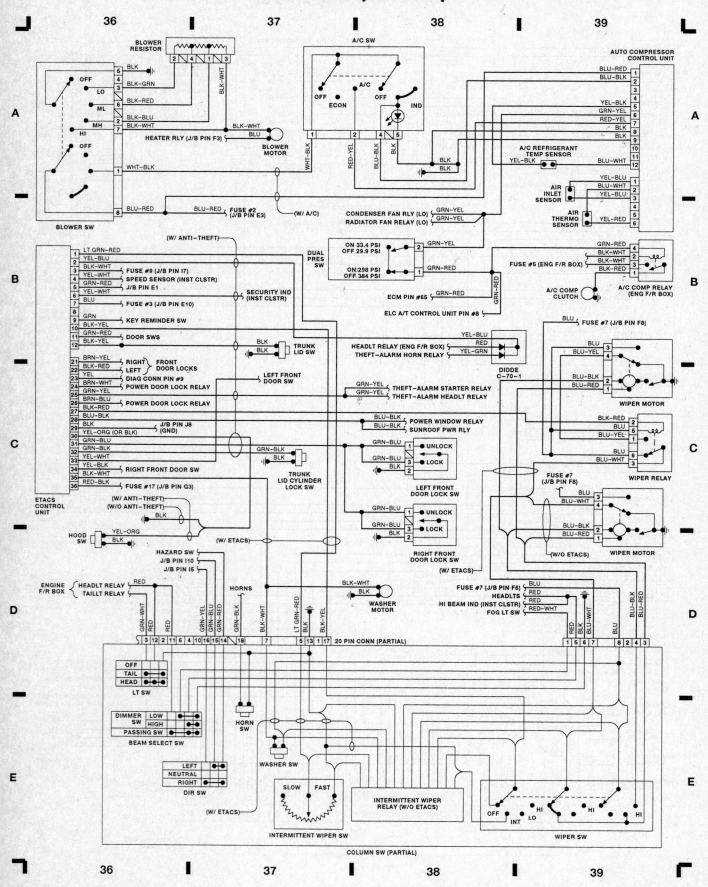

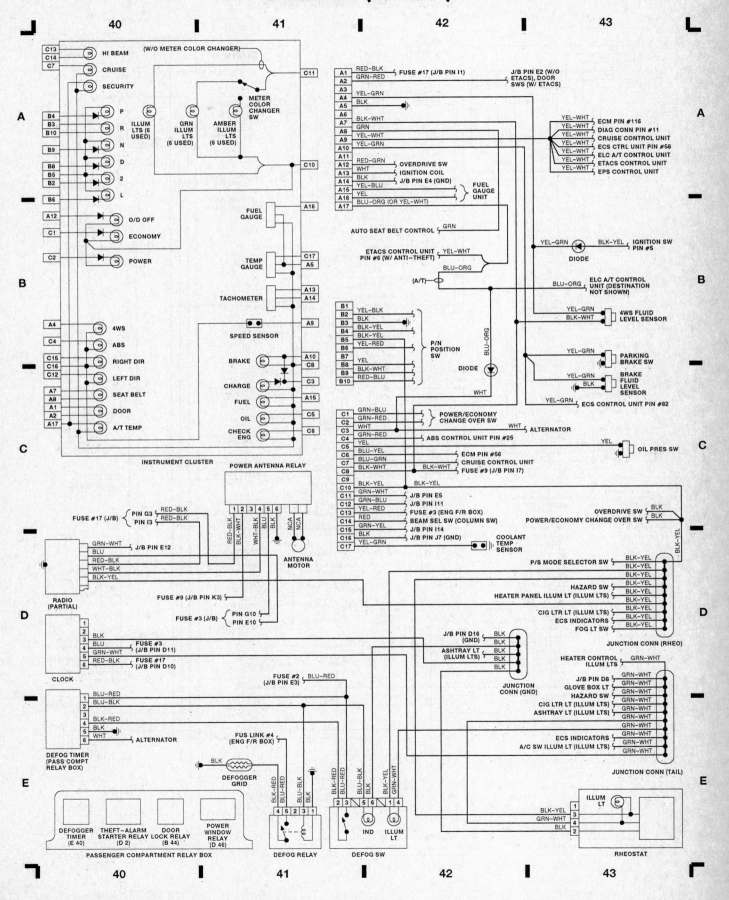

1993 WIRING DIAGRAMS
Galant (Cont.)

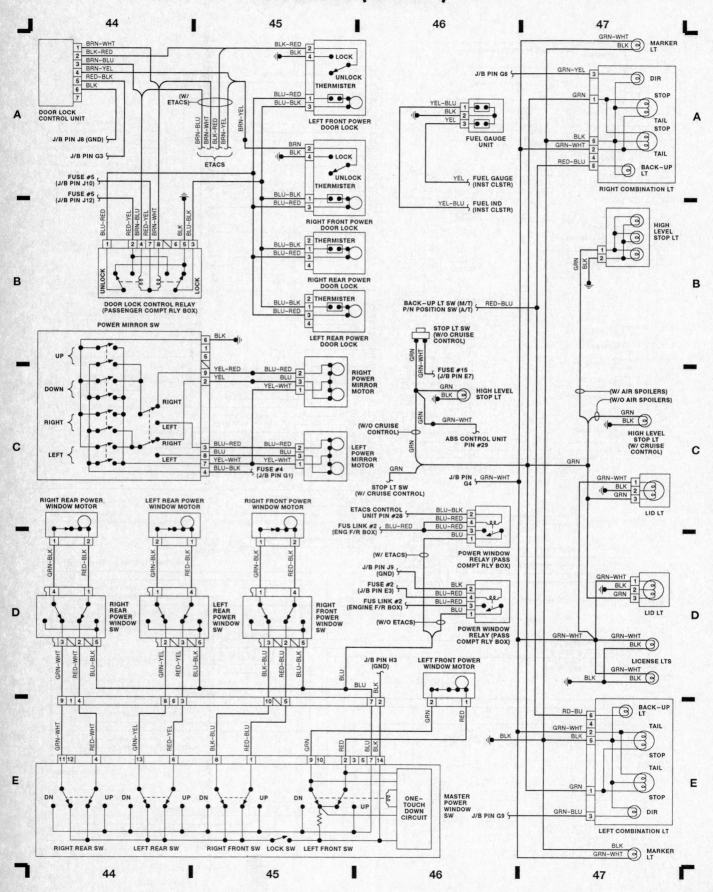

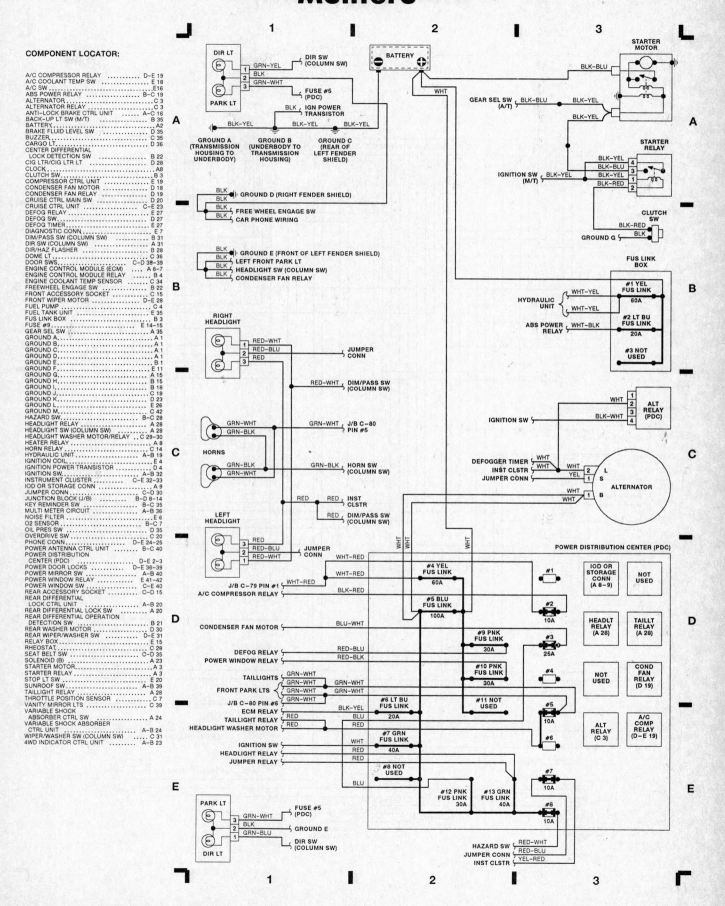

COMPONENT LOCATOR:

A/C COMPRESSOR RELAY .... D-E 19
A/C COOLANT TEMP SW .... E 18
A/C SW E16
ABS POWER RELAY .... B-C 19
ALTERNATOR .... C 3
ALTERNATOR RELAY .... C 3
ANTI-LOCK BRAKE CTRL UNIT ...... A-C 16
BACK-UP LT SW (M/T) .... B 35
BATTERY A2
BRAKE FLUID LEVEL SW .... D 35
BUZZER .... C 35
CARGO LT. .... D 36
CENTER DIFFERENTIAL
   LOCK DETECTION SW .... B 22
CIG LTR/CIG LTR LT .... D 28
CLOCK A8
CLUTCH SW. .... B 3
COMPRESSOR CTRL UNIT .... E 19
CONDENSER FAN MOTOR .... D 18
CONDENSER FAN RELAY .... D 19
CRUISE CTRL MAIN SW .... D 20
CRUISE CTRL UNIT .... C-E 23
DEFOG RELAY .... E 27
DEFOG SW. .... D 27
DEFOG TIMER .... E 27
DIAGNOSTIC CONN. .... E 7
DIM/PASS SW (COLUMN SW) .... B 31
DIR SW (COLUMN SW) .... A 31
DIR/HAZ FLASHER .... B 28
DOME LT. .... C 36
DOOR SWS. .... C-D 38-39
ENGINE CONTROL MODULE (ECM) . A 6-7
ENGINE CONTROL MODULE RELAY . B 4
ENGINE COOLANT TEMP SENSOR ... C 34
FREEWHEEL ENGAGE SW .... B 22
FRONT ACCESSORY SOCKET .... C 15
FRONT WIPER MOTOR .... D-E 28
FUEL PUMP .... C 4
FUEL TANK UNIT .... E 35
FUS LINK BOX .... B 3
FUSE #9 .... E 14-15
GEAR SEL SW .... A 35
GROUND A .... A 1
GROUND B .... A 1
GROUND C .... A 1
GROUND D .... B 1
GROUND E .... B 1
GROUND F .... E 11
GROUND G .... A 15
GROUND H .... B 15
GROUND I .... B 18
GROUND J .... C 19
GROUND K .... D 23
GROUND L .... E 26
GROUND M .... C 42
HAZARD SW. .... B-C 28
HEADLIGHT RELAY .... A 28
HEADLIGHT SW (COLUMN SW) .... A 28
HEADLIGHT WASHER MOTOR/RELAY . C 29-30
HEATER RELAY .... A 8
HORN RELAY .... C 14
HYDRAULIC UNIT .... A-B 19
IGNITION COIL .... E 4
IGNITION POWER TRANSISTOR .... D 4
IGNITION SW. .... A-B 32
INSTRUMENT CLUSTER .... C-E 32-33
IOD OR STORAGE CONN .... A 9
JUMPER CONN .... C-D 30
JUNCTION BLOCK (J/B) .... B-D 8-14
KEY REMINDER SW .... B-C 35
MULTI METER CIRCUIT .... A-B 36
NOISE FILTER .... E 6
O2 SENSOR .... B-C 7
OIL PRES SW .... D 35
OVERDRIVE SW .... C 20
PHONE CONN. .... D-E 24-25
POWER ANTENNA CTRL UNIT ...... B-C 40
POWER DISTRIBUTION
   CENTER (PDC) .... D-E 2-3
POWER DOOR LOCKS .... D-E 36-39
POWER MIRROR SW .... A-B 40
POWER WINDOW RELAY .... E 41-42
POWER WINDOW SW .... C-E 40
REAR ACCESSORY SOCKET .... C-D 15
REAR DIFFERENTIAL
   LOCK DETECTION SW .... A-B 20
REAR DIFFERENTIAL LOCK SW .... A 20
REAR DIFFERENTIAL OPERATION
   DETECTION SW .... B 21
REAR WASHER MOTOR .... D 30
REAR WIPER/WASHER SW .... D-E 31
RELAY BOX .... E 15
RHEOSTAT .... C 28
SEAT BELT SW .... C-D 35
SOLENOID (B) .... A 23
STARTER MOTOR .... A 3
STARTER RELAY .... A 3
STOP LT SW .... E 20
SUNROOF SW .... A-B 39
TAILLIGHT RELAY .... A 28
THROTTLE POSITION SENSOR ...... C 7
VANITY MIRROR LTS .... C 39
VARIABLE SHOCK
   ABSORBER CTRL SW .... A 24
VARIABLE SHOCK ABSORBER
   CTRL UNIT .... A-B 24
WIPER/WASHER SW (COLUMN SW) . C 31
4WD INDICATOR CTRL UNIT .... A-B 23

1993 WIRING DIAGRAMS
Montero (Cont.)

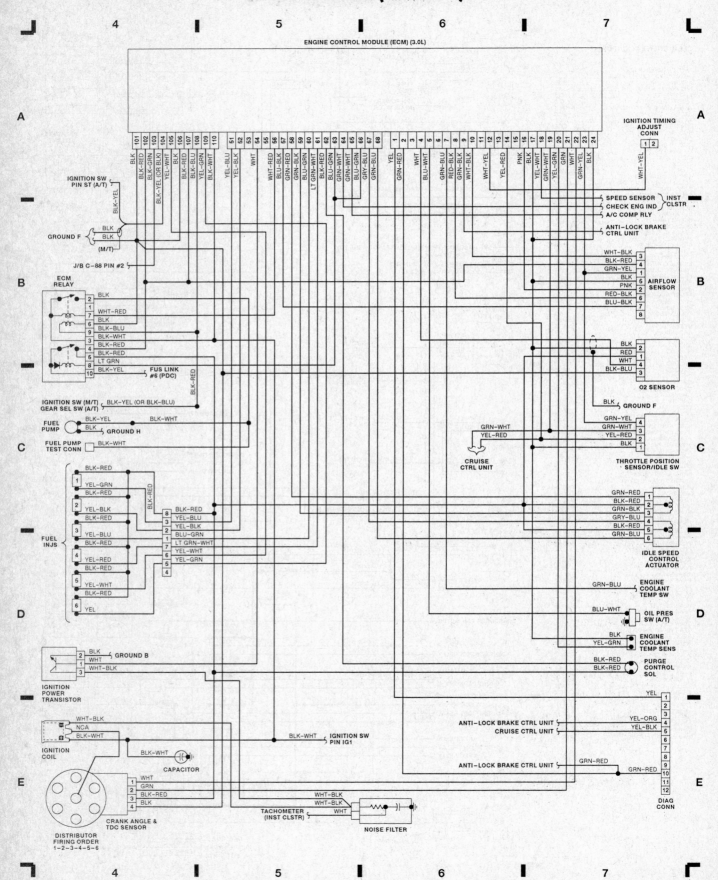

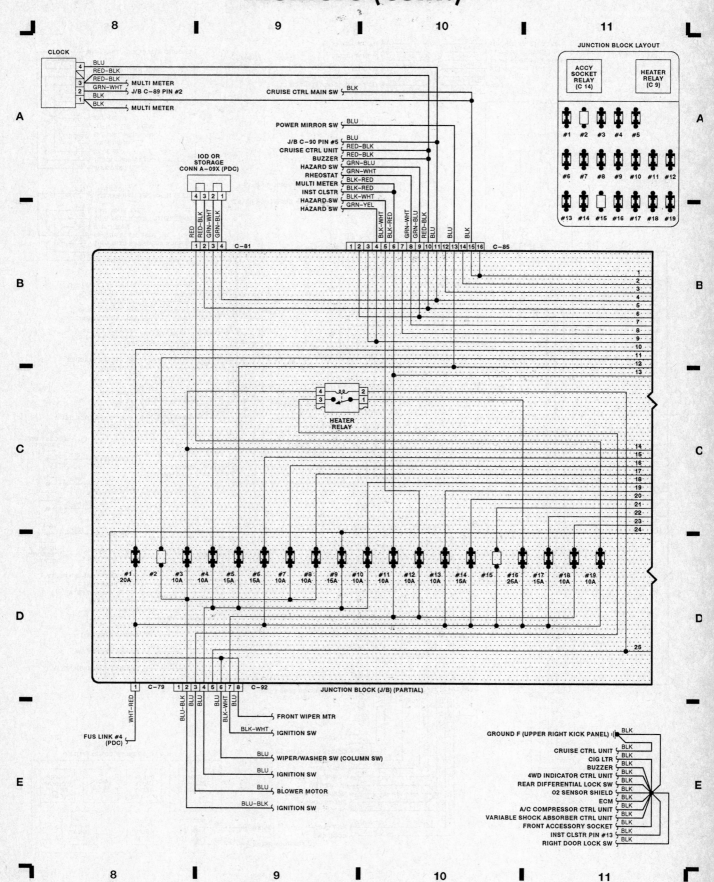

1993 WIRING DIAGRAMS
Montero (Cont.)

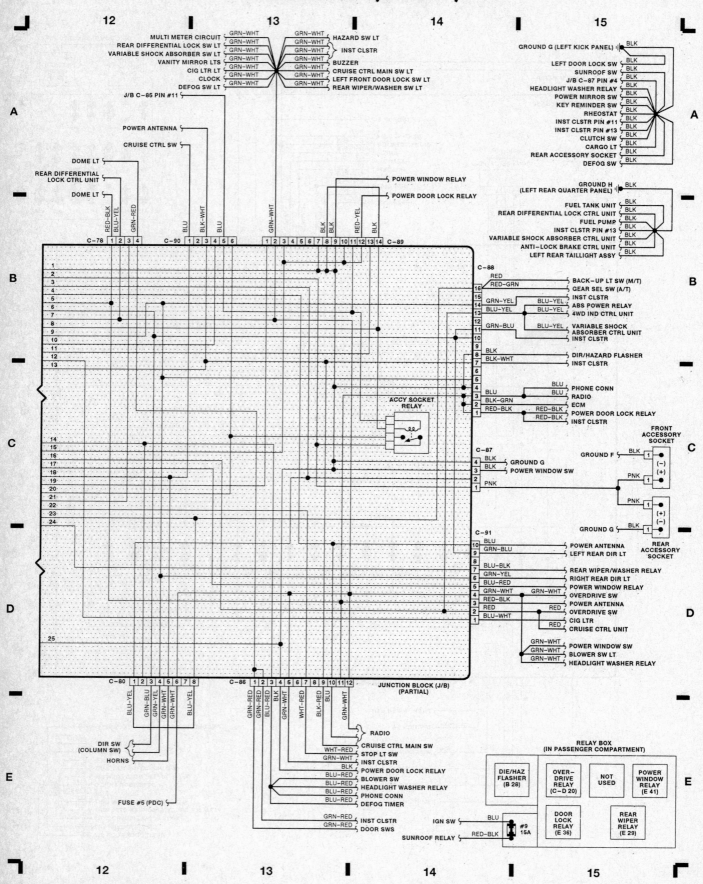

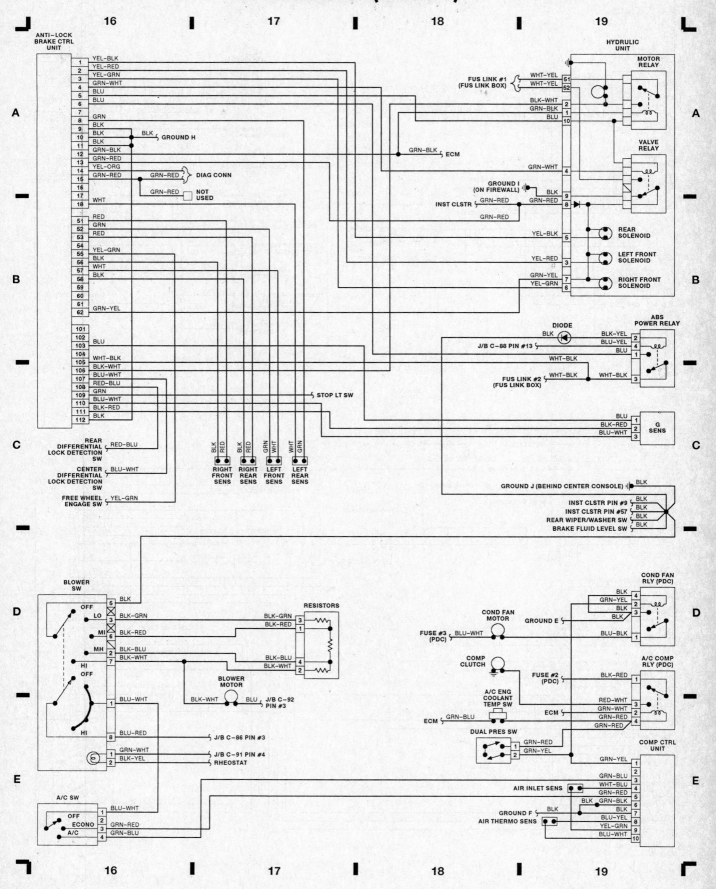

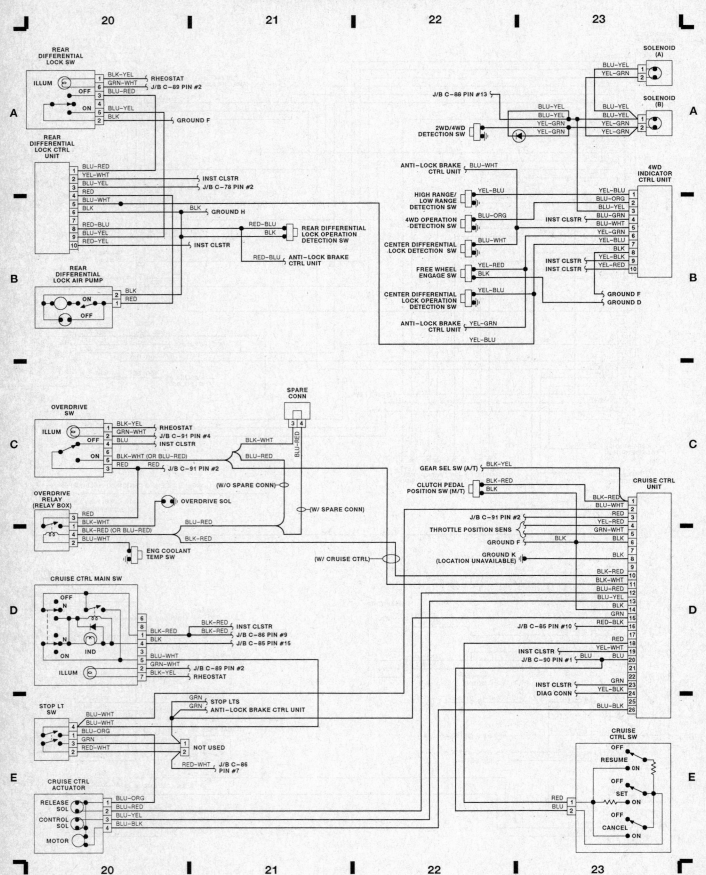

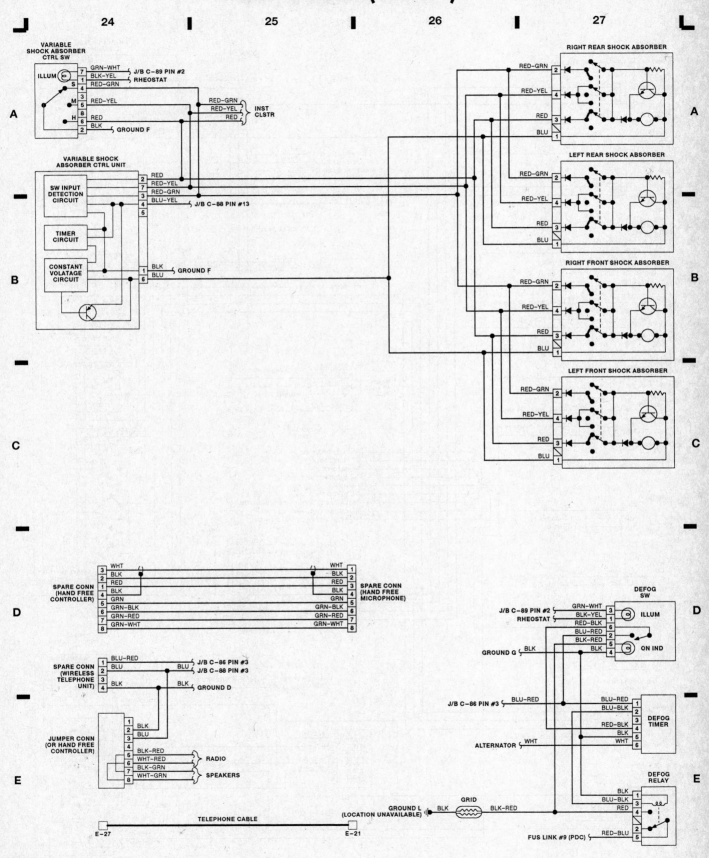

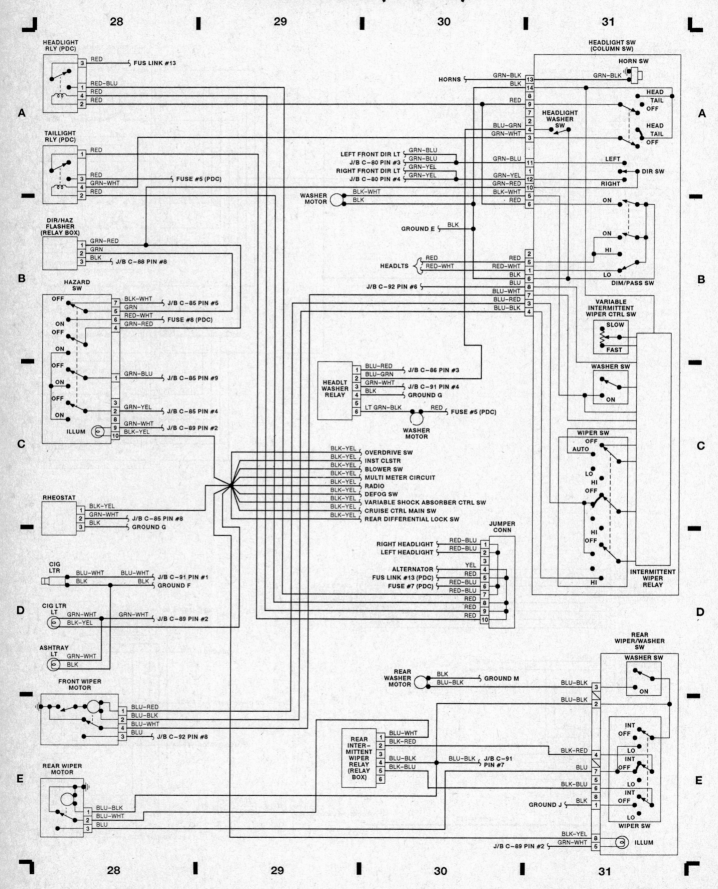

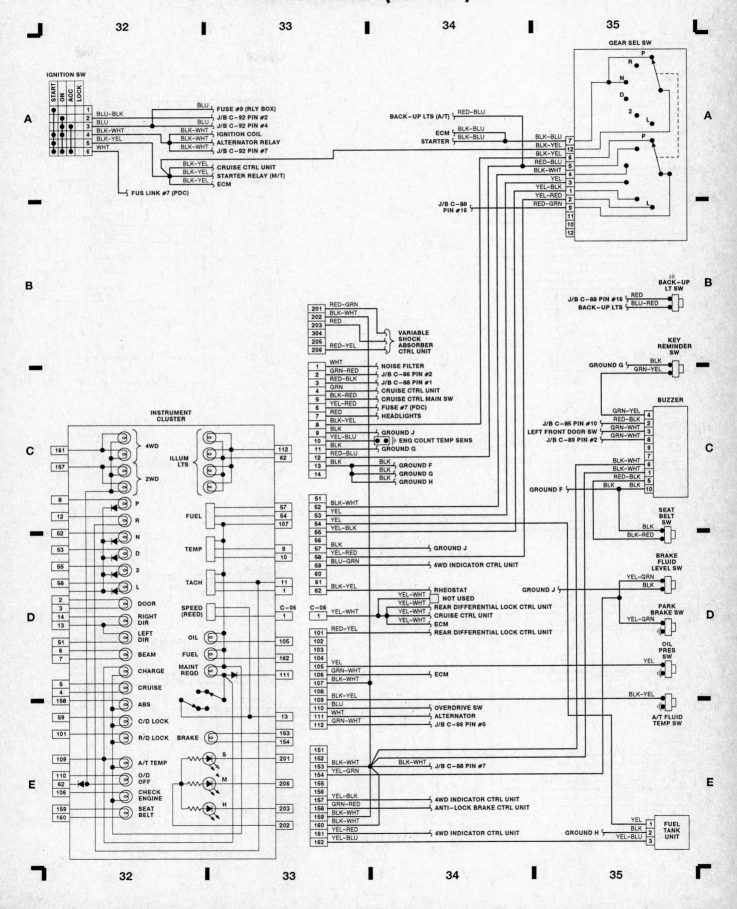

1993 WIRING DIAGRAMS
Montero (Cont.)

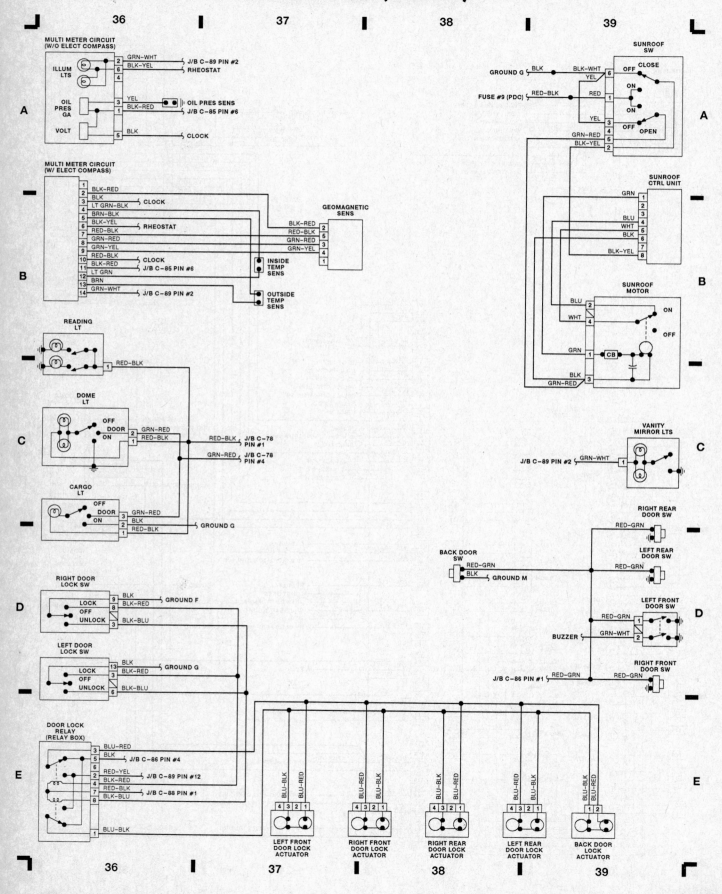

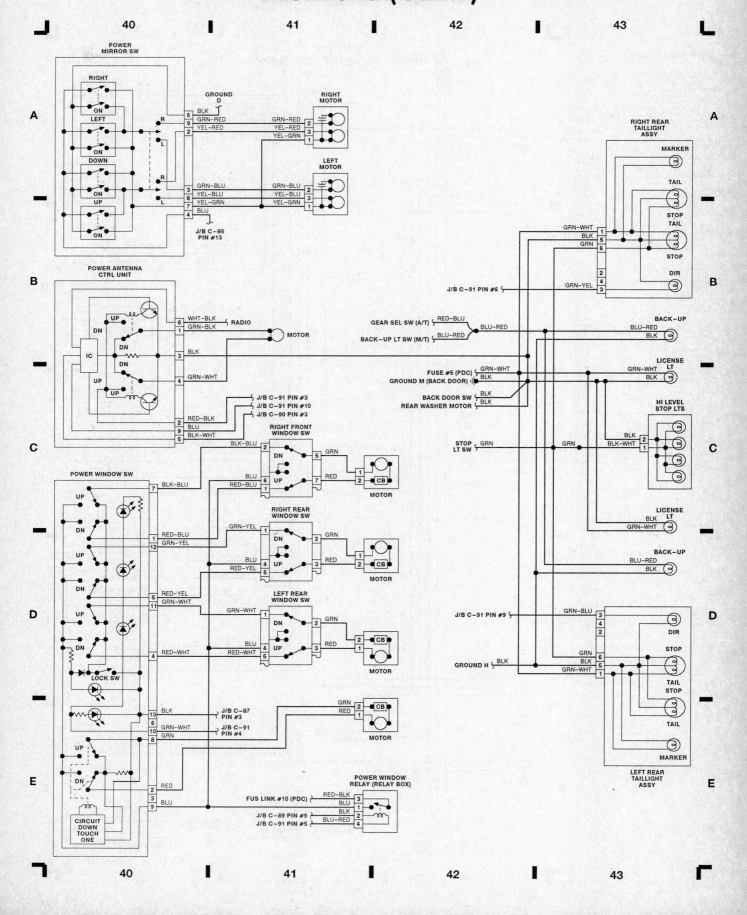

1993 WIRING DIAGRAMS
Pickup & Ram-50

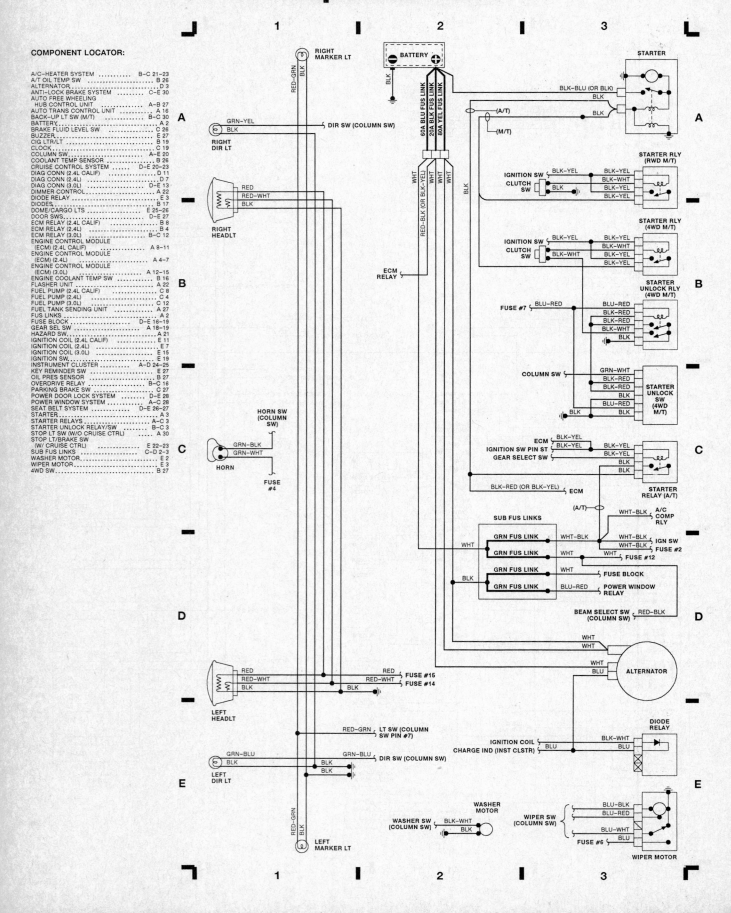

COMPONENT LOCATOR:

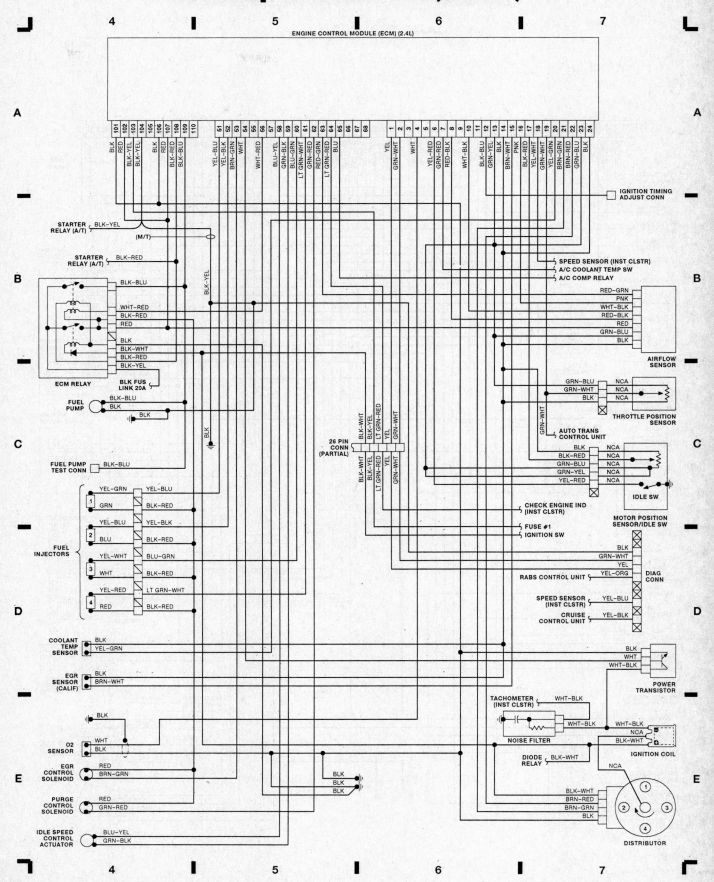

1993 WIRING DIAGRAMS
Pickup & Ram-50 (Cont.)

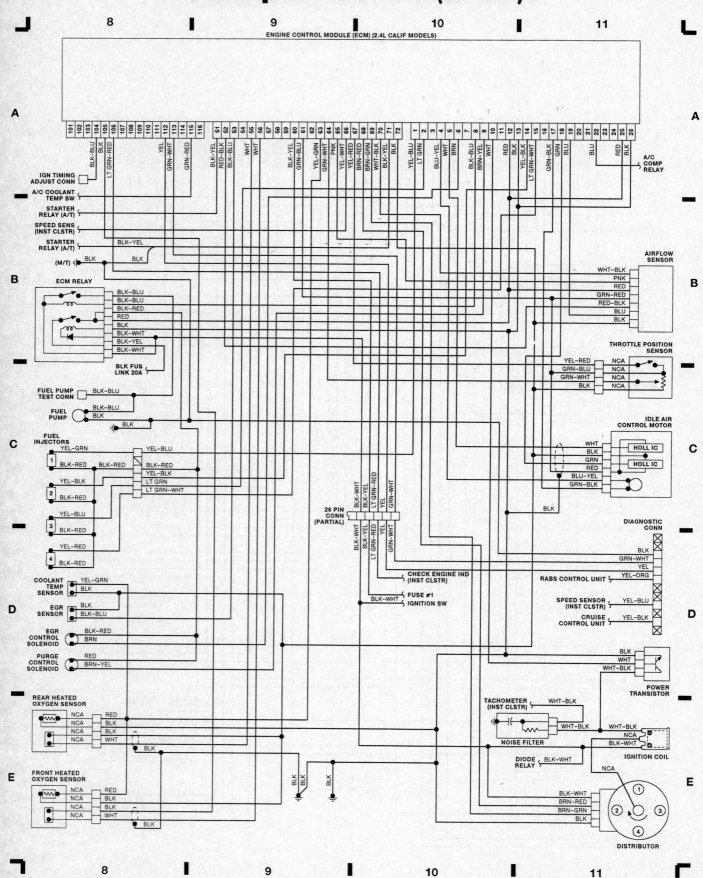

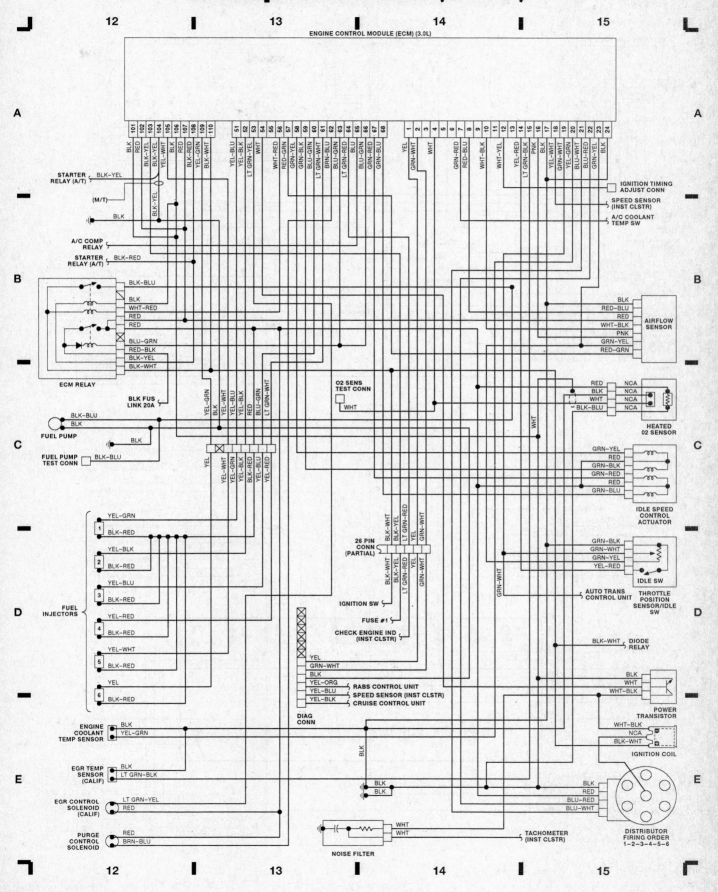

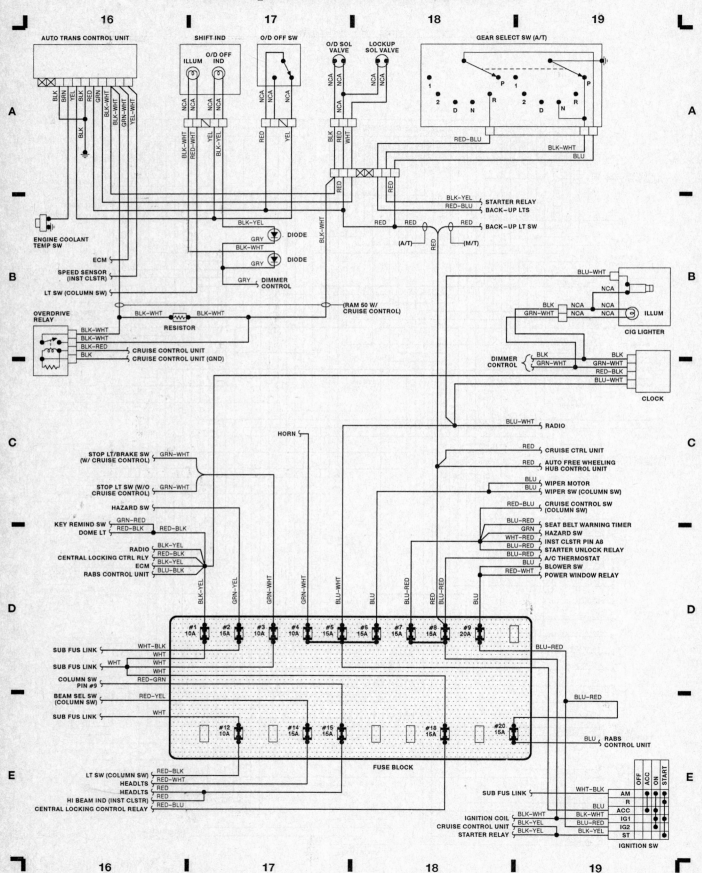

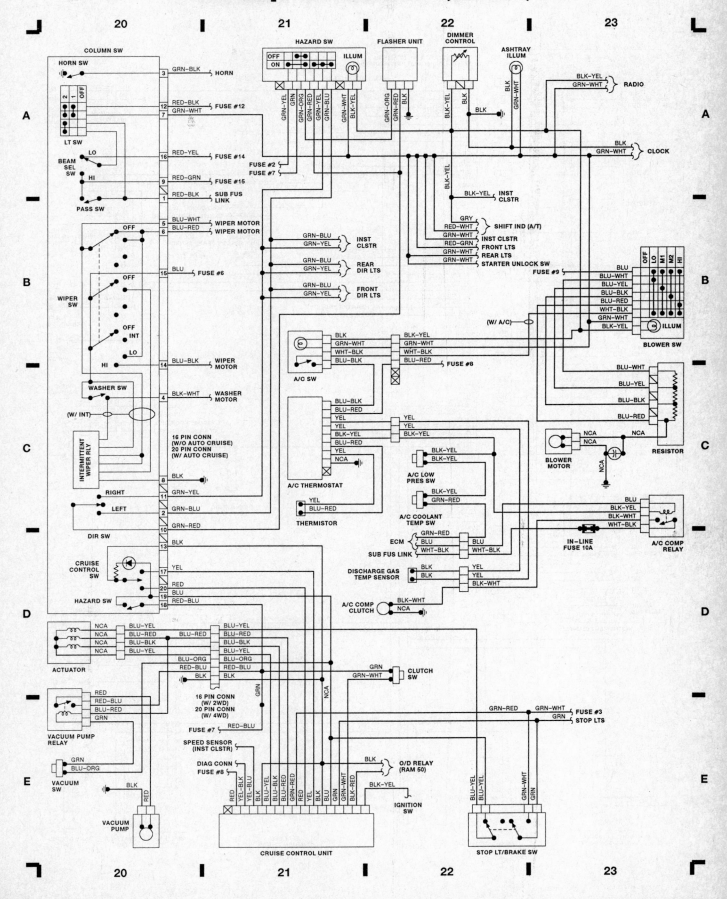

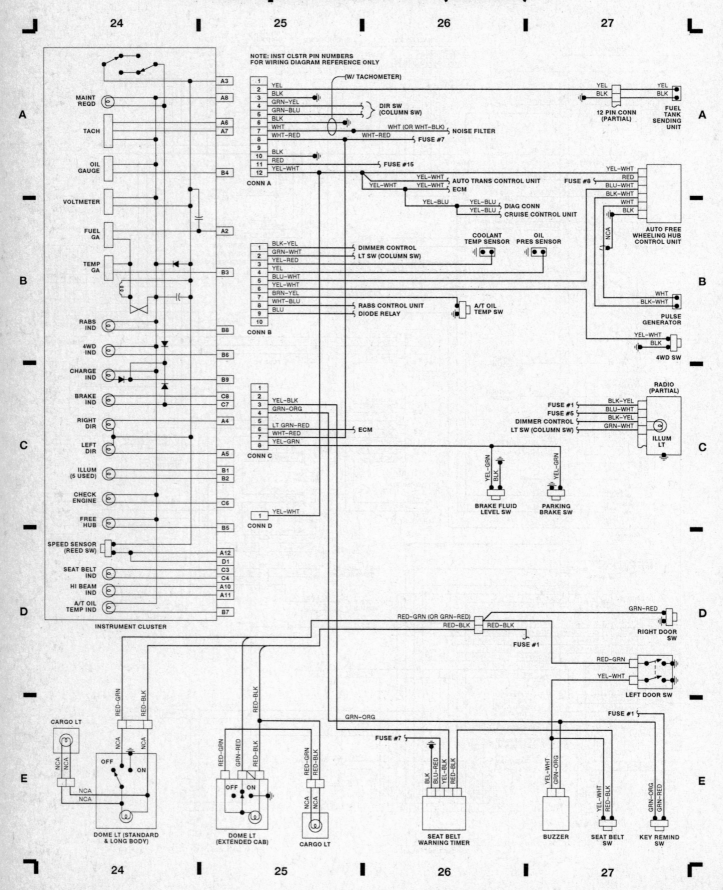

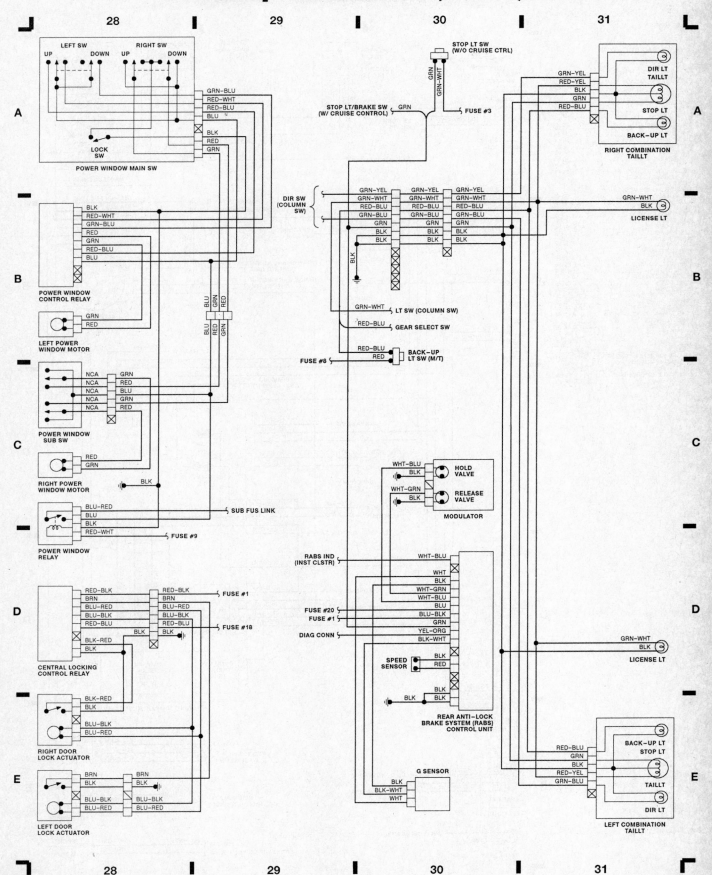

COMPONENT LOCATOR:

A/C-HEATER SYSTEM .... C-E 19
ALTERNATOR .... B 3
AUTO TRANSAXLE KEY LOCK UNIT...C-D 16-17
BACK-UP LT SW (M/T) .... A 16
BATTERY .... A 3
BRAKE FLUID LEVEL SENSOR .... D 23
CHIME .... D-E 20
CIG LTR/LT .... C-D 15
CLOCK .... B 12
COOLANT TEMP SENDER .... C 23
DEFOG GRID .... C-D 21-22
DIAG CONN .... E 7, E 11
DOME LT .... E 23
DOOR SWS .... E 20
DOOR WARNING SW .... D 21
ECM RELAY .... B 4, B 8
ENGINE COMPARTMENT RELAY BOX ...C-D 2-3
ENGINE CONTROL MODULE
   (ECM) (CALIFORNIA) .... A 8-11
ENGINE CONTROL MODULE
   (ECM) (FEDERAL) .... A 4-7
FLASHER UNIT .... D 14
FRONT WASHER MOTOR .... E 3
FRONT WIPER MOTOR .... E 3
FUEL SENDER .... C 23
FUSE BLOCK .... A-B 13-14
IGNITION COIL .... E 4, E 8
IGNITION LOCK SW .... A 2
IGNITION SW .... C 12
INHIBITOR SW .... A 16-17
INSTRUMENT CLUSTER .... A-C 23
JUNCTION BLOCK (J/B) .... D-E 13-14
MAIN FUS LINKS .... A-B 3
MULTI-FUNCTION SW .... A-C 20
NOISE FILTER .... E 5, E 9
OIL PRES SW .... D 23
OVERDRIVE OFF SW (O/D) .... C 16
PARKING BRAKE SW .... D 23
RADIATOR FAN SYSTEM .... D-E 16-17
REAR WIPER/WASHER MTR/SW .... A-C 24
RESISTOR W/ DIODES .... B 1
RHEOSTAT .... E 24
SEAT BELT SWS .... C 21
STARTER .... A 3
STARTER RELAY .... A 2
TAILLIGHT RELAY .... D 13
THROTTLE POSITION SENSOR .... C-D 7, D 11
TIME AND ALARM CONTROL
   UNIT (TACU) .... C-D 20
TRANSAXLE CONTROL UNIT .... A 17-19
TRUNK LT/SW .... D 22-23

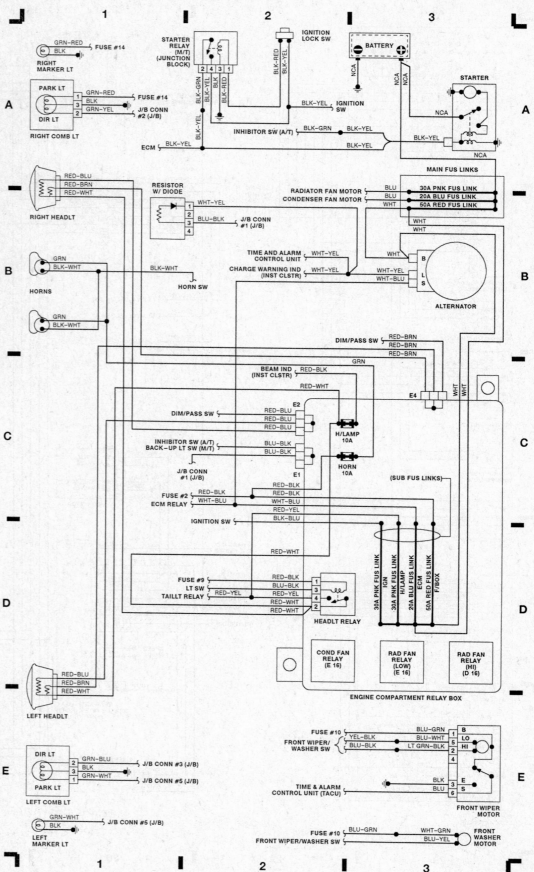

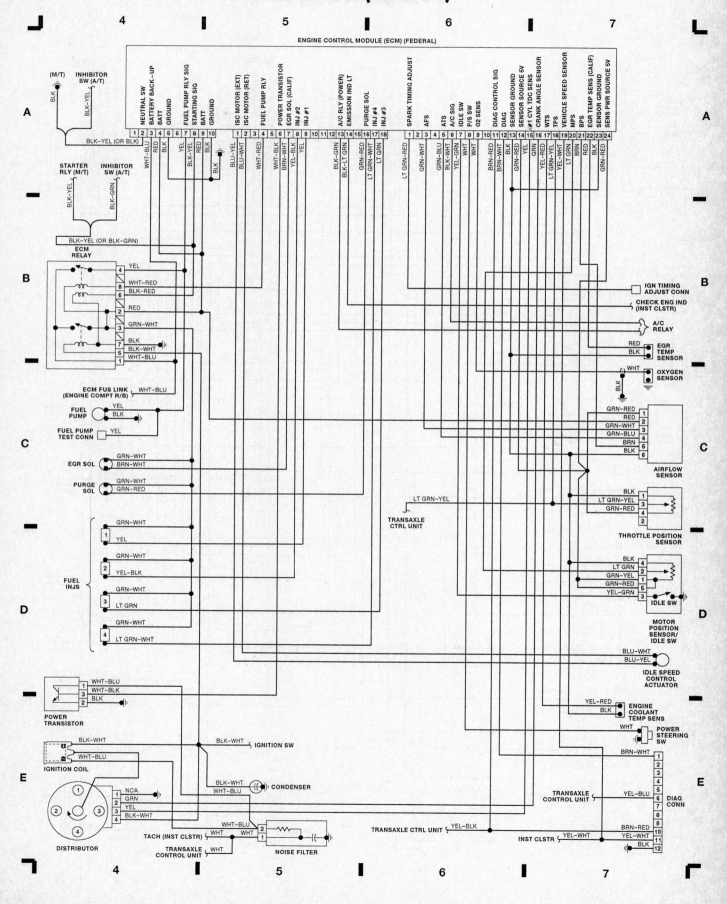

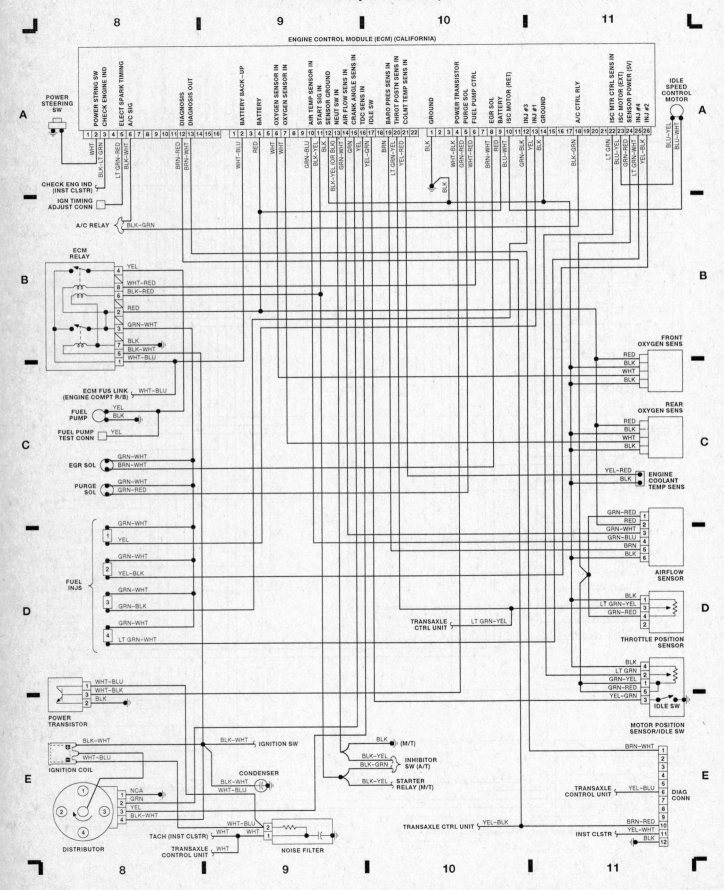

1993 WIRING DIAGRAMS
Precis (Cont.)

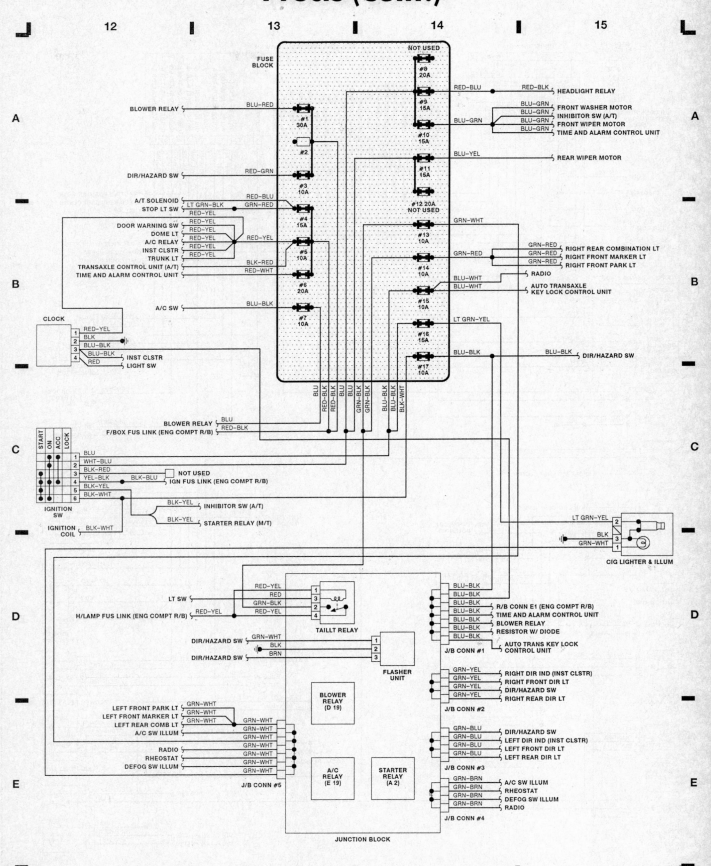

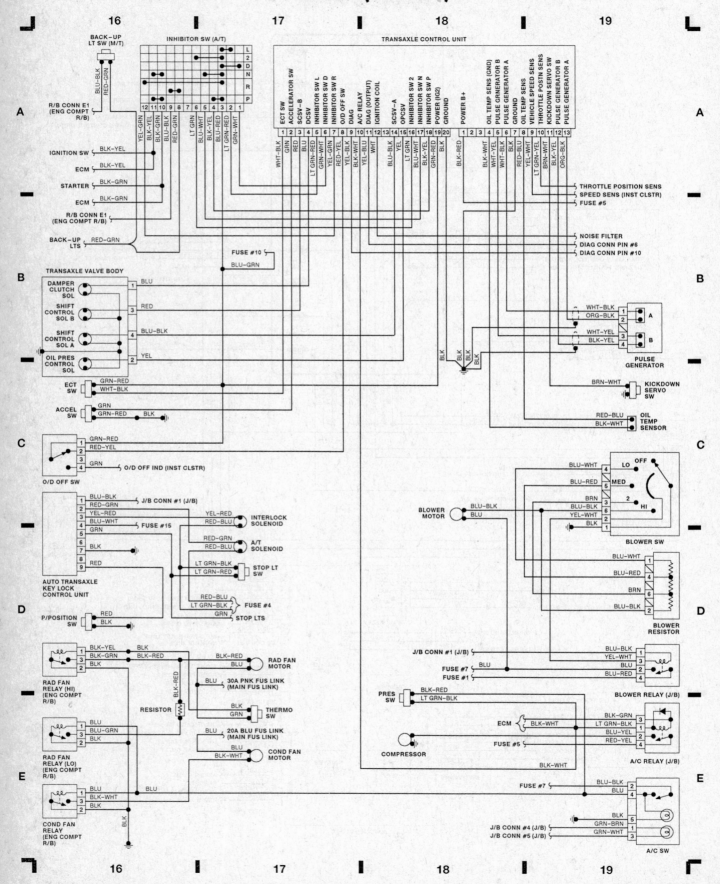

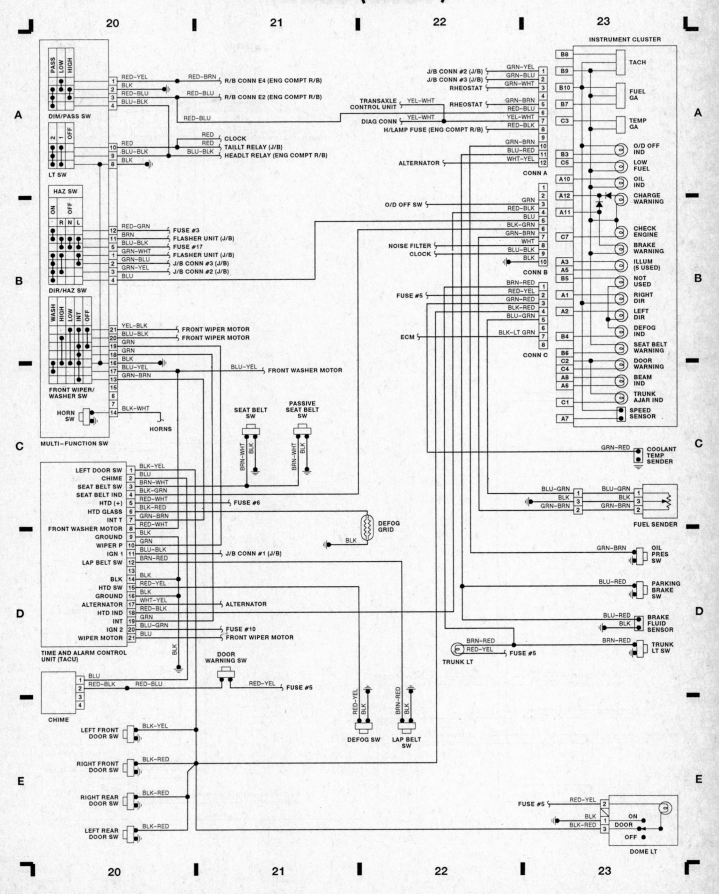

1993 WIRING DIAGRAMS
Precis (Cont.)

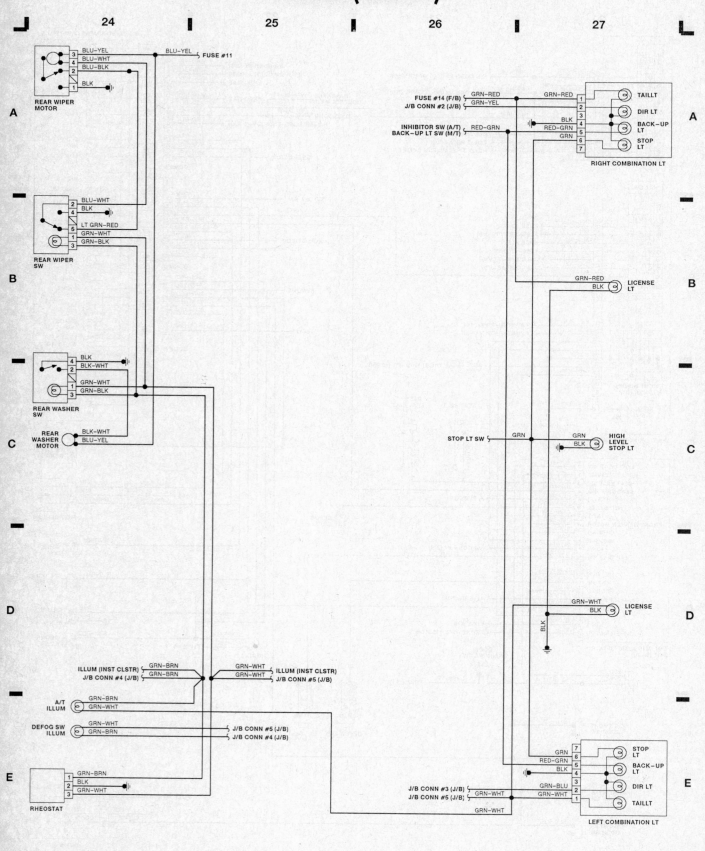